FINANCIAL ANALYST'S HANDBOOK II
Analysis by Industry

Edited by
SUMNER N. LEVINE
State University of New York
Stony Brook, New York

 1975

DOW JONES-IRWIN, INC.
Homewood, Illinois   60430

First Printing, February 1975

Library of Congress Cataloging in Publication Data

Levine, Sumner N.
      Financial analyst's handbook.

      CONTENTS: v. 1. Portfolio management.—
v. 2. Analysis by industry.
      1. Investments. I. Title.
HG4521.L625   332.6   74–81386
ISBN 0-87094-083-X (v. 2)

Printed in the United States of America

Preface

This two part Handbook is intended as a comprehensive guide to the principles and procedures necessary for successful investment management. Security analysts, portfolio managers, corporate financial officers and other professional investors will find these volumes a convenient and authoritative source of information.

The Handbook was originally conceived as a single volume reference. However, the enthusiasm of a singularly capable group of editors and contributors soon overwhelmed the original scenario and the project grew like Topsy. The coverage was increased and a number of contributions turned out to be longer than originally planned. Many of these more extensive sections contained much valuable information not readily found elsewhere. Rather than implore our contributors to cut and prune their sections to accommodate the confines of a single volume Handbook, it was decided to expand the book into two volumes. The first volume provides a discipline oriented coverage of investments while the second deals with the analysis of specific industries.

Because of the rapidly changing hues of the investment landscape, we expect that both volumes will find considerable use by analysts. Such is the tempo of events, that on one occasion the analyst may find it necessary to undertake an in-depth analysis of a specific industry, and hence refer to Volume II, while on another occasion he may seek guidance in Volume I for a critical evaluation of special situations, foreign securities, or municipal bonds. Each section provides the analyst with the expertise of authorities who have devoted years to their subject.

v

A few words should be devoted to the organization and some special features of Volume I. The first sections take cognizance of the growing complexity of government regulations as they impinge on the profession. Recognition is also given to the increasing importance of the examinations administered by the Institute of Chartered Financial Analysts.

Comprehensive coverage is given to the characteristics and analysis of both long term and short term investment vehicles. Indeed, we have leaned over backward in this regard and have included substantial information on special situations, foreign securities, and even venture capital investments. Who can foresee future investment opportunities?

The sections on the Analysis of Financial Reports contain a number of special features. Because of the frequent need to compute earnings per share, we have included, in full, APB Opinion 15, together with relevant supporting material. Another feature worthy of comment is an up-dated outline of the 10-K form. Study of this 10-K form section will inform the analyst what information is available and where in the 10-K form it can be found.

The sections on Economic Analysis and Timing also contain a number of useful features. A very complete account is given of the Federal Reserve System since, as every analyst is well aware, the securities markets exhibit an almost instantaneous reflex reaction to significant changes in the Fed's policies. Also included is a detailed section on the interpretation of National Income and Balance of Payments Accounts. It should be noted too, that technical analysis has also been given its day in court. A useful appendix to the latter section will provide the user with detailed definitions of the more commonly used market averages.

Quantitative methods are presented at a level which should be accessible to most analysts. In order to enhance the usefulness of these sections, fairly comprehensive tables of the more widely used compound interest functions have been provided.

Considerable space has been given to Portfolio Management and Theories. The field of capital market theory has experienced an explosive development in recent years. As with most new ideas, some of these developments (efficient markets, random walk, and others) have been the subject of considerable controversy. One point seems clear, however, it is not enough for analysts to evaluate a company, an industry and even future economic trends, as important as these matters may be. He must also attempt to determine whether the market has already discounted his prognostications; for what one analyst knows, so may others. In any case, a broad spectrum of views concerning portfolio management has also been provided, including a section which gives a very comprehensive and objective assessment of current opinions.

The second volume of the Handbook covers the analysis of specific industries. The material in this volume is intended to provide examples of how leading industry specialists proceed. A large selection of industries is represented. The coverage is not exhaustive since it is assumed that the reader has a good familiarity with security analysis: Each section emphasizes only the specific considerations relevant to the industry. Contributors have attempted to point out the economic, social, marketing, regulatory, taxation, accountancy, and other considerations of significance in each instance. The length of the sections varies and is not necessarily proportional to the economic significance of the industry. This is due, in part, to a contributor's style and emphasis, but it also reflects the nature of the industry. For example, somewhat more space is given to highly regulated industries with rather special accounting practices (banking, insurance, and utilities) than is given to the manufacturing industries.

Familiarity with key government and trade publications is a vital aspect of investment analysis. Several sections are devoted to information sources including one on site visits. A list of some of the more important trade publications relating to a variety of industries has been included. Such publications number in the thousands, and complete listings are available in the compendia referred to in the section on Information Sources.

Security analysis and the management of investments is surely one of the more exciting and, we hasten to add, precarious professions. Perhaps it may be likened to cardiac surgery; a vital and necessary business involving substantial survival risks. We hope that the information provided in these volumes will help the user reduce his risk and increase his returns—more we cannot wish fellow analysts.

December 1974   SUMNER N. LEVINE

Contributors

Peter L. Anker, C.F.A. First Vice President, Smith, Barney & Co., Incorporated, New York, New York.

James Balog Chairman of the Board, William D. Witter, Inc., New York, New York.

W. Scott Bauman, D.B.A., C.F.A. Executive Director, The Institute of Chartered Financial Analysts and The Darden Graduate School of Business Administration, University of Virginia, Charlottesville, Virginia.

Nathan Belfer, Ph.D., C.F.A. Vice President, Wood, Struthers & Winthrop, Inc., New York, New York.

Martin Benis, Ph.D., C.P.A. Baruch College, The City University of New York, New York, New York.

Peter L. Bernstein Peter L. Bernstein, Inc., New York, New York.

Robert P. Black, Ph.D. First Reserve Bank of Richmond, Richmond, Virginia.

Charles P. Bonini, Ph.D. Graduate School of Business, Stanford University, Stanford, California.

Clarence W. Brown Senior Investment Analyst, H. C. Wainwright & Co.. New York, New York.

Jerome H. Buff, C.F.A. First Vice President, Smith, Barney & Co., Incorporated, New York, New York.

Gordon L. Calvert, J.D. Vice President and General Counsel (Washington), The New York Stock Exchange, Washington, D.C.

Arthur K. Carlson Vice President, First National City Bank, New York, New York.

Glenelg P. Caterer, C.F.A.   Advisor to Corporate Information Committee, Financial Analysts Federation, New York, New York.

David C. Cates   President, David C. Cates & Co., Inc., New York, New York.

Abraham Charnes, Ph.D.   Center for Cybernetic Studies, University of Texas at Austin, Austin, Texas.

William E. Chatlos   Principal, Georgeson & Co., New York, New York.

George H. Cleaver   First Vice President, White, Wild & Co., Incorporated, New York, New York.

Stuart H. Clement, Jr., C.F.A.   Ernst & Company, Rye, New York.

Jerome B. Cohen, Ph.D.   Senior Editor, *Bankers Magazine,* and Emeritus Professor of Finance, Baruch College, The City University of New York, New York, New York.

William W. Cooper, Ph.D.   School of Urban and Public Affairs, Carnegie Mellon University, Pittsburgh, Pennsylvania.

Thomas J. Donnelly, C.F.A.   Vice President, Kuhn, Loeb & Co., New York, New York.

Edwin J. Elton, Ph.D.   Graduate School of Business Administration, New York University, New York, New York.

Herbert E. Goodfriend   Vice President—Research, Paine, Webber, Jackson & Curtis, Inc., New York, New York.

Eileen M. Gormley, C.F.A.   Vice President and Senior Institutional Analyst, Thomson & McKinnon Auchincloss Kohlmeyer, Inc., New York, New York.

Martin J. Gruber, Ph.D.   Graduate School of Business Administration, New York University, New York, New York.

Charles H. Hanneman, C.F.A.   Vice President, Argus Research Corporation, New York, New York.

David R. Hathaway   Vice President, Director of Technology Research, G. A. Saxton & Co., Inc., New York, New York.

Erich A. Helfert, D.B.A.   Assistant to the President, Crown Zellerbach, San Francisco, California.

Kenneth Hollister, C.F.A.   Vice President, Dean Witter & Co., Inc., New York, New York.

Arvid F. Jouppi   Senior Vice President, Delafield Childs, Inc., New York, New York.

Robert A. Kavesh, Ph.D.   Graduate School of Business Administration, New York University, New York, New York.

Martin A. Keane, Ph.D.   Research Laboratories, General Motors Corporation, Warren, Michigan.

Saul B. Klaman, Ph.D.   Vice President and Chief Economist, National Association of Mutual Savings Banks, New York, New York.

Dennis A. Kraebel   Manager of Preferred Stock Trading, Donaldson, Lufkin & Jenrette, New York, New York.

Charles D. Kuehner, Ph.D., C.F.A.   Director—Security Analysis and Investor Relations, American Telephone & Telegraph Co., New York, New York.

Dennis H. Leibowitz   Partner, Coleman and Company, New York, New York.

Martin L. Leibowitz, Ph.D. Vice President and Director of Investment Systems, Salomon Brothers, New York, New York.

Sumner N. Levine, Ph.D. State University of New York, Stony Brook, New York.

A. Michael Lipper, C.F.A. Lipper Analytical Services, Inc., Westfield, New Jersey.

Herbert W. McNulty Senior Security Analyst, Hornblower & Weeks-Hemphill, Noyes, Inc., New York, New York.

Joseph A. Mauriello, Ph.D., C.P.A. Graduate School of Business Administration, New York University, New York, New York.

Rose Mayerson Security Analyst, Bear, Stearns & Co., New York, New York.

Sylvia Mechanic Business Librarian, Brooklyn Public Library, Brooklyn, New York.

Edmund A. Mennis, Ph.D., C.F.A. Senior Vice President and Chairman of the Investment Policy Committee, Security Pacific National Bank, Los Angeles, California.

Robert D. Milne, C.F.A. Partner, Boyd, Watterson & Co., Cleveland, Ohio.

Francis A. Mlynarczyk, Jr. Investment Officer, First National City Bank, New York, New York.

Franco Modigliani, Ph.D. Sloan School of Management, Massachusetts Institute of Technology, Cambridge, Massachusetts.

Geoffrey H. Moore, Ph.D. Vice President-Research, National Bureau of Economic Research, Inc., New York, and Senior Research Fellow, Hoover Institution, Stanford University, Stanford, California.

J. Kendrick Noble, Jr., C.F.A. Vice President, Auerbach, Pollack, and Richardson, Inc., New York, New York.

William C. Norby, C.F.A. Senior Vice President, Duff, Anderson & Clark, Inc., Chicago, Illinois.

Thomas L. Owen Vice President, National Securities and Research Corporation, New York, New York.

Jackson Phillips, Ph.D. Vice President and Director, Municipal Bonds Research Division, Moody's Investors Service, Inc., New York, New York.

Robert B. Platt, Ph.D. Economist, Delafield Childs, Inc., New York, New York.

Gerald A. Pogue, Ph.D. Baruch College, The City University of New York, New York, New York.

B. U. Ratchford, Ph.D. First Reserve Bank of Richmond, Richmond, Virginia.

Robert B. Ritter Institutional Research, L. F. Rothschild & Co., New York, New York.

Benjamin Rosen Director of Research, Coleman and Company, New York, New York.

Terry W. Rothermel, Ph.D. Arthur D. Little, Inc., Cambridge, Massachusetts.

Stanley M. Rubel President, S. M. Rubel and Company, The Vencap Fund, Chicago, Illinois.

Part II   Analysis by Industry Categories

ties. Summary. Exxon Corporation: A Case Study. Salient Factors of Investment Significance. Profile. Earnings and Prospects: *Cash Income. 1973 versus 1972. 1974 and 1975 Earnings.* Operations: *Exploration and Production. Refining. Marketing. Chemicals. Transportation. Other.* Financial: *Capital Expenditures. Dividends.*

The Industry: *Its Definition. Its Structure.* Factors Affecting Industry Performance: *Constraints on Growth. Price and Profit Determinants.* Costs and Economics: *Costs for the Supplier. Economics for the Customer. Legislation and Regulation.* Financial Considerations. Illustrative Case Study: New Ventures.

Introduction: *Historical Background. Common Factors.* Structure and Scope of the Industry: *Newspapers. Book Publishers. Magazines Education.* Factors Affecting Growth of Revenues and Price Structures of Various Market Segments: *The Impact of the Population Wave. Personal Consumption Expenditures. Federal Expenditures. State and Local Expenditures.* Business Expenditures: *Inflation and Controls. Pricing versus Costs. The Consumerism Movement. Social Changes. Alternative Media. Technology. Labor and the Unions. Seasonality.* Federal and State Regulation: *Copyright: National and International.* The Federal Trade Commission. Analysis of Cost Factors (Including Special Tax Considerations): *Newspapers. Book Publishers. Periodical Publishers. Educational Services.* Market Behavior of Securities. Illustrative Case Study: Prentice-Hall, Inc.: *Background.* Prentice-Hall (ASE-PTN).

Investor Sponsorship. Growth Pattern. Factors Affecting Growth. Recent Trends. Industry Characteristics. Regulatory Agency. Cost Structure. Outmoded Work Practice. Allocation of Operating Expenses. Other Operating Costs. Passenger Service Operations. Railroad Income Account. Trend of Industry Earnings. Quality of Reported Earnings. Nonrail Income. Railroad Industry Finances. Industry at Crossroads. Future Potential. Market Performance of Rail Stocks. Case Study: Union Pacific Corporation: *Summary and Recommendations. Railroad Operations. Oil and Gas Operations. Exploration and Production.*

How Are REITs Organized? *Trustees. Advisors. Declaration of Trust. Operating Capital.* The Market for REIT Shares. Regulation of REITs: *The SEC and Stock Exchanges. State Securities Commissioners. Frequent Public Offerings. Other Monitoring of REITs.* Types of Real Estate Investment Trusts. REITs: History and Recent Developments: *Early History. Recent Developments.* Types of Investments Undertaken by

Factors—Electric. General Factors—Natural Gas. General Factors—Telephone. New Pricing Techniques. Uses and Problems of Extrapolation. Analysis of Cost Factors: *Equipment. Size and Quality Problems. Fuel Conversions and Environmental Control. Capital Cost. Labor. Fuel. Depreciation. General Taxes. Income Taxes. Nonregulated Income. Senior Security Coverages.* Federal and State Regulation: *Rates. New Developments. Rate Making. Legislation.* Accounting Considerations: *Sources. Uniform System of Accounts. Balance Sheet. Income Account.* Market Behavior: *Bonds. Stocks.* Case Study: *Construction. Operating Expenses. Balance Sheet. Other Market Considerations.*

Part III   Information Sources

Sources of U.S. Governmental Technical and Trade Information. Summary of World Technical and Trade Literature. Sources of Foreign Investment and Business Information. Case Study. Computerized Services.

Information Sources—General Business and Economic Conditions: *Newspapers, Periodicals, etc. Books, Reports, Monographs, etc. Statistics.* 2 Information Sources: Industry Analysis. 3 Sources of Information: Company Analysis. Reference Sources.

VOLUME I   METHODS, THEORY, AND PORTFOLIO MANAGEMENT

Part I   Introduction

The Role of the Financial Analyst in the Investment Process: *The Financial Analyst. The Investment Process. Company and Industry Analysis. Portfolio Management. Ancillary Functions of the Financial Analyst.*

Introduction. Basic Characteristics of the Corporate Bond: *Issuer. Management. Analysis of the Security. Principal Amount (or Face Value). Coupon Rate. Maturity Date. Quality. Call and Refunding Features. Sinking-Fund Provisions.* Conventional Measures of Absolute and Relative Value: *Pricing of Corporate Bonds. The Yield Book. The Many Facets of Yield to Maturity. The Yield to Call.* Investment Analysis of Bonds: *The Future Value of a Bond Investment. The General Role of Time Valuation. Future Value per Opportunity Dollar. The Analysis of Principal Return. The Volatility Factor. Analysis of Yield Relationships. Analysis of Yield Changes. The Future Value Measure and Component Yield Changes. A Numerical Example: Future Value per Dollar. Other Investment Measures.* Bond Swaps and Their Evaluation: *Bond Swaps and Net Future Value per Dollar. Investment Implications of the Net Future Value per Dollar Expression. A Numerical Example of a Bond Swap.* Glossary of Symbols.

The Structure of a Convertible Security. The Convertible's Response Pattern. The Convertible as a Stock Substitute. The Conversion Premium. The Response Pattern of the Conversion Premium. The Premium over Investment Value. Key Convertible Levels in Terms of the Stock Price. The Current Yield Advantage. Break-Even Times for a Dollar-for-Dollar Swap. Break-Even Times for an Equity Maintenance (Pay-Up) Swap. Total Return over Time. The Threshold Common Level. Short-Term Opportunities. Other Approaches.

U.S. Government Debt. Federal Agency Obligations. The Government Securities Market. Comparative Yield Experience. Forecasting the Level of Interest Rates. The Term Structure of Interest Rates. International Money and Securities Markets.

Types of Bonds: *General Obligations. Revenue Bonds. Special Types.* General Form and Price Quotation. Regulation and Procedure in Sale: *Role of the SEC. Procedure in Sale by Issuer.* Tax Exemption. Analysis of Municipal Credit: *Ratings. Availability of Information. Factors in General Obligation Bonds. Factors in State Bonds. Factors in Revenue Bonds.* Appendix A. Appendix B. Appendix C: *Data Required by Standard & Poor's. Data Required for General Obligation Bond Rating. Data Required for Revenue Bond Analysis.*

Holders and Security Holdings of Management. Item 12. Directors of the Registrants. Item 13. Remuneration of Directors and Officers. Item 14. Options Granted to Management to Purchase Securities. Item 15. Interest of Management and Others in Certain Transactions.

Part V   Economic Analysis and Timing

Mean Deviation. The Standard Deviation. Relation between Measures and Dispersion. Characteristics of Measures of Probability Distributions: Basic Definitions. Rules of Dealing with Probabilities. Random Variables. The Binomial Distribution. The Poisson Distribution. The Normal Distribution. Multivariate Probability Distributions.

Economic Models for Financial Analysis. Using Regression Analysis to Study Other Relationships. Essentials of Regression Analysis. Goodness of Fit. Forecasting. Problems with Residuals. Multiple Regression. Summary. Appendix: *Simple Regression Calculations. Least Squares Method.*

Time Series Analysis—An Introduction. Time Series Models with Seasonal and Trend: Time Series Model with Trend. Adding a Seasonal. Illustration of Techniques: Exponential Smoothing Model with Additive Trend and Seasonal. Exponential Smoothing Model with Multiplicative Trend and Seasonal. Regression Models. The Parameterization of the Models. Evaluation of Forecasting Techniques: *Geometric Analysis. Numeric Evaluation.* The Accuracy of Time Series Forecasts—A Case Study.

The Financial Analyst, Financial Data, and Computers: Concept of Financial Data. Use of Financial Data. Use of Computers. Choosing a Computer-Use Philosophy. Examples of Computer and Financial Data Use: *Economic Forecasting. Security Analysis. Screening. Equity Valuation. Bond Valuation. Portfolio Policy Analysis. Security Analyst Evaluation. Portfolio Performance Measurement. Statistical Report Generation.* Economics of Computer Use. Organizing for Computer Use.

Part VII   Portfolio Management and Theories

General Characteristics of the Organizational Structure: Scope and Diversity of Functions. Structure of the Organization. Evaluation of the Investment Management System: *Philosophies of the Organization and the Senior Administration. Evaluation of Portfolio Management Plans. Investment Research System. Portfolio Management Process. Internal Interrelationship of the Professional Staff. Qualifications of the Portfolio Management Staff. Evaluation of Portfolio Performance.* The Institutional Characteristics of Different Categories of Investment Portfolio Accounts: *Individual/Family-Type Investors. Formal Retirement Funds. Insurance Companies. Foundations, Endowments, and Charitable Trusts.*

Economic Projections: *Economic Information Needed.* Derivation from Economic Projections: *Interest Rates. Profits and Stock Values. Industry Expectations.* Input from Security Analysis: *Industry Studies. Company Reports. Other Information from Research.* Inputs from Investment Policy: *Economic and Market Assumptions. Portfolio Objectives. Stocks to Be Analyzed. Portfolio Mix. Industry Diversification.* Function of the Portfolio Manager: *Account Objectives. Stock Selection. Executions. Performance Evaluation.* Traditional versus Academic Portfolio Theory.

Introduction. Requirements for an Efficient Market. Situation Prior to Emergence of the Efficient Market Concept: *Technical Analysis. Fundamental Analysis.* Three Forms of the Efficient Market-Random Walk Hypothesis: *The Weak Form. The Semistrong Form. The Strong Form.* The Weak Form of the Efficient Market-Random Walk Hypothesis: Survey of Evidence: *Kendall—Serial Correlation: The Next Move. Weintraub—Serial Correlation: The Next Move. Osborne—Brownian Motion. Granger and Morgenstern—Spectral Analysis. Fama—Serial Correlation: 1 to 10 Days Lag. Roberts—Random Numbers. Cheng and Deets—Rebalancing. Fama—Runs. Shiskin—Runs. Alexander—Filters. Cootner—Random Walk with Barriers. Levy—Relative Strength—200 Stocks. Jensen and Bennington—Relative Strength: All NYSE Stocks. Jen—Relative Strength: Long Term versus Short Term. Kruizenga and Boness—Options.* The Semistrong Form of the Efficient Market-Random Walk Hypothesis: Survey of Evidence: *Fama, Fisher, Jensen, and Roll—Splits. Ball and Brown: EPS Announcements. Niederhoffer and Regan—News Reporting Lag. Zeikel—Adjusting to New Information. Scholes: Secondary Distributions. Kraus and Stoll—Block Trades.* The Strong Form of the Efficient Market-Random Walk Hypothesis; Survey of Evidence: *Miller—Low P/E Portfolios versus High. Breen—Low P/E Portfolios versus High. Diefenback—Research Advice versus Performance. Niederhoffer and Regan—EPS Forecasts versus Market Price Changes. Friend, Blume, and Crockett—Mutual Funds versus Random Portfolios. Black—Value Line Rankings versus Performance. Kaplan and Weil—Beta Versus Value Line Performance. Wallick—Stock Price Gyrations versus Intrinsic Values. Morton—Relationship between Risk and Investor Returns. Edesess—Beta versus Portfolio Performance. Fouse—Integrating Fundamental Security Analysis with Efficient Market Theory.* Implications, Challenge, and Conclusion. *Implications. Challenge to Security Analysis. Malkiel—A Middle Road. Molodovsky—Needed: A Good Idea.*

1. Introduction. 2. Investment Return: *Single-Interval Portfolio Return. The Arithmetic Average Return. The Time-Weighted Rate of Return.*

The Dollar-Weighted Return. 3. Portfolio Risk. 4. Diversification. 5. The Risk of Individual Securities. 6. The Relationship between Expected Return and Risk: The Capital Asset Pricing Model. 7. Measurement of Security and Portfolio Beta Values. 8. Tests of the Capital Asset Pricing Model: *Other Measures of Risk. Empirical Tests of the Capital Asset Pricing Model. Results for Tests Based on Securities. Results for Tests Based on Portfolio Returns. Summary of Test Results.* 9. Measurement of Investment Performance: *Performance Measures from the Capital Asset Pricing Model. Problems with the Market Line Standard.*

Primal Dual Relations. Linear Programming Formulations of Capital Budgeting Problems. Portfolio Selection. Chance and Other Risk Constraints via Chance Constrained Programming.

Is There a Difference between Personal and Institutional Portfolio Management? Defining Investment Objectives. How Should Risk Be Considered? Hedging against Risk. A Case Study. Tax Considerations. Professional Considerations. Appendix—Quantitative Aspects.

PART I

Introduction

1

Overview of Financial Analysis

WILLIAM C. NORBY, C.F.A.
Senior Vice President
Duff, Anderson & Clark, Inc.
Chicago, Illinois

THE ROLE OF THE FINANCIAL ANALYST IN THE INVESTMENT PROCESS

FINANCIAL ANALYSIS is an exciting occupation. Its subject matter encompasses not only business and finance but also science, government, and society around the world. Its perspective is both broad and deep. It is future oriented. It has a strong influence on the direction of capital investment and hence on the shape of business and industry. It employs a wide diversity of analytical techniques including economics, mathematics, accounting, and psychology. No wonder financial analysis holds such fascination for so many able people.

The Financial Analyst

The term *financial analyst* has broad usage throughout business and government to identify anyone who analyzes financial data for internal or external purposes such as capital expenditure programs, current operating budgets, or long-term financial plans. This book is concerned with financial analysis *as related to security investments*. In this context it is synonymous with *security analyst* or *investment analyst*—that is, one who analyzes securities and makes recommendations thereon.

Even within the field of investment, financial analysis is sometimes used to describe the entire field of investment management but at other times is confined to the narrower function of company and industry

3

analysis. Continuing the definition then, this book uses the term financial analysis *as comprehending the entire function of securities investment management,* including both analysis of companies and industries and the management of investment portfolios.

A financial analyst thus is one who: (1) analyzes companies and industries and makes recommendations thereon, or (2) as a principal or advisor selects securities for purchase or sale in an investment portfolio to achieve the objectives of the fund, or (3) manages all or part of the organization responsible for those functions.

These functions have been a part of the investment process since the beginning, but they have become increasingly specialized and institutionalized in the postwar period coincident with the expansion of savings intermediaries, increased capital investment in a growing economy, and a rising confidence in common stocks as a medium of investment. These developments stimulated a rapid growth in the emerging profession of financial analysis. Today the typical profile of the financial analyst is that of a relatively young and well-educated man who has moved up in his organization fairly quickly. His mean age is 41 years but 36 percent are under 35. A high educational attainment is indicated by the fact that over 90 percent have college degrees and half have one or more graduate degrees. The average experience in investments is almost 13 years. More than 40 percent of financial analysts have attained a high organizational level—either vice president or above in the corporate sector, or partner in the noncorporate sector. Women have been attracted to the field in recent years, but as yet they number only 5 percent of the total.[1]

The Investment Process

The investment decision process may be thought of as a three-legged stool. One leg is the analysis of the company and its securities and of the industry in which it operates. The second is the assessment of the economic environment which includes the business outlook, financial markets and interest rates, and international trade and finance. The third is the portfolio decision in which these two streams of information are integrated into an investment appraisal related to the objectives of the fund. Portfolio decisions sort out expected rates of return (income and appreciation) relative to risk as the portfolio manager seeks that combination of securities which will produce the highest total return available within the risk constraints established for the fund. In this continual

---

[1] William C. Norby, *Compensation in Professional Investment Research and Management* (New York: The Financial Analysts Federation, 1972), p. 8. This study was based on a survey of members of the Financial Analysts Federation in October 1971. The federation's membership (13,500 at the time of the survey; about 14,000 at the beginning of 1974) is considered to encompass substantially all financial analysts in the United States and Canada.

winnowing process, investment funds tend to flow toward the most favorably situated companies and industries and away from the weaker and less promising areas. Economic theory tells us that this free market direction of investment capital leads to the most efficient employment of scarce economic resources.

The financial analyst plays a key role in this capital allocation process. As a security analyst he studies and selects industries and companies, interacting with the economist who provides the general economic framework. As a portfolio manager he integrates the work of the economist on the outlook for business and the financial markets with the securities recommendations of the analyst to make portfolio selections. These roles are interdependent; each contributes a necessary element to the investment decision.

Company and Industry Analysis

Subsequent chapters in this book will examine in detail the methodology of analyzing companies and their securities. It is useful here, where we are broadly defining the functions of the financial analyst, to put that methodology in broad perspective. The primary objective of any security analysis is the determination of future earning power because earning power is the source of cash flow to the investor (interest or dividends). Capitalized earning power is the primary basis of wealth. In the long run, the quality of any security rests on earning power and so the essentials of analysis are the same for all types of securities although the areas of emphasis may differ. Investment analysis concentrates largely on common stocks to which the residual earnings accrue and therefore where change and risk are greatest.

The methodology of investment analysis is directed to identifying change and change in the rate of change in the earning power and financial position of a company. A typical analysis begins with a review of the company's history, products, markets, operations, earnings, and financial position. Data for the firm are then related to information about the industry in which it operates, to its competitors within that industry, and to the general economy in order to determine the dynamic relationships between the firm and its environment. Analysis of the individual firm must also encompass management and its decision-making philosophy, marketing capabilities, production facilities, and changes in all of these elements as they have occurred over time.

The many elements of an investment analysis must be summarized and expressed in quantitative terms. Investors generally consider net earnings as the best measure of a company's performance and the indicator of value in most continuing enterprises. The quality of earnings is tested by the concepts of normality (i.e., what a company might earn under normal economic conditions absent strikes, floods, wars, and the like); extraordinary earnings from special nonrecurring events in the company; the trend over a 5- or 10-year period or a succession of business cycles; and stability or variability from year to year around the trend line.

All these facets of earnings add up to the concept of *earning power* which may be defined as the ability of the company to produce continuing earnings from the operating assets of the business over a period of years. It encompasses the foregoing concepts of normality, stability, and growth. It is not fixed but will change with changes in management, the life cycle of industries, and other long-term factors. Investors are constantly on the alert to catch incipient shifts in the direction of earning power, and consequently, even small variations in earnings, depending upon their cause, can have a magnified impact on investor expectations.

This historical record is the basis for an evaluation of management's ability to plan and to take advantage of economic opportunity or defend against economic adversity. It also is the basis for the analyst's estimate of earning power over future periods—one, three, and perhaps five years. The estimating process moves from the general to the particular, starting with the outlook for the economy and the industry. Detailed analysis of new markets, new capital investment, new technology, regulatory changes, price trends, and many other factors follows. Their impact on the company is measured through the financial statements. The analytical conclusion usually is cast in the form of a forecast of earnings, dividends, and financial requirements for the period ahead. In a dynamic economy, the margin of error in such forecasts is bound to be considerable, but nevertheless, investors base their decisions on expectations of the future.

This kind of future-oriented information is not readily available to the analyst in convenient brochures or corporate plans. Much of it must be pieced together from various sources, making inferences based on past experience. Projective information is subject to considerable error and must be checked against other information. Thus the task of the analyst is difficult and strenuous. Ingenuity is required to collect and organize all of this data. Yet these analytical procedures must be repeated many times since the investor is faced with continually shifting investment alternatives. Investment analysis is comparative between companies in the same industry, between different industries, and over time.

Portfolio Management

The methodology of portfolio management lagged behind economic and security analysis as a discipline but in recent years has developed rapidly. If all the portfolio manager had to do was select the companies with the most optimistic earnings projections, his task would be relatively easy. In fact, it is far more complex.

First, he must indeed weigh the evaluations and projections of several security analysts to develop an array of estimated future returns and attendant risks. Individual security analysts are skilled in regard to companies and industries they follow, while the portfolio manager (or perhaps the research director) must integrate these segments into a comparative list of all securities followed.

Second, the portfolio manager must temper the collective outlook for individual companies with macroeconomic factors provided by the economist. This is especially important at turning points in the economic cycle, since impending change is usually perceived in macro factors before it appears in individual companies. Hopefully, the security analyst has also been able to sense economic change and apply it to his estimates, but the portfolio manager (or the chief investment executive in large organizations) must insure that this integration is complete.

Third, the portfolio manager must consider financial markets. There is no simple sequence of earnings changes and market price changes. Various security instruments compete with each other for investment funds—bonds versus stocks, short-term notes versus long-term bonds, or bonds versus mortgages. To some degree, the price of each security is affected by supply and demand within its sector of the market, but the sectors are interconnected so that developments in one sector affect all others. Therefore the portfolio manager must take into account all developments in the financial markets, such as the structure of interest rates, monetary policy, and the volume of new offerings of stocks and bonds.

The portfolio manager may sometimes avail himself of so-called technical analysis. Technical analysis attempts to infer the supply and demand conditions for a stock or for the market as a whole from the pattern of price movements, trading volume, short position, and the like. This is thought to be a more direct approach to predicting price than analysis of the underlying economic and investment factors, but numerous statistical studies indicate that technical analysis does not produce results significantly different from chance. Technical analysis is not usually considered a part of the discipline of investment analysis and management, but because of the widespread interest in the subject, it is discussed in a later chapter in this handbook.

Finally, all of these investment and economic factors must be related to the objectives of the fund and the amount of risk it can accept. The manager selects from the broad array of investment opportunities those securities that are expected to provide the best relative returns (income and appreciation) within the risk constraints, i.e., the acceptable degree of uncertainty of the returns. The decision might be a combination of treasury bills and commercial paper for low return and low risk at one end of the spectrum or common stocks of a diversified list of small, fast growing, high-technology companies for high potential return and high risk at the opposite end of the spectrum. And since these factors are constantly changing, the portfolio manager must monitor the financial markets and investment opportunities to continually optimize portfolio return and risk.

Ancillary Functions of the Financial Analyst

From the foregoing brief sketch we can readily see that the financial analyst—either the security analyst or the portfolio manager—engages in a rigorous and demanding intellectual endeavor in his primary function of allocating investment funds. In the process he serves other important functions tangential to portfolio management.

The security analyst is frequently a reporter and interpreter of corporate financial information to a wider investing public. This is particularly true of analysts with brokerage firms, since their reports are publicly distributed. The security analyst reports on a current basis factual and interpretive corporate information which is frequently more understandable than the company's own reports. Although the analyst's primary responsibility is to his clients rather than to a more general investing public, his reports must be prepared with the same standard for accuracy and completeness of the facts and objectivity of his interpretation that is required for general publication.

The experienced financial analyst has a breadth and depth of comparative knowledge of company finance and financial markets which can make him an especially valuable advisor to corporations on mergers and acquisitions, capital structures, new financing, and valuations. Such work may be performed on a professional fee basis or as a supplementary service to important clients of the firm.

Similarly, experienced investment managers may be retained to consult with large investors on the organization structure for management of their funds, or on the criteria for determination of investment objectives, or on the measurement of investment results. These subjects are appropriate aspects of the broad function of investment management. Both financial analysts and econometricians have contributed to the newly developing disciplines supporting these subjects.

Is Financial Analysis a Professional Discipline?

The complexities of investment decision making as suggested in this brief summary confirm the status of present-day investment research and management as a professional discipline. Yet when we observe the ups and downs of the stock market or the seeming perverse responses of stock prices to company developments, we might well ask whether the net impact of all of this analytical effort on the stock market is any greater than almost 50 years ago, when investment analysis first gained identity as a specialized activity.

In the final analysis, prices of securities, especially common stocks, attempt to discount expected future returns. The future is unknowable, and we can only speculate on the outcome of events based on the best information available. While we attempt to apply rigorous discipline to this speculation, human emotions also play a role in market trends. The two emotions which tend to dominate investors are greed and fear— among the most powerful known to man. As a result of these psychological elements, market prices show wide dispersion around the trend line of value. There would seem to be room for another intellectual discipline in the panoply of investment management, namely the psychology of markets, for we find ever present in financial markets the twin strands of "logical" investment analysis and "illogical" investor emotions.

These twin strands are reflected in the following summary of views of business executives as issuers of corporate reports:

> While security analysts in particular were regarded as the focal point of the financial community audience, their rights to financial information were viewed in sharply differing ways. They were portrayed on the one hand as public servants interpreting business performance for the layman, and on the other as incompetent and ruthless profiteers seeking only to "find a reason to trade." Despite this divergence, managements, on balance, regarded the power of this audience as significant and failure to recognize its needs was seen as shortsighted.[2]

Clearly the profession of financial analysis must aim to further expand and deepen its discipline in the public interest and to submerge illogical emotions and "incompetent and ruthless profiteers."

CAREER PATHS OF FINANCIAL ANALYSTS

The career opportunities open to the financial analyst can be best understood in the context of the institutional structure of investment management. Professional financial analysis occurs almost entirely in an institutional setting. After giving an overview of the institutional framework, the specialized facets of investment research and portfolio management will be described in detail. Finally compensation will be sum-

---

[2] Booz Allen & Hamilton, *The Businessman's View of the Purposes of Financial Reporting* (New York: Financial Executives Research Foundation, 1973), p. 13.

marized. This section is based largely on two studies of the Financial Analysts Federation.[3]

Overview of Institutional Structure of Investment Management

While investment research of some sort has always been an aspect of investment management, the first professional organization did not appear until 1925, when the Investment Analysts Society of Chicago was organized. However, research did not begin to achieve independent stature until the advent of increased corporate disclosure stemming from the Securities Acts of 1933 and 1934, and rapid growth did not begin until after World War II.

Development of investment research has proceeded in tandem at both institutional investors and broker-dealers during the postwar period. The larger investing institutions, such as banks, mutual funds, and advisory firms, were the first to go beyond published reports to visit company managements and do other field work, and to practice industry specialization. Prior to the early 1950 brokerage research was generally limited to elementary statistical comparisons and answering questions; the primary sources were the financial services and an occasional call to company management. Research was neither intensive nor continuous. Specialization by industry was rare, being practiced only by a few investment houses largely, but not entirely, retail oriented.

Starting in the mid-1950s specialized institutional brokerage firms started to appear. These firms covered industries intensively and on a continuing basis and aimed largely at institutional markets. By the early 1960s the universe of brokerage houses doing intensive continuing research had expanded substantially.

Concurrently the research staffs of major investing institutions continued to grow, and more institutions moved into the major size category. The growth in staff was not commensurate with the growth in assets and rising standards of investment performance, however, and so increasing use was made of the greatly expanded institutional research services of broker-dealer firms. The larger institutions utilized broker research to supplement field work by their in-house staffs and also to originate new investment ideas. The expansion of assets, coupled with some increase in turnover, provided ample commission dollars to pay for this research and created incentives for rapid expansion of broker-dealer research.

As institutionalized savings spread more widely through the economy and the acceptability of common stocks continued to grow, many new and smaller investing institutions entered the investment management field. They were able to meet their requirements for basic investment re-

---

[3] Walter P. Stern and William C. Norby, "Investment Research and Market Structure—Today and Tomorrow," *Financial Analysts Journal*, January–February 1972; and Norby, *Compensation in Professional Investment Research*.

search through the services of broker-dealers. Typically the staffs of such organizations consisted of one to a few analysts to digest and check outside research reports, and several portfolio managers. Commission dollars generated by funds under their management were sufficient to acquire the necessary research services from brokers and thereby keep internal overhead costs low.

The "performance era" of 1967–69 lowered research discipline substantially on the part of both brokers and institutions. Many smaller securities houses entered the institutional business by covering new industries, "concept stocks," and a variety of other investment vehicles which grew up in this speculative period. This was facilitated by the great increase in "soft" dollars available as institutional turnover increased rapidly and the spreading use of the "give-up."

As the search for new common stocks spread to smaller companies, some strong regional broker firms perceived an opportunity to provide specialized research of institutional caliber on companies in their region. This service enabled them to develop commission business with institutional investors outside of their region.

The market decline of 1969–70 brought about some change in attitudes of institutional investors. The shake out of performance stocks led them to rely somewhat more on their internal sources, and many institutional investors increased their analytical staffs between 1970 and 1973. Nonetheless they continued to utilize broker research because the commission dollars available were ample. In 1970 there was much shifting of research personnel in the broker-dealer community and probably a net reduction in number, but in 1971, some rebuilding of broker research staffs occurred.

The 1973 market decline and the ensuing financial crisis in the brokerage industry has brought further changes. The consolidation of brokerage firms and the drive to reduce overhead costs have reduced the size and number of research staffs in the brokerage industry. Institutional quality research has been maintained reasonably well, but regional and small company research has been sharply curtailed due to evident lack of investor interest. Research for retail clients has also been curtailed.

To some extent these recent developments are typical of the highly volatile brokerage industry, but they portend a longer run shift in the structure of investment research which cannot yet be fully evaluated.

The market pattern of 1970–73 has also produced shifts in the structure of investment management. Bank trust departments, by far the largest sector of funds under management, regained stature during this period as their investment results were generally more favorable than other types. This reflects their tendency to concentrate on the large capitalization growth companies which performed well in the market, and their efforts to modernize their investment management organizations. Mutual funds as a group experienced continuous net redemptions as their investment results suffered in comparison with market averages. The new small institutional advisory firms seem to have survived for the most part, but the rate of new entrants has dropped. In any case, the size of funds under institutional management today is so large that structural change comes slowly.

Employment and Compensation Profile of Analysts

The overall structure of institutional investment can be described in terms of the membership of the Financial Analysts Federation. The aforementioned survey in late 1971 showed the following:

One third of all members work for broker-dealers and 62 percent for institutional investors such as banks (25 percent), investment counselors, insurance companies, mutual funds, and others.

By function, 43 percent are engaged in research and analysis; 25 percent, in portfolio managment; and 11 percent have executive responsibility for the investment function. The balance are salesmen, economists, and academicians.

About half of all research members are employed by broker-dealers. Research is heavily concentrated in New York, which accounts for 49 percent of all research members.

Portfolio management members are more dispersed. Only 19 percent of portfolio management members work in New York, while about 26 percent are in Boston, Chicago, San Francisco, and Philadelphia. Trust investment accounts for 38 percent of such members, other institutional investors together total 48 percent, while brokers employ only 8 percent.

This profile has probably changed marginally in the last two years but is still broadly representative.

In terms of career paths, the normal progression is from entry as an investment analyst up through research to supervisory responsibilities and director of research. Some analysts may develop substantial seniority

TABLE 1

Age, Experience, and Function (mean years)*

	Age	Experience
Analyst	36.3	9.2
Supervising analyst	39.3	12.8
Director of research	41.8	15.2
Portfolio manager	39.5	12.2
Supervisor portfolio management	41.4	14.7
Director portfolio management	45.1	18.3
Chief investment executive	45.5	17.9

* Norby, *Compensation in Professional Investment Research* as specialists without supervisory responsibilities. Lateral moves may be made from research to portfolio management and then by normal progression to director of portfolio management. Progression is often fairly rapid, and beyond the entry level positions there is not much difference in age or experience in the managerial positions. (See Table 1.)

Structure of Investment Research

Investment research is a fixed cost function and therefore tends to be concentrated in larger institutions and firms. Most large research departments are located in the major financial centers. Almost half of research is performed by brokers whose product is distributed over a more widely dispersed portfolio management function. Brokers are compensated largely by commissions. This arrangement enables institutions to gear their investment management costs more directly to the volume of funds under management and to reduce fixed research costs. This structure of investment research may change if the brokerage industry continues under economic pressure or when fixed minimum commissions are abolished.[4]

Broker investment research covers a broad range of activities designed to provide the investor or portfolio manager with information and ideas for investment decision making. There are probably some 10 to 20 firms which consider themselves "broad service" institutional firms; some 40–50 more specialized firms including regional firms and small firms covering a few industries intensively; and an additional 10 to 20 largely retail houses with a small institutional group.[5]

Many other brokerage firms offer so-called retail research. This is less intensive research drawn largely from secondary sources such as other brokers' reports and statistical services, but supplemented with an occasional company check.

Among institutional investors, many large banks, a few of the large advisory firms and mutual funds, and some of the insurance companies maintain large research staffs although there is somewhat less emphasis on original field work or company contact and more on evaluating the flow of investment information from outside sources. A number of large banks have begun to offer their investment research materials to other institutions for a fee either in cash or deposit balances.

The research staffs of medium and smaller institutional investors rely largely on outside sources for information and confine their efforts to assimilation and evaluation. They will do occasional original research on special situations or important concentrations.

---

[4] Chairman Garrett of the SEC announced the present intention of the SEC to end fixed commissions by April 1975. *Wall Street Journal,* October 4, 1973.

[5] Data as of late 1971. The numbers had declined somewhat by mid-1974.

Most research departments of any size are organized by industry specialties, and many analysts are classified as specialists in one or more industries. It is probable that each major industry grouping has some three to six key analysts, well known in the field, at leading brokers and perhaps one or two at leading institutions. There may be another 20 to 30 industry specialists spread around various brokerage firms and a number of larger institutions. Other analysts are generalists, applying standard research techniques to a variety of companies over a period of time.

No research staff is really large. In the largest institutions, with $4 to $12 billion of funds under management, the number of analysts doing specific industry and company work does not exceed 30 to 40. In organizations with $1 to $3 billion under management, these analysts will number 20 to 25. In medium-sized and smaller organizations, the typical number will be three to seven, and some may rely entirely on outside sources for company and industry information.

Research staffs in broker-dealer firms doing institutional research show a similar size range with the exception of one firm having a larger staff for both institutional and retail research. The SEC Institutional Investor Study showed that research expenses attributable to commission business for all NYSE member firms was only 1.4 percent of all commission expenses. However, the expense ratio for the median institutional firm was 3.3 percent (with some up to 10–15 percent) but only 1.0 percent for the retail firm.[6]

It is evident that broker institutional research now makes an important contribution to the investment management function of institutional investors. The research-for-commission-dollars system is embedded in their costs and operations, although reliance on it varies among institutions, primarily by size.

The intensive specialization of top industry analysts makes it economic for them to work in an organization serving more than one institution. Many institutional users of broker research regard the work of these specialists as excellent. Frequently they allocate commission dollars to these individual analysts rather than to the firm as such and often follow them as they move from one firm to another.

The largest banks, insurance companies, and investment counselors rely on broker research for 5 to 35 percent of their total research input (based on informed judgment since this is hard to quantify). They value broker research for the stimulus of new ideas and the work of particular industry specialists.

Medium-sized organizations of all types, with management responsibility for $250 million to $2 billion of investment funds, may rely on

---

[6] Securities and Exchange Commission, *Institutional Investor Study Report,* 1971, p. 2,265.

broker research for up to 75 percent of total research input. For the smallest organizations, the degree of reliance may be even higher. Most smaller organizations rate broker research a "significant addition."

Specialized research services available on a fee basis provide only a small fraction of research input—typically 5 to 10 percent. Today there are only two independent firms whose principal business is investment research on a cash fee basis. There are a few exceptions where fee services provide up to 50 percent of input with broker research the balance. There are a few isolated cases of cash fee—i.e., "hard dollar"—payments for broker research and also a few cases on nonbroker research for commissions through "soft dollar" conduits, i.e., brokers.

Will the structure of investment research change in the evolving structure of the brokerage industry due to economic pressure and competitive determination of commissions? The FAF study indicated that most broker-dealers would continue to provide present research services in order to maintain industry position. Research is an important marketing tool. Most large institutional investors, especially those acting as fiduciaries, have indicated that, given "best execution," they would continue to allocate business on the basis of research services. Some institutions such as endowment and pension funds and insurance companies might place some business at higher than pure transaction cost as compensation for research. Typically, these are organizations without a large internal staff which pay commissions out of their own resources. Thus there appears to be sufficient common ground in the present hopes or intentions of institutional investors and broker-dealers to warrant supposing that some broker research will continue to be a viable service and that investors will be willing to pay for it through the commission structure. But, until these considerations interact in the marketplace, no confident prediction can be made.

Should there be, contrary to expectation, a sharp curtailment of brokerage research, institutional investors have a combination of alternatives. These alternatives are: purchase of fee services either (1) from present institutional brokers or (2) from new research consulting groups which might be formed or (3) expansion of the internal research staff.

The financial feasibility of these alternatives varies largely by size of institution. Many large and medium-size institutions would have no problem in utilizing these alternatives, assuming that structural changes were phased in over a period of time. A good many smaller institutional investors of all types, which are now heavily dependent on the present broker-research-for-commissions system, might have some difficulty in moving to any of these alternatives, all of which require the displacement of variable costs with fixed costs, a change that is more burdensome for the smaller firm.

The financial analyst would be well advised to understand and follow these possible structural changes in investment research as they may affect his career development.

Structure of Portfolio Management

Most portfolio managers begin their investment careers in investment research and after several years of training move across to portfolio management. In banks and counseling firms where there are many client accounts to manage, the portfolio manager will have 10 to 50 accounts assigned to him depending on their size and complexity. He will have relatively little discretion to deviate from institutional policy. In due course he may supervise several portfolio managers and finally, in large organizations, may become the director of portfolio management or chief investment executive. In these positions, he will be concerned largely with development of policy rather than actual management of accounts.

In such institutional investors as insurance companies there are only one or a few accounts to manage, and portfolio managers will tend to be both policy makers and managers. There will be little of the hierarchal organization necessary to administer a multiplicity of accounts. Consequently over 60 percent of portfolio managers are employed by banks and counseling firms. Brokers also provide portfolio management services and employ over 8 percent of portfolio managers.

Only 19 percent of portfolio managers are located in New York, in contrast to 49 percent of investment analysts. Other concentrations of portfolio managers occur in Boston and Chicago, but otherwise they are more widely dispersed, reflecting the decentralization of investment funds throughout the country.

Compensation

The best information available on compensation in investment research and management is the Financial Analysts Federation (FAF) survey of October 1971. General trends in compensation since then make the actual figures obsolete, but the compensation *structure* can be assumed to be still indicative. The comparative data may be useful to financial analysts in their career planning.

Investment research and management is a highly compensated professional activity. The median salary in 1971 was almost $27,000. Close to one fourth made $40,000 or more and about 15 percent received $50,-000 and above. The range was great—from under $10,000 to over $100,000.

There is a wide diversity in compensation by type of employer, functional responsibility, and geographic location. Such factors as age, experience, and education are also present, as in any similar professional group. By type of business, brokerage-investment banking is the most remunerative and trust investment the least, with a spread in median salaries from $33,660 for brokers to $19,700 for bank trust departments. Geographically, New York shows the highest median compensation, but Boston and Chicago also rank relatively high. Investment research and portfolio management are approximately equal at the first two levels, but research is more highly compensated at the director level. Directors of research and New York Stock Exchange supervising analysts show the highest compensation in the entire field with medians of $43,000 and third quartiles of $65,000.

Compensation normally tends to rise with experience and investment management is no exception. Most of the rise takes place in the first 15 years, after which there is a further slight gain and then a leveling off.

PROFESSIONAL ORGANIZATION AND DEVELOPMENT

Individuals engaged in a common pursuit usually find it worthwhile to band together for mutual advantage in the performance of their work and to enhance their status as an occupational group. Financial analysts are no exception. Much thought and organization effort has been invested in establishing financial analysts as a professional body with a public identity.

The analyst interested in his own advancement and concerned for the public recognition of his occupation will find it worthwhile to participate in the activities of the professional organization, which for financal analysis and investment management is the Financial Analysts Federation and its constituent bodies. Since substantially all eligible analysts and most portfolio managers are members, the new analyst entering the profession should be familiar with its structure and activities and how they relate to professionalism.

The Attributes of a Profession

The first attribute of a profession is a common body of knowledge that has an intellectual content which can be mastered only after a period of study. We often use the term "profession" loosely to refer to baseball players, or politicians, or lawyers, or investment managers. Sometimes the term simply means that one is doing something on a full-time basis for pay rather than on a part-time, amateur basis. Sometimes it means that the person excels at the activity and at the same time is knowledgeable as to its structure and techniques.

In regard to investment management or financial analysis, we should use profession in the strict sense as a subject of some difficulty requiring training and study to master. It is often argued that investment management is an art and not a science and that one can be successful without any particular training simply because he has a certain shrewdness or insight. Fortuitous events do play an important role in investment success but certainly one should not hold himself out to serve the public on this basis. And when we speak of something as "art," we usually overlook the fact that the artist has indeed gone through a long period of training and study and has mastered the basic techniques of his art before he undertakes his own self-expression. It is somewhat the same in investment management.

The second attribute of a profession is qualification for entry to practice before the public. The legal qualifications for financial analysis-investment management have been minimal and not subject oriented, in contrast to law, accounting, or medicine for example. Supervising research analysts of New York Stock Exchange member firms are required to be qualified as such and investment advisers must register with the Securities and Exchange Commission. Otherwise anyone can hold himself out to be a financial analyst.

Qualification for entry presumes mastery of the body of knowledge. An individual can give evidence of his mastery of the body of knowledge in various ways. One is through an examination program. However, an examination program by itself is not sufficient in the investment field. Practical experience in research or portfolio management is also desirable to assure thorough training, for not all investment knowledge can be reduced to book learning and examination.

The third important attribute of a profession is a code of ethics and professional conduct which the members understand and apply in the daily conduct of their affairs. As members of a professional group they hold themselves out to the public to follow that code and to be subject to professional discipline for infractions.

A fourth attribute of a profession is service to society above monetary gain; a belief or a goal beyond making a living. In law we think of justice; in medicine, life and health. In investment management and financial analysis, the public service element is more difficult to define since the apparent objective is an increase in personal or institutional wealth. It can be argued that professional financial analysis improves the efficiency of the capital allocation function in the economy by enhancing the quality of judgments which direct savings flows. This is a worthy but abstract goal and it must be conceded that the investment process of necessity will always have an element of speculative gain which seems antithetical to service.

The fifth attribute is public recognition. The public must know about, understand, and respect the profession and the members must live up to the image of the profession. Financial analysis has gained much public recognition in the last 25 years but not yet to the same extent as, say, law or accounting.

Not all of these rigorous requirements for true professional status have been met but in early 1974, after active debate, financial analysts adopted significant measures in furtherance of that objective. These will be explained in the context of the Financial Analysts Federation. Whether the ultimate goal can be attained will be known only in the future but in a larger sense the striving for professional status may be just as important as its achievement. It is in striving for larger goals that we make progress by setting a tone, raising standards, enhancing competance, and expanding knowledge.

The Financial Analysts Federation

The Financial Analysts Federation is an organization of member societies located in 46 cities in the United States and Canada. The Federation is governed by a board of directors and officers elected by delegates appointed by the societies. An analyst can become a regular member in a society if he is engaged in investment research, portfolio management, or certain ancillary functions, and has completed three years experience in these qualifying activities. Some societies admit provisional or junior members upon completion of two years work as an analyst.

There are many important activities that comprise a professional organization—information and service, education, enlargement of the relevant body of knowledge, and promotion of the public interest. Specific activities of the FAF and its constituent societies provide examples of these professional endeavors.

Information and Service. The society meetings and periodic FAF conferences are the principal public forums at which corporate executives report to investors on their progress. Other meetings provide information on industries, or special topics such as the "energy crisis," or new techniques of portfolio management. Over the course of a year these programs provide a vast flow of information to professional investors.

Education. Continuing education is an obligation of every professional because new techniques of analysis and management are constantly appearing. Of course, the nature of the work itself and of many information programs is educational in a sense. Formal programs available to members include an annual seminar in association with the University of Chicago Graduate School of Business, a Canadian seminar in association with the University of Western Ontario, and a workshop for portfolio managers at Harvard Graduate School of Business Administration.

Body of Knowledge. Much of the research and thought is done by individual practitioners and by academicians. Up to this time the Federation has not sponsored major research projects. However its *Financial Analysts Journal* is the leading professional journal in the field and every FAF member receives a subscription. Almost all of the ideas that have become permanent additions to the body of knowledge have appeared in the *Journal* at one time or another.

Promotion of the Public Interest. The public interest is not always easy to identify; inevitably there are many conflicts of interest and divided loyalties in business and finance. One area of the public interest on which investment analysts and managers can agree, regardless of their business affiliation, is full and fair disclosure of corporate information to the investor. This is the primary thrust of the legislation that established the Securities and Exchange Commission.

The efforts of the FAF and of individual analysts have contributed much to the improvement of corporate disclosure. The FAF Corporate Information Committee for many years has evaluated company reports and sought more and better quality information about important aspects of the company's business. Its Financial Accounting Policy Committee has recommended changes in accounting policies to the accounting profession to ensure more accurate measurement of corporate earnings.

Through FAF position papers, the views of financial analysts on corporate disclosure issues are presented to regulatory bodies. In 1973, for example, the Federation recommended to the SEC some guidelines on the definition and disclosure of inside information. This is a subject of great concern to individual analysts as well as to the investing public at large.

In these cases the real interests of professional investment managers and the public at large are the same. This fortunate curcumstance, if effectively articulated by analysts and their organization, can serve to enhance the stature of the profession and give members a greater voice in financial affairs. All benefit when analysts can give thought and consideration to broad questions and speak out with their views.

The FAF Plan for Professional Self-Regulation

In becoming a member of a constituent society, the analyst commits himself to know and follow the Code of Ethics and Standards of Professional Conduct adopted by the society and the Federation. These are reproduced in their entirety in Appendix A and every analyst should be familiar with them.

While analysts as a group have demonstrated exemplary conduct, there have been isolated failures to meet these standards. Enforcement has been the responsibility of the societies rather than the FAF and has been ineffective because it is difficult and burdensome. Consequently, during 1974, the FAF and its member societies actively debated alternative methods of strengthening enforcement proceedures. At its 1974 annual meeting, FAF Delegates adopted a plan for self-regulation of professional conduct on a national basis. The three key features of this plan are:

Enforcement of Standards. Means of effective enforcement of standards of practice and ethics are provided by:

a. a "dual membership" plan by which regular and junior members of electing societies become direct "fellows" and "juniors" of the FAF in addition to being members of the society, and

b. establishment of a national centralized Professional Conduct Committee which will investigate and adjudicate possible violations of standards of professional conduct by fellows and juniors.

Standards of Practice. The "Investment Analysis Standards Board" was established to review continuously the standards of practice and ethics of the profession. It supersedes and greatly expands the work of the Professional Ethics Committee.

Entry Standards. Commencing July 1, 1976, in order to become a regular member of a member society or a Fellow of the FAF, an applicant must have passed Chartered Financial Analysts Examination I. This means that applicants will be required to demonstrate certain minimum professional knowledge before being eligible for membership.[7]

This plan will give the Federation direct responsibility for those individual members who become fellows of the FAF and in due course, by a complex process, these should be substantially all regular members of societies. The staff and resources of the FAF will provide stronger support to the Professional Conduct Committee for disciplinary proceedings. Through the new Standards Board, there will be continuous development of standards of practice in financial analysis. Most important is the establishment of an examination for entry. Thus, the FAF plan marks substantial forward movement toward full public recognition of the profession. It is hoped that the designations of *FAF Fellow* and *Chartered Financial Analyst* will become well known and widely used marks of distinction in the field, and necessary for individual recognition.

Self-regulation has proven difficult in almost all professional fields. The FAF plan does not have the force of law and cannot prohibit an individual from practicing financial analysis—although not as a society member. If, however, public recognition of FAF Fellows and C.F.A.s makes these designations sine qua non for public practice, then society membership will become necessary for entry to the profession and self regulation could work. Should this expectation prove optimistic, then some form of government involvement might become necessary.

---

[7] From letter of E. H. Vaughn Jr., chairman, The Financial Analysts Federation, to the members dated May 15, 1974.

The Institute of Chartered Financial Analysts

After years of debate and discussion within the FAF on profession-alism and a professional designation, the Institute of Chartered Financial Analysts was established by the Federation in 1962. Its purpose was to develop an examination program leading to the award of the profes-sional designation of Chartered Financial Analyst or C.F.A. The first C.F.A.s were awarded in 1963 and ten years later over 3,200 analysts held this designation. Another 3,000 were registered in the study pro-gram.

The C.F.A. designation connotes high achievement in mastery of the body of knowledge of financial analysis and a commitment to high standards of professional conduct. It is not yet a requirement for public practice, as is a CPA certificate for example, but is a foundation for such legal sanction in the future.

The Institute is now an independent organization within the Financial Analysts Federation. Its principal functions are to administer the ex-amination program and maintain the ethical standards of C.F.A.s. It has a Code of Ethics and Standards of Professional Conduct similar to those of the FAF shown in Appendix A. It also publishes the *C.F.A. Digest*, a quarterly summary of important academic articles on aspects of financial analysis. All C.F.A.s become members of the Institute, and since they already are members of a society, there is a close identity of interest between the FAF and the Institute.

For the new financial analyst the examination program is the key aspect of the Institute of Chartered Financial Analysts. Three examina-tions, taken at intervals of at least a year, must be passed in order to receive the C.F.A. designation. In addition, the candidate must con-form to the Code of Ethics and Standards of Professional Conduct, must be engaged in a qualifying aspect of financial analysis as related to security investment, and (for Examinations II and III) must be a mem-ber in good standing of a constituent society. The examinations are given once each year in June and require about 5½ hours each.

Altogether these requirements probably are the most rigorous of any professional designation. They combine comprehensive examinations with a lengthy experience requirement in well-defined activities in financial analysis. The examinations are not easy; failure rates range between 25 percent and 35 percent on each examination. The experi-ence requirement is a practical minimum of five years, which is longer than any other similar professional qualification program and is one of the strengths of the C.F.A. program.

The occupational definitions are carefully applied to insure that the experience is in acceptable aspects of financial analysis and investment management. There are many closely allied activities in the investment business, such as sales or underwriting, which require some degree of analytical ability as well as other skills. However, none of these activities require a consistent application of the techniques of investment research and management, and it is for that reason that these individuals are not considered eligible for the C.F.A. program. There is no question that many of them, with an appropriate study program, might be able to pass the examinations. However, they would not have evidenced the complete commitment to the field of investment research and management or perhaps would not be committed to the C.F.A. ethical standards. Therefore it would not be fair then for them to hold themselves out as professional investment managers along with those who are fully qualified.

The C.F.A. Examinations[8]

The examination program is worth review by the new financial analyst seeking an outline of the fields of study. There are five basic areas: (1) accounting, (2) economics, (3) financial analysis, (4) portfolio management, and (5) ethical standards. Each area is covered in all three examinations, but initial emphasis in Examination I is on principles and techniques. Examination II places more emphasis on analytical use of these techniques; Examination III moves on to policy applications. A schematic outline of the subject matter of the examination program and information on the contents appears in Appendix B.

The Institute has prepared study guides, supplemental readings, and textbook references which together make up a graduate course of study in financial analysis. The serious student will find these materials valuable as he pursues his career in financial analysis.

Financial Analysts on an International Scale

We conclude this chapter with the observation that professional financial analysis and investment management has become worldwide in scope. This development came later abroad than it did in North America, but now analysts societies circle the globe. As capital markets become increasingly international in character, standards of financial analysis and corporate reporting must become more uniform from country to country if investment funds are to flow freely and confidently. The accounting profession has taken initial steps toward international standards, and this movement is bound to accelerate in the next five years.

Financial analysts are developing an organization structure which will enable them to move in the same direction. There is a European Federation of Financial Analysts Societies composed of societies in 10

---

[8] A sample set of C.F.A. examinations is given in Appendix C.

countries. There are active societies in Japan, Australia, and South Africa. A society has been formed in Brazil where there is a newly developing capital market. These analyst organizations are already cooperating on projects such as field trips, and an international congress of analysts' organizations is likely to develop within a few years in concert with the increase in international capital movements.

A financial analyst can take pride in the professional growth of his profession in the past 26 years, but still more exciting opportunities lie ahead!

APPENDIX A: Code of Ethics and Standards of Professional Conduct of the Financial Analysts Federation

CODE OF ETHICS

WHEREAS, the profession of financial analysis has evolved because of the increasing public need for competent, objective and trustworthy advice with regard to investments and financial management; and

WHEREAS, those engaged in this profession have joined together in an organization known as The Financial Analysts Federation; and

WHEREAS, despite a wide diversity of interest among analysts employed by banks, brokers and security dealers, investment advisory organizations, financial relations counselors, insurance companies, investment companies, investment trusts, pension trusts and other institutional investors and corporate bodies, there are nevertheless certain fundamental standards of conduct which should be common to all engaged in the profession of financial analysis and accepted and maintained by them; and

WHEREAS, the members of The Financial Analysts Federation adopted a Code of Ethics and Standards on May 20, 1962, and it is now deemed appropriate to make certain amendments to this Code.

Now, THEREFORE, the members of The Financial Analysts Federation hereby adopt on October 19, 1969, the following Code of Ethics, and Standards of Professional Conduct:

A financial analyst should conduct himself with integrity and dignity and encourage such conduct by others in the profession.

A financial analyst should act with competence and strive to maintain and improve his competence and that of others in the profession.

A financial analyst should use proper care and exercise independent professional judgment.

STANDARDS OF PROFESSIONAL CONDUCT

1. The financial analyst shall conduct himself and encourage the practice of financial analysis in a manner that shall reflect credit on himself and on the profession. The financial analyst shall have and maintain knowledge of and shall comply strictly with all federal, state and provincial laws as well as with all rules and regulations of any governmental agency governing his activities. The financial analyst also shall comply strictly with the rules and regulations of the stock exchanges and of the National Association of Securities Dealers if he, or his employer, is a member of these organizations.

2. The financial analyst shall ascertain that his employer is aware of the existence and content of the Code of Ethics and of these Standards of Professional Conduct.

3. The financial analyst shall conduct himself in such manner that transactions for his customers, clients, or employer have priority over personal transactions, that personal transactions do not operate adversely to their interests, and that he act with impartiality. Thus, if an analyst has decided to make a recommendation as to the purchase or sale of a security, he shall give his customers, clients, and employer adequate opportunity to act on such recommendation before acting on his own behalf.

4. The financial analyst shall, in addition to the requirements of disclosure required by law and rules and regulations of organizations governing his activities, when making recommendations, disclose to his customers, clients, and employer any material conflict of interest relating to him and any material beneficial ownership of the securities involved which could reasonably be expected to impair his ability to render unbiased and objective advice.

5. The financial analyst shall be objective in his opinions in advising his customers, clients, and employer, and when making a recommendation must have a basis which can be substantiated as reasonable. He must be accurate and complete when reporting facts.

6. The financial analyst shall inform his customers, clients, and employer of compensation arrangements in connection with his services to them which are in addition to compensation from his employer or from the customer or client for such services.

7. The financial analyst shall not pay any consideration to others for recommending his services unless such arrangement has been appropriately disclosed.

8. The financial analyst shall not undertake independent practice for compensation in competition with his employer unless he has received written consent from both his employer and the person for whom he undertakes independent employment.

9. The financial analyst shall not, in the preparation of material for distribution to customers, clients, or the general public, copy or use in substantially the same form material prepared by other persons without acknowledging its use and identifying the name of the author or publisher of such material.

APPENDIX B: The C.F.A. Candidate Study Program*

The Specific content of the C.F.A. study materials and examinations are subject to modifications in order to keep pace with changing emphases and techniques in financial analysis.*

Candidates who have been approved for a particular study program and who have paid the applicable enrollment fee will receive a Study Guide containing a detailed reading list prepared specifically for C.F.A. candidates.

---

* In Canada, examinations for C.F.A. candidates will recognize the differences in regulatory procedures.

Source: The Institute of Chartered Financial Analysts, *C.F.A. Study Programs, 1973–74,* pp. 6–9.

There is no additional charge to such candidates for this material. A limited number of copies is available for purchase by non-candidates.

While the Institute itself does not offer classroom-type courses of instruction, it does assist in the organization of local study groups in conjunction with the C.F.A. Educational Coordinators of local analyst societies and universities. Of special assistance to candidates are the Study Guides, textbooks, and books of readings published periodically by the Institute.

The C.F.A. is awarded to those candidates who have successfully completed the examinations and other requirements established by The Institute of Chartered Financial Analysts. The candidate must pass three examinations: Examination I—Investment Principles; Examination II—Applied Financial Analysis; and Examination III—Investment Management.

The Main objective of the C.F.A. Candidate Study Program and examination series is to assure the investing public, employers, and fellow analysts that a C.F.A. possesses at least the fundamental knowledge necessary to practice his profession. There are seven basic topical areas extending through the study series: Economics, Financial Accounting, Quantitative Techniques, Fixed Income Securities Analysis, Equity Securities Analysis, Portfolio Management, and Professional Standards. The C.F.A. study program necessarily continues to be of an evolutionary nature, reflecting as it does the changing emphasis and techniques of financial analysis and portfolio management in the dynamic economies of the United States and Canada. The logic and objectives of the program may best be illustrated by the following brief review of the seven main subject areas. More specific study guidance to candidates is provided in each of the three Study Guides published annually by the Institute.

The C.F.A. Competency Standards

Although the subject matter and skills needed by a C.F.A. continue to evolve the principal areas and topics to be mastered by C.F.A. candidates are suggested by the topic areas described below and listed in the *General Topical Outline*. The candidate level I study program is designed for the junior analyst, while the program at levels II and III is intended for analysts at progressively more advanced stages of professional development. Consequently, the candidate study program emphasizes the continuity of required subject matter over the three different levels as well as a progression to higher levels of sophistication involving more complex financial problems. In addition, at the progressively more advanced levels, the experienced candidate is expected to deal with an expanded number of topics.

Area One—Economics

Pre-Candidate Requirements. The candidate should be familiar with the basic principles of macroeconomics and the monetary system. The analyst should have minimum knowledge equivalent to one academic year of principles of economics as reflected in an elementary economics textbook. The examination, however, emphasizes practical application of economic concepts rather than abstract economic and monetary theories.

Candidate Level I. The candidate should be familiar with the tools of economic analysis and forecasting and have a perspective of the history of economic and industrial activity and of the structure of money and capital markets. Primary emphasis is placed on the relevance and application of economics to the practice of financial analysis as related to securities investment.

Candidate Level II. The candidate should be able to apply the basic economic techniques and concepts, studied under candidate level I, to an evaluation of the prospects for specific industries and companies. Emphasis is placed on forecasting broad economic forces and understanding their implications for forecasts of interest rates, aggregate corporate earnings, and equity prices.

Candidate Level III. At this level, the candidate should be able to interpret economic conditions, government policies and actions and their effects on growth, inflation, and employment. The analyst is expected to understand the implications of these policies and conditions and to relate them to the conduct of a penetrating analysis of aggregate corporate earnings, of earnings trends in specific industries and companies, of interest rates, and of security prices. This analysis should be used to formulate investment policy decisions.

Area Two—Financial Accounting

Pre-Candidate Requirements. The candidate should understand the basic principles of accounting equivalent to at least one year of college level accounting.

Candidate Level I. A candidate should be able to apply accounting principles and techniques to basic financial analysis. Emphasis is placed on skill in using published accounting data, including corporate financial statements and reports, in a meaningful analysis of the firm.

Candidate Level II. The candidate should have a sufficiently thorough understanding of financial accounting, including such complex areas of accounting as mergers, acquisitions, asset valuation, and pension plans, to interpret financial statements for use in the proper evaluation of companies and securities. Candidates are expected to be familiar with current opinions and decisions of the FASB, AICPA, and regulatory authorities.

Candidate Level III. In addition to the knowledge required at levels I and II, the candidate is expected to be able to relate accounting data to the investment decision-making process with emphasis on portfolio management.

Area Three—Quantitative Techniques

Pre-Candidate Requirements. It is assumed that the candidate has some knowledge of elementary statistics and basic mathematics.

Candidate Level I. The candidate should have a sufficient understanding of elementary statistics, mathematics of finance, and probability theory to be able to work with statistical data and apply a knowledge of statistical techniques to basic problems in finance and in financial analysis.

Candidate Level II. In addition to the knowledge at level I, a candidate is expected to be familiar with more advanced techniques such as hypothesis testing, and simple and multiple regression and correlation analysis, and to be able to apply these techniques to problems of financial projections, portfolio analysis, and security valuation and risk.

Candidate III. At this further advanced level, the candidate is expected to understand the application of more sophisticated statistical techniques and systems to problems in financial analysis, capital markets, and portfolio selection.

Area Four—Fixed-Income Securities

Pre-Candidate Requirements. The candidate is assumed to have the equivalent of at least two years of college exposure to business administration, including business finance, corporate financial analysis, and either money and banking or money and capital markets.

Candidate Level I. The candidate is expected to be able to analyze and understand the basic features and characteristics of various fixed-income securities, such as preferred stocks, corporate bonds, and national and local government bonds, including convertible securities. The analyst should be able to determine the basic investment quality and value of such securities in terms of yield and exposure to the risk of corporate illiquidity and insolvency. The candidate should understand the basic nature and cause of bond price fluctuations and the exposure of fixed income securities to interest rate risk and purchasing power risk.

Candidate Level II. At this level, the candidate should have an understanding of the financial and investment implications of all of the usual elements and characteristics commonly present in fixed income securities. The candidate is expected to be able to conduct a penetrating analysis of government and corporate issuers and of the major types of fixed income securities. In the selection of such securities, the analyst should understand the implications of the interest rate structure or yield spreads, and of the term structure of interest rates or yield curve. The candidate should be able to analyze bond swaps and problems of marketability.

Candidate Level III. In addition to the knowledge required at levels I and II, emphasis at this level is placed on the management of fixed income securities in a portfolio situation and their suitability to objectives and constraints of different investors under changing economic and market conditions.

Area Five—Equity Securities Analysis

Pre-Candidate Requirements. The prerequisite requirements for the candidate correspond to those under Area Four, above.

Candidate Level I. The candidate should have the ability to conduct a relatively basic appraisal and evaluation of industries and companies from a financial and investment point of view. The analyst should be able to understand and interpret ordinary types of financial data and demonstrate an ability to appraise the risks and values of common stocks, warrants, rights, and options.

Candidate Level II. Emphasis is placed on a rigorous and complete appraisal and evaluation of industries, companies and their common stocks with respect to their current position and outlook, and on an appreciation of the investment implications of such an analysis for different investors. The candidate should be able to apply the techniques of security analysis including quantitative measures for valuation and risk, and the analyst should have an appreciation of controversial issues in capital market theory.

Candidate Level III. In addition to the requirements at prior levels, emphasis is placed on the analysis and selection of equities consistent with the financial circumstances of different types of individual and institutional investors and consistent with changing economic and market environments.

Area Six—Portfolio Management

Pre-Candidate Requirements. Because the task of portfolio and investment management involves to a considerable extent the integration of economics, financial accounting, quantitative techniques, and security analysis, the pre-candidate requirements for this area are the same as those for the five areas previously specified.

Candidate Level I. The candidate is expected to understand the basic financial circumstances of different individual and institutional investors, to be able to formulate appropriate fundamental portfolio account objectives and constraints and to be able to select specific investment instruments that are suitable for such portfolios.

Candidate Level II. The candidate should, at this level, be able to construct portfolios and to formulate portfolio strategies based on the candidate's analysis of the outlook of the economy and of conditions in the securities markets. Emphasis is placed on security selection, concepts of diversification, risk, return, and modern portfolio and capital market theory.

Candidate Level III. Based on knowledge gained at previous levels and in the other topical areas, the candidate is expected to interrelate economic and market conditions, securities analysis, analysis of the requirements of individual and institutional investors, and portfolio concepts, and be able to develop suitable investment policies and construct appropriate portfolios. The candidate should have an understanding of the investment management process including how to organize and implement the security analysis and portfolio management effort and how to evaluate the results.

Area Seven—Ethical and Professional Standards

Pre-Candidate Requirements. Candidates are required to show evidence of sound character and to agree, in writing, to abide by the I.C.F.A. Code of Ethics, Standards of Professional Conduct, and related rules at the time of candidate registration. Character references are an integral part of the registration requirement. Violations of professional standards may cause suspension from the candidate program or revocation of the charter.

Candidate Level I. The candidate should be familiar with ethical and professional standards and security laws and regulations and be able to deal

The C.F.A. Candidate Study Program—General Topical Outlines

	Candidate Level		
	I	II	III

ECONOMICS

Tools of analysis and
forecasting:
—National income accounts
—Flow of funds and money
supply indicators
—Input-output analysis
—Leading indicators
Historical and structural
perspective:
—Economic trends and cycles
—Flow of funds and relationship to national income
accounts
—Economic price indexes
—Aggregate profit trends by
types
—Trends and cycles in stock
prices and interest rates
Forecasting broad economic
forces:
—Quantitative and qualitative aspects of forecasts
—Implications for forecasts
of:
 interest rates and the
 structure of interest
 rates
 corporate profits and
 earnings of stock price
 indexes
 aggregate equity price
 indexes
 industry and company
 prospects
Economic policy:
—Government policies and
actions regarding:
 growth, inflation and
 employment
 monetary and fiscal
 policies
 social goals
 antitrust and industry
 regulation
 international policy, including balance of
 payments
—Implications of policy
decisions for:
 profit outlook
 interest rates
 equity prices
 industry and company
 analysis

	Candidate Level		
	I	II	III

FINANCIAL ACCOUNTING

Principles and construction of
accounting statements:
—Income statements
—Balance sheets
—Sources and uses of funds

Content and usefulness of
accounting reports to regulatory agencies

Financial analysis of accounting
statements:
—Adjustments for
comparability
—Ratio analysis
—Adjustments for sub-
sidiaries, affiliates and
foreign operations
—Stock splits and dividends
—Rights, warrants and
convertible securities
—Effect of price level
changes

Areas of judgment:
—Inventories
—Depreciation
—Tax treatment
—Intangibles
—Consolidation
—Acquisitions and mergers
—Deferred assets and
liabilities
—Off balance sheet financing
—Pension plans

Current accounting principles
and practices:
—AICPA and FASB opinions
—Regulatory decisions

The C.F.A. Candidate Study Program—*Continued*

Candidate Level
I   II   III

APPLICATION OF QUANTITATIVE TECHNIQUES

Elementary statistics:
—Averages and measures of dispersion
Mathematics of finance:
—Compound growth
—Present value of stocks and bonds
—Performance measurement techniques
Probability theory:
—Expected values
—Strategies
Hypothesis testing:
—Sample testing and confidence limits
—Analysis of variance
Simple and multiple regression and correlation
Matrix algebra
Mathematical programming in portfolio theory
Applications of computer systems to financial analysis

TECHNIQUES OF ANALYSIS— FIXED INCOME SECURITIES

Classification of fixed income securities:
—By issuer
—By maturity, if any
—By security
—By contractual obligation
—By tax status
—Convertible features, if any
Special characteristics:
—Call features
—Sinking fund provisions
—Security
—Protective covenants
—Taxable features
Fixed income security selection and management:
—Quality ratings
—Interest or preferred dividend coverage, past and future
—Coupon and maturity
—New issues, discount and premium bonds
—The yield curve and interest rate structure
—Marketability
—Bond swaps

Candidate Level
I   II   III

TECHNIQUES OF ANALYSIS— EQUITY SECURITIES

Sources of information

Financial instruments:
—Stocks, warrants, rights, options

Industry appraisal and evaluation:
—Interindustry competition, supply-demand, product prices, costs and profits
—Security market evaluation of profits, historical and projected

Company appraisal and evaluation:
—Sales volume, product prices, product research, intraindustry competition
—Ratio analysis-balance sheet and income statement and analysis of corporate profitability, liquidity, solvency, operating and financial leverage
—Management appraisal
—Earnings and dividend evaluation and projection, near and long-term
—Valuation techniques-long and short-term: discounted cash flow earnings multiplies, absolute and relative growth stock valuation
—Risk analysis-quantitative and qualitative
—Efficient capital market hypothesis

Candidate Level
I   II   III

Candidate Level
I   II   III

OBJECTIVE OF ANALYSIS—
PORTFOLIO MANAGEMENT

Investor Objectives and
  constraints:
  —Individuals
  —Institutions:
    investment companies
    foundations and endow-
      ment funds
    pension funds and profit
      sharing plans
    trust funds
    property and liability
      insurance companies
    life insurance companies
    commercial banks

Portfolio strategy and con-
  struction
  —Policy inputs:
    assumptions regarding
      the short and long-
      term outlook for the
      economy and the
      securities markets
    types of investments to
      be used regarding
      quality, liquidity, risk
      and other characteris-
      tics
    portfolio diversification
      by type of investment
      and diversification by
      industry
  —Account objectives and
    constraints:
    specific definition of ob-
      jectives, e.g., risk and
      return, liquidity re-
      quirements, legal and
      regulatory constraints
    the time horizon for the
      investment
    aggressive and specula-
      tive properties
  —Investment selection:
    selection of specific
      investments suitable
      for objectives
    comparative evaluation
      of alternative invest-
      ments
  —Modern portfolio theory
    and the construction of
    "efficient portfolios"
  —Tax planning
  —Execution of purchases and
    sales
  —Evaluation of account
    performance

CONDUCT OF ANALYSIS—
ETHICAL AND PROFESSIONAL
STANDARDS, SECURITIES LAWS
AND REGULATIONS

Ethical standards and profes-
  sional responsibilities:
  —Public
  —Customers and clients
  —Employers
  —Associates
  —Other analysts
  —Corporate management
  —Other sources of informa-
    tion

treatment of ethical issues:
  —Identification of ethical
    problems
  —Administration of ethical
    policies
  —Changing structure of
    financial markets and the
    participants therein and
    the consequent develop-
    ment of new ethical issues

Security laws and regulations:
  —Nature and applicability
    of fiduciary standards
  —Pertinent laws and regula-
    tions
  —Treatment of insider
    information

with these standards as they pertain to his responsibilities with the public, clients, employer, his fellow analysts, and corporate management.

Candidate Level II. The candidate should be able to identify poor professional practices and violations of standards in a variety of areas, including conflicts of interest and use of insider information, and to understand appropriate corrective actions.

Candidate Level III. The candidate should understand how to administer a program of professional and ethical standards within an organization in terms of internal disciplinary controls and of compliance with the I.C.F.A. standards and rules and security laws and regulations. The candidate should understand the full meaning of the public interest, professionalism of financial analysts, and ethical issues associated with changes in the financial system.

Eligibility Requirements for C.F.A. Candidates

C.F.A. Candidate Level I

Education: A candidate should have a bachelor's degree from an accredited academic institution. In the absence of a degree, other educational training or work experience may be accepted for C.F.A. candidacy. The candidate must submit credentials in proper form evidencing his education.

Occupation and Experience: In order to qualify for this examination, the candidate must be currently and primarily engaged in the occupation of financial analysis as related to securities investment as outlined on page 15 and must have completed *at least* one year of experience in one or more of these occupational categories by the end of the calendar year preceding the year in which the examination is to be taken.

C.F.A. Candidate Level II

Occupation and Experience: In order to qualify for this examination, the candidate must be currently and primarily engaged in the occupation of financial analysis as related to securities investment as outlined on page 15 and must have completed *at least* three years of experience in one or more of these occupational categories by the end of the calendar year preceding the year in which the examination is to be taken.

Society Membership: A candidate must be a member in good standing of a constituent society of The Financial Analysts Federation. Membership in a constituent society must be obtained by April 15 of the year in which the examination is to be taken.

C.F.A. Candidate Level III

Occupation and Experience: In order to qualify for this examination, the candidate must be currently and primarily engaged in the occupation of financial analysis as related to securities investment as outlined on page 15 and must have completed *at least* five years of experience in one or more of these occupational categories by the end of the calendar year preceding the year in which the examination is to be taken.

Society Membership: A candidate must be a member in good standing of a constituent society of The Financial Analysts Federation.

C.F.A. Occupation and Experience Requirement

A candidate for the C.F.A. designation must be currently and primarily engaged in the occupation of financial analysis *as related to securities invest-ment*. This statement is sufficiently comprehensive to include the following occupational categories:

a. A person who is engaged in financial analysis as related to securities investment for a bank, insurance company, investment counsel firm, investment company, securities firm, financial publishing house, or other similar organization.

b. A person occupying the position of professor (including assistant and associate professors) or dean of a college or university who is currently teaching or conducting research in the field of securities investment.

c. A person engaged as an economist in the field of financial analysis as related to securities investment.

d. A person who is engaged in portfolio management.

e. A person who is engaged in financial analysis as related to securities investment for a public agency.

f. A person who is engaged in financial analysis as related to securities investment for a corporate pension, profit sharing, or similar fund.

g. A person who previously would have qualified for candidacy as a financial analysts or portfolio manager, but is curently engaged in the professional supervision of financial analysts or portfolio managers as related to securities investment.

Change in Employment Status

In order to meet the occupational requirement for C.F.A. candidacy, it shall be the responsibility of a C.F.A. candidate to notify the Institute im-mediately of any change or termination in his company affiliation or position, *giving the details of the duties involved in the new position*. The candidate should include the *date* on which he terminated his previous employment and the effective *date* of his new affiliation.

Ethical Standards

The professional conduct, of a candidate must conform to the Institute's *Code of Ethics* and *Standards of Professional Conduct*. The Institute will obtain confidential reports on each candidate.

APPENDIX C: Recent I.C.F.A. Examinations

THE INSTITUTE OF CHARTERED FINANCIAL ANALYSTS

C. F. A.
EXAMINATION I

(June 9, 1973)

SECTION 1

9:45 A.M. – 12:00 P.M.

There are five questions in this section of the examination. The weighting used to grade each question is equal to the amount of time allocated to answering each question.

The time allocated for answering each question is:

Questions	Minutes
1	60
2	20
3	25
4	15
5	15
Total	135

INSTRUCTIONS TO CANDIDATES

1. All questions must be answered.

2. Write legibly and in ink.

3. Begin each question on a new page.

4. Write your identification number in the two spaces indicated on the front cover of your answer book. Fill in the other required information on the cover of your answer book.

I-1-2

1. Zeller's Limited and Metropolitan Stores of Canada Limited are two medium-sized department and variety store chains which operate across Canada. Table I below shows the net sales of each of these companies, the value of retail trade and Canadian Disposable Personal Income.

   (a) Based solely on the data in Table I, characterize the growth and stability of retail sales, the value of retail trade, and the relative position of Zeller's and Metropolitan in the Canadian retail industry. Illustrate your conclusions numerically by using 1962, 1966, and 1971 statistics.

(15 minutes)

TABLE I

	Net Sales* (Current $ in Millions)		Canadian Value of Retail Trade**	Canadian Disposable Personal Income
Year	Zeller's	Metropolitan	($ Billion)	($ Billion)
1971	201.4	75.7	30.6	58.9
1970	176.6	69.0	28.0	53.6
1969	157.6	64.7	27.3	50.5
1968	142.9	60.7	25.4	46.4
1967	132.7	50.0	23.8	41.7
1966	117.2	37.7	22.4	38.6
1965	102.8	32.7	21.0	35.0
1964	86.0	28.8	20.1	31.6
1963	74.0	25.9	18.8	29.9
1962	68.8	23.2	17.9	28.1
1960	--	--	16.5	24.8
1955	--	--	13.1	18.2

*Fiscal years end January 31 of the following calendar year.
**Includes automobile sales at retail.

Zeller's Limited, directly and through subsidiaries, operates a chain of department and variety stores across Canada and offers credit facilities to its customers. In mid-1972, there were 62 suburban department stores and 84 variety stores in operation. W. T. Grant Co. owns 50% of the company's common stock and thus Zeller's has access to the experience of Grant in matters of real estate, store development and general administration. The company added eleven new department stores in the 1972-73 fiscal year and the same number is expected to be opened in the 1973-74 fiscal year. Variety store operations are being phased out. The merchandise sold ranges from high-turnover variety items to clothing, camper trailers and camping supplies, floor coverings, major appliances, home entertainment units, cameras, sporting goods, and home furnishings. In addition, auto service bays, food service, beauty salons, etc., are offered.

I-1-3

Metropolitan Stores of Canada Limited, directly and through subsidiaries, operates a chain of 171 variety and junior department stores in all provinces of Canada. At January 31, 1973, there were 171 stores in operation, with twenty stores opened February 1, 1972 through January 31, 1973. An aggressive expansion program is planned for future years. The more important merchandise handled includes textiles, ladies dresses, infants wear, sports wear, mens' and boys' wear, notions, toys, toiletry and crockery items. Restaurants and bakeries operated at many locations.

Both companies write-off store opening expenses as incurred.

(b) Using the information below and in Table II, on the following page, compare the progress of the two companies from 1962 to 1972 and their respective positions at January 31, 1972.

(25 minutes)

The following paragraph summarizes the appraisal of the retail store industry by a prominent Canadian research-oriented brokerage house early in 1973:

In 1972, we estimate that total retail sales, excluding autos and fuel oil sales, were up 11%. This compares with the annual average increase from 1967-72 of only 7.7% . . . . Our estimate of a 9½% increase in retail trade in 1973, excluding autos and fuel, is a very bouyant one and above the five year average gain. Our estimate assumes a decrease in the rate of personal savings, which was extremely high last year, and some further stimulus to the economy by the federal government to combat the high level of unemployment . . . .

The expected continued growth in the merchandising sector in 1973 will help minimize the adverse effect that some investors have been anticipating from the rapid store expansion programs being undertaken by many of the major retailing companies . . . . We do not feel that overstoring is going to be a universal problem though some areas of the country may periodically experience some overstoring. Probably a more difficult obstacle to overcome will be rising costs, particularly labor costs. This factor, combined with a continuing price awareness by the consumer, may tend to further enhance the price advantages that genuine discounters are able to offer consumers . . . .

The merchandising sector has been popular with investors for almost two years now and as a result, multiples are generally high reflecting investors anticipation of the good results that 1972 is expected to provide, particularly in the fourth quarter. The earnings outlook for most companies continues to be favorable in 1973, but it is unlikely that these prospects will stimulate upward multiple revision for this group generally. The long-term economic outlook to the mid-1970's for merchandisers is attractive considering the forecasts produced by the Economic Council of Canada; thus the earnings multiples for this group are probably quite realistic for the longer-term view . . . . We do not feel that this is the time for portfolios to move out of the merchandising field as their outlook over the next two or three years continues to be favorable.

(Question 1 continues on next page)

I-1-4

TABLE II
Zeller's Limited vs. Metropolitan Stores

Year (1)	Earned on Net Worth Zel %	Met %	Oper. Profit Margin Zel %	Met %	Asset Turnover Zel X	Met X	Total Debt: Net Worth Zel %	Met %	Current Ratio Zel X	Met X	Acid Test Ratio Zel X	Met X	Sales per Store ($ Million) Zel $	Met $
1973	-	-	-	-	-	-	-	-	-	-	-	-	-	-
1972	-	-	-	-	-	-	-	-	-	-	-	-	-	-
1971	15.7	13.1	8.2	8.0	2.1	2.2	88.8	57.2	3.5	2.0	1.9	.3	1.47	.48
1970	16.6	11.1	9.4	5.7	2.1	2.0	82.3	75.9	2.5	1.7	1.3	.4	1.37	.44
1969	16.5	11.1	9.7	6.9	2.2	2.0	72.1	79.5	3.1	1.6	1.9	.3	1.32	.40
1968	17.0	12.0	9.9	7.6	2.1	1.9	79.5	88.0	3.0	1.5	1.8	.3	1.20	.39
1967	18.1	12.5	10.3	8.0	2.3	1.7	73.3	89.0	3.7	1.5	2.2	.3	1.19	.34
1966	16.3	10.1	8.8	7.8	2.2	1.8	76.7	90.9	4.0	2.0	2.3	.2	1.07	.29
1965	15.9	10.4	8.8	7.8	2.3	1.6	67.1	100.6	3.0	2.0	1.7	.2	.97	.26
1964	12.7	8.7	7.7	7.1	2.3	1.5	55.0	112.5	4.2	1.9	2.3	.1	.84	.25
1963	9.6	8.0	6.1	6.9	2.2	1.4	54.4	102.3	4.6	2.4	2.4	.2	.74	.23
1962	8.9	7.7	5.7	7.5	2.1	1.4	54.0	103.7	4.9	2.6	2.4	.3	.69	.21
1961	9.1	4.2	5.8	4.8	2.2	1.4	38.0	107.7	3.1	3.0	1.4	.4	.67	.24

Year (1)	Sales per Share Zel $	Met $	Earnings per Share Zel $	Met $	Dividends per Share Zel $	Met $	Payout Ratio Zel %	Met %	Price/Earn. Ratio Zel X	Met X	Div. Yield on Common Zel %	Met %
1973 e	-	-	.96	1.60	.35	.28	36.5	17.5	-	-	-	-
1972 e	-	-	.81	1.30	.30	.24	37.0	18.5	20.4	15.8	2.1	1.5
1971	15.86	29.58	.61	1.00	.28	.10	45.9	10.0	26.7	14.9	1.7	0.7
1970	13.94	26.96	.59	.73	.26	Nil	44.0	Nil	18.6	12.0	2.4	Nil
1969	12.47	25.27	.53	.65	.24	"	45.3	"	25.3	20.8	1.8	"
1968	11.36	23.71	.50	.65	.22	"	44.0	"	26.3	23.0	1.7	"
1967	10.53	19.55	.48	.54	.18	"	36.5	"	17.9	16.1	2.0	"
1966	9.48	14.75	.37	.45	.15	"	40.5	"	17.4	11.6	2.3	"
1965	8.38	12.77	.33	.33	.13	"	37.9	"	14.9	11.3	2.5	"
1964	7.07	11.24	.23	.24	.10	"	43.5	"	13.1	13.1	3.3	"
1963	6.12	10.14	.15	.21	.09	"	58.0	"	14.7	12.7	3.9	"
1962	5.71	9.06	.13	.18	.09	"	66.9	"	15.7	15.1	4.3	"
1961	5.23	9.32	.13	.03	.09	"	66.9	"	18.5	18.6	3.6	"

COMPOUND GROWTH RATES

Years (1)	Sales Per Share Common Zel	Met	Earnings per Share Common Zel	Met	Dividends per Share Common Zel	Met
1961-71	11.7%	12.2%	16.7%	42.0%	12.0%	N.A.
1964-71	12.2%	14.8%	15.1%	22.6%	15.7%	N.A.
1968-71	11.7%	7.6%	7.0%	15.4%	8.3%	N.A.

(1) Fiscal years end January 31 of the following calendar year
e - Estimates
N.A.- Not applicable

I-1-5

(c) As the manager of a medium-sized pension fund, you are planning to make a new commitment of up to $250,000 in the Canadian department store industry. Early in January, 1973, you are considering the stocks of these two companies. There is room for one—but not both—of these stocks. Price data is as follows:

Market Close	Zeller's	Metropolitan
1/19/73	19½	25¾
Range of Market		
Year 1972	20-13	25-16

Based on the information supplied in (a), (b), and (c) above, state which of the two stocks you would have selected for inclusion in the portfolio of January 31, 1973. **Explain.** (Ignore interest equalization tax in this problem.)

(20 minutes)

2. Ed Updike has been an analyst for two years in a medium-sized brokerage firm. The firm derives its business primarily from retail accounts but is now making an effort to gain institutional clients. He has completed a review of ABC Corporation, a small company in one of the industries he follows, and is reporting to his supervisor and research manager, Mr. Owens. In his verbal report, Updike has concluded that there is little likelihood of future improvement in ABC's record of below-average sales and earnings growth within its industry, and that ABC's stock is unattractive as an investment. The stock has been strong recently.

Owens tells Updike that his conclusion regarding the continued slow sales growth is incorrect. Owens' argument rests on his knowledge that one of ABC's new product development projects has been successful. Owens cites another brokerage firm's recent buy recommendation as the source of that information. The meeting ends with Owens asking Updike to read that recommendation and then to prepare his own buy recommendation on ABC stock.

(a) Identify those provisions of the *C.F.A. Code of Ethics* and *Standards of Professional Conduct* which are pertinent to this situation.

(8 minutes)

(b) Based on your answer in (a) above, state what action Updike should take on Owens' request. **Explain** your reasons.

(12 minutes)

(Please Turn Page)

I-1-6

3. Company A's common stock had a market value of $72.00 immediately prior to the announcement of a merger with Company B. There were 6,100,000 shares outstanding and earnings just reported were $3.50 per share.

    Company B had 800,000 shares of common stock outstanding. Immediately prior to the merger announcement, its stock sold at 10 times most recent earnings per share.

    Company A acquired Company B on a pooling of interests basis with Company A being the surviving corporation. Company A exchanges one share of its stock for three shares of B's stock. The exchange ratio was determined solely on the basis of the market prices of the two stocks immediately prior to the merger announcement.

    (a) Calculate the per share earnings of Company A after the merger.

                                    (20 minutes)

    (b) Based on your calculation in (a) for Company A, explain why post-merger EPS for Company A differs from its pre-merger EPS.

                                    (5 minutes)

4. The following tabulation gives pertinent data on the bonds of two electric utility companies early in January, 1973. Both of these bonds are rated Aa by Moody's. The yield to maturity for Moody's Aa-rated Utility Bond Index was 7.40% at this time.

    Bond No. 1 - Toledo Edison - First 9s of 11/1/2000

    Bond No. 2 - Pacific Gas and Electric - First 4 1/4s of 6/1/1995

	Bond No. 1	Bond No. 2
Current Price	110 1/4	68
First Call Date	11/1/75	Currently callable
Call Price	107.33	103.39
Yield to First Call Date	7.36%	Not applicable
Yield to Maturity	8.07%	7.12%

    Discuss the price fluctuations of these two bonds if the interest rate on Moody's Aa-rated utility bonds:

    (a) Decreases to 6.40%.

    (b) Increases to 8.40%.

                                    (15 minutes)

5. Corporate management has considerable freedom of action in selecting from generally acceptable accounting procedures that have a material effect on reported results. List 5 such procedures relating to different areas of accounting, and explain in a sentence or two how each might be used to report higher current earnings per share.

(15 minutes)

END OF SECTION 1

THE INSTITUTE OF CHARTERED FINANCIAL ANALYSTS

C. F. A.
EXAMINATION I

(June 9, 1973)

SECTION 2

1:45 P.M. – 4:45 P.M.

There are six questions in this section of the examination. The weighting used to grade each question is equal to the amount of time allocated to answering each question.

The time allocated for answering each question is:

Questions	Minutes
1	20
2	25
3	20
4	30
5	35
6	50
Total	180

INSTRUCTIONS TO CANDIDATES

1. All questions must be answered.

2. Write legibly and in ink.

3. Begin each question on a new page.

4. Write your identification number in the two spaces indicated on the front cover of your answer book. Fill in the other required information on the cover of your answer book.

I-2-2

1. A linear regression study was made using a sample of 72 common stocks over an eight year period. The following variables and equations were used:

   The dependent variable Y = the annual rate of return (market price change and dividends) for each stock.

   The independent variable X = the annual growth rate in earnings per share for each stock.

   $$Y = a + bX$$

   The results of the study produced these findings:

   The intercept $\underline{a}$ = 0.05

   The slope $\underline{b}$ = 1.17

   The standard error of estimate $S_{y.x}$ = 0.08

   The coefficient of correlation r = 0.67

   The coefficient of determination R^2 = 0.45

   The average annual rate of return for the average stock in the group was 0.12 (12%).

   (a) **Describe** the relationship which existed between rate of return and the growth rate of EPS for this 72 stock sample.

   (10 minutes)

   (b) **State** how well this equation explains the relationship between rate of return and growth of EPS for this sample. **Discuss** in statistical terms.

   (10 minutes)

2. The United States International Balance of Payments has deteriorated in the last decade.

   (a) **List** the major factors contributing to the declining strength of the dollar.

   (10 minutes)

   (b) Beginning in 1971, **discuss** briefly the changes which have been made in the effort to reverse the adverse trend in the U. S. Balance of Payments.

   (15 minutes)

3. Following are financial data for three corporations. **Select the most attractive invest-**
ment under stated assumptions. Dividend payout ratios and P/E ratios will remain
constant. The growth rate in earnings per share from 1967 through 1972 is presumed
to continue indefinitely. Investor's required rate of return is adjusted for the different
risk characteristics of each security. Show all calculations.

	Albemarle Co.		Nelson Co.		Orange Co.	
	1967	1972	1967	1972	1967	1972
Earnings per share	$2.00	$ 2.94	$2.30	$ 3.70	$1.20	$ 2.10
Current market price		40.00		60.00		40.00
Current dividend rate		1.60		1.80		1.00
Investor's required rate of return		10%		12%		14%

Compound Sum of $1 for N Years

Year	6%	7%	8%	9%	10%	12%	14%	16%
4	1.26	1.31	1.36	1.41	1.46	1.57	1.69	1.81
5	1.34	1.40	1.47	1.54	1.61	1.76	1.93	2.01
6	1.42	1.50	1.59	1.68	1.77	1.97	2.20	2.44

Compound Sum of an Annuity of $1 for N Years

Year	6%	7%	8%	9%	10%	12%	14%	16%
4	4.64	4.75	4.87	4.99	5.11	5.35	5.61	5.88
5	5.98	6.15	6.34	6.52	6.72	7.12	7.54	7.98
6	7.39	7.65	7.92	8.20	8.49	9.09	9.73	10.41

(20 minutes)

(Please Turn Page)

I-2-4

4. Based on the information below, **outline** and **explain** briefly your recommendations as an investment counselor in each of the following cases. Also, list what additional information you would like to have.

   (a) Mr. Adams, aged 40, with a wife and two teen-age children, approaches you with the following questions:

   "I have been investing in stocks for the past ten years. Recently I've been having doubts about placing all of my investment funds there. I have about $100,000 in stocks and own my home. I am gainfully employed. What do you suggest about bonds as an investment vehicle?"

   (15 minutes)

   (b) A recently divorced woman, age 32, with one child seven years old teaches technical writing at a large university. The university has a retirement program and a group insurance program covering life insurance, basic medical and major medical expenses. She participates in both of these programs. In the divorce settlement, she was awarded the home and furnishings worth $50,000 and cash of $30,000. In addition, the husband was required to pay her a total of $50,000 in installments of $4,000 per year for the first five years and $3,000 a year for the following ten years. She can live on her salary. She does not understand investments, but she wishes to invest aggressively.

   (15 minutes)

5. Badger Company is being organized to manufacture and sell a product which is produced on machines each having an installed cost of $300, a life of three years, and zero salvage value. Pre-depreciation pre-tax income from each machine is $200 per year. The company plans to install one machine each year in the first three years but none thereafter. The effective tax rate on income is fifty percent.

   The company is considering different methods for the treatment of depreciation expense and income accrual in reporting to stockholders. The data in Table I show results using straight-line depreciation, and Table II shows results using sum-of-the-year's digits depreciation.

I-2-5

Table I
Straight-Line Depreciation

	Year				
	1	2	3	4	5
Pre-depreciation pre-tax income	200	400	600	400	200
Depreciation expense:					
Machine No. 1	100	100	100		
Machine No. 2	–	100	100	100	
Machine No. 3	–	–	100	100	100
Total Depreciation Expense	100	200	300	200	100
Pre-tax income	100	200	300	200	100
Tax on income - 50%	50	100	150	100	50
Net Income	50	100	150	100	50

Table II
Sum-of-the-Year's Digits Depreciation

	Year				
	1	2	3	4	5
Pre-depreciation pre-tax income	200	400	600	400	200
Depreciation expense:					
Machine No. 1	150	100	50		
Machine No. 2	–	150	100	50	
Machine No. 3	–	–	150	100	50
Total Depreciation Expense	150	250	300	150	50
Pre-tax income	50	150	300	250	150
Tax on income - 50%	25	75	150	125	75
Net Income	25	75	150	125	75

(a) **Explain** why Badger Company might use the sum-of-the-year's digits method of depreciation instead of straight-line depreciation.

(10 minutes)

(b) Suppose Badger Company were to use "flow-through accounting." Using the data in the above tables, calculate the income after taxes in each of the five years.

(10 minutes)

(c) **Explain** the "normalizing method" of determining depreciation, using the data supplied above.

(10 minutes)

(d) **Identify** the advantages and disadvantages of the "normalizing method" of depreciation compared to the use of "flow-through accounting."

(5 minutes)

(Please Turn Page)

I-2-6

6. **SHORT ANSWER QUESTIONS**

(4 Questions — 50 minutes)

Answer briefly **ALL** of the following questions. (The answers must appear on consecutive pages in the answer book.)

6-1. These data are for the Cavalier Company:

Ratio	Forecasted 5 Year Average
Pre-tax operating income (loss) / Sales	15.5%
Pre-tax non-operating income (loss) / Sales	(1.5%)
Sales / Operating assets	1.3
Income taxes / Net income before taxes	50%
Dividends / Net income	40%
Operating assets / Shareholder's equity	1.4

Based on these data, calculate the expected growth rate of earnings per share for this company. **Show** all calculations.

(10 minutes)

6-2. APB Opinion No. 15 covers the calculation of earnings per share.

(a) In accordance with the Opinion, **list** four categories of common stock equivalents which must be used to determine primary earnings per share.

(10 minutes)

(b) **Explain** how primary EPS is modified to determine fully diluted earnings per share.

(5 minutes)

6-3. The variance, standard deviation and coefficient of variation have been calculated for these numbers: $2, 3, 5, 7, 8$.

$$\text{Variance} = \frac{(2-5)^2 + (3-5)^2 + (5-5)^2 + (7-5)^2 + (8-5)^2}{5} =$$

$$\frac{(-3)^2 + (-2)^2 + 2^2 + 3^2}{5} = \frac{26}{5}$$

$$\text{Standard Deviation} = \sqrt{\frac{26}{5}}$$

$$\text{Coefficient of Variation} = \frac{\sqrt{\frac{26}{5}}}{5}$$

(a) Explain what analytical purpose is served by these statistical measures.

(5 minutes)

(b) Identify one useful application in financial analysis for each of these statistical concepts.

(5 minutes)

6-4. "An analysis of the growth record and growth prospects of an industry or a company frequently can be conducted within the framework of the so-called 'industrial life cycle.' Many students of economic history have argued that industries, like people, go through fairly well-defined stages of development."

(a) Explain what is meant by the concept of the "industrial life cycle" of a company or an industry.

(5 minutes)

(b) Explain the implications of this approach for achieving investment success.

(5 minutes)

(c) Explain the limitations of this concept.

(5 minutes)

END OF SECTION 2

THE INSTITUTE OF CHARTERED FINANCIAL ANALYSTS

C. F. A.
EXAMINATION II

(June 9, 1973)

SECTION 1

9:45 A.M. – 12:00 P.M.

Five questions must be answered in this section of the examination. You may choose between Question 5 or 6, but you must answer Questions 1 through 4. The weighting used to grade each question is equal to the amount of time allocated to answering each question.

The time allocated for answering each question is:

Questions	Minutes
1	25
2	30
3	30
4	30
5 or 6	20
Total	135

INSTRUCTIONS TO CANDIDATES

1. Questions 1 through 4 must be answered. Answer either question 5 or 6, but not both.

2. Write legibly and in ink.

3. Begin each question on a new page.

4. Write your identification number in the two spaces indicated on the front cover of your answer book. Fill in the other required information on the cover of your answer book.

II-1-2

1. The following quotation from an article written by Leopold Bernstein highlights the issue concerning the use of reserves to recognize future costs and losses—are they valid or merely a means of further clouding reports?

    "The growing use of reserves for future costs and losses impairs the significance of periodically reported income and should be viewed with skepticism by the analyst of financial statements. That is especially true when the reserves are established in years of heavy losses, when they are established in an arbitrary amount designed to offset an extraordinary gain, or when they otherwise appear to have as their main purpose the relieving of future income of expenses properly chargeable to it.

    "The basic justification in accounting for the recognition of future losses stems from the doctrine of conservatism which, according to one popular application, means that one should anticipate no gains, but take all the losses one can clearly see as already incurred."

    (a) **Discuss** the merits of Bernstein's arguments and apprehensions.

    (b) **Explain** how such information may be factored into your review of past trends, the estimates of future earnings, and valuation of the common stock.

    (25 minutes)

II-1-3

2. Three years ago, you established an investment counseling organization which achieved substantial success in the bull market from mid-1970 through 1972. A brokerage firm, which includes several of your friends, has recently established an advisory service for corporations to recommend the types of managers which should be used in handling their pension accounts. Both you and the principals of the brokerage firm are C.F.A.'s.

Two members of this brokerage firm recently informed you that your record was good—but not more spectacular than several other counseling organizations. They pointed out that their work necessitated making many contacts and numerous presentations—many of which did not result in a new business relationship. After many inferences, it became evident that their recommendations about your management ability were somewhat dependent upon your willingness to provide them with substantial brokerage commissions.

This brokerage firm was continuing a modest research effort and had, in past years, been valuable in helping you select stocks for customers.

Because you and your associates realize that the amount of your future counseling business may be dependent upon the recommendations of these "advisors," you and your associates decided to discuss the entire situation and any ethical problems which were inherent in it.

(a) Review the situation as it pertains to the *C.F.A. Code of Ethics* and *Standards of Professional Conduct.*

(b) List and explain your recommendations for handling the situation as a principal of the investment counseling organization.

(30 minutes)

(PLEASE TURN PAGE)

II-1-4

3. Robert Graham has come to your office for investment counseling. You have been
    acquainted socially with him and his family for several years, but only today were you
    told of the details concerning his family situation. He is 38 years old, is married and
    has three children. The oldest child, a 10 year old boy, has a physical deformity which
    may limit his work potential. Mr. Graham is concerned that his son may need some
    type of income supplement for the remainder of his life. The other two children, a boy
    and a girl, appear to be doing well in school; Graham expects that each will go to
    college. He carries a $40,000 ordinary life policy on himself and $15,000 on his wife.

    Robert Graham has an executive position with a small manufacturing corporation. He
    earns $35,000 per year, from which he is saving approximately $3,000 annually at the
    present time—but savings are becoming increasingly more difficult as he tries to meet
    some of the social obligations which have been necessary in the business. He feels his
    job is very secure and enjoys working for the company, but any chance of
    advancement is limited. He expects regular though modest salary increases but no
    promotions. Mrs. Graham's mother, age 58, recently became paralyzed and has limited
    financial resources. Mr. Graham believes that she will need approximately $3,000 per
    year for the remainder of her life.

    The parents of Mr. Graham were recently killed in an automobile accident and he
    inherited $200,000. The inheritance is in savings accounts and readily marketable
    securities.

    (a) Outline your recommendation for a general investment plan for Robert Graham.

    (b) Indicate the type of investments (not necessarily the specific securities) which
         would suit his needs and requirements best.

    (c) List and discuss the factors which you must consider in making these decisions.

                                    (30 minutes)

4. "There are those who believe that the time is at hand to abandon the experiment with controls and to rely entirely on monetary and fiscal restraint to restore a stable price level. This prescription has great intellectual appeal; unfortunately, it is impractical." (Arthur Burns, Chairman of the Federal Reserve Board of Governors, December 29, 1972).

   (a) **State** the intellectual appeal of using only monetary and fiscal policies.

   (b) **Explain** why Mr. Burns thinks it is "impractical" to rely only on monetary and fiscal policies in 1973.

   (c) **Discuss** briefly "Phase III" and evaluate its potential effect on controlling wages and prices, and on corporate profits.

   (30 minutes)

(PLEASE TURN PAGE)

II-1-6

(ANSWER EITHER NO. 5 OR NO. 6. IF BOTH ARE ANSWERED, ONLY THE FIRST ANSWER APPEARING IN THE ANSWER BOOK WILL BE GRADED.)

5. The chart below is a schematic illustration showing the historical relationship between rate of return on bonds and stocks. It shows a probability distribution of rate of return with the rates on the horizontal axis, and the probabilities on the vertical axis. (The probabilities are based on the frequencies of observed occurances.) Assume that distribution "A" represents AAA-rated corporate bonds, while distribution "B" represents the rate of return on the common stocks of large, established corporations.

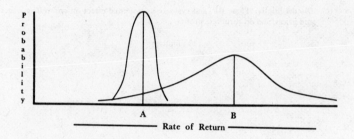

(a) Reproduce the chart in your answer book. For each type of security listed below (C, D, and E), place a vertical line to indicate the mean and sketch the shape (width and height) of the frequency distribution. Label with the appropriate letter.

Type of Security	Letter
Long-term U. S. Treasury bonds	C
Common stock warrants	D
Convertible bonds	E

(b) Justify your answer to (a) above by discussing each type (C, D, and E) in terms of its expected return and dispersion of returns relative to securities A and B. Explain your placement of distribution C, D, and E.

(20 minutes)

6.

(ANSWER EITHER NO. 5 OR NO. 6. IF BOTH ARE ANSWERED, ONLY THE FIRST ANSWER APPEARING IN THE ANSWER BOOK WILL BE GRADED.)

You are managing a $100 million pension fund portfolio and have received the following probability distribution, based on an econometric model, for the expected one-year total return (including income) on the Standard and Poor's 500 Index.

Market Prediction	One-year Total Return S&P 500	Probability
I	+20%	0.15
II	+10%	0.30
III	+ 5%	0.20
IV	- 5%	0.20
V	- 10%	0.10
VI	- 20%	0.05
		1.00

There are three possible portfolio strategies available, A, B, and C. Under each portfolio strategy is displayed the percentage return for each of the three market predictions.

PORTFOLIO STRATEGY

Market Prediction	A	B	C
I	7%	50%	20%
II	7	30	12
III	7	10	10
IV	7	-10	4
V	7	-25	0
VI	7	-40	-8

(a) State the expected one-year total return for the S&P 500. Compare this return with the mode of the distribution, explaining the difference, if any.

(b) Assuming that you are an expected-value decision maker (linear utility curve), select the proper strategy. Explain.

(c) Assuming a "risk-averter" utility curve, select the proper strategy. Explain.

(20 minutes)

(END OF SECTION 1)

THE INSTITUTE OF CHARTERED FINANCIAL ANALYSTS

C. F. A.
EXAMINATION II

(June 9, 1973)

SECTION 2

1:45 P. M. — 4:45 P. M.

There are three questions in this section of the examination. The weighting used to grade each question is equal to the amount of time allocated to answering each question.

The time allocated for answering each question is:

Questions	Minutes
1	60
2	60
3	60
Total	180

INSTRUCTIONS TO CANDIDATES

1. All questions must be answered.

2. Write legibly and in ink.

3. Begin each question on a new page.

4. Write your identification number in the two spaces indicated on the front cover of your answer book. Fill in the other required information on the cover of your answer book.

II-2-2

> This section of the examination consists of 3 questions based upon:
>
> 1. the annual report of Walt Disney Productions (enclosed)
>
> 2. a research memorandum (accompanying the questions).
>
> Base your answers on the information contained in these materials.

---

1. You have been granted a one-half hour interview with the top management of Walt Disney Productions. You may presume that those present will be able to answer your questions concerning the company and its operations, but you wish to <u>concentrate on basic policy-level topics,</u> since another interview with the financial staff has been arranged for later in the day.

    (a) **List** the subjects you would try to cover pertaining to this annual report and the particular questions which you feel would be most important from the standpoint of a stockholder.

    (b) **State** your reasons for asking these questions.

    (60 minutes)

II-2-3

2.
                                    M E M O R A N D U M

To: Herbert Standish,   Date: March 15, 1973
          Research Director

From: Lawrence Miller,   Subject: An Analysis of
          Staff Analyst   Research Reports on
                                                            Walt Disney Productions

This analysis summarizes two of the better research reports published in February on Walt
Disney Productions. In brief, Report A continues to rank the stock as a "definite candidate
for accumulation" while Report B states purchase of Disney should be deferred at this time
"in light of the possibility of poor first-half earnings."

Both reports discussed four major areas to provide a rationale for their recommendations:

                        (1)   Earnings
                        (2)   Motion Pictures and T. V.
                        (3)   Parks
                        (4)   Ancillary Operations

REPORT A: DEFINITE CANDIDATE FOR ACCUMULATION

(1)   Earnings:

      (a)   First quarter earnings down from $0.19 in the prior year to $0.18.

      (b)   Table 2 (under Financial Data) indicates a 17.9% increase in revenues but a 6.1%
            reduction in net income for the first quarter.

      (c)   Second quarter earnings could be lower than in prior years.

      (d)   We anticipate earnings of $1.65 - $1.70 for fiscal 1973 (down from our previous
            $1.80 forecast), but still a 19% annual gain.

      (e)   Long-term growth is expected to be in the area of 15% to 20% per year.

                                                            (PLEASE TURN PAGE)

II-2-4

(2) Motion Pictures and T. V.:

    (a) Disney continues to regard motion pictures and T. V. as its main business.

    (b) Revenues from these sources should increase but there should be a small decline in profit margins.

    (c) *Mary Poppins,* Disney's most successful film, is scheduled for reissue in mid-1973.

    (d) It will be difficult to attain last year's income in this area because of the great success Disney had with foreign films in 1972.

    (e) Disney will release one more motion picture this year than it did last year.

    (f) Disney, over the years, has been the most successful motion picture production company. It is important to realize that quarterly earnings from motion pictures are quite volatile.

    (g) The company's major motion picture release, *Snowball Express,* is going well and the company forecasts about $7,000,000 in revenue from it.

(3) Parks:

    (a) There is "no convincing evidence that things are not going well at Walt Disney World."

    (b) Attendance at Walt Disney World is up 5-6%, less than the 10% forecast. Local attendance is down, but there were record crowds of out-of-state visitors at Christmas-time.

    (c) Attendance at Disney World is expected to reach 12 million and per capita expenditures are rising at roughly a 6% rate.

    (d) Disneyland attendance was up 10% last year over the previous year and per capita expenditures were up. The corporation is expecting a 5% attendance increase and 5% increase in expenditures per capita for 1973.

(4) Ancillary Activities:

    (a) Disney has announced a residential development of conventional homes.

    (b) Continued development of the company's vast Florida land holding is expected.

    (c) Long-term growth in ancillary activities is expected but no significant impact is anticipated for 1973

II-2-5

REPORT B: PURCHASE SHOULD BE DEFERRED AT THIS TIME

(1) Earnings:

Overall evaluation: $1.60 EPS forecast. This long-term forecast is for 20-25% annual rate of growth. Current problems are unrelated to areas of expected future growth.

    (a) Films dominate near-term prospects

        — Foreign films are down compared to last year

        — There is one less film in the first quarter for the domestic market compared to last year.

    (b) Nevertheless, increases were shown at Walt Disney World, at Disneyland, and in the ancillary activities. The long-term prospects are exciting.

(2) Motion Pictures and T.V.:

Overall evaluation: Films dominate earnings in the first two quarters of the year. EPS from films will be flat to up moderately compared to last year.

    (a) While first quarter EPS is affected by fewer films than last year, the second quarter will benefit from one added film. Also, the fourth quarter reissue of *Mary Poppins* (with no negative costs to be amortized) is expected to have a substantial positive affect on EPS.

    (b) No precise breakdown on the impact of the decline in foreign film earnings is available, but the impact will lessen throughout the year.

(3) Parks:

Overall evaluation: Parks dominate earnings in the third and fourth quarters. Increases here will offset possible declines or flat performance in other areas of operations.

    (a) Walt Disney World attendance is up 6% during the first quarter, with a 10% increase expected for the year. Spending per capita could be up 5-10%. Revenues will also benefit from the increase in ticket price. Revenues will also benefit from the increase in ticket price. Revenues are expected to be $160-$180 million. Operating margins may hit 17% this year, compared to 13% last year, with 23-25% in the future.

    (b) Disneyland attendance is up 19% in the first quarter. A 3-4% increase is expected for the year. Revenues will be up 5-6%. No change in profitability is expected.

(4) Ancillary Activities:

Overall evaluation: A 20% gain this year in both revenues and earnings.

(PLEASE TURN PAGE)

II-2-6

FINANCIAL DATA FROM REPORTS A AND B

TABLE 1

1972-73 Range	Recent Price	Indicated Dividend	Yield	1972 Earnings Per Share	Common Shares Outstanding	Market Value ($ Million)
124-66	$104	$0.12	0.1%	$1.41	28,564,000	$2,970

TABLE 2

	First Quarter of Fiscal Year Ended		
	12/31/72	12/31/71	% Change
Revenues (000)	$68,916	$58,433	+ 17.9
Cost and Expenses (000)	60,442	48,880	+ 23.7
Net Income (000)	5,024	5,353	- 6.1
After-tax Margin	7.3%	9.2%	
Earnings Per Share	$ 0.18	$ 0.19	- 5.3

TABLE 3

	Report A	Report B
Estimated EPS - 1973	$1.65 - 1.70	$ 1.60
Estimated EPS - 1974	$1.95 - 2.00	N.A.*
P/E Ratio - Recent	74	74
P/E Estimated - 1973	62	65
P/E Estimated - 1974	53	N.A.*

*Not Available

___

End of Memorandum

II-2-7

The above memorandum was prepared by Lawrence Miller, an analyst in your research department:

(a) **State** your opinion of the recommendations, based on the 1972 Annual Report and the memorandum.

(b) **State** the various methods which could be used in placing a value on the stock. **Explain.**

(c) **State** the time horizon that you are using for each valuation method. **Explain.**

(d) **Compute** the return on total capitalization for 1972 and **discuss** its significance.

(60 minutes)

3. In preparing for your interview with Disney's financial staff, **review** those areas in the annual report which could be presented in greater detail. After reading the financial statements, the letter to stockholders on pages 28 and 29, the Summary of Significant Accounting Policies on page 30, the Notes to Consolidated Financial Statements on pages 36 and 37, and the historical material on pages 38 and 39, **list** the factors which, in your opinion, need close appraisal and will provide the basis for your questioning. **Explain** carefully using numerical data to **substantiate** your reasoning where it is appropriate.

(60 minutes)

END OF SECTION 2

THE INSTITUTE OF CHARTERED FINANCIAL ANALYSTS

C. F. A.
EXAMINATION III

(June 9, 1973)

SECTION 1

9:45 A.M. - 12:00 P.M.

There are five questions in this section of the examination. The weighting used to grade each question is equal to the amount of time allocated to answering each question.

The time allocated for answering each question is:

Questions		Minutes
1		30
2		30
3		25
4		30
5		20
	Total	135

INSTRUCTIONS TO CANDIDATES

1. All questions must be answered.

2. Write legibly and in ink.

3. Begin each question on a new page.

4. Write your identification number in the two spaces indicated on the front cover of your answer book. Fill in the other required information on the cover of your answer book.

III-1-2

1.　During 1972 the United States imported about $7 billion more goods than it exported. This trade deficit was much larger than had been expected after the realignment of currencies at the Smithsonian meeting in December, 1971. A rather prompt reversal in the deterioration of the trade balance had been expected.

　　Identify and discuss the factors which were present in the world and U. S. economies that negated or slowed the "expected" effect of devaluation.

(30 minutes)

2.

GREAT LAKES MANUFACTURING COMPANY
Lorain, Ohio　44120

March 31, 1973

Mr. Arthur G. Hopewell
Vice President, Trust Department
Ohio State Bank and Trust Company
Cleveland, Ohio

Dear Art:

Your year-end report on the performance and status of our pension fund was reviewed at yesterday's meeting of the Pension Fund Advisory Committee of the Board of Directors. A serious question was raised about the continued shift to common stocks.

Under policies you have been following, and with which the Committee has concurred, the bank has raised the percentage of common stocks in the fund from 40 to 75 percent (at market) over the last ten years. The question we would like to discuss with you at our April 15th meeting is whether this policy should be reversed, or at a minimum modified to place all new money (contributions plus investment income) in bonds. Based on the past five years, our rate of return on common stocks appears to be lower than the return now available on high-grade bonds (7¼%-7½%). From your year-end report:

III-1-3

Overall Rate of Return (% per annum)

	Great Lakes Mfg. Common Stock Fund	S & P 425 Industrials
1967-72	6.9	6.5
1962-72	8.5	8.4

As you know from the actuary's report, a copy of which you received, the forecast for excess of contributions over outlays will slow from its present rate of 20 percent to 10 percent over the next ten years.

We look forward to seeing you shortly.

Sincerely,

James S. Gans
Vice President - Finance

(a) **State** your recommendation to the Committee.

(b) **Substantiate** your recommendation by **discussing** the major points, pro and con.

(30 minutes)

3. As a highly respected senior investment official in the financial community, you have been approached by the chief executive officer of one of the largest industrial corporations in the world. He has asked for your advice about the establishment of a corporate policy to estimate earnings, as permitted by SEC rulings.

Prepare a carefully reasoned recommendation **discussing** points in favor of and opposed to such a policy.

(25 minutes)

(PLEASE TURN PAGE)

III-1-4

4. The trust department of Inner City Bank has decided to monitor the investment performance of its portfolio managers due to a recent increase in the number of performance-related complaints from clients. As Director of Portfolio Management of the bank, you are reviewing two performance measurement techniques proposed by a committee established to investigate the problem and to recommend solutions. A basic stumbling block has arisen because the bank's clients require portfolios with a diversity of investment objectives.

One group has proposed that the portfolio performance be measured by comparing portfolio performance with the performance achieved by the market as a whole. In its opinion, this approach should be sufficient since most investors normally relate their portfolio's performance to that of the general market.

An opposing body of opinion—led by several "beta theorists"—argues that the general market approach does not adequately take into account the degree of risk assumed by portfolio managers in achieving performance.

(a) **Describe** how the beta theorists might take investment risk into consideration by **outlining** a possible portfolio performance measurement technique.

(b) **Discuss** briefly some of the weaknesses of the measurement technique described in (a) above.

(c) Without using either the "beta technique" or the general market approach, outline another approach to the measurement of performance.

(30 minutes)

5. Several commentators on the state of the bond market during 1972 and early 1973 have pointed to the increased activity in the secondary market, much of it due to the greater emphasis placed on bond performance by institutional investors.

Cite at least **four** different kinds of trades or switches that are used by bond investors (not necessarily within the last 12 to 15 months) who attempt to increase "performance." **Explain** clearly how each, if successful, will benefit a portfolio.

(20 minutes)

END OF SECTION 1

C. F. A.
Examination III
Section 2

THE INSTITUTE OF CHARTERED FINANCIAL ANALYSTS

C. F. A.
EXAMINATION III

(June 9, 1973)

SECTION 2

1:45 P.M. - 4:45 P.M.

There are five questions in this section of the examination. The weighting used to grade each question is equal to the amount of time allocated to answering each question.

The time allocated for answering each question is:

Questions	Minutes
1	30
2	60
3	35
4	25
5	30
	180

INSTRUCTIONS TO CANDIDATES

1. All questions must be answered.

2. Write legibly and in ink.

3. Begin each question on a new page.

4. Write your identification number in the two spaces indicated on the front cover of your answer book. Fill in the other required information on the cover of your answer book.

III-2-2

1. Arnold Hornby is the head of research and a partner of a medium-sized investment counseling organization located in a large eastern city. Most of the firm's accounts are managed with the firm having full discretion for transactions. Peter Spencer, the youngest of the firm's four analysts, rushes into Mr. Hornby's office and makes this statement:

> "Let's get on the wire to account managers and sell General Manufacturing out of all accounts right now—I've just received some very unfavorable news. The salesman for one of our prime brokers is friendly with an outside director of that company who told him that development costs on their new product are running much higher than expected, earnings for 1973 will be sharply lower than the $3.20 that most people are using, and that, in addition, the new product is likely to be abandoned soon. The stock has been selling pretty full even on the $3.20, with a lot of hope given to the long run potential of the new product. When this news gets generally known that stock is going to plummet. We have an obligation to our clients to get them out now!"

Mr. Hornby knows that Peter keeps in touch with the treasurer of General Manufacturing on a regular basis.

Discuss thoroughly what Mr. Hornby should do.

(30 minutes)

2. The El Camino Press publishes a daily newspaper in a medium-sized U. S. city. Its printing press is more than ten years old and will need replacement in about ten years. The estimated replacement cost will be $4,000,000 in ten years, including building renovations needed to accommodate the press. The best estimates are that the salvage value of the printing press will be $200,000 ten years from now.

The management of El Camino Press has decided that depreciation on the old equipment and building will be funded into an investment account, with augmentation from retained earnings annually. The depreciation charges can provide $100,000 annually, while an average of $50,000 annually is available from after-tax operating earnings. The El Camino Press is a corporation, and usually has a net income before tax

III-2-3

in excess of $100,000. It is owned by a relatively small number of civic-minded citizens who are not primarily interested in large dividends each year, but who think that some cash payment should be made. The editor-publisher draws an adequate salary.

The portfolio accumulated to date is listed below:

	Approx. Mkt. Value	Est. Income
100 shrs. I.B.M. common	$ 43,000	$ 560
400 shrs. Gulf Oil common	10,400	600
400 shrs. U.S. Steel common	12,000	640
1,200 shrs. Sears, Roebuck common	133,000	1,680
100 shrs. Merck common	9,600	118
500 shrs. General Motors common	36,000	2,225
1,000 shrs. Litton Industries common	10,000	—
$100,000 P.V. U.S. Treas. 6¼%, 2-15-78	99,000	6,250
$100,000 P.V. G.M.A.C. 7¼%, 3-1-95	99,000	7,250
Total	$452,000	$19,323

In making the analysis, ignore the capital gains already in the portfolio. Otherwise, assume a capital gains tax rate of 25%.

(a) Without performing the calculations, **outline** in detail the analytic approach you would use in determining the capital accumulations required for the printing press and building improvements.

(b) **Perform** the calculations outlined in (a) above.

(c) **Present** a general long-range investment plan, including any specific changes you would make now to implement the plan. **Explain** carefully all of your reasoning. (You need not name specific securities for purchase. Instead, **indicate** classes and types; bonds, preferreds, and commons by industry or other category.

(60 minutes)

(PLEASE TURN PAGE)

III-2-4

3. On January 17, 1973, the following new issues were publicly offered by underwriting
    syndicates:

    (a) Vermont Yankee Nuclear Power Corporation 7.70%
         First Mortgage Bonds due January 15, 1998 --
           $20 million
         Offered at 101.375 to yield 7.58% to maturity
         Rated "A"
         Redeemable on 1/15/78 beginning at $107.26.

    (b) Vermont Yankee Nuclear Power Corporation 7.48%
         Cumulative Preferred stock -- 250,000 shares,
           $100 par value
         Offered at 101.355 per share to yield 7.38%
         Rated "BBB"
         Redeemable on 3/1/75 beginning at par

    (c) State of New York General Obligations (a tax-exempt security)
           due serially February 1, 1990-95
         Offered as part of a $129,500,000 issue of serial
           bonds due 1974 to 2003
         Rated "AA"
         Non-redeemable prior to maturity

Amount	Year of Maturity	Coupon	Price	Yield to Maturity
$4,975,000	1990	4.75%	99.42	4.80%
4,975,000	1991	4.80	100	4.80
4,975,000	1992	4.80	99.79	4.85
4,975,000	1993	4.80	99.79	4.85
900,000	1994	4.90	100	4.90
900,000	1995	4.90	100	4.90

    (d) Pan American World Airways, Inc. 7½%
         Convertible Subordinated Debentures due
           January 15, 1998 -- $75 million
         Offered at 100 to yield 7.50% to maturity
         Rated "B"

III-2-5

Convertible on and after January 16, 1975 into common stock. The initial conversion price equals 80% of the market price—but the initial conversion price may not be less than $7.00 or more than $13.50 per share.

Not redeemable prior to February 1, 1976: then at 107-1/2. Market price of common stock on 1/17/73: 9-1/8.

Common Price Range	Earnings Per Share
1968 30 - 19-1/2	$1.46
1969 31-3/4 - 11-3/8	.77 (deficit)
1970 14-1/2 - 8	1.38 (deficit)
1971 20-1/4 - 9-1/2	1.19 (deficit)
1972 17-3/4 - 8-5/8	.72 (deficit)

As head of a portfolio management unit in a large investment counseling firm, you are responsible for a number of accounts with varying investment objectives and requirements. These include:

- individual clients whose investment assets range from moderate to large size
- educational endowment funds
- a $10 million pension fund
- the $15 million investment portfolio of a rapidly-growing and profitable casualty insurance company.

Your firm's established policy is to make continuous use of fixed-income securities rather than investing entirely in equities. At a meeting early in January, 1973, the management committee of the firm advised all portfolio managers that, while there were some uncertainties in the outlook for the bond market, the acquisition of fixed-income securities would be approved, consistent with on-going investment programs for the accounts under supervision.

Discuss the suitability and attractiveness of each of the four newly-issued securities for each type of client listed above.

(35 minutes)

(PLEASE TURN PAGE)

III-2-6

4. "The principal question on the economic outlook for 1973 is not whether, but how
    fast, output and employment will expand. For policy, there are two issues. The first is
    to find and implement the set of policy actions which will maximize the likelihood
    that the economy will move to its full potential level of output and employment. The
    second is to do so in ways that will serve both to eliminate the vestiges of the
    post-1965 inflation and to place the economy squarely on a sustainable path of
    subsequent non-inflationary growth.

    "This is an ambitious set of policy goals, but there is a good prospect of achieving
    them, or at least approaching them closely. The year ahead is the first in a long time in
    which there is reasonable hope of closing in on full prosperity without serious inflation
    and without war."*

    Economic Report of the President, 1973, p. 71.

    Identify the fiscal and monetary actions, excluding "Phase III" controls, which the
    Report recommends for realizing these goals. Explain the impact that each of these
    fiscal and monetary actions is expected to have on the stock market and the bond
    market.

                                    (25 minutes)

5. As senior vice-president of the trust investment division of a large commercial bank,
    you are chairing a meeting of the investment committee in March, 1973. The
    vice-president for research holds a viewpoint regarding investment policy which is the
    polar opposite of the view held by the vice-president for portfolio management. The
    research V. P. wants to stress basic stocks of the type in Group A below, which was
    recently prepared by an analyst on his staff. The portfolio management V. P. wants to
    continue to stress the leading high-quality growth stocks such as those in Group B
    below.

    (a) **Summarize** carefully the case which can be made for each of the two viewpoints.

    (b) **Discuss** in detail how you would resolve the two viewpoints, and substantiate
        your reasoning.

III-2-7

	Group A			Group B		
	Am.Elec.Power	G.M.	Goodyear	Avon	Coca Cola	IBM
EPS Growth Rate						
Average Past 10 Years	6.3%	0.2%	8.4%	18.1%	14.1%	15.3%
Average Next 5 Years (estimate)	4%-6%	4%-6%	4%-6%	14%-16%	10%-12%	12%-15%
Dividends						
Payout Ratio	68%	59%	35%	65%	51%	49%
Current Yield	6.7%	6.0%	3.4%	1.0%	1.1%	1.2%
Return on Equity						
Average Past 5 Years	11.9%	16.0%	12.2%	34.3%	23.8%	18.6%
Price/Earnings Ratio						
Average Past 10 Years	19	15	15	43	31	41
Current	10	9	9	56	40	34

(30 minutes)

END OF SECTION 2

2

Inside Information and the Analyst

WILLIAM E. CHATLOS
Principal
Georgeson & Co.
New York, New York

AN AREA of rapidly growing concern for the analyst is liability under the various antifraud provisions of the federal securities law and in particular Rule 10b–5. Applications of Rule 10b–5 now appear quite frequently in reported cases and represent about one third of all current cases, both public and private, under the whole array of SEC statutes. This dramatic increase in the number of cases being brought before the courts or the commission is attributable, in significant part, to the loss of small investor confidence in the market system due to repeated violations of the rules covering material nonpublic information.

In the Treasury Department's recently released report entitled *Public Policy for American Capital Markets,* George P. Schultz, former Secretary of the Treasury, points out that "The loss of public confidence in our securities markets can be directly attributed to the relatively low returns on equity investment in recent years and to the feeling that institutions have an advantage over individual investors." Put another way, the average investor simply feels that he cannot compete equitably in the marketplace if he does not have access to the same lexicon of information that his more formidable counterparts do. As is typical of our democratic system, these feelings have been transformed into actions to bring the courts and the administrative agencies to full bearance on this now popularly perceived problem of the day. In this environment, analysts face increasingly serious difficulties in going about their ordinary tasks. Bradford Cook, former chairman of the SEC, has stated emphatically that the commission intends to become much more stringent in its dealings with analysts. In a recent decision, an industry specialist in the research department at Merrill Lynch, Pierce, Fenner & Smith received a formal censure and 60 days' suspension without pay for selectively distributing inside information. Also, there is the now famous *Equity Funding* case in which analyst Raymond Dirks was indicted for inadvertently committing a fraud while attempting to uncover and expose fraudulent activities which had been committed by others. Fortunately, thus far, citations of actual incidences of infractions by analysts have been few. But the momentum of court and commission activities indicates that there will be an increasing amount of accountability on the part of the professional financial analyst. In addition to civil penalties such as censure and suspension, criminal penalties of up to $10,000 or two years in jail are specified in the 1934 act for willful violation of the act and rules like 10b–5 issued under it.

As it stands now, the analyst in the course of his everyday work can, inadvertently or otherwise, come into the possession of material nonpublic information and in so doing becomes exposed to action from many sources if it can be determined or inferred that he has distributed or used this information. The action can come from the SEC through the initiation of proceedings for suspension, license revocation, and so forth, by the courts through injunction, by his own or his company's clients for issuing misleading advice or discrimination in issuing advice, by an issuer company or its shareholders claiming misappropriated company property, and by buyers and sellers of particular securities at the time when the information is possessed, distributed, or used alleging damages on the basis of same.

While total protection for the analyst is impossible, especially at present when there is as yet no definitive set of guidelines on what is specifically permitted and prohibited, there are reasonable considerations that the prudent analyst should make in order to effectively protect both himself and his profession. In addition, the survival of the marketplace will depend, in no small way, on the curtailment of the frequency of abuse of inside information by individuals and organizations occupying a favored position not available to all.

The next few years will determine direction of rule 10b–5's development. What we endeavor to do here, during this intervening period, when the SEC is developing the definitive set of guidelines on the responsibilities and obligations imposed by the rule is to sketch a general picture of where some of the lines have been drawn and where they may be drawn in the future. The area of greatest need for the analyst is a delineation of what separates good analytical inquiry from inside information. Many who seek useful private information are not fully informed of the intricacies of securities law and their responsibilities under such law. All that we have at present is a spectrum on one end of which there appears an emerging body of case law with citations of specific infractions of Rule 10b–5 with their far-reaching implications. At the other end of the spectrum, we have a host of real, everday hypothetical situations involving bona fide research and analysis, not yet determined as lawful or otherwise. The entire scope of the rule has not yet been fully defined but its growing implications for the analyst are outstanding. In the brief space of this chapter, we shall attempt to describe some of the more obvious practical considerations which the analyst should entertain in the course of his work.

The term *insider* has been defined in a number of ways but has come to include any person with material information not yet disclosed to the public. The question of exactly what constitutes inside information is a more difficult one. The two major elements are materiality and publicity. Under what circumstances is information material and when is it considered to be public? Although, as yet, there is no universal agreement as to what exactly constitutes liability for the analyst under rule 10b–5, it can be safely said that the potential for liability exists when an analyst distributes or uses information in his possession which is (1) material, (2) nonpublic, (3) known to be nonpublic and possibly obtained improperly, and (4) a factor in a decision to act. Information is material when in and of itself it would reasonably be expected to have a marked impact on the stock or would be considered important by the average investor in making his decision to buy or sell a security. Information is nonpublic when it has not been channeled through any of the various mass media or when knowledge of such information is in the possession of an extremely limited number of individuals. Information is obtained improperly when it is of a confidential nature, and is transmitted or received by unauthorized or unethical means. Information is a factor in a decision to act when it is received before the execution of such actions, and when it has some bearing or relevance to that which is acted upon.

In order to present as clear a picture as is possible of both the nature and direction of the law, it is necessary to undertake a brief examination of some of the more significant cases which have come before the court and the commission. Insofar as the judicial decisions are concerned, it should be noted that most have been on the pleadings. Typically then, a 10b–5 decision has been only a holding by the court that a cause of action has been stated well enough to withstand a motion to dismiss. This is far from a decision on the merits, where adequate proof of the relevant assertions has been made. It should also be noted that most of 10b–5 law has come from the district courts. The circuit courts have come to approve many of their principles, but many remain unconfirmed by any higher court, and as of this writing the Supreme Court has yet to speak on 10b–5.

The SEC has been the initiator in three landmark cases under the rule. The first is the *Cady Roberts* case of 1961 where a quarterly dividend was reduced and one of the directors ordered a trade in advance of public dissemination. The second case was the now famous *Texas Gulf Sulfur* case of 1968 where directors and officers and employees of the company purchased large amounts of shares and calls and tipped off others to do the same in advance of a public announcement regarding a mineral discovery. The third was the 1968 matter involving Merrill Lynch, Pierce, Fenner & Smith where the employees of that firm received information as prospective underwriters of an issuing company which was used to trade with and distribute to others for the same purposes prior to public disclosure.

In the *Cady Roberts & Company* case a partner in a brokerage house heard of an impending dividend cut from one of the company's directors.[1] Trading had taken place before the news of the dividend reduction had reached the market. In this case, a special relationship with the source of information was determined. It was also determined that the information was properly designated for corporate purposes alone. It was determined, therefore, that there was an "inherent unfairness" in using information for a purpose other than that for which it was intended. It was reasoned that analytically the obligation to disclose material public information prior to trading rests on two principal elements; first, the existence of a relationship giving access directly or indirectly to information intended to be available only for a corporate purpose and not for the personal benefit of any individual and, second, the inherent unfairness involved where a party takes advantage of such information knowing it is unavailable to those with whom he is dealing (in the market).

In the case of the *Securities and Exchange Commission* v. *Texas Gulf Sulfur Company*,[2] the information involved knowledge of a discovery of a substantial, commercially exploitable mineral deposit on a piece of company owned land. Officers and directors of the company who became aware of this discovery purchased the company's stock in the market before the information was made public. When the information finally became public, the market knew that the value of the company's assets and its earning power would become substantially augmented and the price of the stock adjusted to reflect the increase in the value of the company. Purchase of the stock by directors and officers of the company, under these circumstances, violated the antifraud provision of rule 10b–5, and the court's decision confirmed judicially the Cady Roberts' rule that trading with material undisclosed information violated 10b–5. In addition, the Texas Gulf decision made new law by determining that tipping, the selective transmission of material inside information,

---

[1] In the matter of *Cady Roberts & Co.*, 40 Securities and Exchange Commission 907, 912 (1961).

[2] *Securities and Exchange Commission* v. *Texas Gulf Sulfur Co.* 401 F.2d 833, 849 (2d Cir. 1968).

was a violation of the law. This case also initiated the classic discussion about proximity to the originating source of information as a determinant of liability. "As information becomes more diffuse in terms of its specificity and its remoteness from a corporate source, the appropriateness of applying Rule 10b–5 diminishes."[3]

The case of *Investors Management Co., Inc.* (Merrill Lynch–Douglas)[4] was the first where the commission held a tippee in violation of rule 10b–5. In this instance, it was determined the information was nonpublic because it was not available to investors generally; some analysts had reached negative conclusions regarding Douglas' profitability, but the information passed out by Merrill Lynch was much more specific than that which was generally possessed by the investment community at the time. It was also determined that the tippees either knew or should have known that the information was from an inside source. That source was a prospective underwriter for a proposed Douglas debenture offering. Finally, it was determined that the tippees knew or should have known that the information was inside nonpublic information intended for corporate purposes only and not for external distribution. Conclusions handed down in this case included a set of general guides for disclosure which encouraged discussion between management and analysts while stressing the need for adequate and timely disclosure of any material nonpublic corporate information which might come out during the course of such discussions. This case was the first instance where the SEC considered whether tippees are subject to prohibitions on trading and distribution when they receive material nonpublic information about a company. The SEC said that liability can be incurred if the tippees "know or have reason to know that [the information] was nonpublic and had been obtained improperly by selective revelation or otherwise."[5] Since this case, the term *insiders* has come to include those persons who come into possession of inside information even though they do not fall within the traditional categories of insiders.

The case involving Faberge Inc. was another clear example of an instance in which information about a company came into the possession, use, or distribution of certain individuals but had not been generally disclosed.[6] Had it been disseminated, it would have likely affected the market price of the company's stock because it would have been considered important by reasonable investors in determining their position. What specifically happened in this instance was that a report for a third quarter became known to the company's vice president of finance and this report indicated a substantial loss for the third quarter

---

[3] Ibid.

[4] In the matter of *Investors Management Co., Inc. et al.* (Securities and Exchange Act Release No. 9267. Investment Advisers Act Release No. 289. July 29, 1971.)

[5] Ibid.

[6] In the matter of Faberge, Inc. (Release No. 34–10174, May 25, 1973).

due to disappointing sales. The information was transmitted privately through telephone calls between the vice president and a number of persons who consequently acted on the basis of it and effected large sales of the stock of the company. The formal public dissemination of the information via communications wire systems was not made until some time after this preliminary selective disclosure.

Another case similar to that of the *Faberge* case was that of the *SEC* v. *Lum's Inc.*[7] In this instance the president of the company had informed a group of security analysts in a seminar that the company's earnings would fall within a certain definite range. Some time later he revised his estimate sharply downward. The information was telephoned to an employee in a Wall Street firm who, in turn, telephoned it to a portfolio manager who informed another portfolio manager of the same firm. Both subsequently sold their entire holdings in the company. Later in the day, when revised earnings were publicly released, the stock dropped substantially in price. Many of the individuals involved in this chain of selective distribution and use of what was material nonpublic information were found by the court to be involved in a common enterprise to misuse confidential information.

In a case involving Bausch & Lomb, actions were commenced through the SEC against the company, its chairman of the board, certain Wall Street brokerage firms, and others.[8] The actions alleged, among other things, violation of disclosure requirements under federal securities laws. It was alleged that various individuals failed to make timely public disclosure of adverse information and made disclosure of certain information including projected earnings of the company on a selected basis. This information was subsequently used by others to effect sales prior to its dissemination to the public. During 1973, the SEC commenced action against the company and others relating to these same events and seeking injunctive relief.

One of the most recent additions to the body of case law has been a case involving Liggett & Myers Inc.[9] The diversified tobacco and consumer products company was enjoined, upon consent, for violating an antifraud provision of federal securities laws. The SEC had charged that L & M's director of corporate communication gave several security analysts nonpublic inside information about a decline in the company's earnings before the figures were made public. The disclosure, in this instance, was alleged to have triggered trading activity by the analysts' firm and their clients.

---

[7] *Securities and Exchange Commission* v. *Lum's Inc.* __F. Supp.__ (S.D. N.Y. 1972) 70 Civ. 5280 (HRT) CCH Fed. Sec. Law Reports, #93659.

[8] *Hawk Industries Inc. et al.* v. *Bausch & Lomb, Inc. et al.* 59 F.R.D. 619 (S.D. N.Y. 1973).

[9] *Securities and Exchange Commission* v. *Liggett & Myers, Inc. et al.* (S.D. N.Y. 1973) 73 Civ. 2796, CCH #94204.

The *Equity Funding* case was another case where infraction of rule 10b-5 occurred as a result of tipping.[10] An analyst received a rumor in a phone call from a disgruntled former employee of the company. The rumor was that at least 66 percent of the total underwriting of the company's insurance operation was bogus. While the analyst investigated what he termed "sensational rumors," he discussed those rumors with various clients who began to unload their stock. News of the scandal did not become public until three weeks later, long after several large accounts, with whom the analyst had been in contact, dumped their stock. The analyst contended that unsubstantiated rumors cannot be considered inside information and that to publicly disseminate such "hearsay information" would have been irresponsible and improper. Essentially, he was caught in the middle of an incredible predicament. First, he was trying to learn the truth behind the rumor of fraud. Second, he was trying to keep his institutional clients informed of what he had learned. Third, he wanted to expose the fraud to the public. Unfortunately, because of his ignorance of the finer points of the law with regard to material information, he got himself into considerable difficulty. Partly as the result of this case, the New York Stock Exchange stated on May 10, 1973, that analysts have "an obligation to the public which must take precedence over the duty to clients or employers".[11]

Liability under the law has been determined to exist even in cases where the information distributed and acted upon is misleading and inaccurate. An example of this is the recent case involving Merrill Lynch, Pierce, Fenner & Smith and sales of Scientific Control Corporation stock.[12] In this instance, Merrill Lynch allegedly disseminated research reports and wire flashes which contained erroneous information about the company. The commission determined that despite the fact the information selectively disseminated was misleading and inaccurate, Merrill Lynch was nevertheless culpable for the misuse of inside material information.

The case of the *SEC* v. *Shapiro* involved a proposed merger between two companies (Harvey's Stores Inc. and Ridge Manor Development Corporation), in which two financial analysts acting as consultants encouraged the merger while at the same time accumulating shares of stock in both companies.[13] While the merger did not go through and the defendants subsequently contended that their knowledge of the negotiations was therefore not material, the court still determined that they were guilty of abusing material nonpublic information.

---

[10] *Securities and Exchange Commission* v. *Equity Funding Corp. of America* (C.D.C. 1973) 73 Civ. 714, CCH #79417.

[11] New York Stock Exchange release dated May 10, 1973.

[12] In the matter of Merrill Lynch, Pierce, Fenner and Smith, Inc., Exchange Act release 10233, June 22, 1973.

[13] *Securities and Exchange Commission* v. *Shapiro et al.* 348 F. Supp. 46 (S.D. N.Y. 1972).

Once it was established by the commission that there were limitations on trading by both corporations and their employees during any period of material nondisclosure, two extensions of the law followed logically— liability of tippors and tippees. It became clear that a corporate official or employee who was not allowed to benefit directly from the use of material undisclosed information should not be able to benefit indirectly by passing on the information to someone else for the same purpose. This was determined to be a violation in the *Texas Gulf Sulfur* case.[14] While in that case the commission proceeded only against the tippor, the commission subsequently held that the tippee is equally bound to refrain from the use of material undisclosed information, at least under circumstances in which the tippee has reason to know the information is nonpublic and improperly obtained. In the broadest terms, the tippee's responsibilities depend upon how the information was acquired, from whom it was acquired, how reliable it was, whether he reasonably believed it was already public, and his degree of financial sophistication. Naturally, this is a very unsettled environment with many potentially conflicting viewpoints. There will be questions of fact in each case which must come to bear on any determination.

Separate from the distinction of tippor as corporate insider is that of the *outside-insider*. Corporate personnel are not the only persons having access to confidential corporate information for legitimate purposes. Such information is obtained by many other persons including analysts, underwriters, lawyers, accountants, government officials, investor relations counselors, and financial printers. While these people have little, if any, control over the disclosure machinery, if they trade upon such information or distribute it in an unauthorized way, they can violate rules of expected confidentiality. It follows logically, then, that they are also bound in a way that is similar to the way corporate officials are bound. Under present circumstances, the analyst should also be wary of using material nonpublic information which comes to him from outside the company, but which he has reason to believe comes from the company itself. Although less risky than information coming directly from the company, it still carries possible violation and liability implications.

In the *Texas Gulf* case as well as the *Investors Management Co.* case and the *Faberge* case, the court determined that the tippee who does trade upon such information is a participant after the fact in the tipping corporate official's breach of fiduciary duty and so may be held responsible for the consequences of any illicit trading activity. A separate but related issue is whether or not a tippor can be held liable for the trades of a tippee, on the theory that such instances fall into the same category as conspiracy or aiding and abetting.

Under certain circumstances, more commonly referred to as the "mosaic" pattern, a securities analyst or other professional obtains from

[14] *Securities and Exchange Commission v. Texas Gulf Sulfur Co.*

the sources within an issuer items of information which standing alone would not be material, but which become significant to the security analyst in light of his familiarity with the full mosaic of individual bits of information about that particular issuer or its industry. This is obviously a result of the application of professional expertise which is normally unavailable to the average investor. It seems only right that the analyst's capacity to obtain individually nonsignificant items of information from issuer sources and to utilize this information despite the absence of public dissemination should not be held to be improper or illegal. This type of information is what Philip Loomis, a commissioner of the SEC called "a link in the chain of information." The SEC feels that the kind of research which produces this type of information should not be discouraged. Whether the information is a link in a chain or whether it is one small bit of data which nobody else knows and which gives the recipient a distinctly unfair (potentially illegal) advantage is a fine but important distinction.

While the courts have given certain legal direction as a result of the cases involving inside information, i.e., information originating with the issuer, both the courts and the SEC have been slower in dealing with market information which, while providing the same self-interest advantage, does not fall specifically under the semantic terms associated with materiality in known cases.

> One might conclude that notwithstanding its historical development, thus far, the application of Rule 10b–5 to the unfair use of material nonpublic information should not be restricted to information which emanates from a corporate source, nor need it necessarily deal with a corporate issuer or its affairs. It should apply with equal force to the use of any information in the securities marketplace which either should be or is about to be made public, as long as the publication of the information might effect the decision of a reasonable investor.[15]

If, for example, an analyst has a close relationship with a company giving him possession of certain material nonpublic information, he can become both a tippor and a tippee, subject to legal action even when he, in fact, has done no tipping, but especially, of course, if he has. If his employer or client makes a trade in the issuer company's stock, then he can find that he is in trouble. Another example would be an instance where an analyst is engaged by a company to evaluate a merger or acquisition offer by or for the company. The information he receives in that capacity is inside information, at least that which has not been publicly disseminated. If he passes on the information to friends or clients, both he and they could be potential violators of the law. In

---

[15] Peloso, SEC rule 10b–b5, and outside information, 168N.Y.L.J., December 11, 1972, at 32, 34.

other cases, an analyst may learn that a tender offer for a target company will shortly be made at a premium over the present market price or he may know that some organization or group intends to purchase or sell a sufficiently large number of shares to substantially affect the present market price of a stock. He may, on occasion, learn that a given company may shortly split its stock. Any of these cases could be instances where, if the information is used and/or distributed in advance of public dissemination, the analyst can be held in a violation of the rule.

Let us now consider for a moment the types of liability which might ensue in the course of an analyst issuing his research report. Analysts are, in fact, restricted in the distribution of their own conclusions as a result of analysis. The *Merrill Lynch-Douglas* case is a good example of where selective distribution of a research opinion can be held to be in violation of the SEC rules. Another case, that of *SEC* v. *Alex N. Campbell,* involved a situation where a financial writer, who authored a column which had marked impact, traded on his own recommendation prior to the publication of his column.[16] The case is still under consideration, but the SEC has alleged that the writer was in violation of rule 10b–5.

Let us sketch yet another hypothetical case where infractions of rule 10b–5 can inadvertently occur. Suppose an officer of a company learns from a brokerage firm's analyst interviewing him about his company, that the brokerage firm will shortly publish favorable analysis of his company, including a recommendation to buy the stock. Despite the fact that the report may be based on generally available facts, if the stock is so thinly traded that the appearance of the brokerage report and recommendation is "reasonably certain" to have a substantial impact on the price of the stock, both the officer of the company and the analyst may be in a position where they could be held in violation of rule 10b–5. In this case nothing has happened which affects the value of assets or earning power of the company. However, anyone with advance information as to the brokerage firm's report and recommendation will have an advantage over sellers of the stock who are unaware of the situation. This is just another example of a situation where undisclosed information is market information. In short, information about events or circumstances which affect the market for a company's securities, but which do not necessarily have anything to do with the company's assets or earning power, place the analyst at a potential disadvantage, not only for using and/or distributing such information, but even for the mere possession of it.

It has been argued quite frequently that market information is only important to short-term traders and not so much to long-term investors. It is doubtful, however, that courts will make much of a distinction

---

[16] *Securities and Exchange Commission* v. *Campbell,* Civil Action 72–1684, (C.D. Cal. 1972).

between market information and information about the company. The case of Texas Gulf Sulfur determined that short-term traders are entitled to the same legal protection that is given to conservative traders.[17]

Among the precautions a prudent analyst should take are the maintenance of careful records, kept as complete as possible, showing the time, source, and character of the information received, the basis for the recommendations, and the time and extent of the distribution of such advice and recommendations. In addition, he should be alert and informed as to what news has already been disseminated about the corporation in question so that he can recognize material nonpublic information when he is confronted with it. If inside information is inadvertently disclosed, he should not allow himself to be compromised in the hope that perhaps the news will slip by unnoticed. News should be disseminated broadly, following at least the minimum guidelines established by the New York Stock Exchange. All rumors should be reported to the appropriate authorities.

The simplest method for an analyst to obtain information concerning a corporation under study is through the use of publicly issued reports, current news reports, and trade publications. In-depth study, however, may involve personal contacts with management, with suppliers, bankers, and other third parties, and possible sources within the analyst's own firm, such as partners who are corporate directors. While verbal communication is necessary and fruitful to the analyst as he probes the company in depth, it is also the most vulnerable and the most difficult to control. Analysts' meetings, splinter group meetings, and especially one-to-one conferences, during which only the analyst and one corporate officer are present, provide fertile ground for planting or inadvertently revealing inside information. It can consist of a mere nod or smile of confirmation. It can be a statement that inadvertently slips out. Nevertheless, the analyst involved has just become an insider.

A suggested protective procedure would be to include a member of the press at all meetings. From a purely logistical standpoint, however, this would obviously be impossible. Not only would the number of meetings have to be severely curtailed as a result of the relatively small number of competent financial reporters available, but one-to-one meetings would become nonexistent. Corporate officers tend to be more formal and constrained in the presence of a member of the press; there is a certain, probably well-warranted, nervousness about possible slips of the tongue (especially concerning personalities) which the press has a great love of publishing and which severely curtails the free give-and-take that small groups have traditionally enjoyed. Those sessions to

---

[17] A fuller description of the SEC's concern with the unfair use of market information appears in Securities and Exchange Act release no. 9950 at 114–29 (January 16, 1973).

which the press is not included tend to have a more conducive business atmosphere. However, these meetings are a perfect opportunity for marginally material information to slip out. In addition, the presence of the press at a meeting is no real defense. The analyst is the expert; if he is not aware of the divulgence of a material fact, how can the member of the press be expected to recognize it?

Regardless of how many analysts are in attendance at such a session, if a material bit of information inadvertently is mentioned, the analysts should not consider the information public. The two alternatives open to him are either to insist upon or arrange for immediate disclosure or to bury the information until the company or someone else releases it. Recommending that the company release the information is perhaps the best choice. Release by an analyst without company authorization could create more legal problems than it would solve. However, it should be considered as a last resort, should all other attempts at prompting public disclosure (including reporting to the SEC or exchange) fail.

A significant problem associated with assuring adequate dissemination of corporate information is that of timing. There is no way of assuring promptness and accuracy. While dissemination is most often sought through the facilities of the major financial news wire services, these do not assure effective dissemination in instances where the wire services are carrying large numbers of releases and are operating under space and time limitations. Perhaps the commission will establish guidelines based on the American Bar Association's suggestions, relating to "waiting periods." These will require those with knowledge of material information to wait until a specified time after dissemination before its distribution or use can be presumptively lawful. In the meantime, the prudent analyst should wait a reasonable length of time after a disclosure, say 24 hours after it has been published on the wire or in the press, in order to be sure that he is not jumping the gun.

Some brief mention should be made in these closing paragraphs about some areas of inquiry for the analyst which have more recently been suggested as areas which fall under the domain of material information. The biggest revelation thus far has been that the seeking out of a firm or person that is the main supplier of an essential part in the production process of a company and asking for information concerning the issuer's orders for parts may be illegal. SEC spokesmen have informally suggested that this type of information could be considered material and nonpublic. Other areas where information could be judged material include information about competitive patterns such as market share, orders and backlogs, sales trends, the significant expansion or curtailment of operations, the status of litigation, extraordinary borrowing, and even, believe it or not, changes in dividend policy and earnings estimates or revisions. This list is by no means complete, either. In the meantime, pending issuance of the definitive guidelines, caution should be exercised in obtaining information in all of these areas.

Indications of the direction of the law thus far point to the objective of achieving equality of information among investors. What is perhaps more realistic is an equal access to that information. This has been termed an "informational access parity" by Harvey Pitt, assistant to the chairman of the SEC.

Until the unlikely time where an effective method of assuring simultaneous receipt of all material information by all interested persons, a strong and healthy capital market will continue to be dependent upon the efforts of security analysts and others to ferret out, analyze, and decipher all of the relevant information that is available in order to make a legitimate profit for themselves and their firm from the application of their resourcefulness and ability in these efforts.

Until precise legal definitions are available, analysts would be well advised to exercise discretion and caution in an attempt to conform not only to the letter of the law and SEC regulations, but also the *intent* and *spirit* of the SEC pronouncements. The advice given by former Chairman William J. Casey of the SEC could well be applied to analysts and should be framed and hung in every financial research department. Speaking about institutional trading, Chairman Casey said that [an analyst] should satisfy himself that all of the information that comes into his possession is available to the public prior to distributing or using it.

3

Securities and Exchange Commission

INTRODUCTION

The Securities and Exchange Commission (SEC) was created by an act of Congress entitled the Securities Exchange Act of 1934. It is an independent, bipartisan, quasi-judicial agency of the United States Government.

The laws administered by the Commission relate in general to the field of securities and finance, and seek to provide protection for investors and the public in their securities transactions. They include (in addition to the Securities Exchange Act of 1934) the Securities Act of 1933 (administered by the Federal Trade Commission until September 1934), the Public Utility Holding Company Act of 1935, the Trust Indenture Act of 1939, the Investment Company Act of 1940, and the Investment Advisers Act of 1940. The Commission also serves as advisor to Federal courts in corporate reorganization proceedings under Chapter X of the National Bankruptcy Act.

Organized July 2, 1934, the Commission is composed of five members not more than three of whom may be members of the same political party. They are appointed by the President, with the advice and consent of the Senate, for 5-year terms, the terms being staggered so that one expires on June 5th of each year. The Chairman is designated by the President.

The Commission's staff is composed of lawyers, accountants, engineers, security analysts and examiners, together with administrative and clerical employees. The staff is divided into Divisions and Offices (including nine Regional Offices), each under charge of officials appointed by the Commission.

The Commission reports annually to the Congress. These reports contain a review of the Commission's administration of the several laws.

SECURITIES ACT OF 1933

This "truth in securities" law has two basic objectives: (*a*) to provide investors with material financial and other information concerning securities offered for public sale; and (*b*) to prohibit misrepresentation, deceit and other fraudulent acts and practices in the sale of securities generally (whether or not required to be registered).

Registration of Securities

The first objective applies to securities offered for public sale by an issuing company or any person in a control relationship to such company. Before the public offering of such securities, a registration statement must be filed with the Commission by the issuer, setting forth the required information. When the statement has become effective, the securities may be sold. The purpose of registration is to provide disclosure of financial and other information on the basis of which investors may appraise the merits of the securities. To that end, investors must be furnished with a prospectus (selling circular) containing the salient data set forth in the registration statement to enable them to evaluate the securities and make informed and discriminating investment decisions.

Exemptions From Registration

The registration requirement applies to securities of both domestic and foreign private issuers, as well as to securities of foreign governments or their instrumentalities. There are, however, certain exemptions from the registration requirement. Among these are: (1) private offerings to a limited number of persons or institutions who have access to the kind of information registration would disclose and who do not propose to redistribute the securities, (2) offerings restricted to the residents of the State in which the issuing company is organized and doing business, (3) securities of municipal, State, Federal and other governmental instrumentalities, of charitable institutions, of banks, and of carriers subject to the Interstate Commerce Act, (4) offerings not in excess of certain specified amounts made in compliance with regulations of the Commission discussed below, and (5) offerings of "small business investment companies" made in accordance with rules and regulations of the Commission. The anti-fraud provisions referred to above, however, apply to all sales of securities involving interstate commerce or the mails, whether or not the securities are exempt from registration.

Purpose of Registration

Registration of securities does not insure investors against loss in their purchase, nor does the Commission have the power to disapprove securities for lack of merit—and it is unlawful to represent otherwise in the sale of securities. The *only* standard which must be met in the registration of securities is an adequate and accurate disclosure of the material facts concerning the company and the securities it proposes to sell. The fairness of the terms of securities (whether price, promoters' or underwriters' profits, or otherwise), the issuing company's prospects for successful operation, and other factors affecting the merits of securities, have no bearing on the question whether securities may be registered.

The purpose of registration is to provide disclosure of these and other important facts so investors may make a realistic appraisal of the merits of the securities and thus exercise an informed judgment in determining whether to purchase them. Assuming proper disclosure, the Commission cannot deny registration or otherwise bar the securities from public sale whether or not the price or other terms of the securities are fair or the issuing company offers reasonable prospects of success. These are factors which the investor must assess for himself in the light of the disclosures provided; and if the facts have been fully and correctly stated, the investor assumes whatever risks may be involved in the purchase of the securities.

Nor does registration guarantee the accuracy of the facts represented in the registration statement and prospectus. The law does, however, prohibit false and misleading statements under penalty of fine or imprisonment, or both. In addition, if an investor suffers loss in the purchase of a registered security, the law provides him with important recovery rights if he can prove that there was incomplete or inaccurate disclosure of material facts in the registration statement or prospectus. These rights must be asserted in an appropriate Federal or State court (not before the Commission, which has no power to award damages); and if such misstatements are proved, the issuing company, its responsible directors and officers, the underwriters, controlling interests, the sellers of the securities, and others (or one or more of such persons) would be liable to the purchaser of the securities for losses sustained in their purchase.

The Registration Process

To facilitate the registration of securities by different types of issuing companies, the Commission has prepared special registration forms which vary in their disclosure requirements to provide disclosure of the essential facts pertinent in a given type of offering while at the same time minimizing the burden and expense of compliance with the law. In general, the registration forms call for disclosure of information such as (1) a description of the registrant's properties and business, (2) a description of the significant provisions of the security to be offered for sale and its relationship to the registrant's other capital securities, (3) information about the management of the registrant, and (4) financial statements certified by independent public accountants.

The registration statement and prospectus become public immediately on filing with the Commission; but it is unlawful to sell the securities until the effective date. After the filing of the registration statement, the securities may be offered orally or by certain summaries of the information in the registration statement as permitted by rules of the Commission. The Act provides that registration statements shall become effective on the 20th day after filing (or on the 20th day after the filing of the last amendment thereto); but the Commission, in its discretion, may advance the effective date if, considering the adequacy of information theretofore publicly available, the ease with which the facts about the new offering can be disseminated and understood, and the interests of investors and the public, such action is deemed appropriate.

Registration statements are examined by the Division of Corporation Finance for compliance with the disclosure requirements. If a statement appears to be materially incomplete or inaccurate, the registrant usually is informed by letter and given an opportunity to file correcting or clarifying amendments. The Commission however, has authority to refuse or suspend the effectiveness of any registration statement if it finds, after hearing, that material representations are misleading, inaccurate or incomplete. Accordingly, if material deficiencies in a registration statement appear to stem from a deliberate attempt to conceal and mislead, or if the deficiencies otherwise are of such nature as not to lend themselves readily to correction through the informal letter process, the Commission may conclude that it is in the public interest to resort to a hearing to develop the facts by evidence and to determine on the evidence whether a stop order should issue refusing or suspending effectiveness of the statement.

A stop order is not a permanent bar to the effectiveness of the registration statement or sale of the securities, for the order must be lifted and the statement declared effective if amendments are filed correcting the statement in accordance with the stop order decision. The Commission may issue stop orders after the sale of securities has been commenced or completed. Although losses which may have been suffered in the purchase of securities are not restored to investors by the stop order, the Commission's decision and the evidence on which it is based may serve to put investors on notice of their rights and aid in their own recovery suits.

This examination process naturally contributes to the general reliability of the registration disclosures—but it does not give positive assurance of the accuracy of the facts reported. Even if such a verification of the facts were possible, the task, if not actually prohibitive, would involve such a tremendous undertaking (both in time and money) as to seriously impede the financing of business ventures through the public sale of securities.

Small Issue Exemption

Among the special exemptions from the registration requirement is one adopted by Congress as an aid primarily to small business. The law provides that offerings of securities not exceeding $500,000 in amount may be exempted from registration, subject to such conditions as the Commission prescribes for the protection of investors. The Commission's Regulation A permits certain domestic and Canadian companies to make exempt offerings not exceeding $500,000 in amount. Offerings on behalf of controlling persons are limited in amount to $100,000 for each such person, not to exceed $500,000 in all. Offerings on behalf of persons other than an Issuer or its affiliates are limited to $100,000 for each such person, not to exceed a total of $300,000, which is not included in the $500,000 ceiling limitation. Under certain circumstances an estate may offer up to $500,000 of securities. The exemption is available provided certain specified conditions are met, including the prior filing of a "Notification" with the appropriate Regional Office of the Commission and the use of an offering circular containing certain basic information in the sale of the securities. A similar regulation is available for offerings not exceeding $500,000 by small business investment companies licensed by the Small Business Administration. Other exemptions of a more limited nature are available for other types of offerings.

Interpretations and Rulemaking

As a part of its activities under this Act, the Division of Corporation Finance also renders administrative interpretations of the law and regulations thereunder to members of the public, prospective registrants and others, to help them decide legal questions about the application of the law and the regulations to particular situations and to aid them in complying with the law. This advice, for example, might include an informal expression of opinion about whether the offering of a particular security is subject to the registration requirements of the law and, if so, advice as to compliance with the disclosure requirements of the applicable registration form. Other Divisions render similar advice and assistance.

The Commission's objective of effective disclosure with a minimum of burden and expense calls for constant review of the practical operation of the rules and registration forms adopted by it. If experience shows that a particular requirement fails to achieve its objective, or if a rule appears unduly burdensome in relation to the benefits resulting from the disclosure provided, the Division of Corporation Finance presents the problem to the Commission for consideration of possible modification of the rule or other requirement. Many suggestions for rule modification follow extensive consultation with industry representatives and others affected. In addition, the Commission normally gives advance public notice of proposals for the adoption of new or amended rules or registration forms and affords opportunity for interested members of the public to comment thereon. The same procedure is followed under the other Acts administered by the Commission.

The scope and importance of the Commission's work in the accounting field under the several statutes are discussed below under "Office of the Chief Accountant."

Fraud Prohibitions

Generally speaking, the fraud prohibitions of the Securities Act are similar to those contained in the Securities Exchange Act of 1934, under which topic the Commission's investigation and enforcement activities are discussed.

SECURITIES EXCHANGE ACT OF 1934

By this Act, Congress extended the "disclosure" doctrine of investor protection to securities listed and registered for public trading on our national securities exchanges; and the enactment in August 1964 of the Securities Acts Amendments of 1964 applied the disclosure and reporting provisions to equity securities of hundreds of companies traded over-the-counter (if their assets exceed $1 million and their shareholders number 500 or more).

Corporate Reporting

Companies which seek to have their securities listed and registered for public trading on such an exchange must file a registration application with the exchange and the Commission. A similar registration form must be filed by companies whose equity securities are traded over-the-counter if they meet the size test referred to. The Commission's rules prescribe the nature and content of these registration statements, including certified financial statements. These data are generally comparable to, but less extensive than, the disclosures required in Securities Act registration statements. Following the registration of their securities, such companies must file annual and other periodic reports to keep current the information contained in the original filing.

Since trading by and between public investors, whether involving listed or over-the-counter securities, involves transactions between holders of outstanding securities (not an offer of securities for sale by the issuing company), there is no provision for dissemination of the reported data to investors through use of a prospectus or similar medium. However, the reported information is available for public inspection, both at the offices of the Commission and the exchanges. It is also used extensively by publishers of securities manuals, securities advisory services, investment advisers, trust departments, brokers and dealers in securities, and similar agencies, and thus obtains widespread dissemination. In addition, as indicated below, copies of any of the reported data may be obtained from the Commission at nominal cost.

The law prescribes penalties for filing false statements and reports with the Commission, as well as provision for recovery by investors who suffer losses in the purchase or sale of registered securities in reliance thereon.

Proxy Solicitations

Another provision of this law governs the solicitation of proxies (votes) from holders of registered securites (both listed and over-the-counter), whether for the election of directors or for approval of other corporate action. In any such solicitation, whether by the management or minority groups, disclosure must be made of all material facts concerning the matters on which such holders are asked to vote; and they must be afforded an opportunity to vote "Yes" or "No" on each matter. Where a contest for control of the management of a corporation is involved, the rules require disclosure of the names and interests of all "participants" in the proxy contest. Holders of such securities thus are enabled to vote intelligently on corporate actions requiring their approval. The Commission's rules require that proposed proxy material be filed in advance for examination by the Commission for compliance with the disclosure requirements.

Tender Offer Solicitations

In 1968, Congress amended the Exchange Act to extend its reporting and disclosure provisions to situations where control of a company is sought through a tender offer, or other planned stock acquisition of over 10 percent of a company's equity securities. The amount was reduced to 5 percent by an amendment in 1970. These amendments and Commission rules thereunder require disclosure of pertinent information, by the person seeking to acquire over 5 percent of the company's securities by direct purchase or by tender offer, as well as by any persons soliciting shareholders to accept or reject a tender offer. Thus, as with the proxy rules, public investors who hold stock in the subject corporation may now make informed decisions on take-over bids.

Insider Trading

The protection provided the investing public through disclosure of financial and related information concerning the securities of registered companies, is supplemented by provisions of the law designed to curb misuse of corporate information not available to the general public. To that end, each officer and director of such a company, and each beneficial owner of more than 10 percent of its registered equity securities, must file an initial report with the Commission (and with the exchange on which the stock may be listed) showing his holdings of each of the company's equity securities. Thereafter, they must file reports for any month during which there was any change in such holdings. In addition, the law provides that profits obtained by them from purchases and sales (or sales and purchases) of such equity securities within any 6 months' period may be recovered by the company or by any security holder on its behalf. This recovery right must be asserted in the appropriate United States District Court. Such "insiders" are also prohibited from making short sales of their companies' equity securities.

Margin Trading

The statute also contains provisions governing margin trading in securities. It authorizes the Board of Governors of the Federal Reserve System to set limitations on the amount of credit which may be extended for the purpose of purchasing or carrying securities. The objective is to restrict the excessive use of the nation's credit in the securities markets. While the credit restrictions are set by the Board, investigation and enforcement is the responsibility of the Commission.

Market Surveillance

The Securities Exchange Act also provides a system for regulating securities trading practices in both the exchange and the over-the-counter markets. In general, transactions in securities which are effected otherwise than on national securities exchanges are said to take place "over the counter." Designed to protect the interests of investors and the public, these provisions seek to curb misrepresentations and deceit, market manipulation and other fraudulent acts and practices and to establish and maintain just and equitable principles of trade conducive to the maintenance of open, fair and orderly markets.

While these provisions of the law establish the general regulatory pattern, the Commission is responsible for promulgating rules and regulations for their implementation. Thus, the Commission has adopted regulations which, among other things, (1) define acts or practices which constitute a "manipulative or deceptive device or contrivance" prohibited by the statute, (2) regulate short selling, stabilizing transactions and similar matters, (3) regulate the hypothecation of customers' securities and (4) provide safeguards with respect to the financial responsibility of brokers and dealers.

Registration of Exchanges and Securities Associations

In addition, the law requires registration with the Commission of (1) "national securities exchanges" (those having a substantial securities trading volume); and (2) brokers and dealers who conduct an over-the-counter securities business in interstate commerce.

To obtain registration, exchanges must show that they are so organized as to be able to comply with the provisions of the statute and the rules and regulations of the Commission and that their rules contain provisions which are just and adequate to insure fair dealing and to protect investors. Among other things, exchange rules must provide for the expulsion, suspension or other disciplining of members for conduct inconsistent with just and equitable principles of trade.

While the law contemplates that exchanges shall have full opportunity to establish self-regulatory measures insuring fair dealing and the protection of investors, it empowers the Commission by order, rule or regulation to "alter or supplement" the rules of exchanges with respect to various phases of their activities and trading practices if necessary to effectuate the statutory objective. For the most part, exchange rules and revisions thereof, suggested by exchanges or by the Commission, reach their final form after discussions between representatives of the exchange and the Commission without resort to formal proceedings.

By an amendment to the law enacted in 1938, Congress also provided for creation of a self-policing body among over-the-counter brokers and dealers. This measure authorizes the registration with the Commission of an association of such brokers and dealers provided it is so organized as:

> "to prevent fraudulent and manipulative acts and practices, to promote just and equitable principles of trade, to provide safeguards against unreasonable rates of commissions or other charges, and, in general, to protect investors and the public interest, and to remove impediments to and perfect the mechanism of a free and open market . . ."

To enforce these objectives, the rules of such an association also must provide for the disciplining of members (including suspension or expulsion) for misconduct. The establishment, maintenance and enforcement of a voluntary code of business ethics is one of the principal features of this provision of the law. (Only one such association, the National Association of Securities Dealers, Inc., is registered with the Commission under this provision of the law.)

Not all broker-dealer firms are members of the NASD; thus, some are not subject to supervision and control by that agency. To equalize the regulatory pattern, Congress provided in the 1964 Amendments that the Commission should undertake to establish investor safeguards applicable to non-NASD firms comparable to those applicable to NASD members. Among the controls adopted by the Commission is a requirement that persons associated with non-NASD firms meet certain qualification standards similar to those applied by the NASD to its members.

Broker-Dealer Registration

Applications for registration as broker-dealers and amendments thereto are examined by the Office of Registrations and Reports with the assistance of the Division of Market Regulation. The registration of brokers and dealers engaged in an interstate over-the-counter securities business also is an important phase of the regulatory plan of the Act. They must conform their business practices to the standards prescribed in the law and the Commission's regulations for the protection of investors (as well as to the fair trade practice rules of their association); in addition, as will be seen later, they may violate these regulations only at the risk of possible loss of registration with the Commission and the right to continue to conduct an interstate securities business, or of suspension or expulsion from the association and of the benefits of such membership. (The broker-dealer registration requirement does not apply to firms engaged solely in a municipal securities business.)

Investigation and Enforcement

It is the duty of the Commission under the laws it administers to investigate complaints or other indications of possible law violations in securities transactions, most of which arise under the Securities Act of 1933 and the Securities Exchange Act of 1934. Investigation and enforcement work is the primary responsibility of the Commission's Regional Offices, subject to review and direction by the Division of Enforcement.

Most of the Commission's investigations are conducted privately, the facts being developed to the fullest extent possible through informal inquiry, interviewing of witnesses, examination of brokerage records and other documents, reviewing and trading data and similar means. The Commission however, is empowered to issue subpoenas requiring sworn testimony and the production of books, records and other documents pertinent to the subject matter under investigation; in the event of refusal to respond to a subpoena, the Commission may apply to a Federal court for an order compelling obedience thereto.

Inquiries and complaints of investors and the general public provide one of the primary sources of leads for detection of law violations in securities transactions. Another is the surprise inspections by Regional Offices of the books and records of brokers and dealers to determine whether their business practices conform to the prescribed rules. Still another is the conduct of inquiries into market fluctuations in particular stocks which appear not to be the result of known developments affecting the issuing company or of general market trends.

The more general types of investigations concern the sale without registration of securities subject to the registration requirement of the Securities Act, and misrepresentation or omission of material facts concerning securities offered for sale (whether or not registration is required). The anti-fraud provisions of the law also apply equally to the *purchase* of securities, whether involving outright misrepresentations or the withholding or omission of pertinent facts to which the seller was entitled. For example, it is unlawful in certain situations to purchase securities from another person while withholding material information which would indicate that the securities have a value substantially greater than that at which they are being acquired. Such provisions of the law apply not only to transactions between brokers and dealers and their customers but also to the reacquisition of securities by an issuing company or its "insiders."

Other types of inquiries relate to the manipulation of the market prices of securities; the misappropriation or unlawful hypothecation of customers' funds or securities; the conduct of a securities business while insolvent; the purchase or sale of securities by a broker-dealer, from or to his customers, at prices not reasonably related to the current market prices therefor; and violation by the broker-dealer of his responsibilty to treat his customers fairly.

The most common of the latter type of violation involves the broker-dealer who, on gaining the trust and confidence of a customer and thereby establishing an agency relationship demanding the highest degree of fiduciary duty and care, takes secret profits in his securities transactions with or for the customer over and above the agreed brokerage (agency) commission. For example the broker-dealer may have purchased securities from customers at prices far below, or sold securities to customers at prices far above, their current market prices. In most such cases, the broker-dealer subjects himself to no risk of loss, since his purchases from customers are made only if he can make simultaneous sales of the securities at prices substantially in excess of those paid to the customers, and his sales to customers are made only if he can make simultaneous purchases of the securities at prices substantially lower than those charged the customer. Or the firm may engage in large-scale in-and-out transactions for the customer's account ("churning") to generate increased commissions, usually without regard to any resulting benefit to the customer.

There is a fundamental distinction between a broker and a dealer; and it is important that investors should understand the difference. The *broker* serves as the customer's *agent* in buying or selling securities *for* his customer. As such, he owes the customer the highest fiduciary responsibility and care and may charge only such agency commission as has been agreed to by the customer. On the other hand, a *dealer* acts as a *principal* and buys securities *from* or sell securities *to* his customers. In such transactions, the dealer's profit is measured by the difference between the prices at which he buys and sells securities. Since the dealer is operating for his own account, he normally may not charge the customer a fee or commission for services rendered. Even in the case of such dealer transactions, however, the Commission and the courts have held that the conduct of a securities business carries with it the implied representation that customers will be dealt with fairly and that dealers may not enter into transactions with customers at prices not reasonably related to the prevailing market. The law requires that there be delivered to the customer a written "confirmation" of each transaction disclosing whether the securities firm is acting as a principal for its own account or as an agent for the customer (and, if the latter, the broker's compensation from all sources).

Statutory Sanctions

It should be understood that Commission investigations (which for the most part are conducted in private) are essentially fact finding inquiries. The facts so developed by the staff are considered by the Commission only in determining whether there is *prima facie* evidence of a law violation and whether an action should be commenced to determine whether, in fact, a violation actually occurred and, if so, whether some sanction should be imposed.

Assuming that the facts show possible fraud or other law violation, the laws provide several courses of action or remedies which the Commission may pursue:

    a. *Civil injunction.* The Commission may apply to an appropriate United States District Court for an order enjoining those acts or practices alleged to violate the law or Commission rules.

    b. *Criminal prosecution.* If fraud or other willful law violation is indicated, the Commission may refer the facts to the Department of Justice with a recommendation for criminal prosecution of the offending persons. That Department, through its local United States Attorneys (who frequently are assisted by Commission attorneys), may present the evidence to a Federal grand jury and seek an indictment.

c. *Administrative remedy.* The Commission may, after hearing, issue orders suspending or expelling members from exchanges or the over-the-counter dealers association; denying, suspending or revoking the registrations of broker-dealers; or censuring individuals for misconduct or barring them (temporarily or permanently) from employment with a registered firm.

Broker-Dealer Revocations

All of these sanctions may be applied to any person who engages in securities transactions violative of the law, whether or not he is engaged in the securities business. However, the administrative remedy is generally only invoked in the case of exchange or association members, registered brokers or dealers, or individuals who may associate with any such firm. In any such administrative proceeding, the Commission issues an order specifying the acts or practices alleged to have been committed in violation of law and directing that a hearing be held for the purpose of taking evidence thereon. At the hearing, counsel for the Division of Enforcement (normally a Regional Office attorney) undertakes to establish for the record those facts which support the charge of law violation, and the respondents have full opportunity to cross-examine witnesses and to present evidence in defense. The procedure followed in the conduct of such proceedings is discussed below under "Administrative Proceedings." If the Commission in its ultimate decision of the case finds that the respondents violated the law, it may take remedial action as indicated above. Such action may effectively bar a firm from the conduct of a securities business in interstate commerce or on exchanges, or an individual from association with a registered firm—subject to the respondents' right to seek judicial review of the decision by the appropriate United States Court of Appeals.

In its investigation and enforcement actions, the Commission cooperates closely with other Federal, State and local law enforcement officials, as well as with such private agenices as the Better Business Bureaus.

The many instances in which these sanctions of the law have been invoked present a formidable record. However, of perhaps greater significance to the investing public is the deterrent or prophylactic effect of the very existence of the fraud prohibitions of the law and the Commission's powers of investigation and enforcement. These provisions of the law, coupled with the disclosure requirements applicable to new security offerings and to other registered securities, tend to inhibit fraudulent stock promotions and operations. They also have a tendency to increase public confidence in securities as an investment medium, thus facilitating financing through the public sale of securities, which contributes to the industrial growth of the nation.

Commission Not a Collection Agency

Communications from the investing public are very helpful to the Commission in connection with its statutory duties and the Commission appreciates receiving them. However, because the Commission receives many inquiries and complaints from investors urging it to intercede in their behalf in an attempt to recover losses in the purchase of securities, it is appropriate to point out that the

Commission in no sense is to be considered a collection agency. While the laws provide investors with important recovery rights if they have been defrauded, and although the Commission's administration of the laws operates in many instances to uncover facts indicating the possible existence of such rights, recovery may be sought only through the assertion of claims by investors before a court of competent jurisdiction. Further, the Commission cannot give advice as to the merits of securities, whether or not they are registered. Through enactment of the securities laws Congress sought to provide disclosure of much of the basic information on which the merits of particular securities, and the risks inherent in their purchase, might be realistically appraised. But the responsibility for examining the information and determining the investment merit of securities and the risks involved in their purchase rests with the investor.

Administrative Interpretations and Rulemaking

As previously indicated, the Commission not only consults and advises with industry representatives and others concerning legal interpretative problems arising under the securities laws and with respect to the adoption of new or amended rules and regulations, but also gives public notice of suggested rules and invites comments and criticisms which are considered in determining the nature and scope of rules to be adopted. The Commission constantly reviews its rules in light of the experience gained in their administration, to the end that they will provide maximum investor protection with a minimum of interference with the proper functioning of the securities markets.

The examination of the periodic report and proxy statements of companies whose shares are listed or traded over-the-counter (except those of investment companies), as well as the reports of insiders, is conducted by the Division of Corporation Finance, while the investigative, enforcement and regulatory work under this law is carried on by the Division of Trading and Markets, assisted by Regional Offices—both under supervision and direction of the Commission.

PUBLIC UTILITY HOLDING COMPANY ACT OF 1935

Purpose of Act

This statute was enacted by Congress to correct the many abuses which Congressional inquiries had disclosed in the financing and operation of electric and gas public-utility holding-company systems.

When the Act became law in 1935, some 15 holding-company systems controlled 80 percent of all electric energy generation, 98.5 percent of all transmission of electric energy across State lines, and 80 percent of all natural-gas pipeline mileage in the United States. Many of the huge utility empires then in existence controlled subsidiaries operating in many widely-separated States and which had no economic or functional relationship to each other. Holding companies were pyramided layer upon layer, many of them serving no useful or economic purpose; and many systems had very complicated corporate and capital structures, with control often lodged in junior securities having little or no equity. These conditions ranked high among the abuses which the Act was designed to correct.

Registration

Interstate holding-companies which are engaged through their subsidiaries in the electric-utility business or in the retail distribution of natural or manufactured gas are subject to regulation under the statute. The Act requires that they register with the Commission and file initial and periodic reports containing detailed data about the organization, financial structure and operations of each such holding company and of its subsidiaries. Once the holding companies are registered, they and their subsidiaries become subject to regulation by the Commission in accordance with statutory standards designed for the protection of investors, consumers, and the public interest. If, however, a holding company or a subsidiary thereof meets certain specifications, it may be exempted from part or all the duties and obligations otherwise imposed on it by statute.

Integration and Simplification

From the standpoint of their impact on the electric and gas utility industries, the most important provisions of the Act are its requirements for the physical integration and corporate simplification of holding-company systems. The integration standards of the statute restrict a holding company's operations to an "integrated utility system," which is defined in the Act as one capable of economical operation as a single coordinated system confined to a single area or region in one or more states and not so large as to impair (considering the state of the art) the advantages of localized management, efficient operation and effectiveness of local regulation. Additional systems or incidental businesses are retainable only under certain limited conditions. The corporate simplification provisions of the Act require action to insure that the capital structure and the continued existence of any company in a holding-company system do not unduly or unnecessarily complicate the corporate structure of the system or unfairly or inequitably distribute voting power among security holders of the system.

The integration and simplification provisions of the Act direct the Commission to determine what action, if any, must be taken by registered holding companies and their subsidiaries to comply with these requirements; and the Commission may apply to Federal courts for orders compelling compliance with Commission directives made on the basis of such determinations. However, many divestments of nonretainable subsidiaries and properties, recapitalizations, dissolutions of companies and other adjustments required to comply with the Act have been accomplished by the holding-company systems through voluntary reorganization plans for which the Act also provides. If a voluntary plan is found by the Commission to be fair and equitable to all affected persons and to be necessary to further the objectives of the Act, the Commission may approve the plan. Thereafter, if the company requests, the Commission applies to a Federal district court for an order approving the plan and directing its enforcement. All interested persons, including State commissions and other governmental agencies, are accorded full opportunity to be heard in proceedings before the Commission and before the Federal courts.

The overall effect of the Commission's administration of the integration and simplification provisions of the law has been far-reaching and unparalleled.

During the 34 year period from 1938 to 1972, about 2,500 companies have been subject to the Act as registered holding companies or subsidiaries thereof at one time or another. Included in this total were over 227 holding companies, 1,046 electric and gas utility companies and 1,210 other companies engaged in a wide variety of pursuits. Among the latter were brick works, laundries, experimental orchards, motion picture theaters and even a baseball club. Today the picture is strikingly different. Only 17 active holding company systems are now registered. They are comprised of 13 registered holding companies which function solely as holding companies, 7 holding companies which also are engaged in utility operations, 91 electric and/or gas subsidiary companies, 57 nonutility subsidiaries and 16 inactive companies, making a total of 184 companies with aggregate assets of $19 billion. Further, these 17 systems now account for only about one-fifth of the aggregate assets of the privately-owned electric and gas utility and gas pipeline industries of the nation. Most electric and gas utility companies, which formerly were associated with registered holding companies, now operate as independent concerns.

The Commission's Continuing Jurisdiction

In enacting the statute, the Congress recognized that certain electric-utility holding company systems and certain groups of gas utility and transmission companies, which constitute physically integrated systems and are not too large or scattered to meet the integration and simplication requirements of the Act, may offer operating economies and other advantages which justify the continuation of holding-company control. Thus, the 17 systems referred to above are expected to be subject to the regulatory provisions of the Act for the indefinite future.

Financing Transactions

The issue and sale of securities by holding companies and their subsidiaries are subject to regulation by the Commission under prescribed standards of the law. The tests which a proposed security issue must meet are: (1) the security must be reasonably adapted to the security structure of the issuer and of other companies in the same holding company system; (2) the security must be reasonably adapted to the earning power of the company; (3) the proposed issue must be necessary and appropriate to the economical and efficient operation of the company's business; (4) the fees, commissions and other remuneration paid in connection with the issue must not be unreasonable; and (5) the terms and conditions of the issue or sale of the security must not be detrimental to the public interest or the interest of investors or consumers. In certain cases where there has been an approval by a State regulatory commission, the law directs the Commission to exempt security issues of subsidiary companies, subject to imposition of such terms and conditions as the Commission may deem necessary for the protection of investors or consumers.

To implement these objectives and to eliminate investment banker control and assure maintenance of competitive conditions as required, the Commission has promulgated a rule requiring (with certain exceptions) that in the sale of new securities by registered holding companies and their subsidiaries, as well as in the sale by such holding companies of securities held in their investment portfolio, the issuer or seller shall invite sealed competitive bids for the securities.

Purchases and Sales of Utility Securities and Properties

The acquisition of securities and utility assets by holding companies and their subsidiaries may not be authorized by the Commission unless the following standards are met:

1. The acquisition must not tend toward interlocking relations or concentration of control to an extent detrimental to the public interest or the interest of investors or consumers;

2. Any consideration paid for the acquisition, including fees, commissions and other remuneration, must not be unreasonable;

3. The acquisition must not complicate the capital structure of the holding company system;

4. The acquisition must not be otherwise detrimental to the public interest or the interest of investors or consumers, or to the proper functioning of the holding company system; and

5. The acquisition must tend toward the economic and efficient development of an integrated public utility system.

Sales of utility assets or securities may not be made in contravention of Commission rules and orders regarding the consideration to be received, maintenance of competitive conditions, fees and commissions, disclosure of interest and similar matters.

Other Regulatory Provisions

Other phases of the Act provide for the regulation of dividend payments (in circumstances where such payments might result in corporate abuses), intercompany loans, solicitation of proxies, consents and other authorizations, and insiders' trading. "Upstream" loans from subsidiaries to their parents and "upstream" or "cross-stream" loans from public-utility companies to any holding company in the same holding-company system are expressly forbidden. The Act also requires that all services performed for any company in a holding-company system by a service company in that system be rendered at cost fairly and equitably allocated. Thus, the Act deals effectively with the problem of excessive service charges levied on operating electric and gas companies by their parent holding companies, a problem with which State commissions had experienced considerable difficulty.

Administrative Interpretations and Advice

The Commission is assisted in the administration of the Holding Company Act by its Division of Corporate Regulation, which analyzes legal, financial, accounting, engineering and other problems arising under the Act. The Division participates in hearings to develop the factual records; where necessary, files briefs and participates in oral arguments before the Commission; and makes recommendations with respect to the Commission's findings and decisions in cases which arise in the administration of the law. All hearings are conducted in accordance with the Commission's Rules of Practice discussed below under

"Administrative Proceedings." The Division also confers with and renders advisory assistance to holding-company representatives to aid in the solution of their problems under the Act.

TRUST INDENTURE ACT OF 1939

This Act applies in general to bonds, debentures, notes, and similar debt securities offered for public sale which are issued pursuant to trust indentures under which more than $1 million of securities may be outstanding at any one time. Even though such securities may be registered under the Securities Act, they may not be offered for sale to the public unless the trust indenture conforms to specified statutory standards of this Act designed to safeguard the rights and interests of the purchasers.

The Act was passed after studies by the Commission had revealed the frequency with which trust indentures failed to provide minimum protections for security holders and absolved so-called trustees from minimum obligations in the discharge of their trusts. It requires that the indenture trustee be free of conflicting interests which might interfere with the faithful exercise of its duties in behalf of the purchasers of the securities. It requires also that the trustee be a corporation with minimum combined capital and surplus; imposes high standards of conduct and responsibility on the trustee; precludes preferential collection of certain claims owing to the trustee by the issuer in the event of default; provides for the issuer's supplying evidence to the trustee of compliance with indenture terms and conditions such as those relating to the release or substitution of mortgaged property, issuance of new securities or satisfaction of the indenture; and provides for reports and notices by the trustee to security holders. Other provisions of the Act prohibit impairment of the security holders' right to sue individually for principal and interest except under certain circumstances, and require the maintenance of a list of security holders which may be used by them to communicate with each other regarding their rights as security holders.

Applications for qualification of trust indentures are examined by the Division of Corporation Finance for compliance with the applicable requirements of the law and the Commission's rules thereunder.

INVESTMENT COMPANY ACT OF 1940

This legislation, together with the Investment Advisers Act of 1940, discussed below, resulted from a study of the activities of investment companies and investment advisers conducted by the Commission pursuant to direction of Congress contained in the Holding Company Act. The results of this study were reported to Congress in a series of reports filed in 1938, 1939 and 1940, the legislation being supported both by the Commission and the investment company industry.

Under this Act, the activities of companies engaged primarily in the business of investing, reinvesting and trading in securities and whose own securities are offered and sold to and held by the investing public, are subject to certain statutory prohibitions and to Commission regulation in accordance with prescribed standards deemed necessary to protect the interests of investors and the public.

It is important for investors to understand, however, that the Commission does not supervise the investment activities of these companies and that regulation by the Commission does not imply safety of investment in such companies.

In addition to a requirement that such companies register with the Commission,* the law requires disclosure of their financial condition and investment policies to afford investors full and complete information about their activities; prohibits such companies from changing the nature of their business or their investment policies without the approval of the stockholders; bars persons guilty of security frauds from serving as officers and directors; prevents underwriters, investment bankers or brokers from constituting more than a minority of the directors of such companies; requires management contracts (and material changes therein) to be submitted to security holders for their approval; prohibits transactions between such companies and their directors, officers, or affiliated companies or persons, except on approval by the Commission as being fair and involving no overreaching; forbids the issuance of senior securities by such companies except under specified conditions and upon specified terms; and prohibits pyramiding of such companies and cross-ownership of their securities.

Other provisions relate to sales and repurchases of securities issued by investment companies, exchange offers, and other activities of investment companies, including special provisions for periodic payment plans and face-amount certificate companies.

With respect to plans of reorganization of investment companies, the Commission is authorized to prepare advisory reports as to the fairness of their terms and provisions if requested by the company or 25 percent of its stockholders; and it may institute court proceedings to enjoin a plan of reorganization if it appears grossly unfair to security holders. The Commission may also institute court action to remove management officials who may be guilty of gross misconduct or gross abuse of trust.

The securities of investment companies are also required to be registered under the Securities Act; and the companies must file periodic reports and are subject to the Commission's proxy and "insider" trading rules.

The Division of Corporate Regulation assists the Commission in the administration of this law, as well as the processing of investment company registration statements under the Securities Act as well as their proxy statements and periodic reports.

INVESTMENT ADVISERS ACT OF 1940

This law establishes a pattern of regulation of investment advisers which is similar in many respects to Securities Exchange Act provisions governing the conduct of brokers and dealers. It requires, with certain exceptions, that persons or firms who engage for compensation in the business of advising others about

*A list of registered investment companies, showing their classification, assets size and location, may be purchased from the Commission in photocopy form (cost furnished upon request).

their securities transactions shall register with the Commission and conform their activities to statutory standards designed to protect the interests of investors.

The registration of investment advisers may be denied, suspended or revoked by the Commission if, after notice and hearing, it finds that a statutory disqualification exists and that such action is in the public interest. Disqualifications include a conviction for certain financial crimes or securities violations, the existence of injunctions based on such activities, a conviction for violation of the Mail Fraud Statute, the wilfull filing of false reports with the Commission, and wilfull violations of this Act, the Securities Act or the Securities Exchange Act. In addition to the administrative sanction of denial, suspension or revocation, the Commission may obtain injunctions restraining violations of this law and may recommend prosecution by the Department of Justice for fraudulent misconduct or wilfull violation ot the law or rules of the Commission thereunder.

The law contains anti-fraud provisions, and it empowers the Commission to adopt rules defining fraudulent, deceptive or manipulative acts and practices and designed to prevent such activities. It also requires that investment advisers disclose the nature of their interest in transactions executed for their clients; and, in effect, it prevents the assignment of investment advisory contracts without the client's consent. The law also imposes on investment advisers subject to the registration requirement the duty to maintain books and records in accordance with such rules as may be prescribed by the Commission, and it authorizes the Commission to conduct inspections of such books and records.

The Commission is aided in the administration of this law by the Office of Registrations and Reports and the Division of Investment Management Regulation.

BANKRUPTCY ACT, CHAPTER X

Under Chapter X, the Commission serves as adviser to United States district courts in connection with proceedings for the reorganization of debtor corporations in which there is a substantial public interest. It participates as a party to these proceedings, either at the request or with the approval of the courts. It renders independent, expert advice and assistance to the courts, which do not maintain their own staffs of expert consultants.

Representatives of the Commission follow closely the progress of reorganization proceedings in which it is a participant, and confer with the court-appointed trustees and their counsel and with other interested parties in the s   tion of the various problems which arise in the administration of the affairs of the debtor corporation and in the formulation of plans of reorganization. In addition to the advice and assistance which the Commission renders, both to the court and to the parties, in connection with the preparation of plans of reorganization, the Commission also presents its views and recommendations on such matters as the qualifications and independence of trustees and their counsel, fee allowances to the various parties, including the trustees and their counsel, sales of properties and other assets, interim distributions to security holders, and other financial or legal matters. The Commission has no independent right of appeal from court rulings.

Of primary importance is the Commission's assistance in the formulation of plans of reorganization of the debtor corporation which will provide fair and equitable treatment to the various creditors and other security holders and which will help to assure that the corporation will emerge from bankruptcy in a sound financial condition and able to carry on without the continued threat of bankruptcy. Underlying the Commission's recommendations concerning the fairness and feasibility of reorganization plans, is a thorough study and analysis of the debtor's past operations, its financial condition, its past earnings record and prospective future earning power, its competitive position in the particular industry, and related matters. In cases in which the scheduled liabilities of the debtor exceed $3 million, the plan of reorganization must be, and in other cases may be, referred by the court to the Commission for preparation of an advisory report on the fairness and feasibility of the plan. This advisory report is filed with the court for its assistance and is distributed among the creditors and security holders to enable them to exercise an informed judgment in considering whether to vote for or against acceptance of the plan. In cases where no formal advisory report is prepared, the Commission's views are stated orally at the hearing on the plan before the court.

Because of the predominantly local character of reorganization cases, court appearances, consultations with the parties, investigations and examinations are handled primarily by the Commission's Regional Offices, subject to supervision by the Division of Corporate Regulation and approval by the Commission.

ADMINISTRATIVE PROCEEDINGS

All formal administrative proceedings of the Commission are conducted in accordance with its Rules of Practice, which conform to the Administrative Procedure Act and are designed to establish procedural, "due process" safeguards which will protect the rights and interests of parties to each such proceeding. Among these are requirements for timely notice of the proceeding and for a sufficient specification of the issues or charges involved to enable each of the parties adequately to prepare his case. All parties, including counsel for the interested Division or Office of the Commission, may appear at the hearing and present evidence and cross-examine witnesses in much the same manner as in the ordinary trial of court actions. In addition, other interested persons may be permitted to intervene or be given limited rights of participation. In some cases, the relevant facts may be stipulated in lieu of the conduct of an evidentiary hearing.

Hearings are conducted before a Hearing Officer who is normally an Administrative Law Judge appointed by the Commission; he serves independently of the interested Division or Office and rules on the admissibility of evidence and on other issues arising during the course of the hearing. At the conclusion of the hearing, the parties and participants may urge, in writing, specific findings of fact and conclusions of law for adoption by the Hearing Officer. Thereupon, the Hearing Officer prepares and files an initial decision (unless waived), setting forth his conclusions as to the facts established by the evidence and including an order disposing of the issues involved in the proceeding. Copies of the initial decision are served on the parties and participants, who may seek Commission review thereof. If review is not sought and the Commission does not order review on its own motion, the initial decision becomes final and the Hearing Officer's order becomes effective.

In the event of Commission review of the initial decision, the parties and participants may file briefs and be heard in oral argument before the Commission. On the basis of an independent review of the record, the Commission prepares and issues its own decision; the Office of Opinions and Review aids the Commission in this decisional process. The laws provide that any person or firm aggrieved by a decision or order of the Commission may seek review thereof by the appropriate United States court of appeals. The initial decisions of Hear-ing Officers as well as the Commission's decisions are made public. Copies of Commission decisions and announcements that the initial decisions of Hearing Officers have become final also are distributed to the Commission's mailing lists. Ultimately, the Commission's decisions (as well as initial decisions which have become final and are of precedential significance) are printed by the Government Printing Office and published in the Commission's "Decisions and Reports"

OFFICE OF THE GENERAL COUNSEL

The General Counsel is the chief legal officer of the Commission. The duties of his office include representing the Commission in judicial proceedings; handling legal matters which cut across the lines of work of the several operating Divisions; and providing advice and assistance to the Commission, its operating Divisions, and Regional Offices with respect to statutory interpretation, rule-making, legislative matters and other legal problems, public or private investigations, and Congressional hearings and investigations. The Office also reviews cases where criminal prosecution is recommended. The General Counsel directs and supervises all contested civil litigation (except United States district court proceedings under Chapter X of the Bankruptcy Act) and represents the Commission in all cases in the appellate courts, filing briefs and presenting oral arguments in behalf of the Commission. In addition, in cases between private parties involving the statutes the Commission administers, the Office represents the Commission where it participates as a friend of the court in cases involving legal issues of general importance.

The Commission from time to time recommends revisions in the statutes which it administers. In addition, it prepares comments on any proposed legislation which might affect its work or where it is asked for its views by Congressional Committees. The Office of the General Counsel, together with the Division assisting the Commission in the function which may be affected by such legislation, prepares this legislative material.

OFFICE OF THE CHIEF ACCOUNTANT

The Chief Accountant is the Commission's chief consulting officer on accounting matters, advising the Commission with respect to accounting problems which arise in the administration of the Acts, particularly in matters involving new accounting policy determination. The Chief Accountant has general supervision over the execution of Commission policy with respect to the accounting principles and procedures applicable to the financial statements filed with the Commission and to the auditing standards and practices observed by the independent public accountants who examine and render an opinion on these statements.

A major objective of the Commission has been to improve accounting and .auditing standards and to maintain high standards of professional conduct by the independent accountants through cooperation with the accounting profession and by the rule-making process. In furtherance of this policy the Chief Accountant consults with representatives of the accounting profession regarding the promulgation of new or revised accounting and auditing standards and drafts rules and regulations which prescribe requirements for financial statements. Many of the rules are embodied in a basic accounting regulation entitled Regulation S-X adopted by the Commission which, together with a number of opinions issued as "Accounting Series Releases," governs the form and content of most of the financial statements filed with it.

The Chief Accountant also has supervisory responsibility for the drafting of uniform systems of accounts for public utility holding companies, mutual service companies and subsidiary service companies under the Holding Company Act; for accounting requirements for investment and broker-dealer companies; and for the general administration of those systems and accounting requirements.

The Chief Accountant administers the Commission's rules which require that accountants who examine financial statements filed with it be independent of their clients, and makes recommendations on cases arising under the Commission's Rules of Practice which specify that an accountant may be denied the privilege of practicing before the Commission because of lack of character or integrity or qualifications to represent others, or because of unethical or unprofessional conduct. He also supervises the procedures followed in accounting investigations conducted by the Commission's staff.

OFFICE OF ECONOMIC RESEARCH

The principal functions of this Office are three-fold: (1) to assist the Commission by analyzing legal, economic and industrial developments affecting the securities markets and by recommending to the Commission the institution or modification of programs commensurate with such developments; (2) to prepare statistical data and analyses related to the capital markets for Commission use as well as for general economic analysis and (3) to compile and publish data furnished to the general public as part of the overall Government statistical program.

Some of the more important projects of this office include: (1) development of analytical framework for anticipating developments in the securities industry and a continuing analysis of the economic and financial condition of the securities industry; (2) analysis of the impact of competitive rates on the economic and legal structure of the securities industry and on the investment process; (3) review of trends in corporate capital structure; (4) analysis of trends in capital markets worldwide, the impact of internationalization of these markets; and (5) continued study as to the role of self-regulation in the securities industry, and the possible need for change in regulatory rules or the industry itself to make the capital markets more efficient.

The Office of Management and Budget has designated the Commission as the agency best suited to make and publish certain financial studies including: (a) The Net Working Capital of Nonfinancial Corporations; (b) The financial activities of Private Noninsured Pension Funds and (c) New Security Offerings and related studies.

PUBLIC INFORMATION

Financial and other data included in registration statements, reports, applications and similar documents filed with the Commission are available for inspection in the Public Reference Room of the Commission's Headquarters Office in Washington, D.C. Copies of portions or all of any such public document may be obtained at nominal cost (the amount of the fee is established by an annual contract between the Commission and the copier who reproduces the documents. Estimates as to the cost of copies of specific reports or other information may be obtained on request to the Section of Public Reference, Office of Records and Service, Securities and Exchange Commission, Washington, D.C. 20549.

Current annual and other periodic reports (including financial statements) filed by companies whose securities are listed on exchanges also are available for inspection in the Commission's New York, Chicago and San Francisco Regional Offices, as are the registration statements (and subsequent reports) filed by those companies whose securities are traded over-the-counter which register under the 1964 Amendments to the Exchange Act. Moreover, if the issuer's principal office is located in the area served by the Atlanta, Boston, Denver, Fort Worth or Seattle Regional Office, its filings also may be examined at the particular Regional Office in question. In addition, prospectuses covering recent public offerings of securities registered under the Securities Act may be examined in all Regional Offices; and copies of broker-dealer and investment adviser registrations, as well as Regulation A notifications and offering circulars, may be examined in the particular Regional Office in which they were filed.

PUBLICATIONS

The publications described below are compiled by the Commission but printed and sold by the Superintendent of Documents. Requests for single copies or subscriptions, accompanied by the correct remittance, should be addressed to the Superintendent of Documents, United States Government Printing Office, Washington, D.C. 20402. THE COMMISSION DOES NOT MAINTAIN A MAILING LIST FOR THESE PUBLICATIONS.

NEWS DIGEST. A daily report of Commission announcements, decisions, orders, rules and rule proposals, current reports and applications filed, and litigation developments.

SEC DOCKET. A weekly compilation of the full texts of SEC releases under the following Acts: Securities Act, Securities Exchange Act, Public Utility Holding Company Act, Trust Indenture Act, Investment Advisers Act, and Investment Company Act. Also included will be the full texts of Accounting series releases, corporate reorganization releases, and litigation releases.

OFFICIAL SUMMARY.

A monthly summary of security transactions and holdings reported under the provisions of the Securities Exchange Act of 1934, the Public Utility Holding Company Act of 1935, and the Investment Company Act of 1940 by officers, directors, and certain other persons.

STATISTICAL BULLETIN.

A weekly publication containing data on odd lot and round lot transactions, block distributions, working capital of U.S. corporations, assets of noninsured pension funds, 144 filings, and 8æ reports.

ACTS AND RULES AND REGULATIONS:

Rules of Practice and Rules Relating to Investigations and Code of Behavior Governing Ex Parte Communications Between Persons Outside the Commission and Decisional Employees.

Securities Act of 1933.

Rules and Regulations under the 1933 Act.

Securities Exchange Act of 1934.

Rules and Regulations under the 1934 Act.

Public Utility Holding Company Act of 1935.

Rules and Regulations under the 1935 Act.

Trust Indenture Act of 1939 and Rules and Regulations.

Investment Company Act of 1940.

Rules and Regulations under the Investment Company Act.

Investment Advisers Act of 1940 and Rules and Regulations.

Chapter X, National Bankruptcy Act,

Regulation S–X (form and content of financial statements under 1933, 1934, 1935 Acts and Investment Company Act of 1940).

ACCOUNTING SERIES RELEASES:

Compilation of Releases Nos. 1-112, inclusive.

Compilation of Releases Dealing with Matters Frequently Arising under the Securities Act of 1933.

Compilations of Releases Dealing with matters arising under the Securities Exchange Act of 1934 and Investment Advisers Act of 1940.

Compilation of Releases Dealing with matters arising under the Investment Company Act of 1940.

SEC ANNUAL REPORT TO CONGRESS:

First through Thirty-fourth (out of print) (Available only for reference purposes in SEC Washington, D.C., and Regional Offices.)

SEC JUDICIAL DECISIONS (Buckram bound)—Vols. 1–5, covering period 1934–48, available only for reference purposes in SEC Washington, D.C., and Regional Offices.

SEC DECISIONS AND REPORTS (Buckram bound)—Vols. 1–41, covering period 1934–64, available only for reference purposes in SEC Washington, D.C., and Regional Offices.

Directory of Companies filing Annual Reports with the Commission under the Securities Exchange Act of 1934. Lists companies alphabetically and classified by industry groups according to the Standard Industrial Classification Manual of the Bureau of the Budget. Published annually.

A Study of Mutual Funds (Prepared for the SEC by the Wharton School of Finance and Commerce) (1962)—595 pages H. Doc. No. 2274 (87th Cong.) (Available only for reference purposes in SEC Washington, D.C., and Regional Offices.)

Report of SEC Special Study of Securities Markets (1963).

Part 6 of the Special Study Report contains the Index to Parts 1, 2, 3, 4 and 5, Tables of statutes, rules, cases, persons or securities mentioned in the Special Study.

Commission Report on Public Policy Implications of Investment Company Growth H. Rept. No. 2337 (89th Cong.), available only for reference purposes in SEC Washington, D.C., and Regional Offices.

Institutional Investor Study Report of the Securities and Exchange Commission (1971)—Eight Parts, H. Doc. No. 64 (92d Cong.).

Part 8 of the said Institutional Investor, containing the Text of the Summary and Conclusions drawn from each of the fifteen chapters of the report.

Study on Unsafe and Unsound Practices of Broker-Dealers, H. Doc. 231, (92nd Cong.)

Report of the Real Estate Advisory Committee to the SEC.

The Financial Collapse of The Penn Central Company, Staff Report of the SEC to the Special Subcommittee on Investigations, August, 1972.

SECURITIES AND EXCHANGE COMMISSION

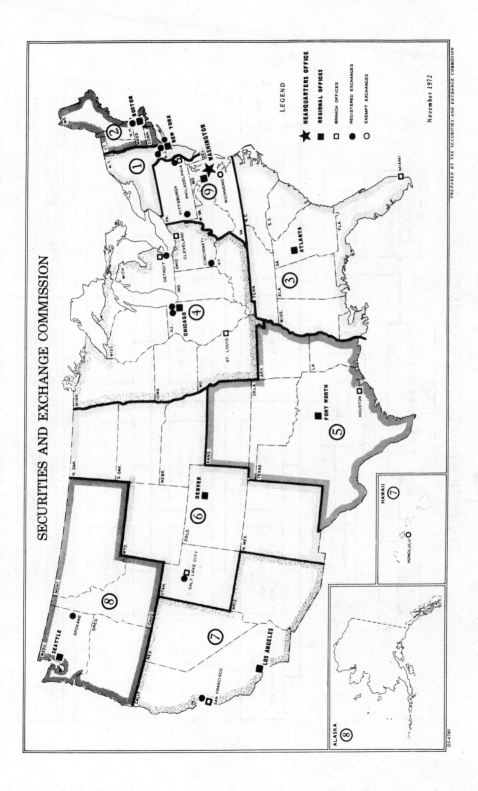

November 1972

PREPARED BY THE SECURITIES AND EXCHANGE COMMISSION

DS-4780

LEGEND

★ HEADQUARTERS OFFICE
■ REGIONAL OFFICES
□ BRANCH OFFICES
● REGISTERED EXCHANGES
○ EXEMPT EXCHANGES

SECURITIES AND EXCHANGE COMMISSION

THE COMMISSION

- THE SECRETARY
- THE OFFICE OF ADMINISTRATIVE LAW JUDGES
- THE OFFICE OF OPINIONS AND REVIEW
- THE GENERAL COUNSEL

THE EXECUTIVE DIRECTOR

- THE OFFICE OF POLICY PLANNING
- THE DIVISION OF CORPORATE REGULATION
- THE DIVISION OF CORPORATION FINANCE
- THE DIVISION OF ENFORCEMENT
- THE DIVISION OF MARKET REGULATION
- THE DIVISION OF INVESTMENT MANAGEMENT REGULATION
- THE CHIEF ACCOUNTANT
- THE OFFICE OF ECONOMIC RESEARCH
- THE OFFICE OF PUBLIC INFORMATION
- THE OFFICE OF REGISTRATIONS AND REPORTS
- THE OFFICE OF DATA PROCESSING
- THE OFFICE OF COMPTROLLER
- THE OFFICE OF PERSONNEL
- THE OFFICE OF RECORDS AND SERVICE

THE REGIONAL OFFICES

NEW YORK REGIONAL OFFICE	BOSTON REGIONAL OFFICE	ATLANTA REGIONAL OFFICE	CHICAGO REGIONAL OFFICE	FORT WORTH REGIONAL OFFICE	DENVER REGIONAL OFFICE	LOS ANGELES REGIONAL OFFICE	SEATTLE REGIONAL OFFICE	WASHINGTON, D.C. REGIONAL OFFICE
		Miami, Fla. Branch	Cleveland, Ohio Branch, Detroit, Mich. Branch, St. Louis, Mo. Branch	Houston, Texas Branch	Salt Lake City, Utah Branch	San Francisco, Calif. Branch		Philadelphia, Pa. Branch

January 1973

DS-8067

PART II

Analysis by Industry Categories

4

Aerospace

STUART H. CLEMENT, JR., C.F.A.
Aerospace Analysts of New York
(Past President)
Ernst & Company
Rye, New York

THE NATURE OF THE INDUSTRY

THE aerospace industry is a most exciting and challenging one for the security analyst because, by its nature, it is the leader of the advanced technologies and therefore the pacesetter for all other major industries based on high technology. In the author's opinion the name "aerospace" industry is a misnomer. It used to be called the aircraft industry, but the name was changed when the development of missiles and the exploration of space beginning in the early 1960s became a major part of the industry. Because it promotes the advancement of technology for the benefit of many major industries such as transportation, aircraft building, electronics, computers, and all aspects of national defense, and because it is a major contributor to the industrial strength and leadership of the country and the improvement in the quality of life of developing nations around the world, it could appropriately be called the national survival industry. Aerospace is really no longer a fitting title because the industry has become so widely diversified during the past two decades. It is now a mature and basic industry essential to the economic health and progress of the free world.

To begin with, the so-called aerospace industry is still the nation's largest manufacturer employer as well as one of the leading exporters and one of the largest contributors to the balance of payments, in spite of the fact that since 1968 total employment in the industry has dropped by 33 percent. Nearly 950,000 people were employed in the industry in June 1973, according to the Aerospace Industry Association of America, Inc.; but by June 1974, which the association expected would be the point where an upturn might begin again, payrolls would have been further cut by about 32,000.

As mentioned above, the industry has become widely diversified in the past 20 years. Its products generally are relatively high-priced, extremely complex products including aircraft, submarines, space vehicles, missiles, electronics and electronics systems, and, more recently, ships of very advanced design—not only for defense but for the shipment of petroleum, liquefied gases, and containers. Most of these products are highly automated and extremely flexible in capability and operation and represent extremely complex systems design. In producing such products, the aerospace companies have become unique as major systems developers and managers. This capability has brought about an outstanding level of cooperation among major contractors who work together to design, produce, operate, and manage enormously effective and efficient systems. Led by the management teams of the major contractors, thousands of companies may work well meshed together through several tiers of subcontractors and suppliers to an extent unknown in other industries. This complex systems management capability has developed extreme flexibility to tackle more and more diversified projects in recent years.

The industry's major market components consist of ships, submarines, spacecraft, aircraft, missiles, and other weapons systems for national defense and international peace keeping. They also include commercial aircraft, airline equipment, and support systems for the major passenger transportation systems of the world. A third major market component is general aviation which includes all flying other than that done by the military and commercial airlines. The final broad market components consist of development and operation of a wide variety of nonmilitary major systems such as satellite communications, specialized transportation systems, special purpose computers, and many services for the government, military, and private industry. Incidentally, the aerospace industry probably has installed the largest and most versatile digital and analog computer equipment in the world. In fact, it was the aerospace industry that was responsible for the development and use of large-scale computer systems in order to meet the enormous demands of the government and Department of Defense for data handling and advanced design work.

In time of war or periods of concern for national defense, many of the major contractors devote 90 to 100 percent of their efforts to defense. However, in recent years, particularly since the coming of the commercial jet airliners in 1959 and the rise in general aviation and diversification of the industry, the ratio of defense to commercial business has declined to nearly 50–50. Boeing's business today, for example, is 90 to

95 percent commercial. Lockheed, McDonnell Douglas, and United Aircraft, the major producers (along with Boeing) of jet aircraft and engines, currently have backlogs of commercial business amounting to nearly 50 percent.

The industry is very definitely a cyclical one and for some very definite and understandable reasons. First of all, business depends upon the state of major defense and commercial programs. Since it takes from five to eight years (or even more) to develop a new aircraft, an engine, a ship, or a major system, the business cycle, particularly for an individual company, is a rather long one involving research, development, production, and continuous growth of the product to its ultimate maturity.

Longevity of a program, of course, is the major source of profitability for a prime contractor and his chain of subcontractors and suppliers. Longevity depends upon a continued need for the product or system and continued growth in the product's capability and usefulness and productivity. Since major programs are extremely expensive to initiate, finance, and develop, profitability is often postponed until production is well established. Not until then does return on investment become maximized. Continued prosperity over a period of time, therefore, depends on continuity of advanced research and development, both government and company sponsored. It also depends on the ability of a company to develop a number of programs properly phased to succeed one another with a minimum decline of sales between maturing programs.

Boeing, for example, has been extremely successful until quite recently because of its ability to bring along a series of bombers and tankers and transports for the military followed by an evolution of these products into a very successful series of commercial jet airliners including the 707, 727, 737, and finally the 747. Boeing has been a relatively minor defense contractor since its last B-52 bomber was delivered in 1963, and the minuteman ICBM passed the production peak. The company suffered a serious stretchout in orders for the 747 jumbo jet after the initial wave of about 200 because of the airlines' economic difficulties around the world. However, as is usually the case, follow-on or second-wave orders are being received now that the plane has proved itself in service and the inevitable initial deficiencies have been ironed out. The airplane seems destined for many more years of production of derivative aircraft, including military versions such as the Airborne Warning and Control System (AWACS) which is presently a derivative of the KC-135 jet tanker plane. The 747 jumbo jet may also become an airborne command post, a tanker, or be adapted to other military uses. It has already become a commercial all-cargo plane.

Grumman Corporation is another example of a company which has successfully modified and changed its basic aircraft designs to make them adaptable for a number of different uses. Shifting from fighter aircraft in the late 1950s, Grumman has produced antisubmarine carrier-based aircraft which have also become carrier-based cargo planes and airborne early warning and command-and-control aircraft. The latter have greatly extended radar surveillance range and protection of the fleet at sea by placing search radars high in the air where they can see around the curvature of the earth, and have revolutionized fighter direction by moving the command post from the deck of the carrier to the aircraft where operations can be much more efficiently carried out. This system is now being developed by the air force in its AWACS program by Boeing. Both Boeing and Grumman very successfully contributed to the exploration of space, and Grumman is now engaged in a major new fighter program, the F-14 Tomcat, the long-postponed successor the 25-year-old McDonnell Douglas F-4 Phantom, which has now been made obsolete by new generation triple supersonic fighter and reconnaissance aircraft built by the Soviet Union.

Contrary to the belief of some, competition is extreme at all levels in the aerospace industry, be it on the defense or commercial side. A fighter builder, for example, must keep his product growing in capability and productivity, as must a commercial airline builder, in order to prevent its competitors from replacing it with a better one. Competition comes not only from within the United States but in recent years has been developing more and more from the outside. The Europeans and even the Japanese are now beginning to become major competitors, developing new types of aircraft such as vertical and short takeoff and landing (V/STOL) aircraft, fighters, helicopters, and short-range commercial aircraft.

The most outstanding competitive threat to the United States aerospace industry is the supersonic transport or SST. The reason is that this aircraft represents a whole new generation of technology which the Europeans and Soviet Union are pressing hard and which the United States has made the unfortunate decision to at least postpone. Involved in such an undertaking is a whole generation of scientists, engineers, and aircraft workers who are developing new materials, hydraulic, electronic, and electrical systems, new aerodynamics principles and management techniques which will revolutionize air transport and create a huge fallout for other industries. The fact that we have elected not to go forward does not mean that we can prevent it since our allies and our enemies are determined to use the SST to regain aerospace industry primacy. This represents international competition at a high level, and the SST will undoubtedly be one of the most important revenue producers in international trade for its builders. Even more important, the development cycle for this program is much longer than usual, and development is being heavily subsidized in a competitive way by the nations involved. Furthermore, such a program is highly dependent on a very broad subcontractor and supplier base and a team approach among prime contractors, so that the failure to go forward with such a program of national commercial evolution can have a very serious effect on the economy some years from now.

Production in the aerospace industry is characterized by and differentiated from other major industries by a relatively low volume of relatively high-priced products that require a relatively long time span to produce. Although such programs can be quickly stopped by congressional action, bringing a program into being is a relatively slow process highly dependent upon continuity of funding, management, employment, research, development, testing, and engineering.

The aerospace industry is composed of a large number of companies in three major classifications: prime contractors, subcontractors, and suppliers. Prime contractors, as the name implies, hold the overall contract for a program, oversee and manage it, perform a major part of research, design, engineering, test, assembly and production. They also are responsible for the coordination of all the subcontractors and are ultimately responsible for the integration of all elements of the system involved and for its successful and reliable operation. Subcontractors are assigned to engineer and develop and produce major pieces or sections of an aircraft or a rocket such as fuselage sections, wings, engine pods, fuel tanks, electronics systems, and guidance systems. Suppliers provide materials, individual components, and services.

Among the prime contractors are a number of companies that can be considered "dedicated" prime contractors whose managements have been traditionally dedicated not only to the support of the major market components of the industry, especially defense, but also to commercial air transports, general aviation, and major subsystems. Such companies, for example, are Boeing, Grumman, McDonnell Douglas, Lockheed, General Dynamics United Aircraft, Rockwell International (formerly North American Aviation), and Northrop. Other prime contractors whose main business lies elsewhere or who also have the capability to act as prime contractors in times of stress or national defense are, for example, General Electric, IBM, and Eastman Kodak. Most major industrial companies find it absolutely necessary to stay involved in, and current with, the aerospace industry in order to benefit from the advance technology fallout that is essential to their own growth, prosperity, and leadership in their individual endeavors. For example, the highly miniaturized electronic components and systems that have made the computer industry such a fast growing business have come directly from such programs as the Minuteman and Polaris ICBM programs.

Finally, the aerospace industry activity cycles can be greatly influenced by international developments affecting national defense or international commerce. Such events, past and present, include: launching of the U.S. program in the early 1960s, for the exploration of space meant instrumented and later manned vehicles in response to the technological surprise of the Soviet Sputnik satellite in 1957; the ascendency of the Soviet navy during the past decade to become among the largest and most modern in the world; the emergence of Communist China and the Soviet Union as nuclear powers; the Middle East oil situation, the worldwide growth in air traffic, the emerging energy crisis, the responsibilities of the United States to support its treaties and international agreements; the rapidly rising cost of major weapons systems; and the opportunities opened up by the emergence of new technologies, such as satellites, for communications, surveillance, weather forecasting, navigation, and earth resources management.

Important domestic developments that are also currently having a strong influence on the aerospace industry include the Merchant Marine Act of 1970 to rejuvenate this country's neglected Merchant Marine; the Clean Air Act of 1970 which is challenging the industry to develop methods for monitoring and detection of sources of pollution of the atmosphere; the recent adoption of volunteer armed forces which will require a great increase in automation and productivity of weapons, vehicles, ships, and systems; and lastly, the nation's reordering of its spending priorities which we believe have now been largely accomplished and which will lead to even greater diversification of the aerospace industry. In short, the industry has become so broad and mature and important that the security analyst choosing this field can hardly consider himself a restricted specialist. In fact, a considerable number of major specialties now exist within the industry upon which the analyst can focus nearly full time.

The industry can also suffer from adverse mass psychology. A wave of antimilitarism in recent years has tended to obscure the true value of the aerospace industry as an investment medium. In the author's opinion this influence is already beginning to wane, as the realities of the domestic and international scenes are brought back into focus by such events as the Middle East war and as the increasing buildup of foreign military forces and foreign aerospace industries, friendly and enemy, threaten this country's safety and economy.

REGULATION AND RESTRAINTS

Besides the severe competitive aspects outlined above, the aerospace industry also operates under severe regulatory, budgetary, and supervisory restraints. In recent years, concern for environmental protection has led to severe public pressures to reduce noise and engine emissions. The Federal Aeronautics Administration is responsible for licensing and certification of aircraft, engines, systems, and equipment as airworthy. The FAA also regulates safety most stringently. Pressure for noise reduction, for example, has led to new FAA regulations setting noise limits for all new aircraft and engines, and efforts are also being undertaken to reduce the noise levels of existing aircraft. As a result, rather startling results have been achieved in the new engines for the Boeing 747, the McDonnell Douglas DC-10, and the Lockheed L-1011. Even the Anglo-French Concorde SST has had its sound level brought down to that of current 707 and DC-8 type air transports—quite an engineering achievement, since the SST engines are approximately twice as powerful.

Defense expenditures are rigidly governed by congressional appropriations and Congress often waits until the last moment to give funding approval. The Government Accounting Office acts as a congressional watchdog over the progress of defense contracts, closely tracking the progress of contractors to assure that they adhere to delivery schedules and do not exceed contract costs. The Department of Defense itself constantly overhauls its procurement rules, regulations, and policies in response to problems as they arise. Public sentiment can be fickle, much to the consternation of the investor, and is capable of extreme pressures on the procurement process. Allowable profit margins are tightly controlled and over the postwar years have averaged lower than those of any other major industry as a percentage of sales. Renegotiation of profits has always been an issue in wartime or during periods of buildup or modernization of the armed forces. However, in recent years it has become a relatively insignificant factor, although always a threat. Return on investment in the aerospace industry is quite variable and often arguable because it is dependent upon the degree of reliance on government facilities used by the contractors. In recent years there has been a trend by the major contractors to provide more and more of their own facilities in an effort to increase return on investment. United Aircraft, for example, now owns virtually all its facilities.

MAJOR CURRENT PROBLEMS

Uncontrollable inflation during the past decade has been a major problem with the aerospace industry because it has been a major cause for astronomical cost increases for the Department of Defense, the airlines, and for the country as a whole. This has been especially severe in the past few years during which the Defense Department's now discredited "total package procurement" policy was in effect. Under this concept, major procurement programs, starting from the research and development stage and carrying on through production, have been conducted under fixed prices with relatively small allowance written into the contract for inflation. For example, Lockheed was nearly driven to bankruptcy, largely because of the excessive cost overruns the company was forced to absorb under this policy on several programs including the well-publicized C-5A Galaxie military jet transport program. The company itself was partly to blame for technical problems that arose requiring costly changes in design. Yet often the design changes were required in order to meet stringent and inflexible specifications set forth under the fixed-price contracts. On top of that, inflation allowed for by approximately 3 percent in the contract actually approached a rate of 10 percent shortly following the signing of the C-5A contract, and the difference was not allowable under the contract.

Several other total procurement package programs in the aerospace industry were similarly affected, finally leading to the scrapping of this procurement concept and overhauling of the procurement system in favor of the prototyping and milestone testing approach, popularly known as the "fly before buy" policy. Under this plan, established development and production milestones have to be passed, one by one, in order that funding may continue. This procurement policy has given much greater recognition to inflation and is much fairer and more flexible from the point of view of both parties. It also improves profit potential for the industry and tends to give the customer a superior product.

Another serious current problem of the industry is the rising technological competence of both friendly and potentially unfriendly nations. Japan and the major European countries have gradually rebuilt their aerospace industries since World War II, with the help of the United States, to the extent that they are now becoming major competitors. The SST in England, France, and the Soviet Union is probably the most outstanding example. Placing major restrictions on the American aerospace industry for political reasons and ignoring the progress of the rising aerospace industries of other nations threatens the loss of U.S. leadership in the next generation of technology and subsequently the loss of major markets. For example, since the war the United States has provided about 85 percent of all the world's commercial air transports, piston types and jets. Successors to all types of U.S. built commerical transports are now being designed, produced, and flight tested in Europe, Japan, and the Soviet Union.

Another aspect of this problem is that all the governments of the above named countries are giving substantial subsidy support to their rising aerospace industries. The United States does not do this to any significant degree. For example, the British and the French and, of course, the Russians have completely subsidized the development of their SSTs, while United States advances for the development of the cancelled Boeing SST prototypes were required by law to be repaid through a system of royalty payments on delivered aircraft. The new European A-300 airbus, a short-range, wide-body jet for use on high-density routes, has been heavily subsidized. The British government came to the rescue of Rolls Royce when the cost of development of the RB-211 quiet jet engine for the Lockheed L-1011 far exceeded original estimates. That government is continuing to pay for further development of this engine—which happens to be one of the finest available. The United States only guaranteed Lockheed's commercial bank loans for which it is being well recompensed by fees and generous interest rates. The cost of development of a new jet engine of the size of the RB-211 or the United Aircraft JT9D used in the Boeing 747 is extremely high. The latter cost over $1 billion to develop and to put into service. The cost of each of the U.S. wide-body jet airframes alone ran well over $1 billion to develop. Such development costs are making it extremely difficult for U.S. prime contractors to continue development of aircraft engines as private ventures without some form of government assistance, such as the foreign competitors are now receiving.

In an effort to solve this problem, U.S. companies have begun soliciting partnership with foreign companies to undertake the development and building of the next generation of engines and aircraft. Boeing, for example, has been negotiating in Japan for assistance in financing and building its next jet transport, and United Aircraft and General Electric have been doing the same thing in Europe in order to continue their engine development business.

Finally, a distinct trend towards isolationism in this country and a continuing, but hopefully waning, antimilitary sentiment most popularly expressed as a reordering of priorities has driven the U.S. defense budget to the lowest percentage of the gross national product since 1950, although the actual dollar amount has appeared to remain large. This is an historical postwar trend which unfortunately is part of the cyclical nature of the aerospace industry.

OUTLOOK FOR THE INDUSTRY—FAVORABLE FACTORS FOR GROWTH AND SPECIFIC OPPORTUNITIES

Because the industry is a cyclical one, the pendulum will undoubtedly swing back as the industry's major problems described in the preceding paragraphs are contained or resolved. To begin with, there has been a strong, underlying growth trend in general aviation which, although cyclical itself because of its dependency on the business cycle, has shown extraordinary health and has achieved outstanding growth and maturity in the past few years as the use of aircraft as an efficient and essential tool for conducting business has been proven more and more.

The end of U.S. participation in the Southeast Asian war has given the Department of Defense an opportunity to divert its attention to modernize and reequip the armed services. The strategic and tactical forces' major weapons systems are well along on the obsolescence curve. For example, new fighter aircraft for the Air Force and the Navy and a new strategic bomber are considered urgent items, because the Soviet Union now has far superior fighter aircraft in rapidly growing operational numbers as well as supersonic bombers and a huge airlift capacity which was demonstrated in the recent Middle East war. Our last B-52 subsonic bomber was built and delivered 11 years ago, and our major fighter, the F-4 Phantom used by both the Air Force and the Navy has been in production 20 years and has reached the end of its development potential. Although we have provided our best fighter to our allies in the Middle East, it has been proved incapable of intercepting such Soviet aircraft as the new Mach-3 80,000-foot-altitude MIG-23 and MIG-25 on reconnaissance missions. As a result, Iran is negotiating for procurement of our newest fighters, the Grumman F-14 and the McDonnell Douglas F-15 now under development but not yet operational in our own armed forces. Both of these programs have suffered intense procurement opposition, primarily because of their high cost; but it now appears that they are necessary and the Congress has approved funding for limited production of both planes.

The rise of Soviet naval, air, strategic missile, merchant marine, space, and commercial aircraft capabilities is being viewed with increasing alarm by the Department of Defense and the more responsible members of Congress. It is now being recognized that the United States has lost its superiority in military deterrent power and that a detente with Russia can only be achieved by at least maintaining parity. Finally the aerospace industry is accelerating its efforts at diversity to increase its commercial business, thereby lowering its dependence on defense business. The result should be a trend toward higher profit margins.

The Nixon Doctrine, established as this country prepared to extricate itself from the Southeast Asian conflict, should have a favorable effect on the aerospace industry in that the doctrine calls for this country to supply its allies' material defense needs without doing the fighting for them. Already many countries have been turning to the United States to fulfill their requirements for antisubmarine aircraft, helicopters, fighters, attack aircraft, defensive missiles, communications systems, and other equipment. The growth of airline traffic, while temporarily stalled, will undoubtedly begin to advance again as the aerospace industry develops new technology and new aircraft to generate new traffic. The jumbo jets seem destined to play an important role in the further development of air freight. The 10- to 12-year airline and the 20-year military equipment cycles have recently begun again and should provide major opportunities for the industry.

Because the aerospace industry forcefully develops advanced technology under the pressures for defense, cost reduction, performance productivity, and efficiency, many new specific opportunities are available to the industry which continue to make it an exciting one for the analyst and potentially profitable for investors. Relieved of the pressures and restraints of the Vietnam war and spurred by foreign competition and renewed requirements for defense and mass transportation, a rebirth of the industry during the remainder of the 1970s seems definitely on the horizon. We believe the following areas of endeavor will be actively pursued and can develop into major, long-term programs.

Vertical and short takeoff and landing (V/STOL) aircraft, long under development for commercial and military use, are now beginning to capitalize on technological breakthroughs. The British Royal Air Force and the United States Marine Corps are currently pioneering the tactical use of the V/STOL fighters now in their respective inventories in limited numbers. The Navy, in order to offset increasing ship costs and to replace and modernize its aging and rapidly diminishing fleet, and to meet new threats, is well along in the development and early procurement of such new vessels as gas turbine destroyers, high-speed surface effect and hydrofoil craft, and the new Trident ballistic missile submarine system necessary to preserve the balance of deterrent forces. The energy crisis is creating a rapidly growing market for liquid natural gas tankers whose complex design has been made possible by the cryogenics technology fallout from the missile and space programs. The worldwide drive for noise reduction is bound to produce a new generation of aircraft and engines for military, commercial, and general aviation use. The aerospace industry has entered the mass transportation field on several fronts with new technologies and new ideas for airport transportation systems, high speed trains, subways, and rapid transit systems. Satellite reconnaissance and communications have achieved primary importance as guarantee for disarmament negotiations and pacts. NASA's Skylab and Shuttle programs should redirect the space program along lines offering more direct benefits to the inhabitants of the planet Earth. Remotely controlled aircraft are now approaching the advanced development stage for a wide variety of uses. The supersonic transport revolution will open new opportunities for a large number of aerospace companies, large and small. And finally the opening of Red China has already begun to develop what may ultimately be a vast new market for the aerospace industry.

FINANCE AND ACCOUNTING

The fact that return on investment in the aerospace industry can be highly variable and the return on sales historically low has already been referred to. Investments credit can be of considerable importance to earnings since capital requirements are very large. Because of the long-term nature of most aerospace programs, progress payments from the customer, either military or commercial airlines, are a necessary and important part of financing and accounting and must be considered by the analyst. Financing of new commercial programs is growing increasingly difficult, as noted, and may require government assistance in some form. Most probably payback arrangements out of production revenues will ultimately prevail. Long-term development, testing and tooling before production results in considerable inventory buildup prior to initial deliveries, particularly for commercial aircraft, and results in very high interest costs which must be taken into account. The write-off of current expenses for research and development, testing and engineering on major new commercial programs is extremely important and has the result of postponing substantial amounts of earnings. The industry has learned through bitter experience the extreme danger of deferring such charges in any appreciable amounts. This is perhaps the most important accounting factor for the analyst to understand. Correct assessment of this factor, along with an early investment decision on a sound, major commercial program, is one key to successful investment in the aerospace industry.

RESEARCHING THE INDUSTRY

Because of the high degree of technology involved in the aerospace industry, the analyst must have an understanding of its importance and its organization and management. This can only be acquired through constant study, interviews with management at several levels, and frequent plant visits.

When interviewing management, advanced preparation is most important. Being knowledgeable about the industry saves a tremendous amount of time, improves the analyst's reception and elicits more and better information, and encourages trust. The analyst must do his homework on the company's history, the technology being used, the research and development work, and the major programs underway. He must make every effort to understand the industry, its problems, and the particular problems of the company he is interviewing. He must keep current on foreign and domestic developments affecting the industry and the company being researched. It is important to show a positive and unprejudiced interest in the company and its problems. The analyst should prepare a list of key questions in advance and go through it efficiently and quickly without wasting the interviewer's time. He should show appreciation for courtesies extended by personal thanks and through follow-up letters of thanks. The analyst will also do well to encourage investor and analyst relations to the extent he can. He will also find it helpful to offer what background information he can in return. Above all he must respect government classified information and company confidential matters and should offer to submit any written reports before publication to prevent any slipups in this respect.

When making visits to plants, which is extremely important to understanding a particular company, the analyst should again be prepared as well as possible and demonstrate knowledgeability about manufacturing processes. Otherwise he will waste too much time having unimportant things explained to him and may miss out on the important things. In short, the more an analyst can demonstrate that he knows, the more he will be told. It is important to observe such things as employee morale, plant efficiency, the quality of tooling and equipment, status of serial production, production rates, and special manufacturing techniques and advantages the company has developed to improve its profitability and competitive position. The analyst should avoid asking special favors of his tour guide on his initial visit or until he has begun to develop the trust of his host. After concluding a plant visit or an interview with the management, it is important to write up notes quickly in order to retain as much information as possible.

Other research sources of considerable importance to the aerospace analyst to maintain and develop his understanding of the industry's technology include company, industry, and armed forces technical periodicals. Joining and attending occasional meetings of related industry organizations such as the American Institute for Aeronautics and Astronautics will be extremely helpful. An important source of industry statistical information is available from the Aerospace Industries Association of America. Attendance at major air shows and product displays is also a must. Finally, acquiring a knowledge of flying and the basic theories of flight will give the analyst an appreciation of the unique aspects of the industry that he can gain in no other way except through long association with it.

INVESTMENT IN THE AEROSPACE INDUSTRY

Because the aerospace industry is largely oriented to long-term programs, it is important for the analyst and the investor to identify major new programs early, selecting the company or companies which will receive the major benefit from the program, and to make investment decisions early at the low prices that usually prevail at the start of a new program. The analyst should not wait for market confirmation which always seems to be rather late in this industry. Market confirmation usually comes at or close to the production phase and after prices have gradually crept up during the development and tooling phases. Appreciations in price of several times are not uncommon for aerospace stocks if the analyst has been correct in judging the value of a program to a company and has made his decision early while the stock is being ignored. This is particularly important when a company has been out of favor because of a gap between the completion of an earlier program and the phasing in of a new one or after a company has suffered losses or reduced earnings or "bad press" from a previous problem. This is the essence of successful analysis of the aerospace industry.

It is also extremely important for the analyst to take the long-term view in his investment approach to aerospace stocks. Certainly in recent years the stock market has tended to be very short-term minded and not geared to the long development period of an aerospace program cycle. Complex major programs take time to develop and mature but can be well worth waiting for. The analyst should be prepared to accept low earnings at the start of a new program if earnings growth can be projected as the program matures through the production phase.

The aerospace industry is perhaps different from other major industries in that the analyst must be very selective in his choice because of the program orientation of the industry. Buying across the board in the industry can often result in neutralization of gains by losses. The industry seldom develops as a whole except in times of emergency. In fact, excellent investments can often be made when the general industry conditions appear poor. We are presently facing such an example where two new badly needed fighter programs are maneuvering their way through political flak at a time when overall defense spending has been under considerable pressure. In fact, one of the companies involved has achieved a nearly 50 percent increase in the price of its stock in spite of poor earnings and much controversy. This is because major roadblocks to the program's progress appear on the way to being overcome. Investments should be based on a particular company's participation in a major program and its degree of reliance on it as well as the mix of other programs the company may have. The analyst must, of course, carefully monitor the programs being carried out by the companies he has selected and do so both from within and from without the company.

Other criteria for selection of individual companies should be based on past records of program management, current management's ability, and product design superiority which will enable it to grow in usefulness and productivity, as has been previously described. Other very important considerations include diversity of the company's business, the pattern of phasing of major programs to minimize earnings valleys, and the company's experience and competence in specific areas or skills as opposed to those of competitors.

Finally the analyst should be prepared to recommend sale of a particular aerospace investment after its price/earnings ratio has grown to historically high levels and as company programs reach and pass production peaks. The aerospace analyst will also discover that his horizons will be tremendously broadened as the fallout from the advance technology of the aerospace industry inevitably leads him into other areas and greater responsibilities.

5

Airlines

CHARLES H. HANNEMAN, C.F.A.
Vice President
Argus Research Corporation, New York, New York

INDUSTRY STRUCTURE AND OVERVIEW

THE AIRLINE INDUSTRY consists of a number of distinct company groups. The 11 major trunks[1] account for by far the largest part of the business and stock market valuation. The eight regional carriers[2] started out as local feeder airlines, but their horizon has steadily expanded. Then there are three all-cargo carriers,[3] several charter airlines,[4] a number of inter-state operators,[5] and at least one foreign airline (KLM) available for investment. This chapter concerns itself only with the analysis of the 11 trunks, but its outline is generally applicable to the other entities as well.

A few of the carriers constitute the major part of holding companies, and several others have sizable nonairline interests, typically in hotel and related areas. While the airline is the key to an investment analysis in each case, it is nevertheless necessary to evaluate the other operations as well. Occasionally, the industry experiences major consolidation movements—usually at the bottom of the economic cycle. In the past, this has never gone beyond providing a new home for marginal, failing carriers.

---

[1] American, Braniff, Continental, Delta, Eastern, National, Northwest, Pan American, TWA, United, Western.

[2] Allegheny, Frontier, Hughes Air West, North Central, Ozark, Piedmont, Southern, Texas International, plus two Hawaiian and several Alaskan carriers.

[3] Airlift, Flying Tiger, Seaboard World.

[4] Overseas National, Saturn, Trans International, World.

[5] Air California, PSA, Southwest Airlines.

But while the movement is in progress, investment values are affected, and it is necessary to study the intricately interrelated effects on all other carriers of each merger proposal.

Evaluation of an airline should be accompanied by appreciation of some general principles:

1. Airlines are a very homogeneous group in both operating and stock market experience. There is a strong tendency to move together.

2. For this reason, and to guard against the common experience where the sum of individual projections equals much more than 100 percent of the industry, it is highly desirable that a company analysis be accompanied by at least a general industry review.

3. Despite industry homogeneity, carriers have distinct characteristics, reflecting their route system, traffic mix, level of competition, seasonality, etc., which affect current results and explain historical earnings patterns. Moreover, at any point in time some carriers are in a "phase" which differentiates their short-run prospects from the rest of the industry. Such a phase may be based on route awards or additional competition, a particularly good or bad cost experience, success or failure of marketing or equipment strategies, or the like.

4. The airline industry operates under a unique combination of circumstances: It is both highly regulated and very competitive; the areas of competition are narrow; airlines are both labor and capital intensive; they have a high degree of operating and financial leverage; their product is either consumed or perishes the instant it is produced; on either side of the breakeven point, most of the marginal revenues go directly to the bottom line of the income statement. As a result of these factors, airline results are highly volatile and most difficult to project within a reasonably narrow range. Stock prices are similarly unstable.

Data

As a regulated industry, airlines provide vast amounts of statistical information, and the only problems are discrimination and timeliness. Carriers submit to the Civil Aeronautics Board (CAB) detailed operating reports monthly and financial reports at least quarterly. The CAB makes condensed versions available on a subscription basis but with a time lag of several months. The time lag can be eliminated by subscription to commercial services which copy and send out any desired data as soon as it is submitted to the CAB. Drawing on the same basic source, a number of organizations provide data in varying detail and/or analyzed form on a continuing basis: the Air Transport Association (ATA), McDonnell Douglas, the International Air Transport Association (IATA), as well as Standard & Poor's and Moody's. Most of these sources have directories detailing their publications and the cost.

Airline managements have in the recent past become much more helpful to the analyst. A number have established executive positions for the principal purpose of dealing with analysts. The scope and timeliness of monthly traffic reports (some also report earnings monthly) and quarterly financial reports have improved greatly. Still, quarterly and annual stockholder reports do not provide sufficient data for a proper analysis.

For a thorough, ongoing coverage of the airline industry, a number of other data sources will be found essential. Among trade publications, *Aviation Daily* and *Aviation Week & Space Technology* are virtual necessities. Internal company newspapers and magazines contain much useful information and provide a "flavor" and "feel" for an airline and its management. The *Official Airline Guide* contains the details on route coverage and competitive schedules. Some airport authorities regularly release their operating statistics which can be used to gauge the strength of market areas. The CAB makes available on a subscription basis the preliminary reports and final decisions of its regulatory proceedings. The copies of Board members' public speeches frequently contain useful clues to regulatory policy.

Most airline data are derived from Form 41, the basic reporting framework from the carriers to CAB. This being a prescribed system, the data are generally comparable and usable for the analyst without routine adjustments. However, the financial statistics do reflect existing differences in the carriers' accounting policies, which are discussed in a later section of this chapter. Much of an airline's daily statistical output, especially that covering operations and revenues, is based on sampling techniques. This means that the initial monthly operating figures are apt to be revised within several subsequent weeks. It also means that interim earnings reports, particularly monthly reports, should be considered with the knowledge that significant amounts of revenue and/or expense can be shifted inadvertently or deliberately from one accounting period to another.

Regulation

Airlines are a regulated industry, and their freedom of action is circumscribed by various governmental bodies. The technical side of the business is under the authority of the Federal Aviation Administration (FAA) which is an executive agency under the Department of Transportation. This aspect of regulation need not be of particular concern to the analyst except where special matters such as new safety regulations or environmental rules affect the economics of the carriers.

The economic side of all airlines in interstate commerce is subject to regulation by the CAB, an independent, quasijudicial body nominally responsible to Congress but in practice more attuned to the executive branch. The CAB controls entry into the business and the exit from it as well as combinations of existing firms. It controls the prices charged by the airlines, and it controls the expansion or contradiction of their service through the power of route awards. In the international area, regulation is less clearly defined but no less restrictive. It involves not only the CAB but also the State Department and the counterparts of both in each foreign country. Issues are typically resolved by diplomatic negotiations rather than judicial proceedings. In addition, there is IATA of which all free-world airlines are members and which acts as a self-regulating body. International fares are determined through negotiations among IATA members subject to approval of the various governments.

The CAB's mandate is unique among regulatary authorities in that it is charged not only with guarding the "public convenience and necessity" but also with promoting air transportation and fostering a healthy industry. As a result, CAB regulation is generally considered to be of higher quality than is the case with other regulated industries. It would appear that in the past the CAB has usually acted as arbiter among contending factions, mainly individual carriers, while the industry was in its high-growth developmental phase. More recently, the board has frequently been the instigator of new approaches. This probably reflects not only unique economic circumstances but also the increasing maturity of the industry.

The analyst should be concerned first, with assessing the current and prospective regulatory climate and second, with digesting the continuous flow of factual information. The overall climate reflects, on the one hand, the current condition and economic needs of the industry (though with a variable "regulatory time lag") and, on the other, the politics and economic philosophy of the current administration as well as the qualifications and personalities of the five CAB members. The daily flow of data is valuable because it contains much information not regularly available. This would include analyses of the past and projections into the future for route and fare cases.

Competition

Most of the major air-travel markets (that is, routes between city pairs) are served by two or more competing airlines. Given the economics of the industry, competition for the incremental passenger tends to be fierce. Yet, the tools are limited since all carriers fly identical airplanes at the same speed for the same price. Competitive efforts fall into two broad categories: service amenities and image building, and scheduling and frequencies. The former involves anything from food service to in-flight piano lounges and a carriers' association with experience, class of traveler, or particular destinations. The latter concerns the scheduling of flights at times most desired by travelers and reflects the historical experience that a disproportionately large market share tends to go to the carrier offering the most capacity in a market.

Because carriers' route systems have multiple overlaps, seemingly successful competitive moves often spread throughout the industry and then lose their effectiveness. They are frequently expensive and wasteful, but they have, no doubt, stimulated the growth of air travel. The details of carriers' current competitive positions are surrounded with secrecy by the industry, but the data are available with considerable time lags. The analyst can approximate an appreciation of current relationships by observing differential traffic growth rates (keeping in mind the differences in route systems), industrywide market shares, and schedule adjustments. The overall competitiveness of a carriers' route system is of significance because it bears strongly on profitability.

Regulatory efforts, economic circumstances, and resource limitation have recently combined to restrain the more wasteful and nonproductive forms of competition in the United States. This has not been the case on international routes where competitors are foreign airlines. Regulation here is more diffused and involves diplomatic negotiations more than judicial proceedings. Since most foreign carriers are owned by their respective governments, national interests often overwhelm sound commercial practice, and U.S. carriers suffer from many discriminatory practices. Prime routes have too many competitors, others are controlled by methods considered distasteful or illegal in this country. The discounting of published fares has become rampant in many parts of the world.

Earnings Factors

In analyzing airline earnings it is useful to oversimplify the income statement in the following manner, adding detail and elaboration as the circumstances require:

$$\text{Traffic} \times \text{Yield} = \text{Revenues}$$

$$\text{Capacity} \times \text{Unit Cost} = \text{Operating Expenses}$$

The other items necessary to arrive at net income—nonoperating expenses (mainly interest) and the tax rate—can be determined with comparative ease since they reflect known parameters and remain largely fixed within a fairly wide range of operating results. Before discussing the key operating variables, it should be pointed out that they are interrelated and interdependent. Different rates of traffic growth are often associated with changes in the revenue mix and hence affect the yield. Changing the seating configuration of aircraft may vary both capacity and unit cost (in opposite directions), although total expenses and profits remain the same. Also, the industry's very high leverage produces inordinately large swings in operating results from only small variations in these four variables.

Traffic. Traffic is usually measured in scheduled revenue passenger miles (RPM) which means one paying passenger flown one mile in scheduled service. For some carriers or special purposes it may be more appropriate to use revenue ton miles (RTM) which covers the total weight carried, including cargo. Past data are available on a monthly basis by division, that is, domestic and one or more international break-downs. In assessing traffic trends, it is important to consider the location of the route system in question, its seasonality, share of business versus pleasure travel, competitors, and the like.

The projection of traffic trends is perhaps the most important, and also the most troublesome, task for analyst and industry alike. There is general agreement on the positive or negative impact of the many determinants such as general economic variables, fare elasticity, or changes in schedules and service. But reasonably accurate forecasts on a consistent basis continue to elude the experts within and outside the industry. This has been costly for managements (because major decisions often involve long lead times) and investors (because the stocks are very volatile) alike. Other revenue items, which vary in importance from one airline to another, are cargo traffic, charters (both military and commercial), and contract operations (the provision of ground or overhaul service for other carriers).

Yield. This term refers to the average fare received per RPM. Yields vary greatly among airlines, between routes, and over time. Personal pleasure travel is associated with below-average yields because of its heavy use of discounted promotional fares. Long-haul yields are typically lower than short-haul yields, reflecting the operating economies of jet aircraft. Some routes are notorious for their low yields (East Coast–Puerto Rico, West Coast–Hawaii, the North Atlantic) because of competition and/or a preponderance of pleasure travel. Yields change not only from official fare changes but from variations in the mix, as noted above, as well. It is therefore useful to evaluate differential growth rates among the various traffic sectors.

Capacity. Similar to traffic, capacity is usually measured by available seat miles (ASM) in scheduled service. Again, it may be desirable to use the overall weight measure, available ton miles (ATM), where cargo or charter traffic is significant. The volume of capacity is dependent on the number of aircraft, their seating configuration, and their utilization in revenue service. The latter is commonly expressed as hours per day, and for detailed calculations it is also necessary to know the average speed of the aircraft.

The schedules for the delivery of new planes and the retirement of old ones have become increasingly well known and can now be treated as given facts. Configurations and utilization rates used to be reasonably stable, so that prospective levels of capacity (and their cost implications) could be independently developed by the analyst with tolerable accuracy. Since the late 1960s, however, the industry has been in a position of significant overcapacity. Increasingly, managements have cut back from theoretically maximum levels through early retirements of older planes, temporary groundings, reduced seating densities, or lower daily utilization. Future capacity levels have thus become highly discretionary, and the usefulness of independent calculations in assessing expense trends has diminished. Nevertheless, certain capacity indicators do provide valuable insights for the analyst. Instead of seat miles or ton miles, the plane mile numbers provide clues to expense patterns. The relationship of seat miles, plane miles, and number of departures often suggests competitive strategies or the outline of basic operating plans.

The load factor, the percentage of available seats or weight tons that is actually sold, is one of the most frequently cited airline statistics. The standard presumption is that higher load factors are more profitable than lower ones. This is obviously true—assuming all else remains the same. Rarely is this the case, however, which explains why some carriers with low load factors are more profitable than others with high load factors. Load factors vary substantially by route, by season, by day of the week, and even by hour of the day. Moreover, they can be manipulated. Increasing or reducing the number of seats per aircraft, for example, lowers or raises the load factor but has essentially no effect on expenses or profits. An important corollary statistic is the breakeven load factor which indicates the number of seats (or tons) which must be sold to cover expenses. The spread between actual and breakeven more appropriately indicates profit potential and also reflects the interrelationship of the key operating variables.

Unit Cost. This number indicates, most commonly, total operating expenses per unit of available capacity (ASM or ATM). Because of the capacity developments discussed earlier and the fact that expenses do not vary proportionately with the volume of either capacity or traffic, the usefulness of unit cost statistics has also declined greatly, especially for forecasting purposes. It seems instead more meaningful to deal with aggregate costs broken down by major category or function.

Using the total-cost approach, it is important to recognize that roughly 75 percent of airline operating expenses are concentrated in three major categories: employment (46 percent), fuel (12 percent), and depreciation (15 percent). Further, airline operations involve numerous lead times which can vary from several years for new aircraft to a few weeks for seasonal employees. Therefore, the relationship of fixed to variable costs—often generalized as being 50/50—is subject to much qualification. In analyzing total costs, analysts should consider, among other items: employment levels and average compensation (including union contracts), depreciation based on known fleet composition and depreciation rates, and interest expense reflecting anticipated debt levels and specified interest rates.

Financial Factors

The financial aspects discussed in this section highlight the distinction between airlines and other enterprises as well as the differences among carriers. A useful starting point in an airline financial review is the *equipment position*. This should consider the current composition of the fleet, preferably in detail, by aircraft type and engine used, and the scheduled addition of new planes as well as the planned disposition of older equipment. The simplicity or complexity of the fleet are not only a reflection of the route structure requirements, but they also provide clues to capacity trends, cost patterns, management strategies, and financial flows. It may be noted that aircraft have historically been subject to continued and significant technological changes which have induced new investment, not because old planes wore out physically but because competition and/or better economics forced a change.

The next logical step is an analysis and projection of the *flow of funds*. The principal items on the inflow side are: retained earnings, depreciation, deferred taxes, and additional debt which may have been arranged but remains unused. The major outflows are capital expenditures for new aircraft (including advance payments for future deliveries) and ground facilities, and debt maturities. Analysts should be alert to the details of lease financing (for both aircraft and major ground facilities) because this has become a major source of funds for airlines and because company-provided funds' flow statements often net out lease transactions. While some numbers in this analysis are by their nature highly uncertain, others are relatively fixed (depreciation and equipment commitments), and their relationship provides valuable insights into the financial flexibility or restraints facing a carrier under various assumptions of future trends.

Closely related is a familiarity with a carrier's *capitalization*. Aside from such overall indicators as debt/equity ratios, it is most desirable to know the details of the various debt issues because their interest rates, maturity schedules, or restrictive covenants may impinge on management's actions currently or in the future. Many airlines have outstanding large issues of convertible debt which, at this writing, are far below their conversion points and are thus antidilutive in share calculations, but which may be the source of massive equity dilution at some future point. Airlines have also made heavy use of intermediate-term debt for long-term investment. The cost of revolving credits is typically tied to the prime rate which, in time of sharply rising rates, introduces a significant cost element into the income statement. The increasing use of off–balance sheet financing (leasing) has already been referred to. For the purpose of intraindustry comparison or to assess financial flexibility, it may be useful to capitalize leases. It may also be noted that leasing distorts some income statement figures in that rental payments are submerged in operating expenses which makes depreciation and interest expense appear relatively low. Airlines differ from most other enterprises by conducting their business essentially on a cash basis and by not having products in inventory. They can therefore operate with comparatively small—and sometimes negative—working capital.

The format of airline *accounting* is fairly uniform for stockholder purposes, and reports to the CAB are prescribed in great detail. There are, however, differences in accounting policy among the carriers which results in identifiable variations in the quality of reported earnings. The analyst should, as a minimum, be aware of the differences. For some analytical purposes, it is desirable to adjust the numbers to a common level, but historically the stock market does not seem to have been significantly discriminating as to the quality of earnings. There has been a trend over the years toward more liberal (that is, earnings boosting) accounting policies. As a generality, the least profitable airlines tend to have the most liberal accounting practices. Major differences exist in the following areas:

1. *Depreciation:* Variations exist among carriers (and equipment types of the same carrier) as to depreciable lives as well as assumed residual values. For tax purposes, depreciation rates are nearly identical at the maximum permissible rate.

2. *Overhaul reserves:* Some carriers charge current expenses and credit overhaul reserves on the basis of actual flight operations for new equipment placed in service. Others charge off such expenses only as incurred, which means that they get "a free ride" in the early part of ownership.

3. *Preoperating costs:* The introduction of new types of equipment, the start-up of service on major new routes, or special training programs usually involve significant expenses which are of a "nonrecurring" nature. Some airlines capitalize such costs for amortization over several years, while others expense them as incurred.

4. *Investment tax credit:* Through their massive equipment purchases, airlines have generated large amounts of tax credits. Some carriers defer the credit to the extent it is "earned" on the tax books and amortize it over, usually, eight years. Others flow through the maximum amount even where it has not yet been "earned" on the tax books. As a result, the nominal tax rate is theoretically 48 percent for the former group and 24 percent for the latter. In practice, even the amortizing carriers now have tax rates well below 48 percent as their annual amortizations have built up.

A further note on taxes: A number of carriers have accumulated very large amounts of tax-loss carryforwards and unused (for tax purposes) investment credits. Sizable earnings are necessary over the intermediate future to utilize these amounts and, in some cases, validate current tax credit flow-through practices.

In assessing interim, and particularly monthly, airline earnings reports, analysts should recognize that there are numerous ways in which both revenues and expenses can shift from one period to another inadvertently or deliberately. Substantial year-end adjustments are not uncommon. Relatedly, the occasional difficulty of allocating revenues and expenses between domestic and international operations might be noted. Historically, international operations have tended to be more profitable than the domestic business. This reflects, of course, the greater efficiency of jets over the longer stage lengths typical in international service. But it is also probable that managements shifted income into this area which is under reduced CAB influence.

The high degree of financial *leverage* inherent in airlines deserves special attention because it aggravates the difficulty of projecting financial results, affects the investment standing of airline securities, and varies within the industry. High fixed costs of equipment ownership reflect the capital intensive nature of the business and the relatively low investment quality as illustrated by a usually high cost of capital. For the industry as a whole, depreciation and net interest expense were 3.5 times pretax profits during a recent 12-month period, while the aggregate balance sheet showed $1.30 of long-term debt for every dollar of equity. These numbers understate the real leverage to the extent that substantial lease commitments do not appear on the balance sheets and current rental payments are not included in the depreciation and interest accounts in the income statements. Variations in leverage among carriers tend to correspond to longer-run profitability levels. The more consistently profitable airlines were able to fund a larger portion of their investment from internal sources, and they could raise outside capital on more advantageous terms.

Stock Market Considerations

Before arriving at an investment judgment it is useful to consider some stock market aspects of the airline industry. The intense coverage of airlines belies the industry's small size. The aggregate number of shares and the total market value of all carriers are less than those of numerous individual prominent U.S. companies. Individual share capitalizations are often relatively small and exhibit high turnover rates. Airline stocks usually move as a group with the market, but they have high "beta" factors. The wide dissemination of current operating statistics and the usually prominent coverage of events affecting airlines typically result in quick and sharp stock market reaction to real or apparent changes in the industry's prospects. Moreover, in the short-to-intermediate run at least, the market tends to focus on earnings per share without much regard for qualitative differences. In addition to high short-run volatility, airline stocks have experienced extreme secular price swings.

The huge amount of available statistics enable the analyst to project airline operations in elaborate detail and to estimate results with great arithmetic precision. While this is desirable from the standpoint of understanding the dynamics of the industry or a company, it easily leads to a false sense of accuracy. Even minor deficiencies in key assumptions are quickly magnified by the large operating and financial leverage of airlines into substantial variations from estimates. History indicates that airline analysts and managements alike have more often than not been well off the mark with their projections. Thus, it is well to recognize explicitly the low confidence factor attached to earnings estimates and to think of them as most likely numbers in a realistic range.

Due to highly volatile stock prices, low confidence in earnings estimates, and generally poor financial quality, airline equities have increasingly come to be regarded as inherently speculative and low-quality securities. Accordingly, their principal attraction is thought to lie in their high leverage potential in a favorable operating environment. For intra-industry comparisons it is useful to calculate the carriers' revenues per share and per dollar of market value. This will indicate that airlines with relatively high and consistent earnings have, for example, about one dollar or less of revenues per dollar of market value, while others with marginal or irregular profitability may have several dollars of revenue per dollar of market value. The analyst might then assess the carriers' ability to raise their profitability in a comparable operating environment (but reflecting their differing degrees of leverage) or through competitive strategies (that is, internal turnarounds).

Recent Developments

The United States has been in the initial stages of a unique, new experience. The "energy crisis" limited the availability of fuels and sharply increased the price. Governmental policies limited jet fuel consumption to a level roughly 25 percent below industry plans. As a result, airlines have gone through a program of massive schedule reductions and employment cutbacks. Price increases, though cushioned by long-term contracts, amounted to 20 percent or more.

Over the intermediate future, the availability of jet fuel will, no doubt, improve, although it may be some time until fuel is again in unlimited supply as has been the case historically. The price, which has historically been both low and quite stable, could well double over a one-to-two-year period. In addition to these operating restraints—which could affect the marketing efforts of airlines—the market for air travel itself might change. The economy is increasingly forecast to be entering a prolonged period of unusually high inflation. Initially, at least, real discretionary incomes are declining. Since an estimated 50 percent of airline traffic consists of personal (pleasure) travel and most of the industry's future growth has to come from this market, the factors affecting discretionary income are of obvious importance.

The format and methods of airline analysis as outlined in this chapter are likely to remain applicable for the future. Analysts will probably have to shift the emphasis of their inquiry along the lines indicated above and consider some new questions: If fuel limitations lead to much higher average load factors, will operating leverage be reduced and, if so, will the industry's investment attraction be affected? If cost and capacity pressures reduce the airlines' competitive and promotional spirits, will longer-term growth prospects be diminished and how will profits fare?

6

Automotive and Related Industries

ARVID F. JOUPPI
Senior Vice President
Delafield Childs, Inc., New York, New York

STRUCTURE AND SCOPE OF THE INDUSTRY

SECOND to the United States government, the auto industry is the biggest business in America. In the five years through 1972 alone, the multinational Big Four of Detroit—General Motors, Ford Motor, Chrysler, and American Motors—had combined sales of approximately $250 billion. In the half decade from 1973 to 1977 when our nation will be 200 years old, Detroit's sales could well reach $400 billion—including inflation and allowing for more small, but as expensive, cars. By our estimates, Big Four world sales in 1973 exceeded $70 billion, with sales outside the United States outpacing the domestic growth rates; following an off year in 1974, sales growth should resume, aided importantly by overseas performances.

Large homogenous industries which supply materials, components, or parts for the auto industry include steel, chemical, glass, and the tire and rubber fabricating industries. In this study, we will consider especially the rubber industry and a less homogenous group of companies which we will identify as the parts industry. The machinery industry—which includes companies such as Caterpillar Tractor, Deere & Co., and Clark Equipment—is discussed elsewhere in this handbook. Many other industries depend for a small or large fraction of their markets on the auto-related industries.

In 1974, the total U.S. labor force crossed over the 90 million mark, and more than 14 percent of those employed were directly in the auto-

141

motive industry or in fields which were almost wholly auto dependent, such as in the trucking industry. Well over half of the total labor force used automobiles to go to and from work, and almost all of the things we consume are to a small or large degree dependent on motor transportation.

The rubber fabricating industry's Big Six are Goodyear Tire and Rubber, Firestone Tire and Rubber, Uniroyal Corporation, B. F. Goodrich Company, General Tire & Rubber, and Armstrong Rubber. These companies, representing well above 90 percent of the entire U.S. rubber fabricating industry, account for about one fifth as much annually in sales as do the Detroit Big Four. In the 1968–1972 period, aggregate Big Six sales were near $50 billion. We anticipate the 1973–1977 aggregate to exceed $75 billion.

There are in use, by our early 1974 estimates, approximately 90 million passenger cars, 22.5 million trucks and busses, and many millions of motorcycles, snowmobiles, and motorized carts. Parts for these provide an immense aftermarket, as Wall Street has labeled the market for replacement parts for vehicles in use. There is no accurate aggregate total for this market, but we judge it to be near $35 billion annually, and growing at a rate approximately twice the growth of the vehicle population itself. Cars in use have been increasing at an annual rate of nearly 4 percent and in view of domestic scrappage of some 97 million cars over the next decade and big changes coming in our cars, we believe the growth will continue but below recent rates, perhaps at 3 percent.

Superimposed on the basic markets for automobiles, trucks, busses, tires, batteries, and accessories is a fast-rising—and so far largely unprofitable—need for safety and ecology devices. Vehicles must be made safer, less air polluting, and more quiet. We expect this industry to develop into a half-profit expansion of the motor industry.

The automobile is part of a dynamic world system. It is dependent on fuel supplies and upon an adequate and improving world highway system. The U.S. highway system alone should during the next five years move across the half quadrillion dollar value level. Our highways, roads, and streets are the largest resource in our nation which is shared fairly equally among all of our people. Rising safety and ecology standards for automotive vehicles must compete with another socially desirable standard: to make good highway transportation available as far as possible down the economic ladder of our population's income-generating capabilities. The automobile "liberated" especially the lower-income groups during the first half century of its existence.

In recent years, pressures of the industry, of the citizenry, and of the government have demanded higher standards of automobiles themselves.

It takes considerable capital to get into auto-related and product manufacturing—and immensely more capital to survive and prosper. Severe domestic and overseas competition has brought economic destruction to scores of companies which sought to establish rich niches in making cars, trucks, busses, tires, and farm and other heavy machinery. Of economic necessity, these companies have assumed some of the marks of oligopolies. Both the auto and rubber industries have seen today's survivors outsell and outprofit literally scores of other companies which did not have enough competitive strength to produce satisfactory profits for their owners and had to go out of business or move into other fields. Since the auto industry began at about the turn of the 20th century, more than 2,500 different car names have disappeared from the American scene and scores of rubber-fabricating companies have failed. The nation is so big, the highway system is so vast, the people's needs and abilities to buy are so insatiable and strong that it has required and continues to require very great capital resources and strong corporate staying power to remain viable through the rather large ups and downs in demand.

Car demand seems to fluctuate plus or minus 10 percent in units from a rising trendline. Most of the companies which have failed have made expansion plans for facilities and/or products during above-trend periods, and by the time the capacity and products were ready for the market, the economy was in a down cycle. Expensive plans developed during prosperity could not be sustained during lean times.

The cyclicality of the industry has caused managements of the auto industry itself and of those industries which supply it to diversify outside the industry. Thus, we find General Motors as a major developer and marketer of Frigidaire household products, B. F. Goodrich the world's largest producer of polyvinyl chloride, and Borg Warner a major factor in air conditioning. The examples of diversification out of the automotive industry are present in almost every company commonly declared to be auto related.

FACTORS AFFECTING GROWTH OF REVENUE AND PRICE

Seasonal Character

In a quarter century of study of the automotive industry, the writer has found no better outline of the seasonality of automotive demand than one which came from a veteran floor salesman in a Chevrolet dealership in Rochester, Michigan:

> When the new cars come out all the people with money and means rush in and buy high on the price ladder. At the same time, the fleets grab off the low-priced cars. Through the winter you work harder than at any other time to get sales. When spring comes you get a fair number who are stirred because winter is over and buy what the fall and winter have proved to be the popular cars. In the summer you grub for every

sale—to attract the bargain hunters late in the model year. Then in the fall the cycle starts all over again.

Even with the change in emphasis occurring in an energy conscious age, the percentage distribution of car sales at retail probably will remain near this historic pattern:

March quarter........................	24.6
June quarter........................	27.6
September quarter...................	22.1
December quarter....................	25.7

The third quarter calendar generally absorbs much of a new model-year start-up expense. Car-a-minute plants generally begin new car assembly at a rate of one per hour and gradually work up to the car-a-minute pace.

While a car-a-minute has somehow become the most standard "design speed" for car manufacturing, the pace varies. Up to 1974, efforts to raise the pace to a hundred cars per hour have succeeded only at the Lordstown, Ohio Chevrolet Vega plant of General Motors Corporation. There, strong opposition to the high line speed developed among rank-and-file union workers—members of the United Auto Workers, formed by the late Walter Reuther. The Vega line was rather highly automated, with automatic welding techniques, for example, not before used in production. Car-a-minute became a car each 36 seconds.

In any event, heavy expense of many kinds "bunches up" into a model-year start up. Likewise, customer demand tends to "bunch up" into the fall and spring. Employment agreements which have become rather standard throughout the auto-related industries since 1946 place profit premiums on steady operations. Advertising, price concessions (for which reserves are established at the beginning of production each model year and continue throughout the year), and what we call "jaw boning" by the factory representatives cause dealers to keep a reasonably good sales flow from their outlets. The flow from dealers to retail customers is, by any standard, uneven, while, in our automated age, automotive vehicles are most profitable to the manufacturer when they are made with unvarying steadiness. Such matters as overtime disturb the profit process.

In our view, accounting procedures have been firm enough to keep the balance sheets of auto-related industries sound even at the expense of making the income statements appear to have rather large swings.

Both successes and failures over the longer term in automotive investments have been determined by the degree of research accuracy in six areas. These are stated below:

1. Is there a market for the new product or changed product which is planned or in existence? How big is the market? Where? Can it be reached? What are the competitive factors within the market?

2. What products are there for these markets? Are they right or must

the company make changes or price concessions? Are new products coming?

3. What plants and facilities are there to make the products and distribute them quickly enough to build up a cash flow? Does depreciation cover modernization and replacement expense?

4. Does the company have at hand the human skills and organization to monitor the markets, develop products faster than they obsolesce, and maintain our facilities? If we do not employ all the needed human skills can we obtain them at reasonable costs? Is there an adequate plan for succession from senior management down to the least skill level needed to make the business successful? Are our labor relations satisfactory and competitive?

5. Does the company have sufficient money on hand to operate the business effectively? Is there prospect of a cash flow to meet the problems and opportunities present in our markets, products, facilities, and payrolls? Can the company pay its creditors according to agreed upon timetables and collect from our customers in a timely manner? Are the bank lines for short-term credit satisfactory? Is there a need to raise long-term money, is the market valuation satisfactory to sell common stock? Can the company sell regular debentures at competitive rates or sell convertible debentures?

6. Is it profit-prone to or is the record one of spending too much money on product, plant, personnel, or otherwise to deliver a proper return on not only stockholders' equity but on the total capital invested? What does the future look like purely on an earnings basis? Can the dividend increase as earnings move up or must all or almost all of the earnings be invested?

The auto-related companies are attempting to expand their sales by entering overseas markets. General Motors, for example, produces one vehicle outside the United States for each three domestic vehicles; Ford Motor, one for each two domestic; and Chrysler Corporation, one for each two and one half.

The companies also have sought to enter related industries—General Motors, the bus and engine markets and most recently the motor-home market; Ford Motor, the farm machinery and home electronics field (its Philco Division); and Chrysler, the chemical and air conditioning markets. The major rubber companies have moved into chemicals, plastics, and other areas—General Tire and Rubber into broadcasting, for example. The so-called automotive supplier companies have occupied the halfway position of trying to out-perform the major end-product producers in making components (generally with cheaper and as-skilled labor) with half of their corporate energies and using the other half to "run away from Detroit" into other more stable markets. Permanent survival for auto-related companies and for the basic producers themselves has depended largely upon proper management of money and other assets—drawing upon large Detroit markets and, at the same time, seeking other profit opportunities which would smooth out the ups and downs of Detroit. Diversification may be geographic, and into like and unlike fields: An analyst must study the ultimate earnings consequences.

ANALYSIS OF COST FACTORS

Automotive vehicles are priced with a large degree of sophistication gained from accumulated experience which by now has become a tradition.

Market studies indicate approximate size factors which may be present four years hence. Costs are figured on current dollars, and each company makes assumptions as to the spread of the market from lowest to highest priced models. An automobile takes shape for a target volume of sales; target unit prices and all design parameters must fit into the economic mold. At some late point in a development, engineers will make very big issues over items as small as a fraction of a cent. It is very easy to design all of the profit out of a car through unwise decisions along the four-year path from that first design pencil stroke to the first signed agreement signature of the first buyer of the car in a dealership.

We have found many methods of analyzing cost on a pragmatic quarter-by-quarter basis. These methods prove quite useful for general analysis but are particularly useful for studying the Big Four auto makers.

1. Fixed and variable costs will continue approximately as they have appeared on audited income statements during the recent past unless unbalancing forces are introduced.

2. Work from raw materials upward through fixed charges and value added as the end product in precreating earnings statements. Yet, do *not* rely on a single method.

3. As a *first order* projection, accumulate the interim earnings statements since the last audited annual statement and *then* add *last year's* remaining statements as though they were for the remainder of the *current year*. This projection, of course, is only a rough estimation.

4. As a *second order* projection, determine year-to-year changes in the elements of interim statements for the part year already reported and simply extend them through the year. Be assured that this projection also will be only an approximation.

5. Use estimates gained from the "cost ladder"—adding value to purchased materials—and from first-order and second-order estimates arrive at one's own analysis. If possible, talk with dealers, suppliers, and of course with the company officers. Armed with evidence of "homework" a company officer will feel freed from the thought that he must simply be a "source" for the analyst. A management interview immediately leaps above the interrogatory level to being a serious discus-

sion about raw material prices (published data), supply and demand factors, and value added factors.

6. Especially seek information from individuals who do not place themselves into an "insider" role. Ethical data from a privately owned supplier or a dealer often can be far more precise than getting the same type of information from an inside company official. None of the regulations governing the securities industry bar careful and far-reaching fact gathering and careful statistical analysis of them. No analyst has the right to reject consideration of a company because "they won't tell me anything."

7. In gathering data, share noncompetitive information on a company gathered from noncompany sources. Never, however, carry one company's secrets to its competitor—even though your research may have uncovered matters of great value to competitors. In servicing clients, weigh carefully the ethics of disclosing a company's trade secrets, legally obtained, with the true value to the client. Ordinarily it is better *not* to disclose such information unless *failure* to disclose would deny a client facts on which to base true value of equities under review.

8. In making projections into the next fiscal or calendar year, use identical techniques as moving from quarter to quarter. Always work toward precreating the financial statements—try to anticipate auditors' decisions and allow for them.

9. Finally, be honest. Don't pretend that you can forecast with precision. Automotive demand fluctuates plus or minus 10 percent in units above a given trendline. This means that sales could be off as much as 20 percent from a given year's total. We have observed that as sales go up earnings go up from one and one half to two times as fast, and the reverse is true as sales go down.

FEDERAL AND STATE REGULATION

As noted above, the automotive industry is becoming more and more controlled by legislation. Legislation has created clean air, safety, and now energy-consumption standards. These standards are administered at the federal level by the Department of Transportation and the Environmental Protection Agency.

Factors in reduced profit margins, less noticeable "styling" changes, and relative unpopularity of auto-related stocks have been mandated changes in the automobile, trucks, and busses of today. "Too many cooks spoil the broth" is an old kitchen phrase. When Detroit alone determined vehicle standards it was possible to "engineer in" the needed profit more easily than when Washington, another cook with ideas of how the ingredients should be used, entered at the designer's elbow. The extra factor has caused increased vehicle cost, detoured designers and engineers away from elements which might help to sell cars and toward elements which satisfy Washington's very serious and rightful standards, and generally frightened squeamish investors away from the motor stocks. Our research role should be to study the factors, keep in close touch with the Washington individuals who are setting the ground rules, and keep clients advised.

It has been our view that each person who speaks through the media represents a specific interest. Automobile company officials say things which are calculated to protect their freedoms and prerogatives as much as possible. Government figures say things that are calculated to win public approval for their own views. Spokesmen for the various federal agencies tend to enhance the importance and value of their particular agency. We occasionally find it necessary to analyze the true meaning of diametrically opposing viewpoints. A rather difficult one in 1973 was when the Environmental Protection Agency and the Department of Transportation were requiring higher ecology and safety standards, and the Cost of Living Council was indicating that costs could not be passed through. In 1972 it was common for Washington to be indicating that Detroit must do something in some future year to make the car safer or more compatible with the environment, and Detroit was insisting through its spokesmen that the demanded equipment could not be produced. Under those conditions the analyst had to beware of becoming an advocate instead of serving as a "judge" to keep investors advised on where the probable truth lay.

ACCOUNTING CONSIDERATIONS

As noted above, annual and interim reports of auto-related companies are quite directly usable in analysis. Additional data, such as that published by Ward's Automotive Reports, Automotive News, and various economic services are useful.

A major pitfall in making interim analyses between statements is to overlook—or not expect—the flow in and out of reserve cash accounts. A lesser pitfall is to assume that public relations statements are translatable into earnings statements and balance sheets.

Recently an automotive chief executive learned that during the past week car sales had slumped 15 percent below standard expectations. He thought a moment and said, "We cranked $50 per car into our production beginning last August. It's now February and we have not used any of that reserve. We've got to keep the plants going or take a penalty there. Figure out a way to give the dealers $150 to $200 per unit to get those sales up." A contest was ready and announced within hours; sales picked up; and the March quarter results came in stronger. This example has been typical of practice for years, and discounts continue to this day. Such a reserving feature of the automobile industry is a way of "moving the merchandise into the bargain basement without taking it off the main floor."

Each year the automotive industry changes models. The new look for decades has tended to stimulate sales and to cause what Detroit called "dynamic obsolescence." Engineers have an annual opportunity to introduce their improvements which may have been in development for a number of years. In the late 1960s and early 1970s these changes included mandated items for safety and ecology purposes. Such changes are foreseen through the 1970s. There are only so many dollars which can be economically introduced into the money stream of the automotive companies. For a number of years, appearance changes were minimal because of the cost of the mandated changes. By 1971 a group of companies which served the major producers became almost extinct. They were the small "tool and die shops" which made the wooden and metal patterns for changing the shapes of everything from the roof to the little bezels that go around side lights. There simply was not enough money to go around to keep these small suppliers economically healthy. That industry was concentrated in the Detroit area, but over the years skilled craftsmen in Canada and overseas began outbidding the Detroit area producers who had higher labor rates for tool and die makers. As Detroit minimized design as a sales feature, overseas car producers accelerated their "styling changes," and by the mid 1970s Detroit was again forced to accentuate the year-to-year changes on its cars. Rather strict accounting procedures have developed for amortization of the tools, dies, jigs, and fixtures for each model year's vehicles. This amortization has proved sufficient—in spite of the temporary malaise which did affect the small shops in 1969–1972—to maintain a healthy tool and die industry.

Conventional accounting procedure is to charge current car sales amortization approximately as follows:

Appearance tools (A tools): Used for *only* one model year specifically to identify, highlight, or mark that year's vehicle. These must be amortized 100 percent in that model year—an equal charge against each unit which has assigned to it a "standard volume."

Body tools (B tools): Used often for three model years to change the basic shape of the car—as, for example, moving from a finned look to a rounded look. These tools form the basis for what industry observers call "a three-year cycle." The promotion people call the first year of B tools an all-new look. In the second year A tools help to give the basic shape a changed look. In the third year A tools again give to the model what car men call "a face-lift." B tools conventionally are written off 40 percent in the first year, 35 percent in the second year and 25 percent in the third.

Chassis tools (C tools): Used anywhere from 5 to as long as 18 years. These are the bread-and-butter internal changes—engines, drives, chassis. A new engine might be used for well longer than a decade. The famous Chrysler slant-six engine was introduced in 1959 and remains standard with small variations. Chevrolet once used the same basic engine with minor changes for 18 years. Frames often go unchanged for six to nine years. C tools are amortized annually in equal amounts over a five-year period.

What happens when sales fall off and standard volume is not achieved? Generally the car companies write off, or amortize, tooling (a general term to include also jigs, dies, and fixtures) on a time basis, month by month. The result is that earnings in a down month or two are depressed additionally by allocation of fixed charges on a time rather than unit basis. What happens when sales exceed standard volume? Generally the car companies write off tooling faster than normal. The common rule is to amortize on a unit or time basis, whichever is faster. What then happens toward the end of a model year when all tools are written off, reserves for dealer incentive and warranty expense have been filled? Profit flows through to the bottom of the earnings statement with fewer absorption points.

The sense of the accounting procedures is to smooth out as much as possible the ups and downs of this up-and-down industry. In an ideally planned production flow, year after year each company would produce exactly as many of each model year's products as the market could comfortably absorb. Each manufacturing tool would be used up to its economic life. There would be a constant flow of new ideas into new vehicles through the use of tooling. In 1972, amortization charges for General Motors were $874 million; for Ford Motor, $465 million; and Chrysler Corporation, $196 million. Considering the number of shares involved—GM's 287 million, Ford Motor's 101, and Chrysler Corporation's 52—the reduction in "would have been" pretax earnings was substantial for each company.

Few car models have been able to maintain a long life without change. Notable exceptions were the famed Ford Model T and the Volkswagen Beetle. In time the Ford Model T became a money loser, and because it had moved from a superb and apparently everlasting profitability to a loss position it made an indelible imprint on Detroit management thought. A Ford Motor executive of those earlier years later moved to General Motors and helped usher in the annual model change. Later, his son followed him as a GM executive and now heads a major truck manufacturing company. There he has increased annual engineering expenditures more than 20-fold in his two-year tenure. "I've never forgotten what he told me," he said pointing to a fatherly portrait. "You need a good set of tools to succeed in business. It costs money, but they pay off very fast when you have them; and if you don't have them, you fail."

It is dangerous for an analyst to become an advocate of directions an industry should take, unless his advice is sought. An analyst's job is to get at the facts, analyze them, predict the earnings and balance sheet consequences, and recommend proper action regarding the stocks. Generally, the industry is so large that there is room for opposing viewpoints; and each becomes successful, or each fails.

An accounting strength or weakness, depending upon the viewpoint, is that depreciation and amortization charges are unevenly spread with respect to the earning capability of the asset employed. A substantial portion of reported profits are reported without depreciation charges or amortization charges, for these charges have already been allocated to previous sales. Many old automotive plants continue to provide excellent earnings even after they have been fully depreciated.

We have found public relations statements on the expenses involved in developing this or that model or innovation are of little value in security research. Political purposes and self-serving "image building" lead companies often to say that this or that amount has been spent on safety, ecology, training of ghetto workers, expansion of fringe benefits, or for new car introduction. The analytical facts seem to be that specific expenses cannot be unilaterally allocated. There is a vast area left for analytic judgment. Thus, the best procedure in our view is to work forward from the most recent audited statements, including statements submitted to the Securities and Exchange Commission, using whatever data and facts can be obtained to analyze toward the next published statement. It is well to watch production data as it emerges and also the dealer sales figures, which are announced at ten-day intervals. Canadian production figures also are useful. Overseas data generally must be privately obtained.

Whether for an automotive, rubber, or parts company a useful research tool is to attempt forecasts of six quarterly statements ahead—building upon a *macro*economic model to include five- to ten-year historical "tracks" of as many indicators as an analyst feels necessary to fit his companies into the general business outlook. Economic data is quite freely available in most companies, and the analyst who taps this intelligence flow in a large number of companies soon finds himself becoming an "expert" in those economic series most useful to him.

In gathering economic data, a useful method is to provide one's economic model for use or comment to company or union officials. Again, the best research is not interrogative; it is a sharing of business experience. In time the analyst gets to know an industry from his Wall Street vantage point as well as the officers sitting in the chairs making the decisions. Overconfidence in this respect, however, may well be the largest research pitfall of all.

FORECASTING AUTO SALES

Short-term forecasting should begin by determining as accurately as possible the pattern of current sales, using industry sales information such as the latest ten-day data. Caution is required when special circumstances may be influencing results, that is, sales contests, the introduction of new models, or supply shortages. Thus, with new models when style changes occur, sales may be stimulated; while less pronounced style change in subsequent years may dampen sales. Consequently, the future implications of current sales information may be interpreted with caution. (Energy availability may well dominate all sales forecasting considerations.)

Certain other factors should next be considered:

a.   The trend in used-car prices may influence demand, since customers rely on the trade-in value of their old models to reduce cost.
b.   It is helpful to consider various surveys of customers' buying intent such as those published by the University of Michigan Consumer Survey Center, the Bureau of the Census, and the more current reports of Sindlinger and Co.
c.   The trends in credit conditions are of importance.
d.   The trend in fleet purchasing, leasing, and sales to government should also be taken into account.
e.   Estimate the trend in overseas markets.
f.   Project the "massive factors": economic and social transportation needs, highway availability, mass transit as supplemental and competitive modes, energy availability and changes in sources and types, and international commerce and comity.

Vehicle size, price, energy need, and freedom from air pollutants are current factors which must be projected. These projections for the basic vehicle producers have immediate current-year affect on the auto supplier companies and on the rubber-fabricating companies. The ripple effect in future years may well have marked effect on many other industries: metals, petroleum, railroads, mass transit, and others.

MARKET BEHAVIOR OF AUTO-RELATED EQUITIES

As a generality, auto-related equities have been extremely cyclical in market price.

In recent years earnings have been strong, but stock prices have deteriorated. In 1973, stock prices for the automotive Big Four fell to their lowest price-earnings ratio in modern times. There were extreme fears regarding the nature of the market, the appropriateness of the products for the markets, and the ability to shift facilities to keep pace with market preferences for cars. The companies were regarded as most burdened by energy shortages and by the upward push of employment cost rates. There were fears that the Big Four did not have the financial resources to bring forth the new vehicle concepts which the public, including environmentalists and zero-growth and antibigness advocates, thought it wanted.

7

Banking

DAVID C. CATES
President
David C. Cates & Co., Inc.
New York, New York

STRUCTURE AND SCOPE OF THE INDUSTRY

To DEFINE the "banking industry" today requires us to look beyond commercial banks alone. Because of the growing importance of bank holding companies—which compete in more markets than do banks—the analyst is obliged to concern himself with the entire financial spectrum across which these companies operate.

Though most financial holding companies have so far been organized by and around a "flagship" bank, it is important to understand that the flagship need not be a bank. For example, CIT Financial is the "flagship" owning National Bank of North America, and more recently Walter Heller has acquired American National Bank of Chicago. Such cases may be expected to multiply in the future, especially if savings and loan associations and banks are permitted to cohabit the same holding company.

Definition of Banking

Despite the proliferation of holding companies, analysts should not forget that banks comprise the overwhelming percentage of holding company assets and earning power. We will therefore attempt to render a very basic definition of banking, though it is getting harder to be precise about the essentials of banking.

Commercial banking is a system of institutions which (a) accept

153

deposits, (b) *create money through credits to checking accounts,* (c) *are owned by their stockholder(s),* (d) *are regulated by at least one of a tightly cooperating network of examining agencies, and* (e) *own and operate, together with the Federal Reserve, the funds-transfer machinery through which all other financial institutions so far clear their transactions.*

Early History of Industry

It is important to understand the history of U.S. banking in order to grasp not only the peculiar evolution of financial subindustries in this country, but also to appreciate the historic context from which has sprung the recent movement to form holding companies.

In the early days of the republic, Alexander Hamilton sponsored the creation in 1791 of a nationwide bank, 20 percent owned by the government and 80 percent by private investors. Dominated by eastern interests, the First Bank (later the Second Bank) of the United States was angrily perceived by capital-short western and southern settlers as an oppressive agent inhibiting locally determined development.

In the political overthrow of 1832 led by Andrew Jackson, the charter of the Second Bank was allowed to lapse, and a free (if not wildcat) system of state-chartered banking flourished. Poor supervision, no central bank, and lack of a national currency (banks issued their own notes thinly backed by specie) led to several panics prior to the War between the States.

Beginning in 1863, Congress passed several National Banking Acts designed to induce "state" banks to switch to "national" charters, largely by a punitive tax on the issuance by state banks of their own notes. National banks were to receive financial benefits in return for (a) underwriting the war debt, (b) issuing a national currency instead of their own notes, and (c) submitting to national examination. By 1870 the conversion was more than half accomplished, leaving a banking system of small local units competing for the same customers on a two-charter basis, that is, state versus national. Meanwhile, the "checkbook" had been invented as a means of avoiding the tax on bank notes, thus stabilizing the balance between the two kinds of charters.

Perhaps if the industry had remained fully state chartered, banking would have followed the path of insurance companies and finance companies, which today operate interstate by virtue of reciprocal agreements between states. But the two-charter basis of banking set the stage for a chronic "states rights" issue, whereby Congress jealously preserved the privileges of small local bankers against the imagined threats of a national chartering/supervisory body.

The legacy of 1832 and 1863 has left marks on banking which we will describe in the section following.

Structural/Regulatory Characteristics Pre-1962

Though 1962 is not the only watershed year separating the "old" from the "new," it is a useful threshold by which to organize this review of structure and regulation. *Prior to 1962, we can discern the development of four industry characteristics which together bound a tight harness around the entrepreneurial initiatives of bankers:* (a) local nature of banking; (b) complex regulatory matrix; (c) regulatory "style"; and (d) nominal competition for customers.

Though challenged by events of 1962 and later years, these four industry characteristics are still widely prevalent.

The Strong Identification of U.S. Banking with Local Interests. Banking is the only major national industry which contains a preponderance of locally owned and managed units. This structural fragmentation (which makes it difficult for banking to respond to certain kinds of change) is primarily rooted in two factors:

a. The great political power of suburban and rural interests in state legislatures has enabled local banking interests to limit the incursion of their territories by city banks. Moreover, the issue of "states' rights" has been utilized in Congress to force the federal regulatory authorities to defer to state legislation.

b. Large city banks and their country correspondents have historically shared a certain communality of interests. The city banks can profitably employ the deposit balances of their correspondents, while the country banks benefit from the services offered by their city banker.

The multiplicity of banks (14,000 today and 29,000 in 1924) is, however, no simple tapestry. Heavy attrition from failure and/or merger occurred in the 20s and 30s. Since the 50s began, heavy attrition due to merging has been approximately offset by a high rate of new-bank entry, especially in suburban neighborhoods and "growth" regions. The large gross number of banks, furthermore, conceals a prevalence of "chain banking," where common family or syndicate control links a group of banks. Finally, some states (for example, California) allow full statewide branching, others (for example, Minnesota) permit only holding companies, and others (for example, Illinois) restrict banks to home offices only.

Complex Regulatory Matrix. It helps to be an archeologist to make sense out of the dense regulatory apparatus that monitors and restrains the banking industry. In general, each regulatory body is a specific response to some specific crisis brought about by the economic vulnerability of a highly fragmented industry.

Thus the germ of state supervision was sown in the Jacksonian period. The office of Comptroller of the Currency was created when the Lincoln administration tried to facilitate war finance by encouraging charter switching. The Federal Reserve System was created in 1913 as a direct response to the uncontrolled credit bubble that burst in the Panic of 1907. The Federal Deposit Insurance Corporation (FDIC) was a daring answer in 1935 to the rash of bank failures which culminated in depositor panic just prior to the Bank Holiday of 1933. The Federal Reserve role in the effective supervision of bank holding companies was articulated in 1956, when Congress first moved to prevent nonbank commercial interests from gaining control of banks.

Lest it be thought that the regulatory mantle prior to 1962 was a seamless garment of restrictions, let us look at a few areas that escaped regulation, in whole or in part.

First, banking until 1962 was held to be exempt from antitrust statutes (and is still exempt from FTC, but this itself may change).

Second, banks won an exemption from regulation under the SEC. This exemption (not even partly closed until 1969) had profound consequences for financial reporting and for the status of minority and/or dissatisfied shareholders.

Third, the overwhelmingly *domestic* preoccupations of Congress left U.S. banks with considerable freedom of maneuver in overseas banking markets. Only a handful of banks, to be sure, were interested, but they have had wide latitude in liquidity, capital, branching, and affiliate acquisitions. Often, this freedom was contingent upon the domicile state (notably New York and California) granting reciprocal privileges to foreign banks wishing to operate in the United States. As a result, states have found themselves concluding treaties with foreign powers (see Article One, Section 10 of the U.S. Constitution)!

Regulatory "Style." The large number of banks, coupled with the large number of regulatory agencies (50 states, plus three federal-level bodies: Federal Reserve, Comptroller of the Currency, FDIC), has powerfully affected *how* banks get regulated.

a. The first characteristic of bank regulation is its vast scope and inter-agency cooperation. Bank regulation is, first and foremost, a preventive maintenance apparatus designed to forestall (and if not possible, to quickly neutralize) bank failure. When necessary, the agencies work quickly, powerfully, cooperatively, and very quietly. This was recently illustrated in the near failure of Bank of the Commonwealth (1971) and in the 1973 failure of the U.S. National Bank of San Diego (whose offices opened the next day as branches of Crocker National Bank amid great public apathy).

Another example of inter-agency operation is the complex procedure established by Congress in the Bank Merger Act of 1966, where each merger proposal must clear not only the federal regulatory body of primary jurisdiction but also the two sister federal agencies *as well as* the Antitrust Division of the Justice Department (who register advisory opinions).

b. The second characteristic of bank regulation is its conservatism. Just as the Maginot Line was planned to forestall the recurrence of trench warfare, many regulatory concepts are rooted in the fear of widespread bank failure. By 1962, two generations of examiners had taught two generations of bankers that "soundness" primarily meant high ratios of liquidity and capital, with only secondary emphasis on competitiveness, earning power, internal reporting systems, and other management skills.

c. A third characteristic of bank regulatory style is its procedural inertia in solving problems. Three drawbacks of the system are evident. First, the various parts of the system can only work on the problems they were each created to solve, which may not be the problems of tomorrow. Second, liberalizing initiatives in one agency (for example, the Comptroller's office in the 60s under Saxon) must run the gauntlet of the whole regulatory system, Congress, and trade-group adversaries such as Savings and Loans Associations (S&Ls). Third, the need for inter-agency cooperation has tended to foster similar routines and similar concepts. In fact, bank regulation is a good example of the historian's adage that social institutions are, in part, a blueprint for the future and, in part, an historical junk shop.

One example of this inertia is the administration of Federal Reserve Regulation "Q" (the rules by which interest-rate ceilings are set). Participating in Q deliberations are the Federal Reserve for state member banks and all national banks), the FDIC (for state nonmember banks and all mutual savings banks), the FHLB (for federally chartered S&Ls), and Congress (which now and then changes the ground rules).

Another example is the far more informal system by which liquidity and capital standards are set (see later discussion). Despite some inter-agency disagreement, liquidity and capital judgments are based on rather primitive and methodologically obsolete ratios generated almost entirely from balance-sheet data as reported in prescribed financial reports. This process is understandable, but only when one realizes that (*a*) some standard set of simplistic guidelines is necessary to lead armies of examiners through the maze of banking, and that (*b*) double standards— as between large and small banks, or between one agency and another —are politically awkward.

Industry Undercompetitiveness. From the Bank Holiday of 1933 until 1962, the growth of bank profitability—within a climate of diminishing financial risk—was widespread throughout the industry, regardless of management. World War II saw an enormous expansion of the money supply, with riskless bank financing of the war. After the war, although growth of the deposit base was limited, bank profits rose steadily year by year, in response to four factors:

a. The strength of private loan demand, coupled with the Fed's 1950 refusal to continue to "peg" interest rates by money supply creation, led to a steady annual rise of bank lending rates;

b. This postwar loan demand was financed largely by banks selling off their low-yield Treasury securities, thus causing continued enhancement of overall earning asset yield;

c. The banking system had not encouraged interest-bearing deposits since 1933, and paid low rates on such deposits; as a result, interest expense increments did not nearly offset the increments of interest income;

d. "Back-office" costs in this precomputer era were low, partly because the gains in income were not based on gains in volume, and partly because a loyal depression-bred work force was willing to settle for low wages in return for the job security of banking.

The "automatic" nature of bank earnings growth in the 50s allowed bankers to postpone a number of challenges. In short, they did not compete aggressively for personnel, for capital, or for new customer markets. Let us now consider the latter problem.

In the 19th and early 20th centuries, bankers forged an understandable identity of interest with the proprietor class (whether farmers, merchants, or manufacturers). The "working man" of that era was not a borrower, and his paltry savings were solicited not by bankers but by mutual savings banks and cooperatives.

Because of this commercial preoccupation, the rise of the "consumer" as a financial force totally bypassed banks. The development of the installment loan in the 20s was left almost entirely to the fledgling sales-finance and personal loan companies and the self-amortizing mortgage loan was pioneered by S&Ls.

Far more important in separating the consumer from commercial banking was the legislation of 1932 creating a federally chartered savings and loan system, complete with a "central bank" (the Federal Home Loan Bank), an "FDIC" (the Federal Savings and Loan Insurance Corporation), and tax incentives on the accumulation of loss reserves.

Thus a regulated financial subindustry was born to perform two consumer-oriented functions which banks had more or less repudiated: attract savings and make mortgage loans.

The installment loan, the mortgage loan, and the savings deposit were not the only financial instruments which bankers overlooked in their preoccupation with the "credit worthy" business borrower. Over the years, other financial specialists had grown up alongside banks (but borrowing from them) to finance leases, accounts receivable, mortgage portfolios, builders, and other credits where technical skill, shirt sleeves, and a willingness to accept occasional losses were essential.

With very few exceptions, bankers entered the 1960s with great com-

placency based on their postwar earnings performance and their acknowledged ability to finance established businesses. Few seemed to
notice that their industry was losing market-share of the total spectrum
of financial opportunity. Probably no one could then guess that by the
end of the decade the industry would be on the threshold of trying
to buy back into the markets it had sacrificed.

Two Watershed Years: 1962 and 1969

By stretching only a little bit, it is possible to place in either 1962 or
1969 the start of almost every aspect of the complex revolution that looms
over the industry. The fascinating thing about this revolution is that
each of its component elements—technology, entrepreneurship, free-
floating money, etc.—initially arose as a rather small-scale challenge to
the solidity of established order. The residual vitality of the *status quo*,
in fact, is so widespread and enduring that it is sometimes hard to
realize how sweeping the ultimate changes are likely to be.

The Events of 1962. The three revolutionary developments of 1962
were (*a*) the recasting of Regulation Q as a stimulative tool of monetary
policy and of bank growth; (*b*) the decision of the Supreme Court that
the Clayton Act did, after all, apply to banking; and (*c*) the work of
James J. Saxon, appointed by President Kennedy in 1961, as Comptroller of the Currency.

Regulation Q as an Expansion Tool. In a conscious act of economy
policy, the Federal Reserve—acceding to Kennedy economics—used
Regulation Q in two ways. First, by raising the maximum interest ceiling
on savings deposits (from 3 percent to 4 percent in January 1962), the
Fed hoped to accelerate the flow of savings-type money into financial
institutions (including banks) which would in turn be pressed by
higher costs to make long-term investments in the national plant (for
example, term loans, mortgages, municipal facilities, etc.). Second, by
encouraging First National City Bank—and others—to develop in 1961
the certificate of deposit (C/D) as a negotiable money-market instrument, the Fed hoped to sop up the excess liquidity which was felt to be
responsible for the low level of short-term rates and hence the dollar outflow impacting the U.S. balance-of-payments.

Though bankers at first complained about the higher cost levels imposed on them (the Regulation Q announcement of 4 percent came in
the middle of a stock offering by Bank of America!), the new uses of Q
quickly became accepted. In the past, rate ceilings had been a way of
not having to compete. In the 60s, however, every new upward ratchet
of the "ceiling" quickly became the "floor" for the next round.

The conversion of Q from a lid to a prod had far-reaching effects on
bank management. The new game, clearly, was to be one of volume
growth, since it was evident that "per dollar" margins were going to fall

from the artificially high levels of the 50s. Most of this growth, further-more, had to come from time deposits (both household and corporate), since rising interest rates, coupled with the new availability of C/Ds, put a premium on cash management (that is, minimizing demand deposit balances). Finally, the fledgling art of "interest-differential banking" or "spread management" was born out of the recognition that interest costs would be rising faster than interest income in the "catch-up" years ahead.

To be sure, only a few bankers then grasped the full implications of the new game. Those who did responded by: (a) bidding aggressively for savings and C/D funds; (b) exploring new—and/or higher yield—lending markets in order to maximize spread; (c) extending the cor-porate planning horizon to match the longer investment cycles which the new banking implied; (d) initiating precise accounting for depart-ment, product, and customer profitability in order to control the tide of declining margins; (e) recruiting personnel for ability, imagination, and drive; and (f) managing the capital structure—debt utilization and breadth of markets for new securities—with careful attention to its essential role in sustaining volume growth. Only by doing all these things could declining margins be converted from nemesis to oppor-tunity.

Though these six characteristic post-1962 bank management prin-ciples may seem like truisms to observers of other industries, in banking virtually each one meant a wrenching break with established traditions.

Supreme Court "Philadelphia" Decision. In 1962 the Supreme Court reviewed—and overruled—a lower court decision in favor of the Phila-delphia National Bank combining with the Girard Trust. Until this de-cision, banks had freely merged within their mutual "service areas," regardless of the concentration of resources that resulted. Actually, banks had little choice in most states: State laws tended to limit the geographic range over which banks could branch or merge, and thus the only available partners were often local.

Since 1962, antitrust doctrine affecting banks and bank holding companies has flowered into a rich complexity, with bank regulatory agencies (state and federal) applying *their* own procompetitive theories alongside those of the Justice Department. One such is the "potential competition" doctrine, whereby a bank merger is enjoined because the two *might* someday compete. Though this doctrine is still strong among regulators, as of late 1973 the courts have repudiated the Justice Depart-ment in several attempts to apply it against bank mergers.

Perhaps the most important effect of the 1962 decision, however, was to show the smaller banker that his profitable opportunities to sell con-trol would diminish *unless state legislatures broadened the geographical arena of merger.* Before 1962, any two banks could merge. After 1962 (and the string of Justice victories flowing from that precedent), banks could merge only on a "procompetitive" basis—and that means "at a distance."

The downtown banker, meanwhile, was coming to recognize the value of suburban and country deposits. A sufficient identity of economic interest was created between large and small banks so as to change laws in several states. The Virginia banking law was modernized to a state-wide basis (but only for holding companies) in 1962, New Jersey opted for statewide holding companies in 1969, Florida eased its interpretation in 1967, Texas in 1971, Michigan in 1971, and New York in 1971 (for full implementation in 1976). The above is not a complete summary, and change is fast moving at the state legislative level.

Emergence of Saxon. Our citation of Saxon as a truly innovative force in regulatory circles may appear to contradict our earlier argument about inter-agency regulatory "style." He was, certainly, the exception that proves the rule.

Saxon was a gadfly to regulatory habits—and even industry tradition —in many ways. His emergence was very timely for those in the industry searching for guideposts and leadership centering on "competitiveness" and "leverage."

His several contributions can be summarized as follows: (*a*) He carefully researched and endorsed the issuance of preferred stock and capital notes by national banks; (*b*) he stimulated inter-bank competition by relatively lenient approvals of branch applications and new bank charters; (*c*) he pioneered a "can-do" regulatory style that encouraged more than a few banks to switch from state to national charter (including Chase Manhattan in 1965); (*d*) he taught his field force of examiners—and the banks they examined—to de-emphasize standard ratio guidelines on liquidity and capital analysis, in favor of emphasizing earning power and management characteristics; (*e*) he encouraged and authorized substantial diversification for national banks; and finally, (*f*) he pioneered in extending to shareholders of smaller banks beyond the reach of SEC some minimal protection based on fuller disclosure.

The Events of 1969. The chemistry unlocked in 1962 "worked" powerfully until a second catalytic year (1969) brought further changes. These were: (*a*) the failure of Regulation Q as a credit control tool; (*b*) the de facto emergence of broadly diversifying "one-bank holding companies"; (*c*) the reform of bank accounting, the new role of the SEC, and the advent of CPA certification; (*d*) the emergence of the "back office" as a front line of technology, marketing, and organizational design; and (*e*) the listing of bank and bank holding company stocks on major exchanges.

Failure of Regulation Q. In the first credit crisis of the postwar years (1966), the Federal Reserve almost provoked a liquidity emergency among major C/D-issuing banks by refusing to raise the Q ceilings on large-denomination time deposits. The resulting deposit outflow was "planned" to inhibit inflationary credit expansion, but served only to divert demand to the commercial-paper and Eurodollar markets, squeeze out small business and home builders, and teach the banks to find alternate funds sources the next time around.

When it happened again (1969), the big banks were ready with (*a*) an efficient Fed funds-gathering machine (Fed funds are inter-bank lending of excess reserves); (*b*) a sufficient network of offshore branches to borrow huge volumes of Eurodollars; and (*c*) commercial paper through holding company parent companies.

These funds-gathering vehicles (which one Fed governor called "loopholes") were survival tactics used to offset the clumsy impact upon individual banks which was inevitable when the Fed nervously switched Q from stimulant to depressant.

As a consequence of the 1969 credit crisis, Q was gradually discarded as a tool of credit control, since the resourcefulness of bankers had found other sources to meet loan commitments. A secondary effect was to stimulate the growth of holding companies, if only to broaden access to commercial paper as still another C/D substitute.

Holding Company Diversification. The growth ethos that was reborn in banking during the 60s found a culmination in 1969: a rush to form "one-bank holding companies" (OBHC) as a diversification vehicle. Curiously, this corporate avenue had always existed (except in those states forbidding holding companies, as did Michigan until 1971). In fact, the Bank Holding Company Act of 1956 had exempted the hundreds of single-bank holding companies from the burdens of "registration," since they existed primarily as shells by which the ownership of small banks could be leveraged with debt by individuals.

Led by Unionamerica Corporation and First Union National Bancorporation (now Cameron Financial) in 1968, expansion-oriented bankers quickly realized that the single-bank holding company was almost a totally unregulated vehicle for acquiring nonbank businesses and financing such operations with commercial paper. More than 200 such companies were organized around banks in 1969, comprising roughly half of banking system assets! The process worked the other way too: The almost successful effort of Leasco Corporation to gain control of Chemical Bank was a startling revelation of the vulnerability of banking institutions to raids by nonbank interests.

Since this politically unacceptable threat was similar to that which led Congress to write the 1956 act, it was inevitable that Congress would again move, as it shortly did in the Bank Holding Company Act of 1970.

The critical sections of the Act are Section 3, which establishes the "convenience and needs of the community" as the primary criteria for

Fed approval of holding company acquisitions, and Section 4.c.8, which delegates to the Fed the responsibility to determine the list of "financially related" areas (Regulation Y) into which bank holding companies may move, that is, those areas "closely related to banking as to be an incident thereto." *All* holding companies must file with Fed and clear their acquisitions, and those companies owning impermissible businesses must either divest those affiliates or sign irrevocable letters of intent to divest the bank affiliate(s) by January 1, 1981. Some industrial companies (for example, Great American Transportation) will sell their banks (for example, LaSalle National of Chicago), while only one major bank holding company (Unionamerica) has so far decided to spin off its bank (Union Bank of Los Angeles, to be owned by a holding company Union Bancorporation).

Shareholder Reporting and SEC. The Securities Acts Amendments of 1969 brought larger bank holding companies (initially, those with 750 stockholders or more; since then, 500 or more) under the direct and full regulation of SEC. The federal banking agencies were given the task of similarly supervising the shareholder reporting of banks.

One immediate result of this was the appearance of CPA firms to audit bank holding company statements, and another was a modest reform of bank accounting which became the new standard for banks and bank holding companies (see *1968 Bank Audit Guide,* published by the AICPA). The two chief characteristics of the 1969 accounting reform were: (*a*) the recognition that loan loss was a normal cost of doing business and that a "provision for loan loss" must be included among operating expenses, and (*b*) the recognition that "realized gain/loss on sale of securities" was a special category of transaction and must be handled *after* "income before securities transactions" (IBST) but *before* truly extraordinary items.

Financial analysts of bank securities quickly seized upon IBST as a more accurate measure of year-to-year operating results than "Net Income." Meanwhile, many analysts—and a few CPAs and bank managements—continued unsuccessfully to argue that realized gain/loss on securities should be amortized into interest income as "adjustments of yield" in an ongoing portfolio rather than be treated as "completed transactions" allocable solely to the year of realization (see later discussion).

Listing of Bank Shares. The new audited, SEC-registered status of at least the larger bank holding companies made their shares attractive merchandise for the NYSE and its member firms. Despite the warnings of some specialist dealers, a trickle of "listings" in 1969 has since expanded into a fair-sized stream of larger companies with substantial capitalizations, though it is important to remember that the historic fragmentation of U.S. banking—the Jacksonian fossil of American business—has produced an industry whose leaders, with very few exceptions, are relatively small corporations within the "big business" spectrum.

The initial reaction of managements to the listing of their shares was disappointment. Volume did not pick up, market depth did not improve, nor did the P/E ratios behave as hoped for. Only later did some of these managements realize that listing is merely a "gate pass" entitling the players to a slightly more attentive audience from NYSE member firm analysts, research directors, stock salesmen, and clients, than is normally accorded OTC stock groups. The chief reason for this extra attention toward a major industry is that a listed-stock trade is internally a lower-cost execution for a brokerage firm than an OTC trade.

"Back Office." In the late 60s, bank technology and production problems began to get more farsighted attention. The coming logjam in paper-check flow was clearly foreseeable and led to task forces within the Fed and the industry to plan for more efficient funds flows, freed wherever possible from a paper base. Meanwhile, some major banks were experimenting with untraditional techniques in adapting their back-office organizations from a "bookkeeping" mentality to a "factory" mentality. Banker reluctance to fire/hire freely and to innovate new organizational styles was challenged by rising turnover, inner-city employee problems, steeply escalating costs, and rapidly emerging technology.

Major Problems: 1973 and Beyond

The foregoing historical presentation gives us a basis for appreciating the complexities of current issues facing the bank industry and its regulators, to say nothing of analysts and investors.

Technology. Far-seeing students of the impact of technology upon banking define the future of banking within the context of a "financial knowledge" industry whose function is to generate financial flows, whether debit or credit. According to this view, traditional "deposit" and "loan" functions—in the coming world of paperless entries—will merely be by-products of the banking industry's ability to capture data about an elusive mass market, both corporate and household.

Although the current inclination of analysts may be to postpone consideration of such seemingly conjectural matters until they show up in EPS, we urge even the beginner to become familiar with the technological wilderness through which this fragmented industry will surely pass. These issues also form the basis for a series of questions which any analyst can pose to managements, in order to ascertain technological and policy readiness at given companies.

Our review of technology—by which we largely mean data processing

—will cover the subject from three perspectives: (*a*) the in-bank perspective; (*b*) the bank/customer perspective; and (*c*) the bank/bank link. There are dramatic (if not revolutionary) events taking place at all three levels—events which will profoundly affect earnings, share of market, and industry structure.

In-Bank Technology. From the mid-50s to the late 60s, electronic data processing, or EDP, in banking grew to encompass virtually all accounting functions—for example, demand deposits, trust operations, etc. But with few exceptions, EDP merely substituted machine for manual procedures. In other words, the computer was used as a bookkeeper.

In the late 60s, a few progressive banks began to widen and elevate their use of EDP: (*a*) They made their data and their programs mutually interactive; (*b*) they increased the expertise, flexibility, and policy awareness of their EDP supervising staffs; and (*c*) they linked the operations function closely to product development, market research, financial analysis, and corporate strategy.

To illustrate, one problem that most large banks are trying to solve with computer analysis is the determination of profitability by administrative unit, by product or service, and by customer. Since all are wrestling with the effort to synthesize this complex equation, an analyst may find this a useful lever for gauging the status of EDP at particular companies.

Bank/Customer Technology. Though banks were leaders in accustoming the public to plastic cards as transaction instruments, they are not the leaders in the next phase of card-based transaction systems. Food and merchandise retail chains have recently developed point-of-sale (POS) equipment specifications which manufacturers are beginning to produce against sizable order backlogs.

These retailers need partly to gain computer access to a wide variety of inventory, credit, and personnel data for corporate use, partly to automate the point-of-sale environment, and partly to reduce the burden of taking checks (a rising percentage of which are uncollectible).

In food stores, there is an opportunity for card-activated cash dispensers or automatic tellers to be owned by financial institutions, but in merchandise retail stores, it is less likely that financial institutions will own or control the card-activated equipment that is being developed (which uses optical-scan technology, not magnetic stripe).

Since retailers want to get the paper check off their backs, they are welcoming the issuance of plastic transaction cards (which may or may not have a credit and/or overdraft feature). These so-called "shopper" or "debit" cards activate an immediate transfer of funds from the customer's account to the retailer's account.

The savings and loan industry (including the Federal Home Loan Bank Board) views the debit card as a major strategic opportunity to enlarge consumer share of market, especially among younger savers. The U.S. Savings and Loan League, in fact, has recently developed a translucent debit card for its members. Commercial banks are apt to follow suit, though reluctantly, since most would be in the awkward position of sponsoring two cards—one for credit, one for debit purposes.

Other efforts to by-pass the check are being conducted by banks in Los Angeles, San Francisco, and other selected cities. These groups have formed "automated clearing houses" (ACH) with Federal Reserve participation (and subsidization) to handle checkless payroll credits and preauthorized bill payments.

Bank/Bank Technology. The Federal Reserve, from its inception in 1913, has a mandate to oversee and to some extent operate the inter-bank funds transfer system of the United States. The problems of shifting to paperless transfer are manifold. (See Federal Reserve Regulation J, with proposed changes as of November 1973.)

By 1980, paper-check volume (most of which is under $100 per check) will have risen to 45 or 50 billion items a year, and unless something is done to develop check substitutes, the payments system will cease to be acceptably efficient. The debit card (with or without a credit feature) appears to be part of a universal remedy, but requires a system of community, regional, and national clearing which would exist *parallel to* the paper-check clearing machinery. Since thrift institutions are likely to be major issuers of debit cards, what participation should they have in local, regional, and national switches? The position of the Fed is that they should come in *through* commercial banks, not as *direct members*. The position of the Antitrust Division of the Justice Department is that local clearing houses should not exclude competition.

Meanwhile, retail stores may well wind up owning a major share of card activated (POS) systems. What role should they have? And the new world of data transmission—over state lines—may bring the FCC into jurisdictional partnership with the Federal Reserve. Will the Fed be granted a de facto monopoly over data transmission of money, or will competition from private sources be encouraged to emerge? Finally, how swiftly and evenly will all relevant supervisory jurisdictions cease to define off-premises bank-owned equipment as "branches"? As of this writing, the Federal Home Loan Bank Board has given clearance to such terminals within 50 miles of a head office, but the FDIC and the Comptroller of the Currency have not, nor have the states followed a consistent pattern!

Management Style. Technology challenges bank organization by the speed of its evolution and the necessity for quick adaption to challenge. The banking "subculture," however, has been slow to shift from a hierarchic, title-based, seniority-oriented system of management to the shirt-sleeves "task force" style of management which is implied by the technological challenge.

Money Flows. Partly because of the technology of funds transfer, partly because of high and volatile interest rate levels (which serve to alter rather quickly and significantly the "opportunity cost" of any given use of money), and partly because of the broad new repertory of liquidity instruments, money flows have accelerated from "trickle" to "slosh."

The De-localization of Money. One consequence is that local money pools—the accumulated liquidity and savings of a neighborhood or town —no longer "stay at home" in the simple form of demand and time deposits. Even in small communities, a growing fraction of local money can be rented by outside issuers of commercial paper, Treasury bills, and other liquidity instruments. This has profound implications, in our opinion, for the viability of the present structure of deposit-gathering institutions (55,000 offices of banks and thrift units). Does the delocalization of money pools threaten the profitability of a significant fraction of the physical plant of banking and thrift companies? Is that threat greater for the small independent than for the diversified branch system? In our opinion, the ultimate answer to both these questions is *yes.*

The Decline of Federal Reserve Control. With the interpenetration of worldwide money supplies (mediated largely by multinational banks and borrowers), it is harder than formerly for the central bank of a given country to insulate its credit system. Certainly for the Fed to use Regulation Q as a tool of control would provoke either a liquidity emergency or an easy switch by major banks to alternate funds sources, or both.

This problem of decreasing control should, we think, be viewed as more paramount than the debate over what the FRB should actually try to control. The "interest rate" school believes that FRB policy should aim for given levels of interest rates, regardless of the money supply consequences. The "monetarist" school urges a steady rate of money supply increase, with relative disregard of the interest-rate volatility that would surely result from these policies.

A further type of control which may well flower in the capital-short, high-rate decade of the 70s is credit allocation. Tax benefits (or other subsidies) on student loans, residential mortgages, ship mortgages, etc., are early examples. In 1973, to illustrate further, the Committee on Interest and Dividends (CID), chaired by Arthur Burns, worked out a politically acceptable formula on the "prime rate": *Large* borrowers may be charged a market-determined (that is, a cost-plus) lending rate, while *smaller* borrowers are to pay rates whose fluctuations are far more gradual.

The Effect of Velocity on Circulation. In June 1967, the annualized turnover of demand deposits in 233 leading SMSAs was 56.5 and was 120.0 in New York. In June of 1973 these turnover rates had risen to 99.8 and 245.0 respectively. Technology, coupled with opportunity cost considerations, is a stimulant to this steady rise in velocity. Unfortunately, the inflationary impact of a *velocity* increase is the same as that of a *supply* increase, since the two factors multiplied together make up the "circulation" of money (which in turn impacts goods and services and prices). Though admittedly "demand deposits" are only part of total money, the increase of velocity poses a serious challenge to inflation management.

Capital. Despite the hand wringing of bank examiners, this was a capital-surplus industry in the 50s. Since then, banking has become not only capital short but capital intensive, increasingly tapping the markets for equity, debt, and short-term funds.

Capital Availability. Whereas smaller banks in the mid-60s could compete with larger companies for debt capital, the situation today is far different. Professional debt capital placement—by high-quality New York and regional firms—is available only to companies of, say, $150 million of assets or more. This excludes more than 13,000 banks!

In addition, the shift of bank stock merchandising from dealers to brokers, coupled with a steeper performance-differential (in EPS growth and stability) than formerly, has greatly widened the P/E ratio distances among bank stocks. Those bank stocks that have emerged as widely attractive investment vehicles possess a powerful cost-of-capital advantage over the low-multiple majority. If this split persists, capital will flow selectively rather than generally to the industry, with profound implications for financial industry structure.

Regulatory Attitudes. There are three problems emerging in the regulatory attitude toward capital.

Data Base for Analysis. The process of inter-agency cooperation has affected capital analytic techniques. In short, the conceptual basis of regulatory thinking is considered by keen students of capital to be highly inadequate. The most sophisticated of these analytic formats (Federal Reserve Form ABC: *Form of Analyzing Bank Capital*) fails to make quantitative provision for earnings coverage, loan commitments, seasonal characteristics, growth trends, and market access (for money-market liabilities); nor does it distinguish among types of loans for either credit or market risk. Unfortunately, any explicit recognition of these factors would appear to establish a double standard according to bank size and/or capability.

Legitimacy of Debt Capital. Stimulated by Comptroller Saxon, the regulatory agencies during the 60s accepted long-maturity debt as a fair substitute for equity capital, up to 30 or 40 percent of total capital funds. Since the Bank Holding Company Act of 1970, however, which gave the Fed control of all acquisitions, the Fed has used its power to argue forcefully for strong *equity* ratios (in relation to loans, deposits, etc.) in the underlying *bank(s)*, regardless of their charter. The Fed position has been that *holding companies* may capitalize with debt so long as some of the proceeds flow into the *bank(s)* as equity.

Recent Fed thinking on capital has bewildered bankers, investment bankers, and other regulatory bodies as to *who* has primary jurisdiction and by *what* standards. As of late 1973, there was some hope that the Fed attitude on debt capital would be clarified as that agency thought through its total regulatory posture over holding companies.

Intraindustry Relative Cost of Capital. When bank regulators imposed capital requirements only on a few banks during the era when banks were undercompetitive with sister subindustries, nobody got hurt. Today, the growing inter-industry competition for capital (including competition for "acceptable" leverage ratios, P/E ratios, and "ratings") points to a collision between private-market standards and government standards. Some questions: (*a*) What will the Fed do to recognize—or offset—the steepening gradient between large-bank and small-bank access to capital and even capital quality? (*b*) Will Fed interest in capital be focused only on "banks," or will it extend to "parents" and "affiliates"? (*c*) To the extent Fed thinking impacts on the cost-of-capital of bank holding companies, what positive or negative implications are there for independent competitors in bank-related fields? Certainly the "merging toward the middle," foreseen (and advocated) by the Hunt Commission on Financial Structure and Regulation, will be heavily skewed by Fed capital guidelines (whether strict or lenient) imposed on banks or bank holding companies alone.

A thoughtful "antiregulatory" position paper on capital adequacy was written in 1973 by George J. Vojta of First National City Bank, stressing profitability and earnings quality as key factors in capital analysis and singling out loan loss experience as the single most relevant factor in designing a theoretical definition of bank capital adequacy. One of the elements of Vojta's paper reviewed research on banks that failed. This research established that balance-sheet ratios of apparent *capital* to *assets* and/or *loans* were not reliable in predicting failure.

Banking Structure. The inertia of U.S. financial history has left the nation with 14,000 banks, 5,400 S&L Associations, 480 mutual savings banks, and countless credit unions, to say nothing of other bank-related subindustries. Technology, money flows, and capital access problems pose enough threats to the structural status quo to make the merger "escape valve" highly desirable. This threat will emerge even sooner if Congress amends the National Banking Act of 1933 to permit, once again, the payment of interest on demand deposits.

Will Branching Laws Be Further Liberalized? With state law changes since 1962 as a clue, it is safe to say that many more states will indeed liberalize. In Illinois, for instance, the branching fight has exploded into the open, with the Illinois Bankers' Association repudiating the study proposals of larger banks, and these banks withdrawing to form their own state association.

Interstate Branching or Affiliation? The 1970 act permits interstate operation of *nonbank* affiliates of holding companies, and the Comptroller's regulations have long permitted national banks to operate interstate "loan production offices," as several large banks have done, and as more now plan to do. In addition, the 1956 act contemplates reciprocal interstate treaties governing bank acquisitions across state lines. Though this is being conjectured (New York/California; Maine/New Hampshire/Vermont; Virginia/D.C./Maryland), the only actual instance is the 1972 Iowa law permitting "any bank holding company" (doing business as of 1971) to control up to 8 percent of Iowa bank deposits as of each June 30. Since Northwest Bancorporation of Minnesota is a qualifying company, it is now able to add to its Iowa banking affiliates!

Some farsighted bankers predict nationwide banking by 1985, with a few truly national companies, many interstate regional companies, foreign banks active throughout the nation, and small "neighborhood" banks stressing aggressive, personal banking. By this time, thrift institutions would be free to convert to stock status and/or to affiliate with bank holding companies, or vice versa. (In 1974, the FRB was considering the application of American Fletcher Corporation to acquire a Phoenix, Arizona S&L.)

Are Machines Branches? The trend toward "point-of-sale" banking poses a challenge to the franchise value of a manned facility. Yet banking law has not come to grips with the definition of unmanned facilities. In all probability, they will be construed differently than branches, and this will in turn undermine still further the value of bricks and mortar.

Who Will Regulate Foreign Bank Entry? Under present law, foreign control of U.S. banks is quite unsupervised at the federal regulatory level, though states have various permissive or prohibitive laws. The successful efforts of major Japanese and English banks to become major interstate operators in this country may lead to reasonable federal regulation of foreign acquisitions.

Will Bank Holding Companies Swallow Whole Subindustries? Mortgage banking companies, finance companies, and factors are high on the popularity list for bank holding company acquisition and appear to be vanishing as independent industries. Regulation Y of the Federal Reserve Board (created to fulfill Sec. 4.c.8 of the 1970 act) summarizes permissible "bank-related" industries, and (in our opinion) may be broadened shortly to include S&Ls. With the relative P/E ratio advantage enjoyed by successful holding companies, it is hard to see how this momentum will be blunted. Furthermore, some observers feel that the mandate of the Federal Reserve to retain control over (*a*) credit and (*b*) funds-transfer will tilt that agency toward maintaining the primacy of bank holding companies within the total financial structure.

On the other hand, the competitive power of the plastic card and the point-of-sale terminal in the hands of aggressive nonbank merchandisers is potentially enormous. What if a broad-line retailer (say, Sears Roebuck) were to offer a plan to finance a more costly way of life for young families (to be repaid as income rose), on the condition that the financing be obtained through that retailer?

Regulation. With the Fed in control of holding companies, the delicate historic equilibrium among the three Washington agencies (FRB, Comptroller, and FDIC)—and the 50 states—has been breached. The ultimate outcome may be a single federal agency. Certainly any legislation to put in place Hunt Commission recommendations would alter the jurisdictions—or at least the relative importance—of agencies, very probably in favor of Fed primacy.

It is important to consider, therefore, how the Fed will regulate holding companies. Today, Fed regulatory practice with holding companies must be deemed tentative and transitional, with full-company reviews occurring only when acquisitions are proposed to the Board. Since there are 1,500 holding companies, this is hardly a permanent answer to the regulatory challenge, and the January 1973 failure of Beverly Hills Bancorporation to meet its commercial paper obligations renews and intensifies this challenge.

Strict Regulation. One alternative openly discussed by Fed officials is to treat parents and nonbank subsidiaries *as if they were banks* and to mount a full-scale field army of examiners conducting regular visits, checking loan quality, management, liquidity, capital, etc. Many observers feel that this is not feasible, given the kaleidoscopic variety of industries, functions, markets, management styles, etc. Could the Fed recruit, train, and manage such a force? Is it desirable even to try to impose a negligible failure rate on nonbank enterprises? How would competition within financial subindustries be affected? How would overall financial industry structure evolve under such a "mother hen" approach?

Separateness. The extreme opposite approach is virtually to ignore the affairs of parents and nonbank subsidiaries, permit these the "right to fail," but at the same time tighten the present "wall" which bank regulation has already built around the assets and earning power of banks. The attitude of the Fed toward the Beverly Hills failure suggests that this is a tempting approach.

What are these walls? The National Bank Act and/or the Federal Reserve Act (*a*) limit(s) bank dividends to one year's earnings plus two prior years of retained earnings, subject to modification in exceptional cases, and (*b*) limit(s) *any* affiliate from borrowing more than

10 percent of the bank's equity capital, and *all* affiliates together from borrowing more than 20 percent—these loans to be secured, furthermore, by specified forms of collateral having a then market value of at least 100 percent of the loan(s). In addition, examiners—armed with "cease and desist" powers, if need be—can criticize excessive management fees, prepayment of debt, transfer of profitable operations *from* bank (and/or transfer of unprofitable operations *to* bank), and, finally, bank guarantees of affiliate obligations.

Some observers feel strongly that this iron curtain approach would violate the "unity of enterprise" and throw upon the private capital markets an industry of bank holding companies whose *effective* "capital" and "liquidity" were far less than a consolidated statement might imply.

"Composite" Approach. A third alternative being discussed is some blend of the two extremes. In our opinion, it makes sense to consider a highly professional, relatively small examiner staff whose explicit function is to monitor problems and problem companies, not with a view to eliminate the failure rate, but to make responsible judgments about new diversification areas, specific acquisition proposals, and the occasional requests of well-managed holding companies to utilize bank assets and earning power beyond the strict limits of administrative rules.

Necessary to this style of regulation would be (*a*) supplementary financial reports of real value to the examiner force and (*b*) heightened sophistication of private market factors—rating agencies, underwriters, analysts, and large investors—as to the financial fundamentals of bank holding companies.

Financial Reporting. The simplicity and profitability of banking from 1950 until the 60s, coupled with industry exemption from SEC regulations (hence from CPAs), resulted in a tradition of extremely poor financial reports, both internal and external. The consequences of these exemptions are serious ones since they affect the very ability to manage.

Internal Reporting. Only in the last ten years has there even been discussion of sophisticated profitability analysis. Even today, only a handful of banks know (*a*) the profitability of administrative units, (*b*) the profitability of products, *and* (*c*) the profitability of customers. Analysts, of course, should make a point of learning whether all or part of such a unified system is in place at the companies they follow.

Another dimension of profitability analysis is isolating the "interest-differential function" from the rest of the accounts. At its minimum, interest-differential reporting involves (*a*) daily averages of financial assets and liabilities, (*b*) functional breakdowns according to affiliate, produce line, and/or markets served, (*c*) tax-equivalent yield rates and cost rates, and (*d*) tax-equivalent dollars of interest income and interest expense, leading to a "net interest margin."

At its maximum, interest-differential reporting also allocates overhead (staff, occupancy, etc.) to every interest-differential category in order to produce a true "gross profit." *Only a tiny handful of banking companies are able to generate such data about themselves, though perhaps several hundred are capable of generating an "uncosted" funds equation.* It is safe to say that the next major reform of bank accounting will center around allocating overhead to the net interest margin.

Related to the analysis of interest income, of course, is the analysis of funds sources and uses. In this era of "spread management," where "bought" money supports a major fraction of earning assets, it is necessary for banks to construct "liquidity models" of themselves. A liquidity model and a statement of condition are only distant cousins: The model estimates (*a*) asset maturities, by type and by time period; (*b*) liability maturities; (*c*) volatility of both sides; (*d*) secular growth; (*e*) loan commitments; and (*f*) funds availability.

A good savings bank (a much simpler operation than a complex bank) typically does have a liquidity plan which takes the above factors into account. But it is hard for commercial banks. Perhaps the key reason is that *stated* loan maturities and loan commitments bear no relation to *effective* values. For example, the "90-day loan" gets renewed, so that its effective maturity may be two years! Again, some "commitments" are merely back-ups to commercial paper and are unlikely to be drawn upon (as opposed to a construction loan commitment). Thus statistical (or actuarial) techniques must enter into the liquidity model of a large, complex bank.

External Reporting. If one of the objectives of financial statement disclosure is to permit an outside analyst to roughly simulate company earnings under varying conditions of environment and strategy, then the certified financial statements of banks and bank holding companies must be deemed failures.

The regulatory apparatus is partly to blame, since (*a*) the Fed in 1964 enshrined in Regulation F a standardized version of 1960-model bank accounting designed to summarize "demand-deposit" banking, not "interest-differential" banking; (*b*) other federal agencies adopted this format as a reporting requirement (at least for larger banks); (*c*) in 1969, when SEC first got involved, it was easier for that agency to defer to the Fed's "specialized knowledge" than to oppose; and (*d*) the AICPA, called for advice in 1969, had to cope with the long-established inertia of regulatory concepts of "proper" reporting.

The current solution to this problem (that is, the gap between analyst data needs and that body of data supplied by certified statements) is only partly satisfactory. Stimulated by analysts, many managements supply "supplementary" data—either in published annuals and quarterlies or in limited-circulation mailings.

In a later section we will return to the question of data. For the present, analysts interested in reviewing reasonably good supplemental presentations may inspect the annuals, quarterlies, and/or quarterly analyst mailings of the seven companies recently selected to receive awards for excellence in 1972 corporate reporting (by the Banking and Financial Industries Subcommittee, Corporate Information Committee, FAF). These companies are: NCNB Corporation, Continental Illinois, First Bank System, First Chicago, First Tennessee National, Harris Bankcorporation, and Philadelphia National Corporation.

MARKET HISTORY OF BANK STOCKS

History from 1950 through 1969

It is hard today to realize how sweeping has been the postwar evolution of bank stocks as trading and investment vehicles.

In the early 50s, the public image of bank stocks was worse than zero, since this industry—a high-flyer stock group in 1929—was not only battered by loan losses (1929–33) and by its panicky propensity to call loans but, in addition, the investing public remembered that bank stock was assessable! (Shareholder liability was cancelled in the 30s.)

The first renewal of interest skittishly treated bank equities as though they were a kind of high-risk preferred stock, with "book value" standing for "liquidating value." It was a rare stock that traded "over book," and invariably caused ripples of anxiety among the cautious.

As the 50s progressed, the emergence of *P/E ratio* as a general yardstick of equity value by-passed bank stocks, partly because the regulator-endorsed secretiveness of bankers made EPS unavailable or unreliable or noncomparable. Only toward the end of the decade did there occasionally appear the bare skeleton of an earnings statement which yielded "net operating earnings" (and usually ignored bond losses, loan losses, reserve reconciliations, accruals, accounting definitions, etc.).

In the early 60s, this version of EPS (which would be totally unacceptable even by today's standards) was widely reported by larger banks. Analysts—most of whom then were employed as handmaidens to OTC dealer operations—began to concentrate on the P/E ratio, as against the book-to-market ratio. *The purpose of this analytic effort, however, was not to single out particular stocks for heavy emphasis over others, but rather to assist arbitrage-type trading based on minor differences in relative P/E ratio.* To put it another way, the research style in bank stocks was more like convertible-bond analysis than growth-stock analysis.

This orientation had some unusual by-products: (*a*) it accorded investment-grade status to a wide repertory of stocks (perhaps 100 in mid-1964); (*b*) it caused a rather narrow spectrum of P/E ratio differences to be considered "normal"; (*c*) it focussed research on the extreme short run, such as "next quarter" or "full year estimate"; and (*d*) it almost entirely overlooked (for purposes of pricing stocks) the very real differences among companies as to strategy, management, technology, etc.

Since 1969, when banks began to list on NYSE, research style in bank analysis has shifted drastically, to correspond with the merchandising style of member-firm brokers. In this type of merchandising, salesmen are rarely connoisseurs of a many-company industry and prefer to single out a handful of "story stocks" per group. Since the "story" in banking has more to do with strategy, management, and technology than with P/E ratio arbitrage, one can appreciate how sweeping are the implications of moving bank stocks from a dealer to a broker matrix! Finally, the ponderous logistics of turning a large sales force onto a "stock story" preclude a connoisseurship based on narrow price movements.

Post-1969 Characteristics

In Figure 1 we illustrate the bank stocks' P/E as it was perceived by investors on November 11, 1964 (close to the pinnacle of P/E ratios

FIGURE 1

P/E Ratio: November 11, 1964

```
                        61
                        51                      78
                        48                      75
                57      32      59      65
                56      30      55      45
                54      24      53      25                      44
                50      22      40      20                      42
                33      21      16      18                      37      73
                31      14      15      17                      36      72      76
                29      13      11      12      60      8       71      70      80
        52      27      7       10      5       39      6       47      66      79      67
        28      19      3       9       2       1       4       35      26      77      64                      69
       ─────────────────────────────────────────────────────────────────────────────────────────────────────────────
         10.9    11.0    12.1    13.2    14.3    15.4    16.5    17.6    18.7    19.8    20.9    22.0    23.1    24.2    25.3
SCALE    and
         Below   12.0    13.1    14.2    15.3    16.4    17.5    18.6    19.7    20.8    21.9    23.0    24.1    25.2    and
                                                                                                                        Above

SCORE     0               1       2               3       4       5       6       7       8       9               10
```

for this industry). The numbers refer to the predecessor companies of the 80 companies comprising the Bancompare universe.[1] Earnings are 12 months through September 30, 1964.

[1] Bancompare is comprised of 80 large banks and bank holding companies. Bancompare is a research tool produced by Comparative Systems, Inc., an affiliate of David C. Cates & Co., Inc. Each number (from 1 through 80) corresponds to a company (see Appendix A for number key). The principle behind Bancompare is that approximations of a "normal distribution"—per ratio, per time period—are a useful way of organizing data. One by-product of this technique is "scores," which function as ratio substitutes as well as comparative benchmarks. Thus a score 8 in Figure 1 stands for (*a*) a P/E between 20.9 and 21.9, and (*b*) a relatively high position within that universe for that time period. It is important to note that all numbers along the horizontal axis are *percentage* figures, that is, ratios.

In Figure 2 we illustrate the bank stock universe in 3Q73, where prices are the mean of third-quarter hi/low and where earnings are 12 months through September 30, 1973.

Several contrasts are apparent: (*a*) The 1964 curve is clearly uni-modal suggesting "one market," while the 1973 curve looks suspiciously bi-modal, suggesting a split market; (*b*) the 1964 ratio spectrum is rather

FIGURE 2

P/E Ratio: 3Q1973

```
                                80
                  74            76
                  73            58
                  60            55
                  59            54
                  50            51              78
                  33            49    77        75
                  32            31    71  79    72
                  28            29    67  56    65
                  27            22    39  48    46                                    68
                  25            16    30  36    45              70                    64
         62       21            15    26  23    44    69        63              53    41
         57       17            11    12  20    19    66        61              42    35
         52       14             3     5  18     9    40        47                    34
         24       13             1     2   4     7    38  37    10  43            8     6
```

SCALE	3.3 and Below / 4.4	3.4 / 4.4	4.5 / 5.5	5.6 / 6.6	6.7 / 7.7	7.8 / 8.8	8.9 / 9.9	10.0 / 11.0	11.1 / 12.1	12.2 / 13.2	13.3 / 14.3	14.4 / 15.4	15.5 / 16.5	16.6 / 17.6	17.7 and Above
SCORE	0			1	2		3 4	5	6		7	8 9			10

tight, while the 1973 spectrum is dispersed; (*c*) the 1964 P/E median is 16.6, while the 1973 median is 9.6; and (*d*) the relative standing of companies is greatly altered.

Still another contrast is evident when we look at recent price movement differentials within this large-company universe (Figure 3).

The distribution in Figure 3 shows, over almost a three-year period

FIGURE 3

Price Change: 3Q73/1Q71

```
                                74
                  80            69
                  76            60
                  73            59
                  71            58    79
                  62            52    77
                  54            51    72
                  50            33    67    66
                  28            32    57    48
                  26            29    55    47
                  25            27    49    46
                  22            21    44    45                    78                    68
                  14            17    40    42                    75                    64
                  13            16    30    39    70              63                    41
                   5            15    12    38    56              61                    34
                  24             3    11     7    31    36        43    53    65        10
                  20             1     2     4    18    19    9   37    23    8           6
```

SCALE	-78.0 and Below / -64.0	-77.9 / -64.0	-63.9 / -50.0	-49.9 / -36.0	-35.9 / -22.0	-21.9 / -8.0	-7.9 / 6.0	6.1 / 20.0	20.1 / 34.0	34.1 / 48.0	48.1 / 62.0	62.1 / 76.0	76.1 / 90.0	90.1 / 104.0	104.1 and Above
SCORE	0		1	2	3		4	5	6	7	8	9			10

from 1Q71 through 3Q73 (using mean prices in each of the two quarters), that the rate of price dispersal within the universe is high. By inspection, furthermore, the reader can easily see that the "top 15 price-move" stocks of Figure 3 cluster toward the high end of the Figure 2 distribution, while the "bottom 15" of Figure 3 cluster toward the low end of Figure 2! In our opinion, this points to an ongoing split within the bank stock market that has not yet run its course.

Though some argue that this split is entirely the product of the "two-tier" (or institutionalized) market, we believe that two extra factors are active:

1. *Shift from Dealer to Broker Sponsorship.* We have commented already on this process.
2. *Company Performance Differentials.* As margins narrow and risks multiply, management is more deeply challenged. As a result, performance differentials are becoming wider, illustrating the adage, "There are more banks than bankers."

To illustrate, Figure 4 shows EPS growth rate 1968–72 (simple compound annual method with 1968 restated to a 1969 accounting basis for

FIGURE 4

EPS Growth: 1972/68 (simple; restated)

```
                        80              78
                        79              69
                        74              61
                        73              57
                        58              56
                        54        75    46
                   76   52   62   72    39
                   51   49   60   70    38
                   33   30   59   67    36
                   32   25   55   66    35           77
              50   24   18   45   47   27           68
              28   21   13   43   44   10           65
         71   26   14   12   17   40   9    53      64
         5    22   7    11   16   31   8    48   37  63   41
    20   3    2    1    4    15   29   6    42   23  19   34
   _____

         -6.0  -5.9  -3.9  -1.9  0.1   2.1   4.1   6.1   8.1   10.1  12.1  14.1  16.1  18.1  20.1
SCALE    and                                                                                   and
         Below -4.0  -2.0  0.0   2.0   4.0   6.0   8.0   10.0  12.0  14.0  16.0  18.0  20.0      Above

SCORE    0           1     2     3     4     5     6     7     8     9           10
```

loan loss provision *and* for pooling). Whatever one might have once meaningfully said about "group average" performance should be destroyed by this picture of wide diversity.

The 1972/71 picture shows an even more diverse pattern of EPS performance (see Figure 5.), and the 1973/72 picture is shaping up similarly.

Can fundamental performance characteristics of market favorites be discerned? Table 1 singles out some rather striking characteristics of the 15 top and 15 lowest price performers from 1Q71 through 1Q73.

FIGURE 5

EPS Change: 1972/71

```
                              80   76
                              60   75   69
                              58   72   68
                              51   70   64
                              50   66   62   79
                              32   47   55   78
                              28   46   53   77
                    73   27   45   43   67
                    57   21   24   40   65
          59   52   18   17   39   61   63
     74   30   38   16   15   37   42   49
     54   29   25   13   11   31   35   48
71   22   26    7   12    8   19   33   44   56
20    5   14    1    4    3    2    9    6   10   41   36              34
                                                                      23
```

SCALE	-15.5 and Below	-15.4 -12.0	-11.9 -8.5	-8.4 -5.0	-4.9 -1.5	-1.4 2.0	2.1 5.5	5.6 9.0	9.1 12.5	12.6 16.0	16.1 19.5	19.6 23.0	23.1 26.5	26.6 30.0	30.1 and Above
SCORE	0	1	2	3	4	5	6	7	8	9				10	

TABLE 1

The Fifteen Highest and Fifteen Lowest Price Performers (1Q71–1Q73)

| | Stock Price Performance | | | |
| | Highest | | Lowest | |
Ratio*	Ratio	Score	Ratio	Score
EPS Change: 72/71	16.7	8	−4.6	2
: 71/70	11.1	8	−7.4	4
EPS Growth: 72/68	13.6	8	1.9	2
NOI to EA : 1972	12.3	7	8.7	2
NOI to SE : 1972	1.11	7	0.73	2
P/E Ratio : 1Q73	17.6	9	9.8	3
Price Change: 1Q73/71	87.4	10	−18.0	3
EA Change: 72/70	43.1	8	22.4	3
EA Yield : 1972	7.33	7	6.85	4
Overhead Change: 72/70	26.1	7	16.0	3
Overhead to NOI: 1972	2.76	4	4.95	8
Overhead to EA: 1972	3.02	5	3.24	5
Dividend Payout: 1972	34.2	3	53.3	7

* Guide to abbreviations: (a) EPS is After tax Income before Securities Transactions, on Primary Basis; (b) NOI is the same, before division into shares; (c) EA is Earning Assets (Loans and Investments) carefully defined on a daily average basis and other criteria; (d) SE is Stockholders Equity plus Loan Loss Reserve in full; (e) Overhead is all Operating Expenses other than Interest Expense and Loan Loss Provision.

Though most of the performance differences indicated in Table 1 are self-evident, some require a special understanding of ratio relationships in bank analysis. We will treat this in the next section.

In concluding this review of market characteristics, we show turnover in bank stocks, that is, what percentage of the outstanding shares were traded (across exchanges and/or NASDAQ, where available) in the third quarter of 1973 (Figure 6).

FIGURE 6

Percent Shares Traded: 3Q1973

```
                        80
                        79
                        61        74
                        59        70
                        56        60
                        54  78    53
                        47  57    42    77    75
                72      37  50    40    76    64
                71      28  46    38    67    63    73
        65      62      26  41    22    36    30    48    68
        55      58      23  33    9     32    29    25    44
        43      51      18  31    7     19    24    14    39
        27      49      10  17    6     8     21    11    35                    66
        16      12      3   15    1     5     13    4     2     69        45    34
─────────────────────────────────────────────────────────────────────────────────
SCALE   0.1   0.2  0.8  1.4  2.0  2.6  3.2  3.8  4.4  5.0  5.6  6.2       6.8   7.4
        and                                                                     and
        Below 0.7  1.3  1.9  2.5  3.1  3.7  4.3  4.9  5.5  6.1  6.7       7.3  Above
SCORE    0     1    2    3    4    5    6    7    8    9                    10
```

PRINCIPLES OF RATIO ANALYSIS

Introduction

The first step in bank (and bank holding company) analysis is to realize that this is a multicompany, multiproduct, multimarket and multi-environment industry (and becoming more so). Only occasionally can the analyst identify salient "swing factors," and even these are apt to be different from company to company and from year to year.

Thus the *difficulty* of bank analysis is to properly grasp the relative significance of all the items in the lengthy "laundry list" which must be checked off before valid earnings forecasts can be made. Correspondingly, the *art* of bank analysis is to simplify this complex routine for the benefit of salesman, portfolio manager, and investment committee.

The second step in efficient analytic coverage of even a few companies is to learn to "screen" those companies which form one's reference group for purposes of understanding performance. Once the performance characteristics of a reference group are grasped in skeletal outline, the analyst is better prepared to move from "screen-level" to "interview-level" routines. We can safely say that analysts who do not appreciate (*a*) the enormous complexity of bank data and/or (*b*) the necessity of sorting out essentials, will tend either to remain dangerously superficial or else waste time on improperly digested detail.

The third step in bank analysis is to realize that this intrinsic functional complexity poses an even more formidable challenge to managements. Thus the analyst should be alert for the "decision quality" within organizations, to ascertain whether managements function well on all fronts, on only a few, or perhaps on none at all. A good management team may perhaps be characterized as one that plays hard and cooperatively, winning more points than it loses, year after year.

Finally, the analyst of a *holding company* must always remain aware of the *unconsolidated* structure and the possible financing problems of parent and individual affiliates.

Screen-Level Analysis

The most primitive type of screen is based on "final performance" data such as earnings, and upon ratios such as EPS growth, EPS stability, return on equity and on assets, P/E ratio, etc. These are, however, common to the analysis of any industry, and by themselves tell us virtually nothing about the "how" and "why" of banking.

The Primacy of Earning Assets. The next level of sophistication is to develop a ratio framework based upon one or more "master aggregates" against which a maximum number of significant ratios can be generated. Of course, ratios carefully connected by common data elements are (provided the data are good) far more useful than unrelated ratios. This is so because it makes the "game of 20 questions" easier to play, first between analyst and data, and then between analyst and management.

In bank analysis there is only one such aggregate: that is, the sum of all interest-producing loans, investments, and other vehicles for earning a spread. Admittedly, some analysts and many bankers prefer "total assets" or "total deposits" or even "total income." *We argue, however, that Earning Assets is the only master aggregate upon which interest-differential analysis can be based.* That is, the gross yield rate less the interest-cost rate equals the net yield rate—all figured against Earning Assets! How to deal with "trading account" presents problems, since (*a*) the gross yield rate should logically not be modified by *nonyield* factors of profit/loss, and (*b*) since the offsetting liabilities (with their specific cost rate) cannot easily be segregated for separate analysis of net profitability.

This is not to deny the importance of other kinds of assets, but rather to assert the analytic primacy of interest-producing assets. Two "memo-type" ratios—Earning Assets to Total Assets, and Fixed Assets to Earning Assets—can easily be built to screen irregular bulges of float, concrete, or hardware, without cluttering up the intricate ratio system which can only be based on Earning Assets. Some analysts treat Trading Account on a memo basis, too, and carve out an exactly offsetting aggregate of liabilities, to which they assign a hypothetical cost rate, for example, average Fed funds rate in each quarter.

To put it another way, Earning Assets analysis permits the analyst to isolate the interest-differential function from the rest of total operations and gives him a framework for tracking critical components such as growth, mix, yield sensitivities, cost sensitivities, spreads, and loan loss (both the "provision" and the "net charge-off"). Finally, this master aggregate permits insights into productivity. To illustrate, suppose that Company A and Company B both have identical gross yields, gross cost rates, loss ratios, and—therefore—net spreads; yet Company A returns 1.1 percent on Earning Assets while Company B returns 0.95 percent. *Only when Earning Assets is used as the master aggregate is it possible to isolate this important difference for further analysis.* Before continuing this presentation of a screen-level ratio matrix, however, we should digress to consider the problem of data availability.

The Problem of "Certified" Data. Put simply, the certified financial statements of banks and bank holding companies are largely useless to the diligent analyst. In fact, the only data of really sound value are "operating expenses." There are several reasons for analyst wariness of certified accounting for banks and holding companies.

Lack of Averages. The relatively volatile funds flows through banks can only be usefully summarized on a daily average basis, whether annually, quarterly, or monthly. They cannot be summarized by the statements of a single day, especially at year end, when "window dressing" is likely to occur. Since accountancy has not yet come up to certifying "averaged" statements, analysts must ask for such data on a noncertified basis.

Misclassification of Interest Income. Four problems may be singled out.

First, regulatory agencies—with the acquiescence of accountants—have ruled that bank holdings of bank C/Ds is properly a "cash and due from banks" item. The consequence of this is that the interest income does not fall within "loan" or "investment" income, and often appears lumped within "other income" (by implication, therefore, noninterest income).

Second, leases have not been defined as loans and are often lumped within "other assets" (producing once again "other income").

Third, since some interest income is tax sheltered (notably, that on tax-free municipals), roughly half of the yield benefit consists of a reduction of tax. Bank portfolio managers, however, internally add this benefit back to "coupon income" in order to calculate a "fully tax-equivalent" income (and yield rate) in order to have a common denominator for comparing investment alternatives. Though this calculation is a necessary step for any analyst in computing the total interest-differential equation, the ingredients for doing so are not present in financial statements. At best, analysts can only estimate tax-adjusted income, by taking tax-exempt investment income and applying to it the *reciprocal of state, federal, and any local income tax rates.*

Fourth, realized gains and losses on securities are treated as quasi-extraordinary transactions below the level of EPS. Since bond-switching programs of banks are undertaken to improve true portfolio yield, sophisticated internal analysis always amortizes the prospective gain/loss over the remaining life of the bond to be sold, *as a yield offset to the gross yield on the new bond.* Only in this way can managements properly plan—and track—the interest income contribution from the portfolio operation. The same principle applies to sales of mortgages and loans. Financial statements, however, ignore these internal operating disciplines, thus distorting not only "interest income" but—even worse—also creating EPS confusion. That is, *two final EPS numbers* (Income before Securities Transactions and Net Income) are mandated in a clumsy effort to deal with a relatively small problem within securities accounting!

Insufficient Breakdowns of Assets/Liabilities and Income/Expense. Normal standards of "materiality" are inadequate to summarize the multi-product, multimarket nature of banking. Most statements contain un-differentiated "loan income" totals and fail to dissect "other income," "other expenses," and "interest on deposits" into functional subsections corresponding to real differences in markets and/or products. Further-more, statements do not properly group types of income. For example, a major asset category has emerged in recent years to which the label Temporary Investments (or Money-Market Instruments) is often ap-plied. These include federal funds, repurchase agreements, and Euro-dollar and currency positions. *These typically comprise arbitrage-type operations, in the sense that a money desk is trading to maximize the spread between large volumes of offsetting assets and liabilities.* Unless analysts can quickly identify these volumes *on both sides of the balance sheet and income statement,* false inferences as to asset growth, mix, risk, yield rates, and income are sure to occur! At present, it is not pos-sible to sort out from statements this new and unprecedented type of income/expense. (Gross treatment of leveraged leases presents a similar type of problem.)

Definition of Good Data. In general, good data from banks and holding companies should be such as to facilitate screen-level and inter-view-level analytic routines. More specifically, data should have complete consistency at each corporate level: (*a*) Consolidated figures should be adequate to form a ratio screen; and (*b*) "banks-only" or "domestic bank" should be analyzable *in the same form,* so that ratio disparities with "consolidated" can act as a flag. Too often, a *worldwide* balance sheet will be supplemented, say, by a *domestic* yield rate, presenting analysts with incompatible data. Finally, (*c*) special types of operation such as trust, mortgage banking, sales finance, and other nondeposit services should be presented in appropriate detail (though the hetero-geneity of these functions makes screen-level analytic routines difficult).

The characteristics of good data texture at each of the two corporate levels (*a*) and (*b*) described above, are as follows:

a. Average Balance Sheet. The groupings within assets and liabilities should be functional, as subheadings and items. By *functional* we mean discriminations according to product, market, maturity, and/or risk. (See Appendix B for an adaptation by Standard & Poor's Corporation of the disclosure format articulated in 1973 by the Banking and Financial Industries Subcommittee of the FAF.)

b. Yield Rates and Cost Rates. These should be on a tax-adjusted basis, and absolutely compatible with (*a*) above, for each corporate level.

c. Dollars of Income and Expense. Similarly, these should flow from (*a*) above, with some "memo" summary of tax-adjusted gross income. Some compression of headings is acceptable.

d. Memo Items. Arbitrage-type assets/liabilities and income/expense should be shown "net," together with tax-adjusted gross income from the arbitrage operation.

e. Historic Restatement. All the above should be reported in reasonably full detail for at least five (and preferably six) years.

Data and Ratios as Developed in Bancompare "Screen Techniques." To the best of our knowledge, Bancompare is the only explicit system of investment-oriented ratio analysis available for discussion. If there were others of rival complexity, we would not have failed to mention them. Within a strictly banking (as opposed to bank stock) context, however, two other systems are worthy of mention. Bank Administration Institute publishes for its members' use an annual *Financial Diagnostic Profile* which makes interesting reading, and First Bank System applies to the analysis of its 88 bank affiliates a "distribution and profile" method (which was the original model for the Bancompare concept).

Appendix C contains a blank data base and item definitions for a ratio review of Company A and Company B. Note the great care with which it is necessary to define Earnings Assets (item N).

From this reasonably spare data base, it is possible to develop over 55 ratios (many of which are merely different time periods). A distribution analysis of the 80-company universe for each ratio, furthermore, yields a set of scores for each company which facilitates the grasping of ratio interrelationships, or, to put it another way, visualization of the "field properties" of ratios. In Figure 7, for example, a scored distribution of Market-Sensitive Liabilities to Earning Assets is illustrated. This ratio clearly interacts with many other ratios, such as yield, cost, overhead, EPS, etc.

This interactive technique of analysis can be illustrated by performing a screen-level analysis of two companies. Company A (Fig. 8) is a large "growth regional" bank holding company, and Company B (Fig. 9) is a large far western regional.

Note the following: Ratios 1–17 are final-performance type ratios;

FIGURE 7

Market-Sensitive Liabilities as Percent of Earning Assets: 1972

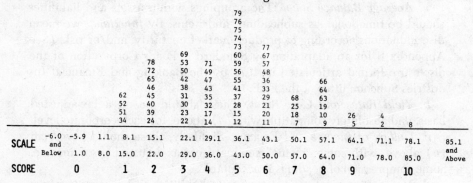

FIGURE 8

Company A

		Ratio	Score
1.	EPS Change (9 mos.) 1973/1972	−4.10	1
2.	EPS Change (6 mos.) 1973/1972	8.30	4
3.	EPS Change (3 mos.) 1973/1972	17.40	6
4.	EPS Change 1972/1971	14.40	7
5.	EPS Change 1971/1970	0.00	5
6.	EPS Change 1970/1969	9.80	5
7.	Net Income per Share Change 1972/1971	13.80	8
8.	Net Income as Percent of NOI 1972	1.04	8
9.	Effective Tax Rate 1972	34.80	8
10.	Effective Tax Rate Change 1972/1971	−2.90	5
11.	EPS Growth Rate 1972/1968 (simple, restated)	10.90	7
12.	EPS Growth Rate 1972/1968 (least squares)	9.00	7
13.	EPS Growth Rate 1972/1968 (as reported)	11.80	7
14.	EPS Growth Rate 1971/1967 (simple, restated)		
15.	NOI/Average Stockholders' Equity 1972	12.80	8
16.	NOI/Earning Assets 1972	1.38	10
17.	NOI/Earning Assets 1971	1.38	9
18.	P/E Ratio 3Q 1973	19.60	10
19.	P/E Ratio 3Q 1973 DILUTED	20.60	10
20.	P/E Ratio 2Q 1973	22.80	10
21.	P/E Ratio 1Q 1973	24.00	10
22.	Price Change 3Q1973/1Q1971	23.20	6
23.	Price Change 2Q1973/1Q1971	43.30	8
24.	Price Change 1Q1973/1Q1971	44.80	7
25.	Percent Shares Traded 3Q 1973	6.10	9
26.	Percent Shares Traded 2Q 1973	2.80	5
27.	Percent Shares Traded 1Q 1973	N.A.	
28.	Earning Asset Change 1972/1970	27.00	4
29.	Earning Asset Change 1971/1969	13.00	3
30.	Loan Change 1972/1970	27.00	6

FIGURE 8 (*Continued*)

		Ratio	*Score*
31.	Loans/Earning Assets 1972	82.82	9
32.	Loans/Earning Assets 1971	81.55	9
33.	Market Liabilities/Earning Assets 1972	35.20	4
34.	Market Liabilities/Earning Assets 1971	35.40	5
35.	Consumer Time/Earning Assets 1972	21.00	3
36.	Consumer Time/Earning Assets 1971	24.00	4
37.	Earning Asset Yield 1972	7.79	9
38.	Earning Asset Yield 1971	7.88	8
39.	Loan Yield 1972	7.94	8
40.	Loan Yield 1971	7.97	7
41.	Interest Expense/Earning Assets 1972	2.75	2
42.	Interest Expense/Earning Assets 1971	2.90	4
43.	Loan Loss Provision/Earning Assets 1972	0.32	9
44.	Loan Loss Provision/Earning Assets 1971	0.27	8
45.	Net Charge-off/Earning Assets 1972	0.38	10
46.	Overhead Change 1972/1970	31.00	8
47.	Overhead Change 1971/1969	39.00	8
48.	Staff Expense Change 1972/1970	30.00	9
49.	Staff Expense Change 1971/1969	38.70	9
50.	Staff Expense/Overhead 1972	60.90	7
51.	Overhead/NOI 1972	3.54	5
52.	Overhead/Earning Assets 1972	4.90	9
53.	Avg. Stockholders' Equity/Earning Assets 1972	10.80	8
54.	Long-Term Debt/Total Capital 1972	12.00	3
55.	Dividends/NOI 1972	43.20	5

Earning Asset Notes.................... 0
Loan Notes.......................... 0

ratios 18–27 focus on market performance; 28–45 isolate the interest-differential function of the company; 46–52 are concerned with non-financial overhead; and 53–55 examine capital factors.

Earnings and Profitability. EPS growth—with the exception of 1972 —has slipped, both absolutely and relatively, from the high levels of prior years. Especially in 1973, quarterly performance has deteriorated badly (lines 1–6).

The company appears to be a profit taker in its bank portfolio operations (7,8). The effective tax rate scores high (9), suggesting low municipal holdings.

Return on equity and on earning assets is extremely high, especially in view of the strong equity ratio (15,16,53).

Market Factors. The premium P/E ratio of Company A (18–21) has not been supported by relative price action (from a base of 1Q71). In fact, the relative action score has slipped to the "6" level in 3Q73 (22), while stock turnover has jumped to the "9" level (25), suggesting investor concern about the EPS pattern (1–3).

Interest-Differential Factors. Earning assets and loan growth have not been strong (28–30), but loans are a heavy fraction of earning assets (31,32), suggesting that a significantly richer mix is not possible. Meanwhile, market-sensitive liabilities (items T and U of the data base) are fairly high for a regional bank (33,34), while consumer-type time deposits are fairly low (35,36).

Earning asset and loan yields (37–40) are not only high in score but show relative insensitivity to money-market and price-rate shifts. This is in contrast to the proportionately greater interest-rate sensitivity shown on the cost side (41,42; also see 33,34). Could this contrast be the adverse element in 1973 EPS?

The basic financial spread is very high: EA yield scored "9" in 1972, while EA cost scored "2," for an indicated gross spread of 5.04 percent (37–42). Loan loss provision, however, runs high, and the 1972 net charge-off is similarly out of line (43–45).

Overhead Factors. Company A is overhead intensive (52), staff intensive (50), and has been increasing its outlays for staff (46–49) at a percentage rate quite disproportionate to its growth of Earning Assets and loans (28–30). This could, of course, be toward non-funds-using sources of income.

The profitability of "nonfunds" income, in fact, is probably quite substantial. Despite the very high spread (37,42) and the high overhead input (52), how else to account for the strong productivity of overhead in relation to earnings (51) and of earnings to assets (16)?

Capital Factors. Though a high loan ratio (31) requires heavy capital support, the equity ratio is good (53) and debt usage is low (54).

Summary. The critical questions might follow this path. Has a funds-availability slowdown occurred? If so, has corporate strategy chosen to emphasize a non-funds-using type of earnings? If so, is the incremental overhead expense incrementally profitable, or will a narrower margin emerge? Will continued loan growth be financed disproportionately by market-sensitive liabilities? If so, what will happen to EPS stability? Is high loan loss chronic, and does this—coupled with the loan ratio—imply need for more equity capital?

FIGURE 9

Company B

		Ratio	Score
1.	EPS Change (9 mos.) 1973/1972	10.10	5
2.	EPS Change (6 mos.) 1973/1972	14.70	5
3.	EPS Change (3 mos.) 1973/1972	18.20	6
4.	EPS Change 1972/1971	13.50	7
5.	EPS Change 1971/1970	4.50	6
6.	EPS Change 1970/1969	1.10	3
7.	Net Income per Share Change 1972/1971	34.20	10
8.	Net Income as Percent of NOI 1972	1.01	5
9.	Effective Tax Rate 1972	29.70	6
10.	Effective Tax Rate Change 1972/1971	−3.80	5

FIGURE 9 (*Continued*)

		Ratio	*Score*
11.	EPS Growth Rate 1972/1968 (simple, restated)......	5.70	4
12.	EPS Growth Rate 1972/1968 (least squares)........	5.10	4
13.	EPS Growth Rate 1972/1968 (as reported)..........	5.70	4
14.	EPS Growth Rate 1971/1967 (simple, restated)......		
15.	NOI/Average Stockholders' Equity 1972............	8.80	2
16.	NOI/Earning Assets 1972.........................	0.63	1
17.	NOI/Earning Assets 1971.........................	0.65	2
18.	P/E Ratio 3Q 1973.............................	10.00	5
19.	P/E Ratio 3Q 1973 DILUTED....................	10.30	5
20.	P/E Ratio 2Q 1973.............................	10.10	4
21.	P/E Ratio 1Q 1973.............................	12.30	5
22.	Price Change 3Q1973/1Q1971.....................	3.60	4
23.	Price Change 2Q1973/1Q1971.....................	2.40	5
24.	Price Change 1Q1973/1Q1971.....................	19.50	5
25.	Percent Shares Traded 3Q 1973...................	2.20	3
26.	Percent Shares Traded 2Q 1973...................	3.00	5
27.	Percent Shares Traded 1Q 1973...................	4.30	5
28.	Earning Asset Change 1972/1970..................	31.00	5
29.	Earning Asset Change 1971/1969.................	16.00	4
30.	Loan Change 1972/1970..........................	31.00	6
31.	Loans/Earning Assets 1972.......................	77.13	8
32.	Loans/Earning Assets 1971.......................	75.91	8
33.	Market Liabilities/Earning Assets 1972............	40.50	5
34.	Market Liabilities/Earning Assets 1971............	34.20	5
35.	Consumer Time/Earning Assets 1972.............., :	42.70	7
36.	Consumer Time/Earning Assets 1971..............,	45.40	9
37.	Earning Asset Yield 1972.........................	6.83	4
38.	Earning Asset Yield 1971.........................	7.04	4
39.	Loan Yield 1972.................................	6.99	4
40.	Loan Yield 1971.................................	7.22	5
41.	Interest Expense/Earning Assets 1972..............	3.98	8
42.	Interest Expense/Earning Assets 1971..............	4.08	8
43.	Loan Loss Provision/Earning Assets 1972..........	0.13	3
44.	Loan Loss Provision/Earning Assets 1971..........	0.12	3
45.	Net Charge-off/Earning Assets 1972...............	0.15	5
46.	Overhead Change 1972/1970......................	26.00	7
47.	Overhead Change 1971/1969......................	26.00	5
48.	Staff Expense Change 1972/1970..................	23.50	7
49.	Staff Expense Change 1971/1969.................	27.10	5
50.	Staff Expense/Overhead 1972.....................	61.10	7
51.	Overhead/NOI 1972.............................	4.92	8
52.	Overhead/Learning Assets 1972..................	3.12	5
53.	Avg. Stockholders' Equity/Earning Assets 1972.....	7.20	2
54.	Long-term Debt/Total Capital 1972...............	26.00	6
55.	Dividends/NOI 1972.............................	40.70	4

Earning Asset Notes..................... 8
Loan Notes........................... 2

a. Earnings and Profitability. The relative strength of year-to-year EPS has gained sharply from 1970 through 1972, and has held steady at a "5" level throughout 1973 (1–6). Profitability on equity and on assets, however, appears very low (15–17).

b. Market Factors. With the exception of a lower level of share turnover in 3Q73, the market position of Company B is "5" or "4" throughout (18–27).

c. Interest-Differential Factors. There is a great similarity with Company A in the low-to-moderate growth, high loan ratios and dependence on money-market liabilities (28–34). This company, however, has a far greater stake in consumer time deposits (35,36), though the 72/71 ratio decrease is more a function of the big 1972 jump in market-sensitive liabilities.

Also in sharp contrast to Company A are all the major spread characteristics: EA yield is a 4, while EA cost is an 8 (for an indicated spread of only 2.85 percent); asset yield sensitivity appears greater than liability cost sensitivity; and loan loss is low (37–45).

d. Overhead Factors. Overhead expansion is once again disproportionate to earning asset and loan growth (46–49). If this is to enlarge non-funds-using sources of earnings, the base does not appear large, judging from the merely average level of overhead to earnings assets (52). Meanwhile, due to a narrow spread (and possibly to unprofitable non-funds-using activities), the ratio of overhead to earnings is high (51), indicating a high level of operating (nonfinancial) leverage.

e. Capital Factors. Equity capital looks quite low, especially in view of the loan ratio (31); and debt usage is reasonably advanced (54).

Summary. Three kinds of leverage—financial, operating, and capital —seem to be present in above-average degree. At the same time, overhead increases appear disproportionate against underlying growth. An analyst might wish to explore which one of these leverages is considered by management to be most out of line, and what the remedial strategy is to be.

APPENDIX A

The Numbering System of BANCOMPARE

Company and Region	No.

MONEY CENTER —
NEW YORK AND CHICAGO:

Bank of New York Company, Inc.	01
Bankers Trust New York Corporation	02
Charter New York Corporation	03
Chase Manhattan Corporation	04
Chemical New York Corporation	05
First National City Corporation	06
Manufacturers Hanover Corporation	07
J. P. Morgan & Co., Inc.	08
Continental Illinois Corporation	09
First Chicago Corporation	10
Harris Bankcorp, Inc.	11
Nortrust Corporation	12

ATLANTIC:

Baystate Corporation	13
C B T Corporation (Hartford)	14
Fidelity Corporation	15
Fidelity Union Bancorporation	16
First Empire State Corporation	17
First National Boston Corporation	18
First Pennsylvania Corporation	19
Franklin New York Corporation	20
Girard Company	21
Hartford National Corporation	22
Industrial National Corporation	23
Lincoln First Banks, Inc.	24
Marine Midland Banks, Inc.	25
Mellon National Corporation	26
Midlantic Banks, Inc.	27
New England Merchants Co., Inc.	28
Philadelphia National Corporation	29
Pittsburgh National Corporation	30
Provident National Corporation	31
Shawmut Association, Inc.	32
State Street Boston Financial Corporation	33

APPENDIX A (*Continued*)

Company and Region	No.
SOUTHERN:	
Barnett Banks of Florida	34
Citizens & Southern and Subsidiaries	35
First National Holding Corporation (Atlanta)	36
First Tennessee National Corporation	37
Cameron Financial Corporation	38
First & Merchants Corporation	39
Maryland National Corporation	40
NCNB Corporation	41
Southeast Banking Corporation	42
Trust Company of Georgia	43
United Virginia Bankshares Inc.	44
Virginia National Bankshares	45
Bank of Virginia Company	46
Wachovia Corporation	47
MIDWEST:	
American Fletcher Corporation	48
BancOhio Corporation	49
Centran Bancshares	50
CleveTrust Corporation	51
DETROITBANK Corporation	52
First Bank System, Inc.	53
First Union, Inc.	54
First Wisconsin Bankshares Corporation	55
Indiana National Corporation	56
Manufacturers National Corporation	57
Mercantile Bancorp, Inc.	58
National Detroit Corporation	59
National City Corporation	60
Northwest Bancorporation	61
Society Corporation	62
SOUTHWEST:	
First City Bancorporation of Texas	63
First International Bancshares, Inc.	64
First Security Corporation	65
Republic of Texas Corp.	66
Southwest Bancshares, Inc.	67
Texas Commerce Bancshares	68
Valley National Bank of Arizona	69
FAR WEST:	
BankAmerica Corporation	70
BanCal Tri-State Corporation	71
Hawaii Bancorporation	72
Crocker National Corporation	73
Marine Bancorporation	74
Seattle-First National Bank	75
Security Pacific Corporation	76
Unionamerica, Inc.	77
U.S. Bancorporation	78
Wells Fargo & Company	79
Western Bancorporation	80

APPENDIX B

STANDARD AND POOR'S CORPORATION

Bank and Bank Holding Company Financial Data Questionnaire

PART I — BANK HOLDING COMPANY — FULLY CONSOLIDATED

The following pages have been designed to give Standard & Poor's a data base for ratio analysis of fully-consolidated holding company operations. A companion questionnaire (Part II) applies to banking subsidiaries only. We have made every effort to stay within standard classifications widely used in good financial reporting.

Please note the following:

1. With the exception of Table E, the formats of Parts I and II are similar. Part I requests a *fully-consolidated* history, Part II requests a consolidated history of *bank(s) only*, including all divisions and subsidiaries thereof.

2. Averaging of balance-sheet items is necessary, on a daily and/or weekly basis. Where monthly or quarterly averages only are available, please indicate approximate fraction of each year's data so computed.

3. Italicized captions refer to selected data closely related to the data aggregate immediately above.

4. All data should be consolidated on a line-by-line basis.

5. All data for all years should be on a fully-pooled basis, and *pro forma* where acquisitions on a purchase basis have occurred.

ALL DATA SUPPLIED BY YOU WILL BE HELD IN STRICTEST CONFIDENCE FOR THE SOLE USE OF OUR CORPORATE FINANCE DEPARTMENT.

Please return your completed questionnaire to Mr. Norman Johnson of our Corporate Finance Department, together with a copy of each of (a) your 1972 annual report, (b) your 1973 quarterlies to date, and (c) your most recent 10-K and any prospectuses filed in 1973. Your management will be supplied with a computer printout of the ratios we develop for your company, together with median and/or mean ratios for our comparative universe.

Any definitional questions should be directed to Mr. Johnson (212-924-6400).

APPENDIX B (*Continued*)

Table A / AVERAGE ASSETS — CONSOLIDATED HOLDING COMPANY				
	1972	1971	1970	1969
1. Cash and due from banks*				
2. *Items in process of collection*				
3. Investments:				
4. U.S. government securities				
5. U.S. agency obligations				
6. State and municipal obligations				
7. Securities held in foreign branches				
8. Other securities				
9. Trading account				
10. Federal funds sold and repos				
11. Certificates of deposit—domestic				
12. Certificates of deposit—international				
13. Customers acceptances held				
14. Loans (gross of loss reserve and unearned income):				
15. Broker/Dealer				
16. Commercial				
17. *Term Loans*				
18. Consumer—instalment				
19. Consumer—credit card				
20. Real estate—short term/interim				
21. Real estate—permanent				
22. Mortgages held for sale				
23. International loans				
24. Direct lease financing				
25. (less: supporting liabilities)				
26. Bank premises and equipment				
27. Other assets				
28. Total Assets				

*Exclude interest earning assets, e.g. CDs and Eurodollars

Comments:

APPENDIX B (*Continued*)

Table B / AVERAGE LIABILITIES AND CAPITAL — CONSOLIDATED HOLDING COMPANY				
	1972	1971	1970	1969
1. Total Deposits:				
2. Demand: (Total)				
3. IPC				
4. Banks				
5. U.S. government				
6. Public funds				
7. Foreign				
8. Time: (Total)				
9. Regular Savings				
10. Savings certificates				
11. Large-denomination certificates (domestic):				
12. IPC				
13. Banks				
14. Public funds				
15. Foreign				
16. Federal funds purchased and repos—under 1 year*				
17. Federal funds purchased and repos—1 year and over				
18. Borrowed funds—under 1 year*				
19. Mortgages payable				
20. Unearned discount				
21. Liability on acceptances				
22. Accrued taxes and other expenses				
23. Other liabilities				
24. Contingency Reserves				
25. Loan Loss Reserve:				
26. Valuation				
27. Contingency				
28. Deferred tax				
29. Long-Term Debt:*				
30. Holding Company:				
31. Senior				
32. Subordinated				
33. Bank(s)				
34. Non-Bank Subsidiaries:				
35. Senior				
36. Subordinated				
37. Preferred Stock:				
38. Holding Company				
39. Bank(s)				
40. Non-Bank Subsidiaries				
41. Common Stock				
42. Surplus				
43. Undivided Profits				
44. (Less Treasury Stock)				
45. Total Liabilities and Capital				

*Maturity classification should be by original maturity

APPENDIX B (*Continued*)

Table C / OPERATING STATEMENT — CONSOLIDATED HOLDING COMPANY				
	1972	1971	1970	1969
1. Revenues:				
2. Interest and fees on loans				
3. Interest and dividends on taxable securities				
4. Interest and dividends on tax free securities				
5. Trading account income—interest				
6. Trading account income—net profits				
7. Income on federal funds and repos				
8. Income on certificates of deposit				
9. Trust income				
10. Service charges on deposits				
11. Other income				
12. Expenses:				
13. Salaries and employee benefits				
14. Interest on time deposits				
15. Interest on federal funds and repos				
16. Interest on other borrowed funds—under 1 year				
17. Interest on other borrowed funds—over 1 year				
18. Net occupancy expense				
19. *Rental income*				
20. Equipment expense				
21. Provision for loan losses				
22. *Gross charge-offs*				
23. *Recoveries*				
24. Other expenses				
25. Income (before extraordinary items):				
26. Income before taxes and securities transactions				
27. Applicable income taxes				
28. Income before securities transactions				
29. Securities gains (losses)				
30. Net income				
31. Extraordinary items (if any)				
32. Dividends Paid:				
33. Common				
34. Preferred				

Comments:

APPENDIX B (*Continued*)

Table D / RATES EARNED/PAID AND OTHER DATA — CONSOLIDATED HOLDING COMPANY				
	1972	1971	1970	1969
1. Rates Earned (tax-equivalent):				
2. Loans:				
3. Broker/Dealer				
4. Commercial				
5. *Term Loan*				
6. Consumer-instalment				
7. Consumer-credit card				
8. Real estate-short-term/interim				
9. Real estate-permanent				
10. International loans				
11. Federal funds and repos				
12. Certificates of deposit—domestic				
13. Certificates of deposit—international				
14. Securities:				
15. Tax free				
16. Taxable				
17. Rates Paid:				
18. Time deposits:				
19. Regular savings				
20. Savings certificates				
21. Large-denomination certificates (domestic)				
22. Foreign time				
23. Federal funds and repos				
24. Borrowed funds—under 1 year				
25. Borrowed funds—all other				
26. Other Data (at year-end):				
27. Number of employees (full-time equivalent):				
28. Banking-domestic				
29. Banking-international				
30. Bank-related				
31. Number of locations:				
32. Banking-domestic				
33. Banking-international				
34. Bank-related				

Comments:

APPENDIX B (*Concluded*)

Table E / LOAN LIQUIDATION ANALYSIS AND DEBT MATURITY SCHEDULE — CONSOLIDATED HOLDING COMPANY				
Loan Liquidation Analysis as of 12/31/72				
	Parent	Bank(s)	Non-Bank	Consolidated
1. Commercial—Demand(1)				
2. —Contractual(2)				
3. Consumer—Demand(1)				
4. —Contractual(2)				
5. Real Estate—Demand(1)				
6. —Contractual(2)				
7. International—Demand(1)				
8. —Contractual(2)				
9. Other—Demand(1)				
10. —Contractual(2)				

(1) All loans on demand or 90-day basis
(2) All other loan repayment proceeds due in 1973

Debt Maturity Schedule as of 12/31/72				
Year	Parent	Bank(s)	Non-Bank Subsidiaries	Consolidated
11. 1973				
12. 1974-1978				
13. 1979-1983				
14. 1984-1988				
15. 1989-1993				
16. Beyond				

Comments:

APPENDIX C

Primary Data Base

A. NOI per Sh
01_____/_____ 1972
02_____ 1971
03_____ 1970
04_____ 1969
05_____ 1968
06_____ '1968'
07_____ 1967

B. Net Inc per Sh
08_____ 1972
09_____ 1971

C. NOI
10_____ 1972
11_____ 1971

D. Gross Oper Inc
12_____ 1972
13_____ 1971
14_____ 1970

E. Tot Oper Exp
15_____ 1972
16_____ 1971
17_____ 1970
18_____ 1969

F. Interest Exp
19_____ 1972
20_____ 1971
21_____ 1970
22_____ 1969

G. Loan Loss Prov
23_____ 1972
24_____ 1971
25_____ 1970
26_____ 1969

H. Net Chge Off
27_____ 1972
28_____ 1971

I. "Overhead"
29_____ 1972
30_____ 1971
31_____ 1970
32_____ 1969

J. Sal and Emp Ben
33_____ 1972
34_____ 1971
35_____ 1970
36_____ 1969

K. Pre-tax NOI
37_____ 1972
38_____ 1971

L. App Inc Tax
39_____ 1972
40_____ 1971

M. Dividends Paid
41_____ 1972
42_____ 1971

N. Earn Asset Notes
43_____

O. Earn Assets
44_____ 1972
45_____ 1971
46_____ 1970
47_____ 1969

P. Loan Notes
48_____

Q. Loans
49_____ 1972
50_____ 1971
51_____ 1970

R. Earn Asset Yield
52_____ 1972
53_____ 1971

S. Loan Yield
54_____ 1972
55_____ 1971

T. Foreign Deposits
56_____ 1972
57_____ 1971

U. Other Mkt Sens Liabs
58_____ 1972
59_____ 1971

V. Savings-Type Deposits
60_____ 1972
61_____ 1971

W. Stk Equity and Res
62_____ 12/72
63_____ 12/71
64_____ Avg 72
65_____ 1973

X. Long Debt
66_____ 12/72
67_____ 1973

Y. Tot Cap
68_____ 12/72
69_____ 1973

Z. NOI per Sh
70_____/_____ 3mo73
71_____/_____ 6mo73
72_____/_____ 9mo73
73_____/_____ 12mo73

74_____/_____ 3mo72
75_____/_____ 6mo72
76_____/_____ 9mo72
77_____/_____ 12mo72

AA. Price
     hi   lo   ·mean
78____ ____ ____ 1Q71
79____ ____ ____ 1Q73
80____ ____ ____ 2Q73
81____ ____ ____ 3Q73
82____ ____ ____ 4Q73

BB. Shs Traded
83_____ 1Q73
84_____ 2Q73
85_____ 3Q73
86_____ 4Q73

CC. Shs Outstanding
87_____ 1Q73
88_____ 2Q73
89_____ 3Q73
90_____ 4Q73

DD. Marginalia

APPENDIX C (*Continued*)

Item Definitions

A. NOI per Sh
Income before securities transactions, on fully-restated basis *except* line 06, where use originally reported '1968 EPS' of core company, restated only for subsequent stock dividends, splits, exchange ratios other than 1:1 in holding company formations, and loan loss provision. In line 01 please provide fully-diluted per share amount, if any.

B. Net Inc per Sh
Excludes extraordinary items.

C. NOI
Items (C) through (M) on a fully-pooled basis, with consistent accounting definitions throughout. Suggest marginal notation if otherwise.

E. Tot Oper Exp
Excludes income taxes.

F. Interest Exp
Includes long-term debt interest, but suggest marginal notation of same. See (V) below.

I. Overhead
Total operating expense *less* interest expense, loan loss provision and (where possible) goodwill amortization.

J. Sal and Emp Ben
Suggest marginal notation of relevant statement footnotes.

M. Dividends Paid
Suggest use "declared" where "paid" unavailable.

N. Earn Asset Notes
Exceptions to the following model definition (see *Description of BANCOMPARE* for reference) should be noted numerically.

1. Daily or weekly average basis.
1a. Average, other than daily or weekly.
2. Investment securities adjusted for amortization of premium and accretion of discount.
3. Trading and/or dealer position excluded.
4. Fed funds, repos (and other temporary investments) included on a gross basis.
5. Revenue-producing obligations of banks—overseas and/or domestic—included on a gross basis (check ___ if none).
6. Loans net of unearned income.
7. Loans gross of loss reserve.
8. Direct lease equipment included (regardless of valuation method).
9. Fully consolidated. (Indicate function or company excluded, if any: _____).
10. Prior years on pooled basis.

P. Loan Notes
Exceptions to the following model definition should be noted numerically.

1. Excludes all temporary investments of a market-sensitive nature, such as fed funds, repos, short term obligations of banks and commercial paper.
2. Direct lease equipment *included*.

R. Earn Asset Yield
Fully-taxable equivalent, and on same basis as Earn Asset Notes. *If yield is on different basis, add "Z" to E/A Notes.*

S. Loan Yield
On same basis as Loan Notes. *If yield is on different basis, add "X" to Loan Notes.*

T. Foreign Deposits
On average basis.

U. Other Mkt - Sens Liabs
Defined to include all time deposits other than savings-type deposits, plus all short-term borrowings and commercial paper. Please provide averages.

V. Savings-Type Deposits
Defined to include both 'passbook' and 'certificate' savings, on average basis.

W. Stk Equity and Res
Shareholders' equity includes all capital-type (loan and contingency) reserves. Convertible preferred classified as equity. Straight preferred classified as debt and dividends to be grouped with interest expense. Suggest marginal notation of preferred capital and dividend [See(F) above.]

X. Long Debt
Includes, in addition to capital debt, all mortgage indebtedness (consolidated) and all non-deposit borrowings whose original maturity is seven years or more. Suggest marginal notation of annual lease rentals.

Y. Tot Cap
Consists of Stock Equity and Reserve (W) and Long Debt (X). *Please note: W, X + Y should be updated on a pro forma basis throughout 1973.*

Z. NOI per Sh
Restated as per press release. Full-year 1972 should be as restated against 1973, rather than as originally reported (but compare Line 77 with Line 01). Please also provide fully-diluted amounts, if any.

AA. Price
Adjusted for stock dividends and splits. Use "mean" in all calculations. Carry *any* adjustments to *all* per share figures in (A), (B) and (Z).

BB. Shs Traded
Defined to include all market transactions, but excludes non-market transfers (e.g., estate distribution, gifts, etc.). Suggest marginal notation of treasury stock and employe trust purchases, by quarter.

CC. Shs Outstanding
Use quarter-end shares.

DD. Marginalia
This section is provided to record marginal notes re stock dividends, splits, acquisitions, goodwill amortizations, special comments about Earn Asset Notes, etc.

8

Chemicals

HERBERT W. McNULTY
Senior Security Analyst
Hornblower & Weeks-Hemphill, Noyes, Inc.
New York, New York

STRUCTURE AND SCOPE OF THE INDUSTRY

America's Largest Chemical Companies: Similarities and Differences

GENERALIST SECURITY ANALYSTS and many portfolio managers find it convenient to approach stocks in similar businesses (steels, autos, etc.) as *groups* and to generalize about their earnings response to the economy and about their price response to projected changes in the economy. Such generalizations are completely out of order when one attempts to understand the dynamics of chemical companies. Table 1 includes data on the product mix of America's large chemical companies. These data have been taken from 1972 annual reports. As companies do not have consistent definitions of business areas, this table should be viewed as a rough approximation of the business area described, rather than a precise definition. For example, some firms regard the nylon or polyester fiber sold to build tire ply as a textile end-use, while others classify it as a rubber end-use. From Table 1 it is evident that demand for synthetic fibers and other textile products is vitally important to the welfare of such firms as duPont, Celanese, and Monsanto, but less important to Allied Chemical, and hardly important at all to Dow or Union Carbide. In the second quarter of each year, agricultural products such as weed killers, insecticides, and especially fertilizers are very important to the fortunes of Allied Chemical, American Cyanamid, Monsanto, and Stauffer, but are not very important to the earnings performance of Celanese,

199

TABLE 1

Chemical Companies Have Widely Different Marketing Mixes (shown by percent)

	Allied Chem.	American Cyanamid	Celanese	Dow	duPont	Hercules	Monsanto	Stauffer	Union Carbide
Fibers and textile	13	*	62	*	39	23	23	*	*
Plastics, coatings, rubber, packaging	8		11	33	21	23	34	13	14
Agriculture	7	19		*		6	10	20	*
Chemicals	39	29	13	49	19		13	64	28
Energy	23			*			6		
Metals, alloys, electrodes									20
Industrial gases and equipment									14
Paper				*		10			
Pharmaceuticals, etc.		20							
Building, consumer, paint		32	14						22
Export, foreign									
Other	10			18	21	38	14	3	2
Percent of sales	100	100	100	100	100	100	100	100	100
1973 Sales (millions)	$1,665	$1,472	$1,609	$3,068	$5,276	$1,155	$2,648	$780	$3,939
Approximate common shares outstanding (millions)	27.6	47.7	13.9	92.3	47.9	41.7	33.4	9.7	60.8

* Signifies participation, usually small, classified elsewhere.

Dow, or Union Carbide. Among the larger chemical firms, Union Carbide has a considerably heavier involvement in the steel and metals industries through its sales of oxygen, oxyacetylene welding gases, and alloying materials. Further examination of the product mixes of the oil and smaller companies will reveal still more differences which will tend to discourage gross generalities.

Large, Diversified Companies with Important Chemical Operations

In the 50s and early 60s, market research departments abounded. Most large, well-established companies recognized the limitations of their own product lines and searched diligently for high return on investment opportunities. The chemical business was enjoying high growth rates and high profit margins, so it naturally attracted a good deal of competition. Milk companies, distillers, shipping lines, and others rushed into this business. Aided by technology offered on a turnkey basis by engineering firms, many conglomerates were formed with an important thrust in chemical technology. Some of these movements were successful, but, in general, their plants were less efficient than the established firms and their marketing was too much directed toward price cutting and deal making. Profit margins fell for new and old companies.

A good deal of these poorly planned product lines have fallen by the wayside. Some companies have sold their chemical division; others are trying to sell them. In any event, the security analyst should look carefully at the chemical groups of all these companies, both from the point of view of analysis of the company itself and, most importantly, in relation to the competitive advantage or disadvantage some of these companies may have in selected product lines.

A very large list of diversified chemical companies could be offered to the reader. In order to save space, he is referred to the *Directory of Chemical Producers*, published by Stanford Research Institute. Tables 2 and 3 carry a list of some of the larger producers who manufacture key chemicals—producers which are not generally regarded as chemical companies. These lists, naturally, include several petroleum and natural gas companies.

From the generalist analyst point of view, a good deal of caution should be used in drawing up earnings estimates for broad-line companies having chemical content in their product lines. Frequently, chemical groups of conglomerate companies have considerably greater capital intensity in their manufacturing business than does the parent. Consequently, response of earnings to volume changes in the chemical group might be considerably greater than that of the rest of the business. As chemical operators, multiproduct companies' plants are often smaller than those of the pure chemical companies. Their competitive position may be somewhat weaker. The security analyst should carefully investi-

TABLE 2
Several Chemical Products Where Conglomerate Companies Hold Important Positions

Company	Important Chemical	Approx. Share of U.S. Capacity (percent)	Rank of* Company	Major Use of Chemical
Eastman Kodak Co.	Polyester fibers	14	3/23	Textiles
U.S. Steel Corp.	Ammonium sulfate	5	8/39	Fertilizer
The B. F. Goodrich Co.	Polyvinyl chloride Resins	20	1/26	Plastics
Borden, Inc.	Formaldehyde	16	3/18	Plastics, adhesives
The Upjohn Co.	Organic Isocyrates	18	2/10	Urethane plastics
Borg-Warner Corp.	A B S Resins	31	2/8	High-impact plastics

* 3/19 means that the company is the third largest among 19 manufacturers.
Source: *1974 Directory of Chemical Producers,* Stanford Research Institute, Menlo Park, California.

TABLE 3
Several Chemical Products Where Petroleum or Natural Gas Companies Hold Important Positions

Company	Important Chemical	Approx. Share of U.S. Capacity (percent)	Rank of* Company	Major Use of Chemical
Standard Oil Co. (Indiana)	Dimethyl terephthalate	11	4/5	Polyester fibers
Standard Oil Co. (Indiana)	Ethyl benzene	12	4/16	Styrene plastics
Shell Chemical Co.	Isopropyl alcohol	36	2/5	Solvent, intermediate
Gulf Oil Corp.	Polyethylene Resins	8	5/20	Packaging

* 3/5 means that the company is the third largest among 5 manufacturers.
Source: *1974 Directory of Chemical Producers,* Stanford Research Institute, Menlo Park, California.

gate the raw material and process economics of important products to establish the competitive position of a non chemical company operating in chemical areas.

Small and Medium-Sized Companies

Over 100 chemical companies have their stocks traded on the two major stock exchanges or over the counter. At the time of this writing, price-earnings ratios run as high as 30 to 50 times earnings for well-managed marketers (for example, National Chemsearch) or innovative technical-type companies (for example, Lawter Chemicals). A good number of other firms are selling in the 5 to 8 times range. For purposes of this article, we are able to divide the smaller companies into four classifications: marketing intensive companies, technology intensive companies, diversified companies, and commodity companies. Although small commodity companies generally are not frequently of interest to the marketplace, in the fall of 1973 almost any company with a line of commodity fertilizers is having its multiple bid up because of shortages.

The marketing intensive companies are probably the most interesting. In addition, it is probable that each year or so a new marketing intensive company will arise and attract investors' attention. A search for profits in the market would certainly be aided by an understanding of how already successful marketing intensive companies grew in the early stages of their history.

National Chemsearch is probably the best example of a marketing intensive company. Their product line has been characterized by one writer as janitorial supplies. Call their products chemical specialties, and you have a better description, but not an explanation of their phenomenal success. National Chemsearch is a people-oriented company. Their key to success is the continued location, selection, training, and deployment of salesmen. They may be characterized as "The Avon Products of the Chemical Industry." The major job of management is to continue to motivate its 2,000-man sales force while locating 200–300 new salesmen a year to continue the dynamism. While selection and training of personnel is vital to business continuity, so are new products. The 300 products in the line include cleaning compounds, waxes, maintenance material, and other products that can be sold by its commission sales force. Through proper selection of products and people, National Chemsearch has been able to grow at over 14–15 percent per year in earnings per share, and this growth has earned a price earnings multiple of as high as 50X. The dependability of earnings growth has been most important in the market evaluation of the stock.

By marketing intensive companies we mean those whose technology is readily duplicated but whose marketing techniques, sales organization, distribution network, or brand leadership has given the firm a real advantage over competition. Many marketing intensive companies have been able to show extremely high growth rates and have thereby been able to hold on to a relatively high price earnings multiple for several consecutive years.

Standard Brands Paint Company manufactures and sells paint through company-owned stores in the southeastern part of the United States. Since World War II this firm has been able to grow at or above 15 percent per year and has often commanded price/earnings multiples over 50 times—over five times the multiple of the average paint company. In this case, a firm applying chemical technology similar to its competitors has gained a high multiple through exceptional marketing.

Although technology has played an important part in the growth of Air Products and Chemicals Company (P/E-25X), we believe that its creative marketing of on-site oxygen and other gas plants has been a major reason for the company's success. The analyst who may be examining companies like Air Products would be well advised to carefully distinguish between the technical and economic reasons for success.

Two companies which have proven to be exceptional marketers but where technology is a major reason for success are Rohm and Haas (P/E-16X) and Lawter Chemicals (P/E-48X). Both of these firms have selected a very narrow area of technology, spent comparatively large amounts of research money in these areas, and have been immensely successful. Their technology, engineering, and products are far ahead of their competitors. Rohm and Haas has lead the acrylic plastics field for years, while Lawter is the major manufacturer and vendor of fluorescent and other ink materials.

In the chemical area, highly specialized companies manufacturing basic commodities often produce very fine investment opportunities if the timing is right. At the time of this writing, fertilizer sales prospects are excellent, while supply is very limited. Beker Industries, which bought several old fertilizer facilities from other firms, is attracting investor attention.

Synthetic Fibers

The worldwide development of the synthetic fiber industry has probably been the most dramatic example of the abilities of the chemist to manipulate molecules to serve the needs of a growing population. Nylon, polyester, acrylic, and other synthetic fibers have replaced natural materials in many end uses. In 1970, U.S. noncellulosic fiber consumption passed cotton, and this replacement appears to be continuing at an accelerating rate as cotton export opportunities increase and acreage demand to produce other crops, such as soybeans, tend to abort cotton supply increases.

Synthetic fiber content in the product mix of chemical companies has proven to be a difficult factor for the security analyst and institutional analyst to cope with. The reason for this is that there is a very large difference between the marginal cost of synthetic fibers and their selling price. When fiber demand drops, fiber prices drop considerably faster, as suppliers with overcapacity scramble for the remaining share of the business. Security analysts in touch with textile manufacturers see inventory buildups and hear of price concessions by major manufacturers. Advertising allowances increase, and a surprising amount of very fine "off-grade" material comes to the market at a cut price. News of building inventories and declining sales is reported in *Textile Organon* and elsewhere. All of this makes the holders of fiber intensive companies (such as Akzona, Celanese, Monsanto, and even duPont) insecure. Blocks of stock come to market and must be discounted to be sold.

The situation described above may seem to be somewhat dramatic, and it may not repeat itself again. A look at the record of fiber stocks during the "credit crunch" year of 1966 shows both Celanese and Monsanto dropping to less than half their January values and both duPont and Akzona stock recording material declines. Before buying fiber intensive securities, the investor is cautioned to look carefully into consumer buying intentions, especially in home furnishings, and to appraise the inventory/sales ratios not only for producers, but also the inventories on hand at the mills and in the stores. Table 5 illustrates the varied fiber mix of the major companies. Table 6 should be useful in illustrating the large marginal profitability in the synthetic fiber business and the reasons for the high amplitude in earning cyclicality of these products. Table 4 illustrates how in 1973 short-term growth for many fibers ran far ahead of the long-term growth rate. When will this trend reverse itself? Stockholders are necessarily interested.

Plastics

It is no coincidence that the larger chemical companies that have achieved the highest institutional confidence and price/earnings ratios generally dominate one or more areas of plastics. Dow Chemical is the leader in styrene plastics and their intermediates, has a large position in polyethylene here and abroad, and is a key vendor of vinyl chloride monomer. Rohm and Haas pioneered acrylic plastic market development in the United States. Hercules did pioneering research on catalytic systems for polypropylene and led in the development of markets for the products.

Plastics are still in the earlier stages of the replacement cycle for paper, wood, metals, concrete, and other classical products. They are the only large sector of the chemical business that can still grow at over 10 percent per year over an extended period of time. In most cases plastics used in furniture, automobiles, appliances, and elsewhere allow

TABLE 4

Shipment Growth of Major Synthetic Fibers (first six months 1973 versus 1972)

Product	Shipments (millions of pounds)		Percent Change	Possible Long-Term Growth Rate (percent per year) 1971–1976
	1972	1973		
Industrial rayon...............	82.6	67.9	−18	−3
Textile rayon..................	60.8	39.1	−36	−3
Rayon staple and tow..........	368.4	365.8	− 1	+6
Total rayon...............	511.8	472.8	− 8	
Cellulose acetate...............	207.1	228.6	+10	+2
Nylon yarn...................	738.7	805.7	+ 9	+5
Nylon staple and tow..........	232.6	304.9	+31	+8
Total nylon...............	971.3	1110.6	+14	
Polyester yarn................	421.7	673.6	+60	+9
Polyester staple..............	659.9	828.8	+26	+7
Total polyester...........	1081.6	1502.4	+39	
Total acrylic..............	311.3	390.3	+25	+8
Olefin yarn...................	158.3	202.2	+28	
Olefin staple..................	421.7	673.6	+60	
Total olefin...............	580.0	875.8	+51	+7

Source: *Textile Organon*, Vol. XLIV, No. 7, July 1973 (New York: Textile Economics Bureau, Inc.).

TABLE 5

An Illustration of Differences in Product Mix of Larger Chemical Companies (productive capacity—millions of pounds per year)

Product	Allied	Dow	duPont	Hercules	Monsanto	Stauffer	Union Carbide
Fibers:							
Acrylic and modacrylic.		44	245		220		30
Nylon..............	230	86*	965		397		
Polyester............	80	95*	660		115		
Polyolefin...........				100			
Plastics:							
Polyethylene (HDPE and LDPE).........	275	1290	939	none	310		1380
Polypropylene........				700			
Polystyrene..........		890			440		280
Polyvinyl chloride.....	none				150	175	400

Note: Data obtained from *1974 Directory of Chemical Producers* (Menlo Park, Calif.: Stanford Research Institute, 1974), and *Chemical Economic Handbook*, Stanford Research Institute, Menlo Park, California.

TABLE 6

Acrylic Fibers and Acrylonitrile—Marginal Profit Analysis (assuming a 10 percent decline in volume, no drop in selling price)

Company	Acrylic Fibers						Acrylonitrile						(13) Combined Marginal Profit Loss per Share (Pretax)	(14) Earnings per Share (most recent 12 months)
	(1) Approx. 1973 Capacity (millions of lbs.)	(2) Cyclical Sales Loss (millions of lbs.)	(3) Marginal* Profit Loss ($ million)	(4) No. of Shares Outstanding (millions)	(5) Marginal* Profit Loss (per share)	(6) Pounds per Share	(7) Approx. 1973 Capacity (millions of lbs.)	(8) Required for Fibers (millions of lbs.)	(9) Cyclical Sales Loss	(10) Marginal Profit Loss ($ million)	(11) Marginal Profit Loss* per Share Pretax	(12) Pounds per Share		
duPont	255	26	7.7	47.9	$0.16	5.4	380	245	25	1.8	$0.04	7.8	$0.20	11.25
Monsanto	240	24	7.2	33.0	0.22	7.3	370	230	23	1.6	0.05	11.2	0.27	6.32
Am. Cyanamid	130	13	3.9	48.0	0.08	2.7	175	125	13	.9	0.02	3.6	0.10	2.41
Dow Badische	45	5	1.5	—	—	—	—	—	—	—	—	—	—	—
Eastman Kodak	45	5	1.5	161.6	0.01	0.3	—	—	—	—	—	—	0.01	4.04
Union Carbide	30	3	0.9	60.8	0.01	0.5	—	—	—	—	—	—	0.01	4.54
Standard Oil (Ohio)	—	—		13.5	—	—	350	—	35	2.5	0.19	25.9	0.19	4.45
	745	76					1,275	600						

* "Marginal Profit Loss" (30 cents per pound for fibers) is calculated by subtracting marginal cost (22 cents per pound) and freight (2 cents per pound) from the selling price (54 cents per pound). The 30 cent per pound figure is then multiplied by the cyclical sales loss which assumes a 10 percent decline in volume for each company. The reader can easily adjust this loss, upward or downward, in line with his own expectations for the textile economy. The marginal profit loss for acrylonitrile is simply the 7-cent per pound difference between the 12-cent per pound price used in the fiber cost calculations and the marginal cost for acrylonitrile of 5 cents per pound.

Note: The marginal profit losses in column (13) may appear small to the reader when they are compared with the earnings per share figures in column (14). It is important to stress that these figures are really quite large when compared with the longer-term growth rate of the companies involved. Thus, if one assumes that none of these companies, except Kodak, can grow faster than 10 percent per year over the longer term, column (13) should be compared with 10 percent of column (14). In this case, a 10 percent fall in volume for acrylic fibers could wipe out 27 cents of pretax earnings for Monsanto, where 10 percent of the last 12 months (after tax) is 63 cents.

for a lower labor component of total costs than is experienced with older materials. Given raw material availability, plastics should continue to be the major reason why premium multiples will be accorded and maintained in the marketplace.

The largest problem in the plastics sector for the next several years will be raw material availability. Virtually all plastics, except those based upon cellulose, are derived from hydrocarbon raw materials which originate in petroleum or natural gas. In the 20s and 30s, coal was a large starting point for plastics rather than gas and oil which are used today. A return to coal may take place in the late 70s and thereafter. The huge plastics materials production gains recorded in the first half of 1973 (see Table 7) stands in contrast with the smaller gains in raw materials

TABLE 7

Production Growth of Major Plastics Products (first six months 1973 versus 1972)

Product	Domestic Production (millions of pounds) 1972	Domestic Production (millions of pounds) 1973	Percent Gain	Exports Percent Gain
Polyethylene, low density	2,532	2,830	12	23
Polyethylene, high density	1,103	1,288	17	13
Polypropylene	788	1,017	29	96
Polystyrene and copolymers	2,197	2,454	12	—
Polyvinyl chloride and copolymers	2,027	2,276	12	—

Source: U.S. Department of Commerce.

production during the same period. This raw material squeeze was in 1973 and early 1974, aggravated by various price control proposals that tend to restrict productive capacity. Raw material supply will be a major consideration in the projected growth of the plastic industry.

Agricultural Chemicals

Following the election of President Kennedy in 1960 and before the tragedy of Vietnam became evident, America went on a "feed the world" campaign. Large programs were initiated to improve South American and Oriental agriculture through the use of give-away farm machinery, fertilizer, pesticides, and technical assistance. These programs were never fully funded, but the promise of the American Agency for International Development did catch the imagination of the stock market. Spearheaded by some real shortages, International Minerals' stock rose from a low of 12 in 1962 to a high of 58 in 1966. The current price is $40. Earnings rose from $1.02 to $2.56 in the same period. Comparable rises in other "starvation stocks" were:

	Low 1962	High 1967–68	Today
Freeport Minerals	15	78	$33\frac{3}{4}$
Texas Gulf	4	54	$29\frac{3}{8}$

Although mineral discoveries helped these stocks, a major factor in the movement was the expectation that potash, phosphate, and sulfur use in fertilizers would skyrocket.

Some believe that the response to the wheat deal with Russia, the cotton deal with China, and high food prices here may be the cause for the fact that agricultural content companies were reappraised upward by the stock market in 1973. Some price movements confirm this reappraisal.

	1972 Close	Price (Oct. 73)	Gain (percent)
Allied Chemical	29	44	52
International Minerals	26	$36\frac{5}{8}$	41
Freeport Minerals	28	$33\frac{3}{4}$	21
Texas Gulf	17	$29\frac{3}{8}$	73
Monsanto	50	$69\frac{5}{8}$	39
Dow Jones Industrial Average	1020.02	960.57	6

These firms are not wholly dependent upon agriculture. The case is that a relatively high agricultural content may have supported these companies' earnings and stock prices over the short run. Future expectations are bright.

Among the large companies, heavy agricultural involvement is found at Allied, International Minerals, Monsanto, and Stauffer. Allied's involvement is principally in fertilizers and sulfuric acid sold to others to manufacture fertilizers. Monsanto and Stauffer are in fertilizers, sulfuric acid, and pesticides.

There is a great deal of misunderstanding in relation to the impact of fertilizer demand and supply upon the fortunes of major chemical companies. It should be recognized that there are three important fertilizer elements (nitrogen, phosphorous, and potassium) which have widely different supply situations and differing demand considerations.

Nitrogen fertilizer is almost always based upon ammonia synthesis which obtains nitrogen (N) from the air and hydrogen (H) from either natural gas or petroleum. Thus, nitrogen-type fertilizers are intimately tied up with the energy crises. Nitrogen is useless to most plants in its elemental form, but in various chemical combinations it becomes available to plant life as the key building block in their synthesis of vegetable amino acid materials which become vital to man and animals. The widely varied nature of nitrogen fertilizer materials is illustrated in

Table 8. The rapid increase in ammonia consumption is indicated in Table 9. The fertilizer mix of some major companies is given in Table 10.

In calculation of the projected earnings of fertilizer companies the analyst must distinguish between manufacturers of nitrogen, phosphorus,

TABLE 8

Producers of Nitrogen Fertilizers

Product	Form	Capacity (thousand tons)	No. of Producers	Important U.S. Producers*
Ammonia.............	Gas	18,243	60	Allied Chemical, American Cyanamid, Atlantic Richfield, CF Industries, Commercial Solvents, W. R. Grace & Co.
Urea.................	Solid	4,310	34	Allied Chemical, American Cyanamid, Standard Oil (Ohio), Triad Chemical Union, Union Oil
Ammonium Nitrate.....	Solid or Solution	7,837	40	Allied Chemical, Cooperative Farm Chem., W. R. Grace & Co., Witco, Hercules, Mississippi Chem., U.S. Steel
Ammonium Phosphate..	Solid or Solution	9,000	31	Allied Chemical, Atlantic Richfield, CF Industries, Cities Service
Ammonium Sulfate.....	Solid or Solution	2,915	39	Allied Chemical, Dow Badische, Lykes Youngstown, U.S. Steel

* In some cases, smaller companies are included to emphasize the diversity of origin.
Source: Stanford Research Institute.

TABLE 9

Growth of U.S. Fertilizer Production (thousands of tons, product wt)

Product	1946	1971	Approximate Percent to Agriculture 1971 Fertilizer	Fertilizer and Feed
Ammonia.................	986	14,701	80	83
Phosphate rock............	8,029	38,886	78	84
Potash...................	1,688	4,543	95	95

Source: Chemical Economics Handbook, Stanford Research Institute, Menlo Park, California.

TABLE 10

Domestic Fertilizer Content of Seven Companies (units—thousands of tons, product wt. per year, except as noted)

Producr	Allied Chemical	Dow	du-Pont	Her-cules	Monsanto	Stauffer	Union Carbide U.S.A.
Ammonia*.................	960	115	780	140	450		16,680
Ammonium nitrate.........	365		270	760	635		8,302
Ammonium phosphate, solid...................	0				10	195	10,525
Ammonium sulfate.........	650	Dow Badische, 250	§			§	2,878
Nitric acid†..............	375		1,104	658	803		9,900
Phosphate rock‡..........					3,000	2,400	48,510
Phosphoric acids, ortho (P$_2$O$_5$ basis)‡............	160				455	380	8,099
Phosphoric acids, super, poly (P$_2$O$_5$ basis)‡........	127				neg.	56+	934+
Phosphorus, elemental‡.....					232	110	572
Super phosphate, normal (tons per day)..........						300	15,395
Super phosphate, triple.....						35	4,970
Urea....................	440	neg.		135			4,485

* Ammonia is the basic starting point for nitrogen fertilizers such as ammonium nitrate, phosphate, and sulfate. At all of these companies, a good deal of the ammonia is diverted to other end uses such as nylon or acrylic fibers (ACD, DD, MTC), explosives (DD, HPC) and other end uses.

† As noted in (*) above, ammonia oxidized to nitric acid finds nonagricultural uses in explosives, plastics, fibers, etc.

‡ Phosphate rock, elemental phosphorus, and phosphoric acids find nonagricultural uses such as in detergent builders.   § Company produces product; capacity figures not available.

Source: *1974 Directory of Chemical Producers*, Stanford Research Institute, Menlo Park, CA.

and potassium fertilizers. It is important to be thoroughly familiar with the sources of oil or gas in the case of nitrogen fertilizers. Raw material regulation of Canadian provinces have been particularly important in the case of potash. In 1973, phosphorus production was restricted because of energy shortages in Florida. On the demand side, the farmers planting intentions are important. Since soybeans fix their own nitrogen, acreage moving into soybeans could be bearish for nitrogen fertilizers but could generally be good for phosphorus fertilizers. The export situation is a particularly important consideration for analysts in the agricultural chemical area. Not only are fertilizer exports most important to producers, but export plans for specific crops are also useful. Commodity price changes in the futures market also affect the fortunes of specific fertilizer material. They should be followed by analysts of fertilizer companies.

Specialized Companies

In addition to the large, broad-line chemical companies, there are dozens of specialized companies which play an important role in the American economy. Often due to cyclical anticipation, either favorable, these specialized companies become under or overpriced. These situations may produce really unique profit opportunities for the astute investor. In this section we will illustrate some of these specialized companies and point out some of their unique features.

In the area of industrial gas production and sales, there are Air Products, Airco, Big Three, and Chemetron. Although Air Products has had a much more successful record of growth, there are times when the more cyclical companies prove to be better investment opportunities.

In the synthetic fiber area, duPont, Monsanto, and Allied Chemical may be too diversified to benefit or suffer from large changes in the demand/supply balance for synthetic fibers. Akzona and Celanese earnings' swings are more dependent upon the synthetic fiber business.

Inmont and Sun Chemical earnings are dependent upon changes in demand for printing ink.

Dow Chemical's earnings are more dependent upon the plastics area than the other large chemical companies. Among the medium to smaller plastics-dependent companies are Rohm and Haas, Reichhold, and a good number of over-the-counter stocks.

Lubrizol is a company specializing in the lubricating oil additives business.

Both Great Lakes Chemical and Michigan Chemical are heavily involved in bromine chemistry. Bromine chemicals are finding increasing usage in flameproofing textiles, plastics, etc.

In the area of water purification, there are a number of companies, such as Nalco Chemical, Betz Laboratories, Mogul, and Chemed Corporation.

Fast-growing companies engaged in merchandising chemical specialties to industry and commercial accounts include Chemed and National Chemsearch. Both of these firms have found ways to motivate commission salesmen to produce a superior growth record.

Future Trends in the Industry

The principal trends likely in the chemical industry are a tendency to greater concentration and a major adjustment to raw material shortages and to energy shortages.

The return to greater concentration is most evident. At the end of World War II companies like Allied Chemical and Dye, duPont and Union Carbide dominated the industry. Their technology, developed over several decades, was regarded as the best in the country. However, high growth, large profit margins, and available European technology attracted competitors into the industry. W. R. Grace, National Distillers, Borden, and others joined a few dozen oil and gas companies in expanding the size of the industry's capacity far in excess of demand with the inevitable collapse of profit margins in many areas.

The nonspecialist analyst may be interested in the large number of domestic suppliers currently involved in some commodity businesses:

	Suppliers
Ammonia	60
Chlorine	34
Nitric acid	47
Polyester fibers	19
Nylon fibers	16
Polystyrene	31

Our feeling is that raw material availability constraints and failure to develop competitive manufacturing technology will cause a reconcentration of the industry in the period 1974–1984. Especially in the area of petrochemicals, massive changes may be coming. These changes will probably result in reconcentration—fewer suppliers and possibly considerable foreign production of basic organic chemicals. Reconcentration will take place since only the largest firms can afford the kind of engineering research required to develop the most efficient processes. In addition, only the largest firms can deal with governments such as Saudi Arabia, Indonesia, and Algeria as equals. We believe that the oil-rich nations will insist on production of the first-step products in their countries. There is considerable economic logic in this move, especially in the case of natural gas derivatives, since such derivative materials as ammonia are much more readily stored and shipped in ships than is natural gas.

Over the next several years, the chemical industry should be a major beneficiary of the emerging processes to reclaim and recycle used materials such as metals, plastics, paper, fibers, etc. However, this is a mixed blessing for the industry as a whole, since massive reclamation will result in less usage of virgin products. Without quantifying those effects, we will offer some examples of reclamation processes which will conserve energy, utilize some chemicals (usually inorganic), and thereby reduce demand for virgin products.

1. *Polyester fibers*—It is possible to reclaim the acid and polyalcohol used to make polyester fibers by cooking up used garments in an aqueous alkaline solution.
2. *Urethane foam*—One company is recovering one of the ingredients of urethane foam by a hydrolytic process similar to the one above used for polyester fibers.

The chemical industry's response to energy shortages may dictate a reconcentration of manufacturing into large energy conservative plants. As evidenced by Dow Chemical practice, large plants favorably affect energy economies by self-generation of electric power and by use of the low-pressure steam or gas from turbines for process heating purposes.

TABLE 11
Costs of High-density Polyethylene (table of incremental and total production costs)

Product	Capacity (millions of pounds a year)	Process	Market Share (percent)	Plant Gate Cost (cents per pound)	Incremental Cost (cents per pound)	Incremental Cost as Percent of Plant Gate Cost	Remarks
Ethylene............	500	From ethane	50	2.52	1.45	58	Propylene credited at 2.2 cents per pound.
		From propane	50	2.29	1.11	48	
		Composite*	100	2.40	1.28	53	Ethylene charged in at 3 cents per pound.
High-density polyethylene......	200	Ziegler catalyst	33⅓	10.15	5.24	52	1.03 pounds of ethylene per pound of polymer is assumed.
		Phillips (Slurry)	33⅓	11.47	6.03	53	
		Phillips (Particle)	33⅓	6.87	3.84	56	
		Composite*	100	9.50	5.04	53	

* Composite refers to our best evaluation of the best single figure to use in view of process differences, etc.

Note: In this analysis we have used incremental costs rather than fully allocated factory costs or costs which include overhead expenses. We believe incremental costs are most useful in determining earnings response to changes in volume, especially over the short term.

ANALYSIS OF COST FACTORS

The reader should recognize that a good deal of the products of the industry—inorganic chemicals, fibers, plastics, fertilizers—are highly capital intensive. Like the product lines of steel companies, paper companies, etc., the chemical plants pour forth extraordinarily high profits during periods of high operating rates and suffer large declines in profits when operating rates fall. Sensitivity to operating rate changes is exaggerated in those cases where a good deal of fixed changes for interest is put on top of the depreciation charges for the huge plants. When demand, prices, and operating rates are all favorable, chemical companies can bring in very large profit increments. At the time of writing (fall 1973), third-quarter results for the large chemical companies illustrate this point.

In building up an earnings estimate, the cost factors for each major product should be included in the appraisal. These factors can then be factored into earnings estimates for the company as a whole. An extended example of such a study follows.

The analysis of cost factors in the heavy chemical industry is not too different from those procedures used in other capital intensive commodity companies such as paper, steel, aluminum, etc. The industry may be regarded as a noncollusive oligopoly, acutely aware of its kinked demand curve. Price decreases, over the short term, do not often result in demand increases. Over the long term they certainly do. In the more concentrated sectors of the industry, during times of slack demand, price seldom gets anywhere near marginal cost. In some of the less concentrated areas, especially where technology differs, price has often fallen below some producers' marginal cost, resulting in abandonment of businesses.

It is impossible to offer a typical cost sheet for a chemical. Tables 11

TABLE 12

High-Density Polyethylene: Incremental Profit Calculations

	Cost of Process Employed (cents per pound)		
	Ziegler Catalyst	Phillips (Slurry)	Phillips (Particle)
Marginal ethylene cost (1.03–1.04 lbs. required because of yield loss)	1.33	1.33	1.33
Conversion cost (ethylene to polymer)	2.24	3.03	0.84
Marginal manufacturing cost	3.57	4.36	2.17
Average freight-out	2.00	2.00	2.00
Delivered marginal cost	5.57	6.36	4.17
Selling price	12.50	12.50	12.50
Less (delivered marginal cost)	5.57	6.36	4.17
Marginal profit	6.93	6.14	8.33
Average of three processes		7.13	
Deviation from average	–0.20	–0.99	+1.20

Note: Each process shown accounts for one third of the market share in the United States.

TABLE 13

High-Density Polyethylene (U.S.): Calculation of Marginal Profit Growth

Company	No. of Shs. Outstanding (millions)	U.S. Capacity (millions of lbs.) 1967	1972	Annual Sales Potential — At 12.5¢ per lb. ($ millions)	As % of Total Sales of Co.	Per Share Potential — Pounds	Sales at Capacity
Northern Natural Gas‖,¶	10.9	—	500	63	10.8	45.9	$5.73
Celanese¶	13.9	140	260	33	2.7	18.7	2.34
Phillips Petroleum‖,¶	74.8	160	260	33	1.4	3.5	0.43
Natl. Petrochemicals*,‖,¶	—	125	240	30	—	—	—
Union Carbide‡,‖,¶	60.6	125	240	30	1.0	4.0	0.50
Allied Chemical¶	27.6	175	230	29	2.2	8.3	1.04
Dow Chemical‡,‖,#	45.5	100	200	25	1.2	4.4	0.55
Monsanto#	32.8	50	180	23	1.1	5.5	0.69
Sinclair-Koppers‖,#	—	50	180	23	—	—	—
Chemplex†,‖,¶	—	—	170	21	—	—	—
duPont‡,‖,¶	47.4	75	150	19	0.5	3.2	0.40
Standard Oil of Indiana#	69.7	—	100	13	0.3	1.4	0.18
Gulf Oil (2,L,Z)†,‖,#	207.6	—	100	13	0.2	0.5	0.06
Hercules#	20.0	80	90	11	1.4	4.5	0.56
Dart Industries‖,#	19.4	—	60	8	1.0	3.1	0.39
Total		1,080	2,960	374			

     * National Distillers and Owens-Illinois Glass Co.
     † American Can and Skelly Oil.
     ‡ Important producer outside United States.
     ⌀ At an estimated intermediate-term growth rate of 12 percent per year. Some companies may have a more advantageous position than others because of technology, integrated facilities, or raw materials. We have not attempted to discriminate among these firms on a product-cost basis.

through 13 develop some cost data for high-density polyethylene. Since these computations were made, there have been large increases in natural gas costs which have been passed through to the customers. Table 13 brings these cost data into an analysis of impacts of change upon company earnings.

The impact of domestic price rise of earnings per share would vary according to pounds per share manufactured. Table 13 allows us to calculate this effect. Revenue estimates, which are derived from capacity figures, are used to compute marginal profit gains, which in turn can be used to determine the influence of high-density polyethylene on swings in earnings of the companies included.

The reader should note that there is a good deal of difference between full or marginal cost and price. This difference does not descend to the bottom line since marketing, research, and administrative costs have to be carried by the product. Over the past several years, process technology advancements have allowed significant cost reductions to be effected in this and other plastic products.

Table 13 shows how marginal cost data can be used in earnings per share analysis. In composing Table 13 several assumptions are made allowing for the adjustment of figures. The assumptions are as follows:

1. Plant capacity data provided by published sources are reasonably accurate.

| Annual Sales Gain (at 12%) (millions of lbs.) | Annual Marginal Profit Gain | | | Effect of a 1¢ per lb. Price Increase on Aftertax Earnings per Share | Reported Earnings per Share (last 12 mo.) |
	$ Millions	Pretax (¢ per share)	100% Minus Tax Rate	After Tax (¢ per share)		
60	4.2	38.5	62.0	23.9	28.5	$4.55
31	2.2	15.8	60.0	9.5	11.2	3.90
31	2.2	2.9	72.0	2.1	2.5	1.89
29	2.0	—	—	—	—	—
29	2.0	3.3	56.5	1.9	2.3	2.82
28	2.0	7.2	68.0	5.0	5.6	2.06
24	1.7	3.7	63.5	2.4	2.8	3.79
22	1.5	4.6	58.0	2.6	3.2	3.19
22	1.5	—	—	—	—	—
20	1.4	—	—	—	—	—
18	1.3	2.7	55.0	1.5	1.8	8.26
12	0.8	1.1	75.0	0.9	1.1	5.09
12	0.8	0.4	43.0	0.2	0.2	2.46
11	0.8	4.0	55.0	2.2	2.5	2.90
7	0.5	2.6	51.5	1.3	1.6	2.29

|| Firm or an affiliate also produces LDPE.
¶ Phillips Process.
# Ziegler Process.
Source: Kidder, Peabody & Co., Inc.

2. The delivered price of high-density polyethylene is 12.5 cents per pound. Since this price has risen, adjustments can be made to the data in the table when necessary.

3. Demand for high-density polyethylene will grow at 12 percent per year.

4. Freight-out is two cents per pound paid by the supplier. This figure was confirmed by large suppliers.

5. Incremental manufacturing costs for high-density polyethylene and its precursor, ethylene, are indicated in Tables 11 and 12.

FEDERAL AND STATE REGULATION

In this section we will confine our remarks only to those areas of federal and state regulation which seem to affect the operations of the chemical industry more critically than they do other industries. We will not consider those areas that are common to all companies such as anti-trust problems, advertising claims, etc.

In the area of import tariffs, the chemical industry has a preferred position versus all other American industries. Following the critical shortages brought about by the British blockade of German shipping during World War I, Congress voted in a unique American Selling Price clause for chemical import evaluation. Benzenoid chemicals (those having a benzene or related chemical ring in their molecules) are to be valued for tariff calculation on importation not according to the invoice value, but according to the "American Selling Price." This value, often larger than import invoice value, was designed to allow the American dyestuff companies to become insulated from the volume advantages possessed by I.G. Farbenindustrie and other European exporters. Sixty years later, American Selling Price still protects some manufacturers in the chemical industry.

Many chemical processes involve discharge of solid, liquid, or gaseous waste products. Although most companies have done a really competent job to diminish this waste contamination, some unsalable by-products are a necessary result of the chemical process used. The conventional process for making soda ash from salt and limestone produces approximately one pound of calcium chloride for each pound of soda ash produced. Only a fraction of this waste material can be sold for melting ice or laying dust. Ninety percent of the production has been collected on waste beds for the past several decades. Occasionally these beds break their dams and leak into rivers, lakes, and streams. Legal problems and public disapproval result. Problems with such waste disposal situations often appear in the newspapers and depress stock values.

Other areas where federal or state action has influenced the operations of chemical companies, and probably their stock values, are covered in the following examples which should guide the analyst in searching for opportunities and problems in ownership of chemical stocks. Although the earnings impact of most of these problems were small, the market tended to exaggerate the effects of regulation on the fortunes of the companies.

1. Witco Chemical, the largest, private, label packager of detergents, experienced extraordinary start-up expenses with enzyme-containing formulations only to have their products outlawed by health authorities because of danger to factory workers.

2. Monsanto and W.R. Grace both suffered losses in research engineering and construction work aimed at replacement of phosphates in detergents by a chemical called NTA. Some preliminary data indicated that NTA caused birth defects in laboratory animals. The soap companies indicated that the products would not be used, and plants had to be scrapped. Later data have partially vindicated NTA and this product may be used at some point in the future.

3. At the time of this writing a favorable federal action has enhanced the value of some stocks in the eyes of the market. Phase IV price control regulations were tending to force export of fertilizers because the foreign market price was radically higher than the domestic price. Price controls were eliminated on fertilizers, thus allowing for greater profits for the companies.

4. The federal government's attitude on hydrocarbon feed materials for the chemical industry is not clear at the time of this writing but will

CHART 1

Price Earnings Ratios of Chemical Stocks*

P/E Ratio	Stocks
6	RCS
7	IKN, GAF, EYC
8	WIT, SNL, RCI, KOP, CTN, CZ, CBT
9	AN
10	EI
11	UK†, OLN, DIA†, ACY
12	STF†, AXO, GRA
13	PSM, MTC†
14	PRC, ACD†
15	
16	TG, IGL
17	UOP, DD†
18	DEX, CV
19	
20	ROH, HPC†
21	
22	
23	DOW†
24	BIG
25	NSC
26	FT
27	
28	
29	
30	
31	LZ, APD

* Based on latest 12-month earnings and prices as of October 22, 1973.

† Companies covered in this report.

Stock symbols used in this report:

AN	Airco
APD	Air Products and Chemicals
AXO	Akzona
ACD	Allied Chemical Corp.
ACY	American Cyanamid Co.
BIG	Big Three Industries
CBT	Cabot Corp.
CZ	Celanese Corp.
CTN	Chemetron Corp.
CV	Commercial Solvents Corp.
DEX	Dexter Corp.
DIA	Diamond Shamrock Corp.
DOW	The Dow Chemical Co.
DD	E. I. duPont de Nemours & Co.
EI	Emery Industries
EY	Ethyl Corp.
FT	Freeport Minerals Co.
GAF	GAF Corporation
GRA	W. R. Grace and Co.
HPC	Hercules
IKN	Inmont Corp.
IGL	International Minerals & Chemical Corp.
KOP	Koppers Co.
LZ	Lubrizol Corp.
MMM	Minnesota Mining & Manufacturing Co.
MTC	Monsanto Co.
NLC	Nalco Chemical Co.
NCH	National Chemsearch Corp.
NSC	National Starch and Chemical Corp.
OLN	Olin Corp.
PSM	Pennwalt Corp.
PRC	Products Research and Chemical Corp.
RCI	Reichhold Chemicals
RCS	The Richardson Co.
ROH	Rohm and Haas Co.
STF	Stauffer Chemical Co.
SNL	Sun Chemical Corp.
TG	Texasgulf
UK	Union Carbide Corp.
UOP	Universal Oil Products Co.
WIT	Witco Chemical Corp.

Source: Hornblower & Weeks-Hemphill, Noyes, Inc.

CHART 2

Price Book Value Ratios of Chemical Stocks*

0.4	0.5	0.6	0.7	0.8	0.9	1.0	1.1	1.2	1.3	1.4	1.5	1.6	1.7	1.8	1.9	2.0	2.1
					SNL												
					RCS												
					RCI												
					PRC												
					KOP			WIT							PSM		
		IKN			GAF			EI		EY		UOP			IGL		
CTN		AN	CBT	OLN	CZ	CV	GRA	AXO	UK†	ACY	ACD†	STF†	MTC†	DIA†	DEX	FT	

* Companies covered in this report.
* Based on book values as of latest fiscal year and prices as of October 22, 1973.

CHART 3

Yields of Chemical Stocks*

0.4	0.6	0.8	1.0	1.2	1.4	1.6	1.8	2.0	2.2	2.4	2.6	2.8	3.0	3.2
					PRC							MTC		
				ROH	MMM							EY	IKN	
NCH				NSC	IGL				TG			DD†	CV	
APD			LZ	NLC	DEX	DOW†		SNL	HPC†	BIG	FT	CBT	ACD†	EI

.† Companies covered in this report.
* Based on prices as of October 22, 1973

be critical to the earnings of the companies involved. Thus, should oil and gas usage be radically decreased in the private sector of the economy, feed stock availability would be more certain for chemical companies.

MARKET BEHAVIOR OF SECURITIES

Although many institutional investors tend to refer to chemical securities as a "group" there is very little evidence of similar market behavior among even the very large chemical company securities. For example, the betas of the various chemical companies vary over a fairly wide range as shown below. The reader should relate the wide variation of betas to similar dispersions of price/earnings ratios and price/book value ratios shown in Charts 1 (p. 219) and 2.

Betas of Chemical Stocks

Allied Chemical	1.17
American Cyanamid	1.00
Dow Chemical	1.04
duPont	0.85
Hercules	0.92
Monsanto	1.06
Stauffer	0.87
Union Carbide	1.11

Source: *Value Line*, November 2, 1973.

2.2	2.3	2.4	2.5	2.6	2.7	2.8	2.9	3.0	3.1	3.2	3.3	3.4	3.5	3.6	3.7	3.8	3.9	4.0	4.1
TG			ROH				HPC†	DD†	BIG	APD								DOW†	

Source: Hornblower & Weeks-Hemphill, Noyes, Inc.

3.4	3.6	3.8	4.0	4.2	4.4	4.6	4.8	5.0	5.2	5.4	5.6	5.8	6.0	6.2
		STF†	RCI							WIT	GRA			
GAF		DIA†	AXO			PSM	CTN	ACY	UK†	OLN	CZ	KOP	AN	RCS

Source: Hornblower & Weeks-Hemphill, Noyes, Inc.

Stability of earnings and better-than-average growth appear to have given such firms as Dow Chemical and Air Products superior price earnings ratios (see Graph I). Similarity of product lines does not appear to be a major determinant of price/earnings ratio which would be the case if the companies were a homogeneous group. Wide disparities between chemical companies' yields (Chart 3) and price/book value ratios (Chart 2) also exist.

9

Communications Media

ROBERT B. RITTER
Institutional Research
L. F. Rothschild & Co.
New York, New York

THE SUBJECTS covered in this section are media or entertainment oriented, based on programming. With statistics indicating that the average television set is used over six and a quarter hours per day, only sleep takes up a greater portion of the average week. Since all major spectator sports, motion pictures, and variety forms count television as a major profit area, it must clearly be labeled as the mass entertainment media. It is free only in the sense that there is no box office. Its cost is borne through advertising dollars added to the price of consumer goods and services. Television occupies the position once held by the motion picture, now a selective media. Just as the film industry is dependent upon television for so much of its existence, so does Cable TV rely on television for its economic start, even as a potential competitor. Radio is still related to television through ownership, network affiliation, and a complementary position as an advertising vehicle. Records and tapes, a major industry in its own right, is dependent on radio as its greatest source of programming, as well as on television and motion pictures through ownership and other financial interests.

NETWORK TELEVISION

The Advertisers

Network Television comprises three networks (ABC, CBS, and NBC) capable of full-time programming, each with a line-up of affiliated sta-

222

tions throughout the country. Revenues are generated through the sale of time to advertisers, with the unit of sale one minute in segments of 30 seconds. Time charges include program expense. In prime time (essentially 8:00 P.M.–11:00 P.M. eastern time, Monday through Friday; 7:00 P.M.–11:00 P.M. eastern time, Saturday and Sunday) the maximum units for sponsorship are six minutes per hour; at other times it varies up to 12 minutes per hour. Each of the three networks have between 180 and 200 affiliates connected by coaxial cable, provided by AT&T, and microwave, by various interests, and sent over the local air by a transmitter. Satellite systems now contemplated should substantially lower costs for the networks. The network pays its affiliate for carrying its program as would any advertiser. This is called *station compensation.* The line-up of affiliates is presented to the advertiser for each program to be sold, since all affiliates do not necessarily clear (transmit) each show. The local station may prefer to delay it to a less suitable time or else substitute one of its own shows.

The advertisers on network television are generally the largest companies in the United States. In 1972, the 100 largest advertisers accounted for 78.4 percent of all network billings, according to an *Advertising Age* study. Major advertisers include auto, food, drug, soaps, household furnishing, appliance, soft drink, cosmetic, and oil companies. The advertisers generally buy time on more than one show and, in many cases, on different days and during different time periods, according to their marketing needs. This type of buying is called *scatter plan.* The advertiser looks to place his messages on the most advantageous programs. They might require a broad general market such as one that a popular series might provide, or a specific market of, say, sports enthusiasts that an athletic event might receive. Advertisers generally use two methods of buying time. The first is six months in advance, the second can almost be up to a few weeks before the show is scheduled. In buying time made available on an existing program, the advertiser acquires a *measured audience,* at least by recent standards.

In buying time on a new program, the advertiser hazards opinions as to both the success and the demographic makeup of his audience. Commitments are generally made in 13-week cycles with 52-week contracts not uncommon. The latter is generally more prevalent among the advertisers of staple items such as foods and household cleansers. Existing sponsors are generally given the first option on renewal of a program or a time period at the start of a new season. This new season commences the week following Labor Day. Special selling periods of the year are generally reserved for advertisers with products specific to holidays—products such as perfumes and greeting cards. Auto companies are very active during new model seasons, while airlines accelerate advertising around vacation periods.

Prices are usually negotiated even though rate cards are prepared by the networks. During periods of strong economic demand (and assuming a discontinuance of federally imposed controls), bidding is strong, more long-term contracts are written, and large amounts of time are sold well in advance. Income is recognized by the networks and stations upon the showing of a commercial. When economic activity weakens, price cutting is generally prevalent, with the weakest network initiating the cycle. However, with the three networks finally closely competitive, greater stability might result in the future.

Programming

The networks finance virtually all programming taken by their affiliates. Ideas and formats are developed with television production companies, including most of the motion picture industry's television subsidiaries and divisions. While the production companies incur some early development expenditures, the financing of the bulk of the project is undertaken by the networks. Prime-time programs are made in time lengths of 30, 60, and 90 minutes. The development of a new 60-minute show with scripts including a pilot episode cost a network around $600,000 by late 1973. A half hour cost about $300,000. Each new episode would run about $225,000 per hour and about $115,000 per half hour, if the program makes the schedule as a regular series. If a program succeeds and a firm 52-week contract is signed, it will generally call for 24 originals and 26 reruns. (Two weeks are usually occupied by special programming.) The rerun price is generally about 25 percent of the original, whereas the cost per minute to the advertiser is about 75 percent of the original cost.

Motion Picture Programming

The programming content of prime time also includes the rental of theatrically exhibited motion pictures, movies made specially for television, the anthology or three-in-one 90-minute series and the special. During the early 1970s there were as many as a dozen regularly scheduled nights for movies, either rented from the major studios or made specially for television. The rentals averaged around $800,000–$1,000,000 for two showings on TV, but features that had done well at the box office often brought much higher prices. (*My Fair Lady* reportedly brought $3 million.) The specially made movies cost around $500,000–$800,000 for two showings and draw ample audiences. In 1973, some of these special films sold for less than $500,000. These movies are often used as pilots in themselves to develop continuing series for a subsequent season. Often a pilot that has been rejected is exhibited as a movie as part of an overall package in order to recover some of its cost.

Long-Form Series

The anthology or three-in-one series runs 60 or 90 minutes per segment, usually in groups of three. These series, each based on a different character, alternate during the same time period each week. The cost may be higher than the average made-for-television movie, due to the fact that the key actor or actress for each major character, as well as the writers, etc., must be compensated to be available for series renewal.

The Special

A prime-time special can run between $200,000 and $400,000 per hour. Specials can take any format, that is, drama, comedy, variety, historical narrative, news, etc. Specials preempt continuing series and are often sponsored by a single advertiser for a specific sales objective, such as a new product or a particular seasonal event.

Sports

Athletic events have long been a part of prime-time television. Football and baseball have become regular additions to programming schedules, while basketball championships, both professional and collegiate, are seasonal events. Every fourth year the Olympics become an important television event. These programs are costly, and negotiating is done directly with the leagues or governing bodies of the sport.

News

Regular evening news and special events are important economic factors in television since they often penalize earnings (revenues rarely cover expenditures). While it is not a regular prime-time event, news does influence the period during important occasions. In the past, elections, assassinations, space shots, presidential messages, and various occurrences of similar import have caused preemptions. Time preempted must be made good in a future period of equal quality or else be refunded. Every four years, national elections affect schedules by both network news coverage and paid political broadcasts. Costs are extensive and are only partially covered by sponsors. The news budget revolves around the nightly half-hour network evening news, broadcast between 6:00 and 7:30 P.M. eastern time to the affiliates. Estimates are that a major network news effort would run about $60 million per year.

Daytime

Daytime programming between 10:00 A.M. and 4:30 P.M. eastern time is a most important segment of the network operation. It is by far the most profitable part of the business. Program costs are considerably cheaper, and the network may sell six minutes per half hour. There are two formats used, drama and game shows. The drama or soap opera is preferred since it delivers a more demographically advantageous audience, women between 18 and 49. During the 1973–74 season, some game shows were becoming demographically attractive. The average production cost of a successful half-hour daytime drama for the 1973–74 season was $60,000 per week. The average cost per minute charged to the advertiser was around $11,000 to $13,000. The reason for lower costs was the simplicity of the operations. Tape rather than film is used, as the raw material is cheaper and editing is virtually nil. Performers, directors, and writers receive substantially less compensation than prime-time counterparts, production is quick with brief rehearsal, sets are generally static. Game shows are even cheaper, averaging about $45,000 per week to produce, with cost per minute to the advertiser around the $8,000 level.

Weekend

Weekend programming has also developed various formats. The major categories are sports and children's fare. The former has become a tremendous source of revenue for the leagues and teams involved. Professional football carries the highest price tag. For the 1973–74 season it was estimated that the National Football League would receive $40 million from the three networks for the regular season, $6 million for the play-offs and Super Bowl, and $350,000 for preseason games. Advertisers pay from $50,000 to $125,000 per minute for regular season and play-off games, $210,000 per minute for the Super Bowl. Most of these games are played on Sunday afternoons, a few on Saturdays. (The Monday night prime-time rate is reported to be $80,000 per minute.) Under terms of the new contract, these prices will escalate. College football, baseball, basketball, hockey, tennis, and golf have all become regular entries, drawing meaningful audiences and advertising dollars. Special programs relating to sports have now been regularly scheduled by all three networks on weekend afternoons.

Saturday morning has generally been reserved for children's programming. Differing attitudes among various groups—especially in the educational and consumer areas—may produce a considerable change in network schedules and revenues from this period. This area has been an important profit center for the sale of time to advertisers of cereals and toys, etc. The period features cartoons, movies, and music programs relatively inexpensive to produce. Advertisers are charged according to a formula, about one third of the price of adult viewing programs, escalating up to two thirds around Christmas.

Other Peripheral Time

Both early morning, 7:00–9:00 A.M., and late night, 11:30 P.M.–1:00 A.M. eastern time, have proven to be profit centers. In certain cases, such as NBC's "Today" and "Tonight" shows, the time periods have been so successful that it would appear to be a growth area for the industry. Since it is not prime time, the affiliates are not limited to two minutes of commercials per hour. With the cost of the popular "Tonight" show reportedly less than $150,000 per week in 1973 and the charge to advertisers around $20,000 per minute from the network, the cost of the week could virtually be recouped during the first day. Movies and low-cost specials are also run during this time. In lieu of station compensation, affiliates receive ten minutes to sell locally, making it advantageous to carry network programming at this late hour. Early morning telecasts such as "Today" have also proven highly profitable, and a post-"Tonight" show is planned by NBC.

Audience Measurement (Ratings and Shares)

Audiences are measured by a variety of means, mainly electronic devices (attached to the television set) and diary. The samples are selected by demographic analysis, so as to best represent the age, sex, education, geographical (urban, suburban, etc.), and income level in the total television homes. A. C. Nielsen Co., the best-known rating service, has used as small a sample as 1,200 audimeters and 2,200 diaries to judge the viewing habits of better than 200 million television viewers. They claim a standard error of 1.5 percent. Using 70 million TV households as a hypothetical base, a program received by 25 million would have a rating of 35.7 ($25 \div 70$), which is quite acceptable. If 60 million of those 70 million homes were tuned in, the share of our hypothetical program would be 41.6 percent ($25 \div 60$), which would be its competitive position against the other network affiliates as well as nonnetwork or independent station offerings at that time. Shares of 30 or below have generally been the level at which a prime-time program would be seriously considered for replacement. However its rating would be a major factor (17 being the general point of demarcation) as would its trend from prior rating and share reports. Its demographics, or audience makeup, would also be an important consideration. An advertiser or group of advertisers might buy a show that would deliver a specific audience no matter what the rating. Realistically, a sponsor buys an audience, not a program. Daytime television drama ratings rarely surpass 10, yet since these programs deliver the 18–49 age group of housewives, they are a natural for soap and household products companies. Adventure plots deliver a male audience; variety shows, an entire family; and comedies attract both younger and older viewers. Each night has its particular audience characteristics. Sunday is the largest overall; Monday is the next; Tuesday, Wednesday, and Thursday all are lower than Monday but about equal to each other. Friday goes more to the younger and older segments, as does Saturday, except that Saturday has larger audiences. Time periods also are different—the earlier hours drawing the younger viewers with the adult becoming more predominant as the evening draws on. By 11:00 P.M. eastern time the adults are assumed to comprise about 80 percent of the audience with the 18–49 age group reaching 50 percent.

A more sophisticated approach to audience measurement has been the Neilsen *70 Market Reports*, or *MNA*, which isolate the largest markets in the country. Other reports analyze the demographic breakdown—18–49 age group; male and female; urban, suburban, and rural; and income category—outlining to advertisers the type of audiences available. These measurements determine the cost that the advertiser is or will be paying. A significant proportion of sales are made on the basis of demographics.

Cost Analysis (Cost per Thousand)

Using an hypothetical example of $50,000 per minute, if an audience of 10 million households was reached, the advertiser would be paying $5 per thousand households. Cost per thousand households or *CPM* is the common advertising method of reckoning expenditure. The average CPM for network television during the early 1970s was between $4.50 and $4.75. If the audience was less, say 5 million, a $10-CPM figure would simply be unacceptable, and the price would be lowered or the program dropped. This would penalize the network's earnings, especially if a new series were involved. (A higher than $5 CPM, say up to $8 CPM, may be within reason if specific audiences are being reached.) A lower figure would ordinarily bring an increase in price, assuming no federal price controls. A program is very often switched to another time or another night where it may succeed. Very often it may benefit from the audience of the program immediately preceding it. The casualty rate of new shows is very high, close to 70 percent. Ratings are the most important determinants of network profits. A satisfactory balance in prime-time ratings supplies tremendous financial leverage and is very helpful in attracting other daypart contributions. The proper demographics are of great importance to advertisers. A poor combination of ratings will produce the need for many costly substitutions and impose an impediment to earnings.

The American Broadcasting Company is an excellent example of how improvements in ratings are translated into higher earnings. In the 1968–69 season during prime time, ABC averaged a 15.6 Neilsen rating, compared to 20.3 for CBS and 20.1 for NBC. By the 1971–72 season ABC had improved to an 18.7, with CBS at 20.4 and NBC at 19.5. In the MNA ratings, or major market areas, ABC improved over the same period from 16.0 to 19.6. The daytime improvement was just as dramatic, from 6.2 to 7.6 (In 1967–68 ABC's average daytime rating was 4.9.) In addition, the evening news increased its audience by almost 50 percent. As a result, their share of network billings, as reported by Broadcast Advertiser Reports (BAR), rose from 26.2 percent to 30.6 percent. Reported pretax broadcast earnings (inclusive of owned and operated television stations and radio operations) went from the $10 million to the $70 million level in this time period. Most of the gain was accounted for by the television network, which had been losing money consistently for close to a decade. The improvement in broadcast earnings was certainly an important factor in ABC's stock market action in 1971 and 1972.

Owned and Operated Stations

Each of the networks own and operate five stations on a VHF frequency. All three networks have stations in New York, Los Angeles, and Chicago. Other cities with network-owned affiliates are Philadelphia, St. Louis, Cleveland, Washington, San Francisco, and Detroit. The stations are important contributors to earnings. They carry the entire schedules of their network parents, although on a rare occasion they substitute their own programs.

During prime time they sell two minutes per hour within and adjacent to the show. They receive about 30 percent of their rate card during prime time—and a lower amount during daytime—from the network as station compensation. During nonprime time when the stations are originating programming, they may sell five minutes per half hour. Local shows generally cost in the area of $25,000–$35,000 per week. At times, the five stations will buy as a *group* from a producer or *syndicator*. The group buys movies, game shows, variety shows, and, especially for the 7:30–8:00 P.M. eastern time period, inexpensive adventure series or documentaries. The group also buys syndicated shows. These programs may have previously run on the network, although not necessarily on the parent network.

The stations have their own news operations. In certain cases, these report directly to the network news departments.

Audience measurements are made, among others, by A. C. Nielsen Co. and the *American Research Bureau* (Arbitron). The latter conducts "sweeps" three times a year to rank all the stations in the area. As with the network, points determine dollars. Adjacencies to top-ranking network shows sell for premium prices. National advertisers aiming for specific markets often try to supplement their network messages.

While it is difficult to document, the three networks utilize different accounting methods in applying overhead to the stations. This complicates the job of comparative analysis.

Regulations

Broadcasting is regulated by the Federal Communications Commission. Recently, various other elements of the government have taken action with regard to the media. The White House, Congress, and the Justice Department have or are considering matters pertaining to broadcasting, as are some of the other regulatory agencies.

The FCC maintains most of its control over the networks through their stations and affiliates. The FCC could, if it desired, modify or revoke the license of a station if it should violate public service obligations, fairness, or commercial time limits. The FCC initiated the prime-time access rule by limiting to three hours the amount of programming that a station can receive from a network between 7:30 and 11:00 P.M. eastern time. (In early 1974, the FCC announced a modification of the rule, eliminating it for Saturdays and Sundays. Pending challenges, the change was to take effect in either the fall of 1974 or 1975.)

Congress legislated against the advertising of tobacco over the airwaves, thereby removing close to a quarter of a billion dollars of billings, mostly on the network. Congress has been debating restrictions on over-the-counter drug advertising. The Justice Department is contemplating a suit charging the networks with monopolozing programming.

The Office of Telecommunications Policy (OTP), a super-agency created by the White House, has made known a distaste for the method of analyzing and reporting news practiced by the networks. It has encouraged stations to challenge the networks. The OTP is suggesting the possibility of a five-year license period, rather than the current three-year period. On network programming, the OTP has indicated to the FCC that the ratio of originals to reruns be greater, in order to increase employment in Hollywood. This would add to network costs.

Various regulatory and consumer groups are pressing for legislation to curb children's advertising and that of particular products.

The broadcasting industry is one in which legislation must be carefully evaluated.

The National Association of Broadcasters (NAB) is the industry's self-regulating body. It is NAB code that restricts nonprogram (advertising) material each hour to 10 minutes during prime time and 16 minutes per hour in nonprime time. It also bars the advertising of hard liquor on television or radio.

TELEVISION STATIONS (Including Network Owned)

Advertisers

Advertising on television stations is divided into two categories, national spot and local spot. Advertisers use national spot in order to supplement network expenditures, to increase coverage in weak areas, or to introduce new products in test marketing. Local advertisers include retail stores and automobile dealers. Local advertising is the fastest growing segment of the industry.

	1967 (millions)	1972 (millions)	Growth (percent)
Network..............	$1,455	$1,802	+ 23
National spot..........	988	1,310	+ 32
Local spot............	466	960	+106

Source: Robert J. Coen, "Estimated Annual U.S. Ad Expenditures," *Advertising Age*, August, 1973.

Premium rates are generally paid for spots adjacent to highly rated programs on the station.

Network Affiliates

Most of the nation's television stations are affiliated with one of the three major television networks. In 1972, 413 of the 473 VHF (Very High Frequency) stations, and 110 of the 173 UHF (Ultra High Frequency) had an affiliation. An affiliate may take all or most of the network's programming for a negotiated rate of around 30 percent of its network hourly rate card during prime time, and a lower percentage during other dayparts. This is called *station compensation*. During prime time, the stations are permitted to sell two spots per hour to national or local advertisers. During nonprime time they may sell up to ten spots per hour. In the top ten markets during 1973, the cost of rating points (A. C. Neilsen, Arbitron, etc.) during prime time approximated $83 per 30 seconds. In New York City, affiliate spots for 30 seconds were selling as high as $180 in prime time. Spots are sold on a preemption basis. The highest price is paid for those least liable to preemption, the lowest for those most likely to be replaced.

An affiliate rarely refuses a prime-time network offering. It is most likely to happen when a controversial show may be deemed unfit by the station for the market. Occasionally, profitability may be a factor. A type of show most often refused is the movie, since an affiliate can buy its own package of films and run them off-network with additional spots to sell for itself. Late night shows are another area of frequent affiliate programming. On occasion, an affiliate may delay a program to a later time in order to present its own program, one it has obtained from a syndicator.

In a two-station city, of which there are very few, a station may have both a major and a secondary network affiliation. The latter's best programs are shown on a delayed basis.

Affiliate Programming

Affiliates must do their own programming during certain parts of the day. The networks program only one half hour of news between 4:30 and 8:00 P.M. eastern time. The affiliates either originate a program themselves or else buy one from a syndicator. The latter is often a series originally programmed by the network which, after a run of several years or more, has not been renewed. The affiliates generally "strip" these shows, exhibiting them during the same time period every day from Monday through Friday. The best examples of these are "Perry Mason" and "I Love Lucy." Another popular type of syndicated show is the 90-minute talk show. Movies already exhibited on the network are also run during nonnetwork time. They are acquired in various packages from syndicators or motion picture companies; usually both are part of the same company. Another method of program acquisition is "barter." Under this plan, an advertiser or advertising company offers a free program to the station. It receives in return two or three free spots, which it sells to its clients. This type of transaction is not frequently used.

Stations generally utilize companies with offices in New York to do their acquiring for them. These companies are known as "station representatives," and receive a commission for their services.

Groups

Many television stations are parts of corporations which own other television stations. These multistation operations are known as "groups." Groups are limited by the Federal Communications Commission to owning seven stations but no more than five of the VHF type.

Groups may own cable systems, but not in their own service areas. Groups often buy or produce some programs for their stations and syndication to others. They are not required to have uniform network affiliations. Most have various affiliations and an occasional station without affiliation, known as an "independent." Among the groups are Westinghouse Broadcasting, General Electric, Capital Cities, Taft, Storer, Wometco, and Metromedia.

Independent Stations

An independent station has no network affiliation and must, therefore, program its own schedule. The independents are heavy users of syndicated shows, movies, and rerun series. They originate their own news, often much more extensively than their affiliated station competitors. They also originate extensive local sports programming, since network obligations make this inconvenient for affiliates. Local baseball and basketball, professional football exhibitions, and special sports network

TABLE 1

Revenue and Expense Items of Three National Television Networks, 1972 (in thousands of dollars)

Broadcast Revenues of Networks

Network Revenues:

Revenues from sale of time when program is supplied by advertiser	$ 45,505
All other advertising revenues	1,637,094
Revenues from stations for cooperative programs	4,110
All other broadcast revenues	57,618
Total gross broadcast revenues	$1,744,327

Deduct:

Payments to stations	219,625
Commissions to advertising agencies, representatives, brokers, and others, and cash discounts	253,399
Total deductions	$ 473,024
Net Broadcast Revenues	$1,271,302

Network Broadcast Expenses

General Categories of Expenses:

Technical expenses	*
Program expenses	$1,026,077
Selling expenses	29,196
General and administrative expenses	105,152
Total broadcast expenses	1,160,425

Selected Expense Items:

Salaries, wages, and bonuses of officers and employees engaged in following categories:

Technical	*
Program	152,920
Selling	13,389
General and administrative	45,748
Total (all officers and employes)	212,057

Depreciation of tangible property	20,819
Amortization expense on programs obtained from others (total):	571,860
Feature film shown or expected to be shown in U.S. theaters	132,182
All other feature film	15,230
All other programs	424,447
Records and transcriptions	3,091
Music-license fees	9,000
Other performance or program rights	70,904
Cost of intercity and intracity program relay circuits	63,792
Total expense for news and public affairs†	146,586

Broadcast Income

Broadcast revenues	$1,271,303
Broadcast expenses	1,160,425
Broadcast operating income (or loss)	110,878

* Because methods of treating technical and program expense differ among the networks, the two figures have been combined.
† This figure contains costs already shown above. Costs of sports programs are not included.
Source: Federal Communications Commission.

TABLE 2

Broadcast Financial Data of Three National Television Networks and 690 Stations, 1972 (in millions of dollars)

Broadcast Revenues, Expenses, and Income	Networks	Percent Change over Previous Year	15 Owned-and-Operated TV Stations	Percent Change over Previous Year	675 Other TV Stations*	Percent Change over Previous Year	Total Three Networks and 690 Stations*	Percent Change over Previous Year
Sales to advertisers for time, programs, talent, facilities, and services.								
Network sales..........	$1,682.6	13.1						
Deduct: Payments to owned-and-operated stations..........	34.3	(3.9)						
Deduct: payments to other affiliated stations..........	185.4	(3.1)						
Retained from network sales..........	1,463.0	16.1	$ 34.4†	(4.2)	$ 190.1†	(2.0)	$1,687.5	13.2
Nonnetwork sales								
To national and regional advertisers..........	—		272.7	15.4	904.7	15.0	1,177.4	15.1
To local advertisers..........	—		84.2	22.7	725.9	21.6	810.1	21.7
Total nonnetwork sales..........			356.9	17.0	1,630.6	17.9	1,987.5	17.7
Total sales to advertisers..........	1,463.0	16.1	391.3	14.8	1,820.7	15.4	3,675.0	15.6
Sales to other than advertisers..........	61.7	6.9	6.1	15.1	26.9	24.0	94.7	11.8
Total sales..........	1,524.7	15.7	397.4	14.8	1,847.6	15.5	3,769.7	15.5
Deduct: Commissions to agencies, representatives, etc..........	253.4	13.1	70.3	14.5	266.6	17.1	590.3	15.0
Total Broadcasting Revenues..........	1,271.3	16.2	327.1	14.9	1,581.1	15.3	3,179.4	15.6
Total Broadcast Expense..........	1,160.4	11.5	224.6	16.0	1,242.3	10.2	2,627.3	11.3
Total Income (before federal income tax)..........	110.9	106.5	102.5	12.4	338.8	38.7	552.2	41.9

* Includes 59 satellites, 27 of which filed combined reports with their parent stations.
† Includes payments from networks other than ABC, CBS, or NBC.
Note: Last digits may not add because of rounding. ( ) indicates decline.
Source: Federal Communications Commission.

TABLE 3

Broadcast Expenses of Three Networks and TV Stations in 1972* (in thousands of dollars)

Item	Technical	Program	Technical plus Program	Selling	General and Administrative	Total Broadcast Expenses
3 Networks..........................	††	††	$1,026,077	$ 29,196	$105,152	$1,160,425
15 Network owned-and-operated stations......	$ 37,265	$115,920	153,184	28,053	43,335	224,573
413 Other VHF network-affiliated stations.....	110,375	344,114	454,489	108,474	297,552	860,515
110 UHF network-affiliated stations...........	16,219	32,922	49,141	14,174	38,223	101,539
Total 538 network-affiliated stations..........	163,859	492,956	656,814	150,701	379,110	1,186,627
33 VHF independent stations.................	19,839	95,379	115,218	18,519	40,193	173,930
53 UHF independent stations.................	12,810	40,304	53,114	14,436	29,533	97,083
Total 86 independent stations................	32,649	135,683	168,332	32,955	69,726	271,013
Total 624 stations..........................	196,508	628,639	825,146	183,656	448,836	1,457,640
Total 3 networks and 624 stations............	—	—	$1,851,223	$212,852	$553,938	$2,618,065

* Excludes part-year stations, satellite stations, and those with less than $25,000 of time sales.
† Because methods of treating technical and program expenses differ among the networks, the two figures have been combined.
Note: Last digits may not add to totals because of rounding.
Source: Federal Communications Commission.

offerings are popular on independent station schedules. Special sports networks are created on an ad hoc basis for individual events not carried by the three major networks. Among these would be such events as the NCAA regional basketball tournaments, professional basketball play-offs, golf matches, etc. Independents and some affiliated stations are lined up for each telecast. The best example of an independent group is Metromedia, with five stations (four VHF and one UHF) of this type.

Federal Regulations

The FCC has had direct responsibility for licensing television and radio stations, since virtually the beginning of commercial broadcasting. Licenses must be renewed every three years. Though licenses are just a small fraction of a station's worth, much of a financial nature rides on renewal. A station's "value" reflects plant and equipment, affiliation, program inventory, and goodwill. The major determinants for licensing include local involvement, programming directed at children, religion, education, public affairs, editorializing, agriculture, politics, news and weather, minorities, sports, and entertainment. In only one recent case has a license been revoked, that of WHDH in Boston. This was actually due to circumstances involving its original issuance in the 1950s. At this writing, the license of WPIX, New York, is in jeopardy due to charges of irregularities in news programs.

Various bills are currently in the Congress or its committees pertaining to license duration, prohibiting advertising of certain products, children's advertising, and equal time. Since so much is changing in this area, we suggest the analyst familiarize himself with these restrictions, as well as regulation from such agencies as the Federal Trade Commission which may be pertinent to broadcast advertising.

RADIO

Radio through 1972 was the second most important media for local advertising. It ranked second only to newspapers and had billings of over $100 million more than television. According to Robert Coen, McCann-Erickson Inc., 70 percent of radio expenditures were on the local level, the remainder spot and network.

Programming on radio comprises mostly music, news, sports, and talk shows. There are over 4,300 AM stations and 2,000 FM stations in operation. In 1950 there were 2,050 AM and 733 FM stations in operation.

Radio is a selective medium, using entertainment forms based on demographic analysis. Specific music tastes—rock, country and western, middle-of-the-road, etc.—are catered to. Periods devoted to news, sports, and talk shows are calculated to fit with selected audience groups.

Economics

Stations as a whole make roughly 10 percent pretax on net billings. Some of the more successful AM operations make as much as 25 percent. Programming is mostly local. News feed is taken from networks or local news wires. Four networks—ABC, CBS, NBC, and Mutual Broadcasting Co.—supply programming to affiliates, mostly news and features. ABC, with four types of network feed, has 1400 affiliates; Mutual Broadcasting, 560 in addition to 60 taking a black-oriented service; CBS has close to 250; and NBC about 240. Network rates range from $800 for an evening 30-second spot to $1,100 for the same period between 7:00 A.M. and 7:00 P.M. eastern time, Monday through Friday. Similar one-minute spots run in the range of $1,050–$1,450.

Audience Measurement

Individual stations use rate cards competitive with other media on a cost per thousand basis. The most important audience-measuring company servicing radio is "Pulse." Ratings are done periodically by daypart and season. Prime time is during the day from 6:00 A.M. to 6:00 P.M. The automobile radio use is particularly heavy. A study by the Radio Advertising Bureau, a trade association, indicates that the average individual spends 70 percent as much time listening to radio as to television.

Regulation

Radio is regulated by the Federal Communications Commission. Any one individual or group may own no more than a maximum of seven stations. In the case of radio, this means seven AM and seven FM stations. Many groups are involved in radio ownership. They include ABC, CBS, and NBC, Storer, Taft, Capital Cities, Metromedia, Westinghouse, Lin, Sonderling, and Cox. The National Association of Broadcasters, the industry's self-regulating body, specifies a maximum of 18 minutes of commercial time per hour.

MOTION PICTURES

Production and Distribution

The major motion picture production companies all distribute their product to theaters and television. The majors include: Paramount (Gulf & Western), Warner Bros. (Warner Communications Inc.), Twentieth Century-Fox, United Artists (Transamerica), Universal Pictures (MCA), Columbia Pictures, and Walt Disney.

Product for theatrical production is financed by the company. This is generally accomplished through cash flow and revolving credit arrangements from a group of banks, often specializing in this type of loan. Loans are generally collateralized by the negative of the film.

In making a movie, the motion picture production company finances a producer who is frequently an independent. Often the producer has his own company which takes an equity interest in the film. This is in addition to the fee paid by the major to the producer or his company. The financing arrangements involve a loan to the producer. The company or major often supplies space, sets, crew, and other forms of overhead for which the producer is charged. Either the major or the producer may supply the script, select the director, the cast, the locations, etc. The company has the responsibility of controlling the budget.

Producing a motion picture for theatrical exhibition is highly speculative. Budgets often run over estimates, and revenues are often short of anticipation. Motion picture budgets have been averaging $2 to $3 million in recent years. A rule of thumb is that a picture should make *two and one-half times* its negative cost in *distributors' gross*. The distributors' gross is that amount received by the distributor after the theater owner or *exhibitor* has taken his share.

Once the film is completed, the motion picture is released for theatrical distribution. The distributor earns a fee, generally 30 percent, from the receipts. The next share of the receipts goes toward the amortization of the negative, that is, the cost of production. This may include guarantees to one or more performers against the distributors' gross. A performer may demand a percentage before distribution and/or amortization. Compensation for the performer—and in certain cases the director, writers, and others—may be a percentage of the profits after distribution, amortization, and other costs. There are various methods of amortization. Some majors use a fixed formula to *television residual*. For example, if a film cost $3 million, and its television worth is judged $600,000, $2.4 million is amortized over, say, a two-year period. This is referred to as the Periodic Table Computation method. Then the $600,000 would be left as an inventory item against which amortization is charged during subsequent licensing or release to television. Another and increasingly utilized method of amortization is the Individual Film Forecast Computation. This method amortizes film costs in the same ratio that current gross revenues bear to anticipated total gross revenues. In effect, costs are written off against forecast gross receipts. The formula must be under constant scrutiny to compensate for incorrect forecasting, a common occurrence. This method is recommended by the American Institute of Certified Public Accountants. The Periodic Table Computation is to be used only if it accomplishes the same result. The American Institute of Certified Public Accountants has published a booklet "Accounting for Motion Picture Films" to cover this complex subject.

The analyst should keep in mind that amortization is proportional to the flow of estimated income. Poor forecasting results in inventory write-downs, a condition that has in the past plagued the industry. This is especially true in the case of films that have run considerably over budget. Outstanding examples of this include *Cleopatra* and *Mutiny on the Bounty*. During the early 1970s United Artists, Paramount, MGM, CBS, and ABC took substantial inventory write-downs which affected their profits.

The vast majority of domestic films are produced by companies best described as *financier-distributors*. There are, and have been, companies which produce and obtain their own financing but do not distribute. Until recently, the American Broadcasting Company and the Columbia Broadcasting System were in this category. They made distribution arrangements with others, giving up a substantial part of their distributors' fee. These companies have since closed their operations, although others start up periodically. They include combines of broadcasting station groups, producers, directors, and artist companies, and advertising and industrial companies.

International Production

Distribution of films also involves foreign language films. Foreign films find acceptance in higher-income and university areas. They result from an active international market, often developed by government subsidies and favorable labor conditions. American companies have taken advantage of these benefits by using foreign locations. Changing monetary conditions, escalating foreign labor costs, and U.S. tax incentives may negate these foreign advantages. The United States now permits its film makers to apply a 7 percent investment credit to films as well as equipment.

Theatrical Distribution

Traditional distribution is through motion picture theatres or exhibitors in the United States and abroad. Distribution is managed through regional branches established by the majors.

Motion pictures have various methods of release. These include a first-run exclusive situation for important pictures and could be on a reserved-seat basis, known to the industry as a "hard-ticket" situation. This usually involves a single theatre. There is a first multiple run, which involves different areas of a metropolitan region. Others include a limited multiple run and a second and third multiple run, often referred to as "show case." There is, additionally, the rerun, from one to many years after the original run (for example, the series-type "James Bond" films, a period-piece favorite such as *Gone with the Wind,* or old Walt Disney productions). There is also a flat fee basis in which the theatre pays a fee to the distributor, or the distributor takes over the theatre for a fee.

The distributor and exhibitor share revenues on a percentage basis. In the early part of a film's run, the distributor's share may run as high as 90 percent after the exhibitor's basic expenses are covered. The distributor's share then declines. Contracts between distributors and exhibitors include length-of-run guarantees, advance payments to the distributor, and local exclusivity for exhibitors. Advertising and promotion is usually the responsibility of each party in relation to his percentage participation in the gross receipts. Exhibitor concessions such as popcorn and soft drinks do not enter into the negotiations. They accrue only to the benefit of the exhibitor.

The success of a theatrical release can best be gauged by weekly analysis of distributors' gross revenues in *Variety.* This service presents an excellent sampling.

Income Recognition

The licensor should recognize revenues on the dates of exhibition for both percentage and flat-fee engagements. Nonrefundable guarantees should be deferred in the accounts and recognized as revenues on the dates of exhibition, except for guarantees in foreign countries which are, in substance, outright sales. Outright sales should be recognized as revenues on execution of a noncancellable contract. (American Institute of Certified Public Accountants.)

Foreign Distribution

International receipts, which at one time equaled those of the United States and Canada, are now only about 35 percent of the market. The distributor's overseas fee is about 35 percent or more, since costs are higher. Most U.S. distributors have joint efforts to exploit foreign markets —for example, Paramount and Universal, Warner Bros. and Columbia Pictures. The industry uses the DISC program to defer for an indefinite period taxes on one half of foreign earnings.

Television Distribution

Television has severely impacted the traditional movie-going habits of the United States. As an example, in 1948, movie box offices sold 80 million tickets per week; by 1972 the figure had shrunk to 18 million per week. The network and stations have become the most important source of income for the motion picture industry. Theatrical film licensing is just one facet of this relationship. Except in unusual cases, a film made for theatrical distribution and exhibition is *licensed* to a network two years after initial release. Deals are generally made for a package of films with an overall price. The price averaged $800,000 per film during the late 1960s. Internally, individual films must be priced on an actual, rather than an average, basis for residual purposes. The residuals are paid to participants who may include actors, directors, producers, etc. Films must be played during a specific time span of, say, one or two years. Each film is usually played twice. Following the network exhibition, a film generally goes into *syndication* to the individual television stations. All of the major film producers have their own syndication operations. Syndication and distribution costs amount to 35 percent of the receipts. For accounting purposes, the companies are advised by the AICPA to recognize income as soon as the license for a film's showing commences. The greater the company's library of films, the more stable should be its income from licensing and rerelease.

Special Films for Television

The networks have all become users of full-length motion pictures specially made for their medium. The average cost is between $450,000 and $800,000. Either the network or the motion picture producer supply the script. The network is the major financier, so the risk of the motion picture producer may be limited to script development costs. The network controls the budget. Costs are lower, both *over-the-line* (for example, actors, director, script) and *under-the-line* (for example, staff, locations, studio time, editing), and expenses are kept down. After showing, TV films are syndicated, usually by producers. Occasionally they are exhibited in theaters, especially overseas. They are often used as pilot films to develop characters for a continuing series.

Continuing Series for Television

All the major companies have television production units that present projects to the networks for continuing series. Often they form joint efforts with the independent producer. Once a program is accepted, the network will place an order for 13 episodes. During the life of the series, while it is being renewed by the network, the producer makes little money, as income barely covers expenses. In certain cases money is lost. Increases in costs have been averaging 8 percent a year. Major recognition of revenues takes effect when the series is licensed through syndication after a long network run. Such series as "Bonanza," "Perry Mason," "I Love Lucy," and "Mission Impossible" are licensed to individual stations. The greater the number of episodes, the more profitable the series is to the producer.

Continuing series also include such anthology or "three-in-one" series as MCA's "Mystery Movies," with "Columbo," "McMillan and Wife," etc. These are often syndicated to stations as movies, since 90-minute entertainment is difficult to "strip" on a Monday through Friday basis, especially to a network affiliate.

New Technologies

The motion picture industry is looking to the developing technologies of CATV and audio-visual cassette for new markets. With recent emphasis in CATV on *premium* or *subscription cable,* movie producers are forming subsidiaries to exploit these markets—by supplying film either for a fixed monthly fee or on a per movie basis to cable companies. This would occur *after* first-run theatrical exhibition but *before* conventional television. Opposition has begun from both theater and television interests.

Audio-visual cassette technology involves the use of a player attached to a television set. A cassette or disc containing a movie is placed in the player and the image projected on the screen. Several cassette systems have already failed. Current thought is that a disc system, such as the MCA Disco-Vision may eventually prove to be successful. Costs for players-changers are estimated at below $500, while disc albums are being designed to sell between $2 and $10.

Neither of these markets have yet proven successful. Both systems may face copyright legislation currently in congressional hearings.

CABLE TELEVISION (CATV)

Cable is the newest and the most controversial of the leisure-time media. As of 1973, it barely covered 10 percent of the country. It utilizes a *broad-band* (many channels) *coaxial cable* to bring an image to the television screen. Originally, this method was a way to bring television to areas where conventional "over-the-air" wave reception was unsatisfactory, due to unfavorable terrain or atmospheric conditions. Called CATV for *Community Antenna Television,* a system constructs a master antenna in a position favorable to receiving conventional television signals. The signal is often amplified by *microwave* and fed by the cable to the *head end.* From there, cable is deployed either via telephone pole (in suburban and rural areas) or *underground* (in most urban areas where it has been introduced). The cable is made available to homes or buildings along its various routes. Such dwellings are known as *passed* homes. The major companies operate more than one signal and are called Multiple Signal Operators (MSO). They include Teleprompter, Cox Cable, American TV & Communications, Warner Communications, and Viacom.

Economics

The cost of a mile of cable in an average nonurban (central city) area was between $7,000 and $10,000 in 1973. In some of the major urban areas such as Manhattan in New York City, the cost was estimated at up to $105,000 per mile. Cable has to be especially insulated, run underground, and then run up through the high-rise apartments. The height of these urban buildings produces a need for cable since it distorts reception of atmospheric signals. Each home passed by the cable is calculated to cost around $150, based on the average homes per mile. If a system is able to connect half of the homes in its jurisdiction, it is deemed to have a 50 percent penetration factor with a cost of $300 per subscriber (for example, 2 × $150). The installation charge to the subscriber is between $6 and $12, although the cost may be over $100 per home—especially for more sophisticated two-way systems. The industry averages a $5 per month subscription fee, or $60 per year per subscriber. *Franchise fees* are paid to municipalities and state commissions after licenses have been granted by them. Duration of the licenses varies, averaging 15 years. The television set is connected to the cable via a *converter* (cost to the system is $35, included in the installation fee) which takes the amplified signal from the head end and feeds it through the set.

The Converter and Broad-Band

The original converter has a 12-channel capacity, duplicating the conventional television set tuner. Systems in areas with poor reception generally duplicate the areas' signals. If the system services a one- or two-station market, it often brings in the closest second or third network. This additional service is an added incentive for a passed home to subscribe. In major urban areas, such as Los Angeles and New York City, seven stations occupy the channels, leaving five out of the twelve converter channels for system use. New technology has developed converters with over 20-channel capacity. Some systems in smaller markets bring in or import nonnetwork independents to add further service. They also offer the weather, news, stock market reports, *local* athletic events, discussions of local interest, and old movies.

Regulation and Signal Importation

In 1966, the FCC banned the importation of distant signals into the 100 largest markets. Judicial proceedings resulting from that step had the effect of placing a temporary freeze on the industry. In 1968, the FCC modified its stance, and by 1972 it had authorized minimum service standards for all markets whereby the importation of distant signals was permitted, if necessary, to reach the minimum standards as follows:

1. In the top television markets (1–50), three full-network stations, three independent stations.
2. In the next tier of television markets (51–100), three full-network stations, two independent stations.
3. In markets below 100, three full-network stations, one independent station.

In all markets, cable operators are obliged to carry all stations licensed in communities within 35 miles. In the top 100 markets, they are permitted to import two *distant* signals, even if such importations bring service above the minimum standards. Smaller markets must be content with minimum service. The proposed rules also include "leap-frogging" conditions. These provide first, that in the top 100 markets, the first distant signal that may be imported must be a UHF station from within 200 miles, if such a station is available; in the absence of such a station, any VHF station within 200 miles or any UHF station may be imported. Second, in those few markets where a third independent signal may be imported, that signal must, if possible, be in-state or within 200 miles. Beyond those restrictions, importation is unrestricted up to the level of the "minimum service standard" as established above. The cable operator is not permitted, under the FCC proposed rules, to select the distant station that would most appeal to viewers in his vicinity. In many instances he is obliged to carry a UHF station which is likely to carry weak programming.

According to the Sloan Commission on Cable Communications, an advocate of the industry,[1] this compromise frees cable television to expand in urban centers, but limits the amount of competition it can offer. The FCC requires the cable companies in the top 100 markets to set aside three free nonbroadcast channels for noncommercial use—one for state and local government, one for education, and one for public access.

Leased Channels and Premium Cable

The cable company is also obligated to lease channels for any legal purpose. These would include the use of *subscription* or *premium-charge* cable for exhibitors of movies, theater, ballet, and athletic events, for examples. A special converter or "black box" would be placed by the operator or leasor alongside the conventional instrument. The viewer would make a selection for which an extra fee would be charged, either

---

[1] See Sloan Commission on Cable Communications, *On the Cable* (New York: McGraw-Hill, 1971), pp. 55–56.

by month or event or combination. It is this facet of cable that puts it squarely into the leisure-time category. Currently, experiments in subscription or premium cable are being conducted with various results. The most successful of these is in San Diego, a market with relatively poor over-the-air television reception. It has a 75 percent cable penetration. Cox Cable has leased through its Mission Cable system a pay-TV channel to Optical Systems Corporation. The latter operates the system and pays Mission 10 percent of its gross. In 1973, it charged a viewer $6.50 per month for a season pass to all movies—or $2.75 a week for unlimited use. Various combinations for athletic events and phone-in requests are listed. The converter requires a $20 deposit plus $1 per month maintenance in advance.

Operations of a similar type are being conducted in hotel and motel rooms on a per movie basis. Columbia Pictures and M-G-M are among the companies participating in this experiment.

Obviously, there is substantial opposition from free television and motion picture theater interests. The FCC has utilized the same restriction imposed on pay-TV, a so-far unsuccessful over-the-air predecessor of premium cable. Under these "antisiphoning" arrangements, premium cable may carry no picture films more than two years old, and no athletic event that has been carried in the area during the past five years.

Copyright Considerations

The U.S. Supreme Court has ruled that cable television does not infringe on copyrights when it rebroadcasts programs picked up from distant signals. Legislation to require royalty payments of some form may be introduced in Congress.

Two-Way Capability

The FCC requires all systems to have two-way capability. The operator must provide the capacity for two-way communications. This would allow the receiver to signal the system. Such services as burglar alarm protection, catalogue type advertising, and educational feedback are examples of two-way signalling.

The Impact of Capital Requirements

The degree of capital intensity required by the cable industry is high. Debt/equity ratios are often inordinate by normal standards. Depreciation is rapid and often leads to partnership with private interests for tax purposes. Teleprompter had such arrangements with buy-back provisions. This permitted individuals to take depreciation-induced tax losses during building stages. Investment tax credits accrued to the company.

For typical reporting purposes, a new system is not consolidated for 18 months after the first subscriber installations, or until 25 percent of the homes in the market have subscribed, whichever comes first.

During periods of monetary restriction, the high cost of money may penalize earnings or cause a slowdown in construction. Interest charges have, in certain cases, been capitalized rather than expensed for reporting purposes.

An expansion of cable systems and technology will cause higher expenditures on more sophisticated equipment, such as two-way cable and more complex converters. Methods that might cover these costs and those of programming are currently being considered. Among them is "satellite technology." Such systems would be controlled by the cable operators, such as American TV and Communications, Cox Cable, Telecommunications, Warner Communications, and Viacom. This would enable the cable companies to organize networks, as in the case of television, and thereby effect substantial economies. Competition with the networks is anticipated, since television networks are not permitted to own any cable systems. In addition, the Justice Department opposed a proposed merger between Cox Cable and American TV and Communications. Since those companies are two of the largest, a competitive environment is guaranteed. It should also be noted that the major phone company operators are forbidden to participate in the industry. A broadcast station operator may own all or part of a cable system, provided it is not in any of the broadcaster's reception areas, as in the cases of Cox and Storer Broadcasting.

Cabinet Committee Report

On January 21, 1974, the Cabinet Committee on Cable Communications, appointed by the president three years earlier, made recommendations that, if adopted, would remove many of cable's restrictions.

Among the changes suggested were some which would encourage television industry involvement in programming, pay, or subscription cable, and a separation of programmer-operator combinations. There would be no restrictions on either cross-media ownership or multiple ownership of cable systems. Under certain limited conditions an operator would be able to program his own system.

The commission argues for a single industry regulatory jurisdiction, preferably on the municipality level. This would eliminate overlapping agencies of the federal, state, and local bureaucracies.

The recommendations of the cabinet committee were made to facilitate the growth of the cable industry, with its enormous capital requirements a major consideration.

RECORDS AND TAPES

The record and tape industry has been one of the fastest growing segments in the leisure time field. Between 1967 and 1972, the sales of prerecorded records and tapes at retail list price almost doubled. Actual figures for the industry are difficult to ascertain; for the most part, they are estimated. In 1972, the trade publication *Billboard,* estimated that close to $2 billion worth of records and tapes at retail list were sold in the United States. This compares to $1.2 billion in 1967. Retail list is considered an inflated figure, since very few outlets do not discount to some extent, especially in metropolitan areas. Of the total dollar sales, records are thought to account for 70 percent and prerecorded tapes for 30 percent. Foreign markets are believed to be equal to, or larger than, those in the United States, with U.S.-owned products estimated to average around 33 percent of these markets. Albums account for roughly 90 percent of record revenues, single records 10 percent.

Production

The major producers of records in the United States are Columbia Records, division of CBS; Warner Record & Tape, division of Warner Communications, Inc.; Capitol Records, owned by England's Electrical and Musical Industries (EMI); Victor Records, division of RCA, MCA; and Polygram, a subsidiary of Dutch Phillips. Two important privately held companies are A&M and Motown.

Economics

Artists are contracted to record by the production company on an exclusive basis over a fixed period of time. A recognized artist will usually sign for five years, a new artist for one- and four-year options. Compensation varies, but it is generally a percentage of net record sales, either at the distributor's (wholesale) or the retail level. Since a *return* privilege of unsold records and tapes is granted to distributors and retailers, the net figure is important. Percentages of wholesale prices vary between 15 percent and 20 percent and retail between 5 percent and 10 percent. To sign the more successful artists, a *guarantee* against that figure is often a necessity. There is a great deal of risk in a guarantee, since an album may fail to reach the break-even point after the guarantee payment. A few outstanding performers, and producers, insist on *label* arrangements. In this case they record under their own label, such as the Beatles did on the Apple label, distributed by Capitol. In a few cases, an outstanding artist may sign a contract calling for a guarantee, or front money, against a high percentage, or half the profits of the album. In deals of this type, the artist/producer assumes production costs; but unless the albums have extraordinary sales, the profit potential to the company is limited. Another type of arrangement involves a major company assuming distribution for a smaller company. An example of this is the Columbia Records arrangement with Philadelphia International and Mums. This method is used by the majors to acquire the talents of outstanding producers or particular types of music. Music is broken down into several important categories including contemporary (rock during the late 1960s and early 1970s) with about 40–50 percent of the market, country and western with a stable 15 percent, middle-of-the-road, rhythm and blues, jazz, and classical. Many versatile artists known for specific categories often cross over to a more popular style.

The success of a record is best judged if it reaches the top playing *charts*. These are published weekly by the industry's trade papers. Other barometers, also found in trade publications, are the lists of records most often played by radio stations. As the charts and stations are classified by *sound*—that is, contemporary, soul, country and western —one can develop a feel for the trend of a company's sales. For earnings evaluation, one must have knowledge of the various artists' contractual arrangements and the actual sales figures.

Distribution

Most major recording production companies operate their own distribution or wholesale organizations. These include Columbia, Warner, Capitol, RCA, and MCA. They service subdistributors, "rack jobbers," and large-volume retailers. They distribute their lines and, as shown above, may also distribute other products.

Independent distributors handle the products of companies without such an outlet. Among the independents are ABC of American Broadcasting Company, Handelman, and Pickwick. Among their lines are those of A&M, Motown, Buddah, and ABC Records. They sell to the same outlets as the record company distributors. Subdistributors obtain their products from either a record company or another distributor and service small retail accounts in specified regions.

A rack jobber services department stores and large retailers who cannot merchandise records and tapes with the same expertise as the rack jobber. The latter arranges for inventory and promotions and is compensated by a margin of profit over his cost of goods sold.

The largest chain department and discount stores may, if volume warrants, buy directly from record company distributors. The multiunit free-standing store is becoming the most important factor in the retailing of records and tapes. Pickwick and Tower Stores are among the leaders.

Gross profit margins for the various classes of distributors are: independent distributors, 15 percent; rack jobbers, 18–20 percent; and large-volume retailers, 35–40 percent.

Return Policy

Restrictions on returns of unsold albums to the manufacturer were instituted by industry leaders in early 1974. Manufacturers had permitted virtually unlimited returns during the growth period of the late 1960s and early 1970s. Most manufacturers maintained a 25 percent reserve against returns, a figure that was often exceeded. Under the new policy, returns from rack jobbers and subdistributors are limited to 18 percent, and those from retailers to 13 percent. Single records still have the unlimited return privilege.

Clubs

A method of distribution utilized by the record companies is the record *club* (for example, Columbia, RCA, Longines, and Record Club of America). Such clubs have lost their share in the industry as a consequence of the increase in retail outlets. Mailing lists are being used to sell other merchandise and services.

Catalog

One of the most important assets of a record company is its catalog of past records. The greater the depth (amount of specific artist releases) and diversity (jazz, country and western, middle-of-the-road, soul, contemporary, classical), the more the value. Outstanding records from an individual artist on a new album often stimulate the sales of old releases. A dormant performer's return to popularity can lead to a demand for past hits. A frequently used merchandising effort is the pressing of an album of the best songs from several past releases (for example, the "Greatest Hits" recordings) of an artist.

Special Products

A new form of record merchandising is *special product promotion*. This includes old records repackaged. They are promoted by television, radio, newspaper, and magazine advertising. The major companies, as well as marketing specialists, are involved in these activities.

Repackaging has become more profitable as the result of various periods of nostalgia that affect the country. When repackaging was not as important, Pickwick was a dominant factor, buying up old record rights from the majors. The latter are currently establishing their own profit centers in this market.

Technology

Various audio-technological developments have, in the past, proved to stimulate record sales. They include the long-playing album (LP), high fidelity, and stereophonic sound. In addition, magnetic tape produced the cartridge and cassette which permitted mobility of pre-recorded music, especially in the auto. The transistor radio has proven a boon to the record industry. Its mobility, combined with the heavy music orientation of radio, is a great stimulant to record sales. This is also the case with FM and stereo broadcasts. The development of "quadraphonic sound," once the industry agrees on a compatible form, may be of similar importance.

MARKET AND ECONOMIC CONSIDERATIONS

The comparative performance of leisure-time, entertainment-based stocks is inconclusive. Many of these companies are involved in conglomerate situations. Factors other than the market or the economy may not be enough to counter a trend. Broadcasters are consumer-advertising oriented, and now that they are approaching a maturity, they should become increasingly sensitive to the business cycle. In the 1970–73 period, they outperformed the market on both the downside and the upside. Leverage may be a factor, especially in the networks. Motion pictures are involved with television, so licensing and syndication are important variables. Theatergoing for films is discretionary, and prices are high. Monetary restrictions could curtail motion picture companies. Record and tape sales are also a product of discretionary income. They are a relatively inexpensive form of entertainment, since buyers tend to play their records and tapes many times. They are also very faddish, and that, plus a technological change, could produce some contra-cyclicality. There are few "pure" investments available. Cable companies, due to their capital intensiveness, are affected by high money costs. Alternately, they have been perceived as growth stocks and cyclical stocks. The former perception would relate to their program or software potential, the latter to their construction period.

Analyst's Summary

The entertainment analyst must always be aware of trends in public taste. One should be sure in observing television that one recognizes a mass-culture audience against a more select market in motion pictures or records. The ability of a company to be in the forefront of changes in public taste would be reflected in its earnings statement.

Balance is an integral requirement of an enduringly successful company. Overemphasis on any one program, movie, or music type would be detrimental once a trend terminated. Therefore, the analyst must carefully scrutinize ratings and revenues to see what percentage may depend on any one style or time period or appeal to any one group at the expense of another.

The economic factor is quite naturally of paramount importance. Consumer spending produces advertising to attract more of the spending. The demographics of industrial activity may lead to investment opportunities. Particular geographic areas may be stimulated by certain economic influences, thereby benefitting the areas' advertising media. This would also apply to age groups or products. In this manual there are chapters dealing at great length with these and other factors such as projecting business and monetary changes. As far as industry and company projections are concerned, the important element in entertainment is cost. The analyst should be an avid student of trade publications, which often are the best sources of news relating to costs, prices, and negotiations.

Statistics emanating from the industry relating to revenues, costs, earnings, unit sales, and attendance are more often late or subject to substantial interpretation. For example, Federal Communication Commission figures are late, while television and record trade industry statistics often require meaningful revision.

Accounting procedures are becoming more meaningful. Analysts should become familiar with the new rules concerning revenue recognition and amortization policies.

The evaluation of management is often difficult. Entertainment is "show business" and advertising is "hard sell," and both can be disconcerting in analysis. Creative management has often both sensitivity and ego, and too much of either can impair an earnings statement. Marketing strategy is important, and the analyst should know the objective of the company's activities.

ANALYST SOURCES

Periodicals:

Broadcasting Magazine (weekly)
Television/Radio age (biweekly)
Television Digest (weekly)
Variety (weekly)
Billboard (weekly)

Record World (weekly)
Advertising Age (weekly)

Books:

Television, Les Brown, New York: Harcourt, Brace & Jovanovich, 1971.
About Television, Martin Mayer, New York: Harper & Row, 1972.
Television and the Public, Robert T. Bower, New York: Holt, Rinehart &
    Winston, 1973.
Survey of Broadcast Television, duPont-Columbia University, New York:
    Grosset & Dunlap (Annual).
On the Cable, Sloan Commission, New York: McGraw-Hill, 1971.
The Movie Business, A. W. Bluem and J. E. Squire, New York: Hastings
    House, 1972.

Regulatory Agency:

Federal Communications Commission

Trade Organization:

Television Bureau of Advertising—New York, N.Y.

APPENDIX

The annual report of the American Broadcasting Companies (shown in the Appendix) is an excellent example of detailed disclosure in a leisure-time company. Covering broadcasting, theatres, records, and motion pictures, the statement details revenues and earnings by operation. Inventories are segregated, amortization and depreciation policies are stated. This presentation to shareholders is virtually identical to that submitted to the SEC in the 10-K form. It's source is the American Broadcasting Companies, Inc.

APPENDIX

American Broadcasting Companies, Inc. and Subsidiaries

Statements of Consolidated Earnings		1972	1971
Revenues:	Broadcasting	$637,349,000	$528,020,000
	Theatres	105,916,000	95,887,000
	Records	82,501,000	87,345,000
	Motion Pictures	14,619,000	13,320,000
	Publishing and Other	29,064,000	31,923,000
	Total revenues	869,449,000	756,495,000
Expenses:	Operating expenses and cost of sales	638,437,000	587,996,000
	Selling, general and administrative	134,932,000	111,831,000
	Depreciation and amortization of property and equipment (Note A)	15,124,000	16,044,000
	Interest	6,344,000	9,028,000
	Total expenses	794,837,000	724,899,000
Earnings from Operations Before Income Taxes and Extraordinary Items		74,612,000	31,596,000
Provisions for Income Taxes (Notes A)	Federal	32,509,000	13,700,000
	State, foreign and local	7,062,000	2,956,000
	Total provisions for income taxes	39,571,000	16,656,000
Earnings from Operations Before Extraordinary Items		35,041,000	14,940,000
Extraordinary Gains (Losses), net of applicable Federal income tax (Note G)		596,000	(1,740,000)
Net Earnings for the Year		$ 35,637,000	$ 13,200,000
Primary Earnings Per Share	From operations before extraordinary items	$ 2.06	$ 1.05
	Extraordinary gains (losses)	.04	(.12)
	Net earnings for the year	$ 2.10	$ .93
Fully Diluted Earnings Per Share	From operations before extraordinary items	, $ 2.03	$ .96
	Extraordinary gains (losses)	.04	(.10)
	Net earnings for the year	$ 2.07	$ .86

Statements of Consolidated Retained Earnings		1972	1971
	Balance at beginning of year	$110,256,000	$105,575,000
	Net earnings for the year	35,637,000	13,200,000
		145,893,000	118,775,000
	Deduct dividends on common stock— ($.60 per share in 1972 and 1971)*	9,753,000	8,519,000
	Balance at end of year (Note D)	$136,140,000	$110,256,000

See accompanying notes to consolidated financial statements.

APPENDIX (*Continued*)

Five Year Financial Summary (Dollars in thousands, except per share amounts)

	1972	1971	1970	1969	1968
Revenues					
Broadcasting	$637,349	$528,020	$523,221	$507,807	$454,704
Theatres	105,916	95,887	99,918	94,774	97,627
Records	82,501	87,345	78,074	69,365	49,079
Motion Pictures	14,619	13,320	16,703	18,509	7,683
Publishing and Other	29,064	31,923	30,346	30,469	24,901
	$869,449	$756,495	$748,262	$720,924	$633,994
Earnings (Losses) from Operations Before					
Income Taxes and Extraordinary Items					
Broadcasting	$ 69,644	$ 27,477	$ 26,071	$ 29,407	$ 9,728
Theatres	10,444	9,714	10,120	11,892	14,083
Records	1,001	6,418	3,456	4,622	3,873
Motion Pictures	(11,781)	(15,993)	(8,310)	(7,521)	(2,412)
Publishing and Other	5,304	3,980	3,793	1,256	1,708
	$ 74,612	$ 31,596	$ 35,130	$ 39,656	$ 26,980
Net Earnings					
Operations	$ 35,041	$ 14,940	$ 15,979	$ 17,639	$ 12,679
Extraordinary gains (losses), net	596	(1,740)	818	(878)	3,661
	$ 35,637	$ 13,200	$ 16,797	$ 16,761	$ 16,340
Primary Earnings Per Share					
Operations	$ 2.06	$ 1.05	$ 1.13	$ 1.22	$ .89
Extraordinary gains (losses), net	.04	(.12)	.06	(.06)	.26
	$ 2.10	$ .93	$ 1.19	$ 1.16	$ 1.15
Fully Diluted Earnings Per Share					
Operations	$ 2.03	$ .96	$ 1.04	$ 1.12	$ .85
Extraordinary gains (losses), net	.04	(.10)	.05	(.05)	.23
	$ 2.07	$ .86	$ 1.09	$ 1.07	$ 1.08
Dividends					
Total	$ 9,753	$ 8,519	$ 8,503	$ 7,675	$ 7,581
Per share	$ .60	$ .60	$ .60	$ .54	$ .54
Financial Position at Year End					
Working capital	$206,534	$176,950	$188,225	$177,140	$151,581
Property and equipment, net	151,855	146,925	146,148	133,872	129,024
Total assets	537,031	496,076	479,045	468,419	434,563
Long-term debt	106,669	159,729	177,393	163,101	143,527
Stockholders' equity	264,491	177,515	172,044	163,376	160,286
Number of common shares outstanding					
at year end	16,943,210	14,231,564	14,177,806	14,145,590	14,387,190

APPENDIX (*Continued*)

Consolidated Balance Sheets

Assets		December 30, 1972	January 1, 1972
Current Assets:	Cash	$ 27,142,000	$ 26,869,000
	Marketable securities, at cost (approximate market)	55,334,000	21,803,000
	Receivables, less allowance for doubtful accounts of $4,249,000 in 1972 and $3,456,000 in 1971	119,657,000	113,733,000
	Television and theatrical motion picture rights, production costs and advances, less amortization (Notes A, B and I)	115,974,000	126,037,000
	Inventory of merchandise and supplies, at cost or less	18,795,000	16,315,000
	Prepaid expenses (Note A)	10,833,000	6,901,000
	Total current assets	347,735,000	311,658,000
Investments, less reserve of $3,222,000 in 1972 and $3,868,000 in 1971 (Notes A)		7,528,000	6,541,000
Property and Equipment, at cost (Notes A and B):	Land	28,447,000	29,751,000
	Buildings	71,592,000	71,424,000
	Operating equipment	84,727,000	77,054,000
	Leasehold and leasehold improvements	53,569,000	43,489,000
		238,335,000	221,718,000
	Less—accumulated depreciation and amortization	86,480,000	74,793,000
	Property and equipment—net	151,855,000	146,925,000
Other Assets:	Intangibles, at cost (Note A)	22,859,000	22,859,000
	Deferred charges	2,550,000	2,249,000
	Other	4,504,000	5,844,000
	Total other assets	29,913,000	30,952,000
Total Assets		$537,031,000	$496,076,000

See accompanying notes to consolidated financial statements.

APPENDIX (*Continued*)

Liabilities and Stockholders' Equity		December 30, 1972	January 1, 1972
Current Liabilities:	Accounts payable and accrued expenses	$113,261,000	$105,878,000
	Federal income taxes (Note A)	25,902,000	13,358,000
	Loans payable within one year (Note B)	2,038,000	15,472,000
	Total current liabilities	141,201,000	134,708,000
Long-Term Liabilities:	5% convertible subordinated debentures (Note B)	—	49,969,000
	Loans payable (Note B)	106,669,000	109,760,000
	Other (Note A)	19,084,000	18,632,000
	Total long-term liabilities	125,753,000	178,361,000
Deferred Income		5,586,000	5,492,000
	Total liabilities	272,540,000	318,561,000
Stockholders' Equity			
	Common stock, par value $1 per share, authorized 30,000,000 shares	17,443,000	7,367,000
	Capital in excess of par value	117,871,000	67,372,000
	Retained earnings	136,140,000	110,256,000
		271,454,000	184,995,000
	Less—common stock held in treasury, at cost	6,963,000	7,480,000
	Total stockholders' equity	264,491,000	177,515,000

Commitments and Contingent Liabilities (Note I).

Total Liabilities and Stockholders' Equity	$537,031,000	$496,076,000

APPENDIX (*Continued*)

Notes to Consolidated Financial Statements

Note A: Summary of Significant Accounting Policies:

Consolidation: The consolidated financial statements include the accounts of American Broadcasting Companies, Inc. and its majority-owned domestic subsidiaries. Substantially all investments in other companies which are at least twenty percent owned are reported at cost plus equity in undistributed earnings. The remaining investments are stated at cost less applicable reserves. All significant intercompany transactions are eliminated in consolidation.

Television and Theatrical Motion Picture Rights, Production Costs and Advances:
Television program rights, production costs and advances primarily represent amounts paid less amortization based on usage for network programs and rental periods for local station programs. Management estimates that a major portion of the costs will be charged to operations within one year and substantially all of the remaining balance in the subsequent year.

Theatrical motion picture costs are stated at the lower of cost or estimated realizable value. Amortization of these costs is based on the estimated flow of income. When it is determinable, based on such estimates, that a motion picture will result in an ultimate loss, the entire loss is reflected immediately.

The composition of inventory values is as follows:

	December 30, 1972	January 1, 1972
Television program rights, production costs and advances	$ 90,099,000	$ 83,411,000
Theatrical motion picture costs	25,875,000	42,626,000
Total	$115,974,000	$126,037,000

Depreciation: Property and equipment is depreciated principally on a straight-line basis for financial reporting over the estimated useful lives of the various classes of depreciable assets. Properties acquired after 1967 are depreciated on an accelerated basis for tax purposes where permitted and the resulting reduction in current tax liabilities is classified as deferred income taxes.

Leasehold improvements are amortized on a straight-line basis over the period of the lease or over the estimated life of the improvements, whichever is shorter.

Intangibles: Intangibles as shown in the accompanying balance sheets represent the excess of cost over underlying net tangible assets at dates of acquisition of companies, all of which occurred prior to 1970. Such intangibles are currently considered to be of continuing value and, therefore, are not being amortized.

Income Taxes: Income tax expense differs from amounts currently payable because certain items are reported in the statement of consolidated earnings in periods which differ from those in which they are subject to taxation. The principal differences in timing between statement of consolidated earnings and taxable income involve (a) future tax benefits arising from audit and settlement of Federal income taxes through fiscal year 1964, and certain accrued costs deducted from income in the financial statements but deferred for tax purposes, and (b) deferred taxes payable arising from depreciation expense reported on a straight-line basis in the financial statements and on an accelerated basis for tax purposes. Deferred tax items are classified as current or non-current according to the classification of the related asset or liability. At December 30, 1972, net estimated future tax benefits of $9,499,000 are classified as prepaid expenses and net deferred taxes payable of $1,974,000 are included in other long-term liabilities in the accompanying balance sheet. Similiar amounts at January 1, 1972 were $5,365,000 and $908,000, respectively.

Investment tax credits are accounted for on the "flow-through" method.

Pension Plans: The unfunded past service costs of the Company's contributory retirement plans are amortized over a period of thirty years commencing in 1965. It is the Company's policy to fund pension cost accrued.

Note B: Debt: In 1972, the Company's 5% convertible subordinated debentures due July 1, 1993 were called for redemption at 104¼ %. Debentures in the amount of $49,715,000 were tendered for conversion into 1,145,771 shares of common stock at

APPENDIX (*Concluded*)

$43.33 per share (before the two for one split) and cash in lieu of fractional shares.

	December 30, 1972	January 1, 1972
Debentures:		
5% convertible subordinated debentures	$ —	$ 49,969,000
Loans:		
4.55% notes payable semi-annually $1,625,000 to January 1, 1985 and $10,750,000 on July 1, 1985.	$ 49,750,000	$ 53,000,000
7% subordinated notes less unamortized debt discount of $3,386,000 with purchase warrants and options expiring January 2, 1982 for the purchase of 833,332 shares of the Company's common stock at a price of $24 per share. Notes are payable $2,940,000 on January 1 in each of the years 1976 to 1991 inclusive and the balance on January 1, 1992.	46,614,000	—
Bank loans, secured by motion picture film rights, at prime rate plus ½ of 1% per annum, paid during 1972.	—	23,250,000
Bank loans at prime rate plus ¼ of 1% per annum, paid on February 24, 1972.	—	32,500,000
First leasehold secured note payable in quarterly installments with interest at 7½% per annum commencing in 1973 and the remaining balance on January 1, 1997.	12,000,000	9,000,000
Other mortgages and loans payable at various interest rates and maturity dates.	343,000	7,482,000
Total loans payable	108,707,000	125,232,000
Less current installments	2,038,000	15,472,000
Total long-term loans payable	$106,669,000	$109,760,000

Aggregate maturities of long-term loans payable for the five years subsequent to December 30, 1972 were as follows:

Year	1973	1974	1975	1976	1977
Amount	$2,038,000	$3,444,000	$6,399,000	$6,415,000	$6,433,000

Note I: Commitments and Contingent Liabilities: The Company is liable under real property leases in effect at December 30, 1972 for minimum annual rentals totaling $8,233,000 of which $1,610,000 relates to leases expiring before 1976, $2,511,000 to leases expiring during 1976-1980, $1,616,000 to leases expiring during 1981-1990, and $2,496,000 to those expiring after 1990. Total rent, including rentals based on percentage of revenues, charged to operations in 1972 amounted to $9,260,000 and $8,884,000 in 1971.

Under contracts covering rentals of feature films for future telecast, the Company is obligated for payments aggregating approximately $108,000,000 during the next five years.

There are contingent liabilities under pending litigation including antitrust suits. However, in the opinion of counsel, the Company will not suffer any material liability in connection therewith.

(Notes incomplete: See 1972 Annual Report, American Broadcasting Companies, Inc.)

10

Computer and Office Equipment

DAVID R. HATHAWAY
Vice President, Director of Technology Research
G. A. Saxton & Co., Inc.
New York, New York

THE electronic data processing and reprographics industries are unique in the annals of American industry. In less than two decades both have become major segments of the international marketplace and neither gives any indication of maturation or significant slackening in rate of expansion. While there are notable dissimilarities between the two industries, the parallels are remarkable as well. For instance, both industries owe their preeminent stature largely to the foresight and skill of two corporations—International Business Machines and Xerox— which, in turn, have become multinational giants and dominant powers within their respective markets. Both industries have benefited from the exploitation of technology, especially the field of electronic componentry. Both demand enormous financial resources, in terms of capital outlays, for rental equipment and continuing expenditures on research and development and marketing and support. Finally, both are largely immune to the cyclicality and perturbations of normal economic growth.

Despite these and many other similarities, the circumstances which surround the data processing and reprographics industries are sufficiently different to warrant separate discussion in this chapter.

ELECTRONIC DATA PROCESSING INDUSTRY

Historical Perspective

It has become increasingly difficult to discuss data processing as a single industry. The computer has penetrated and continues to penetrate every element of our economic framework. Certain areas have emerged as particularly attractive avenues of growth: data communications and transmission; data collection and reduction; time sharing; data processing services; and special purpose industrial/commercial applications. While it is widely acknowledged that the EDP marketplace has been the most rapidly growing segment of the U.S. economy for the past 15–20 years, accurate measurement of that growth has been problematical. Primarily due to IBM's historic dominance, there have been no reliable market statistics by which to measure the industry's expansion. While IBM's revenue growth (19 percent compounded for the past decade) provides a useful proxy for the industry's growth, the increasing differentiation of submarkets will make this measurement less satisfactory in the future. Similarly, the dramatic increase in the number of companies deriving revenues from the EDP industry (1,733 in 1970 as compared with 13 in 1952) and the growth in EDP revenues ($48 million in 1952 to more than $15 billion in 1972) simply reflect the tremendous expansion in demand, without providing a precise measurement of growth.

The pace of technological change that has characterized this industry has been staggering, and it gives no sign of abating. In 20 years, IBM has introduced more than 600 products and freely licensed over 10,000 patents. The first commercially built EDP system, the UNIVAC I, was delivered in 1951 to the Bureau of the Census. By comparison, one of IBM's most advanced systems, the System/370 Model 168 which was announced in August 1972, has approximately 700 times the real memory capacity, executes addition more than 4,300 times faster, multiplication more than 3,100 times faster, and division more than 2,000 times faster than the UNIVAC I but costs less than 7 times as much. Such strides in the price/performance ratio have been made possible by innovation in electronic component technology. During the next five to ten years, we can expect even greater advances in technology to be introduced.

Industry Structure

Definition of Industry. The data processing industry is worldwide in scope. The absence of reliable statistics on all the industry participants complicates the task of measuring market size. Consequently, a considerable amount of estimating is required. These estimates must be founded on field surveys and extensive research at the user level. On this basis, the worldwide data processing industry surpassed $15 billion in revenues in 1972, with a further 17 percent growth in 1973 to $17.6 billion.

A typical general purpose computer system consists of several component parts: (1) the central processing unit (CPU) or mainframe;

(2) main memory; and (3) input/output devices such as disk drives, tape drives, printers, card readers, and terminals. Depending on the size of the system and the application, the CPU and main memory normally account for 50–70 percent of the system's value, with the balance being peripheral devices. In addition to hardware, however, operating software and applications programs are required in order for the system to function.

The key segments of the industry are:

1. General purpose systems, including minicomputers;
2. Peripheral equipment;
3. Data processing services, including contract programming; and
4. Data processing supplies.

Of these, the most rapidly growing market segment for the past few years has been minicomputers, defined as basic processor configurations with a sales value below $25,000. This definition does not include peripheral equipment which can increase the value of a minicomputer system to in excess of $100,000. This definition would incorporate all Digital Equipment Corporation's current product line, with the exception of the large-scale PDP-10. The total estimated market for minicomputers (including peripheral equipment) approached $600 million in 1972 and is growing at a 30–35 percent annual rate. These computers have found widespread use in research, education, medical, and process control applications. In contrast to the more general purpose applications of larger, commercially oriented systems, minicomputers can often be thought of as serving a dedicated application.

There is considerable overlap of participants between the different segments identified above. In addition, with the present trends of technology, there is a tendency for the hardware portions of the market to merge. Consequently, the lines of division are not precise. The major portion of data processing industry revenues accrue to the systems manufacturers, as shown in Table 1.

Estimates of IBM's market share vary widely. Clearly, IBM is the dominant industry factor, regardless of the standard of measurement. In addition to data processing revenues (which understate IBM's position to a certain extent due to the generally higher mix of rental revenues than is the case with its competitors), a useful measurement of market power is the value of installed equipment in view of the rental nature of the marketplace. On this basis, IBM's share is approximately 65 percent, with Sperry Rand (Univac) and Honeywell having 9 percent and 7 percent respectively.

The International Market. The non-U.S. portion of the data-processing market has grown more rapidly than the U.S. portion for the past several years. This is generally attributed to a lower level of maturation and sophistication in the use of computers. The lag varies between two

TABLE 1

Data Processing Industry—1972 Revenues (in $ millions)

	Estimated 1972 EDP Revenues	*Percent Total*
International Business Machines Corp	$ 7,530	50
Honeywell (Honeywell Information Systems)	1,060	7
Sperry Rand (Univac)	985	7
Burroughs	675	4
Control Data	670	4
International Computers, Ltd	370	2
Siemens	350	2
Fujitsu, Limited	340	2
Compagnie Internationale pour l'Informatique	260	2
Hitachi	250	2
NCR	250	2
Digital Equipment Corp	215	1
Nippon Electric Company (NEC)	210	1
Philips Gloeilampenfabrieken	150	1
Nixdorf Computer Corporation	130	1
Xerox (Xerox Data Systems)	70	–
Other	1,635	11
Total	$15,150	100

Note: Revenue comparisons between companies are not strictly comparable due to difference in accounting policies concerning revenue recognition.

Sources: Estimates of G. A. Saxton & Co., Inc. Based, in part, on published information where available. Foreign currency values translated at average exchange rates.

to five years, depending on the country, with the more industrialized nations of Western Europe and Japan being the most advanced foreign countries in computer applications. Demand is expected to grow at a more rapid rate outside the United States over the next several years as this gap continues to narrow. In contrast with a projected 12–14 percent annual growth in demand in the United States, foreign demand is expected to grow at a 16–17 percent rate.

Approximately 39 percent of the computers installed worldwide (as measured on a value basis) are installed outside the United States. The development of foreign markets has largely been due to the U.S. manufacturers, although there are local competitors as indicated above. IBM operates in 114 foreign countries, with West Germany, France, the United Kingdom, Italy, Canada, and Japan being IBM's largest markets outside the United States. As a measure of importance, IBM's foreign operations (IBM World Trade Corporation) contributes approximately 47 percent of IBM's total revenues and in excess of 50 percent of total profits. In 1973, IBM World Trade Corporation's total revenues exceeded $5.1 billion.

The foreign markets are also of considerable importance to the other American manufacturers, although their respective penetration and market positions are not uniform across all markets as is the case with IBM. In general, however, the non-IBM U.S. manufacturers have fared better against IBM outside the United States. Burroughs (in the United Kingdom), Honeywell (in France), and Univac (in Japan especially but also throughout Western Europe) have market positions that are greater than their respective U.S. shares. In addition, throughout Europe and Japan, IBM is confronted with indigenous competition which often has local government support. Despite this, IBM's market share in non-U.S. markets generally exceeds 50 percent (as measured by value of installed equipment), with the two major exceptions being Japan and the United Kingdom where IBM's shares of market are approximately 24 percent and 38 percent respectively.

Economic Nationalism. Growing sensitivity to American dominance of the worldwide computer industry has led to government sponsorship of local computer manufacturers throughout Europe and especially in Japan. The constraints on American manufacturers have been most overt in Japan where the Japanese government supplies capital (Japan Electronic Computer Company, Ltd., a government-sponsored joint venture which leases all Japanese manufactured systems to users) and technical direction and limits the participation of foreign (that is, non-Japanese) manufacturers. The official agency of the Japanese government that controls the Japanese computer industry is the Ministry of International Trade and Industry (MITI). Its policies have sheltered the Japanese industry from U.S. domination. IBM, Univac, and NCR actually manufacture in Japan, with the remaining U.S. manufacturers having technological ties, joint ventures with Japanese computer companies, and relying on trading companies to handle the marketing. As a consequence, the six Japanese computer manufacturers (NEC, Fujitsu, Hitachi, Toshiba, OkiDenki, and Mitsubishi Electric) supply approximately 70 percent of the small- and medium-scale computers installed in Japan. Since 1966, the "foreign" share (including computers manufactured in Japan by U.S.-based companies) has declined from 63 percent of the total value of computers installed to approximately 43 percent presently. The only market segment where "foreign" manufacturers have a dominant position is in large-scale systems with a 54 percent share. The rapid growth and size of the Japanese market (the installed base, in terms of value, is approximately one seventh the size of that of the United States), however, have meant that the U.S. manufacturers have prospered in Japan despite these constraints.

In Western Europe, the impact of economic nationalism has been less noticeable due to the absence of cooperation (until recently) between the various countries. Rather, government sponsorship has been manifest primarily in research and development contracts and favored status for the local manufacturer in government installations. Consequently, European manufacturers are strong only in their home countries. Recent efforts to develop cooperative ventures and joint marketing arrangements must cut across local nationalism in order to be successful.

Thus, the competitive environment outside the United States is considerably more complex than the one which exists within the United States. It is essential to recognize the heterogeneous mix of economies, markets, and political considerations which are markedly in contrast with the more homogeneous U.S. framework.

Factors Affecting Growth of Industry

Although the growth of the general purpose computer hardware industry has been universally recognized, the sources of that growth have been the subject of considerable speculation. While macroeconomic factors, especially capital goods expenditures, have played a meaningful role in the expansion of the industry, other, noneconomic factors such as "product cycles" and the pace of technological change have been more important determinants of growth on a year-to-year basis. Longer term, there are several factors which will influence the industry's development:

1. Technological change and progress
2. New applications and market opportunities
3. Economic considerations and budgetary constraints
4. Management understanding
5. Availability of skilled personnel

Short-term Factors. Over the short term (2–3 years), the growth in demand for computer hardware adheres to a fairly predictable growth rate. There are three factors which explain this rate of growth (defined as the gross sales value of computer system shipments, since this coincides most closely with the physical production process and, therefore, with demand):

1. The level of general economic activity;
2. The effect of technological progress; and
3. The effect of the "product cycle."

Economic Factors. The relationship between the activity of the general economy and the activity of the computer industry was largely discounted until the recession of 1970–1971 coincided with the end of a product cycle. The rental nature of the industry was thought to render it "recession resistant." During 1970–1971, however, IBM and other manufacturers experienced a sharp drop-off in new orders; and IBM, especially, a high level of discontinuances of previously rented equipment.

Using the technique of regression analysis, it is possible to identify the correlation between the economy and the shipments of computer hardware. Letting S represent the year-to-year growth of computer shipments and letting M represent the year-to-year growth of a chosen macroeconomic indicator, the relationship to be regressed is:

$$S = a + b(M)$$

Where: a = average growth due to factors other than M; b = coefficient of economic growth (M); and a and b are calculated in the regression analysis.

The highest correlation is obtained using real investment in producers' durable goods, the wholesale price of durables being used as the deflator from money to real terms. The results were $S = .1275 + 1.397(M)$. This means that 12.75 percent of the growth of computer system shipments was not explained by the real investment in producers' durables and, therefore, not subject to the normal cyclical influences of the economy. Out of the total 21.75 percent average yearly growth of shipments, the remaining 9 percent is, therefore, explained by the chosen economic indicator—in this case, real investment producers' durable goods. Clearly, this is a significant factor when attempting to predict the growth of hardware shipments. The following graph (Fig. 1) shows the actual system shipments compared with the shipments which would be pre-

FIGURE 1

Annual Growth of Computer Shipments (actual and predicted)

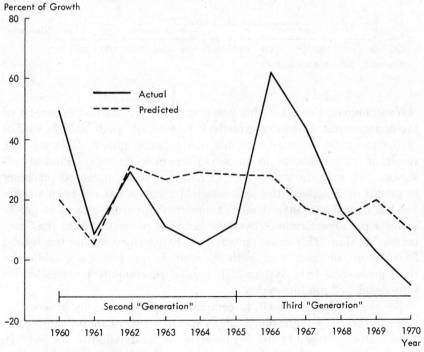

Source: G. A. Saxton & Co., Inc.

dicted by the above regression formula, pointing out that factors exogenous to real economic growth played a significant role in determining industry growth.

That the predicted results do not correspond exactly to actual shipments is not unexpected. The formula was designed only to separate out the economic effects, leaving the other (unexplained) effects lumped together in an average 12.75 percent per year growth. By computing the difference between actual shipments and predicted shipments year by year, we obtain an extremely interesting time series, as shown in Figure 2.

FIGURE 2

Difference between Actual and Predicted Computer Shipment Growth

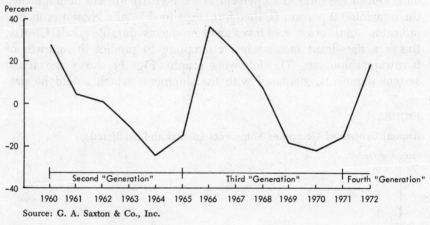

Source: G. A. Saxton & Co., Inc.

Noneconomic Factors. This graph must be viewed in the context of the noneconomic sources of growth. It is generally postulated in studies of the computer industry that this noneconomic growth is largely the result of improvements in price/performance through technical advances. Yet, with the appearance of new and more advanced machines in groups or "families," this technological progress has not been smooth but has moved in spurts. A new "generation" provides a large improvement in price/performance over the last, but progress within the "generation" is slow. This situation was only half-formed during the second "generation" of computers, with its multiple product lines, while the third generation IBM System/360 "family" of computers represented a fully developed product cycle.

So, essentially the growth of computer shipments can be broken into three factors. The regression formula specifies two of these factors. The third factor, pictured in the Figure 2, is the modulation of the average noneconomic growth into the product cycle. A reasonably accurate formula to describe shipment growth, on an annual basis, over the past 11 years would thus be:

$$S = (.1275 + PCE) + 1.397(M),$$

where *PCE* is the "product cycle effect." Note that this effect is a modulation of noneconomic growth around its average, caused by the distortions in the process of technical change in the computer industry. As such, the sum of all the "product cycle effects" is zero.

In order to refine further this analysis, it is necessary to approximate mathematically the product cycle effect which is shown in the Figure 2. The function (P) selected was $\cos(\pi y/4)$, with y cycling from 0 to 5 and then returning to 0 again. This function has the advantage of reaching its minimum in the fourth year of the cycle and then jumping from a low level in the last year of a cycle to a very high level in the next year, as shown in Table 2. This regression was performed with the following results:

$$S = 0.110 + 1.867M + 0.259(P)$$

with R-square = .937;
standard error of regression = 0.064.

TABLE 2

Year	y	Value of P	
1960	0	1.0	
1961	1	0.7	
1962	2	0	Second generation
1963	3	−0.7	
1964	4	−1.0	
1965	5	0.7	
1966	0	1.0	
1967	1	0.7	
1968	2	0	Third generation
1969	3	−0.7	
1970	4	−1.0	

Thus, the product cycle appears to have a definite effect upon shipment growth. The deviation of noneconomic factors from their average coincides exactly with hardware generations. By 1960, volume shipments of second-generation machines were underway. In 1963 and 1964, there was a lull as new product production was limited to refined and improved models of older machines. When the IBM System/360 began volume shipments in late 1965, the cycle turned around. Volume shipments throughout 1966 and 1967 kept the cycle high. Delivery schedules for IBM systems were nearly two years long. By 1968, a new plateau had been reached. The firms which could profitably employ computers with third-generation price/performance had apparently done so. In 1969 and 1970, the bottom of the cycle had again been reached, with new products limited to improved older models. Similarly, the surge in shipments in late 1972 and throughout 1973 reflects the favorable coincidence of a favorable part of the product cycle with a strong economic recovery.

Long-Term Factors. In this section, five factors which will determine the long-term growth of the industry are assessed. While each is analyzed separately in this section, all are closely interrelated. Of the five, two (technological progress and new applications development) clearly exert positive influences on the growth of demand, while two (economic and budgetary considerations and skilled personnel) may introduce a dampening effect on growth. The influence of the fifth factor (management understanding) will be a function of a particular manufacturer's marketing prowess.

Technological Change and Progress. As discussed above, rapid technological progress in the design and operation of computer systems has been a key ingredient in the growth of the computer industry over the past two decades, both as a determinant of year-to-year trends and aggregate demand over the long term. The most dramatic examples of technological progress have been catalogued into families of products which were commonly called "generations." Even greater advances in technology are expected over the next five to ten years. The Large Scale Integration (LSI) of semiconductor components is the seminal development which permits projections of dramatic improvements of the cost/performance ratio in computer systems over the years ahead. Published papers from the IBM Research Laboratories indicate that component costs may drop by factors of five to ten by 1976–1977 from those of equivalent functional ability today. Table 4 shows the expected densities and expected costs of several types of LSI hardware. The table also reflects the sensitivity of cost to production quantities. The costs are projected to be attainable in the mid-1970s.

The practical effect of the projected costs shown in Table 3 may be demonstrated in the following comparison (Table 4) of the component

TABLE 3

Future Component Technology

Semiconductor Hardware	Circuits or Bits per Chip	Mfg. Cost* per Circuit or Cell Chip Production Quantities		
		10	100	10,000
Read-only memories	64,000	0.16	0.02	0.008
Random-access memories	16,000	0.66	0.09	0.032
Logic circuits	2,000	13.00	1.50	0.260

* Cost expressed in cents.
Source: IBM T. J. Watson Research Center and estimates of G.A. Saxton & Co., Inc.

costs of a large-scale computer central-processing unit in 1970 versus the late 1970s:

TABLE 4

Comparison of Component Costs

	1970		Late 1970s	
	Cost	Percent of Total	Cost	Percent of Total
Main memory (1 MB)....	$120,000	35	$2,400	4
Special memories.......	40,000	11	2,000	3
Logic circuits..........	50,000	15	2,600	4
Special circuits........	20,000	6	8,000	12
Packaging.............	30,000	9	10,000	15
Power and cooling......	30,000	9	15,000	23
Other.................	50,000	15	25,000	39
	$340,000	100	$65,000	100

Source: IBM T. J. Watson Research Center and estimates of G. A. Saxton & Co., Inc.

For comparison purposes, no functional redesign of the system was assumed. However, the reduction of the cost of logic and memories to 11 percent of the total from the previous 62 percent clearly indicates the strategy of including significant additional functional capability in the systems of the future, rather than just reducing the total price. As will be discussed later, the added functions will be designed to make systems more reliable and easier to use by low-skilled and untrained people.

The most likely implications of lower-cost memory is that future computer memory capacity will be significantly larger. In the past, because memory was the most expensive of the system resources, considerable overhead in the form of special processor design, operating systems software, input/output access methods, and user programming time, was spent in attempting to conserve memory utilization. If memory is available to users at, say, $300 per megabyte per month in the future, the data processing function could be carried out in a much simpler and more orderly way. By comparison, the current cost of a megabyte of memory on the 370/168 is $5,200 per month.

This dramatic decline in the cost of main memory has myriad implications for future growth of the industry. Main memories large enough to contain all programs and frequently used data could greatly improve the operating characteristics of interactive, on-line systems applications. Response times could be improved because mechanical file accesses would be reduced. Programming would be simpler because the logic required to manage the movement of program segments into and out of main memory would be eliminated. Other ways in which larger main memories could improve the operations of computer systems are: providing faster checkpoint and restart capabilities, more tables and indices for complex data base structuring, more memory available for queueing input/output messages, and more resident service programs for on-line hardware maintenance.

New Applications and Market Opportunities. Although the future growth of the computer industry will be influenced by continued penetration of traditional (that is, clerical or bookkeeping) applications, expansion beyond that associated with general economic growth must come from new applications made possible by the reduced costs of computing brought about by technological change. In the most general sense, computer applications can be divided into two types: (1) clerical or reporting functions and (2) operational or decision-making functions. To date, the vast majority of applications performed fall into the "clerical or bookkeeping" category, such as payroll, accounts receivable, inventory, demand deposit, and so forth. The common denominator among these applications is that all are performed after the transaction or event takes place.

The second general group of applications (operational or decision making) is expected to gain increasing acceptance in the future. Unlike clerical applications, utilization of a computer in an operational environment implies the computer process takes place *before* the subject event or transaction. Examples of this type of application are forecasting, scheduling, and process control. A second characteristic of this set of applications is the requirement to look outside the process itself and to consider ambient factors. Automation and forecasting also involve sensing, feedback, and control. These requirements impose severe demands on computer systems in terms of memory capacity, communications capability, and system reliability.

Economic Considerations and Budgeting Constraints. As computers move more into operational applications, it will become increasingly difficult to measure their benefits in terms of "cost displacement." Rather, benefits derived from the newer applications will be measured in terms of improved return on investment and asset management. While such benefits are perhaps less tangible and clearly are more difficult to measure than in the case of "cost displacement," there are, nonetheless, growing economic pressures to accelerate the pace of new applications development. Field surveys of computer users indicate three major reasons for continuing growth in demand for computers: (1) new applications; (2) management demand for more information; and (3) increasing volume of business.

As discussed earlier, the sensitivity of EDP demand to economic perturbations has been the subject of considerable speculation. Our studies have indicated that a major portion of demand for data processing is related to noneconomic factors. A significant number of domestic users (28 percent) contacted during the trough of the 1969–1970 recession, however, indicated that the state of the economy had a negative effect on their EDP progress.

Skilled Personnel. The critical factor on the growth of the computer industry has persistently been the shortage of adequately trained programmers and operators. This manifests itself in the failure of software to keep pace with hardware. Following the introduction of System/360 by IBM in 1964, enormous delays were encountered in computer deliveries and acceptance as a result of problems with the 360 Operating System. This compounded the problem of conversion from the second generation to the third generation, resulting in the majority of third-generation systems being run in an emulation mode well into the late 1960s.

Persistent problems with software efficiency and compatibility have led to a more rapid rate of gain in personnel expenditures than in hardware expenditures over the past decade. During the 1960s, the number of EDP employees (at user sites) increased at an 8 percent compound rate which, combined with wage and fringe benefit increases, resulted in personnel expenditures accounting for approximately 40–45 percent of the typical computer user's budget, as compared with 35–38 percent for hardware. Five years ago the percentages were almost exactly reversed.

Consequently, while this is a potential limiting factor in growth, it also can be regarded as an opportunity for the systems manufacturers. Much of the expected technological improvement discussed earlier is aimed at making the computer "easier to use." As the price/performance ratio of systems continues to improve, hardware becomes a less scarce (and less expensive) resource than personnel. For this shift in balance to come about, however, the industry must continue to make progress in the fields of high-level (and problem-oriented) languages and generalized application packages, both of which will alleviate the programming bottleneck. In addition, progress in the fields of intelligent data bases, automatic programming, and artificial intelligence will help move the industry toward this goal.

Management Understanding. As the computer shifts from an (essentially) accounting workload to broader usage in operational functions, a broad view of the role of data processing becomes more critical. Although this awareness is increasing gradually among the upper echelons of corporate management, continued progress on this front is essential in order to foster new applications growth in the years ahead. Education in the use of computers is becoming much more common in colleges and even in high schools. As the "mystique" of computer use is removed from future management discussions, three results are predictable: (1) New applications will be chosen which have the greatest return on investment for the enterprise as a whole; (2) computers will be used in ways which cannot be foreseen today; and (3) executives will understand computers better and will demand higher quality results from EDP managers. This may result in increased demand for the more sophisticated applications over the long run. In the interim, however, the generally low level of top management familiarity with computer-aided management techniques will shift the burden of proof in justifying a new installation to the marketing prowess of a particular manufacturer's sales organization. In essence, this represents little change from the environment which has prevailed over the past decade.

New Markets

Eastern Europe. For the past several years, U.S. computer manufacturers have viewed the Eastern European countries (including Russia) as a potentially huge market. This interest had been further spurred by the stress on automation and EDP equipment in the current Five-year Plan of COMECON ("Council for Mutual Assistance," a loose economic association of the Eastern European countries). The plan calls for increased population of 15,000 computers between 1971 and 1975.

Despite this demand, several obstacles must be overcome:

1. Export controls in most Western countries are quite limiting in the area of strategic goods.
2. Eastern European countries lack large amounts of free foreign exchange.
3. The Soviet manufacturing facilities lack proven capability.
4. The nonscientific user in the Soviet Union is unsophisticated and lacks the stimulus of the aggressive U.S. style computer salesman.

In addition, the Soviets have stressed their preference for establishing joint production ventures with Western computer manufacturers. The most recent (April 1973) formal joint venture was between Control Data and Romania for a peripherals manufacturing plant (card readers, card punches, and line printers).

Legal Considerations

Given the industry's dynamic growth and its dominance by IBM, the computer industry analyst must be thoroughly familiar with U.S. antitrust laws. IBM has been confronted with government antitrust suits at three different times (1936, 1952, and 1969). In addition, with the accelerating trend toward private antitrust suits in recent years, IBM has been faced with 12 private antitrust suits since 1968. Although many were settled out of court, two have come to trial. In addition, the important Justice Department suit is scheduled to come to trial after December 2, 1974.

U.S. Antitrust Law. The controlling laws in most antitrust cases are the Sherman Act of 1890, the Federal Trade Commission Act of 1914, and the Clayton Act of 1914. The majority of antitrust actions against IBM have come under the Sherman Act. Section 1 of the Sherman Act covers business "conduct" or "behavior" and is aimed at unlawful restraints of trade in the form of a "contract, combination . . . or conspiracy." Section 2 is normally viewed as a supplement to Section 1, and is an all-inclusive prohibition of monopoly and attempt to monopolize. The issue of monopoly power turns on the determination of the "relevant market." This is usually argued in "percent of the market" terms. In general, courts feel fairly comfortable with a monopoly ruling if a defendant can be found to have a market share of 75–80 percent or more. A market share of 50 percent generally requires evidence of "intent to monopolize" or some other evidence of illegal action. A market share below 50 percent normally is not a monopoly. In antitrust cases, however, the definition of market is subject to gerrymander and manipulation on both sides. Plaintiff normally argues for an extremely narrow market, while the defendant does the opposite.

United States v. IBM. Although numerous private antitrust suits have been filed against IBM in the past four years, the Department of Justice suit filed on the last business day of the Johnson administration in 1969 represents the most serious threat. The relief requested by the Department of Justice in its Preliminary Memorandum on Relief, dated October 16, 1972, would, if granted, result in a significant restructuring of the U.S. data processing industry. The government stressed the need for divestiture in order to create "several discrete, separate, independent, and competitively balanced entities. . . ."

The possible ramifications of such an outcome are innumerable. It is clear, however, that a more fragmented industry would require some external (government) standard setter, a function heretofore performed by IBM setting de facto industry standards that have fostered rapid growth in the use of computers. Although the implications of government involvement are unclear, in other industries it has tended to inhibit rapid change which accompanies high growth.

Cost and Profitability Factors

Although the data processing industry has experienced rapid growth in terms of revenues, consistent and satisfactory profitability has been more elusive. While IBM has enjoyed pretax margins in excess of 20 percent (the range for the past ten years is 24.3 percent to 27.7 percent) and a return on equity of almost 20 percent, the other U.S. manufacturers have experienced more marginal performance. Only Burroughs and Digital Equipment have pretax margins above 10 percent. This disparity, in part, reflects IBM's dominance and greater economies of scale, but it also indicates the underlying cost structure which characterizes this industry.

Cost Structure. Unlike most other manufacturing industries, data processing is heavily rental oriented. As a result, cash flow, rather than reported profitability, is a more useful measurement of operating performance. Cash flow, in turn, is determined by depreciation of the installed rental base and profitability. Given the rental nature of the industry, profitability is a function of: (1) the initial investment in a product (development, manufacturing, marketing, and so forth); (2) continuing expenses in the areas of support, maintenance, and refurbishment; and (3) product life measured in rental months. The most important variables affecting the last-named factor are technological obsolescence and the rate of new product introductions. The earlier discussion on product cycles mentioned the periodicity of new product introductions on a fairly predictable basis. Coming, on average, every five to six years, the normal average product life ranges 60–70 months, although there clearly are innumerable exceptions.

Consequently, the cost structure of companies must be viewed over a sufficient length of time to eliminate the distortions inherent in cost

TABLE 5

Company X—Computer Division (dollar values in thousands)

Computer A-Shipments	Year 1	Year 2	Year 3	Year 4	Year 5
Beginning of year (units)...	—	100	230	400	620
Additions (units)..........	100	130	170	220	285
End of year (units..........	100	230	400	620	905
Average installed (units)....	50	165	315	510	762
Average yearly rental per computer (000)......	$ 156	$ 156	$ 156	$ 156	$ 156
Estimated total annual rentals (000)............	$ 7,800	$25,740	$49,140	$79,560	$118,872
Expenses (000)					
SG & A...................	$12,000	$15,600	$20,400	$26,400	$ 34,200
R & D...................	1,000	3,000	5,000	7,800	12,000
Depreciation..............	4,000	12,200	20,900	30,200	40,160
Other overhead...........	2,000	3,000	4,000	4,000	4,000
Total expenses........	$19,000	$33,800	$50,300	$68,400	$ 90,360
Pretax income (loss).......	(11,200)	(8,060)	(1,160)	$11,160	$ 28,512
Taxes (50 percent rate)....	$ 5,600 cr.	$ 4,030 cr.	$ 580 cr.	$ 5,580	$ 14,256
Net income (loss).........	($ 5,600)	($ 4,030)	$ (580)	$ 5,580	$ 14,256

Assumptions:
1. Computer A-sales value—$600,000
        Book value—$200,000
        Average monthly rental—$13,000
2. One hundred percent lease—no outright sales
3. Shipments increase 30 percent a year
4. Depreciation 4-yr. SYD
5. No deferral of expenses
Note: All dollar amounts are shown with 000's omitted.
Source: G. A. Saxton & Co., Inc.

TABLE 6

Capital Expenditures and Cash Flow Comparisons*

	Year 1	Year 2	Year 3	Year 4	Year 5	Cumulative
			($millions)			
Cash Flow						
Net income (loss)..............	($5.6)	($ 4.0)	($ .6)	$ 5.6	$14.3	$ 9.7
Depreciation..................	4.0	12.2	20.0	30.2	40.2	106.6
Total cash flow...............	($1.6)	$ 8.2	$19.4	$35.8	$54.5	$116.3
Capital Expenditures						
Rental equipment.............	$20	$26	$34	$44	$57	$181
Plant and equipment..........	13	17	23	29	38	120
Total capital expenditures......	$33	$43	$57	$73	$95	$301
Working Capital Deficit........	$34.6	$34.8	$37.6	$37.2	$40.5	$184.7

* Due to the limitations of this presentation, normal working capital requirements have been ignored.
Source: G. A. Saxton & Co., Inc.

and revenue matching for a rental base business over the short term. Tables 5 and 6 are helpful in illustrating these cost profitability and cash flow relationships. Table 5 is the income statement of a hypothetical computer company. Table 6 illustrates the cash flow considerations. It is assumed that this computer company is the division of an established corporation which has other operations and thus has the cash flow necessary to absorb all the research and development expenses necessary to enter the business.

While such an analysis cannot, for obvious reasons, be precise, it does illustrate:

1. The enormous capital investment and continuing cash flow requirements required to build a rental base.
2. The heavy front-end expenses in terms of marketing and product development.
3. The marginal profitability on a cumulative and on an annual basis until Year 5.
4. The marginal cumulative return on equity (7.5 percent after five years, assuming the capital requirements are financed 70/30 equity/debt).

The previous analysis also illustrates the need for manufacturing economies of scale. The assumed 200 percent markup over manufacturing cost results in marginal profitability and return on investment due to the continuing requirement for heavy expenditures on marketing, support, and product development.

Accounting Considerations

Implications of a Rental Base. The cash flow and earnings drain of building a computer rental base have resulted in the use of significant accounting variations which, in turn, often have distorted the comparability of reported earnings. It is generally accepted that IBM follows the most conservative accounting practices. While recent FASB opinions, combined with the general trend toward conservative accounting, have reduced the latitude available to corporate treasurers, variances and discrepancies still exist. The degree of accounting conservation in the industry appears primarily to be a function of two factors: (1) the sales/lease ratio, and (2) the diversification of the company in combination with its ability to throw off significant cash flow to finance the growth of the computer operation. While it can be argued that IBM, with a unique ability to finance growth through the large internal generation of cash flow, has set the industry accounting standards at an excessively conservative level, there clearly were numerous abuses of generally accepted accounting practices in the late 1960s, especially by the smaller companies, in two major areas:

1. Treatment of operating (short term) leases as sales.
2. Deferral of research and development and/or marketing and support costs.

Both had the effect of lessening the margin pressures which accompany the build-up of a rental base. While this, more liberal, accounting approach did not alleviate the continual hunger for capital, the equity markets were more than accommodating.

Deferral of Expense. Control Data, Honeywell, and Sperry Rand (of the major manufacturers) utilize deferral accounting. Control Data presently capitalizes certain product and software development costs, systems applications costs, and marketing expenses relating to operating leases. The costs are amortized over three years. Honeywell and Sperry Rand capitalize hardware engineering expenses for leased computer systems. In addition, Honeywell capitalizes R&D associated with leased computer equipment. The costs are then included in the depreciation of that equipment over a five-year period. While the rationale for this treatment lies in the accounting principle of matching costs and revenues, deferral of such expenses gives rise to potential exposure to unexpected equipment returns. Memorex Corporation's write-off of $90 million of previously capitalized expenses (both research and development and lease acquisition costs) illustrates the risk of this accounting technique in the extreme.

Depreciation. In the area of rental equipment depreciation, the methods utilized (straight line, sum-of-the-years' digits (SYD), and double declining balance), as well as the determination of equipment life, vary widely within the industry. The most conservative practices (followed by IBM) accelerate, or front load, the expenses in the first years. For example, using a four-year useful life, under the SYD method, the charge-off would equal 40 percent of book value; while using straight line, the first-year charge would amount to only 25 percent of the book value. Clearly, in a period of rapid expansion of shipments, the straight-line method would have a lesser immediate impact detrimental to earnings. However by "normalizing" expenses, the swing in profitability of the rental base is rendered less dramatic. In addition, a company's ability to finance the transition from one product cycle to another without adversely affecting earnings is restricted in the absence of the lower depreciation charges in later years which occur under an accelerated method. It should be noted that in most cases where a company is using straight-line depreciation for book purposes, an accelerated method is employed for tax purposes, thereby increasing cash flow through deferred taxes.

Treatment of Leases. The two most common methods of accounting for leases are the operating method and the finance method (including the sale of lease rights). Under an operating lease, the conservative method most often used for short-term leases (generally under four years), the rentals due from such leases are included in revenue as earned over the term of the lease. This results in revenues being substantially understated relative to shipments. On the other hand, the finance method is usually only employed with long-term, noncancellable leases (four or more years). Finance leases are intended to cover the selling price of the equipment, with the aggregate rentals due (less unearned finance, maintenance, service, and other charges) recorded as sales in the period in which the equipment is delivered. This variation shows up on the balance sheet in the long-term receivables account. The finance method not only tends to result in an overstatement of current year's earnings relative to the operating method but distorts the stability of a rental base. Reported earnings instead are more closely related to the shipment level. Again, however, under the finance method, for tax purposes revenue is usually recorded as earned.

Because several companies resorted to selling lease rights and accounting for the transaction in an inappropriate fashion, the Accounting Principles Board issued Opinion No. 27 in November 1972 on "Accounting for Lease Transactions by Manufacturer or Dealer Lessors." This significantly curtailed the practice by setting rigid requirements concerning the remarketing commitment and treatment of lease residuals.

Other Variations. In addition to the previously mentioned variations, there is another area which deserves attention but is more difficult to document. This aspect relates to the timing concerning when rental revenues are initially accrued (at the time of shipment, invoicing, installation, or acceptance of the equipment?) and, subsequently, the initiation of depreciation charges. Related to the above concerns is the recognition of when equipment reaches the work-in-process stage in a rental-base business. If it is transferred directly from the raw materials account to the rental equipment account (as is normal in a lease-oriented business), the current ratio may, in effect, be understated. Depreciation, however, may not be initiated until well after shipment. In other cases, notes to the financial statements may reveal that, for book purposes, sales are recognized upon shipment of products to the customer but before notification of final acceptance. The timing between the two can range from a month to as long as six months.

Several other general accounting areas, which are not necessarily peculiar to office equipment companies, should be watched closely in any analysis. The following list points out some of the more common areas of divergence: the utilization of reserves (both segregated on the balance sheet, as well as hidden in the inventory and accounts receivable accounts); foreign dividends (for example, IBM World Trade); expense recognition on a quarter-to-quarter basis; patent amortization; inventory valuation (FIFO versus LIFO) and overhead absorption; and the method of consolidating or not consolidating subsidiaries (for example, Honeywell's finance subsidiary). Although the impact is difficult to document, each of these last-named accounting options is utilized by the companies in the data processing industry.

Case Study: Memorex Corporation

Memorex Corporation, once a high-flying glamour stock that sported a lofty price/earnings ratio and a high price of $173 per share in 1969, is presently struggling to remain solvent. Its stock is trading around $2 per share. The corporate development of Memorex during this period illustrates many of the issues and factors discussed herein:

1. The continuing requirements for capital associated with building up a rental base.
2. The distortions interjected by utilizing liberal, or nonstandard, accounting practices.
3. The dominance of IBM and resultant impact of pricing changes and new product introductions.

Background. Memorex was founded in 1961 to concentrate in the field of magnetic tape. The first year was focused in researching tape coatings and developing tape manufacturing and process procedures. Memorex surpassed 3M Company in the late 1960s as the leading supplier of magnetic tape to the computer market. In 1967 Memorex entered the equipment business by manufacturing disk drives for original equipment manufacturers (OEMs). The line of peripheral equipment was broadened in 1968 to include microfilm printers and terminals. From

1964 to 1969 Memorex sales increased from $8 million to $74 million.

The Plug Compatible Phenomenon. The key change in Memorex's method of doing business came in 1970 when management shifted from selling basically to OEMs to the end user, bringing the company into direct confrontation with IBM. The primary vehicle was the 2314-type disk drive, a disk subsystem with a total storage capacity of 233 million bytes and originally introduced by IBM in 1965 (first customer shipment did not occur until 1967). The Memorex subsystem was "plug compatible" with IBM's product, meaning it required no hardware or software changes to operate with an IBM computer. It rented for 4 percent less than IBM's product on a monthly basis, although considerably greater discounts (usually in the range of 10–20 percent) were available for longer leases and large installations.

Plug compatible devices became an industry-wide phenomenon and several companies, including Telex Corporation, Century Data Systems, and Marshall Computer, as well as Memorex seized the opportunity of marketing to IBM's captive base of installed peripheral equipment. At their peak in 1972, the plug compatible manufacturers (PCMs) accounted for almost 12,000 installed units and 22 percent of the total installed base, all of this penetration coming at IBM's expense. IBM had terminated new production of its 2314 drive in 1970 and was satisfying demand from returned equipment. The PCM success was based on an ability to:

1. Duplicate IBM's product with a substantially lower investment in product development and marketing where the pioneering had been done by IBM.
2. Attract sufficient capital due to the (then) euphoric state of the stock market (at its peak, Memorex' total market value exceeded $600 million).

The downfall of the PCMs was the result of:

1. The impact of a series of unexpectedly aggressive moves by IBM with regard to pricing of existing products, forcing all PCMs to reduce their own prices, ultimately at or below breakeven in some cases.
2. The PCMs failed to keep pace with technological change and new product advances by IBM.
3. A general move to more conservative accounting policies throughout the industry.

Creative Accounting. Memorex was both the most successful and the least well managed of the PCMs. Its management team, composed largely of former IBM employees, attempted to superimpose a big company mentality on a small enterprise. The company grossly overexpanded beyond the point of prudence. When equity capital no longer was available, debt was added in a wanton, albeit highly creative, fashion.

In order to finance its tremendous growth, Memorex settled on a plan of establishing an independent leasing company (ILC) that would be 10 percent owned by Memorex and the balance owned by institutional investors. Banks would supply medium-term and short-term debt. Total capital raised in this fashion was $142.5 million. For a time, Memorex tried to preserve the best of both worlds by not consolidating ILC and counting sales to ILC as normal commercial transactions, which would result in extremely strong earnings performance. A lawsuit by the SEC terminated this practice. Memorex changed its accounting policies and began treating the transactions as if ILC were "transparent." All leases were then treated as operating leases. Earnings which had been reported as $1.87 per share in 1969 fell to $0.83 per share in 1970, with this decline itself understated due to Memorex' liberal accounting policies with regard to expense deferral. In addition, between the end of 1969 and 1971, long-term debt increased from $22 million to $230 million. At the end of 1971, equity was $30 million. A cash flow analysis of Memorex for 1970 illustrates the problem.

TABLE 7

Cash Flow Analysis (in $ millions)

Sources		*Uses*	
Net income	$3.2	Capital expenditures	$75.1
Depreciation and amortization	9.4	Deferred cost	18.7
Deferred taxes	2.4	Reduction of debt	18.1
Cash flow from operations	$15.0	Increase in working capital	22.4
Additions to long-term debt	129.2	Other	16.7
Sale of common stock	.9		
Other	5.9		
Total	$151.0		$151.0

Initially, the only concession Memorex was willing to make to conservative accounting was use of the operating lease, which was forced upon it by the SEC. Accounting policies employed by Memorex included:

1. Deferral of "lease acquisition and marketing costs" and subsequent amortization over 48 months.
2. Deferral of start up costs associated with building a sales organization.
3. Deferral of research and development costs of products in a preproduction stage and subsequent amortization over 36 months.

Each of these resulted in the overstatement of current earnings since recognition of the expense was deferred until a later period. At the end of 1972, total deferred costs from these sources *exceeded* Memorex' equity base of $32 million. As a result of these accounting practices, rental revenues built up sharply, and the margin pressure normally associated with building up a rental base was postponed by deferring recognition of most of the costs.

Memorex' accounting failed to consider the changing industry environment. An inability to attract new capital precluded Memorex from keeping pace with new technological advances, fostered primarily by IBM. As Memorex' financial position became more precarious, morale worsened and several key employees departed. Finally, in August 1973, Memorex elected to abandon its deferred accounting and also to terminate its planned entry into the computer systems business. Write-offs exceeded $90 million, giving Memorex a negative net worth.

REPROGRAPHICS INDUSTRY

This portion of the chapter will only highlight aspects related to the market structure and competitive environment of the office copying industry. Most of the issues concerning the lack of reliable market data, accounting practices, and profitability that are relevant to the analysis of investments in this industry can be viewed in a framework similar to the one presented earlier.

Historical Perspective

The dominant position which Xerox enjoys today in the office copying market can be traced to patent license and other agreements with Battelle Memorial Institute, beginning in 1947. Prior to 1950, Xerox was known as Haloid Corporation. The agreements with Battelle covered xerography, a technology which permitted the copying of documents by electrostatic means. Xerography had been invented by Chester Carlson in 1938. Prior to the agreement with Battelle in 1944, Carlson offered the process to more than 20 major corporations, including IBM, RCA, and Kodak. From 1960, when the first xerographic copier was introduced, to 1972, Xerox revenues increased more than 43 times.

The Reprographics Market

During the 1960s, the domestic office copying industry experienced dramatic growth of revenues, reaching $2 billion in 1972. The introduction of the first plain-paper copier by Xerox, followed by the proliferation of electrofax (coated paper) copiers (which were designed to compete on a price basis), provided a means to make good-quality copies, conveniently and at a low cost. Growth of the xerographic copying process was at the expense of the earlier, less effective methods (diffusion transfer, dye transfer, and thermofax.) Xerography and electrofax opened up new markets in the 1960s by providing simple, convenient methods of producing high-quality copies. The plain-paper copier is a prime example of a product which has virtually created its own market through introduction of a convenient, simple method to reproduce copies from an original.

The domestic reprographics market can be divided into two distinct segments: office copying and duplicating. The copier segment is defined here as including all copiers from desktops through high-speed consoles to copier/duplicators. The duplicating market includes offset, mimeograph, and spirit processes serving high-volume needs characterized by long runs and low cost per copy.

TABLE 8

Estimated U.S. Copying and Duplicating Market

	Copying		Duplicating		Total Market	
	Volume*	*Dollars† (millions)*	*Volume**	*Dollars† (millions)*	*Volume**	*Dollars† (millions)*
1960...................	2	$ 125	98	$ 750	100	$ 875
1965...................	15	500	200	1,000	215	1,500
1970...................	50	1,500	310	1,250	360	2,750
1975...................	120	3,000	360	1,500	480	4,500
	Annual Compound Growth (percent)					
1960–1965.............	50	32	15	6	17	11
1965–1970.............	27	25	9	5	11	13
1970–1975.............	19	15	3	4	6	10

* Billions of copies.
† Includes equipment sales, rentals, and supplies.
Source: Estimates based on field research performed by G. A. Saxton & Co., Inc.

Virtually all copiers are installed on short-term rental agreements with monthly rentals supplemented by a per copy cost. However, at the low end of the market, most non-Xerox copiers are sold outright.

Industry Structure

There are in excess of 40 office copier companies presently marketing equipment in the United States. Prior to 1970 when IBM introduced a plain-paper copier, Xerox was the only company to manufacture copiers utilizing the process. This position was based in large part on the original xerographic patents. Although some of these have expired, Xerox has established a web of patents that have complicated entry into this market.

Consequently, in terms of revenues Xerox dominates the U.S. office copying market to a greater extent than IBM dominates the EDP industry. However, in terms of machine placements, 3M, due to the large

base of installed thermofax machines, approximately equals Xerox'
base, with roughly 400,000 copiers of all types installed. Xerox also
dominates the foreign office copying markets. However, competition
exists in both Japan and in Europe from local as well as U.S. manufacturers.

TABLE 9

Office Copying Industry—1972 Revenues*
(U.S. only—in $ millions)

	1972 Revenues	Percent of Total
Xerox Corporation.....................	$1,315	66
3M Company.........................	170	9
Apeco...............................	60	3
A. B. Dick Company, Inc...............	50	3
Dennison Manufacturing...............	45	2
Addressograph-Multigraph Corp.........	40	2
Savin Business Machines Corp..........	35	2
SCM Corp...........................	35	2
Pitney-Bowes........................	30	1
Saxon Industries.....................	30	1
Other...............................	170	9
	$1,980	100

* Including supplies.
Source: Estimates of G. A. Saxton & Co., Inc. Based, in part, on published
information, where available.

11

Containers

CLARENCE W. BROWN
Senior Investment Analyst
H. C. Wainwright & Co., New York, New York

THE CONTAINER INDUSTRY is frequently defined to include all forms of packaging materials such as metal cans, glass bottles and jars, plastic containers, flexible films, collapsible tubes, paper bags and boxes, and a wide variety of component materials such as closures, labels, and adhesives. This chapter, however, will deal principally with metal and glass containers. A brief discussion of plastics is also included; but detailed reference to paper and paperboard packaging materials is covered in another chapter entitled "Forest Products."

STRUCTURE AND SIZE OF THE CONTAINER INDUSTRY

Present Value and Shares of Market

Valued at the point where its products leave their suppliers' factories, the U.S. packaging industry's annual sales volume has grown from an estimated $12 billion in 1960 to about $25 billion today. Table 1 outlines the shares of the total packaging market held by various types of packaging materials in 1960 and 1973. Packaging machinery and certain other miscellaneous packaging specialties are excluded from the tabulation.

From the foregoing figures, it is apparent that the relative importance of the four major types of packaging materials—that is, paper, metal, glass, and plastic—has remained virtually unchanged during the past 13 years. In dollar terms, paper still ranks first, metal second, glass third, and plastic fourth.

284

TABLE 1

Share of Packaging Market Held by Various Types of Materials

	1960		1973 (estimated)		Annual Growth Rate 1960– 1973 (percent)
	Dollars (millions)	Percent of Total	Dollars (millions)	Percent of Total	
Paper and paperboard boxes, bags, shipping containers, wrapping materials, and fibre cans........	$ 5,058	47	$ 9,570	42	+ 5.0
Steel and aluminum cans, drums, collapsible tubes, foil, and aerosols..............	2,414	22	5,785	25	+ 7.0
Glass containers and closures......	1,202	11	2,850	12	+ 6.9
Plastic containers and flexible packaging materials (including cellophane).............	567	5	2,210	10	+11.0
Wood, textile, and bulk containers.......................	701	6	1,085	5	+ 3.4
Component and cushioning materials—for example, labels, adhesives, tapes, etc......	923	9	1,450	6	+ 3.5
Total....................	$10,865	100	$22,950	100	+ 5.9

Source: Various government and industry organizations.

Competition, Diversification, and Integration

Competition within the container industry is intense and involves not only the invention of new packaging forms—for example, seamless cans, aerosols, plastic tubes, flexible pouch packages, etc.—but also competition among different materials, such as steel, aluminum, glass, paper, and plastic. Most rigid containers, however, are insulated from foreign competition because of their abnormal bulk and low unit value.

Although most metal and glass container companies purchase their basic raw materials from external sources, a few diversified producers, such as American Can, Continental Can, and Owens-Illinois, produce a substantial percentage of their own plastic resin and paper fibre requirements. All three of these major container producers, as well as many of their principal competitors, offer a diversified line of packaging products and services—for example, metal or glass containers, plastic bottles and films, paperboard boxes, etc. A diversified company is better equipped to supply its customers not just with containers but with an entire packaging system of creative design service; prompt and reliable deliveries; a choice of packaging materials and forms best suited to the customer's product; and supplementary packaging materials and services, such as, labels, closures, filling and sealing machinery, shipping containers, etc.

Raw material suppliers have further intensified competition within the packaging industry during recent years either by integrating forward into the manufacture of finished containers or by helping other container manufacturers to expand their sales of products made from a particular raw material. Reynolds Metals, for instance, has constructed aluminum-can assembly plants near the sites of its customers' packing plants and now sells cans at prices competitive with those of nonintegrated producers.

Other examples of inter-industry subsidies include millions of advertising dollars spent by major steel companies to promote the sale of beverages in steel cans and the free fabrication advice and low-cost resin supplied by certain petrochemical companies to their plastic packaging customers.

Factors Governing Demand for Container Products

The basic functions of packaging have changed little over the years. Preservation, protection, sanitation, and mobility are still among the prerequisites a package must meet in order to be a commercial success. Self-service retailing has added three others: brand identification, merchandising ability, and convenience.

Consumers have repeatedly demonstrated their preference for aesthetics or convenience and their disdain for cost whenever they are offered a choice of packaging forms. Containers with easy opening or resealability features usually cost more than similar containers with standard closures; portion-packed foods cost more than bulk packages; aerosols add substantially to product cost; and beverages usually cost more in nonreturnable (NR) bottles or cans than they do in returnable bottles. Yet all of these more costly packaging forms are among the industry's most popular products.

Retailers likewise have demonstrated their preference for nonreturnable containers of all types. Durability, ease of handling, and merchandising appeal remain the principal container characteristics sought throughout the retail trade. Among brewers and soft-drink bottlers, container cost also represents only one of several considerations that determine the choice of container form. Shipping weight, filling-line efficiency, and seal integrity are additional factors that are invariably considered.

Product Substitution

Many packaged products have evolved in the marketplace through a series of different packaging materials. Liquid detergents, for example, first appeared in glass bottles, then in metal cans, and finally moved into blow-molded polyethylene. Fresh milk, once distributed in ten-gallon cans, next appeared in returnable glass bottles, then in paperboard cartons, and can now frequently be purchased in plastic jugs, especially in gallon sizes. Some products, such as noncarbonated soft drinks, can often be found simultaneously in a wide variety of different materials and forms—for example, returnable and nonreturnable glass bottles; rigid plastic containers; steel, aluminum, and fiber composite cans; paperboard cartons; and flexible plastic pouches.

Sensitivity of Demand to Changes in General Business Activity

Today, approximately two thirds of all packaging materials are used to serve consumer markets which include food, beverages, drugs, and toiletries. In the case of metal cans, the percentage is above 85 percent; for glass containers, it is close to 100 percent. Metal and glass container shipments to the beer and soft-drink markets alone now approximate half of all such containers produced. Such end-markets lend unusual stability to container demand.

Foreign Manufacturing and Licensing Agreements

Due to their extraordinary bulk and low unit value, most rigid containers cannot be transported economically more than a few hundred miles from their point of manufacture. Overseas markets, therefore, can best be served by foreign manufacturing subsidiaries or licensees, rather than by export from the United States.

Several leading U.S. packaging companies derive important and growing benefits from such foreign participation. In addition to the highly profitable, worldwide can and closure operations of Crown Cork & Seal, Owens-Illinois and Continental Can have also become multinational packaging suppliers. Owens-Illinois, through its West German subsidiary, Gerresheim, and its English affiliate, United Glass Ltd., is now the largest glass container producer in the European Common Market. Similarly, two Continental Can subsidiaries in West Germany and the Netherlands, with combined sales volume approximating $525 million a year, make that company the largest metal container producer on the European continent. Both Owens and Continental Can also derive significant royalty income and technical assistance fees from scores of container manufacturers throughout the world who license American technology for their own domestic plants. Such licensees often provide attractive acquisition opportunities for their U.S. sponsors.

THE ROLE OF GOVERNMENT IN PACKAGE DESIGN AND DISPOSAL

Labeling and Safety

Recent consumerist pressures have prompted our federal government to enact the Fair Packaging and Labeling Act which empowers the Federal Trade Commission (FTC) to adopt and enforce national standards for clarity, completeness, and accuracy in the labeling of such packaged consumer products as food, toiletries, and proprietary drugs. Other laws, such as the Federal Hazardous Substances Act and the Comprehensive Drug Abuse Prevention and Control Act, authorize the Food and Drug Administration (FDA) to promulgate and enforce rules governing the safety and integrity of container closures, particularly those used on products which could prove harmful to children. The FDA also is responsible for the safety and sanitation characteristics of aerosol containers, dairy packaging, and certain food-grade plastics. The recently formed federal Consumer Product Safety Agency will eventually assume some of the regulatory authority now divided between the FTC and the FDA.

Litter Control and the Solid Waste Problem

During recent years, the increasing industrialization of our country and the growing affluence of its inhabitants has been accompanied by commensurate growth in environmental pollution of all sorts, including increased volumes of litter and other consumer wastes. Although metal, glass, and plastic containers combined represent only about 1 percent (by weight) of all solid wastes generated today in the United States, they remain among the most visible and identifiable elements of roadside litter, as well as an important component of collectible household and commercial solid waste.

In response to the urging of their ecology minded constituents, political authorities in dozens of states and hundreds of municipalities have given serious thought to legislation that would ban, tax, or restrict the use of nonreturnable containers. Although some such proposals are still pending, and others may yet be considered at the federal level, only three states (Oregon, Vermont, and South Dakota) and a few local communities have enacted punitive packaging laws. Most of these are being challenged in court on constitutional grounds or have already been rescinded voluntarily by the same authorities which imposed them.

Under the Oregon law, pull-tab opening devices on beer and soft-drink cans that separate from their original containers are banned altogether. In addition, a mandatory five-cent deposit must be collected by beer and carbonated soft-drink distributors on each can or bottle of such product sold to a consumer in a nonreturnable container. A minimum deposit of two cents per bottle must be collected on beverages sold in returnable glass bottles. Noncarbonated beverages, fruit juices, fluid milk, and other packaged food products are exempt. Although there is some preliminary evidence that the above-mentioned restrictions may have helped to reduce roadside litter, it has also become obvious that the economic consequences of the legislation upon container manufacturers, brewers and soft-drink bottlers, grocers, and beverage consumers have been almost totally negative.

Relative Magnitude of Household and Commercial Wastes

As revealed in Table 2, household and commercial wastes amount to about 7 percent of our country's total solid waste, and only about four-fifths of this 7 percent (that is, about 5.5 percent) is actually collected

TABLE 2

Sources of Solid Waste by Proportion of Weight Generated

Types of Waste	Percent of Total
Animals	41
Mining	34
Agriculture	15
Household and commercial	7
Industry	3
	100

Source: Anheuser-Busch, Inc. and the Council on Environmental Quality.

and disposed of. Table 3 reveals that glass, metal, and plastic combined represent only 20 percent of the collectible 5.5 percent, or slightly more than 1 percent of total solid waste.

TABLE 3

Components of Collected Solid Waste by Proportion of Weight

Material	Percent of Total
Paper	49
Organic garbage	16
Glass	9
Metal	9
Lawn and garden	8
Wood	3
Textiles	2
Rubber and leather	2
Plastic	2
	100

Source: U.S. Environmental Protection Agency—Solid Waste Management Office and Council on Environmental Quality.

Recycling Potentials of Various Packaging Materials

Many environmental control authorities are convinced that commercial recycling systems will eventually provide the solution to our nation's solid waste problem, and that legislative restrictions against disposable containers will solve nothing. Other authorities suggest that new waste incineration technology may someday help alleviate the world's growing energy shortage. All agree that the present market for salvageable packaging materials—that is, paper, glass, steel, and aluminum—far exceeds their segregated supply.

An increasing number of municipalities across the nation, therefore, are beginning to employ magnetic, mechanical, and optical separation techniques for at least part of their collected solid wastes; while the National Center for Resource Recovery, funded by private industry and labor organizations, is planning various "demonstration" recovery systems in many additional U.S. cities. Profit-oriented solid waste management companies, such as Browning-Ferris Industries, Inc., represent another rapidly growing vehicle for the collection and disposal of residential and commercial trash.

SPECIAL CHARACTERISTICS OF THE METAL CONTAINER INDUSTRY

Size and Concentration

Exclusive of steel drums, collapsible metal tubes, and flexible metal foil, steel and aluminum can shipments during 1973 totalled approximately 75 billion cans, worth an estimated $4.8 billion. The industry's four largest producers currently account for slightly over 70 percent of this volume.

Capital Requirements

Since can making is essentially a converting operation, and not a continuous process raw materials industry like glass or paper, its capital requirements are modest relative to these latter packaging forms. Similarly, entry by new producers is relatively easy. Nevertheless, a minimum investment of at least $4 million is needed for a modern two-piece drawn-and-ironed (D&I) can line capable of producing about 125,000,000 12-ounce cans per year, valued at about $6 million; and between $1.5 and $3 million for a somewhat less productive conventional three-piece line. The industry's annual expenditures for new plants and equipment have recently been averaging more than $100 million.

Can-Making Technology

For decades prior to 1960, metal can bodies were fabricated from sheets of tinplated steel, seamed along their sidewalls with solder, sealed at the ends with separate disks of metal, and wrapped with paper labels. The manufacture of such three-piece cans was facilitated and improved during the 1960s by a series of innovations which included:

1. Shearing the body "blanks" from continuous coils of tinplated steel.
2. Lithographing the sheared "blanks" before converting them into cans.

3. Substitution of double-reduced "thin" (that is, lighter weight) tin-plate for heavier, thicker can stock.
4. Development of lower cost tin-free steel for beverage cans.
5. Cemented and/or welded side seams.
6. Easy opening aluminum ends.

Within the past several years, a revolutionary new can manufacturing technique known as the drawn-and-ironed process has been widely adopted throughout the industry, primarily to produce two-piece, seamless aluminum cans for the beverage industry. Such containers are usually lighter in weight, require less metal to manufacture, cost less to transport and store, and are thought to possess certain aesthetic advantages. Although the capital cost of a D&I can line is higher than for conventional three-piece equipment, most D&I lines are built to operate 24 hours a day, six or seven days per week, versus only 8 or 16 hours a day, five days per week for conventional lines. The annual productivity of a D&I line, therefore, is greater, and its unit production cost is competitive with most other can-making techniques. An estimated 30 percent of total beverage can production is currently represented by D&I products, and the percentage continues to escalate as rapidly as new D&I equipment can be installed.

Specialty Can Products

Foil and fibre composite cans, developed in recent years for such markets as frozen citrus juice concentrates, refrigerated dough, and motor oil, represent perhaps the only type of rigid container that can be produced at lower cost than its metal or glass counterparts. Although composite-can sales have grown since 1960 at about 10 percent annually, future growth may be blunted somewhat by the increasing acceptance of lightweight steel and all-aluminum cans, or by all-plastic containers.

Another major contributor to can industry growth during recent years has been the aerosol can. Developed initially during World War II as a dispenser of insecticides, aerosols have steadily enlarged their share of the can business from less than 1.5 percent in 1960 to almost 3.5 percent in 1972. Annual dollar sales of aerosol containers (principally metal) are currently estimated to exceed $475 million. As shown in Table 4, despite their higher cost, the unique and convenient dispensing properties of aerosols have enabled them to capture important segments of certain product markets, such as hair sprays, shaving lather, and personal deodorants.

Analysis of Costs

Raw material cost, principally that of the steel or aluminum used in the can body and ends, represents by far the largest single element of

TABLE 4

Consumption of Aerosol Containers, by End Use (1972)

	Percent of Total Aerosol Sales
Product Category	
Hair sprays	19
Personal deodorants	17
Starches and laundry products	10
Coatings and finishes	9
Household waxes, polishes, and cleaners	9
Industrial and automotive	6
Colognes and perfumes	6
Shaving lather	6
Insect sprays	4
Miscellaneous	14

Source: Chemical Specialties Manufacturers Association, Inc.

cost in can manufacture—that is, about 60 percent. Metal cost alone represents almost 50 percent. Other major costs include direct labor, an estimated 20 percent; selling, general, and administrative expenses (including freight) of about 15 percent; and capital costs—for example, depreciation and interest—about 5 percent. Table 5 illustrates the extent

TABLE 5

Changes in the Wholesale Prices of Selected Metals and Metal Containers

Metal or Container	Percent Change 1967–1973
Tinplate	+35
Tin-free steel	+40
Black plate steel	+45
Aluminum beer can stock	+14*
No. 303 x 406 food cans	+40
12-oz. beer cans	+37

* Since 1968 only.
Source: Bureau of Labor Statistics.

to which various can-making material costs and can product selling prices have increased during recent years.

Although the great majority of metal cans are still made from tin-plated steel, aluminum's share of the total metal consumed by the can industry during the past decade has grown substantially and now accounts for about 20 percent of total can production. Aluminum's non-corrosive properties and lighter weight seem to have been principally responsible for its rising popularity. The metal's continued growth as a packaging material, however, may be more affected in the future by economic considerations—for example, rising cost—and by energy constraints. Obviously, far more Btu's. are required to produce a ton of aluminum than are needed to produce a ton of steel.

During the early 1960s, unit labor costs in the can industry remained rather stable, as productivity gains approximately offset increases in wage rates. Within the past five years, however, the cost of new wage agreements reached throughout the industry has far exceeded productivity gains and has thereby helped to erode industry profit margins.

Pricing Practices

The commodity nature of most metal cans tends to keep their selling prices highly competitive, and also to prevent any one supplier from becoming a price leader. Price increases in the industry are usually geared to increases in raw material and labor costs, while price cutting has occasionally been triggered by more efficient can-making technology or temporary periods of excess fabricating capacity.

The nominal selling price of standard 12-ounce beverage cans currently averages about $47 per 1,000. In a buyer's market, however, nominal prices are often modified significantly by free storage privileges, freight allowances, deferred payment terms, and other sales concessions.

On-Site Can Making and Self-Manufacture

During recent years, certain major food processors, soup canners, and national brewers have found it economical to manufacture part or all of their metal can requirements. By the mid-1960s, more than 20 percent of total can industry production was being manufactured by can users themselves. Since then, forward integration by major aluminum companies has pushed the independent can companies' share of the market down further, to less than 70 percent. Such developments have been a deterrent to higher selling prices among the independents.

Within recent years, the industry's two major independents, American Can and Continental Can, have offered their major beverage customers the privilege of buying their can requirements on a contractual basis from supplier-owned-and-operated can lines located at the site of the customer's brewery or bottling plant. Cost savings from such on-site lines as well as from the use of lower-cost tin-free steel have been shared with their related customers through price discounts of about 8 percent.

While such contractual arrangements, which presently account for about 15 percent of total beverage can production, effectively slowed the trend toward self-manufacture among brewers and aborted it altogether among soft-drink bottlers, they also triggered a wave of price cutting by competing can producers who had previously elected not to construct on-site can lines for their customers. Such price competition has continued throughout the marketplace during most of the past three years.

End-Use Markets and Factors Affecting Their Growth

Table 6 outlines the growth in domestic shipments of metal cans since 1960, by end use. Annual per capita consumption of metal cans during this period grew from 246 in 1960 to an estimated record high of 360 in 1973.

TABLE 6

Domestic Shipments of Metal Cans by End-Use Market (millions of base boxes of metal consumed*)

	Food (incl. fruit juice and coffee)	Beer and Soft Drink	Pet Food	Aerosol	Nonfood	Total
1973E	68.8	84.6	7.5	6.0	13.5	180.4
1972	65.9	75.6	6.7	5.9	15.8	169.9
1971	67.9	67.8	6.0	5.3	14.9	161.9
1970	68.5	64.2	6.5	5.4	15.3	160.0
1969	69.4	56.9	6.2	5.1	15.0	152.6
1968	69.3	50.7	6.2	4.8	14.9	145.9
1967	67.3	42.1	5.8	4.4	14.4	134.0
1966	68.1	37.2	5.5	3.8	14.8	129.4
1965	67.3	30.4	5.1	3.8	14.8	121.4
1964	66.4	27.4	4.9	3.0	14.5	116.2
1963	64.7	23.7	4.6	2.5	15.4	110.9
1962	68.6	21.5	4.7	2.2	17.6	114.5
1961	66.2	20.0	4.5	1.7	17.1	109.4
1960	63.4	19.4	4.5	1.4	16.4	105.1
Compound annual growth rate: 1960–73E (percent)	1	12	4	12	(2)	4

* A base box includes 112 sheets, 14″ x 20″ size, equivalent to 31,360 sq. in.
Source: 1960–72, U.S. Department of Commerce—Bureau of the Census; 1973, writer's estimates.

From Table 6, it is obvious that virtually all of the can industry's growth during the past 12 years has come from one market: the beverage industry. Although aerosol cans have shown the most rapid percentage growth, they represent less than 3.5 percent of total can shipments. Beer and soft-drink cans, on the other hand, accounted for about 45 percent of total can shipments in 1972 and rose to an estimated 47 percent in 1973.

Although nonreturnable beer and soft-drink containers have accounted for virtually all of the can industry's production gains during the past decade, Tables 7 and 8 reveal that about 21 percent of all packaged beer and about 39 percent of all packaged soft drinks are still being marketed in returnable bottles.

TABLE 7

Beer Packaged and Marketed in Metal or Glass Containers (percent of total market)

	1967	*1968*	*1969*	*1970*	*1971*	*1972*	*1973E*
Cans	47	54	50	53	55	57	59
NR bottles	20	17	21	20	21	20	20
Returnable bottles	33	29	29	27	24	23	21

Sources: Glass Container Manufacturers Institute, National Can Co., and writer's estimates.

TABLE 8

Soft Drinks Packaged and Marketed in Metal or Glass Containers (percent of total market)

	1967	*1968*	*1969*	*1970*	*1971*	*1972*	*1973E*
Cans	19	25	29	31	34	35	36
NR bottles	9	12	18	23	24	25	25
Returnable bottles	72	63	53	46	42	40	39

Sources: Glass Container Manufacturers Institute, National Can Co., and writer's estimates.

Since a returnable "deposit" bottle is designed with a stronger neck and thicker walls than the lighter-weight, "no-deposit," nonreturnables, the returnable can be refilled and capped many times before it eventually breaks or is destroyed by a consumer. Recent experience reveals the average number of "round trips" made during the life of a returnable soft-drink bottle to be about 16; for a typical returnable beer bottle, the number approaches 25. Although lighter-weight, NR bottles can, of course, be collected and reused as crushed glass by a glassmaker, their design and fragility prevents them from being filled and capped more than once. Every time a beverage consumer shifts his container preference from returnable bottles to NRs, therefore, significant new demand for both metal and glass containers is created, in a ratio of at least 16 to 1 (that is, the average number of new NRs required to duplicate the delivery capability of one returnable bottle).

On the other hand, demographic forces which boosted soft-drink consumption in the United States during the 1960s at a compound annual rate of 7 percent are expected to generate only about a 5–6 percent annual growth rate during the 1970s. As the millions of Americans who swelled the ranks of our 10- to 24-year age group during the past decade move up to beer-drinking age during the 1970s, however, beer consumption is expected to accelerate from the 3 percent per year growth it enjoyed during the past decade to at least 4 percent during the current one.

In light of the above-mentioned circumstances, unit demand for beer cans and NR beer bottles should grow at least 4.5 percent a year for the balance of the current decade, and demand for NR soft-drink containers should grow at about 6.5 percent during the same period.

The second most important market for metal cans—food products—accounts for about 38 percent of all domestic can shipments and has grown since 1960 at an annual rate of less than 1 percent. General line (nonfood) cans, the industry's third largest product group serving such markets as paint, motor oil, and antifreeze, still account for about 8 percent of total shipments, but have actually declined slightly since 1960. Reasonable future growth expectations for food and general-line can shipments, including aerosols, seem to fall within a range of zero to 1 percent per year.

All of the above growth estimates, of course, are expressed in physical terms and apply only to domestic markets. Growth in dollar volume should be moderately higher in all product categories, and the growth rates for all types of convenience packaging materials in foreign markets should be much higher than the domestic rate.

SPECIAL CHARACTERISTICS OF THE GLASS CONTAINER INDUSTRY

Size and Concentration

Shipments of glass containers during 1973 totaled approximately 39 billion units, worth an estimated $2.2 billion. The crowns and closures used to seal these glass containers probably added an additional $600 million to their value.

The glass container industry today employs more than 75,000 men and women at about 120 plants located in 27 states. Although the industry still includes 40 different producers, a number of mergers and other structural changes within the industry have gradually brought its productive capacity into the hands of fewer, more efficient, and financially sound producers. The three largest—Owens-Illinois (with an estimated 34 percent market share), Brockway Glass (10 percent), and Anchor Hocking (9 percent)—presently account for over 50 percent of the industry's total production. The eight largest producers account for about 78 percent.

Capital Requirements

An estimated $2 of capital is now required to produce $1 of new sales at a totally new glass container plant. Such heavy investment requirements, together with the "continuous process" character of glass-making technology, have long tended to discourage the self-manufacture of glass containers by beverage bottlers or food processors, as well as to discourage the entry of new independent producers into the glass industry.

However, by concentrating their capital expenditures upon productivity improvements at existing plants rather than upon the construction of totally new plants, established glass container companies have been able to maintain reasonably stable capital turnover ratios during recent years, as well as adequate returns on stockholder equity and pretax profit

TABLE 9

Selected Financial Data of Two Leading Glass Container Companies

	Capital Turnover Ratio*		Return on Equity†		Pretax Profit Margin	
Year	Anchor	Brockway	Anchor (percent)	Brockway (percent)	Anchor (percent)	Brockway (percent)
1973.	1.83	1.58	10.8	8.0	9.7	7.4
1972.	1.80	1.58	12.6	11.9	12.0	11.9
1971.	1.79	1.59	12.8	12.0	12.2	12.7
1970.	1.81	1.63	13.8	14.2	13.1	14.7
1969.	1.90	1.66	17.2	15.8	16.2	17.5
1968.	1.81	1.52	15.0	9.6	14.1	11.2
1967.	1.81	1.46	12.4	6.4	9.5	6.3
1966.	2.07	1.53	14.3	8.3	11.0	8.1
1965.	2.20	1.92	11.6	6.9	9.4	6.9
1964.	2.26	1.65	10.8	11.3	8.5	10.3
1963.	2.20	1.65	9.2	9.1	8.0	9.1
1962.	2.27	1.64	10.2	8.2	8.5	8.5

* Annual sales ÷ average long-term debt and equity outstanding during year.
† Net income available for common shares ÷ year-end common equity.

margins. Table 9 illustrates how two leading glass container producers have recently performed in these vital areas.

Glass-Making Technology

Glass making is one of the world's oldest technologies still surviving as a major industry. Yet the opportunities for glass to contribute to man's comfort and convenience have never been greater than they are today.

The advantages of glass as a packaging material are many. Glass is transparent, chemically inert, and impermeable. Glass containers can be colored and formed into an infinite variety of sizes and shapes. They neither add nor subtract anything from the products they contain.

The basic ingredients of glass have always been essentially the same. Clear bottle glass is made by melting silica sand, one of the earth's most abundant and lowest cost raw materials, in a furnace at 2,700 degrees Fahrenheit and then adding limestone and soda ash to give the mixture hardness and chemical durability. Crushed glass, known as cullet, normally representing between 10 and 15 percent of total raw material, is also usually added to facilitate melting. About 70 percent of the total "batch" (by volume) is sand, while soda ash represents the most important ingredient from a dollar value standpoint. The latter is currently in tight supply and is expected to remain so until, perhaps, 1975.

Substantial productivity gains have been achieved during recent years by the development of faster and more efficient glass-forming machines —including eight-section double-gob and six-section triple-gob equipment. A new electronic device also now controls more efficiently the size, shape, and other physical characteristics of the containers to be molded on a forming machine; and electronic glass inspection gear and automatic case-packing equipment have also begun to replace manual labor at the "cold ends" of many glass-making lines.

Other technological developments favorable to the glass container industry include a variety of easy opening closures now in widespread use throughout the bottling industry, some with a resealable feature. The handicaps once suffered by narrow-necked beverage bottles on filling and closing lines have also been gradually removed. Until a year or two ago, conventional 12-ounce beverage bottles could be filled at only half the speed of 12-ounce cans (that is, 600 per minute versus 1,200 per minute). Recently, however, commercial bottling equipment has been perfected that can fill and cap up to 2,000 bottles per minute —a speed faster than the average bottler requires.

The glass container industry is also improving its competitive posture in the areas of weight and durability. Leading producers are now marketing various types of lighter-weight, chemically strengthened or plastic-reinforced glass containers, such as Owens-Illinois' "Plasti-Shield" or Anchor Hocking's "Anchor-LITE." Such containers are particularly popular in 32-ounce and larger sizes.

Analysis of Costs

Although labor is still the largest operating cost in glass making— that is, an estimated 39 percent of total cost—future productivity gains at existing glass plants should help to stabilize its relative importance.

Raw material costs, on the other hand, including the corrugated shipping containers used to pack finished ware, presently represent about 25 percent of total cost and continue to rise sharply. On a comparable weight basis, however, glass is by far the least costly of the various materials used to manufacture rigid containers. Rapid escalation is likely to continue in fuel costs (principally natural gas) which historically have averaged about 7 percent of the total, but which are obviously headed much higher. Other routine costs and expenses include freight (an estimated 9 percent) and selling, general, and administrative (6 percent).

Pricing Practices

Like their metal and plastic counterparts, most glass containers are priced and sold as commodities, by the gross, in standard sizes and shapes. Usually, the costs of related corrugated container materials, decorating or labeling, and delivery expenses are also included in the selling price. The industry's unofficial, but recognizable, price leader is Owens-Illinois.

To facilitate the introduction of such new or improved products as the nonreturnable beverage bottle or Owens-Illinois' foamed-plastic-jacketed "Plasti-Shield," leading glass container producers also frequently offer cooperative advertising or sales promotion allowances to their customers for limited periods.

Table 10 traces the history of glass container selling prices since 1962.

TABLE 10

Glass Container Wholesale Prices (based upon actual transactions)

Year	Index (1957–59 = 100)	Percentage Increase over Prior Year
1973E	140.0	3.5
1972	135.2	4.0
1971	130.0	6.8
1970	121.7	4.8
1969	116.1	7.1
1968	108.7	7.2
1967	101.1	1.2
1966	99.9	1.8
1965	98.1	1.0
1964	97.1	0.6
1963	96.5	(0.4)
1962	96.9	(1.5)

Source: 1962–72, Bureau of Labor Statistics; 1973, writer's estimate.

It should be noted that the abnormal price increases which ensued during 1968 and immediately thereafter were largely the result of product shortages triggered by an unprecedented 51-day industrywide strike early in 1968. Other factors serving to restrict glass container price increases during more recent years include price cutting among competing metal can manufacturers and government price controls.

End-Use Markets and Factors Affecting Their Growth

As revealed by Table 11, unit shipments of glass containers since 1960 have grown at an annual rate of about 4 percent; and only twice —in 1968 and 1971—have shipments and per capita consumption failed to exceed the prior year.

Much of the glass container industry's stability stems from the food, beverage, and toiletries markets, which account for virtually all of its sales. Shipments of new glass containers to brewers and carbonated soft-drink bottlers alone during 1973 accounted for about 47 percent

TABLE 11

Domestic Glass Container Shipments by End-Use Market (millions of gross)

Year	Food	Beverage	Drug and Cosmetic	Chemical	Total	Units per Capita
1973	82.9	153.7	31.5	4.4	272.6	186
1972	82.8	147.7	29.9	4.2	264.6	182
1971	81.8	141.8	27.6	3.9	255.3	179
1970	83.8	143.0	34.3	4.3	266.0	188
1969	82.6	128.0	35.9	4.5	251.1	180
1968	77.7	107.0	32.8	4.3	221.9	160
1967	82.4	102.1	38.5	5.6	228.8	166
1966	74.9	83.6	39.8	5.8	204.1	150
1965	76.6	73.7	38.8	6.9	195.9	146
1964	73.0	67.7	36.8	7.4	184.8	139
1963	69.9	61.8	35.7	8.9	176.3	135
1962	69.9	56.1	36.8	9.4	172.2	133
1961	66.6	49.6	35.8	12.1	164.0	129
1960	63.8	42.9	34.8	13.1	154.7	124
Compound annual growth rate 1960–73 (by percent)	2	10	−1	−9	4	3

Source: Glass Container Manufacturers Institute.

of total industry shipments, and nonreturnables represented more than 92 percent of this segment (see Table 12).

In addition to the product demand factors already discussed in preceding paragraphs, which relate both to metal and glass containers, other factors of special importance to glass include the latter's ability

TABLE 12

Domestic Shipments of Beer and Soft-drink Bottles (millions of gross)

Year	Beer			Soft-Drink		
	Returnable	NR	Total	Returnable	NR	Total
1973	2.1	57.9	60.0	8.4	62.6	71.0
1972	1.7	52.7	54.4	10.1	60.9	71.0
1971	1.9	51.3	53.2	9.6	57.9	67.6
1970	2.3	50.3	52.6	11.3	57.9	69.3
1969	3.3	47.8	51.1	11.4	44.3	55.7
1968	3.3	41.6	44.9	12.1	32.3	44.4
1967	4.3	40.2	44.5	13.3	24.9	38.2
1966	4.0	34.9	38.9	13.4	13.7	27.1
1965	3.5	32.6	36.1	13.3	7.0	20.3
1964	2.9	30.4	33.3	13.3	4.4	17.7
1963	2.7	26.7	29.4	12.3	3.9	16.2
1962	2.5	23.8	26.2	10.9	3.3	14.2
1961	2.6	19.4	22.0	9.3	2.8	12.1
1960	3.0	13.5	16.5	9.8	1.7	11.5

Source: Glass Container Manufacturers Institute.

to package and reseal larger volumes of carbonated beverages than can be effectively contained in metal cans. Consumer preference for the convenience and economy of 28-ounce and larger resealable beverage bottles has given glass a competitive advantage in such container sizes, and has helped boost the tonnage consumption of glass containers during recent years more rapidly than unit consumption. Between 1969 and 1973, for example, glass container unit shipments increased 8.5 percent, while tonnage shipments rose 19.4 percent.

Another unique advantage of glass containers lies in their ability to be refilled and resealed, a capability not presently possessed by any other carbonated beverage container. In the unlikely event that NR containers were outlawed nationally, and barring unforeseen raw material or energy shortages, the returnable glass bottle might temporarily endure as the only ecologically acceptable beverage container.

The Glass Container Manufacturers Institute

To a greater extent than most other American trade associations, the Washington-based Glass Container Manufacturers Institute (GCMI) performs a variety of useful economic and political services for its more than two dozen glass container and closure members, who collectively produce about 90 percent of all U.S.-made glass containers.

The GCMI's activities in recent years have included such vital services as:

1. National advertising and sales promotion
2. Industrial relations
3. New product development
4. Improved filling and closing technology
5. Development of improved recycling systems for glass containers.
6. Political lobbying for fair and reasonable packaging legislation.

SPECIAL CHARACTERISTICS OF THE PLASTICS PACKAGING INDUSTRY

Size and Concentration

Since 1960, the growth of plastics in the packaging industry has exceeded that of any other material. Sales of plastic containers and flexible packaging materials during this period have grown about 11 percent per year; and in 1973 are estimated to have exceeded $2.2 billion, or about 10 percent of the total packaging market.

Since plastic package manufacture is essentially a converting operation requiring relatively little capital investment or technical skill, it has historically been the easiest for new producers to enter, but not necessarily the easiest in which to make high profits. Moreover, competition within the industry has been further intensified and fragmented by the forward integration of major petrochemical companies into the fabrication of finished packages, the backward integration of package users into self-manufacture, or of container manufacturers such as American Can and Owens-Illinois into the production of their own resin. As a consequence of the above, competition remains widely diffused and product diversity almost infinite.

Contemporary Plastic Packaging Resins

Thanks to its low cost and versatile fabrication properties, polyethylene remains, by far, the most widely used resin in the plastic-packaging industry, both for blow-molded bottles as well as for flexible film. In the form of film, it is roughly half as expensive as waxed paper, one third the cost of cellophane, and less than one sixth the cost of saran. Its limited rigidity, gas barrier properties, and low melting point, however, restrict its use principally to the packaging of perishable foods and a variety of nonfood applications such as apparel products and household chemicals.

Other higher-priced resins more suitable for special packaging markets include:

1. *Polyvinyl chloride* (PVC): For translucent bottles generally used to package toiletries and noncarbonated food products.
2. *Polystyrene:* Used primarily for injection-molded or thermoformed transparent containers or as a foamed cushioning material.
3. *Cellophane:* A cellulosic film used primarily to package baked goods, snacks, candy, and tobacco products. Often coated with polyethylene, saran, or vinyl to improve its moisture and gas barrier properties.
4. *Acrylonitrile styrene:* Special transparent barrier resin being developed for use in all-plastic beverage bottles. Available under such trade names as *Barex, Lopac,* and *Vicobar.*

Economics of Plastics Conversion

Although the high cost of certain plastic resins continues to restrict their use in the packaging industry, the costs of many others have tended to decline in response to the economies of large-scale production. Moreover, large users of semirigid plastic containers or flexible films often find it to their economic advantage to extrude or mold their own packages at the same site where they pack their principal products—for example, fluid milk, etc.

Since the capital cost of a plastic-bottle-making line or a film extruder can be measured in terms of a few hundred thousand dollars, whereas a polyethylene resin plant requires tens of millions of dollars, it is easy to understand why plastics conversion is usually subject to narrow profit margins but frequently yields a better return on invested capital than could be obtained if the converter was fully integrated.

Consumption Trends

Table 13 describes the growth of plastic packaging material sales since 1960. In dollar terms, both plastic bottles and polyethylene film continue to score major sales gains. The former, constructed primarily from high-density polyethylene or polyvinyl chloride (PVC), have cap-

TABLE 13

Value of Plastic Packaging Material Sales: 1960–1972 ($ millions)

Product or Material	1960	1969	1970	1971	1972	Annual Growth Rate (1960–1972) (by percent)
Polyethylene film......	$140*	$ 540†	$ 600†	$ 672†	$ 770†	15.3
Cellophane............	277*	255*	253*	254*	250*	(0.9)
Other plastic films......	N.A.	150†	160†	163†	170†	N.A.
Plastic bottles.........	64	300	345	405	428	17.2
Boxes and baskets......	58	96	105	111	124	6.5
Plastic sheet‡..........	15	71	80	92	101	17.2
Jars and tubs..........	7	54	60	66	68	20.8
Foamed plastics........	4	33	36	43	50	23.5
Tubes................	N.A.	28	34	35	40	N.A.
Totals............	$565	$1,527	$1,673	$1,841	$2,001	11.1

* Does not include value added by conversion.
† Includes value-added conversion.
‡ For thermoformed or fabricated packages.
N.A.: Not available.
Source: Various government and industry organizations.

tured certain segments of the packaging market previously held by glass or metal containers. Plastic containers have become particularly popular in the toiletries, cosmetics, and household chemical markets, which together account for over 70 percent of total blow-molded plastic bottle shipments. Food and beverages, on the other hand, account for only about 15 percent of total plastic bottle shipments, and virtually all of this percentage is represented by such nonpressurized products as syrups, cooking oils, salad dressings, and milk.

Plastic bottles have won consumer acceptance primarily because of their light weight, durability, and because they can be easily molded in an infinite variety of sizes and shapes. Table 14 illustrates how unit shipments of plastic bottles have grown during the past ten years.

Many petrochemical and packaging companies continue to develop and test-market clear plastic bottles constructed from a variety of new resins designed specifically for the beer and carbonated soft-drink markets. Standard of Ohio's *Barex* resin and Monsanto's *Lopac* have thus far been the industry's most promising contenders. Both are physically capable of containing carbonated beverages and nonpasteurized beer. Neither resin, however, is yet available in quantities or at prices that would make it a commercially feasible raw material. Until their cost is reduced to at least $0.30 per pound from present $0.50 per pound levels, and until their total production capacity is substantially increased

TABLE 14
Plastic Bottle Shipments (1963–1973)

Year	Millions of Bottles
1973	7,170
1972	6,900
1971	6,052
1970	5,549
1969	5,032
1968	3,930
1967	3,729
1966	3,356
1965	2,723
1964	2,364
1963	1,989

Sources: Bureau of the Census and Society of the Plastics Industry.

from the presently estimated level of 100 million pounds per year, such resins are not likely to score any significant penetration of existing beer and soft-drink markets.

A new nitrile-based resin, *Vicobar*, is currently being developed by duPont and market-tested by Continental Can Co. This new resin, which it is hoped can eventually be produced and sold for about $0.30 per pound, is said to be capable of withstanding internal carbonation pressure and can allegedly retain its shape at high temperatures. It is light-weight and shatter resistant, and is said to offer the barrier properties needed to preserve product quality and flavor. If forthcoming market tests are successful, Continental could have the new bottle in commercial production by 1975.

Also revealed in Table 13 is the substantial growth achieved since 1960 by such flexible packaging materials as polyethylene film. The total market for plastic films, including cellophane, now exceeds $1.2 billion per year. Major end-uses include fresh produce, baked goods, agricultural and industrial chemicals, and dry cleaning service. Recent forecasts by the National Flexible Packaging Association place the physical growth of plastic film production between 1970 and 1980 at about 8 percent per year, the same rate of growth that prevailed between 1960 and 1970.

The availability of petroleum-based resins represents perhaps the only potential constraint upon the future growth of plastic packaging materials.

THE "SYSTEMS" APPROACH TO PACKAGING

To attract new business and to service properly the packaging requirements of their existing customers, most container manufacturers offer more than just finished container products. In addition to a diverse assortment of different package forms, many suppliers also offer creative design services, filling and sealing equipment, convenience closures, and a wide variety of auxiliary benefits to their customers. Such services and benefits are usually intended to increase the customer's productivity, lower his total packaging and distribution cost, or facilitate the sale of his product.

Package Design

Of particular importance to the packager of a consumer product is the choice of a packaging material and form which will attract maximum favorable attention from prospective buyers prior to its sale in a self-service retail store and will provide the greatest utility and convenience thereafter. Examples of such "custom-built" containers include:

1. Custom-molded wine and liquor decanters, with an accompanying decorative paperboard carton.
2. Sculptured or embossed cans.
3. Vacuum-sealed paperboard and plastic bacon cartons.
4. Seamless aerosol cans decorated with four-color lithography.
5. Reusable polystyrene carrying cases for men's shaving accessories.

Filling and Sealing Equipment

Many diversified packaging materials suppliers facilitate the sale of their primary container products (for example, bottles, cans, plastic containers, closures, etc.) by developing efficient, high-speed filling and closing devices which may be purchased or leased by their container customers. The value of such equipment constructed in 1973 has been estimated by the Packaging Machinery Manufacturers Institute at nearly $100 million. Total packaging machinery shipments in 1973 probably exceeded $450 million. Leading manufacturers of packaging machinery include the Emhart Corporation, Diamond International, Crown Cork & Seal, Owens-Illinois, Anchor Hocking, and Maryland Cup Corp.

Convenience Closures

There can be little doubt that "pull-tab" can tops helped metal container manufacturers capture a larger share of the beverage market during the 1960s than they might otherwise have enjoyed. Although cans must now share this competitive advantage with the glass container industry and its new twist-off and resealable bottle caps, and despite legal prohibitions against detachable "pull-tabs" in Oregon, easy-opening devices continue to proliferate throughout the container industry and are still eagerly sought-after by most consumers. All such features, of course, add to the total cost of a package; but most consumers seem willing to pay something extra for the additional convenience.

SENSITIVITY OF CONTAINER COMPANY STOCKS TO GENERAL BUSINESS CONDITIONS

Historically, because of the stability of its principal end-markets—that is, the food and beverage industries—investors have tended to consider the packaging industry "defensive," much the same as they have appraised the food and beverage industries, the tobacco industry, or electric utilities. Even today, metal and glass container companies do not experience sharp declines in demand for their products during a general business recession, and container-product prices do not fluctuate widely in response to general economic activity.

Container company stocks, however, have developed certain cyclical characteristics, related primarily to the introduction of new products or technology, temporary excesses in new production capacity, the availability and cost of raw materials, periodic wage negotiations, and the degree of ecological constraint currently threatening the industry.

THE ADVANTAGES OF DIVERSIFICATION: A CASE HISTORY

As recently as 1968, domestic metal container operations represented about 58 percent of the sales and earnings of Continental Can Company, the world's largest packaging company. Before the company entered the paper and plastics businesses during the previous decade, metal had constituted an even larger percentage of its total sales and earnings.

Sensing a slowdown in the future growth of U.S. demand for metal cans and a decline in the profitability thereof, Continental accelerated its diversification efforts overseas by acquiring major interests in two packaging companies operating in West Germany and the Benelux countries, increased its minority positions with several other foreign licensees, acquired certain additional North American companies that expanded the sales and earnings of its Diversified Products Group and

TABLE 15

Continental Can Company, Inc.: Operating Summary ($ millions)

| Year Ending December 31 | Net Sales | Net Income | | | Return on Average Common Equity (percent) | Price Range | Price/Earnings Ratio Range | Div'd. per Share | Year-End Shares Outst. (millions) |
		Amount	Percent of Sales	Per Common Share					
1973	$2,540	$95.2	3.7	$3.25	13.3	31–20	10– 6	$1.60	29.2
1972	2,193	80.8*	3.7	2.77*	11.0*	35–27	13–10	1.60	29.1
1971	2,082	72.9	3.6	2.51	9.6	45–26	18–10	1.60	29.1
1970	2,037	91.9†	4.6	3.20†	12.8†	47–35	15–11	1.53	28.7
1969	1,780	90.4	5.2	3.18	13.2	52–41	16–13	1.47	27.4
1968	1,508	83.5	5.5	2.95	13.3	48–30	16–10	1.37	28.3
1967	1,398	78.1	5.6	2.77	13.4	41–27	15–10	1.32	28.2
1966	1,339	70.9	5.3	2.54	13.2	33–25	13–10	1.17	28.0
1965	1,233	59.5	4.8	2.14	11.9	28–22	13–10	0.98	27.7
1964	1,198	48.9‡	4.1	1.77‡	10.2‡	24–19	14–11	0.89	27.4
1963	1,154	40.1	3.5	1.43	8.4	21–18	15–13	0.87	27.3
1962	1,183	41.0	3.5	1.45	8.8	21–17	14–12	0.80	27.9
1961	1,153	36.1	3.1	1.28	8.0	22–16	17–13	0.80	27.9
Compound annual growth rate	6.8%			8.1%					

* Before extraordinary charges of $120,100,000 equal to $4.13/share.
† Before extraordinary charges of $ 15,500,000 equal to $0.54/share.
‡ Before extraordinary charges of $ 21,950,000 equal to $0.81/share.
Source: Continental Can Company Annual Reports to shareholders.

Canadian subsidiary, substantially enlarged its U.S. paper-making capacity, and acquired a well-managed U.S. bag-converting company.

In 1968, 43 percent of Continental's annual capital expenditures were invested in domestic metal operations. In 1971 and again in 1972, only 19 percent was invested in domestic metal. During the past five years, the company has invested nearly $1 billion of new capital, divided approximately as follows:

	Percent
Outside the United States	32
Domestic forest products	30
Domestic metal operations	25
Diversified products (plastics, meat casings, closures, etc.)	13

As a consequence of the above shifts in business emphasis, Continental's 1973 sales and earnings appeared as follows:

	Sales (*percent*)	*Earnings* (*percent*)
International operations	30	30
Forest products operations	19	30
Domestic metal operations	42	25
Diversified products	9	15

The company's sales and earnings performance during the past 12 years is outlined in Table 15. Especially noteworthy is the sharp recovery experienced by Continental's return on common equity and earnings per share between 1971 and 1973, resulting not only from an extraordinary write-off of obsolete plant and equipment in 1972, but principally from a sharp improvement in overseas profits and in domestic forest products earnings. The figures provide convincing evidence of the virtues of intelligent product and geographic diversification.

12

Cosmetics

ROSE MAYERSON
Security Analyst
Bear, Stearns & Co., New York, New York

THE INDUSTRY

THE U.S. cosmetics and toiletries industry achieved rapid growth during the 1960s. According to the U.S. Department of Commerce, manufacturers' shipments rose at a compound annual growth rate of over 10 percent during the census years 1958 to 1967, continuing at this rate to about $3.2 million in 1969 (Table 1). The 1970s started with a slower growth year of an estimated 4 to 5 percent, rebounded to the 8 to 10 percent level by 1972, and, after reaching an estimated $4.2 million in 1973, is currently in another period of moderating volume. It is difficult to document industry trends as the trade association, The Cosmetic, Toiletry, and Fragrance Association, Inc. (CTFA), does not issue figures. The Department of Commerce statistics are fragmentary, late in arrival, and in addition are only estimates, subject to revision, between census years.

The cosmetics and toiletries industry can still be termed "recession resistant" when compared with the more cyclical components of the U.S. economy which either failed to grow or even declined in volume during 1970. A comparison of eight major cosmetics and toiletries companies with total corporate profits bears this out (Table 2). However, 1970 was a difficult year in which the cosmetic industry faced near-term problems largely attributable to conditions present in the U.S. economy. The primary problem was inventory cutbacks. With tight money, interest

TABLE 1

Cosmetics and Toilet Preparations: Trends and Projections 1958–1974 (in $ millions, except as noted)

	1958	1963	1967	1969	1972*	Percent Increase 1972–73	1973*	1974*	Percent Increase 1973–74
Industry†									
Value of shipments	1,059	1,793	2,515	3,163	3,920	8	4,230	4,570	.8
Product‡									
Value of shipments (total)	1,126	1,859	2,794	3,462	4,200	8	4,500	4,900	8
Shaving preparations	75	111	179	242	275	8	300	320	8
Perfumery	103	209	395	509	610	7	650	700	8
Hair preparations	316	593	772	926	1,170	8	1,260	1,360	8
Dentifrices	198	225	323	402	495	8	530	570	8
Other cosmetic and toilet preparations	418	698	1,046	1,326	1,590	8	1,720	1,860	8
Toilet preparations (n.s.k.)	16	20	80	58	50	8	55	60	8
Value of imports	6.5	7.7	12.4	14.3	21.6	-8	20	19	-5
Value of exports	25.0	18.3	25.8	41.8	53.9	4	56	58	4
Wholesale price indexes (1967 = 100)			100.0	105.9	109.5	—	109		—

Compound Annual Growth Rate	Industry—Value of Shipments	Product—Value of Shipments
Census years 1958–1967	10.1%	10.6%
1958–1969	11.2	10.3

* Estimated by BDC.
† Includes value of all products and services sold by the cosmetics and toilet preparations industry (SIC 2844).
‡ Includes value of shipments of cosmetics and toilet preparations made by all industries.
n.s.k.: Not specified by kind.
Source: U.S. Department of Commerce, Census of Manufactures, and "U.S. Industrial Outlook."

TABLE 2

Comparison of Composite-Eight Major Cosmetics and Toiletries Companies
with Total Corporate Projects, 1968–72

	1972	1971	1970	1969	1968
	..............(millions of dollars)...............				
Eight-company composite:					
Net sales..................	$3,278.3	$2,840.5	$2,573.9	$2,300.5	$2,038.8
Percent increase...........	15.4	10.4	11.9	12.8	17.3
Income before taxes........	$ 595.8	$ 510.5	$ 473.8	$ 455.1	$ 423.3
Percent increase...........	16.7	7.7	4.1	7.5	16.8
Net income.................	$ 311.8	$ 268.8	$ 251.9	$ 234.4	$ 208.0
Percent increase...........	16.0	6.7	7.4	12.7	8.2
	...............(billions of dollars)...............				
Total corporate profits:					
Corporate profits before taxes.	$ 98.04	$ 85.05	$ 74.04	$ 84.90	$ 87.64
Percent increase (decrease)..	15.3	14.9	(12.8)	(3.1)	9.8
Corporate profits after taxes..	$ 55.35	$ 47.61	$ 39.25	$ 44.84	$ 47.78
Percent increase (decrease)..	16.3	21.3	(12.5)	(6.1)	2.4
Eight-company averages (percent):					
Pretax margin..............	16.3	16.1	16.0	18.1	18.5
Net margin.................	8.7	8.5	8.4	9.1	9.0
Profits per dollar of sales (percent):					
Nondurable manufacturing...	4.4	4.5	4.5	5.0	5.2
All manufacturing...........	4.3	4.1	4.0	4.8	5.1

Sources: Department of Commerce, Quarterly Financial Reports for Manufacturing Corporations,
Federal Trade Commission, and Securities and Exchange Commission.

rates at all-time highs for that period, and a poor economic outlook, retailers and wholesalers had strong incentives to cut back on inventories.
Also, chain stores had taken on added importance in the channels of
distribution, and they used a sophisticated tool, the computer, to control
stocks. This was subsequently compounded by a reduction in consumer
purchases of expensive gift items at Christmas. Therefore, margins for
the composite declined, since manufacturers used more aggressive marketing methods, incurred increased expenses to finance larger accounts
receivables and inventories, and were subject to other cost pressures
as well. It should be noted, however, that the group has an impressive
record when compared with total corporate profits, and that, in general,
the eight-company average net margin, which was 8.7 percent in 1972,
runs well above those attained by the manufacturing sector as a whole.

With a return to a better economic environment in 1972, the industry
achieved more rapid growth. Inventories do not appear to have been rebuilt to previous levels, although brand proliferation could cause some
slippage. The most recent economic problem, which started late in 1973
and appears to be short term in nature, is the impairment of consumer
demand by high inflation rates and the increase in costs of food and

gasoline—all of which impact disposable income. Industry is also faced with shortages, higher costs of raw materials and supplies due to the energy crisis, and the government's program of price controls.

FACTORS AFFECTING GROWTH OF SALES

The long-term outlook for the industry during the decade of the 1970s remains strong due to the following factors:

1. *Population Trends and Favorable Demographic Mix*. Total U.S. population expanded quite rapidly for the 15 years after World War II, averaging 1.7 percent a year up to 1961. Since that time, the U.S. Census Bureau has noted a decrease in this rate, and, at present, Census E with a projected compound annual growth of 1.0 percent appears to be realistic between now and 1980. Much, of course, will depend upon the attitudes toward timing and family size of the children of the postwar baby boom (who are currently reaching marriageable age), and these estimates may prove to be conservative. While the latest population trends will affect the cosmetics and toiletries industry over the longer term, between now and 1980 the industry will continue to benefit from favorable demographic changes taking place as a result of the earlier wave of new births. Roughly half of the U.S. population will be under 29 years of age from 1965 to 1980; and the 15-to-29-year age group, a prime market area for cosmetics, will continue to expand from 24.5 percent of the total population in 1970 to 27.0 percent in 1975, remaining at this level in 1980 when the 30-to-39-year age group will take on additional importance. Similar trends exist for the U.S. female population (Table 3).

2. *Increased Per Capita Consumption*. The Conference Board's publication, "A Guide to Consumer Markets 1973/1974," confirms that "Toilet Articles, Preparations" has been one of the faster growth areas of consumer spending. Based on previous experience from 1955 to 1970, for each 1 percent rise in disposable income, a 1.5 percent increase in expenditures for Toilet Articles, Preparations is expected. The outlook for income growth is summarized in Table 4; a marked upward shift should take place over the next decade.

3. *Broadened Usage*. Cosmetics have come a long way from the days of grudging acceptance. Certain products, such as lipsticks, are viewed as necessities, and women on both ends of the age spectrum have increased their usage in recent years. Our affluent society has nurtured a greater degree of sophistication at an early age; teenagers are a prime market. Recent fads may raise doubts about this segment, but according to the 1970 cosmetics survey of *Seventeen* magazine, while teenagers are only 12 percent of the female population, they account for 22 percent of all feminine purchases of cosmetics and toiletries. The psychological need to be attractive persists, and evidently teenagers select different products from the more mature woman while striving for a "natural"

TABLE 3

Population by Age and Sex, 1960–80—Census Bureau, Series E (in thousands)

Age and Sex	1960		1970		1975		1980	
	Number	Percent Total	Number	Percent Total	Number	Percent Total	Number	Percent Total
Both sexes:								
Total	180,667	100.0	204,800	100.0	213,925	100.0	224,132	100.0
Under 15 years	56,073	31.0	57,865	28.3	54,143	25.3	52,970	23.6
15 to 19 years	13,455	7.5	19,285	9.4	20,943	9.8	20,221	9.0
20 to 29 years	22,064	12.2	30,934	15.1	36,713	17.2	40,611	18.1
30 to 39 years	24,521	13.6	22,728	11.1	25,406	11.9	31,240	13.9
40 to 49 years	22,593	12.5	24,128	11.8	22,907	10.7	22,504	10.1
50 to 59 years	18,134	10.0	21,051	10.3	22,393	10.5	22,679	10.1
60 and over	23,829	13.2	28,812	14.1	31,417	14.7	33,905	15.1
Female:								
Total	91,349	100.0	104,583	100.0	109,548	100.0	114,893	100.0
Under 15 years	27,569	30.2	28,388	27.1	26,533	24.2	25,936	22.6
15 to 19 years	6,645	7.3	9,492	9.1	10,291	9.4	9,937	8.6
20 to 29 years	11,075	12.1	15,462	14.8	18,249	16.7	20,115	17.5
30 to 39 years	12,479	13.6	11,537	11.0	12,872	11.8	15,732	13.7
40 to 49 years	11,481	12.6	12,409	11.9	11,780	10.8	11,548	10.1
50 to 59 years	9,226	10.1	10,968	10.5	11,751	10.7	11,942	10.4
60 and over	12,874	14.1	16,328	15.6	18,071	16.5	19,684	17.1

Total population:
compound annual growth rates:
1960–1970, 1.3%
1970–1980, 1.0%

Source: Current Population Reports, Series P-25; U.S. Department of Commerce.

TABLE 4

Projections of Income Distribution by Income Class (based on 1970 dollars)

Family Income Class	1970 (percent)	1975* (percent)	1980* (percent)
Under $3,000	8.5	6.0	5.0
$3,000–$5,000	9.5	7.5	6.5
$5,000–$7,000	11.5	9.0	7.5
$7,000–$10,000	18.5	14.5	13.0
$10,000–$15,000	27.5	26.0	23.0
$15,000–$25,000	19.5	27.0	32.0
$25,000 and over	5.0	10.0	13.0
Total	100.0	100.0	100.0

* Projected.
Source: U.S. Dept. of Commerce; The Conference Board.

look. Part of the current popularity of eye makeup is attributable to this group. Since about half of today's women marry by age 21 and have their last child at about 30 years of age, a mother may have 30 or 35 active years ahead of her when her youngest child is in school.

There are almost 35 million women in the labor force today and the U.S. Department of Labor estimates there will probably be more than 39 million by 1980. With the current accent on youth, working women who have both the means and the drive to retain a youthful appearance, present another rapidly expanding area of market demand. It should also be noted that men are placing greater emphasis on personal care.

4. *New Products and Trading-Up.* The cosmetics and toiletries industry has successfully stimulated demand by offering a wide variety of new and improved products. As part of the process, particularly in the case of cosmetics, companies can increase their average realized price by inducing women to trade-up.

Apart from trading-up by the consumer, various items have also registered price gains. This is more apparent in cosmetics than in the price-competitive mass market toiletry line. The current economic environment may slow or reverse this process in the short run, however.

5. *Overseas Expansion.* Similar factors affect the use of cosmetics and toiletries in the overseas market. Foreign sales have thus far been largely concentrated in Western Europe. Japan has also proven to be a lucrative market. As other areas of the world raise their standard of living and continue to stress improvement in the quality of daily life, other growth markets will emerge. U.S. cosmetics enjoy a worldwide reputation much the same as fragrance does from France. American companies operating in foreign markets may encounter local problems such as devaluations, restrictions, and higher taxes by certain foreign governments. Also, the U.S. government placed restrictions on foreign investment a few years ago because of our balance of payments problem. These restrictions have

recently been removed. Through a variety of measures (acquisitions, debt financing in foreign capital markets, and sophisticated monetary and tax techniques), U.S. companies with large foreign sales have thus far benefited from overseas operations, and those companies with well-entrenched positions should continue to do so in the future.

6. *Diversification.* To further bolster growth, some companies have diversified, either internally or through acquisitions, into other product lines such as drugs, jewelry, and food.

INDUSTRY STRUCTURE, COSTS, COMPETITION

The cosmetics and toiletries industry is not labor or capital intensive; gross margins average approximately 60 percent of sales (Table 5). The

TABLE 5

General Statistics for Cosmetics and Toilet Preparations Industry (SIC 2844), 1958–71 (as percentage of value of shipments)

Year	All Employees Payroll	Production Workers Payroll	Cost of Materials	Capital Expenditures	End-of-Year Inventories
1971*	10.4	5.0	30.2	1.8	11.4
1970	10.9	5.2	30.9	2.3	13.0
1969	10.6	5.0	31.4	1.6	12.1
1968	10.2	4.9	31.8	1.7	11.3
1967	10.4	5.0	32.0	2.1	11.1 Census
1966	10.2	5.0	32.1	1.4	10.5
1965	9.8	4.8	32.3	1.6	9.6
1964	9.6	4.8	31.4	1.0	9.5
1963	10.2	5.2	31.5	1.1	9.8 Census
1962	11.6	5.4	32.7	1.0	10.2
1961	12.0	5.8	32.0	0.8	9.9
1960	11.9	5.8	31.8	0.9	10.1
1959	11.9	5.9	32.2	3.7†	10.4
1958	12.7	6.3	33.9	1.4	11.1 Census

* Preliminary.
† Not cosnistent.
Source: U.S. Department of Commerce, 1967 Census of Manufactures, 1970 Annual Survey of Manufactures.

four largest companies account for roughly 40 percent of industry volume; the eight largest, about half; and the twenty largest, three quarters. The major costs are associated with marketing the products: packaging, advertising, promotions, and product development. While it would appear that this industry offers ease of entry, in reality it is becoming increasingly more difficult to establish a position, since marketing costs are rising and a firm must have a special creative flair. In the case of toiletries, where there is little brand loyalty, large advertising expenditures, particularly TV, are usually mandatory; cosmetics, on the other hand, require a longer term investment to build an "image" which establishes brand loyalty.

High return on equity has attracted several drug, chemical, and soap companies into the industry. The structure of the cosmetics and toiletries industry has been changing. While in the 60s there were many more specialized companies, smaller competitors, particularly those heavily dependent on one cosmetic or toiletry line, are now finding it harder to survive. Many acquisitions and mergers have taken place. Drug companies have acquired cosmetic companies, since often these products are sold in similar stores. To name a few—Pfizer acquired Coty; Eli Lilly acquired Elizabeth Arden; Schering and Plough (Maybelline) merged; and Smith Kline & French created Love Cosmetics. Just recently mass merchandisers have moved in—Norton Simon acquired Max Factor; Colgate-Palmolive took over Helena Rubinstein. Soap companies have had large toiletry operations in the past, but Rubinstein is a fashion cosmetic house. It is hard to assess the effect these changes will have on competition within the industry. As a part of a larger corporation, more money may be available for product development and promotion. However, product development and marketing flexibility might only be slowed if all major decisions must be cleared with the executive committee.

MARKETING

Effective marketing and merchandising are the key to industry success. Important differences exist between programs for cosmetics and toiletries, and these are outlined in Table 6. It should be noted that these are broad generalizations which, in most cases, can serve as a framework when viewing the industry. Many areas of the market, however, are not so clearly defined as in the case of low-priced cosmetics, which are marketed as commodity-type products; prestige toiletries (both women's and men's), which are franchised like cosmetics; and hair coloring, sold both ways. Also in recent years, some manufacturers have been trying new methods; for example, Smith Kline & French's Love line of cosmetics was originally introduced with heavy TV advertising and distributed in drugstores only. It has since been phased into department stores as well.

Retail channels of distribution appear to be shifting for the cosmetic industry. The independent drugstore is diminishing in importance, and chain operations are expanding. Retail stores are very cognizant of the cost of labor. These trends are leading to more floor stand displays of medium-priced cosmetics. Manufacturers are still primarily using the department store for prestigious cosmetic lines but are trying to adjust to the new trends in merchandising for medium-priced lines, without a loss of image. This is a gradual process and the industry is approaching it with caution.

Product trends provide opportunities for the creative marketer. While overall retail volume continues to expand, shifts in consumer demand can greatly affect corporate performance, particularly in the case of low-priced toiletries where there is little brand loyalty. Rates of growth vary widely among the industry's different product categories due to age of product line, packaging, and fashion changes; recent retail sales trends are reflected in Table 7 (page 320).

Major *cosmetic* manufacturers have extensive lines which offer a full range of products. Therefore when consumer fashion changes occur, demand for certain items may slow, but the innovative cosmetic company can actually experience more rapid overall sales growth by benefits which accrue in other parts of the line. Also, more aggressive companies create new markets. For example, the "natural" look in makeup has been stressed as a normal extension of the present accent on youth. Unbelievable as it may seem, it actually can take up to 15 products to attain a "dewy" appearance. Since the matte look is out, the demand for face powders has slackened; but makeup bases and eye makeup have registered sizeable gains—in fact, entirely new eye products such as false lashes and liners have come into their own in recent years. Skin care and treatment products are another rapid growth area. Bath lines have done much to stimulate sales of fragrances (toilet water and cologne still dominate). Despite recent gains, however, fragrance—particularly high-priced perfume—remains, to a large extent, a gift item for special occasions. This is evident from the seasonal pattern of sales; the major portion of industry volume still occurs during the Christmas season.

Toiletries

While hair preparations have only been experiencing modest gains, shifts within the various segments have provided both marketing opportunities and problems. The large-volume categories—hair spray and hair coloring—are highly competitive since their growth has declined in the last year or two. A few subcategories within these segments are expanding rapidly, however (for example, men's hair spray and protein shampoos). These changes are attributable to new styles originated by the younger set. Longer hair styles led to the increased use of men's hair spray instead of hair dressing, while the straight natural look for girls expanded the demand for shampoos and conditioners, reducing the use of hair spray. Home permanent kits and refills have been at or near the $50 million level for several years because of the various straight hair styles which have been in vogue.

Aerosol deodorants, aided by the addition of antiperspirants, are continuing to make rapid strides. A new category, feminine spray deodorants, which started from a small base in 1967, achieved dramatic increases but then fell back as the government first eliminated the use of hexachlorophine and then required a warning label be placed on the package.

TABLE 6

General Characteristics of Cosmetics and Toiletries

	Cosmetics	*Toiletries (commodity type)*
Product nature........	Fashion-oriented items of personal adornment, such as lipstick, fragrance, and makeup.	Utilitarian products, including hair spray, shampoos, personal soap, etc.
Corporate reputation...	Over the years, individual companies strive to make their name (or several of their complete cosmetic or fragrance lines) synonymous with glamour and premium-quality, high-fashion products. Image dictates the marketing mix.	While a company's reputation for quality items is a basic requirement, in most instances each brand is promoted separately. Exclusivity is unimportant.
Distribution...........	Principally sold through a controlled distribution system. Aside from Avon's door-to-door method, medium- and premium-priced cosmetics are marketed through franchised specialty, department, and selected drugstores, with distribution narrowing and store reputation becoming more prestigious as the price of the line increases.	Broad distribution through all available outlets which include chain and independent drugstores, food chains, discount operations, and variety stores.
Advertising...........	Usually under the company name, stressing the entire line. Advertising expenditures in measured media are roughly 15 percent of company sales and are largely concentrated in color ads in fashion and other magazines as well as spot and network TV.	Generally, each brand is promoted separately. Advertising expenditures in measured media run about 20–30 percent of sales. Effective use of mass communications is of critical importance; network and spot TV are primarily employed, as well as radio and printed media.
Promotional expenses...	These could range as high as 10–15 percent of sales and include: (1) point-of-purchase displays, (2) special gifts and introductory offers made both in stores and through special mailings to department store charge-account customers, (3) periodic training sessions of store cosmeticians to aid them in properly servicing customers.	"Cents-off" promotions, coupons, sample mailings, point-of-purchase displays.
Product line...........	Broad—can encompass hundreds of items.	Limited

TABLE 6 (*Continued*)

	Cosmetics	Toiletries (commodity type)
Packaging............	Luxurious	Functional, distinctive to spur point-of-purchase sales.
Pricing..............	Medium- to premium-priced products; minimal price competition within each market segment.	Lower-priced items subject to strong price competition.
Brand loyalty........	Usually strong	Slight
New product payout period..............	New products introduced under the corporate name or as extensions of existing lines usually are profitable within a short period of time.	Since each brand is introduced individually with massive advertising and promotional expenditures, new products could take one to two years to become profitable.

While a wide variety of men's toiletries are available in several price categories, men's colognes and aftershave lotions have been the most successful products in this group, thus far. The men's toiletries area tends to illustrate the fact that rapid market expansion does not always guarantee success. Many firms tended to overestimate the sales potential for these products. As a result, too many manufacturers were drawn into the market and a costly shakeout period followed.

GOVERNMENT REGULATION

In this "age of consumerism" the cosmetic industry faces greater government scrutiny and control. This is, however, an ongoing program that has been underway for some time and the following is a brief review of some of the major developments.

Food and Drug Administration (FDA)

The Cosmetic, Toiletry, and Fragrance Association, Inc. (CTFA) has been cooperating with the FDA on a voluntary program of self-regulation which includes: (1) registering of plants, (2) compiling formulas of products and submitting them to the FDA, and (3) reporting of adverse reactions.

Regulations on (1) and (2) were listed in the April 11, 1972 Federal Register. All of CTFA's 180 members have complied, and a total of 775 plants have been registered. Voluntary cosmetic product experience regulations (3) became official in the October 17, 1973 Federal Register. The first filing deadline is March 1, 1974, covering data for the last half of

TABLE 7

Cosmetics and Toiletries: Estimated Retail Sales (major product categories and selected statistics, 1965–72)

	Retail Sales ($ millions)				Percent Change 1972–71	Percent Change 1971–70	Compound Annual Growth 1965–70 (by percent)
	1972	1971	1970	1965			
FACE CREAMS	$ 239.4	$ 228.0	$ 217.0	$ 154.0	5.0	5.1	7.1
MAKEUP PREPARATIONS AND ACCESSORIES	919.1	872.6	823.8	561.3	5.3	5.9	8.0
Lipsticks	300.2	285.4	270.5	182.1	5.0	5.5	8.2
Eye makeup	194.1	173.1	152.7	60.8	12.1	13.4	20.0
Pressed, loose powder and blushers	100.0	97.2	92.2	80.8	2.9	5.4	2.7
Makeup bases	69.5	68.9	69.3	47.9	0.8	−0.6	7.7
Face lotions and astringents	46.1	43.9	42.0	29.2	5.1	4.4	7.6
Liquid facial cleansers	60.0	56.6	52.0	37.3	6.0	8.9	6.8
FRAGRANCES	448.2	409.4	380.2	236.4	9.5	7.7	10.0
Toilet water and cologne	302.9	272.7	249.2	147.9	11.1	9.5	11.0
Perfumes	78.6	75.4	73.5	51.4	4.3	2.5	7.4
Bath salts, tablets, oils	63.1	57.6	53.9	33.5	9.5	6.8	10.0
HAND PREPARATIONS	197.8	184.6	173.5	131.9	7.1	6.4	5.6
Nail polish and enamel	91.2	81.0	74.5	54.4	12.6	8.7	6.5
Hand lotions and creams	81.2	80.6	76.6	60.8	0.7	5.1	4.7
HAIR PREPARATIONS	1,361.8	1,298.5	1,230.0	880.6	4.9	5.6	6.9
Hair spray	276.3	282.8	295.8	239.0	−2.3	−4.4	4.4
Shampoos	441.6	396.0	343.7	220.1	11.5	16.2	9.7
Hair coloring	249.2	249.9	245.7	154.4	−0.3	1.7	9.4
Home permanents kits and refills	50.8	52.9	52.8	62.9	−3.9	0.1	—
Women's hair dressings and conditioners	119.0	95.0	85.8	58.2	25.4	10.7	8.1
Men's hair dressings	99.9	98.8	98.0	87.1	1.1	0.8	2.4

DEODORANTS	426.0	382.7	366.1	175.9	11.3	4.5	15.8
Aerosols	338.3	289.1	272.0	61.0	17.0	6.3	35.0
DENTIFRICES	408.3	390.9	360.6	275.6	4.4	8.4	5.5
SHAVING PREPARATIONS	467.0	452.5	339.9	229.9	3.2	7.0	8.1
Shaving cream	116.0	111.9	108.6	88.2	3.7	3.0	4.3
Aftershave lotions	123.5	118.8	110.7	68.5	4.0	7.3	10.1
Preshave lotions	17.7	16.7	15.4	11.1	5.9	8.6	6.7
Men's cologne	100.2	104.3	94.5	51.4	-3.9	10.4	12.9
SHAVING ACCESSORIES (including razor blades)	651.8	608.7	571.5	400.0	7.1	6.5	7.4
BATH AND DEODORANT SOAPS	365.5	348.1	333.0	299.4	5.0	4.5	2.1
Deodorant soaps	186.8	167.5	163.5	117.6	11.5	2.5	6.8
FEMININE SPRAY DEODORANTS	51.9	67.7	52.1	N.A.	23.3	30.0	N.A.

N. A. Not available.
Source: *Product Management and Drug Topics.*

1973. The FDA has asked for immediate reports (at least within 15 days) on unusual cosmetic product experience, and other reports semiannually. Prior to submission, the companies will have screened the complaints to determine which are spurious or unfounded. The CTFA is about to issue its recommended industry screening procedure. The FDA will then have the right to audit representative samples of complaints in order to ascertain that the procedure is being followed.

The FDA has issued mandatory ingredient labeling requirements. The labeling of every cosmetic product now on the market will have to comply with the regulations which appeared in the Federal Register October 17, 1973 under the Fair Packaging and Labeling Act (1966). All new labeling ordered after March 31, 1974 must conform to the new ingredient disclosure regulations. The cosmetic industry can use up old labeling supplies until March 31, 1975, but after that date all products made or packaged must have the new labeling. The CTFA has compiled a lengthy CTFA Cosmetic Industry Dictionary of uniform chemical terms to facilitate the process. Under the industry's voluntary plan, fragrances and coloring, when shown, would have been identified only as such, since these two categories are regarded as trade secrets by manufacturers. The government's mandatory program included disclosure of colors. Requests for confidentiality can be made and this matter has yet to be resolved. In view of the energy crisis which has affected supplies of product ingredients and packaging, the government may have to extend the March 31, 1974 deadline, most likely to September 30, 1974.

The FDA may require an additional warning label on aerosol products. The Consumer Product Safety Commission will also be holding hearings on aerosols.

Federal Trade Commission (FTC)

This agency has been active in regulating (1) advertising, (2) marketing, and (3) mergers. Manufacturers have recently been called upon to submit ad substantiation on acne preparations, deodorants, and shaving equipment. The legal department at the FTC has been reviewing recent mergers and acquisitions involving drug and cosmetic companies to decide whether to bring suit against these combinations.

PERSPECTIVES

The cosmetic industry, through the CTFA, is working closely with the government agencies involved. Obviously government action should be watched closely. In our interviews with corporate managements and individuals at trade publications, we were advised that the industry has a good reputation, is becoming increasingly careful about advertising claims, and that most firms have batch testing procedures in effect. Certain areas, such as hair dyes, aerosols, and treatment products, may be more vulnerable.

Additional legislation is pending in Congress which would require preclearance of cosmetic and toiletry products. Hearings will be held periodically. Legislation of this type would slow new product introductions. However larger-sized manufacturers with proper laboratory facilities would probably experience volume gains since smaller companies would find it difficult to operate in this environment. The industry's self-regulation program may forestall further legislation; but should consumerism dictate the need for one, it may serve as the basis for a new cosmetic law in future.

Barring a startling event, such as the recent elimination of hexachlorophine (and even these products in the main were allowed to sell through), it would appear that the industry thus far has been adjusting well to developments. While government preclearance of new products remains a possibility, government budgets (FDA $2.2 million for fiscal 1974) suggest that drug and food regulations have much higher priority. Since large manufacturers have been gradually building their research and development efforts, they should be equipped to meet requirements with a minimal effect on earnings.

ACCOUNTING CONSIDERATIONS AND ADJUSTMENTS

The companies engaged in the cosmetics and toiletries industry are heterogeneous in nature. Standard balance sheet and profit-and-loss ratios should be computed. Since the major companies are multinational, it is important to try to identify foreign exposure and the balance sheet and profit-and-loss effects of the swings in monetary exchange rates.

Since marketing is the most important factor, breakdowns of sales and earnings by division or product line contained in Form 10-K or annual reports, if of sufficient detail, offers meaningful information. Identification of past trends will aid in future projections. When possible, an analysis should be made of each company's major product lines to determine the overall market size, growth potential, competitive environment, and the brand position within these areas.

New product activity is important to future volume expansion. A judgment should be made of management's short- and long-term plans for corporate expansion, its capability to recognize new markets, shifts in demand for existing product categories, and for introducing new items to capitalize upon these trends. Advertising and promotional expenditures as well as expected breakeven points and margins should also be reviewed.

MARKET BEHAVIOR OF SECURITIES

Cosmetic industry averages, while used, present a problem. If Avon Products is included in the index, it dominates the average. On the other hand, elimination of the company would not be representative since Avon has such an important position in the industry. A better approach is to compute price/earnings ratios and relative price/earnings ratios (S&P 425) for each of the companies for the last several years. The companies with above-average dependable earnings growth have sold at premiums to the S&P 425. In the two-tier market of 1972, this differential was expanded, while secondary companies did not participate. This trend continued until late in 1973 when, reflecting economic concerns and some slowdown in profits, these multiples declined. However, the major quality companies continue to sell at a premium to the S&P 425 in view of the favorable long-term outlook for the industry.

13

Drug and Health Industries

JAMES BALOG
Chairman of the Board
William D. Witter, Inc., New York, New York

and

DAVID H. TALBOT
Vice President
William D. Witter, Inc., New York, New York

HEALING must certainly be one of the oldest of the arts. For centuries it was performed by one man who was doctor, drug manufacturer, pharmacist, and hospital, all in one. Specialization of the various segments of the healing arts took place over the years. By 1900, the distinction among the various factors providing health care was fairly well developed. The health industry of today is still quite young, although its roots date back to ancient times.

Technological and social changes are the twin vectors of growth for the health industry. Technological innovation is certainly well known to the investor and to the layman. But perhaps even more important is the fact that good health is a basic human desire. The investor must realize that health care is not just any business; it carries special social burdens. In turn, the industry's responsiveness to social and technological change is often limited by the many vested interests that exist within the health system, such as the dominant role of the physician.

INDUSTRY COMPONENTS

The analyst approaching the health care industry must assess technological and social changes in addition to the classical requirements of financial analysis. To begin with, the health industry must be divided into segments in order to comprehend the different factors that influence investment analysis and decision making.

325

Drug companies are by far the most important, from an investment point of view; most of this chapter will be devoted to this sector. *Ethical drugs* are those which are available only under prescription and which are promoted solely to the medical and paramedical professions. *Proprietary drugs* are those available without a prescription and heavily promoted to the individual. There are many other distinctions between ethicals and proprietaries, and these are summarized in Table 1. From

TABLE 1

Distinction between Ethical and Proprietary Drugs

		Proprietary	*Ethical*
I.	Product		
	Ailment...............	Minor	Usually major
	Action...............	Relief of symptoms	Potent, often cures
II.	Communication		
	Image................	Brand	Firm's reputation
	Advertising copy.......	Persuasive, emotional	Factual
	Media................	TV, radio	Direct mail and medical journals
	Package..............	Descriptive	Functional
III.	Pricing	Less than $1.00	Over $3.00
IV.	Distribution	Wide (over 200,000 outlets)	Drugstores, hospitals, and pharmacy depts. of retail outlets

Source: William D. Witter, Inc.

an investment point of view, perhaps the two most important distinctions are that the ethical drug companies rely very heavily upon research and new product development, while the proprietary drug companies rely very heavily upon product promotion. The diversification activities of many ethical drug companies in recent years has clouded these distinctions somewhat. For instance, Schering Corporation's merger with Plough, Inc. greatly expanded its participation in the proprietary drug sector. Despite this, the company's orientation remains primarily toward ethical drug research and development. (See Figures 4 and 5 on p. 346, p. 347).

Medical supply companies are those which design, manufacture, and distribute supplies and equipment that are used in patient care, principally in hospitals but increasingly through other channels such as the clinical laboratory. Often the supply items are disposable, thus offering labor-saving advantages as well as ease of use. Major companies such as Baxter Laboratories and Becton-Dickinson specialize in high-volume manufacturing, while American Hospital Supply Corporation retains a leading position in distribution. (See Figure 6 on p. 348). Some commentary will be devoted to this sector.

Instrumentation companies are those which provide biomedical devices for the diagnosis, treatment, or monitoring of physiological conditions. These companies are often offshoots of electronic technology. Interestingly, most of the major drug companies have not been attracted to this field to any great degree; the instrumentation field is populated by numerous, relatively small companies with specialized equipment. There are relatively few major public companies with capitalizations sufficient to warrant broad investor participation. Little discussion will be devoted to instrumentation companies. Analysis of them follows guidelines given in the chapter on the electronics industry.

Patient care companies encompass hospital management companies, companies with extended care facilities, and nursing home operators. This is, of course, one of the newest and smallest areas for investment because the field is still evolving within the structure of government programs and private health insurance. No commentary on this sector will be contained in this chapter.

SIZE AND SCOPE

The U.S. health care industry is the second largest industry in the United States, now accounting for annual spending on the order of $80 billion. Figure 1 breaks down how the medical care dollar is spent. It is interesting to note that the bulk of this vast health spending stream is beyond the reach of the investment community. For instance, services by doctors and dentists account for somewhat over one fourth of the total health care spending. The biggest source of spending is the hospital care portion, accounting for almost 40 percent of the U.S. health care total. The number of products purchased per se from public corporations is relatively small. Drugs, for example, account for about 11 percent of health care spending. These figures illustrate the limited investment opportunities and suggest that there is a concomitant scarcity factor associated with the equities in the health care industry.

As to sources of funds, Table 2 illustrates that these sources are more and more being shifted toward third-party payments, reflecting a dramatic change since the pre–World War II era when health care was largely an individual expense. The main effect of this, from an investment point of view, is that health policy has become public policy because the public purse has become involved. Thus, health product sales growth and pricing no longer respond merely to the traditional laws of supply and demand. Obviously, the ultimate of government involvement would be the passage of some broad-scale national health insurance, a strong likelihood within the next several years. The United States is the only major economic power not having some form of national health insurance.

FIGURE 1

How the Medical Dollar Is Spent

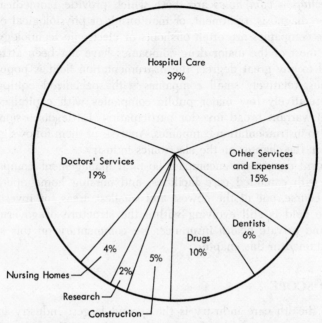

Note: Medical supplies account for 7 percent of the national health dollar and are consumed largely in the hospital care and doctors' service areas (William D. Witter, Inc., estimate).
Source: U.S. Department of Health, Education, and Welfare.

In addition to the demand for products in the United States, there is an important segment of growth abroad. Important overseas activity within health care has been largely confined to the drug companies. American drug companies were among the first, and are currently among the most powerful, of the American-based multinational companies. Of

TABLE 2

Source of Funds for U.S. Health Care

	1950 (percent)	1972 (percent)
Direct.............................	68	35
Third-party		
Public..........................	20 ⎫	37 ⎫
Private insurance and industrial	}32	}65
services........................	12 ⎭	28 ⎭
Total.....................	100	100

Source: U.S. Social Security Administration.

the total sales of American drug companies in 1972 (approximately $8 billion), $2.7 billion was achieved overseas. This represents 34 percent of total sales. Even more importantly, the foreign business has been growing in the past ten years at a compound annual rate of 12 percent versus a compound annual rate of growth in the same period of 8 percent domestically. Further indication of the multinational nature of pharmaceutical companies is the fact that 41 percent or some 240,000 employees of American pharmaceutical manufacturers are employed at overseas locations.

The expansion of the American health care industry abroad in sectors other than drugs has been considerably more modest and for a variety of reasons. The medical supply industry, for example, has made relatively minor inroads abroad. The reason for this may be that disposable medical supplies in the United States represent a relatively new industry, coming into broad hospital acceptance as recently as the mid-1960s. Thus, foreign expansion plans of U.S. medical supply companies have played a subordinate role until recently. Now, foreign sales for the major supply companies are growing very rapidly, and their importance to the industry is beginning to expand.

GROWTH CHARACTERISTICS

The analysis of growth in the health industry involves consideration of numerous complexities. Sheer incidence of disease is one starting point, but sometimes a highly misleading one for assessing growth and demand. The attached tabulation of disease categories shows the tremendous variation between disease incidence statistics, diseases leading to hospital admissions, and diseases causing death. Thus, disease incidence can be a poor indicator for the consumption of products in the health care system, particularly that which occurs in a hospital setting. On the other hand, the incidence ratios might be good indicators of the source of new products since high incidence may reflect a lack of adequate therapeutic approaches. Figure 2 illustrates that one must be very careful to look beneath the surface in the analysis of a specific company or a specific product. Health statistics in this country or abroad are very rudimentary, and many improper inferences can be drawn from them. For one thing, even if the statistics of disease incidence were correct, a number of studies have shown that people will seek treatment for only perhaps one fourth of all the conditions with which they are afflicted.

Having introduced the element of caution in the evaluation of statistics, let us turn our attention to certain macro-industry factors. There is a strong correlation between wealth of nations and spending on health care. This is logical in the sense that once the requirements for food, shelter, and clothing are satisfied, health comes very close behind. The proportion of the gross national product in the United States dedicated

FIGURE 2

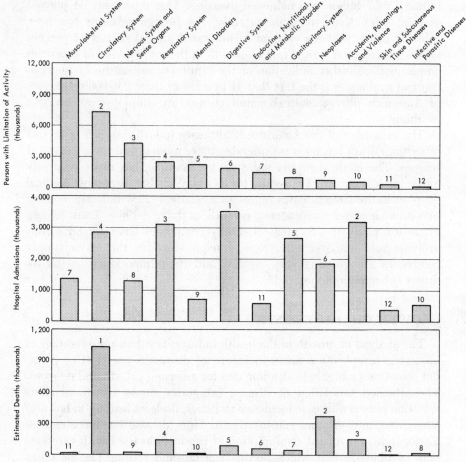

to health care is currently around 7.5 percent, in contrast with 3.8 percent in 1930 and 5.3 percent as recently as 1960.

Another important generalization is that as the spending on health care increases, the amount of government involvement in the health care system also increases. While the United States has a much freer medical economy than most other advanced countries of the world, the ultimate passage of national health insurance should close this gap somewhat.

There is a distinct seasonality to health care expenditures. The incidence of respiratory infections follows the cycle of the weather, showing valleys in the summer and peaks in the winter, as one might expect. How-

ever, these peaks and valleys are not at the same level from year to year
—reflecting the existence of larger cycles of disease generally related to
the fluctuating incidence of influenza infections from year to year. Underlying these cycles of disease is the fact that microorganisms, such as
viruses, have distinct patterns of distribution around the globe. For example, in 1957 a worldwide flu epidemic occurred because of a new
organism, the so-called Hong Kong flu virus. These viruses developed
by a process called mutation; a variation of an existing organism develops
through the processes of natural selection. Because the worldwide population does not have an immunity to that particular organism, it quickly
spreads, causing a large epidemic. Once the epidemic has spread, a
reservoir of natural immunity begins to develop so that the incidence
level will recede. What follows is a lower incidence of disease until another mutation takes place. Unfortunately for the analyst, these cycles
of mutation are not accurately predictable. It is of some help to study
the patterns of the immunity reservoirs around the globe, but there is no
way to predict the development of a new mutant.

Looking at the growth characteristics even more closely, one can
identify five specific stimulants to growth in drugs, medical supplies, and
instruments.

Population

It is obvious that the gradual uptrend in population will lead to the
increased consumption of drugs and supplies. The population of the
United States is expected to grow at an annual rate of about 1.5 percent
over the next ten years, while the worldwide population will grow somewhat faster. Clearly, expansion of this magnitude is not of great excitement to investors were it not for other elements stimulating growth in
health care products. In passing, however, it should be noted that certain sectors of the health industry will probably benefit materially by
efforts to limit population—through the sale of birth control products
and, indirectly, through the upgrading of personal disposable income.
Moreover, the growing complexity of American life produces a greater
incidence of certain disease forms, such as hypertension and emphysema,
and increased urbanization brings additional people in contact with a
more extensive and accessible health delivery system than exists in rural
areas.

Rising Standards of Health Care

With the growing income in the United States and the rest of the
world, more and more of the consumer dollar is being devoted to health
care items. Health care spending tends to rise as disposable personal

income grows. Per capita disposable personal income rose 100 percent between 1948 and 1966 (current prices), while per capita health care expenditures increased 192 percent, roughly twice as fast.

Health Care Plans

The growing use of medical, surgical, and hospitalization plans tends to cause people to allocate more of their income on a *planned basis* for medical care, which in turn tends to raise the level of medical care and the consumption of drugs and other health care products. Hospitalization insurance paid for about 82 percent of all health care in 1973, compared with 37 percent in 1950. However, outside the hospital—where much of American medicine is still practiced—cost reimbursement remains rather spotty. For instance, outpatient drug costs are generally not reimbursable, and dental insurance is still a rarity. Thus, considerable further expansion in third-party coverage in the United States has yet to be enacted; expansion should provide further stimulus to the growth of health care products.

Substitution of Products for People

Drugs and medical supplies should be viewed as labor-saving products, helping to cope with shortages in physicians and other skilled personnel as well as with spiraling wage and salary costs generally. This trend has hardly run its course. In fact, roughly two thirds of all hospital costs are still for payroll and related expenses.

Research Discoveries

The health care industry is very research intensive as voids in existing medical therapy usually represent significant potential markets for new products. Pharmaceutical companies spend about 9 percent of sales on research and development—more than any other sector of U.S. manufacturing. While there is a correlation between research spending, new product development, and earnings growth, it is very difficult to establish the correlation for any particular company over a relatively short period of time.

SPECIAL ROLE OF RESEARCH AND DEVELOPMENT

As drugs extend life spans in conjunction with better nutrition and better general health care, disease entities that were not originally a problem take hold. So long as man continues to extend his life span and the complexities of his life, new products will continue to be required. The adaptability of disease organisms is also reason for continuing emphasis on research and development. Bacteria are particularly adept at devising ways to cope with the antibiotics developed to destroy them. A whole family of diseases caused by so-called gram negative bacteria have surfaced because bacteria of other types have been surpressed through the use of antibiotics. This illustrates the delicate ecological balance that exists among living things that surround us. A therapeutic agent or a medical procedure tends to disturb that balance and a new equilibrium must be reached. It is this constant alteration of the balance that causes the need for new drugs. Many of the new drugs that are developed are not cures but treatments.

Influence of Legislation of Research

Earlier in this chapter we alluded to the interplay between technological change and social change, and nowhere is this more apparent than in pharmaceutical research. Changes in technology and the clamor for legislation have gone hand-in-hand throughout the evolution of the pharmaceutical industry. The basic law governing the conduct of research and the marketing of drug products was the Pure Food and Drug Act passed in 1906. Its primary concern was food adulteration, and its passage grew out of two crises around the turn of the century—excessive use of benzoate of soda as a food preservative and the scandals in the meat-packing industry—which drew attention to the adulteration of food and the unsanitary practices in the food industry. The 1906 law created the Food and Drug Administration, but the FDA at first was largely concerned with food and its purity.

Nothing much happened on the legislative front until 1938 when the Food, Drug, and Cosmetic Act was passed. In the late 1920s and 1930s, much progress took place in the development of chemotherapeutic agents, that is, chemicals used for the treatment of disease. Unfortunately, one of the early sulfa drugs was formulated in liquid which turned out to be unsafe for human consumption, and over 100 children died from ingesting this substance. The laws up to that time were concerned only with adulteration and were not so much concerned with safety. As a result, the new law that was passed in 1938 focused on drugs and their safety. So, another crisis and another step in regulatory control of drug products to keep up with advancing technology was taken.

Then another long interval passed during which there were enormous developments in chemotherapeutic agents, again with practically nothing taking place on a regulatory front. In the early 1940s, we had the tremendous growth of the antibiotics; in the late 1940s and early 1950s, the steroids; and during the decade of the 1950s—probably the most prolific time for drug development—came the antihistamines, diuretics, mental health drugs, and many other major advances.

In the late 1950s, Senator Kefauver began to investigate the economic practices of the pharmaceutical industry; what had been a rather mysterious industry began to be exposed to public scrutiny. Also about this time came the thalidomide episode (a sedative which caused birth defects when used by pregnant women) which raised questions about the testing practices of pharmaceutical products and reopened the whole question of safety in drugs. Finally, the rapid proliferation of drugs in the 1950s and the aggressive promotion of a variety of modifications of basic drugs raised the questions about the benefit-to-risk ratios for the patients. These events led to the passage of the 1962 Amendments to the 1938 Drug and Cosmetic Act. These amendments, in addition to being concerned with whether or not drugs are safe, were also concerned with whether or not drugs were efficacious. In short, did the drugs perform as advertised and was the benefit commensurate with the added risks, since no drug is free from side effects.

Ethical Drug Development Cycle

Figure 3 depicts the manner in which an ethical drug is developed and the influence of regulatory developments—several of which resulted from the 1962 Amendments. Drug development is essentially a trial-and-error process based upon relatively few unique insights into the relationship

FIGURE 3

Development of a New Drug: Proof of Safety and Efficacy

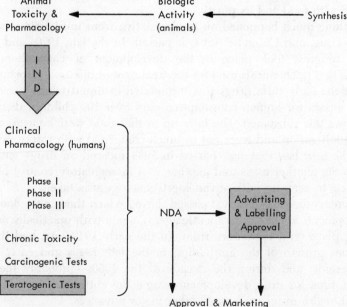

Note: Shaded areas show 1962 amendments.
Source: William D. Witter, Inc.

between chemicals and a living system. As biologists and biochemists study living systems, they begin to get some comprehension of the chemical mechanisms by which tissues exist in the healthy and diseased states. The medicinal chemist then synthesizes chemicals which might alter this chemical process within the living system. Once candidate compounds have been synthesized, they are tested in animals. Careful measurements are made within the animals to determine what desirable biochemical effect the drug is having in the test animal and what undesirable side effects are being encountered. After very exhaustive studies in animals, the chemical compound may be selected for a trial in humans.

The first tests in humans are under very closely controlled conditions and involve sensitive monitoring of the reaction of the substance in the human body. Particular attention is paid to the hazards of use, the biological activity in man, and the dosage that might be used. Sometimes very surprising results occur. For example, one substance that was an excellent contraceptive in rabbits turned out to be a fertility enhancer when given to women, illustrating a research phenomenon called "species differences." This also plagues the drug researcher in that a side effect in an animal may not occur in man, and yet drug regulatory agencies are extremely wary of any side effects observed in any test animals.

Once the drug passes the early tests, Phase I, the drug moves into broader-scale trials in man, with a limited number of clinical investigators and an expanded group of patients. Here, dosage forms are better established and the biological activity can be monitored in a variety of persons —by age, by sex, by ethnic origin, etc. Thus, the applicability of the drug to a broader population is ascertained. If the drug is successful at this stage, it can then move into broad-scale, or Phase III, clinical trials. At this stage, the emphasis is on collecting large amounts of data, in a variety of users, under a variety of actual conditions. Massive data are compiled and submitted for approval by the Food and Drug Administration as a New Drug Application (NDA). In addition to tests for the efficacy and safety of the product, Phase III data also determines the labeling claims and use restrictions for each drug. Among the tests that are conducted are those pertaining to birth defects, an obvious outgrowth of the thalidomide episode.

Once the drug is finally evaluated by the Food and Drug Administration, it is either approved for marketing or additional data is requested. Following introduction, each drug is carefully monitored by the manufacturer, and untoward side reactions must be immediately reported to the Food and Drug Administration. *No drug is completely free of undesirable side effects.* There is always a balance between desirable effects and undesirable effects, between benefit and risk. The ultimate evaluation of the drug is its broad-scale mass use all across the country under a variety of conditions. No structured trial can completely foretell the results in broad-scale use.

The importance of this sequence of events to the analyst is that it takes time and money to develop new ethical drugs, and the odds of success are rather small. It is important to note that less than 1 out of 100 chemical agents synthesized ever reaches the stage of initial human testing, and of these only about 3 out of 100 receives FDA approval for marketing. (Overall ratio: 1 in 5,000.) Thus, the analyst should be extremely cautious on imputing any particular value and probability of success on a compound that is in the animal test stages. Even if the drug gets into human trials, the odds are very poor that it will become a marketable entity. It is a sobering thought that it takes approximately seven years from the time a candidate compound is first selected for evaluation in animals until the time that it becomes a marketable ethical drug. In terms of expense, the development of a new single entity drug would take a minimum of $5–$7 million. True, it is possible that a particular flash of genius could result in a new drug in a very short time period, at a very low expense. But this sort of serendipity was more likely in Pasteur's day than it is at the present time. Analysts should be well armed with skepticism when evaluating new drugs.

Proprietary Drug Development

Proprietary drugs are subject to somewhat the same Food and Drug Administration regulations as are the ethicals. The development cycle is less difficult because the proprietary drug product is based upon a chemical compound that is already generally recognized as safe. Because of the nature of the chemical ingredients, much of the animal testing of the drug itself has been completed, and the drug has been in wide-scale use in humans before it is formulated into a proprietary drug. Nonetheless, the formulation itself and its mode of administration must be tested in human beings. Even though the compound is identical, scientists must be sure that nothing has been altered in the method of preparation of the drug form to change its therapeutic action or introduce new hazards. Thus, a drug company engages in certain aspects of the clinical trials and submits a New Drug Application similar to that for an ethical drug, although far less complex. A major proprietary drug may cost on the order of $500,000 to $1 million to develop and market test. This process consumes two or three years, perhaps longer if a complex NDA is involved.

Medical Supply Product Development

While the origin of a new product idea in the drug field is quite often a biochemical observation, the origin of many medical supply products relates to commercial observations. Medical supply companies are continually attempting to assess the needs of the physician, nurse, and other medical personnel in hospitals and private-practice settings to determine what would be more effective, more convenient, less prone to infections, more comfortable to the patient, etc. Imitation by another manufacturer can be rapid, depending on the complexity of the production and marketing requirements for a given product. Generally, the distinctions among the products are on some minor aspect of design or cost. Thus, marketing and service are vital considerations, and the competitive advantages normally accrue to the more powerful companies such as American Hospital Supply Corporation.

Instrumentation Product Development

Biomedical instruments quite often originate through the joint efforts of a physician and an electronics engineer. The development cycles can be extremely long, simply because prototypes are put into actual use and modified continually as times goes on. Normally, a drug product is developed completely in the laboratory and is put into medical practice in the final form in which it is to be used. On the other hand, a biomedical device is quite often modified frequently as use experience is gained.

The regulatory agencies are also greatly concerned with these new product introductions and are becoming more so. Generally, those products which are implanted within the body will be subject to considerably more examination under any new medical device legislation. Of course, manufacturing practices should be of the highest order, and sterility is continually monitored by most companies and by the regulatory agencies.

GOVERNMENT INVOLVEMENT

As mentioned earlier, the health care business bears special social responsibilities. As such, it has been the target of great interest by governmental bodies for a number of years. The health care system is extremely complex, and the consumer is in a very difficult position in assessing whether or not he is receiving proper treatment and proper value. Consequently, there has been a long history of regulation of the health care industry in its various aspects, and this is bound to blossom with each passing year. Some of the more important regulatory factors involved in the health care industry are discussed in this section.

Food and Drug Administration (FDA)

This agency is part of the Department of Health, Education, and Welfare and is charged with the responsibility of supervising the safety and efficacy of food and drug products sold in the United States. In addition, no drugs may be exported for medical use unless they have been approved for use by the Food and Drug Administration (FDA). The

FDA makes its biggest headlines in the consumers' mind with its seizures of existing products that are found to be defective. But from an industry point of view, the FDA has its greatest influence on premarketing clearance, and this is of greater concern to the analyst than the relatively infrequent seizures that take place for marketed products.

Regulatory activity in proprietary drugs has accelerated in recent years. The FDA, sometimes in conjunction with the FTC, has been attempting to bring the advertising claims for proprietary drugs in line with scientific evidence of safety and efficacy. In particular, the agency is concerned with irrational combinations of ingredients whose primary purpose is to create an advertising claim rather than a therapeutic advantage. Once current investigations and hearings are complete, many proprietary drug products may have been reformulated and relabeled to conform with the more stringent attitudes of the FDA.

The FDA is beginning to expand its authority into the premarket clearance of certain medical devices and instruments. To date, the agency has dealt with only a few products—those which come into prolonged contact with the body, such as specialty contact lenses and intrauterine contraceptive devices impregnated with a chemical. The passage of federal legislation for medical devices should greatly expand the FDA's premarket clearance authority. Until this legislation is enacted, the medical device industry will remain virtually unregulated with respect to premarket clearance, manufacturing quality, and safety standards.

In general, increased FDA regulatory activity produces greater uniformity of products and advertising claims and a more expensive and time-consuming research and development process. It seems likely that the major health companies with established products and financial resources may be better equipped for this changing environment than the smaller companies within the industry.

Federal Trade Commission (FTC)

This agency of the government is particularly important to the analyst reviewing proprietary drugs. The Federal Trade Commission is particularly concerned with whether or not drugs are being advertised correctly and that the claims are not misleading. The FTC has been a relatively ineffective agency in the proprietary sector. In recent years, there has been a closer working relationship between the Food and Drug Administration and the Federal Trade Commission in an attempt to enhance the effectiveness of the Federal Trade Commission. Essentially, the FDA can use medical experts whereas the FTC is, unfortunately, limited to the processes of the law. The FTC is also of interest to the analyst when it comes to mergers that might cause an undue restraint of trade.

Drug Enforcement Agency (DEA)

This agency is part of the Justice Department and is concerned with the control of substances that might cause addiction. The agency was created by federal narcotics control legislation of the late 1960s and was granted broad authority to restrict the prescribing patterns and manufacture of drugs suspected of having abuse potential. DEA has greatly reduced the U.S. market for amphetamine drugs through these measures, and the agency has shown interest in possibly restricting the use of certain analgesics (pain killers). It seems doubtful that analgesics will be as harshly restricted as the amphetamines have been.

Legislative Trends

The health care analyst should keep closely attuned to developments in the United States Congress. A congressional hearing conducted to consider new legislation can have a substantial impact in its own right, causing a strong shift in stock market sentiment. The health industry is assaulted frequently with great enthusiasm by its critics. In this regard, one of the perennial topics seems to be health industry pricing practices and profitability.

Actually, medical cost increases have been strongest for hospital-related services (hospital fees have doubled since 1964), and physicians' fees have been the second fastest growing aspect of medical costs. On the other hand, the cost of drugs and prescriptions has actually declined. The main argument of critics is that net income for drug companies is "too high," while the counter-argument of the industry is that the profit is needed to "finance research." This argument seems to be one that will rage for as long as health care issues are being discussed. Indeed, the drug companies are more profitable as a percentage of sales and as a percentage of net worth than U.S. manufacturing in general. Net income as a percent of sales ranges between 12 percent and 14 percent for typical major drug companies, whereas for all manufacturers it ranges between 4 percent and 6 percent. As a percentage of net worth, the pharmaceutical industry leaders have returns after taxes on the order of 20 percent— reflecting their strong commitment to research and development—while that of U.S. manufacturers in general is on the order of 10 to 12 percent.

From an analyst point of view, it is best to recognize that the main difficulty is that a health care expenditure is unplanned and generally creates a high degree of disruption in the financial planning of the individual. The measurement of the value received is difficult for the individual to comprehend, overwhelmed as he is by this major unplanned expenditure. Observors look at the health delivery system in a statistical sense, whereas change must occur on a human level; and it is far easier to theorize about the health care system than to change it.

Another source of recent congressional discussion has been the question of testing ethics in the health care industry—especially administration of dangerous drugs to individuals and the inadequate disclosure, by hospitals, of patients participating in a new drug trial. By and large, the drug companies and members of the medical profession are extremely aware of the ethical and legal hazards in medical testing. There are very few ironclad rules to guide investigators in new areas, and the investor is forced to rely upon the good judgment and ethical standards of the company in which he is investing. Obviously, a producer of drugs, instruments, or medical supply products has a very important commercial reason to maintain high standards of business and medical ethics, since deviations on his part can have serious commercial consequence.

Generic Drugs and Pricing

Drugs are generally trademarked to identify a particular manufacturer's brand of a basic chemical ingredient. This ingredient is also given a generic name which identifies it in a relatively simple way. For example, the tranquilizer Equanil is the registered trademark of the Wyeth Division of American Home Products. The generic name for Equanil is Meprobamate and, in turn, its chemical name is 2-Methyl-2-N-Propyl-1,3 Propanediol Dicarbamate. It is easy to see why a generic name is given to describe the underlying chemical formula! Once the patent on the substance has expired, any company is free to manufacture and market that substance under its generic name but not the trademarked name. While patents have a 17-year life in the United States, trademarks remain the property of the originator indefinitely.

Many of the critics of drug pricing believe that trademark names create the opportunity for drug companies to charge excessive prices. The feeling is that if substances were available under the generic name from a variety of producers prices would be considerably lower. Of course, this would not be possible until the patent for the original inventor has expired, or if he were forced to license it to others.

The analyst should be very cognizant of the expiration dates of patents that are of importance to the companies that he is analyzing. Obviously, such an event usually ushers in generic competition and lower prices. By this time, however, the company has probably recovered its research and development costs and is in an excellent manufacturing cost position as well. While the profit margin is bound to decrease when the drug "goes generic," the usual case is that the drug can continue to be marketed at an attractive, though lower, profit margin.

VI. THE PROFIT AND LOSS STATEMENT

As one might imagine, the profit-and-loss-statement ratios of ethical drug companies, proprietary drug companies, and medical supply companies are vastly different. While there are very few companies that are "pure" participants in the ethical and proprietary drug sector, shown below are typical examples drawn from each of the three sectors to illustrate the profit-and-loss-statement ratios.

TABLE 3

Profit and Loss Comparisons (shown by percent)

	Ethical Drug (Merck & Co., Inc.)	Proprietary Drug (Amer. Home Products)	Medical Supplies (Baxter Labs., Inc.)
Sales.................................	100	100	100
Cost of goods.......................	34.2	45.9	56.8
Gross margin.......................	65.8	54.1	43.2
Selling, general, and administrative........................	30.1	29.4	26.5
Research...........................	8.3	3.8	5.0
Pretax.............................	28.2	21.6	9.8
Aftertax...........................	15.4	10.9	7.9
Compound 5-year growth rate (1968–1972)			
Sales............................	11	10	22
Pretax...........................	10	12	16
Aftertax.........................	10	11	19
Tax rate...........................	44.0	47.7	18.6

Note: Based on 1972 annual report data. The relatively low tax rate of Baxter Labs. largely reflects unusually high utilization of Puerto Rican manufacturing facilities. This phenomenon is not unique to the medical supply sector. Drug companies have become particularly active in Puerto Rico in recent years.

Assessing Table 3, certain salient factors stand out.

1. Cost of goods sold as a percent of sales ranges from 34 percent to 54 percent for the ethicals and medical supply companies, respectively.
2. Marketing is a major element of each of the three sectors, as indicated by the high percentages of the sales dollar dedicated to selling, general, and administrative expenses.
3. Research and development, as a percent of sales, is the highest for the ethical sector and lower for the proprietary drug and medical supply sector.
4. Profit margins are the highest for the ethical drug companies and lowest for the medical supply companies.
5. Growth rates in sales and profits are generally more accelerated in the medical supply field, where overseas and domestic markets are somewhat more dynamic than in the pharmaceutical sector.

In all three cases, the analyst should be aware of the fact that the health care companies have a sizable fixed-cost component because of the relative importance of selling, general, administrative, and research expenses. Thus, changes in sales can have very dramatic impact on pretax profits. While the overall margin for an ethical company is on the order of 25–30 percent, the *incremental* income from incremental sales can be on the order of 50–90 percent. Therefore, a sudden windfall of sales resulting from such things as withdrawal of a competitor's product or an epidemic of a respiratory disease can dramatically magnify profits. Of course, this leverage also operates in the opposite direction, such as when a product recall produces a collapse in sales.

Pressure on the top line of the profit and loss statement from price changes varies by sector. Ethical drug companies have perhaps the most to gain or lose in terms of profits, depending on whether an important product is being introduced or is losing its patent status. Analysts should be alert for companies that are losing patent protection on one drug and have a flow of new drugs that is insufficient to displace this loss. In the proprietary sector, brand names are generally more important than

TABLE 4

The Economics of Introducing a New Proprietary Drug

	Year 1	Year 2	Year 3
Sales....................................	$5,000	$6,000	$6,900
Growth (percent).....................		+20	+15
Gross profit (70 percent)..............	$3,500	$4,200	$4,800
Marketing...........................	$5,000	$4,200	$3,300
Net profit (50 percent tax rate)...........	($750)	Break even	$750
Cumulative net profit..................	($750)	($750)	—
		Break even	Payout

Source: William D. Witter, Inc.

patents, and the effect of a new prescription drug gaining or losing patent status is buffered by the existence of over-the-counter items that sell on a brand name basis. In the medical supply sector, active price protection is a fact of life, and a product's success depends on manufacturing skills and efficiencies plus the marketing capability and medical reputation of the company involved.

Some special considerations are required of the analyst when assessing a proprietary drug company. This relates to the high cost of introducing new products and the attendant high risks. Shown in Table 4 is an illustration of the introductory costs of a proprietary drug. This tabulation assumes that the targeted sales volume for a proprietary drug to be introduced nationally is on the order of $5 million in the first year, a figure required to bear the burden of a national marketing program. As illustrated, the cost of proprietary drug goods sold is relatively small, on the order of 30 percent; but the first-year marketing expenses can be targeted to equal the first year's sales expectations. As illustrated in Table 4, given the expected growth rate, the product might break even in the second year; and in the third year it might break even cumulatively. It is obvious that the profit-and-loss-statement risks from the introduction of a new proprietary can be very severe. While the marketing *expenditures* might be $5 million for the introduction, the first year's sales might be substantially less than the targeted $5 million. Should this occur, the first-year losses can be substantially higher than the budgeted loss shown in the tabulation. If the product does not show the sufficient introductory acceptance and subsequent growth, the whole venture has to be written off, with possibly great losses. The analyst, therefore, should be very sensitive to new product introductions on a case-by-case basis, but even more sensitive to the *pattern* of new product introductions. Most proprietary drug companies are, or should be, constantly introducing new products—some of which will be successful and others of which will fail. If the new product introductory cycle has been interrupted, it may mean that the profitable products were being "milked" and the profits not being reinvested in the introduction of new products. Once the "daisy chain" of new product introductions—successes and failures—is broken, it can only be reinstituted by taking losses on the first of the new products to start another "daisy chain" going.

As to virtually all of the major companies in the drug and medical supply business, research and development expenses are written off as incurred. This tends to improve the quality of earnings, vis-à-vis other industrial sectors that might capitalize research and development expenditures. Furthermore, health care companies employ fairly rapid write-offs of plant and equipment, partly because the estimated lives of the equipment may be short due to technological change. In short, the quality of health care company earnings—especially given the secular growth of the medical business—is usually markedly superior to industry in general. This perhaps gives one of the reasons why the price/earnings ratio of companies in this field is higher than stocks in general.

The multinational nature of health industry companies is worthy of special comment. Because of this multinational operating characteristic, they have been able to operate in lower tax rate countries and establish offshore subsidiaries to take advantage of tax laws. In particular, manufacturing operations in tax-haven areas such as Puerto Rico, Grand Bahama, and Ireland have become popular. These areas of the world have been anxious to attract health companies because they are relatively "clean" industries whose products are lightweight and high in unit value so that shipping costs are not prohibitive. Moreover, many of these countries are anxious to have an indigenous industry to generate foreign exchange.

Thus, multinational operation tends to manifest itself in low tax rates. During the period since 1960, the American drug and medical supply companies have shown a downtrend in tax rates as a result of expansion in overseas operations. In general, these tax situations are sound and should not cause the analyst particular concern—except that tax preferences have a finite life, and attention should be focused on their expiration dates. So far, and perhaps for the next five to ten years, most health care companies will be able to roll over their tax preferences within a given country or from country to country to preserve their overall tax advantage.

Foreign exchange risks are also a fact of life for multinational companies. For years, leading American drug and medical supply companies have operated globally and have become rather sophisticated in currency hedging operations. Nonetheless, large currency devaluations can have significant impact from year to year. This was particularly true during the 1972–1973 period when the U.S. dollar was effectively devalued relative to several other important foreign currencies, thus producing a favorable impact on sales and earnings gains for American multinational corporations.

TABLE 5

Varying Importance of Debt

Pharmaceutical Industry		*Medical Supply Industry*	
	Approx. Long-Term Debt as Percent of Total Capitalization		*Approx. Long-Term Debt as Percent of Total Capitalization*
American Home Products	10	American Hospital Supply	5
Eli Lilly	5	Baxter Laboratories	45
Merck	5	Becton, Dickinson	30
Pfizer	25		
Schering-Plough	5		

Source: Company-published Annual Reports, 1972.

From a liquidity point of view, drug companies are in particularly strong condition because of their high profit margins and the methods of writing off research and development and most other assets. This has resulted in generally high cash positions, favorable working capital ratios, and excellent debt/equity ratios. Typical recent debt/equity ratios for a variety of drug companies are shown in Table 5, along with those from leading medical supply companies. The medical supply companies offer less internal cash generation, and because of their higher working capital needs generally show more debt leverage in their balance sheets.

INVESTMENT CHARACTERISTICS

One of the first things that the investor must realize about the drug and medical supply industries is that they are relatively small industries in terms of capitalization. The capitalization of all of the drug and medical supply companies listed on the New York Stock Exchange is approximately $54 billion. This contrasts sharply with that of such solitary corporate giants as General Motors ($14 billion) and IBM ($39 billion). Thus, there is a scarcity factor associated with these companies that manifests itself in a high price/earnings ratio.

Drug and medical supply companies sell on the basis of growth rather than yield. With yield typically on the order of only 1 to 2 percent, the health industry is a classic growth-stock investment where the consistency and quality of earnings are key ingredients. We noted the elements of income quality earlier. Consistency can be illustrated by the fact that the drug industry has not had an earnings setback for at least the last 20 years. While not *every* company within the industry has a forward progress in earnings each year, earnings slumps of the reasonably well-managed companies are of relatively short duration. The earnings slumps are usually related to competitive or technological obsolescence of a particular product, such as the oral contraceptives in the case of G. D. Searle; a regulatory change, such as the forced withdrawal of certain combination antibiotics by Upjohn; or a serious side effect in a major product, such as occurred with certain weight-reducing agents marketed by Smith Kline Corporation. Indeed, one of the important areas of investigation for any analyst is to anticipate these periodic disappointments and assess a stock's subsequent recovery prospects. Syntex has been particularly volatile over the past 15 years, but the amplitude of these fluctuations is diminishing as the company appears to be improving the quality and consistency of its earnings. Upjohn endured enormously difficult periods of product withdrawals and regulatory attacks on some of its key drugs. Since then, the company has resumed growth at an attractive rate and has made demonstrable progress in research and development.

Institutional ownership of drug stocks is very high. The better the company and the more consistent its earnings pattern, the more attractive the stock has been to the institutional investor. Indeed, the drug companies are prominent members of the upper tier of the stock market that has developed in recent years. Their stock capitalization, which is small to begin with, is often virtually controlled by institutional investors. Thus, the market for many drug stocks can be quite thin, even with respect to the capitalizations. For example, the average recent trading volume of Merck is 160,000 shares per week, or 0.2 percent of its total capitalization of 74 million shares.

STOCK PRICE BEHAVIOR

In order to gain an impression of the valuation of the stocks in the ethical, proprietary, and medical supply sectors, we have developed composites of these prices and related them to the Standard & Poor's 425 Index. In the accompanying charts, we show the relative evaluations for these three sectors going back to 1960. The Standard & Poor's 425 price/earnings ratio is plotted as a base figure, and the price/earnings ratio of a composite of companies in each of the three sectors plotted relative to it. The shaded area between the S&P 425 line and that of the sector composite is the price/earnings premium for the group.

The ethical drug sector (see Figure 4) has typically shown a price/ earnings premium of 55–65 percent over the S&P 425. This has remained relatively consistent over the years, but note that this premium expanded in the last couple of years. This is obviously a reflection of the esteem in which the drug stocks are held during a period of general market and economic uncertainty, when earnings quality and predictability are key investment criteria. Clearly, any broadening of the market would tend to bring the ethical drug companies down closer to their historical premium to the S&P 425.

Proprietary drug companies have also shown a price/earnings premium increase over S&P 425 for the entire time span (see Figure 5). However, the premium started to expand in the middle 1960s and apparently has achieved a more permanent increase in premium relative to the S&P 425. Indeed, proprietary drug companies are now selling at premiums roughly in line with those of the ethicals. In the 1950s, the ethical drug companies had a higher premium than the proprietaries because of the enthusiasm that investors were willing to attach to the new product prospects of the ethical drug companies. Since the mid-1960s, the new

FIGURE 4

Ethical Drug Industry: Average Price/Earnings Ratios

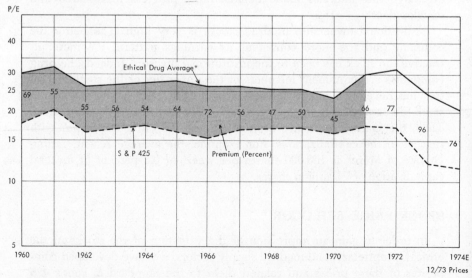

* Includes Abbott Labs, Lilly, Merck, Schering (only to 1970), Searle, SK&F, and Upjohn.

FIGURE 5

Proprietary Drug Industry: Average Price/Earnings Ratios

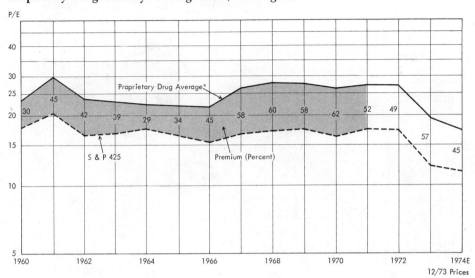

* Includes American Home, Bristol-Myers, Miles Labs, Plough (only to 1970, Schering-Plough after 1970), Pfizer, Sterling Drug, and Warner-Lambert.

product introduction capabilities of ethical drug companies has decreased, and so the investor has been willing to upgrade the proprietary drug company earnings closer to that of the ethicals. It also should be mentioned that the distinction between ethicals and proprietaries has blurred considerably as the ethical drug companies have diversified into proprietaries and other product lines, so that their investment characteristics are becoming more similar to those of the proprietaries.

Medical supply companies have perhaps the most interesting price/earnings development over the past ten or twelve years (see Figure 6). Just prior to the passage of the Medicare legislation, the medical supply companies attained a much higher investor esteem. Indeed, medical supply companies were overvalued because of the great rush of the investor to participate in the Medicare boom. Subsequently, the price/ earnings ratios have come down and the premiums are now in the 130 percent range. It is clear that the medical supply companies are still seeking their "normal" level of price/earnings premium. This will come about as the secular growth trend of the industry becomes more established and more predictable, as opposed to a burst of growth as a result of the passage of new legislation. The medical supply companies have become a definite part of the health care system. Their products are contributing to the expansion of health services in this country and are imparting greater cost efficiency to the medical system.

FIGURE 6

Medical Supply Industry: Average Price/Earnings Ratios

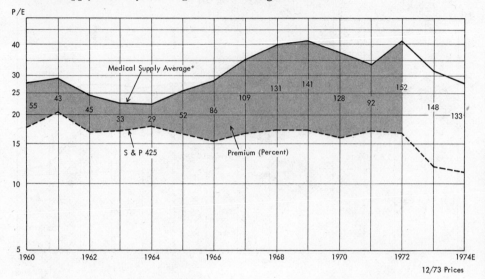

12/73 Prices

* Includes American Hospital, Bard, Baxter Labs, Becton Dickinson, Cutter Labs (to 1971 only), IPCO (to 1970 only), and Johnson & Johnson.

CONCLUDING COMMENTS

Just as the health care industry has gone through its phases of development, the analysis of health care companies has also changed over the years. In the 1950s when drug companies were rapidly developing new products, the burden on the analyst was to track these developments. The typical literature that the analyst would follow would include the *Journal of the American Medical Association* and the *New England Journal of Medicine*. But today, research and development progress is a much reduced part of the analyst's work load. Today, the analyst must continue to follow what goes on in the "Halls of Science," but he must be equally alert to what goes on in the "Halls of Congress." Health industry analysis today includes an analysis of what is going on in government.

In this chapter, we have attempted to describe the health industry as encompassing both research and marketing, and the analyst should monitor these two facts with equal vigor; the health industry *is* a marketing business. True, new product development is required in order to fuel the marketing machine, but essentially the success of the major companies revolves around how well they market the products and how much sales and profits can be extracted from each research discovery. Thus, the analyst should be extremely careful to evaluate the legislative changes that might impact the marketing of drugs. Here, of course, the pressures on price are of prime importance. The analyst, therefore, must look to the laboratory, to the legislatures, and to society all around him. It is changes in these three places which will have major impact on the profit and loss statement, the balance sheet, and the price/earnings ratios these equities will command in the marketplace.

14

Electrical Equipment

IRWIN W. SILVERBERG, C.F.A.
Vice President
Loeb, Rhoades & Co., New York, New York

THE STRUCTURE AND SCOPE OF THE INDUSTRY

THE electrical manufacturing industry (EMI), as defined by the National Electrical Manufacturers Association (NEMA) ranks sixth among all industries in its contribution to both domestic and international economies. The industry's products fall into a variety of categories having differing characteristics as to growth, cyclicality, manufacturing processes, distribution, etc. The participating companies range from small, narrow-line producers to the two broadly diversified industry giants, General Electric and Westinghouse, which had combined revenues of $15.3 billion in 1972. While some 25–30 percent of those combined revenues fall outside of the electrical equipment industry as presented here, their participation still is quite large in relationship to total industry shipments of $52.2 billion, as shown in Table 1.

Another source of statistical information concerning the electrical manufacturing industry besides NEMA is the data compiled by the United States Department of Commerce in its Standard Industrial classification (SIC) Code. Although the subgroupings are slightly different, the eight categories under SIC Code 36, titled Electrical Machinery and Equipment Manufacturers, accounted for 81.6 percent of the value of products comprising the NEMA total in 1970. The remaining 18.4 percent, principally air conditioning and related equipment and electric generating equipment, can be found under SIC Code 35.

Table 1 shows that the growth of sales in current dollars for the EMI

TABLE 1

Value of Electrical Equipment Industry Shipments and Comparison with All Manufacturing Industries and Durable Goods Industries 1963–72

	Value of Shipments ($ billion)										Compound Annual Growth Rate 1963–72 (percent)
	1963	1964	1965	1966	1967	1968	1969	1970	1971	1972	
Consumer products............	$ 6.8	$ 7.5	$ 8.4	$ 9.1	$ 9.4	$ 10.1	$ 10.4	$ 10.0	$ 10.5	$ 11.6	6.2
Lighting equipment............	1.9	2.0	2.2	2.5	2.7	3.0	3.3	3.4	3.5	4.1	8.9
Industrial electronics and communications equipment............	8.5	9.0	9.9	11.7	12.8	13.6	14.6	14.6	15.4	16.9	7.9
Industrial equipment............	4.1	4.6	5.2	6.0	6.1	6.3	6.9	7.1	7.1	7.4	6.8
Building equipment............	0.9	1.0	1.1	1.2	1.3	1.4	1.6	1.6	1.8	2.1	9.9
Insulating materials............	0.5	0.5	0.6	0.7	0.6	0.7	0.8	0.7	0.8	0.9	6.7
Insulated wire and cable.........	1.6	1.9	2.2	3.0	2.9	2.5	2.9	3.2	3.1	3.4	8.7
Power equipment............	2.2	2.4	2.8	3.1	3.6	4.0	4.3	4.9	5.3	5.8	11.4
Total electrical manufacturing industries.....	$ 26.5	$ 28.9	$ 32.4	$ 37.3	$ 39.4	$ 41.6	$ 44.9	$ 45.5	$ 47.4	$ 52.2	7.8
Durable goods industries..........	219.0	235.6	266.6	295.6	302.6	332.3	353.5	336.7	359.4	406.7	7.1
All manufacturing corporations.........	420.4	448.0	492.0	538.4	557.5	603.4	642.7	630.7	671.0	749.6	6.6

Source: NEMA Statistical Department, United States Department of Commerce.

TABLE 2

Profitability of the Electrical Manufacturing Industry versus All Manufacturing Corporations 1963–72

	1963	1964	1965	1966	1967	1968	1969	1970	1971	1972
Percent return on sales after taxes:										
Electrical Manufacturing Industry..........	3.8	4.2	4.7	4.9	4.4	4.3	3.9	3.3	3.5	3.9
All Manufacturing Corporations.............	4.7	5.2	5.6	5.6	5.0	5.1	4.8	4.0	4.2	4.3
Percent return on employed capital after taxes:										
Electrical Manufacturing Industry..........	7.7	8.6	10.1	10.7	8.9	8.4	7.4	5.9	6.1	7.2
All Manufacturing Corporations.............	8.2	9.2	10.1	10.2	8.6	8.7	8.1	6.4	6.9	7.0

Source: Federal Trade Commission.

between 1963 and 1972 has been more rapid than either the total durable goods industries or all manufacturing corporations. As can be seen in Table 2, the net margin on sales of the EMI has consistently been below that for all manufacturing corporations, but the gap was narrower in 1972 than at any time since 1963. The industry's return on total capital in 1972 was comparable to that for all manufacturing corporations.

Labor costs as a percent of sales are substantially higher for electrical equipment manufacturers, generally, than for all industrial companies as shown in Table 3.

TABLE 3

Labor Costs as a Percent of Sales

	1972	*1971*	*1970*	*1965*	*1960*
All industrial companies	26.9	25.9	27.9	27.1	27.8
Electrical/Electronics manufacturers	37.5	37.4	39.4	39.3	41.1

Source: Standard & Poor's *Outlook*. Copyright 1973.

Historically, exports of the EMI have been well in excess of imports. However a substantial increase in imports of home electronics products in the late 1960s and more recent increases in other household appliances as well as transmission and distribution equipment for utilities has served to narrow the favorable balance of trade, as shown in Table 4. Imports have been virtually nonexistent in control and distribution equipment for the important industrial and construction markets, and they have been a relatively minor factor in power generation. It is likely that the recent relative changes in international currency values and foreign reaction to antidumping suits brought by several U.S. manufacturers will serve to slow down imports, with the result that exports should exceed imports by gradually increasing amounts over the next several years.

THE CHARACTERISTICS OF DIFFERENT MARKET SEGMENTS

Industrial electronics and communications equipment, the largest sector of the industry as described in Table 1, is covered in the preceding section of this book. The principal focus of this section will be consumer products, industrial equipment, building equipment, and power equipment.

Consumer Products

Apart from home electronics products, which are discussed in the preceding section, the major area within the consumer sector is house-

TABLE 4

Electrical Equipment versus Imports 1963–72

	1963	1964	1965	1966	1967	1968	1969	1970	1971	1972
					billions of dollars					
Electrical manufacturing industry:										
Exports	$1.7	$1.9	$1.9	$2.2	$2.4	$2.6	$3.1	$3.4	$3.3	$3.9
Imports	0.4	0.5	0.7	1.1	1.2	1.6	2.0	2.4	2.7	3.5

Source: United States Department of Commerce and expanded by the NEMA Statistical Department.

TABLE 5

Growth of Manufacturer's Unit Shipments and Related Retail Value* for Home Appliances 1963–72

	1963		1972		Average Compound Annual Growth 1963–72 (by percent)	
	Number Shipped (millions)	Retail Value ($ millions)	Number Shipped (millions)	Retail Value ($ millions)	Number Shipped	Retail Value
Major appliances						
Air treatment..........	2.2	$ 508	5.1	$ 958	9.8	7.3
Kitchen...............	11.1	2,582	19.8	4,167	6.7	5.5
Home laundry.........	5.7	1,255	9.0	1,901	5.3	4.7
Water heaters.........	3.4	273	5.4	473	5.2	6.3
Total major appliances..	22.3	4,618	39.3	7,498	6.5	5.5
Electric housewares						
Air treatment..........	8.0	245	13.9	398	6.3	5.5
Floor care............	5.3	369	9.3	582	6.4	5.2
Kitchen electrics.......	34.1	559	54.4	1,073	5.3	7.5
Personal care electrics..	20.3	297	20.6	346	–0–	1.6
Total electric housewares..	67.7	1,470	98.3	2,398	4.2	5.6

* Retail value is based upon manufacturer's suggested selling price, rather than actual transaction prices which probably are lower.
Source: *Merchandising Week* Statistical Issue, 1973: Billboard Publications, New York.

hold appliances—divided into major appliances (refrigerators, ranges, room air conditioners, home laundry equipment, water heaters, etc.) and electric housewares (fans, humidifiers, vacuum cleaners, blenders, broilers, can openers, irons, hair dryers, hair setters, make up mirrors, and others). The best single source of statistical information concerning household appliances is *Merchandising Week,* which compiles the data as reported by various trade groups such as the Association of Home Appliance Manufacturers, the Gas Appliance Manufacturers Association, and the Vacuum Cleaner Manufacturers Association, and which publishes an annual Statistical and Marketing Report. Each annual study presents ten-year tables of factory unit-shipments and the related retail sales value for each separate home appliance, along with product saturation patterns, import/export data, and other information of value in investment analysis. Table 5 excerpts some of this data.

Major Appliances

The Bureau of Domestic Commerce estimated the value of manufacturers' shipments of household appliances in 1972 at $6.5 billion—of which three fourths, or about $4.9 billion, is in major appliances. The two dominant companies in this sector are General Electric and Whirlpool which, combined, had sales of major appliances in 1972 of an estimated $2.5 billion, or 51 percent of the total industry shipments. Other full-line producers include Westinghouse, General Motors (Frigidaire), and Fedders (Norge). Appliance companies with a narrower base of products include McGraw-Edison, Maytag, Magic Chef, Tappan, and Hobart.

Major appliances reach the consumer through three distinct marketing channels: local dealer, retail chain, and home builder. It is roughly estimated that each channel accounts for one third of the distribution. Sales through retail chains, best exemplified by the relationship between Whirlpool and Sears, Roebuck, are growing most rapidly, and this trend is expected to continue. Sales through builders are expected to gradually increase as a share of the total market, whereas the local retail dealer in the aggregate is losing share of market.

The major appliance industry was more fragmented and suffered from excess capacity throughout the 1950s, so that highly competitive pricing has been the rule. This pattern began to change in the mid 1960s, as can be seen in Table 6. A number of more marginal producers have been absorbed through mergers and acquisitions; excess capacity has been utilized; and the benefits to cost of material substitutions and new production methods have importantly been employed already, so that pricing in the past several years has begun to increase. In the future, manufacturers should be able at least to pass on higher costs. Further concentration in the industry is likely since participation in the two most

TABLE 6

Wholesale Price Indexes (1967 = 100)

	1972	1971	1970	1969	1968	1965	1960	1955
All commodities	119.1	114.0	110.0	106.0	102.5	96.4	95.3	86.9
Electrical machinery	110.4	109.5	106.4	102.9	101.3	95.1	99.5	82.9
Electrical appliances	107.6	107.2	105.3	103.1	101.8	98.9	107.5	112.9

Source: Bureau of Labor Statistics.

rapidly growing market segments (retail chain and home-builder/home improver) is enhanced by having product breadth.

The demand for major appliances is affected by macroeconomic factors such as the level of disposable income, residential construction activity, interest rates, and the availability of consumer credit. However, while sales have varied with changing economic conditions, the degree of cyclicality has not been severe. Increasingly, major appliances are being viewed as necessities; and with replacement sales roughly half of total shipments, there is reasonable stability. Furthermore, while demand is affected by the saturation levels of individual appliances, it can be stimulated by the introduction of new features, for example, the self-cleaning oven several years ago. In addition, demographic factors (family formations, and the age distribution of heads of households) as well as sociological trends (the growing number of working wives and the increasing use of frozen or otherwise prepared foods) can be important and must be considered. For example, the working wife has less time for accomplishing the household chores and therefore finds the convenience of appliances even more important than otherwise; while at the same time, her earnings can provide the income which permits purchases. The demographics (data which can be obtained from the Department of the Census) and the sociological trends appear favorable with regard to sales growth. In sum, after evaluating the variables and assuming normal expansion of the economy, it appears reasonable to project that the value of shipments of major appliances by manufacturers may, on the average, expand at a rate of 6–7 percent per year from the 1972 level, for the next decade.

Electrical Housewares

The largest manufacturers of electrical housewares are General Electric and Sunbeam, but the industry is more fragmented than is the major appliance industry. Most companies sell through distributors who, in turn, sell to dealers or chains. The Hoover Company is one notable exception because it sells direct. Competition for shelf space has become very keen in the past decade, as a number of previously narrow-line suppliers have attempted to capitalize on well-accepted brand names—for example, Toastmaster (McGraw-Edison) and Hoover —and have broadened their lines.

Demand is principally related to levels of consumer disposable income, family formations, and saturation levels. It tends to be seasonal, with Christmas gift giving very important. Most of the staple items such as toasters, coffee pots, irons, etc. are mature, so that there is a constant quest for new products. In the past decade, most of the new products have come in the personal care area, and they have frequently had short life cycles—a fact which provides a speculative element to this business. The threat of foreign competition may be greater in electrical housewares than in major appliances because shipping cost, as a percentage of selling price, is less.

The demographic factors are favorable over the coming decade. However, the recent increases in food and fuel costs may adversely affect discretionary spending patterns; and this, in turn, may have an adverse effect on demand for electric housewares in the next several years, since many of the electric housewares items are better classified as luxuries than as necessities. Altogether it seems reasonable to extrapolate the rate of gain experienced in the period 1963–72 as shown in Table 5.

Electrical Equipment for the Industrial and Construction Markets

NEMA includes a wide range of electrical components and electrically powered machinery, such as conveyors, ovens, welders, and mining equipment, in its industrial category. For the purposes of this discussion, the principal interest is in electrical components, such as electric motors and generators; current converting apparatus; controls, such as starters, switches, and relays; and automation systems.

General Electric and Westinghouse are generally well represented in this area, but they are not dominant. Reliance Electric is an important manufacturer of integral horsepower motors, as is Emerson Electric in fractionals (one h.p. or less). Square D Company and the privately owned Allen-Bradley Company are leading producers of controls; whereas Cutler-Hammer is a lesser factor in controls. Although varying in the degree of emphasis, all of these companies provide systems to automate various production processes. The demand for products is importantly influenced by capital spending patterns. However, in analyzing any particular company, one must recognize whether its product base is diversified or whether it is more dependent upon one particular area (for example, the capital spending by manufacturers of durable goods as opposed to that of producers of nondurables or to that of the non-manufacturing sector which includes utilities, transportation, etc.). Moreover, despite the cyclical influence of capital expenditures for new plants and equipment, many electrical products have an important replacement market which provides some stability. In this area, as in most where competition is keen, pricing is greatly affected by demand; that is, when demand is soft, the ability to raise prices is diminished. Price competition in industrial controls was particularly severe between 1963 and 1970–71, but some increases have been realized in the past couple of years. Competition in integral horsepower motors and automation systems was quite keen between 1968 and 1972; but conditions began to firm in 1973, reflecting higher capital spending by manufacturers.

The demand for electrical equipment from the industrial sector has benefited from the well-established trend towards automation of manufacturing processes as an offset to increasing labor costs. This should continue. In addition, there should be a further increment to demand as a result of the recent stress on safe working conditions embodied in the Occupational Safety and Health Act of 1972. Similarly, the emphasis on pollution control, which in effect increases the capital intensiveness in manufacturing, also should add to demand. On the other hand, important customers—such as the manufacturers of automobiles and other consumer durables and the producers of industrial durables (for example, the steel industry)—have matured, so that the growth in demand from these markets may be lessened. On balance, the long-term growth in the value of shipments of industrial electrical equipment should be equal to, or greater than, the 6.8 percent annual rate experienced between 1963 and 1972, assuming normal economic conditions.

Another factor which must be considered when analyzing companies in this area is the changing technology which is bringing more and more electronics into the electrical equipment area. For example: (1) The development of solid-state devices for converting AC current to DC reduced the demand for AC motors and DC generators in adjustable speed drive systems; and (2) the growing use of programmable controllers and minicomputers will reduce the demand for relays. Consequently, it is important for the analyst to determine whether or not the particular company of interest is spending sufficiently for research and development in order to keep abreast of the technology trend. He must also be sensitive to the degree to which new products (which frequently carry lower profitability in early years) substitute for more mature, more profitable "bread and butter" products.

The array of electrical products which enters the construction market is quite diverse. Included are wiring devices, conduit and fittings, circuit breakers, load centers, ground fault protectors, busways, and many other items. Again, General Electric and Westinghouse are well represented in this sector, while the Square D Company also is a leader. ITE Imperial, Cutler Hammer, Federal Pacific Electric (division of UV Industries), Crouse Hinds, and Harvey Hubbell are more significant among the many other participants.

The demand for electrical equipment in the construction area, of course, is a function of the level of new-building activity, which very generally runs about 40 percent residential and 60 percent commercial and industrial. Since the cycles within these market sectors frequently are at variance, the total new-building market has demonstrated reasonable stability. Further stability is afforded by the significant level of renovation and repair expenditures. Importantly, the value of electrical work in construction, as estimated by *Electrical Construction and Maintenance Magazine*, has increased from 9.5 percent in 1960 to 12.9 percent in 1972. This pattern of expenditures for electrical construction increasing more rapidly than the total value of construction is expected to continue. It stems, in part, from the following trends: (1) growth in the use of air conditioning and other appliances; (2) increased lighting levels; (3) greater utilization of electric heat; and (4) more office machines and greater factory automation. However, the desire to curb profligate consumption of energy may diminish the rate of gain as compared with the last 12 years. Historical statistics on the construction market can be found in the series entitled "Construction Review" published by the U.S. Department of Commerce. The F. W. Dodge (subsidiary of McGraw-Hill) statistics on contract awards can serve as a leading indicator of demand for electrical equipment from the various segments of the new-construction market.

Price competition in the building area has been less intense than in the industrial sector. Products are sold through independent distributors of electrical equipment throughout the country who, in turn, sell to electrical contractors. Shelf space with the strongest local distributors is ardently sought by the manufacturers, and considerable sales assistance is provided by them. This tends to make breadth of product line important, as it can reduce the unit selling expense. One of the most profitable companies in the industry, Square D, is reputed to have *one* of the strongest distribution systems, if not *the* strongest.

The market for lighting equipment is an adjunct to the building area. According to Bureau of Domestic Commerce figures, approximately 25 percent of the $4.1 billion of shipments in 1972 was in lamps (bulbs)— with General Electric believed to account for about one half of the market, followed by Westinghouse, Sylvania, and a number of manufacturers of specialty bulbs. The market for lighting fixtures, poles, and related equipment is highly fragmented and competitive. Growth in demand in the future should approximate the rate of increase since 1963, as shown in Table 1.

Power Equipment

The sale of equipment for the generation, transmission, and distribution of electric power is the most rapidly growing portion of the electrical manufacturing industry, as is apparent from Table 1. In general, the strong growth in the consumption of electricity, which has been at a 7 percent to 7.5 percent compound annual rate, has provided the stimulus for this trend. Until recent years, projections of the rate of consumption of electricity typically were extrapolations. Now, the growing concern for the environment and the so-called energy crisis have combined to create a call for conservation of energy. Environmental action has resulted in delays in the construction of numerous power plants. These developments have led some to believe that the consumption of electricity will grow at a lesser rate than in the past. On the other hand increased consumption of electricity is required to operate pollution control apparatus and to enlarge mass transit, both of which are beneficial to the environment. In addition nuclear electric power, assuming the environmental and safety concerns associated therewith will be resolved, obviously will result in the saving of scarce and increasingly more expensive fossil fuels. Consequently, some industry observers conclude that the rate of consumption of electricity should, and will, increase in the future. At this time, the various factors seem to be offsetting each other, and it appears reasonable to anticipate that the consumption of electricity will continue to increase at about a 7.0 percent compound annual rate for the next decade or two.

In assessing the different areas within power equipment, it is helpful to examine the trends of capital spending by utilities, as shown in Table 7.

The value of equipment shipments by manufacturers has not grown as rapidly as capital spending by utilities, principally because the latter figures include substantial construction expenditures, the cost of which has escalated dramatically in the past decade. At the same time technological improvements such as larger generating units and higher transmission voltages have provided important economic benefits to utilities. There is abundant published data available to security analysts concerning power equipment. Some of the sources of this data are: (1) the "Annual Statistical Report" of *Electrical World* (a McGraw-Hill magazine) published in the spring of each year and its "Annual Forecast," published in the fall; (2) the "Year-End Summary of the Electric Power Situation in the United States," a report of the Edison Electric Institute; (3) a biennial "Survey of Power Equipment Requirements of the U.S. Electric Utility Industry," sponsored by NEMA; and (4) data from various government agencies compiled in the annual "U.S. Industrial Outlook" and organized according to the SIC Code.

The principal products for power generation in the NEMA power equipment category are nuclear and conventional steam-turbine generators and gas turbines. General Electric and Westinghouse, combined, typically garner close to 90 percent of the large steam-turbine generator market, with foreign sources accounting for the remainder. The industrial and marine steam-turbine markets also are dominated by the two U.S. giants, but there are some other minor U.S. competitors. GE is the largest factor in gas turbines, followed by Westinghouse and United Aircraft's Turbo Power and Marine Division. Other important power generation equipment, not found in the NEMA statistics but available elsewhere, includes: (1) nuclear reactors, where so far Westinghouse and General Electric are dominant worldwide, followed by Combustion Engineering, Babcock and Wilcox, and Gulf General Atomic; and (2) fossil-steam boilers, where Combustion Engineering and Babcock and Wilcox are dominant, followed by Foster Wheeler and The Riley Company. In a

TABLE 7

Total Electric Power System* Capital Expenditures (millions of dollars)

	Generation		Transmission		Distribution		Miscellaneous		Totals	
	Total Industry	Investor Owned	Total Industry	Investor Owned	Total Industry	Investor Owned	Total Industry	Investor Owned	Total Industry	Investor Owned
1963...........	1,743	1,165	853	644	1,672	1,323	244	187	4,512	3,319
1964...........	1,819	1,113	1,056	824	1,800	1,424	267	189	4,940	3,551
1965...........	1,964	1,300	1,197	940	1,991	1,585	294	202	5,446	4,027
1966...........	2,535	1,788	1,438	1,137	2,220	1,770	317	236	6,510	4,932
1967...........	3,503	2,559	1,630	1,328	2,464	1,985	346	268	7,943	6,140
1968...........	4,280	3,201	1,917	1,510	2,719	2,143	394	315	9,311	7,169
1969...........	5,324	4,001	2,010	1,555	3,009	2,437	401	329	10,744	8,321
1970...........	6,860	5,440	2,123	1,681	3,264	2,633	529	426	12,776	10,182
1971...........	8,566	6,716	2,174	1,806	3,673	2,799	717	617	15,130	11,938
1972...........	9,737	7,946	2,151	1,751	3,989	3,101	777	637	16,654	13,435
1973...........	10,924	8,807	2,450	2,050	4,434	3,405	915	717	18,723	14,979
1974†..........	12,230	10,143	2,859	2,393	4,879	3,670	1,205	961	21,173	17,166

Source: *Electrical World* surveys, adjusted to 100 percent of industry. Reprinted from March 15, 1974 issue of *Electrical World*, © Copyright 1974, McGraw-Hill, Inc. All rights reserved.

* All 50 states 1967–72; earlier years contiguous U.S.

† Prospective.

third and related area, nuclear fuel, it appears that in the United States General Electric and Westinghouse will be primary participants, along with possibly Exxon, Gulf Oil, Combustion Engineering, and Babcock and Wilcox. General Electric has projected the future of the world fuel cycle market as follows:

	Free World Nuclear Fuel Market (millions of dollars)		
	1973	1980	1990
Fabrication..................	$200	$1,500	$ 4,650
Reprocessing................	88	600	1,800
Enrichment*................	—	1,425	4,275
	$288	$3,575	$10,275

* This business is currently government controlled, with private industry participation now under study.

Spending for power generation equipment is growing more rapidly than that for all power equipment, primarily because of the development of nuclear power. A nuclear plant is more capital intensive—that is, costs more per kilowatt of installed capacity—than a fossil-boiler plant, but its operating costs are lower; so that, even apart from consideration of the availability of fossil fuels, therein lies its benefit to both utilities and to the suppliers of equipment, fuel, and services. The long-term growth of the nuclear market should be at a substantial rate, perhaps 15–25 percent per year, but the near-term outlook is complicated by environmental considerations which already have caused delays. However the energy crisis of late 1973, precipitated by the oil embargo, may serve to reaccelerate the growth of nuclear-generated electric power. The Atomic Energy Commission publishes an Annual Report which discusses most important aspects of nuclear power.

Gas turbine shipments have grown considerably more rapidly than total power generating equipment, as indicated by new orders for 9,127 megawatts in 1972 compared with 3,525 megawatts in 1968. The early growth in usage of these units stemmed from their advantage in peaking applications. More recently, delays in nuclear base-load plants have created additional demand for these units, which can be brought on line 12–18 months from the date of order. The continued work on combined-cycle plants, where the heat normally dissipated in a simple-cycle peaking unit is recaptured and utilized (thereby improving efficiency), leads some industry observers to anticipate continued growth in the demand for gas turbines by utilities. However, in view of shortages of distillate fuels, significant enlargement of the market may have to await development of an effective method of coal gasification.

Transmission and distribution equipment includes transformers, circuit breakers, switchgear, capacitors, insulators, line hardware, etc. General Electric and Westinghouse are the largest factors in the market, but they are not as dominant here as they are in generation equipment. Other important broad-line companies are McGraw-Edison and ITE Imperial, while more specialized competitors include RTE Corporation, A. B. Chance, and many others. The long-term growth in the value of manufacturers' shipments of transmission and distribution equipment is likely to be on the order of 6–7 percent annually, depending upon the rate of inflation experienced in the United States. The market is cyclical in relation to the programs of utilities as much as it is to general economic conditions, although typically about one half of the demand for distribution equipment is a function of new construction activity. Pricing is on a bid basis and is competitive. Foreign vendors achieved significant penetration of the U.S. market in the 1969–1972 period. However the recent changes in international currency values and the finding by the U.S. Tariff Commission in 1972 that dumping of power transformers by foreign producers was injuring our domestic industry have lessened this competitive force. Nevertheless, it is likely that potential foreign competition, particularly in transmission equipment, will remain a factor to consider.

THE ANALYSIS OF COST FACTORS

In general, the manufacture of electrical equipment is relatively labor intensive, as can be seen in Table 3. One exception here is power generation of equipment, which involves building very large apparatus to extremely precise specifications, thus making it much more capital intensive. The industry's important raw materials are copper, steel, aluminum, and, in certain products, silver. Copper prices can be volatile at times and can have an effect on a company's earnings depending upon the particular company's inventories, its commitments and sources of supply, and its inventory accounting practices.

ACCOUNTING CONSIDERATIONS

The accounting practices of electrical equipment manufacturing is generally straightforward and common. While there are some exceptions, most of the companies: (1) use FIFO inventory accounting; (2) flow through the investment credit; (3) report depreciation to shareholders on a straight-line basis; and (4) expense research and development as incurred. A few companies capitalize tooling, particularly in the appliance area, but they amortize the amounts in a few years. Some companies capitalize a portion of the start-up costs of new plants, but again the amortization period usually is short.

A notable exception to the above generalizations is General Electric which is a model of conservative accounting practices not only within the electrical equipment sector but compared with all companies. Since Westinghouse has a similar business mix and its accounting is typical of a broad cross-section of companies, an attempt to normalize the earnings of one company versus the other by adjusting for their differing accounting practices is a worthwhile exercise. The task is made difficult because certain information necessary to make the adjustments is not provided by General Electric. However the diligent analyst can develop methods which will provide for sufficiently accurate approximation.

In 1972 General Electric reported earnings per share of $2.91, 30 percent higher than the $2.24 per share reported by Westinghouse. The principal adjustments which can be quantified are as follows:

1. GE reports its depreciation on an accelerated basis for both book and tax purposes, while Westinghouse switched to straight-line depreciation for book purposes in 1968 on all assets acquired since January 1, 1968. GE will not disclose what its depreciation would be on a straight-line basis, but other companies such as Caperpillar Tractor, Rohm and Haas, and Ingersoll-Rand, which also report on an accelerated basis, do provide this information. By comparing the aggregate capital expenditures of these companies in the five years 1968–1972 to net plant at the end of 1972 and by determining the percentage by which straight-line depreciation would be lower than accelerated, one can estimate a similar percentage for GE—a fact which leads to the conclusion that its reported earnings, assuming a 48 percent tax rate, would be higher by an estimated $0.14 per share.

2. GE amortizes the investment tax credit, whereas Westinghouse flows it through. If GE flowed it through, its reported earnings in 1972 would have been higher by $12.1 million or about seven cents per share. The information necessary to make this adjustment is in the GE Annual Report.

3. In 1972, U.S. companies were permitted to establish Domestic International Sales Corporations (DISC). These subsidiary corporations were excused from paying one half the tax, otherwise payable, on profits earned by export sales which flowed through the DISC. GE has chosen to reserve this tax reduction rather than to report it as earnings. Westinghouse and most other companies are doing the opposite. GE will not disclose the amount reserved in relation to DISC, but knowing the level of export sales and the earnings associated with its total international sales, a reasonable estimate of the amount could be made. However, for purposes of this discussion it is easier to subtract the roughly four cents per share by which DISC benefited the earnings of Westinghouse in 1972.

4. There are other accounting differences between the companies where it is difficult, if not impossible, for an analyst to quantify the earnings effects. For example, whereas Westinghouse always used com-

pleted contract accounting for its long-cycle products, it chose the percentage-of-completion method for its rapidly growing nuclear reactor business. GE uses completed contract accounting throughout its operations. All other things being equal, the percentage-of-completion method will result in higher reported earnings at any particular time than the completed contract method, assuming a growing, profitable business. In another area, GE's policy is to immediately write off any goodwill related to an acquisition; whereas Westinghouse records it as an asset, with some 90 percent of the $85 million of goodwill on the 1972 balance sheet not being amortized and the remainder being amortized over 40 years.

5. In regard to another aspect which affects the quality of earnings, analysts should attempt to estimate differences in the levels of various reserves carried by the two companies—reserves for receivables, investments, warranties, and seemingly arbitrary miscellaneous items. It appears that the conservative treatment of the latter two types of reserves is in part responsible for GE having accumulated a large deferred tax asset of $130.5 million at the end of 1972. A portion of this asset arises because the company is charging certain expenses by increasing reserves when reporting to shareholders which the Internal Revenue Service is not allowing for tax purposes. A detailed analysis of the treatment of reserves by the respective companies is too lengthy for the scope of this section, but the effect on relative reported earnings can be significant.

6. Finally, the accounting for pension expense may be compared. General Electric now uses 6 percent as the estimated rate of future income—which includes a provision for the systematic recognition of a portion of the unrealized appreciation in the common stock portfolio of the pension trust. Unfunded past service liabilities, which were $323 million at the end of 1972 based on the book value of the trust, are being amortized over 20 years. The market value of General Electric's Pension Trust exceeded its book value by $693 million at the end of 1972. Although not mentioned in its Annual Report for 1972 Westinghouse is believed also to have used a 6 percent assumption of the future earnings of its pension trust. Neither did the company disclose the relationship between the book value and the market value of its pension trust assets. At the end of 1972, Westinghouse had an unfunded prior service liability of $444 million which is being amortized over a period of 30 years. General Electric and Westinghouse had average total employment in 1972 of 369,000 and 184,000 persons, respectively, for a ratio of almost exactly 2 to 1. General Electric pension expense in 1972 at $102.0 million was 2.1 times the $48.7 million pension expense of Westinghouse. While the relative pension expense in 1972 appears appropriate, it is fair to say that General Electric's accounting for its pension programs over the years has been more conservative than that of Westinghouse—at least to the extent that its unfunded past service liability is only three

fourths that of Westinghouse—despite the relative level of employees.

Using only the quantifiable differences, that is, items 1 through 3 above, GE's adjusted earnings in 1972 would have been $3.12 per share or 51 percent higher than the $2.20 per share adjusted earnings for Westinghouse, as compared with the 30 percent difference indicated by reported earnings. The price/earnings ratio accorded GE typically has been higher than that accorded Westinghouse. While a variety of factors enter into the relative valuation of the two companies, the "quality" of earnings undoubtedly is significant.

THE MARKET BEHAVIOR OF SECURITIES

One good way to analyze the price performance of a particular company and its industry—relative to each other, to the overall market, and

FIGURE 1

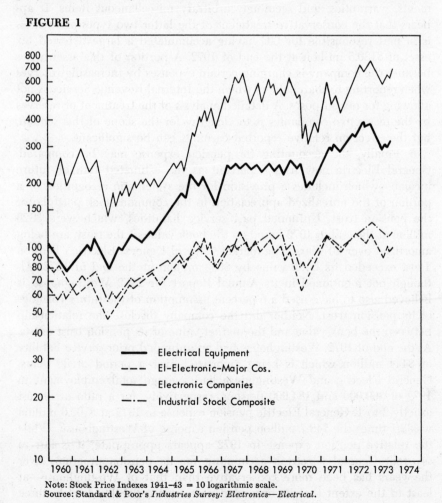

Note: Stock Price Indexes 1941–43 = 10 logarithmic scale.
Source: Standard & Poor's *Industries Survey: Electronics—Electrical.*

FIGURE 2

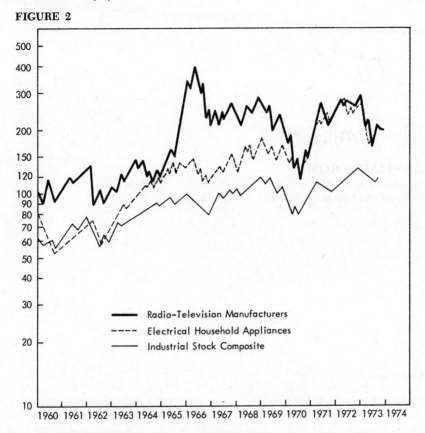

Note: Stock Price Indexes 1941–43 = 10 logarithmic scale.
Source: Standard & Poor's *Industries Survey: Electronics—Electrical.*

to any other desired variable such as capital spending or GNP—is graphically. Standard & Poor Corporation publishes charts and statistics which are useful towards this end. The S&P market price indices of particular interest as regards this chapter are: (1) Electrical—Electronics Major Companies (seven companies, including GE and Westinghouse); (2) Electrical Equipment (five companies); and (3) Household Appliances (three companies). A graphic presentation of these indices can be found in the *Industry Surveys, Electronics—Electrical,* published by Standard and Poor. Price index data is updated every week in the "Outlook" published by S&P. Of course, each stock report by S&P on an individual company graphically shows the monthly price range for that security for the previous four or more years, the appropriate industry index, and the index of the S&P 425 Industrials—making it easy to see the relative price performance of the three items.

Figures 1 and 2 depict the pattern of the pertinent indices for the electrical equipment and electronics industries between 1960 and 1972.

15

Electronics

BENJAMIN ROSEN
Director of Research
Coleman and Company, New York, New York

Overview

LONG a fascination for investors, the electronics industry encompasses a variety of differing subindustries, each with its own growth rates, earnings prospects, and investment outlook. To get a broad picture of just what is entailed in this so-called glamor industry, we summarize below some of its basic characteristics and trends.

Size. In 1972, U.S. electronics industry sales totaled $29.4 billion, or about 2.6 percent of the gross national product.

Growth. As an industry, electronics has grown at 9.0 percent per year compounded over the 20-year period ending in 1972. This overall growth figure, however, masks some sectors, such as government electronics, which are relatively stagnant and others, such as integrated circuits, which are growing consistently at rates of 30–40 percent per year.

Increasing Pervasiveness. Technological innovation, declining costs, and increased performance are sharply accelerating the pervasiveness of electronics into the economy. Whereas a decade ago the principal outlets for electronics were in government applications and computer mainframes, today electronic products are finding their way increasingly into automobiles, cameras, appliances, manufacturing operations, and almost every facet of the consumer and industrial sectors of the economy.

Technological Innovation. The principal reason for the rapid growth rate of the industry is its obsession with innovation. Through research

370

and development funding provided increasingly by the companies themselves, electronics companies typically spend more on new product innovation than most other industry groups.

Relationship to Macroeconomic Trends. As recently as the 1970 recession, the electronics industry demonstrated some sensitivity to overall economic cycles. But with the veritable explosion of new products and with the increasing penetration of electronics into the more mature sectors of the economy, the sensitivity of the electronics industry to macroeconomic cyclicality appears to be decreasing with time.

Declining Costs. Unlike virtually every other sector of this inflationary economy, the electronics industry produces products whose costs *decrease* with time, rather than increase. By pricing products on a decreasing curve parallel to its cost curve, the electronics industry can thus benefit from increasing market penetration and from market elasticity, while maintaining profit margins.

Regulation. Overall, the electronics industry is a relatively unregulated industry. Indeed, in many cases the industry *benefits* from the regulation of other industries, in that electronic products provide the means of solving those other industries' regulatory problems in the pollution and safety areas. Analytical instruments, for example, are used to detect the presence and amounts of pollution; semiconductor seat belt interlock systems are used to solve one of Detroit's safety problems; while electronic ignition systems are both reducing pollution and improving gasoline mileage.

Size and Composition of Industry

As shown in Table 1, the electronics industry reached a size of $29.4 billion in 1972, up from a post–World War II level of under $2 billion. As defined by the Electronics Industries Association, the principal sectors are (1) communications and industrial products, (2) government products, (3) consumer products, and (4) replacement components. Table 1 illustrates that the communications and industrial products sector is the largest of the four (with 40 percent of the total), closely followed by government products (with 35 percent). The latter sector, however, has been relatively stagnant for seven years, while the communications and industrial products category has been growing handsomely.

Aside from the EIA classifications, another useful way of breaking down the industry for analysts is the following:

Components. It is convenient to subdivide this category further into semiconductors (integrated circuits, transistors, etc.) and passive components (resistors, capacitors, connectors, etc.). In the former category, the principal suppliers are Texas Instruments, Motorola, Fairchild Camera, and National Semiconductor, while in the latter category, one might include such companies as Sprague Electric, Mallory, CTS, and AMP.

TABLE 1

Industry Summary: Factory Sales by Selected Years, 1925–72 (in millions of dollars)

Year	Consumer* Products		Communications and Industrial Products	Government Products	Replacement Components		Total
1925	$ 92						$ 180
1926	94						187
1927	95						200
1929	275						465
1931	125						220
1933	73						135
1935	135			$ 20			240
1937	182			28			350
1939	186			37			340
1947	810			680			1,750
1950	1,500		$ 350	655	$200		2,705
1951	1,400		450	1,193	270		3,313
1952	1,300		600	3,100	310		5,210
1953	1,400		600	3,230	370		5,600
1954	1,400		650	3,100	470		5,620
1955	1,500		750	3,332	525		6,107
1956	1,600		950	3,595	570		6,715
1957	1,805		1,300	4,130	610		7,845
1958	1,660		1,405	4,725	475		8,265
1959	2,002		1,676	5,373	530		9,581
1960	1,774‡		1,980	6,124	555		10,433‡
1961	1,757‡		2,585	7,190	580		12,112‡
1962	2,127‡		3,025	8,080	620		13,825‡
1963	2,320‡		3,610	8,841	590		15,361‡
1964	2,643‡		4,268	8,775	620		16,306‡
1965	3,303‡		5,222	8,969	630		18,124‡
1966	4,130‡		5,842	10,330	640		20,942‡
1967	3,916‡	6,373†	9,018	11,720	650	23,121†	25,304‡
1968	4,157‡	6,693	9,941	12,563	675	24,550	27,336‡
1969	4,367‡	7,913	10,843	12,287	718	25,747	28,215‡
1970	3,683‡	7,996	10,935‡	11,295	667	23,898	26,580‡
1971	5,541		10,646‡	10,700	634		27,521‡
1972	6,642		11,652	10,400	710		29,404

* Prior to 1971, data reflects products either produced in the U.S. or imported by U.S. manufacturers for sale with their brand name, excludes foreign label imports. Data from 1971 on reflects products produced or purchased by U.S. manufacturers plus those products imported directly by distributors or dealers for resale. Import statistics are adjusted to U.S. factory values, including U.S. import duties, freight charged from the foreign country to the U.S., and insurance.

† Boxed area represents total prior to inclusion of telephone equipment sales in Communications and Industrial Product category.

‡ Revised from prior publications.

Sources: Electronics Division, Business and Defense Services Administration, Bureau of the Census, and Electronic Industries Association Marketing Services Department.

Instruments. This category includes manufacturers of analytical instruments, test and measurement instruments, medical instruments, nuclear instruments, and a variety of other measuring equipment and systems. Among the principal companies are Hewlett-Packard, Perkin-Elmer, Tektronix, Beckman Instruments, and Varian Associates.

Systems/Diversified. This category includes a large number of electronics companies whose activities span several sectors of the electronics spectrum. Among the companies here would be Raytheon, International Telephone and Telegraph, Litton Industries, Teledyne, and TRW.

Military/Government. Companies in this category derive the principal part of their sales from the government, and include Sanders Associates, Watkins-Johnson, Hazeltine, and Hoffman Electronics.

Consumer Products. The oldest electronics category, the consumer sector, includes such well-known household names as RCA, Zenith, Magnavox, Sony, etc.

The consumer products sector has been dominated by television over the last couple of decades. As recently as 1965, monochrome TV receivers still accounted for the largest single amount of dollar sales. In 1965, however, the lead shifted to color TV, a position it has not relinquished to this day. As of 1972, color TV accounted for 43 percent of the consumer electronics sector, up from 9 percent a decade earlier.

Communications and Industrial Products. In this sector, the Electronic Industries Association includes some computation equipment in its total. Other major categories include communications equipment, control and processing equipment, broadcast equipment, navigational aids, test and measurement equipment, and medical electronics equipment.

Government Electronics. This market has been one of negative to little growth over the last few years. As shown in Table 4, the government market declined from $12.3 billion in fiscal 1968 to $10.2 billion in fiscal 1973 but was budgeted to increase slightly in fiscal 1974.

Electronics as a Growth Industry

The electronics industry is usually viewed as a growth industry. Indeed, from 1952 through 1972 the industry grew at a compound annual rate of 9 percent per year. However, there are certain shortcomings in blindly accepting the tenet that the overall industry is one of growth. One problem arises from the fact that certain sectors, such as government, have stagnated since 1967. A second problem is the type which occurred in 1970—an economic recession adversely impacting technology-related industries. The theory, of course, is that technology industries, because of their heavy investment in R&D to develop new products, should be relatively immune to economic cycles, rather than acting in consonance with them.

Looking at the decade of the 1960s, we see that the electronics industry as a whole grew 8.4 percent per year, or well above the current-dollar GNP growth of 6.8 percent and the constant-dollar GNP growth of 4.0 percent. But as Table 5 shows, the electronics industry's 11.6 percent growth in the first half of the 1960s decelerated significantly to 5.3 percent in the second half, falling even below the growth rate of current-dollar GNP.

Why did this happen in a supposed growth industry? For several reasons. In the early through mid-1960s, there were at least five significant stimuli to the demand for electronics products: (1) capital spending, (2) the emergence of foreign markets, (3) the rapid development of color television, (4) explosive growth of computer industry, and (5) a strong government electronics market. But then at various times during

TABLE 2

Total U.S. Market of Consumer Electronic Products, 1960–72 (in millions of dollars)

Category	Factory Sales plus Imports*											Factory Production plus Imports†	
	1960	1961	1962	1963	1964	1965	1966	1967	1968	1969	1970	1971†	1972
Monochrome TV receivers	$ 50	$ 758	$ 851	$ 841	$ 896	$ 910	$ 756	$ 555	$ 591	$ 554	$ 518	$ 621	$ 649
Color TV receivers	47	56	154	258	488	959	1,861	2,015	2,086	2,031	1,684	2,355	2,825
Radios	190	190	207	179	267	328	346	333	371	422	380	487	606
Auto radios	154	134	181	206	205	248	267	259	330	316	271	315	377
Phonographs	359	304	389	421	440	505	528	480	503	490	376	425	577
Tape equipment‡	21	75	81	110	135	170	159	181	225	278	424	707	861
Electronic organs‡	§	51	56	94	97	103	94	90	101	121	115	147	177
Other electronic musical instruments‡	12	16	19	24	27	42	39	36	37	40	43	46	51
Electronic kits‡	§	29	31	37	34	35	41	40	46	44	42	49	54
Hearing aids‡	§	38	38	35	37	36	37	35	36	37	36	42	48
Other consumer products‡ N.E.C.‖	272	157	183	198	215	241	272	280	304	320	280	347	417
Total electronic	$1,805	$1,808	$2,190	$2,403	$2,841	$3,577	$4,400	$4,304	$4,630	$4,653	$4,169	$5,541	$6,642

* Prior to 1971, data reflects factory sales by U.S. manufacturers plus those products imported directly by distributors or dealers for resale. Import statistics are based on average value as published by the U.S. Department of Commerce, which is F.O.B., and therefore excludes U.S. import duties, freight charged from the foreign country to the U.S., and insurance.

† Data from 1971 on reflects products produced or purchased by U.S. manufacturers plus those products imported directly by distributors or dealers for resale. Import statistics are adjusted to U.S. factory values, including U.S. import duties, freight charged from the foreign country to the U.S., and insurance.

‡ Estimated.

§ Included in "Other consumer products, N.E.C."

‖ Includes estimates for home intercoms, window and door controls, pleasure boating equipment, citizens band transceivers, hi-fi components, and similar home equipments. These data are based primarily upon industry estimates analyzed by the EIA Marketing Services Department and represent the best opinion of the department.

TABLE 3

Factory Sales of Communications and Industrial Products,* 1967–72
(in millions of dollars)

	1967	1968	1969	1970	1971	1972†
Computers and peripheral equipment	3,087	3,328	3,667	3,678	3,201	3,681
Control and processing	1,580	1,591	1,668	1,606	1,615	1,868
Testing and measuring	560	590	613	672	646	692
Communications, broadcast equipment, and navigational aids	1,650	1,835	1,889	1,847	1,615	1,868
Equipment for use by communications common carriers	1,977	2,413	2,807	2,886	3,154	3,258
Nuclear electronic	15	13	13	18	16	17
Medical equipment	149	170	186	228	254	270
Total	9,018	9,941	10,843	10,935	10,646	11,652

* For Industrial Use.
† Estimated by EIA Marketing Services Department.
Source: U.S. Department of Commerce; EIA Marketing Services Department.

the latter half of the decade, all five of these factors diminished in importance or in growth rates. And when combined with the 1970 recession, this had a significant impact on the electronic industry's growth rate during that year. As a result, 1970 was the first year in which the electronics industry as a whole showed negative growth.

This historical analysis is helpful in determining why a supposed recession-resistant industry did, in fact, show a decline. The capital spending boom of the early 1960s decelerated significantly. Rapid increases in penetration of the foreign market were harder to come by after significant penetrations were made. Color television, which was a $47 million market as the decade began, became a nearly saturated product by the end of the decade. Similarly, the computer industry, a major market for electronics products, decelerated in rate of growth as

TABLE 4

Government Electronics Market Expenditures, Fiscal Years 1968–74*
(in billions)

	FY 1968	FY 1969	FY 1970	FY 1971	FY 1972	FY 1973	FY 1974
Department of Defense	10.6	11.1	10.5	9.9	9.4	9.1	9.6
National Aeronautics and Space Administration	1.6	1.6	1.1	1.1	1.0	1.0	.9
Federal Aviation Administration	.1	.1	.1	.1	.1	.1	.1
Total	12.3	12.8	11.7	11.1	10.5	10.2	10.6

* Discrepancies due to rounding.

TABLE 5

Compound Annual Growth Rates: Electronics and GNP
(by percent)

Period	Current $ GNP	1958 $ GNP	Electronics Industry
1960–65	6.3	4.8	11.6
1965–70	7.3	3.2	5.3
1960–70	6.8	4.0	8.4

its size increased. Finally, the government market was stimulated early in the 1960s by the closing of the "missile gap" and the mushrooming Apollo program; spending for these peaked in the 1966–67 period.

In looking ahead, the analyst must determine those forces which will stimulate growth in the 1970s. Clearly, government electronics, computer mainframes, and color television will not be nearly as important as they once were. Instead, new forces of growth will come to the fore.

Technological Innovation. Unlike many of the basic industries, electronics derives more of its growth through new product innovation than

TABLE 6

Five Key Stimuli to the Electronics Industry in the 1960s

Factor	Early 1960s: Boom Period	Late 1960s: Deceleration Period
1. Capital spending	1963–66: +16%/Year	1966–71: +5%/Year
2. Foreign markets	Rapid penetration increases	Modest penetration increases
3. Color television	1960–67: +71%/Year	1967–71: +2%/Year
4. Computer industry	Rapid growth	Modest growth
5. Government sector		
Military electronics	1959–68: +10%/Year	1968–71: −5%/Year
Space programs	1960–66: +57%/Year	1966–73: −9%/Year

it does from cyclical factors. Such innovation, in turn, stems from heavy R&D investment by its member companies. Depending on which sector of the electronics industry one looks at, the percentage of sales allocated for R&D can range from several percent to as high as 10 percent for such instrument companies as Hewlett-Packard and Tektronix.

Creation of New Markets. One path of innovation is the creation of entirely new markets. Coming to mind here are the consumer calculator, the microcomputer (computer-on-a-chip), the laser, and, within a few years, the inexpensive home video recorder and player.

Growth through Displacement of Nonelectronic products. Another important avenue of growth for electronics in the 1970s is that derived from the displacement of electromechanical devices by electronic products. Examples include the replacement of electromechanical ignitions on automobiles by electronic systems, mechanical cash registers by electronic point-of-sale systems, and mechanical watches by electronic ones.

Growth through Technological Obsolescence. Innovation not only provides growth through the replacement of nonelectronic devices but also through the replacement of obsolescent electronic products. As an example, a thriving market for linear integrated circuits has been brought about by the displacement of vacuum tubes in television sets. Similarly, magnetic core computer memories are rapidly being replaced by semiconductor memories. Even in the two-year old consumer calculator field, consumers are beginning to replace their recently purchased calculators with newer and cheaper ones which offer more features.

Growth through Performance Superiority. This factor is interrelated with some of those above. For example, semiconductor computer memories are now becoming not only cheaper than magnetic core memories, but also offer better performance. But some functions, such as the seat belt interlock system, now mandatory on all 1974 model year cars, can be achieved only by electronic systems.

Growth through Lower Prices. Because of the rapid advances in technology, and particularly in semiconductors, the prices of many electronic products are being reduced, rather than raised, with time. These price reductions reflect cost reductions by the manufacturers. As a dramatic example, a high-quality silicon transistor in the late 1950s typically sold for $20. Today, a transistor of higher reliability, found as a part of a semiconductor memory circuit, costs the equivalent of one tenth of a cent. Yet, as a vivid demonstration of the price elasticity of the semiconductor market over this 15-year period (in which the price per transistor dropped by a factor of 20,000), the total dollar market for semiconductors has increased tenfold, from $200 million to $2 billion. A similar dramatic example is seen in the consumer calculator field. In 1971, when the lowest-priced consumer calculator was $249, the total world market was several million dollars. In 1973, as the average consumer calculator price dropped to about $70 (and the minimum price to $20), the number of units skyrocketed to about 8 million—thus yielding a total dollar volume of well over a half-billion dollars.

At any given time it is difficult for the analyst to assay the relative impacts of declining mature markets versus burgeoning new markets. It is our view, though, that the electronic industry's growth over the next five years will be (1) at a higher rate than it has been historically, and (2) less sensitive to economic cycles than it has been. These assertions are based on the fact that the rates of innovation are higher now than they have ever been, and that the erstwhile dependence of much of the industry on just two major markets (government electronics and computer mainframes) has lessened.

Aside from the contention that the electronics market as a whole will grow more regularly and rapidly than it has in the past, companies within the industry have additional opportunities for growth through forward vertical integration. This is materially different from the avenue of growth pursued by so many electronics companies in the 1960s. During that earlier period, many companies attempted to achieve quantum jumps in growth through acquisitions, often in only marginally related fields—and often with unhappy results. Today, such companies as Texas Instruments and National Semiconductor are attempting to accelerate their growth through the manufacture and marketing of electronic end-products, as opposed to just their traditional components and subsystems. This trend, of course, stems from the fact that as electronics accounts for more and more of the value added of an end-product, it makes a certain amount of sense to market the end-product itself and thereby capture more of the added value. Thus, Texas Instruments has begun marketing minicomputers, large-scale scientific computers, and calculators. National Semiconductor has extended its components capability forward into the manufacture of calculators and point-of-sale electronic cash registers.

Analysis of Cost Factors

Decreasing cost of production, alluded to earlier, is one of the major factors permitting electronic products to grow more rapidly than GNP and increasing the pervasiveness of electronics in the economy. These price declines, in turn, are largely due to the rapid technological changes. As an example, the transition from vacuum tubes to transistors to small-scale integrated circuits to large-scale integrated circuits has afforded all users of electronic products remarkable opportunities for lowering their costs.

To the extent that labor content is important—and its importance varies from subsector to subsector within the electronics industry—many manufacturers have taken advantage of low-cost offshore labor in order to compete more equitably with foreign manufacturers. This lesson was dramatically learned by the electronics industry after foreign manufacturers almost captured virtually the entire U.S. home radio market with low-cost manufacturing in the Orient. Until 1957, the U.S. market was almost entirely supplied by the U.S. manufacturers; today, however, the reverse is true, as is shown in Figure 1.

Having heeded this lesson, U.S. semiconductor manufacturers made sure that their labor-intensive assembly operations were performed offshore, where hourly labor is as low as one twentieth of the U.S. rate. By keeping costs down in this manner and by continuing to maintain its substantial technological edge, U.S. leadership in this seminal sector of the electronics industry has never been threatened seriously by foreign

FIGURE 1

U.S. Home Radio Market versus Foreign Production

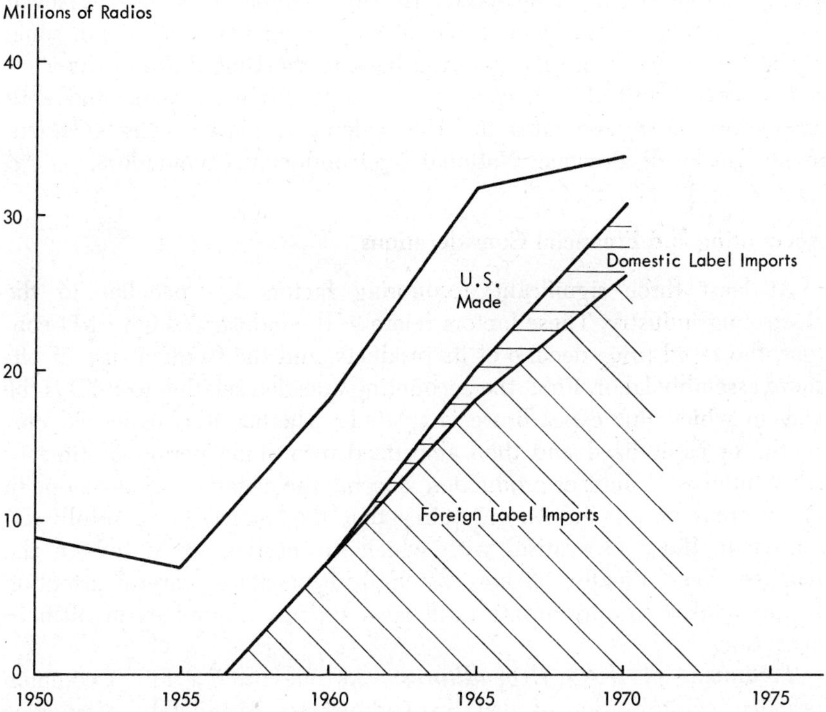

Millions of Radios

suppliers. Thus in 1973, semiconductor imports into the U.S. were only 3 percent of total U.S. consumption.

Further inroads into lowering costs have been achieved by the use of automation and other productivity-enhancing methods. Texas Instruments, as an example, has increased its sales per employee 35 percent in the last ten years—from $13,518 in 1962 to $18,290 in 1972.

As electronics content accounts for an increasing amount of total value of many end-products, and as the degree of semiconductor integration increases year after year, the labor content in many electronics end-products has decreased significantly. The best example of this is seen in the consumer calculator. Originally, in the 1960s, the calculator market was entirely electromechanical and was supplied by such companies as Friden, Marchant, Monroe, and other well-established companies. The Japanese, with no entrenched electromechanical calculator industry, seized the opportunity to dominate the electronic calculator market in its embryonic stages. Even though they had to buy the key components (semiconductors) from U.S. suppliers, the entrepreneurship of the Japanese plus their lower labor costs allowed them to monopolize the early electronic calculator market. Two factors, however, have changed this dominance. First, the labor content for calculators has been reduced, through advances in semiconductors, from hours to as few as seven minutes in some of the newer, less expensive calculators. Second, some of the entrepreneurship has reverted back to the United States. As a result, a new group of U.S. companies, not traditionally associated with calculators, now dominates the U.S. calculator market—Texas Instruments, Rockwell, Bowmar, National Semiconductor, Commodore.

Accounting and Financial Considerations

At least three significant accounting factors are peculiar to the electronics industry. These factors relate to the industry's high R&D content, the rapid price decline of its products, and the frequent use of off-shore assembly labor. First, the accounting question relating to R&D is the way in which this expenditure is treated—whether it is expensed currently, or capitalized and then amortized over some period of time or some number of units of production. Second, the negative pricing slope in many areas of the industry requires that the analyst be carefully attentive to the conservatism with which inventories are stated on the balance sheet. Finally, offshore assembly necessitates careful attention by the analyst to appropriate tariff laws and tax treatments of offshore operations.

Treatment of R&D Expenditures. At one time a fairly common practice, capitalization of R&D expenditures is, fortunately, a practice rarely resorted to nowadays. The argument in favor of capitalizing R&D is that it affords a better matching of revenues with related costs. That is, when the product under development finally goes into production and is sold, its cost of development will then be charged against actual sales of the product. The fallacy in this argument is that R&D is an absolutely essential and regular cost of participating in the electronics business and that a high proportion of R&D products never reach the production stage. Indeed, what has happened in practice with companies which have resorted to R&D capitalization is that they have more frequently than not been forced into sizable R&D write-offs when product expectations did not pan out. In order to compare better the quality of earnings of companies within the same subindustry grouping, it is advantageous for the analyst to make an adjustment to earnings to assume that all R&D funds are expensed on a current basis.

Another factor which virtually demands current expensing of R&D is rapid technological obsolescence. Capitalized R&D which is amortized over anything but the briefest period may be a dubious asset at best. As an example, in quoting from a footnote in the annual report of one manufacturer of calculators, the statement is made that "proprietary design and development costs are capitalized and amortized over a five-year period." Because the state of the calculator art is changing almost daily, it would seem highly inappropriate not only to capitalize such R&D, but to amortize it over such a long period of time.

Also, the analyst should be wary of managements which attempt to convince the investment public that capitalization of R&D is indeed appropriate for *their* business. In case after case, these accounting policies are inevitably changed, much to the chagrin of the investor. Again, to quote from an electronics manufacturer's report to shareholders, the management stated,

> "These R&D expenditures are deferred, which means that they are shown as an asset upon our balance sheet and are not charged against current sales revenues. Investment analysts who question the advisability of this accounting treatment (which is approved by our public auditors and the SEC accounting staff) and infer that R&D expenses should be charged against revenues of existing product lines, are simply naïve or ill informed. . . ."

Two years after this statement was made, the company changed its accounting policy and incurred a substantial write-off.

Inventory Accounting. In the 1960s, when the semiconductor industry was relatively young, the analyst had to be especially wary of inventory accounting by semiconductor manufacturers because of the rapidity of price changes of the end-product. Year-end downward valuations of inventories, to reflect lower prices and also technological obsolescence, were frequent phenomena. Today, however, most companies producing products with negative price slopes tend to value their inventories monthly in order to maintain as conservative a stance as possible. This is not to say, however, that inventory write-downs are a thing of the past or that the analyst should be any less vigilant; it is simply that this is less of a problem than it used to be.

Tariff Regulations and Tax Treatments of Offshore Operations. Many electronics companies employ offshore operations in the Orient, Caribbean, and other low-labor-cost areas in order to reduce their assembly costs. This practice has given rise to two considerations of which the analyst should be aware. Under the tariff schedules of the United States, items number 806.30 and 807.00 are of particular interest to the electronics industry. These items provide that when U.S. components are sent to a foreign country and assembled there into a product, the product may then be imported into the United States with duty paid only on the value added abroad (which is primarily inexpensive labor), not on the total cost. These tariff regulation exemptions have allowed U.S. electronic companies to be cost competitive with foreign manufacturers. Recently, however, items 806.30 and 807.00 have come under fire from various pressure groups within the United States, primarily U.S. labor organizations. Should these exemptions be repealed, it would add a significant cost burden to many U.S. electronics manufacturers. A second pressure, arising from within the Customs Bureau, has been for standardization of the provisions; to date there has been little standardization of tariff rates or documentation from one U.S. port of entry to another. This new standardization and any additional provisions are likely to add some cost to companies using the tariff exemptions, but they are not nearly as serious as repeal of the exemptions would be.

In addition to the Customs Bureau, the Internal Revenue Service has also been scrutinizing foreign operations of American electronics companies. In particular, the IRS is looking at inventory valuations and reallocations of income and expense between parent companies and their foreign subsidiaries.

Other tax considerations related to foreign operations arrive from the use or nonuse of the Domestic International Sales Corporation provision of the tax laws. Some companies, taking the conservative stance, do not flow through the benefits of the tax savings in reports to shareholders, while others use its benefits fully.

Market Behavior of Securities

Because of the electronics industry is made up of a number of quite disparate subindustries—consumer, industrial, and government-related—it is virtually impossible to characterize their market behavior in a generalized fashion. But it does seem valid to contend that electronics securities, relative to the market, have (1) higher multiples, (2) more volatility, and (3) higher growth rates.

For purposes of this discussion we focus on four of the higher quality electronics securities: AMP, Hewlett-Packard, Perkin-Elmer, and Texas Instruments. Over the decade from 1963 to 1973, multiples accorded the earnings of these companies have typically been in the 20–40 range, or well above the P/E ratio accorded the market as a whole.

From the point of view of volatility, these securities have also shown significantly more fluctuation than the overall market. In the 1969–70 recession, for instance, Hewlett-Packard stock dropped, from peak to valley, more than 60 percent, and Texas Instruments more than 50 percent. Both these declines, of course, far exceeded those of the broad market averages over the same period.

Finally, there is no question that the aforementioned four electronics companies have demonstrated what one expects of fine technology companies—above-average long-term growth. Over the 1963–73 decade, this group of four companies had an average stock price increase of 600 percent. By contrast, the Dow-Jones Industrial Average increased by about 20 percent. These four companies are, of course, among the innovative leaders in the electronics industry. This innovation, in turn, has led to successful new products development which has generated the earnings growth to create the commensurate stock price increases.

CASE STUDY: SEMICONDUCTOR INDUSTRY

The semiconductor industry affords an excellent case study of the overall electronics industry. The semiconductor industry is rapidly growing, its prices are rapidly declining, it uses substantial amounts of off-shore assembly labor, and it provides the basic components out of which virtually all electronics equipment and systems are fabricated.

Introduction

The semiconductor industry is a growth industry; over a 15-year period it has grown at a 10.7 percent rate, and in the 1969–74 period at an estimated 12.9 percent rate. We believe its future long-term growth rate will accelerate to over 14 percent because:

1. *Integrated circuits,* the growth sector, are surpassing discretes in size next year.
2. *Discretes* are changing in mix, with the probability that their growth rate is likely to improve somewhat over historic rates.
3. *International markets* are growing faster than the U.S. market, and U.S. companies are increasing their share abroad.
4. *New semiconductor markets* are a new phenomenon, and an important one. Led by new consumer applications, the new markets constitute one of the most powerful forces for semiconductor growth in the 1970s.
5. *Penetration of mature markets,* such as automobiles, color TV, and appliances, offers an additional facet for semiconductor growth to supplement that traditionally derived from end-market growth.

Furthermore, sensitivity of the industry to economic cycles is likely to be diminished in the future because of the accelerating flow of new products and the changing end-market mix.

Long-Term Growth to Accelerate

Because of the severe impact of the economic and technological recession of 1970–71, the semiconductor industry has been criticized in some quarters as no longer being a growth industry. Our contention is to the contrary—not only is the semiconductor industry a true growth industry, but its growth rate is accelerating. We believe that the growth rate of the 1970s will exceed that of the 1960s. More specifically, from 1959 through 1974 we estimate that the total semiconductor industry, as measured by U.S. factory shipments, will have grown at a 10.7 percent rate (least squares logarithmic method). For the five-year period beginning in 1974, we estimate that this rate will accelerate to 14.3 percent per year.

Historic Growth. Figure 2 illustrates the historic growth of the industry. As is clear, the integrated circuit portion of the industry is a truly rapidly growing sector, while discrete devices have grown at a far more modest rate. While overall semiconductors are growing at only a 10.7 percent rate over the 15-year period depicted, discretes are growing at 4.8 percent per year and integrated circuits at 40.1 percent. It should be noted that during the latest five years, 1969–74 (which includes a major recession), the overall growth rate has already increased to 12.9 percent. This stepped-up growth reflects strongly the growing importance

FIGURE 2

U.S. Semiconductor Shipments: 1959–74E

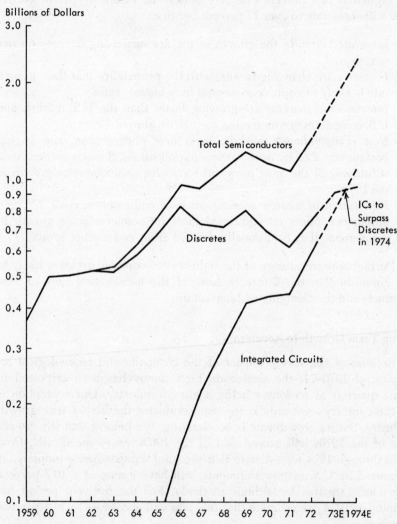

of integrated circuits. The industry, which crossed the billion dollar market in 1968, is likely to cross the $2 billion market next year (see Table 7).

Future Industry Growth to Accelerate. One of our basic theses about the semiconductor industry is that we expect its future growth to accelerate. Following a 10.7 percent rate from 1959 through 1974, we look

TABLE 7

U.S. Semiconductor Shipments: 1959–74E ($ millions)

Year	Discretes	Integrated Circuits	Total Semiconductors
1974E	$950	$1,085	$2,035
1973E	910	890	1,800
1972	754	606	1,360
1971	623	443	1,066
1970	686	433	1,119
1969	805	413	1,218
1968	712	303	1,015
1967	721	221	942
1966	829	148	977
1965	677	79.1	756
1964	586	40.7	627
1963	519	15.8	535
1962	519	—	519
1961	503	—	503
1960	498	—	498
1959	363	—	363

for a 14.3 percent rate from 1974 through 1979. This acceleration, indicated in Table 8, assumes some slowdown in integrated circuit growth and a very modest increase in discrete semiconductor growth.

Five basic reasons underlie our acceleration thesis. We look for IC shipments to surpass discretes in 1974, discrete growth to increase slightly from historic rates, faster-growing international markets to increase in importance, new semiconductor markets to surge, and penetration of mature markets to become a major target of opportunity.

1. *Integrated circuits overtaking discretes in 1974:* Referring again to Figure 2, we note that 1974 will be a significant year for the industry in that it will be the first year in which integrated circuits—the *faster-growing* part of the industry—becomes the *dominant* part of the industry. In prior years, the rapid growth of integrated circuits had relatively modest impact on total industry growth, inasmuch as discretes accounted for such a high percent of industry volume. For instance in 1969, the year before the recession, discrete semiconductor shipments were about twice those of ICs. But by the late 1970s, we expect IC shipments to be more than twice those of discretes.

2. *Improving mix of discretes and devices:* For years, discrete semi-

TABLE 8

Long-term Growth Rates: U.S. Factory Shipments

| Category | Historic | | Recent | | | Future Pro-jected Growth Rate (percent) |
	Period	Annual Growth Rate* (percent) No. of Years	Period†	No. of Years	Annual Growth Rate* (percent)	
Integrated circuits...........	1963–74E	11 40.1	1969–74E	5	23.2	20.0
Discretes...................	1959–74E	15 4.8	1969–74E	5	5.5	6.0
Total semiconductors.......	1959–74E	15 10.7	1969–74E	5	12.9	14.3

* Least-squares logarithmic method.
† Includes a major recession.

conductor growth has been impacted by the steady encroachment of integrated circuits on small signal devices. Much as small signal devices largely replaced vacuum tubes in earlier years, integrated circuits have more recently been replacing small signal devices. Until this year, small signal devices accounted for the majority of the dollar shipments of discretes. In 1973, however, two growth sectors within the discrete domain—power semiconductors and optoelectronic devices—now account for over half the discrete dollar total. This fact is significant, inasmuch as these products are immune to encroachment by integrated circuits and are, in their own right, growth products. As indicated in Table 9, we estimate that power and optoelectronic devices will account

TABLE 9

Changing Discrete Mix

Device Type	Percent of Total U.S. Discrete Shipments						
	1968	1969	1970	1971	1972	1973E	1974E
Small signal..................	61	60	60	53	50	46	40
Power.......................	35	35	35	41	41	41	43
Optoelectronics..............	4	5	5	6	9	13	17
Total discretes...........	100	100	100	100	100	100	100

for 60 percent of the discrete semiconductor mix in 1974, up from 39 percent in 1968.

As a result, the growth rate of discretes—4.8 percent per year from 1959 through 1974, and 5.5 percent from 1969 through 1974—is projected by us to increase to a 6.0 percent annual rate from 1974 through 1979, and thus contribute in a small way to the overall acceleration of the total semiconductor industry growth. Figure 3 illustrates the contrasting growth rates between small signal devices, on the one hand, and power and optoelectronic devices, on the other.

3. *International penetration increasing:* The semiconductor market outside the United States has been, and is expected to continue to be, a faster growing market than the U.S. market. As shown in Table 4, U.S. consumption of semiconductors from 1969 to 1973 has increased at a 10 percent rate, while Europe (at 16 percent) and Asia (at 23 percent) have grown at substantially higher rates. Overall, the world market has been growing at about one and one-half times the U.S. rate. This fact is important to U.S. companies, inasmuch as they have been increasing their penetration of foreign markets in recent years, particularly in the last three. Foreign semiconductor companies have been laggard in recent years, both in technology and in capacity expansion. Thus, the U.S. companies are benefiting twofold: from the faster growth rates of the foreign markets and from the increasing U.S. penetration of them. We look for

FIGURE 3

Changing Discrete Mix

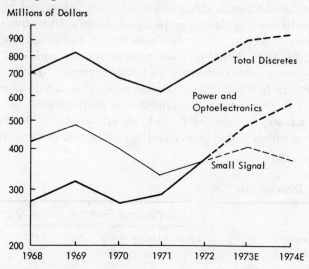

foreign growth in the future to continue at a faster rate than that of the United States and thus to upward bias the total world growth rate above that of the U.S. rate (Table 10).

4. *New markets—a new phenomenon:* The new semiconductor markets are both an *important* phenomenon and a *new* phenomenon. We have quantified nine significant new markets for semiconductors; they are reproduced in Table 11. It should be noted that these by no means constitute all the new markets—examples of some important omitted ones are communications and point-of-sale registers—but they are significant enough to demonstrate a point. That is, just two years ago these nine new markets accounted for only 10 percent of the U.S. semiconductor output; two years from now we expect them to account for almost half.

We see in Table 12 that all other semiconductor markets could be

TABLE 10

**World Semiconductor Consumption Growth:
1969–73E**

Area	Annual Growth Rate (percent)
United States	10.0
Europe	15.8
Asia	23.3
Rest of world	17.9
Total world	14.8

TABLE 11

Forecast of Semiconductor Shipments to "New Markets"

	Value of Semiconductor Shipments ($ millions)*				
	1971	1972	1973	1974	1975
Consumer-related:					
Automotive......................	$ 15	$ 20	$ 50	$100	$ 150
Color television.................	30	50	65	90	125
Calculators.....................	15	35	60	90	100
Photography....................	10	15	30	50	75
Appliances.....................	—	—	10	25	50
Watches/clocks.................	—	—	5	10	40
Subtotal..................	$ 70	$120	$220	$365	$ 540
Industrial/Computer-related:					
Memory........................	$ 15	$ 50	$150	$250	$ 350
Display........................	25	50	70	100	125
Microcomputer.................	—	5	10	25	50
Subtotal..................	$ 40	$105	$230	$375	$ 525
TOTAL................	$110	$225	$450	$740	$1,065

* Figures in table are subject to wide variation and are intended to show general trends rather than absolute magnitudes.

assumed to be flat—as we have done for the 1973–75 period—but the total market would still grow at a very healthy rate (13 percent in 1974 and 16 percent in 1975) because of the new market stimulation. (Though we are assuming for forecasting purposes that traditional markets will be flat, we would not be surprised to see them actually grow during this period.) To cite just one example of this stimulation, in 1971 the total market for consumer calculators (defined as calculators selling for under $150) was zero units and zero dollars. Two years later, the U.S. market alone is 7.5 million units at a factory sales value of perhaps a half billion dollars, with a semiconductor content of about $150 million. These new markets are not trivial!

5. *Penetration of market versus growth of market:* In the 1960s the two dominant users of semiconductors were computer mainframes and

TABLE 12

Increasing Importance of New Semiconductor Markets

	1971	1972	1973	1974	1975
Estimated Shipments ($ millions):					
Nine new markets..................	$ 110	$ 225	$ 450	$ 740	$1,065
Other markets....................	956	1,135	1,350	1,295	1,300
Total U.S. shipments.............	$1,066	$1,360	$1,800	$2,035	$2,365
Percent of Total:					
Nine new markets..................	10	17	25	36	45
Other markets....................	90	83	75	64	55
Total U.S. shipments.............	100	100	100	100	100

government electronics. These markets had been using semiconductors heavily since the early 1960s, and, in the case of mainframes in particular, represented a saturated market for semiconductors. Thus, for semiconductors to grow in the 1960s it was necessary for their two major markets (mainframes and government) to expand. This, of course, turned out to be the case for most of the decade. But as we look into the 1970s, we see an additional, and potentially much more important, factor for growth. In the forthcoming years, semiconductors will derive a large measure of growth from *penetration* of market rather than from growth of the end market itself. Among the best illustrations of this are the automotive, television, and memory markets.

In the automotive market, the traditional application of semiconductors has been for entertainment purposes—radios and tape players. But in the future, stimulated by regulation, legislation, and lower prices, semiconductors will be used to perform a variety of emission control, safety, and performance functions. As a result, we are forecasting that automobiles (and trucks) will become one of the largest users of semiconductors in the second half of the 1970s, despite the fact that we do not anticipate—and need not have—growth in the automotive market itself. The semiconductor market is instead going from essentially zero penetration to small penetration of a huge dollar market. A similar phenomenon is occurring now in color television, as tubes are being displaced, and in computer memory, as semiconductors are displacing magnetic cores.

In summary, then, we feel strongly that semiconductor growth will accelerate in the future as (1) integrated circuits shipments surpass discretes, (2) discretes themselves begin to grow somewhat more rapidly, (3) the faster-growing international sector takes on more importance, (4) the new semiconductor markets begin to take off, and (5) penetration of large, mature markets creates new semiconductor opportunities.

Near-Term Outlook

Demand in 1973 Far Greater Than Shipments Figures Suggest. A standard industry measure of the strength of demand is the ratio of bookings (orders) to billings (shipments), commonly referred to as the book/bill ratio. In 1969, a strong year, the book/bill ratio averaged 106 percent for the year and reached a peak of 109 percent in the second quarter. Based on that strength, and the general expectation of a good 1970, semiconductor manufacturers added a fair amount of production capacity. But as shown in Figure 4, the book/bill ratio in 1969 was not spectacularly high; bokings were just comfortably ahead of billings for the year. In 1970, when demand dried up, the book/bill ratio fell below 100 percent, and the industry found itself shipping more than it was receiving in new orders.

FIGURE 4

Semiconductor Book/Bill Ratios: 1968–1973E

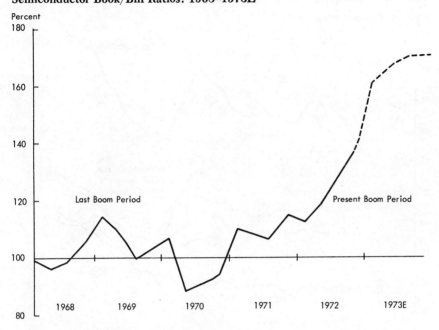

Referring once more to Figure 4, one sees an absolutely startling contrast between the strength of demand (as measured by the book/bill ratio) in 1973 and that in 1970. To say glibly that 1973 is just another strong year, basically the same as 1969, is grossly misstating the case. Instead, book/bill ratios are at historic highs (1973 data is estimated by us, based on discussions with industry sources). Even allowing for double ordering and for long lead-time bookings, the strength of demand is still totally unprecedented. We expect the book/bill ratio to decline in 1974 but, unlike 1970, to average above 100 percent for the year.

Historic versus Future Cyclicality

Shipment Collapse in 1970 Primarily a Demand Shortfall. Figure 5 illustrates that the precipitous decline in industry shipments in 1970 (29 percent, peak to valley) was almost entirely due to a decline in shipments to the computer industry (39 percent, peak to valley). Computer industry use of semiconductors at the time was mainly concentrated on mainframe applications, and this was the cause of the problem. An unprecedented set of adverse circumstances occurred during 1970. Computer manufacturers had been ordering semiconductors in large quantities in 1969 (this surge shows up clearly on Figure 5), anticipating an-

FIGURE 5

Total OEM Semiconductors Breakdown by End Market (dollars in millions)

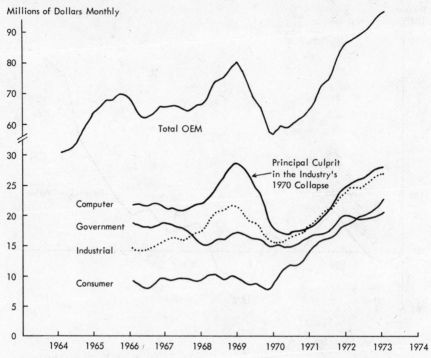

other strong year for computer shipments in 1970. But, as it turned out, 1970 proved to be the first recession year for the computer industry. Also, IBM, a significant outside purchaser of semiconductors, despite its large captive capability, was in the midst of a model change. As a result, computer manufacturers were able to live off bloated semiconductor inventories in 1970 and in 1971 to a significant degree. It should be noted in Figure 4 that 1970 falloffs in shipments to the industrial, government, and consumer sectors were relatively minor, and these markets were not significant contributors to the semiconductor industry's 1970 woes.

Mainframes Far Less Important in 1974. We foresee no repeat of the 1970 mainframe debacle in 1974. First, we believe that mainframe shipments will be stronger in 1974 than they were in 1970. Second, inventories at the computer manufacturers' level are much tighter than was the case in the previous cycle. Third, as Figure 6 illustrates, the importance of mainframes to the semiconductor industry is now sharply lower than it was before. Peripherals and memory, the *growth* sector of the computer industry, are now the *dominant* sector as well, with regard to their use of semiconductors. Thus, even if one uses a worst-case assumption of flat mainframe shipments in 1974—an assumption which we believe unduly pessimistic—we would nonetheless anticipate growth of semiconductors to the computer industry simply because of the increasing use of semiconductors in peripherals and particularly in memory. This forecast stands in sharp contradistinction to the 1970 situation, when peripherals and memory were relatively minor semiconductor users.

FIGURE 6

U.S. Computer Market Semiconductor Sales (dollars in millions)

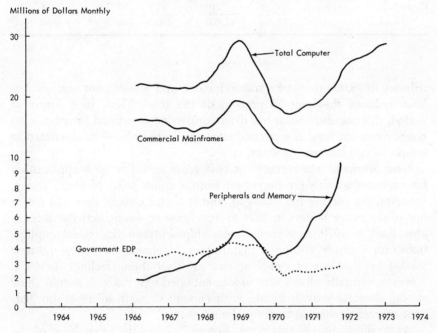

Market Diversification. In 1969, 27 percent of the semiconductor industry's shipments went to the computer sector, while only 11 percent found their way to consumer applications. Since then, the consumer market has improved dramatically in importance. As shown in Table 13, we estimate the consumer sector to be the largest class of semiconductor users. The importance of this fact is that as we enter 1974, the diversification of semiconductor end-markets is much better than it was in 1969 and is thus more immune to the collapse of any single market.

Increasing Pervasiveness of Semiconductors. That semiconductors have dramatically broadened their pervasiveness within the economy is demonstrated by the following. In 1969, Hamilton-Avnet, the largest distributor of semiconductors in the United States, served about 8,000 customers. Of these 8,000 customers, government end-use accounted for about 75 percent of the parts shipped. Today, the same company dis-

TABLE 13

Changing Mix of End Markets

	Amounts ($ millions)		Percent of Total		Compound Annual Growth Rate
Market	1969	1973E	1969	1973E	(percent)
Consumer.................	$ 137	$ 375	11	21	+29
Computer.................	326	335	27	19	+ 1
Industrial.................	255	325	21	18	+ 6
Government..............	172	235	14	13	+ 8
Distributor..............	190	320	16	18	+14
Export..................	138	210	11	12	+11
Total...............	$1,218	$1,800	100	100	+10

tributes to 22,000 users of semiconductors, and government end-use has been reduced to about 25 percent of the total. Thus, in a four-year period, this one distributor has dramatically increased and broadened its nongovernment base as semiconductor applications have mushroomed in industrial and consumer sectors.

New Markets. As recently as two years ago, few new applications for semiconductors were important from a dollar point of view. Today, however, the picture has changed, and it is this change that will act as one of the major buffers in 1974 as aggregate economic activity decelerates. Back in 1970, as semiconductor shipments for traditional applications (for example, computer mainframes) declined, there were no new market applications of sufficient size to offset these declines. In 1974, however, virtually all the nine aforementioned new markets should show strong, absolute growth trends, with enough strength to offset any flatness, or even decline, in traditional markets.

As an illustration of this point, Figure 7 shows the breakdown of the consumer market. The bottom half of the chart shows the three major subsectors: home and portable entertainment (largely color TV), transportation vehicles (largely automobiles), and miscellaneous other applications (appliances, etc.).

The surge in consumer semiconductor shipments, which began in 1970, has resulted primarily from color TV—the beginning of the conversion to all-solid-state by the entire television industry. Only 24 percent of color TV factory production in 1972 was all-solid-state sets. In 1973, about 50 percent was all-solid-state (it was 36.5 percent for the first six months), and in 1974 perhaps 85–90 percent will be, if parts are available in sufficient quantity. These percentages lead us to an important point—that is, even if production of color TV, a relatively mature product, declines in 1974, we anticipate almost certainly that semiconductor shipments to the industry will increase. This follows from the fact that increasing semiconductor penetration, even of a declining market,

FIGURE 7

U.S. Consumer Market Semiconductor Sales (dollars in millions)

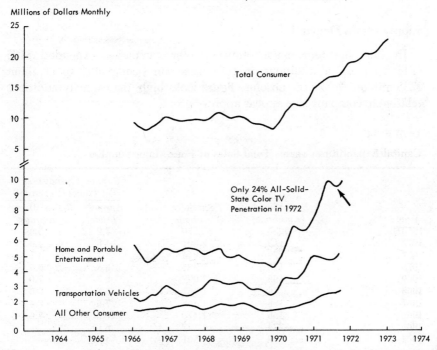

will allow the number of all-solid-state sets to increase from 1.9 million sets in 1972 (24 percent penetration) to perhaps 5.5–6.0 million (85–90 percent penetration) in 1974. These figures assume total U.S. color TV production dropping from 7.8 million sets in 1972 to 6.5–7.0 million in 1974. It's likely that color TV use of semiconductors will peak in 1975, but total consumer semiconductor usage will increase as automotive and other consumer applications begin to reach appreciable size in that year.

To take an example from the computer sector, we can look at the 1103, a 1,024-bit random access memory developed by Intel. In 1973 the industry will ship close to 6 million of these devices at a valuation of about $25 million. In 1974, because of the 1103's increasing penetration of the computer memory market, 1103 unit shipments could reach 15 million with a valuation of perhaps $50 million. This progression is virtually independent of what happens to the mainframe computer market in 1970.

Considering another product area, photographic uses of semiconductors are certain to grow in 1974, again because of increasing penetration. The Polaroid SX-70 will use a substantially greater dollar volume of semiconductors in 1974 versus 1973. Also, Kodak has sharply increased its use of semiconductors in cameras. The pocket Instamatic models 50 and 60 each use three custom integrated circuits, and these are likely to be in strong demand in 1974.

Supply versus Demand

In 1969 the four major semiconductor companies expended $165 million on capital additions; in 1973 these same companies spent about $235 million. While the absolute figure looks high, the capacity additions relative to company size appear appropriate:

TABLE 14

Capital Expenditures versus Total Sales of Four Major Suppliers

Year	Capital Expenditures ($ millions)	Total Sales ($ millions)	Capital Expenditures ÷ Total Sales (by percent)	
			Annual Data	3-Year Moving Averages
1973E	$235	$3,270	7.2	5.6
1972	115	2,391	4.8	4.9
1971	79	1,944	4.1	6.1
1970	110	1,881	5.8	6.5
1969	165	1,998	8.3	7.0
1968	86	1,667	5.2	7.6
1967	106	1,407	7.5	8.4
1966	156	1,476	10.6	7.6
1965	74	1,137	6.5	—
1964	38	891	4.3	—

The moving average data is plotted in Figure 8. The top curve shows the strong upward trend of capital expenditures in 1973 and 1974 (estimated). On the surface, one could get quite disturbed about this steep upward thrust in spending. However, if one divides the moving average of capital expenditures by a moving average of total company sales (bottom curve), one sees that the capital additions in 1973 and 1974 are much more in line with industry size and with company size than one might infer from the top curve alone.

Further, as the chart of book-to-bill ratios indicated (Figure 4), actual *demand*—as reflected by order strength—is really much greater than the shipments figures alone would suggest. Accordingly, these factors give us at least some comfort that plant and equipment additions are not being added at unreasonably high rates.

Historically, each capital expenditure dollar has generated about two dollars in incremental sales. Looking at 1973 and 1974 together, total capital expenditures are projected at $435 million and total sales increases at $1.2 billion. Based on long-term historical relationships, these capital outlays would not seem to be unduly high and, in fact, could be construed as being too low, relative to the expected sales growth.

FIGURE 8

**Capital Expenditures (FCI, MOT, NSM, TXN): Absolute and Relative
(three-year moving averages)**

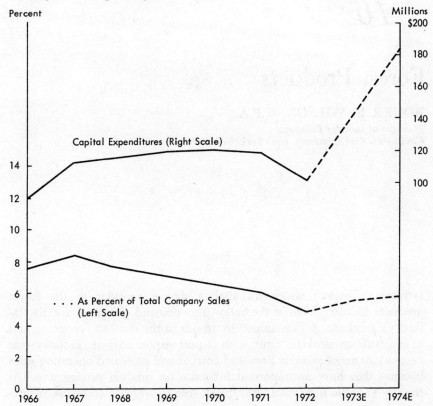

16

Forest Products

ROGER B. WILSON, C.F.A.
Manager of Investor Relations
Continental Can Company, New York, New York

IMPORTANT factors which an analyst should consider in the forest products industry include the following: demand prospects for the industry's products, as determined by trends in the domestic economy and in construction markets, along with import/export outlook; industrywide capacity in major product lines and current and projected operating rates because they have an important influence on product pricing which is the key variable in profitability; the degree to which a company is integrated, especially the percentages of basic raw materials such as wood and pulp that are obtained internally, and the cost of all raw materials; and special accounting considerations such as captial gains on timber. The industry has been cyclical, within long-term uptrends, in the past and is likely to remain so in the future. Several companies have had superior earnings records, and it is the analyst's job to determine which ones will continue to outperform the industry, based in part on an application of the subjects discussed in this section.

STRUCTURE OF THE INDUSTRY

During the past 20 years, the forest products industry has evolved from a preponderance of companies operating primarily in specialized areas, to the present situation of most companies being large, diversified operations. In the years since the Korean War, holders of timberland moved forward into wood products and diversified into pulp, paper, and packaging. Paper and packaging producers diversified within these fields

398

and integrated backwards into woodlands ownership, pulp manufacture, and wood products production. As a result, most companies in the industry are large, broadly diversified, national in scope, and the owners of large tracts of timberland. Many have subsidiaries or divisions in Canada, because of the vast timber resources there, and also have investments in overseas areas which are increasing in size and importance. Despite this trend towards concentration in the industry, it is still relatively fragmented. For example, the largest producers of lumber (Weyerhaeuser Company) and paper products (International Paper Company) account for somewhat less than 10 percent of the output in North America in their respective areas of dominance.

There are two main subindustries within forest products—paper and wood products. The paper segment consists of all pulp, paper, paperboard, and packaging output, which includes such major product categories as printing and writing papers, newsprint, tissue products, linerboard, bags, corrugated boxes, and folding cartons. Lumber and plywood are the principal wood products, as well as newer items such as particleboard.

The industry's products are primarily commodities which are sold to wholesalers or to other industrial firms for use as is or for conversion and resale. Very few products are retail consumer lines, with the notable exception of tissue items, and advertising expenditures are not large. Research and development expenditures are also rather small, accounting for less than 1 percent of sales. Most of the industry's hourly labor force is unionized, usually on a plant-by-plant basis within a company, although there are some multifacility or regional contracts.

The primary factors to examine when analyzing a forest products company are the following: product mix and relative position within principal lines, timberland ownership, degrees of integration (extent to which the company is self-sufficient in principal raw materials such as wood and pulp), exports, foreign operations, labor contracts, location of facilities, and geographical marketing coverage.

DETERMINANTS OF DEMAND AND PRICING

The consumption of paper products in the United States is closely correlated with overall economic activity. The American Paper Institute, a trade association, has compiled data demonstrating that total domestic consumption of paper is closely related to real gross national product. During the last 20 years, consumption in each year has ranged between 76,000 and 81,800 tons per billion dollars of GNP in 1958 prices. Apparent consumption is derived by adding imports to domestic production and then subtracting exports from the total. In 1973, consumption totalled 67.2 million tons—61.7 million tons of production plus 8.5 million tons imported minus 3.0 million tons exported. The industry has benefited from rising per capita consumption of paper on a fairly steady basis to 640 pounds in 1973. Imports and exports have been somewhat more volatile than output, with production declining only four times on a year-to-year basis since 1950.

The consumption of wood products in the United States is determined by overall construction activity. The markets for lumber and plywood, in terms of unit volume, are approximately evenly divided between residential construction (housing) and nonresidential applications (commercial buildings, manufacturing plants, public facilities, containers, furniture, etc.).

Lumber production has advanced less than 2 percent a year over the long term, to about 37.9 million board feet in 1973. Imports, mostly from Canada, have risen over 6 percent annually to 9.5 million board feet, while exports have also increased over 6 percent a year to 2 million board feet in 1973. Lumber consumption has been retarded by competition from other materials such as plywood and other wood-panel products. Softwood plywood production has grown almost 7 percent a year to 18.3 million square feet in 1973, with virtually no imports and very small exports of this product.

In addition to foreign trade in finished products, there are large volumes of imports and exports of raw materials, such as logs, wood chips, and wood pulp, in the forest products industry. Most exports are to the advanced industrial nations such as Western Europe and Japan, while the majority of imports come from Canada and Scandinavia.

Although final consumption is the primary determinant of the level of production in the forest products industry, profitability is importantly influenced by capacity to produce and the resulting effects of operating rates on product pricing. Year-to-year changes in output and capacity have not been very large in either paper or wood products. Profits have fluctuated in a wide range, however, and the key variable has been pricing.

In common with other major manufacturing industries, the forest products industry has high fixed costs that inexorably increase due to inflationary pressures. Therefore, a small decline in production combined with an increase in capacity results in lower operating rates and reductions in product pricing, which has a dramatic impact on earnings when costs are rising. The opposite occurs when operating rates are improving. The decision to add to capacity is usually made by management when the company is doing very well—demand is strong, the utilization of facilities is at a high level, operating efficiencies are improving, product prices are rising by percentages that may exceed increases in costs, and profits are soaring. Unfortunately, most companies in the industry are operating close to maximum capacity simultaneously and decide to expand at about the same time. As a result, additions to capacity tend to come on stream in periodic surges on an industrywide basis, and quite often the bulges in capacity coincide with periods of economic slowdown due to the lag in time between the approval of plans for a new facility and its completion.

The next group of factors to consider in the analysis of a forest products company, therefore, are the following: current and prospective consumption of the industry's products (and, more specifically, the products of the company under review), current levels of capacity and scheduled additions, operating rates at present and over the foreseeable future in major product lines, and the resulting impact on the price structure from these factors.

ANALYSIS OF COST FACTORS

In order to evaluate the impact on profitability of changes in the costs of operating a company, it is necessary to know the relative importance of the components of costs. An analysis of the principal expenses in the forest products industry will provide an overview, but it should be recognized that there may be considerable variation in the cost structures of individual companies.

Raw materials consisting of wood, waste paper, chemicals, pulp, inks, glue, etc. account for varying percentages of total costs, depending on the type of product being manufactured. In the production of wood products such as lumber and plywood, for example, the principal raw material is sawlogs, shipped to the mill directly from the forest. These will account for a relatively high proportion of the finished product's total costs. Paper manufacture, on the other hand, involves a variety of raw material inputs. Pulp is the basic raw material, but the type of paper to be produced will determine the amounts of wood (logs, or chips and sawdust), waste paper, chemicals, clays, and dyes utilized. Converted products such as grocery bags, corrugated shipping containers, envelopes, and folding cartons are produced from paper or paperboard obtained from outside or from within the company. Therefore, it represents to the convertor a commodity whose cost consists of the raw materials input of the basic producer plus many other items such as labor and freight.

Production and distribution costs, other than overhead, consist of items such as hourly labor, transportation, energy, and chemicals. Despite the fact that many types of forest products facilities are capital intensive, the industry also has a rather large labor factor, with hourly wages representing about one fourth of total costs and all wages, salaries, and employee benefits accounting for about one third of the industry's costs. Transportation, both inbound and outbound freight, is also a major cost factor, with the industry absorbing the charges for shipments to its customers. Energy consists of fuel oil, natural gas, coal, and electricity used to operate equipment and process materials, and the rising costs and questions of availability have become a serious problem recently due to the nation's energy crisis. Some energy requirements, approximately one third, are generated internally when waste products in the manufacturing process are burned. Purchased chemicals such as chlorine, salt cake, lime, sulfur, and caustic soda are used primarily in the production of pulp and certain grades of paper.

Overhead expenses in the forest products industry, representing all costs other than raw material and production and distribution costs (and excluding federal income taxes which will be discussed below), consist of items such as depreciation and amortization, interest charges, selling and administrative costs, utilities, social security taxes, state and local income taxes, and insurance. Because of the large capital investments, depreciation often represents a rather large annual expense.

The industry has an unusual item on the income statement, identified most frequently in the past as depletion, which allows a forest products company to deduct as an expense for tax purposes the cost of timber as it is cut. When a company purchases woodlands, it assigns separate portions of the total cost to the land and to the standing timber; with as much value assigned to the standing timber as the Internal Revenue Services will permit, because this cost can be recovered by the purchaser through depletion. On land that has been cleared, the expense of growing a new crop of trees represents the amount that can be charged as depletion expense when this timber is cut. The carrying costs of timberland ownership, such as taxes, interest, fire protection, and insect control, are usually expensed as incurred. Depletion is computed on a tract basis, utilizing cruises of the timberland to estimate the board feet of wood in a tract and to assign a cost (depletion) per thousand board feet. Depletion in this industry, therefore, represents the amortization of the capital cost of standing timber during the future time periods in which it is utilized. In other words, timber depletion has the same purpose as depreciation, but it is the writing-off of costs on a unit of production basis rather than on a time period basis. Because trees are a renewable natural resource, this is a cost depletion that is not the same as depletion in other resource industries such as petroleum and mining. In order to more accurately identify the expense, many forest products companies have begun to label this item "cost of timber harvested" on the income statement.

For a variety of reasons, the overall effective tax rate for many forest product companies is often well below the basic corporate rate for federal income taxes. A unique tax feature in this industry is the capital gains on timber. Section 631 of the Internal Revenue Code allows for capital gains tax rates being applied to profits arising from the difference between the cost of standing timber and its value (stumpage price) when harvested if it is owned for over six months. The capital gain, therefore, takes place when the tree is cut (not yet consumed or sold) and is equal to its fair market value lying in the forest minus its cost (depletion). The computation of this tax is not shown separately on the income statement, even though it is computed independently of profits taxed at regular corporate rates. Therefore, variations in the proportions of earnings (before federal income taxes) derived from capital gains on timber and from ordinary operations will cause different apparent tax rates between companies in a single year or from year to year in a company's historical record.

In common with other industries, forest products companies may reduce their tax rates through items such as the investment tax credit (or job development tax credit) and Domestic International Sales Corporations (DISCs). The investment tax credit represents a percentage of the cost of qualifying capital investments that is directly deducted from federal income taxes payable, and can be an important item in view of the industry's large capital spending. In order to encourage exports, the federal government passed legislation that permits corporations to set up DISCs through which a company's exports can be sold. The profits of a DISC are taxed at one half the ordinary rate for federal income taxes. The growing importance of forest products exports causes DISCs to have a meaningful impact on the tax rate of some companies.

FEDERAL AND STATE REGULATION—ENVIRONMENTAL PROBLEMS

The forest products industry is subject to the usual corporate regulations, of which only pollution control is unique. The industry faces environmental problems that have gained increasing attention in recent years in the following areas: air and water pollution, solid waste disposal, and conservation of forests. Legislation to combat these problems has been enacted at the federal, state, and local levels.

Because the paper-making process requires chemical operations and uses large amounts of water, air and water pollution is a problem at the industry's pulp and paper mills. Capital expenditures to reduce emissions from these mills are running in excess of $400 million a year; the annual operating costs of installed pollution abatement equipment is estimated at approximately $150 million and is in a steeply rising trend.

The disposal of solid wastes generated in the production of paper and wood products at the mill level represents a problem that most companies seem to have brought under control, although at great cost. A more serious question, and perhaps an indirect one, exists regarding how the United States and other countries will deal with solid wastes (or garbage) at the consumer level. Paper, such as newspaper, boxes, cartons, and bags, represents a large portion of the country's mounting volume of solid wastes. There is the possibility that penalties might be legislated which would prohibit or tax products that are disposable. Most industries seem to favor recycling as a solution—at present, over 20 percent of the paper industry's raw materials consists of wastepaper. In addition, paper wastes have a potential value as a fuel that may become increasingly attractive in view of the energy crisis.

Increasing awareness of "the quality of life" has included heightened concern for the preservation of our forests. A conflict has arisen between conservationists (or "preservationists") who often want to prohibit cutting on government land and would like to increase the acreage set aside as wilderness areas, and those who favor a multiple-use policy for timberlands (including tree harvesting and more aggressive forest management) to increase yields. The total amount of forest land in the United States is estimated at about 750 million acres, of which the forest products industry owns approximately 9 percent. Pressure has been brought to bear by environmentalists, primarily through lawsuits, to limit or prevent tree harvesting on government lands; and there has been a negative effect, through delays in arriving at a final decision in the courts, on the availability of this wood—a factor which tends to increase the cost of all wood in a period of tight supply.

The analysis of a forest products company, therefore, must include a determination of its position with regard to pollution control expenditures and the possibility of wood supply problems caused by environmental pressures. In addition, solid waste considerations may influence a company's decisions on new product development and the recycling of raw materials.

ACCOUNTING CONSIDERATIONS AND ADJUSTMENTS

Although most financial data is comparable among companies in the forest products industry, it is necessary to make adjustments in certain items to get a more accurate picture of relative performance. On the balance sheet, the financial data is, for the most part, directly usable. Inventory valuations, for example, are fairly consistent, with average cost the most commonly used method. The first-in, first-out valuation method (Fifo) is not often used, while the last-in, first-out method (Lifo) is used frequently for raw materials inventory valuations. Intangible assets such as goodwill are not significant. Timber assets, however, are often sizable and may require special consideration.

The acquisition of timber resources by a company is usually accomplished by one of the following methods: outright purchase, timber leasing, or timber rights (also known as cutting contracts). Outright purchases are recorded on the balance sheet at cost, while timber leases may or may not appear on the balance sheet, and timber rights—which are usually shorter-term arrangements than leases—are most often not reflected on the balance sheet or in the footnotes. As mentioned above in the section on analysis of cost factors, timber holdings give rise to depletion and capital gains—factors which may also apply to leases and cutting contracts, depending on their terms. As a result, costs, tax rates, and profits will vary among companies in the industry because of differences in their timber holdings with regard to method of acquisition, cost basis, proportion of total wood needs supplied from these holdings, and accounting treatment dictated by the terms of a lease or contract.

Timber holdings that are reflected as an asset are recorded at historical cost. The longer this asset is held the more it becomes understated, when compared to its current economic worth in view of the steady rise in timber values over the years. Therefore, differences in the age of timber assets will cause variations in balance sheet values, costs, profits, and return on investment. In other words, the older a timber holding the more it is undervalued on the balance sheet; costs are lower and earnings are higher than they would be with more recent timber acquisitions; and return on investment is greater than it would be if current asset values were used.

On the income statement, there are several factors to consider, or adjust, in order to improve the comparability of financial reports. The investment tax credit is accounted for either on a flow-through basis, reflecting the entire credit in the year in which it is earned for federal income tax purposes, or amortized over the life of the assets to which the credit applies. Most companies in the industry use the flow-through method. Depreciation is also treated in two different manners; on an accelerated basis for both tax and financial reporting purposes, or accelerated for tax reports and on a straight-line basis for financial reports to shareholders. Almost all forest products companies use the latter method.

The treatment of transportation expenses are not uniform in the industry. This has no effect on net income but causes variations in net sales, total costs, and any financial ratios computed with these statistics. Product prices are the cost to a customer on a delivered basis, with the forest products company absorbing the freight charges. Some companies include this cost in gross sales, which is rarely reported, and deduct it before arriving at the net sales figure, while others carry transportation as an expense item on the income statement below net sales.

Sometimes it is necessary to obtain supplementary financial data from a company. For example, costs associated with the start up of a major new facility, such as a pulp, paper, or paperboard mill, may be treated in different manners, and the details are often not revealed in shareholder reports. There is no set formula to determine when a facility under construction becomes operative and when the amortization of deferred costs and the depreciation of plant and equipment commences. In addition, certain pre-start-up costs, such as interest on money borrowed for the project or employee training, are expensed by some companies and deferred by others to be amortized after the facility is in commercial operation. These variations obviously affect the profits reported by companies at any given time during the life cycle of a new mill.

A relatively new feature in financial reporting is the indication of the sales and earnings contributions of major divisions or product lines. The method of reporting is determined by each company. Therefore, there can be wide variance in the allocation of revenues and costs. In the forest products industry, for example, the transfer price of materials shipped from one division to another within an integrated company may reflect cost, market price, or some other valuation. As a result, divisional reports might have little use for making comparisons of similar units in separate companies, but should have value for analyzing the historical performance of a division within a company over a period of time.

MARKET BEHAVIOR OF SECURITIES

The earnings of the forest products industry have been cyclical in the past (with a gradual, long-term uptrend) and are likely to remain so in the future. As pointed out above, year-to-year changes in unit volume have not been great, but the key variable is product pricing. With high fixed costs, changes in volume and pricing are magnified into wide swings in profitability.

Although total production of paper has declined only four times on an annual basis since 1950, there have been about ten years, depending upon which statistical series is used, in which earnings were lower than in the previous year. Drops in output have taken place in single years and usually coincide with periods of slack overall economic activity, while the slide in profits may last longer until the negative forces are gradually reversed. For example, a recent recession in the United States is generally accepted as having lasted from November 1969 to November 1970. Production of paper declined only slightly more than 1 percent in 1970 and then rose to a new high in 1971. Profits, on the other hand, dropped in 1970 and again in 1971 by a total of close to 50 percent over the two years.

The production of wood products is influenced by construction activity; residential construction obviously follows the housing starts cycle while all other construction activity combined is largely determined by the general economic cycles. Since 1960, lumber output has declined in five of the years; and plywood production, with a stronger growth trend in consumption, has dipped in only two different years. As with paper, the swings in earnings are far more than the changes in the economic aggregates. The pullback in residential construction in 1969–70, when housing starts were off about 5 percent in the two years, overlapped the economic recession of 1970; and the profits of wood products companies, reflecting the same leverage as paper producers, fell sharply in both 1970 and 1971.

The market behavior of forest products stocks should be related to the earnings record, and, in fact, the shares have followed a cyclical pattern. It has been pointed out quite often in financial writings that the stock market is more a reflection of anticipated conditions than a mirror of current operations. This apears to be true especially among basic cyclical industries and seems to apply to forest products companies based on observations of past performance.

In general, forest products shares (both paper and wood products companies) seem to follow the long-term trend of earnings, with cyclical swings getting underway prior to, and presumably in anticipation of, changes in the direction of earnings. Price/earnings ratios are usually higher when earnings are depressed than they are when profits are rising to a cyclical peak. This reflects the anticipation by investors of the inevitable ups and downs in profits. These characteristics are also true in large measure for the overall stock market; and forest products stocks usually move in harmony with the market, as most cyclical stock groups have in the past.

During the slump in earnings in 1970–1971, the sequence of market behavior seemed typical. Forest products stocks, as a group, reached a peak around the middle of 1969 and then fell sharply until they turned upwards in the second half of 1970. Earnings peaked in 1969 and declined throughout 1970 and 1971. Price/earnings ratios were high in 1969, but moved even higher in 1970–1971 as earnings fell more than stock prices; and in 1972, price/earnings multiples receded while profits were undergoing a strong recovery.

It should be recognized that the patterns discussed here are generalizations and that the performance of individual forest products stcoks are as unpredictable as any other group until we apply hindsight to their market behavior.

17

Insurance Issues

HERBERT E. GOODFRIEND
Vice President—Research
Paine, Webber, Jackson & Curtis, Inc., New York, New York

ANALYSIS of insurance stocks is viewed with a mystique and accorded reverence not usually manifest in many other areas of security analysis. While standard gauges of appraisal (for example, P/E multiples, management, growth in new sales, financial stability, and markets served, as well as book value and earning power) are as germane here as elsewhere, their calculation and derivation are considered an enigma enshrouded in a maze. Accordingly, it should come as no surprise to the reader that in the past and until recently, the art of insurance company analysis has remained the arcane province of a relatively small group of investors and professionals. In the past five years, however, a movement towards standardization of reporting in a manner analogous to more conventional industrial accounting has made the task more inviting and interesting from a broader stock market standpoint.

Like Caesar's Gaul, the insurance industry is divided into three major parts: life, accident and health (A&H), and property-casualty coverages. Subsectors or overlapping functions within each category tend to make for more complex analysis, but for purposes of this section, we will focus on (1) *stock life* insurance companies writing ordinary and/or industrial-debit insurance; (2) *A&H* companies underwriting medical coverages to supplement or augment those provided by the federal government or the quasi-public sector—for example, Blue Cross-Blue Shield; and (3) *property-casualty* coverages for commercial and personal property risks.

For many years a single company was not permitted by state laws to write both fire and casualty insurance. This restriction led to the growth

408

of groups or "fleets" of companies operating under common corporate ownership, with each company in the group specializing in a particular type of insurance. Between 1946 and 1955, however, state laws were in large part revised to permit a single company to write both fire and casualty insurance. This change has led to a steady movement away from specialized underwriting toward comprehensive coverage of the field by "multiple-line" companies writing all forms of fire and casualty insurance. A number of these multiple-line companies resulted from the merger of companies formerly operating as fleets. In addition, an increasing number of multiple-line companies have been acquiring life insurance companies and are now able to offer all types of insurance.

FIRE AND CASUALTY INSURANCE

The term "fire insurance" includes not only straight fire, but also such other forms of insurance as extended coverage, ocean, marine, inland marine, and auto physical damage. "Casualty insurance" includes principally accident and health, workmen's compensation, third-party liability, and fidelity and surety. Distribution of premiums written by lines is shown in Table 1 (see p. 412).

Fire and casualty insurance is written by many different types of organizations. *Stock companies,* which are owned by stockholders, are the most important kind and account for the largest part of the industry's volume. *Mutual companies,* which are owned by their policyholders, are the second most important group and compete with reciprocal and inter-insurance exchanges, state funds, self-insurers, nonprofit hospital-medical associations, life insurance companies writing various types of accident insurance, domestic branches of foreign insurers, and, to a relatively limited extent, with agencies of the federal government.

Insurance is an indispensable factor in modern economic life—an investment factor of prime importance. The volume of insurance transactions necessarily increases not only in proportion to the growth of the entire nation but actually at a greater rate, because the increasing complexities of modern industry and social economic requirements constantly give rise to the need for entirely new forms of insurance, and also because the public is constantly becoming better educated to the necessity for carrying adequate amounts of insurance of many different types.

The safety of an investment in insurance stocks is maintained in many ways. The laws of the various states impose sound restrictions with respect to investments and the setting up of reserves for both known and contingent liabilities. The companies are required to file annual statements showing assets, liabilities, premiums, losses, and expenses in great detail. Insurance companies are also subject to examination by insurance departments of the states in which they operate, and these examinations are made at reasonably short intervals as a matter of routine, or more frequently if unusual conditions require that action. The fundamental basis of all insurance operations is the assumption of a moderate amount of liability upon each of a very large number of risks, allowing ample room for the operation of the law of averages, so that in large and well-managed companies, the element of chance is minimized.

The operation of an insurance company of any class involves three major activities: (1) the securing of business; (2) the underwriting of the risks offered (that is, the decision as to which risks are and which are not acceptable); and (3) the investment of the initial capital and surplus and accretions arising from operations. The nature of the business requires the setting up of large reserves, a part of which are invested and earn money. The legal restrictions and the general practice of the business results, at least in the case of fire-marine and casualty-surety companies, in an investment portfolio partially similar to that of a sound investment trust. But certain attractive operating features give insurance carriers advantages over investment trusts. In the latter, the only source of earnings is the contributed capital funds and accretions thereto representing reinvested profits. In a fire-marine or casualty-surety company, however, the reserves accumulated out of premiums collected frequently equal or exceed the contributed resources and accretions through reinvested earnings, with continuing income from the invested portion of such reserves. In addition, an insurance company normally should have a profit through its purely underwriting operations. It is the combination of these three advantages, all necessary to help finance growth, which results in the profits earned by well-managed insurance companies. Also, seldom does a company have an unusually large investment in any one security unless it be ownership of insurance companies which act as running mates.

It is the business of insurance to provide for contingencies of every kind. Against these contingencies the business establishes reserves. These reserves must be ample, as required by law or as dictated by conservatism, and, if ample, they must at all times be calculated upon a basis which affords a comfortable margin of safety. Business conducted along these lines must, in the long run, prove beneficial to all concerned.

The maintenance of such an adequate foundation of financial stability is not merely for practical needs. The purpose is to furnish buyers of insurance with that complete confidence which the nature of the business demands. The fire-casualty business imposes upon itself a self-denying ordinance by which practically the whole of the underwriting profits are plowed back into the business. Dividends on shares are invariably limited to an amount much smaller than the interest earned on the invested funds. The cumulative growth effect of earnings retained for the purpose of assuring stability and future expansion is one of the most important factors responsible for the favorable performance of insurance stocks over a long period of years.

There is a striking difference between operations of a fire or casualty insurance company and almost any other type of business concern. This is the lack of correlation between volume of business and net earnings in insurance operations and the normal direct relationship between these two items in general business or industry.

Two factors are primarily responsible for this peculiarity. The first concerns the making of rates which generally are based on loss experience over periods upwards of five years determined on the basis of the normal duration of the various forms of policy contracts. A profitable period for any class of business, under normal circumstances, becomes the base for a reduction in rates, and an unprofitable period brings about higher rates. Thus, periodic swings in underwriting experience are fundamental, and each trend sets the stage for its counter trend. With the goal of rate making being the establishment of rates sufficient to provide for all losses and assure a reasonable underwriting profit, the business as a whole realizes a margin of profit over a period.

The second factor has to do primarily with the lag in adjusting the amount of insurance carried to changing economic conditions and the long-term decline in the purchasing power of the dollar. Not only are buyers of insurance slow in recognizing changes in property value levels but many policies are written for terms of three or five years and adjustments are customarily made only when a policy is renewed. Bodily injury losses, moreover, may be settled many months after the policy is written.

Investment Philosophy

Although rising stock prices have made an important contribution to long-term growth, it is well to remember that insurance companies have more funds invested in bonds than in stocks, as they have consistently bought bonds to cover their steadily increasing insurance reserve requirements. Record high interest rates have been reflected in investment income. The bond portfolios, during recent years, have shown substantial market depreciation but, under insurance accounting regulations, are carried at amortized values in financial statements. Managements are fully aware of the market values of their bond portfolios, many showing actual market values in a footnote. Nevertheless, state commissioners have been increasingly bringing investment income into rate-making considerations.

Central to the conduct of the insurance business, is the theory of spreading the risk of diversification. Definite selection risks may be interjected and approximated across a broader band of risk measurement. The principle is applied to investments of the underwriter as well as to its risk selection. Life insurance companies are subject to comprehensive controls by regulatory bodies in the selection of their invest-

TABLE 1

Distribution of Premiums Written by Lines—Stock Fire and Casualty Companies (1947 and 1972)

	1947		1972	
	Amount (000)	*Percent of Total*	*Amount (000)*	*Percent of Total*
Fire.............................	$ 998,590	25.9	$ 2,060,239	7.47
Allied Lines.......................	246,160	6.37	764,438	2.77
Homeowners multiple peril...........	—	—	2,551,276	9.25
Commercial multiple peril............	—	—	1,774,426	6.43
Ocean marine.....................	167,919	4.3	528,675	1.92
Inland marine.....................	167,669	4.3	868,440	3.15
Accident and health................	193,190	5.0	979,314	3.55
Workmen's compensation...........	414,904	10.7	3,030,840	10.98
Liability other than auto-bodily injury....................		4.5	—	—
Auto liability.....................	676,499	17.5	6,941,573	25.16
Auto physical damage..............	527,970	13.7	4,111,287	14.90
Fidelity and surety.................	105,283	2.7	633,191	2.29
Glass............................	19,540	0.5	32,002	0.12
Burglary and theft.................	71,980	1.9	118,821	0.43
Boiler and machinery...............	27,448	0.7	114,524	0.42
All other.........................	41,861	1.1	947,397	3.43
Miscellaneous liability..............	203,110	5.26	2,138,614	7.75
Total.....................	$3,862,123	100.0	$27,595,057	100.0

Source: *Best's Aggregates & Averages—Property Liability 1973* (Morristown, N.J.: A. M. Best Company, Inc., 1973), pp. 28–29.

ments. They limit their bond purchases to those meeting specific satisfactory criteria and/or even some limited number of qualified preferred shares as well as secured real estate mortgages. Common stock holdings are also under state jurisdiction and for some states cannot be acquired by life companies directly in excess of 12 percent of admitted assets. Actually, at the end of 1972, equity holdings of life insurance companies were only 9.1 percent of admitted assets, equal to $21.8 billion.

Competition

In the field of insurance, price competition under state price regulation and a marketing system developed over many years through independent agents creates many problems not found in other industries. Competition has driven underwriters to extremes quite unbelievable a decade ago when, in a climate of large investment gains and increasing surplus, there was not quite the urgency to produce underwriting profits. It was virtually impossible to hew to the line when the competition was willing to stray.

Between the unavoidable lag of underwriting experience development, particularly on personal automobile liability business, and the reluctance of some authorities to approve rate increases, many responsible insurance companies have been forced to restrict their underwriting in certain areas and in certain classes of business. An inadequate market for necessary classes of insurance harms the public, the regulatory authorities, and the industry. It fosters the creation of a substandard market, and this inevitably includes a certain number of substandard companies which often get into financial difficulty. Some 50 high-risk companies have failed during the past ten years.

Added to the varied problems of the industry has been general inflation in claim costs due to rising values of materials and services, lower purchasing power of the dollar, increased claim consciousness of the public, and unwarranted delays in securing approval of some needed rate increases, despite so-called "file and use" methods of rate introduction.

Specialization

Orthodox companies, in addition, have had to cope with the more intense aggressiveness of specialty carriers in the private passenger automobile business and their rapidly expanded operations into other fields of insurance. The specialty carriers, with their so-called captive agents, supplement their business-developing marketing programs by pre-selling the customer via newspaper, magazine, billboard, radio, television, and direct-mail advertising.

In another direction, the never ending effort to reduce expenses will encourage the further handling of insurance on a group basis, and insurance agents and companies will face additional competition as oil companies, stores and hotels try to exploit their credit card lists by selling selected classes of insurance on a monthly basis. Among insurance operations, as a step toward further diversification, a few groups are now functioning on a holding company basis. Mutual companies have entered the arena too.

Merger Trend

The relentless squeeze on underwriting profits and the competitive necessity of underwriting broader lines and servicing additional classes of business continue to spark the "urge to merge." Companies have merged, agencies have merged, and companies have taken over general agencies to integrate into their branch office systems. Mergers have been arranged to gain territorial expansion, enlarge multiple-line underwriting, acquire management talent, reduce expenses, improve servicing, increase capital funds, and for many other reasons. Several companies have taken advantage of the generally depressed prices of fire and casualty stocks and purchased some of their own shares in the open market.

Mutual companies are under the same pressures, but have special problems in coping with them. Mutuals, in general, operate on a lower surplus margin than stock companies, so their investment commitments in common stocks have been modest. They therefore did not enjoy the substantial appreciation reported in the stock field, nor have they been able to call on stockholders for additional capital funds. In addition, many operate on a restricted basis as to classes of business underwritten or territory served. Merger into larger units seems an obvious answer, but mergers among mutuals are difficult to accomplish. One solution, which may become increasingly popular, is to form an alliance such as that worked out between the State Mutual Life Assurance Company of America, Worcester, Mass.; the Citizens Mutual Insurance Company, Howell, Mich.; and The Beacon Mutual Indemnity Company, Columbus, Ohio.

The rapid changes and increasing complexities of the business have placed a premium on trained personnel and high-caliber management. Multiperil policies bringing so many lines into a single contract are creating higher catastrophe hazards and are placing greater responsibility on the underwriter who must evaluate all lines. The industry, which has grown up on a by-line basis, has had to convert to multiperil thinking and reorganize some departments accordingly.

Most of the changes that have taken place—the use of the holding company, the employment of mass marketing techniques, the retirement of company stock, another drop in the expense ratio—were visible proof of the fact that insurance managements have been working intensively on their problems.

Group Operations

In June 1898 the control of Mechanics and Traders of New Orleans was purchased by National Fire of Hartford, and early in 1899 Citizens of Missouri was purchased by Hartford Fire. These two purchases marked the beginning of the group or "fleet" operation plan in this country. The original impetus and early development of fleet operations was to secure additional agency representation and make possible more intensive cultivation of territories than was permitted under agency limitation rules covering single-company operation adopted by the industry.

Added to this quest for wider agency representation was another important factor responsible for the later development of group operations—the growth and increasing importance of casualty business. Not only did many fire companies establish casualty subsidiaries, but casualty companies organized fire subsidiaries.

Approval of multiple-line underwriting has not only slowed down the organization of additional subsidiary carriers but has permitted the consolidation of fire and casualty companies. A number of company fleets have consolidated their operations by merging some of their affiliated carriers, while others have made complete consolidations into a single carrier.

Although the two most important reasons for group operations of fire and casualty carriers no longer exist, a plan of operation that has been built up over a period of 75 years still persists. While there is less incentive to start new fleet operations, there are many reasons to continue some of those which are well established. Not all groups are set up on a basis that would lend themselves to physical merger. Some are organized on a management basis, others have strong specific reasons for separate existence, and often it is very difficult to merge companies domiciled in different states. Company names have acquired value through long association and extensive advertising. Numerous special reasons could be cited for specific situations, but, fundamentally, many managements hesitate to go to the trouble and expense of consolidation unless it can be more fully demonstrated that a single, large unit can be operated more efficiently.

The most important recent change in group operation concerns the development of all-lines underwriting through the affiliation of life insurance companies with fire and casualty companies. All but one of the 25 leading fire and casualty underwriters have organized or acquired a life company affiliate.

Special Rate Filings

Rating laws in some states often make it advisable to use a second company for special filings. Some companies have organized or are using a subsidiary or affiliated carrier to operate on a basis of six-month special policies, direct billing of renewals, and lower commission rates so as not to disrupt the overall backlog of business being underwritten on the conventional basis.

The emergence of open competition or so-called "file and use" laws gained significant advocates among state regulation in the 1960s and early 1970s. Under open competition laws, it is assumed that enough price competition exists for state insurance departments to rely upon priced competition to produce a proper insurance premium among insurers. Abuses have been noted in some quarters, and a return to direct rate setting by selective state bodies is being considered in several states including New York but is not an immediate prospect.

Resistance to Economic Recession

Insurance spreads individual risks among a large number of insureds; by reducing the risks of individual insureds in this way, it performs an essential service in the orderly functioning of commerce and industry. Because of its necessary function, demand for insurance remains firm during periods of general economic recession.

The essential role that insurance plays in the economy means not only that premium volume is resistant to recessions but also that fire and casualty companies will continue to grow as our economy expands. Growth in premium volume has been fostered by inflationary increases in insurable values, while, at the same time, the insurance industry has participated fully in the gain of the country's real income and wealth. Premium volume in recent years has also reflected the enactment of financial responsibility laws which have forced many car owners who were previously uninsured to buy insurance.

Distribution

In the United States the sale of insurance is generally effected through local agents. Under this method of distribution, which is called the "American agency system," the underwriting company appoints an agent who agrees to represent the company in accordance with an agency contract. The agent performs preliminary underwriting functions in selecting risks; he also collects premiums, delivers the policy, and, when losses occur, prepares initial loss reports.

The American agency system has been advantageous for insurance companies, enabling them to obtain a large volume of business without investing substantial sums in retail sales offices. The agency system has also proven effective because of the fact that the agent is a member of his local community and is already known to the people to whom he sells insurance. By advising his customers on the type of insurance that they should purchase and by assisting them in receiving prompt and fair claim payments when losses occur, the agent provides a valuable service.

The agency system, on the other hand, has several important disadvantages. In some cases, the agent's representation of the insurance company is incidental to other interests, for he may also act as a real estate broker, a banker, or a merchant. As an independent businessman, the agent does not serve the interests of the insurance company exclusively. Furthermore, in the fire and casualty field, the agent has traditionally controlled the expiration list, which is a record of the names and addresses of his customers and the dates of expiration of their policies. Agents are generally not exclusive agents, and they usually represent a number of different companies. Consequently, a successful relationship between the agent and the company is not essential to continuance of the agent's business because he can place his customers' insurance with a number of underwriting companies.

Recent Developments

For many years, the agents' multiple interests did not impair the efficiency of the American agency system, and the local agent was able to operate successfully as an independent businessman. Operating in this way, each individual agent paid for his own accounting and statistical operation in writing and processing policies and billing and collecting premiums. To perform these and other functions, the independent agent incurred expenses which would otherwise have been borne by the company. To recompense the agent for these expenses, the old-line companies traditionally paid large commissions.

Large commissions opened the door for competing methods of distribution, and in recent years the so-called "direct-writing" companies have become an increasingly important factor in the industry of insurance. The principal direct writers are Allstate Insurance Company, a wholly owned subsidiary of Sears, Roebuck, & Company; Nationwide Mutual Insurance Company; Government Employees Insurance Group; and State Farm Mutual Insurance Company. On new business, their payments to salesmen or agents are at a lower rate than payments by the old-line companies. On renewals, these companies pay a lower rate than for new business, whereas old-line companies pay the same rate. Direct-writing companies bill policyholders directly. By centralizing their accounting operations, they are able to reduce unit costs, whereas under the agency system, each agent maintains a separate accounting operation or billing. Direct-writing companies control the expiration list, and consequently their salesmen are free to concentrate on developing new accounts. Because of their more efficient methods of distribution, the direct-writing companies have been able to sell insurance at an average discount of about 20 percent. They have, consequently, grown much more rapidly than have the old-line companies.

The direct-writing companies' ability to reduce rates has been due not only to their lower expenses but also to their selection of preferred, above-average risks. On such risks, loss experience is more favorable. From 1953 to 1957, for example, Allstate's loss ratio in auto bodily injury liability was 60 percent, compared with an industry average of 61.2 percent. If the industry's rates had been 20 percent lower, its loss ratio would have been 76.5 percent, instead of 61.2 percent. If the direct-writing companies are to continue to grow more rapidly than the old-line companies, however, they will be forced to underwrite average risks to a greater extent.

There are indications that the growth of the direct-writing companies has begun to moderate. Allstate's share of the total amount of automobile insurance written by stock companies increased rapidly in the postwar period. During the past several years, however, the increase in its share of the market has been at a slower rate.

Competition from direct-writing companies has forced old-line companies to improve the efficiency of their distribution methods. Changes have occurred. Some companies have formed new subsidiaries which bill policyholders directly for first-year premiums and control renewals with automatic billing. The first and largest of these is Safeco Insurance Company of America, organized in 1953 by the General American Group of Seattle. Safeco sells a six-month continuous policy on private passenger cars at reduced commissions and reduced rates. A similar type of contract has also been developed by a number of other companies. Insurance Company of North America has, for several years, sold homeowners' package policies at a deviation of 10 percent from standard bureau rates. In New York, Continental Insurance and Fidelity-Phoenix, which together head the America Fore-Loyalty Group, have taken the initiative in reducing commissions for automobile insurance. At its annual meeting in May of 1958, the National Automobile Underwriters Association voted to reduce its allowance for the cost of acquiring new business from 25 percent to 20 percent of the premium. The largest part of this cost is commission expense. In June 1958, the Automobile Rating Committee of the National Bureau of Casualty Underwriters also announced a reduction in production cost from 25 percent to 20 percent. In due course, further price competition led to reduced commissions for auto and spread to a number of other lines.

Although many agents are opposed to reduced commissions, changes in present methods of distribution are having a beneficial effect upon the operations of both companies and agents. Within the framework of the established agency system, adoption of direct billing and automatic renewals are making possible an improvement in operating efficiency and competitive position. With these better methods of distribution, the leading multiple-line companies can be expected to show continued long-term growth in premium volume.

Regulation and Its Purpose

Insurance, like several other of our nation's major industries, is regulated by government authorities. Traditionally, an insurance company's operations have been regulated by the insurance commissioners in each of the states in which it operates. In 1944, the United States Supreme Court in the Southeastern Underwriters Association case held the business of insurance to be commerce and subject to federal statutes when conducted across state lines. By Public Law 15, enacted in 1945, Congress declared that continued regulation by the states was in the public interest, although the federal antitrust statutes are applicable to insurance to the extent that the business is not regulated by state law. State laws and administrative precedures vary greatly, but the insurance statutes and regulatory practices of the different states are similar in many respects and generally have as their primary purpose the protection of policyholders' interests through the supervision of insurance company rates, their solvency, and their trade practices.

State insurance commissioners require companies to file complete financial statements. They prescribe methods of valuing investments and determining reserves, require maintenance of adequate amounts of capital and surplus in relation to premium volume, establish minimum requirements for high-grade investments such as United States government obligations, and direct and fully guarantee state obligations. Furthermore, they discourage excessive purchase of foreign securities, real estate, mortgages, and other investments which do not represent sound, readily marketable assets for the satisfaction of policyholder claims. As a result of these regulatory practices and the conservative operating policies of most prudently managed companies, investments of insurance companies tend to be concentrated in high-grade bonds and stocks. Regulation of this type, as it affects company solvency, thus not only requires that companies be able to fulfill their contractual obligations to policyholders but also tends to enhance the quality of the stockholders' investment.

State insurance commissions regulate trade practices and the provisions of policy forms. Supervision of policy forms is necessary because many policyholders cannot easily analyze the technical provisions of an insurance contract. To prevent incompetent or untrustworthy persons from taking advantage of the public, insurance departments license brokers and agents. State insurance laws, furthermore, prohibit misleading advertising claims and unfair discrimination. That the insurance business is generally conducted according to high ethical standards is thus partly due to state regulation of trade practices.

The third area of regulation, and perhaps the most important, is the supervision of premium rates. Premium rates are determined in the following way: rating bureaus, which are membership organizations owned by insurance companies, gather statistical data showing industry underwriting experience during the past three to five years on both a state and national basis. With this information, the premium rate for each type of insurance is calculated so as to cover claims, expenses, and a reasonable margin for profit and contingencies. When a change is indicated, the rating bureau submits to the state insurance department an application for a revision in rates together with statistical evidence of the need for a change. If the department approves, the revised rates are placed in effect on new policies as they are written, or as "filed and used."

In this way, the insurance department regularly reviews the adequacy of rates at which policies are sold to the public. In the interests of the policyholders, insurance commissioners do not permit an excessive level of premium rates. On the other hand, rates must be adequate so that companies can maintain the solvency necessary to fulfill contractual obligations to policyholders. At the same time, healthy competition within the industry exerts an important influence upon the level of premium rates. If rates are too high, efficient carriers offer insurance at reduced rates. They may do so either by filing rates independently of the rating bureaus or at a "deviation," or discount, from standard bureau rates. Thus, in the long run, competition prevents excessively high rates.

Effects of Rate Regulation

As it is impossible to determine in advance the exact amount of losses that will occur on risks underwritten, it is assumed in rate making that losses will follow actual past experience. The frequency and severity of losses fluctuate, however, and claim costs reflect changes in general business activity as well as inflation or deflation in the price level. Hence, losses during the term of contracts may prove to be smaller or larger than assumed when the contracts were written. The adequacy of rates is continually tested by experience. When losses incurred are small, rates are lowered; when losses are large, rates are raised in order to restore a fair margin of profit. Periods of underwriting loss are followed by periods of underwriting profit, and underwriting operations thus tend to be cyclical but, normally, profitable.

During periods of continuous inflation, the present method of determining rates functions imperfectly. Inflation is expressed, among other ways, in rising costs of replacement and repairs under fire insurance, in higher jury awards in automobile bodily injury liability cases, and in larger benefits provided by workmen's compensation insurance. Inflation thus causes an increase in the dollar amount of losses. There is a lag, however, between this rise in losses and the obtaining of rate increases to offset them. Under the present method of determining rates, time is required for the rating bureau to prepare an application for an increase in rates, and there is some lag between the filing of the application and approval of the increase by the insurance department. Moreover, separate approval must be obtained in each of the different state jurisdictions. Because revised rates apply only to new policies written, increased rates on lines written for a one-year term are not reflected in a full year's premium income until two years after new rates go into effect. The interval for three- and five-year property coverages is even longer. Periods of continuous inflation therefore produce an increase in the dollar amount of losses in excess of the corresponding increase in premium income. For this reason, inflation has an unfavorable impact upon underwriting earnings, even allowing for prompter filings under "file and use."

Under the present method of rate making, rates are based upon an average of loss experience in the preceding three to five years, with the experience of each year receiving equal weight. A recent development having considerable potential significance is the introduction by casualty rating organizations of procedures which give weighted values to the loss experience of previous years. Maximum weight is given to the most recent experience, and factors are employed to provide for inflationary trends. If these "trend factors" become a generally accepted part of rate-making procedures, insurance companies will be in a better position to maintain adequate underwriting profits during periods of continuous inflation, and underwriting operations will become less cyclical.

Regulation and the Investor

The regulation of insurance companies is important to the investor in several ways. As mentioned above, supervision of insurance company solvency tends to enhance the quality of the stockholders' investment. Regulation of rates also tends to be beneficial for the stockholder. As rates are generally set at levels believed large enough to permit carriers a fair return on their underwriting operations, the investor in the stock of an efficient company over a period of years can expect normally profitable operations and a growing value for his equity.

ACCOUNTING

A major difficulty for investors not familiar with insurance stocks is the difference in accounting terminology and practice of an insurance company as compared with the more familiar accounting of a commercial or industrial enterprise.

Underwriting and Investment Exposure

Because of its investment activities, an insurance company is, in a sense, two organizations—an insurance company and an investment company. It is reasonable, therefore, that if risks are allowed to increase in one part of the business, they should be reduced in the other. Companies with a large exposure to insurance risk consequently tend to curtail the amount of their investment risk by limiting their common stock holdings. Companies with less insurance risk can afford to maintain a more aggressive common stock position.

The amount of a company's insurance risk depends upon the volume of business it writes in relation to its capital funds. The degree of this risk may be measured by the ratio of premiums written to policyholders' surplus. Policyholders' surplus is equal to the sum of capital and surplus. For Insurance Company of North America, which had premiums written of $341 million in 1958 and policyholders' surplus of $534 million at the end of the year, the ratio was 0.64—that is, $0.64 of premium written for each dollar of policyholders' surplus.

The risk to which a company is exposed in its investment operations is a function principally of the amount of its investment in common stocks. Since unearned premiums, loss reserves, and other liabilities are fixed-dollar amounts, any fluctuation in the value of the common stock portfolio is reflected directly in the amount of policyholders' surplus and in a company's capital position.

It is therefore customary to measure the degree of a company's investment exposure by computing the ratio of its common stock holdings to policyholders' surplus. For Insurance Company of North America with common stock holdings of $493 million (statutory value) and policyholders' surplus of $534 million, the ratio at the end of 1958 was 92.3 percent. For the ten largest domestically owned stock company groups, this ratio ranged from 109 percent to 68.3 percent.

Dividends

Insurance companies generally pay out less in dividends than the amount of their investment income. Because of this conservative practice and because investment income has shown steady, long-term growth, many fire and casualty insurance companies have records of uninterrupted dividend payments covering many decades. Moreover, the retention of a portion of investment income and all underwriting earnings produces a relatively favorable long-term increase in the value of the stockholders' equity.

Premium Accounting

The premiums which an insurance company receives from its policyholders are analogous to the revenues which a manufacturing company obtains for the sale of its products. The premiums billed are known as "premiums written."

There is, however, a basic difference between a sale made by a commercial enterprise and the sale of an insurance policy. This difference lies in the fact that with the ordinary transaction the sale is complete at the time it is made, whereas with the sale of an insurance policy the service is not completed until the policy has expired. Suppose, for example, that a store sells an item for $100 and that total costs, including a $25 commission for the salesman, are $95. The store knows at once that its profit on this transaction is $5. However, in a similar situation, where an insurance company's agent sells a policy for which the premium is $100 and the agent's commission is $25, the company knows only the amount of the agent's commission and the amount of the premium. It cannot know what its profits will be until the policy expires.

Since the term of a policy extends forward in time, an insurance company does not immediately take into income the amount of premiums written in the same way that an ordinary company does when a sale is made. Premiums are rather prorated over the life of the policy. If a company, for example, writes a five-year policy for which the premium is $500, at the end of the first year it would report $100 as earned, at the end of the second year another $100, and so on until at the end of the five-year period all of the $500 would have been earned.

The principal item of income in an insurance company's income statement is therefore not premiums written but premiums earned. In this respect "premiums earned" occupies the same position in an insurance company's income statement that "sales" does in the income statement of an ordinary company. Premiums earned represent the gross amount of underwriting income before deduction of expenses and losses.

Thus, with each policy an insurance company has written, at any given time a portion of the premium paid by the policyholder has been earned, while the remainder is unearned. The unearned portion is included in a reserve, known as the unearned premium reserve, which appears on the liability side of the company's balance sheet. This reserve represents the unearned portion of premiums on all policies in force on the statement date, and hence it represents premiums that will be taken into income, or earned, as policies age or elapse. Since a company is obligated to return to a policyholder who cancels his policy the unearned portion of the premium which he originally paid, the unearned premium also represents a liability which the company has to its policyholders.

The unearned premium reserve is increased by new premiums written and reduced by premiums earned. The amount of the unearned premium reserve at the end of year is therefore equal to the amount in the reserve at the beginning of the year plus premiums written during the year, less premiums earned during the year. The same fact may be stated in the following way to explain premiums earned. The amount of premiums earned during the year is equal to the unearned premium reserve at the beginning of the year, plus premiums written during the year, less the unearned premium reserve at the end of the year. The way in which an insurance company calculates the amount of premiums it has earned and the relationship of premiums written, unearned premiums, and premiums earned may be illustrated by the following example.

Assume a company's unearned premium reserve was equal to $25 on December 31, 1972 and that all of this amount was earned before the end of 1973. Suppose further that the company on July 1, 1973 wrote a one-year policy for a premium of $120. Premiums written for 1973 would be equal to $60, representing one half of the premium or the unexpired portion of the policy written in July. From this information, premiums earned, as shown in the income statement, would be calculated in the following way:

Unearned premiums December 31, 1972.................... $ 25
Add: Premiums written during 1973........................ 120
                                                         ─────
                                                          $145
Less: Unearned premiums December 31, 1973..............   60
Premiums earned during 1973........................... $ 85

In this example, premiums earned can also be calculated by adding $25 (the amount of premiums written in 1972 but earned in 1973) to $60 (the amount earned on the policy written in 1973).

Expenses

In the insurance company's income statement there are two major items which are deducted from premiums earned in order to arrive at underwriting profits. These two items are expenses and losses.

Expenses consist of agents' commissions and other "acquisition" costs which a company incurs in selling insurance contracts and also include the general overhead expenses of maintaining the home office, paying salaries, etc. State insurance laws generally do not permit insurance companies to amortize prepaid commissions and other acquisition costs over the terms of policies, and these expenses are therefore charged-off in full against income at the time policies are written.

Loss Accounting

To provide for the losses which have occurred on policies it has issued, an insurance company sets up loss reserves. These loss reserves provide for three things: (1) loss claims which have not yet been paid; (2) losses which have not yet been reported to the company, but which the company estimates it has incurred; and (3) expenses which the company estimates it will incur in settling claims. Income is also reduced by a fourth item, namely, the amount of cash actually disbursed during the year in settling claims. The way in which losses are treated is illustrated in the following examples.

Assume that a policyholder filed a claim for $40 in November 1973 but that the company was not able to settle the claim before the end of the year. If the company estimated that the claim might be settled for $25 and that the costs of doing so would be $2, it would have set up reserves at the end of the year for these amounts.

The company, on the basis of past experience, knows that because of delays and laxness of policyholders in filing claims, some losses will have been incurred in the closing days of the year that were not reported by the year end. If the company estimates that the amount of losses incurred but not reported was $5 at December 31, it would establish a reserve of this amount.

On December 31, 1973 the company would therefore show, on the liability side of its balance sheet, total loss reserves of $32, calculated as follows:

Losses unpaid..	$25
Incurred but not reported................................	5
Reserve for losses.......................................	$30
Reserve for loss adjustment expenses......................	2
Loss reserves December 31, 1973..........................	$32

The $32 in the company's loss reserve is not, however, the total amount of losses incurred during the year. Suppose, for example, that during the year 1973 a policyholder filed a claim for $20 and that before the end of the year the company paid this amount in settling the claim. This transaction would be reflected on the company's books in a reduction of its cash and a corresponding charge against income.

Assuming that at the beginning of the year the company had no loss reserves, the total amount of losses shown in the company's income statement for the year, including amounts set aside for loss reserves, would be calculated in the following manner:

Loss reserves December 31, 1973..........................	$32
Add: losses and loss expenses paid during 1973..............	20
	$52
Less: loss reserves December 31, 1972.....................	0
Losses and loss expenses incurred during 1973...............	$52

It is to be observed that loss payments were the only items charged on the books. Insurance company statements are prepared by a system of modified cash accounting. Loss reserves are prepared statistically on the basis of a separate file of loss claims and are not reflected on the ledger. The amount of losses incurred, shown in the income statement, is prepared from the loss reserves calculated at the beginning and end of the accounting period and from losses and loss expenses paid in cash during the period.

It should be noted also that the amount which a company sets aside in its loss reserves is not precisely determined. Unpaid losses represent estimates of the amounts at which claims may be adjusted; incurred but not reported losses represent an estimate of the amount of loss suffered on claims that have not yet been filed with the company. Both are thus based on judgement, and if the company views the trend of claim costs pessimistically, it can increase its loss reserves accordingly. In the example above, if the company determined conservatively that the estimated amount of losses unpaid should have been $30 rather than $25, losses incurred would have been increased by $5 and the amount of net income reduced correspondingly.

Statutory Underwriting Earnings

It has been mentioned that insurance companies charge off acquisition costs in full at the time a policy is written. The premium received, however, is not taken into income immediately but rather over the term of the policy. This practice of writing off acquisition costs immediately while deferring the associated income means that statutory underwriting earnings, which are the earnings reported in accordance with regulations of state insurance commissioners, are not an accurate indication of the profitability of operations in any particular year. If agents' commissions and other acquisition costs were capitalized as prepaid expense and amortized over the terms of the policies to which they applied, statutory earnings would more accurately reflect underwriting results.

To illustrate this problem, assume that a company had earned premiums of $100 in 1973, resulting from contracts written in 1972, and further that it sustained a loss of $85 in 1973 on policies written in the prior year. If the company did not write any policies in 1973 it would report underwriting earnings for the year of $15. Suppose, however, that the company on July 1, 1973 wrote a five-year policy for which the premium was $500 and the agent's commission $200, or 40 percent. The company in 1973 would earn one half of a year's premium, or $50, on this policy, and its statement of underwriting earnings for the year 1973 would be as follows:

Earned premiums		$150
Losses	$ 85	
Expenses	200	285
Statutory underwriting earnings		−$135

In the above example, the one policy written in 1973 was sufficient to change the company's profit for the year to a deficit, despite the fact that it incurred no additional losses in its underwriting. This illustrates the general principle that in periods of rising volume an insurance company's statutory underwriting earnings are depressed by increased acquisition costs, whereas in periods of declining volume statutory earnings are increased by reduced acquisition costs.

Underwriting Ratios

A better indication of the profitability of an insurance company's underwriting operations than is provided by statutory underwriting earnings may be obtained by examining the combined loss and expense ratio. The combined loss and expense ratio, as the name suggests, is the sum of two ratios, the loss ratio and the expense ratio. The loss ratio is the ratio of losses and loss expenses incurred to premiums earned, while the expense ratio is the ratio of underwriting expenses to premiums written.

Losses are related to premiums earned rather than premiums written, because losses are more closely related to the portion of policies that elapsed during the year than they are to the volume of new business written. Underwriting expenses are related to premiums written, because in any particular year the expenses incurred are principally those necessary to obtain the business written in that year. The combined loss and expense ratio may be stated in an alternative form as the underwriting profit margin. The underwriting profit margin is equal to the difference between the combined loss and expense ratio and 100 percent.

In 1972, for example, Insurance Company of North America incurred losses and loss expenses of $670 million, and, after deduction of dividends to policyholders, premiums earned were $990 million. The company's loss ratio was therefore 67.6 percent; that is, for each dollar of premiums earned, $0.676 in losses and loss expenses were incurred. The company incurred underwriting expenses of $310.7 million and booked $1,020 million in premiums written. The expense ratio was therefore 30.4 percent —in other words, it incurred $0.304 in underwriting expense to write one dollar in premiums. Insurance Company of North America's combined loss and expense ratios in 1972 were 98 percent, the sum of its loss ratio of 67.6 percent and its expense ratio of 30.4 percent. Its underwriting profit margin was equal to 2 percent, the result of subtracting the combined loss and expense ratio from 100 percent.

To illustrate this method of interpreting a company's reported statement of underwriting income, Table 2 shows the loss ratio, expense ratio, combined loss and expense ratio, and underwriting profit margin of Insurance Company of North America for the ten years between 1963 and 1972.

TABLE 2

Underwriting Ratios, 1963–72 (in percent)

Year	Loss Ratio	Expense Ratio	Combined Loss and Expense Ratio	Profit Margin
1963	66.6	34.4	101.0	(1.0)
1964	67.7	33.2	100.9	(0.9)
1965	69.9	31.3	101.2	(1.2)
1966	68.9	30.8	99.7	0.3
1967	71.2	31.8	103.0	(3.0)
1968	71.8	32.1	103.9	(3.9)
1969	72.3	31.1	103.4	(3.4)
1970	69.4	30.6	100.0	–0–
1971	65.5	31.2	96.7	3.3
1972	67.6	30.4	98.0	2.0

Source: *Best's Insurance Reports—Property—Liability* (Morristown, N.J.: A. M. Best Co.),Vol. 69, pp. 570–73; Vol. 74, pp. 648–50.

It will be observed in Table 2 that the expense ratio is relatively constant, whereas the loss ratio fluctuates. Wide fluctuations in the loss ratio reflect changes in the frequency and cost of loss claims and changes in the rate level. The small changes in the expense ratio reflect the fact that acquisition costs, which constitute the bulk of underwriting expense, vary with the amount of premiums written. Acquisition costs include commission and brokerage fees, field supervision and collection expense, and taxes (other than income taxes), licenses, and other fees.

In analyzing a company's operations in terms of the combined loss and expense ratio, underwriting results in a particular year are considered to have been profitable if the combined loss and expense ratio was less than 100 percent. If the combined loss and expense ratio exceeded 100 percent, underwriting operations were unprofitable. Expressed in terms of the underwriting profit margin, operations were profitable if the underwriting profit margin was positive, unprofitable if negative. It can be seen from Table 1 that Insurance Company of North America's underwriting operations have been profitable in only three of the past ten years. A company may have a statutory underwriting loss and yet have a combined loss and expense ratio of less than 100 percent.

Adjusted Underwriting Earnings

There are various methods of adjusting statutory underwriting earnings used by insurance stock analysts to obtain what is believed to be a more accurate picture of underwriting profits in any particular year. Moreover, different reasons are given for making these adjustments. The following discussion describes one method of obtaining an earnings figure which appears to be more satisfactory from the stockholders' point of view than the statutory figure. This method is based on the premise that the reason for adjusting statutory earnings is to restate them in such a way that they will approximate the earnings that would have been reported if the costs of selling a policy were amortized over the term of the policy in the same way that premiums are taken into income as they are earned.

If expenses were reported in this way, the expense shown in the income statement would be the proportional part of the expense that was associated with booking the premiums earned in the period. In practice, of course, a part of the cost of booking premiums earned in one year was already charged to expense when the policies were written in a prior year. As was indicated above, however, the expense ratio—that is, the per dollar cost of writing premiums—is relatively constant. A reasonable estimate of the expenses associated with booking the premium earned in a given year can therefore be obtained by multiplying premiums earned by the expense ratio. The result of this calculation is adjusted under-

writing expense. The statement of earnings in the example on page 426
would be adjusted as follows:

Premiums earned.......................................		$150
Losses...	$85	
Adjusted expense 40 percent $\frac{(\$200)}{(\$500)}$ of $150..................	60	145
Adjusted underwriting earnings............................		$ 5

The same adjustment can be made by a different method of calculation. Premiums earned (before deduction of dividends to policyholders)
are calculated as unearned premiums at the beginning of the year, plus
premiums written, minus unearned premiums at the end of the year.
Thus the difference between premiums written and premiums earned
represents the increase in the unearned premium reserve. From the foregoing considerations, it can be shown that adjusted underwriting expense
can also be calculated by deducting from reported expenses an amount
equal to the expense ratio times the increase in the unearned premium
reserve. This is an estimate of the so-called "equity" in the increase in
unearned premiums. This method of calculation applied to the previous
example would be as follows:

Premiums earned.......................................		$150
Losses...		$ 85
Statutory expenses.....................................	$200	
Less: estimated equity in increased in unearned premiums—		
40 percent of $350....................................	140	
Adjusted expenses......................................		60
Adjusted underwriting deductions.........................		$145
Adjusted underwriting earnings...........................		$ 5

In the case of Insurance Company of North America, premiums written in 1958 were $340.5 million and premiums earned $316.9 million (before dividends to policyholders), and the difference of $23.6 million repre-
sented the increase in unearned premiums. The expense ratio was 37.4
percent, and applying this ratio to the increase in unearned premiums
produces an estimated equity of $8.8 million. Adjusted underwriting
earnings would thus be as follows:

		(000)
Premiums earned*...............................		$316,917
Losses and loss expenses incurred...................		$191,361
Other underwriting expenses incurred...............	$127,361	
Estimated equity in increase in unearned premiums....	8,835	
Adjusted underwriting expenses.....................		118,526
Adjusted total underwriting deductions...............		$309,887
Adjusted underwriting earnings before taxes..........		$ 7,030

* After deduction of dividends to policyholders.

Estimated Taxes on Adjusted Underwriting Earnings. A fire and casualty insurance company's federal income tax is determined from its statutory statement of income. If acquisition costs were capitalized as prepaid expense and amortized over the terms of policies to which they applied, and if taxes were based on the resultant amount of income, taxes incurred would be different from those actually reported. If an adjustment is made in underwriting earnings, therefore, it is reasonable also to adjust the amount of income tax incurred. Taxes on adjusted underwriting earnings may be estimated by simply applying the 52 percent corporate rate to the adjusted underwriting earnings figure. This takes into account the adjustment made in underwriting earnings, for adjusted underwriting earnings include the estimated equity in the increase in unearned premiums.

In arriving at adjusted underwriting earnings after estimated taxes, a tax credit at the 52 percent rate can be made in the case of an adjusted underwriting loss, since an underwriting loss reduces the amount of taxable investment income. Moreover, under the present Internal Revenue Code as amended, if an underwriting loss is larger than the amount of taxable investment income, the loss may be carried back three years and used to claim a tax refund. Investment income and taxes on investment income are explained in the next section on investments.

It should be emphasized that the amount of hypothetical taxes estimated in the foregoing manner is not the same as the amount of federal and foreign income taxes incurred which companies report to state insurance departments. In practice, the determination of a company's actual tax liability is extremely complex and technical, particularly in the treatment of losses. The calculation of taxes on adjusted underwriting earnings is simply an estimate of what taxes might have been if earnings were not those actually reported. Although the amount of taxes estimated in this way is not intended to be a precise statement of what taxes on underwriting earnings would in fact have been if acquisition costs were amortized over the terms of policies to which they applied, it appears reasonable to make such an estimate on the basis of the assumptions which have been made in adjusting reported income.

Table 3 shows the calculation of adjusted underwriting earnings after estimated taxes for Insurance Company of North America for the past ten years.

Estimated Normal Earning Power. Methods of interpreting underwriting earnings to provide a reasonable picture of the profitability of underwriting operations in any one year were discussed above. There remains the question of the use of earnings as a basis for appraising the investment value of individual insurance stocks.

Recognizing the possibilities for recovery inherent in depressed earnings of fire and casualty companies, investors generally tend to anticipate an improvement. Conversely, when operations are at an unusually profitable level, investors foresee the likelihood of a decline in earnings when rates are revised downward. Investors' efforts to look into the future in this manner are reflected in a high market capitalization of depressed earnings and in a low multiple of high earnings at the peak of the underwriting cycle.

Because of fluctuations in underwriting results, earnings in any one year do not provide an adequate basis for valuation of a company's stock. To develop a standard for measuring relative values, it is useful to estimate what normal earnings might be when underwriting operations are neither depressed nor unusually profitable.

The use of a ten-year average underwriting profit margin eliminates the distortions of high and low underwriting profits and provides an indication of what can reasonably be regarded as "normal" underwriting profitability. By applying the average profit margin to premiums written, which in effect represent the amount of contracts for future premiums earned, an estimate of normal earnings can be made. For illustration, estimated normal earning power of Insurance Company of North America is calculated in Table 3.

In the fire and casualty insurance business, damage claims—both those litigated and those settled peaceably—are a basic part of the operations. The results for any year and the equity shown for the stockholders will depend in large measure on the method followed in computing reserves for unsettled and unreported losses. The regulatory bodies require that specific formulae be followed in setting up the minimum reserves for personal injury claims in automobile insurance and for workmen's compensation claims. (If the company's own estimate on a "case basis," indicates a larger liability, that figure must be used instead.) Liability under other types of claims is a matter for management to determine, subject to a triennial or quadrennial check by insurance commission examiners. There is room for a considerable degree of either overestimation or underestimation in this field.

The reserves for unearned premiums also play a major role in the accounting of insurance companies. Despite publication by AICPA of an audit guide covering several years on the topic, there is a conflict in this area of accounting treatment which has given rise to much confusion among insurance company investors and has in part served at times to depress unduly the price of their shares. There is also some needless confusion and inaccuracy in the treatment of this item by financial agencies analyzing insurance company statements.

The unearned-premium reserve represents that part of premiums received which is applicable to the unexpired portion of the policies. Under the standard accounting prescribed by the state insurance commissioners, the full amount of unearned premiums must be shown as a liability. There are, however, two different reasons for concluding that the true liability is considerably less than that required to be shown. In

TABLE 3

INA Calculations of Adjusted Underwriting Earnings after Estimated Taxes (thousands)

Year	Premiums Written 000s	Premiums Earned 000s	Statutory Losses and Loss Expenses Incurred 000s	Statutory Other Underwriting Expenses Incurred 000s	Computed Expense Ratio (percent)	Adjusted Underwriting Earnings before Taxes	Taxes
1949	$ 164	$ 152	$ 70	$ 64	38.8	22.2	$ 8.5
1950	176	161	83	69	39.2	14.4	6.1
1951	204	185	106	77	37.7	9.5	4.6
1952	227	209	114	84	37.1	17.6	9.2
1953	239	226	124	90	37.8	17.0	8.8
1954	251	241	139	95	37.8	11.0	5.7
1955	270	254	146	103	38.1	10.7	5.6
1956	288	269	158	111	38.5	7.3	3.8
1957	323	295	184	122	37.8	0.8	0.4 Cr.-
1958	341	317	191	127	37.4	7.0	3.7
1962	450	433	N.A.	N.A.	34.2	—	(3.3)
1963	486	465	N.A.	N.A.	34.2	(12.2)	0.3
1964	517	502	N.A.	N.A.	32.9	(9.5)	0.4
1965	612	597	418	194	31.8	(13.5)	(0.7)
1966	670	654	451	209	30.8	(4.4)	(5.3)
1967	702	699	499	223	31.8	(22.8)	(2.9)
1968	712	726	521	229	32.2	(26.2)	1.7
1969	822	794	572	258	31.0	(38.3)	2.4
1970	882	888	619	279	30.7	(4.9)	3.4
1971	979	974	641	310	31.2	37.3	14.9
1972	1,211	1,189	804	368	30.4	22.1	

N.A.: Not available.

the first place, on the basis of many years' experience, it is known that the losses in many coverages will rarely exceed two thirds of the premiums received; hence there is usually a very considerable equity later realized from the reserve. This equity can usually be turned into cash immediately, if the company so desires, by the process of reinsurance, under which another company assumes the risk upon payment of a percentage of the unexpired premium (for example, 60–65 percent). (This question formed the nub of a controversy over the solvency of Rhode Island Insurance Company in 1949–50, which ended by placing the company in receivership. In the life insurance field the so-called "policy reserves" involve more intricate computations. They are a matter for actuarial, rather than security analysis.)

Second, the chief reason the stockholders have so large an equity in the unearned-premium reserve is that the company has paid out a considerable amount of acquisition expense—mainly in the form of agents' commissions—in order to put the business on the books. In ordinary accounting, such costs paid in advance would be entered as an asset under the title Prepaid Expense. In fact, they would be directly analogous to the unearned premiums themselves, which are a similar asset to a business which has paid them.

The official reports of insurance companies include no prepaid expense or other credit to offset part of the liability for unearned premiums, nor are the financial statements to stockholders presented on different accounting bases. But in the management's comments in the body of the report, supplemental data filed by the companies in behalf of the investment community, in prospectuses and registration statements and in analyses of the results by financial services, it is now the custom to adjust the official figures to reflect an equity in the unearned premiums. This has had been done in a variety of ways.

1. For a great many years, the services credited earnings with 40 percent of the increase in the reserve of five insurance companies and 35 percent of that of casualty companies. Nearly all such companies now operate in both fields.

2. After 1956, *Moody's Bank & Finance Manual* changed from the flat credit basis, to a credit equivalent to the ratio of each company's overall expenses (excluding losses and loss expense) to premiums written.[1] The theory is that this percentage represents the approximate cost of putting additional business on the books. It still runs at about 40 percent for most agency companies but is considerably less for the direct writers. However, this addition to earnings makes no allowance for the tax already saved on the prepaid expense—a fact reflected only in the services' footnotes.

3. A more conservative method is to take credit for the prepaid expense at the overall rate but to reduce this by 50 percent to reflect the

---

[1] *Best's Insurance Reports* have apparently done the same in most cases.

TABLE 4

Comparative Consolidated Statistics: Ten Largest Domestically Owned Stock Groups

	1972 Net Premiums Earned (000,000)	Percent Increase 1968-72	Average Underwriting Profit Margin 1968-72	Net Premiums Written per Dollar of Capital and Surplus	Percent Common Stock to Capital and Surplus	Adjusted Total Operating Earnings per Share after Estimated Taxes 1973	1972	Indicated Annual Cash Dividend	Adjusted Book Value 12/31/72	1973 Market Range
The Aetna Casualty and Surety Company	$ 1,117	21.4	(2.4)	2.02	60.7	$7.32	$6.50	$1.85	$58.41	82–58
Allstate Insurance Co. (Sears Roebuck)	2,090	85.8	2.8	1.83	80.6	1.29	1.09	—	—	—
Continental Casualty Company (CNA)	646	0.9	2.1	1.29	71.9	—	—	—	—	—
The Continental Insurance Company	602	1.9	1.6	0.93	65.2	5.22	4.72	2.40	55.28	44–34
Fidelity-Phenix Fire Insurance Co.	—									
Fireman's Fund Insurance Co. (American Express)	466	52.8	3.0	1.15	80.2	—	—	—	—	—
Hartford Fire Insurance Company (ITT)	1,529	75.9	0.5	1.86	83.9	—	—	—	—	—
The Home Insurance Company (City Investing)	728	38.1	(0.5)	2.55	61.6	—	—	—	—	—
Insurance Company of North America	1,189	63.8	0	1.66	73.0	4.71	4.43	2.10	45.65	50–31
The Travelers Insurance Company	11,552	28.7	(1.5)	.97	103.0	3.93	3.54	0.92	34.72	40–27
United States Fidelity and Guaranty Company	798	57.1	6.0	1.12	96.0	7	3.41	2.40	42.12	45–34

Source: Best's Insurance Reports 1973.

tax benefit already received. An exception could be made, of course, for companies operating at a loss even with the prepaid-expense credit.

4. The fourth method is the Audit Guide approach. The prospectus of Hanover Insurance Company, dated July 1961, makes adjustments of its official earnings substantially in accordance with method 3. The equity in unearned premiums is calculated at rates related to the expense and loss experience of two merged companies and works out at about 30 percent overall. Allowance is then made for the tax effect of this addition to profits. The figures are complicated by a simultaneous adjustment to exclude gains and losses on security sales and by a loss carryforward during the period covered. In the year 1956 the earnings are shown as increased from $1.22 to $1.98 per share, entirely because of the unearned-premium equity.

In some instances, a company's financial statements prepared in conformity with generally accepted accounting principles may show stockholders' equity when its statutory surplus is below the minimum required by law (or where surplus impairment is likely or imminent). While there may be evidence that such a condition is only temporary, the auditor must determine what action, if any, is intended by regulatory authorities. Disclosure of the relevant facts should be made in the financial statements. There may be circumstances where the possible effect of the uncertainties is such that the auditor would need to consider qualification of his opinion, or possible disclaimer of opinion, on the financial statements taken as a whole.

When financial statements are presented on the basis of generally accepted accounting principles, it would be desirable, and in some cases it may be necessary in order to meet regulatory requirements, to include a reconciliation of net income and stockholders' equity determined under generally accepted accounting principles, with net gain from operations and capital and surplus determined under regulatory accounting practices. The reconciliation, in the form of either a note or supplemental financial statements, would include descriptions of differences in the two methods. In addition, it would be desirable, and in some cases it may be necessary in order to meet regulatory requirements, to include a condensed statutory balance sheet in a note to the financial statements. Comparative statistics of 10 large stock companies are given in Table 4.

INVESTMENT POLICIES OF FIRE AND CASUALTY COMPANIES

Fire and casualty companies are subject to partial controls and are more liberal buyers of equities. State laws under which they must operate dictate their investment of specific percentage minimums into higher-grade bonds.

Their total assets approximated $78 billion at year-end in 1972. At that time, total investments lined up as follows:

	(*percent*)
Bonds	48.2
Stocks	36.1
Cash	1.9
Real estate	1.5
Mortgages	0.3
Other assets	12.0

Source: "The Long-Term Outlook for the Insurance Industry,"
Chase Econometrics Associates, Incorp.

A comparison of investment funds (Table 5) of two insurance companies span may be helpful. These may illustrate both a suitable method of procedure and the varying significance of portfolio-value changes for the two types of financial enterprises.

These calculations are based on reported figures, plus certain adjustments deemed desirable. The underwriting results include an equity in increased unearned-premium reserve. The tax allowances assume, in part, an average ordinary rate of 50 percent in the decade. They also deduct a 25 percent tax payable on realization of untaken security profits.

The disparate results of Home and Seaboard are representative of the widely different conditions governing the fire and casualty lines, on the one hand, and the surety lines, on the other, during the decade. More than half of the overall gain of Home Insurance must be attributed to the stock market rise; for Seaboard Surety, the figure is slightly over 20 percent.

In a single-year analysis, the writer would urge grouping together the realized and unrealized portfolio gain or loss. This is done in the standard or conventional form of reporting the income account of insurance companies. The figures for the 12 months should be presented in two parts: (1) ordinary income and (2) portfolio profit or loss. Comparatively little significance will attach to the latter component because it is governed mainly by security-market conditions in the year; but the former may serve as a guide to future projections. Detailed annual statements of uniform standards, known as convention reports, are filed with the insurance departments of the states in which the company does business. In addition, an audit is conducted every three years by the domiciliary state in conjunction with other states. These audits are available for inspection by the public.

As with investment companies, insurance companies provide investors with professional investment supervision. A company's investment managers alter the composition of the portfolio in accordance with their appraisal of the outlook for business and securities, and they buy and sell individual issues as changes occur in relative values.

Growth of Investment Income

For many years, investment income of fire and casualty insurance companies has shown a steady upward trend. Growth in premium vol-

TABLE 5

Income Analysis of Two Insurance Companies

	Home Insurance Company			Seaboard Surety Company		
	Before Tax	Related Tax	After Tax	Before Tax	Related Tax	After Tax
Adjusted underwriting results..........	−$ 5.90	cr. $ 2.95	−$ 2.95	$25.95	$12.98	$12.98
Interest and dividends..............	43.32	6.72	27.60	12.65	2.51	10.14
Capital gains:						
Taken........................	8.32			0.29		
Unrealized....................	28.28			8.43		
Total capital gains...........	$36.60	9.15	27.45	$ 8.72		
Total.....................	$65.02	$12.92	$52.10	$47.32	$17.67	$29.65

CHART 1

Stock Underwriting and Investment Results (1925–1975)

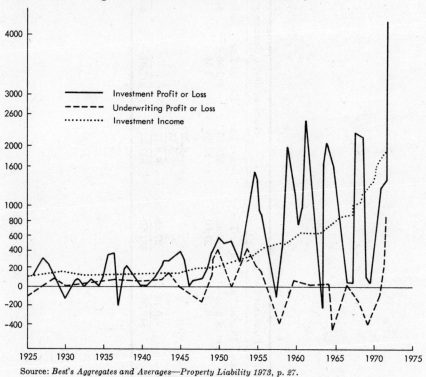

Source: *Best's Aggregates and Averages—Property Liability 1973, p. 27.*

ume has supplied additional funds for investment. Reflecting this increase and the high quality of investment assets, investment income of stock fire and casualty companies has risen in every year but 3 of the past 25. Because investment income reflects the level of interest rates and corporate dividend payments, growth in the postwar period has been rapid. In the years 1963–1972, it was at a rate of 11.9 percent. The steady growth of investment income is illustrated in Chart 1.

TABLE 6

Distribution of Investments (December 31, 1972)

Classification	Market Value (000)	Percent of Total
U.S. government obligations...................	$ 133,805	5.3
State and municipal bonds....................	1,044,054	41.1
Other bonds................................	233,781	9.2
Total bonds............................	1,411,640	55.6
Preferred stocks............................	117,490	4.6
Common stocks.............................	1,008,867	39.8
Total invested assets......................	2,537,997	100.0

In the case of Insurance Company of North America, for example, capital and surplus at December 31, 1972 were equal to $46 per share; but because of the additional funds provided by premiums, the market value of invested assets amounted to $108 a share. Investment income after taxes in 1972 was $4.12 a share.

The company's investments of $2,538 million at the 1972 year-end represented 75 percent of total assets of $3,404 million (with investments at market). Other major assets were cash and agents balances, investments in affiliates, and real estate. (Table 6.)

Insurance company common stock investments, as those of an in-

TABLE 7

Company	Shares	Book Value ($000)	Market Value ($000)
Exxon Corp.	535,053	$ 4,188	$46,817
Eastman Kodak Co.	252,628	4,619	37,484
International Business Machines Corp.	60,380	10,103	24,273
Texaco, Inc.	584,224	1,545	21,908
Mobil Oil Corp.	248,208	1,431	18,367
General Motors Corp.	204,000	5,372	16,549
Merck & Co., Inc.	183,400	368	16,346
Xerox Corp.	100,300	7,933	14,970
Gulf Oil Corp.	478,504	1,273	12,920
Westinghouse	266,600	3,139	11,464

vestment company, are diversified among different industries and are generally concentrated in high-grade issues. The ten largest common stock holdings, based on market value of Insurance Company of North America, as of December 31, 1972 are shown in Table 7.

Estimated Taxes on Investment Income

The effective tax rate on gross investment income is less than the combined normal and surtax rate of 52 percent which applies to underwriting earnings. The reason is that a large part of investment income is derived from tax-exempt bonds and from preferred and common stocks. In the case of dividends on stock, insurance companies, like other corporations, are entitled to the deduction of 85 percent which the Treasury recognizes in order to avoid double taxation of corporate profits. The full 52 percent tax rate applies to taxable interest. Since a portion of interest income is tax-exempt and the rate on taxable dividend income is 52 percent, or 7.8 percent, the effective tax rate on total investment income is substantially less than 52 percent.

Property and Casualty

Insurance shares fluctuate in price for the same fundamental economic reasons that other stock prices move. (See Table 8.) In some respects they are tied even more closely to general overall business and security market conditions than most other stocks. Not only are the volume of underwriting commitments and the experience on many lines of insurance closely linked to general business conditions, but insurance companies also own very substantial blocks of stocks and bonds as investments. This close relationship with general business and the capital markets adds an element of stability because of the wide diversification. The fortunes of insurance are not tied to any one industry or to even a few industries but to the overall economy.

Moreover, property and casualty companies underwrite a number of different classes of business, and this diversification, under normal conditions, lends stability to underwriting returns because the profit cycles of the various classes do not necessarily coincide. Thus, when one class of business enters an unprofitable phase, other lines are usually profitable. Rates are adjusted and the previously unprofitable class enters a change phase usually by the time some other classification has slipped from grace. This basic nature of the insurance business is somewhat unique, with profitable operations setting the stage for lower rates and unprofitable experience automatically calling for higher rates.

Many property-casualty insurance companies' equities tend to sell below asset values, reflecting—at least in part—the difference in market value heavily weighted to bonds, should the portfolio cost be "marked to

TABLE 8

Best's Insurance Stock Indexes: End of Year

	30 Fire & Cas.	30 Life	S&P 500*		30 Fire & Cas.	30 Life	S&P 500*
1941	9.7	8.7	8.7	1957	25.7	134.2	40.0
1942	9.9	9.8	9.8	1958	36.7	191.0	52.5
1943	10.7	12.0	11.7	1959	37.9	190.4	59.9
1944	11.1	14.5	13.3	1960	42.5	193.0	58.1
1945	13.3	17.8	17.4	1961	57.9	375.0	71.6
1946	11.7	18.1	15.3	1962	53.1	348.6	63.1
1947	11.6	17.2	15.3	1963	58.5	413.8	75.0
1948	13.3	19.5	15.2	1964	59.1	399.8	84.8
1949	16.2	25.6	16.8	1965	60.0	393.8	92.4
1950	17.4	33.5	20.4	1966	62.9	293.6	80.3
1951	17.7	41.4	23.8	1967	52.6	253.4	96.5
1952	21.8	60.0	26.6	1968	90.7	324.1	103.9
1953	22.5	68.3	24.8	1969	79.2	286.2	92.1
1954	30.3	129.3	36.0	1970	86.7	271.6	92.1
1955	31.1	163.1	45.5	1971	117.2	351.8	102.1
1956	26.6	140.9	46.7	1972	147.2	444.2	118.1
				1973	118.4	365.2	97.5

* Standard & Poor's Index of stocks (425 industrial, 25 railroad, and 50 public utility stocks combined).
Source: A. M. Best Company, Inc.

the market." Even in bull markets, such anomalies have occurred, suggesting the investment community views portfolios' unrealized appreciation with circumspection and is unwilling to award such accomplishments any premiums.

Until recent years, the price/asset ratios for banks and nonlife insurance companies had a tendency to bunch within a fairly narrow area. Somewhat surprisingly, the model figure stayed below 100 percent for a long period—a fact which called into question the basic profitability of these important enterprises. It was quite rare to find issues selling at more than twice or less than half of asset values. A greater scattering of ratios was discernible among the various types of finance companies. Also, a goodly number of life insurance stocks—as distinct from the casualty companies—have sold at many times their stated asset values.

The valuation of life insurance companies is something of a specialized affair, chiefly because of actuarial complexities. Prior to 1965 it had become customary in this field to ascribe a definite value to the insurance in force—at so much per $1,000 of face value—the rate varying between the different forms of policy. These policy values were then included with the tangible assets in figuring the "adjusted book value" of the shares; and the increase in the policy values for a given year is added to the reported earnings to give "adjusted earnings" for the year. It became typical to add in this way $15 for each $1,000 of net increase in ordinary life insurance in force. The $15 per thousand may properly be added to the capital value of the company's shares, but it should not be added to a year's earnings or earning power. What is involved here is the difference between treating $15 as $15, or as, say, 20 times $15 in valuing the shares. The reader may carry the analogy further by assuming that an ordinary manufacturing or distributing company decides that each new customer has a capitalizable value and adds such capital value to its ordinry earnings per year. Alternatively, it could consider each year's increase in sales and net earnings as adding proportionately to the "net asset value" of the business and then report such increase in capital value as the chief part of the year's earnings or profits. The calculated increase in the value of the business may be justified, but the treatment of such increase as capitalizable earnings would be dangerously incorrect. Analysts and accountants alike consider the latter treatment fundamentally unsound. There are many ways in which increases in capital values can be presented in the guise of capitalizable earnings. The investor must be on his guard against them, and the analyst must oppose them.

LIFE INSURANCE ANALYSIS

Early in this century most of the gains in life expectancy could be traced to medical advances in the treatment of diseases of pregnancy, childbirth, and infancy, communicable childhood diseases, respiratory infections, diabetes, and tuberculosis. As a result, more people began to live into middle age and become victims of diseases associated with that age span. Starting in 1940, with the discovery of the first of the miracle drugs, the diseases and disabilities of middle age began to lend themselves more readily to medical treatment.

This trend toward improved life expectancy showed up dramatically in the death rates of ordinary policyholders. The death rate per 1,000 ordinary policyholders averaged 7.5 during the 1930s, 6.9 in the 1940s, and 6.1 in the 1950s. There has been some stabilization in this rate in the 1960s and 1970s with the rate per 1,000 holding at 6.2 in the first four years of the decade.

Will this favorable mortality experience, a gift to the life industry from the medical profession over the last few decades, cease to play a role in the profit potentials over the next generation? The vast majority of all policies outstanding are held at present by people in the middle years, 25 to 65. Over 95 percent of all males between 25 and 44 have some sort of life coverage, with a rate of 86 percent at ages 45–54 and 82 percent at ages 55–64. These patterns will most probably persist into the next generation since these are the years when life coverage is most needed by growing families. Therefore, it follows that favorable mortality experience can continue to benefit the life companies if medical science can make gains in attacking the causes of death in the 25–64 age group in the years ahead.

Largely as a result of the fact that business machines are so adaptable to the essential tasks of running a life insurance company plus the fact that life company managements were foresighted enough to make early use of these automated tools, the life insurance industry has been about the only major industry to hold the cost line in the postwar years. Despite the fact that life companies are now writing about seven times as much business annually and have about six times as much life insurance in force as at the end of World War II, operating expenses as a percentage of total income have held at around 17 percent. This is higher than the 14.5 percent averaged in the depression years and war years, but it is below the 18.7 percent averaged in the 1920s. Few industries can point to lower operating ratios than they had 40 years ago.

Over the last 30 years, life insurance companies have experienced a substantial increase in their earnings base. This growth has been greatly assisted by the increased life expectancy of all Americans, which has meant that the premiums insuring these lives have remained on deposit longer with the life companies. With more dollars coming in from this expanded earnings base, the costs of acquiring each dollar of income have remained remarkably constant, largely as a result of the widespread use of automation in the home offices. So it can truthfully be said that for the last three decades medical science and scientific management have been the twin generators of the life insurance growth phenomenon.

Some critics of the life insurance industry, while conceding its remarkable progress in the past, say that all of this is just about over; that the industry as a whole, both well-run and poorly run companies, must settle down now to a more routine course. We do not subscribe to these views; however, as this is a critical look at the industry, perhaps it is best to allay some of the ill-founded criticisms that are often raised. Of course, there are some serious problems facing the industry, and we shall consider each of them in turn.

Problems of Life Insurance Companies and Arguments against Life Insurance Stocks

1. Life companies' profitability and growth will probably be killed by regulation.
2. Life stocks lack marketability and sponsorship.
3. The accounting is too complex or leaves too much room for management maneuver.
4. The industry suffers during periods of high money costs.
5. Cash dividend payout is too low.
6. Volume growth is only modest, and the industry is losing its share of the savings dollar.
7. A long-sheltered tax position cannot endure indefinitely.

In partial refutation of these arguments the following comments may prove helpful.

Protection is the basic product of the life industry. Profitability is a part of the pricing of this protection and the cost of providing it. The need for the protection offered by life insurance is widely accepted in our modern economy. Selling a product with a strong, assured demand, the well-managed life company has been able to provide a handsome return on its capital and assets in the postwar years by a careful selection of its risks, an imaginative placement of its investment funds, and a firm control of its costs of operation.

The sharp rise in insurance in force in the postwar period is ample demonstration that the life companies have been doing a fine job catering to the needs of their "frontdoor" customers, the policyholders. The advantages of life insurance ownership are obvious, but the virtues of such commitments have become even greater in our high-tax economy. For many households, a life policy offers the only sure way to amass a worthwhile estate, one that will remain intact and offer support regardless of the state of the business cycle or the current tax needs of federal, state, and local governments. Inflation is the chief corrosive hazard; but life insurance policies, properly integrated in overall estate planning, provide a unique and indispensable building block for anyone who plans for the future.

Why has premium income lagged behind the rise in insurance on the books? Several factors have contributed. The cost to the policyholder for $1,000 of coverage has actually declined over the last 30 years. Also, greater emphasis has been placed on term insurance and group policies in recent years—both of which carry generally lower premiums than straight, whole-life policies. The average household today is getting expanded protection at lower costs. In 1945, the average premium for life insurance was $30 per 1,000. By 1963, the premium had been reduced to an average of approximately $20 per thousand of protection, and today is well below even that level.

While this may partially explain the postwar spurt in life insurance sales, it does not contribute much to an understanding of the greatly enhanced profit position of the industry. How can industry continue to do better profit-wise by selling its product for less? There are no great economies of scale, as in some manufacturing lines, to explain this increase in profitability. As a matter of fact, all other things being equal, the costs of insuring a single life are appreciably the same when 10,000 lives are insured as when 100,000 are covered.

The answer is quite simple: There is a built-in profit factor in every insurance policy sold, and this factor is premium "overpayment" as life expectancy improves. The premium established at the time a life policy is written reflects reasonable expectations of the average life remaining to the policyholder. If medical science makes rapid progress following the date at which the policy is issued, the rate structure will be higher than necessary and each year the life company will pay out lower than anticipated benefit claims. Meanwhile, the difference will remain in the asset structure of the life company, where it will go on earning interest. These interest earnings will be in excess of the obligations under the terms of the contract with the policyholder. Thus when benefits are paid, a windfall residual remains with the company. This windfall can either be paid out to the stockholders, put to work in expanding the sales capabilities of the company, or placed in favorable long-term investments that will spin off earnings for years to come. Under any set of conditions, these benefits from longevity rebound to the stockholders of the company.

As an example, most life insurance policies on the books of the companies today are based on the commissioners' 1941 Standard Ordinary Table, according to which at age 21, 2.51 deaths per 1,000 occur. On the newer commissioners' mortality table of 1958 it takes to age 35 for 2.51 deaths to occur per 1,000 people.

An investor in a life company naturally has a keen interest in profit, but a word of caution appears to be in order: There can be such a thing as too much "profit" in a life company. For if the agents and general agents shut their eyes to the quality and type of risk being undertaken, the apparent vigorous growth of insurance in force and premium income will surely plummet before too many years. When quality and type of risk are ignored, either claims experience will shoot up out of line, or a lot of the present policyholders will prove marginal and be unable to keep up their payments, resulting in a steep rise in the lapse rate.

Whichever of these two circumstances takes place, the rise in policies and premiums will never carry through the early promise. The life company which should be reaping the benefits of earlier underwriting by putting the premiums freed from its initial underwriting costs and commissions to fuller use in its investment program, will have to go back to the starting line again and expend time, money, and effort in putting new policies on the books just to stay even, let alone grow. All of this will be reflected, sooner or later, in the market price of the stock. Investors want a profitable company, but they are most interested in a company that is able to hold on to its profits and use them as a base on which to build later profits.

Investment Returns

Having built a solid earnings base, the next important consideration is how well these funds can be placed. For many investors, this is the critical problem in judging the potential of a life company. An aggressive company, one intent on putting as much sound business on the books each year as possible, may well show little net profit from its underwriting. New business costs money. If it stays on the books it will ultimately pay for itself many times over. But while it is going on the books, it may even register a slight loss over the first-year premiums and take a big bite out of the second-year premiums.

Nevertheless, many aggressive companies manage to show healthy operating profits despite a big chunk of new business. Obviously, these results reflect the investment income from the assets acquired from policies written in earlier years. Often it is the net rate of interest earned on invested funds that determines the overall profitability of a life company in a single year. This rate of return has been the second favorable factor at work in the life industry in the postwar years.

After sinking to a low of 2.88 percent in 1947, this rate started to climb and has kept on the rise ever since. Long-term variations in this rate reflect two factors: the opportunities available to the life company and the general trend in interest rates. Of the two, the long-run trend in interest rates is the most important. At any given time, a life company, like any financial institution, must keep all of its funds which are not needed as a cash reserve fully invested if it is going to perform near its optimum rate. This means that it cannot wait indefinitely for favorable investment terms. At any given time, regardless of how low the rate of return, the funds must be placed in the best available spots. This helps explain the abnormally low 2.88 percent return in 1947 for the industry. Investment portfolios then were reflecting over 15 years of low general rates of return, first in the Great Depression of the 1930s and then the regulated returns of the war years.

But starting in 1948, life companies were able to roll their investments over into higher-yielding placements emerging in the general business prosperity of the postwar years. With this prosperity receiving no serious setback at any time in the last two decades, the insurance companies have been able to place both their new funds and maturing assets at more favorable terms. Due to these circumstances we see no abatement in the upward trend of interest earnings for several years to come.

In modern times the total assets of the life industry have never failed to show a year-to-year increase. This is true even of the depression years of the 1930s. This means that the industry has been able to meet its obligations and participate fully in the benefits to be derived from plowing back investment earnings.

Gross profits of life companies have continued to reflect windfalls from premiums on longevity trends as well as the roll-over of low-yielding investments into higher-yielding placements. Net profits have improved as a result of holding the cost line.

In life insurance, costs reflect an assumed rate of interest, mortality, and expenses. The interest is set in the initial contract with the policy-holder. Expenses can vary after the contract is written and are therefore subject to close scrutiny by the managements of life companies. The expenses in the first two years following the writing of the policy are the critical ones. The third factor, mortality, can only be determined after the passage of years and the actual claim experience checks in. The fact that cost of life insurance can be accurately determined only after the claims are paid is one of the factors that makes the analysis of the common stocks of these companies difficult.

Of the three factors, life companies have the least control over the interest rate written into the initial contract. This rate must be competitive and reflects the going rate in other life policies and in alternative investments at the time. The company has some control over mortality costs by stringent screening of the risks taken, but the progress of medical science also plays a role. Expenses of selling, writing, administering, billing, and paying claims, however, are subject to strict management control.

Holding the cost line in operating expenses has not been easy. Just about everything the life company buys—paper, electricity, office space, even postage stamps—has increased in cost over the postwar years. Yet operating expenses as a percentage of total income (the operating expense ratio, see chart) have remained remarkably level. At present, they are somewhat below the average of the early 1920s.

The reason, of course, is machines; the new data processing office machines are ideally suited to the needs of the large life company with its endless routine of rates, billing, and claims processing. What used to take a battery of clerks hours or even days to accomplish can now be handled in a matter of seconds.

THE TYPE OF PRODUCT—
ANATOMY OF BUSINESS IN FORCE

In absolute dollars, ordinary life policies have accounted for most of the increase of insurance on the books, although the rate of increase here was somewhat below the average of all life lines. The biggest gain in percentage terms was in credit insurance, a line virtually nonexistent in 1945. Industrial insurance, with small face amounts and typical weekly coin payments, was the slowest growth group on all counts. With growing prosperity, life customers upgraded their insurance policies. Group insurance was impressive, in both percentage terms and absolute dollar amounts.

Even this breakdown does not tell the full story of the broad changes in types of coverage that have affected the industry in the postwar years. Although detailed, year-by-year figures are not available for the industry as a whole, term insurance accounted for an increasing share of the ordinary individual life policies in the postwar personnel. For example, in 1950 term insurance represented only about 6 percent of ordinary policies in force, but by 1957 the share of term insurance in total ordinary was over 20 percent. In 1962 the percentage of term had risen to over 26 percent. This sharp lift in the relative percentage of term insurance in total ordinary life in force would indicate that term insurance reflected an even higher percentage of new ordinary life policies being written. Again detailed figures are not available, but in 1956 all types of term policies were accounting for 33 percent of ordinary policies written. By 1964, term insurance was approximately 40 percent of the new business in ordinary life, and even more so today (50+%).

The decline in industrial insurance in the postwar period is less of a problem to the industry. Although the collection expenses were high for the weekly premiums, fewer policies were written to allow for this characteristic. But the face amounts were never large, and even a total disappearance of this business would not greatly affect the industry as a whole. For those companies with a high percentage of industrial business at the end of World War II (there were many such companies in the South), this type of coverage has offered a platform for growth. As the income of the industrial policyholders rose, many of these companies were able to shift industrial policies to bigger ordinary policies, which contributed to a strong growth showing by the companies.

Much has been written about the relative advantages of the varied types of life insurance to a company. All can be profitable when properly written, but the degree of risk varies widely from one to the other. Three factors determine the relative advantages of each; the cost and degree

Percent Increase in Types of Insurance in Force 1945 to 1972

Type of Coverage	Percent Increase	Increase ($ billions)
Ordinary (whole and term).............	735.6	$ 747.0
Group................................	2,744.6	608.5
Industrial............................	44.4	12.3
Credit................................	297.0	108.4
Total life........................	972.7	1,476.2

of effort required to get each type on the books, the costs of servicing—billing, paying claims, etc., and the stability of each type or the average lapse experience with each. Perhaps these differences can be seen easiest in tabular form:

Relative Advantages of the Major Types of Insurance to the
Underwriting Company

	Cost of Selling	Cost of Servicing	Lapse Rate
Ordinary (whole).......................	High	Average	Low
Ordinary (term).......................	Average	Average	High
Group................................	Low	Low	Average
Industrial............................	High	High	Average
Credit................................	Low	Low	High

Based on typical industry experience, whole ordinary life is relatively expensive to get on the books, but once there it tends to be more lasting and, as a result, more beneficial as a contributor to the asset base. Ordinary term, while easier to sell, has a relatively high lapse rate. Group is very favorable in terms of underwriting and servicing, but its big contract size and relatively unstable renewal rate are strong disadvantages for a rationally planned investment program on the part of the life company management. The same is true of credit insurance. Industrial insurance has been known to be most profitable for the companies geared to service it.

But it must be emphasized that while the relative advantages given for each type of life insurance apply to the industry as a whole, individual experience among companies varies greatly. The mix of a given company's type of policies has to be examined carefully before conclusions can be reached about the company's investment merits. What works like a charm for one company often cannot be adapted to the needs of another.

Another factor that often makes a difference in company performance is the type of policy written. Actual rates, of course, are subject to regulation and are not the basis of competition; but the actual terms of the policy—the types of riders and options offered as well as the various conversion features—are very much open to competition. Indeed, this is the chief way inter-firm rivalry expresses itself in the industry. Often a new type of contract that proves popular can give a company a competitive edge, at least for a time. But, as in most fields where patent and copyright laws are not practicable, a good thing is usually copied very rapidly.

Experiments in the type of coverage that can be safely offered can also give a company a competitive edge. With the progress of medical science, many types of insurance customers thought to be uninsurable in the past have become eligible for coverage. To name only one spectacular example, President Lyndon B. Johnson, after a well-publicized heart attack when he was a senator, applied for and received two very large life insurance policies.

As recently as 30 years ago, the victim of a heart attack was generally confined to a bed, or at the most was told that he was through in active employment for the balance of his life. Medical knowledge today, however, dictates that to resume an active life the same victim should be up and around in a matter of months and sometimes weeks. Tuberculosis, diabetes, hypertension, to name but a few of the more chronic diseases which were previously uninsurable, are now considered insurable "at a price."

Growth of the life insurance industry in the past has been closely linked to population increases and the income rises experienced by this growing population. So it will be in the future, and potential for life insurance appears bright indeed. Approximately 350 million people are expected to be living in the United States by the year 2000. Although it is impossible to forecast the actual level of living that will be enjoyed by the average family in the year 2000, no doubt life insurance in one policy or another will figure in protecting this standard of living.

Four broad types of life coverage will probably carry most of this growth. Ordinary whole life policies will probably continue to account for a sizeable share of the total in force. This type of coverage declined in favor during the period of inflation of the early 1950s. In the early 1960s, with the pace of inflation definitely slowing down, this type of coverage made a strong comeback.

Ordinary term insurance has been one of the fastest growing types of insurance in the postwar period. Discovered when inflation fears were widespread, term has earned a niche for itself in the overall investment planning of many. This type of coverage often has a valid use for growing families. It can provide expanded coverage during many of the critical-need years—when a young mother has children under school age, when a family has undertaken greatly expanded commitments such as a new home, or when a son has just entered college. With more and more families coming under industrial pension plans or developing their own investment portfolios, term insurance can provide added coverage as the funds are building in the early years of these programs. For these special reasons, the needs and purchases of term insurance should continue to expand over the next few decades.

Group insurance, up to now, has experienced most of its growth in employer-employee plans which will probably continue to expand in the future. Recently, group plans have been expanded to cover association groups of all kinds, excluding recreational and professional. This expansion into new areas should assure a bright future.

Credit insurance sprang up from practically zero in 1945 and has been the fastest growing type of insurance since the war. With Americans continuing to make liberal use of time plans to purchase everything from a trip to Europe to a new home, this type of insurance may well be in its infancy.

OTHER PRODUCTS OF LIFE INSURANCE COMPANIES

Up to this point we have considered the performance of a life insurance company only with respect to activities in its main field of concentration—the writing and servicing of life policies. But in recent years, life companies have been reaching into new fields in search of premiums, assets, and profits. Some of these diversification efforts have proved successful; others still carry an element of doubt about their ultimate success.

Health and accident policies have been one of the big growth areas for many life insurance companies in the postwar. By 1972 there were 727 life insurance companies offering this line of insurance. Premiums from these policies totaled 14.3 billion in 1963 and accounted for over one quarter of total premium income. This business was two and one-half times larger than in 1968 when health and accident premiums represented less than 17 percent of total premiums. In 1947, the first year for which separate figures are available for the industry, health and accident premiums represented only 8.5 percent of total premium income. This rate of growth was also evident in the benefits paid in the health and accident field by life insurance companies: The total was up about ten times between 1948 and 1963. By 1963, life insurance companies were dominant in the health and accident field; over 70 percent of the premiums for all health and accident insurance were being collected by them, even more so today.

Health departments of many leading insurance companies now offer cancellable and noncancellable coverage in one or more of the following:

1. Health insurance
2. Accident insurance
3. Major medical insurance
4. Hospitalization

There is little doubt that life company managements over the last 15 years thoroughly explored the possibilities in health and accident policies and found them desirable as an additional product line. But should investors give the same favorable verdict to health and accident business?

Some companies fumbled in their health and accident departments, especially in the early years as they gained experience with this new type of risk. But well-managed companies have now proved that health and accident business can be profitable if properly handled.

Nevertheless, the results are less certain than in the life field. For one thing, the science of underwriting is not as well developed in this area. This means that the rate structure in health and accident is hazier than that for life policies. Moreover, sudden catastrophes such as epidemics can play hob with the claims experience for health and accident insurance.

There is another type of underwriting that has tempted many life insurance companies postwar, namely fire and casualty underwriting. Here the results have been less favorable. In general, "department store selling" of insurance protection as yet has not proven itself.

It is difficult enough to teach a salesman of life insurance all there is to know about the product and what it has to offer the public, without his becoming an expert also in fire and casualty.

There are exceptions, of course; but in life insurance, as in the practice of medicine, there is so much research reading to keep in touch with that the really efficient insurance agency must have a staff of competent people in each area. This may not be realized so much at the time of purchase; but when the claims arise, the policyholders find out the real competence of their insurance advisors.

If the complexities of the life and the fire and casualty fields suggest the necessity for specialized staffs in order to do a top-notch job in each field, one of the most common arguments for "department store selling" is greatly weakened. No doubt some life company managements see the increased demand for one-stop service as an opportunity. They argue that as long as more customers expect to have all of their insurance needs cared for by one agent, the life company itself should get into the business of underwriting as many of these insurance needs as possible. Note carefully—this is not to say that if their life customers appear to want it, the company should consider taking on new hands in the agencies to write a greater variety of insurance. This may be sound competitive practice. But the more common argument calls for the life insurance company itself to build in this diversification all the way from the top to the bottom without evidence that customers so demand.

Let's examine this proposition: The life customer is assumed to want fire and casualty coverage as well as life protection; therefore, the life insurance company should *underwrite* this coverage, not just *provide it as an added service.* To make sense, this would have to assume that the money necessary to develop a fire and casualty subsidiary earns at least as much as the same sum spent expanding the existing life business or invested in the portfolio of the life company. Unfortunately, this has just not been the case. For several years now, underwriting experience in fire and casualty insurance has been poor. In fact, if it had not been for their investment portfolios, most of the big fire and casualty underwriters would have run in the red. Consequently, one might ask the managements of life insurance companies—who are, after all, newcomers in the fire and casualty field—how they expect to turn a profit when experts, with years and years of direct experience behind them, have failed?

Admittedly, many of the life managements did not anticipate such a run of bad years when they embarked on their diversification efforts. But it did happen. As a result, too often the better profits available from their life lines have been sacrificed to offset losses in fire and casualty operations. This should give the investor interested in the future of the life insurance industry pause. As a general rule, avoid life companies that are becoming overextended in the fire and casualty field. It might pay off in time, but the most recent experience is very discouraging.

It is interesting to note that in the past decade many fire and casualty companies have developed life insurance affiliates or have merged a life insurance company mainly to bolster the poor profit picture of fire and casualty with the more profitable line of life insurance products.

Health and Accident Lines

Spiraling costs of medical care play a role in the underwriting results from health and accident business. The well-publicized case of the troubled Blue Cross and Blue Shield in making ends meet in a number of states illustrates the problems here. Padded claims contribute to the escalation in hospital costs and raise costs for everyone. Even if the present rate structure on existing policies is high enough to leave some margin of profit, renewals at new higher rates may become a problem and pose a threat to the whole department.

Still most life insurance companies do write health insurance in one form or another—the waiver of premium in case of illness being the simplest form. At the other end of the scale, many life companies write a full line of group and individual accident and sickness coverage.

This business must be judged by the actual experience of each company's health and accident department. One way the company learns to protect itself is to write only health and accident policies that may be cancelled by the underwriter. Understandably, many policyholders strongly resist this change, but experience indicates that this is about the only way to make health and accident policies pay a consistent return. Therefore, it pays to check into the percentage of cancellable business your life company has on its books. If it is large, you can view the prospects more favorably for the health and accident department.

There is another critical percentage figure for the investor interested in an investment in the future of the life insurance industry and that is the share of health and accident business to the total. Health and accident underwriting should be an adjunct to a growing life business, not the other way around. The agency force must be geared to sell the entire line, not just health and accident policies.

If health and accident insurance is simply an added line of business and does not dominate the total activity of the company, it can offer a good, profitable diversification for the life firm. In fact, such a department is necessary for the long-run optimum growth of the modern life insurance company.

Perhaps a word should be said about the future of health and accident policies when further forms of health coverage which have been enacted into the Social Security program of the federal government are implemented. Some observers feel that this will cut into the private business now being written by the life companies. This might be the case, but did Social Security retirement and death benefits as a payroll deduction kill off any noticeable amount of annuity and life insurance sales? Hardly. All types of life insurance have experienced their most vigorous growth since the enactment of payroll deductions for social security. In fact, it might be argued that with a minimum social security built-in, many families had an even greater incentive to bring this minimum of security up to a decent retirement income and death coverage through insurance plans. The same might be the case now that Medicare is law. With a minimum assured, many families may wish to supplement this plan with enough protection to remove all of the hazards from a prolonged illness.

Regardless of governmental developments, there appears to be ample room for private medical insurance, and the life companies will probably continue to supply the coverage needed in this field. For the life investor, the essential question remains: How profitable is this business for the company?

Medicare's effect on life insurance companies has been to stimulate the public to buy additional private accident and health policies, and it will have the effect of prolonging life. Thus, their life insurance premiums will have to be paid longer, and profits of life insurance companies should become greater.

The Disability Income Product

A disability policy provides a monthly cash benefit when the insured is disabled and incapable of pursuing normal employment. The plans are sold either on a group or individual basis. Under group policies, the

employer may assume part or all of the premium cost. Individual contracts are purchased primarily by self-employed and professional people,
by white-collar workers and for those occupations in which defined
skills may be outlined in describing a disability. The cost of the policy
varies greatly, depending on age, waiting period (the time during
which benefits are not paid), amount of cash benefit, and duration of
the indemnity period. The elimination interval may be as short as one
week or extend up to six months or more. The longer the waiting period
for benefits, the lower the cost of coverage. Policies may be short term,
providing indemnity for periods up to two years, or long term with
benefits to age 65.

Today, there is a substantially untapped market for the type of
disability income protection policies that the insured owns and controls.
While over 90 percent of the civilian U.S. population has some form of
private health insurance (primarily hospital and surgical converages),
less than half have any safeguard against the loss of personal income
because of a disability. As noted in Table 9 which illustrates the number
of people enrolled in various types of programs, a majority of the people
has such coverage under group contracts or formal sick-leave programs
at their places of employment. Most plans are subject to termination by
the insurance company or employer. The number of persons with individual coverages has declined over the past several years and today
accounts for less than 25 percent of all programs in effect. The erosion
primarily reflects the high interest in company-sponsored programs and
group insurance because of the relatively low cost of coverage.

While the insurer writes a full range of disability products, the average
individual policy provides a $600 monthly benefit following a 14-day
waiting period for a two-year indemnity period. The average size of the
benefit has increased annually and was about $700 a month in 1973.
Under current underwriting criteria, individual coverages can pay up
to $3,000 a month, with indemnity periods extending to age 65, for those
able to meet the necessary requirements.

Taxes

Life insurance companies are subject to special income tax premiums
which have resulted in their paying considerably less than the regular
52 percent on reported net income—indeed, closer to a 20–25 percent
effective range would be a more realistic figure. They are taxed under a
special provision of the 1959 tax law which increased their tax obligation
to their present level, but still barely at half the regular corporate rate.
This is not to be viewed as an indefinite privilege; indeed, it may well
be that life companies will remain a target of opportunity for tax
revenue seekers in the future seeking to close loopholes and raise tax

TABLE 9

Number of Persons with Disability Income Protection in the United States
(by type of program; 000 omitted)

End of Year	All Programs	Insurance Companies			Formal Paid Sick Leave Plans	Other
		All Insurance Companies	Group Policies	Individual Policies		
1946	26,229	14,369	7,135	8,684	8,400	3,460
1950	37,793	25,993	15,104	13,067	8,900	2,900
1955	39,513	29,813	19,171	13,642	8,500	1,200
1960	42,436	31,836	20,970	14,298	9,500	1,100
1961	43,055	32,055	21,186	14,301	9,900	1,100
1962	44,902	33,602	22,313	14,854	10,200	1,100
Short-Term Disability Income Protection						
1963	44,475	32,475	22,669	12,902	10,900	1,100
1964	45,270	33,270	23,177	13,280	10,900	1,100
1965	49,690	34,160	24,615	12,559	11,700	1,100
1966	50,003	36,403	26,322	13,264	12,500	1,100
1967	51,915	37,515	27,632	13,004	13,300	1,100
1968	55,677	40,777	30,229	13,879	13,800	1,100
1969	57,627	41,027	30,865	13,807	15,500	1,100
1970	57,833	40,833	31,498	12,683	15,900	1,100
1971	58,850	41,250	32,168	12,340	16,500	1,100
1972	61,106	42,346	33,103	12,559	17,660	1,100
Long-Term Disability Income Protection						
1963	3,029	3,029	749	2,280	—	—
1964	3,420	3,420	1,257	2,163	—	—
1965	4,457	4,457	1,903	2,554	—	—
1966	5,002	5,002	2,376	2,626	—	—
1967	6,682	6,682	3,827	2,855	—	—
1968	7,718	7,718	4,710	3,008	—	—
1969	9,076	9,076	5,715	3,361	—	—
1970	10,740	10,740	7,176	3,564	—	—
1971	12,011	12,011	8,209	3,802	—	—
1972	12,774	12,774	8,595	4,179	—	—

Note: Data in the category "Insurance Companies" refer to the net total of people protected—that is, duplication among persons who are covered by both group and individual policies has been eliminated. Any duplication resulting from the combination of numbers covered for short-term and long-term protection has not been eliminated. The category "Formal Paid Sick Leave Plans" refers to people with formal paid sick leave plans but without insurance company coverage. The category "Other" includes union-administered plans and the Federal Mutual Benefit Association.

Source: Health Insurance Council.

dollars. Proceeds from the life insurance policies collected by a recipient are in the main construed tax deductible as received.

Life insurance companies are taxed under provisions of the Life Insurance Company Income Tax Act of 1959. Because of the peculiarities of this act, certain matters of disclosure relative to the accounting for income taxes should be considered. These include, but are not necessarily limited to, the following:

1. The basis upon which current and deferred income taxes have been provided.
2. Disclosures relating to "Policyholders' Surplus" as defined in the Internal Revenue Code and as prescribed by Accounting Principles Board Opinion No. 23.
3. That portion of retained earnings in excess of statutory unassigned surplus upon which no current or deferred federal income tax provisions have been made and the reasons therefor.
4. Unused operating loss carry-forwards (described as operations loss deductions in the code) including amounts and dates of expiration.

Estimating taxes in two parts makes it possible to separate underwriting earnings and investment income on an aftertax basis. This method of interpretation shows clearly that investment income after taxes is usually much larger than underwriting earnings after taxes.

Estimated taxes on investment income may in general be calculated by deducting from investment income earned the amount of tax-exempt interest and the credit for dividends received, and multiplying the difference by the corporate 52 percent rate. As with estimated taxes on underwriting earnings, this estimate is not intended to be an exact statement of taxes actually incurred, but simply an estimate of an amount of taxes applicable to investment income.

Treatment of Participating Department

One of the major areas of concern for the security analyst has been the presentation of earnings from the participating departments of those companies writing both participating and nonparticipating business. Several states, including New York, New Jersey, Wisconsin, and Connecticut, have laws which regulate the amount of earnings from life insurance that can inure to the benefit of stockholders. This is a problem which affects a minority of the companies trading in over-the-counter markets, but it is one which must be faced. We have chosen to treat the participating department as if it were a minority interest in the total corporation. In other words, we have deducted, in figuring the stockholders' interest in earnings and book value, those items that the company allocates to the participating policyholders less the amount transferred to the stock department. In those cases where information is available and the amount of participating business significant, modifications in the expense and interest adjustments have been made for the participating department's interest.

RESERVES

For the reader unfamiliar with the complexities of a life company, this may be the thorniest section in this critique of the industry. Stock life companies and industrial concerns both seek a profit, but that is where the similarity ends. The earnings of the ten large companies are shown in Table 4.) With the life company, even such a basic thing as cost cannot be determined with complete certainty until the last claim on the books has been paid. New business, as in a corner grocery store, is always welcome; but unlike a sale in the corner grocery store, every piece of new business during the first year costs the life company more than it brings in. Just how much profit a piece of new business will bring cannot be determined until the policy has lapsed or the contractual claims have been paid.

It is extremely difficult to determine how well a life company is doing at any given period in the present, as both income and costs are tied to the future. Therefore, it takes a special kind of knowledge and perspicacity to judge the potentials of a life company.

Putting first things first, a legal reserve life company must maintain its policy reserves at a level that will assure payment of all policy obligations as they fall due. (Growth in reserves is shown in Table 10.) This means that at all times there must be a minimum reserve. If a life company is in any way remiss in this fundamental obligation, the interests of its policyholders are clearly endangered and the company is inviting direct intervention into its affairs by state regulatory authorities. This being the case, the stockholders in a life company also have a vital interest in the reserve program of the companies in which their funds are invested.

Total policy reserves, of course, have grown as the dollar volume of policies on the books has grown. By the end of 1972, policy reserves had reached $192.1 billion, or about 80 percent of the $239.1 billion in total assets held by life insurance companies. The purpose of these reserves is to provide the funds that will assure payment of all policy obligations as they fall due.

There are several different methods for calculating the level of reserves. All methods are, of course, actuarially sound and subject to regulation by the state insurance commissioners. The adequacy of these reserves was evident in the 1930s when all life companies managed to operate through the depression quite satisfactorily.

In evaluating the future worth of a life insurance company, the investor should be more interested in a company that has a strong reserve position than one that barely meets the minimum actuarial requirements of the state commissioners. The strongest reserve plan is the net legal reserve method. Under this method, out of the usual level premium payment for life insurance coverage, a "net" is computed that will be large enough to meet claims as they come due under assumed conditions of mortality and interest. In addition, a part of the premium—a much smaller sum—must be set aside for the expenses of (a) keeping policies in force and (b) contingencies that might arise from wars, epidemics, and other calamities. This sum is called the *loading*. Together, the loading and reserve are essential to any life company's solvency.

To skimp in these essential defensive funds is, in effect, to mortgage the future earnings of the life company. If, in practice, loading and reserves prove inadequate, the company will find it necessary to draw on current income flow to meet its obligations, obviously reducing the amount it can report as net from operations.

The temptation is great to pare loading and reserves to the bone. Management can find additional funds for current expansion from these false and illusionary "savings." Furthermore, these earmarked funds must be handled with the greatest of care so that sufficient money is always available to satisfy claims. In no way should these funds be viewed as a surplus. They may be invested, but the type of placement must have a greater stability and liquidity than other assets available to the life company.

Under the level-premium system, the payments by policyholders in the early years of a policy are in excess of the sums needed to meet claims; while in the later years payments dip below the amounts necessary to pay out benefits. The reserve is built up by these excess payments plus the interest earned on these funds.

The actual level of needed reserves can be influenced either by changes in the mortality assumptions or the assumed rate of interest written into the initial policy. Clearly if the rate of return implicit in the claims settlement at the time a life policy is written is increased from 3 percent to 3.5 percent, the reserves per $1,000 can safely be lowered; and this increase in the reserves can take place immediately.

However, any divergence between actual mortality experience and the assumptions about mortality at the time the policy is written can, of course, only be revealed after a period of time has passed. It is well known that mortality assumptions have erred on the conservative side during the 20th century—they have consistently underestimated the progress in medical science.

Although the net level reserve method of setting up reserve requirements is clearly the soundest and strongest, several other methods are acceptable under regulations established by state insurance commissioners. Many younger companies use the so-called modified reserve system, or the Commissioners Reserve Valuation Method. Under this system, in order to offset the very high first-year costs of putting a policy on the books, the full amount that would be set aside under the more conservative net level reserve method is spread over the remaining premium-paying years of the policy.

The methods described above are clearly sound on actuarial grounds —the claims rate is low in the first few years of a new policy. But the results are quite different from the viewpoint of indicated operating results. With less being set aside in the early years, a company using

TABLE 10

Policy Reserves United States Life Insurance Companies (000,000 omitted)

Year	Amount	Year	Amount	Year	Amount	Year	Amount
1890.....	$ 670	1910.....	$3,226	1925....	$ 9,927	1940....	$27,238
1900.....	1,443	1915.....	4,399	1930....	16,231	1945....	38,667
1905.....	2,295	1920.....	6,338	1935....	20,404	1950....	54,946

Year	Life Insurance	Health Insurance	Annuities Individual	Annuities Group	Supplementary Contracts with Life Contingencies	Supplementary Contracts without Life Contingencies	Total
1955...	$54,588	$ 575	°	$13,216	$1,895	$5,085	$ 75,359
1960...	70,791	865	$4,327	14,952	2,674	4,864	98,473
1965...	90,795	1,432	5,028	22,187	3,281	4,897	127,620
1966...	95,316	1,836	5,340	24,029	3,381	4,809	134,711
1967...	100,103	2,144	5,746	26,193	3,483	4,749	142,418
1968...	104,910	2,472	6,264	28,434	3,610	4,618	150,308
1969...	110,041	2,879	6,348	31,213	3,665	4,404	158,550
1970...	115,442	3,474	6,911	33,826	3,726	4,177	167,556
1971...	121,585	3,892	7,606	38,126	3,905	4,136	179,250
1972...	128,257	4,347	8,502	42,948	3,937	4,155	192,146

* Included with "Group Annuities."

Sources: *Spectator Year Book* and Institute of Life Insurance. Before 1947, the business of accident and health departments of life companies was not included. *Life Insurance Fact Book*, p. 66.

the modified reserve plan as opposed to the net level reserve method may appear to be making better progress.

As a general rule, the investor can be certain that steady and sustainable progress is being made if this company has adopted the net level reserve method. In any event, regardless of the method of reserves, a careful check must be made into other factors such as the rate at which claims are being made on the company, the types of risk that are being undertaken, and the overall supervision of the medical inspection methods. Only if these extra backstops are in good operating order should the investor wish to ride with a company that is using less than the maximum security net level reserve method.

Less rigorous reserve methods pose no real threat to the actual survival of the life insurance company—the state commissioners would not approve them if they did. Anything less than the net level reserve method may give a false glow to years in which a lot of new business is going on the books, a glow that may fade as future earnings are mortgaged to make up for high first-year costs or high mortality. In general, the net level reserve method is the safest for the life insurance company as well as its investors.

LAPSE RATES AND MORTALITY EXPERIENCE

Once new business has been put on the books and a sound loading and reserve method has been adopted to assure that the claims contracted for can be met, the next concern of the stockholder should be how well the life company holds on to this new business. Policies go off the books in two ways—either claims are paid or policies lapse. If either the lapse rate or the mortality experience is excessively high, the rate at which new business is being written, however high, is not doing as much for the company as might be otherwise expected. Commissions and underwriting expenses typically absorb all of the first-year premium on a new policy and often a sizeable share of the second-year premium as well. This is what is meant by saying that a life company can reap the benefits of new business only if it stays on the books.

Of the two types of claims paid by life insurance companies, death benefits and living benefits, death payments in recent years have been accounting for a smaller portion of total benefit payments. (See Table 11 and Charts 2 and 3.) As people live longer, they are seeking ways to protect and bolster their income for their old age. As a result, to achieve the optimum in financial security, people will be buying a higher proportion of endowment, disability policies, and annuities than was the case in earlier years. Consequently, living benefits will continue in excess of death payments for years to come. In 1972, for instance, death payments were $8 billion, while living benefits were $10.6 billion.

There are no overall figures concerning the rate of claims payments for the various types of policies written by life companies. However, there are general death rate figures per 1,000 for the total population.

TABLE 11

Life Insurance Benefit Payments in the United States

Year	Death Payments	Matured Endowments	Disability Payments	Annuity Payments	Surrender Values	Policy Dividends	Total
1940	$ 995,000	$269,200	$103,500	$176,500	$652,000	$468,100	$2,664,300
1945	1,279,600	406,700	87,600	216,400	210,900	466,100	2,667,300
1950	1,589,700	495,100	99,600	319,400	592,300	634,600	3,730,700
1955	2,240,700	613,900	110,000	462,300	895,900	1,059,900	5,382,700
1960	3,346,100	673,100	123,800	722,000	1,633,400	1,620,100	8,118,500
1961	3,581,400	714,900	132,700	769,900	1,793,100	1,819,000	8,811,000
1962	3,878,100	713,900	141,700	838,100	1,772,800	1,980,200	9,324,800
1963	4,208,600	809,000	154,500	901,700	1,789,300	2,165,100	10,028,200
1964	4,533,500	898,700	160,600	961,000	1,833,700	2,370,300	10,757,800
1965	4,831,400	931,100	163,000	1,038,900	1,932,300	2,519,900	11,416,600
1966	5,218,200	981,600	169,300	1,152,600	2,120,600	2,699,900	12,342,200
1967	5,665,300	1,017,100	174,600	1,261,300	2,243,100	2,932,200	13,293,600
1968	6,209,300	967,200	195,600	1,401,000	2,456,400	3,155,500	14,385,000
1969	6,758,100	952,600	204,700	1,558,600	2,721,600	3,328,900	15,524,500
1970	7,017,300	978,300	232,900	1,757,100	2,886,400	3,577,400	16,449,400
1971	7,423,300	990,200	256,800	1,944,400	2,881,600	3,680,900	17,177,200
1972	8,007,000	1,000,400	271,200	2,213,200	3,027,400	4,054,900	18,574,100

Source: National Center for Health Statistics, U.S. Department of Health, Education and Welfare. Rates have been computed using the 1940 age distribution of the United States population as the standard population. Figures for 1915–1932 are for Death Registration States only; 1933–1963 are for the United States. *Life Insurance Fact Book 1973*, p. 45.

CHART 2

Life Insurance Benefit Payments: 1942–72 (billions of dollars)

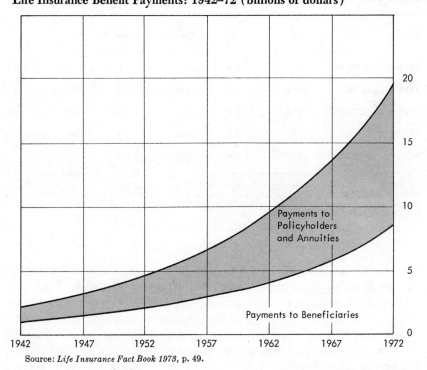

Source: *Life Insurance Fact Book 1973*, p. 49.

CHART 3

Life Expectancy at Birth (1930–71)

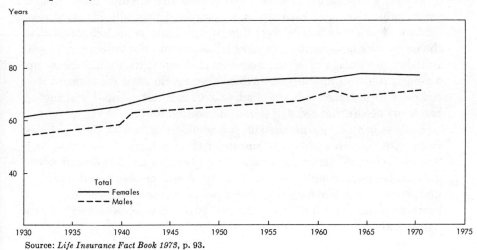

Source: *Life Insurance Fact Book 1973*, p. 93.

TABLE 12

Death Rate in the United Staes (age-adjusted rate per 1,000 population)

Year	Rate	Year	Rate	Year	Rate	Year	Rate
1915	14.4	1940	10.8	1961	7.4	1966	7.5
1920	14.2	1945	9.5	1962	7.5	1967	7.3
1925	13.0	1950	8.4	1963	7.6	1968	7.5
1930	12.5	1955	7.7	1964	7.4	1969	7.3
1935	11.6	1960	7.6	1965	7.4		

Source: National Center for Health Statistics, U.S. Department of Health, Education and Welfare. Rates have been computed using the 1940 age distribution of the United States population as the standard population. Figures for 1915–32 are for Death Registration States only; 1933–63 are for the United States. *Life Insurance Fact Book 1973*, p. 106.

(See Table 12.) The rate of death among the average population may be used as an index of a company's general attitude toward risk. If the mortality among a company's policyholders per 1,000 is way out of line when compared with the experience of the population as a whole, it can only be assumed that this company puts a greater emphasis on new business than on the stability of business on the books. This may be beneficial to the agents (they get their commissions) but it is not favorable for the stockholders. Excessive claims, even if they do not become great enough to endanger the financial soundness of the company, subtract from the rate of asset building that would normally be associated with a given volume of new business underwritten.

Mortality experience is most important in any attempt to determine future projections and earnings of a company. Naturally, a lower percentage of actual mortality over the expected rate is an indication that the company's underwriting of risks is better than the industry average. A higher percentage of actual over expected mortality should throw up a danger signal to investigate further. There is no need for concern if a company experiences only one bad year in mortality; but if a string of bad years occurs, the red flag should be hoisted high.

Each year a certain number of policyholders either let their policies lapse or, if there is cash value, surrender their policies. (See Table 13.) Several factors influence these rates. More policies are terminated when general business conditions are turning down or depressed than in prosperous times. The length of time a policy has been in force also has a bearing on the lapse rate. After the first two years, lapse rates go down significantly.

TABLE 13

Voluntary Termination Rate of Ordinary Policies in Force in the United States

Year	Policies in Force Two Years or More (percent)	All Policies in Force (percent)
1951	2.2	3.2
1952	2.2	3.2
1953	2.2	3.2
1954	2.6	3.8
1955	2.5	3.8
1956	2.8	4.2
1957	3.9	5.4
1958	4.0	5.7
1959	3.7	5.2
1960	3.7	5.2
1961	3.9	5.6
1962	3.5	5.1
1963	3.5	5.1
1964	3.4	5.0
1965	3.5	5.1
1966	3.5	5.2
1967	3.6	5.2
1968	3.7	5.5
1969	3.7	5.6
1970	3.9	5.9
1971	3.9	5.8
1972	3.9	6.0

Source: *Institute of Life Insurance*. The rate is the ratio of the number of policies lapsed or surrendered (for cash, extended term, or reduced paid-up insurance), less reinstatements, to the mean number of policies in force.

Another factor is the type of insurance. Credit insurance, of course, terminates with the credit instrument being insured. Group insurance plans are off the books if the insurance company loses the contract. This type of underwriting has been intensely competitive in recent years. There are no industrywide figures available for the lapse experience in credit and group insurance, but there are figures for the termination rate of ordinary policies.

The rate of termination in ordinary policies may be used, as with mortality experience, as a general index to a company's ability to hold on to its business once it is on its books. If this rate is unusually high, it is a signal that something might be wrong with the sales department and/or the management of the company.

Glowing reports of new business written are hardly sufficient to determine a company's future. Basically, since the cost of writing new business for a life insurance company is generally in excess of its initial premiums the first year, the length of time that business stays on the

TABLE 14

Health Insurance Benefits in United States Paid by Life Insurance Companies (000,000 omitted)

Year	Group	Individual	Total
1948	$ 225	$ 101	$ 326
1950	375	119	494
1955	1,064	326	1,390
1960	2,102	531	2,633
1965	3,572	841	4,413
1966	3,927	1,044	4,971
1967	4,306	1,046	5,352
1968	4,947	1,152	6,099
1969	5,746	1,128	6,874
1970	6,840	1,368	8,208
1971	7,721	1,343	9,064
1972	8,225	1,450	9,675

Source: Institute of Life Insurance and Health Insurance Association of America (figures exclude policy dividends); *Life Insurance Fact Book 1973* (New York: Institute of Life Insurance, 1973), p. 53.

books gives us an idea as to the profitability of that company's overall book of business. Growth data are given in Tables 15 and 16.

The net interest rate is the ratio of the net investment income for the year to the mean invested assets (including cash) decreased by one half the net investment income. Before 1940, the rates were calculated after deducting only such federal income taxes as were deducted by the individual companies in arriving at their net investment income. Beginning with 1940, the rates are calculated before deducting any federal income taxes.

Despite inherent difficulties in determining the true rate of profit, many methods have been devised whereby the basic financial items available in the convention statement, or in the annual statement which the life company must file with state insurance commissioners, are adjusted. All of these methods spring from one important line under the Summary of Operations section: "Net Gain from Operations after Dividends to Policyholders and Federal Income Taxes and Excluding Capital Gains and Losses." There is another important entry under Net Investment Income—"Ratio of Net Investment Income to Mean Assets"—that is often called on for collaborative evidence in arriving at a fuller understanding of the true earnings power of a particular company. None of these figures is exactly comparable to the "profits" as reported by corporations in other industries.

Of the two approaches, the simplest and in many ways the most useful

TABLE 15

Life Insurance in Force in the United States (000,000 omitted)

YEAR	ORDINARY No.	ORDINARY Amt.	GROUP Cert.	GROUP Amt.	INDUSTRIAL No.	INDUSTRIAL Amt.	CREDIT No.†	CREDIT Amt.	TOTAL No.	TOTAL Amt.
1900.....	3	$ 6,124	—	—	11	$1,449	—	—	14	$ 7,573
1905.....	5	9,585	—	—	17	2,278	—	—	22	11,863
1910.....	6	11,783	—	—	23	3,125	—	—	29	14,908
1915.....	9	16,650	•	$ 100	32	4,279	—	—	41	21,029
1920.....	16	32,018	2	1,570	48	6,948	°	$ 4	66	40,540
1925.....	23	52,892	3	4,247	71	12,318	°	18	97	69,475
1930.....	32	78,576	6	9,801	86	17,963	°	73	124	106,413
1931.....	33	79,514	6	9,736	85	17,635	°	85	124	106,970
1932.....	32	75,898	5	8,923	79	16,669	•	69	116	101,559
1933.....	31	70,872	5	8,681	78	16,630	•	63	114	96,246
1934.....	32	70,094	6	9,472	79	17,036	•	75	117	96,677
1935.....	33	70,684	6	10,208	81	17,471	1	101	121	98,464
1936.....	33	72,361	7	11,291	83	18,863	1	138	124	102,653
1937.....	34	74,836	7	12,638	85	20,104	1	216	127	107,794
1938.....	35	75,772	7	12,503	85	20,396	2	256	129	108,927
1939.....	36	77,121	8	13,641	85	20,500	2	307	131	111,569
1940.....	37	79,346	9	14,938	85	20,866	3	380	134	115,530
1941.....	39	82,525	10	17,359	87	21,825	3	469	139	122,178
1942.....	41	85,139	11	19,316	90	22,911	2	355	144	127,721
1943.....	43	89,596	13	22,413	94	24,874	2	275	152	137,158
1944.....	46	95,085	13	23,922	98	26,474	2	290	159	145,771
1945.....	48	101.550	12	22,172	101	27,675	2	365	163	151,762
1946.....	53	112,818	13	27,206	104	29,313	3	729	173	170,066
1947.....	56	122,393	16	32,026	106	30,406	5	1,210	183	186,035
1948.....	58	131,158	16	37,068	106	31,253	6	1,729	186	201,208
1949.....	61	138,847	17	40,207	107	32,087	8	2,531	193	213,672
1950.....	64	149,071	19	47,793	108	33,415	11	3,889	202	234,168
1951.....	67	159,054	21	54,398	109	34,870	12	4,818	209	253,140
1952.....	70	170,795	24	62,913	111	36,448	14	6,435	219	276,591
1953.....	73	184,859	26	72,913	112	37,781	18	8,706	229	304,259
1954.....	76	198,419	29	86,395	111	38,664	21	10,241	237	333,719
1955.....	80	216,600	32	101,300	112	39,682	28	14,750	252	372,332
1956.....	83	238,099	35	117,324	110	40,109	32	17,098	260	412,630
1957.....	87	264,678	37	133,794	108	40,139	34	19,748	266	458,359
1958.....	89	287,834	39	144,607	104	39,646	35	21,474	267	493,561
1959.....	92	315,953	41	159,807	102	39,809	39	26,559	274	542,128
1960.....	95	340,268	44	175,434	100	39,563	43	31,183	282	586,448
1961.....	97	364,347	46	192,202	98	39,451	45	33,493	286	629,493
1962.....	99	389,150	48	209,178	95	39,638	48	38,011	290	675,977
1963.....101		418,856	51	228,540	93	39,672	53	43,555	298	730,623
1964.....104		455,860	55	252,182	92	39,833	58	49,933	309	797,808
1965.....107		497,630	61	306,113	89	39,818	63	56,993	320	900,554
1966.....109		538,992	64	343,362	88	39,663	70	62,672	331	984,689
1967.....113		582,565	68	391,089	84	39,215	71	66,952	336	1,079,821
1968.....116		630,405	72	438,241	81	38,827	76	75,881	345	1,183,354
1969.....118		678,887	75	483,240	79	38,614	79	83,788	351	1,284,529
1970.....120		730,462	79	545,092	77	38,644	79	87,925	355	1,402,123
1971.....122		787,742	82	581,434	76	39,202	77	94,956	357	1,503,334
1972.....125		848,543	84	630,700	76	39,975	80	108,767	365	1,627,985

TABLE 16

Net Rate of Interest Earned on Invested Funds—U.S. Life Insurance Companies

Year	Rate (percent)	Year	Rate (percent)	Year	Rate (percent)	Year	Rate (percent)
1915	4.77	1928	5.05	1941	3.42	1954	3.46
1916	4.80	1929	5.05	1942	3.44	1955	3.51
1917	4.81	1930	5.05	1943	3.33	1956	3.63
1918	4.72	1931	4.93	1944	3.23	1957	3.75
1919	4.66	1932	4.65	1945	3.11	1958	3.85
1920	4.83	1933	4.25	1946	2.93	1959	3.96
1921	5.02	1934	3.92	1947	2.88	1960	4.11
1922	5.12	1935	3.70	1948	2.96	1961	4.22
1923	5.18	1936	3.71	1949	3.06	1962	4.34
1924	5.17	1937	3.69	1950	3.13	1963	4.45
1925	5.11	1938	3.59	1951	3.18	1964	4.53
1926	5.09	1939	3.54	1952	3.28		
1927	5.05	1940	3.45	1953	3.36		

Year	Rate Including Separate Accounts (percent)	Rate Excluding Separate Accounts (percent)
1965	4.61	4.61
1966	4.73	4.73
1967	4.82	4.83
1968	4.95	4.97
1969	5.12	5.15
1970	5.30	5.34
1971	5.44	5.52
1972	5.56	5.69

Source: *Life Insurance Fact Book 1973*, p. 62.

is the ratio of net investment income to mean assets (see Table 16). It is calculated as follows:

> Total interest, dividends, and real estate income
> *less:* Investment expenses
> Taxes, licenses, and fees, excluding federal income tax
> Depreciation on real estate
> *equals:* Net Investment Income
> and

$$\text{Earnings Rate} = \frac{\text{Net Investment Income}}{\text{Mean Assets}}$$

Most state insurance commissioners require some figure comparable to this ratio in the convention statement; therefore, the earnings rate offers one figure that is useful in comparing the relative performance of life companies in at least one important aspect. Of course, this ratio excludes much of what we would call profit from the total operation of the life company; but it does give some indication of the relative financial efficiency of life company managements.

The earnings rate trend has been rising in recent years. (See table of net rate of interest earned on invested funds.) To a large extent, this rise reflects the generally higher rates of return available to the managements as they replace maturing investments with new instruments. If the life insurance company management is ultraconservative, the earnings rate may well dip below average industry experience. On the other hand, an above-average performance would suggest an alert and shrewd management of funds—one that may be reflected in other aspects of the company's business.

While the earnings rate is useful in making comparisons, it is limited. It does not include a full picture of the earnings from all sources. To arrive at an approximation of the overall earnings potential, we have to go to the Net Gain from Operations line of the convention statement.

Even these detailed presentations of operations do not give completely satisfactory answers to the degree of profitability. All premiums are lumped together; so are reserves, commissions on premiums, and general insurance expenses. It is well known that most of these items which are deducted in determining Net Gain from Operations can be traced to new policies being written in the year and, in part, to those written in the immediately preceding year. To use the resulting Net Gain figure as a true indication of "profits" would be, in effect, saying that a life insurance company which is writing the most new business, and thereby upping its deductions, is the least attractive. It might be true that a new burst of business could, in some cases, be a sign of danger—it all depends on the mix of the new business and the quality of the risk being undertaken; but it certainly does not follow that all new business, regardless of type, is to be deplored.

CAPITALIZATION

We have correctly assumed that a life insurance company that does a good job in writing policies, keeps a close tab on expenses, and has a good eye for investment opportunities for its funds will also make a first-rate investment for its stockholders.

But if the investor finds two equally promising life companies, there is another important factor that may give one company an edge over the other in terms of market performance: the number of shares of stock authorized and outstanding, the manner in which this stock is currently held, the various classes of stock issued—in short, the capitalization of the company.

As compared with industrial corporations, the capital structure of life insurance companies is simple. Life companies have very seldom raised new operating funds through bond flotations. This means that the stockholders of life companies will not suffer because of prior claims from senior securities. Some stock companies have mutual departments, and many others write participating policies. If these divisions are segregated —and they should be in any well-run company—they pose no special problem for the stockholder.

Common stock is the typical capital instrument. Preferred stocks (usually convertible) exist, but they are rare. Life companies seldom issue stock warrants; however, rights offerings to stockholders and options to officers and agents are fairly common. At times these can pose a problem to the stockholder, for rights and options dilute the equity. In the case of options to officers and agents, the stockholder derives some benefit inasmuch as these privileges to purchase the common, sometimes at favorable prices, are usually management incentive payments. If not abused, they can help assure continued health and performance in a growing company.

Occasionally, the common stock outstanding will be divided into two classes. Which should the investor seek to hold? The answer depends on the rights and privileges belonging to each class. It is customary for one class to carry voting rights while the other is excluded from all or certain types of corporate voting. Sometimes the voting stock also pays a lower cash dividend. Since life companies in general are stingy cash dividend payers (the cash dividends often being merely token payments) this distinction between classes may be of little practical significance. Of more importance is the presence or absence of voting rights. Here the stockholder may have vital interests at stake. Even if his few votes are unlikely to decide an issue, he and other voting stockholders may be able to block a move that does not seem to be in their best interest.

REINSURANCE

Life reinsurance almost without exception is a direct sales product which, unlike property and casualty reinsurance, is not sold through brokers, probably because the supply has almost always exceeded the demand. This is in contrast to the nonlife reinsurance business where a tremendous capacity is sometimes needed to cover large risks and the role of the broker is a very real one as he arranges the facilities to cover those large risks. However, in the life business which is sold primarily or almost entirely by a company representative, salesmen have tried to sell what the market has needed. Also, companies actively seeking reinsurance are really competing for treaties that will provide them with a steady flow of business, not individual cases. Underwriters, in a sense, may compete for individual cases in situations where risk is submitted to several companies. Although the underwriter may not know all who are appraising the risk, in a sense he's trying to submit a competitive offer. But reinsurance salesmen in representing their companies generally are competing for treaties that will produce a steady flow of business.

During the post-World War II period of new company development, everyone's sales efforts were geared to expansion. Many of the new companies were formed with a small staff and only limited facilities. The reinsurance companies began to step up and offer, in many instances, significant services in return for their business. Meanwhile, some interesting changes were occuring in the underwriting area. Substandard underwriting for example, was becoming less important with the big Eastern companies. Most companies of any size, by that time, had their own very competent underwriting staffs.

There are basically two kinds of reinsurance treaties—automatic and facultative. An automatic reinsurance treaty requires that the reinsurer obligate himself automatically for the excess risk issued by the original company and be bound by the underwriting decision of the original company. In return, the original company agrees to submit to the reinsurer all of the excess risks it encounters, or at least some portion of them that have been specified in advance. Facultative reinsurance, on the other hand, is a situation where the original company submits to the reinsurer, or perhaps reinsurers, its evidence of insurability. The reinsurance company then makes an offer. There is no obligations involved on anyone's part either from the standpoint of the original company or the reinsurer. The original company is usually free to accept the most competitive offer and it is understood that the original company is free to insure the risk in full.

Automatic reinsurance is available only when the original company retains its own retention when it is on the risk. Having done so, it is then entitled to cede within limits the excess coverage. The treaties usually allow for the original company to cede as much as four times the amount of risk it retains. This provides a real convenience for the original company in that it enables it to handle risks as much as five times as much as its retention limit.

It should be clear that automatic treaties also give reinsurers what they want because it is more or less determined in advance where the business is going. A reinsurer with an automatic treaty with a particular client can be sure of a steady flow of business.

Facultative treaties, on the other hand, are purely noncompulsory. The original company is free to submit business to one or more carriers and is under no obligation to cede the risk to any one of them. In the past, facultative reinsurance was considered to be its own reward, from the service standpoint, and reinsurers tended to concentrate their services on their automatic clients. That is perhaps a little less true today. However, the basis for the underwriting competition today is facultative treaties. Many of the foreign reinsurers are seeking business here in the U.S. entirely through facultative treaties. In fact in many instances they freely admit that they have no interest in any treaties.

The first and by far the most common method of reinsurance is risk premium reinsurance (RPR), or, as it is sometimes called, Yearly Renewal Term. Under RPR, the original company pays a pure mortality premium to the reinsurer on the amount of excess risk over its retention limit, usually calculated on a net risk basis or a face amount minus the reserve. There are many variations of RPR available. Probably the most basic version is the experience refunding a nonrefunding basis. As with participating direct insurance experience, refunding premiums are higher, but at the end of the year, the experience in the account is calculated and a refund is paid equal to 50 percent of the profits in the account. If the experience in the accounts turns out to be average or perhaps a little better over a long period of time, refunding insurance is usually cheaper for the original company. But many companies prefer the guarantee cost features of nonrefunding reinsurance. Another variation or series of alternatives offered in RPR is that various companies offer premium scales because the incidence or premiums may vary a great deal each year. Reinsurers are willing to take as low a premium in the early years as possible, recognizing that it is during those years that the original company incurs its acquisition costs. Historically, first year premiums at any given age were one half of the renewal premiums at the same age. All the insurers now operate on the basis of what are called ultimat rates, which incorporate underwriting. These rates may grade upward by duration for as much as five or ten years. The ultimate situation may be that of some grade scale available where the premium in the first year is zero, with renewal rates being adjusted accordingly.

The degree to which the insurer will forego premiums in the early policy years will strongly influence the conditions under which he allows the reinsurer to take back, or recapture, the reinsurance. Obviously, the lower the rates offered in the early policy years, the longer the reinsurer insists the business be left with him so he can recoup his expenses and make at least a nominal profit.

Another important variation is in the relationship between the basic premium per thousand of risk and the policy fee. Low unit premiums and high policy fees are available in some instances, whereas some companies use lower policy fees and higher unit premiums. The other basic method of pricing reinsurance is what we call coinsurance. This is where the *ceding* company buys from the reinsurer precisely the plan of insurance that it has sold to its policy holder and at the same basic gross premium.

The British call this type of reinsurance, quite appropriately, reinsurance on original terms. The basic gross to the reinsurer is the same as that of the original companies. In the reinsurance transaction adjustments are made for commissions and an expense allowance as they are incurred by the original company. Dividends, if any, are also reimbursed to the original company by the reinsurer. It is difficult to discuss coinsurance without discussing modified coinsurance. To define modified coinsurance we have to think of a permanent plan of insurance—e.g., ordinary life— where there is an adjustment element in the premium that is building cash values. To provide for this buildup, reserves are posted by the original company.

From the earlier definition of coinsurance it is clear the savings or adjustment element in the premium is passed on to the reinsurer. He would be posting reserves on the policy. In event of surrender he would be expected to pay his portion of the surrender value. Under modified coinsurance, one additional deduction in the premium is made before it is passed on to the reinsurer, that deduction being the annual increase in reserves. In this way, the adjustment element in the premium is less with the original company, while the assets accumulate with the original company.

Under those conditions, of course, the reserves remain on the balance sheet of the original company. *A key point for analysts is that the impact on the operating statement of both straight coinsurance and modified coinsurance is exactly the same.* In one case, the original company does not have to post a reserve because that obligation has been assumed by the reinsurer. In the other case the original company does post a reserve, but the reinsurer provides the money for it.

The operating statement impact of RPR may or may not be the same. As a general rule if an original company is on a modified reserve basis such as described here, there really is not much difference in surplus impact between modified coinsurance and RPR. Modified coinsurance in a sense is like RPR because in both cases premium income ultimately reaches the reinsurer as nothing more than a pure mortality of net premium. If you take away from a permanent plan gross premium, the commissions, the expense allowance, and remove the investment element, what is left obviously, is the mortality element of the premium. In both modified coinsurance and RPR, the reinsurer receives essentially the same type of premium although how that premium is calculated is quite different. In the one case it comes from adjustments that are made to the original company gross premium. In the other situation it is a pure mortality net premium as quoted by the reinsurer.

Another important point to remember is that RPR competition is essentially a one time thing. When a reinsurance company develops its RPR rate scale, it then competes on the basis of that scale. RPR rates are not individual quotations made on a company by a company and sometimes a plan by plan basis, so that coinsurance price competition is a constant, ongoing thing. RPR rate levels are essentially set for at least a certain period of time.

The standard factors that impact on profits are, interests, expenses, persistency, and mortality. Interest is almost completely unimportant in the reinsurance picture. In a situation where a reinsurer is receiving only pure mortality at premium, his assets are small, yielding returns that will have relatively little influence on his profits.

Expenses are probably more important in the reinsurance business. But in relation to the direct business they are less important. Reinsurance premiums for the most part contain only relatively small expense floatings, and I think the reinsurance business is less vulnerable to inflationary expense trends than the direct business is.

Persistency, of course, is always a problem but again is probably a less important one than on the direct side. Some years ago, when so many new companies were being formed, the persistency of the business in some of these companies was really bad, and reinsurers needed to be aware of poor persistency situations. But as these companies have grown and prospered and succeeded, persistency in general on reinsurance business has improved and is now a less important factor than it once was.

Finally, of course, mortality is the all-important factor. The insurance business is much more sensitive to it from the profit standpoint than the direct business is because the mortality element is dominant in the premium structures. Reinsurance profits are very closely tied to direct profits. Direct profits can be expressed in many ways. Sometimes there is a percentage of premiums. Sometimes there is a certain amount per thousand of insurance in force. But whatever they are, it is important to remember that reinsurance profits are essentially the same kind of *animal*, and that the two are closely related.

Depending on how you might interrelate the various profit-determined factors, a case can be made for reinsurance profits being anywhere from 80 percent of direct profits to perhaps as much as 120 percent. One might be led to the 80 percent figure by saying that the reinsurer should cover both its expenses and its profits objective out of the profit margin of the original company. In that case, the reinsurers profit would probably be about 80 percent of the direct companies' profit. On the other hand, one might make a strong case for this being risky to business from a mortality standpoint and might very legitimately justify a larger premium of profits. Something like the 80 percent to 120 percent range is where reinsurance profits generally will be.

We have to be realistic in recognizing that the basic market is at best a two-to-one and perhaps at worst a declining market. There are few new companies being formed today, so that the new element of the market that gave tremendous growth for so many years is no longer there. On the other hand, mergers do abound, hurting reinsurers. In a sense, reinsurance faces a double risk of loss. A small company might provide a larger reinsurance with a nice continuing volume of reinsurance, then this company decides to merge into a larger company. The larger company might not be an extant client, thus eliminating all future new business. But even if the larger surviving company were a client, the sales capacity of the smaller company is now in a bigger financial environment where the surviving company probably has a larger retention limit and less excess risks. The overall size of the market is certainly not growing much, and perhaps declining a little. The classic graduate business textbook strategy, in such a market is to try to do two things—maintain your share of the market and keep unit profits as high as you can.

Price competition is reasonably stable on the RPR side. The basic competitive factors are set on companies without rate scales, or one adopted several years ago. On the other hand, competition continues at a fierce level in the area of coinsurance. These price structures have to be quoted on a company by company basis. Every time someone changes his own rate pattern in any way, the entire price structure has to be negotiated.

On the matter of services, this whole concept began some 25 years ago. As time has gone on reinsurers have been willing to do more and more for the clients. There have been fewer newer companies and the survivors have been the more successful ones as the nature of services that were asked became more and more sophisticated. In very recent years, some of the services became available only at a specific charge.

Probably the chief development that epitomizes this revolutionary process is that of variable life. There will be significant ways in which reinsurance may be helpful in this area, and elaborate programming will be developed.

COMMENT ON ACCOUNTING

Many differences exist between new methods of accounting and statutory accounting that the industry has historically used. The major difference lies in the treatment of acquisition expenses for new business. Some of the other differences are the use of a more realistic interest rate assumption in computing reserves, the introduction of a lapse assumption (on the statutory basis it was always assumed that all business on the books would stay until maturity), the use of net-level reserves as against preliminary term (under statutory accounting, companies have the option of assuming that the first year policy is a term policy and that a contract really starts to be reserved in its second year—the net level is a higher or more conservative reserving method), and the use of a mortality table based on the company's experience rather than a purely theoretical table. In addition, realized capital gains and losses and profit or loss in subsidiaries flow through income. Nonadmitted (statutory) assets are carried in the balance sheet at recoverable values, and so on. However, the major effect is the ability to amortize the acquisition expenses over a long period of time. In many cases this expense is in excess of the full first-year premium. All the other differences have a minor effect.

Under the Audit Guide it is permissible to amortize these expenses over the lifetime of the policy. Some in management feel however, that it is more conservative to amortize these expenses over no longer than a 20-year period. Inasmuch as the life insurance industry must still keep books for the regulatory bodies on a statutory basis, one method calls for reserves to be merged into statutory over the same period as the amortization of expenses; i.e., 20 years or less. In essence, therefore, any block of business would be on a statutory basis from its 20th year on. Statutory accounting is far more conservative than GAAP. In addition, by the time a block of business has reached its 20th year, there is such a small percentage of the original amount remaining on the books that there will be little effect on the percentage of overall earnings.

The writer concurs with those who believe that a considerable amount of latitude is given to life insurance company managements within which more favorable earnings reports can be constructed via GAAP assumptions. However, this places such companies on a pari passu basis with present day industrial accounting. Those who are involved in this latter endeavor may utilize varied modes of depreciation, leases, loss reserves, et al. Moreover the advance in the state of life accounting art should be placed in the perspective of the vacuum from which it has evolved, leaping from a period when much less scientifically derived, more capricious tools of measuring earning power were utilized. In these terms therefore, GAAP accounting for life insurance companies is a constructive force which can provide the basis for continuing improvement and refinement henceforth.

18

Investment Companies

A. MICHAEL LIPPER, C.F.A.
Lipper Analytical Services, Inc.
Westfield, New Jersey

THE PRINCIPLES which make investment companies attractive investment vehicles are the very same ones that have made their use attractive since they began centuries ago. Essentially the Dutch East India Company and the merchant ship syndicates of the 16th century were the investment companies of their day. The key elements of these companies, both in the 16th century and today, are:

1. A single pool of capital (concentration).
2. Investing in a specific class of investment media (specialization).
3. Reliance on experts (professionalism).
4. A number of different investments (diversification).
5. A commercial life beyond one's mortal own (continuation).

Perhaps even from their earliest beginnings, these concentrators of wealth and controllers of huge amounts of purchasing power have attracted governmental attention. The resulting regulations have made investment companies different from other commercial ventures, which is clearly one of their most distinguishing characteristics.

Investment companies in one form or another are functioning in almost every country of the world that permits easy transfer of investment properties. In each country regulations and operating principles are somewhat different. This section will deal primarily with investment companies as they exist in the United States and, in particular, open-end

475

investment companies—mutual funds. As of June 28, 1974 the total mutual fund assets under management were $41,710.0 million.[1]

ADVANTAGES AND DISADVANTAGES OF INVESTMENT COMPANIES

Advantages

Investment companies have a *legally defined scope of activities.* These are normally more narrowly defined than those of general business corporations. Usually investment companies are permitted to invest only in a *limited type of assets,* for example, stocks, bonds, mortgages, land, horses, etc. Further, the methods of investing, along with their restrictions, are usually spelled out in some detail, for example, investment policies and specified investment restrictions which are discussed in the fund's prospectus. Examples are shown below:

A.

> The Fund provides experienced investment management for investors who seek long-term growth of capital and increase of future income through investment primarily in growth stocks of well-established companies. . . .
>
> The assets of the Fund will ordinarily be invested primarily in common stocks. The Fund's investment program, however, is sufficiently elastic to permit the Fund to establish and maintain reserves, which may be invested in corporate and government bonds and notes, to enable it to take advantage of buying opportunities. The Fund may also invest in convertible securities and preferred stocks, and in securities of foreign issuers. The Fund may invest in securities not listed on a national securities exchange, but such securities generally will have an established over-the-counter market.[2]

B. "Our [Financial Dynamics Fund] investment objective is to provide for our shareholders possible appreciation of capital through speculative investment policies."[3]

C.

> The Fund has adopted certain investment restrictions which are intended for the benefit and protection of its shareholders. So long as these restrictions remain in effect, the Fund may not: (1) Purchase any securities which would cause more than 5% of its total assets at the time of such purchase to be invested in the securities of any issuer, except the United States government; (2) Purchase any securities which

---

[1] Lipper-*Mutual Fund Performance Analysis* (These statistics covered 551 funds, whereas the Investment Company Institute, the industry's trade association, covers only 415 funds with slightly smaller total net assets.)

[2] *T. Rowe Price Growth Stock Fund Prospectus,* May 1, 1973.

[3] *Financial Dynamics Fund Prospectus.*

would cause the Fund at the time of such purchase to own more than 10% of the outstanding securities of any class of any issuer; (3) Purchase the securities of any issuer engaged in continuous operation for less than three years; (4) Purchase any securities which would cause more than 35% of its total assets at the time of such purchase to be invested in the securities of issuers engaged in any one industry; provided, that as a matter of operating policy, the Fund will not concentrate its investments to the extent of more than 25% in any one industry. (5) Purchase or sell real estate, but this limitation does not preclude an investment in the securities of a company whose business involves the purchase or sale of real estate. (6) Purchase or sell commodities or commodity contracts. (7) Acquire the securities of any investment company, except securities purchased in regular transactions in the open market or acquired pursuant to a plan of merger or consolidation; provided, that as a matter of operating policy, the Fund has determined not to purchase the securities of open-end investment companies. (8) Purchase securities on margin or effect short sales of securities. (9) Make loans, except that it may acquire publicly distributed bonds, debentures, notes and other debt securities. (10) Borrow money, except for temporary administrative purposes, and then only in amounts not exceeding 5% of its total assets, valued at market. (11) Act as an underwriter of securities, except insofar as it might technically be deemed to be an underwriter for purposes of the Securities Act of 1933 upon the disposition of certain securities. (12) Purchase or retain the securities of its investment adviser or of any corporation of which any officer, director or member of the investment committee of the investment adviser is a director. (13) Deal with any of its officers or directors, or with any firm of which any of its officers or directors is a member, as principal in the purchase or sale of portfolio securities. (14) Pay commissions on portfolio transactions to its investment adviser, to any officer, director or stockholder of its investment adviser, to any officer or director of the Fund, or to any partnership or company in which any officer or director of the Fund has a financial interest. (15) Invest in companies for the purpose of exercising management or control. (16) Purchase any securities which would cause more than 5% of its total assets at the time of such purchase to be invested in securities which may not be publicly sold without registration under the Securities Act of 1933 or are otherwise illiquid or not readily marketable. As of the date of this Prospectus, the Fund owned no restricted securities. (17) Invest in puts, calls, straddles, spreads or any combinations thereof. (18) Purchase participations or other direct interests in oil, gas or other mineral exploration or development programs. (19) Purchase or retain the securities of any issuer if any officer or director of the Fund or its investment adviser owns more than ½ of 1%, and all officers and directors of the Fund and its investment adviser owning more than that percentage together own more than 5%, of the securities of such issuer.

The restrictions set forth in 1 through 14 above (except those described as operating policies in 4 and 7) are fundamental policies and may not be changed without the affirmative vote of a majority of the outstanding voting securities of the Fund. As defined in the Investment Company Act of 1940, the phrase "vote of a majority of the outstanding voting securities" means the vote of the holders of the lesser of (a) 67% of the shares present in person or represented by proxy and entitled to vote at a meeting of stockholders, if the holders of more than 50% of the outstanding shares are so present or represented, and (b) more than 50% of the outstanding shares. The restrictions set forth in 15 through 19 are operating policies which, like those described in 4 and 7, are subject to change by the Board of Directors without a shareholder vote. As a matter of practice, however, the Fund will not change any of these operating policies without notice to its shareholders.[4]

Disadvantages

Individual issues often have excitement inherent in them due to a new product, merger potential, earnings breakout, etc. As compared with individual issues, investment companies lack this and so may appear to be dull and uninteresting to follow. If one type of investing is thought to be currently unattractive where another area might be considered attractive, *legal and tax restrictions* make a switch difficult, if not impossible, within the same investment company. A fundamental change in investment policy must be approved by the shareholders; a time-consuming and expensive proxy solicitation process. Further, a radical change in policy can cause large-scale selling within the portfolio. This in turn can cause some of the following problems:

1. Unexpected and unwanted tax consequences on realized gains or losses of a materially different magnitude than in the past.
2. Loss of Internal Revenue Service investment company exemption. (Investment companies are exempt from tax if they pass 90 percent of their gains and dividends through to their shareholders and if not more than 30 percent of their gross gains, regardless of losses, come from the sale of securities held under 90 days.)
3. Excessive transactions, proxy solicitation, and other costs will increase the shareholder's expenses and possibly force the management company to reimburse the fund if its expenses are out of line with the provisions of the prospectus, and/or state "blue sky" regulations (see below).
4. "Opportunity costs," for example, large scale sale and purchases, can of themselves effect realized prices, as well as direct the manager's attention away from more effective decisions.

Relative to general business corporations it is *much more difficult to force a change in management* by a proxy fight. Usually there are few concentrated holdings of fund shares to use as a foundation for a proxy fight.

---

[4] *T. Rowe Price Growth Stock Fund Prospectus,* May 1, 1973.

Further, most dissatisfied fund shareholders redeem their shares rather than hold their positions. In addition, with the expense limitations effective in most funds, the victorious side probably has to reimburse the fund for its cost, and the losers have no chance for recoupment of their expenses.

FIELDS OF ACTIVITY

Today investment companies are active in the following fields:

1. Marketable securities (stocks, bonds, etc.).
2. Restricted securities (legal restriction on sale of these assets, for example, letter stock).
3. Natural resources (participations in oil and gas drilling, coal, gold, and diamond mining).
4. Real estate (land, buildings, mortgages, farms, plantations, construction loans, etc.).
5. Venture capital (investments in private companies often at an early stage of their development).
6. Private placements (securities, often of a debt nature, issued to a small number of investors in a public company).
7. Ships (the original, but still used as an investment vehicle today, especially tankers).
8. Others (patents, thoroughbred race horses, theatrical, movie and television productions, stamps, commodities, works of art, currencies).

CLASSIFICATION OF INVESTMENT COMPANIES

There are numerous methods of classifying investment companies. One we have already discussed—the type of assets in which they have invested. A discussion of other methods follows.

Method of Distribution

Dealer Distribution. The fund contracts with a principal underwriter to distribute the shares of the fund continuously through its own efforts and those of associated firms (which have signed a sales agreement). Usually it is a continuous underwriting. Occasionally, particularly in the beginning, there is a fixed period for an initial underwriting.

Direct Distribution by Sales Force. The underwriter employs its own commission salesmen who exclusively distribute only the firm's funds. Both the dealer distribution method and the sales force distribution method embody a sales charge to the buyer. These charges start at about 8.5 percent of the amount to be invested (9.3 percent of the net amount invested). Sales charges scale down sharply as the amount invested by a fund owner increases. From the purchasers' standpoint, the sales charge pays for their general education about funds, suitability determination, fund selection, and administrative assistance.

No-load. Shares of the fund are purchased without a sales charge. Some no-load funds charge a redemption fee payable to the fund if redemption of the shares occurs within a given time period. (There are some low-load funds which have a maximum sales charge of 2 percent; these are often grouped with the no-loads in discussions about the industry.) These funds issue and redeem shares of their net asset value (NAV).

Frequency of Sales and Redemptions

Open-end. This type of mutual fund continuously offers new shares to the public and redeems them on demand.

Closed-end. This type of investment company issues a limited number of shares and does not redeem them. The issues are traded like other shares, and supply and demand determine the price. Often closed-end funds are specialized as to their investments. The chief advantages of these funds are that they have a fixed amount of money to invest, and, while at times their shares will sell at premiums over their net asset or book value, often they will sell at discounts. Dual funds are closed end funds with two classes of stock—an income oriented class (which pays the holder the dividends) and a capital gains oriented class.

Semiclosed Funds. This type of fund has a limited rather than a continuous offering of new shares but will redeem its shares upon demand. These funds combine the best features of the open- and closed-end funds, from the shareholders' standpoint, and the worst from the management company's standpoint (for example, the size will tend to shrink).

Legal Form

Investment companies are organized under state general business acts which are modified to fit the special needs of investment companies. *Investment trusts* fill many of the same purposes as an investment company except they are organized under the trust statutes. Historically, the first investment companies were organized as trusts as they proved to be more flexible than the company charters of the day. *Unit (fixed) trusts* are trusts where the precise nature of the trust assets are fixed (for example, a preselected list of 40 stocks as required by the prospectus of Founders Mutual Fund) or the shares of one mutual fund are acquired through a contractual plan (First Investors Corporation for accumulation of Wellington Fund shares). Because these unit trusts have no discretion as to their investment assets, the Securities and Exchange Commission does not permit a management fee other than operating expenses to be levied on the assets. *Investment partnerships* are organized under the limited partnership acts of the various states. These arrangements permit the general partners, in exchange for unlimited liability, a dispropor-tionately high share of the profits, compared with the limited partners who are liable only to the extent of their invested assets. Typically the limited partners put up the majority of the capital for the general part-ners to manage. Often these partnerships are called "hedge funds" be-cause they can sell short as well as buy securities. The principal ad-vantage of investment partnerships is that the managers will only benefit when the investors do, as they have a profit sharing, rather than a fee, relationship. From the successful manager's standpoint this is attractive, for he can earn a larger amount (if he is successful) than he can on a fee basis. Also, the profit tends to be long term, from a tax standpoint, and therefore is taxed at the lower capital gains rate. The disadvantage of these operations is that if the manager attempts to maximize his profits and is unsuccessful he may find that he worked very hard and has nothing to show for it because there are no profits to share.

Regulations

In the United States, investment companies are regulated under three general jurisdictions: the Securities and Exchange Commission; the In-ternal Revenue Service (Department of Treasury); and agencies of in-dividual states. There are four principal acts (with their amendments) which govern the Securities and Exchange Commission.

Securities Act of 1933. This is primarily a disclosure statute. Registra-tion statements must be filed with the Securities and Exchange Commis-sion for all new issues. With most open end funds in a continuous under-writing, these funds need current (effective) registration statements. These must contain detailed information and be available to the public. Also, severe restrictions are imposed on the advertising and promotion of new issues.

Securities Act of 1934. The 1934 act requires, in addition to the initial registration statement, the filing of annual reports and other periodic re-ports. Also, it governs the solicitation of proxies.

Investment Company Act of 1940. This is the basic regulatory statute for investment companies. It concerns the organization and structure and much of the operation of investment companies. In 1970, the act was amended and brought up to date. The need for revision was brought about by the enormous growth of the mutual fund industry.

Investment Advisors Act of 1940. This act requires Securities and Exchange Commission registration and conformity to statutory standards of all persons or firms engaged for compensation in an advisory capacity with respect to security transactions. This act was amended in 1960.

A very thorough understanding of each of these acts and the regulations promulgated under them is essential for anyone who wishes to comprehend fully the structure of investment company activities.

An investment company qualified under Internal Revenue Service regulations does not pay income taxes on either its income or capital gains. The two most stringent qualifications under Internal Revenue Service rules are that the investment company must pay out at least 90 percent of its income and gains, and that no more than 30 percent of the investment company's income, disregarding losses, can be from transactions held for 90 days or under. The shareholders of the investment company qualified under these provisions (subchapter M) must, of course, pay taxes on the income received.

State Regulations

Each state has "blue sky laws" that cover the characteristics of securities which can be distributed within the individual state. In addition to disclosure and bonding requirements, many states have an expense limitation covering the fund's expenditures relative to its assets. In many cases, this limitation is 1.5 percent on funds below $30 million and 1 percent on those over that amount.

Overseas investment companies are organized in almost every jurisdiction in the free world. Most of these jurisdictions restrict the operations of funds significantly. An attempt to avoid some of these restrictions has led to the establishment of funds in domiciles that have few restrictions (particularly in terms of taxes). These "off-shore funds," as they are referred to, are usually designed to sell to citizens of countries other than the one where the fund is registered. One of the advantages of many off-shore funds is that they can be bought in bearer form. The only record of ownership is the certificate which entitles the unnamed holder (bearer) to any dividends or distributions. The favorite locales for these funds are certain Carribean Islands, Panama, Isle of Jersey, and others. The lack of strong regulation has unfortunately led to improprieties by some of these funds.

Management Company

There are two types of management companies: external and internal. In the external company, professional services are made available through a separate investment advisory company; whereas in the internal one, services are provided by the staff directly employed by the fund.

Investment Objective

Another way to classify mutual funds is according to their investment objectives. There are *growth funds* whose principal objective is capital growth. They invest primarily in common stocks which have a potential for growth. *Growth and income funds* provide a certain degree of both growth and income. They invest in common stocks accordingly. *Income funds* have as their objective to provide immediate income through the receipt of dividend and interest payments. A recent development are the moneymarket investment funds which invest in certificates of deposit, commercial paper, Treasury bills, etc. to provide short term liquidity for investors. The policy of *balanced funds* consists of investing in equities and bonds to provide a balance within their portfolio; whereas *special funds* provide a policy of investment limited to specific types of securities e.g. airlines, aerospace or foreign securities.

Investment Techniques

Long-term investing rests on the ability to recognize prior to their popularity peak, long-term socio-economic trends, and identification of the corporate securities which will benefit from these changes. As these changes are usually evolutionary, securities are often retained for long periods of time (years) until internal company developments require the sale of the security. These buy/hold strategies make sense if the investor is confident he will redeem or sell his shares during a rising market for the manager's decisions are largely based on earnings not prices.

Short-swing investing relies on the manager's belief that specific securities should be valued at a substantially different level than the current price. These buy-low/sell-high funds rely on their ability to separate price and value. Intelligent use of cyclicals can be very profitable for these funds. In addition, securities which are temporarily depressed due to unfavorable news can prove to be excellent purchases under this philosophy. Turnarounds are also useful investment vehicles for them.

Trading funds place reliance on their ability to predict market trends and individual security prices. These funds follow the fashions of whatever is currently moving.

Short selling is an effective trading technique either to make money on a price decline or to take the market price risk out of an existing long position.

Leverage is any technique where a slight price increment creates a significantly greater change in values. Leverage can be accomplished by borrowing on the underlying equity, purchasing warrants, rights, or options, or selling options. In any case, leverage—to be successful—relies on the ability to predict prices on a given day in the future. Leverage also requires a firm understanding of the current interest rates inherent in these devices.

The list of fund characteristics is almost endless. In each category there are numerous gradations. With all of these different methods of characterizing investment companies, it is difficult to find two that are identical in all respects. Thus, comparisons of investment companies are fraught with some of the same dangers as comparisons of industrial companies.

ANALYZING INVESTMENT COMPANIES

The most efficient analysis of any set of facts is dependent upon the purpose involved. Investment companies are continuously analyzed by each of the following groups:

1. Potential investment company investors. (Which fund to buy?)
2. Competitive investment organizations. (How and what is the competition doing?)
3. Sales groups (What is selling? What performed well last?).
4. Management company investors. (Is the underlying asset base keeping up with expenses?)
5. Brokers and other suppliers. (How are my customers doing?)
6. Market analysts. (What is managed money doing?)
7. Academic. (Is the system efficient?)
8. Corporations. (Who is buying our stock? Who should manage the pension fund?)
9. Regulatory authorities. (What is happening?)

While each group will find a different factor of paramount importance to their analysis, the most searching probe should be by the potential investor. (As a practical matter, usually the individual investor is the least qualified person to make such an analysis on the over 650 investment companies that Lipper Analytical Services, Inc. follows regularly.) The techniques discussed below are primarily used to analyze investment companies for an initial investment or for continued holdings.

Key Ratios

Net Asset Value (NAV). The single most important derivative ratio in assessing an investment company is its NAV. This is derived by subtracting total liabilities from total assets and dividing by the number of shares outstanding. (Normally potential tax liabilities on unrealized gains are excluded from consideration in this equation. Also, any possible dilution from warrants or convertibles is not normally recognized.)

Premium/Discount. Premium is the increment over the NAV that the shares are selling for in the open market. Discount is the amount below the NAV at which a fund share is being sold. Premiums and discounts are usually expressed as a percentage from the net asset value. Under normal circumstances, the concept of premium/discount is associated only with closed-end funds. Usually closed-end funds lack enough continuous buying interest in their shares to prevent a significant discount from being created by normal selling patterns.

Performance. The change in net asset or unit value over a period of time is the basis for all performance studies. The purpose of this measurement is to help professional investors analyze comparative results of alternative investments. There are numerous methods of calculating performance. Essentially, the differences between these methods are caused by different approaches to realized gains, dividends, change in size of fund, and time considerations. The method that is used by most institutional investors is the reinvestment of all distributions, capital gains, and income into additional units of the fund similar to any change in cash flow. This is called a time-weighted total-return calculation. Other methods will produce slightly different short-term results which, over long periods, will show considerable distortions to the total-reinvestment or total-return method described.

Turnover Rate. This is calculated by taking aggregate purchase or sales (which ever is smaller) and dividing this amount into the average assets. (A separate calculation can be made for turnover rate of common stocks alone.) The result is usually expressed as an annual percentage. The average fund has a turnover rate of between 30 percent and 50 percent. Many funds which have good long-term results experience low turnover rates of 25 percent and below, whereas funds with high turnover rates have done poorly recently. (This may be a function of the growing illiquidity.) High turnover and poor decision is a very costly combination.

Net Sales/Redemptions. These are measured by the excess of open-end fund share sales or redemptions, usually expressed in dollars. Net sales/redemptions are important to investors in that they may force involuntary purchase or sale of portfolio holdings. At this point in time, there is no evidence that this phenomena hurts the residual investors if the fund's operational (back office) programs are sound. The factors which lead to sales are not the reverse of those that lead to redemptions so that the ratio of sales to redemptions does not measure similar needs except that both are expressed in dollars. Sales, for the most part, are caused by an image created by the fund itself or one of its sponsors. Redemptions are, more often than not, caused by the present need for cash which may have been anticipated at time of purchase. We believe, therefore, sales tend to be volatile, based on waves of images, and redemptions tend to follow actuarial needs. Current (1972–73) net redemptions are due primarily to the relative lack of sales power compared with earlier periods.

Unrealized Appreciation (losses). This is the theoretical difference between current prices of the portfolio and its historic cost. (No tax liability is calculated on the unrealized appreciation, as most investment companies in the United States choose to qualify under "subchapter M" of the Internal Revenue Code, which allows a pass-through of dividends for registered investment companies.)

Management Fee. Management fees are spelled out in the prospectus. They are usually related to asset size, but modifications can be made due to expenses, performance, and brokerage commission paid to an affiliate.

Fund Selection Guidelines

1. Determine first the *investor's needs* in light of the amount of risk the account can sustain, as well as the account objective (for example— growth, income, etc.). Equally important, the level of the investor's financial knowledge and emotional make-up will have a great deal to do with the successful selection of investment companies.

2. Determine financial objectives of the investment company. The prospectus will discuss these. Normally, however, the language will appear to be vague (for example, growth or growth with income, etc.). An analysis of the current portfolio (in the prospectus, annual report, or various portfolio analysis services) will reveal how the management has constructed a portfolio with their objective in mind. (This may be inconsistant with the objective as it is normally interpreted.)

3. If the financial needs of the investor and the objective of the investment company are similar (they will hardly be identical), one should attempt to quantify a mathematical investment goal. Examples of such goals can be any one or more of the following: a return equal to the market; a total return in excess of the savings bank rate; no more than one decline in the last five or ten years; twice any statistical measure on the upside with no more than the measure on the downside; a rating within the top 25 percent of all funds. While the measure is thought of in quantitative terms, it does not have to be precise.

4. Examine the record of the fund along with other funds of similar objectives. This will indicate to the investor the type of periods in the past when a particular investment style has acted well or poorly. Also, this analysis will identify the relative performance of the funds under review during these periods. In this connection, the size and objective report of the Lipper-Mutual Fund Performance Analysis may be useful to professional investors.

Size, under most circumstances, is not as important a determinant of performance as the stated investment objective. At times, size is important. This is particularly true at late stages of an extended move. The small fund can be more flexible than a large fund. Small funds can participate in issues with less liquidity than the larger funds can. Unfortunately, the small funds often get trapped into issues which prove too volatile and illiquid even for them. Another point to consider is that a small open-end fund with a long term mediocre record may not be geared for growth of assets under management and any surge of volume can thus prove costly to the shareholder not only in terms of expenses but also in terms of the quality of the administration.

5. If the fund's objective and record is suitable, the investor himself or his agent must then determine whether the *key elements* which created the record (for example, personnel, market environment, commission generation, capability, etc.) are *still present*.

6. An investor may find it wise to inquire as to the *financial health of the management company* and what it's sources of income are. This will have a lot to do with the amount of time and priority of senior management's effort which were given to the fund.

7. Assuming a purchase is made, the difficult task now begins—*monitoring the investment*. The same procedure should be followed as outlined in step 4. If the fund is holding or improving its position relative to similar funds, one should be encouraged. If the group is not doing well, one should determine whether the investor still believes in the appropriateness of the philosophy. If he does, he should stay with the fund.

Though inherently less volatile than individual securities, funds are subject to both market and specific portfolio risk. As with common stocks, there have been a number of attempts to quantify risk. One which gained considerable notoriety is Beta, a further discussion on this subject is found in Volume I, Chapter 44. While the concept is hardly new, it has cost its adherents substantial sums and opportunities in their search for an acceptable rationalization for poor performance ("I took less risk and therefore performed less; but if you adjust for risk, I did better."). Beta measures volatility (the ratio of price change versus an index of the market over some designated period of time). While these ratios remain relatively constant during certain periods, they do change from time to time as stocks get revalued relative to each other.

SOURCES OF INFORMATION

Readers have already seen that the investment company industry is multifaceted. Therefore, there are many different approaches to the analysis of the industry. Sources of information on the industry are numerous and incomplete. Listed below are the more important sources and the areas where they can be most useful:

Individual Funds

Prospectus
Annual Report to Shareholders
Interim Reports to Shareholders
N–1R (Annual Report to Securities and Exchange Commission)[5]

---

[5] Available on microfiche from Disclosure, Inc., subsidiary of Reliance Financial Services Corp.

N–1Q (Calendar Quarterly Report to Securities and Exchange Commission with portfolios as of the end of the quarter)[6]

Industry Data

Investment Company Institute
Washington, D.C.
Mutual Fund Factbook (size and composition of the industry; monthly sales and redemption data.)

Portfolio Holdings

Vickers Associates
Huntington, New York

Computer Direction Advisers
Silver Springs, Maryland

Performance Data

Lipper Analytical Services, Inc.
Westfield, New Jersey
(Performance data on open-end, closed-end, and dual-purpose funds, and variable annuities. Available only to professional investors and their advisors.)

Wisenberger Services, Inc.
New York, New York
(Performance and other data for investment dealers.)

United Business Service
Boston, Massachusetts
(Performance data and advice for the public.)

Both Barron's and Forbes have extensive coverage of investment companies. Each publishes long-term data periodically.

The different reporting services use different methods of calculation based on their use and the nature of their subscribers (for example, Lipper data reinvests all distributions, where a number of the others either add-back distributions or reinvest only a portion of these dividends).

---

[6] Available on microfiche from Disclosure, Inc., subsidiary of Reliance Financial Services Corp.

19

Lodging

DENNIS H. LEIBOWITZ
Partner
Coleman and Company, New York, New York

THE lodging industry in 1973 was approximately an $8 billion industry, which represented about 15 percent of total tourism in the United States. The industry has evolved into two segments—hotels and motels, and a hybrid of the two, the motor hotel.

The motel-motor hotel sector, which is now the larger of the two, is a relatively recent phenomenon which began in the 1950s and developed with the interstate highway system and growth in pleasure travel by automobile. Motel growth also reflected the shift in population and business activity to the suburbs and the deterioration of downtown urban areas.

The great growth in the motel sector's share of the total industry was also spurred by a much lower room rate than at the downtown hotels. Room rates are initially a function of the cost of building a property; hence, lower cost suburban and highway locations were less expensive, and services were less extensive. In the last few years a "budget" motel industry has developed. A budget property is generally defined as one whose room rates start at $10 or less for a single room. The development of this segment of the industry closely parallels that of the original motel industry in that its raison d'être is the price differential offered, and the lower price reflects location and services. In the last decade, inflationary room rate increases at conventional motels and motor hotels provided enough of a spread to allow builders of budget properties to blossom by offering fairly simple, but modern, accommodations.

In Table 1 we have presented historical data on the size and growth

489

TABLE 1

Lodging Industry Growth

Year	Occupied Rooms per Day	Percent Change	Rooms	Percent Change	Occupancy Ratio	Gross Annual Income ('000)	Percent Change
Hotels:							
1973	749,000	+2.7	1,270,000	+0.4	59.0	$4,350,000	+5.5
1972	729,400	+3.3	1,265,000	+0.4	57.7	4,125,000	+4.0
1971	706,000	−3.8	1,260,000	−0.4	56.0	3,965,000	−0.9
1970	734,000	−6.5	1,265,000	−0.1	58.0	4,002,000	−1.5
1969	785,000	+0.1	1,266,000	+0.5	62.0	4,063,000	+4.3
1968	784,000	−0.5	1,260,000	−0.5	62.2	3,897,000	+1.9
1967	788,000	−1.6	1,266,500	−0.4	62.2	3,823,000	+5.4
1966	801,000	+1.4	1,271,800	−0.2	63.0	3,628,000	+4.5
1965	790,000	−0.2	1,274,280	−0.2	62.0	3,472,000	+2.4
1964	791,600	+1.5	1,276,800	−0.2	62.0	3,389,000	+12.8
1963	780,181	−4.7	1,279,800	−3.1	61.0	3,005,692	+1.0
1962	818,760	−6.6	1,320,580	−3.6	62.0	2,977,214	+0.5
1961	877,040	−5.0	1,370,370	−3.5	64.0	2,962,678	−1.2
1960	923,100	−6.3	1,420,150	−3.4	65.0	2,998,630	+1.1
1958	1,018,210	—	1,519,716	—	67.0	2,794,015	—
1948	1,317,354	—	1,549,823	—	85.0	2,172,756	—
Motels:							
1973	953,700	+5.3	1,445,000	+2.1	66.0	3,810,000	+7.2
1972	905,600	+7.0	1,415,000	+3.7	64.0	3,555,000	+7.7
1971	846,000	−0.6	1,365,000	+1.5	62.0	3,300,000	+2.7
1970	851,000	−3.3	1,345,000	+1.7	63.3	3,212,000	+0.8
1969	880,000	+4.1	1,323,000	+3.8	66.5	3,187,000	+9.3
1968	845,000	+3.3	1,275,000	+3.3	66.3	2,915,000	+7.6
1967	818,000	+2.3	1,234,000	+1.8	66.3	2,710,000	+2.7
1966	800,000	+4.7	1,212,000	+3.1	66.0	2,639,000	+22.9
1965	764,000	+3.2	1,175,700	+3.1	65.0	2,147,000	+9.1
1964	740,600	+4.5	1,139,400	+3.0	65.0	1,968,000	+18.5
1963	708,449	−0.1	1,106,130	+1.3	64.0	1,661,371	+1.4
1962	709,400	+11.4	1,091,450	+14.8	65.0	1,638,300	+16.2
1961	636,700	+10.5	950,350	+12.2	67.0	1,409,800	+12.8
1960	576,000	+16.4	847,120	+19.8	68.0	1,249,500	+21.3
1958	419,343	—	599,061	—	70.0	850,381	—
1948	258,315	—	303,900	—	85.0	195,505	—
Total industry:							
1973	1,702,700	+4.1	2,715,000	+1.3	62.7	8,160,000	+6.3
1972	1,635,000	+5.3	2,680,000	+2.1	61.0	7,680,000	+5.7
1971	1,552,000	−2.1	2,625,000	+0.6	59.1	7,265,000	+0.7
1970	1,585,000	−4.8	2,610,000	+0.8	60.7	7,214,000	−0.5
1969	1,665,000	+2.2	2,589,000	+2.1	64.3	7,250,000	+6.4
1968	1,629,000	+1.4	2,535,000	+1.4	64.2	6,812,000	+4.3
1967	1,606,000	+0.3	2,500,500	+0.7	64.2	6,533,000	+4.2
1966	1,601,000	+3.0	2,483,800	+1.4	64.5	6,267,000	+11.5
1965	1,554,000	+1.4	2,449,980	+1.4	63.4	5,619,000	+4.9
1964	1,532,200	+2.9	2,416,200	+1.3	63.4	5,357,000	+14.8
1963	1,488,630	−2.6	2,385,930	−1.1	62.4	4,667,063	+1.1
1962	1,528,160	+1.0	2,412,030	+3.9	63.4	4,615,514	+5.6
1961	1,513,740	+1.0	2,320,720	+2.4	65.2	4,372,478	+2.9
1960	1,499,100	+1.3	2,267,270	+4.2	66.1	4,248,130	+6.3
1958	1,437,553	—	2,118,777	—	68.0	3,644,396	—
1948	1,575,669	—	1,853,723	—	85.0	2,368,261	—

Source: Harris, Kerr Forster & Co., *Trends in the Hotel-Motel Business 1974* (based on U.S. Census Bureau statistics).

of the industry. Here, the change in share between the hotel and motel sectors can be quite clearly seen. In addition to the factors already mentioned, the advent of jet aircraft in the late 1950s and early 1960s also hurt the hotel industry. Increased speed of travel because of jets allowed businessmen to travel to and from many destinations within a day and no longer required overnight accommodations. The length of stay by others who continued to use commercial facilities was also cut shorter; hence, during this period the negative trends in the hotel sector were exaggerated since most air travelers were hotel patrons, rather than motel users. As can also be seen in the table, the disparity in results between the sectors has narrowed somewhat in recent years.

Ownership Patterns

Hotels and motels are either independently owned and operated, or controlled by chains. Chain ownership offers significant advantages, among them the usual benefits of pooled resources in attracting financing at reasonable rates, quantity discounts because of block purchasing power, the ability to compete for top management, and, most importantly in this industry, the necessary marketing resources. Reservation systems, group-meeting sales capacity, and advertising are among the most important competitive tools in the industry, and only chains normally have the necessary financial resources to offer them.

Table 2 gives some data from the American Hotel and Motel Association as to chain ownership of the industry. Because the data is on a June fiscal year basis, we have averaged the years to approximate the calendar year bases on which data for the entire industry in Table 1 is presented.

The tables indicate that the chains control about one third of all rooms today; that their expansion rate is considerably faster than that of the industry; and that the number of independent rooms is declining.

An important determinant of construction of rooms is the availability of money. The slowdown in overall growth by chains in 1970–1971 reflected the tight money conditions of 1969, given the lag involved, since it takes anywhere from one to three years from the conception to the opening of a property. It appears that the 1970–1971 recession caused an increase in closings as well, a pattern that is fairly evident in past economic cycles also. This resulted in the small net growth seen in 1970–1971.

Within the chain category, there are three basic ownership techniques: The first is complete ownership of units by the chain; the second is the franchise method; and the third is the management contract. Franchising offers the individual investor the ability to own his own property, while at the same time taking advantage of the characteristics and advantages of chain ownership. Normally, a franchisee will pay an initial deposit to a chain and a continuing royalty, which is a percentage of sales. For these fees and royalties, he is given assistance by professionals of the chain in

TABLE 2
Domestic Hotel and Motel Room Ownership, 1969–1973

Year	Total Rooms	Percent Change	Chain Rooms	Average Chain Rooms	Percent Change	All Other Rooms	Percent Change	Average Chain Rooms as a Percent of Total Industry
1973	2,715,000	+1.3	824,810	789,532	+8.1	1,890,468	−0.2	29.5
1972	2,680,000	+2.1	754,254	730,252	+5.8	1,894,748	−1.3	27.8
1971	2,625,000	+0.5	706,249	690,147	+8.0	1,919,853	−3.3	26.4
1970	2,610,000	+0.8	674,044	638,786	+8.8	1,985,472	−1.9	24.7
1969	2,589,000	+2.1	603,528	587,160	—	1,947,840	—	23.5
1968	2,535,000	+1.4	570,791					

Estimated.

site selection, training, procurement, etc. This system gives him the competitive advantage of the chain's brand identification, reservation systems, and other services. From the chain's viewpoint, the franchise method allows more rapid growth than would otherwise be possible, because the investment in developing the system is shared. Rapid development, in turn, aids the chain's own properties by virtue of the referral business generated within the system. Further, the royalties are an important source of income. Ideally, the consumer will come to expect and be attracted by the consistency of service within the chain and will not be aware of whether a property is owned by the parent company or a franchisee.

As the chains have become established, many have begun to buy back franchisees as a means of supplementing growth. While the profit margin on royalties is quite high, the absolute profit dollars from ownership are higher. From the franchisee's standpoint, ownership of a hotel or motel carries with it certain tax advantages due to accelerated depreciation and initial start-up losses, and after a certain number of years, when these attractions are less valid, he may be interested in selling his unit to the parent company and realizing a capital gain as a result of the profitability he has built up over the years.

The management contract is similar to a franchise, except that the chain actually manages the property. For the same reasons that a franchisee, whose background is not normally in the lodging business, seeks professional assistance and a brand name, many hotel-motel developers who wish to profit from ownership but do not wish to actively operate the unit often contract with the major chains to have the latter run the property. The chain is paid a percentage of sales, or a percentage of profits, or a combination of both. As the chains have expanded outside the United States in recent years, the management contract has become more prevalent, particularly where the political climate is unreliable. Since the chains will generally manage only large properties where their income from management is meaningful, the management contract method is almost exclusively used in hotels.

The management contract has also become more prevalent domestically in recent years. The reason is that escalating costs of construction have made it unattractive for the publicly held chains to develop in many downtown locations. Whereas initial start-up costs and heavy depreciation may be an inducement to an individual or private company whose interests are in maximizing cash flow, a chain is interested in reportable earnings and cannot undertake projects which initially will have a significant detrimental effect on those results.

Construction Costs and Financing of a Hotel and Motel

The major cost elements in a hotel or motel are land, building, and furnishings and equipment. For a conventional motel, costs may total

$15,000–$17,000 a room, consisting of $2,000 a room for land, $3,000 for furnishings and equipment, and $10,000–$12,000 for the building.

Hotels are significantly more expensive to build because they are normally downtown, where land is most expensive, and have extensive convention facilities. Costs vary considerably in different parts of the country, ranging from perhaps $25,000 a room in a medium-sized southern city to as high as $60,000 a room in New York City, where land values and union rates are much higher.

A motor hotel, with more extensive facilities than a motel, may cost $20,000–$25,000 a room; while at the other end of the spectrum, budget motels can be built for as little as $8,000–$12,000 a room. The lower costs reflect far less elaborate facilities, and in many cases the fact that the unit does not include a restaurant. Some budget motels are also of modular construction.

Financing Methods

Hotels and motels are normally either fully owned, or leased, or the land may be leased and the building owned, etc. The pros and cons of ownership versus leasing are common to many industries. Under the ownership method, the developer has an asset which may be of growing value if the property is successful. Further, depreciation and interest, while higher in the initial years, is lower over the life of the property than rentals would be.

Normally, rental agreements require a minimum rent versus a percentage of sales, whichever is higher. Therefore, in a successful property, part of the gain in sales is paid to the landlord in the form of rent. Under full ownership, not only is this not true, but depreciation declines in later years and the mortgage is eventually paid off.

Motels are financed by construction loans initially, and then by long-term mortgages upon completion. The mortgage is usually secured by the individual property and may represent 60–70 percent of the total cost, with the balance consisting of the owner's equity.

In a rental, the return on equity is obviously very high versus an ownership, and the capital required for expansion is substantially less, which permits more rapid development. This is the trade-off involved in giving up equity in the asset value.

Factors Affecting Growth

In relating lodging demand patterns to the economy, we find that the variable to which occupancy most closely relates is industrial production; that the next most important determinant is corporate profits; and that consumer disposable income shows little correlation. The reason is that the industry's marketing has always been heavily oriented to the business traveler, a readily identifiable and more locatable customer than the pleasure traveler. Yet the pleasure travel market is considerably larger than the business market, and it has been growing faster. We believe the business orientation marketing of the industry is the basic reason why long-term growth has been relatively slow, even though leisure time and disposable income have been rising.

Table 3 gives some data taken from "The Commercial Lodging Market," published in 1967 by Michigan State University, which illustrates the nature of the lodging customer and his travel patterns.

TABLE 3

Profile of the Lodging Industry

Purpose of Travel by Type of Establishment:

	Convention	Business	Total Business	Pleasure	Personal	Total Nonbusiness
Hotels	17.7%	51.8%	69.5%	27.7%	1.7%	29.4%
Motels	5.3	55.8	61.1	33.8	4.0	37.8

Choice between Hotels and Motels by Purpose of Trip:

	Hotel	Motel
Convention	67.0%	33.0%
Business	36.0	64.0
Mainly business	33.0	67.0
Pleasure	33.0	67.0
Mainly pleasure	31.7	68.3
Personal	20.5%	79.5%

Note: Percentages do not add up due to rounding and nonresponse.

As one can see, hotels are more dependent on the business market than motels. However, even the motel sector still derived 61 percent of its clientele from the business market. Since 1967 when the report was written, however, pleasure travel has probably grown faster than business travel, and the percentage of pleasure travel guests is thus somewhat higher.

Table 4 looks at the total travel market and puts the lodging industry's potential market into perspective.

Table 4 shows that the business market is only 16.1 percent of the total tourism market. It can also be seen that the largest element of pleasure travel is the friends and relatives category, and that such travelers generally do not use commercial facilities. The category "In Own Cabin" includes second homes and recreational vehicles, and the competitive impact from these markets is evident.

In recent years several of the chains have more aggressively begun to market to the pleasure traveler. One method has been the "weekend escape package" where discount package rates are offered people in a local community to use nearby hotels and motels for a mini-vacation,

TABLE 4

Choice of Accommodations by Purpose of Trip (shown by percent)

	Purpose of Trip (percent of all trips)	Number of Person-Nights Spent			
		In Commercial Establishments	With Friends or Relatives	In Own Cabin	In Other Accommodations
Visit friends and relatives.......	40.7	10.2	86.0	2.6	1.2
Business and conventions......................	16.1	72.6	14.2	6.1	7.1
Outdoor recreation............	12.3	31.9	10.6	44.3	13.2
Sightseeing and entertainment...................	14.9	65.6	12.4	15.0	7.0
Other........................	15.8	27.9	43.6	21.9	6.6

Source: *"Travel During 1972,"* National Travel Survey, U.S. Department of Commerce. All data are on trips of over 100 miles, one way.

at the time of week when business travel is lowest. Also, hotels, in conjunction with airlines and car-rental companies, have developed combination fly/drive packages at discount rates. Firms have also begun to develop the rapidly growing foreign tourist market.

Supply Conditions

As was seen in Table 1, the net growth in rooms in the lodging industry has been entirely in the motel side. In Table 2 we showed that the chains were growing faster than the industry and represented about 30 percent of total rooms, and that independent units were closing.

On closer inspection, however, it appears that the major chains actually control a much larger portion of the motel market than of the total industry, and this has been a major factor behind their rapid growth within a slow-growth industry.

In Table 5 we have presented the motel industry in terms of competitive and noncompetitive rooms. We have assumed that the definition given motor hotels below encompasses all units that the major chains own or would be competing with because, by deduction, the "other" motels are very small, probably seasonal, units with limited services. In 1971, there were 7,430 motor hotels which comprised the 803,734 rooms, meaning the average size was 108.2 rooms. There were 43,300 motel rooms in the other category, averaging out to 15.6 rooms.

Since we saw previously that in the overall industry independents are closing on balance, while chains are expanding, it appears that most of the closings in the motel sector are of units that are not in the competitive market for the chains. By our count, in allocating the chains' rooms between those that could be classified as motels or motor hotels rather than hotels, the top 15 chains alone had 422,000 motel-motor hotel rooms

TABLE 5

Motel Industry Rooms

Year	Motor Hotels	Percent Change	Other Motels	Percent Change	Motor Hotel Rooms Percent of Total Motel-Motor Hotel Rooms
1971	803,734	+ 8.3	561,266	−6.9	58.9
1970	742,307	+ 8.7	602,693	−5.9	55.2
1969	682,745	+11.9	640,255	−3.7	51.6
1968	610,023	+10.1	664,977	−2.2	47.8
1967	554,037	+13.9	679,963	−6.3	44.9
1966	486,226	+12.9	725,774	−2.5	40.1
1965	430,679	—	744,321	—	36.7

Source: *Census of the U.S. Motor Hotel Industry*, Hospitality Division, Helmsley-Spear, Inc. A motor hotel is defined as a property with transient lodging facilities, built or completely modernized since 1945, open more than half the year, and containing at least 50 units plus adequate free parking. Alaska and Hawaii excluded.

in calendar 1971, which was 52 percent of the competitive market that year. Considering the top chains probably have above-average occupancy and room rates, they undoubtedly control more than 52 percent of revenues and occupancies in the competitive market. Since 1971, chain expansion has accelerated, indicating that the share has risen even further. Since publicly held lodging companies are chains, the supply situation must be viewed closely in determining growth prospects. Increased market share, along with price increases, has been a major element in the growth of the public companies.

Price Characteristics

Despite increased competition in the lodging industry, prices have rapidly accelerated, rather than declined. There are two basic reasons for this seeming disparity. First, prices reflect the cost of building more than anything else, and increases in construction costs and interest rates caused them to go up. Cost increases also reflected the expansion of services offered, particularly in the motel end. Secondly, since the business traveler is the primary customer, and he is normally on expense account, elasticity to price changes has historically been relatively low. Even in the pleasure markets elasticity is less than one would think because the industry's customer has been relatively concentrated demographically in the higher income brackets. Consequently, when new units opened at high rates, old units lifted prices, and a good portion of the industry's earnings growth in the 1960s reflected rate increases which were greater than cost increases.

By the 1970 recession, resistance was beginning to set in, and this is one of the factors that created the atmosphere which allowed the development of the budget industry. Because we believe the broader aspects of the pleasure travel market are the real growth opportunity in the years ahead, we feel that price will become a far more important factor competitively than in the past. This is an important aspect of the industry's potential which may be in a transition stage and must be monitored for its effect on the public companies.

Operating Characteristics of Hotels and Motels

We have touched briefly on construction costs and financing methods. In Table 6 we have presented data on the revenue and expense characteristics of hotels and motels.

The higher operating profit margins at motels reflects the higher occupancy level and the higher percentage of total sales and income represented by room revenues. Departmental margins (sales less direct costs) on rooms were 70.6 percent for hotels, 73.1 percent for motels and motor hotels with restaurants, and 75.9 percent for motels and motor hotels without restaurants; while departmental profit margins on food and beverage revenues were only 15.7 percent for hotels and 18.7 percent for motels and motor hotels with restaurants at the time of this report. The disparity in margins reflects the relatively fixed cost nature of labor versus the variable cost of food and beverage. One can also see from the table that most of the other cost items are of a relatively fixed nature. This would include depreciation, interest, and rent, which are not separately shown. As a rule of thumb, it is estimated that the flow through to profits of incremental room revenues is about 80 percent, while on food and beverage sales it is about 30 percent. Therefore, one can see that the leverage of a hotel or motel from higher or lower occupancy and/or higher or lower room rates is quite high.

Because the nature of financing can result in wide disparities in results at the pretax level, comparisons of hotels or companies are normally made at the profit-before-other-capital-expenses level. However, as mentioned earlier, the lower the ratio of food and beverage to room revenues, the higher the overall profit ratio, because the departmental margin on room revenues is significantly greater. Since the restaurant department is another profit source for a hotel, two other refinements need to be made for comparative purposes. First, one should look at the ratio of food and beverage revenues to room sales to determine how effective management is in developing profits from the former. While the ratio will be much higher at hotels because of their banquet and more elaborate restaurant facilities, the comparison of the ratios of various hotels and motels indicates how successful this profit center has been developed within similar properties.

The other comparative tool is departmental margins. In looking at margins on this level, one can better compare more dissimilar properties

TABLE 6

Lodging Industry Percentage Cost Analysis

	All Transient Hotels	All Motels and Motor Hotels with Restaurants	All Motels and Motor Hotels without Restaurants
Total sales and income:			
Rooms	54.7	59.5	94.5
Food and beverage	40.5	36.7	
Telephone	2.6	2.8	4.1
Other departmental profit	.5	.1	.1
Other income	1.7	.9	1.3
Total	100.0	100.0	100.0
Cost of goods sold and departmental wages and expenses:			
Rooms	16.1	16.0	22.8
Food and beverage	34.3	29.9	
Telephone	3.8	4.0	5.9
Total	54.2	49.9	28.7
Gross operating income	45.8	50.1	71.3
Deductions from income:			
Administrative and general expenses	7.6	8.1	11.2
Management fees	1.7	1.2	2.3
Advertising and sales promotion	3.7	3.3	3.6
Heat, light, and power	5.0	4.2	6.1
Repairs and maintenance	5.3	4.0	5.0
Total	23.3	20.8	28.2
House profit	22.5	29.3	43.1
Store rentals	1.3	.5	2.8
Gross operating profit	23.8	29.8	46.9
Fire insurance and franchise taxes	.7	.6	1.1
Profit before real estate taxes and other capital expenses	23.1	29.2	45.8
Real estate taxes	5.5	4.1	6.6
Profit before other capital expenses	17.6	25.1	39.2
Percentage of occupancy	62.1	70.6	68.2
Average rate per room per day	$21.13	$17.12	$16.21
Average daily room rate per guest	$15.81	$11.65	$11.47
Number of guests per occupied room	1.34	1.47	1.41
Times real estate taxes earned	4.2	7.2	6.9
Average size (rooms)	438	175	113

Source: Harris, Kerr, Forster, & Co., *Trends in the Hotel-Motel Business 1973.*

and eliminate the bias in overall profit margins caused by a higher percentage of room revenues to total revenues—which, in itself, is not a measure of success.

Accounting Considerations

Accounting at individual properties is relatively standardized, but there are certain adjustments that an analyst needs to make. The major one is in the accounting treatment of preopening and start-up costs. The items involved here include interest on construction loans, allocation of corporate development overhead, and initial operating losses.

Interest on construction loans is usually capitalized as part of the total cost of the unit and amortized over its depreciable life. All other start-up costs, if capitalized, are normally amortized over a much shorter period, normally two to five years. This period theoretically matches the time it usually takes for a unit to reach its mature occupancy level. In some cases, losses incurred in the initial operation of the hotel are included in the figure to be capitalized. More often, only costs incurred prior to opening are counted.

There are differences in depreciation, but they relate more to the length of time a building and equipment are written off, rather than the method of depreciation. From an earnings standpoint, it is to the public company's advantage to use straight-line depreciation for reporting purposes, although accelerated methods are often used for tax purposes. Similarly, preopening or initial losses, which may be capitalized for book purposes, are often expensed for tax purposes. Depreciation lives vary mostly by virtue of differences in the nature of a property. For instance, a downtown hotel will be depreciated over a longer period of time than a budget motel.

One other accounting tool can be used to equate companies which have different ownership arrangements. This is to capitalize the value of lease commitments and discount the value of these leases to the present. By doing this, one can equate leases with assets under the ownership method. Depreciation and interest can be computed on the asset value derived, and results of lessees can then be compared with companies which own properties. The accounting profession has suggested requiring companies to do this, and it may become mandatory for "financing" leases. While hotel-motel leases are often not truly "financing" leases in the sense that companies do not own the property at the end of the lease, the definition could be stretched to say that they "own" the property for its full useful life, if the length of the lease is coincident with actual life or is constantly renewable. Normally, companies which lease units are now required to show minimum lease commitments in footnotes to their balance sheets, so that comparisons with companies which own their own properties can be made.

An Illustration of Hotel-Motel Profits under Various Assumptions

In the first two columns of Table 7, we have used the operating characteristics of hotels and motels in Table 6 to represent a typical property. As one can see, a hotel at current building costs would be unprofitable at the occupancy and room rates given for the industry, and a motel would be only marginally profitable. (See page 502.)

As a rule of thumb, the industry calculates that room rates should average 1/1000 of the building cost per room. In other words, with $35,000 a room construction costs, a hotel today would normally have to average a $35 rate or higher. Even where we have used such a rate in the second part of the table, however, the profitability in terms of return on sales and investment is very low, given the 62.1 percent occupancy level. This is one of the major reasons why there has been so little hotel construction in recent years, and a good deal of growth in the hotel sector by the large chains has been via the management contract route, where fees are on a profit before capital costs basis, or on sales.

In the table one can also see that because of the application of percentage rentals, ownership is more profitable than leasing when occupancy and rate levels are high.

The increased profit ratio before capital costs on higher occupancy and rates reflects the high flow-through to earnings of additional revenues because of the fixed-cost nature of the business. This table actually understates results because depreciation and interest are given at rates in the first year, and these charges would decline over a period of time.

In order to demonstrate the effects of rates, occupancy, and leverage, we have held certain items stable—things like the food and beverage ratio and, as mentioned previously, depreciation and interest. Rent and interest assumptions in the table are based on money market conditions in 1974 but can, of course, be altered to gauge the impact on profits and returns given different assumptions. Depreciation is on a composite basis on buildings and equipment costs, and can also be changed, depending on depreciation and financing policies, etc.

Market Behavior of Securities

In the early 1960s lodging securities sold at very low P/E multiples. For one thing, the hotel sector had gone through a period of overbuilding in the late 1950s, which, when combined with the previously mentioned growth in the motel sector and the impact of jet travel, resulted in a generally poor earnings record in those years. The availability of investment vehicles in the motel sector was somewhat limited, and the companies were still relatively young. On balance, shares in the hotel group sold at five to ten times earnings.

In 1967, there was a clear turn in investor sentiment as it became evident that the hotel sector had begun to turn around, and there was a greater availability of stock on the motel side, which had been experiencing rapid growth. At the same time, the prospects for growing leisure time and disposable income convinced investors that travel was an attractive growth industry, and hotels and motels, particularly the latter, were a way to play this growth. Multiples shot up to an average of 30 times earnings for the major lodging chains, with higher P/Es

TABLE 7
Operating Characteristics of Hotels and Motels

	Standard		Change in Rate		Change in Rate and Occupancy	
	Hotel	Motel	Hotel	Motel	Hotel	Motel
Building cost:						
Number of rooms	500	150				
Total cost per room	$ 35,000	$ 17,000				
Total cost	$17,500,000	$2,550,000				
Financing:						
Own: Mtge. on 70 percent;	12,250,000	1,785,000				
Equity of 30 percent;	5,250,000	765,000				
or						
Lease: Rent at 9 percent of cost	1,575,000	$ 229,500				
versus 20 percent sales	—	—				
Occupancy (percent):	62.1	70.6			75.0%	80.0%
Average room rate	$21.00	$17.00	$35.00	$20.00	$35.00	$20.00
Food, Beverage, and other/room sales (percent)	82.8	68.1				
Sales:						
Rooms	$ 2,380,000	$ 657,100	$3,966,375	$ 773,100	$4,790,625	$ 876,000
Food, Beverage, other	1,970,000	447,500	3,284,375	526,450	3,966,375	596,600
Total	$ 4,350,000	$1,104,600	$7,250,750	$1,299,550	$8,757,000	$1,472,600
Profit ratio before capital costs (percent)	17.6	25.1	25.0	30.0	30.0	35.0
Profit before capital costs	$ 765,600	$ 277,250	$1,812,700	$ 389,865	$2,627,100	$ 515,410
Capital costs:						
Own: Depreciation at 3.5 percent of cost;	$ 612,500	$ 89,250				
Interest at 8.5 percent	1,041,250	151,725				
Total	$ 1,653,750	$ 240,975				
Lease: rental	1,575,000	255,000		260,000	1,751,400	294,520
Pretax profit (loss):						
Owned	(888,150)	$ 36,275	$ 158,950	$ 148,890	$ 973,350	$ 274,435
Leased	(809,400)	$ 47,750	$ 237,700	$ 129,865	$ 875,700	$ 220,910
Pretax return on equity, if owned (percent)	—	4.74	3.0	19.5	18.5	35.9

accorded the motel companies, and with P/Es within both sectors dependent upon the amount of relative expansion rates.

In 1970, the group declined substantially, in line with the market. Stocks then rallied until 1973, when the energy crisis hit, but never got back to previous high levels.

The actual occupancy decline in 1970–1971 was the sharpest since the depression, and the reason the stocks never fully recovered was that this began to erode the basic growth concept on which the group had sold since 1967. As investors more carefully inspected the industry to determine why the occupancy drop should be so much more severe than in previous declines, some of the factors we have discussed became more apparent.

First, the only economic variable which would have predicted the severity of the recession on the lodging industry was industrial production. More investors began to realize that while the growth forecast for the pleasure travel industry did materialize, the lodging industry didn't get its share because its marketing was basically confined to the business market.

Secondly, with the earnings impact of the recession aggravated by price control limits, more investors looked back and realized how much past growth had come from inflationary price increases.

Probably most importantly, more investors began to realize that there was a limit to the chains' ability to capture increased market share in a stagnant market, once it became more clear how much of the "competitive" market they already controlled.

Finally, the growth in motel rooms was seen in proper perspective, and the acceleration in net rooms added after 1971 began to alarm investors about the threat of overbuilding.

When the energy crisis hit, it was a catalyst that shook apart the group because of the accumulated fears just discussed. P/E multiples went to their lowest levels since the early 1960s.

We have no doubt that growth in travel will resume, and we believe a shakeout will occur in the industry, reversing the building cycle. However, it also appears that growth from conventional markets is cyclical and that to return to the old P/E levels requires the development of new markets to supplement growth from conventional sources. Once this occurs, some new P/E level is likely to emerge somewhere between the old lows and the old highs.

20

Machinery

DAVID C. SUTLIFF, C.F.A.
Vice President
E. F. Hutton & Company, Inc.
New York, New York

STRUCTURE AND SCOPE OF THE MACHINERY INDUSTRY

THE MACHINERY INDUSTRY is a large and highly diverse field. Products in this market range in size from small power tools costing only a few dollars to huge earth-moving machines selling for several hundred thousand dollars. Virtually all forms of business utilizes machines of one type or another, although the principal market is with manufacturing firms. The main purpose for the purchase of machines is to improve the productivity of labor by substituting mechanical devices for manual operations. Generally speaking, machinery purchases involve an expenditure which will be capitalized on the books of the user and depreciated over the useful life of the machine. Machinery expenditures are principally a function of industry's production capacity requirements, which mirror economic conditions, and hence outlays are highly cyclical. Other major factors which bear on the level of capital expenditures are the availability and cost of labor, the availability and cost of money, government policies, and technological developments.

Capital expenditures by all businesses for new plants and equipment totaled $88.5 billion in 1972, up 9 percent from the year before. Outlays for plants and equipment in 1972 constituted 7.7 percent of total gross national product, or about the same relationship that prevailed over the preceeding 20 years. Manufacturing firms account for 35.1 percent of the 1972 expenditures, commercial and other firms made up 22.8 percent, and public utilities 19.3 percent. The most rapid growth of capital ex-

504

TABLE 1

Business Expenditures for New Plant and Equipment, 1947–73* (billions of dollars)

Year or Quarter	Total	Manufacturing			Mining	Transportation			Public Utilities	Communication	Commercial and Other†
		Total	Durable Goods	Nondurable Goods		Railroad	Air	Other			
1947	19.33	8.44	3.25	5.19	0.69	0.91	0.17	1.13	1.54	1.40	5.05
1948	21.30	9.01	3.30	5.71	.93	1.37	.10	1.17	2.54	1.74	4.42
1949	18.98	7.12	2.45	4.68	.88	1.42	.12	.76	3.10	1.34	4.24
1950	20.21	7.39	2.94	4.45	.84	1.18	.10	1.09	3.24	1.14	5.22
1951	25.46	10.71	4.82	5.89	1.11	1.58	.14	1.33	3.56	1.37	5.67
1952	26.43	11.45	5.21	6.24	1.21	1.50	.24	1.23	3.74	1.61	5.45
1953	28.20	11.86	5.31	6.56	1.25	1.42	.24	1.29	4.34	1.78	6.02
1954	27.19	11.24	4.91	6.33	1.28	.93	.24	1.22	3.99	1.82	6.45
1955	29.53	11.89	5.41	6.48	1.31	1.02	.26	1.30	4.03	2.11	7.63
1956	35.73	15.40	7.45	7.95	1.64	1.37	.35	1.31	4.52	2.82	8.32
1957	37.94	16.51	7.84	8.68	1.69	1.58	.41	1.30	5.67	3.19	7.60
1958	31.89	12.38	5.61	6.77	1.43	.86	.37	1.06	5.52	2.79	7.48
1959	33.55	12.77	5.81	6.95	1.36	1.02	.78	1.33	5.14	2.72	8.44
1960	36.75	15.09	7.23	7.85	1.30	1.16	.66	1.30	5.24	3.24	8.75
1961	35.91	14.33	6.31	8.02	1.29	.82	.73	1.23	5.00	3.39	9.13
1962	38.39	15.06	6.79	8.26	1.40	1.02	.52	1.65	4.90	3.85	9.99
1963	40.77	16.22	7.53	8.70	1.27	1.26	.40	1.58	4.98	4.06	10.99
1964	46.97	19.34	9.28	10.07	1.34	1.66	1.02	1.50	5.49	4.61	12.02
1965	54.42	23.44	11.50	11.94	1.46	1.99	1.22	1.68	6.13	5.30	13.19
1966	63.51	28.20	14.06	14.14	1.62	2.37	1.74	1.64	7.43	6.02	14.48
1967	65.47	28.51	14.06	14.45	1.65	1.86	2.29	1.48	8.74	6.34	14.59
1968	67.76	28.37	14.12	14.25	1.63	1.45	2.56	1.59	10.20	6.83	15.14
1969	75.56	31.68	15.96	15.72	1.86	1.86	2.51	1.68	11.61	8.30	16.05
1970	79.71	31.95	15.80	16.15	1.89	1.78	3.03	1.23	13.14	10.10	16.59
1971	81.21	29.99	14.15	15.84	2.16	1.67	1.88	1.38	15.30	10.77	18.05
1972‡	88.54	31.16	15.52	15.65	2.45	1.80	2.52	1.41	17.11	11.90	20.18
1973‡	99.99	35.42	18.11	17.31	2.88	1.98	2.41	1.43	19.73	36.14	

* Excludes agricultural business; real estate operators; medical, legal, educational, and cultural service; and nonprofit organizations. These figures do not agree precisely with the nonresidential fixed investment data in the gross national product estimates, mainly because those data include investment by farmers, professionals, institutions, and real estate firms, and certain outlays charged to current account.

† Commercial and other includes trade, service, construction, finance, and insurance.

‡ Estimates based on expected capital expenditures reported by business in October–December 1972. Includes adjustments when necessary for systematic tendencies in expectations data.

Note: Annual total is the sum of unadjusted expenditures; it does not necessarily coincide with the average of seasonally adjusted figures.

Source: Department of Commerce, Bureau of Economic Analysis.

penditures posted in the decade through 1972 was by the airline industry which raised outlays at a compared rate of 17.1 percent, followed by public utilities with a compound growth of 11.7 percent annually. Manufacturing firms expenditures rose at an annual rate of 7.5 percent for the ten years ending in 1972, compared to 8.7 percent for total plant and equipment expenditures. (See Table 1.)

One of the largest machinery markets is for agricultural equipment— sales of which totaled $5.3 billion in 1971. Close behind was the construction machinery industry with sales of $4.5 billion. Other large fields are machine tools, material handling equipment, mining equipment, and oil field equipment. (See Table 2.)

TABLE 2

Selected Machinery Markets Data

	1971 *(sales in $ millions)*
Agricultural equipment:	
Motor vehicles	$2,588.0
Machinery and equipment	2,780.0
Total	$5,368.0
Mining equipment	657.5
Oil field equipment	939.4
Construction machinery	4,499.0
Machine tools:	
Metal cutting	672.0
Metal forming	326.0
Total	998.0

MARKETS FOR MACHINERY—DEMAND DETERMINANTS

The demand for machinery of a particular type is a function of many factors. Basically, changes in purchases of equipment are determined by the rate of growth of the industry using the machinery together with other elements including interest rates, labor cost, government policy, and technological changes.

Construction Machinery

In the construction machinery field, sales of new equipment are tied closely with the level of construction activity. Highway building was once the prime market for machinery, but in the last decade construction of public works, sewer projects, airports, residential construction, dams, and general commercial and industrial construction have expanded into prominent markets as well. Additionally, related fields, such as the strip mining, pipe-laying, and logging industries are increasingly utilizing construction machinery. It has been estimated, for example, that about twice as much earth will be moved in strip mining as in general construction by 1980, due to the rapid shift in coal production to lower cost surface coal mines—now close to 50 percent of total coal output compared to less than 30 percent in 1960.

In projecting the demand for construction machinery the principal source of information is the F. W. Dodge figures on new contracts for construction of all types. Additionally, attention should be paid to congressional action on highway spending under the Interstate Highway Trust Fund program and related annual projections of such activity made available by the Federal Highway Administration of the Department of Transportation. Mining expenditures can be anticipated by coal production estimates released by the National Coal Board, and projected capital expenditures by the mining industry contained in periodic surveys sponsored by McGraw-Hill and the Securities and Exchange Commission. Pipe-laying activity can be gauged by surveys and announced contracts in the *Oil and Gas Journal*. Little direct information is available on the logging industry but changes in equipment demand can be estimated by general projections of lumber and paper production.

Machine Tools

Orders for machine tools show one of the most volatile patterns in the capital goods field and have fluctuated widely over the postwar years. This volatility of orders is due to several factors. First, these machines are most heavily used by basic metal-working industries such as auto, appliance, aircraft, and other capital goods producers, which themselves are highly cyclical. Second, machine tools are relatively small units of capacity with fairly short lead times, and thus orders tend to reflect, and indeed amplify, shifts in business sentiment. As business conditions improve, orders rise sharply; and as the economy slows, many orders are cancelled or postponed. Thirdly, the pattern of machine tool orders shows the effect of snowballing, and as the backlogs of machine tool builders lengthen in the early stages of an upturn, customers accelerate buying plans to assure timely delivery, thereby causing a bunching of orders.

A factor which may tend to dampen the volatility of future cycles is the prospect of a growing replacement demand for machine tools. World War II and The Korean War stimulated substantial purchases of machine tools, an increasing proportion of which are reaching the end of their useful life of 20–25 years either due to physical deterioration or obsolescence by technological innovation. As more of these machines are retired in the years ahead, replacement purchases should constitute a larger proportion of total demand and tend to even out the wide cyclical swings evident in the past 20 years when demand was largely new-capacity oriented.

Sales of machine tools tend to parallel changes in the pace of business as reflected in the FRB Index of Industrial Production, although frequently lagging by a quarter or two. Thus fairly accurate projections of orders can be based on these broad economic indices.

Excellent data on domestic orders, cancellations and backlogs is available monthly from the National Machine Tool Builders Association.

Materials Handling Equipment

The material handling industry, and particularly the lift truck segment, is a fairly stable field with good underlying growth trends and relatively mild cyclical swings. This appears to be the result of several causes. First, lift trucks are widely used throughout the economy not

CHART 2

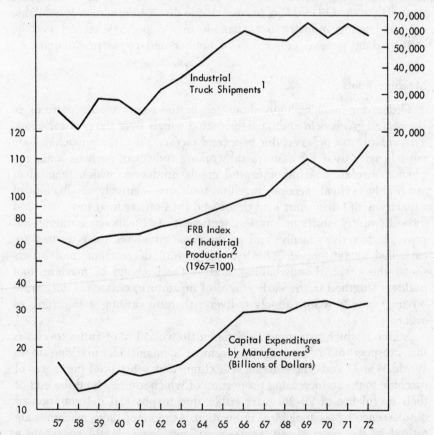

Source: (1) Dept. of Commerce, *Survey of Current Business;* (2) Federal Reserve Board, *Federal Reserve Bulletin;* (3) Dept. of Commerce, Bureau of Economic Analysis.

just by heavy manufactures but also extensively in the distribution of goods and by less cyclical industries such as food processing, publishing, and retailing. Second, the average life of a truck may be about five years, creating a fairly stable replacement demand. Finally, there is an underlying growth of the market due to the steady substitution by lift trucks for manual labor as wage rates rise.

As illustrated in Chart 2, sales of lift trucks correlate closely with the FRB index of production, and this broad index can be used effectively in projection demand for new industrial trucks.

Shipments of industrial trucks are reported monthly in the *Survey of Current Business*. Data on the broader grouping of material handling equipment is reported monthly by the Material Handling Institute.

ANALYSIS OF FACTORS EFFECTING PROFITS

Costs of machinery manufacturers, and hence profit margins, vary widely throughout the industry, depending on the nature of the enter-

TABLE 3

Cost Ratios—1972

	Bucyrus-Erie	Caterpillar	Clark Equip.	Rexnord
Sales...........................	100.1	100.0	100.0	100.0
Labor.........................	32.1	35.2	33.1	41.7
Materials......................	36.8	37.4	47.6	27.2
Selling, general, and administrative..............	16.2	8.9	9.2	21.8
Total.........................	85.1	81.5	89.9	90.7
Gross profit...................	14.9	18.5	10.1	9.3
Depreciation..................	1.8	3.9	1.8	1.9
Interest expense..............	0.5	0.9	2.9	1.5
Total.........................	2.3	4.8	4.7	3.4
Operating profit..............	12.6	13.7	5.4	5.9
Other income.................	2.6	0.4	2.2	0.9
Pretax profit.................	15.3	14.1	7.7	6.9
Income taxes.................	6.6	6.2	3.2	3.2
Net income...................	8.7	7.9	4.5	3.7
Preferred dividends...........	0.0	0.0	0.0	0.5
Net for common..............	8.7	7.9	4.5	3.2

prise and the skills of management. Table 3 shows an income statement of four prominent machinery builders.

Labor is, generally speaking, a fairly large cost factor and typically accounts for 30–35 percent of sales. The labor forces of most manufacturers of machinery are represented by the United Automobile Workers which has been among the stronger unions in attaining higher wages for employees. Labor contracts for machinery builders have generally followed the pattern set first in the bargaining with the Detroit-based auto firms.

Materials costs vary widely, depending on the nature of the operation and the degree of integration. Rexnord performs various engineering and construction services on materials handling systems which tend to lower its materials costs and raise labor expenses relative to sales; whereas Caterpillar is relatively well integrated and manufacturers finished machinery, giving it a reversed cost pattern. Materials costs tend to maintain a fairly constant relationship with sales over the years, while labor costs tend to rise and fall proportionally with volume.

As illustrated in Table 3, selling, general, and administrative costs differ considerably among these manufacturers. SG & A expenses are a function of the amount of selling effort involved in merchandising the product, the amount of cost required to maintain distribution networks, and the level of administration necessary to run the business. Caterpillar, which has a strong dealer network and a high degree of customer loyalty, has relatively low SG & A expenses; while Rexnord experiences a greater costs-to-sales ratio, due primarily to the breadth of its product lines and stronger competition in its markets.

Depreciation for most machinery manufacturers is a relatively minor charge, running under 2 percent of sales. For Caterpillar, however, this item generally is about twice as large, due to several factors: First it uses accelerated depreciation for book purposes; second, it has enjoyed faster growth than most manufacturers and thus has expanded capacity at a higher rate, which, together with the use of accelerated depreciation, tends to enlarge the ratio of depreciation charges to sales well above industry levels.

Interest expense varies as to the debt structure of the individual companies, but generally is a relatively small item. Clark Equipment has higher-than-average interest costs due, in part, to the placement of debt issues abroad in recent years to finance foreign growth. Interest expense may rise during an expansion of business with the increased use of short-term loans for working capital purposes and also as interest rates rise during a cyclical upturn.

Other income may be a relatively large source of earnings for machinery manufacturers. In the case of Bucyrus-Erie and Clark Equipment, for example, other income is increased by dividends or equity interests in subsidiaries, and also by profits from credit subsidiaries. Other income can fluctuate widely due to interest rate changes effecting credit subsidiary earnings, changes in foreign tax policies effecting off-shore subsidiaries, and periodic sales of assets. Because of this, analyses should be based on revenues excluding other income, and a careful analysis of the source of these other earnings to eliminate windfalls or unusual profits may not be repetitive.

Tax rates for machinery companies generally are less than U.S.

corporate tax rates due to the inclusion of other income such as dividends and credit subsidiary net earnings, and also relatively large amounts of foreign earnings which may bear a lower tax rate than domestically. Additionally investment tax credits have been fairly large for machinery builders in recent years, stemming from increases in capital expenditures for expanded facilities. Taxes should be examined closely for factors tending to reduce payments in order to determine a basis for future projections.

In analysing profits statements of machinery manufacturers and projecting future results, two important sources of revenues should be noted: foreign operations and repair parts sales. Foreign sales are fairly important for most machinery builders and may run between 25 and 50 percent of total revenues. U.S. technology in the machinery area is generally superior to foreign equipment because labor cost pressures in the United States have been more pronounced in the postwar era, necessitating strenuous efforts by manufacturing firms to employ labor-saving equipment. Additionally, developing nations have turned to the United States for equipment to expand their manufacturing capabilities, often aided by federal government grants and loans. Finally sales abroad have been helped by U.S. firms establishing manufacturing operations overseas using capital equipment made in this country. Depending on the type of equipment and the geographical despersion of customers, foreign sales may be more or less cyclical than domestic sales. As a general rule, changes in foreign sales tend to lag behind domestic cycles by several quarters due to the dependence of many countries on export trade with the United States. Export sales tend to be more profitable than domestic business due to lower U.S. tax rates.

A second important source of sales for most machinery manufacturers is repair and maintenance parts. Capital goods are used continuously in manufacturing, frequently under rigorous conditions, and as a result machines tend to break down periodically, requiring purchases of repair parts. Further, machines are usually the key element in a manufacturing process, and a disabled machine may tie up substantial amounts of related equipment and idle workers. Thus, manufacturers are in a favorable position to price parts with better margins than obtained on the machine initially. Further, the original manufacturer is usually the only source of parts, although in some cases certain items are interchangeable on different brands of machines. As a result of these factors, repair parts sales tend to grow steadily as a function of the number of machines in operation and also generally carry higher profit margins. In many applications during slack economic periods, users of machines may defer purchases of new machines and operate older equipment beyond normal retirement periods, resulting in higher sales of repair parts and making such sales somewhat contra-cyclical. For most machinery manufacturers, repair parts are 20–30 percent of total sales and 25–50 percent of total profits because of the higher mark-ups. Because of the relative importance and stability of parts sales, this item should be noted in the analyses of total revenues and utilized in projections of profits.

TECHNOLOGICAL, ECONOMIC, AND SOCIAL FACTORS AFFECTING DEMAND

In our complex economy, social, economic, and technical decisions and changes can materially affect the sales of capital goods.

In a broad sense, efforts by the federal government to accelerate or decelerate economic growth obviously bear heavily on corporations' abilities to invest in new equipment. The federal government's two broad techniques for controlling the economy—monetary and fiscal policy— can materially impact the machinery industry.

Federal Reserve programs to stimulate economic activity make funds in the banking system more plentiful and lower interest rates. With an ease in the availability and cost of money, coupled with rising business conditions, firms are encouraged to expand and raise capital expenditures for new machinery. Similarly when the Federal Reserve seeks to curtail the pace of business, interest rates are raised by restricting the flow of funds in the economy, which correspondingly tends to cut capital expenditures either due to the unattractive rates or the inability of firms to borrow for capital expenditures purposes.

Fiscal policies can have a similar impact. Stimulative programs of deficit spending, possibly including tax cuts, make expansion programs more attractive, and tax increases or spending cuts may curtail business spending on new capacity. Certain broad fiscal policy changes can significantly affect particular segments of the capital goods industry; a stimulative program to increase public works and highway expenditures creates a strong demand for construction machinery, whereas a curtailment of defense outlays by the government can cut machine tool orders by the aerospace industry.

In addition to broad measures, socially oriented government programs can change trends for certain segments of the machinery industry. Legislation in recent years regarding water and air pollution have necessitated substantial outlays for equipment to purify air and water discharges from industrial plants, and by the same token have diverted funds away from new productive capacity expenditures. Decreased emphasis on highway expenditures has come about in the past five years as a result of a tightening supply of energy and growing pressure from urban leaders for mass transit facilities—both of which, in turn, have affected sales of construction machinery. Proposed legislation regulating strip mining activities caused a temporary moderation of capital expenditures for new equipment until certain aspects of the bills were clarified.

Technological innovations also can affect capital expenditures. The development of numerical controls for machine tools in the early 1960s added substantially to demand, due to the large increase in productivity made possible by the automation of manual machinery techniques. The development of the low-cost, twin-screw, air compressor created an entirely new segment of the structured compressor market and significantly changed market shares for the major manufacturers. Nuclear power radically altered the demand for power generation equipment and realigned the positions of the major suppliers with the entry of large electrical manufacturers into the utility boiler business.

Because research activities are conducted in secret for competitive reasons, it is difficult to anticipate technological changes. However, it is imperative for analysts to keep abreast of new developments, either directly from companies or as covered in trade journals.

Evaluation

Machinery stocks have traditionally sold at a price/earnings ratio below that of the market in general, although the discount varies widely from year to year.

The discount from the Standard & Poors' 425 Industrial Index assigned to machinery stocks can principally be attributed to the more cyclical nature of the earnings of equipment manufacturers. With a lower degree of predictability of earnings power and concern about an eventual downturn in profits, investors are reluctant to pay up for the earnings of this group. (See Table 4.)

Upward movements in the prices of stocks of machinery manufacturers generally tend to lag behind rises in the general market. This is probably due to the placement of funds into the market, first in areas of the economy where earnings are more visible, then later into more cyclical issues such as machinery manufacturers.

Appreciation in the prices of machinery stocks may preceed actual upturns in earning power as investors discount a predicted rise in capital spending based on forecasts of economic gains and surveys of corporations' spending plans. Because the early discounting of anticipated swings in machinery manufacturers' earnings may occur as current earnings are recovering from a recession, price/earnings ratios may frequently be quite high. Investors also attempt to anticipate declines in earnings resulting from a projected downturn in the economy, and as a cycle matures investors may be reluctant to add to holdings or begin to liquidate positions. This moderating influence on prices, at a time when earnings of machinery builders may be hitting a cyclical peak, frequently results in relatively low price/earnings ratios.

These two trends are evident in Table 4. Profits of machinery manufacturers were at a low in 1960 and the industry's stocks sold at 88.6 per-

TABLE 4

Price/Earnings Ratios

Year	425 Industrials			Machinery Industry Composite			Machinery Composite Avg. P/E as Percent of S&P's 425 Average P/E	Machinery Industry Earnings per Share
	Hi	Low	Average	Hi	Low	Average		
1960	19.12	16.28	17.70	17.67	13.71	15.69	88.6	3.11
1961	22.76	18.06	20.41	18.95	16.02	17.48	85.6	3.32
1962	19.64	14.31	16.97	17.91	12.16	15.03	88.5	3.38
1963	18.69	15.44	17.06	15.35	13.04	14.19	83.2	3.73
1964	18.82	16.44	17.63	15.49	11.44	13.46	76.3	5.10
1965	17.92	15.71	16.81	15.30	11.88	13.59	80.8	6.38
1966	17.14	13.27	15.20	13.75	9.58	11.66	76.7	7.10
1967	18.89	15.18	17.03	17.72	11.86	14.79	86.8	6.14
1968	19.16	15.43	17.29	18.10	13.92	16.01	92.6	6.54
1969	18.96	15.95	17.45	17.35	13.71	15.53	89.0	6.83
1970	19.01	13.97	16.49	15.41	11.36	13.38	81.1	6.71
1971	19.40	16.64	18.02	21.52	16.33	18.92	105.0	6.35
1972	19.55	16.50	18.02	22.28	15.62	18.95	105.1	8.36

cent of the average P/E of the 425 Industrials. Similarly, in anticipation of the cyclical upturn in the late 1960s, the average P/E for machinery stocks rose to 86.8 percent and 92.6 percent of the 425 Industrials average P/E in 1967 and 1968 respectively. The reverse effect occurred in 1966 when earnings peaked for the cycle, and the average P/E dropped to 76.7 percent of the 425 Industrial stocks' average P/E.

CASE STUDY

Bucyrus-Erie is one of the more successful machinery manufacturers evidencing both above-average growth and relatively high profits.

The company holds a leading position in both the construction and mining machinery markets. Bucyrus-Erie is one of two manufacturers of large draglines used in the surface mining of various minerals, sharing the market about equally with Marion Power Shovel. Additionally, BE makes other equipment for the mining industry including blast hole drills and smaller shovels for loading minerals into trucks or trains.

For the construction market, BE produces a broad line of hydraulic excavators and hydraulic and cable-operated cranes. In both categories, the company holds a prominent position but competes with a large number of firms offering products in one or more lines.

The balance of sales comes from industrial products such as gears, chains, electric drive systems, and hydraulic winches. (See Table 5.)

Profit Analysis by Product Line

Product line breakdown analysis can be very useful in projecting profits, especially in a company such as Bucyrus-Erie where significant swings in mix of sales can materially impact earnings. In 1969 the pretax profit margin fell from 15.2 percent (1968) to 14.1 percent. Sales of construction machinery and industrial products both showed gains in sales in 1969 over those in 1968, and margins were maintained. Shipments of mining machines, however, declined 15.3 percent, and, as a result, the pretax return on that line dropped from 15.2 percent of sales to 12.3 percent in 1969 and drew the corporate average down accordingly.

In 1970, the total return again declined from 14.1 percent to 12.1 percent with the pretax margin on both mining machinery and construction machinery falling somewhat. The drop in the rate of return for construction machinery probably can be assigned to the lower volume; the erosion of margins on mining machinery can be attributed to delivery of machines at fairly low prices booked during the slide in new orders during 1968–69.

The overall pretax margin fell slightly in 1971 due to another important shift in mix. Sales of mining machinery spurted 32 percent to a record $101.6 million, and because of the surge in volume and better

TABLE 5
Bucyrus-Erie Product Line Breakdown: Sales and Earnings, 1969–1972 ($ million)

	1968			1969			1970			1971			1972		
	Sales	Pretax Return	Profit Margin	Sales	Pretax Return	Profit Margin	Sales	Pretax Return	Profit Margin	Sales	Pretax Return	Profit Margin	Sales	Pretax Return	Profit Margin
Mining machinery	$67.2	$10.2	15.2%	$56.9	$7.0	12.3%	$77.0	$8.3	10.8%	$101.6	$14.5	14.3%	$70.5	$11.6	16.4
Construction machinery	76.5	12.3	16.1	79.4	12.9	16.2	70.7	9.7	13.7	70.2	6.7	9.5	85.6	11.5	13.4
Industrial products	12.5	1.2	9.6	13.5	1.3	9.6	12.8	1.4	10.9	12.9	0.4	0.3	11.8	0.5	0.4
Total	$156.2	$23.7	15.2%	$149.8	$21.2	14.1%	$160.5	$19.4	12.1%	$184.7	$21.6	11.7%	$167.9	$23.6	14.0%

prices as industry capacity tightened, the pretax margin rose to 14.3 percent in 1971 from 10.8 percent in 1970. However, the profit margin for construction machinery declined sharply to 9.6 percent from 13.7 percent due to the plateau in revenues and, as the company revealed, heavy new-product introduction expenses on several innovative hydraulic excavators. Further adding to the margin pressure in 1971 was a sharp drop in earnings from the small industrial products group due to a number of manufacturing problems.

In 1972 another significant shift in mix took place. Shipments of mining machines fell but the return on sales rose, due to two factors. First, due to better prices and a good mix of products, profits margins on new machines sales continued to be good despite lower volume. Second, and more importantly, repair parts sales for existing mining machines continued to grow, perhaps by 10 percent or more, and because parts tend to be significantly more profitable, the impact on the earnings from total mining machinery operations increased importantly. Specific breakdowns of repair parts sales are not made available, but reasonable assumptions can be made to account for the shifts in profits. For example, if repair parts were 25 percent of 1971 shipments of the mining machinery division and resulted in a 25 percent pretax margin, then by derivation, new machine sales had a pretax return of 10.9 percent in 1971. If in 1972 repair parts sales rose 10 percent to $27.5 million, then again by derivation, new machine sales may have fallen 43 percent to $33.0 million. This rough set of assumptions is supported by the drop in the backlog of orders for the division to $43.1 million at the beginning of 1972, compared to $62.3 million a year earlier—a drop of 31 percent. Assuming further that repair parts continued to return around 25 percent on sales in 1972, then the pretax return on new machine sales apparently was maintained at around 10.9 percent, evidencing the continuation of good price levels and the efforts of management to lower costs quickly in the face of prospective lower shipments.

Total profits for 1972 were also aided importantly by the recovery in margins on construction machinery. Sales of construction machinery rose 22 percent, and together with a reversal of new product expenses, the return rebounded to 13.5 percent compared to only 9.6 percent in 1971. Operations in industrial products continued to be adverse.

Analysis of Cost Ratios

Another approach to the analysis of machinery companies is to look at the elements in the income statement and study the changes from year to year. Costs of goods sold for Bucyrus-Erie have fluctuated in a fairly narrow range from 68.8 percent of sales to 73.4 percent. The proportion of costs accounted for by labor and materials tends generally to vary directly with sales, with the percentage ascribed to "cost of goods sold" rising with gains in volume and declining as shipments fall. (See Table 6.)

Development, selling, and administrative expenses similarly have kept within a narrow range as a percentage of revenues but, being more fixed in the short run, vary inversely with changes in revenue. The sharp rise in the ratio in 1969 and 1970 to 15.1 percent and 15.3 percent respectively is attributable to the surge in new product introductions which raised promotional expenses and, because certain technical problems arose,

TABLE 6

Bucyrus-Erie Cost Ratios

	1968	*1969*	*1970*	*1971*	*1972*
Shipments	100.0	100.0	100.0	100.0	100.0
Cost of goods sold	70.3	69.3	71.3	73.4	68.8
Developmental, Selling, Administrative	13.4	15.1	15.3	14.4	16.2
Total cost	83.7	84.4	86.6	87.8	85.0
Gross profit	16.3	15.6	13.3	12.2	15.0
Depreciation	1.8	1.9	1.8	1.7	1.8
Interest expense	0.4	0.4	0.7	0.5	0.5
Total	2.2	2.3	2.5	2.2	2.3
Operating profit	14.1	13.3	10.8	10.0	12.7
Other income	1.0	0.9	1.3	1.7	1.3
Pretax profit	15.1	14.2	12.1	11.7	14.0
Taxes	7.8	7.4	6.0	5.8	6.6
Net profit	7.3	6.8	6.0	5.9	7.4
Equity Ruston Bucyrus	1.3	1.1	1.2	0.8	1.3
Total net income	8.7	7.9	7.2	6.7	8.7

increased field service costs, particularly in 1970. The rise in the percentage in 1972 is attributable to the 9 percent decline in shipments.

Depreciation and interest charges tend to be relatively small items for Bucyrus-Erie and have held fairly constant over the five-year span. The company uses the straight-line method of depreciating assets for reporting purposes which levels out this expense item. Because the company has largely financed its growth from internal sources, interest expense is small.

Other income fluctuates widely but is generally a small item. The source of other income is from interest, royalties, and miscellaneous areas, and thus is not a very predictable figure.

Taxes on operations have been fairly constant and are about in line with the effective U.S. corporate rate.

The company's equity in Ruston Bucyrus Ltd., its 50 percent owned English subsidiary, has grown about in line with the parent, except for 1971 when profits were depressed by uncertainty in the U.K. economy.

TABLE 7

Financial Ratios

	Net as Percent of Sales	Cash Flow as Percent of Sales	Net per Dollar of Gross Plant	Cash Flow per Dollar of Gross Plant	Net per Dollar of Invested Capital	Cash Flow per Dollar of Invested Capital	Long-Term Debt as Percent of Invested Capital	Sales per Dollar of Gross Plant
Bucyrus-Erie	8.7	10.5	.26	.31	.12	.14	7	2.90
Caterpillar	7.9	11.8	.16	.24	.16	.23	21	1.92
Clark	4.5	6.3	.17	.22	.13	.16	25	2.73
FMC Corp	4.6	6.1	.08	.11	.09	.12	23	1.59
Koehring	2.2	2.7	.16	.19	.09	.11	40	3.02
Rexnord	3.7	5.1	.11	.16	.08	.12	31	2.58

Using a model based on these relationships can be valuable in projecting future profits, especially when matched with a profit projection based on product-line sales and profits breakdown.

Cash Flow and Balance Sheet Analysis

Bucyrus-Erie has been largely able to finance its growth from internal sources because of its relatively high utilization of assets. As illustrated in Table 7, BE in 1972 had a relatively high net return on sales and cash flow return on sales. Additionally, it had the industry's highest net return and cash flow return on gross plant in 1972. Finally its net return and cash flow per dollar of invested capital compared favorably with other industry factors. Because of these good asset utilization ratios, the company's cash flow has been sufficient to pace growth without extensive borrowings, and its long-term debt as a percent of invested capital is well below industry trends at 7 percent in 1972. With consistantly high sales per dollar of gross plant, it seems likely that capital

TABLE 8

CONSOLIDATED
STATEMENT OF CHANGES
IN FINANCIAL POSITION

BUCYRUS-ERIE COMPANY AND SUBSIDIARIES

	Year ended December 31	
	1972	1971
Source of Working Capital		
From operations:		
Net earnings	$14,547,724	$12,295,010
Noncash charges (credits) to earnings:		
Depreciation	3,052,914	3,122,511
Increase in deferred liabilities	340,373	241,627
Equity in net earnings of Ruston-Bucyrus, Limited	(2,074,490)	(1,542,047)
Total working capital provided from operations	15,866,521	14,117,101
Dividends received from Ruston-Bucyrus, Limited	579,844	1,182,333
Decrease in non-current portion of notes receivable	2,208,418	521,796
Stock options exercised	949,240	29,975
	$19,604,023	$15,851,205
Application of Working Capital		
Additions to property, plant and equipment	$ 2,163,695	$ 3,824,012
Cash dividends paid	7,904,675	7,525,877
Decrease (increase) in long-term debt	(840,000)	3,960,000
Addition to working capital	11,295,406	428,810
Miscellaneous	(919,753)	112,506
	$19,604,023	$15,851,205
Increase (Decrease) in Working Capital Components		
Cash	$ 125,420	$(2,134,156)
Notes and accounts receivable	897,275	5,764,619
Inventories	7,828,176	(2,479,944)
Accounts payable and accrued expenses	808,884	(2,247,305)
Federal and state income taxes	2,198,519	272,352
Other - net	(562,868)	1,253,244
Addition to Working Capital	$11,295,406	$ 428,810
Working Capital, End of Year	$86,218,204	$74,922,798

TABLE 9

CONSOLIDATED BALANCE SHEET

BUCYRUS-ERIE COMPANY AND SUBSIDIARIES

Assets

	December 31 1972	December 31 1971
Current Assets		
Cash	$ 3,380,822	$ 3,255,402
Notes and accounts receivable	39,108,004	38,210,729
Inventories	62,849,179	55,021,303
Future income tax benefits	5,122,000	5,402,000
Prepaid expenses	614,983	566,194
Total Current Assets	111,075,288	102,455,628
Investments and Other Assets		
Notes receivable	3,181,671	5,390,089
Ruston-Bucyrus, Limited - at equity in underlying net assets	21,810,451	20,650,820
Other investments	56,839	641,577
	25,048,961	26,682,486
Property, Plant and Equipment - at cost		
Land	2,011,845	2,154,591
Buildings and improvements	17,273,840	18,123,703
Machinery and equipment	37,133,309	39,214,437
Less accumulated depreciation (credit)	(22,604,570)	(24,789,088)
	33,814,424	34,703,643
Excess of Cost of Subsidiary Over Related Equity	1,548,996	1,548,996
	$171,487,669	$165,390,753

Liabilities and Shareholders' Investment

	December 31 1972	December 31 1971
Current Liabilities		
Accounts payable and accrued expenses	$ 19,287,674	$ 20,096,558
Taxes, other than income taxes	2,543,811	2,189,154
Customers' advances in excess of related costs on uncompleted contracts	1,430,611	1,453,611
Federal and state income taxes	1,084,988	3,283,507
Current maturities on long-term debt	510,000	510,000
Total Current Liabilities	24,857,084	27,532,830
Deferred Liabilities		
Pension costs and other compensation	2,333,828	2,413,455
Income taxes	3,609,000	3,189,000
	5,942,828	5,602,455
Long-Term Debt, less current maturities	10,625,000	9,785,000
Shareholders' Investment		
Preferred stock - par value $100 a share Authorized - 300,000 shares; issued - none		
Common stock - par value $5 a share - Authorized 10,000,000 shares; issued and outstanding (excluding 65,037 shares in treasury) - 6,603,331 shares in 1972 and 6,534,345 shares in 1971	33,016,655	32,671,725
Additional paid-in capital	604,310	
Earnings retained in the business	96,441,792	89,798,743
	130,062,757	122,470,468
	$171,487,669	$165,390,753

TABLE 10

CONSOLIDATED STATEMENT OF EARNINGS

BUCYRUS-ERIE COMPANY AND SUBSIDIARIES

	Year ended December 31	
	1972	1971
Revenues		
Net shipments	$167,932,787	$184,703,549
Interest, royalties and miscellaneous	2,366,213	3,169,625
	170,299,000	187,873,174
Costs and Expenses		
Cost of products sold	118,712,829	138,548,012
Product development, selling and administrative expenses	27,230,408	26,670,040
Interest expense	778,529	1,063,159
	146,721,766	166,281,211
Earnings Before Income Taxes and Equity in Net Earnings of Ruston-Bucyrus, Limited	23,577,234	21,591,963
Income Taxes	11,104,000	10,839,000
Earnings Before Equity in Net Earnings of Ruston-Bucyrus, Limited	12,473,234	10,752,963
Equity in Net Earnings of Ruston-Bucyrus, Limited	2,074,490	1,542,047
Net Earnings	$ 14,547,724	$ 12,295,010
Net earnings per share of common stock	$2.21	$1.88

CONSOLIDATED STATEMENT OF EARNINGS RETAINED IN THE BUSINESS

Balance, beginning of year		
As previously reported	$ 70,710,129	$ 66,300,710
Adjustment arising from restatement of investment in Ruston-Bucyrus, Limited to equity method of accounting	19,088,614	18,728,900
As restated	89,798,743	85,029,610
Net earnings	14,547,724	12,295,010
	104,346,467	97,324,620
Cash dividends paid - $1.20 a share	7,904,675	7,525,877
Balance, end of year	$ 96,441,792	$ 89,798,743

expenditures will remain modest relative to growth of sales and probably well within its cash flow generation. Table 8 shows the flow of funds for 1971 and 1972.

The company's financial position at the end of 1972 was excellent. Current assets were 4.4 times greater than current liabilities, compared to 3.7 times a year earlier. Long-term debt totaled only $10.6 million compared to shareholders equity of $130.0 million. Table 9 shows the company's balance sheet for 1971 and 1972, while Table 10 is the income statement for the same period.

As a result of the company's strong balance sheet and favorable profit ratios, it has consistantly been able to pay relatively high dividends. The payout ratio for the last five years has averaged 60.8 percent of net earnings.

Evaluation

The stock of Bucyrus-Erie has not commanded a high multiple relative to its underlying strength and other machinery stocks until recently. For the past five years the stock has sold at an average P/E of 13.2 times current year's earnings in a range of 16.0 to 10.4 times earnings. This compares to an average P/E of four similar companies (Caterpillar, Clark, Koehring, and Rex-Nord) of 15.8 times for the same period. During 1973, however, the P/E for Bucyrus-Erie stock moved up. Based on trailing 12-month earnings through the third quarter of $2.43 per share, the stock, selling at 39, was about 16 times those earnings.

This higher evaluation seems more in line with the company's good record and financial strength. As illustrated in Table 11, the company's growth has exceeded substantially the other major factors in its field.

TABLE 11

Compound Growth Rates 1962–72 (by percent)

	Sales	Operating Income	Net Income
Bucyrus-Erie	6	13	18
Caterpillar	12	11	12
Clark	12	11	9
Koehring	10	5	−1
Rexnord	12	10	9

21

Nonferrous Metals

GEORGE H. CLEAVER
First Vice President
White, Wild & Co. Incorporated
New York, New York

THE nonferrous metal industries are those that mine, smelt, refine, or fabricate aluminum, magnesium, copper, lead, zinc, titanium, and some less important metals such as cadmium and selenium.

Gold, silver, and platinum are often included, partly because these are often by-products of other nonferrous mining. Usually included are nickel and molybdenum much of which is used in conjunction with steel production.

Some companies perform all operations; they mine, beneficiate (mill), smelt, refine, and fabricate metals, and are referred to as integrated companies.

Beneficiate, more often called "milling," refers to the process of upgrading ore, ordinarily a mechanical process. Usually it is crushing, grinding, and otherwise separating waste from the valuable content. The product is called "concentrate." Copper concentrate usually contains 22 percent to 32 percent copper; zinc concentrate 50 percent to 60 percent zinc; and lead concentrate, up to 75 percent lead.

Smelting is ordinarily the next step in purifying the concentrate. It is a furnace or pyro metallurgical process and the product may be about 99 percent pure, not pure enough in most cases to be used by industry. Hydrometalurgical processes are becoming increasingly important. The smelted product is then ordinarily refined to a higher purity. Most commonly this is a form of electrolytic separation of the product from the remaining impurities. Usually it is a form of electroplating; the desired metal passes through an electrolyte and forms on a starting sheet, and

524

the other materials, some of which may be valuable by-products, form a sludge in the electrolytic tanks. There are also other forms of refining.

Companies that mine, smelt, and refine are often called "producers," as are the integrated companies. Some, in addition to producing primary metals, also produce secondary metals. Secondary metal is that recovered from scrap metal. There are a considerable number of "independent" secondary smelters.

Scrap metal is ordinarily classified into two categories: old and new. The former is fabricated metal that has performed the function for which it was intended (for example, a brass radiator from a junked automobile). New scrap is generated in the making of fabricated products (for example, brass sheet trimmings in a plant making automobile radiators).

Some companies mine and mill only. Most of even the small companies mill their ore, that is, they crush the rock and upgrade the ore. They then send the concentrate to a custom smelter.

The smelter usually buys the concentrate from the mining company. Most often it pays the mining company the current price of finished metal, less a smelting and transportation charge and some other adjustments. The current metal price used usually is that published in some periodical such as *Engineering and Mining Journal* (McGraw-Hill) or that established by trading at the London Metal Exchange. A problem sometimes arises when the published price appears to be a "list" price rather than a "realized" price. The "smelter schedule" of payment for ores and concentrates is a rather complex formula showing deductions from the price of finished metal depending mainly on the grade of the concentrate and the impurities contained. In recent years, these smelting discounts (charges) have been rising rapidly, both in the United States and abroad. These charges are likely to rise more, partly because costs will increase considerably from alleviating air pollution.

Returnable Metal

In some cases the metal concentrate is not sold to the smelter-refiner, rather, the mining company pays a "toll" for treatment. The metal is "returned" to the mining company which then sells the metal to the user. Ordinarily this "returnable" metal is actually sold for the mining company by a third company, often a metal merchant or dealer.

The smelter of the concentrate is sometimes not the refiner; in this case the smelted product is shipped to a refiner who will, of course, charge for the refining. The refiner may buy the metal or he may return it to the mining company. Charges in the United States in 1973 for copper smelting and refining were probably about ten to thirteen cents per pound of copper.

The mining company to which the metal is returned usually has a metal dealer sell it; the latter may get one-fourth to one-half cent a pound for selling copper. This may be 0.5 percent to 1 percent of the gross sales price. The mining company may hope for a higher price this way than if it sells it to the smelter-refiner at the producer price. Dealer prices in the United States often differ from producer prices. Producers of copper, and to some extent other metals, tend to maintain a price over a period of months, while dealer prices change often day to day. It is widely believed that producer prices will be less stable than in the past. During periods of tight markets, dealer (merchant) prices are higher than producer prices. When the metal market is soft, the dealer price is lower.

In 1973, the dealer market price (sometimes called the "open market price") was as much as 60 percent higher than the integrated producer price for copper. At times in nonprice controlled periods, the difference was almost as great. The dealer price in the United States as well as elsewhere is ordinarily close to the London Metal Exchange price, for copper, lead, zinc, and tin. The dealer price for lead, zinc, and nickel at times has also been much higher than the producer price. Aluminum prices in some parts of the world are sometimes higher too, but not as much as other nonferrous metals. In some cases, dealer metal is secondary metal; for some uses, some grades of secondary metal are interchangeable with primary metal. In tight markets, secondary metal prices in the United States are usually higher than primary-producer metal prices; usually they are close to the dealer prices of primary metal. In soft markets they are usually a little lower.

The dealer is under almost no pressure to sell his metal in the United States. He is better able to sell metal of U.S. origin abroad where at times prices are higher than in the United States. Foreign prices are usually close to U.S. merchant prices. The integrated U.S. producer is likely to have arrangements with U.S. fabricators which call for about all his metal. Much of his metal, and maybe all of it, is sold on contracts. He may have almost no "spot" metal to sell.[1] The reasons U.S. integrated nonferrous metal producers sell, even in the absence of price controls, at less than the open market price during strong markets are complex and disputable.[2] In the interest of brevity, further discussion is omitted.

In 1973, mining firms that arranged for their copper, lead, or zinc to be returned and sold on the dealer market, rather than selling it to the smelter-refiner at producer prices, benefitted greatly. In at least one case, a sizeable copper-mining firm that ordinarily had returned to it much of its copper was convinced that in 1973 dealer prices would be less than integrated producer prices, and therefore did not sell its return-

---

[1] The metal dealer may also sell metal on long-term contracts.

[2] Copper Range, a medium size U.S. copper mining company, adopted open market pricing early in 1974.

able metal on the dealer spot market or on contracts calling for dealer prices. This company probably "lost" millions of dollars.

Integrated Companies

Many of the large nonferrous metal-mining companies are integrated from the mine through the refinery. The larger copper-mining companies fabricate some of their copper. Phelps Dodge uses about two thirds of its copper in its own fabricating operations; it sells about a third. Most of this two thirds goes into wire mills. The company probably uses only purchased or returned scrap in some of its fabricating plants. Its total use of copper exceeds its mine output—it buys copper. Some of this copper is purchased for others for which it "tolls" the metal into wire rod and possibly other shapes. Some of this copper it buys at the dealer price for the account of its customers.

The importance of the fabrication operation varies from company to company. Kennecott has a smaller fabricating operation than does Phelps Dodge. Anaconda probably fabricates as much or more copper than does Phelps Dodge. Anaconda, in addition to being in the wire and wire rod business as is Phelps Dodge, is also probably the largest producer of brass mill products.

Aluminum Companies Integrated

The aluminum companies mine bauxite, produce alumina from it, and from that produce aluminum metal. Some buy alumina and bauxite. Not much bauxite is mined in the United States. All fabricate products as well as sell the metal to "independent" manufacturers. Some also sell alumina. The aluminum companies have a more certain outlet for their metal if they own their own fabricating facilities. In addition, integration provides an added base for earnings. During the 1950s when the U.S. government bought for the national stockpile all surplus primary ingot at market prices, the markup on ingot was high; since then the move toward fabricating metal has become even more important.

It was at about the time these "put" contracts to the U.S. government ended, that Alcan, the large Canadian aluminum producer, began fabricating aluminum in the United States rather than merely exporting unfabricated metal to U.S. buyers.

The larger companies have tended to remain concentrated in aluminum, in contrast to other nonferrous companies. However, Kaiser Aluminum moved into nickel and strontium and probably regrets it. Kaiser Aluminum also entered a number of nonmetal industries. Alcoa has been involved in a copper development in Mexico and has a large real estate operation. Some nonaluminum companies (for example, Anaconda, American Metal Climax, and Revere Copper and Brass) also produce considerable aluminum. Phelps Dodge is in aluminum via its 40 percent share of Consolidated Aluminum Corporation.

Metal Fabricators

There are a number of large metal fabricators that do not mine metal. One of the largest of these is Western Electric, a subsidiary of American Telephone and Telegraph. The company produces copper from scrap and uses a small amount of aluminum; it uses about 300,000 short tons of copper per year, probably more than any other independent fabricator. General Electric and Westinghouse also use considerable copper and some aluminum but, of course, like Western Electric, are not classed as nonferrous metal companies. General Cable, Essex International,[3] and Revere Copper and Brass are metal fabricators that are usually considered nonferrous metal companies; there are many others.

The U.S. nonferrous metal analyst could find several hundred companies in the United States and Canada to study. As a practical matter, 20 or 30 are about the limit.

These companies change. For example, what was a sulphur company a few years ago is a nonferrous metals company today—Texasgulf and Freeport Minerals.

Much U.S. lead and zinc is produced in relatively small divisions of rather large companies (for example, American Smelting and Refining, Gulf and Western, American Metal Climax, and Kennecott Copper). St. Joe Minerals' major activity is lead and zinc mining.

Depletion Allowances

Controversy breaks out occasionally over the depletion allowances mining companies receive, including nonferrous metal mining companies. With the notion that mining companies are consuming their capital assets and that the income from capital rather than the capital itself should be taxed, mining companies receive depletion allowances; therefore their tax rates appear to be lower than those of manufacturing and other kinds of companies.

Many metal-mining companies pay income taxes between 30 percent and 40 percent. The depletion allowance on copper mines is 15 percent, on lead, zinc and molybdenum 22 percent, and on uranium 23 percent. Assuming the market value of the copper in concentrates is $0.45 a pound,[4] the 15 percent depletion allowance would be $0.0675 a pound. For every pound sold, $0.0675 would be deducted from income in computing the value on which income taxes would be paid. There is an in-

---

[3] Essex was merged into United Aircraft after this was written.

[4] The smelting and refining value is added as a consequence of manufacturing and is not part of the base on which the allowance is calculated.

come limitation; the depletion allowance is not permitted ordinarily to exceed 50 percent of income. Change in the depletion rate can have a substantial effect on a nonferrous mining company's earnings.

Depletion allowances have been under attack as tax loopholes. Awareness of the materials shortage may reduce the success of the attack. If a materials shortage leads to better earnings for mining companies, depletion allowances may be reduced or eliminated with the charge of "excess profits." The major argument against them is applied primarily to mining on public lands where it is claimed the capital put into the project by the mining company is depreciable and therefore there is no sense in also giving depleting allowances. This argument is also used for mining on private land. Reduction in the depletion allowances would increase U.S. dependence on imported metal.

The United States is a net importer of nearly all nonferrous metals (it is a large net exporter of molybdenum). The threat of greatly increased metal prices from foreign, government-sponsored cartels may "save" the depletion allowances.

MAIN PROBLEMS IN NONFERROUS ANALYSIS

For most nonferrous metal companies, product prices dominate changes in earnings, and prices usually reflect changes in supply and demand. In the absence of price controls, prices may move 50 percent in one year.

To forecast changes in earnings of nonferrous metal companies the analyst must be able to forecast changes in product prices and, to a less extent, volume. This requires forecasting supply and demand. Failure to forecast successfully can be illustrated by events in the aluminum industry during 1970–1972. Earnings for the major aluminum companies in 1969 and 1970 were fair to good, and prices for most products were satisfactory. Aluminum ingot prices received by Alcoa rose from $0.236 a pound in 1968 to $0.247 in 1969 and $0.268 in 1970. Average prices realized for fabricated products were about stable during these three years (about $0.51 a pound for Alcoa). Some mill product prices probably rose a little, but this was obscured by changes in the fabricated product mix. Published list prices were, of course, much higher than realized prices. Published "list" prices were $0.28 and $0.29. An analyst rarely accepts published prices for aluminum.

In 1971, earnings of aluminum companies dropped drastically. Alcoa and Kaiser Aluminum earnings fell by about half, and Reynolds Metals earnings to $0.13 per share from about $2.50.

That earnings would fall was indicated in late 1970 and early 1971, though share values did not begin to decline until April or May 1971.

It was evident in mid-1970 that the free world was coming into a period of considerable oversupply of aluminum. During the period

1965–69, aluminum capacity and consumption were approximately in balance. By 1970, data on new capacity being built suggested there was almost no chance consumption could keep up. Free world primary aluminum capacity was due to rise about 9 percent in 1970, 16 percent in 1971, and over 14 percent in 1972. It was clear that overcapacity would be felt in 1971.

It is essential that the nonferrous metals analyst keep current on capacity changes for at least two years ahead and perhaps even longer.

The first nonstatistical indication of approaching trouble occurred in August 1970 when Consolidated Aluminum Corporation, one of the smaller U.S. primary aluminum producers, shut one aluminum-producing pot-line.[5] So far as I know, this was not publicly announced. The following month Kaiser Aluminum did announce closing of a line and others followed.

If the capacity statistics were not a danger signal, these closings certainly should have been. Oddly, these closings were interpreted by many to be bullish. Aluminum is a capital intensive industry, and some important costs continue even when a plant is closed. Moreover, start-up costs are high. Aluminum companies do not want to shut plants unless they have to—ordinarily only after building excessive inventories. A plant shutdown or partial closing means higher average costs and decreased volume. The notion that plant closings were bullish was grasping at straws; it was mistakenly thought to imply higher, or at least no fall in, prices. As the end of 1970 approached, the view that 1971 would be poor for the aluminum industry became more evident. Inventories rose, and other statistics suggested that the 1970 free world consumption increase was small.

By the beginning of 1971, the effect was beginning to show in aluminum prices; new contracts for many aluminum fabricated products were at prices significantly lower than those for 1970. But one still heard presumably bullish news about 1971; the more production was reduced the more people suggested prices would rise. The annual report of one of the major U.S. aluminum companies for 1970, issued early in 1971, stated 1971 would be a better year than 1970.

Other indications of the demand-supply difficulty were showing in early 1971. At a meeting of the European Primary Aluminum Association, a plan was discussed to establish a joint aluminum stockpile to take up $100 million of surplus European aluminum. In spite of all these indications, prices for U.S. aluminum shares actually rose slightly late in 1970 and early 1971. A very careful examination of supply data for U.S. and world aluminum in 1970 and early 1971 would lead one to conclude that a sharp fall in earnings was due in 1971.

---

[5] A pot-line's capacity is likely to be some 20,000 to 40,000 tons per year. A pot-line is a line of small furnaces.

Capacity Studies Important

The nonferrous metals analyst needs data on metal production capacity especially for copper, aluminum, and nickel. The European Primary Aluminum Association and the newer International Primary Aluminum Institute collect detailed numbers on present and planned aluminum facilities. The EPAA data show almost every plant in the free world and its capacity. The U.S. Aluminum Association compiles such numbers for the United States. The major aluminum, copper, and nickel companies have statistical departments that do the same.

If trade associations and companies will not give the analyst data on capacity, the analyst should compile the data from various sources such as the trade literature. Nearly all of the companies that produce aluminum and other metals, and other companies that plan production, announce their plans to build new facilities, indicating expected capacity and the time production is likely to begin. One must keep in mind that such plans change. Four or five metal publications in the United States, as well as some in Canada and Europe and several in Japan, carry these announcements.

The nonferrous metals analyst probably needs to read regularly five or six North American metal and mining publications, several European ones, and at least one from Japan. He will then be able to keep his own statistics on aluminum, copper, nickel, molybdenum, lead, and zinc capacity changes. Of course, if the analyst can get materials from the companies or other sources, he can use them to check his own work. The data he collects will be imperfect, but if done carefully they will likely be sufficient. Surveying existing producers is useful, but it will omit new companies.

The International Lead-Zinc Study Group, sponsored by the United Nations, regularly surveys production capacity.

Need for Demand Forecasts

In the aluminum case cited above, even if demand had increased normally, it is likely prices and volume for the various companies would have fallen. Capacity increases largely dominated the market for aluminum. But the situation was further worsened by the failure of aluminum consumption to rise in 1970 and 1971 as much as normal.

Forecasting nonferrous metal consumption and demand is as difficult as forecasting other economic variables. The various metals correlate unequally with the various macroeconomic series. For example, copper consumption correlates closely with the physical volume of durable goods production; aluminum consumption does not correlate as well. Shipments of metal to users tends to be more volatile than consumption. If the analyst's forecast of metal consumption and shipments must depend on the usual forecast of the major economic variables by economists, he will be confronted with difficulties. Which economist is he to pick?

In some cases, the possibly more easily estimated supply side will play the major part in his problem. It is possible for a shortage to be so severe that even if demand does not rise much the analyst can have confidence in his view of product prices. At present (early 1974), this appears to be the outlook for aluminum for 1974 and 1975; if economic activity is flat, or even declines, and aluminum shipments and consumption fall, aluminum prices and company earnings in the United States are likely to rise. Extraordinary increases in demand can also "swamp" supply increases. This was largely responsible for increased copper prices and company earnings in 1973.

The analyst will do well to forecast demand by each major consuming area (for example, by early 1973 it was evident housing starts would fall in 1974 and even in late 1973). Residential housing in 1972 took about 20 percent of total aluminum shipments to U.S. markets. Some major using industries do not themselves correlate well with GNP or the other major economic series. By working with each consuming industry, one can possibly obtain a sufficiently accurate demand forecast even if the major economic series are forecasted incorrectly.

The problem is complicated by the ease with which metals move across international boundaries. One must forecast for the world, or at least for the free world.

Forecasting Cyclical Changes

The above focuses on the major problem for the nonferrous metals analyst; he must accurately forecast the industry's cyclical movements.[6] Probably the best measure of the ability of an analyst of a cyclical group is his success in forecasting these major changes. If he does not try, he is abrogating his responsibility. If he does not at least try, he will most likely be a reporter of current events rather than an analyst. If the analyst is to make money for his client, or to save money for him, he has to forecast. If he does not, he is asking his customer to do the forecasting.

The nonferrous metal analyst must guard against the common bias toward eternal bullishness, as well as the less common bias of bearishness. Both the bull and the bear will be right sometimes.

Aluminum shares lost from one third to two thirds of their value from early 1971 to late 1972; the analyst should have foreseen this. From the spring of 1973 to early fall they recovered—he should also have foreseen this. He should also have caught the recovery in copper which occurred a little earlier.

---

[6] Since the timing is irregular, this probably should not be called "cyclical."

The nonferrous analyst must guard against the "cheap stock" syndrome. In the summer of 1971, aluminum stocks had fallen considerably; suddenly the cheap stock notion began to circulate and there was a short-lived rash of buying. As it became apparent earnings were falling, this inclination dwindled; so did aluminum share values.

Too much emphasis cannot be put on getting the data. In nonferrous metals there are probably a thousand monthly series. For copper alone there are 300 or 400. Some of these are published in the trade publications, but many are not. In some cases trade associations publish a few series, but the more interesting ones are released only to member companies. In some cases the trade association releases none of its data to the public. Some trade associations do not provide all their data to all member firms; only those firms reporting statistic receive the corresponding numbers from all reporting members. Often series with somewhat similar names are defined differently. The analyst should know the definitions of the statistics.

Trends

The above discussion was concerned with what may be called the "short cycle."

Some longer-term trends can be observed. Aluminum has been called a growth metal, and until some time in the 1960s aluminum companies generally had a high price/earnings multiple. This multiple has been falling; so also has the industry's growth rate. Twelve or fourteen years ago, primary aluminum consumption in the United States was increasing at about twice the rate of increase in the physical volume of industrial production.[7] By the end of the 1960s, it had dropped considerably. In the early 1960s, 4 or 5 percent of the primary aluminum consumed in the United States each year represented market penetration for that year; by late in the 1960s, it was much less.[8] There is a connection between the decline in the growth rate of aluminum and the failure of average aluminum earnings to rise after 1966.[9] If growth had continued at the former rate, there would probably have been more upward pressure on prices. To some extent this might have been offset by even greater increases in aluminum capacity.

---

[7] As measured by the Federal Reserve Board index of industrial production of durable goods.

[8] These are calculated by comparing the increase in the physical volume of industrial production with aluminum consumption. The amount by which aluminum consumption increases exceed industrial production increases is defined as market penetration (a very broad definition). Such data should be calculated using three- or four-year moving averages. This excess (in tons), related to total aluminum consumption for the corresponding year, indicates the extent to which market penetration, in percent, contributed to total aluminum consumption.

[9] Earnings remained at least fair through 1970; 1971 and 1972 were the years of precipitous earnings decline.

For some years there appear to have been reverses in this declining trend; but if three- or four-year moving averages are used, the trend becomes clear. There is no necessity that this or comparable trends continue. It is possible that for aluminum the more moderate growth rate will continue unchanged; it might even increase—one can find reasons for such a view. Presently, many automobiles contain about 70 pounds of aluminum. If bumpers, hoods, engines, and some body work are made of aluminum to save weight and gasoline, it may rise greatly. There are a number of such growth possibilities, including construction. The great consumption increases of 1972 and 1973 may indicate a return to the "old" growth rate, though moderate consumer rebuilding of inventories is probably involved. Some caution is called for though. In addition, some present high aluminum growth areas, such as containers, are threatened (the Oregon effect). Aluminum wiring for construction is under attack.

The decline in the aluminum growth rate has been less outside the United States.

Copper More Complex

The trends are more complex in copper. During the 1950s, copper consumption in the United States dropped sharply relative to the physical volume of production of durable goods; with a one-to-one ratio at the beginning, by the end copper consumption was about 0.75. In the 1960s this changed and copper consumption about kept up with durable goods production.[10] In the United States, substitution by other materials and economization (thinner automobile radiator sheeting, etc.) had probably about run their course by the early 1960s. By 1973 copper consumption had lost only a few percentage points relative to durable goods production.

Europe appeared to lag behind the United States by about one decade —in the 1950s there was almost no copper "saving" but in the 1960s Europe acted much as the United States did the previous decade; industrial production rose sharply, but copper consumption changed little. Japan had a moderate amount of copper saving in both decades.[11]

One may, with some hesitation, expect little further copper saving. The chances are good that copper consumption in the world will increase at close to the same rate as industrial production.[12] But this is merely a

---

[10] Beginning with the mini-recession of 1967 and the nine-month copper strike going into 1968, this was interrupted. For 1973 it appears copper chew-up is almost up to the ratio of 1961–1965. There may, however, be some "stocking" by fabricators' customers, slightly distorting the figure.

[11] These data also require three- or four-year moving averages to see the trends clearly or by calculating trend lines.

[12] In 1972 and 1973 it appeared the increase in copper consumption in the free world exceeded slightly the increase in industrial production. Was this consumer stocking?

hypothesis; it is far from a certainty. Most nonferrous analysts will be mainly concerned with shorter-term changes and will probably not consider long-term movements. There is a tendency, of course, for production capacity in the metals approximately to meet changes in long-term demand trends. If Europe had not "saved" on copper in the 1960s, the world would have needed by the decade's end nearly 1 million short tons more per year—maybe 15 percent more than world capacity.

Materials Shortage

In 1973 one increasingly heard of the materials shortage. The implication is that supply will fail to grow as much as demand. Traditionally it has been maintained that the two always about fit; that prices rise to squeeze off the less intense demand so that the demand which remains will be equal to supply.[13] In this sense, over the long run, it will remain true—assuming prices are permitted to perform this function. Increasing world population and standards of living and decreasing finds of high-grade ore bodies probably mean the equilibrium prices will be considerably higher. Some high-grade ore bodies will probably be found and developed, but the average grade of new mines will probably fall. With aluminum, the ore shortage is less critical, since there are huge known and undeveloped bauxite supplies as well as nonbauxite aluminum-containing ores. However, aluminum production requires considerable electrical power; "aluminum is bauxite plus power." Here, the energy shortage is more significant than the ore shortage.

Most bauxite is in equatorial areas and most aluminum is used in other areas. This may lead to a government promoted bauxite cartel and higher bauxite prices.

Though long-term factors may have less importance for the analyst than the short-term matters, they should not be neglected. The analyst will want to know the grade and amount of ore reserves a company has. If it has high-grade ore that will last for 20 years, the company is in a better position than if the ore grade falls off in 5 years. If a company has a number of high-grade undeveloped ore bodies, it has a possibility of earnings growth as they are brought into production—if ores are low grade, it may be many years before they are developed. The size of the ore deposit and its grade are only some of the factors to be considered. The analyst should also make inquiries about the geology of the deposit.

---

[13] A different emphasis can be placed on the materials shortage. A materials shortage means materials output per unit of input drops sharply—productivity falls rapidly and costs and prices rise drastically. The economy grows less rapidly, or nongoods industries, the prices of which rise much less, grow "at the expense of" goods industries. The latter might even decline. There is a redirection of economic activity away from materials-using industries.

In a more fundamental sense there is no materials shortage—much of the world is useable material. But instead of the U.S. getting its materials for less than 1 percent of the national income it may cost 2 percent.

A copper deposit grading 0.45 percent copper with 25 feet of soft over-burden is likely to be much more profitable than one with 0.65 per-cent copper and 300 feet of a hard rock overburden. Of importance too, are the availability of power, water, and transportation. With foreign mines, the political and investment climate must be weighed, as develop-ments in Chile and other countries have made clear. Several Canadian provinces are so greatly increasing taxes that some describe them as confiscatory. They are accused of unfairness because the "rules are changed after the mines were developed and the funds spent."

Mainly to encourage U.S. companies to invest in countries in need of development, the U.S. government established the Overseas Private In-vestment Corporation. Companies with investments in less developed areas pay an insurance premium for which they are insured against the costs of expropriation. There has been criticism of such measures since they are inclined to reduce care on the part of U.S. companies develop-ing mining and other properties abroad, as well as passing costs onto the U.S. taxpayer if the insurance premiums do not cover fully the costs arising from expropriated properties. In addition, it tends to make the United States less self-sufficient in raw materials and invites dif-ficulties in U.S. relations with other countries. It may also invite ex-propriation. It has been suggested that OPIC has struggled too vigorously to avoid payment of claims.

CASE STUDY: UTAH INTERNATIONAL[14]

Utah International in 1973 probably will have received about 33 per-cent of its net income from copper and by-products, about 42 percent from coal, 12 percent from shipping, and the remainder from iron ore and uranium mining. In a few years it will be involved in other ac-tivities. This is one of the mixed companies referred to above—no prod-uct or service provides 50 percent of its income, and it may be studied by coal or energy analysts, nonferrous metals analysts, "growth stock" analysts, or even shipping analysts.

Utah was selected because it presents some exceptionally interesting analytical problems.

Utah has had earnings increases every year for the past ten. Its pub-licity emphasizes a sales backlog of billions of dollars which, at the current sales rate, extends for seven or eight years.[15] Some of its long-term contracts have highly sophisticated cost-price escalation terms. Odds favor an earnings increase through 1977 and possibly longer.

---

[14] This is a summary of a 58-page report on Utah International written in Septem-ber 1973. The detail on calculating earnings for the various earnings sources is omitted here.

[15] Often overlooked is the fact that buyers as well as sellers may declare "force majeure"—in some cases they can refuse to accept shipments.

What price/earnings multiple does it deserve? In recent years the multiple averaged about 26 but has often exceeded 30. The common stock reached about $57 in October 1973. Its fiscal year ends October 31.

Some believe Utah's earnings will continue to rise for five or six years or longer and by about 15 percent per year. My examination suggests the increases will be less (Table 1, page 540), though owing to the volatility of prices and consumption they might be more than 15 percent per year.

The confusion about the price Utah's shares should have stems from the lack of specific criteria for determining the appropriate price/earnings multiple. Discussions with persons at institutions that hold the stock and with other interested parties suggest the multiple is determined largely by guess or by comparison of the past earnings stream with that of growth companies in other industries. In part, the problem is one of determining what the price of the shares will be if and when the earnings no longer increase.

There is much uncertainty in this area since some investors have learned that about 55 percent of Utah's earnings are in cyclical industries and thereby believe the company has the high multiple due to ignorance of this fact. These volatile earnings could drop so sharply in a world recession that the company's earnings advance could be set back several years.

No methodology appears to be used in dealing with this matter. Probably if and when the earnings advance ceases, and especially if earnings drop considerably and stay low for more than one year, Utah's share values will approach those of other companies in the same industries. To find this level, one should estimate earnings for each source and find the price/earnings multiple the market normally gives to each. A weighted average multiple for each year can be calculated and applied to the total earnings estimate.

Perhaps most important in Utah's high multiple has been its history of earnings increases. They have increased every year since 1963, and there have been only five reversals since 1948. Only once since 1951 has the company failed to raise the dividend. Stockholders' equity per share has increased from $0.41 in 1948 to $9.41 in 1972.

Possibly of equal importance has been the nature of its coking coal contracts. Utah's coking coal earnings can be predicted with some reliability since most of this material is sold on long-term contracts with cost-price escalation that includes not only labor but nearly all other costs. What price/earnings multiple does a company deserve when 35 to 40 percent of its earnings are almost certain to rise and the other 60 percent are highly volatile? The amount of increase in the 40 percent segment can be calculated with some precision.

The major source of Utah's earnings growth is Australia coking coal, most of which is contracted for by Japanese firms. In 1972 about 30 percent of Utah's earnings came from Australian coking coal, with Marcona—a 46 percent owned company, most of whose earnings are from shipping—providing about 23 percent. The percent of earnings attributable to these will in part be determined by the volatile foreign copper price—much of Utah's earnings in some years will likely come from copper. Owing to very high copper prices in 1973, copper and by-product gold is contributing about 33 percent of earnings; coking coal, about 35 percent; and Marcona, about 16 percent. The remainder is from four or five smaller activities, including about 6 percent from U.S. steam coal. If copper prices in future years drop to the 1972 level, coal will contribute a greater percent to earnings, but earnings will then probably be lower.[16]

Utah's Australian Coal

The first mine developed was Blackwater; Peak Downs and Goonyella are also in production, and Saraji will probably begin production in late 1974. It is not certain that Norwich Park, the fifth mine, will be developed. The Australian government has recently instituted a new requirement. An amount equal to 33 percent of the foreign funds for a new mining or other venture must be placed as an interest-free escrow fund in the Australian Reserve Bank. This might not apply to Norwich Park, but uncertainties in the Australian investment climate will probably slow it and other new mining developments there. None of the backlog of coking coal sales used in connection with these estimates is dependent on the development of the Norwich Park mine.

Cost-Price Escalation

The coking coal sales contracts entered into in mid-1972 include cost escalation provisions covering not only labor, materials, and supplies, but rail freight, harbor dues, local taxes, rentals, royalties, and export excises. Some of the contracts limit escalation to $2.20 in five years; this amounts to about 4 percent compounded per year.

Some, and possibly all, new contracts contain currency revaluation offsets.

Some of the contracts are for five years with renegotiation of future sales. Generally, new contracts have been at higher prices—and not only to offset rising costs; very likely they are more profitable.[17] By 1976 Utah's

---

[16] Since this was written, the Arab oil squeeze occurred. This development will probably be beneficial to Utah's coking coal, steam coal, uranium, and small oil and gas business but may adversely affect its shipping, copper, and iron ore income.

[17] Late in 1973 a $1 per ton price increase was "given" by the Japanese in addition to the normal escalation. The Australian government, via taxes, probably gets about 47.5 percent of this—it possibly applied some pressure on the Japanese. In early 1974 there was a $10.60 increase—over 50 percent of the fob Australian port price. Since prices were renegotiated up, can they also be renegotiated down?

annual coking coal capacity will be about 17 million tons, six times its capacity in 1971 and well over double its 1972 capacity. About 16 million will be sold on long-term contracts.

Older coal contracts did not contain provisions offsetting losses from currency revaluation. In April 1973, agreement was reached with Japanese buyers changing prices enough to compensate for those cost increases attributable to exchange rate changes.

Uncertainty Later

Some of the coking coal contracts are to be renegotiated in 1977 or 1978. Some terminate then. Utah's coking coal may then become less profitable. More Western Canadian coal and competing Australian coal may restrict profits.

It seems more likely that the low mining cost of the Australian coal and a continuing increase in metal production in Japan and Europe will mean continued markets for Utah's coal, possibly at even higher prices.

Growing shortage of petroleum will probably spur demand for both coking and steam coal. This may lift the earnings above those indicated here. Utah has enough U.S. steam coal reserves to push this source of earnings well above the $10 million shown in line two of Table 1.

Coal consumption per ton of steel has been decreasing, but it is doubtful this will lead to overcapacity in coking coal. Japan's coke use, per unit of iron output, is very low since it also uses much oil in its metallurgical furnaces. The oil supply problems will probably reverse this.

Utah, though presently showing some signs of hesitation about developing its Norwich Park mine, may bring it and a sixth mine into operation, in which case the tonnage and income shown in Table 1 for 1980 and possibly 1979 will probably be too low.

The Australian income tax is 47.5 percent, and there is no depletion allowance. Utah is not using the Australian fast tax write-off.

Weighted Average Multiple

It is easy to cast doubt on the high UC price/earnings multiple. This can be most easily clarified by showing the company's earnings in three classes. Class A earnings are those from products on long-term contracts, at fixed prices, with cost escalation that covers most costs. These are largely dependable earnings, and even though some of the contracts contain minimum-maximum provisions they give a considerable certainty about earnings growth. Buyers can "escape," though, for part of the shipments by use of "force majeure" Class A earnings can be given a multiple of anywhere from 15 to 40. I cannot go to the higher end, but a case can be made for them.

TABLE 1***

Utah International Earnings (in $ millions, after taxes; by source)

	1972	1973	1974	1975	1976	1977	1978	1979	1980
Coking coal*	11.9	20.6	22.9	27.4	29.4	30.1	22.6*	22.6	22.6
Steam and gas coal	3.4	3.5	3.5	3.5	4.1	6.1	9.0	10.4	10.6
High multiple earnings†	15.3	24.1	26.4	30.9	33.5	36.2	31.6	33.0	33.2
Island Copper	2.1	13.3	11.9	8.2	9.2	12.8	4.3	5.2	8.6
Australian iron‡	2.8	2.8	3.1	2.7	2.3	1.8	1.3	.8	0.0
Cedar City iron	0.7	0.7	0.7	0.7	0.7	0.7	0.7	0.7	0.7
Uranium	2.1	1.0	2.4	3.6	1.0	3.0	3.4	3.8	3.8
Marcona¢	9.2	9.4	11.5	11.7	12.1	12.6	13.1	13.6	14.2
Marconaflo			0.1	0.2	0.3	0.4	0.5	0.5	0.5
Brazil iron							0.2	0.5	0.6
Saudi steel							0.2	0.5	0.6
Waipipi iron			0.3	0.5	0.6	0.6	0.5	0.5	0.5
Total Marcona	9.2	9.4	11.9	12.4	13.0	13.6	14.8	16.0	17.2
Interest income	3.0	3.0	3.0	3.0	3.0	3.0	3.0	3.0	3.0
Lower multiple earnings‖	19.9	30.2	33.0	30.6	29.2	34.9	27.5	29.5	33.3
Pima copper	3.6	5.7	5.4	4.6	4.8	5.7	3.4	3.9	5.3
Utah shipping					1.0	1.0	1.0	1.0	1.0
Land, joint ventures	1.0	2.0	0.0	3.0	3.0	3.0	3.0	3.0	3.0
Low multiple earnings#	4.6	3.7	5.4	7.6	8.8	9.7	7.4	7.9	9.3
Total EAT	39.8	58.0	64.8	69.1	71.5	80.8	66.5	70.4	75.8
Earnings per share**	1.38	2.02††	2.25	2.40	2.49	2.81	2.31¶	2.45	2.63

† Earnings multiple may be 20–30–40, etc.

‖ Earnings multiple assumed to be 10.

Earnings multiple assumed to be 8.

* Drop in contract sales in 1978 of 3.6 million tons per year. New contract may be arranged before then.

¢ Existing operations—shipping and Peruvian iron. Some earnings may be included for 1972 and 1973 for Waipipi and Marconaflo.

** I used 28.772 million shares, as indicated by the company in early 1973. Fully diluted.

¶ This earnings drop comes from the end of the Blackwater coal mine sales contract; it will possibly be renewed or replaced before then. Also, I have assumed we would be at a cyclical low in the highly volatile foreign copper price. This could come in any other year—and might not happen at all. It also reduced Pima's earnings in 1978. I assumed the 1978 foreign average copper price dropped from $0.70 a pound to $0.62—still about $0.14 higher than the 1972 average. For a corresponding reason, Island Copper's 1977 earnings may be too high.

‡ Mt. Goldsworthy sales contracts may be renegotiated by 1976, owing to sharply falling margins. A major contract ends in 1979.

†† I doubt Utah will show $2.02; more likely $1.85. (After this was written Utah's earnings were reported at $1.80 per share. It also set aside reserves of $7 million, $0.24 per share, for contingencies).

*** Coking coal long term contracts were renegotiated early in 1974, first with Japanese customers and later European. Prices were raised $1 per ton and later $10.60. There are a number of reasons customers decided not to hold Utah to the terms of the contract. This price increase will raise earnings in 1974 to over $3 PS and 1975 earnings will be much higher. Utah's share value rose from about $35 to about $45.

Class B earnings are for products sold on long-term contracts in which the prices vary and for which there are no cost escalation provisions. Included also are earnings which for other reasons have gotten higher than minimum multiples. The major income for Utah in this category is from Island Copper and Marcona Corporation, a 46 percent owned subsidiary. The relevant copper prices are those of the London Metal Exchange (a commodity exchange).

Island Copper earnings cannot be put in Class A. I would put a multiple on them of about 10 times earnings. Most metal mining firms get a multiple of 7 to 11, depending on the circumstances and the phase of the business cycle. One can give it two points above Class C earnings, partly because the long-term sales contracts guard against excessive charges if these concentrates had to be sent to a smelter for refining at "spot" prices during a smelter shortage. The contracts though do not provide for fixed smelter costs to Utah. Concentrates are seldom sold except on long-term contracts.

Class C products or services are those getting variable prices and for which some sales are without contracts of a year or more—this includes what the metal trades call "spot" sales. There is no cost escalation. Such earnings deserve and get a slightly lower multiple than Class B. I am somewhat, but not entirely, arbitrary in giving these earnings a multiple of 8. This is about the multiple given to most metal-mining firms by the market. Whether the multiple is 8 or 10 makes little difference in the calculation of appropriate share prices for Utah.

With these three sets of multiples, one can estimate what Utah's stock price should be. Its earnings have been calculated for each of its activities and classified in these three categories. Class A consists of Utah's coking coal business in Australia and its steam coal business in the United States.

It is possible some of the earnings shown here for 1973 will actually apear in 1974. Some, and possibly all, earnings declines shown here for 1978 may not occur; terminating coal contracts may be renewed and foreign copper prices may be maintained. Earnings may decline less than indicated here and just might increase.

After-tax earnings attributable to these three earnings classes are, in millions of dollars:

Earnings for the 12 parts of the company are shown in Table 1. They are assembled in Table 2. By using weights (multiples) of 10 and 8 for Classes B and C, and weights of 20–30–40 for Class A, one can see what the weighted average multiple of the company would be:

These numbers have been rounded; my calculation of relevant share values, therefore, gives slightly different results than those from use of these multiples.

Assuming Table 1 earnings estimates are correct and using the indi-

TABLE 2

Earnings	1971	1972	1973	1974	1975	1976	1977	1978	1979	1980
Class A	10	15	24	26	31	34	36	32	33	33
Class B	18	20	30	33	31	29	35	28	30	33
Class C	6	5	4	5	8	9	10	7	8	9
Total	34	40	58	65	69	72	81	67	70	76

TABLE 3

Weighted Average Price Earnings Multiples*

Class A	1972	1973	1974	1975	1976	1977	1978	1979	1980
Multiple 20**	14	14	14	14	14	14	15	14	14
Multiple 30	17	18	18	19	19	19	19	19	19
Multiple 40	21	22	22	23	24	23	24	24	23

* B multiple = 10; C = 8, in all cases.
** If class A earnings get a multiple of 20, B earnings 10 and C earnings 8, the weighted average multiple will be 14 except in 1978.

TABLE 4#

Utah International Appropriate Share Values Assuming Selected Relevant Price Earnings Ratios for Sources of Earnings ($ millions)

Class A	1972	1973	1974	1975	1976	1977	1978	1979	1980
High multiple 20*	18.8	28.3	31.3	34.2	35.9	40.0	33.6	35.4	37.2
High multiple 30†	24.1	36.7	40.5	45.0	47.6	52.6	44.5	46.9	48.7
High multiple 40‡	29.4	45.1	49.6	55.7	59.3	65.2	55.5	58.4	60.2
Actual range¢	32–	40–	43	57					

* Assumes coal, sold on long-term contracts with "complete" price-cost escalation, gets a price earnings multiple of 20. Other earnings get a multiple of 10 and 8.
† Assumes coal multiple is 30; others are 10 and 8.
‡ Assumes coal multiple is 40; others are 10 and 8.
¢ To October 1973.
Table 3 multiples times Table 1 EPS.

cated weighted price/earnings multiples of Table 3, the share values would be those in Table 4.

These data are set up for the user; you choose your own multiples other than the above 10 and 8, and the 20–30–40 for Class A earnings, and in a few minutes of arithmetic you will have your own appropriate share values.

If one does not apply a different multiple to each source of earnings, one is implying all the earnings deserve the same multiple—in which case Utah's Marcona and Pima earnings have had a multiple of 25 or 30.

Cyprus Mines Corporation, like Utah, owns 46 percent of Marcona— and Cyprus has had an average multiple of about 11. If Cyprus' Marcona earnings are given a multiple of 25 or 30, the rest of its earnings would get an absurdly low multiple. One can attempt to justify giving Utah's Marcona earnings nearly three times the value of Cyprus' Marcona earnings with the notion Utah will use them better.[18] Two times better; three times better? No. More detailed examination shows these are far-fetched. The difference is better explained as a case of imperfection in the securities markets.

Cyprus, like Utah, also owns some of Pima and the situation is similar to that of Marcona.

When Earnings Growth Stops

Utah's high multiple is based partly on the notion its earnings will continue to increase for many years.

To what level will the multiple drop if earnings flatten? To 12 or 15 or 18?[19] Assured flat earnings probably justifies a multiple of about 12. If earnings growth stops at $3 per share in five years, then the stock might be $45, well below its present price. Ought one discount that price to the present?

The recent price of $57 should appear too high in 1973 using the more "reasonable" multiple of 20 or even 40 for Class A products.

The above system merely provides the setting for a judgement, it does not "prove" that the $57 price is too high or too low. The Utah multiple is under that of some other growth stocks. One might say Utah is given a multiple too much influenced by the fact it is a mining company.[20]

The securities market has given stocks a value partly based on the notion that history is repetitious. The handsome chart of UC earnings and share value progressions, it says, are most likely to continue for years. Perhaps the essence of Utah, or the genius of its management, is the great confidence it has created in the investor.

---

[18] Cyprus has had earnings increases every year since 1962.

[19] Early in 1974 the multiple was under 15.

[20] Certainty of earnings growth takes a high multiple, not certainty of earnings.

22

Oil and Gas Industries

THOMAS L. OWEN

Vice President
National Securities and Research Corporation
New York, New York

DURING October 1973, the world oil industry took a dramatic turn, creating consternation in many of the countries of the free world. For it was at this time that a number of Arab oil-producing nations saw fit to cut petroleum supplies to the industrialized nations of the free world in the hopes of gaining concessions stemming from the Arab-Israeli War of October 1973. The dual act of cutting oil production and embargoing oil deliveries to the free world with the concomitant spiralling of crude oil prices has not only set in motion the reshaping of world economics but has caused the necessity of reshaping the oil industry and how its many components are to be analyzed for investment purposes. Thus, the use of oil as a political and economic weapon is changing life styles throughout the world, with the ultimate effects yet unknown. And it has also set in motion the possible use of other commodity items such as bauxite and copper (to name just two) produced in other countries to be used in a similar manner.

What we now have is a setting which is producing untold challenges to oil companies and governments alike. And it is up to the investment analyst to try to perceive the changes taking place and to capitalize upon them in the market place. This chapter will therefore discuss the investment factors critical to analyzing oil securities, particularly as the writer sees things shaping up in early 1974.

STRUCTURE AND SCOPE OF THE INDUSTRY

The oil industry in this country had its beginnings in the middle of the last century with the Drake discovery in Pennsylvania in 1859. It was

544

indeed an historic event because it was the seed that eventually set in motion the industrialized world as we know it today. The human element, of course, is *the* vital force in all activity, but *energy* is *the* nonhuman element which makes the industrialized world tick. If we were to extract energy from the world of economic activity, economies would crumble, because the wheels of industry would come to a halt. There would be no gasoline to move our automobiles; no heating oil to heat our homes and factories; no fuels for railroads, airplanes, trucks, and no natural gas for its innumerable end-products uses. So an oil and gas industry is absolutely vital to economic development.

The world oil and gas industry is composed of many different types of companies. The most well known are the so-called integrated companies—those that explore for oil and gas, produce oil and gas, transport crude oil and natural gas, refine crude oil and gas into products, transport products, and market products. Exxon is the largest such company in the world, and other similar companies are Texaco, Mobil Oil Corporation, Standard Oil Company of California, and Gulf Oil Corporation. Along with the Royal Dutch/Shell Group, they comprise the world's largest oil entities and are referred to as the "international oil companies." There are others, but these are the best known. All of them operate in many, many countries throughout the free world.

In addition, there are a host of other companies which are referred to as the "domestic integrated companies" of which Standard Oil Company (Indiana) is the largest. Others in this category are Shell Oil Company, Continental Oil Company, Cities Service Company, Marathon Oil Company, Union Oil Company, Sun Oil Company, and Atlantic Richfield Company, to name a few. Interestingly, these companies, for the most part, also carry on foreign activities and are often also referred to as the "new international companies" because their foreign operations are a relatively new aspect of their activity.

Then, too, there are a vast number of companies (some quite small and some of good size) which only undertake exploration and production of crude oil and natural gas. Louisiana Land and Exploration Company, Superior Oil Company, and Forest Oil Company are notable examples in this category. And then there are variations—either by size or scope of operation—which fall somewhere in between, such as Kewanee Oil, Tesoro Petroleum, and Mesa Petroleum. And not to be forgotten are a host of Canadian Oil companies which run the gamut of small exploration and producing companies to fully integrated companies, examples being Dome Petroleum and Imperial Oil Company (70 percent owned by Exxon). And then, too, there are a number of foreign companies (many very substantial in size) which should be recognized but which receive no attention by investors because they are owned and controlled by foreign governments. Examples here are the state controlled companies in such countries as France, Italy, Indonesia, Venezuela, Argentina, and Algeria, to name only a few; they are part of a growing breed as the world industry changes.

The composition of the industry also includes several allied industries —allied in the sense that they are vital to petroleum and natural gas operations. Here, the offshore drilling companies such as Sedco, Offshore Company, and Global Marine are notable. And such service companies as Halliburton, J. Ray McDermott, Schlumberger, Williams Companies, and the like must be included; they perform specialized activities vital to the flow of crude oil and natural gas. And not to be overlooked are such service companies which design and construct terminals, refineries, and petrochemical plants. Here, Fluor Corporation, Foster Wheeler, and Universal Oil Products are good examples. Thus, the so-called oil industry has many segments and offshoots. When it comes to the analytical factors vital to company analysis, the writer will devote his attention to the analysis of an integrated company.

Because of its critical role in society, it is not unusual that the oil and gas industry has become one of the largest industries in the world. The vast facilities needed to keep economies in motion dot the globe. The industry in the United States has exploration and production activities in more than half of our states, with Texas being the largest producer of crude oil. Oklahoma, California, New Mexico, and Louisiana (just to mention a few) are also large producers, and crude oil flows from one end of the country to the other with the exception of the New England states. During the last 25 years, offshore crude oil and natural gas production in the Gulf of Mexico has grown dramatically and has become one of our largest producing areas. And late in this decade, Alaska will become one of our most prolific producing states.

To deliver crude oil to the network of refining facilities, an array of pipelines crisscross this country; and tankers and barges also ship the vital crude oil to refining facilities where a multitude of finished and building-block products are turned out. Refining operations, petrochemical facilities, and gas plants stretch from coast to coast and represent a huge amount of capital investment. This same pattern stretches over the free world. Without these facilities we would not have the multitude of end-use products to turn the wheels of industry and provide growth to our gross national product.

The one operation of the industry which is most visible to the average consumer is the gasoline station; and gasoline is the largest profit producer of all refined products. It has been stated that more than 200,000 such stations dot our 50 states. And all of the major integrated companies have a network of marketing outlets selling their own branded products. Most gasoline stations receive their product by tank truck which, in turn, receives its product supply from a refinery directly or from a network of products pipelines and terminal facilities. Home heating fuel oil distribution is the next most visible operation, with the benefits affecting the lives of most Americans and people in foreign countries.

Now the cost of all these far-reaching operations runs into many billions of dollars. That is why the industry is called a very capital intensive industry. Billions of dollars are spent each year to provide for current and future growth of the industry and the world economy. To say the least, oil and gas operations affect the daily lives of every person throughout the industrialized world. And the industry is the backbone of the American economy and any industrialized society. Without energy, no other industry can function; today oil and gas together provide 75 percent of this country's total energy base.

What is highly significant for the future of world development is that oil and natural gas reserves exist in many sections of the world, both onshore and in offshore waters of continental shelves. Based on present technology of extraction, most of the large pools of onshore oil in the United States have probably been discovered. (And for the most part, oil and natural gas are searched for simultaneously.) As technology becomes more advanced and sophisticated, no doubt more reserves will be uncovered in new areas of our country and of the world, and some at very great depths.

Onshore production stretches the globe and occurs in large quantities in such foreign areas as Indonesia, Australia, the Middle East, Russia, China, Canada, Venezuela, and a number of other South American countries, to mention a few. To supplement onshore activities, a new facet of the producing industry had its beginnings about 25 years ago when the first offshore producing well was drilled in the Gulf of Mexico off Louisiana. What has developed over the intervening years has been a credit to the ingenuity of mankind. Today, offshore producing wells (both oil and natural gas) speckle the waters of the world. For the most part, a new industry has sprung up within an industry; and the sophistication of the technology and equipment being used staggers the imagination of even the most knowledgeable industry person.

At this point, it is important to mention that each facet of activity within the industry requires a tremendous amount of planning and capital; and each company plans according to its own set of logistics. Company A with large crude oil production in Texas and the Gulf of Mexico and a network of gasoline stations stretching across the southern tier of the United States does not want a refinery in Montana; it wants it geographically situated close to its producing and marketing outlets for efficiency and cost purposes. As companies expand, and production and marketing become more widespread and possibly international, the planning and erection of refineries and all other oil-operating facilities will have to be undertaken with efficiency and cost as the most significant factors. Exploration and production have always been considered the bread and butter of the industry and the biggest contributors to corporate profits. As companies go beyond the exploration and production facets of the business, they are adding what are called *downstream* investments. Historically, it has been true that the more one does to a barrel of crude oil (transporting it, refining it, marketing products, etc.) the less profit one makes; in other words, the largest profits are made from production. There is now indication, however, that the profit structure is shifting somewhat, and this will be covered later.

One very important item that all students of the industry should be aware of is the fact that prices of crude oil, natural gas, and refined products have been at low levels for a long period of time. For example, the price of gasoline at the service station pump (*excluding* state and federal taxes) has remained remarkably stable and low until just recently. And this has been true for many, many years.

Crude oil and natural gas prices have remained low over the years also, but time has now run out in maintaining such artificially low levels. Until recently, the price of crude oil around the world was set by the price of crude oil in our own Gulf Coast area. Now, the power base has shifted to the Middle East which now, for all practical purposes, sets the price of world crude oil. And until the last few years, the Federal Power Commission allowed only very low prices for natural gas transported in interstate commerce (the price of *intrastate* gas has not been regulated). Such a policy turned out to be self-defeating because there was no profit incentive to search for new reserves, and gas prices in the last few years have begun to rise substantially as a result. Now, since the 1973 war in the Middle East, the price structures for crude oil and refined products have spiralled, and the ramifications and repercussions around the world are now beginning to be felt. The consequences in such overwhelming world crude oil price increases are so staggering that obviously reason must at some point prevail and price levels must be adjusted downward to more economic and political levels.

CRITICAL FACTORS IN ANALYZING OIL SECURITIES

Corporate Operations

The key to an oil company's success and its future prospects is its individual operating segments. In this section of the chapter, the writer will discuss each segment individually.

Production. In an established company, there is a production base, or the amount of barrels of crude oil that is being produced daily. A small company might have 10,000 b/d (barrels a day) or less, whereas a very large international company might have 4 million b/d or more. The analyst should look at the makeup of the base figure and make some judgments from the facts. For example, if total company production is 800,000 b/d, with half of it produced in the United States and the other half produced in the Middle East, Africa, and South America, there is an obvious risk to the shareholder of the stock. That risk is the lack of security of reserves and future production levels. This is particularly pointed out as a result of the October 1973 Middle East war and the embargo on production. Up until relatively recently, there were several areas of the world outside the United States which were considered secure with respect to a production base. Now the winds are shifting, with nationalism spreading throughout the world and the number of secure areas dwindling.

Natural gas is somewhat of a different story. Company production levels usually reflect volumes being produced in the United States and Canada. Other areas of the world can produce gas and do, but for the most part it is *flared* (allowed to burn and escape into the atmosphere) because of a lack of local use. However, liquified natural gas operations appear to be a large factor in the future, and some are already in use. Natural gas production levels are measured in thousands of cubic feet per day (MCF/d).

Exploration. The key to a company's future growth is its exploration program for both oil and natural gas. In this connection, it should be pointed out that rarely does a company explore specifically for natural gas reserves; it does happen on occasion, but normally companies explore for hydrocarbons (oil or gas) and preferably oil, and hopefully the result is the discovery of one or the other.

In order to explore, companies must have acreage spreads—lands or waters on which they have paid for the right to conduct exploration and production operations. Acreage is obtained in the United States through state and federal lease sales and through arrangements with private parties. Obviously, large lease holdings in attractive geological formations in politically secure areas is the best position in which to be. Oil securities continually exhibit market moves based on a company's discoveries (here the size and location of the discovery are most important) and discoveries made on adjacent or nearby acreage. An analyst should study the acreage positions, make judgments on their prospects, and attempt to find out in what new areas a company might be seeking leases. At the moment, the North Sea is probably the "hottest" exploratory area in the world, and an analyst should attempt to learn which company has what acreage positions, their location with regard to known reserves, and possible future potential. As mentioned earlier, a discovery often means a stock market move for the company making the discovery as well as for a stock of a company with nearby acreage positions. Overall, it is important that the analyst assess the potential of the acreage in terms of likely production and how secure production might be.

Crude Oil and Natural Gas Reserves and Their Location. The possession of large and politically secure reserves is the best position in which to be. Because of the difficulty in finding new reserves today, in conjunction with rapidly growing demand throughout the world, company reserve positions have tended to decrease and in some cases rather dramatically. Oil and natural gas reserve positions are measured in the number of years' supply. The analyst should attempt to learn the years' supply of both hydrocarbons, but it should be pointed out that often such data is not revealed, for competitive and other reasons.

For several consecutive years, the oil industry in the United States has produced annually more oil and gas than it has found in new discoveries. This means that the reserve position is sliding for the industry. Massive exploration programs around the world have been instituted to help correct the downtrend. Although an improving reserve trend is anticipated, the quality of the reserves, for political reasons, will tend to come down.

Downstream Operations. Every integrated company has what are called "downstream operations." These consist of pipelines, refineries, chemical plants (in some cases), natural gas plants, tanker fleets, and service station facilities. These facilities handle the basic hydrocarbons and ultimately transform them into building-block or end-use products for the consumer.

In order to distribute crude oil to its refineries, a company transports the crude by tankers and pipelines, for the most part. In many instances, pipeline operations are joint ventures with other oil companies shipping crude oil into the same geographic region. Studies have shown that pipeline transportation is the least expensive way of moving oil. Tankers are used most often to transport foreign oil, and the tendency in recent years has been to build super tankers so as to lower unit costs. Many integrated oil companies own tanker fleets; and because world scale rates have fluctuated rather widely in recent years according to demand and international events, an analyst should study a company's tanker situation to determine the effect on costs and net profits.

Once at the refinery, the crude oil is manufactured into a number of products with gasoline, home heating oil, aviation fuel, and diesel fuel the best known. At certain times of the year, one product will be emphasized more than another so as to build up inventories. Usually during the summer months heating oil is emphasized so as to build inventories for the fall and winter heating seasons. With the aid of catalysts and high-technology equipment (platformers, reformers, etc.), the yield from a barrel of oil can be adjusted. In other words, sometimes more gasoline can be manufactured from a barrel while at other times more home heating oil can be manufactured. But the swing in thruput is not that substantial, although it is enough to make it worthwhile. A large integrated company usually has several refineries, and the analyst should determine the total company capacity, how modern the facilities are, and what plans are being made for future expansion.

Most refineries turn out basic materials for petrochemical operations. And as an adjunct to refinery operations, a number of oil companies have entered the chemical business over the years. Most such plants are usually adjacent to a refinery and work with the building blocks that are eventually turned into synthetic fibers and plastics. An analyst should determine the quantities of petrochemicals being produced, the price structure, expansion plans, and the effect on the overall net profits of the company. Most large producers of natural gas also have plants that strip liquids from wet gas. These products have a number of uses throughout the oil and chemical industries.

Once the products are manufactured at the refinery, they are transported by pipeline, barge, tank truck, etc. to marketing terminals and service stations. The analyst should determine the overall marketing volumes for refined products and the price structures of the principal products such as gasoline and home heating oil. It might also be worthwhile to determine a company's plans regarding adding or eliminating service stations. There are believed to be in excess of 200,000 service stations in this country at this time, and several companies are reducing the number of stations selling their brand. In light of the administration's plan to reduce demand and therefore conserve, it could be that a fair number of smaller stations on less traveled roads will be closed.

Overall Operating Logistics. The most efficient companies are those which have the best operating logistics. Many oil companies in their annual reports to shareholders include a map of their U.S. operations— and those companies which are international also show a map of international operations. The map will indicate the different types of activities which are performed in different areas of the country or world. The analyst should note the coordination or lack of coordination of facilities. For example, with heavy production in the Southwest and a vast network of service stations in the Southwest, a company should have a substantial refinery in the Southwest. (Of the major companies, Texaco has long been considered the company with excellent logistics.) The same type of rationale should be used for international operations. The analyst should attempt to give some sort of qualitative weighting to logistics.

Crude Oil Sufficiency Ratio. This particular ratio is of major importance in anlyzing an integrated company. By way of example, the ratio for a domestic integrated company is determined by dividing the total domestic crude oil production figure by the total domestic refinery runs:

$$\frac{80,000 \text{ b/d production}}{100,000 \text{ b/d refinery runs}} = 80 \text{ percent}$$

"Refinery runs" is a term referring to the crude oil thruput of the facility. It can be the same as refinery capacity, and in some instances can be more than refinery capacity, but in most cases is something less than refinery capacity.

A low percentage, such as 30 percent, suggests that a company's crude production is far short of its refinery needs. If crude oil were selling at giveaway prices, that would be fine for the crude-short buyer. But those days are apparently behind us. It is a general rule that the major companies can produce crude oil at a lower cost than they can buy it. Thus, there is indeed a cost advantage to having a high sufficiency ratio, and most companies aim in this direction. It is a credit to management to have the highest percentage possible.

The analyst should determine the ratio on a worldwide basis for an international company and then determine the domestic percentage. In relation to all other factors necessary in analyzing the company and its stock, the analyst can then make a qualitative judgment on this factor.

Earnings

The many cost factors involved in oil company operations are similar to those of any manufacturing operation in another industry; but there are certain factors that must be studied closely because they have a significant effect on net income and ultimately on the price of the stock. The two factors which affect earnings the most are *pricing* and *volume growth*.

Prices. Prices for crude oil, refined products, and natural gas have been low over the years; and with relatively small demand increases (until the early 1970s), oil company earnings for the integrated companies recorded only modest growth for the most part. The intent was to keep consumer prices down so that energy costs would not be a large part of the average consumer's budget. Politically, of course, this was very palatable.

As it became apparent that domestic supplies of crude oil and natural gas were becoming more limited, prices began to move up—for crude oil, rather slowly, but more rapidly for natural gas. And as a result of the Arab-Israeli war of fall 1973 and the Arab embargo, prices of crude oil and refined products soared. It should be noted that foreign producer governments use *posted prices* (artificial figures used to calculate tax payments by oil companies to foreign producer governments) for crude oil.

In late 1973, we saw quantum jumps in the price of foreign crude oil not only from the Arab countries but also from such areas as Venezuela and Indonesia. At virtually the same time, our government established a two-tier crude oil price system for U.S. production; "old" oil (oil from wells producing from a base period in 1972) was allowed to sell at $5.25/barrel or $1.00/barrel more than the then existing average price, and "new" oil (oil from wells producing from that 1972 base period onward) was allowed to sell at whatever the buyer was willing to pay. ("New" oil averaged out to slightly more than $10.00/barrel.) At the same time, refined product prices both here and abroad recorded dramatic increases, and these were particularly noticeable for gasoline and home heating oil.

The analyst should focus on these price changes very carefully, particularly crude oil changes, as the impact on net earnings can be very dramatic; it should not be forgotten that the big profit segment for any integrated oil company has been the production segment.

In any study on pricing, the analyst should also look very carefully at product prices in Europe and at crude oil prices generally around the world. Over the years, the Federal Power Commission has regulated the price of natural gas and until the last few years has kept it at inordinately low levels. Within the past couple of years, prices for newly discovered natural gas have been allowed to increase rather substantially. And there is even talk that gas prices might be deregulated altogether. This is another area in which the analyst should pay close attention.

Volumes. Historically, refined product volume has fit a pattern. But in the past two years the pattern has been broken on the upside. Demand in the United States has increased faster, due to the new automobiles getting lower mileage per gallon of gasoline and because utilities switched their energy source from coal to oil. So, demand has increased for environmental reasons and increased at a time when domestic crude oil production has been static at best; in fact, domestic crude oil production peaked out in 1971 for the industry. All of this means that from this point on, our imports of crude oil will grow rather dramatically, with the Middle East supplying most of the increment—at least through this decade and probably longer.

The volume effect on net profits of the oil companies began taking place in the last half of 1972, and with such a double-barrelled action (prices and volumes) net incomes soared in 1973.

When an analyst studies a particular company, he or she can obtain a rather quick view as to how earnings are coming along by studying crude oil and natural gas production changes, and pricing changes for crude oil, refined products, and natural gas. A discussion of these items with management should assist an analyst considerably in making an earnings estimate.

Net Income and Cash Flow. As mentioned earlier, the industry is very capital intensive because of the requirement of huge sums of money needed to expand exploration and production and all the downstream operations. Because of very heavy investments in facilities and equipment, depreciation and other noncash charges are high for the individual companies. The total cash flow for an individual integrated company is therefore large. At times, the level of net income is attacked politically, but the analyst should be aware of the need of extensive earnings and cash flow in order that companies have the internally generated funds to provide for the heavy and expensive expansion needed for an expanding industrialized world.

Accounting Policies. Unfortunately, accounting policies for the industry are not uniform, and therefore earnings for the individual companies are not comparable. There is no one accounting approach considered correct and all others incorrect. The accounting profession has been working on this problem for a considerable period of time, and possibly—down the road—some uniform principles will be established and required. At the moment, however, one company might *expense* drilling costs whereas another company might *capitalize* them, for example. This produces different effects on net earnings so that if Company A's accounting policies were imposed on Company B, Company B's earnings could very well be different from earnings developed under its own method. What the analyst should watch for is a *consistency* in accounting policies; if earnings of a company are growing year by year through the use of the same accounting policies, then the company is moving forward and the earnings pattern is consistent with accounting policies. For example, it would be an exercise in futility for the analyst to attempt to reconstruct Company A's earnings using Company B's accounting policies, assuming there are some sizable differences. It is very important for the analyst to learn if a company is contemplating any major accounting changes or if some have already been established. At such point, all prior-year earnings would have to be adjusted by the company under study so as to show a history of comparable earnings.

Taxes. Oil companies pay a lower tax rate on income than many other companies in other industries, and analysts should be aware of this. The industry over the years has been granted a depletion allowance on its producing operations, as is the case for all extractive industries. Originally, this allowance was set at 27.5 percent, the highest rate for any extractive industry. Within the last few years the rate has been reduced to 22 percent because of heavy political pressure. It should be pointed out, however, that the need for such an allowance today is stronger than ever, what with the difficulties in finding new and secure reserves. An oil company is depleting its asset base with each barrel of oil and each MCF of natural gas produced, thereby requiring the search for more oil or gas in order to maintain and hopefully improve its asset base. In effect, a company is allowed to drill up its tax liability on its producing operations but does pay income taxes on its downstream operations within the limits of tax law requirements.

Tax paid to foreign governments can be applied as a *credit* against domestic taxes. In addition to income tax payments, oil companies pay other taxes such as severance taxes and state and federal excise taxes. Thus overall, the amount of money paid to governments for being allowed to do business is very heavy. In their annual reports, many integrated companies indicate separately their tax payments other than income taxes; income taxes can be determined from the profit and loss statement.

Profits Breakdown. An external analyst (one working in the financial community as opposed to one working for an oil company) finds it virtually impossible to break down earnings by operating divisions (production, refining, marketing, etc.) because this information is not revealed for competitive reasons. As mentioned earlier, however, it is generally known that the producing segment of a company historically has produced the bulk of profits; the more that is done to a barrel of oil (refining, transporting, marketing, etc.), the less the return. But companies involved in international operations are inclined to show profit breakdowns by Western Hemisphere and Eastern Hemisphere. It is important for the analyst to study all shareholders' material, including special year-end statistical supplements, as well as statements filed with the SEC (such as a 10-K or a filing in connection with an underwriting) in order to learn as much as possible about the profit structure.

The analyst should then attempt to relate the current corporate picture in relation to the previous year-end figures as an approach to developing an earnings estimate for the current year.

Quality of Earnings. Earnings derived from U.S. operations obviously are of the highest quality because they are the most secure. One can never be sure as to what foreign governments might do to hamper the flow of foreign earnings; and therefore foreign earnings are of a lesser quality. Here, the quality varies by country, according to its governmental and political policies. At the moment, earnings from Indonesia are more secure than they are from Libya. The analyst must adjust his appraisal of a company's earnings according to the earnings' source. Obviously, the stock of a company whose earnings are two thirds foreign and one third domestic is not as attractive (all things being equal) as one whose earnings breakdown is reversed.

Earnings per Share History. To see how well a company has performed its business over the years, the analyst should look at a company's earnings per share history. If earnings have faltered in any particular year due to circumstances beyound management's control, that must be factored into the picture; if it should occur with some frequency, it should raise a red flag.

A consistency in earnings growth is ideal and makes a company's stock an attractive vehicle, all things being equal. Any acceleration of earnings' growth makes the stock even more attractive.

The most important clue, however, relates to current earnings growth and future prospects. Today's integrated oil stocks are selling on the basis of earnings trend, earnings quality, and, most importantly, world political and economic events. The analyst must attempt to relate these factors in his recommendations to investors. The earnings per share history, if negative, should become a lesser factor if current and future prospects have taken on a decided positive tone.

Return on Investment.   Historically, the oil industry has not fared well in this category, particularly when compared with the results of other manufacturing industries. This can be traced principally to a relatively low price structure for crude oil, natural gas, and refined products at a time when costs were rising more rapidly.

There are now some changes in the wind which had their beginnings a couple of years ago with an upward price movement for natural gas. But the Middle East war of 1973 has brought this more shockingly into focus. World crude oil prices have soared, and product prices have also taken quantum jumps. At this writing it is not certain where prices will settle, but the prospect is for a more balanced improvement for rate of return on investment. It seems likely that world crude oil prices will not stay at current inordinately high prices—they should come down to some middle ground (between prewar prices and current levels, and probably nearer current levels). If some of the profit is siphoned away from the producing end by foreign governments and if product prices remain high as expected (low cost energy for consumers is now a thing of the past), then return on investment for downstream investments becomes much more attractive. This looks like the likely scenario over the years ahead. This will foster badly needed refinery construction to meet burgeoning consumer needs and will make attractive and economical alternate energy sources in our quest for energy self-sufficiency in the decade ahead.

But the important item at the moment is the shift in corporate profitability for the oil industry—a fact which should make oil equities more attractive investment vehicles in the years ahead. This better overall rate of return on investment prospect is long overdue. The analyst should watch governmental policy and industry and individual company developments very carefully.

Effect of Federal and State Regulations.   Federal and state policies have tended to become more pronounced in recent years, and many of them have been related to the quality of life or the environmental factor. This is particularly true with respect to offshore lease sales, the construction of the Alaska pipeline, refinery construction, and the content of gasoline.

Historically, there has been no pattern on federal and state offshore lease sales. Presumably, when either government felt it wanted to raise money, it would announce an impending sale. Oil companies were therefore unable to plan, particularly in their capital budgets, for the needed acreage in order to search for more crude oil and natural gas reserves. Now, because of the energy shortage, there is indication that the federal government will schedule lease sales on a continuing basis; the same could hold true for some of the states.

Construction of the Alaska pipeline has also been held up primarily for environmental reasons, and this has hurt the profit outlook for the companies involved. The Prudhoe Bay, Alaska oil discoveries were announced in the late 1960s, but by 1974 the construction of the line had yet to take place. President Nixon signed the bill authorizing construction, but certain legal matters had to be cleared before construction can begin. As a result, production of the much-needed oil will probably not occur before 1977–78.

The lack of sufficient domestic refinery capacity is one of the leading problems for the domestic industry today; and this is the primary problem with respect to probable shortages of gasoline and heating oil over the next several years. It takes approximately three years from the design of a facility to its actual operation, and no new plants are under construction in the U.S. today. Local communities have thwarted construction, primarily for aesthetic and pollution reasons. In addition, the possible design for such a facility has been "up in the air" because design often depends on the source and quality of the crude oil to be used. And this has to be related to the import policy which, until recently, limited imports to a percentage of domestic production. So, for lack of understanding the whole situation, governments have created a problem of immense proportions. Remember, companies must plan ahead for these facilities and they are enormously expensive.

Another environmental problem has been in the manufacture of gasoline: What should the lead content be, if any? And with respect to heating oil, what levels of sulphur will be allowed? The many crude oils from around the world differ in sulphur content: low-sulphur oil being "sweet" crude and high-sulphur oil being "sour" crude. Oil from the Middle East, where the bulk of our domestic requirements will come from over the years ahead, is "sour," and in order to meet air pollution standards, very expensive desulphurization units will have to be constructed. Each community and state appears to be setting up its own standards with respect to clean air, and this goes right back to the manufacture of gasoline and heating oil.

All of these factors create substantial operating problems for the companies and thwart momentum. No oil company is against clean air and clean water, but vacillation and delay cause untold headaches.

It is important that the analyst be aware of these factors as he studies a particular company; profit prospects could hang in the balance.

Statistical Ratios and Judgments

As in the analysis of any security, there are certain ratios which an analyst should ascertain. These ratios are discussed elsewhere in this handbook and should be looked into as another analytical tool. The analyst might particularly want to look at the current ratio and the liquid ratio.

The debt/equity ratio for the integrated oil industry has been historically low over the years, reflecting the abilities of companies to internally generate all or most of their capital needs. But in recent years, the percentage of debt to equity has begun to increase. The reason is now just the opposite: Companies have been finding it more difficult to generate internally all of their needs. What the trend in this ratio will be for the future will depend upon the price structure of the industry (a primary clue to profitability). The analyst should watch this ratio for the industry and for the individual companies because the amount of external financing will hang in the balance. Because integrated oil companies have such vast assets, it is worthwhile to determine the asset value per share. The object here, of course, is to see if the stock is undervalued. During times of inflation and when oil prices are soaring, a stock selling at or below asset value will have a tendency to rise.

Finally, the analyst should take a good look at the items in "Notes to Financial Statements." On occasion, a noteworthy item crops up in that section which could have a significant bearing on the stock. Such items as accounting changes, changes in methods of inventory valuation, and any impending litigation usually appear in such notes.

Other Significant Data

Major Financing Programs. There is strong indication that outside financing programs through the capital markets will be enormous in the years ahead. This means the analyst must screen each company to learn the size of a possible financing, the timing, and the form (whether it be bonds, stock, or some variation). Heavy outside capital needs stem from the fact that companies are no longer able to internally generate all their needs. And here, much will depend upon the level of profitability of the industry and the individual companies in the years ahead. If prices continue to climb here in the United States with profits continuing to soar, there will be tremendous political pressure to place an excess profits tax on the industry or to reduce profits in some way, shape, or form. This would be a negative factor from the viewpoint of investing because negative investment psychology would be rampant. Whatever develops, it seems likely that very large financing programs are in the offing, and the analyst must be alert to them.

Capital Expenditures. Over the years, the oil industry has been one of the largest spenders of capital in the country. The reasons should now be obvious as a result of previous remarks. If anything, these outlays should now begin to accelerate because of shortages, crisis situations, and the long term goal of U.S. self-sufficiency. Expenditures will find their way into every segment of the industry, but the largest portions should be in exploration, production, and refining over the decade of the 1970s; with the exception of refineries, this has historically been true. The major financing programs mentioned previously will be big contributors to the capital expenditure outlays and the two go hand in hand. The analyst will want to study the capital programs of the individual companies so as to get a fix on the future corporate outlook.

Dividends. The integrated oil industry has historically paid out close to 50 percent of its earnings in dividends. With controls in effect in recent years, the percentage has tended to slip, particularly for the year 1973. With the need for heavy capital programs in the future and the concommitant need for outside financing over the decade ahead, it should be recognized that dividends will probably not rise as fast as in earlier years. This is not to say that corporate directors are not cognizant of their shareholders; to the contrary, corporate directors in the oil industry have been well aware of shareholders and their support. It would be prudent to assume, however, that dividend increases might be smaller and more spread out in the years ahead than in the past unless corporate profitability growth exceeds the writer's expectations.

It is essential that the analyst be aware of any possible change in dividend levels and payouts with respect to specific stocks, since many of the big company stocks have afforded a relatively high yield over the years. The level of yield can also be used as a yardstick at times when attempting to determine the "floor" for a stock.

Management

Probably the best way to assess a company's management is to determine earnings growth over a period of management continuity. In other words, it takes time for a specific management to implement its programs with the resulting effects on earnings per share. The one thing that interests the shareholder is the price of the stock, and one of the main determinants of the stock price is the earnings trend.

Once the analyst makes his judgment on management, he should attempt to find out if there are any top management changes pending. The departure of a charismatic chief executive of a company could signal trouble for its stock until the new leader proves himself; and just the opposite, the entrance of a new and vibrant chief executive into a position previously held by someone less inspiring might create a different price movement in the company stock.

MARKET BEHAVIOR OF SECURITIES

The stocks of the major integrated companies have their own market cycles, depending upon events that affect the outlook for oil companies. Thus, movements can occur when stocks of companies in other industries are languishing or when the rest of the market is not decisive or moving downward. The business cycle has little or no bearing, since the demand for oil company products is essentially inelastic. In the past, gasoline price wars had a negative impact because of reduced revenues and profits. Beginning about the middle of 1973, the stocks of the major international companies began to trend downward, reflecting potential problems in the Middle East; the potential problems became a reality when the oil cutbacks and embargo were instituted late last October.

The stocks of Phillips Petroleum, Atlantic Richfield, and Standard Oil (Ohio) have had substantial price moves over the past year, reflecting earnings down the road from secure sources (the North Sea for Phillips and Alaska's North Slope for Standard Oil [Ohio] and Atlantic Richfield). The stocks of these three companies made further moves reflecting the soaring prices for crude oil, thereby indicating even higher earnings potential down the road than originally anticipated.

Oil company stocks also have a tendency to react to oil and gas discoveries announced by managements and to rumors of discoveries. This is particularly true for the smaller exploration company stocks but is also true for the big integrated companies. These moves reflect future increments to earnings from the discoveries.

It is also true that stocks of companies with heavy exposure to foreign earnings have low price/earnings ratios reflecting the risk involved. This explains the low multiples on the international oil company stocks over the years and particularly at the present time. In contrast, the stock of Louisiana Land and Exploration Company has historically had a high P/E ratio reflecting good growth in secure (U.S.) and high-quality earnings. Most of the P/Es of the stocks of the domestic integrated companies fall somewhere in between reflecting security of earnings plus their high quality plus rising domestic potential from crude oil and product price changes. Because of the developments coming out of the Middle East, it could develop that oil stocks will take on higher P/Es, and, coupled with possible higher earnings, there could be a double-barrelled effect on individual stock prices. Possible tax changes should be watched carefully in this connection, however. As is true with stocks in other industries, quality of earnings and consistency of earnings growth is reflected in stock prices, although time lags do occur.

SUMMARY

In summary, the analyst should study the following individual company factors carefully before making his recommendations: exploration acreage holdings and their potential; current production levels for crude oil and natural gas; price changes for crude oil, natural gas, and refined products; crude sufficiency ratio; status of crude oil and natural gas reserves; profit breakdown; quality of earnings; earnings per share history; return on investment; a number of statistical ratios; possible major financing programs; capital expenditures; dividend expectations; management; the current P/E of the stock in relation to its historical pattern and future prospects; and the relative attractiveness of the stock compared with that of securities in other industries. Although not commented upon in detail in the text, it would also be to the analyst's advantage to learn of any possible stock splits and to be aware of the size of company capitalizations.

It is also most important that the analyst be well aware of all industry trends and that he or she have access to as many sources of information as possible, including the company, reference materials, trade publications, and governmental releases.

EXXON CORPORATION: A CASE STUDY

SALIENT FACTORS OF INVESTMENT SIGNIFICANCE

1. Exxon has a broad base from which to establish future growth. The sheer size of the company places it in the forefront of the industry to tap the new energy sources of the future.

2. Future oil and gas production from proven reserves in the North Sea, Offshore California, Alaska, and Canada's Mackenzie Delta provide a source of secure and growing income in the middle to the late 1970s.

3. An extensive position in coal, tar sands, shale oil, and nuclear energy provide potential through the rest of the decade and the 1980s.

4. The company enjoys excellent operating logistics throughout its worldwide operations and has the management talent to provide the dramatic expansion from this point forward.

5. The negative factors of nationalization and possible adverse tax legislation appear to be already reflected in the price of the stock. The current stock price also already reflects a general negative investment atmosphere, particularly toward international oil stocks.

6. Earnings increased dramatically to $10.90 per share in 1973 from $6.83 per share in 1972 and are projected to advance to $11.00 plus and $12.00 per share in 1974 and 1975, respectively.

7. The $4.55 per share dividend provides an attractive yield of 5.6 percent, and dividend increases can be anticipated.

8. The modest P/E of 7.4 on 1974 estimated earnings suggests a low risk factor at the current price. Down the road, some expansion of the multiple can be anticipated.

9. Based on expectations, the stock is attractively priced on a total return basis.

A summary of the pertinent investment statistics for the Exxon Corporation is given in Tables 1 and 2 of this case study.

PROFILE

Exxon Corporation (formerly Standard Oil of New Jersey) is the world's largest oil enterprise. As a result of its vast worldwide operating network, the company ranks as the leader in refining and marketing and near the top in oil and gas production. Importantly, Exxon is also a very significant factor in chemical, tanker, and pipeline operations.

The company's principal consolidated affiliates, with percentage own-

TABLE 1

Exxon Corporation (listed on the New York Stock Exchange as XON)

Price (3/29/74): 81⅜   1973–74 Price Range: 103¼–79⅛
Est. 1975 Earnings: $12.00   Price/Earnings Ratio: 6.8
Est. 1974 Earnings: $11.00 plus   Price/Earnings Ratio: 7.4
Indicated Dividend: $4.55   Yield: 5.6%

Dow-Jones Industrial Average: 846.68 (3/29/74)
Standard & Poor's 500   : 93.98 (3/29/74)

	Book Value ($ millions)	Percent of Total	Market Value ($ millions)	Percent of Total
Capitalization (12/31/73):				
Debt......................	$ 2,670,863	15.7	$ 2,670,863	12.4
Minority interest.............	591,142	3.5	591,142	2.8
Common—223,867,276 shares				
($7 par).................	13,717,691*	80.8	18,217,200	84.8
	$16,979,696	100.0	$21,479,205	100.0

* Book value per share, $61.28.

ership, include Creole Petroleum, 95 percent; Exxon U.S.A., 100 percent; Imperial Oil, 70 percent; and International Petroleum, 99.9 percent. Its nonconsolidated affiliates include Plantation Pipe Line, 49 percent; Interprovincial Pipe Line, 23 percent; Iraq Petroleum, 12 percent; Arabian American Oil Co. (Aramco), 22.5 percent; and Iranian Oil Participants, 7 percent.

Importantly, world operations are well balanced, with crude oil production, refinery runs, and refined products all in excess of 5 million barrels per day. Products are sold under the Exxon and Esso brand names in over 100 countries and in 45 U.S. states. Tanker and pipeline capacities are also growing commensurate with corporate needs.

Like its competitor international oil companies, Exxon's world role will probably change somewhat from here on, due to host country nationalizations and participations. Although ownership of crude oil and natural gas reserves is shifting to the host countries, Exxon's activities will not diminish; in fact, they will expand, since Exxon and its major world competitors will provide the much needed link between the raw material and the end-product.

Exxon's role will also take on added dimension as the company becomes further immersed in the total energy field. Large reserves of coal, tar sands, and shale oil as well as an expanding role in nuclear energy suggest that Exxon will become a major factor in the world energy field. Thus, the seeds for growth have already been planted for the remainder of the century.

As a result of the Middle East war of 1973 with its oil production cutbacks, oil embargo, and spiralling prices, the stage appears to be set for

Exxon to record a somewhat faster rate of earnings growth over the next several years compared with the last decade. The actions of governments, however, will have to be watched carefully in this connection since political decisions sometimes bypass economic reality.

EARNINGS AND PROSPECTS

Over the last decade, Exxon's earnings' record has been satisfactory but not exceptional. A study of earnings by geographical areas indicates that Eastern Hemisphere earnings were essentially in a downtrend from 1965 through the end of the decade, reflecting more than anything else weak product pricing in Europe which is Exxon's largest marketing region; Eastern Hemisphere earnings were considerably less in 1969 than they were in 1965. In contrast, U.S. earnings almost doubled in that time frame, while other Western Hemisphere earnings recorded modest growth (Creole Petroleum provides the bulk of these earnings).

From 1970 through 1973, Eastern Hemisphere earnings reversed the earlier trend and more than tripled, principally due to a burst in profits in 1973. U.S. profits recorded steady gains during this period, while other Western Hemisphere earnings were essentially upward, with the exception of 1972 when the Venezuelan government substantially raised Creole's taxes.

Cash Income

During this time frame, Exxon internally generated substantial funds in order to carry on its many programs. Table 3 illustrates the trend in cash income from 1965 on.

TABLE 3

Exxon Corporation: Cash Income* ($ millions)

	Noncash Charges †	Net Income	Cash Income
1973..............	$1,391.7	$2,443.3	$3,835.0
1972..............	1,324.9	1,531.8	2,856.7
1971..............	1,279.3	1,516.6	2,795.9
1970..............	1,158.8	1,309.5	2,468.3
1969..............	1,070.2	1,242.6	2,312.8
1968..............	1,044.5	1,276.7	2,321.2
1967..............	968.5	1,155.0	2,123.5
1966....:........	926.7	1,054.3	1,981.0
1965..............	897.6	972.7	1,870.3

* Net income plus write-offs.   † Writer's estimate.

TABLE 2

Pertinent Investment Statistics for Exxon Corporation

Year Ended Dec. 31	Gross Operating Income* ($ millions)	Net before Income Taxes† ($ millions)	After-tax Profit Margin (percent)	Net Income ($ millions)	Invested Capital‡ ($ millions)
1973	$25,724.3	$6,316.9	9.5	$2,443.3	$16,979.7
1972	20,309.8	3,958.3	7.5	1,531.8	15,422.8
1971	18,700.6	3,540.7	8.1	1,516.6	14,766.3
1970	16,554.2	2,530.1	7.9	1,309.5	13,865.3
1969	14,929.8	2,321.4	8.3	1,242.6	12,721.3
1968	14,091.3	2,350.7	9.1	1,276.7	12,371.1
1967	13,266.0	2,088.1	8.7	1,155.0	11,297.5
1966	12,191.4	1,874.9	8.6	1,054.3	10,386.3
1965	11,471.5	1,721.3	8.5	972.7	9,921.2

* Excludes excise taxes.
† Includes income applicable to minority interests.
‡ Includes equity of minority interests.
¢ Writer's estimate.

Exxon has already announced a very heavy capital expenditure program for the next four years which will require rapidly growing cash generation from this point forward.

1973 versus 1972

The year 1973 was extraordinary for the oil industry and for the whole world, for that matter, and Exxon fit into the pattern.

It became apparent early in 1973 that company profits were going to record a good gain over 1972, and the earnings' build-up through the first nine months of the year bore this out. But the explosive spurt in the fourth quarter exceeded just about everyone's expectation. The quarterly breakdown is as follows:

	Earnings per Share	
	1973	1972
March	$ 2.27	$1.58
June	2.27	1.48
September	2.85	1.58
December	3.51	2.19
Total	$10.90	$6.83

For the full year, earnings increased 59.5 percent.

Return on Invested Capital (percent)	Cash Income¢ ($ millions)	Per Common Share				P/E Ratio Range
		Cash Income	Earns.	Div.	Price Range	
14.4	$3,835.0	$17.13	$10.90	$4.25	103–84	9–8
9.9	2,856.7	12.73	6.83	3.80	89–68	13–10
10.3	2,795.9	12.24	6.77	3.80	82–67	12–10
9.4	2,468.3	11.02	5.91	3.75	73–50	12–8
9.8	2,312.8	10.23	5.78	3.75	85–60	15–10
10.3	2,321.2	10.67	5.94	3.65	85–67	14–11
10.2	2,123.5	9.38	5.36	3.45	71–59	13–11
10.2	1,981.0	8.31	5.06	3.30	84–60	17–2
9.8	1,870.3	7.78	4.74	3.15	90–74	19–15

A study of the breakdown of earnings by geographical area and operation is more meaningful:

The big contributors (46 percent) to the earnings improvement were Eastern Hemisphere operations, where strong product pricing and good volume gains were the primary factors. In addition, devaluation of the dollar resulted in local currency earnings being translated into higher

TABLE 4

Exxon Corporation: Earnings (by geographical area)

Petroleum and Natural Gas Operations	1973 ($ millions)	1972 ($ millions)	Change ($ millions)	Percent Change
United States.................	$ 829.7	$ 718.9	+$110.8	+ 15.4
Other Western Hemisphere.....	481.6	286.5	+ 195.1	+ 68.1
Eastern Hemisphere...........	988.3	573.4	+ 414.9	+ 72.4
Chemical operations:				
United States................	66.4	31.1	+ 35.3	+113.5
Foreign.....................	135.7	19.7	+ 116.0	+588.8
Other:				
	(58.4)	(97.8)	+ 39.4	+ 40.3
Total....................	$2,443.3	$1,531.8	+$911.5	+ 59.5
Per share................	$ 10.90	$ 6.83		

dollar amounts, adding another $150 million to profits. As an aside, it is interesting to note that the profitability on a barrel of Middle East crude oil dropped to $0.25 from $0.32 in 1972. This suggests Exxon's ability to switch profitability from the production end to the downstream operations.

Another large contributor to the 1973 profit gain was chemical operations. Although profits from U.S. chemical operations more than doubled ($66 million in 1973 versus $31 million in 1972), foreign chemical earnings recorded an even more dramatic increase (to $136 million from $20 million in 1972). Foreign chemical operations are located principally in Canada and Europe.

Other Western Hemisphere operations were also significant contributors to the profit gain in 1973, with Creole's (Venezuela) and Imperial Oil's (Canada) oil and gas operations being the primary reasons.

And last but not least, U.S. earnings from oil and gas activity recorded a respectable 16 percent improvement over the previous year. Total company inventory profits probably amounted to no more than $50 million.

All in all, 1973 was a very unusual year, particularly with the events beginning in October when the Arab-Israeli war broke out, the embargo was imposed, crude production levels in the Middle East were reduced, and crude oil prices were going through the roof.

1974 and 1975 Earnings

Earnings for 1974 are very hazardous to predict at this early point in the year for a variety of reasons:

1. The European and Japanese nations stand to suffer severe balance of payments deficits from the tremendously increased cost of imported oil at a time when their economies are undergoing an adjustment.
2. Shortages in raw materials exist in many of the economies of the industrialized world.
3. Our own Congress is studying crude oil and natural gas pricing, with some legislation anticipated in the months ahead. Congress is also studying tax changes for the oil industry, with new legislation anticipated in the period ahead.
4. Demand for petroleum products is slackening throughout the world because of shortages and substantially higher prices. The net effect on profit margins is not yet clear.

Assuming that Eastern Hemisphere earnings will decline in 1974, that U.S. earnings will increase significantly principally due to about a $2.00/bbl increase in crude oil prices on average this year, and that chemical and Canadian earnings will increase as Venezuelan earnings decline, it is possible for full year 1974 earnings to record a modest increase over 1973, somewhere in the $11.00 per share area. It could very well be higher. This rationale assumes some type of punitive tax legislation against the oil industry in 1974. The big question is: By how much will U.S. earnings' increases offset declining Eastern Hemisphere earnings? It is too early in the year to tell.

By 1975, those items clouding the picture at the moment should be resolved, suggesting an earnings gain in the range of 8–10 percent for the year 1975. A projection of $12.00 per share would fit the pattern, assuming world economic growth is once again moving forward.

OPERATIONS

Exploration and Production

A history of Exxon's gross production of crude oil and natural gas liquids (thousands of barrels daily) by areas is indicated in Table 5. The trend was upward each year, with the exception of 1971 when Libyan production dropped considerably. The bulk of the increase for the period was provided principally by Saudi Arabia, with the United States, Canada, and Iran also providing attractive increases.

However, the year 1973 provided some interesting shifts. Production in the United States declined moderately due principally to decreases in Texas and Louisiana, but declines were more pronounced in the Middle East where the effects of governmental participation and the oil embargo loomed large. Most notable was the dramatic increase in crude oil off-take under special arrangements with the National Iranian Oil Company and Middle Eastern governments through buyback of participation oil. Such special arrangements should become more pronounced in the years ahead. Importantly, other Western Hemisphere production recorded attractive increases, primarily from Canada where Exxon owns 70 percent of Imperial Oil Limited and Venezuela where Exxon owns 95 percent of Creole Petroleum Corporation.

Production levels are difficult to predict for 1974 in light of the embargo and conservation measures by some producing countries. Then, too, reduced demand by consuming nations due to staggering increases in product prices will have an effect. It would not be surprising to see Exxon's worldwide crude oil production level unchanged or possibly down somewhat in 1974. The big question will be: How inelastic is product demand relative to price changes?

An important factor domestically for 1974 is the price of crude oil. By weighting the prices for "old" oil and "new" oil, crude oil prices on average should increase approximately $2.00 per barrel over the average 1973 price. Thus, Exxon's domestic earnings in 1974 should record a substantial increase over 1973 and be the primary factor in the company's expected somewhat better total earnings picture in 1974. Eastern Hemisphere earnings, as mentioned earlier, are expected to be down in 1974.

TABLE 5

Exxon Corporation: Gross Production of Crude Oil and Natural Gas Liquids (thousands of barrels daily)

	1973	1972	1971	1970	1969	1968	1967	1966	1965
United States	1,084	1,114	1,073	1,098	1,015	948	886	814	746
Canada	345	262	213	199	179	173	163	146	132
Venezuela	1,646	1,502	1,658	1,730	1,674	1,654	1,536	1,380	1,448
Other Latin America	20	17	19	18	12	40	51	52	54
Europe	53	59	67	78	82	87	90	83	73
Libya	242	307	398	631	682	677	549	536	520
Saudi Arabia	1,673	1,735	1,364	1,079	911	860	785	721	611
Iraq, Qatar, and Abu Dhabi	158	228	297	258	247	239	199	217	201
Iran	80	320	290	245	217	189	173	141	128
Australia and Far East	224	190	175	94	25	25	26	29	29
Crude oil offtake under special arrangements (Middle East and Africa)	1,193	411	479	663	412	333	372	459	220
Worldwide	6,718	6,145	6,033	6,093	5,456	5,225	4,830	4,578	4,162

A history of natural gas sales by areas is shown in Table 6. At the beginning of the period, the United States provided just about all of Exxon's sales with steady growth continuing to the present. Although on a much smaller scale, Canada's growth has also been on a steady growth trend. But the big increase occurred in Europe, starting about 1968, when the huge Groningen gas field in the Netherlands came on production; sales from this area have increased dramatically ever since. Overall, sales for the entire period have almost tripled. Reflecting a variety of factors, U.S. natural gas sales have flattened in recent years and even recorded a moderate decline in 1973. As a result of higher sales in the Netherlands, Germany, and offshore Great Britain, worldwide gas sales increased 4.8 percent in 1973 aided by higher prices.

U.S. natural gas sales for Exxon will probably record another moderate decline in 1974, but worldwide sales for the company should show another good gain aided primarily by gains in Europe.

Reserves. A history of Exxon's gross proven reserves of crude oil and natural gas liquids (millions of barrels at year-end) and gross proven reserves of natural gas (billions of cubic feet at year-end) is shown in Table 7.

For the period, crude oil reserves (excluding additional crude oil available under special arrangements) remained essentially flat but with some interesting shifts. U.S. reserves declined until 1970, when the Alaskan reserves were included, and have declined each year since. Canadian reserves were essentially flat until 1969 and have declined each year subsequently. In contrast, other Western Hemisphere reserves declined through 1971 but have been in an uptrend the past two years, reflecting principally greater development drilling in Venezuela. And Middle East reserves have recorded a volatile pattern: a large increase between 1965 and 1970, a flat picture from 1970 through 1972, and a dramatic decline in 1973 when participation by foreign governments took its toll. The Middle East figures will continue volatile as Middle East governments continue to increase their participation with ultimate nationalization of assets a probability. However, one should not overlook the amount of crude oil under special arrangements, as it will be growing steadily over the years ahead and has some aspects of "reserves," although obviously much less secure.

For the same period, Exxon's natural gas reserves recorded a moderate increase but, like crude oil reserves, with some interesting shifts. U.S. reserves declined until 1970 (when Alaskan reserves were included) but have been in a downtrend ever since. Canadian reserves climbed through 1969 (except for 1967) and have declined annually since. Other Western Hemisphere reserves declined through 1968 and with the exception of 1970 have been in an uptrend reflecting heightened development drilling in Venezuela. A big shift occurred in Europe when the re-

TABLE 6

Exxon Corporation: Natural Gas Sales (millions of cubic feet daily)

	1973	1972	1971	1970	1969	1968	1967	1966	1965
United States	5,758	5,952	5,885	5,488	4,906	4,280	3,760	3,629	3,174
Canada	477	423	395	386	363	338	301	239	180
Other Western Hemisphere	91	68	60	57	49	56	54	57	48
Europe	3,108	2,641	2,078	1,503	970	611	295	137	61
Other Eastern Hemisphere	333	239	109	57	21	11	9	9	7
Worldwide	9,767	9,323	8,527	7,491	6,309	5,296	4,419	4,071	3,470

TABLE 7

Exxon Corporation: Proved Reserves

	1973	1972	1971	1970	1969	1968	1967	1966	1965
Gross proved reserves of crude oil and natural gas liquids (millions of barrels at year-end):									
United States	5,165	5,510	5,842	6,225	4,470	4,645	4,880	5,058	5,237
Canada	1,338	1,387	1,490	1,567	1,702	1,593	1,517	1,535	1,526
Other Western Hemisphere	7,754	7,513	7,135	7,401	7,996	8,536	8,873	9,416	9,667
Europe	553	400	225	186	207	285	332	355	343
Middle East and Africa	25,929	34,343	34,480	34,359	33,179	32,901	30,945	30,028	26,483
Australia and Far East	914	802	796	833	860	874	252	280	161
Worldwide	41,653	49,955	49,968	50,571	48,414	48,834	46,799	46,672	43,417
Special arrangements	3,600	—	—	—	—	—	—	—	—
Gross proved reserves of natural gas (billions of cubic feet at year-end):									
United States	30,599	33,673	36,835	39,561	34,691	36,134	37,930	38,838	38,882
Canada	2,852	3,044	3,171	3,310	3,322	3,100	2,844	2,944	2,691
Other Western Hemisphere	19,939	18,813	16,267	15,099	15,205	12,212	13,170	14,018	15,912
Europe	25,940	26,855	27,885	24,638	24,966	25,125	24,093	16,209	13,630
Middle East and Africa	22,726	39,328	43,011	39,395	35,318	33,391	32,002	27,848	24,319
Australia and Far East	3,694	4,464	4,429	4,382	4,374	3,562	3,587	3,447	3,026
Worldwide	105,750	126,177	131,598	126,385	117,876	113,524	113,626	103,304	98,460

serve increases from the Groningen Field in the Netherlands became most pronounced in 1967; the trend has been essentially flat since then, however. The widest shift occurred in the Middle East where participation has been the primary factor.

Exxon's exploration and production activities as shown in the tabulations are global. In the United States, the company will probably be concentrating on offshore exploration aided by federal and state offshore lease sales which are expected to occur more frequently than in the past and on a more consistent basis. Substantial sums of money were spent in this connection in 1973. Outside the United States, the company acquired interests in 95 million net acres in 1973 in 12 countries outside North America. At year-end 1973, the company had holdings in 37 countries outside North America totaling 200 million acres, an increase of 67 million acres over the previous year-end, with much of it in deeper water and thereby providing future potential. Seismic surveys were conducted in 26 countries during 1973 in order to locate attractive drilling structures, but, with the high risk involved, only 23 commercial discoveries were made out of 161 wildcat wells drilled in participation with others in 22 countries.

One of the most important factors in Exxon's future is the expected growth in production from new sources considered secure. None of these areas are on production as yet (except North Sea gas in the British waters), but they all should be at varying stages during the 1970s. In this connection, four areas stand out: the Santa Barbara Channel (California), Alaska, the North Sea, and Canada's Mackenzie Delta. In 1968, Exxon acquired a 72 percent interest in the 83,000-acre Santa Ynez unit in the Santa Barbara Channel off Southern California and is the unit operator. The reserves are known to be large, but production has been held up for environmental reasons. As soon as the Department of the Interior gives its approval, development can begin. Production will be large and meaningful.

The story on Alaskan oil is practically household conversation these days. Huge discoveries were made at Prudhoe Bay in the late 1960s, and Exxon owns a sizable portion of these reserves. Development of the field has been delayed because construction of the needed pipeline has been delayed for environmental reasons. The federal permit granting construction of the line was finally issued in January of this year and the state permit is expected momentarily. Exxon has a 25.5 percent interest in the line. Initial construction of the line should begin late this year or early 1975, with completion expected in late 1977 or early 1978. Production would commence sometime thereafter. The oil and gas reserves at Prudhoe Bay are vast, and what is also important is the potential for additional large reserves in Alaska. Exxon has extensive acreage there. Like Santa Barbara, Alaska will provide a future source of secure (domestic) earnings.

The outlook for both the Mackenzie Delta and the North Sea is bright, but the influence of foreign governments (even though from democratic countries) must not be overlooked. Imperial Oil (Exxon's 70 percent Canadian affiliate) is Canada's largest oil company and also has the largest acreage holdings in the Mackenzie Delta of Northwest Canada. Vast natural gas reserves have been discovered as well as some oil, but production is not likely from either until the end of the decade or the early 1980s. A gas pipeline is under study at the moment, and application for the necessary government permits should be filed this year. To the observor, the potential is enormous, but the nationalistic attitude of the Canadian government and of the Provinces leaves much to be desired. It is the writer's opinion, however, that the current political problems will gradually fall by the wayside because the full development of Canada's resources over the next decade and beyond will require a different political view.

The North Sea is probably the most dynamic exploratory area in the world at present, and Exxon is in the thick of it. Large oil and gas discoveries have been made by Exxon and others with the full potential of the North Sea yet to be determined. Significantly, the economic impact on the countries involved as well as on Europe in general should be enormous, particularly when production reaches high rates late in the decade. Needless to say, the impact on a number of companies will be sizable also. Exxon's major successes to date have been in the British sector, both oil and gas, but the company has also been searching in both the Dutch and Norwegian sectors with limited success. Obviously, the North Sea will receive wide attention by the company in the years ahead since Europe is Exxon's largest marketing territory. Importantly, it is becoming widely discussed that both Great Britain and Norway will become self-sufficient in energy by the end of the decade. The ramifications on the balance of payments of both nations and the general effect on their economics is apparent. Exxon will play a large role in this achievement.

Refining

A history of the company's refinery runs (thousands of barrels daily), by areas, is reflected in Table 8.

During the period shown, U.S. refinery runs recorded little growth until 1973. With the exception of 1972, runs in Canada increased each year, although the total was relatively small in overall corporate operations. Other Western Hemisphere runs (primarily in Venezuela and the Netherlands Antilles) were essentially flat. The large gain came in Europe which, as mentioned earlier, is Exxon's largest marketing region. An upward pattern was reflected in the Middle Eastern and Far Eastern areas also. Overall, the year 1973 recorded the largest single year increase of the period.

Importantly, Exxon has a very high crude sufficiency ratio in the

TABLE 8

Exxon Corporation: Refinery Runs (thousands of barrels daily)

	1965	1966	1967	1968	1969	1970	1971	1972	1973
United States	805	816	912	943	992	989	976	1,029	1,202
Canada	330	343	346	354	373	402	408	395	441
Other Western Hemisphere	1,109	1,066	1,112	1,112	1,084	1,171	1,059	1,004	1,147
Europe	1,327	1,550	1,640	1,730	1,934	2,122	2,071	2,015	2,165
Middle East and Africa	109	128	147	179	190	265	233	196	237
Australia and Far East	254	259	280	303	319	321	413	507	569
Worldwide	3,934	4,162	4,437	4,621	4,892	5,270	5,160	5,146	5,761

United States, and a study of production and refinery runs shows excellent overall operating balance worldwide.

The company's five U.S. refineries were operating at virtual capacity at the beginning of 1973, but due to plant expansions during the year, refinery runs increased an exceptional 16.8 percent for the year. Importantly, foreign crude oil provided 21 percent of domestic refinery runs. The plant expansion program could not have happened at a better time since lack of sufficient domestic refinery capacity is a major industry problem today. More importantly, last spring Exxon announced a 350,000 barrel per day refinery expansion program to be completed by 1977. During 1973, Exxon also completed notable refinery expansions in Europe: one in Wales and the other in France.

Because of the expansion programs already planned, Exxon's refinery runs should record further gains in 1974. Then, too, because of the many types of crude oil produced around the world today, it is important that refineries have greater flexibility in the crudes they use. To this end, Exxon is working on a new process called "flexicoking" which is designed to convert heavy residual material from other refining processes into valuable light liquid products and fuel gas. This is just another example of Exxon's research effort to help keep the company in the forefront of the industry.

Marketing

A history of Exxon's refined product sales (thousands of barrels daily), by area, is indicated in Table 9.

Several items stand out. For the period covered, total product sales increased almost 50 percent. Europe is the company's largest single market with the United States a close second. Canada and other Western Hemisphere countries recorded moderate increases while other Eastern Hemisphere volume more than doubled. The United States and Europe together account for more than two thirds of total volume, approximately the same percentage as in 1965. And heavy fuels are the largest selling product, closely followed by heating oil and gasoline.

In 1973, worldwide sales volume increased 8.4 percent over 1972 while, in the United States alone, sales increased an unusual 14.5 percent, reflecting exceptionally heavy demand as well as Exxon's ability to increase refinery runs more than the industry. Sales volume in Europe rose 4.3 percent as a result of heavy demand and Exxon regaining some previously lost market share.

During 1973, the company continued its program of closing uneconomic service stations, and since 1967 the worldwide number of stations has decreased to 82,000—a drop of 14,000 stations. During 1973 alone, more than 1,100 stations were closed in the United States and 1,900 in Europe.

TABLE 9

Exxon Corporation: Marketing (thousands of barrels daily)

	1973	1972	1971	1970	1969	1968	1967	1966	1965
Refined product sales:									
United States	1,980	1,730	1,688	1,753	1,645	1,518	1,485	1,364	1,361
Canada	450	408	412	424	399	395	384	370	367
Other Western Hemisphere	625	613	620	661	671	673	607	570	551
Europe	2,279	2,185	2,155	2,175	1,948	1,720	1,623	1,575	1,496
Other Eastern Hemisphere	844	765	712	671	602	575	548	510	417
Worldwide	6,178	5,701	5,587	5,684	5,265	4,881	4,647	4,389	4,192

The picture for 1974 is cloudy at the moment. Substantially higher product prices around the world will certainly adversely affect volume levels, and conservation measures established in many areas will also adversely affect consumption. These factors alone will ease the pressure on refinery capacity for the industry, but refinery capacity is not an Exxon problem for 1974. At this early date, it would be prudent to be prepared for a flat-to-down volume year in 1974 with the expectation in some cases, particularly in the United States, that higher prices will more than offset disappointing volume levels.

Chemicals

Exxon is one of the country's largest chemical companies, a distinction lost in the company's overall oil and gas activities. As shown in Table 10, revenues have shown good growth over the years; unfortunately, profitability has not kept pace, due to a declining price structure for the industry, but it would seem that the turning point might have occurred in 1973.

TABLE 10

Exxon Corporation: Chemical Revenues* ($ millions)

1973	$1,563.4
1972	1,258.5
1971	1,077.2
1970	1,006.7
1969	1,004.1
1968	932.6
1967	815.1
1966	732.3
1965	587.5

* Excludes products supplied to petroleum affiliates: 1973, $289 million; 1972, $259 million.

More than half of the company's chemical revenues are derived from the United States and Europe, with Canada, the Far East, and Latin America accounting for the remainder. The main product lines include plastics (polypropylene, low-density polyethylene, and polyvinyl chloride), solvents, chemical specialties, synthetic rubber, and a line of chemical additives used in petroleum products.

The year 1973 was an unusually strong chemical year for the company, reflecting improved efficiency, heavy demand, and the recovery of prices from the low levels of recent years. Including revenues from products supplied to petroleum affiliates, total revenues increased 22 percent and net profits almost 300 percent. About 65 percent of revenues were derived from outside the United States. Importantly, return on average total assets increased to 14.2 percent from an inordinately low 3.6 percent in 1972.

The outlook for 1974 is not completely clear, but further sizable gains are anticipated.

Transportation

Exxon's transportation activities can best be described by its tanker and pipeline operations. Table 11 indicates growth in these two areas over the years.

TABLE 11

Exxon Corporation: Tanker and Pipeline Operations

	Oceangoing Tanker Capacity* (thousand dwt/daily avg.)	Pipeline Thruput (thousand bbl/day)
1973	23,804	8,098
1972	19,880	7,569
1971	19,215	7,433
1970	17,550	7,320
1969	14,750	6,811
1968	13,575	6,509
1967	12,765	5,990
1966	10,940	5,521
1965	9,600	5,142

* Owned and chartered.

Pipeline thruput growth of 60 percent over the period reflects the normal expansion of corporate activity feeding the pipeline sector. For many, many years both product and crude oil lines have been considered one of the most attractive modes of transportation for the oil industry. Efficiency and cost factors are the paramount considerations. Total thruputs can be expected to continue their upward pattern for the company and accelerate when large new sources of production come on stream, particularly in Alaska.

Exxon's growth in tanker capacity has been dramatic over the years and particularly during the last four years. This reflects growth in the purchase of supertankers needed to transport crude and products around the world. Reduction in unit cost is the object of such large carriers. During 1973, the company received eight 255,000 dwt tankers at an average cost of $40 million. And at year-end, another 20 tankers of this size or larger were under construction or on order. Overall, the company received 16 new VLCCs (very large crude carriers) during 1973, totaling 2.3 million dead weight tons of capacity. Because of orders on the books, more new tankers will be received in 1974.

Other

In addition to its oil and gas activities, Exxon has positioned itself in other forms of energy, some for the immediate future and some for later in the decade and in the 1980s when oil and gas might very well have reached their full potential.

Coal. Exxon has very large holdings of coal reserves in Illinois, Wyoming, Montana, and North Dakota. During 1973, the company's Carlinville, Illinois mine reached its design capacity of 3 million tons a year, shipping its entire output to Commonwealth Edison Company in Chicago. In addition, Exxon is in the process of negotiating more contracts with utilities for other mines in Illinois as well as in the West. In this connection, a contract was signed early this year with a subsidiary of American Electric Power providing for 5 million tons of low-sulphur western coal annually for 30 years, beginning the middle of 1976, from a new surface mine to be opened near Gillette, Wyoming.

Because sulphur in coal creates an environmental hazard, the company is working on ways of removing sulphur oxides after combustion. In this connection, the company is working on a number of flue gas desulphurization processes and believes it has one ready for large-scale demonstration.

Then, too, the company is planning the development of a commercial coal gasification project based on reserves in Wyoming and using existing technology. It would be possible for a plant to be commercially operative by the early 1980s after an expenditure of more than $400 million. In addition, the company is working on a new coal gasification process. The design work for a 500 ton per day pilot plant is near completion, with construction possible this year; the process calls for several grades of coal.

And as a further extention of its coal activity, Exxon is developing a process for the liquefaction of coal to low-sulphur fuel oil or synthetic crude oil. Pilot plant operations are expected to begin later this year.

Tar Sands and Heavy Oil. The tar sands in Canada are known to hold hundreds of billions of barrels of oil. Imperial Oil (Exxon's 70 percent owned affiliate) holds a 30 percent interest in Syncrude Canada, Ltd. which has announced that it will construct a plant to produce 125,000 barrels per day of synthetic crude oil from the Athabasca tar sands of Alberta. The Syncrude participants have been working on this project for almost 20 years, and with the government giving approval and the economics now being favorable this long awaited project will become a reality. Production will not be meaningful until late in the decade, however.

Not far south of the Althabasca reserves in Alberta, Imperial has been experimenting with its large reserves of heavy, viscous oil in the Cold Lake area. And now it plans to construct a $14 million project to produce about 4,000 barrels per day, with production to begin in late 1974. Reserves total about 160 billion barrels in Alberta, and, importantly, it might be possible for similar technology to be used in other countries where reserves are known to exist.

Nuclear Energy. Exxon is rapidly expanding its efforts in nuclear energy. Its order backlog for uranium, fabricated nuclear fuel assemblies, and related nuclear services now stands at $900 million, compared with approximately $300 million at the end of 1972. All this after only four years in the business! The fabricating plant at Richland, Washington, and the uranium mine and mill at Highland, Wyoming, are already scheduled for expansion after only one full year of operations. In an effort to become further involved in the nuclear field, the company is improving its ability to participate in the uranium enrichment sector of the nuclear fuel cycle. In this connection, Exxon has joined with General Electric Company to develop a program to establish a commercial enrichment plant based on centrifuge technology along with the supporting manufacturing complex to produce the centrifuges and related equipment.

Additional corporate activity in the nuclear area includes work on spent fuel reprocessing, uranium enrichment using laser technology for isotope separation, and gaseous centrifuge technologies for future uranium enrichment plants. The company is also working under contract with U.S. and European electric utility companies to demonstrate the use of plutonium in commercial power reactors as a partial substitute for enriched uranium.

We all know that the age of nuclear energy has not yet arrived, but according to government and business forecasts it will take hold in the 1980s. It would seem that Exxon is becoming well entrenched for future growth in this area.

Shale Oil. Exxon is also active in the development of shale oil. The company is one of 17 participants in the $7.5 million Parano project where two vertical kilns are being installed at the project site near Rifle, Colorado. Additional work is under way at Anvil Point, Colorado, to plan the mine and place supporting equipment in working order.

With world crude oil now dramatically higher in price, the economics of shale oil production are attractive. Exxon, with its partners, is working on ways to improve the technology of production as well as to adequately handle the environmental requirements.

FINANCIAL

Exxon has a strong balance sheet and the selected data in Tables 12, 13, and 14 indicate a strong financial condition. The cash position increased dramatically as of the end of 1973 and so did net working capital. Although current liabilities also recorded a large increase due to substantial increases in accounts payable and income taxes payable, the

TABLE 12

Exxon Corporation: Selected Balance Sheet Data ($ millions)

	1973	1972	1971	1970	1969	1968	1967	1966	1965
Cash and equivalent.	$3,088.2	$1,692.8	$1,619.3	$1,539.4	$1,276.2	$1,366.9	$1,371.3	$1,225.3	$1,346.0
Receivables.	4,062.9	3,328.5	3,130.7	3,076.6	2,765.0	2,546.0	2,361.7	2,109.8	1,832.2
Inventory.	2,225.8	1,745.4	1,676.0	1,566.0	1,323.5	1,367.4	1,233.7	1,145.5	1,043.6
Current assets.	9,793.5	7,098.6	6,790.5	6,527.7	5,634.0	5,524.1	5,213.2	4,721.5	4,441.0
Current liabilities.	6,307.9	4,707.1	4,329.7	4,240.0	3,789.3	3,432.7	3,203.8	2,826.2	2,535.8
Net working capital.	3,485.6	2,391.5	2,460.8	2,287.7	1,844.7	2,091.4	2,009.4	1,895.3	1,905.2
Current ratio.	1.55-1	1.51-1	1.57-1	1.54-1	1.49-1	1.61-1	1.63-1	1.67-1	1.75-1
Ratio of cash to liabilities.	.49-1	.36-1	.37-1	.36-1	.34-1	.40-1	.43-1	.43-1	.53-1
Net fixed assets.	$13,461.5	$12,644.7	$11,930.4	$11,305.3	$10,563.4	$10,077.2	$9,074.9	$8,274.4	$7,797.3
Minority interest.	591.1	536.4	494.2	471.4	454.9	432.6	421.8	409.0	390.8
Long-term debt.	2,670.8	2,616.9	2,679.2	2,443.2	2,173.8	2,082.7	1,500.4	1,036.6	932.4
Common stock and capital surplus.	2,594.6	2,637.2	2,640.6	2,608.4	2,228.8	2,233.1	2,244.2	2,261.6	2,262.1
Earned surplus.	11,123.1	9,632.3	8,952.3	8,342.3	7,863.8	7,622.7	7,131.1	6,679.1	6,335.9
Net worth.	13,717.7	12,269.5	11,592.9	10,950.7	10,092.6	9,855.8	9,375.8	8,940.7	8,598.0
Avg. common shares outstanding (000 omitted).	224,090	224,155	224,045	221,704	215,048	215,097	215,367	215,476	215,537
Debt/equity ratio (percent).	15.7	17.0	18.1	17.6	17.1	16.8	13.3	10.0	9.4

TABLE 13

Exxon Corporation: Sources and Uses of Working Capital ($ in millions)

	1973	1972	1971	1970
Sources:				
Net income				
Accruing to Exxon shareholders.............	$2,443.3	$1,531.8	$1,516.6	$1,309.5
Accruing to minority interests..............	121.9	80.7	62.0	55.3
Depreciation and depletion....................	1,136.3	1,059.7	1,085.9	953.5
Additions to reserves........................	51.8	23.9	36.8	58.4
Additions to deferred income tax credits........	326.2	156.3	41.4	67.1
Extraordinary credits (Charges) to income......	—	—	(55.0)	—
Sale of property..............................	200.7	161.4	96.5	78.8
Proceeds from sales sold.....................	(42.6)	(3.4)	32.2	379.6
Additions to long-term debt..................	624.5	546.7	547.8	522.9
Other..	97.0	(31.6)	(36.9)	51.4
Total sources.........................	$4,959.1	$3,525.5	$3,327.3	$3,476.5
Uses:				
Additions to property, plant, and equipment....	$2,234.9	$1,984.0	$1,810.8	$1,793.6
Additions to investments and advances.........	50.4	115.1	78.8	116.8
Dividends to Exxon shareholders..............	952.5	851.9	851.5	831.1
Dividends to minority interests..............	54.9	41.2	44.1	38.6
Reductions in long-term debt.................	572.3	602.6	369.0	253.5
Total uses...........................	$3,865.0	$3,594.8	$3,154.2	$3,033.6
Net increase (decrease) in working capital.........................	$1,094.1	$ (69.3)	$ 173.1	$ 442.9

current ratio improved moderately to 1.55–1 from 1.51–1 at the end of 1972. Long-term debt was moderately higher; and at year-end, debt, as a percentage of total capitalization, declined to 16.3 percent from 17.6 percent the previous year-end.

Capital Expenditures

As can be seen from Table 15, Exxon has been investing substantial amounts of capital in the Eastern Hemisphere, primarily for manufacturing and marketing activity, in recent years. Since 1965, total corporate capital expenditures have more than doubled on an annual basis; at the same time, exploration costs charged to expense have fluctuated between $190 million and $265 million annually.

In addition, capital expenditures for the years 1965 through 1969 were less each year in the Eastern Hemisphere than in the United States. But over the last few years (1970 through 1973), expenditures were greater each year in the Eastern Hemisphere than in the United States.

Capital expenditures by corporate activity are indicated in Table 16. Historically, the production segment is the largest dollar area, although the tabulation indicates aberrations over the period. Note the strong picture for production in 1973 when the company spent large sums in offshore lease sales in the United States. The pattern has been con-

TABLE 14

Exxon Corporation: Rate of Return (percent)

	1973	1972
Return on assets......................	10.5	7.3
Petroleum operations:.................		
United States......................	12.5	11.4
Other Western Hemisphere..........	13.4	8.7
Eastern Hemisphere................	10.9	7.1
Chemical operations:.................	14.2	3.6
United States......................	11.7	5.6
Foreign............................	15.8	2.2
Return on shareholders' equity...........	18.8	12.8
Return on invested capital..............	14.4	9.9
Return on gross operating income........	9.5	7.5

sistently strong in manufacturing and marketing over the years, while the trend has accelerated in the transportation segment, reflecting the purchase of supertankers for the most part.

More importantly, capital expenditures will expand dramatically from now on. Expenditures of $2.2 billion in 1973 (including $211 million for pollution control) were up 10 percent from the $2 billion level of 1972, and management has already announced that 1974 capital and exploratory outlays will approximate $3.7 billion based on a budget of $6.1 billion. Significantly, the company has also announced a capital investment program totaling $16 billion over the next four years. It would seem that a growing portion of these expenditures would go for oil and gas activity here in North America, as well as for coal, tar sand, shale oil, and nuclear activity in North America. This would fit in with the national objective for self-sufficiency in energy by the 1980s. In this connection, Exxon has already announced that it plans to spend about $200 million over the next six years on research and development programs for coal-conversion processes.

TABLE 15

Exxon Corporation: Capital and Exploratory Expenditures ($ millions)

	Capital				
	United States	Other Western Hemisphere	Eastern Hemisphere	Total	Exploratory
1973...............$	807.0	$429.4	$998.5	$2,234.9	$255.4
1972...............	717.2	392.4	874.4	1,984.0	265.2
1971...............	669.5	332.2	809.1	1,810.8	193.4
1970...............	710.2	354.5	728.9	1,793.6	205.3
1969...............	651.9	401.6	637.2	1,690.7	213.4
1968...............	1,026.4	322.4	595.3	1,944.1	195.3
1967...............	688.2	270.0	660.4	1,618.6	205.9
1966...............	560.0	184.6	460.2	1,204.8	233.9
1965...............	425.9	180.7	364.7	971.3	233.6

TABLE 16

Exxon Corporation: Capital Expenditures ($ millions)

	Production	Manufac-turing	Marketing	Transpor-tation	Other	Total
1973	$820.5	$579.5	$262.9	$491.4	$ 80.6	$2,234.9
1972	497.5	634.5	390.7	323.1	138.2	1,984.0
1971	491.8	539.9	428.4	231.9	118.8	1,810.8
1970	533.0	439.7	452.8	254.1	114.0	1,793.6
1969	521.3	442.8	379.0	264.6	83.0	1,690.7
1968	808.8	581.5	319.6	132.0	102.2	1,944.1
1967	448.1	522.0	403.6	122.1	122.8	1,618.6
1966	321.3	367.7	350.9	68.1	96.8	1,204.8
1965	332.2	195.4	343.9	44.6	55.2	971.3

Part of the expenditure increase for 1974 will go for higher outlays at Aramco. Aramco expended about $500 million in 1973 and has made plans for spending $800 million in 1974. Exxon has a 22.5 percent interest in Aramco at this writing. These monies will be spent on the terminals, pipelines, the refinery, and other facilities. The program is designed to raise Aramco's producing capacity to 11.5 million barrels per day by early 1975 from the current 10.3 million barrels per day. It is obvious, then, that Aramco production will continue to increase in the years ahead but will probably not reach the 20 million barrel per day level by 1980 that had been anticipated a year ago.

It would seem that with the vast sums of money that will be spent in North America over the next decade, the percentage of total earnings from North America should grow, giving overall earnings higher quality and providing the stock with more investment appeal.

Dividends

Until recent years, Exxon's dividend was increased each year. The trend was broken in 1970 when the board declared the $3.75 per share paid in 1969; and again in 1972, the board declared the $3.80 per share paid in 1971. However, the dividend looks again to be on the rise, despite the vast capital expenditure requirements over the next decade. The $4.25 per share payment in 1973 will increase to at least $4.55 per share in 1974 (probably higher) and a further increase in 1975 appears likely if the anticipated earnings trend takes place.

A study of Exxon's payout shows a decline which began in the late 1960s. In 1965, the payout was 70 percent; in 1972 it declined to 55.6 percent; and last year it dropped to 39 percent, reflecting the large increase in earnings. A payout approximating 50 percent appears likely in the years ahead.

RECOMMENDATION

Exxon's past has been both exciting and fascinating, but its present and future look extraordinarily rewarding. Over the years, the company's strong energy base has been confined primarily to expanding oil and gas activities on a worldwide basis, but now the company has positioned itself in the total worldwide energy field for any and all developments that will take place through the rest of the century.

Very importantly, it now appears that corporate earnings will begin to grow faster than in the past decade and be of higher quality. Selling at a very modest P/E of 7.4 times estimated 1974 earnings and yielding 5.6 percent on an indicated dividend that is in a rising trend, the stock is attractively priced on a total return basis, with purchase recommended at current levels.

23

Pollution Control

TERRY W. ROTHERMEL, Ph.D.
Arthur D. Little, Inc.
Cambridge, Massachusetts

THE INDUSTRY

Its Definition

THE pollution control industry is usually defined around companies whose businesses lie in the treatment of major quantities of air, water, and solids pollution. Frequently, other associated or special problems are included in discussions of environmental opportunities—for example, noise pollution, radiation, thermal pollution, or oil pollution.

Air pollution control (APC) is generally associated with preventing emissions from escaping into the ambient air environment. Closely associated businesses not normally included in air pollution control are those of air handling, air conditioning, and the protection of inside living and working environments. The APC business is divided into two major segments: mobile sources and stationary sources. Not only do these segments differ in the physical character of the emission sources but they also differ in their customers, in their relevant technologies, and in their lineup of competitors.

It is further important in the stationary source segment to distinguish between two of its component sectors: particulates and gases. Particulate control is the modern version of what used to be called the "dust collection business." The technologies are largely the same; only the markets have become significantly expanded by legislation. Gaseous removal, on the other hand, is largely a market of the environmental age. Its

586

market potential has been limited by technological constraints, since the traditional particulate removal systems are not relevant to gaseous emission control.

Water pollution control (WPC) is usually divided by its suppliers into its municipal and industrial segments. Municipal wastewater treatment is the old "sewage treatment business" transformed by the promise of large-scale federal monies. The industrial water pollution control business is an even better example of what has been termed a "legislated market." For several reasons, the water treatment business is often associated with that of water pollution control under the broader name of the water and wastewater treatment industry. The first reason is that the companies which supply water pollution control products are also heavily involved in water treatment.

Solids waste management (SWM), of course, dates back to the earliest civilization in which man found it necessary to dispose of waste materials. Here, too, there are municipal and industrial segments to be considered and the different customers which those segments represent. Further, it is important to separate the distinct functions which are part of a solid waste management system: collection, transportation, and disposal (or recycle).

Its Structure

It is, of course, possible to describe a company's overall market position in, for example, air pollution control, water pollution control, or in the larger environmental management business for that matter. It is important, however, to be as specific as possible in defining the market in which a company's position is to be gauged. In that context, one can better evaluate either a company's ability to be selective in its efforts or its inability to penetrate important application areas.

In the *air* pollution control business, a first question is whether the company is involved in particulate or gaseous control or both. Next, it is important to know its position in the different alternative technologies. In particulate control, these would be electrostatic precipitators, fabric filters, wet scrubbers, and mechanical collectors. The historic leadership of Research-Cottrell in the APC business has been built upon its leadership in the sale of electrostatic precipitators. The most important customer industry for the electrostatic precipitator has been the power industry. Hence, a final dimension for describing an air pollution control company's market position is along the lines of its customer industries of specialization. The fact that Research-Cottrell or Joy Manufacturing, by their leadership in electrostatic precipitators, have served the power industry for many years is an important consideration when evaluating their chances in capitalizing on SO_2 control market opportunities in which the power industry is the largest potential market. In short, the market positions of air pollution control companies are as much based upon their familiarity with the problems of a particular customer industry and as they are upon control system technologies.

The most important competitive structure in the APC industry is the lineup of companies which have served the traditional particulate control market. What is viewed as a market share analysis by the analyst or as a concentration analysis by the regulator is displayed in Table 1. The four firms believed to be the current APC leaders in 1971 are Research-Cottrell, Joy Manufacturing, U.S. Filter, and American Air Filter. They were estimated to account for 35 percent of the total market in hardware and associated services. The next eight companies, possibly not in the order indicated, had a combined market share estimated at 25 percent. The last eight companies shown accounted for another 10 percent. Thus, the leading 20 companies accounted for about 70 percent of this market.

TABLE 1

Air Pollution Control Equipment Industry Structure in 1971

	Percent of Company Business in Air Pollution Control	Market Share (percent)
Four Largest:		35
Research-Cottrell.............	50–55	
Joy Manufacturing..........	10–15	
U.S. Filter..................	30–40	
American Air Filter..........	25–30	
Next Eight Largest:		25
Wheelabrator-Frye..........	15–20	
Koppers....................	<5	
Boise-Cascade..............	<5	
Envirotech.................	10–15	
Peabody Galion.............	10–15	
Carborundum...............	<5	
Combustion Engineering.....	<5	
Universal Oil Products.......	<5	
Next Eight Largest:		10
Combustion Equipment Associates................	30–40	
Zurn Industries.............	5–10	
American Standard..........	<5	
Buffalo Forge...............	15–20	
GATX......................	<5	
Babcock & Wilcox...........	<5	
W. W. Sly..................	60–70	
Kirk & Blum...............	40–50	
Total................		70

Source: Arthur D. Little, Inc., estimates.

Probably more than 300 companies shared the rest. There has been a trend toward increased concentration of what has been primarily a particulate control business in recent years, due to mergers and acquisitions on the one hand and the above average growth of electrostatic precipitators on the other. The APC industry, however, is likely to become less concentrated as gaseous (starting with SO_2) emission control becomes a larger part of the total stationary source control effort.

In the *water* and wastewater treatment industry, corporate positions are best defined in terms of their participation in municipal or industrial markets, in water or wastewater applications, or in traditional versus frontier technologies.

On a more general basis, the competitive structure in the water and wastewater treatment equipment business is illustrated in Table 2. There, the four volume leaders—Envirotech, Ecodyne, FMC, and Dorr-Oliver —are indicated to hold about 20 percent of the volume in 1971. Although

TABLE 2

Water and Waste Treatment Equipment Industry Structure in 1971

	Percent of Company Business in Water and Waste Treatment	Market Share (percent)
Four Largest:		20
Envirotech	25–30	
Ecodyne	25–30	
FMC	<5	
Dorr-Oliver	20–25	
Next Eight Largest:		25
Pennwalt	5–10	
Rex Chainbelt	5–10	
Sybron	5–10	
Crane	<5	
Westinghouse	<5	
Neptune Meter	25–30	
Peabody Galion	15–20	
Sunbeam	<5	
Next Eight Largest:		15
Dravo	<5	
Chicago Bridge & Iron	<5	
Davis Water	40–50	
Clow	10–15	
Bird & Sons	5–10	
Komline-Sanderson	50–60	
Roberts Filter	60–70	
Pall Corp.	10–20	
Total		60

Source: Arthur D. Little, Inc., estimates.

the order and membership of the next group of eight companies may not be accurate, this or a similar group was estimated to hold another 25 percent of the market. The last eight of the top twenty firms illustrated by the companies listed in Table 2 accounted for another 15 percent of the market. Probably more than 400 firms share the remaining 40 percent of this business. There has been significant consolidation within the water and wastewater treatment equipment industry. Notable examples are: the merging of EIMCO and Bartlett-Snow-Pacific into Envirotech; FMC's acquisition of both Link Belt and Chicago Pump; the combination of Wallace & Tiernan and Sharples within Pennwalt; and Neptune Meter's acquisition of Microfloc and Nichols Engineering.

Another dimension for characterizing pollution industry structure is along the types of products and services supplied. In air pollution control, the important distinctions are between equipment, associated services supplied with that equipment by the equipment suppliers, instrumentation, and automobile exhaust systems. In water pollution control, the common categories are equipment, instrumentation, and chemicals. In solid waste, the major distinction is between disposal systems (for example, packing trucks, or incinerators) and collection services (illustrated by the growing businesses of Browning & Ferris, Waste

TABLE 3

Pollution Control Markets

	1972 Estimate ($ millions)	1977 Forecast ($ millions)	Growth (percent/year)
TOTAL EXPENDITURES:*			
Air	$ 900	$ 1,800	15
Water†	8,000	12,300	9
Solids	5,000	6,400	5
Total	$13,900	$20,500	8
SPECIALTY PRODUCTS AND RELATED SERVICES:			
Air:			
Products‡	$ 300	$ 650	17
Related services¢	250	600	19
Total	$ 550	$ 1,250	18
Water:			
Equipment‖	$ 550	$ 900	11
Chemicals¶	250	400	10
Total	$ 800	$ 1,300	10
Solids:			
Total	$ 300	$ 400	6
Total	$ 1,650	$ 2,950	12

* Includes both capital and operating costs.
† Includes both water and wastewater treatment markets.
‡ Equipment, instrumentation, and replacement materials.
¢ Services provided by product manufacturers.
‖ Equipment and instrumentation.
¶ Does not include commodity chemicals.
# Equipment only.

Management, Inc., and SCA). The markets for pollution abatement products in 1972 are presented in Table 3 and forecasted for 1977. A major characteristic of the environmental business illustrated in Table 3 is the large proportion of expenditures for products and services which are not special to pollution control applications. Only in air pollution control does the majority of expenditures represent a potential business for the leading suppliers of control systems. In water pollution control, specialty products accounted for less than 10 percent of the total annual expenditures. The remainder of the expenditures are made for civil works construction, including labor and materials. The same is true in solid waste management, where more than 80 percent of the total cost is represented in the collection and transportation steps.

FACTORS AFFECTING INDUSTRY PERFORMANCE

Constraints on Growth

Among the traditional constraints on the control of pollution have been problems related to technology, regulation, organization, priorities, funding, and economics. The relative significance of these factors varies with the pollution problem and will change over time.

Technology. There continues to be considerable debate about the importance of technological constraints upon pollution control progress. The issue of adequate technology is intertwined with that of acceptable economics; available technology may not fall within a reasonable range of control cost. The key test is whether performance in commercial-scale operation has been proven over a sufficient period (for example, a full year) and whether customers are placing orders on other than a demonstration basis.

Generally, the technology to handle most of the nation's pollution problems has been available. The secondary treatment of wastewaters, the removal of particulate emissions, and the sanitary landfill of solid waste have been practical for some time. On the other hand, the lack of proven technology has delayed the widespread control of sulfur dioxide (SO_2) emissions, the control of automobile exhausts, and the development of advanced waste treatment (AWT) methods.

Legislation and Regulation. Principal environmental legislation has had a clear and positive impact on the markets for pollution control equipment. These markets are, to a large degree, legislated ones involving reluctant customers. However, the same set of legislation has also resulted in many uncertainties, unenforceable deadlines, and conflicting objectives. Initial legislation in the 1960s set national sights far beyond national capabilities. Premature expectations of funding and markets have had unfortunate effects upon the planning of municipal sewerage systems and upon the profitability of equipment suppliers. The 1972

Amendments to the Federal Water Pollution Control Act (FWPCA) represented a sophisticated step in improved legislation. Compared to its more idealistic predecessors, the new law is more realistic in setting the timing by which industry is to clean up and the means by which pollution control is to be regulated and enforced. One example of evolution in the regulatory machinery in the 1972 FWPCA Amendments is the combining of what were previously considered alternative approaches: effluent guidelines and stream quality standards.

Manpower and Organization. Our society's relatively recent concern with pollution abatement has led to start-up problems in organizing a national effort. Mobilizing sufficient skilled manpower and organizing federal, state, and local authorities into an efficient regulatory fabric have presented the greatest difficulties. A shortage of manpower trained in pollution control matters has been apparent in the regulatory arena, in the operation of pollution control facilities, and in the pollution control businesses. A number of trends have begun to alleviate this shortage. Universities have begun to produce environmentally oriented engineers with multidisciplinary training; economic recessions have provided an impetus for many to retrain themselves in the environmental field; and the federal and state agencies have carried out extensive programs to train operators of municipal sewage treatment plants.

Until the formation of the U.S. Environmental Protection Agency (EPA) by executive order in late 1970, one of the foremost restraints upon pollution abatement progress was the fragmentation of responsibilities at the federal level. The formation of EPA proved to be a successful step towards eliminating confusion of bureaucratic responsibility; the agency has clearly provided a focal point for information, action, and criticism. This is not to say that organizational difficulties will not continue to frustrate both environmentalists and industrialists. The monumental task of pulling together the responsibilities of this broad societal concern and keeping up with the growing list of legislative objectives will continue to strain EPA's capabilities.

National Priorities. Environmental concern has yet to reach "crisis" proportions. Although pollution often ranks high in public opinion surveys, it holds a more moderate priority when it comes to governmental implementation. Environmental needs have earlier had to be balanced against the competing demands of health care, urban problems, national defense, and numerous other areas. While many of these priorities have diminished, others have gained in strength relative to environmental management. The best example of this, the energy crisis, has clearly forced environmental planners to weave energy requirements into their thinking.

Federal Funding. Municipal sewage treatment is the only sector in which federal funding is a major factor. Figure 1 illustrates the gap between promise and action under the municipal sewage facility grant program. Of about $5.5 billion authorized by legislation for 1968–1972, about 78 percent was appropriated by Congress for use, and about 53 percent was obligated to municipalities. Outlays—the actual repayment of the final bills paid by municipalities—amounted to only about 25 percent of the authorized funds in this five-year period. As a result, the actual investment level of municipal spending in recent years has been less than normal because municipalities have postponed making commitments in

FIGURE 1

Federal Construction Grants for Municipal Wastewater Treatment Plants

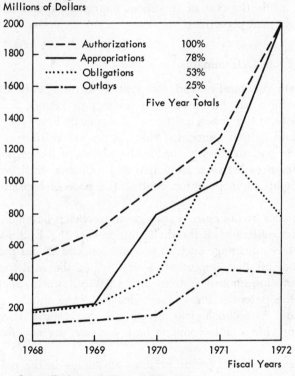

Annual Funding Level,
Millions of Dollars

	Five Year Totals
–––– Authorizations	100%
——— Appropriations	78%
········ Obligations	53%
—·— Outlays	25%

Fiscal Years

Source: Environmental Protection Agency.

anticipation of new government programs. On a constant dollar basis, the associated history of municipal expenditures was disappointing. The average annual real growth between 1965 and 1971 was only 0.6 percent per year—down from a 1958–1965 average growth of 7.6 percent per year.

Control Economics. The pollution control customer is a reluctant one because such investment usually reduces his profitability. Without a legal obligation to invest in pollution control, industry and municipalities would have difficulty in justifying the added costs to investors and taxpayers, respectively. In its early years, a major impediment to pollution control activity was the issue of whether pollution control was an acceptable cost of doing business. Since then, industry has come to recognize, if not quite accept, pollution control as part of doing business. The focus has now become placed upon how much is justified. This new question is of course related to the above issue of competing priorities. It is specifically addressed, for example, in the 1972 FWPCA Amendments which directs EPA to study the relative benefits and costs (i.e., cost-effectiveness) of pollution control in order to evaluate the points of diminishing returns for regulatory policy making. Even the answers of how much is necessary will change in time. The maintenance of a stable level of stream or air quality will require increasing levels of treatment, while the cost of treatment increases exponentially with increased treatment objectives.

Price and Profit Determinants

Corporate profitability and competitive advantage in the pollution control business can be based on a number of factors. Some of these factors relate to the characteristics of the specific firm—for example, its products and its management. Other factors are related to the market environment and are largely outside the control of the corporation, such as the differences between municipal and industrial business and, what is more important in pollution control, the pace of legislation and enforcement.

As the major part of current abatement practice is based on established technologies utilizing off-the-shelf equipment, the traditional sources of proprietary advantage such as product innovation and patent protection are not all that important. Certainly, in the evolving needs for gaseous emission control systems and advanced waste treatment technologies, the potential for technological leverage should grow in the next decade. As technological advantages do become more important they will provide a more common basis for entry by new firms into this business.

The prevailing basis for proprietary advantage in the pollution business lies in the marketing know-how of the leading firms. It is their knowledge of specific industries, their people, and their problems which provides them with repeat business and which gives them an advantage over their competition.

Associated with the roles of technology and marketing in the competitive structure of this industry is the concept of the changing nature of that competition over time. The largest of the traditional pollution control companies may have annual corporate sales of $100 million. Many of the companies which have recently begun to cultivate positions in pollution control or have expressed an interest in it are among the larger billion dollar companies of the *Fortune* 500. As the problems of controlling pollution change from the financial constraints of applying even existing technology to the technological constraints of solving incremental pollution problems, a greater emphasis will be placed upon technological innovation and the R&D budgets upon which they are based. As the traditional leaders in pollution control markets have not needed substantial R&D budgets to support their sales of established technology, their position to supply the frontier technologies required in the future is weakened. The development of these technological breakthroughs, therefore, represents a major vehicle for entry by larger R&D oriented companies—if only by eventual joint ventures with experienced marketing-based leaders in today's markets.

The marketing differences between the municipal and industrial segments of the business are significant enough to affect the overall profitability and growth of participating companies. As municipal business is not a substantial part of the air pollution control segment, these differences are only important in water pollution control and solid waste management. Profitability is lower in municipal markets, primarily because of a multilayered marketing structure extending from the municipal plant operator to municipal authorities to consulting engineering firms to public health authorities to state health agencies and now to federal agencies. Important levels in this structure which impede profitability are the price conscious municipal bidding situation and the role of the consulting engineer as intermediary between the system supplier and the ultimate customer. Although many companies have attempted to deal with municipalities without giving attention to the consulting engineers, most of these efforts have ended in frustration. In the future, so called "turnkey" installations may be constructed by large firms with systems capabilities, but the existing market structure will remain largely unchallenged. Growth, as well, is constrained in both municipal solid waste and water pollution markets. Solid waste management has been practiced for centuries as a matter of necessity. Similarly, municipal sewage treatment has been practiced to some extent for some time in this country. Growth based on upgrading sewerage treatment systems in this country will be further constrained by the availability of federal assistance to accomplish national objectives. In contrast, recent experience has shown that when the cleanup targets for industry are clearly outlined, private corporations can move relatively quickly and thereby supply a faster growing market for pollution control systems suppliers.

Another dimension for gauging potential profitability is a company's strategy for pursuing either product specialization or broad systems capabilities. Actually, profitability can result from effective practice of either strategy. The company with specialized product lines will sacrifice the opportunities for greater volume for higher profit margins. The company with a broad product line can attract a much larger clientele and provide associated services as well.

One of the most difficult, but necessary, requirements for forecasting performance in the pollution control business is the timing of corporate efforts with the timing of market needs. There are many examples where developmental markets in the pollution control are already overpopulated with suppliers competing for limited and, for the most part, unwilling customers. Despite the appeal of the traditional market development effort leading to eventual market acceptance for a new product, the outstanding reality of pollution control is its dependence upon legislation and enforcement for its demand. Enforcement actions have simply not lived up to legislative schedules, and federal funding has simply not matched up with congressional promises. As a result, in its early years as a glamour industry, several pollution control industries have been plagued with overcapacity problems.

COSTS AND ECONOMICS

Costs for the Supplier

The investment requirements to expand facilities to meet a potentially fast-growing demand can be an important constraint upon existing suppliers in the future. The capital resources of companies counting their sales in tens of millions of dollars versus the resources of those that count their sales in hundreds of millions of dollars may be an important factor in restructuring the competitive lineup in the future. It has already been noted that the ability to fund research and development may also be a determinant of future market positions. One cost component which will be a problem for all competitors, both present and future, will be the availability of both skilled and unskilled manpower knowledgeable in pollution control problems and technologies.

Economics for the Customer

From an earlier position that the environment is to be protected at any cost, later legislation has addressed the issue of placing an economic limit on what is reasonable or upon balancing control benefits against control costs. From the early refusals of industry leaders to recognize pollution control as a legitimate cost of doing business, corporate managements have come to recognize pollution control as a new fact of life. As a result, a current challenge of pollution control regulation is to place it in an economic context. Environmental benefits which are difficult to measure must be compared against the accelerating costs of higher degrees of pollution abatement. The seemingly high costs of pollution control must similarly be judged in the context of what may be very high risks of continued pollution.

Pollution control activity has, for the most part, been characterized in terms of so-called tail-end technologies—that is, the control of pollution at the stack or at the pipe. As the cost of incremental pollution control continues to climb, pollutors will increasingly compare these costs to other means of control. Simply stated, the major alternative to collection, treatment, and disposal of pollutants is to prevent the creation of pollutants in the first place. Hence, an increasing amount of pollution control will appear in the form of new processes, process changes, improved maintenance, in-plant recycling, and changes in raw materials and fuel. The pursuit of process and raw material changes represents a very different kind of business opportunity. It is likely, moreover, that much of this activity, although pollution stimulated, will be lost as a specific pollution control market and, of course, diminish the more straightforward market for tail-end technologies.

Another dimension of competition lies between those alternatives which are capital intensive versus those which create higher operating costs. Generally speaking, municipalities have historically favored capital intensive systems for which municipal bonds can be provided and for which federal funds may be used. Schemes to market leased treatment systems have been frustrated by this basic reality in sewage treatment. On the other hand, since the largest cost in solid waste management is the day-to-day cost of transportation and collection, this constraint has been less important in that segment. Industry, on the other hand, has traditionally favored systems involving higher operating costs—expenses which can be added to the price of the product and more directly passed on to the customer.

LEGISLATION AND REGULATION

The federal legislation (Table 4) in air, water, and solids pollution control has had a controlling influence upon the markets for abatement systems. The most impressive result of recent legislation has been the creation of legislated markets over and above the volumes which would otherwise have been enjoyed by companies supplying the relevant systems. In air pollution control, legislation has created a glamour particulate control industry from what was formerly a dust collection business. Without legislation, there would be no great potential market for SO_2 and other gaseous control technologies. Similarly, much of the technological revolution in automobile operation and design is tied to pollution requirements.

While municipal sewage treatment has been around awhile, there was relatively little practice of industrial pollution control until recent federal and state legislation went on the books. With this creation of a new

TABLE 4

Federal Legislation

1899............	Rivers and Harbors (Refuse) Act
1948............	Federal Water Pollution Control Act (FWPCA)
1956............	FWPCA Amendments
1961............	FWPCA Amendments
1963............	Clean Air Act
1965............	Solid Waste Disposal Act
	Water Quality Act
	Clean Air Amendments
1966............	Clean Water Restoration Act
....	Clean Air Amendments
1967............	Air Quality Act
1970............	Resource Recovery Act
	Water Quality Improvement Act
	Clean Air Amendments
1972............	FWPCA Amendments

industrial market for wastewater treatment equipment and products, a more profitable and dynamic market has been legislated. As such, in water pollution control, these industrial customers are as new to the established municipal suppliers as they are to new entrants in water pollution systems generally.

In the already established municipal sewage market, legislation has resulted in a reverse twist of market determination. Compared to the promise of massive federal assistance for municipal plants, the actual obligation of monies (Figure 1) has resulted in a rate of growth in new plant construction or expansion which is less than the rate of increased sewerage facilities construction before the federal statutes were passed.

In solids waste management, legislation has been relatively ineffective in bringing about massive changes in practice and management structure. Promised research and development funds from the federal level have not materialized. There have been all too few insights into better ways of collection, transportation, disposal, or recycling of materials. Consequently, a large part of corporate effort directed at capitalizing on solid waste problems has been frustrated in the marketplace.

To many observers, the national experience in pollution control in the ten years since the passage of the Clean Air Act of 1963 has been a series of blue-sky legislation, unkept promises, and regulatory fumbling. By a more sympathetic view, however, it is not difficult to acknowledge that we should have expected major problems in implementing a national program so broad in its impact and without the promise of commercial benefits for the expenses to be incurred. Writing the legislation has become a challenge in balancing what is ideal environmentally against what is known scientifically and what is possible economically. Regulatory bodies have had to be built from "ground zero" and manpower trained at all levels of the regulatory machinery. Finally, the problems of devising strategies and policies by which to implement the legislation on the books across an endless variety of situations and between different levels of governmental authority had been monumental. In water pollution control, the federal effort initially focused on the establishment and enforcement of water quality standards for streams. The most recent 1972 FWPCA Amendments have now placed the major emphasis upon effluent limitations, subject to overriding requirements of water quality standards. Similarly, air pollution control regulation has shifted back and forth between emission standards and air quality standards.

The issue of the eventual role of federal versus state versus local versus regional authorities in enforcement and management of pollution control programs remains unsettled. To the degree that pollution is a site-specific problem, there are arguments of putting as much power in local hands as possible. To the degree that the air, water, and land environments overlap political boundaries, there is at least one need for regional or federal involvement. To the degree that the load of pollution control costs are more desirably kept equivalent between competitors operating out of different localities, there is further argument for national standards. To the degree that local authorities are presumably more influenced by the politics of large industrial taxpayers, there is another reason for federal involvement. To the degree, however, that the implementation of pollution control is not simply an ecological issue, there is reason for involving the realities of the local situation and the judgment of locally attuned officials.

FINANCIAL CONSIDERATIONS

Among the resources for financial analysis of the pollution control business and the companies in it are the traditional ones of Moodys, Standard & Poors, Dun and Bradstreet, and of course, the 10-K forms required by the SEC. Insofar as pollution control companies have become glamour stocks often earning high price/earnings multiplies, the managements of these companies have typically been fairly open with their views on market trends, their company's position, and their relative participation (on a corporate fraction basis) in environmental systems.

Market estimates are increasingly available from market research firms making periodic surveys on expenditures and projections of those expenditures over a five- to ten-year period. Some associations, like the Industrial Gas Cleaning Institute publish annual summaries of member bookings which are developed from more detailed analyses supplied to their contributing membership. Groups within the U.S. Department of Commerce have also made periodic surveys of shipments in both the air and water pollution control activities.

The Industrial Gas Cleaning Institute statistics have been the best available indicators of particulate control activities but have not been a meaningful source of information relating to activity in gaseous emission control and, more recently, SO_2 control systems. The Department of Commerce has been the best source of estimates of water pollution control activities even with the great difficulty of developing a very confident assessment of that activity.

Another source of information on past and anticipated activity are the McGraw-Hill surveys of pollution abatement expenditures. Unfortunately, these statistics suffer the same problems from which any surveys of corporate intentions suffer. Corporate intentions are of course different than final corporate actions. In pollution control, there is significant political motivation for corporations to overestimate both their actual expenditures and their anticipated ones. Hence, without the raw statistics and without the definition of expenditures used by individual companies, the analyst is left without any reasonable basis upon which to distinguish real from rationalized data.

A similar problem exists in analyzing the published estimates by pollution control companies of their participation in environmental markets. Once again, the analyst has to be careful to define what is meant by environmental business and to determine what a company has included in its own definition. Selling pumps and pipe which happen to be used for wastewater treatment purposes is usually less relevant to the analyst than the equivalent sales of aerators and sludge incinerators. Similarly, air pollution control equipment is a distinct category within the broader product area of air moving and handling systems. More and more, the analyst is faced with an ever-changing definition of environmental matters which may extend from inside the plant environmental control to meteorological or oceanographic activities. This is not to say that these peripheral areas of environmental business may not be as attractive from an investment point of view as the more central pollution control system, but it does teach that one's definition of the business must always be kept close at hand.

The behavior of the stocks of companies involved in pollution control has varied widely. Certainly, companies like Betz Laboratories, Research-Cottrell, and Browning-Ferris have benefited significantly because of a strong and obvious relationship to what has become a glamour industry. One of the first discoveries by analysts was that, for the most part, participating companies enjoyed a very small part of their total volume in this business. Hence, companies like Combustion Engineering, FMC, and Joy Manufacturing have not received strong investor interest because pollution control remains a very small part of their corporate sales.

The new issues market has seen a spate of enterprising companies seeking to capitalize on the natural attraction of capital to what has to be a growing market area. Some of these new companies have been based on a specific system or product invention which appears to solve specific or broad pollution problems. Many of these issues, on the other hand, have been renamed "eco" firms from what were traditional businesses in air, water, or solids.

With the decline of the conglomerate trend, the pollution control industry has become increasingly populated with companies specifically chartered to serve environmental markets. One of the outstanding examples of this trend was the formation of Envirotech by Donaldson, Lufkin, and Jenrette from the research activities and capital of Rockwell International, and the spin-offs of the EIMCO and B-S-P operations from previous corporate parents. Its formation was followed very shortly with a public offering of stock. Since the formation of Envirotech by the vehicle of acquiring divested segments of other companies, many environmentally minded companies have increased their involvement through acquisition of "ugly sister" divisions from other companies.

Another important development has been the spin-off of significant environmental activities into a publicly held corporation. One of the first examples was the public offering of stock in Ecodyne by Trans Union. Although the increased attention and glamour associated with environmental business have increased the tempo of acquisitions in this industry, those same factors have worked to make the acquisition of environmental companies with large price/earnings ratios less practical for acquisition-minded companies, and the number of leading independent firms which can be acquired has been significantly reduced.

A final trend in corporate development activity has been the development of broad-based environmental companies participating in more than just one segment of the air, water, and solids spectrum. Before the pollution control issue became a subject of legislation and potential corporate growth, the leading companies in air, water, and solids businesses were primarily specialists in one segment. Through diversification and mergers, however, several multisegment environmental firms have evolved including Envirotech, Peabody-Galion, Research-Cottrell, Zurn Industries, Combustion Equipment Associates, and Aerojet-General.

ILLUSTRATIVE CASE STUDY: NEW VENTURES

As pollution control increasingly requires new technologies to deal with incrementally more difficult problems, the opportunity for entry by new firms into the present competitive structure has been noted several times above. With this opportunity, there will be increased occurrences in which major companies will announce internally developed systems which are touted to be applicable to well-publicized pollution problems. In many cases, these new systems will have been developed on the basis of research and development programs directed at entering the environmental business. In other cases, the systems will have been the result of a major company's efforts to clean up its own pollution problems. In other cases, a company will have licensed (from a domestic inventor or a foreign source) a technology which has been applied in isolated domestic installations or in a broad range of foreign installations. The problem of the analyst is to effectively gauge the import of these announcements in terms of the technological advantages of the system, the market potential, and the potential impact upon corporate earnings.

In these situations there are many sources of confusion in the information system. A first source of distortion in the viewed potential of a system comes from the inventor or designer of the system who has a natural interest and emotional involvement in its success. A second problem is that inventors, entrepreneurs, and internal engineering staffs solving internal pollution problems may not be sufficiently familiar with competitive systems in the marketplace to competently judge their potential.

In analyzing these situations, the analyst must keep in mind three major kinds of factors important in the pollution control business: technology, marketing, and timing.

The ability to supply technologies which are needed to solve pollution problems has been established as a means for diversification or entry in this business. At the same time, without a sufficient amount of marketing know-how in the relevant markets, the prospects for even the best of technologies are dim. Probably the greatest pitfall for such technologies is for its developers to assume that technology as such will sell itself. With the heavy competition already in this marketplace, no product is going to sell itself against an already profit-shattering noise level of claims and counterclaims. Moreover, customers have been so conditioned by broken promises of past technological breakthroughs that they are inclined to favor the old and proven to the new and promising.

One major lesson of the pollution business is the need to give the marketing of these products the respect it demands. Most of the proprietary advantage existing in the market today resides on the marketing —not the technology—side of the business. The problems of marketing have already frustrated many attempts by large corporations to enter the business, and consequently marketing know-how has been a motivating force behind many acquisitions.

One major kind of difficulty with new ventures in pollution control is that which plagues ventures in any growth area—timing (that is, supplying the right product for the right market at the right time). There are several time-related factors which must be given consideration in order to assess the real market potential of a new pollution control venture. First, potential markets based on identified needs should not be confused with actual markets in which customers are ready to place orders. A second factor is to distinguish between what are available technologies (from the point of view of suppliers willing to deliver) and attractive technologies (from the economic point of view of interested customers).

A final requirement is the need to distinguish between demonstrated and acceptable technology. The difference between demonstrated and acceptable performance lies in its operation in an installation of sufficient size over a sufficient period of time to be acceptable to a cautious and skeptical—reluctant—customer.

24

Publishing and Education Industries

J. KENDRICK NOBLE, JR., C.F.A.
Vice President
Auerbach, Pollak and Richardson, Inc.
New York, New York

INTRODUCTION

VIEWED AS SECTORS of the stock market, the publishing and education industries may be regarded as somewhat small and fragmented. As of September 30, 1973, for example, Media General's *Industriscope* reported on 3,453 companies whose common stocks had a market value of $898,306 million. Of these, 40 were classified as primarily publishing stocks, with a market capitalization of $5,020 million (0.56 percent of the total), and another 7 as educational service stocks, with a market valuation of $194 million (0.02 percent of the total). Thus, if followed, these industries are often assigned to new, young, analysts who rarely follow them exclusively.

Taken seriously, the study of these groups can nevertheless be absorbing and instructive. Almost nothing of significance occurs within our national economic and social framework without affecting one or more publishers, so that the study of the group increasingly broadens an analyst's horizons. Moreover, as the carriers and therefore modifiers of most of the information used by our society, the publishing and education industries play an important role in shaping it. Finally, because of their diversity, it is almost always possible to find both good and poor longer-term investment opportunities within the groups despite changing conditions and differing investment strategies, partly because of a market tendency to lump the stocks of the industry.

Historical Background

Both publishing and education are primarily communication processes, though the latter is increasingly viewed as the communication of skills and attitudes rather than of information alone. Because of the importance of information and education to any civilized society, both can be traced back to the dawn of history and both have commonly been controlled by the authorities of each culture. In our society, education is still primarily, though not exclusively, a governmental function. But publishing has evolved not only as primarily an independent activity but even as one given unusual guarantees of freedom by the state. Both activities are highly decentralized in the United States, however.

The Constitution, and traditions derived from England and Europe, have played key roles in the development of these groups.

The Constitution does not deal with education. Because the Tenth Amendment reserves to the states those powers not delegated to the federal government, they and their local subdivisions have provided the principal financial support and standards for education in this country. Formal educational services are estimated to have absorbed $96.3 billion in 1973, but only small fractions of that amount went for textbooks and other educational materials—perhaps $1.5 billion in all. Statistics are not readily available for such private educational expenditures as for correspondence courses, proprietary schools, preschool education, and the like, but the overall order of magnitude is probably similar to that for educational materials.

Our Constitution embodies two unique provisions affecting publishers. Section 8, Article I, empowers the Congress "To promote the progress of science and useful arts, by securing for limited times to authors and inventors the exclusive right to their respective writings and discoveries" (the rights to copyrights and patents, respectively). The First Amendment, moreover, states in part that, "Congress shall make no law abridging the freedom of speech, or of the press. . . ."

The development of a healthy book publishing industry, and to a lesser extent the expansion of the magazines, can be traced to the legal invention of the copyright. With that development, publishing began to break away from printing. The modern publisher, a marketer comparable to a contractor in many respects, emerged. This publisher, whose assets might be modest:

1. Determined the desire for certain kinds of information.
2. Arranged for that information to be gathered or created by authors.
3. Edited the material for greatest marketability and determined the format of the finished work.
4. Contracted for paper, printing, and binding.
5. Marketed, or arranged for the marketing of, the finished publication.

The new publisher owed his commercial life to the copyright which he obtained by creating the publication or by contracting for its use for some period of time from its authors in exchange for the payments of fees or "royalties" (percentages of sales).

Common Factors

Demographics. As industries, publishing and education have been profoundly affected by the demographic trends of the postwar era. The unit sales of various types of books and periodicals grow relatively slowly with respect to the population groups they serve and are not much affected by short-term economic fluctuations. Thus, of all longer-term factors, the demographics of the markets being served seem to have the greatest influence in publishing.

During the depression, the number of births in this country was relatively static, producing the so-called hollow generation—an absence of growth. Only with the outset of World War II and a reviving economy did the birthrate pick up. The number of births soared after World War II, producing the so-called baby boom, and continued to rise until the late 1950s. Then it began to fall again, reflecting both the coming of age of the hollow generation and a declining birthrate. In late 1973, the birthrate was still falling, so-far offsetting the formation of families by the babies produced during the postwar boom. Sociologists differed on future predictions at that point, but most anticipated a secondary boom of some sort beginning in the mid-1970s.

Children born in one year are potential users of preschool publications two to five years later, are students in elementary schools for the next seven years, and are high school students for the four years after that. From one third to one half of them then go to college for four to six years, and many college graduates become professionals—the greatest per capita users of published materials. Indeed, the 20–35-year age group is generally regarded as the chief book-buying and magazine-buying sector, although newspaper circulation statistics commonly deal with the broader 21–65-year-old workforce.

Figure 1 illustrates the major resulting population trends. If it is appropriate to use demographic factors in calculating industry revenue growth trends as the author believes, then:

1. The preschool market should pick up in the late 1970s and could be a good growth market for years.
2. The elementary textbook and juvenile trade book markets are now soft and will remain so into the late 1970s.
3. The high school and, in the author's opinion, the domestic encyclopaedia markets, both of which have been impacted by other factors, are now in the process of softening, partly due to demographic factors.

FIGURE 1

Demographics Affecting Publishing (thousands)

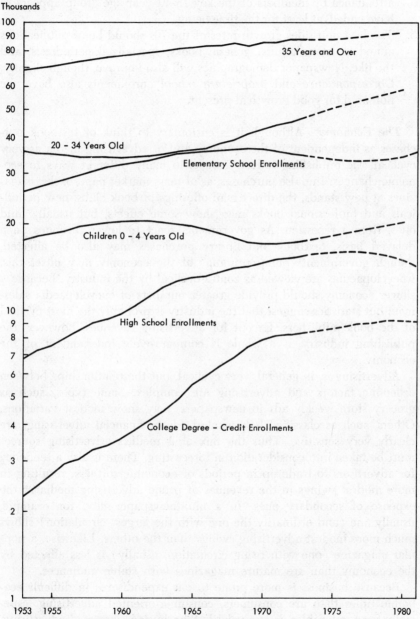

Thousands

35 Years and Over

20 – 34 Years Old

Elementary School Enrollments

Children 0 – 4 Years Old

High School Enrollments

College Degree – Credit Enrollments

Sources: *Economic Report of the President, 1973; Statistical Abstract 1973;* Auerbach, Pollak & Richardson, Inc. estimates; and projections of educational statistics, 1973.

4. The college textbook market's demographics are rising and will for most of the 70s. But a longer-term trend toward greater college attendance by members of the key 18–21-year age group appears to have ended, at least for the time being.
5. The best unit sales growth rates of the 70s should be of publications aimed at young adults: general books, specialized periodicals, and the like. Newspaper demographics will also improve, though slightly. *Correspondence* and *proprietary school* enrollments also have the potential for good growth at present.

The Economy. Although it is customary to think of textbook purchases as independent of the economy and of advertising media as very cyclical, the publishing industry reacts in many different ways to economic changes. Impulse purchases, as of mass market paperbacks, magazines at newsstands, the direct mail offerings of book clubs, new periodicals and professional books may show some effects, but usually mild ones, from a recession. As governments react to lower revenues on a delayed basis, textbook and library purchases may also be affected, though government "pump priming" of the economy may offset this. Encyclopaedias are viewed as contra-cyclical by the industry, because a slower economy should provide greater numbers of encyclopaedia salesmen; but statistics suggest that the industry is probably the most cyclical of the book publishers. Except for advertising revenues, however, the publishing industry as a whole is comparatively independent of the economy.

Advertising is, in general, very cyclical, but the relationships between economic factors and advertising are complex. Some types, such as grocery store weekly ads in newspapers, may show modest variations. Others, such as classified help-wanted ads or financial advertising, are clearly very sensitive. Thus the mix of a media's advertising sources must be taken into consideration in forecasting. There is also a tendency for advertisers to trade up in periods of economic softness, resulting in more modest swings in the revenues of prime advertising media at the expense of secondary ones. In a multinewspaper city, for example, usually one (and ordinarily the one with the largest circulation) shows much more modest advertising swings than the others. Likewise, a popular magazine (one with rising circulation, usually) is less affected by the economy than are mature magazines with stable audiences.

Because business is more prone to cut expenditures in difficult economic times than are consumers, consumer-oriented advertising, especially for nondurables, is less volatile than business-oriented advertising.

In the educational areas, there is a tendency for correspondence course students to withhold periodic payments in recessions, raising bad debt figures substantially, and for businesses to curtail the seminars and payments for student attendance which may mean the difference between profitable and unprofitable years for the proprietary schools.

Social Factors. Both publishing and education are affected by changes in our society. The expansion of education has led to greater literacy and a greater thirst for information—both helpful to the publishing industry. On shorter time-frames, these basic trends may be augmented by changing literary tastes (from detective stories to science fiction or to elaborate novels, for example,) so that general book publishers must be unusually alert to popular whims. On a longer-term basis, some trends appear to be:

1. The search for convenience, which has been a factor in the rise of the *mass market paperback* at the expense of the *cloth trade book*.
2. Greater leisure time, which has meant a boom in sales of books and magazines dealing with sports and other leisure-time activities.
3. The search for self-identification, which has fostered a proliferation of special interest publications and books on psychology, astrology, and some aspects of religion.
4. As of 1973, an interest in the practical at the expense of the theoretical, favoring growth in enrollments in vocational and business subjects in colleges together with declining interest in the humanities.
5. A recognition of the importance of early education, which has fostered the growth of preschool education (that is, at or below the kindergarten level).
6. The rapid expansion of knowledge, which has aided the growth of digest and specialized magazines, newsletters, and the like.

Costs and Problems. Publishing and education, partly because they are involved with the world of ideas, partly because both are served by large numbers of small establishments, and partly because the technologies of both have changed slowly, are unusually labor intensive.

Over 1.1 million people are employed in the printing and publishing industries and about three million in education. Unions are prevalent in the publication production processes and in news gathering, and are increasingly important in education. Only book publishing is free of unionization as an industry, but it tends to compete with the other media and with education for its employees and is thus affected by trends in those fields. Labor costs are the greatest single expense elements for most publishers, directly or indirectly, and the reduction of labor costs is one of the chief elements in margin improvements. Moreover, strikes are the greatest potential threats to the short-term operations of a publisher or school. Fortunately, strikes in these fields tend to be geographically localized, reducing their significance to chains of newspapers or of schools.

For publishers, tied to the printed word at present, the second chief cost problem is paper. In 1973, this became a problem of availability as well, possibly for an extended period of time. Paper costs had been rising about 3–4 percent per year for book quality paper and newsprint, and less for magazine types. Suddenly, in response to heightened demand caused by worldwide economic surges, lower availability due to the actions of environmentalists, low returns on invested capital in the business, and strikes in Canada, prices rose 10–15 percent or more and shortages developed. This event established that large newspaper chains, with a number of suppliers and great buying power, and book publishers who could generally vary the types of papers used in their new books, are the least affected by availability problems. Magazines and smaller newspapers, which often buy papers through intermediaries such as printers and brokers, have the most difficult supply problem.

Distribution problems vary by publication type. A significant factor is postage. Although changes in mail classifications are being studied, at present there are four primary classes of postage and postage rates:

1. First class—letters and other sealed materials.
2. Second class—magazines, newspapers, and unsealed letters.
3. Third class—newsletters, advertising circulars, and other bulk mailings.
4. Fourth class—parcel post—most books.

Books are usually sold with postage charges added. Increases in fourth class rates, while slightly decreasing the funds institutions have to buy books with, have little other effect.

Third class rates are important to all publishers heavily involved in direct mail promotions, including direct mail booksellers, book clubs, and, particularly, magazines. The latter spend large amounts to bring in subscribers.

Second class rates are important to magazines and newspapers serving geographically large areas (for example, the *Wall Street Journal* and some rural newspapers).

First class rates are important to publishers promoting their wares to more important buyers, such as in business press magazine advertising promotion.

After years of relatively steady and modest postal rate increases, in the 1970s publishers were experiencing frequent and somewhat unpredictable changes. The analyst will find these difficult to interpret for any given publisher, but most will summarize their effects for him.

Distribution also presents other problems. Newspapers are finding it harder to attract newsboys and other urban distributors; book publishers are faced with sluggish bookstore growth and competition from other outlets; and encyclopaedias, book clubs, correspondence course producers, and magazine subscription sales agencies have all encountered problems with consumers and the Federal Trade Commission in connection with their distribution and sales techniques.

New distribution techniques are being tried and will likely prove important to these industries in the future.

Technology. As in most other fields, technological advances have two facets: the reduction of industry costs and the creation of new competitors.

Of all technological changes in these information-processing industries, the advent of the computer has been the most important. Introduced as a means of providing better financial controls, the computer has subsequently been used to generate new products such as special editions of magazines and customized information services. In time, its use in this quasi-author/quasi-editor/quasi-teacher mode may have the greatest impact. But, at present, the most important effects are being felt in scheduling, inventory control, and production.

In production, the computer is being allied with *photocomposition* and *offset* printing. Just a few years ago, most publication printing utilized centuries-old techniques. Working from written or typed copy, a *typographer* would use molds to cast characters or lines of metal type. From these, *columns* or *galleys* of type were made, and *proof* copies would be prepared by inking the type and pressing the galleys against paper. The proofs would then be corrected, type reset as necessary, and corrected galleys assembled in *forms* together with engravings of any illustrations. Printing of a few copies could be done with the forms, but commonly *plates* were made for longer runs.

Plates were produced from molds made from forms which were either filled with molten metal or which were first used to prepare metallic or other shells which were in turn filled with metal.

In later days, the galleys might be prepared using special typewriters or machines which produced film images. From these *cold type*, or photocomposed galleys, film images of plates were assembled and then used to chemically produce plates for offset printing. In offset, as opposed to the earlier *letterpress* printing, the thinner, less durable plates transferred their ink to rubber rollers which in turn carried the ink to paper, rather than directly contacting the abrasive paper.

Using the computer, it should soon be possible to produce publications for which whole pages are initially prepared, corrected, and assembled on cathode ray tube displays, without ever creating any intermediate images. Once approved, these computer-generated displays could be used to prepare either films for the preparation of plates or even plates, directly. Thus, the time, labor, errors, and expenses of the production process could be greatly reduced, particularly for the newspapers which generally own their own printing presses.

Special Factors. As noted, there are unique provisions for copyrighting and the freedom of publications in our Constitution. The advent of federal controls in the early 1970s established the fact that the freedom of the press is not absolute; serious questions concerning the rights of copyright holders remain to be resolved, pending Supreme Court decisions and the passage of a new copyright bill.

The salability of a publication depends on its uniqueness in time and place and the value of its information content to its potential user. Thus the only newspaper in a given location has high salability. A weekly magazine has less salability unless protected by copyright; a monthly magazine, still less; a book, even less; and a long-lived reference book, normally expensive and with few pages of immediate interest, the least of all. Since the development of inexpensive mass copying in the 1960s, there has been a growing tendency to ignore copyrights, and the economic effects of this have been felt in roughly the order described above. Many educators, indeed, feel that they should have the right to reproduce materials for nonprofit educational purposes specifically granted by any new copyright bill. Thus the definition of "fair use" in the new bill could be critical to the future of some sectors of publishing. Most publishers would prefer to leave that definition to the courts, which so far have generally agreed with the need for protecting authors and publishers for the public good.

The concept of freedom of the press has, in part, led to some unique privileges for publishers. For example, while cigarette advertising has been banned from the airwaves, so far no restrictions have been placed on printed advertisements. In another connection, the Newspaper Preservation Act permits a failing and a successful newspaper in the same location to combine certain functions, as exceptions to antitrust legislation, in order to preserve both newspapers as independent editorial voices.

Given respect for copyrights, almost every publication is a unique proprietary product. Unit sales growth has been moderate, but price increases have satisfactorily provided for earnings growth, except in periods of unusually rapid changes in the rate of inflation or in serious economic recessions. Thus the freedom to raise prices is very important to most types of publishers—a freedom which was restricted for the first time by the price controls of the 1970s. Future revenue and earnings projections will have to take into account assumptions as to the types of controls, if any, which may be in effect.

STRUCTURE AND SCOPE OF THE INDUSTRY

In 1973, the Department of Commerce estimated the value of publishing industry shipments at about $15 billion: newspapers, $8,310 billion with 8,100 establishments; periodicals, $3,655 billion with 2,400 establishments; and books, $3,077 billion with 1,100 establishments.

The figures for industry shipments over the previous ten years are displayed in Table 1. For comparison, United States Office of Education (USOE) estimates of expenditures for education over the same period are also tabulated.

Newspapers

As of 1974, there were 1,774 daily newspapers with a circulation of about 63.1 million, and 7,641 weeklies with a circulation of over 30

TABLE 1

Receipts of the Publishing Industries and Expenditures for Education
($ billions)

Year	Book Publishing	Periodicals	Newspapers	Elementary and Secondary Education*	Higher Education*
1972	2.861	3.506	8.272	57.5	32.0
1971	2.434	3.239	7.355	53.6	29.9
1970	2.437	3.195	6.967	51.2	28.7
1969	2.417	3.468	6.823	49.8	27.5
1968	2.099	3.342	6.191	46.5	26.1
1967	2.135	3.096	5.757	45.7	25.0
1966	1.996	2.718	5.520	41.1	22.9
1965	1.767	2.626	5.156	39.4	20.6
1964	1.729	2.464	4.820	36.3	18.0
1963	1.535	2.296	4.484	33.6	15.9

* School year beginning in the calendar year cited, in the case of educational expenditures.
Source: U.S. Department of Commerce and U.S. Office of Education.

million. Collectively, they drew gross advertising expenditures (before agency discounts and allowances) of about $8 billion, 30 percent of total advertising outlays. Thus newspapers were, and are, the dominant advertising medium in the United States as well as a major source of information.

As of 1973, five of the ten largest newspaper chains (by circulation) had not yet gone public, though the largest—Tribune Company—was expected to make an offering by 1975. By far, the majority of newspapers were still privately held, an important factor in the aggressive acquisition activities of the public chains. All of the latter had made at least a few acquisitions in the prior decade.

Although the newspapers are grouped into trade associations of dailies and weeklies, the former may be further classified into small-city and large-city papers. The distinction between the latter two groups was, as of 1973, approximately at the 125,000 circulation level. Below that level, competition within the city of origin was unusual, enabling the newspaper to determine the timing and—to a greater degree—the amounts of circulation and advertising rate increases. Moreover, the state of the art in newspaper production currently permitted the paper to make a complete transition from letterpress to offset printing if it wished. Margins tended to be higher and labor costs, though lower per capita than in larger papers, tended to account for larger shares of expenses, while newsprint accounted for smaller shares. Among the larger, competitive newspapers, investors had to be concerned with the possibilities of the eventual elimination of one or more papers in each such city if trends continued.

Circulation revenues account for 20–30 percent of newspaper revenues, and advertising the balance. Typically, 70–80 percent of circulation is delivered to homes and charged for on a weekly or monthly basis, so that newsstand prices are relatively unimportant except to establish home-delivered prices. Home-delivered papers, historically sold at a discount from newsstand prices, seem to be moving toward a premium as part of an effort among the media to shift revenue bases to readers. Although the numbers of readers are growing modestly, circulation revenue growth may exceed advertising revenue growth in the future.

Newspaper advertising revenues, which had held or increased their share of all advertising revenues through the 1963–1973 period, were expected to grow 6–7 percent in the 1970s. Most newspapers tend to view advertising linage as relatively inelastic (as circulation numbers have proven to be), varying their advertising rates on the basis of the state of the economy, competitive rates per thousand viewers in other media, and cost increases. The author has found it preferable to work with estimates of advertising dollar outlays, however.

Newspaper advertising is primarily local in character and thus less affected by national economic conditions than, say, that of magazines.

Book Publishers

In contrast with the newspapers, book publishers depend almost wholly on unit sales. A second factor, especially important as a source of profits to trade book publishers, is royalty income (or "subsidiary rights" income) from granting republication rights to other publishers or media. Mass market paperback publishers and book club operators frequently purchase such rights from conventional trade book publishers for their most successful titles. A third source of income for some book publishers is interest income—particularly important for *subscription reference book publishers* (for example, those who publish encyclopedias) who may collect for their sales over periods of as much as three years. In these cases, interest charges may be included in sales prices or billed separately.

Book publishers' revenue reports deal almost entirely with unit sales, however. For textbook and subscription reference book publishers, most of whom belong to the Association of American Publishers, sales data from that association are believed quite accurate. For other types of publishers, sales data collected periodically by the Bureau of the Census are generally accepted by the industry, subject to minor modifications.

Historically, prices of books have been closely associated with production costs, especially that of paper, while unit sales have tended to be associated with demographics, generally rising modestly on a per capita basis. Rates of growth by sector have therefore differed markedly and have changed with time. In the past several years, sectors associated with children (juveniles and textbooks) have tended to show the least growth, while those associated with young adults (mass market paperbacks and professional books) have shown the highest growth. Volume and growth rates are presented in Table 2.

Approximately 1,000 companies engage in book publishing. Distribution techniques and ultimate purchasers very widely, but certainly among the largest markets is education, with an estimated $1.5 billion in purchases of textbooks and other books in 1973—sold primarily by publishers directly to schools and libraries or through state *depositories* and wholesalers. Direct mail ($221 million of mail-order books, $262 million in book club sales, and approximately $150 million in subscription reference book sales in 1973) is another major sales category. The balance of subscription reference book sales is primarily made door to door; while book, department, and stationery stores account for most other hard-bound book

TABLE 2

Revenues ($ millions) and Growth Rates (percent) of Book Publishing Sectors

	1963	1963–67 Rate	1967	1967–72 Rate	1972
Adult trade books:					
Hardbound	109	9.4	156	11.8	273
Paperbound	17	17.1	32	20.0	80
Total	126	10.5	188	13.4	353
Juvenile trade books:					
Under $1 retail	31	3.1	35	(7.9)	24
$1 and over retail	73	15.6	130	(2.9)	113
Total	104	12.3	165	(3.8)	137
Religious books:					
Bibles, testaments, hymnals, and prayerbooks	35	9.9	51	3.6	61
Other religious	46	5.5	57	3.9	69
Total	81	7.5	108	3.8	130
Professional books:					
Law	58	6.3	74	14.4	145
Medicine	24	12.2	38	8.4	57
Business	15	7.5	20	16.0	42
Technical, scientific, and vocational	69	11.1	105	5.5	137
Total	166	9.3	237	10.0	381
Book clubs	143	5.9	180	14.6	356
Mass market paperbacks	87	10.6	130	14.2	253
University press	18	14.6	31	5.8	41
Textbooks:					
Elementary and secondary	305	8.4	421	3.4	498
College	160	15.7	287	5.5	375
Total	465	11.1	708	4.3	873
Standardized tests	13	14.1	22	4.2	27
Subscription reference books	381	3.0	441	(9.6)	279
Other	102	1.9	110	10.0	177
Total	1686	6.6	2320	5.3	3007

Source: U.S. Department of Commerce and Association of American Publishers.

sales and, joined with news dealers and newsstands, market most paper-backs. Bookstores alone probably accounted for about $219 million in publishers' revenues in 1973, much less than an analyst might suspect.

Magazines

The number of magazines is uncertain. The 1972 Census cited 2,510 publishers, including about 435 in the business press field, but there were about 2,380 business publications alone in print in 1972. There were also over 200 farm publications, and 287 consumer magazines were large enough to be audited by the Audit Bureau of Circulations in that year. Moreover, the Magazine Publishers Association has noted that 818 magazines were introduced from 1963 to 1972, while only 180 publicly folded.

Be that as it may, the periodical publishing field is probably the most fragmented and diversified sector of publishing. Department of Commerce figures underestimate its size, in the author's opinion, by assigning directories, catalogs, newsletters, shopping news publications, and business service publications to the "Miscellaneous Publishing" category (SIC Product Code 2741). Pending the receipt of final 1972 Census figures, receipts of periodical publishers in the broader sense are estimated at about $3,332 million. While it is difficult to draw precise boundaries between publishing sectors, the author views periodicals as publications issued on a regular basis, usually less frequently than daily and sometimes up to annually, with editorial coverage not focussed on local news.

While frequency is certainly of significance, the primary distinctions that we draw among periodicals are two: types of audiences and sources of revenues. Frequently these aspects are related. The two major sources of revenues are readers (through single-copy purchases and subscriptions) and advertisers or other interested parties.

At one extreme, then, are the periodicals which depend solely or almost exclusively on their readers. Examples of these are the proliferating newsletters, the journals, and many business services. *Looseleaf services,* in which obsolete materials are replaced by revised information, tend to fall between periodicals and books. These publications tend to have limited audiences with special interests, may be very expensive unless subsidized by government, nonprofit organizations, or businesses, and are generally sold in advance on a *subscription* basis. Revenues are relatively predictable for periods approximating average subscription lengths, and earnings problems are usually associated with unexpected and/or rapid changes in cost structures. Margins can be quite high, and earnings can be augmented by interest income on prepaid subscriptions which amount to no-interest loans from subscribers. Companies involved in these fields usually grow through adding similar publications rather than experiencing good growth in revenues for particular publications, though prices can be very inelastic for highly useful publications, such as legal, taxation, and financial services. A second reason for growth through proliferation, however, is to avoid the dangers of a rapid loss of interest in a particular specialty area.

Nineteen seventy-two volume in the above areas is estimated at about $100 million.

Consumer magazines, on the surface, appear to fall midway in the subscription/advertising revenue spectrum. In 1972, the Department of Commerce estimated the net advertising revenues of "general periodicals" at $892.6 million and their subscription and sales revenues at $823.2 million. This, incidentally, was one of the lower percentage contributions by advertising to revenues in many years.

At the end of World War II, magazines carried about 20 percent of all national advertising in the United States. Next to direct mail, they were the leading national advertising medium. With the postwar introduction of television, the largest magazines generally sought still larger audiences, with heavy promotional outlays and generous discounts to subscribers, fighting to maintain that role. By the early 1970s, however, that strategy had failed with the death of all the major mass-market weeklies of the 40s—*Life, Look,* the *Saturday Evening Post,* and *Collier's* —and a decline in magazines' national market advertising share to about 11 percent. Survivors were placing increasing emphasis on higher subscription prices, and a new generation of high-priced, often smaller-circulation magazines had entered the competition—frequently intending to be profitable on circulation revenues alone. Related to this, and also affected by rising postal costs, was a tendency to shift distribution toward newsstand sales.

At the other end of the revenue spectrum among periodicals, are the *farm journals* and, especially, the *business press.* Department of Commerce estimates are that the former drew 19 percent of their receipts from circulation in 1972, and the latter drew only 29 percent from readers. These publications, in contrast with consumer magazines, have always been aimed at relatively small and specialized audiences for which advertisers were willing to pay relatively large amounts per thousand ad exposures. At the extreme end are *controlled circulation* business publications: Those sent without charge to audiences of prime interest to certain advertiser groups. Even these will often sell some subscriptions at relatively high prices, but total subscription revenues remain low in proportion to gross revenues.

Total advertising and circulation revenues of these three periodical groups in 1972 were: general periodicals, $1,716 million; farm periodicals, $76 million; and business press, $900 million.

Education

While expenditures for education are an order of magnitude higher than for publishing, the bulk of such expenditures are for public schools, colleges, and services. The book publishers do derive an important portion of their revenues from the educational establishment ($1.5 billion, or 45 percent, in 1972), and the newspaper and periodical industries some much smaller shares, making an understanding of education important to the analyst of book publishing as well as to the publisher. But, more importantly, this understanding—as well as the vastly larger market potential of educational services—and other factors have led many publishers to enter four related fields (together with a host of other types of companies). These auxiliary fields include: correspondence schools; proprietary schools; *preschool centers;* and the publication of nonbook educational materials.

Good historical data are still lacking for all four of these areas, and comparatively little current information is available on the first three.

FACTORS AFFECTING GROWTH OF REVENUES AND PRICE STRUCTURES OF VARIOUS MARKET SEGMENTS

The Impact of the Population Wave

Relationships between the numbers in appropriate population groups and between either units purchased and/or expenditures tend to persist in publishing and education for long periods of time. The analyst will find it useful to search for these relationships, not necessarily accepting prevailing wisdom as to their natures, since many population groups can be easily projected for long periods. If historic data are available, they can be useful in estimating what future changes in demographic trends may produce, since relationships often change with changes in the momentum of population trends. Deviations from relationships are of particular interest.

For example, the textbook publishing industry once used extrapolations of textbook type units per capita to forecast industry growth. In recent years, those trends altered and analysts have found trends in expenditures per capita more useful than unit trends. (See Figures 2 and 3.) The author's work suggests that even better calculations for the elhi field can be derived from relationships between instructional expenditures and textbook expenditures and that instructional expenditures, in turn, are closely associated with expenditures for instructional staff.

In any event, it is probable that sales trends for products serving growing demographic markets will be higher than for products serving shrinking populations. Thus the so-called "postwar baby boom" (Figure 1) led to a rapidly expanding textbook publishing market in the 1950s and early 1960s and more recently has been a factor in the growth of sales of mass market paperbacks and other publications aimed at young adults.

FIGURE 2

Elhi Textbook Sales

Millions of Dollars

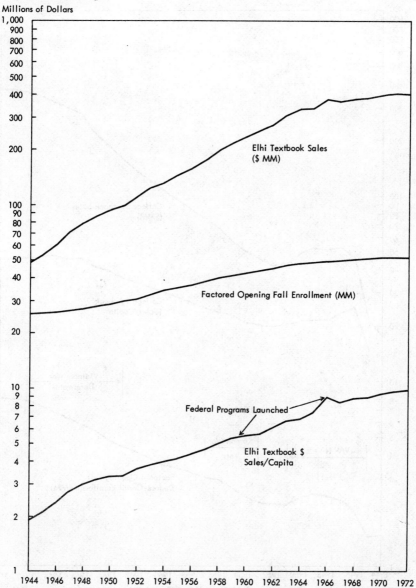

Sources: Association of American Publishers; U.S. Office of Education; and Auerbach, Pollak & Richardson, Inc.

FIGURE 3

College Textbook Sales

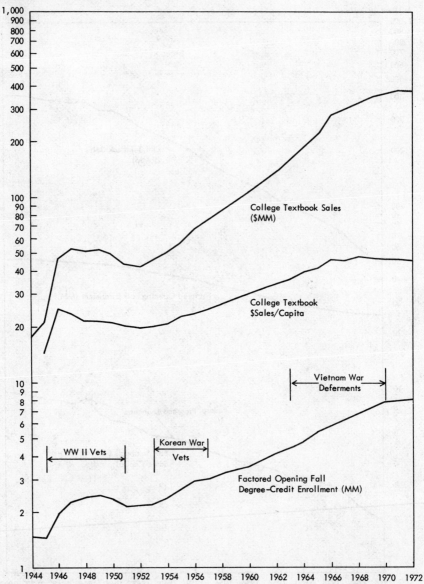

Sources: Association of American Publishers; U.S. Office of Education; and Auerbach, Pollak & Richardson, Inc.

In an unusual example of a periodical's response to these demographic changes, *Ingenue*, directed to teenage girls, was sold and became *New Ingenue* and was to become *Feathers*, directed to young women.

Personal Consumption Expenditures

From 1961 to 1971, books continued a postwar trend to increase their share of personal consumption expenditures. Personal consumption expenditures for magazines and newspapers, combined, merely held their own, although their trend shows signs of improvement. As reading is believed associated with education, affluence, and young adults' share of the population (all of which are rising), the sales of general books, magazines, and newspapers to their readers should take larger shares of personal consumption expenditures in the 1970s. These trends should be augmented by tendencies toward more aggressive circulation pricing by the magazines and newspapers, if not by more rapidly rising paper costs as well.

Advertising expenditures also appear to bear a close relationship to personal consumption expenditures for durables and nondurables (services are not heavily advertised), though the analyst may find more complex economic relationships serve him better in advertising projections.

In the absence of better demographic data, trends of receipts for all types of publications and educational services may be usefully related to personal consumption expenditures for projections—with the exceptions of educational audiovisuals, textbooks, and business publications and services.

Federal Expenditures

With respect to most types of publishing, federal expenditures provide only a small portion of total purchases. But because these expenditures can vary significantly as programs are introduced or terminated, they are worth studying.

There have been over 100 individual programs in recent years with some impact on one or more of the industry segments described above. Trade associations involved usually highlight the few with real impact as they pass through the successive stages of authorization, appropriation, enactment, and fund release. Analysts should be aware that authorizations not only precede funding by long periods but usually authorize spending far in excess of final expenditures. Moreover, what counts is not just how large an appropriation is but how it is to be used and to what degree it truly represents new money and not simply replacement funds.

Insofar as elhi educational materials have been concerned, major programs have included Title III of the National Defense Education Act of 1958, and Titles I, II, and III of the Elementary and Secondary Education Act of 1965. The former specifically excluded textbooks but affected sales of juveniles and audiovisuals; the latter affected all three categories when first funded, usually the year after authorization.

College textbook sales have been indirectly aided by a variety of programs designed to aid college enrollment, including the various "GI" bills to assist veterans. The latter have also helped fund proprietary and correspondence course enrollments.

General book sales have been assisted by the Library Services Construction Act, the Higher Education Act, and specialized programs in medicine and other sciences.

Vocational books and educational programs, particularly the Job Corps programs, have been aided by a variety of specialized vocational education programs.

Repeatedly studied, and perhaps to be funded at some point beyond 1973, are appropriations for audiovisual and other instructional technology programs; for day care centers and other preschool programs; and for equalizing educational expenditures in public schools by raising the general level of such expenditures. Still another potential program would allow students to use vouchers to pick their own schools which might be run for profit. Undoubtedly still other programs will be conceived as time passes.

In general, the effects of new federal funds have been chiefly felt in the calendar year following that in which the authorization has been first approved. Educational materials sales have shown unusually good gains in those years. Apparently, when new funds reach the schools before people have been hired and plans made, abnormally large shares of them are used to buy materials. In consequence, the second year after a new program is approved can be disappointing.

State and Local Expenditures

States and localities provide the bulk of funds for education and libraries. In the 1973–74 school year, the USOE estimated that federal funds accounted for 10 percent of educational spending, up from 9 percent in a decade; state funds for 34 percent, up from 30 percent; local funds for 31 percent, down from 36 percent; with the balance (25 percent) from fees, tuition, and the like. In the elementary and high schools, the ratios were 8, 37, 46, and 9 percent, respectively.

Proposals have been made for the federal share of elhi spending to be raised to one third, while phasing down (or out) the share provided by local real estate taxes. Some momentum to this move has been provided by court decisions in a number of states calling for an equalization of spending per capita for Elhi education within each such state. At the national level, however, the Supreme Court decision in the case of *Rodriguez et al.* (1973) has reduced the momentum of federal efforts; so the move will be long in coming, if it is ever consummated nationally. The effects of equalization could be to equalize upward with greater per capita expenditures for both personnel and materials.

In the elhi textbook market, particular companies and even the industry can be affected by the "adoption cycle." In the southern and western states, educational materials are periodically selected in different fields. Because the lengths of individual state adoption periods vary, collectively they tend to peak in some subjects every few years (about five years on average), producing unusually heavy demand for appropriate books. Most publishers try to schedule new series of books in those fields for such peaks.

About half our state legislatures meet in even-numbered years, while nearly all meet in odd-numbered years. This tends to produce a biennial cycle in elhi textbook purchases (odd-numbered years are currently best) as well as in sales of looseleaf and other legal and tax services (even-numbered years are best).

BUSINESS EXPENDITURES

Advertising. Advertising accounts for a large share of all publishing revenues. It is also a relatively misunderstood subject. For example, advertising is currently viewed as a low-growth, strongly cyclical economic sector. It is associated with corporate profits by analysts, and when profits are expected to soften, advertising-dependent stocks tend to be unusually weak. Figure 4, which traces both corporate profits and advertising expenditures from 1935 to 1972, illustrates the exaggerated nature of that view. In 36 years, corporate profits declined in 11 years (aftertax) or 12 years (pretax), but advertising expenditures declined only in 3 years.

Those in advertising, on the other hand, tend to associate their revenues with GNP—with sales, in other words, rather than profits. Indeed, there is a relatively high correlation between the two. But most advertising is consumer oriented, and most advertised products can be classified as either consumer durables or consumer nondurables. Thus, it is worth examining the relationship between advertising and consumer expenditures in these two categories.

Figure 5 shows ratios of the various factors illustrated in Figure 4.

It can be observed that the ratio of advertising to GNP was essentially the same in 1935–1938 (2.33 percent on average) and 1955–1961 (2.32 percent on average). The advertising ratio trough from 1939 to 1955 can be associated with the relative decline of consumer spending and profits in World War II, and possibly with tax increases as well, followed by a somewhat erratic recovery. The post-1961 advertising erosion can be

FIGURE 4

Advertising and the Economy

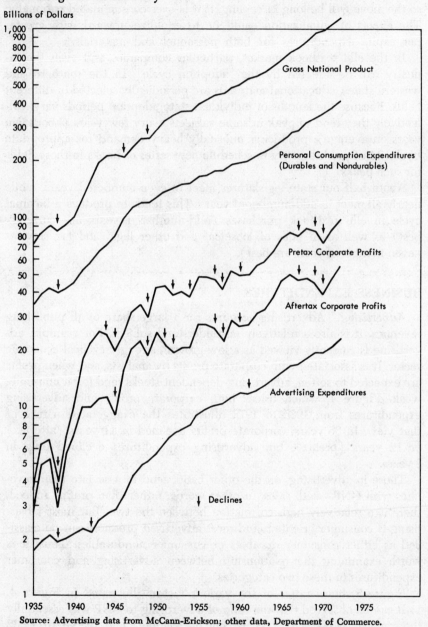

Source: Advertising data from McCann-Erickson; other data, Department of Commerce.

FIGURE 5

Advertising in Relation to the Economy

Percent

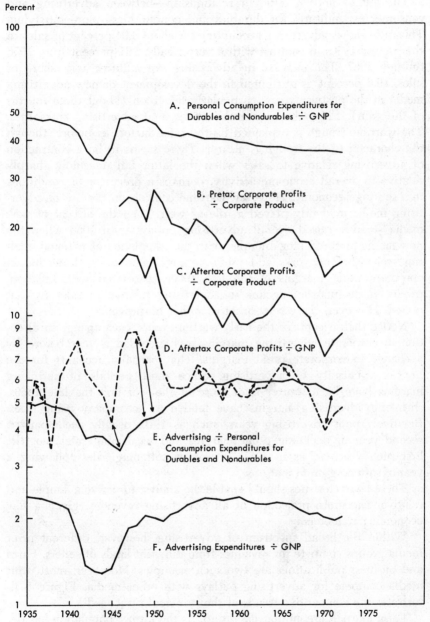

A. Personal Consumption Expenditures for Durables and Nondurables ÷ GNP

B. Pretax Corporate Profits ÷ Corporate Product

C. Aftertax Corporate Profits ÷ Corporate Product

D. Aftertax Corporate Profits ÷ GNP

E. Advertising ÷ Personal Consumption Expenditures for Durables and Nondurables

F. Advertising Expenditures ÷ GNP

Source: Calculated by author (Auerbach, Pollak & Richardson, Inc.) from ad data from McCann-Erickson, Inc., and other data from Department of Commerce.

associated with declines in both corporate profit margins and consumer expenditures for durables and nondurables.

The author finds a different relationship—between advertising and consumer expenditures for durables and nondurables—more satisfying. This ratio shows advertising accounting for about 4.94 percent of sales in the prewar 1930s in contrast with a very steady 5.91 percent from 1956 through 1967. The increase in advertising expenditures as a share of sales, 19.6 percent, is attributed to the development of new advertising media in the postwar years, particularly television (about three fourths of the gain), FM radio, new publications, and advertising specialties. The wartime trough is explained by the same factors as before, though the character of the trough is clearer. There seems to be a contraction of advertising relative to sales when the latter fall unusually sharply relative to overall economic activity, perhaps a precursor of conditions in a shortage economy. However, wartime controls on the use of advertising media evidently played a role as well. Then the advent of new media steadily raised overall advertising outlays until 1956 when the new media matured (for example, with the completion of national, real-time television networks and programming). The unusual decline in corporate profit margins of the late 1960s, associated with inflation, produced the unusual decline in advertising relative to sales in that period. However, these relationships cannot be proven.

Notice that, except for the early wartime years, each change in direction in corporate advertising margins was preceded a year before by a change in corporate profit margins. That partially accounts for the limited cyclicality of advertising. Since most periods of shrinking margins have been shorter than those of the war and the late 1960s, shrinking advertising margins have tended to accompany rising sales. Relatively poor advertising years, such as 1970, usually accompany a second year of declining profit margins and weakening sales, not the first such year; or, as in 1961, a year of softening sales following a year of softening profit margins.

These characteristics should enable the analyst to derive a simple and relatively accurate projection of all advertising revenues, given a few economic parameters.

Within the broad spectrum of advertising, however, different print media groups compete for revenues from different kinds of sellers. Farm and business publications are two such examples. Moreover, most print media compete for advertising outlays with other media. Figure 6 illustrates the competitive trends of the principal print media.

Farm journals are an unusual group. As the farmer population has declined in numbers but increased in affluence, these publications have tended to trim their circulation while raising rates and have remained reasonably profitable despite their declining market share.

The business press depends on advertising revenues more than most

FIGURE 6

Advertising Shares

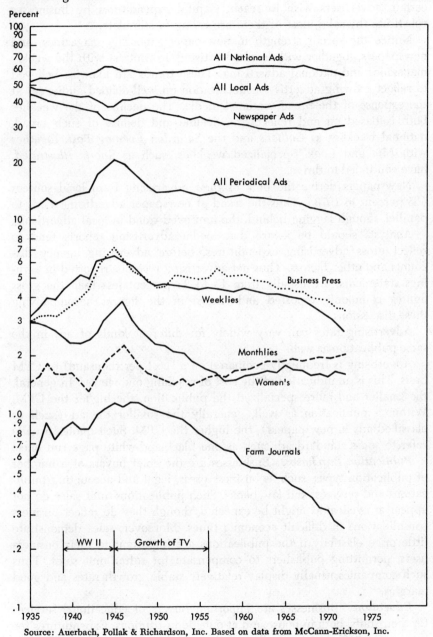

other print media. Many of them have controlled circulation—their publications being sent without charge to carefully defined audiences certain advertisers wish to reach. Capital expenditures by businesses constitute the sales most of them are trying to stimulate.

Notice the recent strength in newspapers, monthly magazines, and newspapers, together with local advertising, in contrast with the weekly magazines and national advertising. These trends are likewise believed to reflect growing advertiser concentration on well-defined audiences at the expense of the broad, national media. The decline of the weeklies both is based on and reflects the decline and demise of such broad, national weeklies as *Collier's* and the *Saturday Evening Post,* together with *Life* and *Look.* Specialized weeklies, such as *Sports Illustrated,* have continued to thrive.

Newspapers derive the bulk of their advertising from local sources (85 percent in 1973). Thus the trend of newspaper advertising tends to parallel, though lagging behind, the improved trend in local advertising.

Analysts should be aware that media advertising reports tend to reflect gross advertising expenditures, before advertising agency discounts and other factors. Thus net advertising receipts, reported in earnings statements, are usually from 15 to 25 percent less than the gross figures commonly reported and shown in the figures accompanying these discussions.

Advertising rates can vary widely for different kinds of ads in the same publication as well.

Advertising is frequently compared on a "cost per thousand" or CPM basis. This is an indication of the cost of reaching one viewer. In general, the smaller and more specialized the publication, the higher the CPM. Within a publication as well, generally the smaller the ad (such as classified ads in newspapers), the higher the CPM. Such quotes usually refer to some standard ad, such as one black-and-white page run once.

Publication Purchases. Businesses are the chief buyers of a number of publication types, such as business press, legal and accounting publications and services, and law books. Such publications' unit sales do not appear as cyclical as might be expected, though they do reflect business consolidations in difficult economic times. Moreover, sales demonstrate little price elasticity if the publications are important to their business users, permitting publishers to compensate for softer unit sales. Thus such companies usually display relatively stable growth rates and good margins.

Education. Businesses are important buyers of educational services for their staffs, both in-house and at outside institutions. Expenditures for these services seem to display cyclical characteristics since they are viewed as fringe benefits or employee upgrading practices by their buyers, rather than as essentials. About one third of the outlays for education outside the formal educational establishment are believed to be of the company-sponsored group type, with still other funds being channeled to regular correspondence and proprietary schools on an individual employee basis.

Inflation and Controls

It is almost a maxim that successful publishers are those offering information (whether for business, education, or recreation) that their customers really want and, subject to the possible erosion of the copyright, can obtain nowhere else. Every product is unique in at least some degree. Accordingly, publishers in general can adapt to, and even thrive in, periods of sustained inflation. Moreover, the desirability of successful products also tends to sustain publishers' sales in periods of recession or depression. Periods most troublesome for the majority of publishers, in contrast with industry as a whole, are times of rapid change in rates of inflation and times in which controls or other factors, such as contracts, act to limit their pricing freedom while not effectively controlling the prices of their chief expense elements.

Because of the industry's diversity, these factors do not affect all types of publishers in equal measure. Under ordinary circumstances, it is the length of time to which a publisher is committed to a fixed price which is the key factor. While the publisher can normally raise prices so as to take effect from one to six months later, depending on his distribution pipeline, he may be locked into an old price on many of his sales— or at least on sales as taken into reported income—for quite long periods. Examples include:

1. The Elhi textbook publisher with his multiyear contracts with states and cities for adopted textbooks (one to six years).
2. The magazine and journal publishers with their multiyear subscriptions (one to five years).
3. The encyclopedia and correspondence course publishers with their longer-term installment purchase contracts and fixed interest charges (one to three years).

There are offsets, of course. For example, the textbook publisher can bring out new books or revisions, and the magazine publisher can invest his prepaid subscription revenues.

Controls which fail to act uniformly on both revenues and expenses can compound the problem and are even harmful to the long-lead-time pricing structure noted above when uniform. Notice that publishers such as those cited above must anticipate expenses in pricing, whereas controls normally allow for expense increases already sustained. Thus when input prices accelerate, as for paper in 1973 and 1974, such publishers may be hurt.

Directly or indirectly, the chief costs of publishers are those of people, paper, printing, and postage; and controls in the early 1970s fell lightly on labor, had little effect on such imports as much of the American paper supply, and were not much of a hindrance to extraordinary increases in postage costs.

Pricing versus Costs

Professional managements in the 1960s and 1970s moved increasingly toward return on invested capital as the criterion for pricing and product development, but competitive pressures in the fragmented, tradition-oriented publishing industry have tended to maintain older pricing philosophies. These are of three types.

One significant form has been pricing based on sales margins. In book publishing, for example, list prices have historically been set so that net revenues would return about three times manufacturing costs. In textbook publishing, where the standard "discount" to school customers has been 20–25 percent, this meant that "list" prices were four times average manufacturing costs. In trade books, on the other hand, where trade discounts averaged 40 percent, list prices ran five times manufacturing costs. On another front, newspaper subscription revenues were once planned to cover newsprint or newsprint and incremental manufacturing costs.

A second significant element has been pricing based on successful precedent and fears of consumer reaction. Once the modern paperback had been successfully introduced at a list price of a quarter, for example, it was many years before any publishers tried to sell paperback books at higher prices, although in recent years paperback prices have successfully soared to the point that they are nearing cloth-bound book prices. By the same token, newspapers have slowly risen through plateaus at the nickel and dime levels.

A third element has been intra- and inter-industry competition, closely related to the second point. Advertising is commonly evaluated by advertisers on a "cost per thousand" (readers, viewers, or exposures) basis, with premiums paid for smaller and better-defined audiences. In this sense, newspapers compete with each other and with magazines (highly competitive), broadcasters, and other advertising vehicles. Again, all newspapers tend to sell at the same newsstand price (about 12 cents in 1973) regardless of content, as do all magazines of a given type, all textbooks of a given type, and many other types of similar publications. Since this tends to produce uniform pricing structures in the face of variable production and other costs, the successful publisher is usually one with very high unit volume or, alternatively, a new and highly priced product which falls into no pricing niche. Examples include the large college textbook publishers, particularly in the mid-1960s (high volume), and *Playboy,* for many years (unique product and high price).

The Consumerism Movement

Growing dissatisfaction with products and services which do not live up to expectations, together with improved education, communications, and political activity have helped spawn consumer activism. This, in turn, has meant a more aggressive Federal Trade Commission and other governmental activities at all levels. In the late 1960s and early 1970s, nearly every sector of publishing and educational services was affected by such factors.

Federal and state regulation is discussed below. Many cities and towns have also passed restrictive legislation (for example, "Green River" laws for Green River, Wyoming) restricting door-to-door sales or have established local consumer affairs authorities, as in the case of New York City.

Most consumerism actions so far have been directed toward selling practices. Exceptions range from the quality of correspondence and proprietary school courses to the locally defined acceptance of pornographic literature. If widely emulated, these have demonstrated the power to affect whole industry sectors and to reduce some companies to bankruptcy.

Potential future problems in this area could include resentment against the quantity of newsprint and other paper waste produced by used publications; against the lack of success achieved using educational materials or courses; and against the content of some publications.

Social Changes

Convenience. Distribution has long been a problem for publications, particularly those purchased on impulse. Bookstores are rarely found in smaller towns; newsstands are often inconveniently located for many people. Thus the industry has sought to make its products more accessible through other distribution channels: direct mail, book clubs, home-delivered newspapers, supermarket racks, vending machines, door-to-door sales, continuity programs, and the like.

The search for convenience by both publishers and consumers has also altered publication forms. For convenience in storage, microforms, microfiche, and microfilm have replaced paper in some applications such as professional journals. The comparative success of the higher-priced paperback suggests that convenience rather than price may be its chief attraction. Recently the *partbook* (a British invention), an encyclopedia sold in magazine-like parts at newsstands, has also achieved success because of its convenience.

Changing Tastes. While publishing is largely a marketing function aided by consumer research and other disciplines, editorial selection in tune with changing tastes appears to be an art. The best indication an analyst has of the future success of a given editor or editorial group appears to be his, hers, or its track record relative to its competition.

While styles and tastes do change, major changes appear to take periods of years to complete. A given magazine or group of magazines, for example, may capture the public imagination and show above-average growth in both subscribers and advertisers for several years. (To advertisers, these are known as "hot books" and attract other advertisers, much as certain streets seem to command the interest of growing numbers of used-car dealers because used-car buyers are also attracted there.) By the same token, certain magazines or groups can lose public favor and progressively lose their circulation or advertising.

Book publishers can vary their product lines in response to these changes. Trade books generally have very short useful lives, six months or so, although successful trade publishers usually have built a reasonably large *backlist* of titles such as "classics" or "standards" which continue to sell for years. Professional books and similar works usually last longer. Textbooks, in revisions and new editions, generally last for many years (though the multidecades of life enjoyed by textbooks in the 19th century are a thing of the past); but versions of the Bible and encyclopedias and other reference works have the longest lives of books these days. Magazines, with greater flexibility, still last for decades as they alter their content and editorial approaches. But the longest-lived publications on the American scene, perhaps because of their great flexibility and keen ears for altered tastes, are the newspapers.

Education. Only in this century did most Americans begin to attend high school, and only in the past decade have most begun some form of higher education. Thus the American citizenry still displays a relatively wide difference in educational levels between young and old, while the young may be approaching maximum participation rates in higher education.

Yet while traditional educational establishments may hereafter grow only with the populations they serve, both preschool and continuing education programs still have scope for expansion and likely will grow (particularly the latter). Education may, indeed, become a lifelong process.

Historically, reading propensity has shown a high correlation with educational attainment. This may not hold true in the future as alternative media appear on the scene. The quest of the educated is for information, not necessarily for the printed word.

Alternative Media

Modern publishing is best regarded as a marketing operation, as we noted at the start of this chapter. The successful publisher should be devoted to communicating and not to the printed word as such. But the printed page is a cheap, handy, culturally acceptable means of communicating, and traditions among consumers as well as among publishers have fostered resistance to change. Moreover, it is probable that different media are best approached in different ways and communicate at different levels. Thus established publishers have not, in the main, been notably successful in nonprint media fields. Within the print medium, however, there have been successful adaptations; and, longer term, the growth of an information industry of multimedia congenerics seems probable to the writer.

Alternative media include such obvious examples as films, tapes, and recordings; such less common but significant variations as microfilm, microcards, and microfiche; and such prospective and actual competitors as computer data banks, with data links, cable television, and copying machines. The latter, at present, are less significant to publishers as competitive distributors of information than as threats to publishers' profits from the unauthorized use of published information by potential buyers.

Mass magazines were early casualties of alternative media: national television networks. There is some evidence that textbook publishers have been impacted by audiovisual materials and copying machines since the mid-1960s, together with publishers of professional and reference books. And newspapers, first hit by broadcast television, are watching cable television with caution. The analyst should watch the development of new media with care, particularly those which compete for the funds of advertisers, education, and other principal customers of established publishers. However, he should be aware that few have had the early impact on publishers generally forecast by their advocates; the printed word seems likely to have a long life yet.

Technology

Publishers have not only encountered new forms of competition from the rise of technology; they have also benefited from it. Future benefits seems likely for their heavily labor-intensive industry.

Technology has had three principal thrusts in publishing:

1. To reduce the costs of manufacturing.
2. To reduce general and administrative costs.
3. To expand sales.

While the computer is probably the most important technological tool yet to affect publishing, earlier technological trends, now involving the computer, are still affecting changes in production. These include the development of photocomposition and offset printing, the *web* (continuous feed) press, simplified binding techniques, and a host of others. In general, production costs have shown the greatest relative decline in publishing in recent decades.

Reductions in editorial, general, and administrative costs, largely initiated by the adaptation of computers, are still in early stages—except in warehousing, accounting, and such specialized, labor-intensive functions as book indexing.

Sales are being expanded through such computer-derived innovations as stock control, in both the publisher's spaces and those of his distributors; the identification of potential customers; *fulfillment* operations; the creation of new products such as specialized editions of books, periodicals, and newspapers; and the development of data banks for customers' use.

Labor and the Unions

Publishing is highly labor intensive, and so long as it continues as a creator of information, it is likely to remain so. Sterile facts are of value but would not meet the desires for interpretation and adaptation of most readers. It is also an old industry with roots in religion, scholarship, and politics. Finally, it is a fragmented industry with relative ease of entry in terms of capital requirements.

For these reasons, its unions are old ones with craft orientations and with an emphasis on the production side. There are many of them, and they tend to act within a given city or region rather than nationally. Strikes may be against the printers or newspapers of a given city rather than all the cross-country plants of a given printing complex or newspaper chain. On the other hand, a given newspaper may have to deal with 10 to 20 unions, any one of which can, in some cities, force suspension of the newspaper on issues relevant to that union alone.

The strength of unions varies from industry to industry and city to city. Unions are rare among book publishers, for example, except among warehouse personnel; and strikes are rare among the unionized employees of magazines (chiefly the Guild, a union of writers, editors, and some photographers). It is the production workers who have proven most militant, and few publishers other than newspapers still do their own production.

The analyst should be aware of scheduled negotiations with the unions of the publishers he follows, particularly with the production unions of the larger newspapers. Stocks of these companies often weaken in the quarters preceding contract termination dates as investors defer purchases until the threats of strikes have passed. Chains offer less risk because of decreased company dependence on particular newspapers. Moreover, in smaller cities and towns a given union may strike without being supported by other employees, permitting continued operations. In general, difficulties with unions in publishing are less significant than analysts, usually located in large cities with militant unions, may believe.

In addition to the publishers' own unions, outside unions can affect their operations. Notable examples are teamsters' strikes in the vicinity of book publishers' warehouses; strikes by employees of printers producing magazines or books; postal strikes, interfering with the delivery of magazines and newspapers; strikes against the paper companies at times of high paper demand; and strikes against major advertisers such as the automotive giants.

Seasonality

Most nondiversified publishers show highly seasonal earnings patterns as labor and other costs continue during seasonal peaks and valleys in sales. Cash flow variations can be even greater; companies with debt-free year-end balance sheets may be heavy seasonal borrowers.

These seasonal patterns vary among segments of the industry, though most show peak sales in the fourth quarter of high consumer purchases and coincident advertising. Elhi textbook sales, for example, peak in the summer months when advertising to educators falls so sharply that most educators' magazines do not publish. College textbook publishers, on the other hand, experience a second, winter peak accompanying the starts of second semesters. Farm journals, in contrast, show a late winter/early spring peak as farmers prepare for spring plantings—perhaps a reason why one textbook publisher (Harcourt Brace and Jovanovich) entered the farm journal business.

Analysts should be aware of the seasonal variations in both reported revenues and actual cash flows experienced by the sectors of publishing in which their companies participate.

FEDERAL AND STATE REGULATION

Copyright: National and International

The United States has had copyright laws since its inception, as noted at the start of this chapter. International copyright agreements are generally of later date, with the Soviet Union only since 1973, for example.

The basic copyright law in the United States at this writing was passed in 1909. Congress began consideration of a new law to deal with the changes wrought by technology in the mid-1960s, but the stakes have been high enough for all sides to prevent an acceptable compromise being reached as this is written.

In its international agreements, the United States has employed either bilateral agreements or the Buenos Aires Convention or the Universal Copyright Convention. In general, these agreements provide that each nation will give the other's works the same protection it gives its own authors' works.

Some indication of the importance of the copyright is provided by history. Until late in the 19th century, the United States had no agreement with the British. While nationalist publications such as textbooks thrived, the American trade book industry was weakened by the greater profits provided by pirating popular British authors than by paying royalties to Americans.

Publishing is a net exporter as an industry. Thus periodic pressures by developing nations for free or almost free use of American-copyrighted books and other works has been of concern. In the postwar era, pirated books have indeed been published and sold beyond the borders of the pirates (for example, Nationalist China [Formosa] for many years), while denying Americans extensive markets (as in the Soviet Union where blocked ruble royalties were paid only to a few authors of its choosing, though pirated Russian language editions were common). Nevertheless, American publishers have worked through such organizations as Franklin Book Programs, Inc., to develop indigenous publishing companies, and purchases of American books have been assisted by federal foreign aid programs.

Most major book and magazine companies have foreign publishing interests, coventures, subsidiaries, or distribution arrangements—particularly the encyclopedia, college textbook, and magazine publishers.

But the domestic copyright problem is the paramount one. In general, the longer the useful life of a publication, the higher its price, and the more limited its audience, the more vulnerable it is to unauthorized reproduction practices.

The copyright laws were not established to enrich publishers or authors but to ensure a thriving intellectual outpouring in a free economy. If works can be freely reproduced, ultimately only those publications subsidized by government, advertisers, nonprofit organizations, the wealthy, and those with special interests may continue to be published. In the writer's opinion, it is in the public interest still to preserve the rights of authors in their works for reasonable periods of time, a fact not always self-evident to readers. Many educators, for example, believe that nonprofit reproduction of textbooks for educational use should be authorized; if achieved, in the writer's opinion, the textbook industry of today would virtually disappear. Thus the progress of copyright legislation and court decisions is of vital interest to the analyst following the publishing industry, although it is not much appreciated at the time of this writing.

Eventually, it is likely that a compromise such as that achieved in the music business—royalties for reproduction rather than purchases of whole works—will be attained.

THE FEDERAL TRADE COMMISSION

While the exact limits on the Federal Trade Commission's rights to establish trade practices appear unclear, it has had a significant impact on sectors of publishing in recent years. Examples of fields affected, usually as regards sales practices, include:

1. *The magazine industry.* Agency sales of magazine subscriptions, usually by door-to-door calls which resulted in lengthy subscriptions for a number of magazines paid for on a periodic basis, have virtually ended. Although receipts to the magazines, themselves, were small, their costs of subscription solicitation have since risen significantly.

2. *The correspondence and proprietary school industries.* Standards for advertising and promotion have been tightened, slowing sales, while more generous refund policies have been adopted with particular impact on the profits of high-dropout correspondence schools.

3. *The encyclopedia industry.* In a round of actions against nearly all of the encyclopedia companies in turn, selling practices have gradually been tightened, with the effect of significantly reducing domestic sales by the major companies in the late 1960s and early 1970s. As a result, the future prospects of domestic companies are still cloudy at this writing, though the industry appears likely to be with us for many years to come.

4. *Book clubs, continuity programs, and other direct mail sales.* The concept that a potential customer should take positive action to avoid a purchase rather than the reverse, known as negative option selling, has been a key factor in the growth of book clubs (and such other institutions as record clubs). Continuity programs, in which a buyer signs up for a series of books as published, can be viewed as falling in close legal territory. In the early 1970s, these techniques and other direct mail sales techniques, notably the "ten-day free return" concept, came under fire by the FTC despite limited consumer protests. These actions do not appear to have led to significant changes in the prospects of companies in these fields, but the questions might be raised again.

In view of the demonstrated impact of past FTC actions against publishers, the analyst should be careful to explore proposed actions. Testimony taken in hearings is available for inspection in Washington, and copies of both proposed and final rules can be obtained from the FTC. Examiners will not discuss rules under study, however.

ANALYSIS OF COST FACTORS (INCLUDING SPECIAL TAX CONSIDERATIONS)

Figure 7 provides comparisons of the revenue and expense breakdowns of the publishing and educational service groups, on the basis of data reported to the Department of Commerce in 1970 and to the Internal Revenue Service in fiscal 1971, which approximately equates with calendar 1970. That was a recession year, which should be taken into account in appraising margins. Also, taxable income frequently is less than that reported to stockholders (and thus tax deductible expenses are higher). But it is the latest year for which such data was available and is useful for identifying absolute and relative cost elements.

FIGURE 7

Revenue and Expense Breakdowns of Publishing and Educational Service Groups

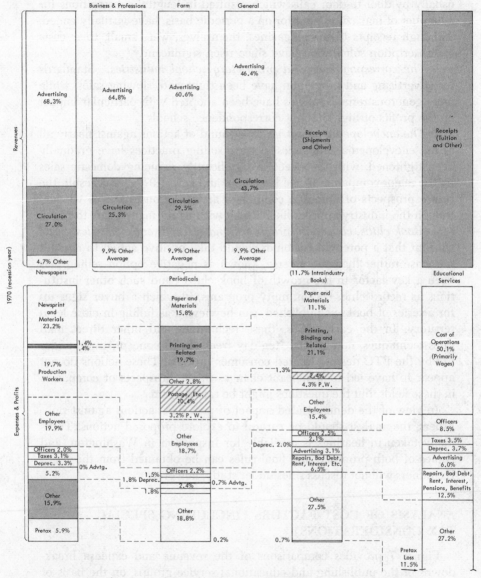

Sources: *Corporate Source Book of Statistics of Income* (IRS, 1971); *Annual Survey of Manufacturers* (Department of Commerce, 1970); and author's estimates.

Newspapers

Labor and Productivity. Labor accounts for the largest share of newspaper expenses, with the balance nearly half production and half non-production wages and benefits. In a seeming oddity, despite lower per capita wages, labor costs run higher as a portion of expenses in smaller newspapers than in large ones. That is because newsprint costs run so much larger for the thicker newspapers of the large cities.

Increases in labor costs are generally established by periodic (usually two-year or three-year) union contracts and the growth of newspapers in size and circulation, offset by productivity gains. Contract settlement dates are worth knowing because of the possibility of strikes at those times if agreements are not reached. Agreements apply to all newspapers in a given location rather than to all newspapers owned by one chain.

One of the main factors improving newspaper margins at this writing is the introduction of labor-saving equipment in the production of newspapers. Until recently, the chief beneficiaries of these improvements have been medium-size and smaller newspapers, though large newspapers are now beginning to show gains. However, the large papers encounter more important union opposition to such changes. The analyst should be aware of the degree to which these improvements can be effected, the timing and amounts of possible benefits, and the more immediate possible earnings problems associated with union opposition, capital requirements, and write-offs of older equipment.

Newsprint. The costs of newsprint are substantial expense elements for all newspapers, but particularly for the larger ones. Additional problems can be posed by unusually rapid increases in the costs of newsprint or by its scarcity. Most newsprint used in America is produced in Canada; thus the analyst must be aware of newsprint capacity and demand in both the United States and Canada, possible paper union strikes in both countries, how newsprint reaches the newspapers of interest to him, and the possibilities of transportation disruptions.

There are three pricing structures for newsprint in the United States: northern (largely set by eastern Canadian suppliers); southern (largely set by domestic suppliers); and western (established by western U.S. and Canadian suppliers). However, percentage increases are usually similar in all three areas. Price increases have followed an irregular pattern.

Newsprint consumption is affected by advertising linage gains (possibly offset by some decline in editorial linage's share of each paper) and circulation. The amount of space devoted to editorial matter is known as the *newshole* and amounts to about one third of the typical large newspaper and a larger share of the smaller paper.

Both advertising linage and circulation show some price elasticity, though the latter is particularly limited. Some reductions in paper consumption, therefore, can be expected from advertising rate increases and circulation price hikes.

Newsprint Subsidiaries. With growing costs and scarcities of newsprint, a number of major American newspapers have invested in newsprint manufacturing to some degree. A captive domestic production operation can be quite profitable since its owner can vary his demands on the mill to keep it operating close to capacity. Minority interests, particularly of Canadian mills, will tend to reflect the varying profitability of ordinary mills accompanied by possible problems involving the American-Canadian dollar exchange rates.

Some newspapers have also invested in equipment to reclaim waste newsprint and convert it into acceptable substitutes for virgin newsprint. The Media General group is the most prominent illustration of this.

The Importance of Circulation. Newspaper circulation numbers have proven highly price inelastic. A commissioned Gallup poll of the early 1970s forecast a 12 percent circulation drop with an increase in newspaper prices of 50 percent (from 10 to 15 cents) and a decline of 30 percent with a doubling in newspaper prices. Even less impact was observed as the newspapers proceeded to raise their prices.

Moreover, an added advertisement requires additional expenses for taking and processing the advertisement, for printing it on purchased paper, and for billing for it. An increase in circulation revenues simply because of higher prices generally costs no more than the normal division of receipts with distributors.

Thus, an increase in receipts due to higher cover and home-delivered prices is normally more profitable than a similar increase in receipts due to greater advertising or even higher advertising rates.

Since most newspapers are home delivered (about 70–80 percent), home-delivered rates are more important than newsstand prices, although the two usually maintain some relationship over time. Historically, however, home-delivered rates have been less than newsstand prices, much as magazine subscription prices have been less than per copy costs at magazine racks. The tendency in both industries now is to eliminate the discount and, at least among newspapers, to charge a premium for the delivery service.

Book Publishers

Outside Printing. As illustrated in Figure 7, outside manufacturing costs are very significant to book publishers, the publishing sector most like contracting in other industries. These outside costs include composition, printing, and binding, each of which is often handled by a distinct "subcontractor." As a result, book publishers tend to deal with a number of outside firms, shifting new books to new suppliers to lower costs but staying with older suppliers who have given them good service.

Printing costs are normally not the subject of long-term contracts because of the variability of different books. However, established relationships and even some contracts exist.

Because of changes in printing technology, because of the fragmented nature of the printing industry, and because of their ability to shift, book publishers have gradually reduced manufacturing costs with respect to sales through the years.

Labor. Except for their warehousing and shipping operations, often organized by the Teamsters, few book publishers have unions. However, they compete with both other media and with education, now increasingly organized, for their editors, salesmen, and other specialists. Thus labor disruptions internally are very unusual, but the growth in labor costs tends to parallel those in the competing fields.

Publishers can be affected by strikes against their printers or against their distributors.

Plate/Plant Costs and Advances on Royalties. Many, though not all, book publishers show balance sheet asset items for plate or plant costs and/or for advances on royalties.

When a book is expensive to produce and ordinarily has a long life expectancy, all its costs of preparation from the time it has been edited until the time its plates are mounted on presses may be capitalized and referred to as its "plate" or "plant costs." These costs are then amortized over a certain sales quantity or in some other fashion, the residue being written off when the book is discontinued. Such costs, then, are more like capitalized research and development costs than like the values assigned inventory or buildings. They may turn out to have no value to their owner. Despite their common name, "plate costs," they may not even involve plates; the plates actually used in offset printing, for example, frequently belong to the printers involved and not to the publishers.

However, the use of plate/plant costs as an accounting item performs the useful function of smoothing out the highly variable expenses of irregularly producing major new book series (as in textbook or encyclopedia publishing) and of assigning costs to the periods in which they produce revenues. It also serves to preserve earnings at higher levels in times of rising sales and inflation.

Amortization of plate costs should proceed at different speeds for different types of books. Trade books and paperbacks, for instance, should normally be amortized in less than a year; textbooks, in three to five years; and encyclopedias or other basic reference works, over ten years or more, depending on the normal useful sales lives of the books.

"Advances on royalties" is another slightly misleading term. While publishers normally do pay portions of gross or net receipts from particular books to their authors and while these payments are called royalties, advances on royalties are not like other prepaid expenses for they are frequently never earned. Royalties prepaid and not earned are seldom reimbursed. Thus advances on royalties are similar to plate costs in that they represent investments in new books which may or may not be recovered.

For tax reasons, some authors prefer to spread their receipts of royalties out into the future. Thus some publishers may have liabilities for deferred royalty payments. For the publisher, these are like long-term, no-interest loans.

Distribution Problems. The problems of acquainting potential readers with one's books and of providing the readers with those books is of continuing importance to the book publisher. For this reason, publishers have experimented with many delivery modes (for example, book clubs, door-to-door sales, supermarket stands, vending machines, and continuing programs). For the most part, the publisher would rather put too many copies on display than lose sales, and this is particularly true when the buying season is short or the likely buyer operating on impulse. Books which have not sold are returned, are sensibly called "returns," and are costly. Returns are normally deducted from gross sales when received, may damage other sales or bookseller relations if sold at low cost ("remaindered") to specialists in that trade, and have few other salvage possibilities. Paperbooks, for instance, cannot be pulped as waste paper until their covers are removed. Thus publishers face a continuing fight to reduce returns, a fight which is particularly costly to paperback publishers whose returns may amount to a third or more of gross sales.

Elhi textbook publishers face an additional distribution problem. In most adopting states, they are required to maintain sufficient stock on consignment in state-approved warehouses, known as depositories, to meet potential local demand. This stock is paid for only after schools have paid the depositories, and then less depository commissions on the order of 8–10 percent. Moreover, they may result in a good deal of unsalable merchandise being returned when it is obsolete. Finally, one or two thinly capitalized depositories have been unable to pay their debts in times past.

Paper. Rapidly rising paper costs can pose problems to publishers with contracts or other long-lead-time problems. Shortages of particular paper types are usually less of a problem because of the flexibilities offered by new books, but such shortages can be troublesome to textbook publishers whose contracts specify certain paper types, and to other publishers with very specific requirements (for example, publishers of high-quality books of art reproductions).

Postage. It is customary in book publishing to pass on postage costs of shipments. Rising fourth-class rates thus hurt publishers most by reducing funds available for books in schools and libraries with fixed budgets. Direct mail booksellers, however, must cope with the rising costs of the third-class mail used to publicize their wares, either raising the prices of books sold by this method or terminating programs with marginal customer order rates.

Installment Sales. Publishers of encyclopedia and other big-ticket books commonly sell on the installment plan. Indeed, encyclopedia publishers are believed to have earned more on interest charges than on book sales as such.

In book installment sales, as in such sales of other items, the seller ordinarily takes the full purchase price into his reported revenues when the sale is made (the accrual method), while the installment method is used for tax purposes. Thus some income taxes on collections are deferred and shown as such. Subsequent reporting periods can be adversely affected if the provision for bad debts in accounts receivable fails to allow sufficiently for defaults.

Currency Losses. Some publishers, including most college textbook publishers and, particularly, encyclopedia publishers, are exporters to a significant degree. Thus their earnings can be importantly affected by variations in currency exchange rates between the United States and their markets.

Periodical Publishers

The Treatment of Subscription Revenues. The treatment of subscription revenue receipts by periodical publishers is almost the reverse of the treatment of installment sales of books discussed above. Most important, of course, the subscriber pays in advance for periodicals he will later receive; while the installment buyer receives in advance books for which he will later pay. The subscriber thus makes a no-interest loan to the publisher, while the installment buyer borrows at relatively high interest rates from his publisher.

So far, so good. But many general magazines incur high sales expenses in obtaining new subscriptions and, in fact, will likely incur greater expenses in delivering the magazines than they have received in subscribers' payments. The attraction of the subscriber in this instance is not his own money but what the advertiser will pay to reach him. In such cases, the subscription is really a liability: a long-term agreement to provide a product below cost.

On their balance sheets, most magazine publishers show as current or intermediate liabilities both amounts for unexpired subscriptions and amounts for deferred taxes payable. A check of footnotes should disclose that the unexpired gross subscription liabilities are far larger than the balance sheet item—the latter having been reduced to reflect the costs of obtaining those subscriptions—and that those costs have been deducted as incurred from federal income tax reports, resulting in much of the deferred taxes payable item. In other words, should the company cease to publish, it will be left with a much larger liability than that shown on the balance sheet itself. This fact posed problems in the termination of the *Saturday Evening Post, Look,* and other mass magazines in the 1960s and 1970s.

Subscription revenues are normally taken into the income stream as earned, gross, less the expenses incurred in obtaining them, for stockholder reports.

Postage Costs. Rising postage costs now constitute a significant cost element for magazine publishers not only for the second-class fees paid to distribute the magazines but for the third-class fees paid to solicit subscriptions. As one consequence, we will probably see greater emphasis on magazines sold at newsstands and the like, reducing both costs substantially. New subscriptions delivery techniques are also being tried.

The postage costs paid by a given magazine publisher will vary so much with his distribution pattern and rates that the analyst should ask for those costs by class and seek to obtain some indication of the magnitudes of expected rate changes as they affect each publisher from that publisher.

Distribution Problems. Newsstand distribution is handled by a number of specialist firms. One problem faced by the magazine publisher is obtaining adequate display space from such distributors (for example, Curtis) and from the outlets themselves. He ordinarily has a substantial returns problem as well, on the order of that of the paperback publishers described above.

New-subscriber solicitation is also a substantial cost for most publishers, to the extent that many receive income in excess of solicitation costs only from renewal subscribers. Renewal rates are jealously guarded secrets for most publishers, but some effort needs to be made to ascertain promotion costs. As a rule of thumb, a magazine with rising circulation numbers in experiencing a higher renewal rate than one with flat circulation and is more profitable. The more popular magazine will usually also be raising its subscription rates more aggressively than the less popular one, increasing the disparity in margins.

Circulations of most magazines are audited for the benefit of advertisers. Audited numbers are the basis of comparative CPM analyses of advertising costs. To count as paid for audit purposes, a magazine must have been sold at no less than half its official subscription price; thus this limit has tended to be approached by most larger magazines with good advertising receipts.

Labor. Magazine editorial workers are frequently organized by the Guild, but strikes are uncommon. More important can be strikes of the printers used by given magazines. Labor cost increases are similar to those for nonproduction workers elsewhere in publishing.

Paper. With established formats and relatively low consumption rates, individual magazines are particularly vulnerable to shortages of certain paper grades. Moreover, with circulation revenues fixed for given subscribers for a year or more, magazines are also impacted by rapidly rising paper costs.

With the sluggish growth of magazine paper consumption prices in the late 1960s and early 1970s—and the special needs of magazines for lightweight, opaque paper and the like—magazine paper production was relatively unprofitable for paper producers. This has heightened the scarcity problem which will probably continue to harass the publishers of smaller magazines for some time.

The Question of Printing Subsidiaries. As did the book publishers, most magazine publishers began as printers seeking captive business. Today, however, like the book publishers, most magazine publishers have divested themselves of their printing operations.

One key reason for the change is probably the accelerated pace of change in the printing field, itself. Publishers often found it better to switch from one outside printer to another to get the best combination of quality and cost, rather than to stick to the in-house printing operation once the concept of separate profit centers took hold.

Another was likely the toughness of printing unions. To protect magazines from disruptions by printers, it made sense to produce them at several plants. Geographic postal cost differences also led to the use of multiple printing facilities.

In sum, only large, multiplant printing operations with substantial outside printing contracts are likely to continue under the corporate wings of large magazine publishers, and there aren't many of those.

Where a diversity of printing techniques is less important, as in the case of all-type journals and looseleaf publications, in-plant printing operations continue to thrive.

Educational Services

The Treatment of Receipts. Proprietary schools, in particular, proliferated through the use of franchises in the late 1960s. Thus, tightening of reporting requirements in the franchise field, coupled with declines in sales and surges in bad-debt experience by correspondence schools using the installment method, helped convert an apparent high-growth industry into one with economic difficulties. FTC-imposed or initiated changes in refund practices are still possible at this writing, raising possible questions about the adequacies of bad-debt reserves. Complexities in accounting also exist in this field, and analysts should be sure that they understand the current accounting techniques and the adequacy of reserves in both good and bad years in the past for any company they follow. They should also attempt to learn the possible effects of new regulations on this industry as they are proposed.

Bad Debt or Dropouts. Companies operating on an installment basis in this area normally provide significant reserves for bad debts in their accounts receivable. Historically, the correspondence course publishers are believed to have experienced both high dropout rates and relatively consistent bad-debt losses. Thus the troubles experienced by the industry in the recession of 1970 may have reflected as much the consumerist outcries against paying for courses which were not being completed as they did the higher unemployment rates of the young adults taking the courses. The tighter acceptance procedures for new students now followed by most companies in the field may mean better bad-debt experience in the future.

FTC Rules—Actual or Proposed. The Federal Trade Commission has acted to moderate industry advertising claims and techniques and, in action still pending at this writing, to institute pro rata refund policies for dropouts. Meanwhile, the National Home Study Council, the trade association of correspondence schools, has acted on its own to tighten refund policies, perhaps foreclosing further FTC moves. The analyst should be aware of FTC proposals (available from the FTC), the rules of regulatory authorities including the trade associations, and the possible impacts of these changes on the companies he follows.

MARKET BEHAVIOR OF SECURITIES

The New Group Syndrome. Publishing and education, as we have observed, are far from monolithic industries. Many sectors are primarily privately owned. Thus there has been a tendency, each few years, for a new group of companies from a new sector of these industries to seek public capital. Examples include the textbook publishers in the late 1950s and early 1960s, the correspondence and proprietary schools in the mid-1960s, and the newspapers in the late 1960s and early 1970s.

These public offerings tend to be fostered by a good recent record of growth in the industry sector, a legitimate need for capital to finance further growth, and the desires of private holders to cash in on market enthusiasm. One company after another tapping these new resources tends to encourage still others to make an offering; and one good prospectus after another tends to build institutional interest and the formation of an analytical specialty. Thus each of these waves of public offerings has tended to be followed by good relative moves by the stocks in question for a few years, followed by a reassessment as industry conditions change and as the stock group matures. This does not mean that long-term investments in new publishing groups will not work out, but it does suggest that the analyst should be cautious about high multiples in a relatively unseasoned industry sector.

Cyclical Aspects. The Standard & Poor's Publishing Stock Index does not currently reflect the industry market weights noted at the beginning of this chapter. In the 1950s it was essentially an index of magazine stocks, while since then it has been primarily an index of book publishing stock prices. But Figure 8, which compares it with the S&P 500 and with the S&P Low-priced Common Stock Index, does illustrate some points.

First of all, the publishing stocks tend to parallel the low-priced stocks more consistently than stocks as a whole. That's not surprising since most have small capitalizations and low prices by institutional standards. Second, they are more volatile than the market averages and particularly vulnerable to episodes of lost confidence in the marketplace— as in 1962, 1970, and 1973—probably because of their thin capitalizations. Such episodes seem actually more important to these stocks than economic conditions as such, although usually accompanying them. Third, they are slow to recover relative strength once confidence in them has been lost. Thus they may lag behind initial bull market moves. Fourth, they may peak out before the market as a whole. Fifth, they tend to accelerate as general economic and market strength persists, and vice versa. Sixth, they are subject to their own periods of market interest or disinterest which tend to persist for three years or so.

P/E Ratios. While theories as to the determinants of P/E ratios differ, most commonly they are associated with anticipated earnings growth rates. The author surveyed a group of professional publishing analysts each January from 1970 through 1973 and found a consistent relationship between these two factors in the opinions of those analysts. It may be approximated as:

$$P/E = 1\tfrac{1}{3} \times R + 6.5$$

where P/E is the P/E ratio applied to the anticipated earnings of a given publisher, R is the anticipated five-year earnings growth rate, and 6.5 is a residual factor. Thus, a publisher with anticipated earnings growth of 10 percent might normally be expected to carry a multiple of about 20 (that is, $1.33 \times 10 + 6.5 = 19.83$). However, this seemed to apply only to market favorites in 1973.

Volatility/Liquidity. As is clear from Figure 8, publishing stocks show great volatility. Generally speaking, the lower their liquidity, the greater their volatility. For those who use both positive and negative betas, moreover, their 1973 betas in down markets appeared greater than their betas in up markets.

Great Differentiation among Groups and Stocks on Fundamentals. This chapter was intended, in part, to demonstrate to the analyst that there are great differences in the fundamentals of different groups within the publishing industry. Historically however, the groups have tended to follow similar market paths. This may be attributable to the overriding importance of general market confidence and the thinness of most publishing stocks. Lacking liquidity by market standards, they tend to be sold as a group in periods of general uncertainty and only regain followers as the general market rises and a search begins for attractive stocks

FIGURE 8

Market Behavior of Securities

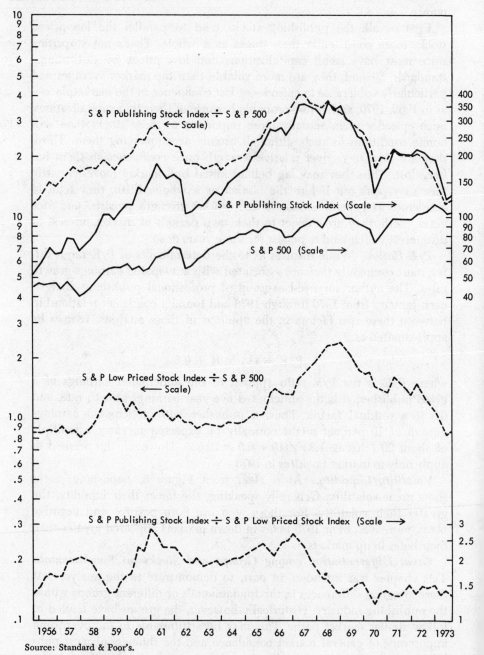

Source: Standard & Poor's.

which have been overlooked. Once that search begins, fundamental differences play a more important role.

There are exceptions in this general rule. Particular stocks in recognized specialty areas (for example, greeting cards, clothing patterns, and business services) may develop sufficient interest so that they are isolated from the general group and may even be followed by analysts not otherwise interested in publishing stocks.

One can hope that an increasing level of market sophistication will ultimately lead to greater recognition of these industry and company differences. For example, the fragmentation of publishing means that superior companies even within sectors displaying modest or deteriorating growth can themselves attain good growth through market penetration. However, the analyst should be careful not to assume that this recognition will be granted in the future; historically, few publishers have managed to sustain superior stock market performance when investors have lost interest in their industry.

ILLUSTRATIVE CASE STUDY: PRENTICE-HALL, INC.

Background

Space does not permit comprehensive description of the approach to a basic study of institutional quality of a publishing company. Accordingly, to illustrate the writer's techniques, he will review the evolution of a progress report on Prentice-Hall which he published on March 22, 1973. In the process, he will draw on some documents issued later than that date in order to identify tools for future analysis, at the risk of possible confusion as to the author's earlier conclusions. He shall also comment on some of the changes in the real world which subsequently modified his estimates and recommendations.

Prentice-Hall has long been regarded as an outstanding book publisher. Before an extraordinary loss, its 1972 return on sales was 11.9 percent after taxes, nearly twice the industry average. Subsequent to the

TABLE 3

Prentice-Hall, Inc. and Consolidated Subsidiaries: Percentage Contributed to Revenues

	1968	1969	1970	1971	1972
College textbooks	40	39	40	39	37
Elhi textbooks	7	7	7	8	8
Professional services*	31	31	32	32	33
Professional books*	15	16	15	15	16
Trade books*	4	4	4	4	4
Miscellaneous	3	3	2	2	2
	100	100	100	100	100

* And related products and services.
Source: Management estimates.

early 1960s spin-off of certain subsidiaries, the company's 1963–72 least-squares revenue growth rate was 10.7 percent, and its least-squares growth rate in earnings was 16.0 percent. It is one of the two largest college textbook publishers, one of the two largest publishers of loose leaf business services, and a major publisher of elhi textbooks and professional books.

TABLE 4

Prentice-Hall, Inc., and Consolidated Subsidiaries
Statement of Consolidated Income and Earnings Surplus for the Years Ended December 31, 1972*

	1968	1969	1970	1971	1972
Sales and other revenue.........	$107,924	$120,128	$128,301	$134,711	$144,059
Cost of operations:					
Cost of sales..................	39,601	42,290	45,760	46,782	49,953
Selling, general and administrative expenses.......	40,305	46,487	51,010	55,368	59,375
Depreciation and amortization†..	958	1,002	1,030	1,169	1,186
Total cost...............	$ 80,864	$ 89,979	$ 97,800	$103,319	$110,514
Income from operations.........	27,060	30,149	30,501	31,392	33,545
Interest and other income (net)..	216	512	895	1,327	484
Income before income taxes and extraordinary item...........	$ 27,276	$ 30,661	$ 31,396	$ 32,719	$ 34,029
Income taxes:					
Federal.......................	12,636	14,109	14,532	14,609	15,083
State and local................	1,297	1,292	1,428	1,546	1,871
Total income taxes.......	$ 13,933	$ 15,401	$ 15,960	$ 16,155	$ 16,954
Income before extraordinary item........................	13,343	15,260	15,436	16,564	17,075
Extraordinary item (Write-down to estimated net realizable value of investments in and advances to Responsive Environments Corporation and E.R.E. Laboratory, Inc., less income taxes of $2,674,000)....					2,815
Net income...................	$ 13,343	$ 15,260	$ 15,436	$ 16,564	$ 14,260
Earned surplus at beginning of year......................	28,766	26,560	34,479	42,832	51,306
Earned surplus of companies acquired in pooling of interests....................	214				
Total..................	$ 42,323	$ 41,820	$ 49,915	$ 59,396	$ 65,566
Per share data (adjusted for 1968 stock dividend) Income per share based on average shares outstanding					
Average shares outstanding......	10,287	10,313	10,324	10,348	10,339
Income before extraordinary item........................	$1.30	$1.48	$1.50	$1.60	$1.65
Extraordinary item.............					$(0.27)
Net income...................	$1.30	$1.48	$1.50	$1.60	$1.38
Cash dividends...............	$0.61	$0.68	$0.68	$0.74	$0.79

* 000 omitted.
† Section on dividends and stock transactions omitted.
Source: Prentice-Hall, Form 10-K.

Corporate annual reports and 10-Ks are relatively sparse, but the company does provide analysts with the percentage contributions to revenues of its various sectors (the 10-K for 1971 described them all as "publications in various fields and services attendant thereto"). These percentages for 1968–72 were as shown in Table 3.

Tables 4, 5 and 6 provide additional information on the company available in its Form 10-K for 1972.

While techniques vary, the writer takes the percentage revenue con-

TABLE 5

Prentice-Hall, Inc., and Consolidated Subsidiaries
Statement of Changes in Consolidated Financial Position for the Two Years Ended December 31, 1972

	Year Ended December 31	
	1972	*1971*
Funds were provided by:		
Income before extraordinary item..............	$17,075,000	$16,564,000
Charges not requiring working capital—		
depreciation and amortization..............	1,186,000	1,169,000
Funds provided from operations exclusive of		
extraordinary item........................	$18,261,000	$17,733,000
Extraordinary item less applicable tax reduction..	(2,815,000)	—
Extraordinary charges not requiring working		
capital—write-down of investments and notes		
receivable...............................	5,489,000	
Stock options exercised......................	163,000	325,000
Decrease in cash value of life insurance.........	—	457,000
Total funds provided...................	$21,098,000	$18,515,000
Funds were applied to:		
Additions to property, plant, and equipment....	$ 1,620,000	$ 1,520,000
Insurance policy loans......................	—	629,000
Increase in investments and notes receivable....	823,000	1,311,000
Increase in deferred charges..................	353,000	1,046,000
Purchase of treasury shares..................	2,374,000	—
Dividends paid.............................	8,173,000	7,657,000
Other (net)................................	(11,000)	(19,000)
Increase in working capital..................	7,766,000	6,371,000
Total funds applied...................	$21,098,000	$18,515,000
Increases (decreases) in components of working capital:		
Cash....................................	$ 1,220,000	$ 2,007,000
Marketable securities and certificates of		
deposit.................................	2,529,000	3,328,000
Receivables (net)..........................	1,803,000	1,303,000
Inventories...............................	1,009,000	1,580,000
Prepaid expenses..........................	131,000	(200,000)
Total.................................	$ 6,892,000	$ 8,018,000
Accounts payable...........................	(125,002)	(666,000)
Accrued royalties and expenses...............	(653,000)	(964,000)
Federal income taxes........................	1,983,000	721,000
Advance payments, etc......................	(331,000)	(738,000)
Total.................................	$ 874,000	($1,647,000)
Increase in working capital..................	$ 7,766,030	$ 6,371,000

Source: Prentice-Hall, Inc., Form 10-K.

TABLE 6

Prentice-Hall, Inc., and Consolidated Subsidiaries
Consolidated Balance Sheet, December 31, 1972 and 1971

	1972	*1971*
Current Assets:		
Cash..	$ 7,563	$ 6,343
Marketable securities and certificates of deposit—at cost, which approximates market...........................	10,944	8,415
Receivables—trade (less allowances for doubtful accounts: 1972—$3,673; 1971—$3,348) (Schedule XII).............	39,854	38,051
Inventories (note 2)*..................................	21,617	20,608
Prepaid expenses.....................................	1,501	1,170
Total Current Assets.............................	$ 81,479	$ 74,587
Property, Plant and Equipment—at cost (Schedule V) (Note 1)*:		
Land and land improvements...........................	$ 3,457	$ 3,106
Buildings..	11,296	11,296
Building equipment...................................	1,143	1,053
Furniture and equipment..............................	6,610	6,351
Construction in progress..............................	420	—
Leasehold improvements...............................	964	909
	$ 23,890	$ 22,713
Less accumulated depreciation and amortization (Schedule VI)...................................	8,747	7,971
Property, plant, and equipment (net)................	$ 15,143	$ 14,742
Investments and Other Assets:		
Cash value of life insurance...........................	$ 1,260	$ 1,238
Investment in wholly owned subsidiary not consolidated—at cost (equity in net assets: 1972 and 1971—$505,000) (Note 1)*..	500	500
Investment in and notes receivable from other companies (Note 3)*...	4,904	9,570
Deferred charges (cost of services to be rendered, advances to authors, etc.).....................................	8,720	8,367
Excess of cost over net value of assets acquired (Note 1)*....	1,340	1,340
Total, investments and other assets.................	$ 16,724	$ 21,015
Total Assets.................................	$113,346	$110,344
Current Liabilities:		
Accounts payable—trade..............................	$ 7,123	$ 6,998
Accrued royalties.....................................	7,324	7,139
Other accrued expenses................................	5,316	4,848
Accrued federal income taxes...........................	1,780	3,763
Advance payments on subscriptions, unexpired subscriptions, etc....................................	13,554	13,223
Total Current Liabilities............................	$ 35,097	$ 35,971
Stockholders' Equity (Note 5)*:		
Common stock—authorized 15,000,000 shares of $0.33—⅓ par value; issued 10,427,388 shares.....................	3,476	3,476
Capital surplus.......................................	21,375	21,375
Earned surplus.......................................	57,246	51,306
Total...	$ 82,097	$ 76,157
Less treasury stock—at cost (1972—120,619 shares and 1971—70,619 shares).................................	3,848	1,784
Stockholders' equity...................................	$ 78,249	$ 74,373
Total Liabilities..............................	$113,346	$110,344

* Notes omitted.
Source: Prentice-Hall Form 10-K.

tributions noted above and sets each up as a range (for example, 39 percent = 38.5 percent −39.5 percent). He then plots these ranges by product line on semilogarithmic paper and superimposes on each a similar plot of industry sales by sector (except for the miscellaneous and professional services categories). Using these, together with management comments on sales changes by categories, he arrives at specific revenue estimates by category.

The assumption is that company sales variations tend to parallel industry sales changes and that trends in market share changes tend to persist (within the bounds indicated by the company).

Reference industry revenues, taken from releases of the Association of American Publishers, are as follows:

TABLE 7

Industry Sales by Category ($ millions)

	1968	1969	1970	1971	1972P
College textbooks..............	$324	$347	$363	$379	$375
Elhi textbooks.................	444	455	479	499	498
Professional books*............	134	145	150	179	191
Trade books (adult, hardbound).................	179	199	214	233	243

* Excluding law and medicine.
Source: Association of American Publishers.

Miscellaneous revenues (those of the New York Institute of Finance and The Prentice-Hall Corporation System) are assumed to parallel other company sales, except as indicated by the company. The reference figures for professional services are based on summing estimates of the combined services sales of Prentice-Hall and Commerce Clearing House, its leading competitor, which the author also follows. However, an independent analysis of this category appears feasible because of its consistency.

The author's resulting estimates of Prentice-Hall's revenues by category were as follows:

TABLE 8

Prentice-Hall, Inc. and Consolidated Subsidiaries: Estimated Contributions to Revenues ($ millions)

	1968	1969	1970	1971	1972P
College textbooks............	$ 43.7	$ 47.5	$ 50.7	$ 52.4	$ 54.0
Professional services.........	32.9	37.2	41.7	43.4	47.7
Professional books...........	15.6	18.6	18.6	19.7	22.7
Elhi textbooks...............	7.5	7.8	9.1	10.7	11.1
Trade books.................	4.5	4.8	5.0	5.7	5.2
Miscellaneous...............	3.7	4.2	3.2	2.8	3.4
Total.................	$107.9	$120.1	$128.3	$134.7	$144.1

Source: Author's estimate.

With these estimates of revenues by category, the author then looked for patterns of revenue changes with respect to industry sales. While some analysts prefer to estimate company sales by category by working up from individual company factors, the author has found that working down from industry estimates works well, except for small companies, magazines, and specialty divisions for which he has no industry data.

For Prentice-Hall, these patterns during the 1968–1972 period were estimated as follows:

1. In college textbooks, Prentice-Hall's pattern was one of nearly steadily improving growth relative to the industry. This could be codified in a number of ways. But relative to what? At the beginning of 1973, a declining pattern of college enrollments and college textbook sales suggested that the industry might experience a sales change of (0.3) percent to 6.6 percent (it actually was 6 percent, as enrollments picked up in late spring). Conservatism seemed warranted for Prentice-Hall's revenues in this sector in 1973, and the author used a range of 0–4 percent for Prentice-Hall's own revenue growth, particularly as he was recommending that the stock be held.

2. In professional services, Prentice-Hall's revenue growth relative to Commerce Clearing House (and thus, evidently, the industry segment) appeared to be slowing. On a longer-term basis, the author estimated the growth of this area as 12–13 percent, with modest biennial swings tied to biennial peaks in state legislative activity. A good indication of year-ahead revenue growth was provided by the "backlog" reported by the 10-K. When the report was written, this backlog and subsequent revenue growth were estimated up 5–8 percent (it was actually up 4.8 percent).

3. In professional books, a blend of book club sales (one third) and direct mail sales (two thirds), the pattern is similar to that of business advertising: stronger than average in good years, below average in poor economic years, and displaying some lag. The average in good years had been about 15.4 percent and the author was relatively confident of a 15 percent gain in 1973.

4. In elhi textbooks, coupled with audiovisual materials, the Prentice-Hall trend was again one of nearly consistent market share expansion. Though some erratic variations were noted against industry sales gains estimated at 2–5 percent early in 1973, Prentice-Hall's gains were projected at 12–15 percent (they were lower due to some changes in adoptions).

5. Trade sales had shown some erratic variations, but the sector's sales displayed some relative improvement in 1971 after years of relative decline. Bradbury Press, a juvenile publisher, was sold in 1971, and its absence contributed to the lower 1972 sales picture. Nineteen seventy-three estimates reflected the erratic nature of this sector.

6. Miscellaneous operations also displayed cyclical characteristics against a generally rising trend. This sector included the New York Institute of Finance which trains security analysts, among others. Nineteen seventy-three projections again reflected this erratic character and the uncertainties of the stock market in 1973.

These analyses led to the sales estimates shown in the attached exhibit (Table 11).

Estimates of cost of sales and selling, general, and administrative expenses can be derived in at least three ways:

1. Estimating allocations of expenses by publishing sector. This also produces estimates of margins by sector, of course. Such estimates can be based on comparisons with reports of companies specializing in those sectors, with data released by the Association of American Publishers and with ratios provided in older editions of *The Bowker Annual*. These estimates should be made, at least periodically, to establish the effects of changes in sales mix. Prentice-Hall, for example, was estimated by the author to derive nearly half its operating income from college textbooks with pretax sector margins of about 29 percent.

2. Estimating expenses in terms of such basic elements as paper consumption and costs and labor consumption and costs. This method is particularly useful for such single-product publishers as newspaper publishers. It is also a necessary cross-calculation for such companies as Prentice-Hall in times of rapidly rising paper or labor costs.

3. Estimating expenses in terms of patterns of expense changes under varying conditions, checked with managements and modified by judgement and periodic experiences. In the case of Prentice-Hall, for example, as for other book publishers, the writer observed that there had been a long-term trend toward declining costs of goods sold. In 1972, this trend for Prentice-Hall flattened at 34.7 percent of sales, leading to a seemingly reasonable estimate of a similar ratio in 1973. Meanwhile, the pattern of selling, general, and administrative costs—costs which are more amenable to control—displayed a pattern of lagging sales increases within certain constraints, as illustrated by Table 9.

This pattern led to initial estimates of increases of 7.4 percent in S, G, and A given a sales increase of 4.5 percent, and a gain of 9.9 per-

TABLE 9

Prentice-Hall, Inc. and Consolidated Subsidiaries: Percentage Changes in Sales versus Percentage Changes in Selling, General, and Administrative Expenses

	1966	1967	1968	1969	1970	1971	1972
Sales gains	13.6	12.1	14.8	11.3	6.8	5.0	7.0
Increases in S, G, and A	9.2	13.9	15.8	14.8	9.8	8.6	7.6

Source: Company reports and author's estimates.

cent given a sales rise of 8.7 percent. However, the pattern of declines in the past few years and management's evident determination to hold the line led to revised estimates of S, G, and A increases of 5.6 percent and 8 percent, respectively. These amounts are largely expenditures for people, while cost-of-sales figures reflect largely paper and printing costs.

Depreciation and amortization figures were based on the data in the preceding tables plus discussions with management, as were estimates of interest and other income and the corporate tax rate. This left the special effect of tax benefits from the company's adoption of a Domestic International Sales Corporation (DISC). A substantial portion of the company's sales are to Canada and abroad, but the former apparently would not benefit from a DISC while the latter evidently would contribute only a few cents a share.

So much for estimates. The next problem was to determine the appropriate recommendation in view of the stock's price. To aid in this analysis, let us review the stock's recent price history in Table 10.

TABLE 10

Prentice-Hall, Inc. and Consolidated Subsidiaries: Market Performance

Year	1968	1969	1970	1971	1972
High price	46	51	52	50¼	49½
High P/E	35.4	34.5	34.7	31.4	30.0
Average price	38¾	42½	39¾	43½	39
Average P/E	29.8	28.7	26.5	27.3	23.6
Low price	31⅜	34	27½	36⅞	28½
Low P/E	24.6	23.0	18.3	23.0	17.3
E.P.S.	$1.30	$1.48	$1.50	$1.60	$1.65*

* Before extraordinary charge.
Source: Standard & Poor's, company reports, and author's estimates.

When the analysis was prepared, Prentice-Hall was selling at $23 with a price/earnings ratio of 13.9. What should the recommendation be?

The author applied several rules of thumb:

1. He had observed that Prentice-Hall's earnings were regarded as deriving roughly half from the textbook market and half from the professional services area. In times of uncertainty, its P/E ratio appeared to equal ½ (prevailing P/E ratio for Elhi stocks + 20). The then P/E ratio for Elhi stocks was about 8, suggesting a P/E ratio for Prentice-Hall of 14 and a Hold recomendation.

2. Recent and prospective earnings growth approximated 6 percent in the author's opinion. Applying the formula for publishing P/E ratios discussed earlier, suggested a P/E ratio of about 14.5, again suggesting a Hold recommendation.

3. If the college textbook market were to resume a growth rate of 3–4 percent, the most commonly accepted industry projection at the

time, Prentice-Hall's own earnings growth could be reasonably projected at nearly 8–10 percent in the author's opinion, suggesting a P/E ratio of 17–20 and that the stock was a long-term Buy recommendation. But the problem at the time was that college enrollments appeared to be falling below expectations, and their future trend was in doubt. Moreover, this even left doubt about the 1973 earnings estimate. Thus, despite favorable demographic and historic trends, the author believed that aggressive accounts might wish to sell the stock.

4. The author's firm's strategy was to increase cash reserves but to hold stocks with above-average longer-term earnings/growth prospects.

These observations led to the actual recommendation of the following report. Subsequently, on April 19, following receipt of a survey by the National Association of State Universities and Land Grant Colleges

PRENTICE-HALL (ASE-PTN)*

1972–1973 Range	Recent Price	Ind. Div.	Yield	Earnings per Share		P/E Ratio	
				1973E	1972A	1973E	1972A
50–21	$23	$0.84	3.7	$1.75	$1.65	13.1	13.9

indicating a 4.2 percent decline in applications for college enrollment, he recommended that Prentice-Hall, then at $22, be sold for the short term but held for the longer term. In late June, as rising college textbook sales indicated better-then-projected college enrollments, he changed that short-term Sell to a Hold. On November 16, subsequent to an acquisition, he raised Prentice-Hall's 1973 earnings estimate to $1.80 and its 1974 estimate to $2.00. At year's end, while retaining his Hold recommendations, a turn for the better in college enrollments was leading him to consider switching to a short-term Buy recommendation: The stock was then priced at $18.

At year-end, Prentice-Hall reported a special charge of $2.8 million ($0.27 per share) reflecting the write-down to estimated net realizable values of its investments in, and advances to, Responsive Environments Corporation and E.R.E. Laboratory, Inc. Thus, when Prentice-Hall joined recently in calling for Responsive Environments to be placed in bankruptcy, the news should not have been unexpected, nor do we

---

* Auerbach, Pollak & Richardson, Inc. Research Notes (3/22/73).

Note: Officers and members of our staff may from time to time have positions in the securities mentioned herein. The statements herein contained, while obtained from sources which we consider reliable, are not to be regarded as representations by us, nor do we guarantee their accuracy. They should not be relied upon as a complete statement of all material facts. The foregoing is not an offer to sell or a solicitation of an offer to buy these securities. It is sent to you for your information only.

anticipate any further losses to Prentice-Hall as a result. Its loans to Responsive Environments ($7.1 million due July 1, 1975) were secured by approximately $8.0 million of collateral—primarily, we believe, accounts receivable under rental or lease agreements executed by public schools which are sound. The final decision to cease efforts to turn Re-

TABLE 11

Estimated Revenues and Income, 1970–1973* ($ millions)

	1970A	1971A	1972A	1973E
Sales and other revenue:				
College textbooks	$ 50.7E	$ 52.4E	$ 54.0	$ 54.0– 56.2
Professional services	41.7E	43.4E	47.7	50.1– 51.5
Professional books	18.6E	19.7E	22.7	26.1
Elhi textbooks	9.1E	10.7E	11.1	12.4– 12.8
Trade	5.0E	5.7E	5.2	5.0– 6.0
Miscellaneous	3.2E	2.8E	3.4	3.0– 4.0
Total	$128.3A	$134.7A	$144.1A	$150.6–156.6
Cost of operations:				
Cost of sales	$ 45.8	$ 46.8	$ 50.0	$ 52.3– 54.3
Selling, general, and admin	52.4	56.9	61.2	64.6– 66.1
Depreciation and amortization	1.0	1.2	1.2	1.3
Total	$ 99.2	$104.9	$112.4A	$118.2–121.7
Income from operations	$ 29.1	$ 29.8	$ 31.7	$ 32.4– 34.9
Interest and other income	0.9	1.3	0.5	0.6
Pretax Income	$ 30.0	$ 31.2	$ 32.2A	$ 33.0– 35.5
Federal income taxes	14.5	14.6	15.1A	15.5– 16.6
Net income	$ 15.4	$ 16.6	$ 17.1A	$ 17.5– 18.9
Net income per share	$1.50	$1.60	$1.65A	$1.69–1.82
Best estimate				$1.75

* Totals may not add, due to rounding.

sponsive Environments around was probably based in part on the anticipated curtailment of the federal educational funds to which it was very sensitive.

Thus, we believe that the key to Prentice-Hall's growth and its stock's performance continues to be the prospect of the college textbook market. This segment accounts for an estimated 37.5 percent of corporate revenues and probably 51–52 percent of corporate income. Relatively, the company is again doing well (an estimated 3 percent sales gain versus an estimated 1 percent sales decline for the industry in 1972). But relative to what?

We continue to think that the weakness in the college textbook market reflects weakness in college enrollments, up only 1.3 percent last year versus an early estimate of 6 percent. We also now think that the problem is short term in nature and a reaction to the end of the draft as an incentive to go to college; a recent Bureau of the Census study found black male and female and white female enrollments still growing, with respect to eligible age brackets, while white male enrollments were falling. Thus, once white males have been reduced in number to those who would go to college under any circumstances, the total should rise as it continues to do for the other three groups. But we cannot be sure when that will occur.

We still think the best indication will be the mid-April release of the applications for enrollment reported by the National Association of State Universities and Land Grant Colleges (also up 1.3 percent last year). However, we have seen one published report that New Jersey's colleges were experiencing a notable decline in such applications already. Thus, the odds on a turn in 1973 so far appear low. On a longer-term basis, however, a 3–4 percent compounded increase in both enrollments and college textbook sales still seems the most reasonable estimate.

While we do not yet have a precise breakdown of Prentice-Hall's 1972 revenues and expenses, our best estimates of recent years and 1973 results are shown in Table 1a.

Some modest further gain in 1973 may result from the company's expanded benefits from DISC operations for a full year. However, we believe the benefit would be on the order of $0.03 per share.

Under the circumstances, *we believe Prentice-Hall is best considered a Hold for the intermediate and longer term, although aggressive accounts may still wish to switch*—particularly if the mid-April applications figures suggest a further softening in 1973 college enrollments. We consider the stock a Hold in view of the growing indications that college enrollments will begin to increase at a faster pace within the next two to three years.

25

Rails

THOMAS J. DONNELLY, C.F.A.
Vice President
Kuhn, Loeb & Co., New York, New York

Investor Sponsorship

IF EVER there was an industry that exemplified changes in investor interest, the railroad group certainly would be one of the leading contenders. A century ago, or 50 years ago for that matter, the rails were prime investment vehicles. The group has gone full cycle in the interim. Except for perhaps 10 to 12 carriers, there is limited sponsorship today for railroad stocks.

The promise of the past for the industry gave way to the undeniable fact that the rails over the past two decades failed to grow as fast as the economy. Most of the factors contributing to this unfavorable showing will be outlined subsequently. It is only necessary to point out here that this basic change came at a time when the general stock market was willing to pay premium multiples for the earnings of companies showing above-average growth trends. Subpar performers have been neglected or, in effect, have received low valuations. For example, institutions have been willing to pay 30 to 50 times the earnings of a company with superior growth characteristics. Companies within industries that were expanding at relatively slow growth rates have accordingly been awarded subpar earnings multiples of perhaps 8 to 12.

Can the basic position of the railroad industry change or be changed? What has happened to this once vibrant group? Without exercising any undue prejudice, it is safe to state that we will always have a railroad industry in this nation. The questions of the moment are whether the railroads will remain a free enterprise system within the transportation

660

spectrum of our nation and whether the rails can recapture some of their lost investment charisma.

While lack of growth has been the prime factor behind the demise of the industry, from the standpoint of investor sponsorship, there is no question that the failure of Penn Central in 1970 has further undermined the industry's investment stature. Several other eastern railroads have followed this major system into bankruptcy. The fate of these roads is now in the hands of Congress. The solutions found in Washington will go a long way toward determining not only the fate of these roads but the future of the industry as well. This is based on the fact that while each carrier is a separate entity, it is dependent on neighboring roads for the interchange of traffic. If one arm is infected, it only is a matter of time before the entire system catches the disease. Thus, there is great concern among investors currently as to what solutions will be found to resolve the fate of the eastern railroads. Current problems, if resolved successfully from an economic standpoint, could go a long way toward revitalizing the basic position of the industry.

Growth Pattern

The basic measure of growth in transportation is the revenue ton-mile performance of a carrier or of one of the major segments making up the transportation industry. A ton-mile is a physical unit of transportation representing the movement of one ton one mile. It ignores the value of the goods moved, the cost associated with moving different commodities, as well as the quality of service rendered by the particular transportation entity. These factors must be analyzed separately. Table 1 will point up the dramatic changes that have taken place in the distribution of traffic among the leading transportation modes.

Table 1 indicates that the railroad industry has fallen from a pre-eminent position among the major transportation modes to an important, but less dominant, role. From a positive standpoint, there is no disputing the importance of the railroad industry. It currently accounts for some 38 percent of this nation's inter-city ton-mile traffic. On the other hand, the industry's share of market has slipped from over 60 percent of the freight market of the 1940s. Also, the rails have failed to keep pace with the growth of our economy in recent years. Generalities are dangerous, however, and it is well to note that there have been dramatic differences within the industry. Eastern railroads have been distinct laggards, whereas carriers in the West and South have fared reasonably well from a traffic growth standpoint.

Factors Affecting Growth

Forces that have adversely affected traffic growth may be classified as internal and external. The internal forces include the pressure pre-

TABLE 1

Traffic Distribution among Leading Transportation Modes

Year	Railroads Millions of ton-miles [1]	Railroads % of total	Motor Trucks Millions of ton-miles	Motor Trucks % of total	Inland Waterways Millions of ton-miles [2]	Inland Waterways % of total	Pipelines (oil) Millions of ton-miles	Pipelines (oil) % of total	Airways Million of ton-miles [3]	Airways % of total	Total Millions of ton-miles [4]
1940	379,201	61.30	62,043	10.03	118,057	19.08	59,277	9.58	14	.00	618,592
1945	690,809	67.26	66,948	6.52	142,737	13.90	126,530	12.32	91	.01	1,027,115
1950	596,940	56.17	172,860	16.27	163,344	15.37	129,175	12.16	331	.03	1,062,650
1955	631,385	48.53	223,254	17.51	216,508	16.98	203,244	15.94	465	.04	1,274,856
1960	579,130	44.06	285,483	21.72	220,253	16.76	228,626	17.39	891	.07	1,314,383
1965	708,700	43.25	359,218	21.92	262,421	16.01	306,393	18.70	1,911	.12	1,638,643
1967	731,216	41.43	388,500	22.01	281,400	15.95	361,041	20.46	2,590	.15	1,764,747
1968	756,800	41.16	396,300	21.55	291,409	15.85	391,300	21.28	2,916	.16	1,838,725
1969 r	780,000	41.02	404,000	21.25	302,901	15.93	411,000	21.61	3,574	.19	1,901,475
1970 r	771,012	39.83	412,000	21.28	318,560	16.46	431,000	22.26	3,295	.17	1,935,867
1971 p	746,000	38.11	445,000	22.73	315,030	16.09	448,000	22.89	3,500	.18	1,957,530
1972 e	781,000	38.05	470,000	22.90	330,000	16.08	468,000	22.80	3,800	.19	2,052,800

1 Includes express and mail until 1970.
2 Including Great Lakes, but excluding deep sea ton-miles between mainland and Alaska, Hawaii and territories.
3 Domestic revenue service, including express, mail and excess baggage. Intra-Alaska and intra-Hawaii ton-miles included beginning in 1959 Effective January 1, 1970, operations between the 48 states and Alaska/Hawaii were reclassified as domestic operations. Data for the years after 1969 has been adjusted in accordance with the new definition.
4 Components may not add to total due to rounding.
r — Revised.   p — Preliminary.   e — Estimated, ATA Research.

Sources: Interstate Commerce Commission, U.S. Corps of Engineers, Association of American Railroads, Civil Aeronautics Board.

sented by rising wage costs and outmoded work rules which forced the industry to raise freight rates on a regular basis during the 1950s and 1960s. While management was forced to this position, it should be noted that there was limited attention to possible alternatives, including a more realistic approach to labor. Also, rate increases generally were on an across-the-board basis. This gave virtually no recognition to areas of vulnerability from a competitive standpoint. In effect, increased rates on certain commodities only tended to accelerate the loss to competing modes of transportation.

Some competitive inroads were inflicted by factors outside the control of railroad managements. These included the trend toward the decentralization of industry and the construction of excellent highway networks. These gave the trucking industry a high degree of flexibility, far greater speed of service than had been available previously, and the potential for increased reliability. The trucking industry was fast to learn the importance of service. The importance of this is well demonstrated by the willingness of shippers to pay premium rates vis-à-vis those charged by the rails or barge lines to assure consistent delivery schedules.

Recent Trends

One of the most encouraging factors that has developed from the railroads' standpoint in recent years is a leveling off in their share of ton-mile traffic. The consistent slippage of the previous two decades has given way to a stabilization period. During the past three years, the rails' share of market has held at about 38 percent. The importance of this change is significant. It would once again indicate that the industry is growing hand-in-hand with this nation's general economy.

Traffic benefits undoubtedly have been derived from improved marketing techniques, especially such innovations as piggyback service, unit trains of coal and grain, and run-through trains. The latter refers to improved connecting service between two or three individual railroads, whereby crew changes are made but the diesel locomotives cross normal property lines. The leveling-off process in the share of market may also reflect a more national distribution of the available traffic. From an economic standpoint, the rail industry is best geared to carload type business which is scheduled to move over long distances. Trucking companies are best suited to relatively short-haul volume, primarily consisting of small type shipments.

Industry Characteristics

The most relevant point that can be made in covering factors that affect the railroad industry is that it is highly sensitive to fluctuations in general business activity. This is readily shown in an examination of

TABLE 2

Comparison of Principal Revenue-Producing Commodities of Major Class 1 Roads (in thousands of dollars)

	1972 Tot. Freight Revs.	% of Tot.	1971 Tot. Freight Revs.	% of Total	1970 Tot. Freight Revs	% of Tot.	1969 Tot. Freight Revs	% of Tot.
ALL CLASS 1 ROADS								
Farm Products	$1,235,000	9.5	1,042,088	8.5	1,068,180	9.4	908,251	8.4
Wheat	310,000	2.4	248,030	2.0	275.822	2.4	218,798	2.0
Forest Prods. & Lumber	1,145,000	8.8	1,015,871	8.3	845,730	7.4	817,317	7.5
Lumber & dimension stk	585,000	4.5	501,907	4.1	406.276	3.6	397,793	3.7
Mineral Products	2,175,000	16.7	2,010,383	16.4	2,128,449	18.7	1,913,496	17.7
Iron ores	265,000	2.0	240,002	2.0	241.508	2.1	235,852	2.2
Bituminous coal	1,400,000	10.8	1,306,836	10.6	1.354.088	11.9	1,164,198	10.7
*Manuf. & All Other	8,450,000	64.8	8,145,837	66.5	7,308,696	64.2	7,162,476	66.1
Food & kindred products	1,518,000	11.7	1,471,579	12.0	1,362.779	12.0	1,267,498	11.7
Pulp, paper & allied prods	870,000	6.7	801,811	6.5	729.941	6 4	690,497	6.4
Chemicals & allied prods	1,350,000	10.4	1,242,932	10.1	1.136.631	10.0	1,087,815	10.0
Stone, clay & glass prods	585,000	4.5	557,244	4.5	512.178	4.5	514,015	4.7
Primary metal prods.	860,000	6.6	819,169	6.6	813.220	7.1	819,291	7.6
Transportation equipt.	1,043,000	8.0	1,028,952	8.4	733.791	6 4	800,807	7.4
L.C.L. Traffic	30,000	0.2	32,922	0.3	36,488	0.3	35,020	0.3
Grand Total	13,035,000	100.0	12,247,101	100.0	11,387,543	100.0	10,836,160	100.0

Source: Interstate Commerce Commission.

industry freight traffic (Table 2) which accounts for virtually all of railroad revenues.

Changes in the level of steel mill operations, auto industry output, and capital spending trends will immediately be reflected by weekly railroad carloading results. Certain roads will be less directly affected, however, depending on the importance in their traffic mix of such items as agricultural products or lumber. Eastern roads, serving a mature section of our nation, also have fared less well than carriers in the West and South where industrial development has been more robust. Traffic in the East for the rails has been especially hurt by the development of highway systems that facilitated the loss of short-haul volume, as well as high-rated type traffic. The divergent trends are pointed up in Table 3.

TABLE 3

Class 1 Revenue Ton-Miles (by region)

Year	Total Ton-Miles (billion)	Eastern District (billions)	Eastern District (percent)	Southern District (billions)	Southern District (percent)	Western District (billions)	Western District (percent)
1972	780.7	231.1	29.7	148.7	19.1	398.3	51.2
1971	739.7	225.6	30.5	139.7	18.9	374.5	50.6
1970	764.8	254.5	33.3	140.0	18.3	370.3	48.4
1969	767.8	259.8	33.8	139.3	18.1	368.8	48.0
1968	744.0	259.4	34.9	130.7	17.5	353.9	47.6
1967	719.5	258.4	35.9	128.0	17.8	333.1	46.3
1966	738.4	265.5	35.9	125.5	17.0	347.4	47.1

Source: Interstate Commerce Commission.

Regulatory Agency

The Interstate Commerce Act of 1887 created the Interstate Commerce Commission. The aim of the law was to prevent discrimination in commerce, and the three main provisions of the act may be summarized as: first, the ICC was given power to set reasonable maximum rates; second, the ICC was given authority over railroad accounting procedures; and, third, the commission could require reports as it saw fit.

Over a period of time, Congress also gave the ICC authority to exercise greater power in the freight rate area, to regulate the issuance of security issues, and to have veto power over consolidations or mergers within the industry. The ICC today is comprised of 11 members. They are appointed by the president, subject to Senate confirmation. No more than six members are to be selected from one of the political parties, and the term of office is seven years.

Cost Structure

Since the railroads are regulated, there is an abundant supply of statistics on the industry, as well as for individual carriers. From an expense standpoint, wage costs and related fringe benefits represent the largest factor. About 45 percent of the average revenue dollar is consumed by wages, while an additional 7 percent represents health and welfare benefits and payroll taxes.

The railroad industry necessarily was under great pressure in the late 1940s and early 1950s and again in subsequent inflationary periods. This is perhaps best pointed up by the fact that in the three-year labor agreement of 1970–1973, wage rates advanced by approximately 10 percent per year. While the industry has made great strides in increasing productivity, it has been impossible to come close to offsetting inflationary pressures.

One way of indicating the gain in productivity is to relate industry ton-miles to the total employee count. Between 1965 and 1972, railroad ton-miles expanded by over 11 percent. Meanwhile, the number of industry employees declined from 640,000 to 526,000, or by 18 percent. This has not been sufficient, however, since wage boosts have been reflected in an expansion of wage and fringe benefits from $4.8 billion to $6.4 billion, an increase of 34 percent. The wage and fringe benefit ratio rose from some 50 percent of revenues to over 52 percent during this period.

Outmoded Work Practices

Are there featherbedding or make-work practices in the railroad industry? Without going into a great many examples, it might be sufficient to point to the fact that long after diesel locomotives replaced steam engines, the industry continued to have firemen employed in the head end of their trains. There are some offsetting circumstances, including safety considerations at times. The fact is, however, that railroads were saddled with needless operating expenses for many years after the steamer was gone. There are many other ways in which the industry has been unable to capitalize on new operating methods or more modern operating facilities.

The lack of success in bargaining with labor may be attributed to several factors. These include the difficulty in negotiating with as many as 18 to 20 separate unions, unenlightened labor relations programs, and different needs on individual railroads and consequential divided fronts. Another consideration has been the weak financial position of many railroads. This precluded the ability to take lengthy strikes.

Labor relations have improved somewhat in recent years, though more progress is essential if the industry is to meet the challenges of the future. Encouragement may be drawn from the fact that both management and labor agreed to a joint study of existing work rules. Changes in outmoded practices would be highly constructive from a longer-term standpoint. Progress in formulating a solution to the rail problem in the Northeast could also facilitate changes in the future. It is worth noting, however, that changes generally evolve slowly, and that potential savings are realized over a period of time.

Allocation of Operating Expenses

Wages account for more than half of the operating revenues realized by the average railroad. The three major operating expenses are the maintenance of way and structures, maintenance of equipment, and transportation accounts. These comprise total operating expenses of the industry which currently consume about 78 percent of railroad operating revenues.

Transportation expenses include all the costs of running trains over the railroad network. These include fuel, loss and damage, as well as train crew salaries. The latter are by far the most important part of this cost area. Transportation expenses average about 39 percent of revenues. This ratio is influenced by the level of traffic as well as the changes in wage rates. While this ratio may be used as a measure of efficiency, weight should be given different operating environments, various traffic mixes, and decisions by management as to whether it should run long trains or short ones. This can be an important influence on the level of traffic service.

Maintenance ratios (ratio of maintenance cost to operating revenue) may be used as guides to the relative conditions of railroad properties and the condition of individual freight car fleets. The maintenance-of-way ratio equals somewhat over 14 percent for the industry, while the equipment maintenance ratio equals about 16.5 percent. These accounts obviously provide management with a fair degree of flexibility. However, failure of a given road to maintain its property in satisfactory condition over a period of time will result in "deferred" maintenance work. This will eventually have to be done. If it is not, the service capability of the road will be affected by a slowdown in train speeds or by an increase in freight train derailments.

Unfortunately, the weakened financial positions of certain roads, particularly in the East, have resulted in substantial deferred maintenance for several railroads. In addition to the guide presented by the equipment maintenance ratio, the ICC requires annual reports from the railroads on the status of their respective freight car fleets. This indicates total ownership, as well as the number of freight cars in need of repair. Historically, about 5 to 6 percent of the industry's car fleet is sidelined for repair work.

Other Operating Costs

In examining the railroad industry's income account, the impact of inflationary pressures on wage and fringe benefit totals can be readily seen. Another account that has advanced rapidly, however, is the one labeled "hire of equipment." This one item totaled about $850 million in 1972, up from $535 million in 1967 and substantially above the $350 million level that prevailed in 1961–1962. The sharp rise reflects increased "per diem" schedules, which are the charges paid by one road to another for the use of its freight cars. There is, of course, a wide disparity among the roads in this category, reflecting the ability to have financed individual requirements as well as various operating differences. Another important factor has been a substantial increase in new car purchases through investment tax credit "lease" arrangements. In effect, roads that couldn't fully utilize Investment Tax Credits used this method of financing. Finally, the equipment rental account also reflects greater use of private car leasing pools, especially for piggyback operations.

Passenger Service Operations

Until the quasi-public National Railroad Passenger Corporation (Amtrak) was established by the federal government in May, 1971, the railroad industry incurred substantial losses in its passenger service operations. In addition to the obvious impact these deficits had on profits results, there was another negative consideration. In effect, the freight operations of the industry were forced to subsidize passenger losses. This obviously had a negative influence on the competitive position of the industry.

One of the questions raised prior to Amtrak was whether the railroads really lost substantial sums on long-haul passenger operations. Reported deficits ranged from $250 million to $475 million in 1970, depending on whether certain related costs were allocated to this service or freight service. There can be no question today that the losses were significant. This is best pointed out by relating that Amtrak incurred a deficit of $147 million in 1972, even though it reduced long-haul passenger operations by about 50 percent.

Unfortunately, it appears that most of the indicated savings expected to be realized by the industry were eroded by the particularly large wage rate increases of the early 1970s. On the other hand, absence of this burden has been constructive in that it has reduced employee totals on a permanent basis, and equipment requirements also have been reduced from the standpoint of the individual railroad.

Some eastern and midwestern railroads are still engaged in commuter service. Losses on these operations are more severe in the East. There has been a decided trend to local subsidization of these essential, but unprofitable, operations. The current fuel crisis may well result in greater federal and local subsidies over the near term.

Railroad Income Account

Table 4 is a capsule summary of the industry's operating record over an extended period of time. The purpose of this table is not to elaborate on the industry's earnings trend, for this will be done subsequently. However, it is worth noting that the overall income totals are distorted by the heavy losses sustained by eastern roads, particularly Penn Central, in recent years. These deficits totaled $157 million in 1972 and $250 million in 1971.

Aside from the amount of detail that is readily available, one other noteworthy fact is the position of federal income taxes in the income account under ICC accounting procedures. These are included in the total tax accrual account, even though they are determined by the going corporate tax laws. One important difference affecting reported railroad earnings is that relating to utilization of accelerated depreciation and other rapid write-offs permitted for tax purposes.

While industrial companies establish reserves for the deferred taxes related to the rapid write-offs, the railroads are not permitted to do so under ICC regulations. In effect, railroad earnings are consequently inflated. However, with many railroad companies taking the holding company route in recent years, most railroads now report to stockholders on the basis of generally accepted accounting policies. Even the roads that have not set up a holding company are now reporting earnings both on an ICC basis and after establishing reserves for deferred income taxes. It should also be noted that all railroads, including those that are holding

TABLE 4

Condensed Income Account for Class I Railroads in the United States
(amounts in millions)

	1955	1966	1971	1972
Total operating revenues...............	$10,106	$10,655	$12,689	$13,411
Freight...........................	8,538	9,281	11,786	12,572
Passenger........................	743	544	294	257
Mail.............................	287	304	123	94
Express..........................	118	67	11	5
All other revenues.................	420	459	475	482
Total operating expenses..............	7,646	8,118	10,055	10,550
Maintenance of way................	1,387	1,304	1,813	1,918
Maintenance of equipment...........	1,788	1,844	2,351	2,393
Traffic...........................	235	265	282	292
Transportation....................	3,770	4,139	4,890	5,209
Miscellaneous.....................	108	66	22	12
General...........................	357	500	698	727
Total tax accruals....................	1,080	968	1,090	1,143
Payroll taxes......................	284	439	578	622
Federal income taxes................	414	186	108	114
All other taxes....................	382	343	404	407
Equipment and joint facility rent........	252	523	848	883
Net railway operating income..........	1,128	1,046	696	835
Other income.......................	$271	$399	$422	$395
Miscellaneous deductions..............	57	78	141	101
Rents for leased roads.................	60	60	64	62
Interest deductions...................	311	360	532	539
Amortization of discount..............	3	5	5	5
Contingent interest...................	40	38	29	24
Ordinary income.....................	927	904	347	500

Source: Association of American Railroads.

companies, use the flow-through method for handling benefits of the 7
percent investment tax credit.

Trend of Industry Earnings

As noted previously, the profits trend of the railroad industry has been
distorted by the large deficits sustained by the Penn Central and other
bankrupt eastern carriers. The deteriorating position of some midwestern
roads also is part of the overall picture. The point is that the industry
trend appears quite poor from a long-term standpoint, but there are
significant differences within the industry. For example, a few carriers
did report record earnings for 1973 frollowing two or three successive
peaks. The following tabulation (Table 5) will point out the general
differences in industry trends, based on geographic location.

The very different trends in each of the three districts in part reflect
the more mature state of industry in the East, as well as the beneficial
effects of the decentralization of industry outside this area. Increasing

TABLE 5

Regional Incomes* (amounts shown in thousands)

	United States	Eastern District	Southern District	Western District
1929	$896,807	$486,978	$ 73,059	$336,769
1939	93,182	110,405	11,668	def. 28,892
1944	667,188	266,208	97,251	303,729
1947	478,875	161,178	55,192	262,505
1951	693,176	234,970	110,703	347,503
1955	927,122	349,288	153,805	424,029
1957	737,431	256,563	117,665	363,203
1958	601,737	140,874	98,747	362,117
1959	577,719	142,471	101,814	333,434
1960	444,640	81,013	81,650	281,977
1961	382,444	def. 2,709	84,003	301,150
1962	571,017	81,609	117,989	371,419
1963	651,637	132,662	114,780	404,196
1964	698,184	176,057	117,386	404,742
1965	814,629	243,767	124,175	446,687
1966	903,783	285,054	141,399	477,330
1967	553,789	94,146	126,079	333,564
1968	569,402ʳ	67,393ʳ	117,123	384,886
1969	514,238	21,329	139,366	353,543
1970	226,583	def. 276,291	159,508	343,366
1971	347,097	def. 249,662	178,957	417,802
1972	499,916	def. 157,079	207,734	449,261

* Ordinary income before extraordinary and prior period charges and credits.
def. = Deficit.
r = Revised.
Source: Association of American Railroads.

demand for lumber, low-sulphur coal, and agricultural products has also facilitated better traffic trends for western and southern carriers. Also, eastern roads have incurred a stronger impact from motor carrier competition because of their shorter average traffic hauls combined with the development of excellent highway networks in recent years.

Quality of Reported Earnings

In appraising the earnings results of individual roads, several factors bear on the quality of reported profits. One obvious area is the federal income tax account. Accrual rates range from 10 percent to about 37 percent, even under generally accepted accounting rules. The reduced rates reflect benefits of the 7 percent investment tax credit, as well as nontaxable income and depletion allowances for nonrail interests.

Less tangible quality measures include the condition of the property. Cutbacks in needed maintenance-of-way expenses, for example, will result in higher earnings in a given period, but this "deferred" maintenance will eventually penalize results. Another important consideration is the percentage of income realized from nonrail sources. This would be significant if it represents a reasonable percentage of overall income and if it is in potentially rapid growing areas.

Nonrail Income

While railroad operations account for the bulk of income in the industry, some carriers are generating increasing income from various nonrail activities. These include oil and gas operations, natural resource interests, and real estate developments. Increasing concern over this nation's future energy requirements should facilitate more rapid development of railroad holdings in coal, as well as oil and gas. Progress made by individual railroads has varied greatly through the years, though there is no questioning the fact that efforts have intensified in more recent years.

Railroad Industry Finances

The railroad industry is capital intensive. Capital expenditures totaled about $1.2 billion in 1972, with about 70 to 75 percent of annual outlays usually expended on new equipment. One of the problems of the industry has been the inability to raise equity capital in over two decades, with the only exception being some isolated convertible debentures. Balance sheets vary greatly. As might be imagined, eastern roads have weak cash and working capital positions. These roads also have been hard pressed to find capital to finance their equipment needs.

For the industry, the prime method of financing new equipment has been through equipment trust certificates and conditional sales agreements. These debt instruments have been well regarded in the financial community over an extended period. This reflects the extremely small losses of principal suffered by holders of these certificates and the fact that they are supported by equipment which is indispensable for railway operations.

The cash and working capital positions of the industry have deteriorated significantly in the last decade. Overall totals are particularly hindered by the weakened positions of roads in the East. Nonetheless, the trends are not encouraging, and this points to the need for a revitalization of industry operations.

Industry at Crossroads

Major developments are currently unfolding which will determine the financial outlook and profitability of the railroad industry for some time to come. Congress currently is weighing measures that will determine the ultimate status of the bankrupt Penn Central and the other bankrupt eastern roads. The fate of Penn Central is important from an industry standpoint, since the road is involved in handling 20 percent of the nation's freight volume.

The industry also has been seeking remedial legislative changes that would help solve some basic problems and handicaps. These include the right to abandon unproductive branch mileage without undue delay, the elimination of discriminatory state tax practices, and government assistance in helping the industry finance the purchase of new equipment. It also is hoped the railroad rate-making process eventually will be modernized.

Efforts of the industry to upgrade and update the level of operations also are contingent on further progress in the labor area. Some encouragement may be drawn from the more improved negotiating climate for wages and work rules. Changes in these outmoded practices would be highly constructive from a longer-term standpoint.

Future Potential

There is no disputing the vital role that the railroad industry plays in this nation's transportation system or in the economic service that it performs. Based on future traffic growth potentials and the more acute fuel shortages that have come to the foreground recently, the role of the railroad industry will become more important than ever. The question is in what form will it survive.

Favorable resolution of the northeastern railroad problem and nearby enactment of remedial legislative changes would greatly strengthen the industry's basic position. Improved labor relationships also would be distinctly constructive. These changes would come at a time when more piggyback and inter-modal business should develop because of fuel shortages, and at a time when bituminous coal traffic could begin to turn higher because of our energy requirements.

Nonrail interests should continue to increase in importance for several roads, and it would not be surprising to see a resumption of merger discussions over the intermediate term. This would help eliminate much of the present duplication of rail mileage and uneconomic competition. Given these changes, there is every reason to believe that a significant revitalization of the industry would materialize.

Market Performance of Rail Stocks

Reflecting the absence of a revenue or earnings growth trend, rail stocks, as a group, have lagged well behind their industrial counterparts. A high degree of operating and capital leverage for the railroads has resulted in noticeable price swings at times, however. Also, allowance should be made for the superior showings of certain western and southern roads, which have demonstrated improved profits trends in recent years. Prospects for an upward evaluation of railroad stocks hinges on the outcome of the northeastern rail problems, remedial legislative changes, and the other factors previously cited.

An illustrative study of one approach to appraising a railroad stock follows.

TABLE 6

Union Pacific Corporation (NYSE–UNP), January 1974

Recent price.................. 85

	Primary	Diluted
Per share earnings:		
1972.........................	$4.62	$4.44
1973.........................	5.61	5.37
E1974.........................	6.00	5.65
E1974 P/E Ratio..............	14.1x	15.0x
Indicated dividend.............	$2.40	
Current yield.................	2.8%	

Capitalization—December 31, 1972

	Amount (millions)	Percent of Total
Long-term debt*..............................	$ 513.1	21.6
Deferred federal income taxes...................	294.0	12.4
Stockholders' equity:		
4.75 percent conv. preferred stock (678,480 shares).............................	6.8	0.2
Common stock (22,500,000 shares)..............	225.6	9.4
Paid-in surplus.................................	53.7	2.2
Retained income.............................	1,283.6	54.2
	$2,376.8	100.0

* Includes $68.0 million of 4.75 percent debentures due 1999, convertible at $57.14 per share until April 1, 1999. Recent price was 146.

CASE STUDY: UNION PACIFIC CORPORATION[1]

Summary and Recommendation

Union Pacific has taken on a new look since it established a holding company in 1969. Several key management changes have taken place

[1] The factual information contained herein has been obtained from sources which we regard as reliable, but we do not represent that it is accurate or complete. The expressions of opinion are subject to change without notice. The statements contained herein are not made in connection with any sale or offer for sale of securities or any solicitation of orders for the purchase of securities. We, or our partners and employees, may from time to time own securities of any of the issuers mentioned herein and may sell or buy such securities.

Written by Thomas J. Donnelly (railroads) and Thomas J. Kramer (oils). Copyright © 1974 Kuhn, Loeb & Co.

and there has been a noticeable change in the direction of the company, amply demonstrated by the impressive breakout in the earnings growth pattern. Profits have reached successive peaks in each of the past three years and earnings are up 50 percent since 1970.

Union Pacific, long renowned for its excellent railroad operation, has added a new dimension to its future through its integrated oil and gas operation, Champlin Petroleum. Railroad income accounts for some two thirds of profits and this area has been fully contributing to the impressive earnings uptrend. Champlin has broadened the scope of its interests and expanded its contribution to earnings. Recent crude oil discoveries in the North Sea and in Wyoming hold significant long-term potential. Champlin is continuing to pursue an aggressive exploration program as demonstrated recently by successfully bidding with Exxon and Mobil Oil on offshore acreage in the Gulf of Mexico, near Pensacola, Florida.

There is promising potential in Union Pacific's extensive bituminous coal reserves which are estimated in excess of 10 billion tons. Other material resource interests include trona (soda ash ore) and uranium. The company also is developing extensive land holdings in the West. Moreover, the company has the financial backing to capitalize on the potential in the railroad, oil, and other promising areas under development. Earnings last year were reported at a new peak of $5.61 a share, up 21 percent from the previous record of $4.62 a share in 1972. We believe earnings can expand to around $6.00 per share this year and to as much as $8.50 per share by 1977 when nonrail earnings may contribute 40 percent of the total.

Investors in the past several months have been stimulated by the promising outlook for Union Pacific, particularly following new oil discoveries in the North Sea and Wyoming. The stock has soared about 50 percent from last September to its current price of 85, which is about 14 times estimated 1974 earnings. We believe Union Pacific shares represent excellent long-term value and purchases made on that basis should prove rewarding.

Railroad Operations

Background. Among the accomplishments that contribute to Union Pacific's outstanding image in the railroad industry are: top-level operating efficiency, a large and modern equipment fleet, fast freight schedules, and dependable service. While some of these qualities may be attributed to management and a strong financial backing, part of the company's well-deserved reputation also has been derived from some natural geographic and operating advantages.

Union Pacific, the seventh largest U.S. railroad in terms of revenues, operates over approximately 9,500 miles of road in 13 western states. About 65 percent of the tonnage hauled is originated, but the road also serves as an important bridge line. Heavy freight volume moves between Omaha and Kansas City on the eastern end of the system to Granger, Wyoming or to Utah, from which points traffic moves over Union Pacific lines to the Pacific Northwest or to Southern California. Substantial volume also is interchanged with Southern Pacific and Western Pacific for shipment to the Bay area from the Utah junctions.

Revenues of the railroad amounted to $770 million in 1972. Nearly 97 percent of this total was derived from freight operations. Passenger business was discontinued in May 1971 when Amtrak assumed responsibility for inter-city service for most railroads. A summary of Union Pacific's major freight traffic sources and their contribution to 1972 revenues can be found in Table 7.

TABLE 7

Major Freight Traffic Sources and Their Contributions to 1972 Revenues

Commodity Group	Tons Carried (thousands)	Percent of Total	Freight Revenues (millions)	Percent of Total
Farm products	14,259	18.7	$105.5	14.0
Iron Ore, metallic ore, and coal	12,936	16.9	46.4	6.2
Lumber and wood products	9,324	12.1	112.2	14.9
Food and kindred products	9,621	12.5	114.8	15.3
Chemicals and allied products	6,942	9.0	77.4	10.3
Nonmetallic minerals	6,915	9.0	16.1	2.1
Miscellaneous	16,645	21.8	279.7	37.2
Total	76,642	100.0	$752.1	100.0

The commodity grouping of Union Pacific reveals a better diversified revenue base than that of the average railroad. For example, farm products accounted for 14 percent of Union Pacific's freight revenues in 1972 compared with 9.5 percent for the industry. This imparts somewhat greater resistance to fluctuations in the general economy, especially since another 15 percent of revenues is derived from relatively stable food products. Meanwhile, lumber and wood products equaled about 15 percent of Union Pacific's freight revenue base, well above the industry average of some 9 percent. Changes in housing starts, therefore, will have more significance than for most carriers. Coal and metallic ores loom far less in importance in Union Pacific's freight picture than for the industry as a whole, but bituminous coal is beginning to increase in importance. This area will be discussed in greater detail subsequently.

This more diversified freight traffic picture is not meant to imply that Union Pacific is immune to fluctuations in general business conditions. Chemicals, various manufactured goods, including automotive shipments, and other general merchandise items still heavily influence the level of freight volume. However, Union Pacific's broader traffic mix does make the carrier less vulnerable to the economic cycle than the average railroad.

Another constructive consideration is the areas of the nation that Union Pacific serves. The Midwest and West continue to benefit from above-average industrial growth, as well as from more intensive development of mineral and agricultural resources. The road's Kansas City gateway continues to benefit from heavy volume moving to and from the South and Southeast. Union Pacific has been actively participating in the development of "run-through" trains. This refers to the operation of a freight train in conjunction with neighboring roads. Switching is unnecessary at interchange points and locomotive power is pooled. This reduces operating expenses and improves service. Special run-through trains of coal and iron ore also are used over long hauls to the Midwest and to California. The accompanying table will point up Union Pacific's superior growth of revenue ton miles relative to the industry and to the roads within its region. (See Table 8.)

TABLE 8

Revenue Ton-Miles (1957–59 = 100)

Year	Union Pacific	Railroad Industry	Western Roads
1972	155	134	151
1971	139	127	142
1970	145	131	139
1969	142	132	140
1968	134	128	134
1967	125	124	126
1966	127	127	132
1965	118	120	122
1964	116	113	116
1963	107	107	109

Operating Position. Union Pacific boasts the longest average haul in the industry at 660 miles, compared with the industry average of 512 miles. In addition to this favorable operating advantage, the road also benefits from the need to have relatively few yards or terminals. This reduces freight train switching delays, helps speed schedules and reduces manpower requirements. In effect, Union Pacific is a relatively simple railroad operation—consisting of fast freight trains moving over long distances and not encumbered with the need to interrupt schedules for switching purposes.

These natural operating advantages have been further enhanced by the strong financial position of the company that has permitted it to continually upgrade and modernize its operations and property, motive power, rolling stock, right-of-way, and communications capability. Union

Pacific owns some of the nation's most powerful locomotives and it has one of the youngest fleets in the country. Locomotives average 11.9 years and freight cars about 11.5 years in age. These compare with an industry average of about 14 years in each instance.

Utilization of the diesel fleet and rolling stock is kept at a high level, reflecting a sound maintenance program. The roadbed is in excellent condition; derailments are held to a particularly low level. The railroad also has been able to take advantage of the latest computer technology. A private microwave communications network is being expanded. The computer system being developed, together with the road's communications network, has facilitated the development of a real time reporting and analysis system, as well as an improved car tracing and car distribution operation. These help increase equipment utilization, boost efficiency, and improve service performance.

Level of Efficiency. One of the most significant measures of railroad operating efficiency is the revenue "carry-through" ratio. This is the percent of operating revenues carried through to pretax net railway operating income. Union Pacific ranked fifth in 1972 in this key measure, with a percentage of 19.3 percent compared with the industry average of 5.9 percent. What is equally important is the fact that the company has been able to maintain a consistently superior carry-through ratio over an extended period. Its performance is outlined in Table 9.

TABLE 9

Revenue Carry-Through Ratios*

Year	Union Pacific	Railroad Industry	Western Roads
1973E	19.6%	—	—
1972	19.3	5.9%	9.3%
1971	18.3	6.3	7.2
1970	17.3	4.8	7.7
1969	15.8	6.6	8.0
1968	15.6	6.9	8.4
1967	16.5	7.2	8.1
1966	18.7	11.6	12.8
1965	16.9	11.0	11.6
1964	14.5	9.7	10.4
1963	17.2	10.1	11.5

* Percentage of railroad revenues retained as net operating income before federal income taxes.
E = Estimated.

The consistency of Union Pacific's superior efficiency rate is also reflected in its operating ratio, which equalled 73.7 percent in 1972. This was the third, successive, annual improvement and the best showing since 1966. Considering the industry's problem in obtaining timely freight rate increases during an intensely inflationary period, Union Pacific's operating performance has been outstanding. While some slippage in the operating ratio (to about 74.3 percent) was looked for last year due to further delays in receiving adequate rate relief, this does not dull the overall excellent showing of the system.

Table 10 traces Union Pacific's "railroad" operating results since 1961. It gives an overview of the company's record by highlighting the principal items that comprise the income account.

In appraising the above record, several background developments should be taken into account. First, the revenue trend is impressive with only one down year noted, namely 1967. Secondly, revenues were penalized through 1970 by the steady decline in passenger revenues from $26.7 million in 1961 to $9.8 million in 1970. This unprofitable service was finally terminated in mid-1971 when the quasi-public Amtrak operation took over.

The noticeable shift in the equipment rental account from a debit position to a credit balance in recent years reflects benefits from the impressive equipment acquisition program of recent years plus an improved per diem rental schedule. Other factors over the period covered included increased rentals for equipment leased to Pacific Fruit Express and the Chicago, Rock Island and Pacific, as well as reduced mileage payments for refrigeration cars. The particularly large gain in 1973 rental credits may be attributed to the sharp rise in grain loadings which kept more of UP's cars off line and comparison with a somewhat depressed period a year earlier. Tax accruals, excluding Federal income taxes, have reflected more liberalized fringe benefits. The particularly sharp rise estimated for 1973 is due to the industry's absorption of a larger share of railroad retirement taxes. However, an offset to this has been provided by legislation which, in effect, calls for the ICC to permit compensatory rate relief.

In appraising Union Pacific's railroad operating record, the most noteworthy factor has been the apparent breakthrough in the earnings potential of the carrier. Prior to 1970, the record could best be characterized as relatively stable with an upward bias. However, beginning with 1970 a distinct uptrend has developed. This may be attributed to a good degree by the more aggressive attitude of a revitalized management team following the establishment of a holding company in 1969. This stimulus came at a time when general economic conditions were favorable and benefits from sound practices of the past could be capitalized upon. Despite the inflationary pressures that have plagued the industry, Union Pacific has been able to hold expenses under good control and to take advantage of the prosperity in the areas served. Allowing for cyclical swings in the economy, there is good reason to believe that a superior rate of earnings growth will be maintained for the railroad in the future.

Summary of 1973 Results. With 1973 over and nine-month results released, the following observations may be made for the railroad. Revenues probably reached a new record of about $865 million, some 12 per-

TABLE 10

Union Pacific's Operating Results, 1961–1973E (000s omitted)

Year	Operating			Tax Accruals*	Equipment and Joint Facility Rentals	Net Railroad Operating Income
	Revenues	Expenses	Ratio			
1973E	$865,000	$643,000	74.3%	$64,000	$12,000†	$170,000
1972	769,623	567,162	73.7	54,994	1,236†	148,704
1971	691,571	516,610	74.7	52,759	4,310†	126,512
1970	669,617	502,572	75.1	53,082	2,234†	116,017
1969	630,407	477,072	75.7	49,390	4,391	99,554
1968	595,031	450,001	75.6	49,117	2,874	93,039
1967	574,020	428,966	74.7	45,654	4,842	94,558
1966	589,138	425,002	72.1	43,040	10,739	110,357
1965	549,190	403,683	73.5	40,683	12,180	92,644
1964	529,079	395,192	74.7	39,736	17,383	76,768
1963	519,104	372,131	71.7	36,780	20,981	89,212
1962	512,125	370,157	72.3	37,869	21,723	82,376
1961	499,324	360,799	72.3	36,480	20,732	81,313

* Before federal income taxes.
† Net Credit.

cent above the previous year's peak. The gain reflected a 10 percent gain in carloadings and a 15 percent increase in revenue ton miles. In line with the robust economy, all commodities moved at a high level. Particular strength was noted for manufactured products, wheat and feed grains, coal and soda ash.

Operating expenses rose at a somewhat faster rate than the gain in revenues, with an estimated increase of 13 percent. Consequently, the operating ratio is believed to have edged up to 74.3 percent from 73.7 percent in 1972. Management has cited the fact that "the 3 percent freight rate increase which became effective in mid-August was too little and too late to offset the cumulative effects on Union Pacific of rapidly climbing costs for labor, diesel fuel, track supplies, and other materials." From a constructive standpoint, the company accelerated its maintenance program to keep equipment and the roadway at optimum conditions. While higher payroll taxes also were restrictive, a substantial rise in equipment rental credits paved the way for the estimated 14 percent rise in net railway operating income in 1973.

Outlook for 1974. We look for further expansion in Union Pacific's railroad operating income this year, possibly in the order of 13 percent. Our assumptions are that real growth in the economy may approach only 1 percent in 1974, that capital spending will expand by some 10 percent and that agricultural production will remain at a high level. While fuel shortages may develop at times, we believe the railroad industry will not be seriously hampered.

Railroad revenues are initially projected at $950 million, up nearly 10 percent from the estimated $865 million of 1973. Other transportation revenues would boost the respective totals to $960 million and $877 million—as reported to stockholders. Of the 10 percent revenue gain, 2 percent would represent an expansion of revenue ton-miles, and the balance would be derived from freight rate increases. The relatively small projected advance in ton-miles is related to the less robust economic outlook, as well as to the prospect of substantial slippage in housing starts which will impact lumber traffic. On the other hand, domestic and international demand for basic agricultural products will provide an important prop, along with the flow of goods related to capital spending programs. Steel industry output is expected to remain at a high level. Bituminous coal volume will increase in importance, based on widening demand for the large reserves of the low-sulphur variety found in the West and benefits from the opening of new mines this year in Wyoming.

Of the 8 percent rise projected for freight rates this year, 4 percent already is assured based on previous ICC rulings. This includes the carryover benefits from the 3 percent boost effected in mid-August 1973, as well as the rate increases authorized to directly offset the rise in railroad retirement payments. It also now appears that the ICC will approve a 5 percent rise in rates March 1 recently requested by the industry. After holddowns on selected items, the overall increase would approximate 4 percent.

Union Pacific's operating expenses are expected to rise by about 8.5 percent this year, a somewhat lesser increase than the 10 percent gain projected for revenues. Wage costs advanced 4 percent on January 1, 1974, while another 1.5 percent will reflect carryover increases from 1973. Margins also will reflect the impact of the rapid rise in the cost of ties, wheels, steel, fuel, and other purchases that are expensed. Costs also will be inflated by higher contributions to the railroad retirement fund, though this will be offset by compensating rate relief.

One area of flexibility for Union Pacific this year is the maintenance account. With the property and equipment in excellent condition, less-than-expected traffic gains or shortfall in the rate category could be compensated in part by reduced maintenance outlays. This is not looked for currently, based on the overall railroad income picture for 1974. Equipment rental credits are expected to approximate the record level of 1973. Interest costs probably will rise by some $6 to $8 million, reflecting the recent $121 million bid for new oil leases off the Gulf coast of Florida.

Long-Term Potential of the Railroad. Factors that bear favorably upon the future growth of Union Pacific are: the ability, demonstrated in recent years, to break out of the relatively dull earnings pattern of the past; the more aggressive attitude of management toward the development of earnings power; and the nation's greater reliance on railroad transportation for long-haul traffic movements as a result of the energy situation. Union Pacific is well poised to benefit from this new development considering its strategic position in the West, its current long average haul, and its strong financial resources. Other traffic and earnings potential lies in the furtherance of run-through trains, new unit train movements of coal and grain, and further development of container freight volume between the Far East and East Coast cities of this country. Union Pacific provides service to more major West Coast ports than any other railroad.

Rock Island Situation. Over ten years ago, Union Pacific proposed a merger with the Chicago, Rock Island & Pacific Railroad. This merger application has been slowly grinding its way through the ICC. The consolidation would give Union Pacific its own line to Chicago from Omaha, as well as to extend its line from Kansas City to St. Louis. The plan also calls for Union Pacific to sell 3,500 miles of Rock Island trackage south and southwest of Kansas City to the Southern Pacific. Opposition to the consolidation proposal has come from several railroads.

After lengthy delays, an administrative law judge of the ICC released the third and final volume on the Rock Island proposal. While the judge recommended that the ICC approve the Union Pacific–Rock Island merger, he went far beyond the initial proposal. As a condition to the takeover, he recommended the restructuring of all western railroads into four major systems. Union Pacific, as well as most western roads, are opposed to the basic recommendations. A decision from the full ICC is now awaited. Therefore, it is still uncertain how the case will be resolved and how long a period of time will be required for resolution of the matter. In any event, the original merger exchange ratio agreed upon with Rock Island in 1965 will be renegotiated at the proper time.

Union Pacific has had a long-standing stock interest in Illinois Central Industries. Ownership consists of 2,149,000 shares, or 17 percent of the shares outstanding (or 11 percent after allowing for conversion of two Illinois Central preferred stocks). Union Pacific's stock interest has been placed in three voting trusts. Under the Rock Island merger proposal, Union Pacific will sell its interest in Illinois Central Industries by August 10, 1982.

Oil and Gas Operations

Background. Union Pacific's petroleum interests date back more than half a century. In 1904 it acquired property in California which was later to become the Wilmington oil field of Los Angeles and Long Beach. Oil was discovered there in 1936 and the field is still productive. Over the years net income before federal income taxes from non–Land Grant lands has totaled more than $600 million.

The scope of petroleum operations was expanded considerably in 1970 through the acquisition of Champlin Petroleum Company for $240 million in cash. At the time of this important acquisition, Champlin held 2.2 million acres under oil and gas leases, including more than 400,000 acres held by production and 1.8 million leasehold acres not under production. As a result of the purchase Union Pacific achieved full integration in the petroleum industry—from producing well to refinery to the gasoline pump.

In an effort to bolster crude oil supplies, Champlin has greatly expanded its principal areas of exploration which currently includes: the Gulf Coast of the United States, the Rocky Mountain area, Canada, Indonesia, the North Sea, Peru, and the Philippines. Particularly encouraging oil discoveries have already been made in the British sector of the North Sea and in Wyoming in which Champlin holds a major interest of 22.5 percent and 41.5 percent, respectively.

Champlin operates three domestic refineries, with a combined capacity of 137,000 barrels daily. The largest unit, located at Corpus Christi, Texas, has a rated capacity of 62,000 barrels daily. The Enid, Oklahoma refinery produces 45,000 barrels a day; the Wilmington, California refinery, 30,000 barrels daily.

Marketing operations are conducted in 18 states with major market positions held in Oklahoma, Nebraska, Kansas, Arkansas, Minnesota, North Dakota, and South Dakota. Motor gasoline sales in 1972 totaled approximately 300 million gallons, a 10.7 percent increase over 1971 volume. This placed Champlin in 29th place in relation to total national gasoline sales. Approximately two thirds of the company's product sales is distributed through wholesale channels, since virtually all output of the Corpus Christi and Wilmington refineries are marketed wholesale.

Exploration and Production

Domestic. In making the Champlin purchase, Union Pacific's management fully recognized that a major exploration effort would be necessary since many of Champlin's producing properties, as well as the railroad's own wells, were experiencing declining production rates. As a producer of approximately 50,000 barrels of crude oil daily and a refiner of approximately 137,000 barrels daily, Champlin had to purchase as much as 87,000 barrels per day of crude oil to fill the imbalanced requirement. Faced with this challenge management took the following steps: (a) exploration expenditures were increased sharply; (b) domestic drilling emphasis was shifted from numerous shallow and medium depth wells to selected deep and expensive wells in west Texas, onshore Louisiana, and offshore Louisiana; and (c) concessions in foreign areas with high political stability and favorable geology were aggressively sought.

Thus far, the results of those measures have proven highly successful and sizable petroleum reserves have been added. As of January 1972, net proven reserves of crude oil and condensate totaled 95 million barrels, natural gas liquids amounted to 20 million barrels, and natural gas aggregated 1.1 trillion cubic feet. These reserves estimates, however, do not include a major oil discovery in the North Sea and in Wyoming made subsequent to the reserve study.

Production of crude oil, natural gas liquids, and natural gas is derived from 13 states and Canada. Table 11 shows 1972 volumes and acreage.

TABLE 11

Production and Acreage by Geographic Area—1972

Location	Crude Oil and Natural Gas Liquids (barrels daily)	Natural Gas (mmcf/day)	Net Acres
California	19,600	2.0	12,335
Canada	3,400	10.0	350,760
Gulf Coast	8,600	172.0	128,690
Mid-Continent	12,400	94.7	343,440
Rocky Mountains	8,700	63.0	752,520
Total	52,700	341.7	1,587,745

Current production of both crude oil and natural gas has declined from the above levels due to further loss of reservoir pressures in producing fields. However, an accelerated water-flooding program in the Wilmington field of California and new production from other states is expected to reverse the decline by 1975 and possibly sooner. Champlin began a major water-flooding operation of the Wilmington field in 1972 and the full benefit of this secondary recovery program is expected in 1974, 1975, and probably 1976.

Wilmington Field Production
(barrels per day)

1971	22,940
1972	21,991
1973E	21,000
1974E	25,000
1975E	32,000

E = Estimated

It is readily apparent that the major production stimulus is expected in 1975 when output should increase by over 7,000 barrels daily. The rate of decline that will be experienced thereafter is expected to be slow, and it is possible that production could level out around the 28,000–30,000 barrels per day level for several years after 1976. Thus, the incremental volumes resulting from the waterflood will contribute to earnings at a time when larger foreign expenditures will be necessary in preparation of building sizable production from the North Sea in late 1976 and beyond.

In other domestic exploration developments, Champlin's discovery in October 1972 at the Brady unit in Sweetwater, Wyoming must be classified as quite significant. The Brady unit area comprises approximately 39,000 acres. Ownership in the Brady unit wells, and in approximately 13,700 acres of pooled lands surrounding the well sites, is shared 41.25 percent each by Champlin and Mountain Fuel Supply Company, and the remaining 17.5 percent is held by Amoco Production Company. The most important drilling results thus far involve the Weber formation in which several wells have been completed. Flow tests on small chokes ranged from 800 to 1,200 barrels per day with gas-oil ratios ranging from 3,500–4,700 cubic feet per barrel. The wells tested from intervals ranging from 420 feet to 486 feet of formation with net pay zones in the order of 300 feet. Industry sources estimate a productive area for the Weber of at least 3,000 acres and oil reserves in excess of 100 million barrels as reasonably proven. During the third quarter of 1973 two additional Nugget Formation oil wells and a Dakota Formation gas well were also completed. Further drilling will be required, however, to delineate the full extension of the Brady Unit. Obviously, estimates of possible production volumes at this stage could be wide of the mark in either direction. Taking into account the drilling successes and the probable magnitude of reserves found we have assumed that production will commence on a full year basis in 1975 at roughly 7,500 barrels daily, of which approximately 6,500 barrels daily will be working interest oil while the remaining 1,000 barrels daily will represent royalty oil. Since all of this output will qualify as "new" oil, the contribution to annual income should exceed $6 million.

In other areas of the Rocky Mountains, Union Pacific's farm out of acreage to Amoco Production Company has resulted in total production of approximately 1,600 barrels per day oil and 3.7 billion cubic feet of natural gas per day. This production is mostly from shallow depths and is characterized by rapid decline which is typical of Rocky Mountain pools. Deeper drilling could prove a notable exception, however.

As part of its changed drilling program Champlin, as part of a group, is presently developing a deep gas discovery in eight sections of West Texas. It is expected that drilling will be completed by mid-year 1974, and pipeline connections will be made in time to contribute fully to earnings in 1975.

Champlin's most ambitious domestic exploration stake by far was undertaken on December 20, 1973 when it acquired a 17 percent interest in nine tracts in the eastern Gulf of Mexico. Its partners in the bidding were Exxon Corporation and Mobil Oil Company. This group spent $700 million for these parcels. The highest bid of the sale was an astonishing $211.9 million which the Champlin group paid for Block 83. This group also made winning bids on the next four high tracts with bids of $126.8 million for Block 76, $91.8 million for Block 84, $81.8 million for Block 90, and $76.8 million for Block 77. The total overbid by the Champlin group on these tracts amounted to $294 million. It is generally believed that these parcels are situated on the Destin anticline just offshore from the Florida panhandle. The tracts are located in shallow water depths of approximately 120 feet and drilling objectives are in the 8,000–10,000 feet range. Exxon, as operator for the group, is expected to commence drilling within 60 days, and the first drilling results should be available four to five weeks thereafter. Considering the sums paid and the high quality of Champlin's partners, prospects of finding substantial reserves of hydrocarbons on this acreage must be considered quite high.

Foreign. Champlin's largest and most visible source of future oil earnings lies in the recently discovered Thistle Field in North Sea Block 211/18. Four consecutive successful exploratory wells have now been completed and the fourth tested at the rate of 5,200 barrels daily. Preliminary development plans for the field provide for the handling of up to 200,000 barrels daily. At the present time it is believed that production could commence toward the end of 1976, with the first full year of operation no sooner than 1977. These dates could prove somewhat optimistic since operations in these deep waters of 550 feet can be hampered by adverse weather conditions. In addition, the setting of permanent drilling platforms in these waters is no simple accomplishment. Meanwhile, exploratory drilling on the remainder of Block 211/18 will continue in 1974. Champlin's net interest in this tract is 22.5 percent.

Based on future production estimates of 200,000 barrels daily, Champlin's net interest will be equivalent to 45,000 barrels daily. Since the quality of this oil is relatively high, it could be exchanged at a favorable rate for domestic crude oil and, as such, could go a long way to closing the company's crude-oil deficiency. Projections as to future earnings contributions from this discovery are dependent on incalculable variables, not the least of which are changing tax rates, operating costs, and market prices. Taking these factors into consideration we believe that per barrel profits could approach the $1.25–$1.50 range and could thus contribute more than $20 million to earnings once full production is achieved.

In other foreign areas, Champlin has increased its interest in a production sharing contract offshore West Irian in Indonesia to 53.8 percent from its initial interest of 15 percent. Under the agreement Champlin will drill an initial exploratory well by March 1975 at a location to be determined.

In Peru, Champlin has become a partner in two groups; one, headed by Sun Oil Company and the other, by Union Oil Company of California. Seismic work has been completed on several tracts and four to five wells will be drilled in 1974, the first of which will be spudded this spring.

Last August, Champlin signed a service contract with the Philippine Petroleum Board for exploration covering 1.4 million acres in offshore Palawan, a large western island of the Philippine Republic. Champlin holds a 70 percent interest in the contract group and has commenced a geophysical program.

Earnings. Champlin Petroleum came through with an excellent earnings performance last year. Indications are that operating income probably expanded to $48–50 million. This was some 60 percent above the $29 million total of 1972. The upswing reflected price strength for refined products, crude oil, and gas. Refinery throughput was maintained at near capacity, though it probably was somewhat tight at times toward the end of the year.

Our initial forecast for 1974 calls for a relatively stable showing in terms of operating income. Benefits from the recent new discoveries will not be a factor this year. Meanwhile, the company faces the problem of keeping its refinery capacity in full usage in the light of current crude oil shortages. Also, the prices of purchased crude will be up sharply from 1973 levels. Thus, we are forecasting oil and gas operating income at approximately the same total as the $48–50 million of 1973. The longer-term picture is decidedly more encouraging, however, as new crude sources increase in importance.

Long-Term Potential. We have attempted to estimate in the following table a possible progression of earnings from oil sources for the 1973–1977 period. These estimates are predicated on certain assumptions which follow: (a) The response to the water-flooding operation in the Wilmington field will be as expected; (b) oil and gas reserves will be discovered on the recently acquired tracts in the eastern Gulf of Mexico sufficient to generate a reasonable rate of return on this sizable investment, with production to start in 1975; (c) there will be no unreasonable delays in developing North Sea oil reserves; and (d) there will be no material changes in existing tax rates or concession agreements.

Year	Projected Pretax Oil Income ($ million)
1972	$29*
1973	50
1974	50
1975	65
1976	70–80
1977	90–100

* Figure for 1972 is actual; figures for 1973–77 are estimated.

Thus, by 1977, we would expect oil earnings after taxes to equal approximately $3.50 per share and contribute an estimated 38 percent to 40 percent of total earnings, versus 30 percent in 1973. Our estimates of aggregate earnings are predicated on a 7 percent annual growth rate for the railroad. This would bring the railroad's contribution to 55 percent to 60 percent ($5.25 a share) of potential 1977 earnings of $8.50 a share. Allowance also has been made for somewhat higher income from land operations and higher interest expenses.

Rocky Mountain Fuel Energy Company.   Union Pacific formed a new subsidiary company, Rocky Mountain Energy Company, a few years ago to accelerate the development of the corporation's extensive coal holdings. Union Pacific is believed to rank second in the nation in coal reserves, with an estimated 10 billion tons. At least half has a sulphur content of less than 1 percent. The company's coal lands are located primarily in southern Wyoming along the main line of the railroad.

This is Land Grant acreage, with Union Pacific owning every other square mile in checkerboard fashion for 20 miles on both sides of the railroad across the 400-mile width of southern Wyoming. The coal is essentially "steam coal," with no substantial deposits of metallurgical coal. Perhaps as much as 95 percent or more of the coal eventually will have to be mined by underground methods. The balance of about 500 million tons is believed to be comprised of surface reserves. This, in itself, is a substantial total.

Based on the current energy situation, prospects have brightened considerably for the development of this nation's western coal reserves. Many problem areas must be resolved, however. These include environmental considerations, health and safety questions, and the commercial feasibility of developing these vastly untapped coal reserves.

Union Pacific does not realize a material amount from its coal interests today, either through production or royalty payments. A gradual expansion is likely, however, and this area could be quite meaningful beginning four or five years from now. Union Pacific's approach is to lease coal lands to other producers in return for royalty payments. This essentially applies to stripable coal which is only 5 percent of the company's total interest. When deep coal is developed, Union Pacific will have an equity interest.

Several new lease agreements have been signed within the past year or so. These include new leases by Rosebud Coal Sales Company and Arch Mineral Corporation, both of whom had been shipping coal over the railroad. A new joint venture was initiated with Arch Mineral and Rocky Mountain Energy, and they expect to be surface mining 3 million tons of coal annually by late 1974.

Union Pacific obviously stands to benefit in the years ahead both from an expansion of royalty payments and from the hauling of coal to Midwest power utilities. However, new research projects may well change the way in which coal income is realized. The company is participating in several coal gasification projects. In cooperation with Continental Oil Company and 12 other firms, Rocky Mountain Energy is participating in the world's first commercial scale demonstration of upgrading coal gas to the quality of natural gas by methanation. A year ago, Rocky Mountain Energy joined with FMC Corporation and four other companies in a venture to develop the technological potential of the FMC "Cogas" process for converting coal to pipeline-quality gas and synthetic crude oil. Union Pacific also has contributed land to the U.S. Department of the Interior for tests on the technology and economics of gasifying coal in place underground.

Union Pacific Mining Corporation. This is the third operating unit of Union Pacific's natural resource area. Its major income is derived from the development of the company's extensive reserves of trona (natural soda ash). Other minerals under development include uranium, nickel, and copper.

Trona. Union Pacific has the world's largest deposit of trona, the ore from which natural soda ash is obtained. These resources are being developed by Stauffer Chemical Company of Wyoming, in which Union Pacific has a 49 percent interest and by FMC Corporation and Allied Chemical Corporation. Each of these three companies lease the trona reserves from Union Pacific.

Demand for natural soda ash obtained from trona has been growing at about 12 percent a year. Soda ash is used in the manufacture of glass, soap and alkaline cleaners. The three companies cited above are increasing trona mining and expanding soda ash production facilities. Total production capacity of the three firms totaled 3.8 million tons per year at the end of 1972. Output is expected to double that rate in a few years. Trona royalty income before taxes amounted to some $3.8 million in 1972.

Uranium. The Mining Corporation has been conducting an extensive exploration program for uranium. Its partner is Mono Power, a subsidiary of Southern California Edison Company. Under the agreement, Mono Power provides the funds for the program, while Union Pacific is the operator. A recent update of this contract calls for an eight-year exploration venture, requiring the expenditure of up to $16 million. Mono will receive a 60 percent interest in any new discoveries in return for funding the program. As additional nuclear power plants are completed in the years ahead, the need for more uranium ore will grow proportionately.

Upland Industries Corporation. This operating subsidiary is responsible for the company's real estate acquisition and development activities. Under the original Land Grant Act, Union Pacific received 11.5 million acres of land in a checkerboard pattern between Omaha and Promontory Summit, Utah. Subsequent railroad acquisitions boosted the total to about 18.5 million acres. A balance of 900,000 acres is still owned in fee, primarily in Wyoming. Some of this land is used for commercial and industrial sites, though a major portion is primarily leased for grazing. Union Pacific also owns mineral rights on 7 million acres of land.

Sale and lease of this land is a prime responsibility of the land company. A major share of attention also is devoted to attracting industrial companies to the railroad. This would include the development of industrial parks. The land subsidiary also has been engaged in the sale of property for residential developments. From an overall corporate standpoint, net income of the land company in 1973 probably moderately exceeded the $3.7 million total of 1972. No significant change is looked for this year.

Financial Position. Union Pacific Corporation has a strong balance sheet. At the end of 1972, long-term debt amounted to $513 million, while stockholders' equity totaled $1.6 billion. The current ratio was 1.2 to 1. The financial position of the company was further strengthened during 1973. At the end of September, $100 million of commercial paper borrowings that were outstanding at the end of 1972 were paid off in full. Repayment of this short-term borrowing reflected the strong 1973 earnings performance and favorable cash flow picture. In view of this and other debt repayments, the balance sheet position of the company undoubtedly exceeded the particularly strong showing of 1972.

Based on the recent major successful bids of Champlin Petroleum in the Gulf of Mexico, the balance sheet picture was altered at the beginning of 1974. Champlin's share of the total bids amounted to $121 million. Union Pacific Corporation utilized its bank credit lines to cover the major outlays. It is apparent that the latest bid by Champlin is further evidence of the change from past policy.

Capital expenditures for 1974, which had been estimated at $250 million, will therefore be swelled by the latest $121 million exploration total. Of this year's budget, $175 million is for railroad capital outlays. In 1973, capital programs totaled about $170 million including $130 million for railroad equipment and plant.

Cash flow of Union Pacific Corporation approximated $275 million in 1973, up from $240 million a year earlier. These totals have permitted the company to internally finance a good part of capital requirements, as well as debt maturities and other corporate needs. Sale of equipment trust certificates were partially utilized in the rail equipment program. The next sizable debt obligation maturing is the $32 million 2⅞ percent debenture issue of 1976. Another $43 million comes due in that year via a maturing equipment trust obligation. It is too early to determine what, if any, form of debt financing may be ahead to cover this maturity and the recent more ambitious exploration program. In any event, these do not appear to be formidable undertakings.

Dividends had been at a $2 rate from 1965 through 1972. The quarterly rate was increased to $0.54 a share at mid-1973, the most allowed under previously set federal guidelines. With these rules liberalized subsequently, the company raised the quarterly rate to $0.60 a share beginning in the fall. Based on the comfortable finances of the company and the promising outlook, further liberalization may be expected in the years ahead.

TABLE 12

Union Pacific Corporation—Outline of Profits Picture (in millions)

	1972	1973E	Percent Change	1974E	Percent Change
Revenues and Sales:					
Transportation Revenue	$ 779	$ 877	12.5	$ 960	9.5
Sales	315	315	—	330	4.5
Total	$1,094	$1,192	9.0	$1,290	8.0
Operating Costs:					
Transportation Operating Expense	$ 635	$ 710	11.8	$ 770	8.5
Cost of Sales	286	265	− 7.3	280	5.5
Total	$ 921	$ 975	5.8	$1,050	7.5
Operating Income	$ 174	$ 217	25.0	$ 240	10.5
Other income—net	20	15		15	
Interest expense	34	31		38	
Income before federal income taxes	$ 160	$ 201	25.5	$ 217	8.0
Federal income taxes	$ 55	$ 74	37.0*	$ 82	38.0*
Net income	$ 105	$ 127	21.0	$ 135	6.2
Per share of common stock:					
Assuming no dilution	$4.62	$5.60		$6.00	
Assuming full dilution	4.44	5.30		5.65	

* Tax accrual rate.
E = Estimated.

26

Real Estate Investment Trusts

PETER A. SCHULKIN, Ph.D.
Director of Research
National Association of Real Estate Investment Trusts, Washington, D.C.

REAL ESTATE INVESTMENT TRUSTS (REITs) have grown rapidly during the past five years, and they now represent an important investment medium for the general public. As mutual funds invest in a diversified portfolio of corporate stocks and bonds, REITs invest in a diversified portfolio of real estate and mortgage investments.

The real estate investment trust industry today includes more than 208 different trusts, with total assets in excess of $20 billion. Their shares are owned by nearly one million people, and their activities extend to every corner of the nation. REITs have invested in or financed structures in virtually all major cities of the United States and many smaller communities as well.

Real estate investment trusts provide both large and small investors with a unique means of obtaining a share in a professionally managed portfolio of real estate properties and mortgages. Because the shares of almost all REITs are traded on the major stock exchanges or over the counter, they are a highly liquid real estate-oriented investment which can readily be purchased or sold in large or small amounts.

REITs are similar to mutual funds in that a REIT does not have to pay federal corporate income taxes on that income paid out to shareholders, providing that the REIT meets certain requirements, including one which states that REITs must distribute at least 90 percent of net income to shareholders.[1] In practice, REITs generally distribute 100 percent of their net income to shareholders.

---

[1] These requirements are spelled out in Sections 856–858 of the *Internal Revenue Code*. Among the requirements are that: (1) At the end of each quarter, 75 percent

691

HOW ARE REITs ORGANIZED?

Trustees

The investment decisions of a REIT are made by trustees who are elected by, and responsible to, the shareholders. The trustees are generally respected members of the real estate, business, professional, and academic communities.

Advisors

The trustees of most REITs contract with an invesment advisor to run the REIT's day-to-day operations and to present investment opportunities to the trustees for approval or rejection.

Many REIT investment advisors are mortgage banking companies or affiliates of financial institutions such as banks and life insurance companies. Other advisors are owned and operated by individuals with real estate backgrounds. In return for its services, the advisor is generally compensated with a basic fee, usually with some provision for limited incentive compensation if a specified earnings performance is exceeded.

Declaration of Trust

REITs are usually founded by the individuals or company which will serve as its investment advisor. The founders carefully compose a document called the "declaration of trust." Among other things, the declaration of trust specifies the investment objectives that are to guide the trustees and whatever restrictions on the trust's operations that are deemed prudent, such as limitations on the trust's debt/equity ratio.

Operating Capital

While most REITs have obtained their initial funds with a public offering of securities, a few have started with private placements. Once a REIT is operational, it normally obtains additional funds for investment through such means as bank borrowings and the sale of commercial paper (short-term debt). In addition, many REITs have had one or more additional public offerings of debt or equity securities to finance their growth, often employing various financing techniques to raise capital at lowest cost.

---

of the value of the REIT's total assets must consist of real estate (including mortgages), cash, cash items, and government securities; (2) at least 100 persons must own shares, and 5 or fewer persons cannot own more than 50 percent of the shares during the last half of any tax year; (3) at least 75 percent of the gross income of the REIT must be derived from rents, mortgage interest, and gains from the sale of real estate.

THE MARKET FOR REIT SHARES

REIT shares are traded on the major stock exchanges and over the counter in the same manner as those of corporations and closed-end funds. Consequently, the price of a REIT's shares is determined by supply and demand in the marketplace, and at any time it may be above or below the net asset value per share.

In March 1974, 54 REITs representing $13.6 billion in assets—approximately two thirds of the total REIT industry—were traded on the New York Stock Exchange, and 35 other REITs were traded on the American Stock Exchange. In all, more than 80 percent of the industry's assets were listed on these two exchanges.

Shareholder lists of REITs indicate that on an industrywide basis the majority of REIT shares are held in small amounts by individuals. Institutions such as pension funds, bank trust departments, and mutual funds also hold sizable amounts of REIT shares.

REGULATION OF REITs

The SEC and Stock Exchanges

While REITs are not formally regulated by a specific federal agency, they are indirectly regulated by a number of different government groups. For example, trusts are subject to the same Securities and Exchange Commission disclosure requirements that are imposed on corporations. And if a trust is listed on a stock exchange, it is also subject to the various disclosure requirements of the exchange. In addition, REIT shareholders, as well as corporate shareholders, are protected by the various securities laws such as the regulation and disclosure required of insider trading.

State Securities Commissioners

If a trust's shares are sold within only one state or if they are sold on an interstate basis, they must be approved for sale by the state securities commissioners of the states in which they are to be sold. These state securities commissioners have tended to play a very important role in the regulation of REITs, in contrast to the SEC's monitoring of disclosure practices. The state securities commissioners go beyond disclosure requirements and may refuse to allow securities to be sold in their states unless specific limitations are met in such areas as advisory fees and portfolio composition.

The Midwest Securities Commissioners Association, a group of state securities commissioners, has been particularly active in formulating policies which are applied by its members as guidelines in determining whether or not to permit the sale of a REIT's securities within their states. Such policies deal with, for example, permissible advisory fee charges and investment portfolio restrictions.

Frequent Public Offerings

Since the REITs cannot retain more than a very minor amount of earnings, they tend to have many more public offerings of debt and equity securities than do corporations. In doing so, they are subject repeatedly to the strong disclosure requirements of state and federal agencies, as well as the watchful eyes of the state securities commissioners.

Other Monitoring of REITs

In addition to the aforementioned securities-oriented regulators, a number of private institutions have an interest in monitoring or are paid to monitor the activities of REITs. These include commercial banks which extend lines of credit and term loans to REITs, accountants who are paid to audit REIT financial statements, and commercial paper-rating services, paid by most trusts which issue commercial paper to rate their paper.

Banks and the commercial paper-rating services receive and carefully study detailed financial reports from REITs. These reports are supplemented with direct contacts with the trusts. By decisions on whether or not to extend credit and what ratings, if any, to assign to REIT paper, these two groups have a moderating influence over REIT activities, generally and specifically. The influence by banks and commercial paper-rating services cannot be avoided by that part of the REIT industry which relies on short-term borrowings to finance investments in construction and development loans.

Accountants play a crucial role in the monitoring of REITs because they certify that the financial statements of the REITs which they audit are accurate and that the statements are presented in accordance with generally accepted accounting principles.

TYPES OF REAL ESTATE INVESTMENT TRUSTS

Within the scope of investment in real property and mortgages, investment objectives may vary widely from one REIT to another. Some REITs concentrate on one type of loan or investment, while others have broader portfolio objectives.

In the past, most REITs were relatively specialized, and it was useful to categorize them according to their investment objectives such as construction and development loan (C & D) trusts and property ownership (equity) trusts. Today, however, most REITs make use of their investment flexibilities to seek a variety of loans and investments.

REITs: HISTORY AND RECENT DEVELOPMENTS

Early History

The forerunners of today's REITs were the 19th century Massachusetts real estate trusts with transferable shares which were purchased by the general public, often by small investors. When prospective returns from local properties were relatively low, these trusts invested in properties outside of Massachusetts.

After the start of World War II, the corporate income tax rate soared, and the small number of existing trusts tried to obtain the same tax benefits that had been afforded mutual funds. Their efforts came to fruition in 1960 when Congress approved the necessary changes in the tax laws.

From 1961, when the new tax law became effective, through 1968, about $350 million of new REIT securities were sold to the public, bringing the total number of REITs to over 50. Most of these early REITs were relatively small in terms of asset size, and they specialized in investment in real property; only a few specialized in construction and development loans.

During the 1969–1970 tight-money period, the traditional real estate lenders such as savings and loans, banks, and life insurance companies were forced to greatly curtail their mortgage lending activities. REIT mortgage lending, on the other hand, grew rapidly during this period as stock market conditions permitted REITs to raise large amounts of funds through the sale of REIT equity securities. The formation of new trusts and the growth of existing ones pushed total REIT assets from $1 billion at the start of 1969 to about $5 billion by the end of 1970.

Recent Developments

During 1971 and 1972 the monetary situation eased considerably, but REIT assets continued their rapid growth, reaching about $13 billion at the end of 1972. Among the factors responsible for the strong growth of REIT holdings of mortgages during these two years are:

1. Many REITs were actively making types of loans and investments not sought after by most traditional real estate lenders;
2. Strong growth in new construction activity enabled all real estate lenders to show increases in outstanding loans and investments.

REIT ownership of properties has also been increasing. Since 1971 a number of new REITs were formed to make such investments, and many existing mortgage REITs have used their investment flexibility to acquire ownership interests in properties. Existing trusts which specialized in property ownership have continued to add to their holdings.

During 1973 the monetary climate changed to a much tighter one, with the prime rate moving as high as 10 percent. REIT assets continued to grow, reaching more than $20 billion by year-end 1973, as REITs remained competitive lenders in the short-term mortgage markets.

TYPES OF INVESTMENTS UNDERTAKEN BY REITs

The Internal Revenue Code requirements that must be met by organizations wishing to qualify as REITs are such that REIT investments and income must be confined predominantly to property ownership and mortgage holdings. The property ownership of REITs generally represents the ownership of income-producing buildings and the land on which the structures are situated. REITs own very little unimproved land.

The mortgage investments of REITs are predominantly (92 percent) first-mortgage investments, although they need not be so. The types of mortgages vary widely in maturity and purpose. See the aggregate REIT balance sheet at the end of this section for the dollar magnitude of the different types of mortgages.

The pie graph in Figure 1 points up the fact that today REITs as a group have most of their funds invested in mortgage loans, with prop-

FIGURE 1

Percentage Breakdown of REIT Investments in Properties and Mortgage Loans (third quarter, 1973)

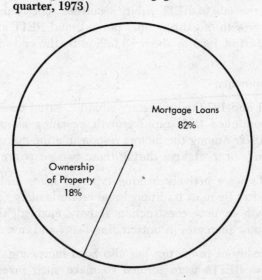

Mortgage Loans
82%

Ownership
of Property
18%

Source: National Association of Real Estate Investment Trusts.

erty ownership accounting for only 18 percent of all REIT assets. This is a result of the strong movement of trusts into construction and development mortgages since 1969. Prior to 1969, property ownership was the dominant type of REIT investment.

A BRIEF OVERVIEW OF REIT MORTGAGE LENDING

The various types of REIT mortgage loans can be categorized into the five groups which follow. This categorization does not take account of the fact that there exists a limited amount of mortgage lending which is not adequately described by the particular grouping to which it is assigned.

FIGURE 2

Percentage Breakdowns of Mortgage Loans (third quarter, 1973)

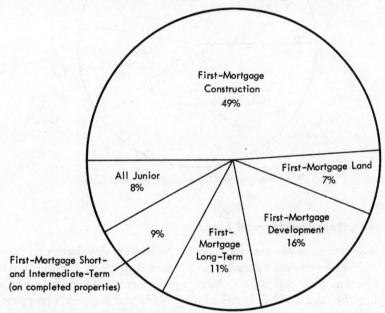

Source: National Association of Real Estate Investment Trusts.

First-Mortgage Construction Loans

Construction loans represent the largest single category of REIT mortgage loans, approximately 49 percent of the total. Construction loans are short-term mortgage loans obtained by real estate developers to finance the construction phase of their projects. This phase may last from less than a year to three years or longer. When the construction is completed, the construction loan is generally paid off with the proceeds of the long-term mortgage. The average construction loan has a maturity of about one to one and a half years.

REIT construction loans are concentrated in the residential area, primarily financing the construction of apartment buildings and condominiums. Office buildings and shopping centers are the next most common types of construction financed by REITs.

FIGURE 3

REIT Construction Loans by Type of Construction (third quarter, 1973)

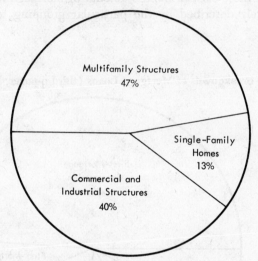

Source: Department of Housing and Urban Development.

First-Mortgage Development Loans

Development loans are obtained by real estate developers to finance the site improvements necessary to prepare a property for the building construction that will follow. Site improvements include clearing and leveling the land and the installation of roads and utilities. The property under development is the primary collateral for this type of mortgage loan. A REIT usually makes a development loan on a project for which it will also make the construction loan.

First-Mortgage Long-Term Mortgage Loans

REIT long-term mortgages are generally conventional mortgages with maturities of 20 to 30 years. Almost all long-term mortgage loans made by REITs are on apartment or commercial properties.

REITs were not active in making long-term mortgage loan commitments during 1973 because the rates on long-term mortgages were low relative to the cost of funds of REITs.

First-Mortgage Short- and Intermediate-Term Mortgages on Completed Properties

The short- and intermediate-term mortgages on completed properties are usually regarded as having a maturity of less than ten years. Developers generally use this type of financing to provide the time required to build up a successful operating history for a project. The developer hopes that once his project is a proven success, he will be able to obtain significantly better long-term mortgage financing than he could obtain at an earlier time.

Some developers seek intermediate-term financing at times when long-term rates are historically high, in the hope of obtaining less costly long-term financing at a later date.

Junior Mortgages (second mortgages)

REITs as a group hold very limited amounts of junior mortgages, although a few REITs specialize in this type of lending. These mortgages take several forms including wrap-around mortgages which usually arise in connection with the refinancing of an existing structure.

All of the circumstances must be known before the relative risk of a second-mortgage position can be assessed. The true risk position of a junior mortgagee depends upon such factors as the loan-to-value ratio, the financial strength of the borrower, and the economic soundness of the mortgaged property. A carefully underwritten second mortgage can be a relatively secure investment.

From another perspective, it might be noted that a property's equity investor has an interest in the property which is junior to that of a junior-lien holder. In fact, a junior-mortgage position is on occasion referred to as a "preferred equity" interest.

Specialized Mortgage Lending

There is a small amount of mortgage lending which is included in the above categories for classification purposes but which is atypical in purpose or design. For example, on occasion, mortgages are convertible into an ownership interest in the mortgaged property.

AN OVERVIEW OF REIT OWNERSHIP OF PROPERTY

Investments in Improved Properties

About 18 percent of total REIT assets are invested in real estate ownership positions. Many different types of properties are owned by REITs, but apartment buildings, shopping centers, and office buildings dominate the list. Less common are such properties as warehouses, hotels, and motels.

In addition to providing a REIT with current rental income, the ownership of properties may benefit REIT shareholders in other ways: Appreciation of property values and increase in rental income are two of the possibilities. Also, when a property is mortgaged, a REIT gradually builds up its equity in the property as the mortgage is paid down.

REITs have their largest amount of equity investments in apartment buildings, more than one-half billion dollars at current book value. Shopping centers and office buildings represent the next two largest categories of REIT equity investments, at $410 million and $333 million of book value respectively. Total REIT equity investments of all types amount to more than $2 billion, not counting $500 million of land purchase-lease-backs.

REITs may acquire their improved properties in any of several ways. They may buy existing improved properties for their portfolios,[2] they may hire a contractor to construct improvements on land which they own, or they may invest in a joint venture with a developer who will construct the improvements. REITs may also acquire improved properties by foreclosing on a mortgage or by receiving a deed in lieu of foreclosure. And REITs may become the owner of improvements on properties when a land tenant of the trust defaults on the terms of his land lease.

In keeping with the mutual fund intent that Congress had for REITs, the Internal Revenue Code does not permit trusts to hold property for sale as part of their operations. Consequently, REITs cannot, for example, improve properties and sell them shortly after completion as a real estate developer might. Trusts must retain properties in their investment portfolios for a reasonable amount of time before selling them (if, in fact, they are sold) for prudent portfolio reasons.

In order to maximize the return to their shareholders, REITs, like other real estate investors, usually mortgage the improved properties which they own. When REITs mortgage their properties, the terms of the mortgage may indicate that the mortgagee can look only to the particular property which is mortgaged as his security, or the terms may indicate that the credit of the trust stands behind the mortgage in addition to the mortgaged property.

REITs depreciate their buildings according to generally accepted accounting practices to reflect a gradual loss of a building's value over its anticipated economic lifetime. The money allocated to depreciation can be paid out to shareholders as a nontaxable return of capital or retained by the REIT for the improvement of the depreciated properties or for investment in new properties.

---

[2] Properties may be purchased with cash or, in some instances, with trust shares on tax-free exchange basis.

Investments in Improved Land

As mentioned earlier, REITs hold very small amounts of unimproved land. However, sometimes REITs own the land under buildings which they do not own (improved land), and they lease this land to the owners of the buildings. This type of property ownership is usually known as a land purchase-leaseback. While many REITs have one or more land purchase-leaseback investments, only a few REITs specialize in this type of investment.

Land purchase-leaseback investments usually arise when a REIT purchases the land for (or from) a real estate developer and leases it back to him on a long-term lease. The developer prefers to lease the land rather than own it, in order to reduce his cash investment in the project, while still retaining ownership of the improvements. The improvements on the leased land may be structures such as apartment buildings and shopping centers.

Normally the trust making a land purchase-leaseback subordinates its position to that of the first-mortgage holder. If the trust did not subordinate, the owner of the improvements would lose the advantage of the extra leverage possibilities offered by the land purchase-leaseback transaction because the owner would not be able to obtain as good a first-mortgage loan. In return for subordinating its position, the trust usually obtains a rental participation in the gross receipts of the property (or a participation in the gross receipts above some specified minimum base amount) in addition to a fixed return on its investment.

SOME GUIDELINES FOR THE FINANCIAL ANALYSIS OF REITS

Today most REITs have investments which are very diverse—different types of mortgage and property ownership investments all contained in one portfolio. For simplicity, the discussion which follows will be confined to two types of REIT investments: (1) construction and development lending and (2) equity investments (property ownership investments).

Construction and Development Loan (C & D) Lending

Management. Management is crucial in all phases of C & D loan operations—loan underwriting, loan administration, and the workout of problem loans. In addition, due to the use of leverage to increase potential profitability, liability management is also important to the success of a C & D lending operation.

A standard method for assessing management calls for a review of the track record of the trust, which may include its performance in the handling of problem situations. This method is of value even in the case of trusts with relatively short operating histories because the average C & D loan matures in 18 months. After three years, most C & D portfolios will have probably turned over completely. The review of the track record is, of course, usually supplemented with management interviews.

The C & D Mortgage Portfolio. When a REIT is only making a construction loan on a project, it normally has no interest in the project once it is completed and its construction loan is paid off. Consequently, a review of the long-run prospects of the individual projects financed by construction loans is of limited value to C & D REIT analysts. However, the *current* economic viability of a project being financed by construction loan is of interest because the collateral value of the project is, of course, dependent upon its current economic value and not upon replacement cost.

To help assess the risk in a C & D portfolio, an analyst will probably want to examine it for diversification. Among the different aspects of diversification are the size of the largest loans relative to the portfolio, the concentration of loans to any one borrower, diversity in type of construction financed, and geographic diversity.

Industry Background Analysis. The analysis and projection of money market rates is often relevant in predicting the profitability of C & D lending. To apply this analysis to a REIT, the methods and costs of the REIT's borrowings would have to be known, as well as the way the REIT has structured its interest rate charges on construction and development loans.

A review and projection of developments in the residential and commercial construction areas also provide a good background for assessing the prospects of individual trusts. Since most large trusts operate over many states, if not nationally, a regional analysis is usually not as pertinent here as a national analysis.

C & D Accounting. In the accounting area, an analysis of loan loss reserves is a difficult one for REITs with C & D loans. There are basically two possible components of these loss reserves: (1) that part associated with some actuarially based anticipation of losses as a normal part of doing business and (2) that part (if any) associated with a particular project (or projects) in difficulty.

Part of the problem in determining the adequacy of REIT loss reserves arises from the fact that since the REIT industry as a whole has a limited operating history, it is not clear what constitutes an actuarially sound loss reserve (Type 1 above). Another difficulty lies in the fact that if a trust has a specific problem situation (or situations) which requires a special addition to the loss reserves (Type 2 above), it is not easy to determine what constitutes an adequate reserve for this purpose until the problem is completely resolved.

Of course, the investment policies of a REIT might lead it to justify a higher or lower Type 1 reserve than the average. Thus, for example, the more conservative the investment policy relative to the average, the lower might be the Type 1 loss reserve.

Equity Investments

The Properties in the Portfolio. Since REIT holdings of improved properties are for long-term investment, the analysis of the long-run prospects of a REIT's major property holdings is an important consideration for analysts. For example, if a trust has a major investment in a shopping center in Cleveland, one might consider the attractiveness of the particular location in Cleveland, both currently and for the future (is the area in which it is located changing character, etc.); and one might consider what the prospects are for shopping centers generally.

Management. Management plays an important role in property investments, both for its ability to assemble a desirable portfolio of properties and for its ability to manage the properties owned. Here the performance of management must be judged over a long-run period since investments in improved properties are normally made with long-run objectives in mind.

Real Estate Accounting. There are two related areas of real estate equity accounting, one from the balance sheet and one from the income statement, which pose problems to analysts of REITs (and analysts of real estate companies generally). They are the problems of asset valuation and cash flow accounting.

Accounting principles dictate that properties on the balance sheet

FIGURE 4

REIT Industry Balance Sheet
Third Quarter, 1973

Assets (billions of dollars):		Liabilities (billions of dollars):	
First mortgages:		Commercial paper	$ 3.92
Land loans	$ 1.07	Bank term loans in use	1.51
Development loans	2.26	Bank lines in use	4.36
Construction loans	7.02	Other nonconvertible debt	1.05
Completed properties:		Convertible debt	0.72
0–5 years	1.17	Mortgages on owned property	1.44
5–10 years	0.19	Other liabilities	0.35
10+ years	1.55		$13.35
Junior mortgages:			
Land, devel. and const.	0.30		
Completed properties	0.81		
Land leasebacks	0.51		
Improved property owned	2.67		
Cash and other assets	1.60	Shareholders' equity	5.80
	$19.15		$19.15

Source: National Association of Real Estate Investment Trusts.

cannot be written up in value until they are sold. In addition, accounting principles require that properties on the balance sheet be depreciated over some estimated useful economic life. Consequently, the REIT balance sheet may show properties owned at amounts which are substantially below the current appraised values of the properties.

The problems of cash flow accounting are related in that the crux of the matter revolves on to what extent the accounting depreciation represents true economic depreciation. If the analyst looks only at net income after depreciation, he may undervalue the income of the REIT if the properties are actually appreciating or if the economic depreciation is less than the accounting depreciation.

These two accounting problems are thorny ones with no simple answers. Analysts of REIT stocks should, however, be prepared to grapple with them if they are examining REITs with investments in improved properties.

27

Retail Trade

JEROME H. BUFF, C.F.A.
First Vice President
Smith, Barney & Co. Incorporated,
New York, New York

STRUCTURE AND SCOPE OF THE RETAIL TRADE INDUSTRY

Basic Characteristics of Retailing

RETAILERS, as middlemen, have characteristics significantly different from manufacturers. Although retailers do operate from fixed facilities, they essentially perform a service function. Retailers do not change the form of the goods they handle. They buy from manufacturers, add time and place utility, assume an ownership risk, and sell to consumers. Their "fee" for this service is their gross margin, the difference between their cost and selling price. This gross margin must cover the expenses of providing the service, including labor and occupancy costs, and produce a profit.

Retailing is a very dynamic business. There are few protected positions. The "consumer franchise" of a retailer must be earned constantly. Locations can become obsolete or outflanked. Most goods are readily available to competitors. Thus, the capability of the management of these fluctuating elements becomes of utmost importance.

Management challenges are many in retailing. *People* are very important. Often the customer's only contact with the store is the retail clerk who has the power to make or break the sale. People at a great number of locations must be motivated and measured.

From the customer's point of view, retailing is a local business.

Through a series of systems and procedures, management often must control the operation of a great number of these separate units, constantly receiving and sending information and merchandise. Coordinating the centralized, risk-taking buying function with the decentralized, selling function is a complex and subtle task.

While formulation of business strategies and implementation of new concepts are important management tasks, at least equally important is the management ability to *execute* strategies and concepts. This involves great attention to detail at the local level. Success in retailing has been described, simply, as having the right goods in the right place at the right time.

Because of their local orientation and the need for a constant management presence, many retailers remained family businesses long after other industries had made the transition to professional management. While some retailers have long histories of professional management, others are in the midst of transition. Professional staff support in such areas as long-range planning, consumer research, real estate strategy, and computer technology is of growing importance in retailing.

The Retail Market

The Battle for Market Share. Retail sales are very large relative to the economy. In 1972, total United States retail sales of $448 billion amounted to 39 percent of the gross national product. Historically, because of an increasing percent of the consumer dollar spent for services, retail sales have grown at a slightly lower rate than the economy as a whole. For example, between 1965 and 1972 the gross national product increased at an average annual rate of 7.8 percent a year; personal consumption expenditures, at 7.7 percent; and total retail sales, at 6.7 percent.

The most significant fact about the total retail market, however, is not its growth rate but its *very large size.* Within this market certain components can grow faster than others, as is shown by the data on personal consumption expenditures in Table 1. Within these large segments there are considerable crosscurrents of faster and slower growth rates of individual retail firms.

From this discussion a key principle of retail analysis emerges. *Retailing is a constant battle for market share.* For any given retail firm, growth in excess of the economy usually involves increasing its share of the retail market. Thus, analysis of the structure and strength of competition in the firm's particular product and geographical market segments is of the greatest importance.

The Changing United States Consumer. Much has been written in recent years to document that consumers in the United States are becoming more wealthy and better educated. Also, the consumer continues

TABLE 1

Data on United States Personal Consumption Expenditures

	1972 ($ billion)	1965–72 Average Annual Increase (by percent)
Gross national product.	1,155	7.8
Personal consumption expenditures:		
Services.	309	8.4
Goods		
Food and beverages.	145	5.7
Gasoline and oil.	25	7.6
Autos and parts.	53	8.3
General merchandise*.	194	8.0
Total goods.	417	7.1
Total personal consumption expenditures.	726	7.7

* Author's term for goods other than the first three categories.

to have a youth orientation. There are several implications for retailers in this "smarter, richer, younger" population. With a higher living standard, consumers have *upgraded* their purchases somewhat. They have shown *greater fashion consciousness* in a wider range of goods, including goods for the home as well as clothing. With greater education and income, more customers can take the longer view of gaining better value by paying somewhat more and have placed more emphasis on *quality*. Young-thinking and well-educated consumers have the self-confidence and openness to try new retail formats. Thus there is *less consumer loyalty*, and "consumer franchises" must be constantly earned.

The consumer market has its crosscurrents, however. The consumer is faced with an ever-expanding array of new wants, from expensive audio equipment to winter tennis club memberships. A self-confident and well-educated consumer is willing ruthlessly to "unbundle" service from goods on items regarded as basic and undifferentiated in order to gain a lower price on these items and, thus, free spending for new wants. As a consequence, there is a wide receptivity to good value at all levels of income today. Currently, factors acting to reinforce this tendency are higher prices for basic food and energy requirements.

Segments of Retailing

Classification of Retailers. The field of retailing is wide and diverse. The analyst should avoid easy generalizations. Often analysts divide retailing into separate segments such as department stores, drug stores, discount stores, grocery stores, etc. While classification and cross-classification is an essential part of analysis, its limitations must be recognized as well. First, many segments of retailing compete with each other. Second, there are wide variations within individual segments.

There are two ways to gain greater perspective on the different retail segments and the firms comprising them: first, by an understanding of the mix of quality, service, and fashion that they offer; and second, by the characteristics of retail facilities in each segment.

Retailers can be classified by the level of *quality, service, and fashion* they offer. In a competitive market, price should vary with the mix of these elements and so is not regarded as a separate classification factor. *Quality* refers to the materials and workmanship of the goods handled. *Service* includes personal help with selection, breadth and depth of assortments, delivery, and the general ambience of store facilities. *Fashion* reflects "newness," responsiveness to changes in tastes, and uniqueness.

Although these three elements are found in varying combinations among retailers, they *tend* to vary together. Thus for purposes of classification, the analyst should think in terms of a continuous spectrum of quality-service-fashion, representing a range from maximum to minimum elements of these factors. It should be emphasized that this method of classification describes stores, not customers. One of the most important characteristics of today's consumer is his ability to move up and down the quality-service-fashion spectrum for various distinct needs and wants.

A second way of classifying retailers is provided by their *facilities.* We may classify retail facilities as either *shopping* or *convenience* in nature. Shopping facilities are those in which the customer wishes to take the time to compare offerings of goods. Convenience facilities tend to offer more standardized goods in easily accessible locations. Naturally all types of retailers do not fit easily into these two categories, since most offer some elements of both. Nevertheless they can be classified as to the major thrust of their business. Shopping facilities include traditional department stores, national general merchandise chains, and certain specialty stores such as those dealing in apparel, jewelry and gifts, furniture, and appliances. Convenience facilities include drug, variety, and grocery stores. Discounters appear to bridge the two categories. The relatively new catalog-showroom format combines certain elements of both the discounter and the specialty store.

The *location* of retail facilities has undergone a radical change in the past two decades. The wave of population movement to the suburbs of metropolitan areas created the basis of dynamism in retail locations. Further facilitating such change have been the new highways around most metropolitan areas. Thus, the focus of retailing has moved from downtown and neighborhood facilities towards stores along highways and in suburban shopping centers. Shopping centers span a wide spectrum from small neighborhood convenience centers with well under 100,000 square feet of retail space to superregional centers of over 1 million square feet of retail space. Many of these superregional centers have assumed the aspects of "new downtowns," with apartments and business office buildings locating near them. The pre–World War II "downtown" is regarded by some retail observers as one of many major shopping centers in a region.

The major department stores in a region have opened branches in the larger shopping centers, and some have pushed beyond the confines of their immediate regions to "invade" new areas, with locations in new superregional centers. The national general merchandise chains also have been active in expansion in major shopping centers, as have specialty stores with a shopping goods orientation. Although some convenience goods stores are found in the larger centers, they have tended to locate in smaller centers to be closer to customers. Discounters often have opened on a freestanding basis, together with grocery supermarkets, to create their own "convenience centers." Catalog showrooms have tended to open on a freestanding basis to date.

The most significant analytical fact about retail locations is that the "board" upon which the "game" of retail strategy is played has become much larger and more complex. There are many avenues to success, and the analyst should avoid "formula approaches" to analysis of locations, keeping constantly in mind the diversity and great size of the retail market.

Comments on Selected Segments of Retailing. Having discussed the quality-service-fashion mix of retailers and the dynamics of retail facilities over the last two decades, we can turn to a brief discussion of some of the separate retail segments.

Traditional Department Stores. The particular merchandise emphasis of the traditional department store is in apparel and home lines such as furniture, home furnishings, linens, and domestics. In the past two decades, many successful department stores have moved up the quality-service-fashion spectrum. In terms of location strategy, many department store organizations have opened suburban branches in large shopping centers and have moved from a single-store orientation to that of a regional chain.

The department store faces competition from the national general merchandise chains, from specialty stores, and from discount stores. The national general merchandise chains have upgraded to the middle of the quality-service-fashion spectrum; a number of specialty chains have been successful emphasizing deep inventories and depth knowledge in one product area; and some discounters have been efficient competitors in the lower end of the quality-service-fashion spectrum.

Successful department stores have moved up the quality-fashion-service spectrum and either function as "headquarters stores" for their regions in goods which they emphasize, or have built special upgraded quality-service-fashion niches. While such organizations continue to do well, department stores with a third or fourth position in their areas, or with a heavy merchandising overlap with national general merchandise chains or discounters, have done poorly. Thus, in studying a department store company, it is significant that the analyst carefully study the type of stores the company operates in each community, rather than relying on a generalization about all department stores.

Large corporations operating traditional department stores include: Allied Stores Corp.; Associated Dry Goods Corp.; Carter Hawley Hale Stores, Inc., Dayton-Hudson Corp.; Federated Department Stores, Inc.; R. H. Macy & Co., Inc.; Marshall Field & Co.; and May Department Stores, Co. Department stores, as defined by the United States Department of Commerce, accounted for $46.6 billion in sales in 1972. This definition includes, however, many stores operated by national general merchandise chains and by discounters. As another reference point, volume of the eight department store companies noted above totaled $10.6 billion in 1972. Some of these corporations operate other types of retailers as well as groups of department stores operating in various regions. In studying these companies, the analyst should attempt to assess the relative competitive strength of each department store group in its particular region.

National General Merchandise Chains. Included in this category are three companies: Sears, Roebuck Co., J. C. Penney Co., and the Montgomery Ward segment of Marcor, Inc. Together they accounted for $19 billion of sales in 1972, representing a substantial and dynamic section of general merchandise retailing. Although the three companies have catalog operations and some smaller stores not classified as department stores, their major expansion thrust in recent years has been in large, full-line department stores. As mass merchandisers, the range of goods in their large stores is wider than that of traditional department stores and includes such items as auto accessories, hardware, paint, garden items, major appliances, and sporting goods. Although fashion emphasis has increased over the years, apparel emphasis could be said to be on more staple items than the traditional department store. These organizations operate with buying centralized and the selling function organized on a regional basis. Organizational structure and systems are important factors in their performance.

With the growing affluence of the mass market, these companies have moved up to the middle of the quality-service-fashion spectrum over the past two decades. These firms have followed a national expansion strategy, as opposed to the regional expansion of department store groups. An important aspect of expansion in recent years has been the opening of large stores in large superregional shopping centers, often with another national general merchandise chain and one or more traditional department stores.

A distinctive aspect of these national general merchandise chains is specification buying where a high percentage of goods handled is made to the companies' own specifications and sold under their own brands. In effect, these companies have created distribution systems serving the broad, middle ground of the United States market.

Specialty Stores. Specialty store organizations concentrate merchandising and management talent on one type of goods, and usually one particular mix of quality, service, and fashion. Specialty stores have long been on the retail scene and operate in all segments of the quality-service-fashion spectrum. Long-established types of specialty stores, together with 1972 sales when available, include women's clothing ($8.4 billion); men's clothing ($5.2 billion); shoes ($3.8 billion); jewelry, paint, hardware ($4.1 billion); furniture ($11.0 billion); and appliances ($6.2 billion). Most of these are shopping goods stores rather than convenience goods stores. Locations vary with the type of business, from downtown, to roadside, to superregional shopping center. Many of these stores tend to operate as multiple-unit chains of stores, and systems and controls are important.

The great population movement to the suburbs of metropolitan areas has provided new location opportunities for specialty stores. The large, superregional centers, representing, in effect, new downtowns, have provided particularly favorable location opportunities for a number of specialty chains. As discussed in a previous section, consumer demand for breadth and depth of stock, and product knowledge in specific goods has risen over the years. Traditional types of specialty stores have evolved in different directions to meet changing consumer demands for quality and service, on the one hand, and efficiency and low price, on the other. New types of specialty chains also have grown in the last decade, including furniture and appliance warehouses, stores specializing in "do-it-yourself" building materials and hardware, and consumer electronics stores.

Discounters. The advent of the discounters in the late 1950s dramatically enlarged the scale of convenience retailing and added lines of merchandise formerly associated primarily with shopping facilities. Important lines relative to other retailers are appliances, apparel staples, hardware, paint, garden items, auto accessories, sporting goods, toys, cameras, drugs, toiletries, books, and housewares. Including food, discount store sales increased from $2 billion in 1960 to $29 billion in 1972, according to *The Discount Merchandiser.* Of the $29 billion in 1972, general merchandise accounted for $22.3 billion and food, $6.7 billion.

The discounters brought a large-scale, self-service, price-promotional approach to the lower end of the quality-service-fashion spectrum. They were quick to fill gaps in retail space in rapidly growing suburban locations. They located in large facilities with large parking lots easily accessible by auto and were pioneers in evening hours and Sunday openings. They tended to open either in free-stand locations, together with an owned or leased food supermarket, or in small centers containing a supermarket and other convenience stores. Although the opening of clusters of stores in metropolitan markets was an important thrust of discounters in the 1960s, discounters have been active in smaller markets as well.

Discounters initially drew sales from lower-end, specialty apparel stores; from undifferentiated, middle-of-the-road department stores; from hardware, drug, and variety stores; and from a host of other small specialty retailers. Those discounters that had food supermarkets followed a promotional approach that further intensified competition in food retailing. In recent years, the discount business itself has become intensely competitive: (1) as many entered the discount business, (2) as the stronger conventional merchants adopted some new techniques and "counterattacked," and (3) as new price-oriented specialty stores have expanded.

The leader in the discount industry has been the S. S. Kresge Company. At the end of 1972 it operated 580 K-Mart discount stores, and its K-Mart division accounted for $3.3 billion of general merchandise sales in 1972.

Catalog Showrooms. At this writing a relatively new retail format is the catalog showroom. This new format fits between the specialty store and the discounter in the retail spectrum. Companies operating these showrooms send out major catalogs once a year to potential customers, supplemented by periodic fliers and perhaps a smaller catalog. Their appeal is price, convenience, and depth of stock. Over 90 percent of sales are usually made at the showroom rather than by mail. The customers preselect by catalog and pick up their purchases at the showroom. Newer showrooms are usually freestanding with adequate parking.

In 1972 total catalog-showroom volume in the United States was $1.8 billion, according to the National Association of Catalog Showroom Merchandisers. Principle merchandise lines include jewelry and silverware, housewares (including small appliances and gift items), cameras, consumer electronics, sporting goods, toys, and luggage. They compete directly with discounters and with retailers handling the above types of goods.

As these operations develop into chains covering wide geographic areas, a key factor in their success will be the development of management, systems, and controls.

Variety Stores. The traditional appeal of the variety store has been in notions, toys, hardware, and housewares available on a convenience basis, although an important business also is done in apparel staples. Generally these stores adopt a quality-service-fashion approach towards the lower end of the spectrum. In recent years, traditional convenience items of variety stores have come under intense attack by discounters, drugstores, and nonfood sections of grocery supermarkets. Many variety

chains have attempted to evolve into junior department stores or discounters. Variety store volume was $7.5 billion in 1972, according to
the United States Department of Commerce.

Drugstores. The analyst should be aware that the drugstore category
covers a wide range of retailing approaches. The basic "reason for being" of a drugstore revolves around dispensing of prescriptions by a
pharmacist, supplemented by sale of packaged medicines, cosmetics, and
toiletries. According to *Chain Store Age,* these four categories accounted
for 58 percent of chain drugstore sales in 1972. Other important merchandise lines can include tobacco, candy, stationery, and photography
items. Drugstore formats can range from small prescription specialists,
to bantam units stressing price-promoted health and beauty aids, to
traditional stores handling the items mentioned above, to super drugstores handling wider lines of general merchandise. A basic appeal is
convenience. Merchandising can vary across the range of the quality-
service spectrum.

A significant change in the drugstore business over the past decade has
been the increased market share of the drug chains. Chains of 11 or
more stores accounted for 36 percent of the $14.5 billion sales of drug
and proprietary stores in 1972, up from a 21 percent share in 1962.

Competition in the drugstore business comes from discounters and
grocery supermarkets with large drugstore departments. Success for
a given company depends more on its individual approach to its markets
and more on its ability to execute and control basic merchandising fundamentals, than on any generalities about this widely diverse segment of
retailing.

Grocery Stores. This is a very large retail segment, with 1972 sales of
$88 billion. Chains of 11 or more units accounted for 56 percent of this
total, and the smaller organizations were largely grouped into affiliated
relationships with food wholesalers. The self-service supermarket format
is widespread, and competition has been intense for a number of years.
Although attempts have been made to differentiate store formats over
the years, the primary consumer appeals continue to be convenience and
price. According to *Supermarketing* magazine, foods, per se, accounted
for 78 percent of 1972 grocery store sales; with grocery products such as
household paper goods and other supplies, pet foods, and tobacco products accounting for 12 percent; and general merchandise items, including
health and beauty aids, 10 percent. In this 22 percent of their business,
grocery stores compete with variety stores, drugstores, and discounters.

In recent years, a number of grocery chain organizations have developed a new format, the "superstore." This represents a significant
escalation in the scale of the supermarket to a store size averaging about
40,000 square feet, from the industry average of under 20,000 square
feet. Emphasis is on massive volume on standard items, based on promotion of low prices, enough room for specialty departments such as

delicatessen and bakery, plus additional general merchandise staples to enrich the gross margin mix. This trend should be watched closely by analysts. Also the analyst should seek out organizations that have continued to do well year after year because of solid merchandising techniques, good controls, and superior management development programs.

Summary. The discussion of these retail segments should serve to underscore that they do not exist independently but compete vigorously with one another. This is particularly true in sales of convenience goods at the lower end of the quality-service-fashion spectrum where we have noted the cross-competition between variety stores, drugstores, grocery stores, and discounters. Many mergers of these types of units have occurred in recent years, and new types of formats to serve this segment of the market are still evolving. The analyst should follow trends in this area carefully.

FACTORS INFLUENCING SALES GROWTH

Sales Growth of the Retail Firm

Retailing is unlike many industries in which a prime determinant of a company's sales growth is the growth of the industry itself. We have discussed in a preceding section that although total retail sales have grown at a slightly lower rate than the economy, the very large size and diversity of the retail industry permit many firms to grow faster than the economy by gains in *market share*. Excluding acquisitions, there are two principle ways a retail firm can gain market share, *expansion* and increased *productivity*.

Often, both expansion and productivity improvement are discussed in quantitative terms which might lead the observer to believe these functions are mechanistic in nature. The importance of management decisions, however, is great. A wide range of choices is available to management in executing policies of both expansion and productivity improvement, with significant variations in rewards and pitfalls.

Expansion

The decade of the 1960s and the early 1970s provided great opportunities for executing strategies of expansion by retail managements. The fast-growing suburbs were initially underservices by retail facilities. A new highway network and almost universal availability of television were drawing regions more closely together and opening retail expansion opportunities farther out from center cities. Long-term mortgage money was available to developers, and the new enclosed-mall superregional shopping centers were creating "new down-towns" through metropolitan regions.

Expansion provided some organizations the opportunity to improve their market position with new facilities, as opposed to the difficult task of transforming the consumer image of an old store.

In recent years some of the larger retailers have taken more initiative in *developing* expansion opportunities through their own real estate staffs or real estate subsidiaries, rather than waiting for locations to be brought to them by outside developers.

Given good locations, the analyst should also consider the following factors when examining a retailer's expansion plans:

1. Financial resources,
2. Development of store management, and
3. Systems and procedures to maintain control of the enlarged organization.

Table 2 presents an example of an analysis of a company's expansion program.

At present the conditions for future retail expansion appear less permissive than those of the past decade. Constraints on expansion include possible federal and state restrictions on shopping center development because of environmental impact; the rising costs of both land and construction labor; and higher interest rates in the 1970s than in the 1960s. Also, having placed great management effort on expansion programs, some retail managements are directing greater energy towards making existing facilities more productive.

Productivity

One of the key tests of a retail management is its ability to increase sales in existing facilities, as contrasted with increasing sales by expansion. With continued increases in expenses, increasing the productivity of established stores is an important ingredient to maintaining a retailer's rate of profitability. The analyst should be aware that, over the short run, an accelerating rate of expansion can mask a deterioration in the productivity of existing stores. Thus, one of the questions most frequently asked of managements by retail analysts concerns the progress of sales in "identical stores" (stores in operation more than one year).

A proper rate of growth in sales productivity will vary with several factors, including overall economic growth, the rate of inflation, the relative maturity of the mix of stores, the intensity of promotional activity, and the rate of store space additions, both of the firm and its competition. Table 2 presents an example of an analysis of store space productivity.

Another way of looking at sales productivity is to regard each new store as an "annuity of sales." This concept is illustrated in Chart 1 (page 718). At the top of the chart may be seen a traditional pattern in which

TABLE 2

Federated Department Stores, Inc., Traditional Department and Specialty Stores—Analysis of Sales and Square Footage Expansion (1965–72)

	1972*	1971	1970	1969	1968	1967(*)	1966†	1965†
Sales ($ millions)	2,157	1,969	1,792	1,732	1,591	1,496	1,409	1,331
Year to year increase (percent)	+9.5	+9.9	+3.5	+8.9	+6.4	+6.2	+5.9	
Total traditional department and specialty store sq. ft. (000)	25,592	24,461	23,459	22,595	21,078	20,528	19,369	18,203
Year to year increase (percent)	+4.6	+4.3	+3.8	+7.2	+2.7	+6.0	+6.4	
Average of beginning and ending sq. ft. (000)	25,027	23,960	23,027	21,837	20,803	19,949	18,786	17,752
Year to year increase (percent)	+4.5	+4.1	+5.4	+5.0	+4.3	+6.2	+5.7	
Sales per average sq. ft.	$86.19	$82.18	$77.82	$79.31	$76.48	$74.99	$75.00	$74.98
Year to year increase (percent)	+4.9	+5.6	-1.9	+3.7	+2.0	nil†	nil	

* Fifty-three weeks.
† Sales for the two years 1965–66 include Ohio Appliances, accounting for about 1.5 percent of sales. Thus 1966–67 gains in sales per square foot are understated slightly.

a store opens, builds volume, levels out, and declines as newer stores enter the market. In the center of the chart may be seen the pattern of the store that continues to offer a unique blend of quality, service, and fashion. It continues to build volume, often requiring a number of physical expansions. At the bottom of the chart is a store with very little uniqueness that builds volume, reaches a peak, and, offering little distinction versus competition, quickly begins to decline.

One of the basic jobs of the retail analyst is to determine the "shape of the store annuities." Often this is not apparent in a five-year record of sales and earnings. For example a company operating stores with little uniqueness can rapidly expand from a small base, given availability of financing. The momentum of expansion can cover over the developing weakness of individual units. Eventually management span of control, finances, or sheer arithmetic limits the *rate* of expansion, and the deterioration of the base becomes apparent. If investor expectations have been built on "bottom line performance" without analysis of the *components* of that performance, the adjustment in expectations can be severe. Thus, as in other industries, the retail analyst must search for *sustainable* earnings growth.

Acquisitions and Entry into New Businesses

Internal versus External Growth. As in the analysis of other industries it is of utmost importance for the retail analyst to break out the *sources* of sales and profit growth so that they can be weighed as to their sustainability and continuity. Acquisitions tend to be more random than internal growth and less predictable. It is important to know what the company's performance has been, excluding the immediate effects of acquisitions on sales, earnings, and earnings per share.

Pro forma figures for the year before the acquisition often are available in company reports filed with the Securities and Exchange Commission, proxies, and prospectuses. Often the figures can be estimated, if not precisely available. One approach to analyzing the effects of acquisitions on company internal sales growth is shown in Table 3.

A significant amount of judgment must enter into assessing the "internal or external" growth effect of acquisitions on earnings after the initial statistical impact of an exchange of shares or a cash purchase. For example, a large retailer might buy a smaller one as an entry into a new geographical area or entry into a different type of retail business. In this case, it buys a foothold in a new area and creates an area for growth that was not there before. The same can be said of buying a low-profit-margin retailer and improving its profitability. In both cases, management has *created opportunities* for profit growth.

Regulatory Constraints on Acquisitions. At this writing the Federal Trade Commission and the United States Justice Department have taken

CHART 1

Retail Stores as Annuities

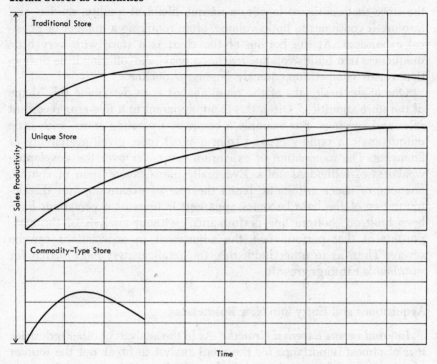

a rather restrictive view of acquisitions by large retailers of companies in their principal lines of business, even if they are located in different geographical areas. All such mergers receive very careful scrutiny, and the pace of such mergers in the 1970s, to date, has decelerated. "Invasions" of new operating territories by retailers from other territories have become more frequent.

Entry into New Businesses. Perhaps because of the more restrictive attitude by federal regulatory authorities mentioned above, there has been a trend by retailers in recent years towards "widening of corporate scope" into other types of retail business. For example, in recent years new divisions added to existing general merchandise and department store operations have included specialty apparel stores, discount stores, bookstores, catalog showrooms, mail-order operations, furniture warehouses, drugstores, food stores, jewelry stores, and consumer electronics stores. Some of these have been accomplished by acquisition (usually of a small company) and some developed by the organization itself.

At this time the success records of such widening of scope have been mixed. Some retailers have turned from such widening and returned to the basic area of retailing they know best, in an attempt to intensify

TABLE 3

Federated Department Stores, Inc., Traditional Department and Specialty Stores—Comparisons of Year-to-Year Internal Sales Growth and Square Footage Expansion (1959–65)

	1965	1964	1963	1962	1961*	1960	1959
Sales (consolidated) ($ million)	1,331	1,257	968	930	886	812	749‖
Excluding sales of companies acquired in year ($ million)		212†			10‡	4¢	76¶
Total, excluding estimated sales of acquisitions ($ million)		1,045			876	808	718
Year-to-year internal sales growth (percent)	+5.9	+8.0	+4.1	+5.0	+7.9	+1.8	
Total traditional department and specialty store space#	18,203	17,300	13,870	13,321	12,559	11,624	11,389
Estimated store space acquired in year#		3,185			270**	130††	1,020‡‡
Total, excluding store space acquired#		14,115			12,289	11,494	10,369
Year-to-year internal expansion (percent)	+5.2	+1.8	+4.2	+6.1	+5.7	+0.9	

* Fifty-three-week year.
† Estimated sales of Bullock's-I. Magnin.
‡ Estimated sales of A. Harris.
¢ Estimated sales of Levy's (Tuscon, Arizona).
‖ Includes Goldsmith's on estimated pro forma basis for full year (addition of $10 million).
¶ Estimated full year sales of Rike's ($52.5 million) and Goldsmith's ($23.5 million).
\# In square feet (000).
** A. Harris, 270,000E (main 155,000E; branch 115,000E).
†† Levy's (Tuscon, Arizona), 130,000 (main 70,000; branch 60,000).
‡‡ Rike's, 655,000 main; and Goldsmith's, 365,000 main.
Note: Estimates by Smith, Barney & Co. Incorporated.

resources and improve productivity. These cross trends should be watched closely by the retail analyst.

FACTORS INFLUENCING PROFITABILITY OF RETAILERS

The Structure of Retail Profits

In examining the profit structure of retailers, it is essential to focus on their position as *middlemen* rather than *manufacturers*. As we noted in the first section retailers buy from producers, add time-and-place utility and assume an ownership risk, and sell to consumers. Their "fee" for this service is their *gross margin*, the difference between their cost and selling price. Retailer profit results consist of a series of interplays between gross margins and expenses, and offsetting relationships within the components of each. We shall examine some of those interplays and offsetting relationships.

Gross Margin. With constantly rising expenses, one retailer profit strategy involves maximization of gross margin. Given the high degree of competition at all levels of retailing, such a strategy rarely involves charging more for an item than available elsewhere at a given quality-service-fashion level. Improvement in gross margin can be achieved by changing the *mix* of items handled to achieve a higher proportion of higher margin items. One important element in such a strategy is to emphasize unique items not available elsewhere. Such a policy can also involve stressing sale of the higher-priced items in each product line. It should be emphasized, however, that maximization of gross margin must be achieved within the limits of the particular store reputation with the consumer established over the years.

Gross margin is the result of *initial markup* less *markdowns*. Items carrying a high degree of style risk usually carry higher initial percentage markups than staples, since the probability of markdowns is higher. Although markdown experience in style merchandise runs higher over time, results can vary significantly from year to year. This degree of fluctuation is offset somewhat in many stores by a broad diversified "portfolio" of merchandise with different style risks. One way a retail management can show superior profit performance is through better buying, better inventory management, and, consequently, lower markdowns.

Inventory shrinkage can also affect gross margin. Shrinkage can be a product of three factors: (1) shoplifting, (2) internal employee dishonesty, and (3) other differences between inventory records and actual inventory count such as unrecorded markdowns.

The Interplay between Gross Margin and Expenses. Dollar expense levels rise as we move up the quality-service-fashion spectrum. A higher position in this spectrum provides a framework for a higher gross margin structure. Thus, we often have higher gross margins at higher expense levels. Conversely, the trend to self-service at the lower end of the quality-service-fashion spectrum permits a lower gross margin structure. The constant interplay between gross margin and expenses presents a challenge for capable managements to maximize profitability.

Promotion. A promotional strategy can involve lowering percentage gross margins by price reductions in an attempt to create enough increase in sales to produce increased gross margin dollars at little increase in expense. The risk in such a strategy is that it will not create enough sales to cover the lower margin and will result in lower profits. Certain companies plan such promotional policies as part of their overall appeal to the consumer. However, the analyst should carefully examine sudden spurts in sales volume to check whether the sales are being "bought" at little profit.

Promotion can also be stressed through increasing advertising expenses. The same risks as in a price-promotion strategy apply. Will the promotional expenses produce enough additional gross margin dollars to cover the expenses and add to profitability?

Inflation. Retailing is basically a "pass-on" business conducted in *current dollars.* A steadily rising rate of inflation results in a higher cost of goods and, at a constant gross margin percent, produces higher *gross margin* dollars. Under these conditions, *if* expenses can be maintained at the same or lower rate of increase as the cost of goods, then profit margins can be maintained. A significant percentage of retail expenses involve labor, or the purchase of services with a heavy labor component. In recent years there has been a tendency for increases in such expenses to outrun increases in the cost of goods sold. Thus, retailers have been faced with the necessity of increasing gross margin percentages. Both price increases and the change of the gross margin *mix* have been utilized. The pressure of inflation on retailers' expense structures has encouraged the trend to self-service, where applicable, and other means to secure high employee productivity.

Price Controls. In the years 1971–73 retailers were regulated under federal government price and wage control programs.[1] These programs recognized the middleman position of retailers and, except for periods of freeze, tended to control the gross margin percent rather than the selling price. As discussed in the preceding section, problems can arise when the rate of expenses is rising faster than the cost of goods sold. Retailers, like other industries, also were controlled on their pretax profit margins relative to a base period.

Interest. Interest rates on short-term borrowings to support inventories and accounts receivable can show very great year-to-year fluctuations. The analyst must ascertain which retailers have significant interest costs and allow for these in his earnings estimates.

---

[1] These controls were substantially removed from most general merchandise retailers in February 1974.

Cyclical Aspects of Retail Profitability

Retailer profitability does exhibit some cyclical characteristics. It is a function of the *rate of change* in sales growth. Retailers operate from fixed facilities that must be kept open and at least minimally staffed. This implies fixed costs and semivariable costs as well as variable costs. If expenses are planned for a sales level that does not materialize, they must be absorbed with resulting lower pretax profit margins. Inventories, too, must be purchased in advance of sales. If anticipated sales do not materialize, they must be marked down and moved out, with resulting lower profit margins.

While retailers can be affected in the initial stages of a sales deceleration, they have the ability to adjust inventories and semivariable expenses faster than many manufacturing segments. Thus, profit pressure for retailers is usually less intense than that for overall corporate profits, and profits tend to recover earlier than corporate profits for the economy as a whole.

Within a given retail segment, the level of profit margins to some extent determines the degree of profit leverage in a cycle. Assume that among operators of department stores Company A has pretax margins of 8 percent and Company B, 4 percent. If a deceleration of sales produces a 1 percent profit margin decline for each company, Company A's profitability is off 12.5 percent and Company B's, off 25 percent.

Seasonality of Retail Profits

Profits in general merchandise retailing are highly seasonal. On average, about 50 percent of earnings are concentrated in the final (Christmas) quarter of the fiscal year ending about January 31, with only about 25 percent in the first half. This reflects the operating leverage inherent in having certain basic costs expensed evenly on a quarterly basis with uneven volume in the quarters. The example in Table 4 of Federated Department Stores quarterly profits for the year ended January 29, 1972

TABLE 4

Quarterly Earnings of Federated Department Stores, Inc. (year ended January 29, 1972)

Quarter Ending	Sales ($ millions)	Pretax Earnings ($ millions)	Pretax Margin (percent)
April	542	28.4	5.3
July	582	27.7	4.8
October	627	49.2	7.8
January*	914	98.2	10.7
Total for year	2,665	203.5	7.6

* Of following year.

illustrates this. The first through fourth quarters accounted for, respectively, 20, 22, 24, and 34 percent of the year's sales, and 14, 14, 24, and 48 percent of the year's profits.

When examining year-to-year comparisons in quarterly earnings, the analyst must be aware of this quarterly earnings pattern of retailers and the operating leverage it creates. Percentage swings in earnings of the first two quarters tend to be great but of less significance than earnings changes in the important second half. In the final quarter, great profit leverage can depend on the very high volume days before Christmas when expenses have been set, inventories are in the store, and fluctuations in gross margin dollars can carry through almost directly to pretax income.

Expansion and Profitability

Retail expansion affects not only sales but the pattern of expenses as well. In its initial stage, expansion is costly, involving the *preopening* costs of hiring in advance of opening and preparing the store for opening. Operating profits are usually low or nonexistent until the store builds adequate volume. Full profitability may not be reached until several years after opening.

Expansion programs of retailers are often uneven, heavy in one year and light in another. This can create a pattern of heavy expansion costs and low operating profitability of new stores, followed by light expansion costs combined with a buildup of profitability from past expansion. The analyst must place such cost/benefit patterns in proper perspective.

On a longer-term basis, expansion creates the occupancy costs of interest on long-term debt, depreciation, and rents. The analyst must examine the trend of such costs. Rising occupancy costs as a percent of sales have been the rule in recent years as land and construction costs have mounted. In some cases, managements have felt the return on such expansion was still quite favorable in view of the substantial volume and good gross margin mix created by such expansion. In other cases, significant efforts are being made to curb this trend of rising costs through construction of smaller, more productive units and by redesign of units to reduce construction and fixturing costs.

MEASUREMENTS OF FINANCIAL STRENGTH

Relation of Financial Strength to Earning Power

In retailing, financial strength and the management of financial resources are important foundations of a company's earning power. In Table 5 are presented the balance sheets of Federated Department Stores, Inc. for the years ended February 3, 1973 and January 29, 1972—

together with a presentation of year-to-year changes in the balance sheet items. The importance of the current asset items, *inventories* and *accounts receivable*, is readily apparent, as is the importance of the *property and equipment* account.

Once having determined that the financial viability of the corporation is not a problem, the analyst must examine the financial position of a retailer from two points of view: first, the *efficiency* with which management utilizes the assets; and second, how the assets are financed. Inadequate financial resources can inhibit managements' flexibility in taking advantage of growth opoprtunities and also can cause dilution of earnings through the necessity of raising additional money.

In the following sections, we shall examine the analysis of current assets, property, and capitalization.

Current Assets

Inventories. Inventory Turnover. As seen in the illustration of a department store company's balance sheet in Table 5, inventories are a very important factor in the financial position of a retailer. In determining the efficiency with which this asset is used, some measure of inventory turnover is necessary. For the analyst using publicly available data, sales divided by the average of beginning of year and end of year inventory provides a useful measure of the productivity of the inventory investment.[2] Calculation of this measure for a number of years can provide useful analytical insights:

1. One retailer can be compared to another in a similar segment of retailing.
2. The trend of sales relative to inventory for a given retailer over a period of years can be studied.
3. Sharp rises in inventory relative to sales can be highlighted, perhaps foreshadowing higher markdowns in subsequent years.
4. Given certain sales expectations, a study of past trends, and discussion with management, future inventory requirements can be forecast.

---

[2] Since inventories are stated at the lower of cost or market, a strict calculation of turnover of inventory requires cost of goods sold rather than sales to be divided by average inventory. It can be difficult, however, to obtain a cost of goods sold figure, excluding such items as occupancy and buying costs, and to obtain it on a comparable basis for all companies studied. Thus, the sales to average inventory figure provides a useful starting point for analysis, although it can be distorted somewhat over time by variation in the gross margin percentage.

It should also be noted that an average of beginning of year and end of year inventories is rather a rough guide as compared to monthly averages and other more sophisticated measurements, but it serves the purpose of highlighting items for further study and questions.

TABLE 5

FEDERATED DEPARTMENT STORES, INC.
Comparative Balance Sheets
February 3, 1973 and January 29, 1972
($ million)

	Year Ended		$ Increase (Decrease)
	2/3/73	1/29/72	1971–72
Current Assets:			
Cash..	42.4	51.7	(9.3)
Accounts receivable...........................	425.7*	428.2†	(2.5)
Merchandise inventories......................	309.8	276.5	33.3
Supplies and prepaid expenses.................	11.5	8.6	2.9
Total Current Assets....................	789.4	765.0	24.4
Less: Current Liabilities:			
Notes payable and long-term debt			
due within one year........................	20.2	46.7	(26.5)
Other current liabilities......................	349.7	302.6	47.1
Total Current Liabilities.................	369.9	349.3	20.6
Net Working Capital.........................	419.5	415.7	3.8
Other Assets:			
Real estate not used in operations..............	31.1	32.0	(0.9)
Investment in unconsolidated finance			
subsidiary................................	15.1	1.5	13.6
Deferred tax charges and miscellaneous...........	14.2	24.8	(10.6)
Total Other Assets.....................	60.4	58.3	2.1
Property and Equipment:			
Land.......................................	66.3	59.7	6.6
Buildings, substantially all on owned land........	267.4	234.0	33.4
Buildings on leased land, improvements			
to leased properties and leaseholds.............	150.7	123.7	27.0
Store fixtures and equipment...................	248.5	218.8	29.7
Total Property and Equipment..........	732.9	636.2	96.7
Less: Accumulated depreciation			
and amortization..........................	202.3	179.7	22.6
Net Property and Equipment.............	530.6	456.5	74.1
Total Net Assets......................	1010.5	930.5	80.0
Deferred compensation........................	66.6	61.1	5.5
Long-term debt..............................	117.6‡	113.9	3.7
Common shareholders' equity..................	826.3	755.5	70.8
Total Capitalization...................	1010.5	930.5	80.0

* Net of $42 million accounts receivable sold to Federated's unconsolidated finance subsidiary.
† Net of $13.5 million accounts receivable sold to Federated's unconsolidated finance subsidiary.
‡ Includes $50 million, 8⅜ percent sinking fund debentures of 1995; $50 million, 7⅛ percent sinking fund debentures of 2002; $13.6 million, 4.5 percent convertible debentures of 1985; and $4.0 million of other long-term debt at an average interest rate of about 6 percent.

It should be noted in studying inventories relative to sales that there can be a number of explanations for changes in turnover rates. Among these are the following:

1. The mix of business can change. For example, a traditional department store that starts a discounting division might show a rising

inventory turn as the discount division becomes a greater proportion of sales.

2. Management can elect a competitive strategy of wider and deeper assortments, in the expectation that the increase in inventory investment will create greater profitability on *total* investment.

3. An expanding *rate* of new store openings can lower inventory turn since stores must be fully stocked when they have not yet approached sales maturity.

Year-end Adjustments.   Most retailers usually take physical inventory once a year, and adjustments from book inventory must be made. Reserves are usually set up for inventory shortages (discussed under gross margin in the previous section), and adjustments are made at the year-end. When attempting to place fourth-quarter profitability of a given year in perspective, the analyst should ask management about the degree of positive or negative inventory reserve adjustments in that quarter.

FIFO and LIFO Methods.   Retailers vary as to their use of the FIFO (first-in, first-out) and LIFO (last-in, first-out) methods of valuing inventory. Those that use LIFO usually disclose the effect on earnings of using the LIFO method. For example, in its annual report for the year ended February 3, 1973 Federated Department Stores stated in its "Notes to the Consolidated Financial Statements": "At February 3, 1973 and January 29, 1972, inventories were $48,608,000 and $45,487,000 lower than they would have been had the retail method been used without the application of the last-in, first-out basis." In other words, pretax earnings in the year ended February 3, 1973 were $3.1 million less than they would have been under the FIFO method. In Federated's case this difference amounted to 1.5 percent of pretax earnings for the year.

Retailers that use LIFO also vary as to whether they *reserve* for LIFO every quarter or make one adjustment at year-end. In periods of rapid acceleration or deceleration in retail prices, the analyst should be aware of the impact of such adjustments.

Accounts Receivable.   Off-Balance Sheet Financing.   Accounts receivable, like inventories, are a very important financial asset for retailers. This can be seen in Table 5. It can also be noted in footnotes (*) and (†) of Table 5, that all of the company's accounts receivable do not appear on the balance sheet. As of February 3, 1973, $42 million had been sold to the company's unconsolidated finance subsidiary, compared with $13.5 million the previous year. Thus, while *net* accounts receivables had declined $2.5 million, year-to-year, *gross* accounts receivable, before sale of receivables, actually had risen by $26 million from $441.7 million to $467.7 million, or by 5.9 percent. In the case of some retailers, the percent of accounts receivable sold can be much higher than this. In others, none are sold, or the credit subsidiary is consolidated. In making comparisons of accounts receivable relative to sales, both over time for a given company or between companies, accounts receivable sold should be added back by the analyst to produce comparable figures.

In the example of the Federated Department Stores balance sheet in Table 5, the accounts receivable sold to the wholly owned, unconsolidated Federated Acceptance Corporation were supported by short-term notes of the finance subsidiary of $27 million and an equity of Federated in the finance subsidiary of $15.1 million. This represents financing of 2.8 times equity investment. This is a relatively young subsidiary and from examination of other, more mature credit subsidiaries, a financed receivables to equity ratio of 6–7 to 1 seems acceptable.

Earnings of unconsolidated credit subsidiaries are usually consolidated on a "one-line" basis. In the case of Federated, earnings of the credit subsidiary are applied as a reduction of consolidated company interest expense.

Just as the accounts receivable sold should be added back by the analyst for comparative purposes in calculating sales/accounts receivable relationships, a case could be made that for comparisons between retailers the debt of the credit subsidiary should be added back to appropriate short-term and long-term debt categories.

Accounts Receivable Relative to Sales. Meaningful comparisons of accounts receivable relative to sales are difficult because of a constantly changing mix. First, the percentage of sales made on credit and for cash can change from year to year. Second, the mix of credit sales can change as between 30-day charge, revolving charge, and installment sales. Payment terms are different for each. Certainly the analyst must start with figures from the company on percent of credit sales to total and utilize these sales in calculating ratios of sales to average receivables. (Unless breakdowns of sales for various categories of credit plans are available over time, more sophisticated aging techniques involving receivables outstanding in terms of average daily sales are not too meaningful.) A rough figure of the trend of credit sales to average receivables can produce a framework for a more incisive discussion with management regarding trends in this area. It can also provide some framework for projecting future financial requirements for receivables.

Credit Charges. Retailers have maintained that operating a credit business is expensive and is justified primarily in that it helps create greater sales volume. In recent years, however, a number of "class action" suits have been instituted against retailers in several states, predicated on the claim of excessive credit service charges relative to state laws. These primarily involve revolving charge accounts. Most managements discount the longer-term significance or impact of such suits, but the retail analyst must stay aware of legal and regulatory trends in this area.

Liquidity Ratios. In analyzing a retailers' financial flexibility and possible need for long-term financing, several liquidity ratios can be of help. These are:

1. Current ratio. Current assets divided by current liabilities.
2. Short term debt as a percent of current assets.
3. Cash and equivalent as a percent of current liabilities.

Before making these calculations, the analyst should add back accounts receivable sold to current assets and the appropriate amount of short-term debt supporting these receivables to current liabilities. (If the accounts receivable are sold to a wholly owned subsidiary, the short-term debt of the subsidiary should be added back to current liabilities. If the accounts receivable are sold to an outside organization, the analyst could add the whole amount sold to current liabilities.)

Calculation of these ratios from the Federated Department Stores balance sheet for the year ended February 3, 1973 (Table 5) are shown in Table 6.[3]

Liquidity ratios for a given company can be compared over a period of years. Ratios for a given year can be compared with other retail companies operating in similar segments of retailing to aid in assessing relative financial strength.

Property and Equipment

Variations in the Property and Equipment Account. As shown in the balance sheets in Table 5, the property and equipment account is a third very important asset of retailers. This account includes land, buildings, and fixtures and equipment. The account can show year-to-year fluctuation for reasons other than store expansion:

1. Land can be purchased well in advance of building a store.
2. Companies may build up ownership of properties preparatory to sale and leaseback arrangements.
3. Companies may take ownership positions in shopping centers in which their stores are located.

Policies toward owning and leasing of property vary widely among retailers. Thus in examining the return on total capitalization in the following section, the analyst must make some adjustment for the debt that would have been incurred to support leased properties had they been owned.

Securities and Exchange Commission Requirements for Lease Disclosure. In October 1973, the Securities and Exchange Commission adopted a proposal requiring companies to submit to it (in annual 10-K reports and other material filed with the SEC) substantial data about their lease commitments. Such data include both the present value of certain rental obligations and the impact on earnings of owning, rather

---

[3] Since Federated is on the LIFO (last-in, first-out) method of inventory accounting, the LIFO reserve (see page 726) would have to be added back to inventories for strict comparability with companies on the FIFO (first-in, first-out) method.

TABLE 6

FEDERATED DEPARTMENT STORES, INC.
Liquidity Ratios
Year Ended February 3, 1973

($ million)

1. Current Ratio:
   Total Current Assets.. $789.4
      Add: Accounts receivable sold............................ 42.0
         Adjusted Total Current Assets....................... $831.4
   Total Current Liabilities.................................... $369.9
      Add: Short-term debt of finance subsidiary.................. 27.0
         Adjusted Total Current Liabilities..................... $396.9

   $831.4 ÷ $396.9 = 2.1x
   Current ratio = 2.1

2. Short-Term Debt as Percent of Current Assets:
   Short-term debt.. $ 20.2
      Add: Short-term debt of finance subsidiary.................. 27.0
         Adjusted short-term debt............................ $ 47.2
   Adjusted Total Current Assets (See 1, above)................. $831.4

   $47.2 ÷ $831.4 = 0.057
   Short-term debt as percent of current assets = 5.7%.

3. Cash and Equivalent as Percent of Current Liabilities:
   Cash and equivalent....................................... $ 42.4
   Adjusted Total Current Liabilities (See 1, above)............. $396.9

   $42.4 ÷ $396.9 = 0.107
   Cash and equivalent as percent of current liabilities = 10.7%

than leasing, property. The capitalized value figures given by companies probably will be utilized by analysts in place of the rough approximations such as those in Table 7, discussed in the following section. At this writing we understand that both the present value of leases and the impact on earnings will be in the form of footnotes to the financial statements rather than in changes in the financial statements themselves.

The effect on earnings of owning, rather than leasing, property is not particularly significant *over the life of the lease*,[4] but does tend to create greater expense in the early years of a lease and less expense in the latter years. Excluding percentage rentals, the *basic rental expense* is usually *level* over the life of the lease, with payments including both return of principal to the lessor and interest. When the property is owned, the corresponding expenses are *interest* and *depreciation*. Depreciation is usually level for reporting purposes, but the interest payments are higher in the early years and decline as the debt is repaid.

At this writing our preliminary calculations indicate that the negative effect on earnings of such a calculation would be under 10 percent for most major retailers. Although considerable controversy surrounds the

---

[4] The interest factor in leasing can be somewhat higher than in regular borrowing.

effects of this calculation on basic earning power, the analyst should study this data for each retailer.

Capitalization

Capitalization and Return on Equity. Capitalization consists of the long-term liabilities and stockholders' equity that support the net working capital and long-term assets of the corporation. An illustration of the components of a return on common equity calculation for Federated Department Stores is presented in Table 7. The adjusted capitalization

TABLE 7

FEDERATED DEPARTMENT STORES, INC.
Analysis of Return on Equity
Year Ended February 3, 1973*

Sales and earnings ($ millions):	
Sales.	$2,665.0
Pretax earnings.	203.6
Interest on long-term debt.	7.9
Imputed interest on capitalized rents (8%).	15.2
Pretax, preinterest.	$ 226.7
Adjusted capitalization ($ millions):	
Capitalized rentals (8x).	190.4
Long-term debt.	117.6
Deferred compensation.	66.6
Common shareholders' equity.	826.4
Total adjusted capitalization.	$1,201.0
Ratios:	
Sales/adjusted capitalization.	2.22x
Pretax, preinterest/sales.	8.5%
Return on adjusted capitalization.	18.9%
Common equity as percent of adjusted capitalization.	68.8%
Pretax earnings as percent of common equity.	24.6%
Effective tax rate.	46.7%
Net return on common equity.	13.1%

* Fifty-three weeks.

figure includes rentals capitalized at 12.5 percent (8×) to approximate roughly the debt equivalent of leases. In adding back interest on long-term debt to pretax earnings, imputed interest on capitalized leases is added back as well.

Having calculated an adjusted capitalization figure to facilitate comparisons with past years or comparisons with other retailers, ratios can be calculated for turnover of adjusted capitalization (sales divided by adjusted capitalization), pretax, preinterest return on sales, and return on adjusted capitalization (pretax, preinterest earnings divided by adjusted capitalization). For purposes of analysis it should be noted that return on adjusted capitalization (18.9 percent) is a product of turnover of adjusted capitalization (2.22 ×) times pretax, preinterest earnings as a percent of sales (8.5 percent). Thus one can examine trends in the *components* of return on total capitalization to understand more fully what has happened in the past and to help project the future. Also performance comparisons between companies can be made.

The addition of capitalization *leverage* translates return on adjusted capitalization to return on common equity as shown in Table 7. In this case, Federated has a relatively high 69 percent common equity as a percent of total capitalization. In comparing return on common equity for a given company over time, it is important to note whether changes are the result of changes in return on total adjusted capitalization or the result of changes in capitalization leverage. In comparing companies with one another, it is important for the analyst to note whether differences in return on equity are the product of differences in return on total capitalization or of differences in capitalization leverage.

Capitalization and Long-Term Financing Needs. In attempting to assess the probable need for long-term financing, a study of the company's capitalization leverage can be helpful along with an examination of liquidity ratios (discussed in a preceding section) and coverage of occupancy costs (long-term debt interest, depreciation, and rents).

COMMON STOCK PRICE ACTION AND VALUATION

Common Stock Price Action

The stock price action of any group is most significant relative to the movement of stocks in general. Chart 2 presents the price action of the Standard & Poor's Department Store Index on semilog paper (on which a straight line indicates a constant rate of change) from 1953 through late 1963. The index itself is presented at the top of the chart and indicates a generally upward trend with downward moves in 1955 and 1956, 1966, 1970, and 1973. The bottom of the chart shows the performance of the department store index relative to the Standard & Poor's Index of 425 Industrials. This shows a decided downtrend from 1953 to 1957 and then a general uptrend, with interruptions in 1963, 1966, and 1973.

As was noted in the first section, retailing is a broad and many-faceted industry, and in using any particular index the analyst must satisfy himself that the stocks within the index are roughly comparable and affected by the same economic forces. If not, it might be preferable to merely compare the relative price action of a given retailer with a broad index of the overall market.

Valuation

Price/Earnings Ratios. Analysis of relative price/earnings ratios can give the analyst valuable perspective in forming a valuation judgment. Since earnings of retailers have some cyclical aspects, it is im-

CHART 2

Trend of S & P Department Stores Stock Index and Performance Relative to the S & P 425 Industrials (1953–September 1973)

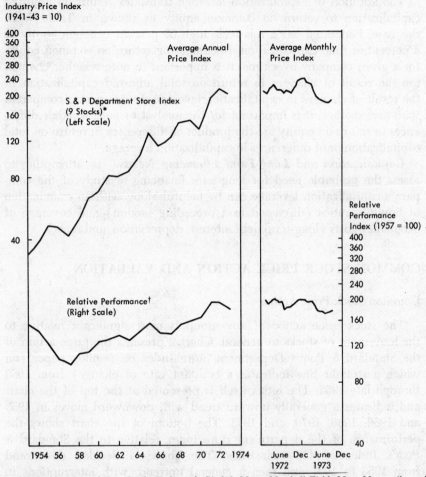

* Allied, Associated Dry Goods, Federated, Gimbel, Macy, Marshall Field, May, Mercantile, and Penney.

† Ratio of Department Store Index to S & P 425 Industrial Index, 1957 = 100.

portant that the analyst consider basic earning power when making price/earning ratio comparisons. Otherwise the ratio may be distorted by cyclically high or cyclically low earnings.

Two very important factors in stock valuation are the rate of expected future earnings growth and the certainty surrounding such growth. Thus, given identical single-point expectations of future five-year growth, one retail stock may sell at a higher price/earning ratio than another if there is greater investor confidence surrounding future growth expectations, or if it is believed that growth prospects are superior for one company beyond the five years.

The concept of an "average industry multiple" has severe limitations, in our opinion, if one takes it to imply that stocks selling in excess of the average multiple are "expensive" and those selling below the average multiple are "cheap." However, as shown in Table 8, the average multiple can be utilized to examine the valuation of a segment of the retail industry relative to the market as a whole over a number of years.

Book Value. Retailing is essentially an operating business rather than an asset business, and in most cases valuation of earnings is much more important than book value. In other words, what can be earned on the book value is more important than what the book value is.

At times of very depressed stock prices or when a retailer is in financial difficulty, book value can be a significant reference point. In analyzing book value, however, several questions should be asked by the analyst. First, what would the inventories and receivables bring if sold in liquidation? Second, in addition to the debt liabilities, what liabilities exist to lessors? On the favorable side the analyst should examine alternative uses and current market value of owned retail properties, especially those in downtown areas. Current value of such properties might be in excess of book value.

TABLE 8

Price/Earnings Ratio Comparisons of Eight Selected General Merchandise Retailers and Standard & Poor's 425 Industrials

	Price/Earnings Ratios		
	S&P 425 Industrials (x)	Eight Selected General Merchandise Retailers* (x)	Eight Retailers Premium or (Discount) (percent)
1972	18.0x	20.0x	11
1971	18.0	18.8	4
1970	16.5	16.4	(1)
1969	17.5	18.2	4
1968	17.3	19.1	10
1967	17.0	16.2	(5)
1966	15.2	16.2	7
1965	16.8	19.6	17
1964	17.6	19.0	8
1963	17.1	18.1	6
Average:			
1968–72	17.5x	18.5x	6
1963–67	16.7	17.8	7
1963–72	17.2x	18.2x	6

* Associated Dry Goods Corp., Carter Hawley Hale Stores, Inc., Federated Department Stores, Inc., R. H. Macy & Co., Inc., Marshall Field & Co., May Department Stores Co., J. C. Penney Co., Inc., Sears, Roebuck & Co.

28

Steel

PETER L. ANKER, C.F.A.
First Vice President
Smith, Barney & Co., Inc., New York, New York

THE U.S. steel industry has long done an effective job of supplying steel in abundant amounts to an American industry which has taken it for granted. In the past ten years, it has faced competition from a world that regards steel as an area providing an opportunity for economic growth. Japan has long had a national policy to make its steel industry one of the largest in the world. The Soviet Union is still building up steel-making facilities. The "third world" has long considered a steel mill as necessary to begin to improve its standard of living. While steel is recognized as a critical national asset for any strong economy, only the industrial nations have been able to collect the capital, raw material, and labor necessary to produce this product in the volume that industry demands.

The steel-making process and steel's markets are the ultimate dictator of the economics of the industry.

TECHNOLOGY

Steel making begins with the manufacture of pig iron. The basic raw material ingredients, iron ore, coking coal, and limestone, are combined in a smelting process. In the 1970s the industry required 1.607 tons of iron ore, 0.027 tons of scrap, 0.235 tons of limestone and agglomerates, 0.608 tons of coal, and 0.049 tons of miscellaneous products to produce one ton of pig iron. The coke furnishes the energy that fuels the smelting process which takes place in a blast furnace. Unfortunately, the coke

734

does not arrive at the furnace site ready for consumption as does the iron ore. Metallurgical coal differs from the coal used to fuel utility boilers because of its coking capability. Before it can be used in the iron-making process it is baked in large coking ovens. During this process, the unwanted chemical properties and high-volatile gases are driven off. In the 1970s 1.38 tons of coal were required for each ton of coke that went into a blast furnace.

The smallest of the big seven integrated steel companies produced 3.033 million tons of coke in the 1970s. The huge tonnage requirements of the industry create the economic facts of life that the analyst must live with. There is no efficient means of producing pig iron on a small scale. In 1955, blast furnaces of 1,700 annual tons of capacity were common. In 1972, blast furnaces in the United States were in the 7,000 annual ton size, with the average furnace producing 4,000 tons of pig iron and ferroalloy, and blast furnaces twice that size are in everyday use in Japan and the Soviet Union. Units of such size do not come cheaply. Furthermore, they consume large quantities of material on a round-the-clock basis (blast furnaces are only shut down for relining and maintenance, or strikes or a slump in demand). As a result, a steel-making complex requires ore and coal-handling facilities, and it must have access to the materials.

A company that controls its iron ore reserves and owns its own coal mines is in a vastly superior position to one which must purchase part or all of its materials. Because the difference between a fully integrated, semiintegrated, and nonintegrated company is great, the industry is divided into these three categories, and companies are analyzed together with their peers. Bethlehem and U.S. Steel control huge reserves of coal and iron ore at a number of different locations many of which are wholly owned. Republic, Inland, and Armco achieve their reserve position through partnership agreements and joint ventures. Companies like Jones and Laughlin have been in a relatively poorer raw material posture and have had to build up their positions in recent years.

The American steel industry was built around the rich iron ore deposits of the Mesabi Range. The mills were located in proximity to the Great Lakes and good river transportation networks. In the early years of steel making, the U.S. industry had a clear advantage over many of its competitors—proximity to rich ore. Eventually the rich 60 percent iron ore was consumed, leaving ore grading about 40 percent. The Midwestern mills could be, and indeed were, supplied with rich ores from South America, Africa, and other geographic areas. Costs of ocean shipping were low, but shipments into the Great Lakes were limited by the size of boat the locks could accommodate. The incentive to use the Minnesota, Michigan, and Eastern Canadian areas continued strong because of the location of the existing facilities. Other mining industries had faced similar problems and developed methods to upgrade the ore by further concentration at plants close to the mine site. Steel in the United States, however, is consumed in 100 million ton amounts, not in amounts of 10 million tons as in aluminum or 3 million tons as is true for copper. Attempts at ore beneficiation took several forms, but in the 60s modern techniques of pelletizing the ore were developed. The grade was increased, the resulting concentrate formed into a marblelike pellet, and this now premium-priced product was shipped to the mills. Pellets soon developed a record for improving the yield of pig iron from the blast furnace and served to revitalize the midwestern ore fields—Not, however, without substantial capital cost. A new pelletizing plant today will cost about 60–70 dollars per ton of annual capacity.

Contrast the ore direction of the American industry with that of Japan. The Japanese home islands provide a very small amount of the raw materials that industrial country requires. Virtually everything must be imported. Shortly after Japan embarked on a program to expand its steel-making capacity, ore deposits yielding up to 64 percent iron were discovered in Australia. While much of the capital required to develop these deposits came from the West they helped make Japan the third largest steel maker in the world, after the Soviet Union and the United States. During this period, the Japanese were experimenting with much larger bulk ore and oil carriers. Today ships of 300,000 tons capacity are common, five times the capacity of the lake boats. Better ore grade and low-cost transportation could achieve considerable cost savings.

In the United States, the scope of iron ore owned by Bethlehem and U.S. Steel extends beyond that of its competition. A company like Bethlehem with its ore reserves and a modern mill, Sparrows Point, on deep water should, if all other things were equal, outproduce a company like Jones and Laughlin. All U.S. mills today use a mix of pellets and lump ores, but the cost of raw materials can vary greatly. If, as we believe, the current environment will create raw material shortages in the United States, it is not unlikely that more attention will be given to the raw materials position of the steel producers. Raw material analysis must extend to coal as well as iron ore. Abundant supplies of coal with coking properties are limited. Even reasonably good coking coal found in Western Canada and Australia must be blended with Appalachian coal to produce the necessary blast furnace fuel.

The pig iron together with scrap and limestone is fed into one of three basic types of steel-making furnaces: an open hearth, a basic oxygen (BOF), or an electric furnace. Steel-making technology has undergone dramatic changes during the past 15 years. In 1958, 84.3 percent of the steel made in the United States was poured from open-hearth furnaces. By 1972, open-hearth steel had dropped to 26.2 percent of the total; BOFs produced 56.0 percent and electric furnaces, 17.8 percent. Table 1 graphically tabulates the shift in production technology. The six- to eight-hour tap-to-tap requirement of the open hearth cannot compete with 30-ton-capacity BOFs that take less than an hour for a heat. Both the open hearth and basic oxygen furnaces require pig iron as part of their feed. The resulting capital investment in blast furnaces and coke ovens can be sure to raise the capital cost of the steel-making facility. An electric furnace uses a 100 percent scrap charge and thus does not require the blast furnace complex. The lower capital cost is not an unmixed blessing, however. Power costs are increasing. In addition, a sizable electric furnace shop is dependent upon scrap purchased on the open market. High scrap prices can penalize an otherwise efficient electric furnace shop.

Operating costs for individual steel companies depend upon a number of factors directly related to the choice of steel-making technology and the age of the furnaces. A company with BOFs and electric furnaces will, in general, fare better than one with even the most efficient open hearths. The age and type of equipment in use can be an important guide to operating costs.

One must, however, be careful not merely to dwell on the negatives. A company with older open-hearth furnaces could be an attractive investment if it were in the middle of a program of modernization. The increase in profitability could be greater for such a producer after the conversion than for one who has a more modern steel-making plant.

The steel-making process requires natural gas, fuel oil, and electric power in addition to the raw material ingredients mentioned. An analyst cannot, in this era of concern over energy, ignore an investigation of how well an individual company has protected itself against shortages in this area.

However, despite some of the criticism launched against the managements of the steel industry, a shortage of supplies has rarely been a cause for a downturn in production. Steelmaking is a complicated exercise in logistics. Large and able staffs are in the employ of most of the major companies for the express purpose of preventing downtime through a lack of material.

From the steel-making furnace, the molten metal is poured into ingot moulds in the conventional process or into the receiving end of a continuous caster called a "tundish." If ingots are poured, they must be reheated and reformed into slabs, billets, or bars before they move to the finishing mills. During the process, considerable steel becomes scrap in the trimming of the various shapes. For this reason, steel shipments fall short of steel production. In 1972 the U.S. steel industry poured 133.2 million tons of raw steel but shipped 96.1 million tons for a yield of 72.1 percent. Such scrap is not lost; it is recycled through the steel-making process. Continuous casting does not require as much trimming. Consequently, yields of 85 percent have been experienced with the use of this process. Casting of semifinished shapes (slabs or billets) has eliminated several steps in the production process and theoretically

TABLE 1

Raw Steel Production and Index by Type of Furnace and by Carbon, Alloy, and Stainless Grades

											(Thousands of net tons)
	Open Hearth *			Bessemer	Basic Oxygen Process			Electric			
Year	Carbon	Alloy	Total	Carbon	Carbon	Alloy	Total	Carbon	Alloy	Stainless	Total
1972	32,036	2,900	34,936		69,231	5,353	74,584	16,431	5,726	1,564	23,72
1971	32,612	2,947	35,559		59,472	4,471	63,943	14,923	4,755	1,263	20,94
1970	44,361	3,661	48,022		58,889	4,441	63,330	14,161	4,722	1,279	20,16
1969	55,530	5,364	60,894		55,927	4,309	60,236	13,375	5,188	1,569	20.13
1968	59,572	6,264	65,836	‡	45,706	3,106	48,812	10,991	4,391	1,432	16.81
1967	64,265	6,425	70,690	‡	38,811	2,623	41,434	10,114	3,524	1,451	15,08
1966	77,395	7,630	85,025	278	31,892	2,036	33,928	9,167	4,052	1,651	14,87
1965	85,861	8,332	94,193	586	21,787	1,092	22,879	8,417	3,894	1,493	13,80
1964	90,763	7,335	98,098	858	15,045	397	15,442	7,776	3,459	1,443	12,67
1963	82,621	6,213	88,834	963	8,484	60	8,544	6,646	3,070	1,204	10,92
1962	77,569	5,388	82,957	805	5,503	50	5,553	5,283	2,645	1,085	9,01
1961	79,525	4,977	84,502	881	3,961	6	3,967	4,971	2,556	1,137	8,66
1960	81,171	5,197	86,368	1,189	3,344	2	3,346	5,158	2,217	1,004	8,37
1959	76,436	5,233	81,669	1,380	1,864		1,864	4,859	2,543	1,131	8,53
1958	71,869	4,011	75,880	1,396	1,323		1,323	4,003	1,757	896	6,65

* Basic and acid open-hearth production shown separately in previous Annual Statistical Reports, 1972.
† Based on average production of the year 1967 as 100.
‡ Included with open hearth.
Source: American Iron and Steel Institute, 1972.

should result in some cost savings. The method's use is escalating. Today most of the major companies have had experience with one or more units. The process has yet to prove itself for all products. There have been cases of some mills experiencing unusual start-up costs and delays that have affected their competitive position. In time, the early experimenters with this method may have a significant advantage over the late comers. An observer of the industry should monitor carefully what is being done by the companies in this area. Continuous casting has not so proven itself that it provides the certain cost savings common to the BOF furnace. As a result, the shift to continuous casting has been much slower than the changes in steelmaking furnaces.

FABRICATION

Thus far the steel product we are discussing is used primarily within the mills. From the semifinished state the slabs, billets, and blooms move to the rolling mills to be turned into sheets, plates, and bars in varying degrees of finishes. It is probably here that the customer has made himself felt most vividly. The American's love affair with his automobile and his care of the highly polished surface demanded techniques that could produce a flawless finish. These needs required the most modern computer-operated mills. Once one company had the facility, the others were forced to follow along. In the mid-60s, the industry was spending upwards of $2 billion annually to achieve a

							(Thousands of net tons)			
	Total All Grades				Per Cent of Total			Steel for Castings (Included in Total Production)		
Carbon	Alloy	Stainless	Total	Index †	Carbon	Alloy	Stainless	Carbon	Alloy	Stainless	Total
117,698	13,979	1,564	133,241	104.5	88.3	10.5	1.2	80	54	2	136
107,007	12,173	1,263	120,443	94.7	88.8	10.1	1.1	92 R	52 R	2	146 R
117,411	12,824	1,279	131,514	103.4	89.3	9.7	1.0	98	62	2	162
124,832	14,861	1,569	141,262	111.0	88.4	10.5	1.1	116	54	2	172
116,269	13,761	1,432	131,462	103.1	88.4	10.5	1.1	116	55	2	173
113,190	12,572	1,451	127,213	100.0	89.0	9.9	1.1	134	59	1	194
118,732	13,718	1,651	134,101	105.4	88.5	10.2	1.3	245	70	2	317
116,651	13,318	1,493	131,462	103.3	88.8	10.1	1.1	198	67	2	267
114 442	11,191	1,443	127,076	99.6	90.1	8.8	1.1	159	62	2	223
98,714	9,343	1,204	109,261	85.9	90.3	8.6	1.1	126	51	1	178
89,160	8,083	1,085	98,328	77.3	90.7	8.2	1.1	129	50	1	180
89,338	7,539	1,137	98,014	77.0	91.1	7.7	1.2	138	47	1	186
90,862	7,416	1,004	99,282	77.8	91.5	7.5	1.0	153	61	3	217
84,539	7,776	1,131	93,446	73.5	90.5	8.3	1.2	130	47	2	179
78,591	5,768	896	85,255	67.0	92.2	6.7	1.1	134	44	3	181

competitive position in furnishing mills that would meet the needs of the customer. Today the major steel mills have quite comparable facilities. Many of the smaller mills do not have the large, flat-rolled facilities and have had to carve a special niche for themselves. This is another reason why the companies are classified by size as well as by extent of integration. They are then compared to their peers.

LOCATIONAL CONSIDERATIOS

Raw materials, fuel, water, and finished products are all consumed or shipped in huge amounts. The location of the mills and their ability to utilize inexpensive transportation conduits are critical to the profitability of the companies. Water transportation is by far the cheapest means to move materials in bulk. Iron ore comes to the mills from Michigan, Minnesota, Canada, and South America; coal, from West Virginia and Kentucky and, to a lesser degree, from the Midwestern fields. For years the inland waterways provided by the Great Lakes and the Mississippi and Ohio Rivers provided the U.S. industry with a competitive advantage over foreign producers. Barge traffic and 40,000–60,000-ton ore boats brought U.S. mills the lowest cost raw materials in the world. After World War II, Europe's and Japan's steel industries were rebuilt largely in coastal locations on deep water. New, rich ore deposits that did not require beneficiation were discovered in Australia. Ship-building technology underwent significant changes. Today 150,000- and 200,000-ton oreboats are not at all unusual. As a result, the raw material advantages of the United States were curtailed. It is important to note the access a mill has to inexpensive transportation. Bethlehem Steel with its

Sparrows Point Plant possesses the deepest port facilities of any U.S. mill; it can only handle 70–80,000 ton vessels. Most U.S. mills depend on United States, Canadian, and South American ores.

At the other end of the steel-making process, transportation also plays an important part. Steel users have generally let the mills inventory their needs, while they kept perhaps a 30-day supply on hand under normal conditions. However, in a year of labor negotiations, inventories will be built up. Mills, therefore, have to be in a position to ship products on call. Since most manufacturers (steel users) do not require water transportation, shipments of finished products go overland, by rail, or, increasingly, by truck. The mill closest to the market is in the preferred position.

As the population of the United States has spread westward, so, too, has the nation's manufacturing facilities. The component manufacturing of the appliance, automotive, machinery, and farm equipment industries is clustered around the Chicago area. As a result, a steel maker with all of its facilities near Chicago is in a better competitive position than one who has only a small percentage of its facilities there. Mills whose plant locations are in Pittsburgh, western New York, Youngstown, or Cleveland are at a disadvantage in market location over the Chicago and Ohio Valley mills. New facilities have gone up in the Southwest as that area becomes more important in consuming steel.

Undoubtedly location has helped give Chicago-based Inland its strong industry showing in return on sales and equity and in increasing market share during the past five years. It is for this reason that Bethlehem once attempted to merge with Youngstown Sheet and Tube. Failing that, the eastern Pennsylvania company built an entirely new mill in the Chicago area at Burns Harbor. National, Youngstown, and Jones & Laughlin all built new facilities to serve this Midwestern market. Location still is an important characteristic of analysis both from the viewpoint of costs and ability to serve the customer. Steel service centers that buy products in large quantities from the mills to sell it in smaller amounts to the low-tonnage user account for about 20 percent of shipments. A small mill can do a good business serving one or two major customers at these centers.

IDENTIFIABLE COSTS

In 1972 total employment costs accounted for 38.7 percent of revenues. Materials, selling, general and administrative expenses, and transportation costs together were slightly more than 43 percent of the total (these figures represent about 91 percent of U.S. steel production). In only a few other manufacturing industries is labor such a high percentage of cost of goods sold (40 percent). The costs related to hourly workers are uniform throughout the industry. The labor force is represented by the

United Steel Workers. Not all plants however, have elected to have that
union represent them. The Weirton Steel Division of National Steel is
represented by a company union. Still, wages are generally comparable.
The advantages of non-USW representation are generally confined to
strike years, since orders will flow to the plant which is least likely
to be struck. The significance of this may be reduced considerably with
the new labor contract signed early in 1974 that agreed to bar nationwide
strikes through 1980.

In the past ten years, hourly wages in the steel industry have risen in
annual increments. Table 2 illustrates the performance. The base wage

TABLE 2

**Total Employment Cost per Hour—Wage Employees in the Iron and Steel
Industry (covering only those employees engaged in the production of iron
and steel products as reported on AIS 1)**

Year	Total Payroll Cost per Hour	Employee Benefits Cost per Hour	Total Employment Cost per Hour
1972	$5.877	$1.198	$7.075
1971	5.215	1.046	6.261
1970	4.767	.910	5.677
1969	4.566	.809	5.375
1968	4.303	.729	5.032
1967	4.069	.689	4.758
1966	4.017	.616	4.633
1965	3.935	.540	4.475
1964	3.796	.559	4.355
1963	3.687	.560	4.247
1962	3.622	.533	4.155
1961	3.501	.488	3.989
1960	3.349	.471	3.820
1959	3.417	.381	3.798
1958	3.181	.332	3.513
1957	2.917	.299	3.216
1956	2.700	.254	2.954
1955	2.509	.213	2.722
1954	2.333	.179	2.512
1950	1.746	.162	1.908
Incr. 1972 vs 1950	$4.131	$1.036	$5.167
Percent Incr. 1972 vs. 1950	236.6%	639.5%	270.8%

Source: *Annual Statistical Report 1972*, American Iron and Steel Institute.

has risen 52 percent. At the same time, fringe benefits have soared. Holidays and vacations have increased, costing the companies more than
twice the 1963 amount. The total cost of all benefits has more than
doubled over the period. According to the Bureau of Labor Statistics,
the average annual increase in labor productivity is 2.1 percent per year.
This is a somewhat misleading figure in that it does not take into account the capital contribution made to productivity since there has been

some extensive new technology applied to the industry (the BOF and continuous casting, for example).

An industry observer must be aware of the potential changes in the cost of labor. While base-rate changes have not been particularly onerous, the heaviest pressure will continue in the fringe area. The idea of increased medical coverage is a part of every negotiation. The steel industry now has an early retirement rule. With the "30 years and out" provision now in effect, care must be taken to examine the age of the work force. At year-end 1971, 18.4 percent of the hourly work force had 25–34 years of service. The companies with older plants could be in a more vulnerable position in terms of potential pension liability and in terms of loss of key operating employees. Further, considerable attention is being given to legislation to change pension fund requirements to make benefits far more portable. Such legislation could have an impact on labor and pension costs. Even if it is not passed, it is worthwhile to recognize that ideas spawned in legislative halls can sometimes be more easily and quickly put into effect through the superior bargaining power of a union than by a legislative body.

The saving characteristics of wage rates is that they affect all companies in like manner. For purposes of comparing one company's efficiencies with another, a simple calculation is the number of wage and salaried employees per ton of steel shipped. In that way, use of personnel can be readily calculated.

It is interesting that for the industry as a whole employment costs as a percent of total revenues have not increased, despite the escalations which have been discussed. More significantly, tons of steel per employee have increased; or put another way, the number of man hours required to produce a ton of steel has declined.

TABLE 3

Man-Hours per Ton of Steel (1963–1972)

1972	11.1	1967	12.4
1971	11.8	1966	12.0
1970	12.2	1965	12.2
1969	11.8	1964	12.7
1968	11.9	1963	13.3

The steel industry has been accused of bureaucratic practices and excessive employment in the white-collar area. To estimate the efficiency of the nonunion force, several types of information are necessary. One is the calculation of salaried employees per ton of steel shipped. Obviously, the lower the ratio the more efficient the use of personnel. A second is the ratio of total compensation paid all officers and directors (as stated in the corporate proxy statements) to tons of steel shipped.

Interest and Depreciation

Other costs that need to be compared are interest and depreciation. Interest cost comparison is quite straightforward and should prompt the analyst to take a good look at the corporate capitalization. If debt maturities are relatively short term, analysts might expect increased interest cost as the debentures are rolled over. The status of the short-term borrowings and the current costs of lines of credit and bank loans that may be outstanding should be carefully checked by the analyst. U.S. Steel's balance sheet contains several issues of over $100 million bearing interest rates under 5 percent and $140 million due to banks at rates that are pegged to the prime. At present none of these are cause for concern because the maturation dates are some time off. However, it is important to recognize the need to refinance.

In the past, steel companies generally pursued conservative accounting procedures with regard to depreciation. Accelerated write-offs were taken for both book and reporting purposes. After the conglomerate bid for steel companies, which resulted in the LTV purchase of most of Jones & Laughlin and the take-over of Youngstown Sheet and Tube by Lykes Shipping, steel companies switched to straight-line depreciation for reporting purposes. The changes helped inflate earnings during the year in which they were undertaken and also eliminated one important potential accounting benefit for an acquiring company. Reported depreciation figures may, as a result, increase in a more regular pattern than in the past. Still, a new capital addition may have an impact on rising total depreciation charges. There is nothing unique to the steel industry about the way in which depreciation affects financial statements. The distinctive feature in the case of the steel industry is the massive amount of capital required and until recently the relatively low absolute amount of earnings. Together they can make the impact of depreciation significant.

Other Cost Factors

We have commented on the importance of location in regard to transportation costs. Analysts cannot, however, ignore some of the built-in expenses relating to rail and truck transport. A particularly arduous teamster settlement can substantially affect the wage demands of the steel haulers who are part of that union.

Similarly, raw material costs must be evaluated. A buyer of iron ore and coal can expect to have his costs relate to market price quotations for that product. What about the integrated company which gets much of this material from its own sources? Here, the analyst needs to keep current on the United Mine Workers labor demands. At present, coal costs are escalating not only because of increasing economic demands but because coal miners are involved in jurisdictional disputes for control of the union. In addition, the Mine Safety Act has contributed to lower mine productivity. It is not the analyst's place to judge the merits of these issues, but it is his responsibility to recognize them and attempt to place them in some realistic financial perspective.

Tax changes and moves to nationalize properties such as are being presently discussed in Canada and Venezuela may have an impact on the cost of iron ore and must be considered in an analysis.

In its early years, the steel industry was a significant contributor to air and water pollution. Because it is a large and highly visible industry it was pressured to make changes even before the Environmental Protective Agency became a household word. For example, in the Pittsburgh area stringent antipollution rules have been enacted. The costs of modifying and adapting equipment to conform to environmental standards have been very great. Obviously a great deal remains to be done in the environmental area throughout the country. Many companies are contesting environmental suits. No new plant is being considered without attention to cleaning up the particulate matter that is expelled into the air and/or the effluent that escapes into streams. Still these changes have not had a material impact on operating costs. While they may cut down efficiencies of some installations, they are more often than not placed on newly expanded or entirely new facilities which by themselves afford some cost saving. The newly installed clean facility may not be as efficient as a newly installed facility with out pollution control devices but such pollution control facilities will probably not add substantially to operating costs. However, capital costs may be materially increased.

Identifiable Costs—Capital

Apart from the capital that will always be needed to replace worn out equipment, changing technology and the need to meet customer demands are perhaps the primary causes for capital expenditures. The massive capital programs of the 60s resulted in record expenditures. Table 4 illustrates the industry's outlays.

The striking characteristic of the heavy capital outlays of the middle 60s is that they did not result in expanded capacity. The U.S. steel industry had a capability of pouring 150–155 million tons in 1963 and has about the same capacity today. The programs usually began with a recognition on the part of some managers that customers were demanding wider sheets in larger roll sizes with more precise surface tolerances. A company could increase its market share by providing the product. Once the 80-inch computer-driven mill was installed, new steel-making furnaces would be needed. In the course of this shift, BOF furnaces with their much higher yields were installed. They, in turn,

TABLE 4

Balance Sheet, Capital Expenditures (covering the consolidated statements including all the affiliated interests of the parent companies rendering these reports; millions of dollars)

ASSETS	1972	1971ᴿ	1970	1969	1968	1967	1966	1965	1964	1963
Current Assets:										
Cash	$ 505.0	$ 561.8	$ 592.2	$ 659.3	$ 682.0	$ 694.0	$ 782.7	$ 939.3	$ 854.1	$ 881.3
United States Government securities including tax notes and other marketable securities	508.9	557.9	318.8	517.4	1,001.1	1,104.4	1,214.9	1,511.6	1,246.7	1,747.3
Receivables, less allowances for doubtful accounts	2,930.4	2,201.3	2,358.7	2,329.7	1,901.6	1,710.2	1,684.7	1,501.7	1,576.7	1,227.3
Inventories	4,092.7	3,932.1	4,063.5	3,737.8	3,561.9	3,740.8	3,616.6	3,228.3	3,184.7	2,908.4
Other Current Assets	145.2	170.8	178.8	108.6						
Total Current Assets	8,182.2	7,423.9	7,502.0	7,352.8	7,146.6	7,249.4	7,298.9	7,180.9	6,862.2	6,764.3
Miscellaneous investments and other assets	1,990.6	1,790.6	1,714.3	2,014.7	1,951.5	1,768.5	1,589.0	1,489.7	1,414.5	1,081.5
Fixed Assets:										
Property, plant and equipment	32,548.2	31,858.6	30,839.2	29,325.1	28,055.7	26,054.3	24,669.9	23,029.5	21,493.8	20,146.2
Less—Depreciation, depletion and amortization	18,169.2	17,396.6	16,694.1	15,914.1	15,352.1	14,682.4	13,991.5	13,056.8	12,189.0	11,302.8
Net Fixed Assets	14,379.0	14,462.0	14,145.1	13,411.0	12,703.6	11,371.9	10,678.4	9,972.7	9,304.8	8,843.4
Intangibles	56.1	57.0	50.7	46.3	16.8	3.2	2.9	5.7	1.2	1.3
Deferred charges	167.7	156.7	173.5	179.5	268.1	238.9	175.4	121.9	143.8	147.3
TOTAL ASSETS	24,775.6	23,890.2	23,585.6	23,004.3	22,086.6	20,631.9	19,744.6	18,770.9	17,726.5	16,837.8

LIABILITIES AND STOCKHOLDERS' EQUITY

	1972	1971ᴿ	1970	1969	1968	1967	1966	1965	1964	1963
Current Liabilities:										
Accrued taxes, including Federal income taxes	890.3	755.1	655.0	672.4	640.4	852.4	858.3	974.5	902.2	890.6
Long-term debt maturing within one year	258.9	270.2	208.9	206.7	124.5	98.6	138.4	111.8	130.6	149.4
All other current liabilities	3,155.0	2,886.3	3,070.3	3,252.0	2,822.3	2,374.7	2,234.3	1,878.7	1,782.5	1,441.3
Total Current Liabilities	4,304.2	3,911.6	3,934.2	4,131.1	3,587.2	3,325.7	3,231.0	2,965.0	2,815.3	2,481.3
Long-term debt less amount maturing within one year	5,226.8	5,144.4	5,133.9	4,608.2	4,601.4	4,205.3	3,782.3	3,120.1	2,874.2	2,694.8
Reserves for future Federal income taxes, insurance, contingencies, deferred credits, etc.	1,574.6	1,530.0	1,433.8	1,400.1	1,269.1	919.0	677.3	650.3	634.7	651.1
Minority interest in companies not wholly owned	18.7	22.8	67.1	28.9	11.4	13.4	8.9	3.6	2.9	2.3
Stockholders' Equity:										
Preferred stock	117.5	118.6	120.1	123.8	143.3	126.8	152.5	524.8	535.8	639.5
Common stock	3,100.2	3,069.7	3,016.7	3,027.1	3,072.3	3,140.8	3,239.5	2,508.5	2,485.6	2,476.0
Capital surplus	1,280.5	1,273.1	1,224.3	1,179.4	1,146.4	1,118.8	1,100.5	1,027.4	1,016.7	1,005.2
Income reinvested in business	9,153.1	8,820.0	8,605.5	8,505.7	8,255.5	7,782.1	7,552.6	7,971.2	7,361.3	6,887.6
Total Stockholders' Equity	13,651.3	13,281.4	12,966.6	12,836.0	12,617.5	12,168.5	12,045.1	12,031.9	11,399.4	11,008.3
TOTAL LIABILITIES AND STOCKHOLDERS' EQUITY	24,775.6	23,890.2	23,585.6	23,004.3	22,086.6	20,631.9	19,744.6	18,770.9	17,726.5	16,837.8
Capital Expenditures	$ 1,164.2	$ 1,425.0	$ 1,736.2	$ 2,046.6	$ 2,307.3	$ 2,145.7	$ 1,952.7	$ 1,822.5	$ 1,699.5	$ 1,040.0
Estimated cost to complete construction in progress (In millions)	$ 1,837.1									

Source: *Annual Statistical Report 1972*, American Iron and Steel Institute.

demanded more slabbing capacity, and consideration was given to using continuous casting machines. The cost of this equipment was huge. Once Company A had the capability to supply 80-inch material to the auto and appliance industries, Company B would be forced to build a comparable complex. Management was thoroughly familiar with the potential demands of the environmentalists, and most of the new equipment came with all the antipollution devices that were available.

The analyst's function during this period was to be very familiar with the timetable of the new finishing facilities. He also had to have a complete appreciation of the age of the open hearths that would be replaced by BOF or electric furnaces. In that way he could pinpoint whether there was a possibility to increase market share and profitability. National Steel recorded its best performance relative to the industry in the early part of the 60s because it was the first company to see the need for the change. Inland made the changes at intervals that enabled it to hold on to its premier position in the Chicago market. However, most of the industry's management approved similar changes.

While these capital programs did not materially increase capacity, they did meet the needs of the marketplace and were able to increase the output of finished steel. As Table 4 points out, capital expenditures peaked in 1968 and began to trend downward in 1970. Expenditures dropped further in 1972, indicating that the program of the 60s had been completed. There are certain clean-up steps that still have to be taken. Coke ovens have defied technologists' efforts to find a cheap solution to pollution problems.

The next probable step in increased capital outlays will be directed to the addition of new capacity. Price action by the industry has begun to generate capital to permit expansion of existing capacity. It is important to identify companies which are likely to have the largest amount of new product available the soonest. To be on top of that, will demand continual monitoring of steel management's corporate decision-making process.

MARKETS

The major markets for steel products embrace the breadth of the economy. In Table 5 we have indicated shipments of steel, by market.

The volume of steel production depends heavily on the vigor of the automotive industry. Much time is spent on predicting what will happen in these areas. A decline in auto shipments can be offset with a pickup in the capital sector.

There is no easy way to obtain an accurate handle on these developments. The analyst must develop a demand model which indicates the type and magnitude of shipments. Once he is confident that conditions will be propitious for the industry, he must translate the markets into specific shipments of steel products. Table 6 provides a very useful breakdown for this purpose. As to timing, the trends in the leading economic indicators are useful (that is, new orders in the durable goods industries, contracts and orders for new plants and equipment, etc.).

The next step is to determine which company is strongest in which product. In some instances the answer is easy. Companies like Jones & Laughlin and Inland give a breakdown of shipments by market. Others like U.S. Steel will give a breakdown by product grouping as part of their regular reporting to stockholders. Some like Bethlehem Steel give the analyst little help in product breakdown or shipments by market. In the latter case, the *Works* directory published by the American Iron and Steel Institute gives a discription of the plants and type of equipment, from which some understanding of the company's manufacturing capability can be determined. From this information, the analyst can determine which company should benefit from the demand pattern.

Within the markets it is helpful to have a good grasp on steel's strength relative to other materials. Smaller cars can have an impact on steel shipments to the auto industry. Plastics have been making some inroads in the amount of steel used in cars. Aluminum has captured a sizable sector of the beverage can market. To keep track of such developments, it often pays to calculate shipments by unit. Pounds of steel per car help clarify what has been happening in the battle for materials. Containers can be measured by base boxes of tinplate versus aluminum. Individual company vulnerability then depends on which steel maker is dependent on a strong or weak market. In 1973 the companies which served the automobile and appliance market (Armco, National, and Inland) reported better results than U.S. Steel and Bethlehem which are more heavily oriented toward the capital goods sectors.

PRICING

Steel is sold in large quantities directly from the mills and in smaller amounts from steel service centers which are either owned by the mills or operated independently. Price changes are generally presented by one or two industry leaders whose action may or may not be followed by their competitors. While aluminum makers have had long-term contractual relations for tonnage sales with their large customers, steel producers have consistently shipped products using the price in effect at time of delivery. Steel pricing has not had the volatility associated with copper, whose price swings are determined by world commodity markets. Copper prices suffer sharp spurts when supplies are tight and even sharper declines when demand falls off. Steel prices show little of that volatility. There have been times when prices have hardly risen over a year, but price cuts are rare indeed. Concessions for freight and extra services are common in weak markets.

TABLE 5

Net Shipments of Steel Products by Market Classifications: All Grades, including Carbon, Alloy, and Stainless Steel (thousands of net tons)

Market Classifications	1972 * Ship-ments	%	1971 * Ship-ments	%	1970 * Ship-ments	%	1969 Ship-ments	%
Steel for converting and processing	4,199	4.6	3,593	4.1	3,443	3.8	3,237	3.4
Independent forgers (not elsewhere classified)	1,007	1.1	1,018	1.2	1,048	1.2	1,256	1.3
Industrial fasteners	1,030	1.1	956	1.1	1,005	1.1	1,090	1.2
Steel service centers & distributors:								
Oil and gas supply houses	1,801	2.0	1,760	2.0	1,653	1.9	1,782	1.9
All other	16,797	18.3	14,424	16.6	16,025	17.6	15,783	16.8
Total	18,598	20.3	16,184	18.6	17,678	19.5	17,565	18.7
Construction, including maintenance	9,299	10.1	9,541	11.0	10,565	11.6	11,402	12.1
Contractors' products	5,055	5.5	4,946	5.6	4,440	4.9	4,768	5.1
Subtotal construction and contractors' products	14,354	15.6	14,487	16.6	15,005	16.5	16,170	17.2
Automotive:								
Vehicles, parts, etc.	17,639	19.2	16,980	19.5	14,011	15.4	17,649	18.8
Independent forgers	578	0.6	503	0.6	464	0.5	627	0.7
Total	18,217	19.8	17,483	20.1	14,475	15.9	18,276	19.5
Rail transportation:								
Freight cars, pass. cars & locomotives	1,511	1.6	1,855	2.1	2,005	2.3	2,309	2.5
Rails and all other	1,219	1.3	1,149	1.3	1,093	1.2	1,035	1.1
Total	2,730	2.9	3,004	3.4	3,098	3.5	3,344	3.6
Shipbuilding and marine equipment	872	1.0	1,161	1.3	859	0.9	907	1.0
Aircraft and aerospace	63	0.1	53	0.1	56	0.1	84	0.1
Oil and gas drilling	278	0.3	257	0.3	245	0.3	339	0.4
Mining, quarrying and lumbering	502	0.5	478	0.5	497	0.5	455	0.5
Agricultural:								
Agricultural machinery	962	1.1	788	0.9	809	0.9	839	0.9
All other	477	0.5	342	0.4	317	0.3	328	0.3
Total	1,439	1.6	1,130	1.3	1,126	1.2	1,167	1.2
Machinery, industrial equipment & tools	5,396	5.9	4,903	5.6	5,169	5.6	5,690	6.
Electrical equipment	2,824	3.1	2,593	3.0	2,694	3.0	2,813	3.
Appliances, utensils and cutlery	2,362	2.6	2,148	2.5	2,160	2.4	2,248	2.
Other domestic & commercial equipment	1,816	2.0	1,720	2.0	1,778	2.0	1,938	2.
Containers, packaging & shipping materials:								
Cans and closures	5,128	5.6	5,808	6.7	6,239	6.8	5,603	5.
Barrels, drums and shipping pails	748	0.8	732	0.8	823	0.9	761	0.
All other	740	0.8	672	0.8	713	0.8	781	0.
Total	6,616	7.2	7,212	8.3	7,775	8.5	7,145	7.
Ordnance and other military	899	0.9	861	1.0	1,222	1.3	1,758	1
Export (reporting companies only)	2,555	2.8	2,433	2.8	5,985	6.6	5,004	5
Nonclassified shipments	6,048	6.6	5,364	6.2	5,480	6.1	3,391	3
TOTAL SHIPMENTS	91,805	100.0	87,038	100.0	90,798	100.0	93,877	100

Similar data not available prior to 1940.
* 1970, 1971 and 1972 data are not strictly comparable with those of previous years.

Source: *Annual Statistical Report 1972*, American Iron and Steel Institute.

Steel makers have cut production when demand falls off rather than cut prices. If 8 million cars are sold in a year following 10 million unit sales, steel requirements are down. Cutting steel prices does not increase consumption. When inexpensive Japanese and European steel was imported to the United States, the lower prices enabled foreign steel to capture a large share of the U.S. market, prevented price increases among the U.S. producers, and sharply restricted profitability.

In the 60s when foreign steels were abundantly available, economic arguments that U.S. steel should move offshore because of the lower wage

1968		1967		1966		1965		1964		1963	
Ship-ments	%	Ship-ments	%	Ship-ments	%	Ship-ments	%	Ship-ments	%	Ship-ments	%
2,909	3.2	2,837	3.4	3,153	3.5	3,932	4.2	2,687	3.2	2,612	3.5
1,197	1.3	1,208	1.4	1,323	1.5	1,250	1.4	1,062	1.3	899	1.2
1,116	1.2	1,128	1.3	1,320	1.5	1,234	1.3	1,229	1.4	1,160	1.5
1,990	2.1	1,493	1.8	1,536	1.7	1,556	1.7	1,719	2.0	1,522	2.0
14,109	15.4	13,370	15.9	14,864	16.5	14,813	16.0	13,845	16.3	11,627	15.4
16,099	17.5	14,863	17.7	16,400	18.2	16,369	17.7	15,564	18.3	13,149	17.4
12,195	13.3	11,375	13.6	11,862	13.2	11,836	12.8	10,992	12.9	10,051	13.3
4,922	5.4	4,582	5.5	4,969	5.5	5,018	5.4	4,646	5.5	4,339	5.7
17,117	18.7	15,957	19.1	16,831	18.7	16,854	18.2	15,638	18.4	14,390	19.0
18,664	20.3	15,932	19.0	17,302	19.2	19,423	21.0	17,767	20.9	16,339	21.6
605	0.7	556	0.7	682	0.8	700	0.7	620	0.7	550	0.8
19,269	21.0	16,488	19.7	17,984	20.0	20,123	21.7	18,387	21.6	16,889	22.4
2,088	2.3	2,337	2.8	3,159	3.5	2,875	3.1	2,633	3.1	1,915	2.6
960	1.0	888	1.0	1,173	1.3	930	1.0	836	1.0	648	0.8
3,048	3.3	3,225	3.8	4,332	4.8	3,805	4.1	3,469	4.1	2,563	3.4
1,006	1.1	943	1.1	1,017	1.1	1,051	1.1	805	0.9	712	0.9
90	0.1	102	0.1	129	0.1	94	0.1	72	0.1	77	0.1
387	0.4	315	0.4	377	0.4	380	0.4	415	0.5	295	0.4
457	0.5	345	0.4	392	0.4	392	0.4	368	0.4	284	0.4
1,015	1.1	1,090	1.3	1,317	1.5	1,169	1.3	1,100	1.3	952	1.2
385	0.4	319	0.4	388	0.4	314	0.3	269	0.3	273	0.4
1,400	1.5	1,409	1.7	1,705	1.9	1,483	1.6	1,369	1.6	1,225	1.6
5,469	6.0	4,994	6.0	5,747	6.4	5,873	6.3	5,338	6.3	4,498	5.9
2,897	3.2	2,808	3.3	3,021	3.4	2,985	3.2	2,654	3.1	2,284	3.0
2,292	2.5	2,092	2.5	2,311	2.6	2,179	2.4	2,168	2.6	2,010	2.7
2,070	2.2	2,060	2.5	2,215	2.5	2,179	2.4	2,034	2.4	1,892	2.5
6,278	6.8	5,762	6.8	5,035	5.6	5,867	6.3	5,231	6.1	5,101	6.8
855	0.9	810	0.9	827	0.9	810	0.9	847	1.0	818	1.1
769	0.9	683	0.9	735	0.8	654	0.7	474	0.6	545	0.7
7,902	8.6	7,255	8.6	6,597	7.3	7,331	7.9	6,552	7.7	6,464	8.6
2,025	2.2	1,622	1.9	686	0.8	289	0.3	214	0.3	289	0.4
2,147	2.3	1,407	1.7	1,541	1.7	2,078	2.3	2,749	3.2	1,831	2.4
2,959	3.2	2,839	3.4	2,914	3.2	2,785	3.0	2,171	2.6	2,032	2.7
91,856	100.0	83,897	100.0	89,995	100.0	92,666	100.0	84,945	100.0	75,555	100.0

structures available abroad were plentiful. At that time it was easy to interpret price data that supported the concept that prices were administered by the steel companies and that they did not reflect market, competitive, or economic conditions. Little attention was paid to the industry's continuous need for capital to modernize, maintain, and expand plants to meet a growing economy.

U.S. steel consumption, despite the continuous inroads of substitute materials and a secular growth rate that was projected at less than that of the GNP, could not be satisfied from U.S. mills. After the currency revaluation of 1973, foreign steels were priced above the U.S. product—

TABLE 6

Shipments of Steel Products by Market Classification, 1972; All Grades Including Carbon, Alloy, and Stainless (net tons)

Products	Steel for Converting and Processing			Forgings (not elsewhere classified)	Industrial Fasteners
	Total Shipments	Less Shipments to Reporting Companies	Net Shipments		
Ingots, blooms, billets slabs, sheet bars and tube rounds	1,062,596	871,195	191,401	589,771	424
Skelp	286,527	284,645	1,882		
Wire rods	1,116.441	439,727	676,714	689	265,744
Structural shapes (heavy)	6,554	2,020	4,534		
Steel piling	88	88			
Plates	204.931	131,615	73,316	12,401	40,488
Rails—Standard (over 60 lbs)	1,789	267	1,522		
—All other	286	286			
Joint bars	1,099	21	1,078		
Tie plates	48	20	28		
Track spikes	720	4	716		
Wheels (rolled and forged)	215	215			
Axles					
Bars—Hot rolled (including light shapes)	1,176,036	777,623	398,413	397,220	402,857
—Reinforcing	70,094	49,427	20,667		
—Cold finished	10,457	3,474	6,983	3,520	44,363
Tool steel	1,176	1,012	164	3,102	62
Pipe and tubing—Standard	155,530	107,934	47,596		
—Oil country goods	37,185	35,063	2,122		
—Line	18,108	13,865	4,243		
—Mechanical	22,370	19,068	3,302		
—Pressure	751	383	368		
—Structural	2,258	615	1,643		
—Stainless	910	282	628		
Wire—Drawn	645,166	34,035	611,131		167,293
—Nails and staples	25,312	5,939	19,373		
—Other merchant wire products	20,915	927	19,988		
Black plate	123,506	82,398	41,108		
Tin plate—Electrolytic and Hot Dipped	6,276		6,276		
Tin free steel	194		194		
Tin Mill products—All other	457		457		
Sheets—Hot rolled	2,605,823	1,150,312	1,455,511		63,559
—Cold rolled	554,235	100,173	454,062	19	5,646
Sheets and strip—Galvanized	67,498	12,426	55,072		1,455
—All other metallic coated	9,721	3,710	6,011		9
—Electrical	3,795		3,795		
Strip—Hot rolled	231,015	175,278	55,737		32,611
—Cold rolled	38,024	4,793	33,231		4,933
TOTAL—ALL GRADES	8,508,106	4,308,840	4,199,266	1,006,722	1,029,444
%			4.6	1.1	1.1

Source: *Annual Statistical Report 1972*, American Iron and Steel Institute.

even when landed here. U.S. consumers turned toward U.S. mills; but the mills were booked up, and shortages accrued in several product lines.

Historically the industry posture on prices had been to achieve levels high enough to generate sufficient cash flow to support the capital requirements of an industry that had to meet a secular growth rate of 2.5 percent. To do that, prices had to meet costs or at least keep up with inflation. Recognizing that markets could change, the price increases that are possible in good years help smooth out the lack of price increases in poorer years. The progression of the composite price for finished steel proved relatively smooth. See Table 7, (page 754).

Steel Service Centers and Distributors	Construction Including Maintenance	Contractors' Products	Automotive	Rail Transportation	Shipbuilding and Marine Equipment	Aircraft and Aerospace	Oil and Gas Drilling
71,196	52,992	1,954	458,450	12,238	6,285	18,773	30,468
94,279	44,952	88,902	87,867	446	5,522	21	...
1,185,976	2,788,706	68,927	152,758	265,969	123,356	60	21,184
68,275	327,913	...	...	2,481	1,496	...	...
1,397,555	1,471,483	635,528	280,534	548,522	636,158	8,705	66,038
7,528	22,168	...	...	784,970	9	...	...
7,411	8,433	...	...	7,653	516	...	...
575	1,326	...	...	9,539	5	...	...
2,031	3,637	...	...	190,308	...	...	...
2,809	1,484	...	...	76,802	...	...	...
56	3,101	...	...	200,258	16	...	...
...	791	...	...	129,628	...	...	...
1,180,622	410,248	238,084	2,580,343	210,535	39,181	14,267	89,920
459,873	1,716,146	33,623	...	...	55	...	...
391,502	3,802	17,334	222,589	3,812	4,688	6,596	5,760
17,858	643	3	10	...	...	123	...
1,432,489	293,389	101,334	1,632	2,767	2,926	29	2,782
1,130,851	827	...	...	...	...	...	22,116
923,960	753,750	4,777	196	61	211	...	7,665
211,819	27,929	20,068	224,485	1,382	304	1,417	20,270
50,329	1,532	1,076	74	69	395	6	617
323,093	126,747	2,811	435	84	706	...	3,596
12,664	665	327	187	27	449	55	492
244,801	46,542	305,640	148,677	2,981	591	464	339
308,552	9,065	83	63	628	12	...	...
285,928	7,232	...	...	899	...	...	...
82,761	22,824	47,984	12,703	224	...	...	...
129,720	811	6,316	70,846	164	46	...	8
10,571	21	214	1,323	48	...	...	...
19,195	46	1,917	38,296	...	...	...	...
3,459,435	535,750	733,619	4,938,093	225,544	35,127	1,384	1,808
3,195,678	103,945	979,357	6,915,157	11,359	2,481	1,786	2,304
1,506,809	421,640	1,608,069	900,112	15,546	4,894	444	98
101,839	22,010	46,230	368,328	60	4,514	2,721	...
30,354	...	208	10,278	3,378	...	326	591
155,982	64,626	68,797	603,636	20,997	2,284	3,363	2,029
93,500	1,851	42,182	199,683	1,112	122	1,959	56
,597,876	9,299,027	5,055,364	18,216,755	2,730,491	872,349	62,499	278,141
20.2	10.1	5.5	19.8	3.0	0.9	0.1	0.3

The steel industry has always been a highly visible sector of American business life. Ever since the Kennedy confrontation, the industry has had to contend with the political impact of its price action. During the 60s this sometimes resulted in price rises that did not meet the general increase in inflation and fell behind the increases in steel wages. Then steel was in oversupply, and new capacity was not needed. The industry could and did raise sufficient capital to modernize and make many of its plants competitive with mills in other parts of the world.

These modernized mills are now producing at capacity and have helped raise the steel industry's rate of return on capital in 1973. The increase has been sharp because the earlier performance was so low. It

TABLE 6 (Continued)

Products	Mining, Quarrying and Lumbering	Agricultural	Machinery, Industrial Equipment and Tools	Electrical Equipment
Ingots, blooms, billets slabs, sheet bars and tube rounds	4,254	28,069	237,238	1,266
Skelp	...	...	...	...
Wire rods	...	17,452	335,650	4,150
Structural shapes (heavy)	26,349	48,696	237,647	17,319
Steel piling	4,050	...	...	...
Plates	78,126	161,545	1,488,181	214,185
Rails—Standard (over 60 lbs)	10,723	...	2,978	...
—All other	3,980	...	1,751	...
Joint bars	518	...	22	...
Tie plates	440	...	...	...
Track spikes	457	...	...	...
Wheels (rolled and forged)	1,310	...	5,858	33
Axles	28	...	442	...
Bars—Hot rolled (including light shapes)	330,995	313,878	1,099,345	132,171
—Reinforcing	872	276	...	...
—Cold finished	5,729	66,189	339,569	25,254
Tool steel	107	...	10,028	...
Pipe and tubing—Standard	2,817	9,426	18,298	236,639
—Oil country goods	5,336	136	258	...
—Line	1,268	2,543	8,550	47
—Mechanical	2,845	20,879	345,430	7,806
—Pressure	54	...	78,784	370
—Structural	...	10,959	1,610	1,574
—Stainless	97	13	3,977	1,784
Wire—Drawn	4,476	6,284	161,742	17,963
—Nails and staples	74	194	10,641	240
—Other merchant wire products	66	418	...	12
Black plate	136	45	9,328	6,167
Tin plate—Electrolytic and Hot Dipped	58	342	10,195	19,159
Tin free steel	...	...	28	25
Tin Mill products—All other	16	...	1,592	1,428
Sheets—Hot rolled	9,027	324,743	464,108	298,061
—Cold rolled	2,538	44,972	240,471	946,699
Sheets and strip—Galvanized	1,181	278,926	50,207	102,687
—All other metallic coated	201	6,785	16,462	32,779
—Electrical	333	...	20,001	602,686
Strip—Hot rolled	3,262	90,336	149,241	78,436
—Cold rolled	109	5,378	46,020	75,192
TOTAL—ALL GRADES	501,832	1,438,484	5,395,652	2,824,132
%	0.5	1.6	5.9	3.1

still does not compare with the average of U.S. industry and does not provide a sufficient return to generate the capital necessary to build new mills. This was not relevant in past years when steel was in oversupply, but it becomes significant as fewer steel products are readily available and the need for new capacity becomes obvious.

Following the end of price controls the steel industry raised prices in an effort to raise its return to that of the average of U.S. industry with which it must compete for capital. The results of such an improvement would be measured in higher earnings for the industry and higher potential dividends—both of crucial importance to investors.

FOREIGN COMPETITION

Steel has not been a fast growing commodity. This has made it painful for the U.S. industry to see such a large percentage of its consumption

Appliances, Utensils, and Cutlery	Other Domestics and Commercial Equipment	Containers, Packaging and Shipping Materials	Ordnance and Other Military	Export (Reporting Companies Only)	Non-classified Shipments	Total	%
...	10	7,002	414,244	401,309	465,162	2,992,506	3.3
				3,654		5,536	
3,640	113,423	7,961	191	136,938	34,203	1,918,744	2.1
518	6,867	762	1,364	80,489	205,479	5,236,960	5.7
				15,029		419,244	0.5
2,657	29,650	27,049	35,833	130,207	215,109	7,553,270	8.2
...	...	...	...	91,622	...	921,520	1.0
...				6,455		36,199	
...				1,772	2,976	17,811	
...				2,190		198,634	0.2
...			40	693	529	83,530	0.1
...				1,861		212,493	0.2
...				335		131,224	0.1
15,456	69,192	6,011	35,821	108,488	1,226,239	9,299,286	10.1
	161			15,855	2,206,422	4,453,950	4.8
26,893	34,911	94	32,226	4,547	428,532	1,674,893	1.8
...	2	...	4	69	58,055	90,230	0.1
3,160	20,209		212,116	33,369	22,403	2,443,381	2.7
		691	...	113,871	658	1,276,866	1.4
24	344			137,512	97,541	1,942,692	2.1
8,629	18,572	215	5,044	11,574	287,049	1,219,019	1.3
		3,172	...	3,696	44,304	184,846	0.2
	1,834			4,343	33,683	513,118	0.6
46	907	39	58	732	5,625	28,772	
24,678	204,496	19,811	3,415	14,776	284,113	2,270,213	2.5
14	254	5,735	393	91	...	355,412	0.4
...	...	2,314	6,411	2,498	1,103	326,869	0.3
27,940	54,361	256,753	3,181	39,527	...	605,042	0.7
29,266	28,127	3,946,047	4,383	211,839	...	4,463,603	4.9
43	987	974,198		546	...	988,198	1.1
5,199	6,309	3,011		792	...	78,258	0.1
228,591	162,326	397,637	65,795	635,583	521	14,036,222	15.3
1,561,476	804,920	647,788	59,151	142,928	...	16,122,737	17.6
287,184	132,617	44,928	6,969	98,303	...	5,517,141	6.0
30,322	13,884	4,329	834	33,304	...	690,622	0.7
6,511	1,396			28,730	293	708,880	0.8
18,393	41,213	120,392	7,480	14,601	...	1,533,416	1.7
81,530	69,061	140,245	4,336	25,300	427,431	1,253,231	1.4
2,362,170	1,816,033	6,616,184	899,289	2,555,428	6,047,430	91,804,568	100.0
2.6	2.0	7.2	1.0	2.8	6.6	100.0	

move to foreign mills. Since 1959 there has been an increased tonnage of imported steel from Europe, Japan, and Canada. Table 8 tells the story.

An important factor in the penetration of the American market has been the uncertainty in supply and the consequent building of inventory positions associated with the steel labor negotiations such as occurred in 1965, again in 1968, and in 1971. A steel customer's need to protect himself against loss of domestic steel prompted the initial sales, if prices and quality were acceptable. Once the customer had experience with the foreign product, he tended to regard the offshore mill as a permanent source. The fact that quality met his standards and that import prices were $20 to $40 a ton cheaper for a product that was priced at $180 accelerated the growth of imports.

The foreign mill may not be as efficient as the U.S. producer, but foreign workers are paid less, often by a large margin. Japanese steelworkers earn less than half the wage of their American counterparts.

TABLE 7

Composite Finished Steel Price (1963–72)
(cents per pound)

	Price	Percent Change
1972	9.01	+ 6.8
1971	8.44	+10.3
1970	7.65	+ 7.9
1969	7.09	+ 7.4
1968	6.60	+ 2.2
1967	6.46	+ 0.1%
1966	6.40	+ 0.5
1965	6.37	+ 0.5
1964	6.37	—
1963	6.27	+ 1.6

The foreign mills have been built since the end of the war and generally incorporate the latest steel-making and finishing equipment (some of which is manufactured here) which provides a product of quality equal to U.S. requirements. The exporter has one further advantage. He does not have to supply a full line of steel products that may have grown over the years. He can install capacity tailored to the highest volume production runs. Since volume is related to profitability, the exporter often deals in high-profit products without the service responsibility that a U.S. mill may have because of a long-time relationship with a customer. As a result, the domestic steel industry is losing the highest profit markets. For this reason, the U.S. industry has begun lobbying hard to have some kind of control over imports. Early in 1972 a voluntary agreement which hammered out a series of quotas were developed and signed by the participants. That helped, but not greatly.

In mid-1973, the United Steel Workers agreed to the terms of a new labor contract that would not go into effect until August 1974. The contract further provided that any issues that were still to be adjudicated should be submitted to binding arbitration. These terms convinced customers that they would not need to build up inventory prior to the contract expiration date as had been the case in prior periods. The 1972–73 period witnessed two devaluations of the dollar and a steel consuming boom in Europe and Japan. As a result it cost more to bring steel from Japan to the West Coast of the United States than to buy U.S.-made steel there. Competitive conditions had changed.

There has been little geographical change in the sources of steel imported to the United States. The largest supplies have come from Europe, followed by Japan and Canada.

With imports a sizable factor, an analyst must keep abreast of the conditions that spawned the increase and carefully note changes. At the moment the trend is down. What would happen if there were significant excess production in Europe and Japan together with threats of domestic

TABLE 8

Imports of Steel Mill Products (net tons)

Months	1972	1971	1970	1969	1968
January	1,093,184	1,304,726	780,996	509,790	1,101,972
February	1,129,337	1,229,584	696,664	567,528	1,058,236
March	1,095,494	1,253,897	859,311	875,974	1,241,268
April	929,875	1,363,434	962,117	1,504,929	1,480,257
May	1,603,175	1,791,944	1,065,735	1,727,292	1,769,799
June	1,598,803	2,111,638	1,082,153	1,431,848	1,507,249
July	1,531,098	1,688,307	1,133,951	1,412,312	1,504,677
August	1,787,250	1,554,015	1,111,313	1,249,229	2,137,597
September	1,569,825	1,779,731	1,277,071	1,310,965	1,698,426
October	1,910,435	1,437,299	1,333,823	1,297,115	1,485,044
November	1,823,991	1,471,900	1,714,439	1,008,188	1,550,496
December	1,608,540	1,335,878	1,346,901	1,139,117	1,424,865
TOTAL *	17,681,007	18,303,959	13,364,474	14,034,287	17,959,886

Months	1967	1966	1965	1964	1963
January	781,850	668,430	346,746	481,836	234,368
February	743,637	537,953	451,774	428,330	339,620
March	882,032	775,960	1,025,200	473,667	386,630
April	828,409	715,119	908,385	495,464	424,770
May	1,030,079	918,875	1,014,425	544,173	516,171
June	962,524	1,013,645	1,191,872	603,757	466,816
July	965,297	1,082,160	1,094,171	582,349	598,875
August	984,790	1,090,270	1,061,437	525,147	547,191
September	955,752	1,089,281	786,329	493,243	470,921
October	998,839	939,973	891,568	555,139	549,795
November	1,308,159	1,151,401	939,138	733,634	518,945
December	1,013,134	769,955	671,917	523,118	401,779
TOTAL *	11,454,502	10,753,022	10,383,021	6,439,635	5,446,326

* Revised totals include adjustments not shown in monthly figures.
Similar data not available prior to 1950.

Source: *Annual Statistical Report 1972*, American Iron and Steel Institute.

labor difficulties is an open question. Now the currency relationships favor the United States. That, too could change. On the other hand, a continued boom abroad could help American steel makers. Imports continue as an important area of observation.

ACCOUNTING PRACTICES

We commented earlier on interest costs and depreciation. Because of both labor and capital intensive characteristics of this industry, the pension fund liability and the treatment of the investment tax credit can be significant factors. There have been occasions when steel managements recognized the appreciation in their internally managed pension funds and used such appreciation in lieu of a contribution. There have been some cases where actuarial requirements have been changed, reducing the annual corporate contribution. However, the recent changes in fringe benefits have materially affected pension contributions. These provisions, calling for a full pension after a man has worked 30 years, a partial vesting after 15 years, and larger benefits have increased company liabilities. Interest in pension funds by both labor and management has served to underscore their visibility. Managements are now required to spell out what they have done in the footnotes to the annual report. Further-more, the difference in pension fund performance and past contributions varies from company to company. Some companies have heavy past service liabilities. Others made heavy contributions in past years and have fully funded plans. Future pension contributions will be much smaller for the latter than the former.

At one time the steel industry was divided on the use of the invest-ment tax credit. Now, however, most companies flow the credit through to income in the year in which the asset to which it applies is put into service. The analyst should consider the positive impact of the credit in the year in which it is taken and recognize that in the year following the flow through, the tax rate may increase.

Many of the major steel companies are also mining companies. As such, they are entitled to depletion allowances on iron ore, coal, limestone, and other by-products. In addition, preproduction expenses *may* be capi-talized prior to the development of a new mine but *can* be expensed in the year in which the mine begins operations. Both of these provisions are in common use in the mining industry. Analysts should note the time when a new property will be put into use. He should also try to ascer-tain any change in the company's depletion allowances. Both of these factors can have important bearing on the effective tax rate of the com-pany. The tax rate can sometimes be useful to determine the source of corporate earnings. A low rate would indicate that the mining operations are a major factor in the company's performance. A tax rate approaching 50 percent would indicate that the steel-making operations are the major contributors to the company's earnings.

There are numerous financial ratios for comparing the performance of two steel companies. It is important that an analyst identify those ratios that he finds most useful and maintain them on a regular basis. We would include the following:

1. *Pretax earnings as a percent of revenues*—the closest thing to operat-ing profit margins available that gives some indication of relative efficiency.
2. *Net income as a percent of revenues*—by itself not as important as pretax margins, but a means to analyze and compare profitability.
3. *Effective tax rate*—taxes as a percent of pretax income. A guide to the source of income.
4. *Return on stockholders' equity*—a measure of how well the corpora-tion is performing.
5. *Debt/equity ratio*—Is the fact that the company is borrowing more still a good measure of financial strength?
6. *Tons of steel shipped per employee*—a test of whether the bureauc-racy is under control.
7. *Market share*—the company's shipments as percent of total industry

shipments. A test of corporate competitive strength. If share is rising and other relationships do not compare favorably, watch out—the company may be expanding its market share by unsound practices.

8. *Sales per ton of steel shipped*—a rough measure of what has been happening to product mix. For some highly diversified companies, not too meaningful.

9. *Profit per ton of steel shipped*—a means of determining whether improved prices have been realized by the company.

There are other standard comparisons such as interest depreciation and general and administrative expenses, as a percent of total costs, that help to keep tabs on whether any of these factors are out of line.

As indicated in other sections of this handbook, these ratios—kept systematically and on a regular basis—can quickly enable the analyst to spot any variations of performance of the company or companies under study.

STOCK MARKET PERFORMANCE

Steel stocks have been out of investor favor for so long that no meaningful discussion of market performance is really possible. Chart 1 illustrates both the absolute performance of the Standard & Poor's Index and steel's performance relative to the market. Only a few industries can demonstrate like records.

A CASE STUDY

As a means to illustrate some of the points we have been making, we have chosen to compare the performance of U.S. Steel, the largest steel maker operating from a variety of plants throughout the country, with that of Inland, which operates a number of plants at a single site in Chicago. In 1972, Inland Steel shipped 5.2 million tons versus 20.8 million tons for U.S. Steel. Shipments were divided as shown in Table 9.

During the year, Inland had the product mix that was in greatest demand. Light flat-rolled products were heavily bought to satisfy the con-

TABLE 9

Shipments by Product—1972

	U.S. Steel (percent)	Inland (percent)
Sheet and strip	40	65
Plates and structurals	20	22
Bar and semifinished	18	13
Pipe and tubing	10	—
All other	12	—
	100	100

CHART 1

Trend of S & P Steel Industry Stock Index and Performance Relative to The S & P 425 Industrials, 1953–September 1973

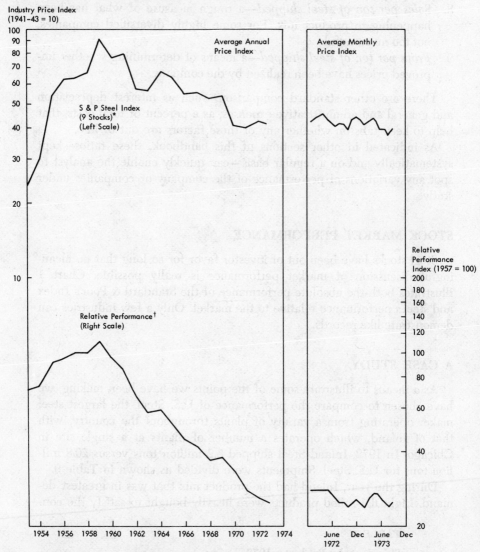

* Armco Steel Corp., Bethlehem Steel, Inland, Interlake, Lykes-Youngstown, National Steel, Republic Steel, U.S. Steel, and Wheeling-Pittsburgh.

† Ratio of Steel Index to S & P Industrial Index. 1957 = 100

TABLE 10

Share of U.S. Steel Shipments (by percent)

	U.S. Steel	Inland Steel
1972	22.7	5.7
1971	22.2	5.4
1970	23.1	5.2
1969	23.9	5.1
1968	24.5	5.2
1967	23.6	5.4
1966	24.0	5.2
1965	24.3	4.9
1964	25.0	5.1
1965	24.0	4.9

sumer durable market. It was not a particularly good year for pipe and tubing. Plates and structurals are a function of capital spending and both companies had similar performance. A further illustration of the relative attractiveness of the product mix can be expressed in the share of the steel market each has held over the past ten years. Our comparison is shown in Table 10.

From 1963 to 1965 and again from 1967 to 1969, Inland's share of market declined. Over the ten-year period, however, the company has held its position. Such fluctuations can sometimes be related to equipment problems, etc. U.S. Steel, on the other hand, has experienced a continuous erosion of market share.

Obviously Inland has been in a better competitive posture, and that may be explained by product mix or by location. Inland is in a steel deficit area. Within that Chicago market many new mills have been built during the past ten years. The fact that Inland could withstand National's expansion at Great Lakes, Youngstown's new Indiana Harbor works, Bethlehem's new facility at Burns Harbor, and Jones & Laughlin's move to northern Illinois says something for Inland's ability to retain customer loyalty.

Table 11 compares the two companies as to profitability.

There is little argument as to which company has had the best performance. It is interesting to try to determine why one company should

TABLE 11

Comparison of Profitability—1972

	U.S. Steel (percent)	Inland (percent)
Pretax profit margin	3.7	7.8
Net profit margin	2.9	4.5
Return on equity	4.4	8.2

do so much better than another. Several tests of efficiency have been applied. A cursory comparison of the tax rate which in 1972 was 21.9 percent for U.S. Steel and 42.3 percent for Inland only confirms a suspicion that there were no unusual allowances. Inland has been making money from its higher taxed assets (that is, steel making) which U.S. Steel has not. Efficiency ratios are shown in Table 12.

TABLE 12

Comparison of Efficiency—1972

	U.S. Steel	Inland
Tons of steel/employee	117.9	155.9
Profit/ton	$ 7.55	$ 12.67

It takes Inland fewer people to make steel, and the smaller company makes more money doing it. The above ratios are important and should be compiled over a period of time. It is certainly true that the product mix has favored Inland and that in an environment that leans toward the heavier steel product, the larger company might come out best.

The one remaining piece of analysis is probably the most critical— the current price of the stock. The steels in the fall of 1973 were valued at six to eight times our estimate of what they may earn. Nothing can compensate for a poor recent past so effectively as a low price. If a case can be made that this difficult industry might yet show a spark of some of its old strengths, these are the prices from which stock market gains can be made.

29

Textiles

EILEEN M. GORMLEY, C.F.A.
Vice President
Thomson & McKinnon Auchincloss Kohlmeyer Inc.
New York, New York

INDUSTRY CHARACTERISTICS

Changes over the Years

BEFORE World War II, the industry was comprised of many small family-owned units, each performing a separate phase of the fabric manufacturing process. It was common practice for mill owners to make production decisions without regard for merchandising considerations and to use independent selling agents to dispose of their output for whatever the market was willing to offer.

In recent years, the industry has undergone a change in orientation. Traditionally, emphasis was placed on maintaining a high rate of production. Now merchandising strategies determine the mix of fabric output, based upon the outlook for demand with respect to a specific product and for growth in the related market area. Despite the higher risk with respect to potential inventory write-downs, fashion and style considerations today are more important than just the production of commodity or staple goods. New equipment in the knitting field along with the application of the computer in purchasing, dyeing, finishing, warehousing, shipping, and billing have resulted in a shorter time interval between receipt of an order and final shipment of goods.

The textile industry is a major consumer of natural and synthetic fibers as well as an important purchaser of plastics, chemicals, and dyestuffs. In the early 1970s, mill consumption of man-made fibers rose to 65 percent of total fiber requirements, up from 54 percent in 1968. Further-more, cotton represented 33 percent of all fibers used, versus 42 percent in 1968; while wool accounted for a meager 2 percent, down from 4 per-cent. According to the Commerce Department, by 1978 the share of mar-ket held by the various types of fibers will be about 19 percent for cotton, 1 percent for wool, and 80 percent for synthetics. Reasons for the shift to synthetics are their relatively greater price stability and availability of supply, along with superior wear and care properties of garments made from these fibers.

The industry's customers are the apparel and related consumer prod-ucts fields which account for about 34 percent and 13 percent, respec-tively, of fabric consumption. Home furnishings represent about 33 percent of textile output, and industrial applications take up 20 percent of mill production. While suppliers of fabrics to the foregoing markets, many mills are themselves manufacturers of such consumer products as carpet-ing, furniture, hosiery, blankets, and towels. Examples of broadly di-versified companies serving most, if not all, of the above markets are Burlington Industries, J. P. Stevens, and West Point-Pepperell.

Since the mid-1960s woven goods have experienced a loss in market share to knitted fabrics. During this period, there also has been a shift away from woven carpets to tufted and needle-punched floor coverings. Wool yarns have lost market share in ready-to-wear to yarns made from synthetic fibers, especially textured polyester.

In 1971, about 70 percent of mill employment was concentrated in North Carolina, South Carolina, Virginia, Georgia, Tennessee, and Ala-bama. Since other industries also have relocated to the South, a scarcity of skilled labor is a new challenge for many mills.

Through consolidation and expansion, small factories are giving way to efficient vertically integrated concerns which operate with improved control of inventories and quality. Typically, a broad range of fabrics and consumer textile items are produced, with the emphasis placed on overall profitability rather than on the results of one specific operation. Marketing has become a factor of critical importance as mills now stress only the production of fabrics which will satisfy consumer demand. Highly skilled managements at the leading companies are deploying financial resources for increased levels of advertising, research, and capital expenditures than in the past.

The trend to consolidation is expected to continue as textile companies diversify in an attempt to satisfy the requirements of larger customers and to counteract the effects of softening demand in any one segment of the market. Consolidation is resulting in larger, better-managed com-panies with greater resources for marketing, financing, and technological improvements. Further integration in operations—from the production of raw yarn (and in the case of Texfi Industries of polyester fiber) to finished fabrics (and in the instance of United Merchants and Manufacturers to the retailing of apparel in its Robert Hall stores)—should lead to improved control of output and greater profits. On the other hand, some apparel companies such as Jonathan Logan, Leslie Fay, and Aileen, Inc. have textile operations which produce part of their requirements for knitted fabric.

Despite the wave of mergers and acquisitions, the industry remains highly competitive. There are approximately 5,500 textile concerns in existence. However, the five largest companies account for about 20 percent of total industry sales.

Cyclical Factors

The inherent cyclicality of profits in the textile industry stems from the long inventory pipelines—from yarn processing to sale at retail—which are characteristic of this field. Since inventory levels expand and contract at each stage of the manufacturing and distribution process, changes in final demand are magnified back at the mill level.

In the past, mill customers, during periods of rising business, made commitments far in advance of needs, a practice which resulted in heavy inventory accumulation. When sales slowed, orders evaporated and inventories were liquidated at marked-down prices all the way back to the mill. The build-up of additional capacity when demand was strong and the emphasis on production rather than profitability increased problems during such periods. Table 1 sets forth sales and earnings data for the textile mill products industry for the 1962 to 1972 period.

TABLE 1

Textile Mill Products Sales and Earnings Data

	Sales* ($ million)	Net Profits† ($ million)	Profits per Dollar of Sales (percent)	Profit on Stockholders' Equity‡ (percent)
1972	$25,616	$659	2.6	7.5
1971	22,938	558	2.4	6.6
1970	21,598	413	1.9	5.1
1969	21,780	621	2.9	7.9
1968	20,841	654	3.1	8.8
1967	18,672	540	2.9	7.6
1966	19,513	702	3.6	10.1
1965	18,028	694	3.8	10.8
1964	16,249	507	3.1	8.5
1963	15,092	354	2.3	6.1
1962	14,449	354	2.4	6.2
Annual percent growth (1962 to 1972)	5.9	6.4		

* Sales are net returns, allowances and discount.
† After federal income tax.
‡ Annual data are quarterly averages.
Sources: Federal Trade Commission; Securities and Exchange Commission.

Although prospects for the industry still are closely geared to overall business conditions, profits for this group are much less cyclical than formerly. As a result of improved market analysis, closer inventory controls, and vertical integration, mills are not as sensitive as before to changes in demand for textile products. Skilled managements now cut back production quickly when demand slackens in an attempt to keep trade inventories at moderate levels. In addition, there is a reduced willingness on the part of mill owners to dump goods on the market without regard to price. Broadened consumer lines which often afford higher profit margins as well as more stable levels of production and the development of synthetic fibers are enlarging the market for textile items. Increased advertising along with favorable demographic and income factors are resulting in more stable levels of operation and improved profitability.

MARKETS

Apparel

While the apparel industry's position as the major market for textiles has been declining on a percentage basis in recent years, ready-to-wear consumes about 34 percent of all textiles produced. The allied field of other consumer products, such as piece goods for home sewing, has been

TABLE 2

Apparel and Related Products: Sales and Earning Data

	Sales* ($ million)	Net Profits† ($ million)	Profits per Dollar of Sales (percent)	Profit on Stockholders' Equity‡ (percent)
1972	$28,684	$679	2.4	11.1
1971	23,695	559	2.3	11.0
1970	22,011	426	1.9	9.3
1969	22,687	523	2.3	11.9
1968	20,718	507	2.4	12.9
1967	18,170	420	2.3	11.9
1966	18,110	432	2.4	13.3
1965	16,263	377	2.3	12.7
1964	14,880	318	2.1	11.7
1963	13,696	189	1.4	7.7
1962	13,055	212	1.6	9.2
Annual percent growth (1962 to 1972)	8.2	12.3		

* Sales are net returns, allowances and discount.
† After federal income tax.
‡ Annual data are quarterly averages.
Sources: Federal Trade Commission; Securities and Exchange Commission.

growing in importance and now represents 13 percent of output. Table 2 details revenue and profit data for apparel and related products during the 1962 to 1972 period.

In 1972, consumers spent $62.0 billion on clothing and footwear. As can be seen in Table 3 the percentage flow of personal consumption expenditures directed at apparel and shoes has declined from the 9–10 percent range recorded in the early 1950s to a low of 8.2 percent for 1963.

A strong domestic economy and military purchases for the Vietnam war boosted apparel expenditures on a percentage basis in the late 1960s until outlays rose to a peak of 8.7 percent for 1969. The economic reces-

TABLE 3

Total Personal Consumption Expenditures and Consumer Spending for Apparel and Shoes

Year	Total Personal Consumption Expenditures ($ billion)	Consumer Expenditures for Clothing and Shoes* ($ billion)	Apparel and Shoe Expenditures Percent of Total Personal Consumption Expenditures
1972	$721.0	$62.0	8.6
1971	664.9	56.9	8.6
1970	616.8	52.0	8.5
1969	579.6	50.3	8.7
1968	536.2	46.3	8.6
1967	492.1	42.3	8.6
1966	466.3	40.3	8.6
1965	432.8	35.9	8.3
1964	401.2	33.5	8.3
1963	375.0	30.6	8.2
1962	355.1	29.6	8.3
1961	335.2	27.9	8.3
1960	325.2	27.3	8.4
1955	254.4	23.1	9.1
1950	191.0	19.6	10.3

* Includes standard clothing issued to military personnel.
Sources: Department of Commerce; Bureau of Economic Analysis; Economic Report of the President, January 1973.

sion in 1970 and the fashion controversy over the hemline length caused the clothing and footwear portion of total personal spending to decline to 8.5 percent in that year. In 1971 and 1972 apparel and shoe outlays stabilized at 8.6 percent of all consumer expenditures.

In nonrecession years, consumers have exhibited a willingness to spend a larger portion of their disposable incomes for ready-to-wear. In the future, greater style awareness and the force of fashion could lead to a rising percentage of overall outlays being directed at clothing. This expectation gains support from the tendency of a growing proportion of apparel to be distributed through chain discount and department stores versus specialty stores.

Consumer expenditures for attire and footwear are expected approximately to double in the current decade, as they almost did in the last one. Rising levels of disposable personal income and the projected increase in the 20- to 34-year-old age group (the largest apparel- and textile-spending segment of the population) of 27 percent to 58 million by 1980 also bode well for ready-to-wear sales. One trade association source projects per capita expenditures for clothing to reach $388 per year by 1980, up from $257 in 1970 and $152 in 1960.

The emergence of larger apparel firms and retailing outlets is leading to the further consolidation of the textile manufacturers into concerns which can meet the requirements for quality, fashion, and service. Also, the closer relationship between mills and garment producers is resulting in improved market forecasting and inventory control. Major producers of apparel fabrics include J.P. Stevens, Burlington Industries, Dan River, M. Lowenstein & Sons, and West Point-Pepperell.

Home Furnishings

The home furnishings market currently consumes about 33 percent of all fabrics produced and, as a category, is expected to grow percentage wise as an end-use for textiles.

Carpeting, representing about one third of this market, has particularly good growth potential. According to the Carpet and Rug Institute, carpeting sales were estimated to exceed $3 billion in 1973, up 11 percent from $2.83 billion a year earlier. About 90 percent of the 901 million square yards produced in 1972 was made on tufting machines. The dominant portion of all carpet delivered for commercial and residential use is made of synthetic fibers, of which nylon is most in demand. The industry is giving priority to the further development of contract carpeting for use in schools, hospitals, supermarkets, and other nonresidential establishments. Textile producers active in the carpeting market include Burlington (Burlington House, Lees, and Monticello), Fieldcrest (Laurelcrest and Karastan), Collins & Aikman (Painter), and Stevens (Gulistan).

Demand for home furnishings is related to new-housing starts, but replacement purchases are growing in importance. Family formations, the level of interest rates, mobility in the population, style considerations, and second homes also influence business in this market area.

In addition to carpeting, products of importance in the home furnishings category include upholstery, bedspreads, sheets, pillowcases, towels, and draperies. Leading producers in this field include Lowenstein (Wamsutta and Pacific), West Point-Pepperell (Martex and Pepperell), Stevens (Utica), Springs Mills (Spring Maid), Cannon, and Fieldcrest.

Industrial Fabrics

Representing about 20 percent of textile consumption, industrial fabrics are produced and engineered for a wide variety of applications. Particularly important items in this area include substrates for vinyl coatings (used in upholstery fabrics), tire cord, hosing, and belting for the automotive market. Other items include sewing threads, glass fibers, twine, and filters.

The production of industrial fabrics is dominated by Stevens, Burlington, West Point-Pepperell, and Collins & Aikman.

NEW DEVELOPMENTS

Although fabric production is one of the world's oldest manufacturing activities, the industry just recently has been undergoing important technological changes. However, only the major companies in the field have been leaders in fostering and exploiting these developments which should aid profits over the longer term. In evaluating prospects for specific mill securities, the product mix as well as management's application of technological break-throughs are important considerations. A willingness not only to accept change but also to invest for the future is essential if a fabric manufacturer is to maintain and advance its standing in the field.

A discussion of the various technological changes underway in the industry is presented below.

Knits

Knitted goods have become an important fabric category. Accordingly, many major fabric and apparel producers have positions in this market. Companies with especially good expertise in knitting include Texfi Industries, Burlington Industries, Collins & Aikman, Jonathan Logan, and Leslie Fay. Modern equipment, skilled managements, and an understanding of the advantages and applications for knitted goods are important ingredients for success. Because of the favorable growth prospects for knits in the years ahead, a company's operations in this field can be an important contributor to future profits.

Knitted fabrics have been produced in the United States for quite some time, but it is only in recent years that they have gained wide popularity. Currently, knits represent about 20 percent of all apparel produced, and some trade sources project that by 1975 substantially more than 50 percent of all ready-to-wear manufactured will be knitted. New applications for knits in automobile seat covers and home furnishings are just beginning.

In 1971 and 1972, a growing supply of polyester from the United

States and abroad drove filament prices for this fiber down. Accordingly, double knit polyester fabrics replaced a large part of the market for acetate-bonded single knits. Acetate is finding some applications in children's flame-retardant sleepwear, knitwear, and in linings of men's suits. As output of domestic polyester textile filament yarn increased 53 percent to 700 million pounds in 1972, prices for this fiber eroded about 8 percent.

The decline in fiber prices, compounded by both a high level of imports and many new domestic entries into textured yarn and knitted goods production, led to lower selling prices and a shake-out in the U.S. knitting industry. However, knits still are very important; and it is estimated that domestic mills in 1972 had about 20,000 double knit machines in place, up from 3,500 in 1966. Despite adverse industry conditions, shipments of knitted cloth, as reported by the U.S. Department of Commerce, Bureau of the Census, rose to 1,018 million pounds in 1972 from 989 million pounds a year earlier. The increase was due to a recovery in the women's sportswear business and some strengthening in textured polyester yarn prices reflecting a shortage of texturizing facilities. Nevertheless, profits for many of the publicly held knitting companies fell sharply in 1972.

Because of strong worldwide demand for yarn, this item will probably remain in tight supply through most of 1974. Some trade sources project that fiber producers increased production of textured polyester yarn in 1973 by 150 million pounds. Furthermore, these trade sources also estimate that producer-textured yarn will account for 50 percent of total textured yarn produced domestically by 1975.

In the fashion world, controversy reigns between the popularity of knits versus wovens. Certainly, there has been some switching from knits to wovens, but knits were never claimed to be a replacement for wovens. While knits have been one of the most important developments in the textile industry during the last decade, in the future they will coexist in the fashion marketplace with wovens. The shortage of wovens arising from a scarcity of spindels, import controls, and a shortage of chemicals used in the production of man-made fibers, may result in a greater application of knits in the quarters ahead as a substitute for goods made on looms.

Despite the mixed near-term outlook with respect to demand for garments made from double-knit fabrics, longer-term prospects are still good for this growing segment of the textile industry. Over the next three years, a growth rate in pounds of about 10 percent for double knits appears attainable. The anticipated increase in consumption of textured woven fabrics should not completely be derived from the double-knit share of the fabric market. It is expected that textured wovens more importantly will be a replacement fabric for nonstretch or traditionally woven goods.

Nonwovens

A material manufactured by interlocking fibers with a bonding agent, nonwovens possess the advantages of good shape retention, high porosity and bulk, and nonravelling edges. Although accounting for a small percentage of textile fabrics, nonwovens are being used in the production of apparel particularly for hospital-medical applications. It is anticipated that the total value of nonwoven disposable materials will grow about 15 percent annually to $1.6 billion in 1976 from $800 million in 1971.

Riegel Textile is using a nonwoven rayon fabric in a flushable sanitary napkin. The major producers of nonwovens are Kendall, (Colgate-Palmolive) and Chicopee Manufacturing Co. (Johnson & Johnson). Because of the high level of technology involved and the long lead time required before profitability is reached, few entrants into this field are expected in the years ahead.

Stretch Wovens

Expansion is underway for increased production of textured woven goods made of polyester. These fabrics combine the stretch and return characteristics of knits with the more durable wearing qualities of woven goods. Stretch wovens should enjoy especially good growth in men's slacks, suits, and sport coats.

Flame Retardants

The 1967 amendment of the Flammable Fabrics Act empowered the Secretary of Commerce to issue flammability standards covering interior furnishings as well as ready-to-wear. Two product standards for carpeting were issued in 1970, a standard for children's sleepwear was promulgated a year later, and one for mattresses was issued in 1972.

Currently, all children's sleepwear in the 0 to 6X size range must be flame retardant. Moves are underway to extend these standards to cover children's sleepwear in sizes 7 to 14 as well as children's apparel. The burden of meeting these requirements initially falls upon textile mills who in turn charge apparel producers a premium price for children's wear fabric which is specially treated to comply with flammability requirements. There has been some consumer resistance to the higher prices they must pay for these treated items. Lowenstien has been important in the development of these chemically treated goods.

The Commerce Department is considering the imposition of standards for blankets and upholstered furniture. Although marketing, styling, and testing problems have arisen with respect to flame-retardant goods, the larger mills are attempting to comply with the new regulations. In addition, some states are issuing their own flammability requirements which could lead to more stringent regulations at the local level. It is believed that imported fabrics and garments which also must comply with the new regulations may lose some of their price advantage, relative to goods made in this country, as flame retardant items become accepted more widely in the United States.

Durable Press and Soil Release

Imparted by means of a process involving the application of chemicals and heat, durable press renders wrinkle-resistant and shape-retaining properties to garments and fabrics. Although widely used in sheets, table-cloths, rainwear, and work clothes, the importance of durable press has been diminished somewhat in outerwear by the advent of knitted goods, and double-knits in particular. Soil release has added potential to the durable press process by affording a finish which reduces the soiling problem associated with polyester.

FACTORS AIDING LONG-TERM GROWTH

Increasing Use of Synthetics

Synthetics, in general, provide a more stable raw material cost structure than wool and cotton, since the supply of man-made fibers is not subject to livestock or crop cycles. The increased use of synthetics provides greater flexibility in mill operations and improves the textile product mix by broadening the variety of cloth constructions. Man-made fibers now account for about two thirds of all fiber consumption, up from 31 percent in 1961.

Demographic and Income Trends

The projected rise in the 20- to 34-year-old age group (the high textile-spending portion of the population) of 27 percent to 58 million by 1980 is a favorable factor for the industry. Also aiding the textile outlook is the fact that average family income is estimated to rise almost 50 percent during this decade with a similar gain in the number of family heads under 35 years of age. Average income for America's 54.5 million families rose to $11,120 in 1972.

Consumer Orientation

Emphasis on merchandising and brand name advertising is affording the industry increased marketing leverage. By directing production toward finished-fabric categories, mills are able to achieve more stable levels of production and higher profit margins than those traditionally associated with the manufacture of gray goods.

Social Changes

Improved living standards, more leisure time, greater fashion consciousness, and the concept of a double wardrobe for work and for play are leading to the demand for a broader variety of fabrics for apparel and home furnishings.

Capital Spending and Research

Continued capital outlays are resulting in larger plants and more efficient equipment, thereby lending to improved productivity and profitability. However, the return on many capital investments for mills currently is so low that a payout period of several years in duration is all that can be expected. In 1973 the industry spent about $830 million for new plants and equipment—of which $67 million will be for employee health and safety, $38 million for water and air pollution control, and $58 million for research and development.

COST FACTORS

Labor Shortages and Rising Wage Costs

Payroll costs generally average about 22 percent of the industry's total value of shipments. The move to the South by many mills over the years has lost many of its cost-saving advantages due to the narrowing in wage differentials. Recently, hourly earnings among mill workers averaged $2.77, versus $3.88 for manufacturing companies in general. High labor turnover and a shortage of skilled labor currently are very important problems for cloth producers.

Labor costs vary by type of fabric produced, the manufacturing process employed, and the extent of automation. Moves by the industry to increase productivity and efficiency and upgrade the product mix have been important in partially offsetting rising outlays for wages.

Approximately 20 percent of the 1 million mill workers are members of the Textile Workers Union of America. Since the labor movement is weakest in the South, J. P. Stevens, one of the largest southern mills, has been the target of union drives. Full-scale unionization is not expected in the near future.

Fibers

The cost of raw materials constitutes about 58 percent of the value of all textile shipments. The industry's dependence upon natural fibers has been reduced, and today synthetics account for about two thirds of all fiber consumption, versus 30 percent in 1959. Presently cotton represents about 30 percent and wool the remainder of fibers used.

Synthetics. The long-term downward trend of prices for synthetics has resulted from increased production and technological improvements. In addition, the development of new synthetics has fostered the use of more sophisticated textile equipment (especially in the knitting area) and the production of fabrics with superior care, wearing, and aesthetic qualities. Furthermore, man-made fibers have been engineered for specific uses in such items as carpeting, hosiery, lingerie, and outerwear. The uniformity of synthetics provides textile manufacturers with a raw material source which requires a smaller investment in inventories and which results in reduced wastage as well as greater efficiencies in production.

Nylon and polyester have been the two fibers enjoying the greatest increase in demand during the last decade. Rayon textile yarn and acetate staple have declined in importance. Recently, prices for many synthetic fibers have been increasing due to strong demand from the textile industry on a worldwide basis, the shortage of hydrocarbons from which some man-made fibers are derived, and the more moderate pace at which new capacity has been coming on stream.

Cotton. Political considerations, wide price swings, uncertainty over crop yields, and the growing supply of synthetic fibers are responsible for the diminishing importance of cotton in cloth production. Cotton prices have risen sharply since 1971 due to low carry-over stocks and increased export demand. The floods in the southern portion of the United States in spring 1973 also hurt crop yields. Cotton textiles primarily consist of commodity goods for which prices are determined by short-term supply-and-demand considerations.

Wool. This natural fiber has declined in importance with the advent of man-mades. Many woolen and worsted mills have closed down in this country to the point where most of these goods now are imported. Recently, prices of wool have risen sharply, but supplies are not expected to increase significantly.

IMPORTS AND EXPORTS

Since the signing in late 1971 of the bilateral import quota agreements with Japan, Taiwan, Hong Kong, and South Korea, textile and apparel imports have entered this country in a less disruptive manner. These quotas provide for a more orderly growth and at lower rates than in the past for textile and apparel imports made from wool and synthetic fibers. Cotton textile imports have been limited since 1962 by the Long-Term Cotton Textile Arrangement.

A new agreement regarding international trade in textiles was approved at the beginning of 1974 by representatives of 50 trading nations. The four-year pact became effective January 1, 1974. It covers cotton, wool and synthetic fibers used in yarns, piece goods, garments and other textile products. The agreement provides for the appointment of a surveillance group which will represent the major trading nations, supervise the agreement and make recommendations when problems arise. Existing quotas must be either eliminated over a three year period beginning April 1 or justified under the pact but new quotas can be introduced under conditions of market disruption. While the domestic industry has mixed attitudes about the new arrangement, the reduction of Common Market restrictions on imports could remove some pressure from the American market.

About 10 percent of all textile yardage consumed in this country is imported. While imports will increase in the future, it seems likely that exports of domestic fabrics also will grow, perhaps at an even more rapid rate. Because of the devaluation of the dollar, strong world-wide demand for fabric, and the governmental controls on increases in selling prices, many U.S. mills are looking at export sales as a new market for growth.

There is a tendency for goods entering this country to be up-graded on a dollar basis per item. This is because the late 1971 quota agreement is set on square yard equivalents rather than on dollar volume. The impact of the devaluation of the dollar on the textile industry depends, in great part, upon the labor intensiveness of the item imported. It appears that the lower the labor content of the item exported from abroad, the greater the impact of the devaluation. Accordingly, in the future, foreign goods entering the United States probably will be concentrated in the garment area rather than in the yarn and fabric categories.

The industry still must conclude import agreements with uncontrolled countries such as, Portugal, Philippines, and many South American nations. Uncontrolled textile and apparel imports account for over 40 percent of all such U.S. imports, and the rate of increase from uncontrolled areas far exceeds that from controlled nations.

RATIOS, ACCOUNTING, AND OTHER CONSIDERATIONS IMPORTANT IN EVALUATING TEXTILE ISSUES

Inventories

Many of the companies in the industry still use the FIFO method of accounting for inventories. Accordingly, there has been and will continue to be an interval of time before their costs reflect the generally increasing level of fiber prices in 1973 and 1974.

The results for textile companies often are influenced by substantial inventory profits in times of growth and inventory losses during recessionary periods. The foregoing stems from the short-term supply-and-demand conditions which impact prices of fibers and fabrics. The magnitude of the effect of inventory profits and losses on the earnings of any specific company depends on the particular mix of its raw materials and finished goods.

The inventory turnover rate (total annual shipments divided by annual monthly average inventories) fluctuates over time. The rate was 7.4 times in 1972, up from 6.2 times in 1970. Turnover rates are higher for knitting companies, wherein the production and shipping cycle is shorter, than for weaving mills. Product mix and marketing policies can have an important effect on turnover rates. A goal of management should be to keep inventories both liquid and profitable.

Excessive inventories which result in competitive pricing frequently are characteristic of this business. In addition, inventory markdown policies vary widely from company to company. They are one of the most important factors in the analysis of mill equities. An explanation of such policies should be requested of management. For example, a company may mark down goods in varying amounts at the end of each season, quarter, or at year-end. The frequency of physical inventory counts also is important in evaluating these securities.

Capitalization

Because of the cyclical nature of the industry and the sometimes wide swings in profits that take place, the ratio of debt to total capitalization for a typical mill should not exceed 25–30 percent. Many companies have used convertible, subordinated, long-term debt to finance capital outlays. Reflecting the slow movement away from family ownership, many mills have small capitalizations, of which the equity portion is to a substantial degree held by management interest.

Cash Requirements

The industry is characterized by the need for large amounts of cash used to carry inventory. Policies as to cash management must be studied in line with a company's pattern of accounts receivable and collection experience. Reflecting modest capital spending programs, cash flow and depreciation are well down in the industry scale for this group.

Return on Investment

In 1972 new plant and equipment expenditures per dollar of sales were 2.9 percent for textiles, versus 3.7 percent for all manufacturing industries. The differential reflects the reluctance of textile managements to invest in weaving facilities on which they cannot earn a sufficient return over a three- or four-year payout period. With new technology, especially in knitting, having a greater impact than in the past, conservative managements are not adding machinery in substantial amounts that cannot be justified in a three-year payback period or less.

Operating Rate

A high operating rate results in better absorption of overhead costs, increased efficiencies in production, and typically higher profit margins. Shorter runs of more highly styled fabrics usually are compensated for by higher selling prices. In 1972 the mill operating rate was 88.5 percent, versus 83.0 percent for all manufacturing.

Profit Margins

Profit margins in the industry are influenced by operating rates and the prevailing price structure. Periods of low operating rates and the consequent underabsorption of overhead costs sometimes take place. Sudden changes in demand and prices, especially for low-margined gray goods, can have a dramatic impact on profits. While new products may enjoy premium prices for a time, increased capacity in these categories can quickly result in steep cuts in selling price. Examples of the latter situation are the production of panty hose and double-knits. Profit margins depend on a company's ability to pass along rising costs for labor and fiber.

Trends in consumer spending and seasonal variations in demand have a direct impact on operating margins. Accordingly, these factors should be taken into consideration in making comparisons of sales and profits on a quarterly basis over a period of years.

Dividends

During the decade of the 1960s, dividends paid by textile companies averaged about 46 percent of earnings. Since profits for the group often can be volatile, a record of consistent dividend payments enhances the attractiveness of a specific textile company.

MARKET BEHAVIOR

Prices for textile shares generally mirror those for the industrial averages, with some variations. The general down drift in Standard & Poor's textile product index since 1966 reflects the growth of imports and the poor profit margins for the group. The disappointment in earnings of many knitting companies since 1972 also has restrained investor interest in the group. Recent behavior has reflected overall stock market activity.

30

Utilities

KENNETH HOLLISTER, C.F.A.

Vice President
Dean Witter & Co., Inc., New York, New York

PUBLIC UTILITIES occupy a special niche in the investment spectrum. They are created and operated under laws that define where they shall serve and control the prices they may charge. Some industries, such as the transportation and insurance groups, are subject to regulation for pricing purposes, but markets are not controlled and they are not considered to be in the same investment category. The public utilities are comprised of electric, gas transmission and distribution, and communications companies. These groups share one other common facet: Taken as a whole, they have the largest annual requirement for new capital of any privately owned industry in the United States. In analyzing the group, it is the two elements of regulation and need for capital that provide the base for investment decisions.

LEGAL CONCEPT

The starting point for modern regulation probably was expressed in two treatises, *De Portibus Maris* and *De Jure Maris*, regarding the common law of England, which were written by Matthew Hale, Lord Chief Justice of the King's Bench, about 1670. These documents found that certain businesses that had been considered privately owned could be considered to "be affected with a public interest," and, therefore, the owners could not charge arbitrary or excessive amounts for the services. Among the services he included were ferries, coaches, and certain port facilities. While it is a long step to modern regulation, the underlying thesis of public service at reasonable rates remains the keystone.

Rate regulation in the United States began about the time of the end of the Civil War and arose mostly from charges of "discrimination." This was the practice of pricing the same service at different prices, either directly or through rebates, to different customers. The United States

776

Supreme Court in the case of *Munn* v. *Illinois*[1] upheld a state law which permitted the fixing of maximum rates for railroad-owned grain elevators. The court found the operation was affected with the public interest and that the operators were using their monopoly position in an unfair manner. Tests such as this were later to be the support for most public utility legislation.

Today, utilities are regulated by administrative bodies created by the legislatures. With the exception of three states which have local regulation, there is in every state a commission which has jurisdiction over the utilities operating within its borders. In addition, there are specialized federal agencies that have concurrent or separate authority over certain aspects of utility operations. Jurisdiction ranges from defining service areas to approving issuance of securities. Rate regulation as it exists today grew gradually, as the early legislation concentrated more on who or what was a public utility and what service had to be provided. Over a period of years the laws and court decisions set forth obligations and rights of utilities. They are:

1. Rights
   a. Entitlement through franchise or other legal grant to a monopoly within a designated area.
   b. Entitlement to appropriate private property at a reasonable fee where it is necessary to provide service to the public.
   c. Entitlement to charge reasonable rates, adequate to cover prudent operating costs and provide the ability to earn a return sufficient to cover financial costs and attract new capital in competition with other industries.
2. Obligations
   a. Service *must* be provided to all who reasonably require it and can pay.
   b. It must be available in sufficient quantity at all times under normal operating conditions.
   c. Rates must not be unjustly discriminatory and must be reasonable.
   d. Service may not be abandoned or extended without express approval of the appropriate regulatory agency.

Legal Monopoly—Service Requirement

Stripped to the bare essentials, regulation requires that utility services be provided at the lowest reasonable price to all who can pay. The price also must be set at a level at which the utility can attract capital in competition with other industries on a competitive basis. Utilities thus are legal monopolies whose prices are set at a level which would exist if there were competition. (They are also called "natural monopolies.") This theory has been set forth and upheld by many court decisions. The

[1] *Munn* v. *Illinois* 94U.S. 113 (1877).

reasons for not having competition, in the generally accepted sense, is the duplication of facilities would be prohibitively expensive. There are numerous examples of attempts to violate this scheme by allowing competition and an equal number of bankrupt utilities to prove it is not feasible. Currently, however, some novel definitions of competition are entering the scene.

Recent Changes in Legal Concepts

In a few recent actions, the courts have somewhat widened the definition of competition in the electric utility industry and the Federal Communications Commission (FCC) has opened certain parts of the communications spectrum to companies that heretofore could not exist. In the electric area, in *Otter Tail Power* v. *United States*,[2] the court found that refusal of a utility to carry power for and to a neighboring municipal system was restraining the ability of the municipal to provide service to new customers even though Otter Tail had offered the power to the ultimate purchaser. This decision reversed an earlier Federal Power Commission decision, and it requires that all contracts between utilities must be reviewed in terms of antitrust proceedings. In another case, the Supreme Court found a utility in violation of antitrust statutes if it sold securities to build such a generating plant without providing a cooperative with the opportunity to join the ownership of the plant.[3]

Other Considerations—New Technologies

More obvious competition has been ordered by the FCC in a series of orders. First, in the so-called *Carterphone*[4] case it was determined that inter-connect equipment could be added to the Bell (American Telephone & Telegraph) System as long as it did not cause degradation of basic telephone service. Prior to that decision only Bell-owned or -approved equipment could be connected. Then in the *MCI*[5] case the FCC authorized a specialized carrier to provide point-to-point data transmission without using Bell System facilities. Before this decision, only Bell and Western Union could offer such service to the public although privately owned systems for use by the owner were in existence. Lastly, with the developing satellite technology, the FCC has opened the communications arena to "all qualified applicants"[6] for both specialized and general services. It begins to appear that the FCC has undertaken the regulation of competition rather than of legal monopolies.

---

[2] Otter Tail Power Co. v. United States, U.S. 97 PUR 3d 209 (1973).

[3] *Gulf States Utilities Co.* v. *Federal Power Commission,* U.S. 98 PUR 3d 262 (1973).

[4] 22 FCC 112 (1959).

[5] FCC Docket No. 18920, adopted May 25, 1971.

[6] FCC Docket No. 16495, adopted December 21, 1972.

TYPES OF UTILITIES

Electric Companies

Electric utilities generate, transmit, and distribute electricity within their franchise area. (Some also distribute natural gas, although the service areas may be different in size, and these are called combination companies.) With few exceptions, equipment is designed by electric equipment manufacturers and construction is completed by contractors. Thus the utility only assumes responsibility after the equipment is completed and in place. As demand for service grew, it was possible for the manufacturers to build larger machines and transmission lines that quite effectively lowered the unit cost of production. Recently, however, rising costs and problems of technology have sharply reduced this capability of cost reductions, and the utilities themselves have come under criticism for not seeking more actively to control such costs.

Along with the operating problems and construction delays of the most recent family of generating equipment, the service obligation of the electric companies has been strained by changes in environmental standards, dislocations of fuel sources, and rapidly rising capital costs. The issues of the environment, however, have caused the greatest difficulties and in some measure may become the basic cause of insufficient power in some areas. It should be remembered that from the late 1940s to 1969 an insufficient supply or interruption (called an "outage"), except for storms and natural disasters, was a truly rare occurrence. The way now seems clear for completion of sufficient facilities to overcome the recent periods of shortage, but the process for locating, constructing, operating and financing new plants has been altered. What this will mean in terms of long-term adequacy and cost of electricity cannot be answered at this time. Growth data is given in Figure 1 (page 784).

Natural Gas Companies

Interstate transmission companies own and operate a network of high-pressure pipelines that move natural gas in large volumes from the producing areas, primarily in the southwestern part of the United States, to distributors who further deliver it to the ultimate consumer. The present status of natural gas pipelines is by far the most confused in the utility area, and the possible directions for solution also are clouded. It is in this group that the concepts of legal and service rights and obligations have been most strained and, in several instances, breached. A number of developments have contributed to the present situation of supply shortages and allocations, but the single event on which the industry turned was a 1954 decision of the Supreme Court[7] which found

---

[7] *Phillips Petroleum Co.*, v. *Wisconsin, et al.*, 347 U.S. 672 (1954).

that producers were subject to price regulation by the Federal Power Commission FPC under the Natural Gas Act. This decision, rendered at a point in time when it was assumed demand for natural gas was increasing at a declining rate, encouraged the FPC to hold down and even reduce field prices of gas to prevent the development of oversupply. With hindsight it is easy to understand the mistakes, but at the time the high saturation of home heating customers and apparent leveling of new-home construction gave credence to the outlook for a lowered growth rate and, thus, little requirement for major new gas reserves. Currently, all interstate pipelines are restricted by the FPC[8] from accepting contracts for new deliveries, and there is a series of priority allocation orders for present customers. The current system is more responsive to political than economic forces and is resulting in further dislocations; however at present the courts have upheld the agency in its actions.

From the standpoint of investment analysis, the wider impact is the change in the legal right to obtain service and the obligation to provide it. In essence the courts have authorized an administrative agency to direct the utility product to certain customers while denying it to others. This will tax analysts for some time to come as it could well portend a change in the basic markets served. The same set of rules are being adopted by the state commissions having jurisdiction over distribution companies operating within the state. The needs of residential and commercial customers are being met, but there are restrictions on the acceptance of new customers, again on a priority basis.

Liquified and Synthetic Gases

Broad-based efforts are being made to augment gas supplies. Domestic prices are being raised, and there is a likelihood of removal of price regulation of producers—although this still poses some legal problems. Other approaches include the liquification (refrigeration) of foreign gas and its movement by ship, and the construction of plants to convert other hydrocarbons, particularly naptha, into synthetic gas. There is also much research and development being directed toward possible gasification of coal, although most current processes require a fortuitous combination of adequate water nearby the coal reserve.

Regulation of these sources has not yet been clarified sufficiently to permit generalizations. The FPC has stated that liquified gases (LNG) and synthetic gas (SNG) will be subject to regulation only after it has entered the interstate gas stream.[9] Thus the production, liquification, transportation, and vaporization are unregulated. On the other hand, some companies have requested that synthetic gas facilities be subject

---

[8] Federal Power Commission order 467, dated Jan. 8, 1973, amended March 2, 1973.

[9] Federal Power Commission orders 622 and 622A, dated June 8, 1972 and October 5, 1972.

to utility regulation. The pricing and possible uses of these gases will be discussed later, but how regulation will affect them is as yet uncertain.

Communications Companies

Telephones. Consisting of The American Telephone & Telegraph Company (AT&T), about 2,000 so-called "independent" telephone companies, and Western Union Corporation (providing telegraph and other specialized services), this industry group also is undergoing changes in its obligations and responsibilities. In the more openly competitive arena of overseas communications, there are, in addition to AT&T: Communications Satellite Corporation, Western Union International, RCA, and International Telephone & Telegraph.

The backbone communications system in the United States is owned and operated by AT&T (the Bell System) and it provides the conduits for practically all local and long distance (toll) and most international voice communication. During recent years the disputes between Bell and the independents centered on the division of revenues for calls using two or more systems, but the increased transmission of data has given rise to a new area of controversy. The Federal Communications Commission has ruled that certain specialized services which are in direct competition with the telephone utilities can be licensed and serve these markets. In itself this might be little cause for concern, but over the years and with regulatory concurrence, the telephone industry has developed an average-pricing concept. Briefly, this permits high-density routes to subsidize those with lower usage so that customers pay the same rates for equivalent usage without regard to location. Under the new rules, specialized carriers are being authorized to serve certain high-density routes without the obligation also to provide service in the higher-cost low-density areas. While the sum total of traffic diverted at present is miniscule relative to the massive size of AT&T, there are investment implications regarding the growth prospects of both groups of companies.

Data—CATV. Methodology for analyzing the specialized carriers is included later in this section. Suffice it to say that the utility obligations and responsibilities of these entities still are to be defined. There does not appear to be any compelling reason to have them franchised and have monopoly powers. On the other hand, to the extent that they infringe on the regulated segment and cause differences in revenue realizations or costs, they will come under some degree of control. We believe the specialized carriers cannot ultimately escape price and service regulation although it is much too early to determine the form that it will take.

Satellites. With the creation of the Communications Satellite Corporation (Comsat) by Congress in 1962, another form of competition was brought to the scene. Originally the organization was to provide overseas communications and supplement fully loaded underseas cables as well as providing service to foreign countries not then served by cable. The FCC subsequently has authorized the use of satellites for domestic toll and specialized services such as data, TV, and education. Further rulings on current applications for use of satellites are expected over the coming several years, and these also will have important meaning in the investment spectrum within the communications group.

· From these comments it may be inferred that regulatory decisions may cause alteration of the past pattern of operation of each of the components of the utility industry. Some of these may be gradual, as in the electric utilities where increased demand may necessitate accomodation to possible restrictions on use, while in the natural gas industry where priorities are already in place the changes may come about more quickly.

FACTORS AFFECTING GROWTH OF REVENUES (SALES) AND PRICE STRUCTURE OF THE VARIOUS MARKETS

There is an historic relationship between the physical facilities of utilities and the rate structures that have evolved. They contain, however, a chicken-and-egg character as each grew somewhat from development of the other. Pervasive in all aspects of the industry is the overriding desire to lower unit cost, and this is in keeping with the public service concept. Over the last several decades the industry has been singularly successful in achieving this goal.

General Factors—Electric

The overall electric generating and transmission system has been designed to provide service to a growing population of increasing affluence. The physical system was constructed to permit a high degree of reliability, and with a very few, but notable, exceptions it has been successful in this regard.

Physical Plant. The physical system of an electric utility consists of:

a. Base load units—large, modern machines (currently 700–1,000 megawatts) designed to operate for extended periods of time and to be stopped for maintenance only once in a 12- to 18-month period. They may use fossil or nuclear fuel. As these units become older they are used to meet day-to-day or anticipated seasonal loads. (In a smaller utility these units may be in the 100–500 megawatt range).

b. Cycling units—small- to medium-size generators (100–400 megawatts) that have the capability of quicker starting and stopping to meet seasonal fluctuations or other anticipated requirements of intermediate term duration. These are fossil fueled and some can benefit from further use of the waste heat from the first part of the cycle.

c. Peaking units—small turbine engines (20–50 megawatts) used to meet sudden or unanticipated demands for power or, in the case of unscheduled outages, of larger machines.

d. High-voltage transmission lines—for the movement of bulk power from the generators to points of division called substations where the voltage is reduced and sent further.

e. Distribution lines—lower-voltage lines that feed the power to service lines and finally to the consumer. In most urban communities service lines now are placed underground, but the technology for burying the larger heavier voltage lines still is far from realization.

Growth of the Electric Utility Industry. The electric utility industry has been growing at the same pace for the last two decades. Figures available starting in 1955 indicate a compound growth rate of kilowatt-hour (kwh.) sales of between 7 percent and 8 percent over the period. More recently, the increasing awareness of heating fuel problems has resulted in a tendency toward electric heating, and this also is contributing to more rapid growth.

Revenues. For rate making, as well as load characteristic purposes, the industry divides its basic sales into three categories: residential, commercial, and industrial as shown in Table 1 and Table 2. While there are other specialized divisions in some instances—such as rural and street lighting—they are minor. Whole sale sales are made to municipal and cooperative distributing companies, generally under special contracts; and in recent years, sales to other electric companies have increased in importance. These latter groups, however, seldom represent more than 5–10 percent of total revenues. Where any one is a significant amount, knowledge of the contract terms becomes a meaningful item.

The anticipated population change of an area remains useful in estimating the future. Generally when an area is growing, there is a balance between industry and commercial and residential use. Put another way, where there is industrial or commercial development, residential construction also occurs. There are a few exceptions, such as parts of Florida, where residential growth far exceeds the industrial category, but there the commercial sales reflect the needs of the increased population. Some big city companies, on the other hand, have static populations and more modest growth in per capita income, and their sales increases are below the average. By studying the population increases in the service area, it is also possible to correlate this to greater demands for power. In addition, if the economic growth of an area is well balanced, there is usually a multiplier effect on residential sales as use of heavy-duty appliances is increased. Geography is also important in terms of temperature differentials and the type of load resulting. Few homes are built in the South today without some form of cooling control, and electric heat is increasingly being used in the South, West, and Northeast. Companies serving areas with extreme temperatures have different load characteristics, and peaks tend to vary more widely than for those operating in more temperate climates. In evaluating both overall load growth and peak load, care must be exercised to account for such abberations. Forecasting generally should be on an assumed normal weather basis.

FIGURE 1

The Electric Utility Industry

Production of electric energy in the United States reached the record total of 1.617 trillion kilowatt-hours in 1971. This represented an increase of 5.5 percent, the lowest year to year increase in the last 10 years, over the 1.533 trillion kilowatt-hours generated in 1970 and may be further compared with an output of 1.445 trillion kilowatt-hours in 1969 and 1.332 trillion kilowatt-hours in 1968. The percentage gains year to year since 1962 have been as follows:

Year	Percent
1971 over 1970	5.5
1970 over 1969	6.1
1969 over 1968	8.4
1968 over 1967	9.4
1967 over 1966	6.1
1966 over 1965	8.7
1965 over 1964	7.2
1964 over 1963	7.3
1963 over 1962	7.3
1962 over 1961	7.6

The compound annual growth rate over the 10 year period was approximately 7.4 percent.

The following tabulation summarizes the output of the various segments of the electric power industry and indicates the relative importance of each to the industry as a whole over the past decade.

Electric utility net generation, United States 1961–71 [a]

Installed generating capacity in the United States also reached a new high of 367,396 megawatts in 1971 compared to 340,353 megawatts in 1970. This represented an increase of about 8 percent.

Installed generating capacity (Kilowatts in Thousands)

Year	Total electric utility industry
1971	367,396
1970	340,353
1969	313,349
1968	291,058
1967	269,252
1966	247,843
1965	236,127
1964	222,285
1963	210,549
1962	191,067
1961	180,668

The percentage gains on a year to year basis since 1961 have been as follows:

Year	Percent
1971 over 1970	7.9
1970 over 1969	8.6
1969 over 1968	7.7
1968 over 1967	8.1
1967 over 1966	8.6
1966 over 1965	5.0
1965 over 1964	6.2
1964 over 1963	5.6
1963 over 1962	10.2
1962 over 1961	5.8

The compound annual growth rate over the 10 year period was approximately 7.4 percent.

Year	Total	Privately owned [b]	Publicly and cooperatively owned			
			Subtotal	Municipal	Federal	Co-ops, power districts, State projects
MILLIONS OF KWH						
1961	794,272	606,736	187,535	38,872	112,375	36,288
1962	854,796	653,076	201,718	41,840	115,926	43,952
1963	916,793	701,253	215,540	46,292	124,340	44,908
1964	983,990	756,183	227,807	50,263	129,935	47,609
1965	1,055,252	809,474	245,778	49,940	145,231	50,607
1966	1,147,364	883,851	263,513	52,627	153,067	57,819
1967	1,217,349	931,423	285,927	57,789	162,399	65,739
1968	1,332,131	1,022,000	310,131	63,804	170,834	75,493
1969	1,445,282	1,105,262	340,020	69,614	183,245	87,161
1970	1,532,796	1,186,069	346,727	71,490	185,755	89,482
1971 [1]	1,617,241	1,253,310	363,931	72,535	194,490	96,906
PERCENT OF TOTAL						
1961	100.0	76.4	23.6	4.9	14.1	4.6
1962	100.0	76.4	23.6	4.9	13.6	5.1
1963	100.0	76.5	23.5	5.0	13.6	4.9
1964	100.0	76.8	23.2	5.1	13.2	4.9
1965	100.0	76.7	23.3	4.7	13.8	4.8
1966	100.0	77.0	23.0	4.6	13.4	5.0
1967	100.0	76.5	23.5	4.8	13.3	5.4
1968	100.0	76.7	23.3	4.8	12.8	5.7
1969	100.0	76.4	23.6	4.8	12.7	6.1
1970	100.0	77.4	22.6	4.7	12.1	5.8
1971 [1]	100.0	77.5	22.5	4.5	12.0	6.0

(a) Exclusive of energy used for pumped storage.
(b) Includes the generation of numerous small utilities accounting for less than 2 percent of the privately owned division of the industry not otherwise represented in this publication.
[1] Preliminary.

Source: Statistics of privately owned electric utilities in the United States, 1971; Federal Power Commission, October 1972.

TABLE 1

Electric Consumers, Sales, and Revenues

Year	Ultimate electric consumers—thousands (average)				Kw.-hr. sales to ultimate consumers—millions				Revenues for sales to ultimate consumers—thousands				Other electric revenues	Total electric operating revenues	Total Kw.-hr. sold, including sales for resale—millions
	Residential[1]	Commercial and industrial[1]	Others[1]	Total	Residential[1]	Commercial and industrial[1]	Others[1]	Total	Residential[1]	Commercial and industrial[1]	Others	Total			
1937	18,925	3,631	986	23,542	14,822	65,202	11,988	92,012	$645,749	$1,105,092	$205,079	$1,955,920	$201,357	$2,157,277	120,835
1938	19,423	3,691	1,013	24,127	16,296	59,183	12,342	87,811	683,341	1,069,932	210,968	1,964,241	204,429	2,168,670	115,254
1939	19,789	3,770	1,239	24,798	17,359	66,972	12,983	97,314	705,608	1,130,970	223,725	2,060,303	211,058	2,271,361	125,470
1940	20,448	3,773	1,290	25,511	18,960	75,926	13,534	108,420	741,918	1,208,198	233,097	2,183,213	220,499	2,403,712	138,190
1941	21,143	3,775	1,358	26,276	20,548	90,669	14,310	125,527	780,635	1,341,669	244,048	2,366,352	255,128	2,621,480	159,360
1942	21,960	3,747	1,393	27,100	21,814	101,129	16,747	139,690	813,661	1,416,825	265,380	2,495,866	263,689	2,759,555	175,262
1943	22,097	3,594	1,403	27,094	23,290	116,417	21,608	161,285	846,040	1,537,789	305,787	2,689,656	281,055	2,970,711	199,424
1944	22,493	3,632	1,406	27,531	24,935	121,546	21,331	167,812	890,426	1,625,669	311,228	2,827,323	280,616	3,107,939	206,892
1945	22,952	3,733	1,457	28,142	27,177	116,472	20,601	164,250	943,910	1,632,414	312,222	2,888,546	282,911	3,171,457	203,541
1946	23,669	3,968	1,557	29,194	30,711	111,546	20,990	163,247	1,010,030	1,672,823	311,462	2,994,315	298,381	3,292,696	202,122
1947	24,664	4,230	1,733	30,627	34,713	127,899	22,235	184,847	1,090,767	1,902,266	336,618	3,329,651	368,247	3,697,898	230,198
1948	25,894	4,421	1,882	32,197	39,582	140,009	23,427	203,018	1,211,861	2,148,427	367,050	3,727,338	439,947	4,167,285	251,775
1949	27,074	4,571	2,056	33,701	44,296	138,957	25,044	208,297	1,332,219	2,226,317	400,010	3,958,546	423,303	4,381,849	256,438
1950	28,316	4,720	2,111	35,147	50,041	158,829	26,011	234,881	1,476,458	2,447,363	424,042	4,347,863	435,997	4,783,860	285,408
1951	29,591	4,785	2,214	36,590	56,530	179,260	27,383	263,173	1,634,443	2,691,601	458,779	4,784,823	453,436	5,238,259	314,073
1952	30,728	4,871	2,253	37,852	63,570	189,530	28,271	281,371	1,813,076	2,888,555	482,625	5,184,256	476,161	5,660,417	332,313
1953	31,956	4,967	2,196	39,119	70,806	209,178	28,690	308,674	2,007,624	3,169,390	515,345	5,692,359	474,898	6,167,257	359,955
1954	32,934	5,060	2,243	40,237	79,071	213,364	29,762	322,197	2,211,683	3,289,865	546,891	6,048,439	500,704	6,549,143	374,917
1955	34,015	5,149	2,301	41,465	87,424	252,151	31,327	370,902	2,411,488	3,656,144	582,848	6,650,480	548,566	7,199,046	431,875
1956	35,218	5,232	2,346	42,796	97,299	277,233	32,668	407,200	2,635,487	3,960,285	615,504	7,211,276	568,871	7,780,147	473,367
1957	36,324	5,298	2,297	43,919	106,599	288,416	34,778	429,793	2,852,819	4,220,598	643,695	7,717,112	591,463	8,308,575	496,929
1958	37,188	5,346	2,319	44,853	115,334	289,172	35,462	439,968	3,068,804	4,360,702	679,569	8,109,075	599,503	8,708,578	506,981
1959	38,266	5,438	2,329	46,033	125,765	323,143	38,551	487,459	3,327,266	4,783,716	753,380	8,864,362	633,302	9,497,664	558,560
1960	39,273	5,512	2,285	47,070	135,641	341,414	41,686	518,741	3,554,839	5,085,652	783,655	9,424,146	691,689	10,115,835	597,107
1961	41,769	5,887	169	47,825	152,899	367,703	24,329	544,931	3,977,408	5,488,069	446,002	9,911,479	754,995	10,666,474	631,279
1962	42,563	5,970	162	48,695	165,071	397,410	24,501	586,982	4,228,981	5,873,148	456,424	10,558,553	833,391	11,391,944	685,711
1963	43,323	6,066	166	49,555	177,591	424,617	26,263	628,471	4,465,108	6,191,108	481,599	11,137,815	880,659	12,018,474	732,894
1964	43,941	6,160	164	50,265	192,318	459,648	26,066	678,032	4,712,606	6,545,330	491,329	11,749,265	923,831	12,673,096	791,201
1965	44,825	6,246	173	51,244	204,981	494,747	28,687	730,432	4,954,412	6,929,223	521,841	12,405,476	994,574	13,400,050	853,826
1966	45,891	6,354	175	51,420	226,298	541,776	30,431	798,505	5,294,620	7,425,228	549,179	13,269,027	1,105,141	14,374,168	942,474
1967	46,733	6,395	181	53,309	243,959	571,349	33,735	849,043	5,625,554	7,827,956	593,551	14,047,061	1,177,870	15,224,931	1,004,762
1968	47,725	6,469	187	54,381	272,337	623,117	36,171	931,625	6,129,275	8,454,641	636,516	15,220,432	1,318,481	16,538,913	1,105,950
1969	48,671	6,528	189	55,388	303,981	672,145	39,556	1,015,682	6,716,512	9,110,391	689,557	16,516,460	1,506,444	18,022,904	1,215,801
1970	49,762	6,613	202	56,577	333,396	707,816	41,821	1,083,033	7,410,788	9,934,904	753,253	18,098,945	1,692,121	19,791,066	1,289,454
1971	50,850	6,734	208	57,792	357,943	747,321	44,119	1,149,383	8,292,951	11,253,756	843,517	20,390,224	1,931,650	22,321,874	1,358,452

[1] Includes rural sales beginning with 1961. Rural classification discontinued in that year.

TABLE 2

Electric Operating Revenue Relationships

Relationship	Year ended Dec.—										
	1971	1970	1969	1968	1967	1966	1965	1964	1963	1962	1961
Residential sales:[1]											
Percent of total customers	88.0	87.9	87.9	87.8	87.7	87.5	87.5	87.4	87.4	87.4	87.3
Percent of total revenues	37.2	37.5	37.3	37.1	36.9	36.8	37.0	37.2	37.2	37.1	37.3
Percent of total kilowatt-hour sales	26.3	25.9	25.0	24.6	24.3	24.0	24.2	24.3	24.2	24.1	24.2
Average annual number of kilowatt-hours sold per customer	7,039	6,700	6,246	5,706	5,220	4,931	4,618	4,377	4,099	3,878	3,661
Average annual bill per customer	$163.08	$148.92	$137.99	$128.43	$120.38	$115.37	$110.53	$107.25	$103.07	$99.36	$95.23
Average revenue per kilowatt-hours sold, cents	2.32	2.22	2.21	2.25	2.31	2.34	2.39	2.45	2.51	2.56	2.60
Commercial sales:[1]											
Percent of total customers	11.2	11.2	11.3	11.4	11.5	11.7	11.7	11.8	11.8	11.8	11.8
Percent of total revenues	27.1	27.0	26.9	27.2	27.4	27.4	27.5	26.8	26.6	26.7	25.8
Percent of total kilowatt-hours sales	20.3	19.9	19.4	19.7	19.7	19.6	19.7	19.0	18.7	18.7	17.9
Average annual number of kilowatt-hours sold per customer	42,594	40,482	37,605	35,009	32,233	30,239	28,093	25,448	23,481	22,378	20,033
Average annual bill per customer	$937.47	$842.51	$773.22	$725.30	$679.94	$643.81	$613.72	$574.60	$549.63	$531.67	$486.81
Average revenue per kilowatt-hour sold, cents	2.20	2.08	2.06	2.07	2.11	2.13	2.18	2.26	2.34	2.38	2.43
Industrial sales:[1]											
Percent of total customers	0.5	0.5	0.5	0.5	0.5	0.5	0.5	0.5	0.5	0.5	0.5
Percent of total revenues	23.3	23.2	23.7	23.9	24.0	24.3	24.3	24.9	24.9	24.9	25.7
Percent of total kilowatt-hour sales	34.7	35.0	36.0	36.7	37.2	37.9	38.2	39.1	39.3	39.3	40.3
Average annual number of kilowatt-hours sold per customer	1,737,985	1,695,774	1,669,728	1,581,801	1,484,617	1,443,952	1,291,746	1,219,650	1,179,158	1,123,281	1,089,660
Average annual bill per customer	$19,127.74	$17,254.42	$16,314.82	$15,399.55	$14,518.37	$14,126.36	$12,865.91	$12,425.65	$12,251.09	$11,794.94	$11,716.71
Average revenue per kilowatt-hour sold, cents	1.10	1.02	0.98	0.97	0.98	0.98	1.00	1.02	1.04	1.05	1.08

[1] Includes rural sales beginning with 1961. Rural classification discontinued in that year.

Source: Statistics of privately owned electric utilities in the United States, 1971; Federal Power Commission, October 1972.

General Factors—Natural Gas

Physical Plant. The history of the natural gas industry essentially dates from the mid-1940s when a process for continuous welding of steel pipe was developed. Prior to that time most pipe was cast iron, and pipelines of any great size or length were prohibitively expensive to install and maintain. Thus most distribution systems were local and manufactured gas from coal or oil. With the introduction of seamless pipe, distance was no longer a factor, and within ten years practically every part of the United States had a supply of natural gas from fields in the Southwest—with Texas, Louisiana, Oklahoma, and Kansas being the major supply areas. There was natural gas in other regions, but relative to the size of the southwestern reserves they were less important.

The trick to operating the pipelines profitably, however, was to operate them at 100 percent load factor—that is, keep them filled to their design capacity all the time. This again allowed for minimum unit cost. Accomplishment of this goal was achieved either through selling gas in the summer for boiler fuel or to certain industrial users at prices which essentially recovered costs (but provided little profit) or through the use of underground storage fields into which gas injected in the summer could be used to meet the profitable winter heating loads.

In this way, over a 20-year period the natural gas industry became the heat source of practically 100 percent of the homes in the Midwest and West and over 80 percent in the industrial areas of the central United States. The saturation (percent of homes served to those in the area) was low only in New England, where fuel cost was competitive; the Southeast, where neither storage nor heavy industry were available; or the Northwest, where hydroelectric power was competitive. (See Table 3.)

Growth of the Natural Gas Industry. With the industry thus growing merrily, field prices of gas began to rise to reflect the higher demand. The pace of the increase was orderly, however, and caused little problem. In 1954 however, the United States Supreme Court found that Phillips Petroleum Company[10] as an "independent producer" was subject to the terms of the Natural Gas Act. The subsequent 20 years of attempts to regulate the price of natural gas at the wellhead (the point at which it leaves the well and enters the interstate stream) have been the proximate cause of current shortages, allocations, and disruptions. Even before this decision, gas was being used at a faster rate than it was being developed, but from that point forward the trend accelerated. As a result, reserves, as shown in Table 4, have declined.

The need for natural gas is painfully obvious. It heats 83 percent of the homes in the country, it is used as feedstock for numerous items, and in some portions of the Southwest is the only source of fuel for electricity until new plants are built or existing ones are modified. The price in the

---

[10] *Phillips Petroleum Co.* v. *Wisconsin, et al.,* 347 U.S. 672 (1954).

TABLE 3

Gas Utility Industry House-Heating Customers, by State (yearly averages for 1965 and 1970–1972)

Division and State	1965 Customers	1970 Customers	1971 Customers	1972 Customers	1972 Percent
United States	26,130.2	30,856.2	31,794.5	32,418.5	82.5
New England	**564.8**	**734.2**	**768.2**	**800.9**	**50.8**
Connecticut	135.1	178.8	183.4	186.2	51.4
Maine	5.4	6.1	5.8	5.5	24.5
Massachusetts	344.1	436.2	463.2	489.7	49.5
New Hampshire	16.2	24.1	24.2	25.3	64.5
Rhode Island	63.8	81.2	82.9	84.9	56.2
Vermont	0.2	7.8	8.7	93.0	64.0
Middle Atlantic	**3,162.9**	**3,762.0**	**3,866.5**	**3,849.0**	**50.9**
New Jersey	537.4	695.9	751.6	783.7	48.5
New York	1,308.7	1,513.5	1,515.8	1,438.6	38.0
Pennsylvania	1,316.8	1,552.6	1,599.1	1,626.8	75.7
East North Central	**6,024.9**	**7,438.7**	**7,698.3**	**7,946.8**	**87.6**
Illinois	1,645.0	2,077.1	2,163.9	2,225.9	79.5
Indiana	577.8	794.5	835.0	872.6	85.4
Michigan	1,295.1	1,641.1	1,712.9	1,771.9	91.3
Ohio	2,103.4	2,353.7	2,385.7	2,444.8	97.1
Wisconsin	403.6	572.3	600.8	631.8	79.6
West North Central	**2,471.9**	**2,902.8**	**2,980.2**	**3,061.7**	**92.5**
Iowa	416.8	517.4	523.9	525.6	91.9
Kansas	512.2	560.7	577.5	589.5	98.0
Minnesota	428.3	508.6	528.5	539.3	88.5
Missouri	757.3	908.3	927.4	973.1	91.9
Nebraska	264.9	298.5	308.2	315.1	93.9
North Dakota	32.8	41.3	44.7	47.9	84.0
South Dakota	59.6	68.0	70.0	71.4	94.8
South Atlantic	**2,056.2**	**2,590.7**	**2,697.3**	**2,844.3**	**82.9**
Delaware	31.0	42.0	40.7	45.7	59.2
District of Columbia	79.1	82.8	84.0	84.9	60.2
Florida	179.7	243.3	259.1	279.2	72.5
Georgia	593.9	721.4	742.9	767.6	97.3
Maryland	351.9	440.8	461.2	486.3	70.9
North Carolina	136.3	208.8	226.0	252.3	89.6
South Carolina	104.0	178.3	191.7	207.5	86.7
Virginia	263.9	335.7	349.2	368.7	77.9
West Virginia	316.4	337.6	342.5	352.2	98.6
East South Central	**1,419.2**	**1,692.7**	**1,727.4**	**1,795.7**	**95.9**
Alabama	449.8	541.4	546.9	557.4	97.3
Kentucky	400.6	488.5	504.4	525.3	93.9
Mississippi	273.3	308.9	315.7	332.8	97.8
Tennessee	295.5	353.9	360.4	380.3	95.2
West South Central	**3,897.8**	**4,264.8**	**4,338.1**	**4,409.2**	**98.8**
Arkansas	317.2	369.6	375.4	388.1	99.6
Louisiana	738.6	735.7	824.7	835.3	99.1
Oklahoma	582.5	625.8	636.6	652.2	99.7
Texas	2,259.5	2,533.7	2,501.4	2,533.6	98.3
Mountain	**1,366.4**	**1,650.1**	**1,715.7**	**1,836.0**	**97.3**
Arizona	319.8	391.6	408.0	439.1	95.5
Colorado	417.9	510.0	531.8	572.8	98.9
Idaho	40.1	66.9	71.7	79.3	99.3
Montana	115.9	126.0	126.9	131.4	92.1
Nevada	43.1	66.4	71.2	77.6	93.4
New Mexico	180.0	203.5	208.8	220.4	98.2
Utah	186.6	217.6	226.8	240.9	99.2
Wyoming	63.0	68.1	70.5	74.7	99.0
Pacific	**5,166.1**	**5,820.2**	**6,002.8**	**5,875.2**	**95.5**
Alaska	5.0	14.0	14.4	16.0	97.8
California	4,908.9	5,403.6	5,549.1	5,404.9	96.0
Hawaii	0.0	0.0	0.0	0.0	0.0
Oregon	105.4	164.0	181.3	187.1	94.2
Washington	146.8	238.6	258.0	267.2	96.2

Note: Percentages refer to proportion of residential gas customers using gas for heating.
Source: *Gas Facts 1972*, American Gas Association, Arlington, Virginia.

field now is in the process of being freed from regulation, but even this does not happen quickly. Whether free pricing will provide adequate supplies, however, remains an unknown.

Revenues and Prices. At the time the technology for pipe construction improved in the late 1940s, natural gas was being flared, or burned off, because there was no place to sell it and it was an unwanted by product of oil development. A number of promotors thus were able to garner supplies of gas adequate to fill a 20- to 24-inch pipeline for a 20-year period, obtain Federal Power Commission authority to construct pipelines to an eastern or midwestern market, and contract for the sale of the gas to manufactured gas distributors in the local areas for the same 20 years. The gas was purchased at $0.03 to $0.05 per thousand cubic feet (mcf.); transported for slightly less than a penny per 100 miles; and sold, after a return of about 6 percent on capital, by the owner of the pipeline at $0.15 to $0.20 in the Midwest and $0.30 to $0.35 in the East. As these prices were one third to one half the price of coal or oil, there was intense demand over a period of 15 years, the other fuels were effectively replaced, and gas has become the principal home heating fuel in the United States.

The realization of lower unit costs also was a factor in the growth of pipelines. With improved technology, pipeline size went to a 36-inch diameter, and there are segments of 48- and 52-inch pipe. The amount of gas that can be put through a larger line increases geometrically. Other developments included "looping," which uses pressure differentials to stimulate a pipeline of larger size, and finally underground storage. The latter was the salvation of the industry as it effectively freed the operator from absolute dependence on weather and on sales (on a dump basis) to large-volume off-peak customers. Gas could be put through the line at a 100 percent load factor, injected in storage fields, and withdrawn for the higher-value heating load in the winter season.

Table 5 showing gas deliveries by classes of customers indicates the changes that have occurred.

Substitutes. Because of the difficulty in obtaining new reserves of natural gas, companies are embarking on new and expensive projects. They include pipelines from Alaska and Canada (subject to that country's approval), at costs estimated to be in excess of $5 billion, and proposals to build facilities to bring gas from the Middle and Far East and Australia. The latter would see fleets of "thermos bottle" tankers carrying liquified natural gas (LNG) to be introduced into the domestic gas stream. Currently there are about five such projects proposed, and the costs are as yet unknown. Tankers, however, are estimated at $100 million each, and nine are required for the importation of 500 million cubic feet per day (which is the smallest size economic pipeline), the liquification plant will cost upwards of $600 million and the regasification facilities, $200–300 million. The delivered cost of Libyian gas with a field price of $0.30 to $0.35 (before the recent Arabian oil embargo) is

TABLE 4

Summary of Annual Estimates of Natural Gas Reserves, 1945–1972 (millions of cubic feet)

| Year | Natural Gas added during year | | | | | | Total of Discoveries, Revisions and Extensions | Net Change in Underground Storage | Preliminary Net Production during Year | Estimated Proved Reserves as of End of Year | Increase over Previous Year |
	Extensions	Revisions	Extensions and Revisions	New Field Discoveries	Discoveries of New Fields and New Pools in Old Fields	New Reservoir Discoveries					
1945	–	–	–	–	–	–	–	–	–	146,986,723	–
1950	–	–	9,122,566	–	2,861,724	–	11,984,290	54,006	6,855,244	184,584,745	5,183,052
1951	–	–	12,942,930	–	3,022,878	–	15,965,808	132,030	7,923,673	192,758,910	8,174,165
1952	–	–	8,885,950	–	5,381,656	–	14,267,606	197,766	8,592,716	198,631,566	5,872,656
1953	–	–	13,298,733	–	7,043,200	–	20,341,933	513,629	9,188,365	210,298,763	11,667,197
1954	–	–	4,607,155	–	4,939,919	–	9,547,074	90,408	9,573,314	210,560,931	262,168
1955	–	–	16,209,610	–	5,688,009	–	21,897,619	87,161	10,063,167	222,482,544	11,921,613
1956	–	–	19,110,250	–	5,605,864	–	24,716,114	133,242	10,848,685	236,483,215	14,000,671
1957	–	–	11,057,936	–	8,950,119	–	20,008,055	178,757	11,439,890	245,230,137	8,746,922
1958	–	–	13,316,094	–	5,580,624	–	18,896,718	57,588	11,422,651	252,761,792	7,531,655
1959	–	–	14,852,007	–	5,769,245	–	20,621,252	160,450	12,373,063	261,170,431	8,408,639
1960	–	–	7,293,016	–	6,600,963	–	13,893,979	281,272	13,019,356	262,326,326	1,155,895
1961	–	–	10,258,693	–	6,907,729	–	17,166,422	159,543	13,378,649	266,273,642	3,947,316
1962	–	–	13,184,795	–	6,299,164	–	19,483,959	159,230	13,637,973	272,278,858	6,005,216
1963	–	–	12,586,733	–	5,577,934	–	18,164,667	253,733	14,546,025	276,151,233	3,872,375
1964	–	–	13,342,837	–	6,909,301	–	20,252,138	195,111	15,347,028	281,251,454	5,100,221
1965	–	–	14,775,570	–	6,543,709	–	21,319,279	150,423	16,252,293	286,468,923	5,217,469
1966	9,224,745	4,937,962	–	2,947,329	–	3,110,396	20,220,432	134,523	17,491,073	289,332,805	2,863,882
1967	9,538,584	6,570,578	–	3,170,520	–	2,524,651	21,804,333	151,403	18,380,838	292,907,703	3,574,898
1968	7,758,821	3,016,146	–	1,376,429	–	1,545,612	13,697,008	118,569	19,373,428	287,349,852	(5,557,851)
1969	5,800,489	(1,238,261)	–	1,769,557	–	2,043,219	8,375,004	107,169	20,723,190	275,108,835	(12,241,017)
1970	6,158,168	(99,721)	–	27,770,223	–	3,367,689	37,196,359	402,018	21,960,804	290,746,408	15,637,573
1971	6,374,706	(1,227,400)	–	1,317,574	–	3,360,541	9,825,421	310,301	22,076,512	278,805,618	(11,940,790)
1972	6,153,683	(1,077,791)	–	1,462,539	–	3,096,132	9,634,563	156,563	22,511,898	266,084,846	(12,720,772)

( ): Denotes negative volume.

Note: Volumes are calculated at a pressure base of 14.73 psi, absolute, and at a standard temperature of 60° F.

Source: AGA Committee on Natural Gas Reserves.

TABLE 5

Gas Utility Industry Sales, by Class of Service, 1945–1972[a] (trillions of Btus.)[*]

Year	Total	Residential	Commercial	Industrial	Other
1945	2,586.7	774.9	249.7	1,452.3	109.8
1950	4,209.1	1,383.9	410.4	2,288.7	126.1
1955	6,658.6	2,238.7	602.9	3,535.1	281.9
1956	7,254.2	2,464.3	655.8	3,868.7	265.4
1957	7,703.5	2,598.5	698.9	4,047.6	358.5
1958	8,028.6	2,812.5	764.9	4,076.4	374.8
1959	8,791.8	2,973.9	827.5	4,563.1	427.3
1960	9,287.7	3,188.1	919.8	4,709.4	470.4
1961	9,589.0	3,321.0	988.1	4,785.6	494.3
1962	10,234.8	3,536.9	1,092.9	5,100.1	504.9
1963	10,766.3	3,668.0	1,136.6	5,438.1	523.6
1964	11,591.2	3,869.7	1,273.5	5,912.0	536.0
1965	11,980.3	3,999.0	1,344.8	6,146.5	490.0
1966	12,859.1	4,175.4	1,462.8	6,653.3	567.6
1967	13,488.3	4,365.3	1,577.6	7,014.3	531.1
1968	14,472.4	4,552.7	1,704.9	7,595.1	619.7
1969	15,391.6	4,820.4	1,878.1	8,135.8	557.3
1970	16,043.5	4,923.7	2,006.6	8,439.2	674.0
1971	16,679.5	5,039.7	2,155.5	8,643.4	840.9
1972	17,109.7	5,148.4	2,280.4	8,797.8	883.1

a. Includes data for Hawaii subsequent to 1959 and Alaska subsequent to 1960.
° Btu is the British thermal unit.
Source: *Gas Facts 1972*.

in the neighborhood of $1.20 to $1.40 per thousand cubic feet. For an industry that developed its markets on five-cent gas only 30 years ago, it is apparent the outlook has changed.

Other approaches to obtaining gas include the production of synthetic natural gas (SNG) and the gasification of coal or oil, including naptha. Pilot projects have indicated that some approaches are commercially feasible, and several such plants are in operation. At present the largest produces only 250 million cubic feet per day and thus, while helpful in a period of extreme shortage, should be relegated to peak-shaving status as pipeline quantities become available.

End-Use Control. While the industry is struggling with the problem of supply, no less than 30 bureaus and agencies of the federal and state governments are attempting to determine where and how the fuels will be used. As there is as yet little or no coordination between these groups, the direction of the final outcome remains clouded. Suffice it to say that the series of priorities effectively creates "end-use control." It is now in existence and seems likely to influence future directions of the industry.

In its present form, the priority system is designed to assure adequate heating service gas for all currently served residential customers. After this need is met, other, but so-called "inferior," uses will be served. Recent recognition of the possibility of industrial dislocations appear to be causing modifications of the early plans, however. At some point economic aspects of this fuel, which presently has the least number of pollution problems, must be considered in directing its use. With only limited knowledge of prospective use and pricing, this set of circumstances provides a challenge for the analyst. In this industry he also must be acutely aware of political and even international developments affecting the worldwide need and movement of energy.

General Factors—Telephone

Growth of the Communications Industry. Both in terms of usage and revenue growth, this industry also has reflected the overall growth of the economy. It also has been influenced by rising per capita income, lowered rates, and technical improvements. In short, it mirrors our .society as much as it affects it, as shown in Table 6.

TABLE 6

Telephones in Service (thousands)

	Bell System	Annual Increase (percent)	Independents	Annual Increase (percent)	Total	Annual Increase (percent)
1972	108,811	4.9	23,187	6.3	131,998	5.2
1971	103,698	3.8	28,107	5.6	125,505	4.1
1970	99,902	4.1	20,650	5.6	120,552	4.4
1969	95,942	5.3	19,559	6.3	115,501	5.5
1968	91,122	5.0	18,393	7.0	109,515	5.3
1967	86,776	4.8	17,195	6.2	103,971	5.0
1966	82,813	5.3	16,193	6.3	99,006	5.5
1965	78,633	5.3	15,233	6.4	93,866	5.5
1964	74,659	4.9	14,317	6.3	88,976	5.1
1963	71,151	4.0	13,468	5.9	84,619	4.3

Source: *Statistics of the Independent Telephone Industry,* United States Independent Telephone Association, Vol. 1, 1973.

The basic long-distance toll pricing policies of the telephone industry have been set over the years by Bell System practices. With the concurrence of the Federal Communications Commission, system average prices have been used. This method provides for equal service and prices between two points regardless of the use characteristics of the stations. In essence the high-density portions of the system subsidize the lower-usage segments. Within a state a similar approach is used for toll and local calls. (Local calls are considered those within one exchange or closely neighboring exchanges, while toll calls are those between more distant exchanges or in other jurisdictions). Complex arrangements exist between the Bell and independent companies on "toll-call settlements." Here the purpose is to divide the revenues between the two handling systems. Currently this is accomplished under the "Ozark Plan" which assigns plant values to each participating carrier. Earlier settlements were made under different plans such as the Denver Plan, the Charleston Plan, etc. The distinctive feature of the current procedure is the use of return on plant or assets rather than solely division of cost, as in the earlier plans. Local rates are set in a manner similar to electric service. There is a minimum charge for service and then a charge for each unit of use.

The telephone industry also is beginning to change its overall basic pricing and instituting "usage sensitive" rates. Here length of the call and time of day relative to the peak requirement is increasingly important, rather than distance being dominant as in the past. Price varies relative to the peak: For the amount of time that the equipment is in use by a caller, especially when near or on the anticipated peak load, there is a higher price, and for that same amount of time, used at an inactive period, there is a lower price.

As noted above, increased competition in the carrier market is creating abberations. The president of American Telephone recently estimated that over $100 million in revenues potentially may be diverted to specialized services over the coming several years. Others recognizing the potential problem of "average pricing" by the telephone industry and prospective diversion of revenues by specialized service companies have begun a counteroffensive. In particular a number of knowledgeable state regulators have spoken out against competition in what is, and I believe should be, a regulated monopoly.

New Pricing Techniques

Electric. Historically, electric rates have been constructed under the theory that the higher the load factor (use related to time) and the greater the total use, the lower was the unit cost of providing the power. For example, if a customer had a load requirement of 50 megawatts (mw.) 24 hours per day for 320 days, this amount of capacity could be built into the machine and the remainder of the equipment structured to handle remaining fluctuations. Thus, the unit cost of service was less than for a residential customer who used two megawatts for only six to ten hours per day for 365 days. What is more important, every residential customer uses the two megawatts during the same time of the day so that much of the equipment necessary to provide for the peak is unused most of the day. If the residential customer demand was constant over a greater time span, the marginal cost of his service would also be lower.

For this reason the first block or minimum charge is designed to recover the highest unit costs. It also recovers the cost of service installation. As total residential load increased, especially with the advent of air conditioning and electric heating, the unit price began in some instances to be brought down to the industrial high-load factor rate, (in part through the use of promotional rates), even though the time of use characteristics were different. Because of development of the air-conditioning market between 1960 and 1970 much of the industry went from a winter peak to a summer peak. This also changed peak-load responsibility and necessitated the addition of more reserve (back-up) capacity than had been anticipated, again adding to cost.

Without regard to outside economic forces, the rapid rise of costs of producing electricity, both in terms of capital and operating expenses, is necessitating a review of rate structures. This is now occurring. It would seem that customers responsible for the peak-associated use or for incremental equipment will bear the brunt of the price rises.

In the meantime, the issue is being clouded by attempts of socially motivated groups to tie the price of electricity to goals unrelated to utility operations. From these sources have come programs to create flat rates (all customers in a class pay the same unit price regardless of use), inverted rates (the greater the use, the higher the unit price), and special interest rates (for example, discounts for the elderly and minority groups). The latter approach has been denied mostly on the basis of unjust discrimination. The state of New York, among others, however, has moved toward flat rates, and Wisconsin adopted peak responsibility rates. It is not appropriate here to attempt judgment but only to note that past practices are being challenged. Finally, regardless of how the charges are allocated, the *basic requirement of the ability to raise capital and provide service is,* in the final analysis, *the determinant of the total revenue need.*

Natural Gas. Retail pricing of natural gas had a history similar to that of the electric industry—a high initial block and successively lower prices as use of load went up. As natural gas replaced manufactured gas, however, pipeline pricing (as opposed to distribution pricing) was developed. Such pricing policy assumed 100 percent load factor operation (that is, full utilization of the entire capacity on a continuous basis). Not only was pricing geared this way, so was financing.

In an oversimplified version, the pipeline was entitled to charge a rate that recovered costs and provided a reasonable return. Costs included the purchased price of gas, operations, depreciation, and taxes. If operations were at a 100 percent load factor, costs did not vary significantly. At one end of the line there was a 20-year supply and at the other, a 20-year market. Under these conditions bond buyers were willing to extend 20-year mortgages for up to 70 percent of the capitalization, and the returns to the equity, fully leveraged, were high. It was characterized as "shooting fish in a barrel."

With the advent of reduced availability of gas, and inflation, the pipelines have come on harder times. With few exceptions, they diversified into other areas or industries so that the pipelines themselves now are primarily a source of cash for other investments.

Many pipelines now are curtailing deliveries, and operation is below 100 percent load factor, necessitating pricing changes. The "Atlantic Seaboard" formula long used by the Federal Power Commission is being modified so that revenues will be more responsive to volumetric sales (commodity portion of the rate) than to the cost of plan dedicated to the service (demand portion of the rate).[11] Thus, despite the return

---

[11] The classic "Seaboard" formula provides for 50 percent of the charge to be dedicated to "demand"—the highest amount of gas taken on any one day during the past year—and 50 percent to "commodity"—the actual amount of gas delivered during any one month.

authorized, there is likely to be greater seasonality in reported earnings. At the present time distributors (retailers) are not changing their price structures, and there is not likely to be any material change until supplies again become adequate to serve a larger market. By that time, however, end-use controls probably will dictate what the incremental uses will be, and prices will be adjusted as necessary to serve them.

Uses and Problems of Extrapolation

As a result of the steadiness of growth in the utility industry, a number of schemes for forecasting had been developed, based on differing mathematical techniques. Each, however, had one common point in that the rate of return, either on rate base or equity, was the independent variable. On a broad industry base the technique was successful, but in making comparisons between companies, problems quite often arose, as returns varied from theoretical levels. As inflation and changes in technology further impinged themselves on the structure in the mid- to late 1960s, these techniques of extrapolation became increasingly less reliable.

Nonetheless there are some areas where the mathematical approaches described in the chapter on forecasting are appropriate in analysis of this industry. Statistical techniques also may gain acceptance in areas such as forecasting the impact of price elasticity and cash requirements associated with nuclear fuel. In general, we would suggest that simple forecasting methods may be best for handling an increasingly complex task. The imposition of mathematical techniques that are subject to unexpected and even irrational forces may distort the series.

ANALYSIS OF COST FACTORS

Operating costs are recoverable in rates for all types of utilities. The functions included in costs are delineated in the Uniform System of Accounts promulgated by the FPC for electric and gas companies and by the FCC for communications corporations. A few states have their own systems, but they closely follow the federal format.

The basic components included in the cost of service are operations, maintenance, depreciation, general (that is, property or ad valorum) taxes, and federal and state income taxes. It is important to remember that in utility accounting income taxes are included in the "above the line" accounts. In rate proceedings such items are considered the recoverable costs. "Below the line" items such as financial costs must be obtained through the authorized return.

Equipment

Utility cost of plant also is a recoverable expense in terms of the return allowed on the investment. The equation provides for a "return" to be calculated by multiplying the cost or value of the plant by a rate that is determined by the appropriate regulatory agency. In past years, cost of plant varied little from expectations, and, for the most part, additions were made in an orderly fashion. There were some notable exceptions, however, brought on by recessions or changes in population growth patterns. Capital costs of debt and equity also changed slowly, so that there was little to disturb the earnings growth record of the industry. Thus regulation generally was leisurely, and there was little damage caused by delays in obtaining rate increases. Most of this has changed in the last several years.

Size and Quality Problems

Coming at a time of serious and prolonged inflation, the additional factors of lower productivity in construction, and mechanical problems of larger and more complex units have added measureably to the capital costs of electric utilities. These difficulties were amplified by passage of legislation controlling air and water emissions, which in many instances required redesign of units under construction and retrofitting existing equipment. The cost of a coal-fired unit rose from around $120 per kilowatt in 1958 to over $300 per kilowatt currently; and one unit in Ohio, to be completed next year, may cost $400 per kilowatt, including $100 per kilowatt for environmental control devices.

The industry also has discovered that construction of larger units has resulted in metallurgical problems that did not exist before, and the move to nuclear fuel has proved particularly frustrating. Costs of the latter, in particular, have escalated more than 100 percent, and in some cases 200 percent, from planning estimates.

All of these developments are straining the industry's need to raise capital at a time when the cost of this commodity also is rising, reflecting the national inflation. Taken together, the rise in prices of equipment and the cost of financing it have increased construction budgets to $16–18 billion annually, compared with $6–7 billion only five years ago and a $3–4 billion ten years ago.[12] One other aspect of increased cost was the need to increase the reserve margins for generation which had become dangerously low. In the mid-1960s, based on then existing units, regional reserve margins were set which were supposed to reduce overall costs for the participating utilities. With lower-than-expected reliability of the larger units, however, the plan failed; and in addition to meeting accelerated growth, reserves had to be augmented on many systems, as shown in Table 7 and Figure 2.

---

[12] *Statistical Year Book of the Electric Utility Industry for 1972,* Edison Electric Institute (November 1972), p. 59, and *Irving Trust Financing Calendar.*

Fuel Conversions and Environmental Controls

One other capital item that came into play as a result of environmental legislation was retraining labor to handle new fuels. A work force trained in a gas-burning station had problems different from those experienced in an oil or coal facility. There have been some spectacular instances such as the multimillion dollar tools that had to be devised to move a piece of loose metal inside a prototype nuclear breeder reactor, but for the most part the need was for retraining to handle more complex work flows. The power-plant manager now is required to monitor sulphur, nitrogen, particulates, and water temperature as well as to produce power. As much of this measuring and control equipment also was newly designed and did not always perform according to specifications, there was a further contribution to the higher costs.

While the factors of inflation and lower productivity have plagued the natural gas and communications industries also, the equipment problem has not been as great. In the case of the gas industry, this reflects lack of product; and in the communications area, a more orderly transition from mechanical to electric-mechanical and electronic devices. For comparative purposes, however, the construction levels of the gas industry for 1973 are estimated at $2–3 billion and for the telephone groups $11–12 billion.

Capital Cost

The cost of plant is included in calculating the "return" allowed by the agency having jurisdiction over rates. The "rate of return" applied to the value of the plant is a judgment amount but must meet a number of legal requirements. The basic decisions of the United States Supreme Court that still guide the agencies are *the Bluefield Water Works and Improvement Co. v. Public Service Commission of West Virginia*[13] and *FPC v. Hope Natural Gas Co.*[14] The decisions outline the requirements that (1) an efficiently managed utility must be authorized a rate of return that will permit the attraction of capital on a basis that will allow it to "maintain and support its credit" and that (2) it will be similar to returns of other business "having similar or comparable risks." There is a lot of latitude in these words, and voluminous litigation followed. But over a period of years the challenges have been overcome and the system has worked. Even in the recent past when inflation has strained the fabric of regulation, and in a few instances caused grave damage, it has provided rates that have attracted capital, and in greater amounts

---

[13] 262 U.S. 679, (1923).
[14] Hope Natural Gas Co., Re, 44 PUR (NS), 1,24 (1942).

TABLE 7

Construction Expenditures—Investor-owned Electric Utilities (excluding Alaska and Hawaii; by type of electric utility plant; millions of dollars)

Year	Total	Produc-tion	Trans-mission	Distri-bution	Other
1972	$13 385	$7 931	$1 748	$3 073	$633
1971	11 894	6 702	1 806	2 774	612
1970	10 145	5 429	1 680	2 614	422
1969	8 294	3 992	1 554	2 421	327
1968	7 140	3 189	1 503	2 135	313
1967	6 120	2 553	1 323	1 977	267
1966	4 932	1 789	1 137	1 769	237
1965	4 027	1 300	940	1 585	202
1964	3 551	1 114	824	1 424	189
1963	3 319	1 165	644	1 323	187
1962	3 154	1 078	609	1 305	162
1961	3 256	1 267	579	1 265	145
1960	3 331	1 342	537	1 300	152
1959	3 383	1 519	554	1 163	147
1958	3 764	1 879	608	1 125	152
1957	3 679	1 647	594	1 270	168
1956	2 910	1 029	455	1 274	152
1955	2 719	1 064	434	1 093	128
1954	2 835	1 280	464	993	98
1953	2 876	1 391	442	938	105
1952	2 599	1 251	379	879	90
1951	2 134	920	300	810	104

Note: In these figures an attempt has been made to eliminate wherever possible capital expenditures made for the purchase of existing properties rather than for actual new construction. Construction expenditures are, in general, the gross amounts spent for construction of all kinds, including the acquisition of real estate and all necessary equipment. The figures include money spent for replacements, additions, and betterments (but not for maintenance of existing plant), as well as for new construction.

Source: Estimated by Edison Electric Institute, based on statistics collected by *Electrical World*.

than ever before. This does not mean to suggest that regulators have been generous. That allegation cannot be made. They have, however, acted responsibly within the framework of the legal requirements on recovery of cost of plant.

To give the reader some insight into the magnitudes involved in the rate problems it should be noted that prior to 1968, the largest annual amount of rate increase authorized in the electric industry was $159 million in 1959 (annual revenues of the industry were then about $9 billion). Subsequent to that, until 1968, rate reductions far outstripped increases. With the onset of serious inflation and the technical problems with equipment, rate increases became necessary and in 1973 are running at an annual rate of $1 billion for the electric utilities ($28 billion of annual revenues); $300 million for gas companies ($20 billion of annual revenues); and $1.3 billion for communications companies ($21 billion of annual revenues for the Bell system and $3.8 billion for the

FIGURE 2

Electric Construction Expenditures—Investor-Owned Electric Utilities
(excluding Alaska and Hawaii; by type of utility plant, 1945–1972)

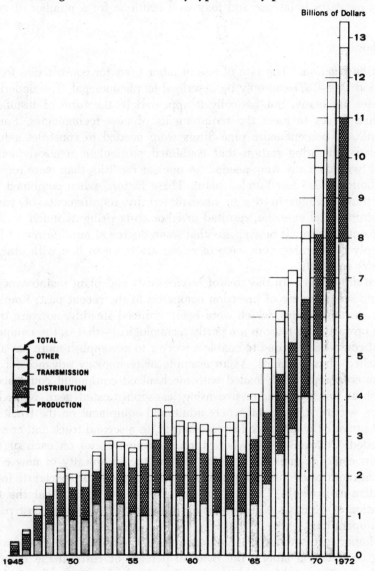

Note: Based on Table 7.

independents). As this is being published the need for higher rates is coming close to crisis proportions because of disarray in the financial markets brought on by inflationary pressure. Thus, the need for further rate increases is intense and may well continue for a number of years.

Labor

Construction. The rate of rise of labor costs for construction for the period 1968–1971 can only be described as phenomenal. The underlying causes are many, but basically it appeared in the form of insufficient skilled forces to meet the requirements of new technologies. For example, 50 percent more pipe fitters were needed to construct a fossil-fueled generating station that contained particulate removal facilities and twice as many were needed for nuclear facilities than were required to build a 1965 fossil-fueled plant. These factors, when combined with constant changes in design necessitated by requirements of various environmental agencies, resulted in labor costs rising as much as 20–25 percent per year. It now apears that some degree of equilibrium of labor supply is returning and wage increases are more in line with other industry contracts.

Maintenance. In the area of service costs and plant maintenance we again see a picture of inversion compared to the recent past. Employee per customer ratios, which were being reduced steadily, now are trending upward. The reasons are partly technological—that is, the equipment that could be provided to enable a worker to accomplish more has about reached physical limits. As an example of technology advances, a two-man crew on a truck loaded with mechanized equipment could accomplish as much as four or five using less-sophisticated gear. Now, however, we are at the point where additional equipment on the truck does not provide the ability to increase output, so a second truck and crew are needed. Concomitantly, where three four-men crews on each of three shifts could operate a generating station, the complexity of new equipment requires five to eight man crews plus a group of specialists for the system as a whole. Thus in the future it would appear that the labor portion of expenses will be a rising rather than a declining cost part of the operation.

Labor cost is about 16–18 percent of electric utility revenues, (excluding construction labor), but over 40 percent of costs in the telephone industry. The need for additional workers has been pressing for the latter, also, but not to the degree that exists in the electric companies. Certainly additional work forces have been required in the gas companies, but thus far this has been in the nonregulated segments of exploration and production. The trends toward greater need for, and cost of, labor seem likely to continue for at least several years.

Fuel

As this chapter is being composed in the beginning of a possibly serious fuel crisis it is difficult to generalize. Suffice it to say it now appears that there will be adequate fuel to keep this country's electric generators operating, although there could be some periods of temporary distress.

Types and Costs. The basic fuel of the electric utility industry currently is coal, and by 1980 we should be well into the age of nuclear power. The history of the industry, however, is coal, as this was the only fuel used—except for natural gas used in plants located in the Southwest near natural gas fields, and hydroelectric source used in the Northwest. A number of events beginning in the late 1950s conspired to reduce the importance of coal. Among them were the promise of nuclear reactors, the low price of imported oil, and the need for companies in highly populated areas to burn cleaner fuel. Mine owners, faced with shrinking markets and the then anticipated onslaught of nuclear units threatening further contraction for their markets, closed inefficient mines and did not develop new ones. In an unrelated way, the growth of the mining industry began to slow as natural gas displaced coal for home heating, and this trend accelerated as rising prices of mine labor resulted in oil becoming relatively less costly, especially in coastal regions.

Despite this trend the great majority of electric utilities still burn coal mined in the Virginias, Georgia, Alabama, Ohio, Indiana, and Illinois. Western coal in Utah and Wyoming was too expensive until recently, but its low sulphur content indicates it will be used increasingly in the future.

Restrictions. Utilities were aware of the need to control particulate emmissions many years ago, and a variety of scrubbers and precipitators were developed and installed. Generally they were designed for a particular plant and grade of coal. Water outlet temperature from plants built up to the mid-1960s was not thought to have a material effect on marine life, although mixing zones were created. Lastly, the size of the plants apparently did not require quantities of water that could in most cases materially affect the characteristics of the water source. Sulphur emissions were recognized but defied solution. In the California basin where air inversions caused smog, gas was substituted for oil as an answer to that problem.

The year 1970 was chaotic. As noted above, the new huge 1,000-magawatt generators came on line and developed mechanical problems. Nuclear plants, also designed on a one-at-a-time basis, stuttered and had to be shut down frequently for repairs. (In passing it should be noted that a few were started up and ran, while a similar machine a few miles away developed all sorts of difficulties.) On top of this came the Environmental Protection Act, the Clean Water Act, and some court decisions, such as the *Calvert Cliffs* case,[15] that changed the face of the industry. All of these laws and decisions are interrelated and imposed upon existing laws, so that descriptions of their impact can become cumbersome. The essence of their effect was a requirement to rebuild a major part of the system practically *with little regard to cost.*

Due to a growing awareness of the need to protect our environment, public utilities systems are faced with a number of problems. Water discharge temperatures have to be controlled, if necessary through the construction of cooling devices, thus reducing a plant's designed output; and intakes must be designed to minimize danger to indigenous fish. As standards for fuel currently are set arbitrarily, there is little consistency. There also will be a period of years before a satisfactory system for sulphur removal can be designed and installed. The cost is unknown but is expected to be high enough that it may be more economical to close down older plants than to retrofit them.

The use of low-sulphur coal is an alternative, but the cost, including thousands of miles of transportation (as this coal is mostly in Montana, Utah, and Wyoming) must be weighed against the probability of development of satisfactory sulphur-removal facilities which permit the use of local or nearby coal. The last problem is that of disposing of the "sludge" that accumulates at sulphur removal facilities. To date there is no satisfactory approach.

The Mine Safety Act has added to the cost of coal and also to the uncertainty of supply. Even though demand for coal is sharply increased as a result of the oil curtailments from the Mideast, the cost of developing new mines or reopening closed ones casts doubt on the probability of a major increase in supply over the next few years. Most Western low-sulphur coal can be strip mined, but the terms of the proposed law governing such activitiy causes questions as to the future availability of these supplies. Labor productivity of the coal mines remains poor because of internal union problems. This causes irregularity of deliveries and higher costs. The utilities in the Southwest use gas for boiler fuel. The Federal Power Commission ruling that this was an "inferior use," however, started a conversion to oil. Progress was made in this process over the past year, but the current shortage of oil has necessitated a partial shift back to gas.

Utilities on coastal areas have converted from coal to oil and in response to air quality rulings are using low-sulphur oil. This is now in short supply, and the air quality restrictions will have to be modified until low-sulphur fuels can be obtained. In a few instances, such as in New England, coal will be burned again.

There are more than 50 commercial nuclear plants operating and reliability rates are improving. The Atomic Energy Commission is striving

---

[15] Cliffs' Coordinating Committee, Inc. v. U.S. Atomic Energy Commission, 449 F. 2d 1109.

to reduce the licensing procedure time, and this should be aided by the dislocations of other energy sources.

Despite rapidly escalating costs, nuclear energy remains the cheapest source of electricity. The main remaining problem, not associated with the reactor, is that of water temperature—the discharge from these plants is warmer than that of a fossil-fueled unit. Cooling towers may provide the answer, but the size of this equipment is causing a problem also.

The need for environmental impact statements, required by the *Calvert Cliffs* decision, has slowed construction of many units and added significantly to costs. Recent actions of the Atomic Energy Commission seem to indicate this will be less of a problem in the future, especially if the utilities and the vendors can settle on a few standardized types of units.

Long-term fuel availability remains an unknown. A price rise for uranium ore should enlarge the potential supply, but there is a finite capacity for enrichment of the ore (currently accomplished by the AEC) which will be reached between 1980 and 1985. As incremental facilities for this purpose could require five to eight years to build, the need is reasonably urgent. Despite this, there is a running debate as to the type of facility (diffusion or centrifuge) to be built and whether it should be accomplished through government or private industry funding.

One of the cost elements involved in construction of electric plants is time. Only ten years ago, a fossil-fueled unit was completed within three years from the time of the original announcement. Lead time is now five to six years for a major size plant and eight to ten years for a nuclear unit. Aside from the capital costs not recovered during the construction period, this time lag is adding heavily to the total cost of completion of the units.

Adjustment Clauses. Fuel cost, as noted, is recoverable in utilities rates. When these costs move gradually there is time to seek offsets from the regulatory agency. When, however, costs escalate from month to month, the regulatory process breaks down. In order to insulate the utility from such rapid changes in costs, fuel adjustment clauses were instituted or, where they existed, time lags were shortened. They permit the utility to change rates to reflect changes in fuel costs—usually without the specific approval of the agency—although the new rates may have to be filed.

When costs moved more slowly, the general approach was to use a 12-month moving average of costs. Now cost recovery can be instituted within one to two months after it is incurred. In a few states, estimates of fuel mix for the future 12 months are being used. As a result of these clauses, the earnings impact of fuel changes have been minimized, but a rapid month-to-month change can still result in nonrecovered costs. At present over 95 percent of the regulatory jurisdiction have authorized fuel adjustment clauses.

Depreciation

Depreciation is at once the simplest and most complex account in the utility world. Basically it recovers the cost of the plant over its useful life, as in any other industry. In the regulatory world, however, it is a device for setting rates, and the amount allowed in rates for depreciation may have little resemblance to either book or tax depreciation. As this also impinges on the amount of recoverable income tax, the impact can be important. *Book depreciation* is generally straightforward and is recorded in a manner to recover the cost of capital items over their lives—usually 30 years for major plant items. The composite rate for electric is about 2.9 percent; for gas distribution companies, 2.5 percent; for gas transmission companies, 3.5 percent; and for telephone companies, 5.2 percent. In recent years these rates have been rising recognizing the factor of obsolescence.

Tax Depreciation. Accelerated depreciation arose during the Korean War and was designed to stimulate plant construction. Major facilities could be written off over shortened periods (for utilities, five years). For book purposes, the tax saving over use of straight-line depreciation was credited to a deferred account and debited in installments equal to the remaining life after the facility was completely depreciated for tax purposes. Most commissions accepted this *normalizing* procedure and there were no meaningful rate changes.

Liberalized depreciation was authorized in 1962 and provided for faster write-offs through two methods: (1) the sum of the years digits (SYD) or (2) double declining balance (DDB). Both had the effect of depreciating 30-year property, for tax purposes, in about 12 to 14 years. In this instance, however, the argument was advanced that this was not a tax deferral but a tax saving, and, therefore, the benefit should accrue to the customer and not the shareholder. In the mid-1960s the disagreement waxed hot, and two methods of accounting evolved for rate making: (1) *normalized* accounting where a deferred tax account was set up and rates were not adjusted and (2) *flow through* accounting which assumes that reduced income taxes, arising from the higher tax depreciation, are a tax saving and, therefore, rates should be reduced accordingly. If the industry had continued into a state comparable to that existing in the mid-1960s it is probably fair to say the differences would not have been meaningful. Unfortunately inflation and all those technical problems imposed themselves, and cash flow differences began to evolve. Some analysts recently have suggested there may even be quality differences in the earnings of the two types of companies.

The Tax Reform Act of 1969 modified the rules somewhat and provides that former flow through companies could, with the approval of their commission, use normalizing procedures on plants constructed subsequent to 1969. A number of companies and commissions have followed this route, and, other things equal, the problem should work itself out over a period of about ten more years. The current need for greater cash flow also is stimulating commissions that historically used *flow through* to adopt *normalization* proceedures.

Asset Depreciation Range. The most recent change in depreciation accounting permits a degree of flexibility in estimating useful lives. For the utility industry it has some advantage of improving cash flow, but in terms of total capital requirements it is of only modest help.

General Taxes

All taxes other than income taxes are included in this category. They are property or sales based and are paid to local taxing authorities. In essence the utility is the tax collector for these municipalities. Also included are franchise taxes. It is rare that general taxes are contested as a recoverable cost.

Income Taxes

Income taxes are levied both by the federal government and some states and cities. As taxes are paid, they are recoverable from the customers of the utilities. As outlined in the depreciation section, however, taxes paid and taxes allowed in calculating rates are not necessarily the same thing. Tables 8 and 9 may help to demonstrate the basic differences.

TABLE 8

Tax Calculation for Federal Income Tax Purposes Using Straight-Line and Accelerated Depreciation ($000)

	Straight-Line Depreciation	Accelerated Depreciation
Revenue..............................	100,000	100,000
Operations...........................	40,000	40,000
Maintenance.........................	8,000	8,000
Depreciation.........................	*12,000*	*16,000*
General taxes........................	10,000	10,000
Interest on debt.....................	12,000	12,000
Operating Expenses..................	82,000	86,000
Taxable income......................	18,000	14,000
Federal income tax (at 50 percent)........	9,000	7,000

If the regulatory agency now finds that $21 million rather than $23 million is the correct return for the flow-through company, the revenue requirement will be reduced commensurately. (It should be noted, however, that in normalizing procedures the deferred taxes included in the capitalization are given zero cost and the unamortized reserve is deducted from the rate base.)

TABLE 9

Regulatory Books for a Company Using Accelerated Depreciation ($000)

	Normalized	Flow Through
Revenue..............................	100,000	100,000
Operations...........................	40,000	40,000
Maintenance..........................	8,000	8,000
Depreciation..........................	*12,000*	*12,000*
General taxes.........................	10,000	10,000
Federal income tax....................	7,000	7,000
Deferred federal income tax...........	2,000	0
Operating Expenses...................	79,000	77,000
Net income...........................	21,000	23,000

In addition to such manipulation of accelerated depreciation, items such as job development credits and asset depreciation ranges may be taken in the year earned, or deferred and amortized over varied periods up to the life of the property. Lastly, some commissions now include the income tax savings applicable to the interest cost of the debt portion of Allowance of Funds Used during Construction (ADC) in the income tax cost, thus enhancing the cash flow.

Tax accounting in the utility industry is a stimulating arena in which imagination and court decisions are the only real restrictions.

Nonregulated Income

Income derived from sources not subject to regulatory agencies is classified as other income or nonregulated income. It is usually from subsidiaries occupied in appliance sales, land companies, mines, railroads, etc. In the electric utility industry there are few companies where it has any real meaning. Among the gas pipelines, with their broadly diversified interests, it is an important portion of income; and in the communications industry, manufacturing income usually is so treated. A few recent agency decisions are suggesting some of these manufacturing operations should be subject to utility type pricing, but it is not possible at present to determine the outcome of this issue.

Senior Security Coverages

The cost of debt has become crucial in the ability of utilities to expand. As the cost of money and plants increased, the margin by which earnings covered interest requirements eroded with amazing speed. On an industry basis, coverage of interest on debt had declined from five to six times only five years ago to about two and one-half times currently. More important than the statistic, however, is the fact that a number of companies have breached indenture requirements, and this precludes sale of additional debt. It has also caused the rating agencies to reduce the quality grading over 50 issues during the past several years. This, in turn, contributes to still higher cost for the new debt of the affected companies. The erosion of coverage for the entire utility industry may be seen in Table 10.

As embedded costs can only rise as older debt is retired and new debt is sold at levels above current costs, rate increases will be needed for some time to come. The importance of protecting coverage requirements cannot be stressed enough. If a company is not freely able to sell debt as it is needed for construction, the only alternative is equity. Sale of common or preferred stock in such quantities then puts pressure on the dividend-paying ability of the utility. The loss of flexibility in financing also threatens the requirement that service be provided to all customers. With only a few years of history of sizable rate increases to guide us, it still maybe said that those commissions that tried to shave rate applications too deeply soon learned the dangers of reduced coverages. This development, more than any other, is aiding in achieving adequate levels of rates.

FEDERAL AND STATE REGULATION

Rates

Jurisdiction. The rates that practically every privately owned utility charges are controlled by either a state or municipal agency. At the present time, only Texas, Nebraska, and Alaska have the control in other than a statewide agency. In Texas, and Nebraska, electric rates are not set by the state commissions; but in Texas, gas rates are. Commissions vary in size, political complexion, length of term, and in competence. Most are appointed by the governor but some are elected. Decisions by a commission at one point in time are not always considered binding on a subsequent group. The staffs supporting the commissions also differ greatly. Some states, such as New York and California, have strong groups of trained specialists, while in other jurisdictions the entire staff may consist of 10 to 20 people. In some states, jurisdiction also extends to rail, truck, airlines, grain elevators, etc. A knowledge of the philosophy and actions of these bodies is essential to analysis of the industry.

Overlapping Jurisdiction. Basically this is a problem of state versus federal regulation. It is also more of a problem in the gas and telephone industries than in the electric area. In an oversimplified version it is a question of where one jurisdiction ends and the other starts.

Gas. Specific legislation, the Hinshaw Amendment to the Natural Gas Act, permits gas utilities that are subject to state regulation to gain exemption from the powers of the Federal Power Commission. Prior to passage of this bill, a number of companies with both intrastate and

TABLE 10

Utility Industry Model—Class A and B Electric Utilities

	1966	1967	1968	1969	1970	1971	1972E
Earnings per share	$2.53	$2.66	$2.71	$2.89	$3.05	$3.09	$3.18
Dividends per share	$1.72	$1.82	$1.92	$2.00	$2.07	$2.07	$2.07
Shares (millions)*	1,000	1,000	1,000	1,000	1,040	1,128	1,195
Capital:							
Debt†	54.9%	54.2%	55.2%	56.4%	56.4%	55.7%	54.9%
Preferred	9.0	9.4	9.3	9.0	9.5	10.4	10.7
Equity	36.2	36.4	35.4	34.6	34.2	33.9	34.4
Total (millions)	$56,106	$58,741	$64,228	$70,756	$79,183	$89,016	$98,390
Gross plant (millions)	$71,116	$77,106	$83,940	$92,048	$93,302	$104,300	$117,125
Depreciation (millions)	16,326	17,685	19,040	20,599	20,253	22,006	23,992
Rate base (millions) (Assumes plant plus 2 percent)	$53,746	$58,331	$63,777	$70,295	$71,796	$80,944	$91,285
Percent return on rate base	6.8%	6.7%	6.4%	6.4%	6.8%	6.7%	6.1%
Equity return	12.5	12.4	12.0	11.9	11.2	10.9	11.2
Payout ratio	67.9%	68.4%	70.3%	69.0%	71.2%	70.8%	65.2%
Tax rate	40.0	38.9	42.2	40.9	34.3	32.5	30.0
Average Cost:							
Debt	3.6%	3.9%	4.2%	4.6%	5.0%	5.3%	5.7%
Interest coverage	*5.0*	*4.6*	*4.3*	*3.8*	*3.1*	*3.0*	*2.6*
Preferred	4.4	4.5	4.7	4.8	4.8	5.3	6.1
Operating rates							
Revenues (millions)	$16,959	$17,935	$19,405	$21,085	$23,127	$26,027	$28,369
Operations	42.0%	41.8%	42.3%	43.1%	45.2%	46.9%	48.0%
Maintenance	6.2	6.3	6.1	6.2	6.6	6.5	7.0
Depreciation	10.5	10.6	10.5	10.4	10.4	10.1	10.0
General tax	10.2	10.4	10.2	10.2	10.8	10.7	10.7
Federal income tax	10.1	9.5	10.2	9.0	6.2	5.4	5.1
Margin (pretax)	31.3	30.9	30.9	30.0	27.0	25.9	24.3
Plant/revenues	$4.19	$4.30	$4.33	$4.37	$4.03	$4.01	$4.13

* Arbitrary assumption on starting shares.
† Includes short-term debt.
Notes: Shares outstanding in the early years are nominally unchanged, since the amount of common stock financing during the early part of the period was nominal.
All ratios are calculated on year-end figures.
Source: Dean Witter & Co., Inc. and FPC Statistics of Privately Owned Electric Utilities in the United States, 1966-1971.

interstate operations were subjected to extensive delays in obtaining needed rate relief because of jurisdictional squabbles.

Telephone. As facilities in this industry may be used by the customer for either intrastate or interstate purposes, rate regulation is complex. The Federal Communications Commission regulates interstate rates and services, but as there is a sharing of the revenues among the companies there is also an impact on intrastate prices. Thus the allocation of plants between the two types of pricing has been subject to many disputes as states sought to force the heavier burden of rate increases on the intrastate market. During the mid- and late 60s the states had a fair degree of success in this endeavor, but more recently the pendulum has begun to move the other way. Very recently a new area of overlapping jurisdiction has occurred in the interconnect markets, also known as the Customer Controlled Service Attachment (CCSA). Various FCC decisions have encouraged development of such units, which a number of states have indicated strong objections—claiming such services are subject to their, and not federal, regulation. This issue is likely to remain contentious for some years to come.

Electric. Problems of overlapping jurisdiction on rate matters in the electric industry are minor. Interstate sales, subject to the Federal Power Commission, are easily identifiable and generally wholesale. Basically, rates in this industry are subject to state or local jurisdiction. The basic decisions ruling this separation is the *City of Colton* case.[16]

New Developments

There are emerging areas of jurisdictional overlap brought on by the passage of new laws such as the Environmental Protection Act, the Clean Water Act, and the newly passed Federal Energy Act. While the requirements of these and other laws, including the Atomic Energy Act, do not provide for rate jurisdiction, they do affect costs—and these, in turn, affect rates. To understand the magnitude of the problem it may be pointed out that in order to build a nuclear fueled electric generating plant in California, 60 different state, federal, and local approvals are needed. Such is bureaucracy at its finest moment.

Rate Making

The art of determining rates has been guided by many court decisions, including the *Hope* and *Bluefield* cases noted above, but also by the economic circumstances of the times and the political nature of the regulators. The principle of a fair return on the value of the plant dedicated to utility use has remained intact. In practice the word "value" has had many definitions.

---

[16] *City of Colton* v. *Federal Power Commission* 376 U.S. 205 (1964).

The underlying issues of the *Hope* case were attempts of the Federal Power Commission to use the "original cost" of plant rather than one assigning a current value in determining the rate base. The court essentially upheld the FPC, and for the ensuing decade all but a handful of states adopted this approach. For many utilities this required write-downs of plant carried on the books in excess of original cost. Certain powers at the FPC carried the concept so far that it came to be known as "aboriginal cost." A few states by law require the use of "fair value" or "current value," and commissions in these jurisdictions have greater leeway in the calculation of the base—although in practice, many of them equate original cost and fair value. Ohio still requires the use of Reproduction Cost New Less Observed Depreciation (RCND) and Texan municipalities use both gross and net plant. Often use of RCND or fair value requires engineering surveys to determine the amount to be allowed as the rate base. When rates were being reduced and economic changes occurred more slowly, the use of historic cost may have been acceptable. With the rapidity of current changes, however, modifications have become necessary. Presently a half-dozen states and the Federal Power Commission are using a "forward looking test year." Thus, estimates finally are entering the regulatory picture. It seems likely this approach will spread and could become the standard method for the future.

In summary, rates must be set to meet the standards of capital attraction and ability of the enterprise to complete necessary construction. The mechanics of achieving this vary with political and economic forces, but the underlying need to maintain a viable utility is unchanged. The analyst must understand the methodology, however, and relate the various systems to each other in making choices regarding securities.

Legislation

Federal regulation of the utilities arises from the commerce clause of the Constitution[17] and enables the federal government to control commercial activities between the states. Most of the earlier legislation was designed to curb abuses that existed at a particular time rather than for a positive future purpose within the economy. Thus in some regards the system in use in today's framework reflects court interpretations during the years rather than the original purpose.

Federal Power Act. This act, as amended, delegated the regulation of interstate transmission of electric energy and its sale in interstate commerce at wholesale, to the Federal Power Commission. It vastly broadened the powers of the commission which had been created by the Federal Water Power Act of 1920, bringing hydroelectric facilities on navigable waters of the United States under federal jurisdiction.

---

[17] United States Constitution Article I, Section 8.

The Federal Power Commission has become and is dominant in the area of utility accounting. The promulgation and use of the "Uniform System of Accounts" is, with minor exceptions, accepted by all regulatory jurisdictions. This was not accomplished without many court battles either, but today it is a sophisticated and comprehensive cost accounting system. As practically all electric utilities sell some power across a state line, they must report annually to the commission on a Form 1. This voluminous record is available at the office of public reference of the commission in Washington. (Practically all companies also publish an abstract called the "Uniform Statistical Report," which can be obtained on request from the individual companies.) In addition the FPC publishes annually a statistical compendium of the financial and operating results of all Class A and B companies (those with revenues in excess of $1 million), called *Statistics of Privately Owned Electric Utilities in the United States.*[18]

Rate actions of the FPC in the electric area deal solely with wholesale sales or those made across state lines. The former category is made mostly to other utilities, municipally owned utilities, or subsidized cooperatives. As these are bulk power sales, they have historically been made at low rates. Recently problems have arisen as the increases necessary to offset fuel and operating costs relative to these low rates has been large. On balance, however, the commission has authorized the needed higher charges.

The commission is also the information-gathering agency for power system reliability and has an advisory voice in planning interconnections. In the past, some of its members have recommended construction of national transmission grids which would facilitate transfer of large amounts of power between geographic regions. The plan, currently dormant, is not dead. It is opposed by the industry which claims that adequate interconnection capacity exists or is being built by the various existing "reliability groups." These groups are confederations of independent companies which plan and operate their systems so that there is protection in the event of emergencies. Viewed in terms of the record, this system works well.

Lastly, the FPC has the responsibility of recommending to Congress whether hydroelectric facilities licensed to a utility should be recaptured by the government at the end of the term. As many of these licenses were granted almost 50 years ago, for that period, it could become important over the coming years. Underlying the issue is a long-simmering threat of nationalization of the utility industry. There remain in the government advocates of this course, and the analyst should be aware of the implications of managerial decisions that are made with this specter in mind.

---

[18] Available each year from Superintendent of Documents, Government Printing Office, Washington, D.C. 20402

Natural Gas Act. Passed in 1938, it delegates to the Federal Power Commission control over rates and service conditions of natural gas sold in interstate commerce for resale. In the late 1940s and the 1950s the explosive growth of the natural gas transmission industry dominated the activities of the commission. At the same time the development of an extremely strong accounting staff set up rate mechanisms that encouraged the use of gas for home heating in practically all areas of the country. When the Supreme Court in 1954[19] brought producers under the mantle of federal regulation, the groundwork was laid for a portion of the current energy difficulties. Currently the Federal Power Commission is striving to encourage development of new gas supplies through the granting of price incentives. With the world political situation regarding oil in a frenzy, this is, at the very least, a trying assignment. Our opinion at this time is that production soon will be greatly free of regulation and that a new agency will be created that will have broader control over energy and that natural gas matters will be included.

Federal Communications Commission. Originally this organization was established to regulate radio (and later television) broadcasting. Later its scope of jurisdiction was extended to telephone and telegraph operations. In that realm it is responsible for rates and service authorizations of interstate voice and data transmission. Until recently this consisted of setting long-distance toll rates of the Bell System and Western Union and negotiating with the state commissions on methods of separating the revenues of toll calls between the Bell System and the independents. For 33 years until 1965, the method of rate regulation used by the FCC was one of "continuing surveillance." Because of technological advances, a number of interstate rate reductions could be, and were, made. Beginning in 1965, however, the FCC undertook a general investigation of Bell System interstate rates and in 1967 found a rate of return of 7–7.5 percent to be just and reasonable. This proceeding resulted in rate reductions of $120 million in 1967 and $150 in 1969. Subsequent cases in 1970 and 1972 have sharply reversed this trend, and the latest return authorized was 8.5–9 percent in November 1972. The aggregate amount of this increase was $320 million.

There remains pending before the commission, however, other issues including, (*a*) amounts properly allowed as net investment, expenses, and taxes and (*b*) reasonableness of prices paid to Western Electric. (Western Electric is a wholly owned manufacturing subsidiary of the Bell System and provides the bulk of the operating companies' equipment. See below under Justice Department.) At one point in 1970, the commission indicated its desire to discontinue this part of the proceeding, stating that manpower available was inadequate to complete the project. The political hue and cry raised caused the commission to

---

[19] *Phillips Petroleum Co.* v. *Wisconsin, et al.,* 347 U.S. 672 (1954).

reinstate the investigation, and we can only presume it is wending its way toward a decision, ultimately.

As noted earlier, the FCC also has authorized the creation and operation of Specialized Communications Carriers for the purpose of providing new point-to-point communications services. The rate controversy in this area is only beginning, but the basic issue of average system pricing used by Bell versus high-load-factor point-to-point rates proposed by the new arrivals is surfacing rapidly. It is being further complicated by proposals of Microware Communications Co., Inc. (MCI), a specialized carrier, that it be authorized to use existing Bell facilities where its lines do not extend to the customers' premises. Other developments include the recent order in the domestic satellite proceeding:

> In March 1970 the commission stated that it would consider applications for domestic satellite communications systems by common carriers and others. A number of applications for such systems have been filed, including a joint application by the American Company and Communications Satellite Corporation for a system to be integrated into the Bell System's nationwide communication network. In June 1972 the commission issued an order adopting a policy of multiple entry which would permit all qualified applicants, including the American Company, to provide domestic communications satellite service but rejected the joint application. Moreover, the commission concluded that the American Company's use of domestic satellites should be limited to providing basic switched telephone services and, with certain exceptions, should not initially include providing specialized communication services. The commission said that if AT&T were permitted unrestricted use of satellites for both monopoly and specialized services, this might . . . curtail any realistic opportunity for entry by others to serve the specialized markets via satellite.[20]

The outcome of this case could have an important bearing on the future expansion of the specialized carriers. The encouragement or discouragement of interstate communications by specialized carriers is, and will be, in a state of flux for a number of years.

Public Utility Holding Company Act. This legislation was an outgrowth of investigations by the Federal Trade Commission into abuses within the utility industry in the 1920s and early 1930s. It specifically dealt with holding companies having control of operating subsidiaries and requires full disclosure of financial transactions between them, including inter-company dividends, proxies, loans, and sales and construction contracts. Geographic integration of systems was required, and, through pursuasion, capital structures were strengthened. Most importantly, administration of the act was lodged with the Securities and Exchange Commission rather than the Federal Power Commission.[21]

---

[20] *Prospectus,* American Telephone and Telegraph Company, November 20, 1972.

[21] *George Washington Law Review,* Vol. 14, No. 1 (December 1945), p. 28.

The abuses of that period have been long corrected, but the SEC bureaucracy remains. In the eyes of some it is an anachronism and the powers should be transferred to another agency. If there should be a broadly based energy agency formed, this could well happen. In the meantime the most apparent manifestations of the Holding Company Act are the restrictions on types of financing allowed companies subject to it. Recently, reacting to the stringencies of the financial markets, the SEC authorized sale of securities on a negotiated, rather than a competitive basis, for the first time since the agency was formed.

Communications Satellite Act. The Congress empowered the Communications Satellite Corporation (Comsat) to own, manage, and operate a global commercial satellite system in conjunction with foreign governments and domestic communications companies. The company represented the United States in the International Telecommunications Satellite Consortium and operated the early family of equipment. Intelesat now operates a global satellite system serving 82 countries. Comsat's participation in the consortium has been reduced to 40 percent, but it remains the operator at the present time.

Revenues of Comsat are derived from leasing of satellite channels under temporary rates approved by the FCC. A formal rate proceeding, designed to set rates, has been before the commission for more than three years. At present there is no decision.

The National Environmental Policy Act of 1969 and the Environmental Protection Agency. This creates a national policy of improving all aspects of the environment and an agency to administer its terms. Since its beginning, it has been active and forceful in the areas of air and water cleanliness, preservation of resources, and esthetic values. The thought has been expressed by some that too much was attempted too soon and with little regard to cost. On the other hand it can not be denied that the agency has worked diligently to carry out the spirit as well as the letter of the law and has successfully curbed deterioration of the environment. The current fuel difficulties are undoubtedly going to slow the process of improving air and water, but it would be foolish to assume that this would be anything more than temporary. Thus, for the analyst, it provides a time to evaluate the costs and impact on the market of the goals of the act, which are to balance our needs against the processes by which we obtain them.

It is in the area of standards that the EPA has caused the utility industry the greatest difficulty. For example, standards have been set for sulphur emissions without regard to availability of fuel or local conditions. Until the recent fuel crisis these criteria were to be met by 1975; now this has been postponed. There has been little study of the cost of attaining these standards (or any other), nor has there been any real consideration as to whether the necessary equipment, if it is available, can be built in sufficient quantity for the entire industry in time to meet the deadline. The discussion could go on, but suffice it to say these major costs will be very important in the future operation of utilities.

Under the NEPA, all construction that could have a material impact on the environment must be approved by the agency. In order to obtain this approval, an "Environmental Impact Statement" must be filed. This document (sometimes four to five volumes) describes the benefit to cost conditions of the project. In relation to nuclear plants it has added 18 to 24 months to construction time. EPA and AEC are working to reduce the period, but progress has been slow. Meanwhile, the cost of a two-year delay is high.

The Atomic Energy Act. This was essentially a postwar document designed to control nuclear weapons. It also was designed to encourage civil uses of nuclear power and other devices, but the military potential was dominant. It is for this reason that various proposals for licensing nuclear generating facilities will probably be shifted to other agencies.

The basic problem facing the AEC is the charge that there could be a condition where radioactive material would be released into the atmosphere. Despite the proliferation of retrofitted safety devices, the argument rages on. It is my view that the weight of evidence on safety is such that nuclear plants will become the base-load units for the electric industry and that capital needs must be viewed in this context.

Antitrust Considerations. Justice Department reviews are another new factor in evaluating utilities. Under the Sherman and Clayton Acts, restraint of trade or interference with competition is prohibited. The United States Supreme Court in the *Otter Tail Power* case[22] rejected the view that regulated natural monopolies are exempt from antitrust considerations. The facts in the case were highly specialized, but there is a body of opinion that believes the decision may be used in the continuing battle of investor-owned versus government-owned power facilities.

ACCOUNTING CONSIDERATIONS

Sources

Primarily as a result of the need for reporting to regulatory agencies, there is an array of statistics available in the utility industry that is adequate for most any need. Companies prepare relatively complete annual and periodic reports, and many publish highly detailed statistical supplements. Most importantly, practically all companies in the industry are readily willing to answer responsible questions from analysts.

In addition to company-prepared reports, the heavy capital needs of the industry cause financing prospectuses to be prepared with a high degree of frequency. These documents are available from the company

---

[22] *Otter Tail Power* v. *United States,* U.S. 97PUR 3d 209 (1973).

or underwriters and aid the analyst in maintaining current information. As noted above, reports are filed and available from the various regulatory agencies and practically every electric, gas, and telephone company files a form 10-K or 10-Q, as well as quarterly reports, with the Securities and Exchange Commission. These are available from various sources and in the form of microfilm or microfiche. Because of the broad range of other reports filed by the utilities, these specific reports may be less valuable to the analyst of this industry compared to others, except where there is diversification, as in the natural gas transmissions companies, or substantial nonregulated income.

Uniform System of Accounts

A highly detailed series of job and equipment titles have been promulgated and are maintained by the Federal Power Commission for electric and gas companies and by the Federal Communications Commission for telephone and telegraph companies. Each account has a specific description of what should be appropriately placed therein. (Several years ago, computer-oriented analysts tried to use these figures for trend analysis and forecasting, but changes in account description from year to year caused failure of the attempt.) With time and patience, any cost or revenue breakdown is available. For industry compilations, the sheer volume of statistics is also a problem, as publication generally requires six to eight months. Thus, including the time for company submission to the agency, the last composite annual figures are ten to eleven months out of date. (Statistics published by the industry organizations, Edison Electric Institute and American Gas Association, are similarly late.) There are a few instances where states require slightly different definitions of the accounts, and these are noted in the annual reports. At present we can think of none that are of major importance. Accounts included in prospectuses accepted by the Securities and Exchange Commission, however, can vary significantly, especially where there is a meaningful amount of nonregulated income.

Balance Sheet

The balance sheet of a utility company has only a few unique characteristics. These include the deduction of the depreciation reserve from the gross plant on the asset side and the frequent appearance of a negative quick or cash ratio. The former arose in recognition of the rate-base approach of setting rates (that is, net cost of plant) while the latter recognized that only minimum cash balances are necessary between the periodic payment by customers and the outlays for fuel or labor. The inventory problem has been minimal. If cash was needed, it was obtained through short-term bank loans.

It is possible that greater cash allowances may be required in the future to stockpile fuel inventories, and the portions of the nuclear fuel cycle for fabrication and reprocessing also may increase the cash need. As some companies are leasing the fuel, rather than owning it, they do not currently include its value on the balance sheet. The Financial Accounting Standards Board and the SEC are reviewing this procedure, however. An example of a utility balance sheet appears in Figure 3. For the sake of simplicity an all-electric, rather than a combination gas and electric, company has been used.

FIGURE 3

Balance Sheet - December 31, 1972 and 1971

Assets	1972	1971
ELECTRIC UTILITY PLANT:		
Electric utility plant other than nuclear fuel:		
In service	$1,087,315,976	$ 942,363,711
Construction work in progress	436,922,188	270,458,350
Total	1,524,238,164	1,212,822,061
Less accumulated depreciation	200,189,742	178,095,896
Net	1,324,048,422	1,034,726,165
Nuclear fuel:		
In service	24,372,864	24,100,348
In process and other	22,886,162	5,968,654
Total	47,259,026	30,069,002
Less accumulated amortization	14,194,823	4,933,371
Net	33,064,203	25,135,631
Electric utility plant, net	1,357,112,625	1,059,861,796
OTHER PROPERTY AND INVESTMENTS	1,698,723	1,746,733
CURRENT ASSETS:		
Cash	5,876,729	6,554,764
Accounts receivable, net	18,690,869	17,528,214
Materials and supplies	28,238,322	22,661,806
Prepayments, etc.	1,661,777	1,323,143
Total current assets	54,467,697	48,067,927
DEFERRED DEBITS:		
Unamortized debt discount and expense	2,662,411	2,069,498
Other	2,863,006	2,343,293
Total deferred debits	5,525,417	4,412,791
TOTAL	$1,418,804,462	$1,114,089,247

See notes to financial statements.

FIGURE 3 (*Continued*)

Carolina Power & Light Company

Liabilities	1972	1971
CAPITAL STOCK AND RETAINED EARNINGS (Note 2):		
Preferred stock	$ 173,800,900	$ 124,375,900
Common stock	352,775,861	227,538,989
Retained earnings	90,673,379	68,153,300
Total capital stock and retained earnings	617,250,140	420,068,189
LONG-TERM DEBT (Note 3)	684,140,242	534,152,633
CURRENT LIABILITIES:		
Notes payable:		
Banks	5,630,000	34,475,000
Other	6,369,702	47,688,288
Accounts payable	22,661,310	14,094,928
Customers' deposits	1,982,665	1,710,874
Taxes accrued	6,619,497	3,397,263
Interest accrued	13,345,867	11,538,446
Dividends declared	13,985,372	9,917,007
Other	1,877,313	1,007,623
Total current liabilities	72,471,726	123,829,429
DEFERRED CREDITS:		
Investment tax credits	7,807,505	6,051,459
Unamortized premium on debt	205,505	222,749
Customers' advances for construction	48,676	48,472
Other	642,396	111,541
Total deferred credits	8,704,082	6,434,221
RESERVE FOR INJURIES AND DAMAGES	563,487	514,405
CONTRIBUTIONS IN AID OF CONSTRUCTION	4,511,328	3,899,712
ACCUMULATED DEFERRED INCOME TAXES	31,163,457	25,190,658
COMMITMENTS AND CONTINGENCIES (Note 4)		
TOTAL	$1,418,804,462	$1,114,089,247

See notes to financial statements.

Assets. The high rate of capital need may be seen in sizable Construction Work in Progress, relative to existing plant. As internally generated funds are a small percentage of the requirement, new securities must be sold to obtain the balance. The nuclear fuel account is essentially for only two plants. Other nuclear facilities now under construction will need a similar amount or more for each unit. There is only a nominal amount of cash on hand, but the company is more than solvent. Signs of cash difficulty in a utility are found in deterioration of cash flow, coverage of senior securities, and/or heavy financing needs relative to capital programs.

Liabilities. On the liability side, the accounts also are clean-cut. Many analysts include short-term Notes Payable in the long-term debt account, on the assumption that it will be funded. Accumulated Deferred Income Taxes include "normalized" differences between the use of straight-line and accelerated and liberalized depreciation. Deferred investment Tax Credits are amounts of tax reductions arising from additions of qualified properties under the Job Development Act. Contributions in Aid of Construction are amounts provided by customers for service lines on their property which cost in excess of the standard amount authorized for such connections. It is repaid by the company over a period of years.

Analysis. Among the more meaningful ratios is the reserve for depreciation at 14.7 percent of electric utility plant. In this case it indicates a vast amount of new plant added in recent years, but a number this low should be carefully examined to determine whether the annual depreciation charge is reasonable. The rate here is about 1.9 percent compared with 2.9 percent for the average electric utility and raises a question about the adequacy of the depreciation charge. (As the company is, and has been, in a number of recent rate proceedings there is evidence that improvement is occurring.)

Rate Base. While stockholder accounts and regulatory books differ, the analyst can use the balance sheet in approximating the rate base. The items included generally are as follows:

Plant in Service December 31, 1972

	(*$000*)
Utility plant	$1,087,316
Less accumulated depreciation	200,189
	887,127
Nuclear fuel—less amortization	10,179
	897,306
Working capital (estimated at 2 percent of net plant)	17,946
	915,252
Deduct reserve for accumulated deferred taxes	31,163
Approximate rate base	$ 884,089

There are many refinements possible, but from the analyst's point of view they seldom are meaningful. One account that is subject to wide variations in rate procedures is that of "working capital." This is loosely defined as the amount of cash necessary to pay for operations and materials other than that associated with construction of facilities. The approaches of the commission range from "no allowance," under the claim that accrued (but unpaid taxes are adequate, and therefore the customer has already paid for the needed cash) to authorization for about 45 days of expenses plus compensating balances required by banks for term loans. As a practical matter, experience shows that an amount of about 2 percent of net plant added to the base is a close indication of the base that will be used. There is no verity to this amount, but over a period of years it has proven to be usable.

Capitalization. Second in importance to the plant figures is the capitalization. In a utility this consists basically of mortgage debt (sometimes debentures) preferred stock, common stock, premiums, and retained earnings. Over a period of many years, and spurred by the persuasion of the Securities and Exchange Commission the ratios of 50–55 percent debt, 10–15 percent preferred stock, and 30–40 percent common equity evolved and became the general industry standard. A company with a common equity ratio below 30 percent of the total capitalization is considered to be of questionable quality.

Different patterns exist in the natural gas companies, with transmission companies having 25–30 percent common equity (although this has been thickened by a number of the transmission companies that have diversified into nonregulated areas), while the distribution utilities tend to have equity ratios of 40 percent or higher. The telephone group has also tended to have greater equity in the capital structure, and until about ten years ago the Bell System standard was close to 60 percent common equity. The rationale behind this was that the telephone industry was more vulnerable to the business cycle and that the market could not absorb such vast amounts of debt. Despite these arguments the Bell System did vary its programs and now has a debt ratio of 47 percent, 3 percent preferred stock (including a convertible issue) and 50 percent common equity. Recently incurred high-debt costs have caused the management of American Telephone again to modify their practices, however, and they now anticipate that the debt ratio will be gradually reduced to 45 percent of capitalization.

Rate of Return. The capital ratios are vitally important in the second half of the rate-making equation—the determination of the rate of return. A fair return under the requirements of the *Hope* and *Bluefield* cases is an amount of dollars that will permit the utility to attract capital. This usually is expressed in a rate applied to the rate base or capital employed in the enterprise. An example follows:

	($000)
Utility plant	$1,200,000
Depreciation	220,000
New plant	980,000
Working capital	20,000
Rate base	1,000,000
Rate of return (percent)	8.0
Return	$ 80,000

Converting this to the income account is accomplished by collecting revenues that will, after the recovery of expenses, permit earning $80 million.

	($000)
Revenues....................	$450,000
Expenses:...................	
Operations.................	200,000
Maintenance...............	30,000
Depreciation...............	45,000
General taxes..............	45,000
Income taxes..............	50,000
Net operating income........	$ 80,000

In other words, rates for service are to be designed to produce $450 million of revenues, based on expected kilowatt-hour (kwh.) sales. If we assume an average rate of $0.012 per kilowatt hour, the sales level would have to be 3.75 billion kilowatt-hours. Over the years the calculation of the rate of return has become increasingly mathematical, based on the assumption that debt and preferred costs had to be protected and that the cost of equity was the judgmental variable. Thus, currently the return allowance is calculated in this manner.

Debt 50% @ 6%...................	= 3.00
Preferred 15% @ 7%...............	= 1.05
Common equity 35% @ 11.57%......	= 4.05
	8.00

or

	(000)
Rate base.........................	$1,000,000
×	.08
Net operating income..............	$80,000

The 6 percent for debt and 7 percent for preferred are the actual incurred, or embedded, cost of interest and dividends as a percentage of the book or stated value of the outstanding securities. The cost of equity is a matter of judgment and must meet minimum legal requirements.

There have been surprisingly few so-called "confiscation" cases (the taking of property without due process) where the court ordered a commission to increase rates. Such cases result from appeals from decisions of the rate-making agency. Recent decisions are not wholly consistent. In Massachusetts, an 11 percent equity return for New England Telephone was found inadequate; while in Georgia, a power company was authorized 11–11.5 percent, and this was found by the Georgia Supreme Court to be adequate, although in *dicta* the view was expressed that it bordered on confiscation.

The basic change that has occurred in the return area is in the change in interest and preferred dividend costs. A decade ago the return calculation for an electric company might have looked like this:

Debt 50 percent @ 3.5 percent.............	1.75
Preferred 15 percent @ 4.0 percent.........	.60
Common stock 35 percent @ 10.43.........	3.65
	6.00

A highly leveraged gas company in 1951 would have required a 21.6 percent return to the equity to have the same overall return, as shown in Tables 11, 12, and 13.

TABLE 11

Transco Industries
(formerly Transcontinental Gas Pipeline Company)

	December 31, 1951		December 31, 1973	
Capitalization ($000):				
First mortgage bonds.....	195,000		566,000	
Debentures..............			120,600	
Notes & bank loans.......	30,000		125,000	
Total Debt...........	225,000	76.8%	811,600	64.7%
Preferred stock (no par)...	27,500	9.3%	155,300	12.3%
Common Stock ($0.50 par)				
3,530,000 shs.........	1,765			
22,300,000 shs........			11,100	
Premium................	29,008		87,200	
Earned surplus..........	9,997		190,200	
Common equity........	40,770	13.9%	288,500	23.0%
Total Capitalization....	293,270	100.0%	1,255,400	100.0%

TABLE 12

Transco Industries
Income Account
($000)

	December 31, 1951		December 31, 1973	
		Percent of Revenue		*Percent of Revenue*
Operating revenues...............	39,300		505,500	
Operating expenses				
Gas purchased.................	9,800	24.9%	230,300	45.6%
Operations and maintenance.....	6,400	16.3	74,900	14.8
Depreciation..................	5,900	15.0	54,200	10.7
General taxes.................	1,300	3.3	16,900	3.3
Charges in lieu of federal income tax........................	5,200	13.2		
Federal income tax.............			3,000⎫	4.0
Deferred F.I.T.................			17,400⎭	
Total..................	28,600	72.8%	396,700	78.5%
Net operating income.............	10,700		108,800	
Other income (net)..............	2,600		3,000	
	13,400		111,800	
Deductions				
Interest & discount expense......	7,700	19.6%	72,300	14.3%
Interest credit.................	(200)		(14,500)	
	7,500		57,800	
Net Income....................	5,900		54,000	
Preferred dividends.............	900	2.2%	9,700	2.0%
Balance for common..............	5000	12.7%	44,300	8.7%
Earned per share...............	$1.41		$1.99	

Note: All figures rounded

TABLE 13

	1951			1973	
	Theoretical	*Actual*		*Theoretical*	*Actual*
Debt:					
76.7% × 3.58%.........	2.76%	2.76%	64.7% × 8.91%.	5.76%	5.76%
Preferred:					
9.4% × 2.55%..........	.24%	.24%	12.3% × 6.25%.	.77%	.77%
Common Equity 13.9%....			23%		
× 21.6%...............	3.00		× 12.0%.....	2.76	
× 12.7%...............		1.70	× 15.3%.....		3.50
Overall return.............	6.00%	4.70%		9.29%	10.06%

The important point for the analyst is the 148 percent rise in interest cost to present levels for debt and a 145 percent increase in preferred cost. In 1951, however, the FPC was using a 6 percent overall return, (which the company was not earning), but now is authorizing a 12 percent return to the equity. Thus, despite the fact that the actual return rose 105 percent, the equity return has declined 8 percent. Coverage of senior securities has been sharply reduced and the quality of the common stock earnings has been eroded.

Income Account

Sales and Revenues. Sales and revenues are divided into similar categories—residential, commerical, and industrial—although the specific titles may vary from company to company. Table 11 from the Federal Power Commission compilation demonstrates quantities and relationships for the entire industry.

There has not been a significant change in the proportion of customers in each of the various categories over the past decade. Kilowatt-hour sales of residential customers have risen at a more rapid rate than the commercial and industrial categories, and commercial has risen faster than industrial. As the latter is designed to be the lowest margin business, this movement has been beneficial. To a lesser degree, this same pattern is evident in revenues. In view of the widespread use of fuel adjustment clauses, which will raise industrial rates by a greater percentage than the other categories, it would seem that kilowatt-hour sales and revenues should rise at close to the same rates in the future. The prospective relationship of sales between categories, however, could well be shaped by government policies that have not yet been delineated.

Nonetheless, some assumptions can be made. Over the past decade sales to ultimate customers have risen at a 7.8 percent compound annual rate.[23] Forecasts made by the industry and federal agencies indicate that until the fuel difficulties, the highly probable outlook was for a continuation, or even modest acceleration, of the rate. The shortage of

[23] Investor-owned utilities: The figure may vary from 7.5 percent to 7.8 percent, depending on the source used.

TABLE 14

Composite Electric Operation Revenues, Customers, and Sales, Year Ended December 31

	1961		1971	
Item	Amount (000)	Percent of Total	Amount	Percent of Total
Number of customers (average per month):	(000)			
Residential............................	41,768	87.4	50,850,340	88.0
Commercial and industrial:				
Small (or commercial).............	5,654	11.8	6,462,624	11.2
Large (or industrial)...............	234	.5	271,608	.5
Public street and highway lighting....	55	1.3	86,607	.1
Other public authorities.............	114	1.0	120,668	0
Railroads and railways...............			71	0
Interdepartmental...................			417	0
Total ultimate consumers........	47,825	100.0	57,792,335	100.0
Resale..............................	4		4,139	0
Total customers..............	47,829	100.0	57,796,474	100.0
Kilowatt-hour sales (thousands):	(000)			
Residential............................	152,874	24.2	357,943,283	26.3
Commercial and industrial:				
Small (or commercial).............	113,259	18.0	275,270,269	20.3
Large (or industrial)...............	254,469	40.4	472,050,616	34.7
Public street and highway lighting....	5,547	.8	9,199,238	.7
Other public authorities.............	15,668	2.3	31,227,145	2.3
Railroads and railways...............	2,545	.4	2,128,100	.2
Interdepartmental...................	569	.1	1,564,999	.1
Total sales to ultimate customers..	544,931		1,149,383,650	84.6
For resale..........................	86,348	13.6	209,068,534	15.4
Total kilowatt-hour sales.......	631,279	100.0	1,358,452,184	100.0
Revenues (thousands of dollars):				
Residential............................	$ 3,976,994	31.2	$ 8,292,951	37.2
Commercial and industrial:				
Small (or commercial).............	2,752,268	25.7	6,058,509	27.1
Large (or industrial)...............	2,736,215	25.6	5,195,247	23.3
Public street and highway lighting....	178,739	1.6	347,695	1.6
Other public authorities.............	229,555	2.1	451,220	2.0
Railroads and railways...............	33,068	.3	34,848	.2
Interdepartmental...................	4,640		9,754	0
Total revenues for ultimate consumers..................	$ 9,911,479		$ 20,390,224	91.4
Revenues from sales for resale........	645,193	6.0	1,634,376	7.3
Total revenues from sales of electricity..................	$10,556,672		$ 22,024,600	98.7
Other operation revenues............	109,802	1.0	297,274	1.3
Total electric operation revenues..................	$10,666,474	100.0	$ 22,321,874	100.0

Source: Statistics of privately owned electric utilities, FPC 1971, Table 15, p. 32.

natural gas has caused anticipation of a discernible increment for the electric heating market. It would now appear that if a full 10 percent reduction requested from anticipated electric load could be achieved, the industry would sustain a 2–3 percent decline in kilowatt-hour sales from 1973 year-end use. Responses by companies to a Federal Power Commission questionnaire indicate, however, that the most likely result of the program in 1974 is that sales will rise about 2 percent. Beyond 1974 the outlook is for a resumption of growth, as a one-year decline in growth of this magnitude should be more than adequate to remove excesses from the system. The growing consensus in that future growth will be in the 5 percent area, but this is in the realm of educated guessing.

Revenue and sales forecasts for the gas industry also are subject to new forces caused by reduced supplies and end-use controls being ordered by various governmental agencies. For the next several years the outlook is for no growth in sales valume, but rapidly rising prices.

Telephone additions reflect the levels of business activity and new-home construction. Long-term trends of stations added and message units seem to be usable for forecasting. Prices are likely to rise, also, but could well have a closer relationship to incurred costs of labor and capital than is true in the other segments of the utility industry.

Expenses. Operating expenses consist basically of labor, fuel, and materials associated with the production, delivery, and maintenance of service of electricity and gas. The relationship to revenues for recent years may be seen in Table 15. The rise in operating and production costs relative to revenues in the later years is a function of lag in recovering fuel and labor costs through higher rates. With automatic fuel clauses now in effect in over 95 percent of the jurisdictions, this ratio should tend to stabilize again and, assuming further rate increases, may well improve, albeit gradually. A more detailed view of recent years shows the trend of the cost increases.

The decline in federal income taxes reflects reduced earnings from the higher costs. As a number of flow-through companies are again normalizing taxes, this ratio should begin to rise. Interest rates are rising rapidly, however, and this will continue. A more detailed breakdown of the operating expense account is shown in Tables 16 and 17.

Another example of the impact of fuel costs may be seen from a comparison of quarterly reports of Carolina Power and Light for the four quarters of 1970 and 1971. (See pages 831–34.) In the earlier period the basic fuel was coal, and the price was rising a total of 16 percent in the year. In the third quarter of 1971 a nuclear unit went into service and weather was moderate so that coal needs were sharply reduced. At that time North Carolina had no fuel adjustment clause.

Capital costs. Previously the rise in embedded cost of debt and deterioration of coverage for the industry was shown. Causes of this condition were the general rise in interest rates and the higher cost of plant which necessitated sale of greater amounts of debt, relative to out-

TABLE 15

Statistics of Privately Owned Electric Utilities in the United States, 1971 (electric operation and maintenance expense relationships)

Relationship	Year ended Dec. 31—										
	1971	1970	1969	1968	1967	1966	1965	1964	1963	1962	1961
Operation and maintenance expenses—percent of operating revenues	50.4	48.8	46.1	45.1	44.8	44.8	44.2	44.0	43.7	43.9	44.3
Maintenance charges:											
Percent of total operation and maintenance expenses	13.5	14.2	14.2	14.3	14.7	14.5	14.8	14.8	14.5	14.7	14.5
Percent of operating revenues	6.8	6.9	6.6	6.4	6.6	6.5	6.5	6.5	6.4	6.5	6.4
Maintenance and depreciation charges—percent of operating revenues	17.6	18.0	17.7	17.7	17.9	17.7	17.9	17.8	17.6	17.4	17.3
Production expenses:											
Percent of operating revenues	33.4	31.0	28.4	27.3	26.6	26.3	25.4	25.0	24.8	24.8	25.0
Per kilowatt-hour sold, mills	5.49	4.76	4.21	4.09	4.03	4.01	3.98	4.00	4.06	4.12	4.22
Transmission expenses:											
Percent of operating revenues	1.4	1.5	1.5	1.4	1.4	1.4	1.4	1.4	1.4	1.4	1.4
Per kilowatt-hours sold, mills	0.24	0.23	0.22	0.21	0.21	0.21	.021	0.22	0.22	0.24	0.24
Distribution expenses:											
Percent of operating revenues	5.9	6.3	6.3	6.3	6.5	6.5	6.7	6.8	6.7	6.8	7.0
Per customer	$22.82	$22.14	$20.56	$19.31	$18.67	$17.84	$17.48	$17.18	$16.36	$16.00	$15.62
Customer accounts expenses:											
Percent of operating revenues	2.5	2.5	2.5	2.5	2.6	2.6	2.7	2.8	2.8	2.8	2.9
Per customer	$9.61	$8.86	$8.11	$7.68	$7.34	$7.18	$7.06	$6.99	$6.77	$6.54	$6.44
Sales expenses—percent of operating revenues	1.3	1.5	1.7	1.7	1.8	1.8	1.8	1.8	1.7	1.7	1.6
Administrative and general expenses—percent of operating revenues	5.8	5.9	5.7	5.7	5.9	6.0	6.2	6.3	6.3	6.4	6.4

standing amounts, at the advanced rates. The counter forces of decreased amounts available for interest coverage and higher interest rates sharply reduced the margin available for protection. Most company indentures under which the debt was issued provide that unless the coverage, under specified conditions, is two times the interest requirement, additional debt may not be issued.

An example of the calculation interest coverage is shown below:

	($000)
Revenues................	$450,000
Operations..............	200,000
Maintenance.............	30,000
Depreciation............	45,000
General taxes...........	45,000
	320,000
Balance for interest....	130,000
Interest................	30,000 ($500,000 @ 6%)
Times interest Covered before Federal income tax	4.3x

For indenture purposes the coverage usually is calculated before federal income taxes. In most instances the item of Allowance for Funds Used During Construction is added to the Balance for Interest before the coverage is computed. To demonstrate the leverage in the coverage figures, let us now assume revenue growth of 5 percent, expense rises of 10 percent, and incremental debt cost of 8 percent.

This is typical of the conditions that struck the utilities in the period 1969–73. Rate increase lag caused serious erosion of the coverage ratios. Some commissions, either through lack of understanding or fear, allowed coverages to decline for the 2x level, which necessitated the sale of equity in order to finance construction. This, in turn, reduced the earnings per share progression and contributed to lower market prices for the company's common stock. Thus the need to maintain and protect coverage ratios has proven to be an extremely important part of regulation of rates.

We do not propose that coverage be maintained near minimum levels. A healthy company has flexibility of financial alternatives, while one that is at minimum coverage has severely reduced capabilities. It should be noted, however, that mere maintenance can produce higher earnings.

	($000)
Revenues................	472,500
Operations..............	220,000
Maintenance.............	33,000
Depreciation............	49,500
General taxes...........	49,500
	352,000
Balance for interest....	120,500
Interest................	34,000 ($500,000 @ 6% + $50,000 @ 8%)
Times covered 3.5x	

TABLE 16

Federal Power Commission Composite Income Account, Year Ended December 31 (privately owned class A and class B electric utilities in the United States; thousands of dollars)

Item	1971		1970	
	Amount	Percent of revenues	Amount	Percent of revenues
Electricity utility operating income:				
Operating revenues	22,321,874	100.0	19,791,066	100.0
Operation expense	9,741,486	43.6	8,287,817	41.9
Maintenance expense	1,516,390	6.8	1,371,801	6.9
Depreciation expense	2,407,425	10.8	2,193,716	11.2
Amortization	4,483	0	3,830	0
Taxes other than income taxes	2,375,790	10.6	2,125,117	10.8
Income taxes:				
Federal	953,085	4.3	1,117,941	5.6
Other	87,454	.4	86,284	.4
Provision for deferred income taxes	245,533	1.1	159,347	.8
Income taxes deferred in prior years—credit	65,347	.3	62,048	.3
Investment tax credit adjustments—(net)	86,604	.4	25,969	.1
Gains from disposition of utility plant	105	0		
Losses from disposition of utility plant	89	0		
Total operating expenses	17,352,887	77.7	15,309,774	77.4
Electric utility operating income	4,968,987	22.3	4,481,292	22.6
Gas utility operating income:				
Operating revenues	3,474,223	100.0	3,137,743	100.0
Operation expense	2,305,712	66.4	2,035,484	64.9
Maintenance expense	142,925	4.1	125,323	4.0
Depreciation expense	192,898	5.6	179,747	5.7
Amortization	3,665	.1	3,899	.1
Taxes other than income taxes	279,411	8.0	255,782	8.2
Income taxes:				
Federal	103,846	3.0	123,093	3.9
Other	9,277	.3	9,929	.3
Provision for deferred income taxes	18,152	.5	13,951	.4
Income taxes deferred in prior years—credit	2,674	.1	1,938	0
Investment tax credit adjustments—(net)	2,872	.1	(1,110)	0
Total operating expenses	3,056,084	88.0	2,744,160	87.5
Gas utility operating income	418,139	12.0	393,583	12.5
Other utility operating income:				
Operating revenues	231,141	100.0	199,131	100.0
Operation expense	156,601	67.8	136,803	68.7
Maintenance expense	21,430	9.3	20,994	10.5
Depreciation expense	18,697	8.1	17,455	8.8
Amortization	530	.2	131	0
Taxes other than income taxes	25,015	10.8	21,888	11.0
Income taxes:				
Federal	(5,571)	(2.4)	(8,074)	(4.1)
Other	(853)	(.4)	(617)	(.3)
Provision for deferred income taxes	1,206	.5	1,173	.6
Income taxes deferred in prior years—credit	814	.3	463	.2
Investment tax credit adjustments—(net)	24	0	(71)	0
Total operating expenses	216,265	93.6	189,219	95.0
Other utility operating income	14,876	6.4	9,912	5.0
Total utility operating income:				
Operating revenues	26,027,238	100.0	23,127,940	100.0
Operation expense	12,203,799	46.9	10,460,104	45.2
Maintenance expense	1,680,745	6.5	1,518,118	6.6
Depreciation expense	2,619,020	10.1	2,390,919	10.3
Amortization	8,678	0	7,860	0
Taxes other than income taxes	2,680,216	10.3	2,402,788	10.4
Inclme taxes:				
Federal	1,051,360	4.0	1,232,959	5.4
Other	95,878	.4	95,596	.4
Provision for deferred income taxes	264,891	1.0	174,470	.8
Income taxes deferred in prior years—credit	68,835	.3	64,450	.3
Investment tax credit adjustments—(net)	89,500	.3	24,788	.1
Gains from disposition of utility plant	105	0		
Losses from disposition of utility plant	89	0		

TABLE 16 (*Continued*)

| | 1971 | | 1970 | |
Item	Amount	Percent of revenues	Amount	Percent of revenues
Total operating expenses	20,625,236	79.2	18,243,152	78.9
Total utility operating income	5,402,002	20.8	4,884,788	21.1
Other income and deductions:				
Other income:				
Nonutility operating income	4,770	---------	4,858	---------
Interest and divided income	136,301	.5	129,673	.6
Allowance for funds used during construction	812,044	3.1	588,406	2.6
Miscellaneous nonoperating income	40,495	.2	45,663	.2
Gain and disposition of property	7,835	---------	4,852	---------
Total other income	1,001,445	3.8	773,452	3.4
Other income deductions:				
Loss on disposition of property	2,617	---------	2,221	---------
Miscellaneous amortization	5,278	---------	4,320	---------
Miscellaneous income deductions	32,145	.2	30,671	.2
Total other income deductions	40,040	.2	37,212	.2
Taxes applicable to other income and deductions:				
Taxes other than income taxes	6,705	---------	6,155	---------
Income taxes:				
Federal	(47,991)	(.2)	(25,720)	(.1)
Other	(3,212)	---------	(2,050)	---------
Provision for deferred income taxes	125	---------	261	---------
Income taxes deferred in prior years—credit	---------	---------	---------	---------
Investment tax credit adjustments—(net)	21	---------	(4)	---------
Investment tax credits	(224)	---------	(149)	---------
Total taxes on other income deductions	(44,576)	(.2)	(21,507)	(.1)
Net other income and deductions	1,005,981	3.8	757,747	3.3
Interest charges:				
Interest on long-term debt	2,423,817	9.3	1,997,365	8.6
Amortization of debt discount and expense	7,917	---------	6,993	---------
Amortization of premium on debt—credit	6,100	---------	6,769	---------
Interest on debt to associated companies	7,616	---------	6,833	---------
Other interest expense	179,539	.7	231,185	1.1
Total interest charges	2,612,789	10.0	2,235,607	9.7
Income before extraordinary items	3,795,194	14.6	3,406,928	14.7
Extraordinary items:				
Extraordinary income	63,531	.2	123	---------
Extraordinary deductions	---------	---------	(1,048)	---------
Net extraordinary items	63,531	.2	1,171	---------
Income taxes—Federal and other	6,730	---------	574	---------
Extraordinary items after taxes	56,801	.2	597	---------
Net income	3,851,995	14.8	3,407,525	14.7
Dividends declared—preferred stock	493,944	1.9	362,370	1.6
Dividends declared—common stock	2,331,914	9.0	2,158,899	9.3

Equity. The "bottom line" for a utility is no different than it is for any other company. Earnings per share are closely watched, and if there is realization of growth it usually is reflected in the security price. Because of the heavy financial needs, however, additions to the amount of common stock are more frequent than in most other industries. This is also advanced as the basic reason for the high payout of dividends relative to earnings. As the regulated nature of the industry tempers the size of possible year-to-year earnings advances, the stock purchaser demands current income in lieu of sizable capital gains prospects. For most of its history, the equities of utilities have sold on a price basis

TABLE 17

Statistics of Privately Owned Class A and Class B Electric Utilities in the United States, 1971 (composite electric operation and maintenance expenses, year ended December 31; thousands of dollars)

Item	1971			1970		
	Amount	Percent of total expenses	Percent of revenues	Amount	Percent of total expenses	Percent of revenues
Production expenses:						
Steam power:						
Operation:						
Fuel	4,366,274	38.8	19.6	3,566,737	36.9	18.0
Other	524,112	4.6	2.3	458,841	4.8	2.3
Total operation	4,890,386	43.4	21.9	4,025,578	41.7	20.3
Maintenance	609,863	5.4	2.7	532,121	5.5	2.7
Total production expenses, steam power	5,500,249	48.8	24.6	4,557,699	47.2	23.0
Nuclear power:						
Operation:						
Fuel	72,845	.7	.3	41,429	.4	.2
Other	25,611	.2	.1	15,459	.2	.1
Total operation	98,456	.9	.4	56,888	.6	.3
Maintenance	15,578	.1	.1	9,398	.1	.1
Total production expenses, nuclear power	114,034	1.0	.5	66,286	.7	.4
Hydraulic power:						
Operation	54,101	.5	.3	50,475	.5	.3
Maintenance	29,452	.3	.1	26,640	.3	.1
Total production expenses, hydraulic power	83,553	.8	.4	77,115	.8	.4
Other power:						
Operation:						
Fuel	218,065	1.9	1.0	145,035	1.5	.7
Other	28,973	.3	.1	8,077	.1	.1
Total operation	247,038	2.2	1.1	153,112	1.6	.8
Maintenance	32,981	.3	.2	19,706	.2	.1
Total production expenses, other power	280,019	2.5	1.3	172,818	1.8	.9

	Amount	Pct	Pct	Amount	Pct	Pct
Purchased power	1,426,106	12.7	6.4	1,234,409	12.8	6.2
System control and loading dispatching	32,878	.3	.1	30,631	.3	.2
Other power supply expenses	27,721	.2	.1	5,484	0	0
Total production expenses	7,464,560	66.3	33.4	6,144,442	63.6	31.1
Mills per killowatt-hour sold	5.49			4.76		
Transmission expenses:						
Operation	198,531	1.8	.9	174,603	1.8	.9
Maintenance	124,171	1.1	.6	116,440	1.2	.6
Total transmission expenses	322,702	2.9	1.5	291,043	3.0	1.5
Mills per kilowatt-hour sold	.24			.23		
Distribution expenses:						
Operation	659,792	5.9	3.0	627,910	6.5	3.2
Maintenance	659,352	5.8	2.9	625,246	6.5	3.1
Total distribution expenses	1,319,144	11.7	5.9	1,253,156	13.0	6.3
Dollars per customer	22.82			22.14		
Customer accounts expenses	555,446	4.9	2.5	501,569	5.2	2.5
Dollars per customer	9.61			8.86		
Sales expenses	291,426	2.6	1.3	306,386	3.2	1.5
Administrative and general expenses:						
Maintenance of general plant	44,993	.4	.2	42,248	.4	.2
Other administrative and general expenses	1,259,605	11.2	5.6	1,120,773	11.6	5.7
Total administrative and general expenses	1,304,598	11.6	5.8	1,163,021	12.0	5.9
Total electric operation and maintenance expenses	11,257,876	100.0	50.4	9,659,617	100.0	48.8

Statement of Income

	Three Months Ended March 31,		Twelve Months Ended March 31,	
	1971	1970	1971	1970
OPERATING REVENUES	$58,041,561	$51,240,605	$211,647,227	$189,984,291
OPERATING EXPENSES:				
Operation and maintenance.........................	36,888,423	25,558,519	133,757,420	95,263,139
Depreciation	5,739,000	4,887,000	20,328,000	18,452,000
Taxes other than income taxes......................	5,333,500	4,738,885	19,647,597	17,872,514
Income taxes	1,057,167	4,744,833	6,106,115	17,921,137
Investment tax credit adjustments..................	183,501	23,751	(1,345,250)	(435,909)
Total operating expenses..........................	49,201,591	39,952,988	178,493,882	149,072,881
OPERATING INCOME	8,839,970	11,287,617	33,153,345	40,911,410
OTHER INCOME:				
Interest charged to construction....................	4,080,062	1,962,108	12,622,890	5,525,069
Income taxes—credit	1,029,437	474,610	3,263,978	1,648,235
Other income (deductions)—net....................	58,489	(27,762)	53,288	(2,432)
Total other income................................	5,167,988	2,408,956	15,940,156	7,170,872
INCOME BEFORE INTEREST CHARGES................	14,007,958	13,696,573	49,093,501	48,082,282
INTEREST CHARGES:				
Interest on long-term debt.........................	6,538,604	4,306,549	21,836,307	15,214,191
Other interest expense.............................	609,365	1,087,937	3,874,170	4,635,916
Total interest charges............................	7,147,969	5,394,486	25,710,477	19,850,107
NET INCOME	6,859,989	8,302,087	23,383,024	28,232,175
PREFERRED DIVIDEND REQUIREMENTS FOR THE PERIOD................................	2,011,490	741,574	5,968,712	2,966,295
BALANCE AFTER PREFERRED DIVIDENDS.............	$ 4,848,499	$ 7,560,513	$ 17,414,312	$ 25,265,880
AVERAGE COMMON SHARES OUTSTANDING.........	13,991,115	12,679,007	13,257,235	12,177,348
EARNINGS PER SHARE COMMON STOCK..............	$ .35	$ .60	$ 1.31	$ 2.07

This income statement and the letter are not, under any circumstances, to be construed as an offer to sell, or as a solicitation of an offer to buy, securities of Carolina Power & Light Company.

more related to yield than earnings advances, although the period of the late 1950s and early 1960s was a notable exception.

The most recent analytical consideration to affect the earnings of utilities is that of "quality." There are serious questions as to whether the reported figures truly represent the earning power. The dispute centers around two accounts: flow through of deferred taxes and Allowance for Funds Used During Construction (ADC). The former was discussed under the tax section of the income account.

Allowance for Funds Used During Construction. Allowance for Funds Used During Construction is a practice whereby a utility capitalizes the cost of raising funds for construction. The debit is to Construction Work in Progress and the credit to the income statement, but "below the line." Until recently this was accomplished by deducting

FIGURE 5

Statement of Income

	Three Months Ended June 30,		Twelve Months Ended June 30,	
	1971	1970	1971	1970
OPERATING REVENUES	$58,598,707	$46,405,881	$223,840,054	$193,410,704
OPERATING EXPENSES:				
Operation and maintenance.........................	34,920,399	27,071,075	141,606,744	101,244,485
Depreciation	5,739,000	4,863,000	21,204,000	18,794,000
Taxes other than income taxes.....................	5,552,360	4,908,252	20,291,705	18,360,631
Income taxes	1,886,699	1,228,780	6,764,034	15,604,195
Investment tax credit adjustments..................	183,501	23,751	(1,185,500)	(396,018)
Total operating expenses...........................	48,281,959	38,094,858	188,680,983	153,607,293
OPERATING INCOME	10,316,748	8,311,023	35,159,071	39,803,411
OTHER INCOME:				
Interest charged to construction.....................	3,263,638	2,362,780	13,523,748	6,846,513
Income taxes—credit	804,502	566,808	3,501,672	1,874,969
Other income (deductions)—net....................	508,540	5,170	556,657	(64,949)
Total other income............................	4,576,680	2,934,758	17,582,077	8,656,533
INCOME BEFORE INTEREST CHARGES...............	14,893,428	11,245,781	52,741,148	48,459,944
INTEREST CHARGES:				
Interest on long-term debt.........................	6,804,973	4,510,767	24,130,513	16,089,192
Other interest expense............................	973,637	1,142,724	3,705,083	4,303,428
Total interest charges............................	7,778,610	5,653,491	27,835,596	20,392,620
NET INCOME	7,114,818	5,592,290	24,905,552	28,067,324
PREFERRED DIVIDEND REQUIREMENTS FOR THE PERIOD.............................	2,119,720	1,109,074	6,979,358	3,333,795
BALANCE AFTER PREFERRED DIVIDENDS.............	$ 4,995,098	$ 4,483,216	$ 17,926,194	$ 24,733,529
AVERAGE COMMON SHARES OUTSTANDING.........	14,023,512	12,691,978	13,589,206	12,437,932
EARNINGS PER SHARE COMMON STOCK.............	$ .36	$ .35	$ 1.32	$ 1.99

This income statement and the letter are not, under any circumstances, to be construed as an offer to sell, or as a solicitation of an offer to buy, securities of Carolina Power & Light Company.

the ADC from interest charges. When the amount of construction was small relative to the capitalization, and plants were completed within about three years, the amounts were insignificant in terms of earnings. Currently, a company with a $1 billion capitalization can be spending $250–300 million per year, or adding 25–30 percent to the capital. Further, this can continue for an extended period of years. Thus the earnings impact also can be sizable. In our display of earnings for Carolina Power and Light on page 835, for example, the ADC was $14,707,389 for the 12 months ending December 31, 1971. This is equal to $1.00 per share of the $1.97 reported. Further, as this company pays a cash dividend of $1, the dividend is barely covered by cash flow as $0.31 of tax deferrals are considered in calculating cash available.

While this would seem to be a prima facie case of questionable book-

Statement of Income

	Three Months Ended September 30,		Twelve Months Ended September 30,	
	1971	1970	1971	1970
OPERATING REVENUES	$71,849,856	$55,209,099	$240,480,811	$198,869,538
OPERATING EXPENSES:				
Fuel	23,824,183	20,473,762	84,936,883	62,878,819
Purchased power	2,899,006	3,581,528	11,775,886	7,775,397
Other operation expense	7,466,895	6,210,660	27,272,098	22,951,856
Maintenance	5,582,636	5,285,468	21,843,178	18,783,091
Depreciation	5,739,000	4,863,000	22,080,000	19,136,000
Taxes other than income taxes	5,458,121	4,685,015	21,064,811	18,715,166
Income taxes	5,528,484	1,450,454	10,842,064	11,095,006
Investment tax credit adjustments	183,501	23,751	(1,025,750)	(191,631)
Total operating expenses	56,681,826	46,573,638	198,789,170	161,143,704
OPERATING INCOME	15,168,030	8,635,461	41,691,641	37,725,834
OTHER INCOME:				
Allowance for funds used during construction	3,257,419	2,776,161	14,005,006	8,552,639
Income taxes—credit	554,524	753,287	3,302,909	2,205,758
Other income (deductions)—net	(36,033)	(176)	520,799	(52,002)
Total other income	3,775,910	3,529,272	17,828,714	10,706,395
INCOME BEFORE INTEREST CHARGES	18,943,940	12,164,733	59,520,355	48,432,229
INTEREST CHARGES:				
Interest on long-term debt	6,805,078	5,180,257	25,755,333	17,633,488
Other interest expense	1,054,472	1,084,066	3,675,489	4,282,533
Total interest charges	7,859,550	6,264,323	29,430,822	21,916,021
NET INCOME	11,084,390	5,900,410	30,089,533	26,516,208
PREFERRED DIVIDEND REQUIREMENTS FOR THE PERIOD	2,119,706	1,474,074	7,674,990	4,016,295
BALANCE AFTER PREFERRED DIVIDENDS	$ 8,964,684	$ 4,476,336	$ 22,414,543	$ 22,499,913
AVERAGE COMMON SHARES OUTSTANDING	15,521,390	12,706,752	14,298,649	12,696,343
EARNINGS PER SHARE COMMON STOCK	$ .58	$ .35	$ 1.57	$ 1.77

This income statement and the letter are not, under any circumstances, to be construed as an offer to sell, or as a solicitation of an offer to buy, securities of Carolina Power & Light Company.

keeping, it is not. It is more to the point to suggest that a perfectly valid system designed under one set of circumstances causes apparent distortions under a different set. If the company has produced, or has a reasonable prospect of producing, an earned return (rate of return on rate base) equal to the credit when the plant is operating, there is no problem. It is prospective lag in recovery of the rates that correctly worries the analyst. Currently there are a number of moves to modify the effects of ADC. Some are attempts to display it more realistically, and others might be called cosmetic. As the capitalized cost consists of debt and equity, this distinction now is being recognized. Also, as the debt charges at current high-interest rates can have a material income tax effect, this now is shown separately as a credit to the ADC. Regulators in a number of jurisdictions have moved this credit "below the line," which

Statement of Income

	Three Months Ended December 31,		Twelve Months Ended December 31,	
	1971	1970	1971	1970
OPERATING REVENUES	$67,152,920	$51,990,686	$255,643,044	$204,846,271
OPERATING EXPENSES:				
Fuel	18,760,643	18,948,350	84,749,177	69,013,927
Purchased power	2,110,675	3,464,863	10,421,698	9,798,741
Other operation expense	7,649,810	6,411,847	28,510,060	23,765,314
Maintenance	6,675,970	5,421,444	23,097,703	19,849,535
Depreciation	5,603,000	4,863,000	22,820,000	19,476,000
Taxes other than income taxes	5,055,492	4,720,830	21,399,474	19,052,982
Income taxes	4,578,988	2,369,714	13,051,338	9,793,781
Investment tax credit adjustments—net (credit)	726,745	(1,576,253)	1,277,248	(1,505,000)
Total operating expenses	51,161,323	44,623,795	205,326,698	169,245,280
OPERATING INCOME	15,991,597	7,366,891	50,316,346	35,600,991
OTHER INCOME:				
Allowance for funds used during construction	4,106,271	3,403,887	14,707,389	10,504,936
Income taxes—credit	1,143,863	914,446	3,532,326	2,709,151
Other income (deductions)—net	(14,307)	(10,195)	516,689	(32,963)
Total other income	5,235,827	4,308,138	18,756,404	13,181,124
INCOME BEFORE INTEREST CHARGES	21,227,424	11,675,029	69,072,750	48,782,115
INTEREST CHARGES:				
Interest on long-term debt	7,754,309	5,606,679	27,902,963	19,604,252
Other interest expense	1,058,673	1,038,014	3,696,147	4,352,741
Total interest charges	8,812,982	6,644,693	31,599,110	23,956,993
NET INCOME	12,414,442	5,030,336	37,473,640	24,825,122
PREFERRED DIVIDEND REQUIREMENTS FOR THE PERIOD	2,119,706	1,424,074	8,370,622	4,698,795
BALANCE AFTER PREFERRED DIVIDENDS	$10,294,736	$ 3,606,262	$ 29,103,018	$ 20,126,327
AVERAGE COMMON SHARES OUTSTANDING	15,542,991	13,648,903	14,776,063	12,933,701
EARNINGS PER SHARE COMMON STOCK	$ .66	$ .26	$ 1.97	$ 1.56

This income statement and the letter are not, under any circumstances, to be construed as an offer to sell, or as a solicitation of an offer to buy, securities of Carolina Power & Light Company.

increases recoverable operating costs and permits the company to seek offsetting revenues before the plant is completed.

Another approach used will add a portion of the Construction Work in Progress (but not in service) to the rate base, which includes it in the calculation of the return and commensurately reduces the amount of ADC. This method has two problems: (1) A number of state laws require the rate base to be plant that is "used and useful," and (2) some regulators balk at the fact that the customer is paying rates for facilities before they are completed.

The importance of ADC could be phased out through the rate-making process or as construction programs become relatively smaller. This may, however, require a decade. Meanwhile, a number of companies must seek sizable amounts of rate relief before current costs are recovered.

TABLE 18

The Mechanics of Coverage* (thousands)

Tax Account

	Year 1	Year 2†	Year 3†
Revenues	$ 50,000	$ 62,500	$ 75,000
Expenses			
Operation and maintenance	$ 25,000	$ 31,250	$ 37,500
Depreciation	5,000	6,250	7,500
General tax	5,000	6,250	7,500
Total	$ 35,000	$ 43,750	$ 52,500
Balance for interest	$ 15,000	$ 18,750	$ 22,500
Interest	6,000	7,500	9,000
Times interest coverage before federal income tax	2.5	2.5	2.5
Taxable income	$ 9,000	$ 11,250	$ 13,500
Taxes (40 percent rate)	3,600	4,500	5,400

Capital structure

	Year 1	Year 2†	Year 3†
Debt at 6 percent	$100,000	$125,000	$150,000
Preferred stock at 6 percent	30,000	37,500	45,000
Common stock	70,000	86,060	102,100
Surplus	—	1,440	2,900
Total	$200,000	$250,000	$300,000

Book Account

	Year 1	Year 2†	Year 3†
Revenues	$ 50,000	$ 62,500	$ 75,000
Expenses			
Operation and maintenance	$ 25,000	$ 31,250	$ 37,500
Depreciation	5,000	6,250	7,500
General tax	5,000	6,250	7,500
Federal income tax	3,600	4,500	5,400
Total	$ 38,600	$ 48,250	$ 57,900
Net operating income	$ 11,400	$ 14,250	$ 17,100
Interest	6,000	7,500	9,000
Net income	$ 5,400	$ 6,750	$ 8,100
Preferred dividends	1,800	2,250	2,700
Balance for common	$ 3,600	$ 4,500	$ 5,400
dividend (60 percent)	2,160	2,700	—
Surplus	$ 1,440	$ 1,800	—
Shares outstanding(000)	2,000	2,460	2,920
Earnings per share	$1.80	$1.83	$1.88
Book value per share	$35.00	$35.56	$35.95

* An example of the effect on earnings per share when coverage of interest requirements is maintained and plant is enlarged.

† Assume construction of $50 million per year.

Note: Assuming the indenture of a particular company requires maintenance of 2.5 times interest charges before federal income taxes, there is a progression of earnings if the coverage is maintained and additional common stock is sold at or above book value. The example is oversimplified and is a portrayal of a theory rather than a display of an actual case. For instance, there is no item for Allowance for Funds During Construction, which would be needed to raise the equity return up to realistic levels. Also, the interest rate is constant, while increases would necessitate further rate adjustments.

Source: Dean Witter.

Looking back to our rate of return example given earlier, but now adding in $200 million of capitalized construction, the allowance for funds is developed in this way.

	($000)	
Construction.......................	$200,000	
Capitalized at 8%..................	.08	
Capitalized interest................	$ 16,000	
Assume it is financed as before		
50% Debt......................	$100,000 @ 6%	3.00%
15% Preferred....................	30,000 @ 7%	1.05
35% Common stock..............	70,000 @ 11.57%	4.05
Return...........................		8.00%

This plant, however, provides no revenues. It has an interest cost of $6 million, a preferred requirement of $2.1 million, and a common cost at least equal to the current dividend rate plus the value of retained earnings. In addition, as there are no revenues, there is an increased deduction from income taxes equal to the incremental interest requirement. Alongside each other, the accounts appear this way:

Tax Accounts

	Before ADC ($000)	With ADC ($000)
Revenues.......................	$450,000	$450,000
Expenses		
Operation......................	200,000	200,000
Maintenance....................	30,000	30,000
Depreciation....................	45,000	45,000
General taxes...................	45,000	45,000
Interest........................	30,000	36,000
Total expenses...............	$350,000	$356,000
Taxable Income..................	100,000	94,000
Tax (at 50 percent)..............	50,000	47,000

Book Accounts

	($000)	($000)
Revenues.......................	$450,000	$450,000
Expenses		
Operations.....................	200,000	200,000
Maintenance....................	30,000	30,000
Depreciation....................	45,000	45,000
General taxes...................	45,000	45,000
Income taxes....................	50,000	47,000
Total......................	$370,000	$367,000
Net operating income..............	80,000	83,000
Interest........................	30,000	36,000
Allowance for funds(cr).............	—	(3,000)
Net income.....................	50,000	50,000

An alternate method of recording ADC, that puts the income tax credit below the line, and thus does not lower taxes for rate-making purposes looks like this:

	(000)
Revenues	$450,000
Expenses	
Operations, maintenance, and depreciation	275,000
General taxes	45,000
Income taxes	50,000
Net operating income	$ 80,000
Interest	33,000
ADC	(1,500)
Credit for income tax	(1,500)
Net income	$ 50,000

MARKET BEHAVIOR

There is an homogeneity to the utility market reflecting its capital intensity and its relative surety of income. To a great degree this is true of the senior as well as the junior securities.

Bonds

When the Federal Reserve pegged government bond rates in World War II, utility bonds were considered the next step in safety. Variations of five basis points between comparable quality issues were worthy of note; and in 1946 the variation between an A^{aa} bond and a B^{aa} bond (using Moody's ratings of A^{aa}, A^{a} A, and B^{aa}) was only 50 basis points. About 1949 a long-term slide in interest rates began, but even today with yields of 8–9 percent quite common, the spread is less than 100 basis points. It must be remembered, of course, that rating changes have occurred with some frequency in the last three years.

Current Position. Utility bonds (and most preferred stocks) still are ranked well in the money markets. They are subject to outside forces affecting the flow of investment, but they still are regarded as a good to excellent credit. In order to maintain this condition, however, in the face of still heavier financing, rate relief will have to be forthcoming in sizable amounts. At present the market prices seem to be anticipating this will occur.

Stocks

Preferred stocks of utilities, closely follow the pattern of bond prices. They are considered good credits and also are responsive primarily to market forces. The range in dividend yields is wider than in the case of bonds, but the gradations are explainable in conditions surrounding the particular company.

Common stocks in the industry must be divided into electric, gas, and telephone categories. Until the recent fuel crisis there was a further division in the electric area of above average, average, and below average growth. All the groups, however, were expected to pay a secure and rising amount of dividends. The frequency and amount of anticipated increase describes the three categories of electric utilities.

Electric Utility Common Stocks. The published averages for prices, earnings, and yields contain companies in all three "growth" categories but, on balance, probably reflect the center group most closely. It should be remembered, however, that in the 1955–65 period rapid growth was considered 12–15 percent annually in earnings per share, while below average was in the 4–5 percent range. Measured by Moody's average, the compound rate for that period was about 6 percent.

The growth continued, although at a lesser pace, until 1969 when price inflation was moving faster than rate relief and earnings declined. The last previous decline was in 1952, caused by imposition of the excess profits tax.

As noted above, during these good years capital needs varied between $3 billion and $4 billion per year. Only after 1966 did the inflation cause the figure to increase rapidly. The typical utility generated 30–40 percent of these capital requirements and sold only enough common stock to generally maintain the equity ratio at 30–40 percent. Practically all the remaining requirement was funded. With capital needs now running at $13–15 billion this year and increases forecasted, the need relative to the total has changed vastly (see case study at the end of this chapter).

Price History. Starting roughly in 1957 and continuing until 1965, the electric utilities were considered to be the growth vehicles in the market. Price/earnings multiples expanded from 15x to slightly over 20x, while yields declined from 5 percent to 3 percent. (In 1958 the yield on the common stock average went below the yield on utility bonds, a condition that persisted until 1973.) At the peaks of the utility market, growth stocks were selling at 35x–40x earnings. Mutual funds and fiduciaries held 60–70 percent of the outstanding shares of many of these companies.

The Long Decline. Subsequent to 1965, utility earnings continued to grow, but new burgeoning industries were growing faster. Thus money began to flow out of the utility group. This encompassed both rapid- and lesser-growth companies, but the multiple spread between the higher- and lower-growth-rate companies continued. The trend toward selling accelerated in 1968, as the earnings trend stuttered reflecting higher operating costs, and capital needs increased.

Present Position. As this is being written, the electric utilities are indeed in a low state. The average multiple is 7x − 9x earnings and the yield is almost 8 − 9 percent, compared to industrials at 11x 1973 earnings. The last time the electric utilities sold on this low a basis was 1942. The market problem was exacerbated in April 1974 when Consolidated Edison of New York omitted a quarterly dividend. The entire market for utility equities dropped between 10 and 20 percent and has not yet recovered. There was immediate fear of other dividend reductions or omissions and the yield spread between companies having better and poorer quality earning widened by 4 percentage points and now ranges between 6–16 percent.

Methods of Financing. The market stability of the 1950s and 1960s for electric utilities favored issuance of common stock to current shareholders under subscription rights. This method also led to speculative opportunities, as rights themselves were purchased on, and exercised under, special subscription privileges permitted by most brokers at low-margin rates. (Practically all senior securities were sold under competitive bids.) Until the need for capital increased, however, the marketing of utility issues was prosaic.

Gas Utility Common Stocks. Gas distribution companies were quite similar to the electric utilities in relative capital needs and market action, although the dispersion of multiples was smaller. The froth that occurred was in the transmission or pipeline sector. These stocks were acquired for potential earnings growth, and yields and dividend payouts were low. With increasing saturation of the market in the early 1960s, managements began diversification efforts; and today there are only two or three companies that are basically natural gas transmission companies. Some, such as Tenneco and Texas Gas Transmission, are broad-based multi-industry companies.

Capital Needs and Financing. At present the capital needs of the transmission companies for expansion of gas operations is directed more to finding new gas supplies than to marketing them. In the future, however, are some very large numbers. A pipeline from Alaska to the United States, for example, is estimated to cost $5 billion. Import of pipeline quantities of liquidfied natural gas has estimated costs of $2 billion per project, and proposed synthetic gas facilities also have very high price tags. Most of the transmission companies have increased the proportion of their equity relative to capital as they diversified, but the difference in risk between the old type of operation and those proposed would indicate the need for significant equity in the new projects. It would seem prudent to view them as unregulated enterprises rather than as utilities with full rights and obligations.

Telephone Industry—Independent Companies. Outside of American Telephone, the industry has a price history based on earnings growth through acquisition and merger as well as on increasing basic telephone service. In the mid 1950s there were over 3,000 so-called independent telephone companies, ranging in size from General Telephone with 12 million telephones, to hundreds of one-community systems having less than 1,000 telephones. These smaller units, often family owned, were not able to afford modernized equipment and sold their facilities to larger independents for marketable securities. Many of these early acquisitions were at favorable prices, and the acquiring system was able to record significant earnings growth. Accounting procedures, such as pooling of interest, also helped. As a number of systems became larger, they also were merged. With the high rate of earnings growth encouraging high multiples, it was quite easy for the acquiring company to minimize dilution. By the late 1960s, however, the larger independents began bidding between themselves for a dwindling number of smaller companies, and dilution from shares issued began to take its toll.

At present merger activity is at a virtual standstill awaiting outcome of an antitrust suit brought by International Telephone & Telegraph against General Telephone & Electronics. A lower federal court has held that GTE must divest itself of a number of subsidiaries and manufacturing operations.[24] The appeals will ultimately be decided in the United States Supreme Court.

Capital Needs. Construction programs of the independents reflect the cost inflation as much as the other segments of the utility area. As the need for equipment can be paced more evenly, however, they are in a somewhat better circumstance. Estimates of amounts are not readily available except from the larger systems, but it would appear the annual need is in the neighborhood of $5 billion per year. Internal generation is good and rate increases have been forthcoming. The relative equity requirement would, thus, seem to be less than for either the electric or gas transmission companies.

American Telephone. As this company is half as big in terms of capitalization as the entire electric utility industry, its position may be considered unique. In many ways its record of operating costs, capital needs, and market price mirrors the electric companies with one difference: The large item in operating cost was labor rather than fuel. At one point in 1973, the system companies had on file $1.3 billion in requests for rate relief—an amount greater than for the electric industry.

There are indications that capital requirements for the system are rising less rapidly and currently are stabilized at about $10 billion. Rate relief and strict cost control programs have improved cash flow, and financing may become less onerous. Still, it will vary between $4 billion and $5 billion per year. A certain amount of this will have to be common stock, although the dilution will be far less than for many electric utilities.

Methods of Financing. American Telephone historically has used convertible debentures and subscription rights to sell incremental common stock. With the market price of the stock currently below book value, they would much prefer to delay any sale of common equity. As a result, the company privately placed a preferred stock and used a convertible preferred. Management is working diligently to improve the earnings and hopes to have this reflected in the common stock price so that additional shares can be sold. This effort is not being aided by publicity regarding potential competition from the specialized carriers.

CASE STUDY

Using a composite of the industry facilitates a general discussion that will not become mired in questions of fuel availability or local regulatory

---

[24] Docket 73–1513–9th Cir. C. of Appeals, dated June 1, 1973.

issues. In some measure, all the electric companies are subject to industry forces and, to a greater or smaller degree, face similar problems and prospects. It might be suggested this is the "average" company.

Construction

At the outset of this chapter it was stated that regulation and capital intensity were the two dominant forces affecting the utilities. From the industry model below, the magnitude of capital needs may be seen. (If one adds $15 billion annually for communications and $3–4 billion for gas utilities to the electric industry requirement, it is roughly 30 percent of the total plant and equipment expenditure by the whole industry of $100 billion in 1973). For the electric companies, two thirds of the requirement will be in the form of new financing.

The amounts for construction in the model are from corporate estimates collected and published by Irving Trust Company.[25] They do not reflect any changes that may occur as a result of energy conservation programs, as it is not possible to evaluate these as yet. We earlier stated, however, that if the rate of sales growth is modified, total construction expenditures can then be extended over a longer time period. For the reader, we believe the methodology is more important than the specific development. The construction estimates are:

	Construction ($ billion)	External Financing ($ billion)
1973	$16.43	$ 8.98*
1974	17.63	11.99
1975	18.68	12.39
1976	21.04	13.90
1977	23.07	14.59

* Excluding short-term bank loans estimated at $1.5–2.5 billion per year.

If these amounts are spent, net plant will rise almost 13 percent per year.

Sales and Revenue Assumptions

A continuation of a 7.5 percent rate of sales growth in terms of kilowatt hours has been used. Revenues are assumed to rise at a comparable pace. The effect of fuel clauses on rates is *not* included in the rates. The growth of each of the categories—residential, commercial, and industrial—remains unchanged from the most recent figures. Rate increases are estimated as follows:

	($ billion)	(percent)
1973	.7	(2.5)
1974	1.6	(5.1)
1975	1.9	(5.4)
1976	2.7	(5.3)
1977	2.5	(5.6)

[25] Irving Trust Company: Financing Calendar, January 2, 1974.

Starting with an assumed overall average rate of $0.018 per kilowatt hour for 1972, the rate at the end of 1977 would be $0.028 kilowatt hours. (If sales are curtailed but capital requirements are not reduced, the revenue requirement would be the same in order to maintain the interest coverage level.)

Operating Expenses

A relative decline is anticipated in operating expenses, as fuel costs will now be offset in revenues (above those shown); and as rates are increased in excess of the amounts needed for fuel recovery, the operating ratio will decline. It is also assumed that nuclear plants now on the verge of completion (and not generally covered by fuel riders) will aid in controlling the rise in operating costs. Labor rates will also continue to increase, but it is assumed that rate increases will fully offset this amount.

Maintenance. As the learning curve for operation of the new machines advances, current excess costs should not recur. Thus, this account also should improve relative to the higher revenues.

Depreciation. Between the recognition of higher cash need and the increasing danger of obsolescence, it is expected that depreciation charges for book purposes will rise more rapidly than revenues. This is an area where regulators are notoriously slow to act, and the lag is likely to continue. It could well be an item that dictates rate increases further in the future, however.

General Taxes. Property and sales-based taxes are likely to rise evenly with revenues. The utilities are too good a vehicle for tax collection for any change to occur.

Income Taxes. Reported federal and state income taxes are increasing as normalization procedures allowed under the 1969 Tax Reform Act are used more and as the tax effects from flow-through accounting are reversed on fully depreciated properties. The tax rate will continue to be sensitive to interest costs and rate actions of the commissions (Table 19).

Balance Sheet

Capitalization. Because of the absolute need to preserve financing flexibility, bond coverage must be at least maintained. This has the dual effect of limiting the amount of debt that can be sold under given rate assumptions and necessitating a gradual rise in the equity component. The ability of the market to absorb up to $3–5 billion a year of equity paper also is a consideration.

Debt is postulated to decline gradually as a percentage of capitalization. We have arbitrarily assumed that interest rates will stabilize at around 7.5 percent. Improvement in the rate could be beneficial; and if it rises to a higher level, the amount of rate increase that must be obtained also rises. In any event, the embedded cost of debt will continue

TABLE 19

Utility Industry Model—Classes A and B Electric Utilities

	1972	1973	1974	1975	1976	1977
				Estimated	*Estimated*	*Estimated*
Earnings per share	$3.18	3.27	3.28	3.41	3.52	3.65
Dividends per share	$2.07	2.08	2.09	2.18	2.23	2.32
Shares (millions)	1,195	1,270	1,344	1,434	1,515	1,600
Capital:						
Debt (%)	54.9	54.0	53.5	53.0	53.0	53.0
Preferred	10.7	11.5	12.0	12.0	12.0	12.0
Equity	34.4	34.5	34.5	35.0	35.0	35.0
Total (millions)	$ 98,890	111,185	124,094	137,574	152,667	169,114
Gross plant (millions)	$117,125	132,705	149,425	167,190	187,140	208,990
Depreciation (millions)	23,992	26,242	28,822	31,767	35,188	39,054
Rate base (millions) (assumes plant plus 2 percent)	$ 91,285	104,061	117,558	131,745	147,669	165,073
Percent return on rate base (%)	6.1	6.0	5.9	6.0	6.1	6.1
Equity return	11.2	10.8	10.3	10.1	10.0	9.9
Requirement (millions)	$ 13,745	16,726	18,538	20,459	22,027	23,941
Internal sources	4,953	5,618	6,307	6,984	7,868	8,705
Additional financing	8,793	11,117	12,237	13,482	14,169	15,246
Debt	4,989	6,071	7,290	8,282	9,025	9,658
Preferred	1,315	2,204	2,105	1,617	1,811	1,974
Common	2,489	2,843	2,841	3,583	3,334	3,614
Percent cash generation	36.0	33.6	34.0	34.1	35.7	36.4
Payout ratio (%)	65.2	63.7	63.5	64.0	63.4	63.4
Tax rate	30.0	30.0	32.0	34.0	36.0	37.0

Average cost:					
Debt (%)	5.7	5.9	6.1	6.3	6.5	6.6
Interest coverage	2.6x	2.5x	2.5x	2.5x	2.5x	2.5x
Preferred (%)	6.1	6.4	6.6	6.7	6.8	6.9
Operating Rates:						
Revenues (millions)	$ 28,369	31,206	35,107	39,320	44,432	50,208
Operations (%)	48.0	47.5	47.0	46.0	45.0	45.0
Maintenance	7.0	6.8	6.8	6.8	6.8	6.7
Depreciation	10.0	10.3	10.5	10.7	11.0	11.0
General tax	10.7	10.7	10.7	10.7	10.7	10.7
Federal income tax	5.1	5.1	5.4	5.9	6.4	6.6
Margin (pretax)	24.3	24.7	25.0	25.8	26.5	26.6
Plant revenues ($)	4.13	4.25	4.26	4.25	4.21	4.16

to rise for the foreseeable future. Recent debt has been sold at costs well above the current embedded rate, and about $1 billion per year of 3 percent and 4 percent debt must be refunded in 1975, 1976, and 1977. By 1977, interest costs will be close to $5.4 billion annually. Increased use of allocation of the interest cost on ADC as a below-the-line credit should aid in the rate-making process.

Preferred stock will remain important as an alternative to debt or common, primarily in that it appeals to different classes of purchasers. Its use also helps to ease the burden on coverage of debt interest.

For *common stock*, under the assumptions set forth, equity dilution would be about 6 percent per year and the progression of earnings per share just under 3 percent, compounded over the 1972–1977 period. A multiple of 11 times the prior year's earnings was used in setting the price for newly added shares. Should the actual multiple be lower, additional shares would be needed; and if it should be higher, a lesser number of shares would be added. Considering the sizable amounts of dollars of rate relief (although modest percentages) needed to provide even this modest amount of earnings growth there obviously are market risks. On the other hand, in a period of possibly slower economic growth, the dividend payout (currently providing about an 8–9 percent yield) plus this growth provides a reasonable 11–12 percent overall return.

Other Market Considerations

Earlier we characterized this as an "average" company. Thus, some part of the sample will have better earnings growth resulting from a combination of lesser equity needs and less onerous rate requirements. Such companies should sell at a higher multiple than the average, as the indicated risk relative to the potential is smaller. As the entire group of almost 200 companies is now selling between 7X and 9X earnings, a wider multiple spread would seem justified. Identification of the better and poorer companies increasingly should be possible.

Conclusion

It is not reasonable to postulate a set of circumstances in which the return to the common stock is declining as this would indicate erosion of the value of the present holders of the equity. As many stocks now are selling below book value, a continuation of this trend would exacerbate the situation. Over the long run the return to the equity must be adequate to add to the book value so that there is a reasonable prospect that the stock will sell above that level. Under that assumption, the industry is twice blessed, as the contribution from the new equity investor (the amount above book value) adds to the ability to further improve earnings. The basic health of a capital intense industry, with its attendant equity need, is inextricable from its need to sell at a price above book.

PART III

Information Sources

31

Site Visits

ALFRED S. RUDD
Standard & Poor's Corporation, New York, New York

SITE VISITS are invaluable to the financial analyst as a means to clarify and to supplement the information which is available from published sources on a company. The focus of the site visit is, of course, an interview with an officer or officers of the company under investigation. Frequently, it is possible, and may be desirable, to supplement the interview with an inspection of the subject company's operating facilities. To arrange for the interview, the analyst should contact the company by letter or telephone, preferably the former, asking for an appointment and outlining his business affiliation and the nature of his interest in the company. In making the contact, the analyst probably would be well advised to address his inquiry to the company's chief financial officer or, possibly, its president. Large corporations, however, usually have a designated spokesman to the financial community and, in such cases, the inquiry would be referred to that person. In any event, the analyst should approach the interview with the primary objective of obtaining answers to the questions which have arisen during his initial investigation. The purpose of the site visit should not be for news gathering.

Before making a site visit, it is essential that the analyst examine thoroughly and analyze carefully all available published information on the subject company. Its annual and interim reports to stockholders for, perhaps, the latest five years should be reviewed in detail, as well as any other releases to stockholders and the press. Its 10-K and other reports to the SEC, and its proxy statements, should be read carefully. In addition, it is advisable to seek any additional information on the company or its industry which is available in publications of the financial statistical

849

services, in reports by industry associations, various trade publications, and by appropriate government agencies.

The analyst should obtain a good working knowledge of the company, its products, its markets, its place in industry, its financial history, and possibly the nature of its competition and of its problems, as well as its aims. At the same time, the analyst will have developed many questions as to "why" certain things have happened, and "why" the company's financial record and present financial standing is what it is. To obtain optimum results from his site visit, the analyst should make a complete listing of all inquiries to be made and organize those inquiries in logical sequence to cover each area of interest and to expedite his investigation. A carefully organized interview featuring precisely worded questions and a minimum of generalizations, stands the best chance of eliciting the full cooperation of the person or persons being interviewed, because it is the hallmark of the analyst who has "done his homework."

With adequate preparation, the analyst has an opportunity through a site visit to round out his knowledge and understanding of a company in several ways. He should be able to obtain a more precise understanding of the interplay of various economic (and sociopolitical) forces as they affect the company in determining (a) the demand for its products or services; (b) the prices received for those products or services; (c) the direct and indirect costs of providing them; and (d) the requirements and means available to finance its operations. A more accurate, or even precise, identification probably can be made of the nature and intensity of the company's direct and indirect competition. A clearer picture may be obtained of the manner in which the company's product mix, operating procedures, and financial policies resemble, as well as differ from, those of its competitors and why. From this, it may be possible to ascertain, and then to discuss, the company's apparent particular strengths and weaknesses. Some questioning is appropriate with respect to the company's operating and financial controls, for subsequent evaluation. If the site visit also includes an inspection of the company's operating facilities, possibly there will be some opportunity to observe if those operating policies and controls are being implemented, as intended.

The site visit also provides an opportunity to canvass at first hand some of the fundamental aspects of the company, such as its broad business policies and its operating and financial philosophies. It is usually pertinent to discuss the company's long-range planning and the direction of its research and development work, if that is important. Also, inquiry can be made about technological, market, or other developments, present and potential, which may have significant influence on demand for the company's products or services, or on their prices and/or costs. Finally, it is conceivable that from his site visit the analyst can begin to obtain some basis for evaluating the calibre of the company's management.

If the site visit extends beyond an interview to an inspection of the company's operating facilities, the analyst should find it valuable to communicate, if the opportunity is presented, with as many as possible of the company's personnel, representing various phases of its activities. Through that communication, he may be able, for example, to broaden his understanding of the company's operating procedures, sales policies and methods, and employee relations. Specific questions with respect to certain products or production methods frequently find their best answers in the plant.

At the conclusion of the site visit, and to supplement his findings, the analyst may find it helpful to discuss some of his questions on the subject company's products or services, and markets, with some of its competitors, suppliers, and customers. Those conversations could provide somewhat better perspective for the answers to those questions. However, the analyst never is justified in discussing with those sources the results of his findings on the site visit. On broader topics, such as industry problems, the analyst may find it advisable to check his conclusions by ascertaining the views held by appropriate industry associations, government departments, and the trade press. Those views may warrant some shading of the emphasis placed on certain problems, or conceivably bring out an entirely different viewpoint.

In evaluating the information obtained from a site visit, and from any subsequent investigation, the analyst should take care to check and recheck for possible errors or misunderstandings if his findings appear to contradict published financial data. If such discrepancies appear, it is more than possible that the analyst's recollections or notes may be at fault. Obviously, all such discrepancies must be reconciled, or the analyst is not warranted in using the information. There is a tendency, all too frequently, for a judgment to be colored by "first impressions," favorable or unfavorable. The analyst is cautioned to beware of any such tendency, insofar as it is possible, and to make his judgments objectively and only after careful consideration. Finally, having weighed all of his findings and drawn his conclusions, the analyst would be well advised to discuss frankly with the company's management the essence of his conclusions and his reasoning in arriving at those conclusions. Management usually welcomes an independent and carefully reasoned assessment.

At all times during his investigation, and particularly at the site visit, the analyst must be constantly aware of his obligation, under the regulations governing transactions in securities, to avoid obtaining any information of a material nature which might be considered "inside information." If, as might happen, any inkling is given at any time to what seems to be significant new information about the subject company (or another), management should be so informed, with the suggestion that the information be made public. Until the latter has been done, the analyst is obligated not to use such information, directly or by implication, either privately or publicly.

32

Information Sources:
An Overview

DOROTHY HENNESSY SUSSMAN
Vice President-Librarian
Goldman, Sachs Co., New York, New York

THERE ARE myriad sources of information for economic, financial, and business analyses: the trade press, national trade associations, financial services, specialized newsletters, marketing research reports, bank letters and reports, computerized services, macroeconomic and industry forecasts, and, finally, the largest single publisher of statistics and general economic information—the United States government. The United States Bureau of the Census is probably the most prolific publisher with its various censuses of agriculture, business, construction, housing, manufactures, mineral industries, population, and transportation—to name but a few. The aim of this chapter is to serve as a guide to the basic sources of information available for examination and study.

An analyst should, of course, be familiar with his company or public library. A tour of the company library, browsing through the catalog and subject files, scanning the periodicals, and inspecting the corporation records will provide knowledge of the scope of the library and the information readily available. Most business analysts are familiar with the *Statistical Abstract of the United States*—an annual comprehensive collection of industrial, economic, and social statistics; the monthly *Survey of Current Business*, with its biennial supplement and a national income supplement giving income by industry and personal consumption expenditures by type (savings and investments); and the monthly *Federal Reserve Bulletin*—the primary source of monetary statistics. The *United States Industrial Outlook*, published annually by the Department of Commerce, is an excellent roundup of over 100 industries. It both sum-

marizes recent trends in the industries and makes projections for five-
to ten-year periods. All are available from the U.S. Government Printing
Office.

Directories of various kinds are often the key for pinpointing particular
information. Familiarity with the several selected directories described
will broaden the horizon for the analyst. Gale's *Encyclopedia of Associations*[1] (1) lists national trade, health, and educational associations with
broad classifications. Brief notations for each association indicate purpose,
functions, membership, publications, staff, and address. *The Directory
of National Trade and Professional Associations of the United States* (2)
similarly guides one to the important trade associations but omits the
detailed annotations. N. W. Ayer's & Sons *Directory of Newspapers and
Periodicals* (3) will provide the analyst with specific titles of trade newspapers and periodicals in his field. This annual publication provides both
an alphabetical and geographical index. The *Standard Periodicals Directory* (4) contains a list of U.S. and Canadian periodicals and annuals
by industry. If foreign information is needed, *Ulrich's International
Periodicals Directory* (5) covers both domestic and foreign periodicals.
The *Standard Rate and Data Service* (6) which lists trade journals by
industry groupings, giving addresses, subscription rates, and frequency
of publication, is another excellent source. Each publication listed in this
directory contains national advertising sold through advertising agencies.

A constant need in business is the demand for biographical data.
Everyone is familiar with *Who's Who in America* (7) but there are numerous other directories to be consulted—for example, *Who's Who in
The East* (7), *Who's Who in The West* (7), *Who's Who in The Southwest* (7), *The Directory of Directors in the City of New York* (8), *Poor's
Register of Corporations and Directors* (9). Undoubtedly, however, the
most important biographical directory for the financial and business
analyst is *Who's Who in Finance and Industry* (7).

Klein's Guide to American Directories (10) which contains an an-
notated bibliography of major industrial, professional, and mercantile
directories is an excellent source of information. *Current European Directories* (11) is a guide of yearbooks, commercial directories, association directories, bibliographical directories, and special industry directories, arranged by country. *Jane's Major Companies of Europe* (12)
contains financial information on the leading companies of Western Europe. *Trade Directories of the World* (13) lists business and trade directories by continent and by country. There is a *Directory of American
Firms Operating in Foreign Countries* (14) and another called *Who
Owns Whom* (15) which lists American parent companies with subsidiaries and affiliates. *Commercial Directories of the United States* (16)

---

[1] See list of Information Sources at the end of chapter 33 for publication information on numbered titles.

contains over 800 listings of U.S. directories, describing the publications, content, and audience. It also contains a breakdown of government Standard Industrial Classification numbers covered by each publication. The *World Guide to Trade Associations* (5) contains 27,000 country-by-country listings—14,500 organizations in Europe and 12,500 in the United States. The list is legion.

Statistical sources can be referenced by consulting Gale's *Statistic Sources* (1) or Gale's *Encyclopedia of Business Information Sources* (1). The *Directory of Business and Financial Services* (17) is another excellent source of information.

Current trends in finance, industry, marketing, and management are best reflected in periodicals, trade press, and various financial services. Access to such articles is vital to acquiring such information. The *Business Periodicals Index* (18), the *Funk & Scott Index of Corporations and Industries* (19), the *Funk & Scott Index-International* (19), and the *Funk & Scott Index of Corporate Change* (19), containing merger and acquisition activities in the United States, reorganizations, liquidations, and bankruptcies, are excellent sources. In-depth studies on various industries are available—*Predicasts* (19), *Frost & Sullivan* (20), *Arthur D. Little Inc.* (21), *Stanford Research Institute* (22), to name but a few—provide data not readily available from the above mentioned sources. However, it is important to note that such research studies are generally expensive.

The primary source of corporate information is obtained, of course, from the company itself. An analyst before writing about a specific company would study the annual reports, interims, news releases, proxies, prospectuses, and listing statements. He would also check the *Disclosure Inc.* service (23) which contains full texts of approximately 100,000 filings released to the public by the Securities and Exchange Commission. Some of the essential reports for accurate financial analysis are the 10-K report which is the annual report filed by a company with the SEC and contains more complete information than the company's annual report to the stockholder, and the 8-K report which contains information of unscheduled events or corporate changes. The *Disclosure Inc.* service also furnishes quarterly reports, registration statements, and prospectuses. Information can be obtained on microfiche or hard copy.

SOURCES OF U.S. GOVERNMENT TECHNICAL AND TRADE INFORMATION

Weekly reports providing a comprehensive overview of technical reports and studies produced or sponsored by government agencies are available at a nominal fee from the *National Technical Information Service* (24). Individual reports are available in the following areas:

Administration
Biomedical Technology and Engineering
Building Technology
Business and Economics
Control and Information Theory
Environmental Pollution and Control
Industrial Engineering
Library and Information Science
Materials Science
Transportation
Urban Technology

The *Business and Economics Report* should be of interest to all analysts.

SUMMARY OF WORLD TECHNICAL AND TRADE LITERATURE

The vast outpouring of technical and trade literature is made somewhat manageable by a useful service which provides weekly tables of contents of all leading U.S. and international scientific and trade publications. Articles can be provided through a tear sheet service. The publication is *Current Contents* (25), published by the Institute for Scientific Information. Individual contents are available for the following topics:

Agriculture, Biology, and Environmental Sciences
Engineering and Technology
Life Sciences
Physical and Chemical Science
Clinical Practice
Behavioral, Social, and Educational Science

SOURCES OF FOREIGN INVESTMENT AND BUSINESS INFORMATION

1. *U.S. Department of Commerce, Bureau of International Commerce, Washington, D.C.*

   The Bureau has a staff studying economic trends, patterns of trade, legislation, and regulation policies in over 100 countries. It provides a checklist of international business publications.
2. *Foreign Chambers of Commerce in the United States*

   Many countries maintain Chambers of Commerce in certain major cities such as New York and Washington. For example, the Japanese Chamber of Commerce has offices in New York, Los Angeles, Chicago, and Honolulu.
3. *U.S. Chamber of Commerce, Washington, D.C.*

Provides information on a variety of publications, for example, *Foreign Commerce Handbook, Guide to Foreign Information Sources,* etc.

Foreign and Government Trade Associations in the United States

4. *Organizations representing foreign governments or private industry have offices in major U.S. cities.* For example:

Japanese Trade Council, Inc. Washington, D.C.; and Japanese External Trade Organizations with offices in New York and San Francisco

5. *United Nations Bookstore, New York*

Distributes a vast number of detailed reports on foreign countries. Of general interest are *Statistical Year Book, Yearbook of National Account Statistics, Industrial Research and Development News, Industrial Productivity Bulletin,* and *World and Regional Economic Surveys.*

6. *U.S. Commercial Banks with Foreign Branches*

7. *Foreign Banks with U.S. Branches*

8. *International Bank for Reconstruction and Development (World Bank), Washington, D.C.*

The staff of experts provides a great deal of published material relating to its function of providing expertise, direct loans, and encouraging loans.

9. *International Monetary Fund, Washington, D.C.*

Publishes *International Financial Statistics,* the standard reference for such information.

10. *Committee for Economic Development, New York*

The committee has available reviews of the economic growth and trade of many countries.

CASE STUDY

Let us suppose an analyst was assigned the task of researching a paper company. He would undoubtedly request from his library the corporate file and also the corporate files on various companies in the same field for purposes of comparison. The files would contain annual reports, proxies, listing statements, prospectuses, newspaper clippings, magazine articles, and studies published by various investment banking and brokerage houses. He would ask for the subject files on the industry such as American Paper Institute's *Statistics of Paper* and the federal government publications, *Printing and Publishing, Pulp and Paper, Pulp, Paper and Board, Paper Manufacturing and Printing.* He might consult Kline's *Marketing Guide to the Paper and Pulp Industry* and Lockwood's *Directory of Paper and Allied Trades.* The analyst might check *Demand and Price Situation for Forest Products,* the *Paper Trade Journal, Forest Industries, Official Board Market,* and newsprint consumption statistics. He would also use Standard & Poor's basic and current surveys on the paper industry. If circumstances warranted it, he might also check the *Official Summary of Securities Transactions and Holdings,* a monthly publication giving changes in stock ownership by officers, directors, and beneficial owners of more than 10 percent of a security. The various trade publications would be located in the references (3, 4, 5) given above.

COMPUTERIZED SERVICES

The computer is being increasingly used as a research tool. The October 1971 issue of *Institutional Investor* contained a tabulation of services available to institutions. The list was admittedly incomplete, and it is very likely that some of the companies mentioned are no longer in the field. However, there are many new services that are currently available.

The article also referred to the SEC's *Institutional Investor Study* indicating that recent statistics show that approximately two thirds of all investment advisers use computers, but that computer usage as a tool for research is considerably less. A list of some of the computer services follows:

1. *Data Resources Inc., Lexington, Massachusetts*—The DRI Economic Information System, designed to implement industry analysis. Macroeconomic estimates aggregated over both eight-quarter and ten-year time horizons for 79 industries. Federal Reserve Board Production Indices for 41 indices. Includes a data bank of nearly 7,000 economic and industry time series.

2. *Bunker-Ramo, Trumbull, Connecticut*—Telequote III—Market monitor displaying up-to-the-second market statistics. Prices on thousands of securities and commodities traded on more than 20 exchanges. Market Decision—System 7 can provide tickers, newswires, statistical recap, volume most active, most advanced, most declines, averages. commodity recap, commodity watch, dividends, ex-dividend dates, and net change. NASDAQ accepts and distributes quotations for OTC securities. Reports each individual bid/ask quote and computes a "representative quotation" based on the median bid and median spread.

3. *Interactive Data Corporation, Waltham, Massachusetts*—Large-scale time-sharing services involving heavy computations and core storage, specialized services provided for finance and treasury departments, portfolio management departments, and economists. Analyzes economic, financial, and user-generated time-series data.

4. *Computer Directions Advisors, Inc., Silver Spring, Maryland*—CDA Composite Filter Report provides flexibility in screening all NYSE and ASE common stocks, that is, dividend yield, earnings growth-absolute, earnings growth-relative, P/E ratio-absolute, P/E ratio-relative, relative price strength, price volatility, beta coefficient.

5. *Wharton Econometric Forecasting Associates, Inc., Philadelphia, Pennsylvania*—Wharton Short-Term Model Forecast extends for eight quarters in the future, provides estimate of GNP categories. Annual Model—long run projections for a ten-year period. Macro model prediction and simulation activities, special studies performed on a contract basis.

6. *Edie Economics—Lionel D. Edie & Company, wholly owned subsidiary of Merrill Lynch, Pierce, Fenner, and Smith, New York, N.Y.* Unique economic data base for both economic and financial analysis. Special programs for company analysis: Confidential written publications and special reports, ranging from general economic environment to specific market and product forecasts.

7. *Dean Witter & Co. Inc., New York, N.Y.* Oracle Information System —monitors every transaction for 2,420 listed common stocks on the NYSE and ASE.

8. *Telerate Systems Incorporated, New York, N.Y.* Computerized Information Network—instant information on current listings of commercial paper rates, secondary markets in CDs, bankers acceptance rates, dealer commercial paper rates, current prime rates of major banks throughout the country, foreign exchange rates.

Many more services could be listed, but the above should give some idea of the wealth of information available. It should be pointed out that many government publications are now available on microfiche and tapes. They are relatively inexpensive and great space savers.

Sources referred to above are given at the end of Chapter 33.

33

Key Reference Sources

SYLVIA MECHANIC
Business Librarian
Brooklyn Public Library, Brooklyn, New York

INFORMATION SOURCES—GENERAL BUSINESS AND ECONOMIC CONDITIONS

Fortunate, indeed, is the financial analyst who can do the bulk of his research in his own company library. He has learned the value of the special files provided by the library staff; he knows the arrival dates of his most needed newspapers and periodicals. In addition, he has had the opportunity to familiarize the librarian with his special interest needs and has established a rapport with all of the members of the library staff. He has also learned that his librarians don't limit themselves to files and printed materials. A telephone call to a colleague in another special library will often elicit an elusive statistic, a company's address, or the name of a newly appointed executive when these facts are not available in his own company library.

Still more fortunate is the financial analyst who works in one of the larger cities such as Boston, Cleveland, Dallas, Detroit, New York, Newark, or Philadelphia where even stronger collections of distinctive materials are maintained in the special business libraries of central public library systems. This analyst has an overwhelming supply of facts and figures at his beck and call. His dilemma soon becomes one of evaluation and selection. He needs to determine the quality and the accuracy of these resources and become aware of the materials which are most current and most comprehensive.

The literature of business and economics is a constantly changing one which must reflect everything from a change in corporate executive structure to the worldwide effects of the devaluation of the dollar in America. The need for up-to-date information is absolutely paramount and accounts for the great dependence of the analyst on "nonbook" materials—newspapers, periodicals, loose-leaf services, reports, and monographs. As a matter of fact, the business world is well noted for its need for specific information "yesterday."

No one article or text can supply the financial analyst with all of the information sources he will ever need. The titles mentioned in this section should serve as a springboard to the literature to be examined and may very well supply the analyst with suggestions for sources for future use. In addition, there are two excellent pamphlets which should be required reading for all financial analysts, businessmen, and executives who are dependent, in any way, on the literature of the business world—*Business Reference Sources* (26), by Lorna Daniells, business librarian of the Graduate School of Business Administration at Harvard University;[1] and the newly revised, fourth edition of the now basic work, *How to Use the Business Library with Sources of Business Information* (27), by Herbert Johnson. Since government publications are so very important in supplying basic statistical and textual information needed by the analyst, he will want to be placed on a free mailing list to receive the *Selected U.S. Government Publications* (28) list issued monthly by the Superintendent of Documents, U.S. Government Printing Office, Washington, D.C. 20402. He will also want to request at least two of the free price lists issued from this same office. These are lists arranged by subject which indicate the titles as well as the prices of publications which are available for sale. *Price List 62* is on commerce and includes, as well, publications which relate to business, patents, trademarks, and foreign trade. *Price List 70*, census publications, includes statistics of agriculture, business, government, housing, manufactures, minerals, population, and maps. The financial analyst will want to find out whether there is now a government documents book store in his city where he will be able to purchase the more popular titles, as well as single issues of many of the more important government periodicals and newspapers. He will want to visit this book store periodically to pick up free book lists, price lists, and other promotional data as well as to note new publications which may be of interest to him. Frequent visits to one of the larger book stores in his city will also enable the alert financial analyst to browse through recently received texts which may prove helpful.

Newspapers, Periodicals, etc.

The successful financial analyst must be an omnivorous reader who knows that almost any event which is reported in the newspaper, whether

---

[1] See list of Reference Sources at the end of this chapter for publication information on numbered titles.

it makes the headlines or not, will reflect in some way the actions of some sector of business, economics, or finance. The analyst should make a daily perusal of the *New York Times* and *Wall Street Journal.* Important too, is the fact that these two dailies have their own indexes. The *New York Times Index* is published semimonthly and cumulates annually into what is undoubtedly one of the most comprehensive, most analytical indexes of any one publication to be found. While delayed, at times, in publication and often very difficult to use quickly, it is an absolutely exhaustive chronicle of world events. The *Wall Street Journal Index* is published monthly and is a divided index. The first part is an alphabetical indexing of corporate news; the second part indexes general news. Book reviews are indexed under the letter *b,* and the last page of each monthly index has a listing of the Dow Jones averages on a daily basis. These monthly issues are cumulated into an annual bound volume. The financial analyst who relies on these two daily newspapers has the very comforting feeling that should he again have to refer to something he remembers reading in one of these dailies, the indexes to them are available. Another Dow Jones newspaper, *The National Observer,* also has its own index, and there is now a monthly *Newspaper Index* (29) published by Bell & Howell which indexes the *Chicago Tribune, Los Angeles Times, New Orleans Times-Picayune,* and the *Washington Post.* The analyst who is concerned with foreign opinion has access to another excellent newspaper index, the index to the *Times* of London. Other daily newspapers of more specialized interest include the *Journal of Commerce* (30), the *American Banker* (31), the *Daily News Record* (32), and *Women's Wear Daily* (32). One of the more recent entries in the newspaper publishing field, *The Media General Financial Weekly* (33), has a veritable treasure house of statistical analysis as well as quotations for the various exchanges and articles featuring financial and economic trends. *Facts on File* (34), a weekly loose-leaf service, is another excellent digest of world events. This index cumulates frequently until the annual volume is completed. One of the most sophisticated of all business indexes, *Funk & Scott Index of Corporations and Industries* (19) is useful for checking periodical articles. However, since it does index the financial pages of the *New York Times* and feature articles appearing in the *Wall Street Journal* and is issued weekly, it is often the answer to an analyst's prayer.

If the number of newspapers dealing with the general and specialized areas of business is a relatively limited one, the same thing cannot be said about periodicals in the field. Indeed, the number of useful business periodicals absolutely staggers the imagination. The busy financial analyst has been reading or skimming *Business Week* and/or *Newsweek* and/or *Time* and/or *U.S. News and World Reports* since his college days. He is most familiar with the economic indicators found in each week's issue of *Business Week.* He knows that business failures and operating ratios appear as a regular feature of *Dun's* (35), and he awaits each monthly issue of *Fortune* and the *Institutional Investor* (36). He tries to find time to look at the table of contents of three of the most basic of all government periodicals which supply him with statistical data. He is absolutely at home with the type of statistics found there; he needs to be aware of the many fine feature articles which appear in the *Federal Reserve Bulletin* (28), the *Monthly Labor Review* (28), and the *Survey of Current Business* (28).

In order to identify the ever increasing number of business periodicals, the analyst should be familiar with the most frequently consulted periodical directories. The *Standard Periodical Directory* (4) now in its fourth edition is a classified listing of about 62,000 periodicals which range over about 230 different subject areas. It is undoubtedly one of the most exhaustive compilations to be found and includes loose-leaf and financial services as well as listings of house organs and U.S. government publications. The *Ayer Directory of Newspapers, Magazines, and Trade Publications* (3) is an annual which lists titles geographically by location of publication. There is a brief description of each state and larger cities, giving much valuable information of an economic and social nature. Basic information is included for each of the more than 40,000 titles listed in over 220 different subject areas. There is, as well, an alphabetical index of titles, lists of newspapers arranged by frequency of publication, maps, statistics on the number of titles published, and other unique information making for a truly outstanding reference book. The *Standard Rate & Data* (6) service is issued in a number of different volumes and is designed primarily to give advertising rates and circulation data. The volume on *Business Publications* and the one on *Newspapers* are useful to the financial analyst who wants to be aware of the leading titles in each field which accept advertising. Included in these two volumes are listings of some of the outstanding titles published abroad. Finally the biennial *Ulrich's International Periodicals Directory* (5) is rich in its listings of foreign as well as domestic titles. It, too, supplies basic information about some 55,000 in-print publications on over 220 subject areas. Especially useful to the financial analyst is the inclusion of foreign bank letters.

Important as these periodicals are as a source of present, past, and future business and economic information here and abroad, their full value is realized and utilized only if they are among the significant titles indexed in one of the many basic periodical indexes. *Business Periodicals Index* (18) is one of the most frequently used of all available sources and is typical of the many periodical indexes published by the H. W. Wilson Co. It indexes about 170 titles, is arranged by subject, and now does include an indexing of book reviews. It is published monthly and then cumulates regularly until the bound volume is available. The special company library and the public business library will try to own as many of the 170 titles as they can handle, simply because of the general excellence of this index. Even more detailed and more analytical is the *Funk &*

Scott Index of Corporations and Industries (19) which is issued on a weekly basis, cumulates monthly, then quarterly, and finally annually. This superb reference tool indexes about 750 titles including newspapers, periodicals, newsletters, bank letters, brokerage house reports, and special industry and corporation reports. The first part of this index is arranged by SIC number and covers industries and products; the second section is an alphabetic arrangement by corporation. An excellent companion volume is the *Funk & Scott Index International* (19), a monthly which cumulates into a bound annual volume. This index is arranged first by SIC number, then by geographic area, and finally by corporation name. These three indexes will undoubtedly supply the financial analyst with the bulk of the periodical references he will need. *PAIS* (Public Affairs Information Service Bulletin (37) and the newly published *PAIS Foreign Language Index* are two more supplemental indexes which are useful in researching recently published books, pamphlets, and government documents in addition to periodicals which, by and large, are not indexed in the other periodical indexes. In addition to these fine general works, there are a great many periodical indexes which cover more specific areas: *Accountants' Index* (38), *Index of Economic Articles in Journals and Collective Volumes* (39), *Index of Supermarket Articles, Insurance Periodicals Index* (40), *Topicator* (41), and countless other indexes, each of which opens a veritable storehouse of information. Few research tools are easier to use or supply more pertinent information than the periodical index since each title includes periodicals usually not indexed elsewhere.

The busy financial analyst needs to be aware of anything and everything which has been published about his corporation and his industry and often needs to know about trends and activities in specific areas of business and economics. The librarian in his own company library will always manage to check and route periodicals to his attention and will try to be on the alert for needed books and reports once he has made known his need for this kind of service. This librarian will also be responsible for the preparation of specialized bibliographies when they are needed.

The financial analyst might be interested in knowing that about a dozen public libraries with special business collections located in such areas as Cleveland, Brooklyn, and Newark issue reading lists and bibliographies on a regular basis. Some of these are available for the asking; others are on a subscription basis. Most of these will be in the special company library as will special accession lists and other useful book aids. Since abstracts are such great time-savers, the financial analyst will want to be aware of the great number of abstracting services and periodicals which help to cut down the time spent in searching and in reading. *Economic Abstracts* (42) and the *Journal of Economic Literature* (43) published by the American Economic Association are two such basic sources. *Boardroom Reports* (44), which is published bimonthly, is a gleaning from hundreds of periodicals and investment advisory services designed to give the busy executive an awareness of the significant articles and trends appearing in some of the most frequently consulted titles. The *Wall Street Review of Books* (45), a quarterly edited by Robert Sobel, will enable even the busiest financial analyst to keep abreast of the many fine books which have been published in the fields of business and finance. *Business/Management Book Reviews* (46) is one of the latest attempts to provide condensations of significant titles. Even as this is written, there is an announcement of the publication of the *Review of the Financial Press* (47), edited by Kandel, which is concerned with the way the nation's press covers the world of business and finance.

The newsletter, that brief but informative kind of literature, has also proliferated to the extent that there is now a *Standard Directory of Newsletters* (4) classifying these publications under some 230 different subject headings. This directory is updated by the monthly *Newsletter on Newsletters* (48). Unfortunately the life span of this genre of publication is often a brief one due to the high cost of publishing. However, such established titles as the *Kiplinger Washington Letter* (49), the *Kiplinger Tax Letter* (49), and the *Whaley-Eaton American* (50), and *Whaley-Eaton Foreign Letter* (50) reflect succinctly, on a weekly basis, trends and happenings in the business and financial world. One of the most recent entries into the field of newsletters of interest to the financial analyst, is *Securities Week* (12) which attempts to cover the industry on a worldwide basis.

Another type of basic reference tool for the financial analyst needing business and economic statistics as well as information on trends in these fields is the bank letter. This is usually a slight publication, issued by the largest banks in the area, reflecting regional as well as national information. It usually includes, as well, comparative statistics for basic economic and financial indicators. To further facilitate the availability of local and regional information, each of the 12 Federal Reserve Banks issues a periodical and/or annual report which may be obtained free by requesting it from the regional office. The Library of the Federal Reserve Bank of Philadelphia has issued an excellent index, *Federal Reserve Bank Reviews Selected Subjects 1950–1970* which is kept up to date by the quarterly index, *The Fed in Print*. These special indexes may be obtained free of charge by requesting them from the Federal Reserve Bank of Philadelphia.

Books, Reports, Monographs, etc.

While the newspaper or periodical article may very well serve as a starting point for a particular study or speech, just as often much more detailed information is required. The financial analyst may then feel that he needs a whole book on a subject which is probably available in his own company library or in the business library of the main public library in his own city. Bibliographic references in the book he is using may then lead him to all of the other titles he will need. However, for additional references, *Business Books in Print* (5) is a basic starting point for still further titles in any business area. This is an invaluable annual volume, arranged by author, by title, and by subject, which supplies the interested financial analyst with price and publisher's name as well.

The astute analyst learned in his college days that some of the finest research in the field of business and economics is still being done at the various graduate schools of business administration throughout the country. He also learned that many of these publications are indexed annually in the *Bibliography of Publications of University Bureaus of Business and Economic Research* (51). This unique index is especially helpful when there is a need for detailed, sophisticated information on a specific geographic area or an industry indigenous to a particular location. At least four prestigious publishers of management and economic literature issue detailed indexes to their own publications which are often basic to the research work needed by the financial analyst. The American Management Association which sponsors many unique seminars and workshops throughout the year, publishes a great many books and monographs under its own imprint. It has an excellent library which is available to members and clients and provides reference assistance as well. Each month this organization issues a book list of recently published titles which is cumulated annually and decennially.

Business International (52), as its name implies, is concerned with events abroad as they affect our country and the world economy as well as the economic affairs of the individual foreign country. *Master Key Index* (52) is an invaluable aid for the analyst who needs information on a country or a company basis. Other monographs on executive compensation in foreign countries substantiate the importance of this series of materials. The Conference Board (formerly the National Industrial Conference Board) also has an excellent library as well as a referral service for its members. It is noted for its very fine publications in the field of business management and business economics. Periodically it issues reports on company practices in such areas as holiday time-off, company benefits, retirement plans, and company giving. Its *Cumulative Index* (53) is an absolute must when this kind of information is needed on a current basis. Finally, the National Bureau of Economic Research which is noted for its many scholarly works issues an annual cumulative index to its publications.

Loose-leaf services published by such basic companies as Commerce Clearing House, Bureau of National Affairs, Institute for Business Planning, and Prentice-Hall provide the financial analyst with data which is as late as the last filing. It would be difficult, indeed, to estimate the number of man-hours spent in libraries all over the country where staff has to put in a new page and remove an old one so that the borrower has the very latest material available. Congressional activity, labor, taxation, and trade are just a few subject areas which lend themselves to loose-leaf topical reporting.

In the routine of research, there is always a need to consult certain categories of books. The dictionary comes to mind immediately and the financial analyst certainly knows the location of the standard abridged and unabridged English and foreign language dictionaries. However, there are always specialized dictionaries which provide definitions in greater depth and help to clarify the meanings of words which might almost be synonyms. One of the best in the field of economics is the recently revised *McGraw-Hill Dictionary of Modern Economics* (12). Part one defines about 1,300 frequently used business and economics terms. Part two gives a description of about 200 organizations which are concerned with various aspects of business and economics. The new, seventh edition of the *Encyclopedia of Banking and Finance* (54) is an absolute *must* for anyone doing work in the field. In addition to giving excellent short summaries of words and concepts, this one-volume encyclopedia supplies the financial analyst with selected titles of additional works which may be consulted. Peter Wyckoff's *Language of Wall Street* (55) may prove helpful for the stricter meaning of an infrequently used investment term.

The special *Dictionary of Economic and Statistical Terms* (28) now in its second edition, issued by the U.S. Department of Commerce, is basic for every financial analyst who ever works with government reports and government periodicals. Here are defined all the terms used to cover such areas as national income and product accounts, balance of payments accounts, economic and statistical indicators, demographic and social terms, and economic and statistical terms as they appear in various government publications. Financial analysts will want to be aware of a most unique new reference work compiled by Disclosure, Inc., now part of the Reliance Group, in connection with their disclosure service. This is the new *Disclosure Financial Thesaurus* (23) which contains some 10,200 terms and is based on actual usage as analyzed through thousands of corporate reports filed with the U.S. Securities and Exchange Commission. Fact books like the *World Almanac, Information Please Almanac,* and the *Official Associated Press Almanac* (formerly the *New York Times Almanac*) are very often absolutely adequate when a simple fact or a statistical table is needed. On an international basis, few titles provide an easier source for quick facts than the *Statesman's Year Book* (56). The *U.S. Government Manual* (28) and the *Congressional Directory* (28) will supply the bulk of all needed, basic facts on the various personnel and agencies which go to make up our complex government.

Handbooks constitute still another favorite source of quick and most succinct information. Usually they include chapters written by noted practitioners in the particular field being covered. Very often these handbooks are most useful when they suggest further readings on a particular subject. *The Stock Market Handbook* (57), and *The Handbook of Business Administration* (12) are typical of the books which the financial analyst may want for his personal book collection.

Statistics

It is a well-known fact that the U.S. Government Printing Office is the largest publisher in the world. Just as apparent is the fact that the various governmental agencies collect and publish more statistics than any other single agency throughout the whole world. Indeed, so great is the total publishing output that there is still no one absolutely complete listing of all available government statistics published nor is there any one absolutely complete subject index to every single government statistical series. Basic to even the most superficial understanding of the whole government statistical program is the pamphlet, *Statistical Services of the U.S. Government* (28). Part one describes the statistical system of the federal government; part two presents brief descriptions of the principal economic and social statistical series collected by government agencies, and part three contains a brief statement of the statistical responsibilities of each agency with a list of its principal statistical publications. An organization chart in the back pocket of the pamphlet presents the whole federal statistical system and aids the user to search intelligently for the particular statistics needed.

The monthly *Statistical Reporter* (28) is another essential working tool for the financial analyst. It reports on current developments in federal statistics and includes notes on surveys, programs, major organizational changes, statistical publications, and federal statistical personnel. Perhaps one of its most important features is the listing of most of the basic economic indicators with an indication of the exact day of the month on which the new figures will be released.

Several indexes are useful in locating the odd or the elusive figure or in helping to substantiate that one has really checked the basic as well as the more sophisticated sources generally consulted. *Statistics Sources* (1) by Paul Wasserman, now in its third edition, is an excellent starting point. This is a subject guide to primary and secondary statistical sources. The recently published *American Statistics Index* (58) is one of the most ambitious projects ever attempted. It is a guide as well as an index to the exhaustive statistical output of U.S. government agencies. Volume I is an index; Volume II contains abstracts of data; and the third volume updates the basic first two. John L. Andriot's *Guide to U.S. Government Statistics* (59), in the newly revised edition, also proves a helpful start when detailed figures are needed.

Without a doubt, the one most important of all government statistics guides is the *Statistical Abstract of the United States* (28). This is an annual publication which first appeared in 1878 as a 157-page book. The 94th annual edition for 1973 has 1,014 pages and is probably the most frequently consulted of all statistical works. Its importance lies in the fact that it is updated annually, covers new subjects and areas in each edition, often gives comparative statistics for a five or ten-year period, and, most important of all, indicates the basic sources from which the statistics have been abstracted. It thus serves as a prime source for recent information as well as a bibliographical guide to sources of basic statistical data. As a matter of fact, one of the many, many outstanding features of this abstract is a listing, in one place, of the sources from which data has been abstracted. In many ways, the *Statistical Abstract* may be said to be constantly updated by a number of government periodicals also published at a regular frequency.

There are about six titles out of the innumerable statistically oriented government periodicals which will probably supply the average financial analyst with all of the basic business and economic statistics, on a current basis, he will ever need for almost any nonspecialized report. These are *Business Conditions Digest* (28) with its *Advanced Business Conditions Digest* (28), needed by the specialist in business cycle analysis; *Defense Indicators* (28), important for its coverage of the relationship of defense spending to the economics of the country; *Economic Indicators* (28), the working tool of the Council of Economic Advisers which has, as well, a supplement giving retrospective statistics; the *Federal Reserve Bulletin* the most comprehensive survey of the banking field available, including articles as well as statistics; the *Monthly Labor Review* (28) which also contains articles as well as statistics including the all-significant Consumer Price Index, broken down by geographic area as well as by component parts; and last, but most important of all, the *Survey of Current Business* with its Biennial supplement *Business Statistics* (28). In addition to up-dating thousands of statistics each and every month, this periodical has articles on National Income, Foreign Investments and other subjects of vital concern to all who deal in any way with business and economics.

When early data is needed, *Historical Statistics of the United States*, from *Colonial Times to 1967* (28) and its supplements may be consulted. *Long-term Economic Growth* 1860–1970 (28) will save the busy financial analyst many hours of tedious work in compiling long-run statistical data.

While business and economic statistics are most frequently needed on a national basis, there is just as often a need for state, county, and even local figures. Interestingly enough, almost every state in the United States and almost every foreign country in the world now issues its own yearbook or statistical abstract. There is a most complete "Guide to State Statistical Abstracts" which appears in each volume of the *Statistical*

Abstract of the United States. Analysts will certainly want to be familiar with the volume which relates to their subject assignment. State and local chambers of commerce, employment offices, and graduate schools of business administration often issue materials relating to economic trends and statistics on a state as well as a local basis. Two government publications, *County Business Patterns* (28), an annual which includes a volume for each state as well as a United States summary, and *County and City Data Book* (28) are absolutely definitive sources for the information they supply.

There are at least two unique annual reports which should be mentioned at this point simply because of the mass of statistical information they contain—material which is often difficult, if not impossible, to find elsewhere. The *Economic Report of the President* (28), together with the *Annual Report of the Council of Economic Advisors,* (28) contains an analysis of current developments in employment, production, and purchasing power, as well as recommendations for policy action. The statistical appendixes present supporting data on a present, as well as a retrospective, basis. The *Manpower Report of the President* (28) reviews the nation's employment situation and reports progress and new developments in manpower programs. Again, the statistical appendix is rich with tables on the labor force, employment and unemployment, projections of population, employment and educational attainment, manpower requirements, and manpower programs. A recently compiled ten-year index to these *manpower reports* becomes still one more tool for the financial analyst. Annual reports of such agencies as the U.S. Federal Communications Commission, the Federal Trade Commission, the Interstate Commerce Commission, and the Securities and Trade Commission provide still further statistical data.

2 INFORMATION SOURCES: INDUSTRY ANALYSIS

One of the very best single sources of information for the financial analyst who is just learning the field or who is going into a new field is, without doubt, the *Encyclopedia of Business Information Sources* (1). The long subtitle best describes its contents—a detailed listing of primary subjects of interest to managerial personnel, with a record of sourcebooks, periodicals, organizations, directories, handbooks, bibliographies, and other sources of information on each topic. The first volume ranges from a review of the literature of the *a*brasive industry to a listing of the basic sources of information on the zinc industry. Volume two is a delineation of the same kinds of basic sources which pertain to each of the countries of the world.

The financial analyst going into a new industry analysis will want to become familiar with as many aspects of this industry as possible. This is most easily done by reading or skimming a history relative to his individual field. A check in any library card catalog, the *Subject Guide to Books in Print* (5), or the somewhat dated but still basic *Guide to Business History* (60), by Henrietta Larson, will make the analyst aware of the people and the companies which are such an important part of the growth and the expansion of any industry. While the financial analyst is certainly not expected to be a scientist or a mathematician or a jack-of-all-trades, he should have more than a nodding acquaintance with the terminology which relates to his specialized industry. An encyclopedia, a dictionary, a handbook or manual, or an individual corporation history are usually available and should be a basic part of the financial analyst's working collection. Again, the *Subject Guide to Books in Print* or a basic bibliography should be consulted. The *Management Information Guides,* (1) a continuing series of basic bibliographies on important business subjects, cover such industries and services as accounting, building construction, computers and data processing, electronics, food and beverage, insurance, packaging, public utilities, real estate, textiles, and transportation.

It would be hard to find a single more important source of basic information on an individual industry than the trade association or the society which pertains to the financial analyst's particular field of interest. This is the group which exists to further the well-being of the industry or profession in every way possible. This is the group which sponsors conventions and is responsible for the publishing of proceedings, annual reports, periodicals, statistics, a membership directory—almost any type of information which assists and furthers the growth of the industry.

The *Encyclopedia of Associations* (1), published by Gale Research and revised every several years, is the standard work in the field. Associations are arranged in some 17 sections by subject, followed by section 18 which lists those organizations which are now inactive, defunct, or have changed their names. The whole work is then pulled together with an excellent alphabetic and key-word index. For each listing there is an address, phone number, date of founding, purpose of the association, an executive listing, membership number, indications of major publications, annual meeting dates, and other pertinent data. Volume two has a geographic listing of all of the associations in the base volume as well as an alphabetic listing of all of the executives mentioned. Volume three is a quarterly loose-leaf updating of this unique service. Also most useful because it is issued annually is the directory, *National Trade and Professional Associations of the United States and Labor Unions* (2). In addition to the standard kinds of information which one would expect to find in such a directory, it provides a special Budget Index arranged in eight budget categories ranging from $10,000 to over $1 million.

Every financial analyst is thoroughly familiar with the Standard & Poor's loose-leaf service, *Industry Surveys* (9). This exhaustive two-volume set has a basic and a current analysis of over 40 major industries, and a fine analytic index which makes information readily available for about 1,000 corporations. *Value Line* (61) is another one of the multitude of financial services which is arranged on an industry basis and helps the financial analyst pinpoint needed information with a minimum of effort. Industry surveys prepared by large banks and by leading brokerage houses add to the mass of information which the financial analyst may peruse.

One of the very fine surveys of industry appears each year in the periodical, *Forbes* (usually in the first January issue). This is called "Annual Report on American Industry" and supplies information in a number of different categories. Another invaluable government publication is the annual *U.S. Industrial Outlook 197– with Projections to 198–*. (28) This volume contains a detailed analysis of more than 200 individual manufacturing and nonmanufacturing industries, or closely related industry groups, arranged in ten major sections. The industries covered in this volume account for about 85 percent of the value of shipments of all manufacturing industries. When basic sources of information prove inadequate for one reason or another, or when time seems to be running out, the financial analyst always has the option of purchasing a detailed, usually very expensive survey of a particular industry. The monthly periodical, *Marketing Information Guide* (62), is an excellent source for finding the names of recently released market surveys completed by such consulting firms as Arthur D. Little, Frost & Sullivan, Predicasts, and a host of other firms who will either sell a prepared study or prepare one to order. *Data Sources for Business & Market Analysis* (63) by Frank, is a veritable gold mine of information in this field.

Trade periodicals and such specialized newspapers as the *American Banker*, the *American Metal Market*, and the *Women's Wear Daily* are among the most important sources for up-to-date information, as well as future trends, for any industry. The periodical guides already mentioned, as well as the specialized indexes for these periodicals, again enable the busy financial analyst to find the specific industry information he needs. There are at least five specialized government periodicals which are just about the most definitive sources in their respective fields: *Construction Review; Containers and Packaging; Copper; Printing & Publishing*, and *Pulp, Paper, and Board* (28).

Statistical data on an individual industry is almost without end. As a matter of fact, it would take a detailed course in the field of government documents to familiarize one with the extent of material available either in hard copy, in microfiche, or on tapes. The *Monthly Catalog of U.S. Government Publications* (28) is, of course, the most comprehensive of all listings of government publications. This is arranged by issuing agency and lists major printed publications with needed bibliographical detail. It has, as well, a separate series of indexes arranged first by subject, then by author, and then by title. The exhaustive annual index appears in the December issue, and the back page of each *catalog* lists the government printing book stores throughout the country. The U.S. Department of Commerce issues an annual index to its publications; the U.S. Bureau of the Census issues a monthly list of its publications which cumulates quarterly and then appears in a cumulative annual. These indexes include, as well, information on the kinds of data available in the agencies which can be provided on an individual basis as needed. These three basic indexes plus those already mentioned should make available to the financial analyst the bulk of the government statistics he will probably ever need. Finally, the *Business Service Checklist* (28), a weekly guide to U.S. Commerce Department publications, is as valuable as a listing of newly issued publications as it is for its inclusion of key business indicators, including comparative data.

Before attempting to delve too closely into government-prepared statistics, the financial analyst must be thoroughly familiar with the *Standard Industrial Classification Manual* (28) or the SIC, as it is popularly called. This is a classification scheme which is widely used in government and nongovernmental reporting and indexing. It covers the entire field of economic activities—agriculture, forestry, construction, manufacturing, transportation, retail trade, real estate, and government. Arranged alphabetically by principal product, process, and service, it lists four-digit codes for each classification. The most comprehensive collections of statistics covering business and industry are, of course, the *U.S. Census of Business* (28) and the *U.S. Census of Manufactures* (28) which is kept up to date by the *Annual Survey of Manufactures*. The *Census of Business* encompasses three distinctive sections—retail trade, wholesale trade, and selected services. The *Census of Manufactures* has two distinctive parts: The area reports provide data on value added by manufacturing, employment, payrolls, new capital expenditures, and number of establishments; the final industry reports are separate reports presenting data on value of shipments, capital expenditure, value added by manufacturing, cost of materials, and employment for some 430 manufacturing industries. These data are shown by geographic region and state, employment size, class of establishment, and degree of primary products specialization.

In addition to the *Annual Survey* which updates the *census* there is a *Current Industrial Reports* (28) series of more than 100 current monthly, quarterly, or annual commodity reports on the production, inventories, and orders for some 5,000 products which represent one third of all U.S. manufacturing. Still another publication which may be said to supplement the *Census of Business* is *Business Statistics*, the biennial supplement to the *Survey of Current Business* which, with the *Statistical Abstract*, supply the bulk of statistics needed on a current basis. Further specialized government documents include *Growth Pace Setters in American Industry* (28), a comprehensive study of 55 U.S. industries whose sales and growth rate set them high above the national average in the decade 1958–1968 and *Industry Profiles,* a comprehensive statistical report providing a comparative analysis of 12 years of performance (1957–1970) by the nation's 409 manufacturing industries.

Other significant U.S. Census reports include the *U.S. Census of Agriculture, U.S. Census of Mineral Industries, U.S. Census of Population, U.S. Census of Transportation,* and related monthlies and annuals which help the bewildered financial analyst in his constant search for latest official figures. A most comforting thought for all who rely on these official statistics is the fact that there is a *Federal Statistical Directory* (28) which is revised frequently. This directory lists, by agency and by appropriate organization unit, the name and location of key persons engaged in statistical programs, whether or not classified as statisticians. When all else fails, and the local field office of the U.S. Census Bureau is unable to supply needed statistics, a telephone call to the Washington, D.C. expert listed in this booklet will provide the caller with the information needed or else the comforting assurance that the statistics he needs are really not made available as requested or that it is just too soon to obtain figures required.

While most statistics of industry are taken from government reports, very often those issued by trade associations are much easier to read and to use. Fact books have always been a favorite kind of reference tool, simply because they are usually published on an annual basis and somehow seem to be arranged just the way one needs them to be in order to obtain certain kinds of information and statistics. The number and range of this type of publication is truly amazing, and one finds the usual gamut from *Automobile Facts/Figures* to *Yearbook of Railroad Facts.* Most of these publications are pamphlets which are either free for the asking or relatively inexpensive. Standard & Poor's *Trade & Securities: Statistics* (9), revised regularly, is still another source of industry statistics on a wide scale, covering thousands of series.

Another type of statistic often needed by the financial analyst involves commodity prices. There is one excellent guide, *Commodity Prices—A Source Book and Index* (1) by Wasserman, which is most helpful in indicating which newspaper or trade periodical regularly publishes prices for specific commodities. The *Commodity Year Book,* an annual which is supplemented by the *Commodity Year Book Statistical Abstract* (64) serves as the most important single volume for listing prices and other basic information on a current and a retrospective basis. The *Journal of Commerce,* on a daily basis, and the *Chemical Marketing Reporter* (65), published weekly, are two of the best sources for current prices.

The financial analyst is always concerned about the financial and the operating ratios of an industry. The Robert Morris Associates, an accounting firm in Philadelphia, publishes an excellent small pamphlet, *Sources of Financial Data* (66). This is arranged by broad industry and has a subject index as well as a listing under the categories of manufacturing, wholesaling, retailing, and services. Again, it is worth pointing out that many of the titles listed in this bibliography are available free simply by requesting them from the organization issuing them. The operating ratios themselves may be found in such general publications as the *Annual Statement Studies* by Robert Morris Associates, the *Barometer of Small Business* (67) issued by the Accounting Corporation of America, various *Key Business Ratios* (35) issued by Dun & Bradstreet, and the *Almanac of Business & Industrial Financial Ratios* (68), a loose-leaf service by Troy.

Of special interest to the financial analyst is still another government periodical, *Quarterly Financial Report for Manufacturing Corporations* (28), issued jointly by the U.S. Federal Trade Commission and the U.S. Securities and Exchange Commission. It covers financial statistics including sales, profits, assets, liabilities, stockholders' equity, and related accounts and ratios, classified both by industry group and asset size. A companion title, *Rates of Return in Selected Manufacturing Industries* (28), covers a ten-year period and gives rates of return on stockholders' investments for 257 identical companies in 21 selected manufacturing industries. Unusual for a government publication, is the delineation of actual company names, with data.

In addition to knowing as much as possible about the present and past status of an industry, the financial analyst must be able to make some sort of forecast about trends and prices and potential earnings for his industry. *Business Forecasting for the 1970* (26), by Lorna Daniells, and *Business Trends and Forecasting: Information Sources* (1), by Woy, are two basic bibliographies in this field.

There is, in addition, *Predicasts* (19), which is a *must* for every financial analyst who ever has to make a forecast. This is a quarterly publication which cumulates into an annual and contains the synthesis of the abstracting of over 500 trade journals, government documents, newspapers, and business and financial services. Statistics are presented for the present base period and projected for a short- and a long-range period on the basis of the articles abstracted. Most important, there is a listing of the sources from which these statistics were taken so that the interested analyst may then read for himself the complete article. Statistics are included for social as well as economic, service, and manufacturing series. Like the other publications prepared by Funk & Scott, the statistics are arranged by SIC number. Of interest, too, is a listing of the names of all publications which have been abstracted. There is, as well, a companion set called *World Regional Casts* (19) and *World Product Casts* (19). These volumes offer the same kind of forecast data on a worldwide basis.

The *U.S. Industrial Outlook* (28) is another excellent source for forecast information on specific industries, as is the *U.S. Occupational Out-*

look Handbook (28) for forecast data on occupations as well as industries. For those looking for some sort of official guidance for an even later period of time, *A Look at Business in 1990* (28) is the summary of a White House Conference on the Industrial World Ahead which took place in Washington in February 1972. Standard & Poor's *Trends & Projections* (9) is a monthly which attempts to forecast industry statistics.

There are a great many organizations which do economic forecasting, and, again, the busy financial analyst may contract for a particular study. One of the most prestigious of the many organizations which issue detailed reports is the National Planning Association. In addition to its monthly *Looking Ahead* (69), it releases at least two very expensive, very sophisticated series: *National Economic Projections Series* and *Regional Economic Projection Series.*

3 SOURCES OF INFORMATION: COMPANY ANALYSIS

There is a veritable storehouse of information available which relates to almost all aspects of the operations of publicly traded companies. This is to be found in the ten different financial reports which each such company prepares. Eight of these ten reports are required by the U.S. Securities and Exchange Commission—the 10-K, 10-Q, 8-K, Proxy Statement, Registration Statement, Prospectus, N1R and N1Q. Two reports are optional—the Annual Report to Shareholders and the Listing Application. It has been estimated that each year about 100,000 reports are filed with the SEC for about 10,000 publicly held companies. These various reports, as outlined, supply the financial analyst with the richest single source of detailed information on the company or companies being researched.

Within the past several years, Disclosure, Inc. (formerly Leasco and now part of the Reliance Group) was made the official agent for handling the reproduction and distribution of all these filings which are now available for sale either in hard copy or microfiche. These reports are made available to subscribers ten days after being submitted to the SEC. In New York City, Washington, D.C., Chicago, and Los Angeles all these reports may be consulted in the field offices of the SEC where copying machines are made available for the quick reproduction of needed items. Basic and important as these various reports are to the financial analyst, the availability of a new title, the *Disclosure Journal* (23) has, for the first time, opened the contents of these ten different filings. Volume one of this set, *Company Resumes*, summarizes the various reports which have been filed by each company; volume two, *Cumulative Index*, cross-references these reports under some 7,000 terms relating to general business, finance, accounting, legal, and social issues. This *Disclosure Journal* is a monthly which cumulates until the bound volume is ready.

Having studied the various corporate reports, visited the company's main headquarters and plant, attended the annual meeting of shareholders as well as the industry's annual convention, the financial analyst now needs to be aware of any and all changes in the company's every activity. On a weekly basis, the financial analyst will want to check the *Funk & Scott Index of Corporations and Industries* through the alphabetic index of companies. Also on a weekly basis, he will want to use the *Wall Street Transcript* which has an alphabetic index to company speeches, brokerage house reports, advisory services, articles, and analysts' meetings. On a monthly basis, the analyst may want to check the company listings which appear in the *Wall Street Journal Index* which will refer him to the date in which pertinent articles appeared in issues of the newspaper.

Since financial analysts are familiar with, and indeed are responsible for, the preparation of special brokerage house reports on companies as well as industries, it seems superfluous to mention that some of the best appraisals are found in these many publications. Obvious, too, are the commercial advisory services issued by such giants of the investment world as Moody, Standard & Poor's, and literally thousands of lesser-known companies and individuals. The *Directory of Business and Financial Services* (17), edited by Mary McNierney, is presently being revised and should prove to be the most important single source of obtaining the names, addresses, prices, and publishers of the basic business and advisory services available. The *Select Information Exchange* (70), edited by Wein, lists smaller, less well-known advisory services. Finally, the *Broker-Dealer and Investment Adviser Directory* (28) issued by the U.S. Securities and Exchange Commission helps to identify brokerage firms and individuals who are registered by this agency.

As the financial analyst does research on his industry or company, he will need to refer to basic directories which will supply him with needed up-to-date facts. The *Guide to American Directories: A Guide to Major Business Directories of the U.S. Covering All Industrial, Professional and Mercantile Categories* (10) is the basic bibliography in the field. It is presently in its eighth edition and contains a classified listing of the major directories being published in this country. One of the most frequently consulted directories is another Standard & Poor's publication, *Poor's Register of Corporations, Directors and Executives of the U.S. and Canada* (9). It is published annually and updated by supplements which provide changes in corporate executive structure. On a more current basis, the financial analyst may consult the *S&P Daily News* part of the *Standard Corporation Records* (9). Executive changes are also reported daily in the *Wall Street Journal* and the financial pages of the *New York Times*. The two annual volumes published by Dun & Bradstreet, the *Middle Market Directory* (35) and the *Million Dollar Directory* (35) make for an almost complete identification of most of the largest corporations in the United States. With these three titles at his disposal, the financial analyst can identify a company, learn its address, phone number, number of employees, SIC number, yearly sales volume, executive officers, products, trade names, and then find these companies arranged geographically as well as by product.

While these three directories are basic for the largest companies, there are literally thousands of directories available to the financial analyst either on a product or a geographic basis or a combination of the two. Each state of the United States and almost every foreign country in the world has at least one industrial directory available, published either as an official document or as a commercial venture. Most of the larger cities also have this kind of industrial directory giving much the same kind of background information. The *Thomas Register of American Manufacturers* (71) includes one volume which is an alphabetic listing of manufacturers giving address, phone number, products, subsidiaries, plant location, and, most important for smaller companies, some indication, by letter coding, of the company's assets. One of the most unique of business services is issued on microfiche by Dun & Bradstreet. This is an alphabetic listing of about 3.5 million firms which have a credit rating with this firm. It lists the firm name, its address, and an indication of whether it has a subsidiary. This is an absolutely invaluable source of identifying a company when one has only the name. Another most important directory for the financial analyst is *30,000 Leading U.S. Corporations* (72) published annually by the editors of *News Front* (73). This directory is arranged both alphabetically and by SIC number and gives about a half-dozen important facts for each of the companies included. Its main claim to distinction is the fact that it includes information about privately held, as well as publicly traded, companies—the kind of information most difficult to find elsewhere. Product directories also prove an assist to the financial analyst who is researching an industry and needs to be aware of the names of companies in the same or in related fields.

Financial analysts are familiar enough with the blue pages of the *S&P Standard Corporation Records* which list subsidiary companies. However, in this day of corporate merger and company takeover, there is need to be aware of other sources which will also supply this information. Again, the publishers of *Funk & Scott* issue a unique reference work, *Index of Corporate Change* (19). This work lists corporate name changes, subsidiaries and parent companies, and hard-to-find listings of companies in reorganization, liquidation, or bankruptcy. The *Standard Directory of Advertisers* (74) has a supplement called *Directory of Corporate Affiliations* which lists "who owns whom." The first part is a listing of parent companies with their divisions and subsidiaries; the second part arranges divisions, subsidiaries, and affiliates in alphabetic order, followed by the name of the parent company. This directory is updated three times a year. There is also a fine series of volumes published in London by O. W. Roskill called *Who Owns Whom* (15). One of the volumes in the series lists international subsidiaries of U.S. companies. The *Directory of American Firms Operating in Foreign Countries* (14) has been supplemented by a reverse volume, *Directory of Foreign Firms Operating in the United States* (14).

Special issues of periodicals have long been favorite sources for statistical information as well as for directory listings. One of the most well known and frequently used appears in several issues of *Fortune* and is, of course, the famous listing of the largest American and foreign firms, with various rankings and indications of changes in ranking over the years. The annual directory issue of *Forbes* also lists largest corporations by revenues, assets, market value, and net profits. It gives, as well, a listing of chief executives with their salaries—a listing which makes it possible to answer the perennial, "Who is the highest paid executive in the U.S.?" A special issue of *Business Week* also supplies listings of executive compensation, as does an expensive service issued by the American Management Association. As a matter of fact, one could devote an entire book to an enumeration of all of the special issues of periodicals which list the largest companies in individual fields, as well as those special issues which supply statistical information on a particular industry.

If there seems to be an absolute abundance of basic sources to research an individual listed or unlisted company, the same thing may be said about the availability of reference tools which give the background of an individual executive, provided he ranks about middle management and higher. Those of lesser responsibility pose a problem, and often the only thing one can find is a listing of their names in a membership directory. *Poor's Register* probably supplies the bulk of needed information, after which the Marquis publication, *Who's Who in Finance and Industry* (7), proves most resourceful. From there on there are literally hundreds of biographical directories which may be consulted, depending on the rank or background or profession of the individual. There is the very familiar *Who's Who in America* (7), *Who's Who in the East* (7), *Who's Who in the West* (7), and many other similar works based on geographic location. On a professional basis there is a *Who's Who in Advertising* (75), *Who's Who in Banking* (76), and *Who's Who in Consulting* (1). There is a *Celebrity Register* (77), *Current Biography* (18), and even a special index of profiles which have appeared in the *New Yorker* magazine. Almost every country in the world is represented through a type of Who's Who. Finally, membership lists prove an invaluable source, when all else fails, to verify the spelling of an individual's name or to ascertain that he is, indeed, in a particular profession.

The range of information in the field of business and finance is almost limitless and, as every financial analyst is aware, there is a whole new field of information retrieval made possible through the use of the computer. Reports and analyses heretofore considered too time consuming and too involved to undertake are now part of the everyday work of the programmer who delights in the completion of a sophisticated project. Hundreds of computer-based advisory and statistical services now monitor every aspect of stock market transaction, supplying further information to an industry already inundated with information.

While the references supplied in these several chapters relate primarily to the United States, just as many titles might be listed again to cover areas throughout the world. As a matter of fact, a whole book might very well be written on each of the units represented here. Sections of the books would have to be revised annually to keep abreast of new titles as well as new sources replacing older ones.

The financial analyst who uses his company and public library will find that the librarian becomes his best ally if he will only make known his special needs.

REFERENCE SOURCES FOR CHAPTERS 32 AND 33

1. Gale Research Co.
   Detroit, Michigan
2. Columbia Books, Inc.
   Washington, D.C.
3. Ayer Press
   Philadelphia, Pennsylvania
4. Oxbridge Publishing Co., Inc.
   New York, N.Y.
5. R. R. Bowker Company
   New York, N.Y.
6. Standard Rate & Data Service, Inc.
   Skokie, Illinois
7. Marquis Who's Who, Inc.
   Chicago, Illinois
8. Directory of Directors Co., Inc.
   New York, N.Y.
9. Standard & Poor's Corp.
   New York, N.Y.
10. B. Klein Publications, Inc.
    Rye, New York
11. C. B. D. Research, Ltd.
    Kent, England
12. McGraw-Hill Book Co.
    New York, N.Y.
13. Croner Publications, Inc.
    Queens Village, New York
14. World Trade Academy Press, Inc.
    New York, N.Y.

REFERENCE SOURCES (*Continued*)

15. O. W. Roskill & Co., Ltd.
    London, England
16. W. M. D. Publications
    Cedarhurst, New York
17. Special Libraries Association
    New York, N.Y.
18. H. W. Wilson Co.
    Bronx, New York
19. Predicasts, Inc.
    Cleveland, Ohio
20. Frost & Sullivan, Inc.
    New York, N.Y.
21. Arthur D. Little, Inc.
    Cambridge, Massachusetts
22. Stanford Research Institute
    Menlo Park, California
23. Disclosure, Inc.
    Silver Springs, Maryland
24. U.S. Department of Commerce
    Washington, D.C.
25. Institute for Scientific Information
    Philadelphia, Pennsylvania
26. Baker Library
    Graduate School of Business Administration
    Harvard University
    Boston, Massachusetts
27. South-Western Publishing Company
    Cincinnati, Ohio
28. Superintendent of Documents
    U.S. Government Printing Office
    Washington, D.C.
29. Bell & Howell
    Wooster, Ohio
30. Twin Coast Newspapers, Inc
    New York, N.Y.
31. American Banker, Inc.
    New York, N.Y.
32. Fairchild Publications
    New York, N.Y.
33. The M/G Financial Weekly
    Richmond, Virginia
34. Facts on File, Inc.
    New York, N.Y.

REFERENCE SOURCES (*Continued*)

35. Dun & Bradstreet
    New York, N.Y.
36. Institutional Investor Systems, Inc.
    New York, N.Y.
37. Public Affairs Information Service, Inc.
    New York, N.Y.
38. American Institute of Certified Public Accountants
    New York, N.Y.
39. Richard D. Irwin, Inc.
    Homewood, Illinois
40. Special Libraries Association: Insurance Division
    Boston, Massachusetts
41. Thompson Bureau
    Littleton, Colorado
42. Library of the Economic Information Service
    The Hague, Netherlands
43. American Economic Association
    Nashville, Tennessee
44. Boardroom Reports
    New York, N.Y.
45. Docent Publications
    Pleasantville, New York
46. Industrial Bookshelf, Inc.
    Murray Hill, New Jersey
47. Review of the Financial Press
    New York, N.Y.
48. The Newsletter Clearinghouse
    Rhinebeck, New York
49. Kiplinger Washington Agency
    Washington, D.C.
50. Whaley-Eaton Service
    Washington, D.C.
51. Association for University Business and Economic Research
    Boulder, Colorado
52. Business International Corporation
    New York, N.Y.
53. The Conference Board
    New York, N.Y.
54. Bankers Publishing Company
    Boston, Massachusetts
55. Hopkinson and Blake
    New York, N.Y.
56. St. Martin's Press
    New York, N.Y.

REFERENCE SOURCES (*Continued*)

57. Dow Jones–Irwin, Inc.
    Homewood, Illinois
58. Congressional Information Service
    Washington, D.C.
59. Documents Index
    McLean, Virginia
60. Harvard University Press
    Boston, Massachusetts
61. Arnold Bernhard & Co., Inc.
    New York, N.Y.
62. Hoke Communications, Inc.
    Garden City, New York
63. The Scarecrow Press, Inc.
    Metuchen, New Jersey
64. Commodity Research Bureau, Inc.
    New York, N.Y.
65. Schnell Publishing Co.
    New York, N.Y.
66. Robert Morris Associates
    Philadelphia, Pennsylvania
67. Accounting Corporation of America
    San Diego, California
68. Prentice-Hall, Inc.
    Englewood Cliffs, New Jersey
69. National Planning Association
    Washington, D.C.
70. Select Information Exchange
    New York, N.Y.
71. Thomas Publishing Company
    New York, N.Y.
72. News Front
    New York, N.Y.
73. Year, Inc.
    New York, N.Y.
74. National Register Publishing Co.
    Skokie, Illinois
75. Redfield Publishing Co.
    Rye, New York
76. Business Press, Inc.
    New York, N.Y.
77. Simon and Schuster
    New York, N.Y.

34

A Guide to Industry Publications

THE following guide to industry publications was compiled by the New York Society of Security Analysts. It provides a list of some of the more important trade publications and organizations. More complete listings are given in the various encyclopedias of trade publications listed in Sections 32 and 33 of this Handbook.

Advertising

Published	Source	Address
PERIODICALS		
Weekly (Magazine)	Advertising Age	740 Rush Street Chicago, Illinois 60611
Weekly (Newsletter)	Gallagher Reports, Inc.	230 Park Avenue New York, N.Y. 10017
Daily (Newspaper)	The New York Times Company	207 West 43d Street New York, N.Y. 10036
The Standard Directory of Advertising Agencies		
Quarterly (Directory)	National Register Publishing Co.	20 East 46th Street New York, N.Y. 10017
BOOKS		
What Advertising Agencies Are— What They Do And How They Do It		
1970 (7th Edition)	Frederic R. Gamble American Association of Advertising Agencies	200 Park Avenue New York, N.Y. 10017
The Advertising Agency Business		
1964	Kenneth Groesbeck Advertising Publications, Inc.—Advertising Age	Chicago, Illinois

Airlines

PERIODICALS		
Air Carrier Traffic Statistics		
Monthly (Statistics)	Civil Aeronautics Board (Publications Services Section)	Washington, D.C. 20428

Published	*Source*	*Address*

Air Carrier Financial Statistics

Quarterly	Civil Aeronautics Board	Washington, D.C. 20428
(Statistics)	(Publications Services Section)	

Airline Industry Data

1. All Cargo Supplemental Carriers
2. Regional Carriers
3. U.S. Trunkline Carriers and Pan American

Quarterly (each)	McDonnell Douglas Finance	3855 Lakewood Blvd.
(Statistics)	Corp.	Long Beach, Calif. 90801
	Airline Credit Analysis	

Airline Industry Economic Report

Quarterly (Booklet)	Civil Aeronautics Board	Washington, D.C. 20428

Airline Industry Financial Review and Outlook

Irregular, Usually	Air Transport Assn. of	1000 Connecticut Ave., NW
Annual (Booklet)	America	Washington, D.C. 20036

Airline Management & Marketing

Monthly	Airline Management &	One Park Avenue
(Magazine)	Marketing	New York, N.Y. 10016

Aviation Daily

Daily	Ziff-Davis Publishing Co.	1156 Fifteenth St., NW
(Newsletter)		Washington, D.C. 20005

Aviation Week & Space Technology

Weekly	McGraw Hill, Inc.	1221 Ave. of the Americas
(Magazine)		New York, N.Y. 10020

Flight Magazine

Monthly	Air Review Publishing	P.O. Box 750
(Magazine)	Corp.	Dallas, Texas 75221
OTHER		

**Forecast of Scheduled International Air Traffic of
U.S. Flag Carriers 1971–1980**

	Civil Aeronautics Board	Washington, D.C. 20428

Aluminum

PERIODICALS
Aluminum

Annual	Bureau of Mines	4800 Forbes Avenue
(Magazine)		Pittsburgh, Pa. 15213

Aluminum Association Yearbook & Releases

Quarterly and		750 Third Avenue
Annually (Reports)		New York, N.Y. 10017

American Bureau of Metal Statistics Yearbook

Annually	American Bureau of Metal	50 Broadway, 30th floor
(Statistical	Statistics Yearbook	New York, N.Y. 10004
Yearbook)		

Published	Source	Address

American Metal Market

| Daily (Newspaper) | American Metal Market Co. | 7 East 12th Street New York, N.Y.   10003 |

Commodity Yearbook Statistical Abstract Service

| Annually (Statistical Yearbook) | Commodity Research Bureau | 140 Broadway New York, N.Y.   10005 |

Engineering & Mining Journal

| Monthly (Journal) | McGraw-Hill, Inc. | 1221 Ave. of The Americas New York, N.Y.   10020 |

Japan Metal Bulletin

| Three times per week (Newspaper) | Sangyo Press, Ltd. | 104 East 40th Street New York, N.Y.   10016 |

Metal Statistics

| Annually (Yearbook) | American Metal Market Co. | 7 East 12th Street New York, N.Y.   10003 |

Metals Week

| Weekly (Magazine) | McGraw-Hill, Inc. | 1221 Ave. of The Americas New York, N.Y.   10020 |

Mining Journal

| Weekly (Newspaper) | Mining Journal, Ltd. | 15 Wilson Street London EC2 London, U.K. |

Mining Journal

| Annually | Mining Journal, Ltd. | 15 Wilson Street London EC2, England, U.K. |

Minerals Yearbook Volumes 1 & 2
Metals, Minerals, & Fuels

| Annually (Yearbook) | Superintendent of Documents U.S. Government Printing Office | Washington, D.C. |

Minerals Yearbook Volume 3, Area Reports—
Domestic; Volume 4 Area Reports—International

| Annually (Yearbook) | Superintendent of Documents U.S. Government Printing Office | Washington, D.C. |

Automotive Industry

PERIODICALS

Automotive Facts & Figures

| Annual (Pamphlet) | Automobile Manufacturers Assn., Inc. | 320 New Center Bldg. Detroit, Mich.   48202 |

Published	*Source*	*Address*

Automotive Market Report

Biweekly (Magazine)	Automotive Publishing, Inc.	127 Pillow Street Butler, Pa. 16001

Automotive News

Weekly (Newspaper)	Slocum Publishing Co.	965 E. Jefferson Ave. Detroit, Mich. 48207

Automotive News Almanac

Annual (Magazine)	Slocum Publishing Co.	965 E. Jefferson Ave. Detroit, Mich. 48207

Sindlinger Automotive Report
Consumer Demand—New Car Dealer Traffic
Domestic/Import

Weekly (Newsletters)	Sindlinger & Co.	Howard & Yale Avenues Swarthmore, Pa. 19081

Ward's Advance Schedule & Inventory Report

Monthly (Statistical Release)	Ward's	28 W. Adams Suite 1805 Detroit, Mich. 48226

Ward's Auto World

Monthly (Magazine)	Ward's	28 W. Adams Suite 1805 Detroit, Mich. 48226

Ward's Automotive Reports

Weekly (Newsletter)	Ward's	28 W. Adams Suite 1805 Detroit, Mich. 48226

Ward's 1972 Indexing Service

Monthly (Index)	Ward's	28 W. Adams Suite 1805 Detroit, Mich. 48226

Ward's Wankel Reports

13 Issues (Special Reports)	Ward's	28 W. Adams Suite 1805 Detroit, Mich. 48226

Books

Planning, Regulation and Competition: Automotive Industry—1968
Hearings before Subcommittees of the Select Committee on Small Business
(U.S. Senate)

1968	U.S. Government Printing Office	Washington, D.C.

Banks and Finance Companies

Periodical

The American Banker

Daily (Newspaper)	American Banker, Inc.	525 W. 42d Street New York, N.Y. 10036

The Bankers Magazine

Quarterly (Magazine)	Warren, Gorham & Lamont, Inc.	89 Beach Street Boston, Mass. 02111

Published	Source	Address
Bankers Monthly		
Monthly (Magazine)	Bankers Monthly, Inc.	1528 Skokie Blvd. Northbrook, Illinois 60062
Banking		
Monthly (Magazine)	Simmons-Boardman Publishing Corp.	350 Broadway New York, N.Y. 10013
Banking Law Journal		
Monthly (Journal)	Warren, Gorham & Lamont, Inc.	89 Beach Street Boston, Mass. 02111
Bank of New York—Finance Company Statistics		
Semiannually (Stat. Abstract)	Bank of New York	48 Wall Street New York, N.Y. 10015
Burroughs Clearing House		
Monthly (Magazine)	Burroughs Clearing House	P.O. Box 418 Detroit, Mich. 48232
Comments on Credit, Bond Market Survey		
Weekly (Newsletter)	Salomon Brothers	60 Wall Street New York, N.Y. 10005
Federal Reserve Bulletin		
Monthly (Bulletin)	Board of Governors Federal Reserve Board	Washington, D.C. 20551
Federal Reserve District Bank Bulletins		
Monthly (Magazine)	Individual Reserve Banks	Atlanta Boston Chicago Cleveland Dallas Kansas City Minneapolis New York Philadelphia Richmond St. Louis San Francisco
Federal Statistical Release H 4.2 (Conditions of Large Commercial Banks)		
Weekly (Bulletin)	Federal Reserve Board	Washington, D.C.
Finance Facts Yearbook		
Annually (Yearbook)	National Consumer Finance Assn.	100 Sixteenth St., NW Washington, D.C. 20003
Finance Magazine		
Monthly (Magazine)	Finance Magazine	5 E. 75th Street New York, N.Y. 10021
First National Bank of Chicago, Finance Company Composite Statistics		
Semiannually (Stat. Abstract)	First National Bank of Chicago	Dearborn, Monroe, & Clark Streets Chicago, Illinois

Published	Source	Address

National Banking Review

| Quarterly (Journal) | Controller of the Currency U.S. Treasury Dept. | Washington, D. C. |

National Economic Trends

| Weekly (Bulletin) | Federal Reserve Bank of St. Louis | St. Louis, Mo. |

New York Clearing House Deposit Statistics

| Weekly (Stat. Abstract) | New York Clearing House Assn. | 100 Broad Street New York, N.Y.   10004 |

Quarterly Bank Survey

| Quarterly (Magazine) | M. A. Shapiro & Co. | 1 Chase Manhattan Plaza New York, N.Y.   10005 |

St. Louis Federal Monetary Trends

| Weekly (Bulletin) | Federal Reserve Bank of St. Louis | St. Louis, Mo. |

BOOKS

How to Analyze a Bank Statement, 4th Edition

| 1966 | F. L. Garcia Bankers Publishing | Boston, Mass. |

Management of Bank Funds, 2d Edition

| 1962 | Roland I. Robinson McGraw-Hill, Inc. | New York, N.Y. |

Management Policies for Commercial Banks

| 1962 | Howard Crosse Prentice-Hall, Inc. | New York, N.Y. |

Brewing and Distilling

PERIODICALS

Beverage Executive

| Bimonthly (Magazine) | Schwartz Publications, Inc. | 222 Park Avenue, South New York, N.Y.   10003 |
| Monthly (Magazine) | Brewers' Digest | 4049 W. Peterson Ave. Chicago, Illinois |

Brewers Industry Survey

| Annually (Annual Report) | Research Co. of America | 654 Madison Ave. New York, N.Y.   10021 |

Distilled Spirits Industry Annual Statistical Review

| Annually (Statistical Yearbook) | Distilled Spirits Institute | 425 Thirteenth St. Washington, D.C.   20004 |

LBI Facts Book

| Annually (Fact Book) | Licensed Beverage Industries, Inc. | 485 Lexington Ave. New York, N.Y.   10017 |

Liquor Handbook

| Annually (Handbook) | Gavin Jobson Associates | 820 Second Avenue New York, N.Y.   10017 |

Published	*Source*	*Address*

Wine Handbook

Annually	Gavin Jobson Associates	820 Second Avenue
(Handbook)		New York, N.Y. 10017

Building Materials

PERIODICALS

Construction Review

Monthly	U.S. Department of Com-	Washington, D.C. 20402
(Journal)	merce	
	Government Printing Office	

Crow's Weekly Letter

Weekly	C. C. Crow Publications,	Terminal Sales Bldg.
(Journal)	Inc.	Portland, Oregon 97205

F. W. Dodge Construction Statistics

Monthly	McGraw-Hill, Inc.	1221 Ave. of the Americas
(Journal)		New York, N.Y. 10020

Economic Services Report

Semiannually	Western Wood Products	Yeon Building
(Journal)	Assoc.	Portland, Oregon 97204

Engineering News-Record

Weekly	McGraw-Hill, Inc.	1221 Ave. of the Americas
(Magazine)		New York, N.Y. 10020

Forest Industries

Monthly	Miller Freeman Publi-	500 Howard Street
(Magazine)	cations	San Francisco, Calif. 94105

Housing Completions

Monthly	U.S. Department of Com-	Washington, D.C. 20402
(Journal)	merce	
	U.S. Government Printing	
	Office	

Housing Starts

Monthly	U.S. Department of Com-	Washington, D.C. 20402
(Journal)	merce	
	U.S. Government Printing	
	Office	

Housing Starts Bulletin

Weekly	National Assn. of Home-	1625 L Street, NW
(Journal)	builders	Washington, D.C. 20036

Mineral Industry Surveys (Var. Materials)

Monthly & Yearly	U.S. Department of Interior	Washington, D.C. 20240
(Surveys)	Bureau of Mines	

Professional Builders

Monthly	Cahners Publishing Co.,	270 St. Paul Street
(Magazine)	Inc.	Denver, Colorado 80206

Random Lengths

Weekly	Random Lengths Publi-	P.O. Box 867
(Journal)	cations, Inc.	Eugene, Oregon 97401

Published	*Source*	*Address*

Rock Products

| Monthly | Maclean-Hunter Publishing | 300 W. Adams Street |
| (Magazine) | Corp. | Chicago, Illinois   60606 |

Short Range Forecasts

| Quarterly | Portland Cement Associa- | Old Orchard Road |
| (Journal) | tion | Skokie, Illinois   60070 |

BOOKS

Directory of the Forest Products Industry

| 1972 | Miller Freeman Publica- | 500 Howard Street |
| | tions | San Francisco, Calif.   94105 |

Timber Trends in the United States

1965	Forest Service, U.S. Dept.	Washington, D.C. 20402
	of Agric.	
	U.S. Government Printing	
	Office	

OTHERS

Building Construction Information Sources

| 1964 | Howard B. Bentley | Book Tower |
| | Gale Research Co. | Detroit, Mich. |

Outlook for The Forest Products Industry

| 1970 | Arthur D. Little, Inc. | Acorn Park |
| | | Cambridge, Mass.   02140 |

Portland Cement Plants—U.S., Canada, & Mexico

| Map of Portland | Pit & Quarry Publications | 105 W. Adams St. |
| Cement Plants | | Chicago, Illinois   60603 |

Chemicals

PERIODICALS

Agricultural Chemicals

| Monthly | Industry Publications, Inc. | 200 Commerce Road |
| (Magazine) | | Cedar Grove, N.J.   07009 |

Chemical Age

Weekly	Benn Brothers, Ltd.	Bouverie House
(Magazine)		154 Fleet Street
		London EC4, England

Chemical and Engineers News

| Weekly | American Chemical Society | 1155 Sixteenth St., NW |
| (Magazine) | | Washington, D.C.   20036 |

Chemical Engineering

| Biweekly | McGraw-Hill, Inc. | 1221 Ave. of the Americas |
| (Magazine) | | New York, N.Y.   10020 |

Chemical Horizons

Monthly	Predicasts, Inc.	200 University Circle Research
(Abstracts)		Center
		11001 Cedar Avenue
		Cleveland, Ohio 44106

Published	Source	Address
Chemical Week		
Weekly (Magazine)	McGraw-Hill, Inc.	1221 Ave. of the Americas New York, N.Y. 10020
Current Industrial Reports—Shipments of Selected Plastic Products Series MA30B		
Monthly (Stat. Release)	Bureau of the Census	Washington, D.C. 20233
European Chemical News		
Weekly (Magazine)	Int'l Publishing Corp., Ltd.	300 East 42d Street New York, N.Y.
Farm Chemicals		
Monthly (Magazine)	Meister Publishing Company	37841 Euclid Avenue Willoughby, Ohio 44094
Industry Reports		
Monthly (Stat. Release)	Superintendent of Documents Government Printing Office	Washington, D.C. 20402
Inorganic Chemicals & Gases (Current Industrial Reports—Series M–28–A)		
Monthly (Stat. Release)	Bureau of the Census	Washington, D.C. 20233
Modern Plastics		
Monthly (Magazine)	McGraw-Hill, Inc.	1221 Ave. of the Americas New York, N.Y. 10020
Modern Plastics Encyclopedia		
Annually (Encyclopedia)	McGraw-Hill, Inc.	1221 Ave. of the Americas New York, N.Y. 10020
Oil, Paint, & Drug Reporter		
Weekly (Newspaper)	Schnell Publishing Co., Inc.	100 Church Street New York, N.Y. 10007
Pilot (formerly Chemical News)		
Bimonthly (Magazine)	Manufacturers Chemists' Assn.	1825 Connecticut Ave. Washington, D.C. 20009
Plastics World		
Monthly (Magazine)	Cahner's Publishing Company	270 St. Paul Street Denver, Colorado 80206
Textile Organon		
Monthly (Stat. Newsletter)	Textile Economics Bureau, Inc.	10 East 40th Street New York, N.Y. 10016

Coal

PERIODICALS

Bituminous Coal Facts		
Biennial (Factbook)	National Coal Assn.	1130 Seventeenth St. Washington, D.C. 20036
Coal Age		
Monthly (Magazine)	McGraw-Hill, Inc.	1221 Ave. of the Americas New York, N.Y. 10020

Published	*Source*	*Address*

Coal Chronicle

| Irregular (Catalogue) | United States Bureau of Mines Publications Distribution Section | 4800 Forbes Avenue Pittsburgh, Pa.   15213 |

Coal Directory

| Annual (Directory) | McGraw-Hill, Inc. | 1221 Ave. of the Americas New York, N.Y.   10020 |

Coal News

| Weekly (Newspaper) | National Coal Assn. | 1130 Seventeenth St. Washington, D.C.   20036 |

Mineral Industry Survey—Bituminous Coal

| Monthly (Magazine) | U.S. Bureau of Mines | 4800 Forbes Ave. Pittsburgh, Pa.   15213 |

Minerals Year Book Vol. 1–2 Metals, Minerals, and Fuels

| Annually (Book) | Superintendent of Documents U.S. Government Printing Office | Washington, D.C.   20402 |

Minerals Year Book Vol. 3 Area Reports—Domestic
Minerals Year Book Vol. 4 Area Reports—International

| Annually (Book) | Superintendent of Documents U.S. Government Printing Office | Washington, D.C.   20402 |

BOOKS

Mineral Facts and Problems

| 1970 (4th Edition) | U.S. Bureau of Mines | Washington, D.C. |

Communications

PERIODICALS

American Growth Story

| Annually (Booklet) | U.S. Independent Telephone Assn. | 438 Pennsylvania Bldg. Washington, D.C.   20004 |

Annual Statistical Volume One

| Annually (Booklet) | U.S. Independent Telephone Assn. | 438 Pennsylvania Bldg. Washington, D.C.   20004 |

Annual Statistical Volume Two

| Annual (Booklet) | U.S. Independent Telephone Assn. | 438 Pennsylvania Bldg. Washington, D.C.   20004 |

From the State Capitals

| Weekly (Newsletter) | Bethune Jones | 321 Sunset Ave. Asbury Park, N.J. |

Naruc Bulletin

| Weekly (Newsletter) | Nat'l Assn. of Regulatory Utility Commissions | 3327 Interstate Commerce Bldg., P.O. Box 684 Washington, D.C.   20044 |

Published	Source	Address

Public Utility Reports—Advance Sheets

| Bimonthly (Pamphlet) | Public Utility Reports, Inc. | 1828 L Street, NW Suite 502 Washington, D.C. 20036 |

Public Utility Reports Executive Information Service

| Weekly (Newsletter) | Public Utility Reports, Inc. | 1828 L Street, NW Washington, D.C. 20036 |

Telecommunications Reports

| Weekly (Newsletter) | Telecommunications Reports | Nat'l Press Bldg. Room 1204 Washington, D.C. 20004 |

Construction Materials

PERIODICALS

Construction Activity—Series C30

| Monthly (Report) | Superintendent of Documents U.S. Government Printing Office | Washington, D.C. 20402 |

Construction Review

| Monthly (Magazine) | U.S. Department of Commerce | Constitution Ave. & E Street, NW Washington, D.C. 20402 |

Crow's Forest Products Digest

| Monthly (Magazine) | C. C. Crow Publications, Inc. | Terminal Sales Bldg. 1220 SW Morrison Portland, Oregon 97205 |

Elevator World

| Monthly (Magazine) | William C. Sturgeon | Box 6523, Loop Branch Mobile, Alabama 36606 |

Engineering News-Record

| Weekly (Magazine) | McGraw-Hill, Inc. | 1221 Ave. of the Americas New York, N.Y. 10020 |

House and Home

| Monthly (Magazine) | McGraw-Hill, Inc. | 1221 Ave. of the Americas New York, N.Y. 10020 |

Housing Starts—Series C20

| Monthly (Report) | Superintendent of Documents U.S. Government Printing Office | Washington, D.C. 20402 |

Industrial Outlook

| Annually (Book) | U.S. Department of Commerce | Constitution Ave. & E Street, NW Washington, D.C. 20037 |

Published	*Source*	*Address*

Minerals Yearbook Vol. 1-2 Metals, Minerals, & Fuels

Annually (Book)	Superintendent of Documents U.S. Government Printing Office	Washington, D.C. 20402

Minerals Yearbook Vol. 3—Area Reports—Domestic
Vol. 4—Area Reports—International

Annually (Book)	Superintendent of Documents U.S. Government Printing Office	Washington, D.C. 20402

Modern Concrete

Monthly (Magazine)	Pit and Quarry Publications, Inc.	105 W. Adams Street Chicago, Illinois 60603

Pit and Quarry

Monthly (Magazine)	Pit and Quarry Publications, Inc.	105 W. Adams Street Chicago, Illinois 60603

Savings & Loan Fact Book

Annually (Fact Book)	U.S. Savings & Loan League	221 N. LaSalle Street Chicago, Illinois 60601

Survey of Current Business

Monthly (Magazine)	U.S. Department of Commerce Office of Business Economics	Constitution Ave. & E Street, NW Washington, D.C. 20402

OTHER

F. W. Dodge Economics Department

		1221 Ave. of the Americas New York, N.Y. 10020

National Association of Homebuilders

		1625 L Street, NW Washington, D.C. 20036

U.S. Department of Commerce

		Constitution Ave. & E Street, NW Washington, D.C. 20402

Defense

PERIODICALS

AIAA Bulletin

Monthly (Bulletin)	American Institute of Aeronautics & Astronautics	1290 Sixth Ave. New York, N.Y. 10019

Aerospace Daily

Daily (Newsletter)	Ziff Davis Publishing Co.	1156 Fifteenth St., NW Washington, D.C. 20005

Aerospace Facts and Figures

Annually (Booklet)	Aerospace Industries Assn. of America	1725 DeSales St., NW Washington, D.C. 20036

Published	Source	Address

Aerospace Magazines

| Quarterly | Aerospace Industries Assn. | 1725 DeSales St., NW |
| (Magazine) | of America | Washington, D.C.   20036 |

Aerospace Market Intelligence Reports

1.   Military and Civil Aircraft
2.   Rockets, Missiles, and Spacecrafts
3.   Aerospace Industry Dossier

| Monthly | DMS, Inc. | 71 Lewis Street |
| (Newsletter) | | Greenwich, Conn. |

Air Force & Space Digest

Monthly	Air Force Assn.	1750 Pennsylvania Ave., NW,
(Magazine)		Suite 400
		Washington, D.C. 20006

Astronautics & Aeronautics

| Monthly | American Institute of Aero- | 1290 Ave. of the Americas |
| (Magazine) | nautics & Astronautics | New York, N.Y.   10019 |

Aviation Daily

| Daily | Ziff Davis Publishing Co. | 1156 15th St., NW |
| (Newsletter) | | Washington, D.C.   20005 |

Aviation Week & Space Technology

| Weekly | McGraw-Hill, Inc. | 1221 Ave. of the Americas |
| (Magazine) | | New York, N.Y.   10020 |

Defense Management Journal

Quarterly	Superintendent of Docu-	Washington, D.C. 20402
(Bulletin)	ments	
	U.S. Government Printing	
	Office	

Drugs and Cosmetics

PERIODICALS

American Druggist

| Biweekly | Hearst Corp. | 224 West 57th Street |
| (Magazine) | | New York, N.Y.   10019 |

Beauty Fashion

| Monthly | Concept Publishing Corp. | 532 Madison Avenue |
| (Magazine) | | New York, N.Y.   10022 |

Cosmetic World

| Biweekly | Concept Publishing Corp. | 532 Madison Avenue |
| (Newsletter) | | New York, N.Y.   10022 |

Drug & Cosmetic Industry

| Monthly | Drug Markets | 101 W. 31st Street |
| (Magazine) | | New York, N.Y.   10001 |

FDC Reports

| Weekly | | 1152 Nat'l Press Bldg. |
| (Newsletter) | | Washington, D C |

Published	*Source*	*Address*

Hospitals

| Bimonthly (Magazine) | American Hospital Assn. | 840 N. Lakeshore Drive Chicago, Illinois 60611 |

Journal of American Medical Association

| Weekly (Magazine) | | 535 N. Dearborn Street Chicago, Illinois 60610 |

Medical Letter on Drugs & Therapeutics

| Weekly (Newsletter) | Drug & Therapeutics Information, Inc. | 305 E. 45th Street New York, N.Y. 10017 |

Medical Tribune

| Weekly (Newspaper) | Medical Tribune, Inc. | 880 Third Avenue New York, N.Y. 10022 |

Modern Drugs Encyclopedia

| Annually (Encyclopedia) | Dun. Donnelly Corp. | 466 Lexington Avenue New York, N.Y. 10017 |

Modern Hospital

| Monthly (Magazine) | Robert M. Cunningham, Jr. | 1050 Merchandise Mart Chicago, Illinois 60654 |

New Product Survey

| Monthly (Magazine) | Paul De Haen, Inc. | 11 W. 42d Street New York, N.Y. 10036 |

Pharmaceutical Newsletter

| Weekly (Newsletter) | Pharmaceutical Manufacturers Assn. | 1155 Fifteenth St., NW Washington, D.C. |

Product Management (formerly *Drug Trade News*)

| Monthly (Magazine) | Topics Publishing Co. | 330 West 34th Street New York, N.Y. 10001 |

Womens Wear Daily

| Daily (Newspaper) | Fairchild Publications | 7 East 12th Street New York, N.Y. 10003 |

OTHER

U.S. Department of Health, Education, & Welfare

| | Nat'l Center for Health Statistics | Washington, D.C. |

Electronics Industry

PERIODICALS

Aviation Week & Space Technology

| Weekly (Magazine) | McGraw-Hill, Inc. | 1221 Ave. of the Americas New York, N.Y. 10020 |

Electronic Buyers' Guide

| Annually (Directory) | McGraw-Hill, Inc. | 1221 Ave. of the Americas New York, N.Y. 10020 |

Electronic Distributing & Marketing

| Monthly (Magazine) | Electronic Periodicals, Inc. | 33140 Aurora Road Cleveland, Ohio 44139 |

Published	Source	Address

Electronic Engineer (formerly *Electronic Industries*)

Monthly (Journal)	Chilton Co.	Chestnut & 56th Sts. Philadelphia, Pa. 19139

Electronic Market Data Book

Annually (Data Book)	Electronic Industries Assn.	2001 I Street, NW Washington, D.C. 20006

Electronic News

Weekly Weekly (Newspaper)	Fairchild Publications, Inc.	7 East 12th Street New York, N.Y. 10003

Electronic News Financial Factbook and Directory

Annually (Factbook)	Fairchild Book Division	7 East 12th Street New York, N.Y. 10005

Electronic Trends—International

Monthly (Magazine)	Electronic Industries Assn.	2001 I Street, NW Washington, D.C. 20006

Electronic Trends—USA

Monthly (Magazine)	Electronic Industries Assn.	2001 I Street, NW Washington, D.C. 20006

Electronic Magazine

Bimonthly (Magazine)	McGraw-Hill, Inc.	1221 Ave. of the Americas New York, N.Y. 10020

Electro-Procurement (formerly *Electronic Procurement*)

Monthly (Magazine)	Mactier Publishing Corp.	820 Second Avenue New York, N.Y. 10017

IEEE Spectrum

Monthly (Magazine)	Institute of Electrical & Electronic Engineers, Inc.	345 East 47th Street New York, N.Y. 10017

Laser Focus

Monthly (Magazine)	International Data Pub- lishing Co.	245 Walnut Street P.O. Box 1 Newtonville, Mass. 02160

NEDA Journal

Monthly (Journal)	National Electronic Dis- tributors Assn., Inc.	343 South Dearborn St. Chicago, Illinois 60604

Television Digest with Consumer Electronics

Weekly (Newsletter)	Television Digest	1830 Jefferson Pl., NW Washington, D.C. 20036

Television Factbook

Annually (Factbook)	Television Digest	1830 Jefferson Pl., NW Washington, D.C. 20036

AVIONICS/ASTRONICS/ELECTRONIC WARFARE

Aerospace Technology

Fortnightly (Magazine)	American Aviation Publica- tions	1001 Vermont Ave., NW Washington, D.C. 20005

Published	Source	Address

Air Force & Space Digest

Monthly	Air Force Assn.	1750 Pennsylvania Avenue,
(Magazine)		NW
		Washington, D.C. 20006

Astronautics & Aeronautics

| Monthly | American Institute of Aero- | 1290 Ave. of the Americas |
| (Magazine) | nautics & Astronautics | New York, N.Y.   10019 |

Market Intelligence Reports

| Monthly | DMS, Inc. | 100 Northfield Street |
| (Reports) | | Greenwich, Conn.   06830 |

DEPARTMENT OF DEFENSE

Military Posture Statement (Secretary of Defense)

| Annually | OASD (Public Affairs) | Pentagon |
| (Newsletter) | | Washington, D.C.   20301 |

Defense Industry Bulletin

| 11 times annually | Business & Labor Division | Pentagon |
| (Bulletin) | OASD (PA) | Washington, D.C.   20301 |

Selected Economic Indicators

Monthly	OASD (Comptroller) Direc-	Pentagon
(Statistics)	torate for Statistical	Washington, D.C. 20301
	Services	

Status of Funds (Monthly Report by Functional Title)

Monthly	OASD (Comptroller) Direc-	Pentagon
(Report)	torate for Financial Analy-	Washington, D.C. 20301
	sis and Control	

Farm Machinery

PERIODICALS

Canadian Farm Equipment Dealer

| Monthly | Southam Business Publica- | 1450 Don Mills Road |
| (Bulletin) | tions, Ltd. | Don Mills, Ontario, Canada |

Current Industrial Reports Series M355

| Monthly | Bureau of Census | Washington, D.C.   20233 |
| (Statistical Bulletin) | | |

Current Industrial Reports Series M35A

| Quarterly | Bureau of Census | Washington, D.C.   20233 |
| (Statistical Bulletin) | | |

Farm Machinery World

| Quarterly | Western Farm Publications, | 251 Kearny Street |
| (Magazine) | Inc. | San Francisco, Calif.   94108 |

Farm and Power Equipment

| Monthly | NRFEA Publications, Inc. | 2340 Hampton Avenue |
| (Magazine) | | St. Louis, Mo.   63139 |

ORFEDA Bulletin

Bimonthly	Ontario Retail Farm Equip-	695 Markham Road
(Bulletin)	ment Dealers Assn.	Suite 27
		Scarborough, Ontario, Canada

Published	Source	Address

Implement & Tractor

| Bimonthly (Magazine) | Implement & Tractor Publications | 1014 Wyandotte Street Kansas City, Mo. 64105 |

Implement & Tractor Redbook

| Annually (Annual) | Implement & Tractor Publications | 1014 Wyandotte Street Kansas City, Mo. 64105 |

Northwest Farm Equipment Journal

| Monthly (Magazine) | Northwest Farm Equipment Journal | 1011 Upper Midwest Bldg. Minneapolis, Minn. 55401 |

Southern Farm Equipment

| Monthly (Magazine) | United Publishing Co. | 735 Spring Street Atlanta, Ga. 30308 |

Western Farm Equipment

| Monthly (Magazine) | Western Farm Publications | 1241 S. Main Street Salinas, Calif. 93901 |

Fixed Income Securities

PERIODICALS

Bond Market Roundup

| Weekly (Market Letter) | Salomon Brothers | One New York Plaza New York, N.Y. 10004 |

Bond & Money Market Letter

| Bimonthly (Market Letter) | Goldsmith-Nagan, Inc. | Nat'l Press Bldg. Washington, D.C. 20004 |

Bond Outlook

| Weekly (Market Letter) | Standard & Poor's Corp. | 345 Hudson Street New York, N.Y. 10014 |

Comments on Credit

| Weekly (Market Letter) | Salomon Brothers | One New York Plaza New York, N.Y. 10004 |

Convertible Fact Finder

| Weekly (Statistical Summary) | Kalb, Voorhis, & Co. | 27 William Street New York, N.Y. 10005 |

Guide to Fixed Income Markets

| Monthly (Market Letter) | Merrill Lynch, Pierce, Fenner, & Smith, Inc. | 1 Liberty Plaza New York, N.Y. 10006 |

Investment Dealers Digest

| Weekly (Magazine) | IDD, Inc. | 150 Broadway New York, N.Y. 10038 |

Kiplinger Washington Letter

| Weekly (Market Letter) | Kiplinger Washington Editors | 1729 H Street, NW Washington, D.C. 20006 |

Moody's Bond Record

| Monthly (Statistical Summary) | Moody's Investors Service | 99 Church Street New York, N.Y. 10007 |

Published	*Source*	*Address*

Moody's Bond Survey

Weekly	Moody's Investors Service	99 Church Street
(Market Letter)		New York, N.Y. 10007

Moody's Convertible Bonds

Monthly	Moody's Investors Service	99 Church Street
(Statistical		New York, N.Y. 10007
Summary)		

Reporting on Governments

Weekly	G. Sumner Collins	Two Fifth Avenue
(Market Letter)		New York, N.Y. 10011

Standard & Poors Bond Guide

Monthly	Standard & Poor's Corp.	345 Hudson Street
(Statistical		New York, N.Y. 10014
Summary)		

Standard & Poors Standard Bond Reports

Weekly	Standard & Poor's Corp.	345 Hudson Street
(Investment Ad-		New York, N.Y. 10014
visory Service)		

U.S. Financial Data

Weekly	Federal Reserve Bank of St.	St. Louis, Missouri
(Statistical	Louis	
Summary)		

The Weekly Bond Buyer

Weekly	The Bond Buyer	77 Water Street
(Newspaper)		New York, N.Y. 10005

The Value Line Convertible Survey

Weekly	Arnold Bernhard & Co., Inc.	5 East 44th Street
		New York, N.Y. 10017

BOOKS

Beat the Market: A Scientific Stock Market System

1967	E. O. Thorp and S. T. Kassouf	New York, N.Y.
	Random House	

A Guide to Convertible Securities

1968	Julius Schwartz, William, and Spellman	New York, N.Y.
	Convertible Securities, Inc.	

Handbook of Convertible Securities

1971	Kalb, Voorhis, & Co.	New York, N.Y.

More Profit, Less Risk—Convertible Securities and Warrants

1971	Robert E. Brown & Ronald D. Bechky	New York, N.Y.
	Arnold Bernhard & Co.	

Food Processing

PERIODICALS

Acreage and Estimated Production of Principal Commercial Corps.

Monthly	Crop Reporting Board	14th & Independence Avenue,
(Catalogue)	U.S. Department of Agricul-	SW
	ture	Washington, D.C. 20250

Published	Source	Address
Agricultural Prices		
Monthly (Bulletin)	U.S. Department of Agriculture	14th & Independence Avenue, SW Washington, D.C. 20250
Agricultural Situation		
Monthly (Mar.–Dec.) Bimonthly (Jan.–Feb.) (Bulletin)	U.S. Department of Agriculture Statistical Reporting Service	Washington, D.C. 20250
Agricultural Statistics		
Annually (Bulletin)	Superintendent of Documents U.S. Government Printing Office	Washington, D.C. 20402
Annual Summary (Fresh Market Vegetables)		
Annually (Catalogue)	Crop Reporting Board U.S. Department of Agriculture	14th & Independence Avenue, SW Washington, D.C. 20250
Annual Coffee Statistics		
Annually (Annual Report)	Pan American Coffee Bureau	1350 Ave. of the Americas New York, N.Y. 10019
Canned Food Report		
Five times per year (Bulletin)	Bureau of Census Business Division Department of Commerce	Washington, D.C. 20233
Commodity Yearbook Statistical Abstract Service		
Yearbook	Commodity Research Bureau	140 Broadway New York, N.Y. 10005
Cotton Situation		
Jan., Mar., May, Aug., Nov.	U. S. Department of Agriculture	14th & Independence Avenue, SW Washington, D.C. 20250
Dairy Situation		
Five times per year (Bulletin)	Economic Research Service Department of Agriculture	14th & Independence Avenue, SW Washington, D.C. 20250
Demand & Price Situation		
Quarterly (Bulletin)	Economic Research Service Department of Agriculture	14th & Independence Avenue, SW Washington, D.C. 20250
Directory of Frozen Food Processors		
Annually (Directory)	Cahner Publishing Co.	205 E. 42d Street New York, N.Y. 10017
Directory of Wholesale Distributors		
Annually (Directory)	Cahners Publishing Co.	205 E. 42d Street New York, N.Y. 10017

Published	Source	Address
Feedstuffs		
Weekly (Newspaper)	Miller Publishing Co.	2501 Wayzata Blvd. Minneapolis, Minn. 55440
Food Engineering		
Monthly (Magazine)	Chilton Co.	56th & Chestnut Sts. Philadelphia, Pa. 19139
Marketing & Transportation Situation		
Quarterly (Catalogue)	Economic Research Service U.S. Department of Agriculture	14th & Independence Avenue, SW Washington, D.C. 20250
National Food Situation		
Quarterly (Bulletin)	Economic Research Service U.S. Department of Agriculture	14th & Independence Avenue, SW Washington, D.C. 20250
Poultry & Egg Situation		
Five times per year (Bulletin)	Economic Research Service U.S. Department of Agriculture	14th & Independence Avenue, SW Washington, D.C. 20250
Progressive Grocers Marketing Guide Book		
Annually (Yearbook)	Progressive Grocers Marketing Guide Book	708 Third Avenue New York, N.Y. 10017
Quick Frozen Foods		
Monthly (Magazine)	Cahners Publishing Co.	205 E. 42d Street New York, N.Y. 10017
Quick Frozen Foods—International		
Monthly (Magazine)	E. W. Williams Publication, Inc.	205 E. 42d Street New York, N.Y. 10017
Sugar Reports		
Monthly (Catalogue)	Agricultural Stabilization and Conservation Service	14th & Independence Avenue, SW Washington, D.C. 20250
Vegetables (Processing)		
Fifteen times per year (Bulletin)	Crop Reporting Board Department of Agriculture	14th & Independence Avenue, SW Washington, D.C. 20250
Washington Food Report		
Weekly (Digest)	American Institute of Food Distribution	28–06 Broadway Fairlawn, New Jersey 07410
Wheat Situation		
Four times per year (Bulletin)	Economic Research Service U.S. Department of Agriculture	14th & Independence Avenue, SW Washington, D.C. 20250
Wool Situation		
Quarterly (Review)	Economic Research Service U.S. Department of Agriculture	14th & Independence Avenue, SW Washington, D.C. 20250

Published	*Source*	*Address*

Glass and Container Industry

PERIODICALS

BDSA Quarterly Industry Reports—Containers & Packaging

Quarterly (Booklet)	U.S. Department of Commerce	Washington, D.C.

Current Industrial Reports—Glass Containers

Monthly (Stat. Summary)	U.S. Department of Commerce	Washington, D.C.

Fibre Box Association Statistical Bulletin

Weekly (Stat. Summary)	Fibre Box Assn.	224 S. Michigan Ave. Chicago, Illinois 60611

Glass Containers

Annually (July) (Booklet)	Glass Container Manufacturing Institute	330 Madison Ave. New York, N.Y. 10017

Modern Packaging

Monthly (Magazine)	McGraw-Hill, Inc.	1221 Ave. of the Americas New York, N.Y. 10020

Modern Packaging Encyclopedia

Annually (July) (Book)	McGraw-Hill, Inc.	1221 Ave. of the Americas New York, N.Y. 10020
Weekly (Newsletter)	Magazine's For Industry	777 Third Avenue New York, N.Y. 10017

Paperboard Packaging

Quarterly (Magazine)	Magazine's For Industry	777 Third Avenue New York, N.Y. 10017

Paperboard Statistics

Weekly (Stat. Summary)	American Paper Institute, Inc.	260 Madison Avenue New York, N.Y.

Home Furnishing Industry

(Including furniture, carpets, and appliances)

PERIODICALS

Advertising Age

Weekly (Marketing Publication)	Advertising Publications, Inc.	740 Rush Street Chicago, Illinois 60611

Appliance Manufacturer

Monthly	Cahner's Publishing Co.	205 E. 42d Street New York, N.Y.

Home Furnishings Daily

Daily	Fairchild Publications, Inc.	7 East 12th Street New York, N.Y. 10003

Merchandising Week

Weekly	Billboard Publications	165 West 46th Street New York, N.Y. 10036

Published	*Source*	*Address*

Current Industrial Reports

Carpets and Rugs	MQ–22Q	
Electric Housewares	MA–36E	
Home Radio Receivers and		
Television Sets, etc.	MA–36M	
Household Furniture	MA–25D	
Major Household Appliances	MA–36F	
Selected Electronic and		
Associated Products	MA–36N	
	U.S. Department of Commerce	Washington, D.C. 20233
(Stat. Reports)	merce	
	Social & Economics Statistics Administration	
	tistics Administration	
	Bureau of the Census	
	Industry Division	

Association of Home Appliance Manufacturers

20 N. Wacker Drive
Chicago, Illinois   60606

Carpet and Rug Institute

208 W. Cuyler Street
Dalton, Ga.   30720

Seidman & Seidman

110 Union Bank Bldg.
Grand Rapids, Mich.   49502

Southern Furniture Manufacturers Association

P.O. Box 951
High Point, N.C.   27261

Vacuum Cleaner Manufacturers Association

1615 Collamer Street
Cleveland, Ohio   44110

Hotels/Motels

PERIODICALS

Lodging & Food Service News

Weekly	Hotel Service, Inc.	131 Clarendon Street
(Newspaper)		Boston, Mass. 02116

Lodging Industry

Annually	Laventhol, Krekstein,	919 Third Avenue
(Survey)	Horwath & Horwath	New York, N.Y. 10022

The Travel Agent

Semiweekly	American Traveler, Inc.	2 West 46th Street
(Magazine)		New York, N.Y. 10036

Trends in the Hotel/Motel Business

Annually	Harris, Kerr, Forster & Co.	420 Lexington Avenue
(Report)		New York, N.Y. 10017

Trends of Business—Hotels

Monthly	Laventhol, Krekstein,	919 Third Avenue
(Newsletter)	Horwath & Horwath	New York, N.Y. 10022

Published	Source	Address

Insurance

PERIODICALS

Best's Review (Life Edition, Fire & Casualty Edition)

Monthly (Journal)	Alfred M. Best & Co.	Park Avenue Morristown, N.J. 07960

Best's Weekly News Digest

Weekly (Journal)	Alfred M. Best & Co.	Park Avenue Morristown, N.J. 07960

Final Report from the Committee on Life
Insurance Earnings Adjustments

1970	The Association of Insur- ance and Financial Analysts c/o Mr. David Seifer Jas. H. Oliphant & Co., Inc.	61 Broadway New York, N.Y.

Insurance Advocate

Weekly (Magazine)	Insurance Advocate	136 William Street New York, N.Y. 10038

Insurance Magazine

Weekly (Magazine)	Insurance Magazine	1100 High Ridge Road Stanford, Conn. 06905

Monthly Bulletin

Monthly (Newsletter)	Insurance Department State of New York	123 William Street New York, N.Y. 10038

National Underwriter (Life Edition, Fire & Casualty Edition)

Weekly (Magazine)	National Underwriter	420 E. 42d Street Cincinnati, Ohio 45202

Spectator

Monthly (Magazine)	Spectator	56th & Chestnut Streets Philadelphia, Pa. 10139

The Tally of Life Insurance Statistics

Monthly (Newsletter) BOOKS	Institute of Life Insurance Div. of Statistics & Research	277 Park Avenue New York, N.Y. 10017

The Economic Theory of Risk and Insurance

1951	Allan H. Willett Richard D. Irwin, Inc.	Homewood, Illinois 60430

General Insurance (8th Edition)

1970	John H. Magee and D. L. Bickelhaupt Richard D. Irwin, Inc.	Homewood, Illinois 60430

Insurance: Principles and Practices

1962	Frank J. Angell Ronald Press Co.	New York, N.Y.

Published	*Source*	*Address*

Life Company Annual Statement Handbook

| 1962 | Chas. H. Beardsley
H. W. Satchell & Co. | Columbus, Ohio |

Life Insurance (Text Edition)

| 1958 | John H. Magee
Richard D. Irwin, Inc. | Homewood, Illinois 60430 |

Sources of Insurance Statistics

| 1965 | Elizabeth Ferguson
Special Libraries Assn. | New York, N.Y. |

Transition to Multiple-Line Insurance Companies

| 1961 | D. L. Bickelhaupt
Richard D. Irwin, Inc. | Homewood, Illinois 60430 |

Leisure Industry

PERIODICALS

R. V. Dealer

| Monthly
(Magazine) | Mobile-Modular Housing
Dealer | 6229 Northwest Hwy.
Chicago, Illinois   60631 |

R. V. Marketing Report

| Monthly
(Newsletter) | Recreational Vehicle Insti-
tute, Inc. | 2720 Des Plaines Avenue
Des Plaines, Illinois   60018 |

Selling Sport Goods

| Monthly
(Magazine) | National Sporting Goods
Assn. | 717 N. Michigan Ave.
Chicago, Illinois   60611 |

Toy & Hobby World

| Semimonthly
(Newsletter-
Newspaper) | United Publishing Co. | 1107 Broadway
New York, N.Y.   10010 |

Toys

| Semimonthly
(Magazine) | Harcourt Brace Jovanovich
Publications | 757 Third Avenue
New York, N.Y.   10017 |

Machine Tool Industry

PERIODICALS

American Machinist

| Biweekly
(Magazine) | McGraw-Hill, Inc. | 1221 Ave. of the Americas
New York, N.Y.   10020 |

Economic Handbook of the Machine Tool Industry

| Annually
(Handbook) | National Machine Tool
Builders Assn. | 7901 Westpark Drive
McLean, Va.   22101 |

Tool Age

| Weekly
(Magazine) | Chilton Co. | Chestnut & 56th Streets
Philadelphia, Pa.   19139 |

Machine Tool Industry: Shipments and Orders

| Monthly
(Statistics) | National Machine Tool
Builder's Assn. | 7901 Westpark Drive
McLean, Va.   22101 |

Published	*Source*	*Address*

Metalworking News (American Metal Market)

Weekly
(Newspaper)
BOOKS

Fairchild Publishing

7 East 12th Street
New York, N.Y.   10003

Machine Shop Theory for Tool, Die, and Machinist Apprentices

1965

Nat'l Tool, Die and Precision Machinery Assn.

Washington, D.C.

Shop Guide for Apprentice Training

1972

Nat'l Tool, Die and Precision Machinery Assn.

Washington, D.C.

Mobile Homes

PERIODICALS

Construction Reports—Housing Starts (C20)

Monthly
(Gov't Stat.
  Bulletin)

U.S. Government Printing Office
Superintendent of Documents

Washington, D.C.   20402

Directory—Mobile & Modular Homes

Annually
(Consumer Product
  Directory)

Hanley Publishing Co., Inc.

1718 Sherman Avenue
Evanston, Illinois   60201

Housing & Realty Investor

Twice Monthly
(Investment Analysis Service)

Audit Investment Research

230 Park Ave., Suite 555
New York, N.Y.   10017

Mobile Home Park Manager & Developer

Bimonthly
(Trade Magazine)

Trailer Dealer Publishing Co.

6229 N. Northwest Hwy.
Chicago, Illinois   60631

Mobile Home Sales Trends

Monthly
(Trade Assn.
  Bulletin)

Mobile Home Manufacturers Assn.

6650 N. Northwest Hwy.
Chicago, Illinois   60631

Mobile-Modular Housing Dealer

Twice Monthly
(Trade Magazine)

Trailer Dealer Publishing Co.

6229 N. Northwest Hwy.
Chicago, Illinois   60631

Supplier News Bulletin

Monthly
(Trade Assn.
  Statistics)

Mobile-Modular Housing Dealer Magazine

6229 N. Northwest Hwy.
Chicago, Illinois   60631

Mobile & Recreational Housing Merchandise

Monthly
(Trade Journal)

Vance Publishing Corp.

300 W. Adams Street
Chicago, Illinois   60603

Woodall's Directory

Annually
(Directory)

Woodall Publishing Co.

500 Hyacinth Place
Highland Park, Ill.   60035

Published	Source	Address

Motor Carrier Industry

PERIODICALS

American Trucking Trends

Annually	American Trucking Asso-	1616 P Street, NW
(Annual Report)	ciation, Inc.	Washington, D.C. 20036

Annual Report (Interstate Commerce Commission)

Annually	U.S. Government Printing	Washington, D.C.
(Annual Report)	Office	

Carrier Reports

Quarterly	Carrier Reports	369 Main Street
(Financial Statistics)		Old Saybrook, Conn. 06475

Daily Traffic World

Daily	The Traffic Service Corp.	815 Washington Bldg.
(Newspaper)		Washington, D.C.

Transport Topics

Weekly	Transport Topics, Inc.	1616 P Street, NW
(Newspaper)		Washington, D.C.

Trinc's Blue Book

Annual	Trinc Associates, Ltd.	485 L'Enfant Plaza, SW
(Company Data)		Washington, D.C. 20024

Trinc's Red Book

Quarterly	Trinc Associates, Ltd.	485 L'Enfant Plaza, SW
(Statistics)		Washington, D.C. 20024

BOOKS

Banker's Analysis of the Motor Carrier Industry

	Peter Douglas	New York, N.Y.
	Chase Manhattan Bank	

Financing the Motor Carrier Industry

	American Trucking Assn.	Washington, D.C.

OTHER

American Trucking Association

		1616 P Street, NW
		Washington, D.C. 20036

Transportation Association of America

		60 E. 42d St., Suite 2232
		New York, N.Y. 10017

Transportation Center

	Northwestern University	619 Clark Street
		Evanston, Illinois 60611

Nonferrous Metals (see also Aluminum)

PERIODICALS

Aluminum Monthly

Monthly	Bureau of Mines	Washington, D.C.
(Statistics)		

Published	Source	Address
American Metal Market		
Daily (Newspaper)	American Metal Market Co.	7 East 12th Street New York, N.Y. 10003
Copper Industry Monthly		
Monthly (Statistics)	Bureau of Mines	Washington, D.C.
Current Industrial Report M 33–2 Aluminum Ingot and Mill Product Shipments		
Monthly (Statistics)	U.S. Department of Commerce	Washington, D.C.
Engineering & Mining Journal		
Monthly (Magazine)	McGraw-Hill, Inc.	1221 Ave. of the Americas New York, N.Y. 10020
Handy & Harman Annual Review of Silver		
Annually (Yearbook)	Handy & Harman	850 Third Avenue New York, N.Y. 10022
Metal Statistics		
Annually (Stat. Yearbook)	American Metal Market Fairchild Publications	7 East 12th Street New York, N.Y. 10003
Metal Statistics		
Annually (Stat. Yearbook)	Metallgesellschaft A.G.	6000 Frankfort A.M. Main Reuterweg 14, Germany
Metals Week		
Weekly (Newspaper)	McGraw-Hill, Inc.	1221 Ave. of the Americas New York, N.Y. 10020
Minerals Yearbook Vol. 1–2 Metals, Minerals & Fuels		
Annually (Yearbook)	U.S. Government Printing Office	Washington, D.C. 20402
Minerals Yearbook Vol. 3 Area Reports—Domestic Vol. 4 Area Reports—International		
Annually (Yearbook)	U.S. Government Printing Office	Washington, D.C. 20402
Mining Journal		
Weekly (Newspaper)	Mining Journal, Ltd.	15 Wilson Street London E.C. 2 England U.K.
Nickel Monthly		
Monthly (Statistics)	Bureau of Mines	Washington, D.C.
Quarterly Industry Report—Copper		
Quarterly (Magazine)	Superintendent of Documents U.S. Government of Printing Office	Washington, D.C. 20402

Published	*Source*	*Address*

Yearbook of the American Bureau of Metal Statistics

| Annually (Statistical Compendium) | American Bureau of Metal Statistics | 50 Broadway New York, N.Y.   10004 |

BOOKS

Minerals Facts and Problems

| 1970 | Superintendent of Documents U.S. Government Printing Office | Washington, D.C.   20402 |

OTHERS

Aluminum Association

| | | 750 Third Avenue New York, N.Y.   10017 |

American Bureau of Metal Statistics

| | | 50 Broadway New York, N.Y.   10004 |

American Zinc Institute, Inc.

| | | 292 Madison Avenue New York, N.Y.   10017 |

Bureau of Census

| | | Washington, D.C.   20233 |

Copper Development of Commerce

| | | 405 Lexington Avenue New York, N.Y.   10017 |

U.S. Department of Commerce

| | BDSA | Washington, D.C.   20230 |

U.S. Department of the Interior

| | Bureau of Mines | Washington, D.C.   20240 |

Office Equipment

PERIODICALS

Computers and Automation

| Monthly (Magazine) | Computers and Automation | 815 Washmaton Street Newtonville, Mass.   02160 |

Computerworld

| Weekly (Newspaper) | Computerworld | 60 Austin Street Newtonville, Mass.   02160 |

Datamation

| Bimonthly (Magazine) | Technical Publishing Co. | 94 S. Los Robles Ave. Pasadena, Calif.   01101 |

Datapro 1972

| Monthly (Reference Supplements) | Datapro Research Corp. | 2204 Walnut Street Philadelphia, Pa.   19103 |

Published	*Source*	*Address*

DMS Electronics & General Support

Monthly (Reference Supplements)	Defense Market Service	71 Lewis Street Greenwich, Conn. 06830

EDP Industry & Market Report

Bimonthly (Newsletter)	International Data Publications Co.	60 Austin Street Newtonville, Mass. 02160

Electronic News

Weekly (Newspaper)	Fairchild Publications, Inc.	7 East 12th Street New York, N.Y. 10003

Electronics

Bimonthly (Magazine)	McGraw-Hill, Inc.	1221 Ave. of the Americas New York, N.Y. 10020

Infosystems Magazine

Monthly (Magazine)	Infosystems Magazine	964 Third Avenue New York, N.Y. 10017

OTHER

Business Equipment Manufacturers Association

                                                       Washington, D.C.

Oil and Natural Gas

PERIODICALS

Energy Memo

Quarterly (Newsletter)	First National City Bank	399 Park Avenue New York, N.Y. 10022

National Petroleum News Bulletin

Weekly (Bulletin)	McGraw-Hill, Inc.	1221 Ave. of the Americas New York, N.Y. 10020

Offshore

Monthly (Magazine)	Petroleum Publications Co.	P.O. Box 66909 Austin, Texas 77006

The Oil Daily

Daily (Newspaper)	Oil Daily, Inc.	59 E. Van Buren Street Chicago, Illinois 60605

Oil and Gas Journal

Weekly (Journal)	The Petroleum Publishing Co.	211 S. Cheyenne Ave. Tulsa, Okla. 74101

Oil Statistics Bulletin

Biweekly (Bulletin)	Oil Statistics Co., Inc.	Babson Park, Mass.

Oil Week

Weekly (Magazine)	Maclean-Hunter, Ltd.	805 Eighth Avenue Calgary 2, Alberta, Canada

Petroleum Engineer

Monthly (Magazine)	Petroleum Engineer Publishing Co.	P.O. Box 1589 Dallas, Texas 75221

Published	*Source*	*Address*

Petroleum Intelligence Weekly

| Weekly (Newsletter) | Petroleum Intelligence Weekly | 48 West 48th Street New York, N.Y. 10036 |

Petroleum Situation

| Monthly (Fact Sheet) | Chase Manhattan Bank | 1 Chase Manhattan Bank New York, N.Y. 10015 |

Petroleum Times

| Biweekly (Newsletter) | IPC America, Inc. | 205 E. 42d Street New York, N.Y. 10017 |

Platt's Oilgram News Service

| Daily (Newsletter) | McGraw-Hill, Inc. | 1221 Ave. of the Americas New York, N.Y. 10020 |

World Oil

| Monthly (Magazine) | Gulf Publishing Co. | P.O. Box 2608 Houston, Texas 77001 |

OTHER

American Petroleum Institute

| | | 1271 Sixth Avenue New York, N.Y. 10019 |

Independent Petroleum Association of America

| | | 1101 16th Street, NW Washington, D.C. 20036 |

National Petroleum Council

| | | 1625 K Street, NW Washington, D.C. 20006 |

Paper

PERIODICALS

Capacity Survey

| Annually (Survey) | American Paper Institute, Inc. | 260 Madison Avenue New York, N.Y. 10016 |

Crow's Weekly Plywood Letter

| Weekly (Newsletter) | C. C. Crow Publications | Terminal Sales Bldg. Portland, Oregon 97205 |

The Demand and Price Situation for Forest Products

| Annually (Nov.) (Survey) | U.S. Forest Service Department of Agriculture | Washington, D.C. 20250 |

Lockwood's Directory of the Paper & Allied Trades

| Annually (Directory) | Lockwood Trade Journal Co., Inc. | 551 Fifth Avenue New York, N.Y. 10017 |

Monthly Statistical Summary

| Monthly (Fact Sheet) | American Paper Institute, Inc. | 260 Madison Avenue New York, N.Y. 10016 |

Paperboard Statistics News Release

| Weekly (Statistics) | American Paper Institute, Inc. | 260 Madison Avenue New York, N.Y. 10016 |

Published	*Source*	*Address*

Paper Trade Journal

| Weekly (Magazine) | Lockwood Trade Journal Co., Inc. | 551 Fifth Avenue New York, N.Y.   10017 |

Photography Industry

PERIODICALS

Audio Visual Communications

| Monthly (Magazine) | United Business Publications | 750 Third Avenue New York, N.Y.   10017 |

Business Graphics

| Monthly (Magazine) | Graphic Arts Publishing Co. | 7373 N. Lincoln Avenue Chicago, Illinois   60646 |

The Communications User

| Bimonthly (Magazine) | Communications Trends, Inc. | 181 S. Franklin Avenue Valley Stream, N.Y.   11481 |

Graphic Arts Progress

| Monthly (Magazine) | Graphic Arts Research Center Rochester Institute of Technology | One Lomb Memorial Dr. Rochester, N.Y.   14623 |

Graphic Communications Weekly

| Weekly (Journal) | Technical Information, Inc. | 6331 Hollywood Blvd. Los Angeles, Calif.   90028 |

Image Technology

| Bimonthly (Magazine) | Acolyte Publications Corp. | 825 S. Barrington Avenue Los Angeles, Calif.   90049 |

Industrial Photography

| Monthly (Magazine) | United Business Publications, Inc. | 750 Third Avenue New York, N.Y.   10017 |

Infosystems Magazine

| Monthly (Magazine) | Infosystems Magazine | 964 Third Avenue New York, N.Y.   10017 |

The Journal of Micographics

| Bimonthly (Journal) | The National Microfilm Assn. | 8728 Colesville Road Suite 1101 Silver Spring, Md.   20910 |

The Journal of the SMPTE

| Monthly (Journal) | Society of Motion Picture and Television Engineers, Inc. | 9 East 41st Street New York, N.Y.   10017 |

Microfilm Techniques

| Bimonthly (Magazine) | Microfilm Techniques, Inc. | 250 Fulton Avenue Hempstead, N.Y.   11550 |

Modern Photography

| Monthly (Magazine) | Billboard Publications | 165 West 46th Street New York, N.Y.   10036 |

Published	*Source*	*Address*

Motion Picture Daily

| Wednesdays & Fridays (Newspaper) | Quigley Publishing Co., Inc. | 1270 Sixth Avenue Rockefeller Center New York, N.Y.   10020 |

Peterson's Photographic Magazine

| Monthly (Magazine) | Peterson Publishing Co. | 8490 Sunset Blvd. Los Angeles, Calif.   90069 |

Photo Dealer

| Monthly (Magazine) | The Gellert Publishing Corp. | 33 West 60th Street New York, N.Y.   10023 |

Photo Marketing

| Monthly (Magazine) | Master Photo Dealers' & Finishers' Assn. | 603 Lansing Avenue Jackson, Mich.   49202 |

Photo Methods for Industry (PMI)

| Monthly (Magazine) | Gellert Publishing Corp. | 33 West 60th Street New York, N.Y.   10023 |

Photo Weekly

| Weekly (Newspaper) | Billboard Publications, Inc. | 165 West 46th Street New York, N.Y.   10036 |

Photographic Applications in Science, Technology, and Medicine

| Bimonthly (Magazine) | Photographic Applications in Science & Technology, Inc. | 250 Fulton Avenue Hempstead, N.Y.   11550 |

Photographic Science & Engineering

| Bimonthly (Magazine) | Society of Photographic Scientists & Engineers | 1330 Massachusetts Ave., NW, Suite 204 Washington, D.C.   20005 |

Photographic Trade News (PTN)

| Semimonthly (Newspaper) | Photographic Trade News, Inc. | 250 Fulton Avenue Hempstead, N.Y.   11550 |

Popular Photography

| Monthly (Magazine) | Ziff-Davis Publishing Co. | One Park Avenue New York, N.Y.   10016 |

Technical Photography

| Monthly (Journal) | In-Plant Photography, Inc. | 250 Fulton Avenue Hempstead, N.Y.   11550 |

Wolfman Report on the Photographic Industry in the United States

| Annually (Magazine) | Modern Photography | 165 West 46th Street New York, N.Y.   10036 |

Books

Fundamentals of Photographic Theory

| 1968 | T. H. James, Ph.D. George C. Higgins Morgan & Morgan, Inc. | Hastings-on-Hudson, N.Y. |

Published	Source	Address

Introduction to Photographic Principles

| 1965 | Lewis Larmore, Ph.D.
Dover Publications, Inc. | New York, N.Y. |

Photographic Chemistry

| 1965 | George T. Eaton
Morgan & Morgan, Inc. | Hastings-on-Hudson, N.Y. |

The U.S. Photographic Industry 1970–75

| 1971 | Ian D. Robinsin
Elliott D. Novak
Arthur D. Little, Inc. | |

World Report of Photography

| 1968 | L.A. M.A. Mannheim
Staples Printers, Ltd. | Rochester Kent, England |

Your Guide to Photography

| 1969 | Helen Finn Bruce
Barnes & Noble, Inc. | New York, N.Y. |

OTHERS

The Encyclopedia of Photography

| | Willard D. Morgan, Editor
The Greystone Press | New York, N.Y. |

Life Library of Photography

| 1971 | The Editors of Time Life
Books | New York, N.Y. |

The Pollution Control Industry

PERIODICALS

Air and Water News

| Weekly
(News Report) | Stanley H. Brams | 801–7 New Center Bldg.
Detroit, Mich.   48202 |

Chemical Engineering

| Biweekly
(Trade Journal) | McGraw-Hill, Inc. | 1221 Ave. of the Americas
New York, N.Y.   10020 |

Environmental Science & Technology

| Monthly
(News Magazine) | American Chemical Society | 1155 16th Street, NW
Washington, D.C.   20036 |

Chemical Week

| Weekly
(Trade Journal) | McGraw-Hill, Inc. | 1221 Ave. of the Americas
New York, N.Y.   10020 |

Water & Sewage Works

| Monthly
(Trade Journal) | Scranton Publishing Co. | 35 E. Wacker Drive
Chicago, Illinois   60601 |

BOOKS

The Budget of the United States Government

| 1972 | U.S. Government Printing
Office | Washington, D.C.   20402 |

Published	*Source*	*Address*

Economic Report of the President

| 1972 | U.S. Government Printing Office | Washington, D.C.   20402 |

A Perspective of Regional and State Marine Environmental Activities, No. PB 177765

| 1968 | National Technical Information Service | Springfield, Va. |

Environmental Quality

(The Second Annual Report of the Council on Environmental Quality)

| Aug. 1971 | U.S. Government Printing Office | Washington, D.C.   20402 |

OTHERS

Subcommittee on Air and Water Pollution

| | Senator Edmund S. Muskie, Chm. | Senate Office Bldg. Washington, D.C. |
| | Copies of Hearings & Bills | |

Federal Register

(The National Archives of the United States)

| Daily | Superintendent of Documents | Washington, D.C.   20402 |
| | U.S. Government Printing Office | |

Public Utility Companies

PERIODICALS

Electrical World

| Fortnightly (Magazine) | McGraw-Hill, Inc. | 1221 Ave. of the Americas New York, N.Y.   10020 |

FPC News

| Weekly (Newsletter) | Federal Power Commission Office of Public Information | Washington, D.C.   20426 |

Federal Power Commission Electric Power Statistics

| Monthly (Bulletin) | Superintendent of Documents | Washington, D.C.   20402 |
| | U.S. Government Printing Office | |

National Electric Rate Book

| Annually (Booklets)50 in all; 1 per state) | Superintendent of Documents | Washington, D.C.   20402 |
| | U.S. Government Printing Office | |

Public Utilities Fortnightly

| Fortnightly (Magazine) | Public Utilities Report, Inc. | 1828 L Street, NW Suite 502 Washington, D.C.   20036 |

Public Utilities Reports

| Fortnightly (Bulletin) | Public Utilities Reports | 332 Pennsylvania Bldg. 425 13th Street, NW Washington, D.C.   20004 |

Published	Source	Address
Statistical Releases		
Weekly-Monthly (Statistical Yearbook)	Edison Electric Institute	90 Park Avenue New York, N.Y. 10016
Utility Spotlight		
Weekly (Newsletter)	Corporate Intelligence	74 Trinity Place New York, N.Y. 10004
Weekly Newsletter		
Weekly (Newsletter)	McGraw-Hill, Inc.	1221 Ave. of the Americas New York, N.Y. 10020
OTHER		
American Gas Association		
		1515 Wilson Blvd. Arlington, Va. 22209
Edison Electric Institute		
		90 Park Avenue New York, N.Y. 10016
Federal Communication Commission		
		1919 M Street, NW Washington, D.C. 20554
Federal Power Commission		
		441 G Street, NW Washington, D.C. 20426

Publishing Industry

PERIODICALS

Published	Source	Address
Advertising Age		
Weekly (Magazine)	Advertising Age	740 Rush Street Chicago, Illinois 60611
Book Production Industry		
Monthly (Magazine)	Book Production Industry	Penton Bldg. Cleveland, Ohio 44118
Education U.S.A. and Supplement Washington Monitor		
Weekly (Newsletter)	National School Public Relations Assn.	1201 16th Street, NW Washington, D.C. 20036
The Gallagher Report		
Weekly (Newsletter)	The Gallagher Report, Inc.	230 Park Avenue New York, N.Y. 10017
Inland Printer/American Lithographer		
Monthly (Magazine)	Maclean-Hunter Publishing Corp.	300 W. Adams Street Chicago, Illinois 60606
Knowledge Industry Report		
Weekly (Newsletter)	Knowledge Industry Publications, Inc.	56 Doyer Avenue White Plains, N.Y. 10605

Published	*Source*	*Address*

Media Industry Newsletter

| Weekly (Newsletter) | Business Magazines, Inc. | 150 East 52d Street New York, N.Y. 10022 |

Printing and Publishing

| Monthly (Newsletter) | U.S. Department of Commerce Superintendent of Documents U.S. Government Printing Office | Washington, D.C. 20402 |

Publishers Weekly

| Weekly (Magazine) | R. R. Bowker Co. | 1180 Ave. of the Americas New York, N.Y. 10036 |

BOOKS

The Art and Science of Book Publishing

| 1970 | Herbert Bailey Doubleday | New York, N.Y. |

Book Publishing in America

| 1966 | Charles A. Madison McGraw Hill Book Co. | New York, N.Y. |

The Bowker Annual of Library and Book Trade Information

| 1972 (latest edition) | Phyllis Steckler R. R. Bowker Co. | New York, N.Y. |

Digest of Educational Statistics

| 1972 (latest edition) | Kenneth A. Simon & W. Vance Grant U.S. Government Printing Office | Washington, D.C. |

A Guide to Book Publishing

| 1966 | Datus C. Smith R. R. Bowker Co. | New York, N.Y. |

The Printing Industry

| 1967 | Victor Strauss Printing Industries of America, Inc. | Washington, D.C. |

Projections of Educational Statistics to 1980–81

| 1972 | Kenneth A. Simon U.S. Government Printing Office | Washington, D.C. |

Railroad and Railroad Equipment Industry

PERIODICALS

Annual Report (Interstate Commerce Commission)

| Annually (Annual Report) | U.S. Government Printing Office | Washington, D.C. |

Daily Traffic World

| Daily (Newspaper) | The Traffic Service Corp. | 815 Washington Bldg. Washington, D.C. |

Published	Source	Address

Modern Railroads

| Monthly (Magazine) | Watson Publications | 5 South Wabash Avenue Chicago, Illinois 60603 |

Railway Age

| Semimonthly (Magazine) | Simmons-Boardman Publishing Corp. | 350 Broadway New York, N.Y. 10013 |

Trains

| Monthly (Magazine) | Kalmbuck Publishing Co. | 1027 North 7th Street Milwaukee, Wisc. 53233 |

Transport Economics

| Monthly (Statistics) | Interstate Commerce Commission | Washington, D.C. |

Yearbook of Railroad Facts

| Annually (Yearbook) | Assn. of Am. Railroads | 1920 L Street, NW Washington, D.C. 20036 |

ASSOCIATIONS, ETC.

American Railway Car Institute

| | | 11 East 44th Street New York, N.Y. 10017 |

Association of American Railroads

| | | 1920 L Street, NW Washington, D.C. 20036 |

Railway Progress Institute

| | | 801 North Fairfax Alexandria, Va. 22314 |

OTHER

"On the Estimation of Railroad Earnings"

| Nov.–Dec. 1966 | Karl Ziebarth Financial Analyst Journal (pp. 54–55) | |

Real Estate and REITs

PERIODICALS

Construction Review

| Monthly (Stat. Review) | U.S. Government Printing Office | Washington, D.C. |

House and Home

| Monthly (Magazine) | McGraw-Hill, Inc. | 1221 Ave. of the Americas New York, N.Y. 10020 |

Housing and Realty Investor

| Twice Monthly (Investment Letter) | Audit Investment Research, Inc. | 230 Park Avenue New York, N.Y. 10017 |

HUD News

| Irregular (News Releases) | U.S. Department of Housing and Urban Development | Washington, D.C. 20410 |

Published	*Source*	*Address*

Mobile-Modular Housing Dealer

| Ten Issues Yearly (Magazine) | Self-published | 6229 North Highway Chicago, Illinois 60631 |

The Mortgage and Real Estate Executives Report

| Biweekly (Newsletter) | Warren, Gorham & Lamont, Inc. | 89 Beach Street Boston, Mass. 02111 |

Professional Builder

| Monthly (Magazine) | Industrial Publications, Inc. | 270 St. Paul Street Denver, Colo. 80206 |

Real Estate Review

| Quarterly (Magazine) | Warren, Gorham & Lamont, Inc. | 89 Beach Street Boston, Mass. 02111 |

Realty Trust Review

| Twice Monthly (Investment Letter) | Audit Investment Research, Inc. | 230 Park Avenue New York, N.Y. 10017 |

BOOKS

Real Estate Trusts: America's Newest Billionaires

| 1971 | Kenneth Campbell Audit Investment Research, Inc. | New York, N.Y. |

OTHER

The U.S. Department of Housing and Urban Development and the U.S. Government Printing Office offer a large variety of Statistical information on request.

Retail Trade

PERIODICALS

Automotive News

| Weekly (Magazine) | Keith Crain | 965 Jefferson Avenue Detroit, Mich. 48207 |

Chain Shoe Stores and Leased Shoe Departments

Operators Directory

| Annually (Directory) | Runpf Publishing Co. | 300 West Adams Street Chicago, Illinois 60606 |

Clothes

| Semimonthly (Magazine) | Prads, Inc. | 380 Madison Avenue Room 507 New York, N.Y. 10017 |

Daily News Record

| Daily (Newspaper) | Fairchild Publications | 7 East 12th Street New York, N.Y. 10003 |

Discount Store News

| Biweekly (Newspaper) | Lebhar-Friedman | 2 Park Avenue New York, N.Y. 10016 |

Financial and Operating Results of Department and Specialty Stores

| Annually (Book) | National Retail Merchants Assn. | 100 West 31st Street New York, N.Y. 10017 |

Published	*Source*	*Address*
Footwear News		
Weekly (Newspaper)	Fairchild Publications	7 East 12th Street New York, N.Y. 10003
Home Furnishings Daily		
Daily (Newspaper)	Fairchild publications	7 East 12th Street New York, N.Y. 10003
Merchandising and Operating Results		
Annually (Books)	National Retail Merchants Assn.	100 West 31st Street New York, N.Y. 10017
Merchandising Week		
Weekly (Magazine)	Merchandising Week	165 West 46th Street New York, N.Y. 10036
Operating Results of Food Chains		
Annually (Book)	Dr. Earl Brown Department of Agricultural Economics	Warren Hall Cornell University Ithaca, N.Y. 14850
Operating Results of Self Service Discount Department Stores		
Annually (Book)	Mr. Kurt Barmard Mass Retailing Institute	570 Seventh Ave. New York, N.Y. 10018
Progressive Grocer		
Monthly (Magazine)	Progressive Grocer	708 Third Avenue New York, N.Y. 10017
Retail Sales Statistics		
Weekly, Monthly, & Annually	U.S. Department of Commerce Superintendent of Documents	Washington, D.C.
Supermarketing		
Monthly (Magazine)	Conover Mast Publications	205 East 42d Street New York, N.Y. 10017
Supermarket News		
Weekly (Newspaper)	Fairchild Publications	7 East 12th Street New York, N.Y. 10003
Women's Wear Daily		
Daily (Newspaper)	Fairchild Publications	7 East 12th Street New York, N.Y. 10003

Rubber/Tires

PERIODICALS

Automobile Facts and Figures		
Annually (Statistics)	Motor Vehicle Manufacturer's Assn. of the U.S.	320 New Center Bldg. Detroit, Michigan 48202
Automotive Industries		
Monthly (Magazine)	Chilton Co.	1 Decker Square Bala Cynwynd, Pa. 19004

Published	*Source*	*Address*

Current Industrial Report—Rubber:
Supply & Distribution for the U.S.

| Monthly (Report) | U.S. Department of Commerce Bureau of the Census Industry Division | Washington, D.C.   20233 |

International Rubber Digest

| Monthly (Magazine) | International Rubber Study Group | 5–6 Lancaster Place Strand London W.C. 2, England |

Modern Tire Dealer

| Monthly (Magazine) | Rubber Automotive Publications | 144 East 44th Street New York, N.Y.   10017 |

Motor Truck Facts

| Annually (Statistics) | Motor Vehicle Manufacturer's Assn. of the U.S. | 320 New Center Bldg. Detroit, Mich.   48202 |

N T D R A Dealer News

| Weekly (Magazine) | National Tire Dealers & Retreaders Assn. | 1343 L Street, NW Washington, D.C.   20005 |

National Petroleum News

| Monthly (Magazine) | McGraw-Hill, Inc. | 1221 Ave. of the Americas New York, N.Y.   10020 |

Natural Rubber News

| Monthly (Magazine) | Natural Rubber Bureau | Hudson, Ohio   44236 |

Quarterly Industrial Financial Reports

| Quarterly (Statistics) | Federal Trade Commission | Washington, D.C.   20590 |

Rubber Age

| Monthly (Magazine) | Palmerton Publishing | 101 West 31st Street New York, N.Y.   10001 |

Rubber & Plastic News

| Monthly (Magazine) | First National Tower | Akron, Ohio   44308 |

Rubber Industry Facts

| Annually (Statistics) | Rubber Manufacturers Assn. | 444 Madison Avenue New York, N.Y.   10022 |

Rubber Red Book

| Annually (Statistics) | Rubber Age | 101 West 31st Street New York, N.Y.   10001 |

Rubber Statistical Bulletin

| Monthly (Statistics) | International Rubber Study Group | 5–6 Lancaster Place Strand London, E.C. 2, England |

Rubber World

| Monthly (Magazine) | Rubber Automotive Publications | P.O. Box 5417 Akron, Ohio   44313 |

Published	*Source*	*Address*

Statistical Highlights

| Monthly (Statistics) | Rubber Manufacturers Assn. | 444 Madison Avenue New York, N.Y.   10022 |

Tire Guide

| Annually (Statistics) | Garfield Publications | 2119 Route 10 Farmingdale, N.Y.   11735 |

Tire Review

| Monthly (Magazine) | Babcox Automotive Publications | 11 S. Forge Street Akron, Ohio   44304 |

Wholesale Prices and Price Indexes

| Monthly (Statistics) | U.S. Department of Labor Bureau of Labor Statistics | Washington, D.C.   20212 |

OTHERS

Rubber Manufacturers Association

444 Madison Avenue
New York, N.Y.   10022

Savings and Loan

PERIODICALS

California Savings and Loan Data Book

| Annually (Book) (Stat. Abstract) | California Savings & Loan League | 1444 Wentworth Avenue P.O. Box R Pasadena, Calif.   91109 |

California Savings and Loan Journal

| Monthly (Magazine) | California Savings & Loan League | Pasadena, Calif.   91109 |

California Savings and Loan Operating Trends

| Annually (Journal) | California Savings & Loan League | Pasadena, Calif.   91109 |

California Statistical Abstract

| Annually (Stat. Abstract) | State of California Documents Section | P.O. Box 1612 Sacramento, Calif.   95807 |

Federal Home Loan Bank Digest

| Monthly (Magazine) | Federal Home Loan Bank Board | Washington, D.C.   20225 |

Monthly Summary of Business Conditions in Southern California, Northern Coastal Counties

| Monthly (Journal) | Security Pacific National Bank (Economic Research Dept.) | P.O. Box 2097 Terminal Annex Los Angeles, Calif.   90054 |

Mortgage Executives Report

| Monthly (Journal) | Banking Law Journal | 89 Beach Street Boston, Mass.   02111 |

Residential Research Reports

| Quarterly (Abstract) | Residential Research Committee of So. California | 433 S. Spring Street Los Angeles, Calif.   90013 |

Published	*Source*	*Address*

Savings and Loan Fact Book

Annually	U.S. Savings and Loan	221 N. LaSalle Street
(Book)	League	Chicago, Illinois 60601
(Stat. Abstract)		

Statistics on State Chartered Savings and Loans, Statistical Release 67–3

Quarterly	Savings and Loan Commis-	3440 Wilshire Blvd.
(Stat. Abstract)	sioner	Los Angeles, Calif.
	(Dept. of Investments)	

BOOKS

California Real Estate Finance

1966	J. W. Pugh and W. H.	New York, N.Y.
	Hippaka	Rt. 9W
	Prentice-Hall, Inc.	Englewood Cliffs, N.J. 07632

Savings and Mortgage Markets in California

1963	Leo Grebler	Pasadena, Calif. 91109
	California Savings & Loan	
	League	

The Savings and Loan Business

1962	L. T. Kendall	Englewood Cliffs, N.J.
	Prentice-Hall, Inc.	

Steel

PERIODICALS

American Metal Market

Daily	American Metal Market Co.	7 East 12th Street
(Newspaper)		New York, N.Y. 10003

Annual Statistical Report

Annually	American Iron & Steel In-	150 East 42nd Street
(Report)	stitute	New York, N.Y. 10017

Inventories of Steel Mills Shapes

Monthly	Commerce Department	Washington, D.C. 20233
(Magazine)	Census Bureau	
	Current Industrial Reports	

Iron Age

Weekly	Chilton Co.	56th & Chestnut Streets
(Magazine)		Philadelphia, Pa. 19139

Iron Ore

Monthly	Bureau of Mines	Washington, D.C. 20240
(Stat. Summary &	Division of Ferrous Metals	
News Sheet)		

Iron and Steel Scrap

Monthly	Bureau of Mines	Washington, D.C. 20240
(Magazine)	Division of Ferrous Metals	

Metal Bulletin

Monthly	Metal Bulletin, Ltd.	46 Wigmore Street
(Newspaper)		London W1, England

Published	Source	Address
Metalworking News		
Weekly (Newspaper)	Fairchild Publications, Inc.	7 East 12th Street New York, N.Y. 10003

Textile

PERIODICALS

Clothes		
Bimonthly (Magazine)	Prads, Inc.	380 Madison Avenue New York, N.Y. 10017
Daily News Record		
Daily (Newspaper)	Fairchild Publications, Inc.	7 East 12th Street New York, N.Y. 10003
Hosiery Statistics		
Annually (Stat. Yearbook)	National Assn. of Hosiery Manufacturers	P.O. Box 4314 Charlotte, N.C. 28204
International Textile Apparel Analysis		
Weekly (Advisory Letter)	International Statistical Bureau, Inc.	156 Fifth Avenue New York, N.Y. 10001
Mill Margins		
Monthly (Statistics)	U.S. Department of Agriculture Consumer and Marketing Service Market News Section—Cotton Division	P.O. Box 7723 Memphis, Tenn. 38117
Textile Highlights		
Quarterly with Monthly Supplements (Booklet)	ATMI	1501 Johnston Bldg. Charlotte, N.C. 28202
Textile Organon		
Monthly (Statistical Magazine)	Textile Economics Bureau, Inc.	10 East 40th Street New York, N.Y. 10016
Textile World		
Monthly (Magazine)	McGraw-Hill, Inc.	1221 Ave. of the Americas New York, N.Y. 10020
Women's Wear Daily		
Daily (Newspaper)	Fairchild Publications, Inc.	7 East 12th Street New York, N.Y. 10003

OTHER

Statistical Bulletin #455; Wool Statistics and Related Data 1930–1969		
(Stat. Booklet)	U.S. Department of Agriculture Economic Research Bureau	Washington, D.C. 20250

Published	*Source*	*Address*

Tobacco and Cigarettes

PERIODICALS

Advertising Age

Weekly (Magazine)	Advertising Age	740 Rush Street Chicago, Illinois 60611

Alcohol and Tobacco Summary Statistics

Annually (Stat. Summary)	U.S. Treasury Department Internal Revenue Service	Washington, D.C. 20224

Annual Report on Tobacco Statistics

Annually (Stat. Summary)	U.S. Department of Agriculture	Washington, D.C. 20250

Monthly Statistical Bulletin

Monthly (Bulletin)	Cigar Manufacturers Assn. of America, Inc.	575 Madison Avenue New York, N.Y. 10022

Monthly Statistical Release—Cigars and Cigarettes

Monthly (Stat. Summary)	U.S. Treasury Department Internal Revenue Service	Washington, D.C. 20224

Tobacco Reporter

Monthly (Magazine)	Tobacco Reporter	424 Commercial Square Cincinnati, Ohio 45202

Tobacco Situation

Quarterly (Stat. Summary)	Economic Research Service U.S. Department of Agriculture	Washington, D.C. 20250

United States Tobacco Journal

Weekly (Journal)	United States Tobacco Journal	145 Ave. of the Americas New York, N.Y. 10003

OTHER

The Cigarette Controversy

	The Tobacco Institute	1776 K Street, NW Washington, D.C. 20006

Federal Legislation Report

Foreign Trade Reports

International Tobacco Report

Leaf Bulletin

Special Reports

State Legislation Report

Tax Letter

Tobacco Barometer

Tobacco Update

	The Tobacco Merchants Assn. of the United States	Statler Hilton Hotel Seventh Ave. & 33d St. New York, N.Y. 10001

Index

Index

All page numbers printed in boldface type refer to Volume II.

All page numbers printed in boldface type refer to **Volume II.**

All page numbers printed in boldface type refer to Volume II.

All page numbers printed in boldface type refer to Volume II.

All page numbers printed in boldface type refer to Volume II.

All page numbers printed in boldface type refer to Volume II.

All page numbers printed in boldface type refer to Volume II.

All page numbers printed in boldface type refer to Volume II.

All page numbers printed in boldface type refer to Volume II.

All page numbers printed in boldface type refer to Volume II.

Computers—*Cont.*
  financial data and use of, 1127–28;
    see also subtopics hereunder
  fixed costs, 1129
  FORTRAN, 1147
  hardware resources, 1128
  highly miniaturized electronic compo-
    nents and systems for, **119**
  industry analysis, 1130, 1132–34
  input/output devices, **261**
  language of programming, 1147
  linear programming codes, 1364–65
  macroeconomic models of forecasting,
    1129–31, 1161
  main memory, **261**
  memory costs, **269**
  microeconomic models of forecasting,
    1130, 1132–34
  modeling software, 1158
  on-line storage, 1128, 1157
  operational functions, **270**
  organization for use of, 1158
  own, use of, 1127–29
  personnel costs, 1156
  personnel resources, 1129
  portfolio performance measurement,
    1155–56
  portfolio policy analysis, 1152–53
  price forecast data system, 1154–55
  program packages, 1128–29
  programmers, 1129
  programming, 1147–48
  publishing and education industries,
    use in, **611, 633–34**
  regression analysis with, 1067, 1071,
    1077–78, 1127
  reporting functions, **270**
  school training in use of, 1158
  screening, 1147–48
  security analysis, 1132–47
  security analyst evaluation, 1152
  simplification of programming, **269**
  software access, 1157–58
  software resources, 1128–29
  someone else's, use of, 1127–29
  special purpose, **116**
  staff specialists, 1158
  statistical report generation, 1155–56
  straight bond valuation, 1149
  technical support, 1129
  terminal connect time, 1157
  terminal input/output, 1128
  terminal rental costs, 1156
  textiles industry use of, **761**
  time-sharing industry, 1128, 1159–61
  total costs, 1129
  usage costs, 1157
  use of, 1127

Computers—*Cont.*
  uses of, 1129 ff.
  variable costs, 1129
  X-11 program, 1136
Comshare, 1159
COMVEST program, 1155–56
Concept stocks, 124
Conditional forecasts of earnings, 167,
    170
Conditional probabilities, 1056–57
Conference Board
  Cumulative Index, **865**
  library, **865**
Conglomerates, divestitures by, 455
Congress (United States), drug and
    health industry discussions of,
    339–40
Congressional Directory, **866**
Conservatism principle, 595, 597
Consistency concept, 595–96
Consolidations
  airlines industry, **129–30**
  equity method of accounting, 600
  financial statements, 599–600
  insurance companies, **415**
  pooling of interest method of account-
    ing, 599–600
  purchase method of accounting, 599–
    600
Construction electrical equipment; *see*
    Electrical equipment industry, *at*
    construction equipment
Construction financing, 385
  commitment techniques, 386
  forward commitments, 386
  interest rates, 386
  standby commitments, 386
Construction loans; *see* Real estate in-
    vestment trusts (REITs), *at* con-
    struction loans
Construction machinery, **506–7**
Construction materials industry, sources
    of information for, **893–94**
"Construction Review," 361
Construction Review, **871**
Consumer calculator, **376–77**
Consumer installment debt changes as
    leading indicator, 792
Consumer Price Index, **868**
Consumer Product Safety Agency, **288**
Consumer products
  electrical equipment industry, **353,
    355–56**
  electronics industry, **371–73**
  total U.S. market, **374**
Consumer spending; *see* Federal Reserve
    System, *at* economy of United States

All page numbers printed in boldface type refer to Volume II.

All page numbers printed in boldface type refer to Volume II.

All page numbers printed in boldface type refer to Volume II.

All page numbers printed in boldface type refer to Volume II.

Costs; *see also specific type*
  computer use, 1127, 1129, 1156–57;
    see also Computers
  defined, 591
  income statement item, 591
Council of Economic Advisers, **868**
  Annual report of, **869**
County and City Data Book, **869**
County Business Patterns, **869**
Coupon bonds, 339
Covariance defined, 1061–62
Credit business in retail trade industry,
  727
Credit insurance, **448, 450, 463**
Credit unions, 690
Credits against income tax, 642–46
Cryogenics technology fallout, **125**
"Cult of equities," 115, 117–18
Cumulative frequency curves, 1044
Cumulative frequency distributions,
  1043–44
Cumulative preferred stock, earnings per
  share on, 716
Current assets, 587–88
Current Biography, **878**
Current European Directories, **853**
Current liabilities, 589
Current ratio, 624
Cyclical fluctuations; *see* Business cycles
Cyclical industries, 127
  aerospace industry, **117, 123**
  automotive, **143–46**
  drug and health industries, **330–31**
  forest products industry, **406–7**
  publishing, **623, 646–47**
  semiconductor industry, **391–96**
  textiles, **763–64**
Cyclical stocks, 120, 125, 127–29
  defined, 127
  top 50, 127–28
  two-tiered market, 127, 129
Cyphernetics, 1159

D

Daily News Record, **861**
Data analysis, 1040–45; *see also* Computers; Financial data; Frequency
  distributions; *and* Ratios
Data communications companies, 503
Data processing equipment; *see* Electronic data processing (EDP) industry
Data Resources, Inc., 165 n, 635, 1159,
  857
Data Resources, Inc., Model, 1130
Data sources; *see* Sources of information
  for financial analysts

*Data Sources for Business & Market
  Analysis,* **871**
Dealer defined, 96, **96**
Dealer paper, 407, 410–11, 425
  bought as sold method of replacement,
    426
  discount on, 426
  outright sale method of placement,
    425–26
Debenture bonds, 187
  covenant of equal coverage, 187
  evaluation of, 187
  governmental issuance, 187
Debit card
  banking industry, **166**
  retail chains, **165**
  savings and loan industry, **165–66**
Debt-to-equity ratio, 1017
Debt ratio, 625–26
Decentralized system of portfolio management, 1189–90
Decision-oriented reports, 1156
Decision process
  elements in, 1347
  forecasting, value of, 1111
  portfolio manager's, 1208, 1215–21
Decision rules, 1370
Defense contractors; *see also* National defense
  aerospace industry, **116–17**
Defense expenditures; *see also* National
  defense
  aerospace industry, **121**
Defense Indicators, **868**
Defense industry; *see* National defense
Defensive stocks, 120, 125, 129
  companies issuing, 129
  defined, 129
  utility stocks, 129
Deferral method of accounting, 643
  conversion to flow-through method,
    666–67
Deferral of taxation, accounting for; *see*
  Tax accounting
Deferred credits, 589
Deferred expenses, 588
  bond discount, 589
Deferred income, 589
Deferred method of tax accounting, 655
Deferred payments, 1006–7
Deferred tax charges, 652–53
  balance sheet classification of, 655–56
  effects on financial analysis, 676–77
  tax rate for measurement of, 655
Deferred tax credits, 652–53
  balance sheet classification of, 655–56
  effects on financial analysis, 676–77
  tax rate for measurement of, 655

All page numbers printed in boldface type refer to Volume II.

All page numbers printed in boldface type refer to Volume II.

All page numbers printed in boldface type refer to Volume II.

All page numbers printed in boldface type refer to Volume II.

All page numbers printed in boldface type refer to Volume II.

All page numbers printed in boldface type refer to Volume II.

All page numbers printed in boldface type refer to Volume II.

All page numbers printed in boldface type refer to Volume II.

All page numbers printed in boldface type refer to Volume II.

All page numbers printed in boldface type refer to Volume II.

G

All page numbers printed in boldface type refer to Volume II.

All page numbers printed in boldface type refer to Volume II.

All page numbers printed in boldface type refer to Volume II.

All page numbers printed in boldface type refer to Volume II.

All page numbers printed in boldface type refer to Volume II.

All page numbers printed in boldface type refer to Volume II.

All page numbers printed in boldface type refer to Volume II.

All page numbers printed in boldface type refer to Volume II.

All page numbers printed in boldface type refer to Volume II.

All page numbers printed in boldface type refer to Volume II.

All page numbers printed in boldface type refer to Volume II.

All page numbers printed in boldface type refer to Volume II.

All page numbers printed in boldface type refer to Volume II.

All page numbers printed in boldface type refer to Volume II.

All page numbers printed in boldface type refer to Volume II.

All page numbers printed in boldface type refer to Volume II.

All page numbers printed in **boldface** type refer to **Volume II.**

All page numbers printed in boldface type refer to Volume II.

All page numbers printed in boldface type refer to Volume II.

All page numbers printed in boldface type refer to Volume II.

All page numbers printed in boldface type refer to Volume II.

All page numbers printed in boldface type refer to Volume II.

All page numbers printed in boldface type refer to Volume II.

All page numbers printed in boldface type refer to Volume II.

All page numbers printed in boldface type refer to Volume II.

All page numbers printed in boldface type refer to Volume II.

All page numbers printed in boldface type refer to Volume II.